From the moment when Swiss teenager Martina Hingis retained her Australian Open crown with such ease, it was apparent that youth was on the march in 1998. The women's game was about to be taken over by kids with braces on their teeth and beads in their hair. But wait a minute. Hadn't Arantxa Sanchez-Vicario read the script? Didn't the 26-year-old Spaniard know she wasn't supposed to win a third French Open? Apparently not, for her win in Paris against fellow geriatric Monica Seles, all of 24, was one of the great matches of the year.

There were others who had not learnt their lines. At Wimbledon Jana Novotna, 29, delayed drawing her pension so that she could remind her 30-year-old opponent Nathalie Tauziat that she could still play a bit. Even at the US Open the teens were repulsed – by an ancient of 22 called Davenport who put young Hingis firmly in her place in a one-sided final.

Meanwhile the older men had also made a good start. In Melbourne there was a new Wizard of Oz – one Petr Korda – an exuberant 30-year-old left-hander from the Czech Republic whose celebratory scissor-kicks and cartwheels had everyone smiling. In Paris there was an all-Spanish final between two mid-twenty-year-olds – the ruggedly handsome 21-year-old first-time winner Carlos Moya and his pal Alex Corretja who is slightly older. At Wimbledon Pete Sampras, the guardian of the grass, had his own way for the fifth time while Aussie No.1 Pat Rafter repeated in New York. By the time it was all over there had been eight different winners of the four major singles titles – a rare phenomenon expertly analysed by Julian Muscat in one of our key features. Elsewhere, John Roberts looks at the ITF's attempts to modernise the game, while John Barrett considers ways of encouraging more of the top men to play doubles.

The main feaure in this 31st edition of *World of Tennis* celebrates 100 years of Davis Cup tennis. Within the nostalgic story by Richard Evans there are photographs of many Davis Cup heroes of yesteryear, resplendent in their long, cream flannels. Immediately following is an eight page colour section of Davis Cup tennis where all the men wear shorts...to bring the story right up to date. A second colour section reflects the highlights of 1998 which proved to be another fascinating year.

There are the usual articles on the four Grand Slams, the two professional Tours, last year's Cup competitions and the main events of the ITF Year involving a growing number of junior, veteran and wheelchair players. Christine Forrest's biographies once again provide a comprehensive career record for the top ten men and women plus the outstanding achievements, year by year, of another 170 players. Tommy Hindley and Michael Cole have provided all the colour pictures and most of the black-and-white photographs that bring to life all the events that have made the headlines. Within these 544 pages there is something for everyone, be they professional observer or keen amateur.

The British Isles Davis Cup team of 1903, the first successful challengers, with the American team they beat 4–1 at the Longwood Cricket Club in Boston. (l to r from back row) George Wrenn (USA), William Collins (BRI Capt.), Mahony (BRI), Robert Wrenn (USA), Laurence Doherty (BRI), William Larned (USA Capt.), Reginald Doherty (BRI). This was the only time that two pairs of brothers appeared in a Challenge Round or final. (Longwood Cricket Club)

World of Tennis 1999

Celebrating the 100th year of the Davis Cup

Edited by John Barrett
Compiled by Joanne Sirman
Biographies by Christine Forrest

CollinsWillow
An Imprint of HarperCollins*Publishers*

Country abbreviations used in this book

AHO	Netherlands Antilles	FIN	Finland	NZL	New Zealand
ALG	Algeria	FRA	France	OMA	Oman
AND	Andorra	GBR	Great Britain	POC	Pacific Oceania
ANT	Antigua and Barbuda	GEO	Georgia	PAK	Pakistan
ARG	Argentina	GER	Germany	PAN	Panama
ARM	Armenia	GHA	Ghana	PAR	Paraguay
AUS	Australia	GRE	Greece	PER	Peru
AUT	Austria	GUA	Guatemala	PHI	Philippines
AZE	Azerbaijan	HAI	Haiti	POL	Poland
BAH	Bahamas	HKG	Hong Kong	POR	Portugal
BAN	Bangladesh	HON	Honduras	PUR	Puerto Rico
BAR	Barbados	HUN	Hungary	QAT	Qatar
BEL	Belgium	INA	Indonesia	ROM	Romania
BEN	Benin	IND	India	RSA	South Africa
BER	Bermuda	IRI	Iran	RUS	Russia
BIH	Bosnia/Herzegovina	IRL	Ireland	SEN	Senegal
BLR	Belarus	ISL	Iceland	SIN	Singapore
BOL	Bolivia	ISR	Israel	SLO	Slovenia
BOT	Botswana	ITA	Italy	SMR	San Marino
BRA	Brazil	JAM	Jamaica	SRI	Sri Lanka
BRN	Bahrain	JOR	Jordan	SUD	Sudan
BRU	Brunei Darussalam	JPN	Japan	SUI	Switzerland
BUL	Bulgaria	KAZ	Kazakhstan	SVK	Slovak Republic
CAN	Canada	KEN	Kenya	SWE	Sweden
CGO	Congo	KGZ	Kyrgyzstan	SYR	Syria
CHI	Chile	KOR	Korea, Republic	TGA	Tonga
CHN	People's Rep. of China	KSA	Saudi Arabia	THA	Thailand
CIV	Cote d'Ivoire	KUW	Kuwait	TJK	Tajikstan
CMR	Cameroon	LAT	Latvia	TKM	Turkimenistan
COL	Colombia	LBA	Libya	TOG	Togo
CRC	Costa Rica	LCA	St Lucia	TPE	Chinese Taipei
CRO	Croatia	LIB	Lebanon	TRI	Trinidad and Tobago
CUB	Cuba	LIE	Liechtenstein	TUN	Tunisia
CYP	Cyprus	LTU	Lithuania	TUR	Turkey
CZE	Czech Republic	LUX	Luxembourg	UAE	United Arab Emirates
DEN	Denmark	MAD	Madagascar	UGA	Uganda
DJI	Dijbouti	MAR	Morocco	UKR	Ukraine
DOM	Dominican Republic	MAS	Malaysia	URU	Uruguay
ECA	East Caribbean States	MDA	Moldova, Republic	USA	United States
ECU	Ecuador	MEX	Mexico	UZB	Uzbekistan
EGY	Egypt	MKD	Macedonia	VEN	Venezuela
ESA	El Salvador	MLT	Malta	YUG	Yugoslavia
ESP	Spain	MON	Monaco	ZAM	Zambia
EST	Estonia	NED	Netherlands	ZIM	Zimbabwe
ETH	Ethiopia	NGR	Nigeria		
FIJ	Fiji	NOR	Norway		

Cover photographs: Front (clockwise from top): *Jana Novotna, Pat Rafter* (both Paul Zimmer), *1903 US Davis Cup team* (Wimbledon Lawn Tennis Museum), *Martina Hingis* (Allsport). Back: *Tim Henman* (Tommy Hindley)

This edition published in 1999 by
CollinsWillow
an imprint of HarperCollins*Publishers*
London

A CIP catalogue record for this book is available from the British Library

ISBN 0 00 218862 7

Printed and bound in Great Britain by The Bath Press

Contents

Abbreviations used throughout this book:

Q	Qualifier	PR	Protected Ranking
WC	Wild Card	def	Default
LL	Lucky Loser	ret	Retired
SE	Special Exempt	w/o	Walk-over

Preface

Besides including all the regular features, this year's edition celebrates 100 years of Davis Cup tennis. As a glance through these pages will show, Dwight Davis's lofty dream has been magnificently realised with 131 nations taking part in last year's competition – a record.

At a participation level, then, all is well. Yet there are worrying signs that television networks around the world will find it increasingly challenging to do justice to the competition because of the indeterminate length of matches and the uncertainty about whether a tie will be alive or not on the third day. If you doubt this, read elsewhere about the decision of the Swedish network to leave this year's final, Sweden v Italy in Milan, just as the long opening rubber had reached its dramatic climax.

At a time when all the forces in the game are working together to enhance the enjoyment level of our sport for the fans around the world, both on site and via TV, perhaps this is the moment to consider ways of updating the format of the Davis Cup to make matches more exciting and ties more accommodating to TV schedules.

However unpalatable it may be to the purists (I can hear them now...'Change the format? Over my dead body...') the truth is that without the wholehearted support of television, international tennis – including the Davis Cup – will wither. For the general good it may be necessary to step over a few dead bodies.

The ITF's Davis Cup committee have been debating this issue long and hard for the past few years without reaching any meaningful conclusions. The tie-break has made little difference – though, equally, it does little harm – but the decision to experiment with sudden death in minor ties is dangerous. To tinker with a scoring system that is such a subtle and clever part of the game is unnecessary.

What are the issues? First, the length of matches. Second, dead rubbers. Third, the lack of worldwide focus on the finals. Fourth, the fact that there is no built-in climax to a tie. Fifth, the lack of success in promoting the Davis Cup as an event to compare with the Olympic Games or Football's World Cup.

Despite being the largest individual ball game in the world, tennis stands way below the great team sports mentioned above in popular appeal. Nor does it compare with the big domestic team sports in America – Grid Iron Football, Baseball, Basketball and Ice Hockey – or those native to Australia – Cricket, Rules and League Football. Yet, we all know that in the team format of Davis Cup ties, tennis can produce excitement and spectacle the equal of anything in sport.

As a contribution to the debate, I make the following suggestions which, I hope, will stimulate discussion and help the decision-makers to produce a formula that will keep Dwight Davis's flame burning brightly far into the next century.

I believe the Davis Cup should be staged as a major outdoor event every four years (in the even year between the Olympics) like the other globally attractive sports already mentioned, so that full world focus can be brought to bear. One country would stage the entire competition, lasting 23 days, and would be selected by rotation to reflect the surfaces on which the game is played – clay, hard and grass.

During the intervening years 'friendly' international matches could be held as well as qualifying competitions to produce the 16 nations who would take part in the final stages. These would consist of four groups of four nations, each playing one another within the groups, with the top two going through to the knock-out stage. Three rounds of knock-out would complete the competition. Nothing particularly new here – but at least we know from other sports that the formula works.

Now to the structure of the ties themselves. All would be three-match affairs (two singles and a doubles) played over two days with teams consisting of up to four players. A new points system would keep excitement alive until the last moment. This is how it would work:

i. There would be two best-of-three-sets rubbers on Day 1 – the 2 v 2 singles followed, after a 30 minute gap (strictly enforced), by the doubles. Both would have tie-breaks in every set. This would enable the No.2 singles player to participate in the doubles if he was one of that country's doubles experts.

ii. Each set won in both matches would earn one point. Thus, at the end of Day 1, the maximum lead one nation could have would be 4–0. The other possible scores would be 4–1, 4–2 or 3–3.

iii. On Day 2 the only match would be the 1 v 1 singles, to be played over the best-of-five sets. Each set won would be worth two points. Thus, a nation trailing 0–4 after Day 1 could still succeed by winning in straight sets (6 points to 4). A win in four sets would produce a draw (6 points all). In this case the tie would be decided by a final tie-break-only doubles match – akin to the penalty shoot out in football. Any other drawn finish would be decided the same way.

iv. There would be a special provision when the player representing a nation leading 4–0 wins the first two sets (now the score is 8–0), but is caught at two sets all by the trailing nation (now the score is 8–4). In this case five points would go to the winner of the last set so that the issue would be alive right down to the wire. Imagine the tension and excitement that would be generated!

There are several advantages to this format. Teams could play ties continuously, day after day if necessary if rain affects the schedule, because no-one plays singles two days running. The length of each day's play would fit comfortably into television schedules. There would be no more dead rubbers and each tie would build to a natural climax on Day 2. Although one great player in a team could theoretically win the tie on his own, that is no different to the present situation, *viz.* Sampras in Moscow in 1995.

Before you howl with derision, remember this. All great institutions remain great by adapting to prevailing economic and social circumstances. The world today is a very different place from the one Dwight Davis knew. It really is a case of adapt or face the consequences.

Adaptation has been the name of the game in producing this 31st volume – an essential requirement when the game continues to grow and yet the number of pages remains the same.

As always there are many people to acknowledge – especially those who have worked through the Christmas and New Year holidays so that first copies can be distributed at the Australian Open.

At the ITF Joanne Sirman stepped into the breach at short notice and performed heroically in providing the bulk of the tournament results and other information with seeming ease. She also charmed, bullied and cajoled her colleagues so that all our tight deadlines were met...well, most of them. In this 16th year of collaboration with the ITF I am more than ever impressed by the knowledge and understanding of Alun James' ever-busy department.

Other key material has been supplied with great speed and accuracy by the two professional Tours. At the ATP Tour Greg Sharko, Joe Lynch and Nicola Arzani have been unfailingly helpful while Joe Favorito's entire team at WTA Tour, both office personnel and those on the road, have been equally charming and co-operative.

To my tennis writing colleagues I can only say how much I have appreciated their contributions. Without their intimate knowledge of the game it would have been impossible to give a balanced picture of the year past, which I hope we have achieved.

Equally, without the dedication and skill of our award-winning snappers, Michael Cole and Tommy Hindley, whose probing lenses seem to have been pointing at all the right people and in all the right places, this volume would have looked very dull indeed. To them both my thanks.

For the third year Roger Walker has brought his design talents to these pages and has assembled the whole jigsaw with deceptive ease. His contribution over the holidays is very much appreciated...so is that of his long-suffering wife Brenda whose egg mayonnaise rolls are second to none.

Christine Forrest continues to amaze with the sheer volume of detail she assembles each year for the biographies, while Tom Whiting's management of the whole enterprise for Collins Willow is masterly. Nothing slips past his experienced eye.

Nor, I am sure, will anything slip past the searching eyes of our dedicated readers whose assistance in pointing out unwitting errors is very much appreciated. Please keep writing.

JOHN BARRETT
January 1999

Foreword

In last year's *World of Tennis* we chose to celebrate thirty years of the 'Open Era' and in 1999 we are recognising an equally significant landmark, one hundred years of Davis Cup.

In *World of Tennis 1999* we have dedicated an eight-page colour picture section to milestones of the Davis Cup over the course of the Twentieth Century supported by the reflections of some of the top tennis journalists on this venerable team competition. This is one element in a comprehensive programme by the International Tennis Federation to celebrate the largest annual team competition in the world of sport – its past, present and future.

To mark the occasion the ITF has devised a new logo for the competition and will be using the famous trophy itself at tennis and sports events throughout the year to raise the visibility of the Davis Cup by NEC. We have invited some of the top names in the sport to act as ambassadors in this special year – among them John Newcombe, Yannick Noah, Stefan Edberg, Boris Becker, Vijay Amritraj, Stan Smith and Nicola Pietrangeli. We have a publications programme that includes *The Davis Cup: Celebrating 100 Years of International Competition* by Richard Evans and *Dwight Davis: The Man and the Cup* by Nancy Kriplen. We have also been working with the BBC on a documentary on the history of the competition.

History is cyclical. At least it proved so in the draw for the 1999 competition because Great Britain will be hosting the United States in the first round of the competition in a repeat of the first ever Davis Cup played in Boston in 1900. In its 100th year, there will be a total of 129 nations competing.

It is also an opportunity to look forward both for the competition and for the ITF. Due in large part to the enormous growth in our organisation over the past ten years, we have in 1998 been preparing for the new millennium with the planning of a revitalised structure and systems. Independent consultants are helping to guide and mould our entire operations to ensure that the ITF is prepared and able to carry out its role as governing body of our sport in the year 2000 and beyond.

I am also pleased to report a closer and more co-operative relationship with the ATP Tour and WTA Tour as we all work together to ensure we have a healthy and prosperous sport.

As ever, John Barrett, publishers CollinsWillow and the team here at the ITF, together with some of the most eminent commentators and photographers of the sport, have worked hard to ensure *World of Tennis* maintains and enhances its reputation as the most comprehensive and definitive work of reference on our game. I hope readers and members of the international media find this edition informative and useful.

BRIAN TOBIN
President, International Tennis Federation

Top: *By successfully defending his US Open title Patrick Rafter joined Frank Sedgman (1951, '52) and Neale Fraser (1959, '60) as the only Australians to achieve that feat.* (Stephen Wake)

Above: *Her 1998 Wimbledon triumph was a special moment for Jana Novotna, who at last won the Grand Slam title her talents have always deserved.* (Tommy Hindley)

The Year in Review

Ronald Atkin

In the end, it was a piece of cake. After labouring for six weeks around the European autumn indoor circuit in search of points to protect his world number one ranking for an unprecedented sixth successive year, Pete Sampras achieved the record without even raising his racket arm.

Sampras was at the ATP Tour World Championship in Hannover, lunching on pasta in his hotel room, when word arrived that Marcelo Rios, the only remaining competitor with a hope of overhauling him, had pulled out of the tournament with a recurrence of back trouble. So, pausing only to don his tennis clothes and notch up a third straight victory in his qualifying group by routing Karol Kucera 6–2 6–1, Sampras launched into full-scale celebration at a media conference. When champagne became shampoo and was poured over his head, Pete seized the bottle and doused the elegantly coiffed Mark Miles, the ATP Tour's Chief Executive Officer, before dribbling the remainder over the wise old head of Ion Tiriac, in charge of marketing at the Hannover event and on the dais as one of the bearers of a giant cake in the shape of a figure six.

Then, once the photographers had exhausted themselves on this picture opportunity, the man who said he had just set a record which would never be broken invited the media to join him at the carve-up. So the journalists managed to have their cake and eat it, which is more than could be said for poor Sampras. Next day, he was doggedly hunted down, overtaken and defeated in his bid for a fifth World Championship by the labours of Alex Corretja, who went on to defeat Carlos Moya the next day in the first all-Spanish final in the 29-year history of the event.

This year, without much doubt, Sampras will set himself a less demanding schedule which will possibly exclude Davis Cup involvement, but he will remain on course for the other summit he is attempting to climb, a record number of Grand Slam victories. Pete pulled level with two of the all-time greats, Bjorn Borg and Rod Laver, on 11 wins when he won Wimbledon for a fifth time – equalling Borg's modern era mark – but remains one short of Roy Emerson's total of 12. However, as Sampras himself acknowledges, the chase becomes more difficult every time he steps up to the line because of the constantly improving level of competition he faces, given extra spice in the minds of his pursuers because they know they are trying to clobber the best player in the game.

There was, as ever in Hannover, much happening behind the scenes as the interested parties got around to thinking about where tennis ought to be heading in the next century. The most prestigious get-together involved the ITF President, Brian Tobin, and Mark Miles – not exactly the most convivial of bedfellows since the formation of the ATP Tour in 1990 – and the International Olympic Committee's President, Juan Antonio Samaranch, an occasion made even more enjoyable for Samaranch because of the presence of two compatriots in the final which he watched afterwards.

Samaranch is anxious to see a coming together of the opposing factions in tennis, with the ATP Tour playing their full part, as tennis attempts to present a long-overdue united front to the world while Tobin, coming towards the end of his term, is also keen to see unity as his legacy, together with the possible award of ranking points for the Davis Cup and for participation in the Compaq Grand Slam Cup. Samaranch is also reportedly keen to see Olympic tennis become a team event, rather than an individual one.

In Hannover a joint venture for the pooling of a larger package of their commercial rights was put forward by the ATP Tour and the Mercedes Super Nine tournaments (which are soon, we were promised, to be renamed). In search of what he called 'progressive evolution rather than revolution', Miles stressed the importance of making the sport 'as important as possible and as user friendly as possible while protecting the integrity of the competition and the traditions of the sport.'

There has been talk, sure to meet fierce resistance from traditionalists, of tailoring tennis to the requirements and timetables of television, with the possible implementation of a no-let rule and a no-ad system, plus an earlier tiebreak. When he was asked for comment on such possible changes Corretja, who expended more sweat than anybody at Hannover, said 'The only thing I would like to change is just to have some rest sometimes.'

The man who has been more responsible than anyone for setting the alarm bells ringing is Boris Becker, in the process of evolving from an outstanding player into one of the sport's leading decision makers. Becker has such control over tennis in Germany that, after declining the upcoming presidency of the German Tennis Federation (DTB) he was asked to nominate who he thought should replace the incumbent, Claus Stauder. As manager of the country's Davis Cup squad, he also tells the captain, Carl Uwe Steeb, who to select for the matches.

Becker is involved with Prisma, a German-owned marketing company who have been awarded the exclusive broadcast marketing rights in Europe for Wimbledon, though the All England Club has excluded United Kingdom rights, at present allocated to the BBC and due for renegotiation this year. Prisma made early overtures to the chairmen of the Grand Slam tournaments at the last Wimbledon about the possible setting up of a new slimline tour in opposition to the ATP Tour but were rebuffed. Hence the need of the sport's present governing bodies to circle the wagons and fight off those who would invade their territory.

The name of Bernie Ecclestone, the head honcho of Formula One motor racing, is mentioned with increasing frequency in connection with the need for change in tennis and it cropped up again in Hannover, where the World Championship will be held for the final time this year before it moves to a different major city every year. Ion Tiriac, in charge of marketing the event, said he would like to see the World Championship go to Moscow in the year 2000 and that he had been talking with Ecclestone about the possibility of staging the event in London's Millennium Dome in 2001.

The ATP Tour is also recommending the buying-out of struggling tournaments in order to slim down the calendar, something which many more players beside Corretja would welcome. The Hannover week provided a graphic example of what happens when tennis players are over-committed. Of the original field of eight, two – Richard Krajicek and Patrick Rafter – did not take up the places for which they had qualified. Krajicek went for a knee operation and Rafter opted to rest so that he could rehabilitate his ailing knee. Both men stated their preference for being fully fit for the first 1999 Grand Slam, the Australian Open.

Then, when the event got underway, both Andre Agassi and Rios pulled out with back problems. These two had won more matches (68 each) than anyone else, so perhaps their collapse was to be expected. Agassi was an undisputed candidate for Comeback Player of the Year after climbing from a ranking of 141 to re-establish himself in the top ten. Rios, who briefly took over as world number one from Sampras in the spring (becoming the first player from South America to do so), had an outstanding year, winning three Super Nine events – Indian Wells, Key Biscayne and Rome – as well as the ultimate cash prize in the sport, the Compaq Grand Slam Cup in Munich. But there were sighs of relief from the ATP Tour's top brass that such a sour and charmless individual was not the man they would be required to present to the world as their top player.

To underline the depth and variety in both the men's and women's game at present, the eight singles titles at the Grand Slams all went to different players. At the Australian Open Petr Korda claimed overdue reward when he lifted the men's singles at the age of 30, saying that his career clock stood at five to twelve. He confirmed that by completing an undistinguished year.

At Roland Garros the Spanish Armada's two biggest galleons, Carlos Moya and Corretja, sailed majestically into Paris to battle for the French Open title. Corretja said beforehand it would be difficult to get motivated against Moya since they were such good pals. He proved it by sinking without trace in straight sets.

Wimbledon rescued Sampras's year, since the 27-year-old American won only three other tournaments. His four-set victory over Goran Ivanisevic – it was the Croatian left-hander's third time unlucky in the Centre Court finale – was closer than it looked. Had Ivanisevic taken his chances to go two sets up he, and not Pete, could have become champion.

At the US Open Sampras was a heavy, and sentimental, favourite to take the title but was run to ground in the semi-finals by the defending champion, Pat Rafter, who had a wonderful autumn on the hard courts of North America. Then Rafter went on to defeat his compatriot, Mark Philippoussis, in the first all-Australian final at the event since Ken Rosewall beat Tony Roche in 1970.

The women's circuit, so frail for so long through over-reliance on Steffi Graf (herself ailing these days), continued to benefit from the arrival, and the rivalry, of Martina Hingis and the other 'teenage phenoms' as they tend to be known in America. The difference in 1998 was that Hingis, winner of three Grand Slams in 1997, had been rumbled by her challengers. They exploited her comparative lack of pace and power to such an extent that Hingis won only one of the majors, the Australian Open, where she defeated Conchita Martinez in the final.

Then the older brigade took over. Arantxa Sanchez-Vicario made it a memorable French Open for Spain by claiming the women's title (for the third time) alongside Moya's men's crown. In the process she wrecked a fairy tale involving Monica Seles, who had just returned from her latest sadness, the death of her father and coach Karolj, to play supremely well and sail into the final.

At Wimbledon it was at last the turn of Jana Novotna at the third attempt. The Czech right-hander had famously lost in 1993, weeping on the Duchess of Kent's shoulder after being over-hauled by Graf, and was again the runner-up in 1997 to Hingis after winning the opening set. But, when faced by an even older opponent, the 30-year-old Frenchwoman Nathalie Tauziat, Novotna seized the moment to achieve the greatest success of her career.

At the US Open it was the turn of Lindsay Davenport to repel the challenge of Hingis and become the first native-born American to win the women's Championship there since Chris Evert in 1982. Though she is a mere 22 years old, Davenport tends to align herself with the 'oldies' rather than the teenage phenoms, one of whom, Venus Williams, helped herself to the title when the women were finally admitted to the Compaq Grand Slam Cup. But, at the end of the year, Hingis popped up again to remind everybody of her class by winning the Chase Championships in Madison Square Garden, New York, though Davenport ended the year at number one.

In the Davis Cup Sweden lifted the giant trophy for the third time in five years, and the seventh occasion in all, by defeating Italy 4–1 in Milan. The win was testimony to the all-round strength of Sweden's players, who can provide a top-notch squad for hard court, carpets or clay, which was the surface Italy opted to prepare indoors in Milan. Sweden, along with Spain, have the most impressive strength in depth of any nation and they could afford to relegate their highest-ranked singles player, Jonas Bjorkman, to the doubles rubber and still win comfortably.

However, the Davis Cup talking points of the year lay elsewhere, in places as far apart as Milwaukee and Mildura. In the most embarrassing setback in their history, the United States – lacking Pete Sampras and Andre Agassi – were beaten 4–1 by the Italians in a Milwaukee semi-final. In the placid surroundings of Mildura, Australia, playing Zimbabwe in what they thought would be a 'no worries' tie (despite the controversial absence of Philippoussis), were beaten 3–2 by the Black brothers, Byron and Wayne.

In the Fed Cup, the women's team event, hopes were high that Switzerland would provide a new winner of the trophy. But the experience of Spain – winning for the fifth time in eight years – proved just too much as Hingis and the fast-rising Patty Schnyder were pipped 3–2 in the deciding doubles by Sanchez-Vicario and Martinez.

On the administrative side of the women's game there were two changes at the top. At the end of 1997 Ric Clarson was brought in from the PGA Tour to replace the outgoing Anne Person Worcester as Chief Executive Officer, only to change his mind almost immediately but not quickly enough to prevent the 1998 WTA Player Guide carrying his face and his message as the new CEO.

Into the breach stepped H. Bartlett ('Bart') McGuire, the Tour's legal counsel and business advisor, who told an early media conference 'I am Bartman, not Batman,' but promised to fly as high as possible. McGuire's special legal skills are in litigation and dispute resolution, so he is well at home in the world of modern tennis.

Right: *Carlos Moya, a first-time winner in Paris.* (Tommy Hindley)

Below: *It was title number five for Pete Sampras at Wimbledon.* (Michael Cole)

Above: *Aussie Pat Rafter repeats in New York.* (Stephen Wake)
Opposite right: *A first for Petr Korda at the eleventh hour in Melbourne.* (Stephen Wake)

Players of the Year

John Barrett

For only the fourth time in living memory there were eight different Grand Slam winners in 1998. Each one deserves to be considered a Player of the Year. But so does Alex Corretja. The serene Spaniard gets an honourable mention for reaching the French Open final in June and then, at the year's end, performing heroically in the ATP Tour World Championship in Hannover. Having beaten the holder and world No.1 Pete Sampras in the semi-final, Alex recovered from two sets down in the final to beat fellow countryman Carlos Moya, the man who had beaten him in Paris. It was a fitting climax to an extraordinary year.

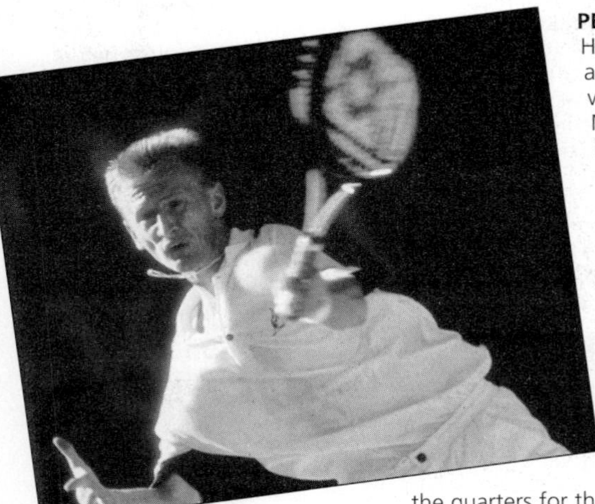

PETR KORDA – Australian Open
He delighted his legion of supporters around the world by high-stepping his way to a first Grand Slam title in Melbourne – not bad for a man who had celebrated his 30th birthday during the Championship. The joy of victory was apparent as he gave the crowd a couple of his famous scissor-kicks before cartwheeling around his end of the arena. The skill of this delightful Czech left-hander has never been in doubt. His ability to conjour winners at will has always reminded me of Rod Laver. But during a frustrating career Petr has seldom matched the Australian's steely resolve in difficult matches. Until Melbourne '98, that is. Sweeping through to the quarters for the loss of just two sets he came back to beat Bjorkman from two sets down, saw off Sampras's conqueror Kucera in four, and then annihilated Rios in a one-sided final. If Petr could never quite match that form thereafter to become the world No.1 – and three chances went a-begging – he can be forgiven. At least he gave us a spectacular start to the year.

CARLOS MOYA – French Open
In Paris this 21-year-old Spanish heart-throb had his many female admirers swooning. His male opponents, too, looked weak at the knees as they scurried to the farthest corners of the court chasing his relentless topspin drives. Losing only three sets on the way to his first Grand Slam title, Carlos made greater use of the faster ball than any of his rivals. His serve and his powerful forehand were his main winning weapons but there was an instinctive ability to win points at the net when the opportunity occurred. This was a victory for all-round ability, the flowering of a talent that had been apparent in Melbourne 18 months earlier when Carlos had beaten Becker and Chang on his way to the final. How ironic, then, that the strong man of Europe, having built a winning lead in the ATP Tour World Championship, should have succumbed to the man he had beaten in the Paris final, his friend and fellow Spaniard, Alex Corretja.

PETE SAMPRAS – Wimbledon
The legend grows. For the last six years the name of P. Sampras has stood at the top of the year-end rankings. It is a formidable record that the great man himself considers may stand for all time. And who would argue? With standards among the middle order players rising all the time it will become increasingly difficult for any individual to dominate his peers. Sampras's own reign is looking increasingly precarious. Only 33 ranking points separated Pete from Marcelo

Rios as the field assembled in Hannover for the climactic event of the year, the ATP Tour World Championship. If Rios had not been forced to default with a back injury who knows what might have happened. As it was, Pete raced through to the semi-finals to clinch his place in history but was thwarted there by Alex Corretja. It was a disappointing end to an average season. The cornerstone of Pete's year was his fifth win at Wimbledon, a magnificently professional performance that left Goran Ivanisevic clutching at straws for the third time in seven years. That was Pete's only Grand Slam win in 1998, his 11th in all, so Roy Emerson's total of twelve successes remains intact at least until this year's Australian Championships.

PATRICK RAFTER – US Open
So he wasn't a one-shot wonder after all. Andre Agassi denies that he ever said it, but the very fact that Pat believed he had, drove the 1997 US Open champion to heights even he had never dreamed of reaching. Arriving in America feeling despondent after a moderate start to the year and a listless performance against Tim Henman at Wimbledon, the athletic Australian put together a string of results that defied belief. Winning 33 of his next 36 matches, Pat won back-to-back Super Nine titles in Toronto and Cincinnati, took the Hamlet Cup on Long Island and then swept through to a second US Open title with victories over Pete Sampras and fellow Aussie Mark Philippoussis in the last two rounds. Pat was in exalted company. Only five times before had anyone successfully defended the US title. But this heroic run had taken its toll. Despite being within reach of the No. 1 ranking Pat relinquished his place in the ATP Tour World Championship so that he would be fit and fresh for the Australian Open in January. He will be strongly fancied to become the first home-bred champion there since Mark Edmondson in 1976.

MARTINA HINGIS – Australian Open
It is hard to believe that the self-assured young woman who won three Grand Slam tournaments in 1997 is still only 18 years old, a precociously talented teenager if ever there was one. Yet, as events would prove over the next twelve months, talent alone is not enough. Well as Martina played throught most of the 1998, on so many of the great occasions others played

Left: *Martina Hingis strode to a second Australian title.* (Stephen Wake)
Above: *A third for Arantxa Sanchez-Vicario in Paris.* (Stephen Wake)
Right: *A deserved win for Jana Novotna at Wimbledon.* (Tommy Hindley)

better. The signs were ominous from the start. When Venus Williams beat her in her first tournament match of the year in Sydney (a red-hot performance on a scorching afternoon from the American youngster), the alarm bells should have been ringing. After that setback Martina had done well to win the Australian Open. Yet as the year wore on there was no indication that Martina or her mother realised that she would have do something to improve fitness, strength and stamina. Semi-final losses at the French Championships and Wimbledon left her with just one more Grand Slam title to defend. Despite playing some of her best tennis of the year in a dramatic US Open final, she failed to upset the attacking rhythm of Lindsay Davenport who then went on to take away her No.1 world ranking. Not until the last event of the year, the Chase Championships, did Martina restore her authority. Besides being sweet revenge for the loss of her US crown, her emphatic defeat of Davenport also reminded the world just how good she can be. The fight for supremacy among the top women in 1999 is certain to be fierce.

ARANTXA SANCHEZ-VICARIO – French Open
With victories over the two Williams sisters in the last two rounds of Sydney, Arantxa made a statement. The bright young things would not have it all their own way in 1998. Nor, for that matter would their seniors. By the time the French Open came around Arantxa was playing from memory. With the glory years of 1989 and 1984 as inspiration, Arantxa found the pace, commitment and intensity that had been missing from her game for so long. Improving with every match, she destroyed Davenport in the semi-final with the precision of a surgeon. Then, in a magnificent final against another great champion, Monica Seles, Arantxa defended and counter-attacked with such skill and determination that her opponent started to charge recklessly to the net, a tactic that was doomed to failure on the slow red clay against a champion who knew that her time had come again. Apart from another win in the Fed Cup, the rest of the season was something of an anti-climax. That did not worry Arantxa. She knew, the world knew, that she was back where she belonged among the top four in the world.

JANA NOVOTNA – Wimbledon
According to the proverb, everything comes to him who waits. Or her, it seems. Jana proved as much at Wimbledon. But it doesn't come without a great deal of effort, in Jana's case a lifetime of dedication to the game she loves. The fact that she was playing at her favourite tournament for the 13th time did not worry her. More important than the numbers was the fact that she had never lost her belief, despite the heart-rending loss to Steffi Graf from a winning position

in 1993 when she had famously been comforted on court by the Duchess of Kent. When Jana had lost in the 1997 final to Martina Hingis the Duchess had no need to offer comfort for Jana knew that she might have won that day if she had not been carrying a minor injury. One year later Jana knew she was ready. So did her coach, Hana Mandlikova, herself twice a Wimbledon finalist in 1981 and 1986. Deploying her skilful serve-and volley game to perfection, Jana lost just one set as she swept to an emotional victory that made up for all the disappointments of the past. By adding the doubles title as well with Martina Hingis (with whom she had already won in Paris and would also win in New York), Jana equalled the 1988 feat of Steffi Graf, the last woman to do the double at Wimbledon. It was the perfect end to an emotional fortnight...and well worth the wait.

LINDSAY DAVENPORT – US Open
It just got better and better. The disappointment of a semi-final loss in Melbourne was immediately balanced by a win over world No. 1 Martina Hingis in the Tokyo final. As the season unfolded it began to dawn on Lindsay that there was no-one on this planet she could not beat. That is what Billie Jean King had been telling her in Atlanta when she had outpaced a full strength field to take the Olympic gold medal in 1996. Ever since, her coach Robert Van't Hof had been giving her the same message. After the frustration of a semi-final loss in Paris and a quarter-final beating at Wimbledon Lindsay decided she'd had enough of coming second. Harnessing all the power at her disposal – and that has always been considerable – she swept majestically through the American summer circuit to annex the titles in Stanford, San Diego and Los Angeles on the eve of the US Open where she was now the logical favourite. Maintaining her form and her nerve, Lindsay won her first Grand Slam title in style without losing a set, only the 15th player to do so since the Championship began in 1887. One month later Lindsay overtook Hingis to become the eighth woman since 1975 to top the world rankings, a position she would hold to the year's end. Not surprisingly she was proclaimed the WTA Player of the Year. It could not have happened to a nicer person.

With intimidating back court power, Lindsay Davenport achieved her dream in New York. (Michael Cole)

Major ITF Events

The ITF Year • Davis Cup by NEC • KB Fed Cup
Hyundai Hopman Cup • ITF Sunshine Cup
ITF Connolly Continental Cup • NEC World Youth Cup
World Junior Tennis

The injury to Italy's No.1 Andrea Gaudenzi on Day 1 of the Davis Cup final against Sweden put paid to any hopes of the home side repeating their 1976 triumph. (Tommy Hindley)

The 18-year-old Russian Marat Safin whose sensational wins over Andre Agassi and the holder, Gustavo Kuerten, contributed to record crowds at the French Open. (Tommy Hindley)

The ITF Year

Wendy Kewley

In 1998, eight different players from five different countries carried away Grand Slam singles trophies – a sharp indicator of the intense competitiveness of the sport. Diversity seemed to be the name of the game. Petr Korda triumphed in Australia, Carlos Moya won at Roland Garros, while Pete Sampras defended his title at Wimbledon and Pat Rafter followed suit at the US Open. The teenage revolution, predicted by many, failed to take off in the women's game – although Martina Hingis did reign in Australia. Instead, the old guard sharpened their rackets and fought back.

'They are calling us veterans but we are a long way from finished yet,' remarked the 26-year-old Arantxa Sanchez-Vicario after defeating Monica Seles in the Roland Garros singles final. The point was further underlined at Wimbledon where 29-year-old Jana Novotna defeated 30-year-old Nathalie Tauziat in the final. Although only 22 herself, Lindsay Davenport kept the teenagers at bay by dethroning the defending champion Martina Hingis at Flushing Meadows.

The quality of the tennis on display encouraged more people than ever to attend the four Grand Slam events. A record crowd of 434, 807 flocked to the Australian Open in Melbourne – an 11 per cent increase on 1997. The Grand Slam websites also attracted attention. The Wimbledon website – the largest of all – had a record 145, 478 hits per minute during the gripping Krajicek/Ivanisevic semi-final. The hit rate was well over 200 million for the fortnight.

The Compaq Grand Slam Cup also set a new record by welcoming female players for the first time resulting in a reduction from 16 to 12 in the men's draw. Set in the historic Munich Olympiapark, the titles were won by Marcelo Rios and Venus Williams.

Competition was intense in the two premier team competitions – the Davis Cup by NEC and the KB Fed Cup which are reported on fully elsewhere.

To mark a hundred years of Davis Cup, a year-long Centennial programme was launched at the 1998 Davis Cup Final. The ITF has invited Vijay Amritaj, Boris Becker, Stefan Edberg, John Newcombe, Yannick Noah and Stan Smith to help promote the Davis Cup by becoming ambassadors for the year.

More than 70,000 fans attended the Hyundai Hopman Cup, the international mixed team competition, held in Perth each year and sanctioned by the ITF since 1996. The popularity of the event was such that in 1998 a play-off was required to select which team would earn a place in the eight-nation main draw. Slovak Republic came through the play-off and then stole the headlines by storming through to take the title.

But the perception of each team event is almost as vital as the quality of on-court play. In 1998, the ITF introduced the Promomatch scheme to share its marketing expertise with the National Associations through detailed workshops and toolkits. Better promoted Davis Cup and Fed Cup ties will create greater impact with tennis fans, players, sponsors and television rights holders.

While the success of top events is crucial to tennis, the ITF is equally committed to the lower tiers of the game. A significant part of the ITF budget is apportioned to the ITF Men's Circuit and the ITF Women's Circuit which both provide entry level events offering valuable ranking points to help promising players reach the elite ranks.

In 1998, the ITF introduced weekly tournaments for men called Futures in order to give players the flexibility to compete in one-week events as well as the more traditional four-week Satellite Circuits. The new Futures have proved extremely successful and have attracted a large number of high quality players. Last year, 209 Futures and 52 Satellite Circuits were held around the world including in Brunei and Vietnam which both hosted new tournaments. In 1999, Futures tournaments will enjoy increased ranking points.

There were 283 tournaments on the ITF Women's Circuit held in 60 countries with a total prize money of $5,025,000. The ITF extended its presence in South America by introducing the Copa Ericsson, a series of seven $25,000 tournaments plus a Masters event which will earn a wild card into the prestigious Corel WTA Tour Lipton Championships in 1999 for the winner.

The Junior Exempt programme is a good example of how players can bridge the gap between junior tennis and the senior game. The scheme offers the top ten girls in singles from the preceding year the chance to enter the main draw of ITF Women's Circuit events.

The ITF continued to promote the junior game through the Junior Grand Slam media service and Tennis Stuff, a popular new 16-page junior magazine launched in January 1998.

The Grand Slam Development Fund (GSDF) is vital in helping the junior game. Each year, the ITF continues to donate $4 million a year to promoting tennis, $2 million of which comes from the GSDF. In 1998, the GSDF enabled 148 players from 62 countries to join ITF touring teams. Team members travel to events outside their region under the guidance of a coach. As in previous years, ITF teams had considerable success in 1998. Jose Antonio De Armas of Venezuela, a member of the ITF International Junior A Team, partnered Chile's Fernando Gonzales to win the boys doubles at the Junior French Championships. Fellow team member, Eleni Danilidou of Greece reached the semi-finals of the girls doubles with Slovenia's Tina Pisnik. Pakistan's Aisam Qureshi won the boys' singles at Roehampton while Danilidou took the girls' singles and partnered Argentina's Erica Krauth to win the doubles.

The ITF Women's Professional Team enjoyed outstanding success at Wimbledon: Cara Black of Zimbabwe and Surina de Beer of South Africa not only qualified for the senior competition but went on to reach the third round with Black eliminating Patty Schnyder in the process.

Begun in January 1996, the ITF School Tennis Initiative continues to introduce mini-tennis to more schoolchildren worldwide. Since 1996, 800,000 children from more than 70 countries have picked up a tennis racket for the first time.

Tennis players obviously need good coaching and over 70 coaches workshops were held in 1998 – with the highlight of the year being the four regional workshops (Central America, South America, Asia and Africa) which attracted a total of over 600 coaches from 60 nations.

Awareness of playing trends is an important factor in ensuring that tennis is promoted effectively to as many people from as many backgrounds as possible worldwide. In December, the second part of the ITF's international research survey into tennis participation and attitude trends was published, releasing valuable marketing data on the following countries: Argentina, Canada, Netherlands, South Africa, Spain and Taiwan.

Wheelchair tennis is one of the fastest growing areas of the sport and is now played in over 70 countries. In January 1998, Marco Polic was appointed as the sport's first full-time Development Officer. Enthusiastic and dynamic, Polic's brief is to conduct coaching clinics and camps worldwide while also overseeing the NEC Wheelchair Tennis Tour.

Affectionately known as vets tennis for some time, in October the ITF Vets Committee announced that veterans tennis would officially be called 'vets tennis'.

On the administrative side, the ITF's AGM took place in Killarney, Ireland where it was decided to allocate a grant of $2,450,000 among all 201 National Asssociations for the game's development. This represents the largest distribution to the National Associations by the ITF.

The AGM also elected Juan Margets as Executive Vice-President to fill the position formerly titled General Manager. ITF President Brian Tobin said, 'I am sure that Juan's depth of experience will be greatly beneficial to the ITF and its member nations as we approach the Millennium.'

In May, the ITF launched a faxback service to provide easy access to tournament information for players, Federations and the media. An Intranet called ITFworldnet was also launched in October to enable ITF staff and National Associations to access information 24 hours a day.

On a regulatory note, in September the ITF, ATP Tour and Corel WTA Tour agreed to have a joint officiating certification programme for the first time in history. The unified ITF/ATP Tour and WTA Tour Anti-Doping Program implemented 1000 player tests throughout 1998.

The ITF's increased involvement in every aspect of tennis has led to staff numbers doubling. In April, the ITF relocated to the Bank of England Sports Club in Roehampton, near London – the venue for the Wimbledon qualifying rounds. The offices also house a permanent equipment testing centre which enables the ITF to achieve a greater insight into the complex technical issues facing the modern game.

Finally, the ITF Philippe Chatrier Award, given for outstanding services to the game, was presented to Rod Laver at the 1998 World Champions Dinner. A double Grand Slam winner and Davis Cup veteran, Laver suffered a stroke earlier this year but has gradually been recovering his health. Given that there were eight Grand Slam champions crowned in 1998, the Rocket's Double Slam record seems safe for some time.

ITF WORLD CHAMPIONS

SINGLES

	Men	Women
1978	Bjorn Borg	Chris Evert
1979	Bjorn Borg	Martina Navratilova
1980	Bjorn Borg	Chris Evert
1981	John McEnroe	Chris Evert
1982	Jimmy Connors	Martina Navratilova
1983	John McEnroe	Martina Navratilova
1984	John McEnroe	Martina Navratilova
1985	Ivan Lendl	Martina Navratilova
1986	Ivan Lendl	Martina Navratilova
1987	Ivan Lendl	Steffi Graf
1988	Mats Wilander	Steffi Graf
1989	Boris Becker	Steffi Graf
1990	Ivan Lendl	Steffi Graf
1991	Stefan Edberg	Monica Seles
1992	Jim Courier	Monica Seles
1993	Pete Sampras	Steffi Graf
1994	Pete Sampras	Arantxa Sanchez-Vicario
1995	Pete Sampras	Steffi Graf
1996	Pete Sampras	Steffi Graf
1997	Pete Sampras	Martina Hingis
1998	Pete Sampras	Lindsay Davenport

DOUBLES

	Men	Women
1996	Todd Woodbridge/Mark Woodforde	Lindsay Davenport/Mary Joe Fernandez
1997	Todd Woodbridge/Mark Woodforde	Lindsay Davenport/Jana Novotna
1998	Jacco Eltingh/Paul Haarhuis	Lindsay Davenport/Natasha Zvereva

ITF JUNIOR WORLD CHAMPIONS

Boys' singles

1978 Ivan Lendl (TCH)
1979 Raul Viver (ECU)
1980 Thierry Tulasne (FRA)
1981 Pat Cash (AUS)
1982 Guy Forget (FRA)
1983 Stefan Edberg (SWE)
1984 Mark Kratzmann (AUS)
1985 Claudio Pistolesi (ITA)
1986 Javier Sanchez (ESP)
1987 Jason Stoltenberg (AUS)
1988 Nicolas Pereira (VEN)
1989 Nicklas Kulti (SWE)
1990 Andrea Gaudenzi (ITA)
1991 Thomas Enqvist (SWE)
1992 Brian Dunn (USA)
1993 Marcelo Rios (CHI)
1994 Federico Browne (ARG)
1995 Marian Zabaleta (ARG)
1996 Sebastien Grosjean (FRA)
1997 Arnaud di Pasquale (FRA)
1998 Roger Federer (SUI)

Boys' doubles

1982 Fernando Perez (MEX)
1983 Mark Kratzman (AUS)
1984 Augustin Moreno (MEX)
1985 Petr Korda (TCH)/ Cyril Suk (TCH)
1986 Tomas Carbonell (ESP)
1987 Jason Stoltenberg (AUS)
1988 David Rikl (TCH)/Tomas Zdrazila (TCH)
1989 Wayne Ferreira (RSA)
1990 Marten Renstroem (SWE)
1991 Karim Alami (MAR)
1992 Enrique Abaroa (MEX)
1993 Steven Downs (NZL)
1994 Benjamin Ellwood (AUS)
1995 Kepler Orellana (VEN)
1996 Sebastien Grosjean (FRA)
1997 Nicolas Massu (CHI)
1998 Jose De Armas (VEN)

Girls' singles

1978 Hana Mandlikova (TCH)
1979 Mary-Lou Piatek (USA)
1980 Susan Mascarin (USA)
1981 Zina Garrison (USA)
1982 Gretchen Rush (USA)
1983 Pascale Paradis (FRA)
1984 Gabriela Sabatini (ARG)
1985 Laura Garrone (USA)
1986 Patricia Tarabini (ARG)
1987 Natalia Zvereva (URS)
1988 Cristina Tessi (ARG)
1989 Florencia Labat (ARG)
1990 Karina Habsudova (TCH)
1991 Zdenka Malkova (TCH)
1992 Rossana De Los Rios (PAR)
1993 Nino Louarssabichvilli (GEO)
1994 Martina Hingis (SUI)
1995 Anna Kournikova (RUS)
1996 Amelie Mauresmo (FRA)
1997 Cara Black (ZIM)
1998 Jelena Dokic (AUS)

Girls' doubles

1982 Beth Herr (USA)
1983 Larissa Savchenko (URS)
1984 Mercedes Paz (ARG)
1985 Mariana Perez-Roldan (ARG)/Patricia Tarabini (ARG)
1986 Leila Meskhi (URS)
1987 Natalia Medvedeva (URS)
1988 Jo-Anne Faull (AUS)
1989 Andrea Strnadova (TCH)
1990 Karina Habsudova (TCH)
1991 Eva Martincova (TCH)
1992 Nancy Feber (BEL)/Laurence Courtois (BEL)
1993 Cristina Moros (USA)
1994 Martina Nedelkova (SLK)
1995 Ludmilla Varmuzova (CZE)
1996 Michaela Pastikova (CZE)/Jitka Schonfeldova (CZE)
1997 Cara Black (ZIM)/Irina Selyutina (KAZ)
1998 Eva Dyrberg (DEN)

Above: *This seventh Davis Cup win for the victorious Swedes was their third in four years, making them the most successful Davis Cup nation of the nineties.* (Tommy Hindley)

Below: *Home advantage was no help to the injury-hit Italians whose dreams of achieving a second Davis Cup success were shattered.* (Tommy Hindley)

Davis Cup by NEC

Wendy Kewley

In 1998, a record 131 countries participated in the Davis Cup by NEC. For the seventh occasion, Sweden earned the right to have its name engraved on the famous sterling silver punch bowl after defeating Italy 4–1 in Milan in early December.

The atmosphere in Milan's Assago Forum was electric as Italy's Andrea Gaudenzi came out on court to face Sweden's Magnus Norman in the opening match of the 1998 Final. The Italian supporters blew klaxons loudly and waved their green, red and white flags while the smaller number of Swedish fans cheered and paraded their blue and yellow banners. The match unfolded into a dazzling display of high quality tennis with both players stretching themselves to the limit. In the decisive fifth set, Gaudenzi played spiritedly reversing a 0–4 deficit before levelling at 6–all. Cruelly, the Italian's recurring shoulder injury flared up and the pain became so unbearable that Gaudenzi was forced to retire, thereby donating Sweden the first tie point. It was an abrupt end to a breathtaking match which had mesmerised the capacity crowd of over 12,000 for nearly five hours – and a bitter blow for Italian hopes.

Magnus Gustafsson defeated Davide Sanguinetti in the second match, giving the Scandinavian visitors a 2–0 lead after the first day of play. Sweden's Jonas Bjorkman and Nicklas Kulti then faced the makeshift Italian pairing of Diego Nargiso and Davide Sanguinetti. It was only the third match for the Italian partnership and the greater experience of Bjorkman and Kulti, who had won seven out of nine Davis Cup doubles matches, proved too much. The Swedes came through 7–6 6–1 6–3 to secure the Davis Cup trophy.

With Sunday's two dead singles rubbers reduced to the best of three sets, Gustafsson dismissed Gianluca Pozzi 6–4 6–2 before Nargiso won Italy's only rubber by defeating Norman 6–2 6–3 to bring the final tie score to 4–1.

Carl-Axel Hageskog, who has captained Sweden to its last three Davis Cup finals, including their triumph in 1997, said, 'This one isn't nicer, it's just different. We never get satisfied with winning. It's a nice feeling and we want it more and more.

'We have eight players who competed for Sweden this year. That depth, and a unique junior system, is the secret to our success.'

Italy's Davis Cup captain, Paolo Bertolucci, a member of the victorious Italian team that won his country's only Davis Cup title in 1976 was obviously less content. 'Andrea's injury made all our plans go up in smoke,' he said. 'We knew that Sweden were favourites. The boys did all they could. I would have preferred to have had a full team.'

Both Italy and Sweden experienced chequered paths to the 1998 Final. Sweden survived a shaky start against Slovak Republic in Bratislava but became more impressive with each round. At the first hurdle, they were without their two best players, Jonas Bjorkman and Thomas Enqvist, but managed to reverse a 0–2 deficit against the Slovaks. Magnus Norman emerged the hero, defeating the higher ranked Karol Kucera in the fourth singles to set up Gustafsson's crucial win against Dominic Hrbaty in the final singles.

Sweden's next trip was to Hamburg where they overcame a German team, led by Boris Becker, 3–2. It was a potentially tricky tie for the Swedes, but confident play from Bjorkman overcame Nicolas Kiefer in a tough five setter to seal the tie after the fourth rubber. Becker applauded the Swedish team's chemistry while Hageskog commented, 'What warms my heart is that the guys are always there when we need them and are ready to play their guts out to win for the team – and they do this without a second thought.'

In the semi-finals, Sweden met Spain in Stockholm. This much-anticipated tie, contested on an indoor court, unfolded into a rather one-sided affair with the Swedes prevailing 4–1. Bjorkman defeated first Alex Corretja and then Carlos Moya while the fast improving Thomas Johansson made a memorable debut by beating the Roland Garros champion, Moya.

The Italians dropped only two rubbers in three ties en route to Milan. In contrast to Sweden's narrow first round survival, Italy began its Davis Cup campaign with a 4–1 victory over an Indian team without the services of Leander Paes.

Competing in the elite World Group for the first time, Zimbabwe had surprised everybody by ousting Australia in the opening round, a victory which Byron Black said he would treasure for the rest of his life. The result was fortuitous for Italy who, as a result, now faced the Africans on clay at Prato instead of the Australians on grass in Australia. Consequently, Italy lived up to their billing as favourites, beating a Zimbabwean team anchored by the Black brothers 5–0.

After exiting at the semi-final stage for the last two years, Italian hearts must have skipped a beat when this year they drew the 1997 finalists, USA, away in Milwaukee. But with Pete Sampras and Andre Agassi elsewhere, American fortunes rested on Jim Courier, Todd Martin, Jan-Michael Gambill and Justin Gimelstob. The Italians were also blessed with a court that was slower than anticipated, favouring them more than the Americans would have wished. Still, few people would have bet on Italy eliminating USA 4–1. Gaudenzi's win over Gambill was followed by Sanguinetti sweeping aside Martin in straight sets. The Americans' fate was sealed when Martin and Gimelstob lost the doubles to Gaudenzi and Nargiso, leaving US captain, Tom Gullikson in shock, 'To lose 3–0 is something I am sure I didn't dream of and I know the players would never have dreamt that they would be in this position.'

There were surprising results elsewhere in the World Group, not least in the opening round. In addition to Zimbabwe's unexpected victory over Australia, Belgium defeated Netherlands 3–2 thanks to Christophe Van Garsse, who scored the vital point for Belgium by defeating Sjeng Schalken in the final rubber. The United States narrowly survived a difficult first round encounter with a Russian team composed of Yevgeny Kafelnikov and Marat Safin. Courier snatched the vital tie point against Safin in the final rubber and afterwards said, 'To clinch a tie is really a special thing. To do it in the fifth set – whew!' Led by Marc Rosset, Switzerland engineered a surprise victory over Czech Republic in Zurich. The Spanish also narrowly edged through their opening round tie against the Brazilians in Porto Alegre. In the second round, they cruised past the Swiss in a tie which reportedly attracted the third largest crowd at a Davis Cup tie held in Spain.

As first round losers, Australia, Slovak Republic, South Africa, Brazil, Czech Republic, India, Netherlands and Russia joined the winners of the Zonal Groups in the World Group Qualifying Round to compete for places in the1999 World Group. The ties involved several top players including US Open champion Patrick Rafter of Australia, Brazil's Gustavo Kuerten, Tim Henman and Greg Rusedski of Great Britain, Russia's Yevgeny Kafelnikov and Karol Kucera of Slovak Republic.

The winning nations were Australia, Brazil, Czech Republic, France, Netherlands, Russia, Slovak Republic and Great Britain who will compete in the 1999 World Group. The losing nations, Uzbekistan, Romania, South Africa, Israel, Ecuador, Japan, Argentina and India will compete in their respective Regional Zone Groups, division one.

In the Euro/African Zone Group I play-off, Croatia and Austria remain in Group I in 1999, while Norway and Denmark are relegated. In the American Zone Group I play-off, Colombia defeated Mexico and compete in Group I, while Mexico move down to Group II. China defeated Indonesia in the Asia/Oceania Zone Group I play-off and stay in Group I.

In the Euro/African Zone Group II final round, Belarus and Portugal earned promotion to Euro/African Zone Group I while Egypt, Georgia, Luxembourg and Monaco were relegated to Euro/African Zone Group III. Venezuela will compete in the American Zone Group I while Guatemala and Jamaica both drop down to American Zone Group III. In the Asia/Oceania Zone Group II, Pakistan earned promotion to Asia/Oceania Zone Group I. China Hong Kong and Pacific Oceania were relegated to Asia/Oceania Zone Group III.

Next year, the Davis Cup by NEC celebrates a hundred years of competition. The Davis Cup began as a challenge match between the United States and the British Isles, held at the Longwood Cricket Club in Boston, USA. It is particularly fitting that Great Britain will play USA in the opening round of the 1999 Davis Cup – a repeat of that first ever encounter in 1900.

Davis Cup – the First 100 Years

Richard Evans

'How many ages hence, shall this our lofty scene, be acted over, in states unborn and accents yet unknown!'

That was Cassius, through the pen of Williams Shakespeare, but Dwight Davis might have done well to utter similar words when he strode on court to receive the first ball ever struck in what would quickly be termed 'Davis Cup play' at the Longwood Cricket Club in Boston on the 7 August 1900. Ernest Black of the British Isles was serving and, for the first time in history, two nations were competing at international lawn tennis.

It had been Davis's idea to offer a cup – a handsome silver bowl crafted by an English immigrant called Rowland Rhodes – so that those nations capable of raising a team could compete for it every year. It was a bold thought from a man of vision who would go on to hold his own lofty positions of state before being appointed Governor of the Philippines. But even Davis did not envisage his dream expanding to encompass more than 130 nations and staging such unlikely matchups as Iceland v Djibouti; Benin v Azerbaijan; Tajikstan v Brunei and Togo v Liechtenstein. Well might Davis have spoken of states unborn...

The birth of Davis's idea had come during a trip he made out West with some fellow members of the Harvard team in 1899. There had been plenty of time to think adventurous thoughts on the long train journey to California and, on his return, Davis, already a man of means, decided to offer a cup to the USLTA so that they could put it up as a trophy to be played for against Britain or any nation which accepted the challenge.

Despite the fact that R.F. and H. L. Doherty, the leading lights of the British game, were not available to make the sea voyage, W.H. Collins, secretary of the LTA, decided that there were players of sufficient stature available to warrant sending a team. So it was that Arthur Gore, already 32, and Herbert Roper Barrett, a 26-year-old London solicitor, left Euston Station for Liverpool where they were to be joined by the third member of the team, Ernest Black, a 27-year-old Scot, for the ocean crossing.

In contrast, the American team of Davis, Malcolm Whitman and Holcombe Ward were still at Harvard. Although they were missing Bill Larned who was suffering from his experiences as one of Teddy Roosevelt's Rough Riders in Cuba where the United States was at war with Spain, this was a strong and vibrant American team that had been practising a twist serve that leapt and kicked off the grass. The British had never seen anything like it and soon found the conditions almost as awkward.

Black began well against Davis winning the first set but was then outplayed 4–6 6–2 6–4 6–4 and Gore proved no match for the 23-year-old Whitman, going down in straight sets. Davis then ensured that he would not be parting with his Cup by teaming with Ward to beat Black and Roper Barrett 6–4 6–4 6–4.

'I have to laugh to myself,' said Roper Barrett. 'I journeyed 6,000 miles to play thirty games.'

By the time he returned home, the future captain of Fred Perry's triumphant team in the thirties was in no laughing mood. He wrote a stinging report on the tie, including such comments as: 'The ground was abominable. The net was a disgrace to civilised lawn tennis, held up by guy ropes that were continually sagging.'

It was not, however, because of the conditions that the British Isles failed to respond to a renewed challenge in 1901. With the Dohertys still unavailable, there was a reluctance to send another sub-par team. However the brothers decided to make the trip in 1902 and, for the first and only time in Davis Cup history, the public were invited to attend the matches at New York's Bay Ridge Club free of charge. Despite the difficulty of getting there by tram from Manhattan, almost 10,000 showed up over the weekend after the opening day had been interrupted by rain.

Larned, fit again, joined Whitman, Davis and Ward on the American team while Dr Joshua Pim, a former Wimbledon champion, augmented the Doherty brothers. To most people's surprise Pim found himself playing singles after Collins, in his role as captain, had decided to rest Laurie Doherty for the doubles. It was a contentious decision for which Collins was roundly criticised but at least this tie went all the way to the fifth rubber where Whitman secured the Cup by beating Reggie Doherty in straight sets.

The following year, back at Longwood, Captain Collins did something even more extraordinary. Having been told that he could not substitute a singles player once the tie had started, he selected the barely fit R.F. Doherty for the singles and forfeited the opening rubber against Larned in which Reggie should have played. The belief was that Laurie could take care of the surprise American choice, Bob Wren, and the younger Doherty did not disappoint. Then, with a rejuvenated brother at his side, he was able to put the British ahead by beating Bob Wrenn and his brother George in a match that remains unique to this day. Never since have two pairs of brothers opposed each other in a Davis Cup Challenge Round or final.

Played side by side, as the singles were in the early ties, the reverse singles provided untold controversy and drama before Collins was vindicated. Laurie Doherty beat Larned in five sets and Reggie proved himself fit enough to beat Wrenn in five. Dwight's 'little pot', as his Harvard pals called it, was heading overseas.

That, briefly, is how it all began. The British victory stimulated interest and, in 1904, with the USLTA too broke to send a team, Austria, France and Belgium took up the challenge. In the end, Austria couldn't get a team together so the original Worple Road site at Wimbledon staged the very first preliminary round between France and Belgium. William Lemaire de Warzee ensured that Belgium would make its only appearance in the final to date by beating France's first great player, Max Decugis, but the length of his name did not stop the Dohertys and Frank Riseley making short work of his team in the final.

The British held the cup for two more years before Australasia, incorporating the New Zealand Cambridge Blue Anthony Wilding as a partner for the superbly talented left hander Norman Brookes, beat Gore and Roper Barrett 3–2 in 1907. For the next four years, the silver bowl spent much of its time residing in splendour on Mabel Brookes' sideboard at her husband's opulent Melbourne home. Given the distance involved, it was amazing that only in 1910 was the Cup defaulted to Australasia. Sending a team Down Under was not only exorbitantly expensive but required little short of a three-month commitment with a sea voyage from Europe or America lasting six weeks.

The unsung British pair of James Parke and Charles Dixon saved everyone many a seasick day by pulling off a sensational victory at the Albert Ground in Melbourne in 1912 when Wilding's absence was compounded after Brookes lost in four sets to Parke in the opening rubber. Two years later, after the Americans had won at Wimbledon, Wilding re-joined Brookes who had just beaten him at Wimbledon to end his four-year reign as champion. Together they beat the United States at Forest Hills. Wilding's victory over Richard Williams, a survivor of the *Titanic*, was his last. Less than a year later he was killed in Flanders.

Two Anglo Saxon giants and a French quartet dominated Davis Cup tennis between the wars. First Bill Tilden, an American with outrageous talent and an equally outrageous personality, teamed with Bill Johnston to keep France at bay before the multiple talents of the Four Musketeers – Renee Lacoste, Henri Cochet, Jean Borotra and Jacques Brugnon – proved too much. Then, as the sheen dulled on the French swords, Fred Perry, an Englishman with a wit as quick and wicked as his running forehand, leapt onto the world stage to revive British fortunes.

The first shift in power had occurred in 1927 where France were meeting the United States in the Challenge Round for the third successive year. Two years earlier they had been swamped 5–0. But now the Musketeers were ready and, with Lacoste beating Tilden to level the tie at 2–2, it required Cochet to beat a tiring Johnston in the deciding rubber for the Cup to change hands. When Cochet closed it out 6–4 in the fourth, Lacoste vividly described what it meant to his team: 'Madame Cochet feinted; our captain Pierre Gillou sprang up like a child; I took off my coat and sweaters (a rare event indeed for this fastidious man); Brugnon dropped his pipe and Borotra...well, you can imagine how the Bounding Basque lived up to his name. Everything after that seemed like a dream.'

For very strange reasons, the dream threatened to become a nightmare the following year when the French prepared to meet Tilden and his colleagues in an eagerly awaited Challenge Round that was to be played in the barely finished Stade Roland Garros. To their horror, the French were told that Tilden had been stripped of the captaincy of the American team and banned as a player for writing unauthorised articles in the press. The French Federation, arrogant enough to believe that they could win even if Tilden played and logical enough to realise that the 12,000 seats in their expensive new stadium would never be sold if he did not, promptly contacted the French Foreign office and demanded that an official protest be handed to the Amer-

Top: *Wimbledon champions Laurie and Reggie Doherty led the British Isles to victory between1903 and 1906.* (Hulton Getty)

Melbourne left-hander Norman 'The Wizard' Brookes (inset right), with New Zealander Anthony Wilding (above), contributed to Australasia's pre-World War One domination of the competition, which brought four wins in six years. (International Tennis Hall of Fame)

The successful American team of 1925: (l to r) Dick Williams, Vincent Richards, 'Little Bill' Johnston and 'Big Bill' Tilden. (International Tennis Hall of Fame)

ican Ambassador. Seldom in sporting history can a team have objected so strongly to its opposition deliberately weakening itself. The protest reached Washington and, in an effort to defuse a diplomatic incident, the Ambassador was instructed to tell the USLTA to have Tilden re-instated forthwith! The French were happy on two counts – the Musketeers won 4–1 despite Tilden gaining revenge over Lacoste in the opening rubber and the Stade Roland Garros was full. Tilden, of course, was totally unrepentant even though he was banned all over again afterwards. Typically, he signed a new contract to write even more articles.

The strain of wresting the Cup away from the Musketeers could be gauged by the fact that Perry passed out twice in the locker room after securing memorable victories over Cochet and newcomer Andre Merlin at Roland Garros in 1933. The team, coached by Dan Maskell and including Bunny Austin, Pat Hughes and Harry Lee, found a telegram from King George V waiting for them at Dover and held the silver bowl aloft at the train window all the way back to Victoria so that people standing in their back gardens could get a glimpse of the prize.

Not until Perry turned professional did Britain relinquish the trophy. In 1937 Don Budge, the man who a year later would become the first player in history to achieve the Grand Slam, led the United States to victory on the Centre Court at Wimbledon but two years later, with a little-known captain called Harry Hopman sitting in the chair, John Bromwich completed an amazing comeback from 0–2 in Philadelphia by beating Frank Parker in the fifth rubber. So once again Australia were left holding the Cup while the world went to war.

By the time hostilities ended Dwight Davis was dying. Sir Norman Brookes, as he had become, visited the Cup's founder at his home in Washington DC shortly before he died in 1946. 'Don't keep the Cup too long, Norman,' Davis told him. 'It is meant to travel. It's appearance in any country brings a flock of exterior implications very beneficial to sporting unity in the tennis world – and the tennis world is a big world.'

That plea – instantly if inadvertently obeyed when Jack Kramer and Ted Schroeder beat the Australians at Kooyong a few months later – poignantly reflected Davis's vision and aspirations for the competition he had created. His intention had always been for the Cup to increase understanding and harmony between nations and it had been one of his frustrations that so few countries had managed to win it. And that was not about to change. Hopman re-emerged to take control of Australian tennis with an assembly line of superstars and America was blessed

The four French Musketeers who captured the Cup from the Americans in 1927 and defended it successfully for five years on the clay at Roland Garros: (l to r) 'Toto' Brugnon, Henri Cochet, Pierre Gillou (Capt.), Rene Lacoste and Jean Borotra.

with home grown talent in Tony Trabert and Vic Seixas, plus some imported inspiration from Peru in the shape of Alex Olmedo. With both nations staging Challenge Rounds on grass courts on which they excelled, it was hardly surprising that no one else got a look in for the next fifteen years.

By then the teenagers, Lew Hoad and Ken Rosewall, had broken attendance records at Kooyong and White City and the term Davis Cup had become synonymous with Australian sporting excellence. But European nations shared Davis's frustration. The Challenge Round concept, whereby the holders simply had to play one match at home to retain the Cup, effectively blocked out any team whose players were not at their best on grass. When Australia were the holders, which was the case fifteen times between 1946 and 1967, geography dictated the need to play the semi-finals and preliminary final round in Australia. Clay courters were put at an immediate disadvantage.

In the sixties, the silken skills of Ramanathan Krishnan, Rafael Osuna and Nikki Pietrangeli plus Manolo Santana's deadly forehand at least ensured that India, Italy, Mexico and Spain got as far as the Challenge Round. But what chance did they have when faced with Neale Fraser, Rod Laver, Roy Emerson, Fred Stolle or John Newcombe on grass? The answer tells a sorry tale. In six Challenge Rounds (Italy and Spain both appeared in two each) visiting teams managed just one victory in a live rubber – Krishnan and Jaidip Mukerjea beating Newcombe and Tony Roche at Kooyong in 1966.

The Hopman era had to end before Davis's dream started to take shape. With the Challenge Round finally abolished in 1972, Romania did its wily best to become the second non-English speaking nation to hold the Cup when the local Fagin, Ion Tiriac, and his artful dodger Ilie Nastase drove Dennis Ralston's team to distraction in Bucharest in one of the most infamous Davis Cup ties of all time. Thanks to the resilience and determination of Stan Smith, Tom Gorman and Erik Van Dillen, the Americans got out of town with a 3–2 victory.

Sadly, politics decreed who would be the first nation outside the big four to win the trophy – the Indian team being forced by their government to default to South Africa in 1974 as a protest against apartheid.

The following year a supreme young athlete with long blond hair ensured that the Cup would be won legitimately in Stockholm when Bjorn Borg, assisted by Ove Bengtsson, outplayed the Czechs at the Kunglihallen. Borg was never in a winning Cup team again but he spawned a dynasty that would see Sweden, led by the likes of Mats Wilander and Stefan Edberg, win six times more in the eighties and nineties.

A big redhead from Leiman burst onto the scene in 1985, winning Wimbledon at the age of 17 and lighting the fire of German national fervour for its Davis Cup team. Boris Becker has remained an icon but much of his popularity derived from leading his country to two Davis Cup triumphs against Sweden, in Gothenberg in 1988 and again in Stuttgart the following year.

By this time NEC had arrived to take on the much needed role of worldwide sponsor of the Davis Cup. There seems little doubt that they had been encouraged to do so by the unwavering commitment of John McEnroe, who not only had become a notorious world No 1 but had stated time and again: 'I will go anywhere, any time to play Davis Cup for America.'

With other top stars of the day less interested in flying the flag, that was what NEC wanted to hear and their own loyalty to Dwight Davis's far sighted idea since 1981 has helped the competition spread its wings and maintain its reputation as the most brilliantly designed and thrilling of sporting competitions – a reputation that was amply endorsed in Malmo in 1996 when, for the very first time in a final or Challenge Round, the tie was extended to the fifth set of the fifth rubber. After over nine hours of unbearable tension on the final Sunday, Arnaud Boetsch eventually beat Niklas Kulti 10–8 in the fifth to write his name into the annals of French sporting history. It was Yannick Noah's second triumph as captain of France, following the 1991 victory over the United States in Lyon and nothing could have been more fitting than for this most cosmopolitan of men – Camerounian father, French mother, half-Swedish children with a home in New York and a lust for the open sea – to become the Davis Cup's outstanding personality in the tenth decade of its existence. At last the founder's dream was being realised.

Above: *Fred Perry was the mainstay of the British team that won the Cup for four years between 1933 and 1936. His decision to turn pro in 1936 spelt the end of British dominance, despite the heroic efforts of British No. 2, Bunny Austin.* (Allsport/Hulton Deutsch)

Left: *The great Don Budge, leader of the American challenge that swept aside the British in 1937 after Perry's departure to the professional ranks and held sway until Budge himself turned professional in 1938.* (Wimbledon Lawn Tennis Museum)

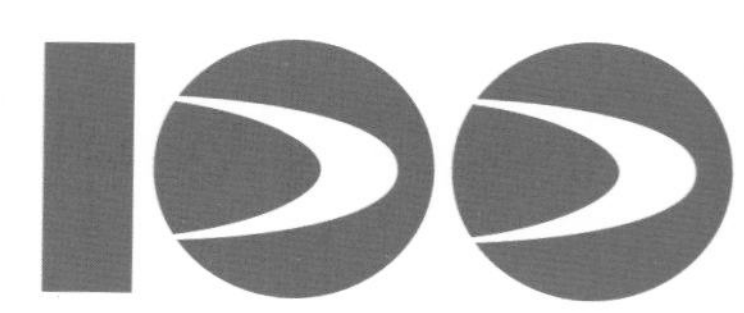

YEARS OF DAVIS CUP®

Right: Walter Pate, the defeated US captain in 1939, is revenged in 1946 when Jack Kramer (left) and Ted Schroeder beat Australia 5–0 at Melbourne's Kooyong Stadium. *(Schroeder Collection)*

Above: President Nixon at Forest Hills with the 1955 US team that lost 5–0 to the same young Australians whom they had defeated so dramatically in Sydney 12 months earlier. (L to R: Australia – Hoad, Fraser, Hartwig, Rosewall, Hopman (Capt.), President Nixon, USA – Talbert (Capt.), Seixas, Shea, Trabert, Richardson. *(Jenny Hoad Collection)*

Right: Ken Rosewall and Lew Hoad, mainstay of Australian teams from 1953 until 1956 when they turned professional and were lost to the competition. *(Gianni Clerici)*

Above: (L to R) The winning US team at Charlotte in 1971, Frank Froehling and Stan Smith, with Ion Tiriac and Ilie Nastase of Romania. *(Russ Adams)*

Left: (L to R) In 1973 Tom Gorman and Stan Smith of the USA were humbled in Cleveland by Australia's John Newcombe and Rod Laver, when the former contract pros were allowed back into the competition. *(Russ Adams)*

Right: Bjorn Borg and Ove Bengtson (right) beat Vladimir Zednik and Jan Kodes in Stockholm en route to the first of Sweden's six Cup wins in 1975. *(Euroverlag)*

Top: Britain's present coach and captain, John Lloyd (left) and brother David, were playing members of the team that reached the final in 1978. *(Michael Cole)*

Above: Captain Nicola Pietrangeli with his Italian team that beat Chile in the 1976 final – Adriano Panatta (second left), Paolo Bertolucci and Corrado Barazzutti. *(Angelo Tonelli)*

Right: John McEnroe in 1978 at the start of a twelve-year Davis Cup career that would earn him 59 wins from 69 matches in 30 ties – a US record. *(Russ Adams)*

Above: The 1980 Czech team that won the Cup for the first time when they beat Italy 4–1 in Prague – ample consolation for their defeat in the 1975 final. *(Euroverlag)*

Right: Arthur Ashe collects the Cup from ITF and FFT President, Philippe Chatrier, in 1982 after America's 4–1 win over France in Grenoble. *(Russ Adams)*

Below: Boris Becker in Gothenburg during West Germany's 4–1 win over Sweden in 1988, the first of their three Davis Cup successes. *(Paul Zimmer)*

Above: Melbourne's Kooyong Stadium, scene of so many Australian Davis Cup triumphs, where Neale Fraser (inset) captained Pat Cash (right) during the 1986 win over Sweden. *(Roger Gould and Ray Giubilo)*

Below: The 1994 Swedish team after their 4–1 win over Russia in Moscow. (L to R) Stefan Edberg, Jonas Bjorkman, John-Anders Sjogren (Capt.), Jan Apell and Magnus Larsson. *(Arne Forsell/Bildbyrån)*

Right: Andrei Chesnokov after beating Michael Stich 14–12 in the fifth set of the deciding rubber as Russia defeat Germany in the 1995 semi-final. *(Clive Mason/Allsport)*

Below: The Germans in Moscow (L to R) Marc Goellner, Boris Becker, Michael Stich, Niki Pilic (Capt.), Bernd Karbacher. *(Paul Zimmer)*

Above: Andre Agassi whose eventful Davis Cup career was temporarily on hold in 1998. *(Russ Adams)*

Left: Despite collapsing after his win against Chesnokov in 1995, Sampras teamed with Todd Martin to win the doubles and then beat Kafelnikov to seal a US victory in Moscow. *(Clive Brunskill/Allsport)*

Right: Stefan Edberg, in his last Davis Cup tie, is hoisted aloft by the victorious French captain Yannick Noah after their 1996 victory over Sweden in Malmo *(Paul Zimmer)*

Below: The moment of victory in Malmo for Arnaud Boetsch whose win over Nicklas Kulti brings the Cup to France for the eighth time. *(Gianni Ciaccia)*

Two South American stars at the start of their Davis Cup careers:

Above: Marcelo Rios of Chile. *(David Leah/Allsport)*

Left: Gustavo Kuerten of Brazil. *(Pascal Rondeau/Allsport)*

1998 DAVIS CUP BY NEC

WORLD GROUP

Seeding: Sweden, Germany, Spain, Czech Republic, Italy, Australia, Netherlands, USA.
FIRST ROUND (3–5 April) – Sweden d. Slovak Republic 3–2, Bratislava SVK: Dominik Hrbaty (SVK) d. Magnus Norman (SWE) 7–6(5) 4–6 6–4 3–6 6–2; Karol Kucera (SVK) d. Mikael Tillstrom (SWE) 1–6 6–1 6–2 6–4; Magnus Larsson/Mikael Tillstrom (SWE) d. Martin Hromec/Jan Kroslak (SVK) 6–2 6–3 6–4; Magnus Norman (SWE) d. Karol Kucera (SVK) 6–3 4–6 6–3 3–6 6–3; Magnus Gustafsson (SWE) d Dominik Hrbaty (SVK) 6–2 5–7 7–5 7–6(4). **Germany d. South Africa 5–0, Bremen GER:** Nicolas Kiefer (GER) d. Grant Stafford (RSA) 4–6 4–6 6–1 6–2 6–2; Tommy Haas (GER) d. Wayne Ferreira (RSA) 7–6(2) 3–6 6–3 6–4; Boris Becker/David Prinosil (GER) d. David Adams/Ellis Ferreira (RSA) 5–7 6–4 6–4 6–3; David Prinosil (GER) d. Wayne Ferreira (RSA) 6–4 6–7(4) 7–6(4); Tommy Haas (GER) d. Grant Stafford (RSA) 6–1 7–6(4). **Spain d. Brazil 3–2, Porto Alegre BRA:** Gustavo Kuerten (BRA) d. Carlos Moya (ESP) 5–7 1–6 6–4 6–4 6–4; Alex Corretja (ESP) d. Fernando Meligeni (BRA) 4–6 6–4 3–6 6–4 6–4; Gustavo Kuerten/Jaime Oncins (BRA) d. Alex Corretja/Javier Sanchez (ESP) 6–1 7–5 3–6 6–2; Alex Corretja (ESP) d. Gustavo Kuerten (BRA) 6–3 7–5 4–6 6–4; Carlos Moya (ESP) d. Fernando Meligeni (BRA) 7–6(4) 6–2 6–2. **Switzerland d. Czech Republic 3–2, Zurich SUI:** Bohdan Ulihrach (CZE) d. Ivo Heuberger (SUI) 6–7(7) 6–0 7–5 6–2; Marc Rosset (SUI) d. Daniel Vacek (CZE) 3–6 6–2 7–6(5) 6–0; Lorenzo Manta/Marc Rosset (SUI) d. Martin Damm/Daniel Vacek (CZE) 6–4 6–7(5) 4–6 6–1 6–4; Marc Rosset (SUI) d. Bohdan Ulihrach (CZE) 6–4 7–5 7–5; Martin Damm (CZE) d. Ivo Heuberger (SUI) 7–6(3) 5–7 7–6(5). **Italy d. India 4–1, Genoa ITA:** Andrea Gaudenzi (ITA) d. Srinath Prahlad (IND) 6–0 6–2 1–6 6–2; Mahesh Bhupathi (IND) d. Davide Sanguinetti (ITA) 6–4 6–4 6–4; Andrea Gaudenzi/Diego Nargiso (ITA) d. Mahesh Bhupathi/Fazaluddin Syed(IND) 6–3 6–4 3–6 6–3; Andrea Gaudenzi (ITA) d. Mahesh Bhupathi (IND) 6–1 7–6(3) 6–1; Davide Sanguinetti (ITA) d. Srinath Prahlad (IND) 6–2 6–3. **Zimbabwe d. Australia 3–2, Mildura AUS:** Jason Stoltenberg (AUS) d. Wayne Black (ZIM) 6–3 6–4 5–7 7–5; Byron Black (ZIM) d. Patrick Rafter (AUS) 3–6 6–3 6–2 7–6(0); Todd Woodbridge/Mark Woodforde (AUS) d. Byron Black/Wayne Black (ZIM) 6–4 7–6(6) 6–2; Wayne Black (ZIM) d. Mark Woodforde (AUS) 6–3 7–5 6–7(3) 6–4; Byron Black (ZIM) d. Jason Stoltenberg (AUS) 6–2 3–6 6–3 6–4. **Belgium d. Netherlands 3–2, Brussels BEL:** Jan Siemerink (NED) d. Johan Van Herck (BEL) 6–4 6–3 4–6 6–1; Filip Dewulf (BEL) d. Sjeng Schalken (NED) 7–5 6–2 7–5: Jacco Eltingh/Jan Siemerink (NED) d. Filip Dewulf/Libor Pimek (BEL) 6–1 6–4 6–4; Filip Dewulf (BEL) d. John Van Lottum (NED) 6–4 6–0 6–4; Christophe Van Garsse (BEL) d. Sjeng Schalken (NED) 6–4 6–4 3–6 3–6 6–3. **USA d. Russia 3–2, Stone Mountain GA, USA:** Yevgeny Kafelnikov (RUS) d. Jim Courier (USA) 6–2 5–7 6–7(2) 6–4 6–4: Andre Agassi (USA) d. Marat Safin (RUS) 6–3 6–3 6–3; Todd Martin/Richey Reneberg (USA) d. Yevgeny Kafelnikov/Marat Safin (RUS) 7–6(3) 6–1 2–6 6–1; Yevgeny Kafelnikov (RUS) d. Andre Agassi (USA) 6–3 6–0 7–6(3); Jim Courier (USA) d. Marat Safin (RUS) 0–6 6–4 4–6 6–1 6–4. **SECOND ROUND (17–19 July) – Sweden d. Germany 3–2, Hamburg GER:** Tommy Haas (GER) d. Jonas Bjorkman (SWE) 6–3 7–6(4) 7–5; Thomas Enqvist (SWE) d. Nicolas Kiefer (GER) 6–3 6–3 7–5; Jonas Bjorkman/Nicklas Kulti (SWE) d. Boris Becker/David Prinosil (GER) 4–6 7–6(5) 7–6(5) 6–4; Jonas Bjorkman (SWE) d. Nicolas Kiefer (GER) 6–3 4–6 6–2 5–7 6–4; Tommy Haas (GER) d. Magnus Larsson (SWE) 6–7(4) 7–5 6–2. **Spain d. Switzerland 4–1, La Coruna ESP:** Carlos Moya (ESP) d. Ivo Heuberger (SUI) 6–1 6–2 6–1; Alex Corretja (ESP) d. Marc Rosset (SUI) 6–1 6–2 6–2; Lorenzo Manta/Marc Rosset (SUI) d. Julian Alonso/Javier Sanchez (ESP) 3–6 6–3 6–4 5–7 6–2; Carlos Moya (ESP) d. Marc Rosset (SUI) 7–5 6–1 7–5; Alex Corretja (ESP) d. George Bastl (SUI) 6–0 7–5. **Italy d. Zimbabwe 5–0, Prato ITA:** Andrea Gaudenzi (ITA) d. Wayne Black (ZIM) 6–3 6–3 6–4; Davide Sanguinetti (ITA) d. Byron Black (ZIM) 6–3 6–3 6–0; Andrea Gaudenzi/Diego Nargiso (ITA) d. Byron Black/Wayne Black (ZIM) 1–6 7–5 7–5 6–3; Diego Nargiso (ITA) d. Genius Chidzikwe (ZIM) 6–0 6–2; Davide Sanguinetti (ITA) d. Wayne Black (ZIM) 6–4 3–6 6–3. **USA d. Belgium 4–1, Indianapolis IN, USA:** Jim Courier (USA) d. Filip Dewulf (BEL) 6–3 7–6(1) 2–6 6–3; Andre Agassi (USA) d. Christophe Van Garsse (BEL) 6–2 6–2 6–2; Jim Courier/Todd Martin (USA) d. Xavier Malisse/Johan Van Herck (BEL) 5–7 6–2 6–7(2) 7–6(5) 6–1; Todd Martin (USA) d. Xavier Malisse (BEL) 7–6(1) 6–3; Christophe Van Garsse (BEL) d. Jim Courier (USA) 3–6 41 ret. **SEMI-FINALS (25–27 September) – Sweden d. Spain 4–1, Stockholm SWE:** Jonas Bjorkman (SWE) d. Alex Corretja (ESP) 6–3 7–5 6–7(5) 6–3; Thomas Johansson (SWE) d. Carlos Moya (ESP) 7–5 7–6(4) 7–6(6); Jonas Bjorkman/Nicklas Kulti (SWE) d. Julian Alonso/Javier Sanchez (ESP) 6–2 6–2 6–2; Jonas Bjorkman (SWE) d. Carlos Moya (SWE) 6–3 7–5; Julian Alonso (ESP) d. Thomas Johansson (SWE) 6–1 7–6(3). **Italy d. USA 4–1, Milwaukee WI, USA:** Andrea Gaudenzi (ITA) d. Jan-Michael Gambill (USA) 6–2 0–6 7–6(0) 7–6(4); Davide Sanguinetti (ITA) d. Todd Martin (USA) 7–6(0) 6–3 7–6(8); Andrea Gaudenzi/Diego Nargiso (ITA) d. Justin Gimelstob/Todd Martin (USA) 6–4 7–6(3) 5–7 2–6 6–3; Gianluca Pozzi (ITA) d. Justin Gimelstob (USA) 7–6(4) 7–5; Jan-Michael Gambill (USA) d. Davide Sanguinetti (ITA) 4–6 6–3 6–3. **FINAL (4–6 December) – Sweden d. Italy 4–1, Milan ITA:** M. Norman (SWE) d. A. Gaudenzi (ITA) 6–7(9) 7–6(0) 4–6 6–3 6–6 ret.; M. Gustafsson (SWE) d. D. Sanguinetti (ITA) 6–1 6–4 6–0; J. Bjorkman/N. Kulti (SWE) d. D. Nargiso/D. Sanguinetti (ITA) 7–6(1) 6–1 6–3; M. Gustafsson (SWE) d. G. Pozzi (ITA) 6–4 6–2; D. Nargiso (ITA) d. M. Norman (SWE) 6–3 6–2.

QUALIFYING ROUND FOR 1999 WORLD GROUP (25–27 September) – Australia d. Uzbekistan 5–0, Townsville AUS: Patrick Rafter (AUS) d. Oleg Ogorodov (UZB) 6–3 6–3 6–4; Jason Stoltenberg (AUS) d. Vadim Kutsenko (UZB) 7–5 6–1 6–0; Todd Woodbridge/Mark Woodforde (AUS) d. Oleg Ogorodov/Dmitri Tomashevich (UZB) 6–3 7–6(3) 7–6(4); Patrick Rafter (AUS) d. Dmitri Tomashevich (UZB) 6–2 6–4; Jason Stoltenberg (AUS) d. Oleg Ogorodov (UZB) 6–3 6–3. **Brazil d. Romania 3–0, Santa Catarina BRA:** Fernando Meligeni (BRA) d. Adrian Voinea (ROM) 6–1 6–4 7–6(3); Gustavo Kuerten (BRA) d. Andrei Pavel (ROM) 7–5 6–3 6–3; Gustavo Kuerten/Jaime Oncins (BRA) d. Andrei Pavel/Gabriel Trifu (ROM) 7–5 6–4 6–4; Gustavo Kuerten (BRA) v Adrian Voinea (ROM) – abandoned due to rain; Fernando Meligeni (BRA) v Andrei Pavel (ROM) – abandoned due to rain. **Czech Republic d. South Africa 5–0, Prague CZE:** Slava Dosedel (CZE) d. Wayne Ferreira (RSA) 6–2 6–3 6–4; Bohdan Ulihrach (CZE) d. Marcos Ondruska (RSA) 6–1 6–2 6–1; Jiri Novak/David Rikl (CZE) d. Wayne Ferreira/Piet Norval (RSA) 6–4 6–2 6–2; Bohdan Ulihrach (CZE) d. David Nainkin (RSA) 6–0 6–1; Slava Dosedel (CZE) d. Piet Norval (RSA) 6–1 6–1. **France d. Israel 4–1, Tel Aviv ISR:** Cedric Pioline (FRA) d. Amir Hadad (ISR) 6–2 6–3 6–3; Guillaume Raoux (FRA) d. Harel Levy (ISR) 7–6(1) 6–2 6–4; Jerome Golmard/Guillaume Raoux (FRA) d. Noam Behr/Eyal Erlich (ISR) 6–1 6–4 6–3; Harel Levy (ISR) d. Cedric Pioline (FRA) 3–6 6–1 6–2; Nicolas Escude (FRA) d. Amir Hadad (ISR) 4–6 6–2 6–1. **Great Britain d. India**

3–2, Nottingham GBR: Greg Rusedski (GBR) d. Leander Paes (IND) 2–6 6–3 3–6 6–2 11-9; Tim Henman (GBR) d. Mahesh Bhupathi (IND) 4–6 6–3 6–3 6–3; Mahesh Bhupathi/Leander Paes (IND) d. Neil Broad/Tim Henman (GBR) 7–6(2) 6–3 7–6(3); Tim Henman (GBR) d. Leander Paes (IND) 7–6(3) 6–2 7–6(5); Mahesh Bhupathi (IND) d. Chris Wilkinson (GBR) 6–3 6–4. **Netherlands d. Ecuador 5–0, Eindhoven NED:** Jan Siemerink (NED) d. Luis Morejon (ECU) 6–3 6–3 6–1; Paul Haarhuis (NED) d. Nicolas Lapentti (ECU) 6–2 6–3 6–2; Jacco Eltingh/Paul Haarhuis (NED) d. Andres Gomez/Nicolas Lapentti (ECU) 5–7 6–1 6–3 6–7(1) 6–4; Jan Siemerink (NED) d. Giovanni Lapentti (ECU) 6–2 6–1; Sjeng Schalken (NED) d. Luis Morejon (ECU) 6–0 6–3. **Russia d. Japan 3–1, Osaka JPN:** Yevgeny Kafelnikov (RUS) d. Gouichi Motomura (JPN) 4–6 6–2 6–3 6–3; Marat Safin (RUS) d. Takao Suzuki (JPN) 7–6(4) 6–2 6–3; Yevgeny Kafelnikov/Marat Safin (RUS) d. Gouichi Motomura/Takao Suzuki (JPN) 7–5 6–3 4–6 6–2; Takao Suzuki (JPN) d. Kirill Ivanov Smolensky (RUS) 6–4 6–4; Gouichi Motomura (JPN) led Alexander Volkov (RUS) 6–3 – abandoned due to rain. **Slovak Republic d. Argentina 3–2, Buenos Aires ARG:** Dominik Hrbaty (SVK) d. Franco Squillari (ARG) 6–3 6–2 6–2; Hernan Gumy (ARG) d. Karol Kucera (SVK) 6–1 6–1 6–4; Lucas Arnold/Luis Lobo (ARG) d. Dominik Hrbaty/Karol Kucera (SVK) 6–3 6–4 6–4; Karol Kucera (SVK) d. Franco Squillari (ARG) 6–3 6–3 3–6 6–7(3) 6–4; Dominik Hrbaty (SVK) d. Hernan Gumy (ARG) 6–2 3–6 6–4 6–2.

The winners of these eight ties qualified for the World Group for the 1999 competition. The losers remained in, or were relegated to, their respective Group I zones for the 1999 competitition.

AMERICAN GROUP I

FIRST ROUND (13–15 February) – Argentina d. Colombia 5–0, Buenos Aires ARG: Lucas Arnold (ARG) d. Mario Rincon (COL) 6–0 6–2 6–2; Franco Squillari (ARG) d. Miguel Tobon (COL) 6–2 6–1 6–1; Lucas Arnold/Luis Lobo (ARG) d. Mario Rincon/Miguel Tobon (COL) 6–2 7–5 6–1; Franco Squillari (ARG) d. Philippe Moggio (COL) 6–1 6–4; Guillermo Canas (ARG) d. Eduardo Rincon (COL) 6–2 7–6(5). **Ecuador d. Bahamas 5–0, Nassau BAH:** Luis Morejon (ECU) d. Mark Knowles (BAH) 6–4 6–0 6–0; Nicolas Lapentti (ECU) d. Roger Smith (BAH) 6–1 6–2 6–2; Andres Gomez/Nicolas Lapentti (ECU) d. John Farrington/Roger Smith (BAH) 6–4 6–0 6–4; Giovanni Lapentti (ECU) d. Bjorn Munroe (BAH) 6–3 7–6(2); Luis Morejon (ECU) d. John Farrington (BAH) 6–2 6–1. **Canada d. Mexico 3–2, Halifax NS CAN:** Alejandro Hernandez (MEX) d. Sebastien Lareau (CAN) 4–6 7–6(4) 6–2 6–1; Daniel Nestor (CAN) d. Luis Herrera (MEX) 6–4 6–7(5) 1–6 6–4 6–3; Sebastien Lareau/Daniel Nestor (CAN) d. Alejandro Hernandez/David Roditi (MEX) 6–1 6–2 6–4; Alejandro Hernandez (MEX) d. Bobby Kokavec (CAN) 6–2 6–0 6–3; Sebastien Lareau (CAN) d. Luis Herrera (MEX) 6–4 6–3 6–3. **SECOND ROUND (3–5 April) – Argentina d. Chile 4–1, Buenos Aires ARG:** Marcelo Rios (CHI) d. Hernan Gumy (ARG) 6–4 3–6 6–3 7–5; Franco Squillari (ARG) d. Hermes Gamonal (CHI) 6–2 6–4 6–2; Lucas Arnold/Luis Lobo (ARG) d. Nicolas Massu/Marcelo Rios (CHI) 7–5 6–3 6–3; Franco Squillari (ARG) d. Fernando Gonzalez (CHI) 6–3 4–6 6–2 6–0; Hernan Gumy (ARG) d. Hermes Gamonal (CHI) 7–5 6–1. **Ecuador d. Canada 3–2, Guayaquil ECU:** Nicolas Lapentti (ECU) d. Sebastien Lareau (CAN) 6–2 6–3 0–6 6–3; Luis Morejon (ECU) d. Daniel Nestor (CAN) 6–2 3–6 7–5 6–2; Sebastien Lareau/Daniel Nestor (CAN) d. Andres Gomez/Nicolas Lapentti (ECU) 4–6 6–4 6–2 6–3; Nicolas Lapentti (ECU) d. Daniel Nestor (CAN) 6–1 7–5 6–2; Jocelyn Robichaud (CAN) d. Giovanni Lapentti (ECU) 6–3 7–6(2).

Argentina and Ecuador were promoted to the World Group Qualifying Round.

RELEGATION FIRST ROUND (17–19 July) – Chile d. Columbia 5–0, Santiago CHI: Marcelo Rios (CHI) d. Philippe Moggio (COL) 6–3 6–0 6–2; Nicolas Massu (CHI) d. Miguel Tobon (COL) 6–2 6–4 6–2; Fernando Gonzalez/Nicolas Massu (CHI) d. Philippe Moggio/Miguel Tobon (COL) 6–7(7) 7–5 7–6(6) 6–4; Marcelo Rios (CHI) d. Miguel Tobon (COL) 6–2 6–2; Nicolas Massu (CHI) d. Jaime Cortes (COL) 6–1 2–0 ret. **Bahamas d. Mexico 3–2, Guadalajara MEX:** Mark Knowles (BAH) d. Luis Herrera (MEX) 6–3 1–6 6–2 6–2; Alejandro Hernandez (MEX) d. Roger Smith (BAH) 6–3 6–1 6–3; Mark Knowles/Roger Smith (BAH) d. David Roditi/Mariano Sanchez (MEX) 7–5 7–6(5) 7–5; Mark Knowles (BAH) d. Alejandro Hernandez (MEX) 4–6 6–3 1–6 6–2 6–1; Mariano Sanchez (MEX) d. Dentry Mortimer (BAH) 6–2 6–0. **RELEGATION FINAL (25–27 September) – Colombia d. Mexico 3–2, Cali COL:** Alejandro Hernandez (MEX) d. Miguel Tobon (COL) 7–6(4) 6–3 6–3; Mauricio Hadad (COL) d. Mariano Sanchez (MEX) 5–7 6–3 6–3 6–4; Mauricio Hadad/Miguel Tobon (COL) d. Marco Osorio/David Roditi (MEX) 7–6(3) 6–4 5–7 6–7(5) 7–5; Mauricio Hadad (COL) d. Alejandro Hernandez (MEX) 6–4 6–3 6–1; Mariano Sanchez (MEX) d. Miguel Tobon (COL) 3–6 6–1 7–5.

Mexico was relegated to American Group II for the 1999 competition.

ASIA/OCEANIA GROUP I

FIRST ROUND (13–15 February) – Uzbekistan d. China P.R. 5–0, Tashkent UZB: Vadim Kutsenko (UZB) d. Yue-Wei Wang (CHN) 6–2 6–2 6–1; Oleg Ogorodov (UZB) d. Yu Zhang (CHN) 6–3 3–6 6–1 6–4; Oleg Ogorodov/Dmitri Tomashevich (UZB) d. Ling Lu/Yu Zheng (CHN) 3–6 7–6(6) 6–4 6–4; Oleg Ogorodov (UZB) d. Lu Zheng (CHN) 6–4 6–4; Vadim Kutsenko (UZB) d. Yu Zhang (CHN) 6–3 3–6 6–0. **Japan d. Indonesia 5–0, Sapporo JPN:** Takao Suzuki (JPN) d. Andrian Raturandang (INA) 6–1 6–4 6–4; Gouichi Motomura (JPN) d. Dede Suhendar Dinata (INA) 6–1 6–3 6–2; Satochi Iwabuchi/Takao Suzuki (JPN) d. Andrian Raturandang/Sulistyo Wibowo (INA) 6–4 7–6(6) 6–3; Gouichi Motomura (JPN) d. Andrian Raturandang (INA) 6–3 6–2; Takao Suzuki (JPN) d. Dede Suhendar Dinata (INA) 6–3 6–4. **New Zealand d. Lebanon 3–2, Beirut LIB:** Alistair Hunt (NZL) d. Ali Hamadeh (LIB) 6–4 6–4 6–4; Jicham Zaatini (LIB) d. James Greenhalgh (NZL) 6–4 6–2 7–5; James Greenhalgh/Alistair Hunt (NZL) d. Ali Hamadeh/Jicham Zaatini (LIB) 6–3 6–4 6–2; Alistair Hunt (NZL) d. Jicham Zaatini (LIB) 7–5 7–6(4) 7–6(8); Ali Hamadeh (LIB) d. James Greenhalgh (NZL) 6–3 6–4. **SECOND ROUND (2–5 April) – Japan d. New Zealand 3–2, Miyazaki City JPN:** Gouichi Motomura (JPN) d. Teo Susnjak (NZL) 6–0 6–0 6–0; Takao Suzuki (JPN) d. Brett Steven (NZL) 7–6(4) 7–6(5) 7–5; James Greenhalgh/Brett Steven (NZL) d. Satoshi Iwabuchi/Takao Suzuki (JPN) 4–6 6–3 6–4 6–3; Brett Steven (NZL) d. Gouichi Motomura (JPN) 3–6 6–2 3–6 6–3 6–4; Takao Suzuki (JPN) d. Teo Susnjak (NZL) 6–4 6–7(5) 6–4 6–1. **Uzbekistan d. Korea 3–1, Seoul KOR:** Vadim Kutsenko (UZB) d. Yong-il Yoon (KOR) 4–6 6–4 6–4 6–2; Hyung-Taik Lee (KOR) d. Oleg Ogorodov (UZB) 7–5 6–2 6–4; Oleg Ogorodov/Dmitri Tomashevich (UZB) d. Dong-Hyun Kim/Hyung-Taik Lee (KOR) 6–2 4–6 6–3 7–6(2); Oleg Ogorodov (UZB) d. Yong-il Yoon (KOR) 6–4 6–7(4) 6–4 7–6(5); Yung-Taik Lee (KOR) v Vadim Kutsenko (UZB) – not played.

Japan and Uzbekistan were promoted to the World Group Qualifying Round.

RELEGATION FIRST ROUND (17–19 July) – Korea d. China 4–1, Seoul KOR: Yong-Il Yoon (KOR) d. Jing-Zhu Yang (CHN) 6–3 6–2 6–0; Hyung-Taik Lee (KOR) d. Yu-Wei Wang (CHN) 6–1 6–2 6–2; Dong-Hyun Kim/Nam-Hoon Kim (KOR) d. Ling Lu/Jing-Zhu Yang (CHN) 6–1 3–6 6–2 3–6 6–2; Yu-Wei Wang (CHN) d. Yong-Il Yoon (KOR) 2–6 6–3 7–6(1); Hyung-Taik Lee (KOR) d. Ling Lu (CHN) 6–4 6–3. **Lebanon d. Indonesia 3–2, Beirut LIB:** Ali Hamadeh (LIB) d. Andrian Raturandang (INA) 7–6(6) 6–3 7–6(5); Jicham Zaatini (LIB) d. Feby Widianto (INA) 6–4 3–6 6–3 6–4; Ali Hamadeh/Jicham Zaatini (LIB) d. Sulistyo Wibowo/Bonit Wiryawan (INA) 7–6(4) 6–4 6–4; Andrian Raturandang (INA) d. Sean Karam (LIB) 6–2 4–6 6–2; Feby Widianto (INA) d. Alex Zakharia (LIB) 6–3 7–5. **RELEGATION FINAL (25–27 September) – China d. Indonesia 5–0, Yanji City CHN:** Yu Zhang (CHN) d. Feby Widianto (INA) 6–1 6–2 4–6 1–6 7–5; Yu Zheng (CHN) d. Andrian Raturandang (INA) 6–3 6–2 6–2; Si Li/Yu Zheng (CHN) d. Sulistyo Wibowo/Bonit Wiryawan (INA) 4–6 7–6(7) 6–4 6–3; Yu Zhang (CHN) d. Andrian Raturandang (INA) 3–6 6–3 6–4; Yu Zheng (CHN) d. Feby Widianto (INA) 6–2 6–1.
Indonesia was relegated to Asia/Oceania Group II for the 1999 competition.

EURO/AFRICAN GROUP I

FIRST ROUND (13–15 February) – Finland d. Croatia 3–2, Helsinki FIN: Ville Liukko (FIN) d. Ivan Ljubicic (CRO) 4–6 6–4 7–5 6–4; Sasa Hirszon (CRO) d. Tuomas Ketola (FIN) 6–4 3–6 6–0 7–6(5); Tuomas Ketola/Ville Liukko (FIN) d. Sasa Hirszon/Ivan Ljubicic (CRO) 6–2 3–6 4–6 6–3 6–4; Tuomas Ketola (FIN) d. Ivan Ljubicic (CRO) 6–3 6–3 6–3; Zelijko Krajan (CRO) d. Ville Liukko (FIN) 7–5 7–6(3). **Ukraine d. Denmark 3–2, Kiev UKR:** Andrei Medvedev (UKR) d. Frederik Fetterlein (DEN) 6–3 6–4 7–5; Kenneth Carlsen (DEN) d. Andrei Rybalko (UKR) 6–2 7–6(4) 6–3; Andrei Medvedev/Dimitri Poliakov (UKR) d. Kenneth Carlsen/Frederik Fetterlein (DEN) 6–3 3–6 6–7(4) 7–6(6) 6–4; Andrei Medvedev (UKR) d. Kenneth Carlsen (DEN) 6–3 6–3 6–3; Frederik Fetterlein (DEN) d. Denis Yakimenko (UKR) 6–2 6–2. **SECOND ROUND (3–5 April) – France d. Finland 4–1, Helsinki FIN:** Guillaume Raoux (FRA) d. Tuomas Ketola (FIN) 6–1 6–1 6–1; Cedric Pioline (FRA) d. Ville Liukko (FIN) 6–3 7–5 7–5; Nicolas Escude/Guillaume Raoux (FRA) d. Tuomas Ketola/Tommi Lenho (FIN) 7–5 4–6 7–6(1) 6–2; Jerome Golmard (FRA) d. Tapio Nurminen (FIN) 7–6(4) 6–4; Tommi Lenho (FIN) d. Guillaume Raoux (FRA) 6–3 6–4. **Romania d. Norway 4–1, Bucharest ROM:** Dinu Pescariu (ROM) d. Jan Frode Andersen (NOR) 7–6(2) 6–4 6–4; Andrei Pavel (ROM) d. Christian Ruud (NOR) 6–2 6–2 6–2; Andrei Pavel/Gabriel Trifu (ROM) d. Lars Hjarrand/Helge Koll (NOR) 6–3 6–2 6–2; Christian Ruud (NOR) d. Dinu Pescariu (ROM) 6–4 4–6 6–4; Andrei Pavel (ROM) d. Jan Frode Andersen (NOR) 6–4 6–4. **Israel d. Austria 4–1, Ramat Hasharon ISR:** Eyal Erlich (ISR) d. Gerald Mandl (AUT) 6–1 7–6(4) 7–5; Amir Hadad (ISR) d. Stefan Koubek (AUT) 7–6(5) 6–4 6–3; Noam Behr/Eyal Erlich(ISR) d. Thomas Buchmayer/Wolfgang Schranz (AUT) 6–4 7–6(3) 4–6 1–6 6–4; Noam Behr (ISR) d. Stefan Koubek (AUT) 7–6(3) 6–1; Wolfgang Schranz (AUT) d Amir Hadad (ISR) 6–4 5–7 6–3. **Great Britain d. Ukraine 5–0, Newcastle GBR:** Greg Rusedski (GBR) d. Andrei Rybalko (UKR) 6–4 6–0 6–4; Tim Henman (GBR) d. Andrei Medvedev (UKR) 6–2 6–7(4) 6–4 1–6 6–1; Tim Henman/Greg Rusedski (GBR) d. Andrei Medvedev/Andrei Rybalko (UKR) 6–4 7–5 7–6(9); Greg Rusedski (GBR) d. Andrei Medvedev (UKR) 6–1 6–4; Tim Henman (GBR) d. Andrei Rybalko (UKR) 6–1 2–6 6–2.
France, Great Britain, Israel and Romania were promoted to the World Group Qualifying Round.
RELEGATION FINAL (25–27 September) – Croatia d. Norway 3–2, Oslo NOR: Christian Ruud (NOR) d. Lovro Zovko (CRO) 7–6(5) 6–4 6–1; Ivan Ljubicic (CRO) d. Jan Frode Andersen (NOR) 6–4 6–4 6–7(5) 6–4; Ivan Ljubicic/Lovro Zovko (CRO) d. Jan Frode Andersen/Christian Ruud (NOR) 6–4 3–6 6–2 3–6 8–6; Ivan Ljubicic (CRO) d. Christian Ruud (NOR) 6–1 6–1 6–3; Jan Frode Andersen (NOR) d. Lovro Zovko (CRO) 6–2 6–3. **Austria d. Denmark 5–0, Portschach AUT:** Markus Hipfl (AUT) d. Kenneth Carlsen (DEN) 6–4 6–0 6–3; Stefan Koubek (AUT) d. Thomas Larsen (DEN) 3–6 3–6 6–4 6–0 6–2; Wolfgang Schranz/Thomas Strengberger (AUT) d. Kenneth Carlsen/Frederik Fetterlein (DEN) 6–3 6–2 6–4; Wolfgang Schranz (AUT) d. Frederik Fetterlein (DEN) 6–3 6–7(3) 6–1; Markus Hipfl (AUT) d. Thomas Larsen (DEN) 6–1 6–3.
Denmark and Norway were relegated to Euro/African Group II for the 1999 competition.

AMERICAN GROUP II

FIRST ROUND (3–5 April) – Venezuela d. Guatemala 4–1, Caracas VEN: Jimy Szymanski (VEN) d. Luiz Perez-Chete (GUA) 6–0 6–3 6–4; Kepler Orellana (VEN) d. Jacobo Chavez (GUA) 6–3 6–3 6–4; Kepler Orellana/Jimy Szymanski (VEN) d. Daniel Chavez/Luis Valencia (GUA) 6–4 6–2 6–2; Jose De Armas (VEN) d. Jacobo Chavez (GUA) 6–2 6–0; Luis Perez-Chete (GUA) d. Ricardo Omana (VEN) 7–6(4) 6–4. **Haiti d. Cuba 3–2, Port-au-Prince HAI:** Ronald Agenor (HAI) d. Armando Perez (CUB) 6–2 6–2 6–0; Lazaro Navarro (CUB) d. Bertrand Madsen (HAI) 7–6(5) 6–7(4) 6–4 4–6 6–3; Lazaro Navarro/Juan Pino (CUB) d. Ronald Agenor/Jerry Joseph (HAI) 6–4 6–3 2–6 6–2; Ronald Agenor (HAI) d. Lazaro Navarro (CUB) 6–2 6–1 6–4; Bertrand Madsen (HAI) d. Armando Perez (CUB) 6–3 4–6 6–2 6–2; **Peru d. Jamaica 5–0, Lima PER:** Luis Horna (PER) d. Jermaine Smith (JAM) 6–1 6–2 7–6(6); Alejandro Aramburu (PER) d. Karl Hale (JAM) 6–4 6–2 3–6 6–3; Luis Horna/Americo Venero (PER) d. Karl Hale/Nicholas Malcolm (JAM) 6–1 6–3 6–3; Alejandro Aramburu (PER) d. Jermaine Smith (JAM) 6–1 6–4; Ivan Miranda (PER) d. Jessi Smatt (JAM) 6–3 6–1. **Uruguay d. Paraguay 3–2, Montevideo URU:** Ramon Delgado (PAR) d. Federico Dondo (URU) 6–0 6–3 6–1; Marcelo Filippini (URU) d. Ricardo Mena (PAR) 6–2 6–1 4–6 6–1; Marcelo Filippini/Gonzalo Rodriguez (URU) d. Ramon Delgado/Ricardo Mena (PAR) 6–3 6–3 1–6 7–6(6); Ramon Delgado (PAR) d Marcelo Filippini (URU) 7–5 3–6 7–5 6–7(2) 6–2; Federico Dondo (URU) d. Ricardo Mena (PAR) 6–7(8) 6–4 6–2 7–6(6). **SECOND ROUND (17–19 July) – Venezuela d. Haiti 3–2, Port-au-Prince HAI:** Ronald Agenor (HAI) d. Keppler Orellana (VEN) 6–2 6–3 7–5; Jimy Szymanski (VEN) d. Bertrand Madsen (HAI) 6–4 6–4 6–1; Keppler Orellana/Jimy Szymanski (VEN) d. Ronald Agenor/Bertrand Madsen (HAI) 6–3 6–4 4–6 6–4; Ronald Agenor (HAI) d. Jimy Szymanski (VEN) 7–5 7–6(4) 3–6 6–0; Keppler Orellana (VEN) d. Bertrand Madsen (HAI) 6–1 6–2 6–2. **Uruguay d. Peru 4–1, Montevideo URU:** Marcelo Filippini (URU) d. Americo Venero (PER) 6–7(1) 7–5 6–3 6–0; Federico Dondo (URU) d. Alejandro Aramburu (PER) 6–4 6–1 7–5; Marcelo Filippini/Gonzalo Rodriguez (URU) d. Ivan Miranda/Americo Venero (PER) 6–3 7–5 6–3; Alejandro Aramburu (PER) d. Alberto Brause (URU) 6–3 ret; Federico Dondo (URU) d. Americo Venero (PER) 6–2 6–4. **FINAL (25–27 September) – Venezuela d. Uruguay 3–2, Montevideo URU:** Marcelo Filippini (URU) d. Kepler Orellana (VEN) 6–2 6–3 7–5; Jimy Szymanski (VEN) d. Federico Dondo (URU) 2–6 7–5 6–4 6–1; Kepler Orellana/Jimy Szymanski

(VEN) d. Marcelo Filippini/Gonzalo Rodriguez (URU) 2–6 2–6 6–2 6–2 6–4; Marcelo Filippini (URU) d. Jimy Szymanski (VEN) 6–3 6–7(2) 6–3 6–3; Kepler Orellana (VEN) d. Federico Dondo (URU) 4–6 6–2 3–6 6–4 6–1.
Venezuela was promoted to American Group I for the 1999 competition.
RELEGATION ROUND (17–19 July) – Cuba d. Guatemala 3–2, Havana CUB: Lazaro Navarro (CUB) d. Alexander Lehnhoff (GUA) 6–1 6–4 6–2; Juan Antonio Pino (CUB) d. Jacobo Chavez (GUA) 6–3 6–3 6–7(5) 1–6 7–5; Lazaro Navarro/Juan Antonio Pino (CUB) d. Daniel Chavez/Luis Valencia (GUA) 6–4 6–4 6–4; Daniel Chavez (GUA) d. Jorge Catala (CUB) 7–6(5) 6–2; Alexander Lehnhoff (GUA) d. Sandor Martinez (CUB) 6–3 6–7(7) 6–1. **Paraguay d. Jamaica 5–0, Asuncion PAR:** Ricardo Mena (PAR) d. Jermaine Smith (JAM) 6–3 6–4 6–4; Ramon Delgado (PAR) d. Karl Hale (JAM) 6–0 6–4 6–2; Ramon Delgado/Ricardo Mena (PAR) d. Karl Hale/Jermaine Smith (JAM) 3–6 6–2 6–2 6–1; Ramon Delgado (PAR) d. Jermaine Smith (JAM) 6–0 6–2; Francisco Rodriguez (PAR) d. Jessie Smatt (JAM) 6–3 6–1.
Guatemala and Jamaica were relegated to American Group III for the 1999 competition.

ASIA/OCEANIA GROUP II

FIRST ROUND (3–5 April) – Thailand d. Philippines 4–1, Manila PHI: Paradorn Srichaphan (THA) d. Adelo Abadia (PHI) 6–1 6–4 1–6 4–6 7–5; Joseph Lizardo (PHI) d. Narathorn Srichaphan (THA) 3–6 6–2 3–6 7–6(2) 6–4; Wittaya Samrej/Danai Udomchoke (THA) d. Robert Angelo/Bryan Juinio (PHI) 1–6 6–4 6–4 6–4; Paradorn Srichaphan (THA) d. Joseph Lizardo (PHI) 6–2 3–6 7–6(5) 6–4; Narathorn Srichaphan (THA) d. Adelo Abadia (PHI) 6–4 2–6 6–4. **Chinese Taipei d. China Hong Kong, 3–2 I-Lan City TPE:** Chia-Yen Tsai (TPE) d. Christopher Lai (HKG) 6–2 6–3 6–3; Melvin Tong (HKG) d. Chih-Jung Chen (TPE) 2–6 6–1 6–4 2–6 8–6; Chih-Jung Chen/Bing-Chao Lin (TPE) d. Christopher Lai/Stephen So (HKG) 6–3 6–1 6–1; Melvin Tong (HKG) d. Chia-Yen Tsai (TPE) 6–7(4) 6–4 6–1 6–0; Chih-Jung Chen (TPE) d. Christopher Lai (HKG) 6–4 6–2 6–0. **Pakistan d. Pacific Oceania 5–0, Islamabad PAK:** Asim Shafik (PAK) d. Lency Tenai (POC) 6–0 6–1 6–0; Mohammad Khaliq (PAK) d. Lawrence Tere (POC) 6–1 7–5 6–1; Mohammad Khaliq/Asam Shafik (PAK) d. Lawrence Tere/Sanjeev Tikaram (POC) 7–5 6–4 6–2; Aqeel Khan (PAK) d. Sanjeev Tikaram (POC) 6–1 6–3; Nasser Shirazi (PAK) d. Lawrence Tere (POC) 6–3 6–4. **(17–19 April) – Iran d. Qatar 5–0, Tehran IRI:** Farhad Tadayon (IRI) d. Mohamed Ali Haji (QAT) 6–3 6–4 6–0; Farshad Talavar (IRI) d. Mubarak Al-Tubaishi (QAT) 6–2 4–6 6–0 6–0; Ramin Raziani/Akbar Taheri (IRI) d. Mohamed Ali Haji/Mohamed Al-Saoud (QAT) 6–3 6–2 6–2; Farshad Talavar (IRI) d. Mohamed Ali Haji (QAT) 6–1 6–2; Farhad Tadayon (IRI) d. Mubarak Al-Tubaishi (QAT) 6–2 6–3. **SECOND ROUND (17–19 July) – Thailand d. Chinese Taipei 3–2, Pattaya City THA:** Paradorn Srichaphan (THA) d. Chih-Jung Chen (TPE) 6–4 6–4 6–2; Wei-Ju Chen (TPE) d. Narathorn Srichaphan (THA) 6–1 7–6(4) 6–1; Wittaya Samrej/Narathorn Srichaphan (THA) d. Chih-Jung Chen/Bing-Chao Lin (TPE) 7–6(6) 3–6 6–3 6–3; Paradorn Srichaphan (THA) d. Wei-Ju Chen (TPE) 6–2 6–3 4–6 2–6 6–1; Chia-Yen Tsai (TPE) d. Narathorn Srichaphan (THA) 7–6(6) 6–2. **Pakistan d. Iran 4–1, Tehran IRI:** Mohammad Khaliq (PAK) d. Farhad Tadayon (IRI) 6–3 6–3 7–6(2); Asim Shafik (PAK) d. Akbar Taheri (IRI) 6–4 6–4 6–4; Mohammad Khaliq/Asim Shafik (PAK) d. Farhad Tadayon/Akbar Taheri (IRI) 6–1 6–4 6–4; Aqeel Khan (PAK) d. Farshad Talavar (IRI) 4–6 6–1 6–4; Shahab-Nafez Hassani (IRI) d. Nasir Sherazi (PAK) 6–3 6–2. **FINAL (25–27 September) – Pakistan d. Thailand 3–2, Lahore PAK:** Aisam Qureshi (PAK) d. Danai Udomchoke (THA) 6–3 6–3 6–3; Paradorn Srichaphan (THA) d. Mohammad Khaliq (PAK) 6–3 6–4 1–6 6–7(6) 10–8; Aisam Qureshi/Mohammad Khaliq (PAK) d. Wittaya Samrej/Narathorn Srichaphan (THA) 6–4 6–3 6–1; Paradorn Srichaphan (THA) d. Aisam Qureshi (PAK) 6–7(5) 7–6(1) 4–6 7–5 12–10; Mohammad Khaliq (PAK) d. Narathorn Srichaphan (THA) 4–6 6–1 6–3 6–2.
Pakistan was promoted to American Group I for the 1999 competition.
RELEGATION ROUND (17–19 July) – Philippines d. China Hong Kong 4–1, Causeway Bay HKG: Joseph Lizardo (PHI) d. John Hui (HKG) 7–6(5) 3–6 3–2 ret; Bryan Juinio (PHI) d. Melvin Tong (HKG) 6–2 4–6 6–3 6–3; Adelo Abadia/Michael John Misa (PHI) d. Shane Barr/Andrew Brothers (HKG) 7–5 7–5 6–4; Melvin Tong (HKG) d. Joseph Lizardo (PHI) 7–5 6–4; Bryan Juinio (PHI) d. Shane Barr (HKG) 6–2 6–2. **Qatar d. Pacific Oceania 4–1, Doha QAT:** Sultan Al-Alawi (QAT) d. Lawrence Tere (POC) 6–4 6–0 6–2; Nasser Al-Khulaifi (QAT) d. Lency Tenai (POC) 6–7(4) 6–4 6–4 6–2; Lency Tenai/Lawrence Tere (POC) d. Sultan Al-Alawi/Nasser Al-Khulaifi (QAT) 6–7(5) 6–3 4–6 7–6(2) 8–6; Sultan Al-Alawi (QAT) d. Lency Tenai (POC) 6–3 6–1 6–2; Nasser Al-Khulaifi (QAT) d. Lawrence Tere (POC) 7–5 6–2.
China Hong Kong and Pacific Oceania were relegated to Asia/Oceania Group III for the 1999 competition.

EURO/AFRICAN GROUP II

FIRST ROUND (1–3 May) – Morocco d. Bulgaria 3–2, Meknes MAR: Karim Alami (MAR) d. Milen Velev (BUL) 7–6(3) 4–6 7–6(2) 6–2; Orlin Stanoytchev (BUL) d. Mehdi Tahiri (MAR) 6–2 2–6 6–3 3–6 6–2; Karim Alami/Mounir El Aarej (MAR) d. Orlin Stanoytchev/Milen Velev (BUL) 6–4 7–5 6–2; Karim Alami (MAR) d. Orlin Stanoytchev (BUL) 3–6 6–3 6–7(5) 6–3 6–1; Milen Velev (BUL) d. Mehdi Tahiri (MAR) 6–2 6–3. **Belarus d. Luxembourg 5–0, Minsk BLR:** Maxim Mirnyi (BLR) d. Adrian Graimprey (LUX) 7–5 6–4 6–4; Alexander Shvec (BLR) d. Sacha Thoma (LUX) 6–1 6–2 6–4; Maxim Mirnyi/Alexander Shvec (BLR) d. Adrian Graimprey/Sacha Thoma (LUX) 6–3 6–2 6–3; Evgeni Mikheev (BLR) d. Roland Theisen (LUX) 6–3 6–2; Maxim Mirnyi (BLR) d. Sacha Thoma (LUX) 7–5 6–3. **Senegal d. Poland 3–2, Dakar SEN:** Jerzy Stasiak (POL) d. Thierno Ly (SEN) 6–3 6–4 6–2; Yahiya Doumbia (SEN) d. Bartlomiej Dabrowski (POL) 6–1 3–6 4–6 7–6(8) 6–3; Yahiya Doumbia/Thierno Ly (SEN) d. Bartlomiej Dabrowski/ Jerzy Stasiak (POL) 6–4 6–7(0) 6–7(4) 6–4 6–4; Yahiya Doumbia (SEN) d. Jerzy Stasiak (POL) 6–2 6–4 3–6 2–6 6–2; Bartlomiej Dabrowski (POL) d. Daouda Senga Ndiaye (SEN) 6–2 6–2. **Cote D'Ivoire d. Egypt 3–2, Abidjan CIV:** Claude N'Goran (CIV) d. Amr Ghoneim (EGY) 6–2 6–1 7–5; Gehad El Deeb (EGY) d. Valentin Sanon (CIV) 6–3 3–6 6–2 5–0 ret; Amr Ghoneim/Karim Maamoun (EGY) d. Claude N'Goran/Nouhoun Sangare (CIV) 7–6(2) 7–6(4) 6–3; Claude N'Goran (CIV) d. Gehad El Deeb (EGY) 6–1 6–4 6–1; Nouhon Sangare (CIV) d. Amr Ghoneim (EGY) 6–7(4) 6–3 6–4 4–6 8–6. **Yugoslavia d. Latvia 3–2, Jurmala LAT:** Andris Filimonovs (LAT) d. Dusan Vemic (YUG) 6–7(7) 7–6(5) 6–4 6–4; Nenad Zimonjic (YUG) d. Girts Dzelde (LAT) 6–0 4–6 6–4 7–5; Dusan Vemic/Nenad Zimonjic (YUG) d. Girts Dzelde/Nils Ivanovs (LAT) 6–4 6–3 6–1; Girts Dzelde (LAT) d. Dusan Vemic (YUG) 6–4 6–3 6–7(8) 1–6 6–2; Nenad Zimonjic (YUG) d. Andris Filimonovs (LAT) 6–3 6–4 6–2. **Portugal d. Georgia 5–0, Braga POR:** Nuno Marques (POR) d. Irakli Kunchulia (GEO) 6–0 6–3 6–2; Joao Cunha-Silva (POR) d. Vladimir Margalitadze (GEO) 6–2 6–3 6–3; Emanuel Couto/Bernardo Mota (POR) d. Vladimir Margalitadze/Givi Samkaradze (GEO) 7–6(3) 6–1 6–3; Nuno Marques (POR) d. Vladimir Margalitadze (GEO) 7–5 6–3; Joao Cunha-Silva (POR) d. Givi Samkharadze (GEO) 6–0 6–3. **Slovenia d. Monaco 5–0,**

Monte Carlo MON: Iztok Bozic (SLO) d. Christophe Bosio (MON) 6–3 6–2 6–2; Borut Urh (SLO) d. Sebastien Graeff (MON) 6–1 6–2 6–3; Andrej Krasevec/Borut Urh (SLO) d. Christophe Bosio/Sebastien Graeff (MON) 6–4 4–6 6–1 6–3; Marc Tkalec (SLO) d. Sebastien Graeff (MON) 6–4 6–2; Andrei Krasevec (SLO) d. Christophe Bosio (MON) 3–6 6–4 6–2; **Hungary d. Ireland 4–1, Budapest HUN:** Norbert Mazany (HUN) d. Scott Barron (IRL) 6–4 0–6 2–6 6–3 9–7; Attila Savolt (HUN) d. John Doran (IRL) 6–1 6–3 6–3; Kornel Bardoczky/Attila Savolt (HUN) d. Owen Casey/Tom Hamilton (IRL) 6–3 6–4 1–6 6–1; Attila Savolt (HUN) d. Scott Barron (IRL) 6–4 6–2; John Doran (IRL) d. Norbert Mazany (HUN) 6–3 3–6 6–3. **SECOND ROUND (17–19 July) – Belarus d. Morocco 3–2, Agadir MAR:** Hicham Arazi (MAR) d. Alexander Shvec (BLR) 6–3 4–6 7–5 6–4; Vladimir Voltchkov (BLR) d. Mounir El Aarej (MAR) 2–6 6–3 6–2 6–4; Maxim Mirnyi/Vladimir Voltchkov (BLR) d. Hicham Arazi/Mounir El Aarej (MAR) 6–7(3) 6–7(5) 7–6(3) 6–3 6–4; Hicham Arazi (MAR) d. Vladimir Voltchkov (BLR) 2–6 6–7(4) 6–3 6–4 6–4; Alexander Shvec (BLR) d. Mounir El Aarej (MAR) 5–7 6–2 3–6 6–4 7–5. **Cote D'Ivoire d. Senegal 3–2, Dakar SEN:** Valentin Sanon (CIV) d. Jean Noel Said (SEN) 6–1 6–1 6–0; Yahiya Doumbia (SEN) d. Claude N'Goran (CIV) 6–4 6–4 6–7(2) 4–6 6–4; Ilou Lonfo/Claude N'Goran (CIV) d. Yahiya Doumbia/Thierno Ly (SEN) 6–4 6–7(9) 6–3 7–6(4); Yahiya Doumbia (SEN) d. Valentin Sanon (CIV) 6–2 6–4 6–3; Claude N'Goran (CIV) d. Thierno Ly (SEN) 6–1 6–4 6–1. **Portugal d. Yugoslavia 3–2, Belgrade YUG:** Dusan Vemic (YUG) d. Joao Cunha-Silva (POR) 7–6(3) 6–3 1–6 6–3; Nuno Marques (POR) d. Nenad Zimonjic (YUG) 3–6 6–0 2–6 6–3 20–18; Emanuel Couto/Joao Cunha-Silva (POR) d. Nebojsa Djordjevic/Dusan Vemic (YUG) 6–7(5) 4–6 7–6(2) 6–2 6–3; Dusan Vemic (YUG) d. Nuno Marques (POR) 3–6 7–6(7) 6–3 6–3; Joao Cunha-Silva (POR) d. Nenad Zimonjic (YUG) 0–6 6–7(2) 6–3 7–5 6–1. **Hungary d. Slovenia 3–2, Budapest HUN:** Attila Savolt (HUN) d. Borut Urh (SLO) 6–2 6–4 6–3; Kornel Bardoczky (HUN) d. Iztok Bozic (SLO) 6–0 6–3 1–6 6–4; Gabor Koves/Attila Savolt (HUN) d. Iztok Bozic/Andrej Kracman (SLO) 6–4 7–5 6–2; Marko Tkalec (SLO) d. Attila Savolt (HUN) 7–5 6–4; Andrej Kracman (SLO) d. Kornel Bardoczky (HUN) 4–6 7–5 6–3. **FINAL (25–27 September) – Belarus d. Cote d'Ivoire 4–1, Abidjan CIV:** Maxim Mirnyi (BLR) d. Valentin Sanon (CIV)6–1 7–6(4) 7–6(6); Vladimir Voltchkov (BLR) d. Claude N'Goran (CIV) 7–5 7–6(6) 7–6(6); Maxim Mirnyi/Vladimir Voltchkov (BLR) d. Ilou Lonfo/Claude N'Goran (CIV) 6–3 6–7(3) 6–3 4–6 7–5; Alexander Shvec (BLR) d. Valentin Sanon (CIV) 7–5 6–4; Claude N'Goran (CIV) d. Evgeni Mikheev (BLR) 6–4 6–1; **Portugal d. Hungary 4–1, Albufeira POR:** Nuno Marques (POR) d. Gergely Kisgyorgy (HUN) 5–7 7–6(4) 6–0 6–3; Joao Cunha-Silva (POR) d. Attila Savolt (HUN) 6–1 6–4 6–3; Emanuel Couto/Nuno Marques (POR) d. Gabor Koves/Attila Savolt (HUN) 0–6 7–6(4) 6–3 2–6 9–7; Nuno Marques (POR) d. Balazs Veress (HUN) 6–3 6–3; Gergely Kisgyorgy (HUN) d. Andre Lopes (POR) 6–3 3–6 6–2.
Belarus and Portugal were promoted to Euro/African Group I for the 1999 competition.

RELEGATION ROUND (17–19 July) – Ireland d. Monaco 5–0, Dublin IRL: John Doran (IRL) d. Christophe Bosio (MON) 6–3 6–3 6–1; Owen Casey (IRL) d. Sebastien Graeff (MON) 6–2 6–3 6–1; Owen Casey/Tom Hamilton (IRL) d. Christophe Boggetti/Sebastien Graeff (MON) 7–6(2) 6–4 6–1; George McGill (IRL) d. Christophe Bosio (MON) 6–3 3–6 7–5; John Doran (IRL) d. Sebastien Graeff (MON) 7–6(1) 6–7(6) 7–6(5). **Latvia d. Georgia 5–0, Jurmala LAT:** Girts Dzelde (LAT) d. Givi Samkaradze (GEO) 6–3 4–6 6–3 6–0; Andris Filimonovs (LAT) d. Irakli Kunchulia (GEO) 6–2 6–3 3–6 6–3; Girts Dzelde/Andris Filimonovs (LAT) d. David Katcharava/Givi Samkaradze (GEO) 6–1 6–3 6–3; Andris Filimonovs (LAT) d. Givi Samkharadze (GEO) 6–3 6–2; Girts Dzelde (LAT) d. Irakli Kunchulia (GEO) 6–3 6–1. **Poland d. Egypt 4–1, Bydgoszcz POL:** Bartlomiej Dabrowski (POL) d. Tamer El Sawy (EGY) 6–2 6–3 6–3; Michal Chmela (POL) d. Amr Ghoneim (EGY) 6–1 6–1 6–4; Michal Chmela/Bartlomiej Dabrowski (POL) d. Tamer El Sawy/Hisham Hemeda (EGY) 6–0 7–6(2) 6–3; Jerzy Stasiak (POL) d. Karim Maamoun (EGY) 5–7 6–2 6–3; Amr Ghoneim (EGY) d. Piotr Szczepanik (POL) 6–4 6–4. **Bulgaria d. Luxembourg 5–0, Sofia BUL:** Milen Velev (BUL) d. Pascal Schaul (LUX) 6–3 6–1 7–5; Orlin Stanoytchev (BUL) d. Mike Scheidweiller (LUX) 6–2 6–2 6–1; Orlin Stanoytchev/Milen Velev (BUL) d. Adrian Graimprey/Pascal Schaul (LUX) 6–3 6–2 6–4; Ivailo Traykov (BUL) d. Pascal Schaul (LUX) 6–3 6–1; Ivo Bratanov (BUL) d. Mike Scheidweiller (LUX) 5–7 6–2 6–2
Egypt, Georgia, Luxembourg and Monaco were relegated to Euro/African Group III for the 1999 competition.

AMERICAN GROUP III

Santa Cruz, Bolivia 29 April–3 May

GROUP A – Antigua/Barbuda, Bolivia, Costa Rica, Puerto Rico.
Bolivia d. Antigua/Barbuda 2–1: Rodrigo Villaroel (BOL) d. Jerry Williams (ANT) 7–6(6) 6–2; Phillip Williamson (ANT) d. Carlos Navarro (BOL) 6–4 6–3; Carlos Navarro/Javier Taborga (BOL) d. Fitroy Anthony/Phillip Williamson (ANT) 5–7 6–4 6–4. **Costa Rica d. Puerto Rico 3–0:** Kenneth Thome (CRC) d. Ernie Fernandez (PUR) 7–5 6–4; Federico Camacho (CRC) d. Luis Haddock (PUR) 6–2 6–4; Rafael Brenes/Kenneth Thome (CRC) d. Ernie Fernandez/Edgardo Rivera (PUR) 6–3 6–4. **Puerto Rico d. Antigua/Barbuda 2–1:** Ernie Fernandez (PUR) d. Fitzroy Anthony (ANT) 6–2 6–1; Phillip Williamson (ANT) d. Luis Haddock (PUR) 6–4 6–1; Ernie Fernandez/Edgardo Rivera (PUR) d. Jerry Williams/Phillip Williamson (ANT) 4–6 7–6(4) 6–3. **Costa Rica d. Bolivia 2–1:** Rafael Brenes (CRC) d. Rodrigo Villaroel (BOL) 6–2 6–4; Jose Antelo (BOL) d. Federico Camacho (CRC) 7–6(2) 6–3; Rafael Brenes/Kenneth Thome (CRC) d. Carlos Navarro/Javier Taborga (BOL) 2–6 6–1 6–4. **Bolivia d. Puerto Rico 3–0:** Jose Antelo (BOL) d. Gilberto Rivera (PUR) 6–2 7–6(5); Carlos Navarro (BOL) d. Luis Haddock (PUR) 6–0 6–1; Javier Taborga/Rodrigo Villarroel (BOL) d. Luis Haddock/Edgardo Rivera (PUR) 6–3 6–2. **Costa Rica d. Antigua/Barbuda 2–1:** Federico Camacho (CRC) d. Jerry Williams (ANT) 6–0 6–0; Phillip Williamson (ANT) d. Fabrizio Golfin (CRC) 6–2 6–2; Rafael Brenes/Kenneth Thome (CRC) d. Fitzroy Anthony/Desney Williams (ANT) 6–4 6–2.

GROUP B – Bermuda, Dominican Republic, El Salvador, Panama.
El Salvador d. Bermuda 2–1: Miguel Merz (ESA) d. James Collieson (BER) 7–5 6–3; Donald Evans (BER) d. Jose Baires (ESA) 6–4 5–7 6–3; Yari Bernardo/Miguel Merz (ESA) d. Ricky Mallory/Michael Way (BER) 6–2 6–4. **Dominican Republic d. Panama 2–1:** Chad Valdez (PAN) d. Sixto Camacho (DOM) 6–3 7–5; Rodrigo Vallejo (DOM) d. Carlos Silva (PAN) 6–4 6–4; Sixto Camacho/Rodrigo Vallejo (DOM) d. Jan Gelabert/Chad Valdez (PAN) 4–6 6–3 6–2. **El Salvador d. Panama 3–0:** Yari Bernardo (ESA) d. Chad Valdez (PAN) 6–4 6–3; Miguel Merz (ESA) d. Carlos Silva (PAN) 7–5 6–2; Jose Baires/Yari Bernardo (ESA) d. Jean Gelabert/Abad Goon (PAN) 6–4 6–7(2) 8–6. **Dominican Republic**

d. Bermuda 2–1: Sixto Camacho (DOM) d. Michael Way (BER) 4–6 6–1 6–3; Rodrigo Vallejo (DOM) d. James Collieson (BER) 6–1 6–0; James Collieson/Donald Evans (BER) d. Victor Estrella/Johnson Garcia (DOM) 4–6 6–3 7–5. **Dominican Republic d. El Salvador 2–1:** Yari Bernardo (ESA) d. Johnson Garcia (DOM) 6–7(4) 6–3 8–6; Rodrigo Vallejo (DOM) d. Manuel Tejada (ESA) 6–2 6–4; Sixto Camacho/Rodrigo Vallejo (DOM) d. Miguel Merz/Manuel Tejada (ESA) 0-30 ret. **Bermuda d. Panama 2–1:** Carlos Silva (PAN) d. James Collieson (BER) 4–6 6–0 6–3; Donald Evans (BER) d. Abad Goon (PAN) 6–3 7–6(2); Ricky Mallory/Michael Way (BER) d. Jean Gelabert/Abad Goon (PAN) 7–5 7–5.

Play-offs for 1st–4th positions: Dominican Republic d. Bolivia 2–0: Johnson Garcia (DOM) d. Jose Antelo (BOL) 2–6 6–4 6–4; Rodrigo Vallejo (DOM) d. Carlos Navarro (BOL) 6–0 7–6(5). **Costa Rica d. El Salvador 2–1:** Miguel Merz (ESA) d. Rafael Brenes (CRC) 6–4 6–2; Kenneth Thome (CRC) d. Jose Baires (ESA) 6–3 6–3; Rafael Brenes/Kenneth Thome (CRC) d. Yari Bernardo/Miguel Merz (ESA) 7–6(4) 6–2. **Final: Dominican Republic d. Costa Rica 2–1:** Johnson Garcia (DOM) d. Rafael Brenes (CRC) 7–6(3) 6–3; Rodrigo Vallejo (DOM) d. Federico Camacho (CRC) 6–2 7–5. Rafael Brenes/Kenneth Thome (CRC) d. Sixto Camacho/Victor Estrella (DOM) 6–4 7–6(3). **Play-off for 3rd/4th positions: El Salvaldor d. Bolivia 3–0:** Yari Bernardo (ESA) d. Javier Taborga (BOL) 7–5 6–4; Jose Baires (ESA) d. Carlos Navarro (BOL) 0–6 6–3 14–12; Jose Baires/Miguel Merz (ESA) d. Javier Taborga/Rodrigo Villaroel (BOL) 5–7 6–2 6–4.

Play-offs for 5th–8th positions: Panama d. Puerto Rico 2–0: Chad Valdez (PAN) d. Ernie Fernandez (PUR) 6–7(6) 6–2 6–4; Carlos Silva (PAN) d. Edgardo Rivera (PUR) 6–0 1–6 10–8. **Antigua/Barbuda d. Bermuda 2–1:** Michael Way (BER) d. Jerry Williams (ANT) 6–2 4–6 6–3; Phillip Williamson (ANT) d. James Collieson (BER) 6–0 6–3; Jerry Williams/Phillip Williamson (ANT) d. Donald Evans/Ricky Mallory (BER) 6–3 6–4. **Final: Panama d. Antigua/Barbuda 2–1:** Chad Valdez (PAN) d. Jerry Williams (ANT) 6–3 6–0; Phillip Williamson (ANT) d. Carlos Silva (PAN) 6–3 6–3; Abad Goon/Chad Valdez (PAN) d. Jerry Williams/Phillip Williamson (ANT) 6–4 6–4. **Play-off for 7th/8th positions: Puerto Rico d. Bermuda 2–1:** Gilberto Rivera (PUR) d. James Collieson (BER) 7–5 2–6 10–8; Luis Haddock (PUR) d. Donald Evans (BER) 6–3 7–6(1); Donald Evans/ Ricky Mallory (BER) d. Luis Haddock/Edgardo Rivera (PUR) 6–3 6–7(6) 6–1.

Final Positions: Dominican Republic 1, Costa Rica 2, El Salvador 3, Bolivia 4, Panama 5, Antigua/Barbuda 6, Puerto Rico 7, Bermuda 8.
Costa Rica and Dominican Republic were promoted to American Group II for the 1999 competition.
Bermuda and Puerto Rico were relegated to American Group IV for the 1999 competition.

ASIA/OCEANIA GROUP III

Kuala Lumpur, Malaysia 15–19 April

GROUP A – Kazakhstan, Singapore, Sri Lanka, Syria.
Syria d. Singapore 2–1: Rabi Bou-Hassoun (SYR) d. Yang-Tat Sherman Lim (SIN) 6–3 6–2; Samir Saad El Din (SYR) d. Ju-Min Adrian Lam (SIN) 6–1 6–2; Jensen Hiu/Leng-Kar Yiu (SIN) d. Lais Salim/Mohamed Jehad Sheet (SYR) 6–2 6–3. **Kazakhstan d. Sri Lanka 3–0:** Pavel Baranov (KAZ) d. Rohan De Silva (SRI) 6–4 6–4; Alexei Kedriouk (KAZ) d. Jayendra Wijeyesekera (SRI) 6–3 6–2; Pavel Baranov/Igor Chaldounov (KAZ) d. Rajeev Rajapakse/Samitha Mahinju Ranaweera (SRI) 6–4 6–4. **Sri Lanka d. Syria 2–1:** Rabi Bou-Hassoun (SYR) d. Rohan De Silva (SRI) 6–3 6–4; Jayendra Wijeyesekera (SRI) d. Samir Saad El Din (SYR) 4–6 6–1 6–0; Rohan De Silva/Jayendra Wijeyesekera (SRI) d. Rabi Bou-Hassoun/Samir Saad El Din (SYR) 5–7 6–2 6–1. **Kazakhstan d. Singapore 3–0:** Pavel Baranov (KAZ) d. Jensen Hiu (SIN) 6–0 5–7 6–4; Alexei Kedriouk (KAZ) d. Yang-Tat Sherman Lim (SIN) 6–3 6–3; Pavel Baranov/Alexei Kedriouk (KAZ) d. Ju-Min Adrian Lam/Yang-Tat Sherman Lim (SIN) 6–2 6–4. **Kazakhstan d. Syria 3–0:** Pavel Baranov (KAZ) d. Rabi Bou-Hassoun (SYR) 7–6(4) 6–2 6–3; Alexei Kedriouk (KAZ) d. Samir Saad El Din SYR) 6–0 6–0; Alexei Kedriouk/Igor Chaldounov (KAZ) d. Lais Salim/Mohamed Jehad Sheet (SYR) 6–2 6–0. **Sri Lanka d. Singapore 3–0:** Rohan De Silva (SRI) d. Yang-Tat Sherman Lim (SIN) 6–1 3–6 6–2; Jayendra Wijeyesekera (SRI) d. Leng-Kar Yiu (SIN) 6–0 6–1; Rajeev Rajapakse/Samitha Mahinju Ranaweera (SRI) d. Jensen Hiu/Len-Kar Yiu (SIN) 6–2 7–5.

GROUP B – Kuwait, Malaysia, Saudi Arabia, Tajikistan.
Malaysia d. Kuwait 2–1: Mohammad Al-Ghareeb (KUW) d. Ramayah Ramachandran (MAS) 4–5 ret; Selvam Veerasingam (MAS) d. Adel Al-Shatti (KUW) 7–5 7–6(1); Vasuthevan Ortchuan/Selvam Veerasingam (MAS) d. Mohammad Al-Ghareeb/Adel Al-Shatti (KUW) 6–1 6–3. **Saudi Arabia d. Tajikistan 2–1:** Bader-Mohamed Al-Megayel (KSA) d. Sergei Makashin (TJK) 6–3 6–2; Mansour Takhjaev (TJK) d. Othman Saleh Al-Anazi (KSA) 6–2 6–3; Othman Al-Anazi/Bader-Mohamed Al-Megayel (KSA) d. Mansour Takhjaev/Bakhrullo Radjabalien (TJK) 6–4 6–0. **Malaysia d. Saudi Arabia 2–1:** Bader-Mohamed Al-Megayel (KSA) d Vasuthevan Ortchuan (MAS) 4–6 6–3 6–2; Selvam Veerasingam (MAS) d. Othman Saleh Al-Anazi (KSA) 6–2 6–4; Vasuthevan Ortchuan/Selvam Veerasingam (MAS) d. Othman Saleh Al-Anazi/Bader-Mohamed Al-Megayel (KSA) 6–4 6–3. **Tajikistan d. Kuwait 2–1:** Mohammad Al-Ghareeb (KUW) d. Sergei Makashin (TJK) 6–3 6–3; Mansour Takhjaev (TJK) d. Adel Al-Shatti (KUW) 6–2 6–3; Sergei Makashin/Mansour Takhjaev (TJK) d. Mohammad Al-Ghareeb/Adel Al-Shatti (KUW) 6–4 6–4. **Tajikistan d. Malaysia 2–1:** Sergei Makashin (TJK) d. Abdul Aziz Shazali (MAS) 6–1 6–1; Mansour Takhjaev (TJK) d. Selvam Veerasingam (MAS) 7–6(6) 7–6(13); Vasuthevan Ortchuan/Selvam Veerasingam (MAS) d. Sergei Makashin/Mansour Takhjaev (TJK) 7–6(2) 6–1. **Saudi Arabia d. Kuwait 2–1:** Bader-Mohamed Al-Megayel (KSA) d. Hussain Al-Ghareeb (KUW) 6–3 4–6 6–2; Mohammad Al-Ghareeb (KUW) d. Othman Saleh Al-Anazi (KSA) 6–3 6–4; Bader-Mohamed Al-Megayel /Fareh Al-Somali (KSA) d. Mohammad Al-Ghareeb/Adel Al-Shatti (KUW) 7–6(4) 6–2.

Play-offs for 1st–4th positions: Kazakhstan d. Tajikistan 3–0: Pavel Baranov (KAZ) d. Sergei Makashin (TJK) 6–2 6–4; Alexei Kedriouk (KAZ) d. Mansoour Takhjaev (TJK) 7–6(2) 6–1; Pavel Baranov/Igor Chaldounov (KAZ) d. Roustam Amonov/Sergei Makashin (TJK) 6–2 6–3. **Sri Lanka d. Malaysia 2–1:** Rohan De Silva (SRI) d. Vasuthevan Ortchuan (MAS) 6–2 6–3; Selvam Veerasingam (MAS) d. Jayendra Wijeyesekera (SRI) 7–5 6–1; Rohand De Silva/Jayendra Wijeyesekera (SRI) d. Ramayah Ramachandran/Selvam Veerasingam (MAS) 0–6 7–5 6–3. **Final: Kazakhstan d. Sri Lanka 3–0:** Pavel Baranov (KAZ) d. Rajeev Rajapakse (SRI) 6–3 6–1; Alexei Kedriouk (KAZ) d. Samitha Mahinju Ranaweera (SRI) 6–3 6–3; Alexei Kedriouk/Igor Chaldounov (KAZ) d. Rajeev Rajapakse/Samitha Mahinju Ranaweera (SRI) 7–5 6–0. **Play-off for 3rd/4th positions: Tajikistan d. Malaysia 3–0:** Sergei Makashin (TJK) d. Abdul Aziz

Shazali (MAS) 6–4 6–1; Mansour Takhjaev (TJK) d. Vasuthevan Ortchuan (MAS) 6–1 6–3; Sergei Makashin/Mansour Takhjaev (TJK) d. Vasuthevan Ortchuan/Abdul Aziz Shazali (MAS) 7–6(4) 6–2.

Play-offs for 5th–8th positions: Syria d. Kuwait 2–1: Rabi Bou-Hassoun (SYR) d. Mohammad Al-Ghareeb (KUW) 6–4 6–4; Samir Saad El Din (SYR) d. Adel Al-Shatti (KUW) 6–3 6–1; Hussain Al-Ghareeb/Ali Hayat (KUW) d. Lais Salim/Mohamed Jehad Sheet (SYR) 7–6(8) 6–3. **Saudi Arabia d. Singapore 2–1:** Bader-Mohamed Al-Megayel (KSA) d. Jensen Hiu (SIN) 6–0 6–2; Yang-Tat Sherman Lim (SIN) d. Othman Saleh Al-Anazi (KSA) 6–3 6–3; Bader-Mohamed Al-Megayel/Fareh Al-Somali (KSA) d. Ju-Min Adrian Lam/Yang-Tat Sherman Lim (SIN) 7–6(3) 6–2. **Final: Syria d. Saudi Arabia 3–0:** Rabi Bou-Hassoun (SYR) d. Fareh Al-Somali (KSA) 6–3 6–2; Sami Saad El Din (SYR) d. Moafa Tawfik (KSA) 6–2 6–0; Lais Salim/Mohamed Jehad Sheet (SYR) d. Fareh Al-Somali/ Moafa Tawfik (KSA) 6–3 6–3. **Play-off for 7th/8th positions: Singapore d. Kuwait 2–1:** Jensen Hiu (SIN) d. Ali Hayat (KUW) 6–2 6–2; Hussain Al-Ghareeb (KUW) d. Leng-Kar Yiu (SIN) 2–6 6–3 6–4; Jensen Hiu/Leng-Kar Yiu (SIN) d. Hussain Al-Ghareeb/Ali Hayat (KUW) 6–4 6–1.

Final Positions: Kazakhstan 1, Sri Lanka 2, Tajikistan 3, Malaysia 4, Syria 5, Saudi Arabia 6, Singapore 7, Kuwait 8.
Kazakhstan and Sri Lanka were promoted to Asia/Oceania Group II for the 1999 competition..
Kuwait and Singapore were relegated to Asia/Oceania Group IV for the 1999 competition.

EURO/AFRICAN GROUP III

ZONE A

Lome, Togo 21–25 January

GROUP A – Ghana, Estonia, Madagascar, Cyprus.
Ghana d. Madagascar 2–1: Isaac Donkor (GHA) d. Harivony Andianafetra (MAD) 6–3 6–3; Frank Ofori (GHA) d. Andriamirija Rajoabelina (MAD) 4–6 7–6(5) 6–3; Jean-Marc Randriamanalina/Germain Rasolondrazana (MAD) d. Gunther Darkey/Tetteh Quaye (GHA) 6–3 7–5. **Estonia d. Cyprus 2–1:** Rene Busch (EST) d. Marianos Baghdatis (CYP) 7–5 2–6 6–3; Demetrios Leondis (CYP) d. Alti Vahkal (EST) 7–6(4) 6–3; Andrei Luzgin/Gert Vilms (EST) d. Demetrios Leondis/Neoklis Neokleous (CYP) 6–4 6–4. **Ghana d. Cyprus 3–0:** Isaac Donkor (GHA) d. Marinos Baghdatis (CYP) 3–6 7–5 6–3; Frank Ofori (GHA) d. George Kalanov (CYP) 6–2 6–2; Gunther Darkey/Tetteh Quaye (GHA) d. Demetrios Leondis/Neoklis Neokleous (CYP) 6–3 6–0. **Estonia d. Madagascar 2–1:** Rene Busch (EST) d. Harivony Andianafetra (MAD) 1–6 6–4 6–4; Andriamirija Rajoabelina (MAD) d. Andrei Luzgin (EST) 3–6 6–4 6–2; Alti Vahkal/Gert Vilms (EST) d. Harivony Andrianafetra/Andriamirija Rajoabelina(MAD) 7–5 7–5. **Estonia d. Ghana 2–1:** Rene Busch (EST) d. Tetteh Quaye (GHA) 5–7 6–2 6–0; Alti Vahkal (EST) d. Gunther Darkey (GHA) 6–3 3–0 ret; Isaac Donkor/Frank Ofori (GHA) d. Andrei Luzgin/Gert Vilms (EST) 6–1 6–2. **Cyprus d. Madagascar 2–1:** Marinos Baghdatis (CYP) d. Germain Rasolondrazana (MAD) 3–6 6–2 6–3; Demetrios Leondis (CYP) d. Jean-Marc Randriamanalina (MAD) 7–6(4) 2–6 6–4; Harivony Andrianafetra/Germain Rasolondrazana (MAD) d. George Kalanov/Neoklis Neokleous (CYP) 6–3 6–1.

GROUP B – Greece, Bosnia/Herzegovina, Kenya, Togo.
Togo d. Bosnia/Herzegovina 2–1: Komi Logo (TOG) d. Merid Zahirovic (BIH) 6–4 6–4; Gerard Gbedey (TOG) d. Kristian Capalik (BIH) 6–2 6–2; Haris Basalik/Capalik (BIH) d. Komi Adeyo/Essenam Loglo (TOG) 6–4 6–3. **Kenya d. Greece 2–1:** Allan Cooper (KEN) d. Nikos Rovas (GRE) 3–6 6–3 6–2; Paul Wekesa (KEN) d. Anastassios Vasiliadis (GRE) 6–4 6–4; Nikos Karagiannis/Anastassios Vasiliadis (GRE) d. Allan Cooper/Norbert Oduor (KEN) 6–4 6–3. **Togo d. Greece 3–0:** Komi Logo (TOG) d. Nikos Rovas (GRE) 4–6 6–3 6–4; Gerard Gbedey (TOG) d. Anastassios Vasiliadis (GRE) 3–6 6–2 6–1; Essenam Loglo/Komi Loglo (TOG) d. Nikos Karagiannis/Yannis Vlachos (GRE) 6–7(7) 6–1 6–4. **Bosnia/Herzegovina d. Kenya 3–0:** Merid Zahirovic (BIH) d. Allan Cooper (KEN) 6–4 6–2; Kristian Capalik (BIH) d. Paul Wekesa (KEN) 6–3 6–3; Haris Basalic/Kristian Capalik (BIH) d. Allan Cooper/Norbert Oduor (KEN) 6–3 6–4. **Greece d. Bosnia/Herzegovina 3–0:** Nikos Rovas (GRE) d. Merid Zahirovic (BIH) 6–1 6–4; Anastassios Vasiliadis (GRE) d. Kristian Capalik (BIH) 6–3 6–2; Nikos Karagiannis/Anastassios Vasiliadis (GRE) d. Haris Basalik/Kristian Capalik (BIH) 6–1 6–4. **Togo d. Kenya 2–1:** Komi Loglo (TOG) d. Allan Cooper (KEN) 6–0 6–4; Gerard Gbedey (TOG) d. Paul Wekesa (KEN) 6–7(5) 1–1 ret; Allan Cooper/Norbert Oduor (KEN) d. Komi Adeyo/Essenam Loglo (TOG) 6–1 7–5.

Play-offs for 1st–4th positions: Togo d. Ghana 3–0: Komi Loglo (TOG) d. Isaac Donkor (GHA) 6–2 7–5; Gerard Gbedey (TOG) d. Frank Ofori (GHA) 6–3 7–6(5); Komi Adeyo/Essenam Loglo (TOG) d. Gunther Darkey/Tetteh Quaye (GHA) 6–1 4–6 6–3. **Greece d. Estonia 3–0:** Nikos Rovas (GRE) d. Alti Vahkal (EST) 7–5 6–2; Anastiassios Vasiliadis (GRE) d. Andrei Luzgin (EST) 6–3 6–4; Nikos Karagiannis/Yannis Vlachos (GRE) d. Rene Busch/Gert Vilms (EST) 6–3 7–5. **Final: Greece d. Togo 2–1:** Komi Loglo (TOG) d. Nikos Rovas (GRE) 7–6(6) 6–4; Anastassios Vasiliadis (GRE) d. Gerard Gbedey (TOG) 7–6(2) 6–3; Nikos Karagiannis/Anastassios Vasiliadis (GRE) d. Essenam Loglo/Komi Loglo (TOG) 7–6(5) 6–4. **Play-off for 3rd/4th positions: Estonia d. Ghana 2–1:** Andrei Luzgin (EST) d. Tetteh Quaye (GHA) 6–3 6–3; Gunther Darkey (GHA) d. Gert Vilms (EST) 7–5 6–1; Andrei Luzgin/Alti Vahkal (EST) d. Isaac Donkor/Frank Ofori (GHA) 6–7(5) 6–3 7–5.

Play-offs for 5th–8th positions: Bosnia/Herzegovina d. Madagascar 2–1: Merid Zahirovic (BIH) d. Jean-Marc Randriamanalina (MAD) 6–2 6–1; Kristian Capalik (BIH) d. Andriamirija Rajoabelina (MAD) 6–1 7–5; Harivony Andrianafetra/Andriamirija Rajoabelina (MAD) d. Haris Basalic/Igor Stjepic (BIH) 7–6(3) 6–3. **Kenya d. Cyprus 3–0:** Norbert Oduor (KEN) d. Marinos Baghdatis (CYP) 4–6 7–6(2) 6–1; Allan Cooper (KEN) d. Demetrios Leondis (CYP) 6–1 6–1; Barry Ndinya/Oduor (KEN) d. George Kalanov/Neoklis Neokleous (CYP) 6–3 6–4. **Final: Bosnia/Herzegovina d. Kenya 3–0:** Merid Zahirovic (BIH) d. Barry Ndinya (KEN) 6–1 6–2; Kritian Capalik (BIH) d. Allan Cooper (KEN) 6–2 6–2; Haris Basalic/Igor Stjepic (BIH) d. Barry Ndinya/Norbert Oduor (KEN) 6–2 6–3. **Play-off for 7th/8th positions: Madagascar d. Cyprus 3–0:** Harivony Andrianafetra (MAD) d. Neoklis Neokleous (CYP) 6–4 6–1; Andriamirija Rajoabelina (MAD) d. George Kalanov (CYP) 7–6(2) 7–5; Jean-Marc Randriamanalina/Germain Rasolondrazana (MAD) d. Marinos Baghdatis/Demetrios Leondis (CYP) 6–3 4–6 6–2.

Final Positions: Greece 1, Togo 2, Estonia 3, Ghana 4, Bosnia/Herzegovina 5, Kenya 6, Madagascar 7, Cyprus 8.
Greece and Togo were promoted to Euro/African Group II for the 1999 competition.
Madagascar and Cyprus were relegated to Euro/African Group IV for the 1999 competition.

ZONE B
Skopje, FYR of Macedonia 20–24 May

GROUP A – Malta, Nigeria, San Marino, Turkey.
Turkey d. San Marino 3–0: Erhan Oral (TUR) d. Cristian Rosti (SMR) 7–6(4) 6–3; Efe Ustundag (TUR) d. Domenico Vicini (SMR) 6–3 4–6 6–3; Mustafa Azkara/Erhal Oral (TUR) d. William Forcellini/Domenico Vicini (SMR) 6–1 6–1. **Nigeria d. Malta 2–1:** Jonathan Igbinovia (NGR) d. Mark Schembri (MLT) 6–2 7–6(5); Sule Ladipo (NGR) d. Christopher Gatt (MLT) 7–5 6–3; Gordon Asiak/Mark Schembri (MLT) d. Ganiyu Adelekan/Yakubu Suleiman (NGR) 6–3 5–7 6–4. **Turkey d. Malta 2–1:** Erhan Oral (TUR) d. Mark Schembri (MLT) 7–5 7–6(6); Christopher Gatt (MLT) d. Efe Ustundag (TUR) 7–6(6) 7–5; Mustafa Azkara/Erhan Oral (TUR) d. Gordon Asciak/Mark Schembri (MLT) 6–4 6–2. **Nigeria d. San Marino 3–0:** Jonathan Igbinovia (NGR) d. Cristian Rosti (SMR) 7–6(4) 1–6 6–3; Sule Ladipo (NGR) d. Domenico Vicini (SMR) 5–7 7–6(4) 6–1; Ganiyu Adelekan/Yakubu Suleiman (NGR) d. Cristian Rosti/Domenico Vicini (SMR) 6–2 6–3. **Malta d. San Marino 2–1:** Gordon Asciak (MLT) d. Cristian Rosti (SMR) 6–2 1–0 ret; Domenico Vicini (SMR) d. Christopher Gatt (MLT) 6–3 7–5; Gordon Asciak/Mark Schembri (MLT) d. William Forcellini/Domenico Vicini (SMR) 6–3 6–3. **Nigeria d. Turkey 3–0:** Jonathan Igbinovia (NGR) d. Mustafa Azkara (TUR) 7–5 6–7(2) 9–7; Sule Ladipo (NGR) d. Erhan Oral (TUR) 3–6 7–5 6–3; Ganyui Adelekan/Yakubu Suleiman (NGR) d. Haluk Akkoyun/Efe Ustundag (TUR) 6–2 6–3.

GROUP B – FYR of Macedonia, Lithuania, Moldova, Tunisia.
FYR of Macedonia d. Tunisia 2–1: Zoran Sevcenko (MKD) d. Selim Baccar (TUN) 6–4 6–1; Oualid Jallali (TUN) d. Ognen Nikolovski (MKD) 6–3 6–4; Lazar Magdincev/Zoran Sevcenko (MKD) d. Selim Baccar/Oualid Jallali (TUN) 6–2 6–3. **Moldova d. Lithuania 2–1:** Iuri Gorban (MDA) d. Aistis Slajus (LTU) 6–0 6–3; Rolandos Murashka (LTU) d. Evgueni Plougarev (MDA) 6–2 6–4; Iuri Gorban/Evgueni Plougarev (MDA) d. Rolandos Murashka/Tomas Petrouskas (LTU) 4–6 6–3 9–7. **FYR of Macedonia d. Moldova 2–1:** Zoran Sevcenko (MKD) d. Iuri Gorban (MDA) 6–4 6–4; Evgueni Plougarev (MDA) d. Dragan Jovanovski (MDA) 6–4 7–6(5); Lazar Magdincev/Zoran Sevcenko (MKD) d. Iuri Gorban/Evgueni Plougarev (MDA) 6–2 6–1. **Lithuania d. Tunisia 3–0:** Aistis Slajus (LTU) d. Selim Baccar (TUN) 6–4 6–3; Rolandos Murashka (LTU) d. Oualid Jallali (TUN) 6–3 6–0; Rolandos Murashka/Aistis Slajus (LTU) d. Aref Jallali/Issam Jallali (TUN) 6–2 6–1. **Lithuania d. FYR of Macedonia 2–1:** Zoran Sevcenko(MKD) d. Aistis Slajus (LTU) 6–2 6–4; Rolandos Murashka (LTU) d. Lazar Magdincev (MKD) 7–6(4) 6–3; Rolandos Murashka/Aistis Slajus (LTU) d. Lazar Magdincev/Zoran Sevcenko (MKD) 3–6 7–5 8–6. **Moldova d. Tunisia 2–1:** Iuri Gorban (MDA) d. Issam Jallali (TUN) 6–1 6–0; Oualid Jallali (TUN) d. Evgueni Plougarev (MDA) 7–5 6–4; Victor Ribas/Oleg Sinic (MDA) d. Issam Jallali/Oualid Jallali (TUN) 7–5 6–3.

Play-offs for 1st–4th positions: FYR of Macedonia d. Nigeria 2–1: Zoran Sevcenko (MKD) d. Jonathan Igbinovia (NGR) 6–1 6–4; Sule Ladipo (NGR) d. Lazar Magdincev (MKD) 6–2 6–4; Lazar Magdincev/Zoran Sevcenko (MKD) d. Sule Ladipo/Yakubu Suleiman (NGR) 6–7(4) 7–6(1) 6–4. **Turkey d. Lithuania 2–1:** Erhan Oral (TUR) d. Aistis Slajus (LTU) 6–0 6–0; Rolandos Murashka (LTU) d. Efe Ustundag (TUR) 6–3 6–1; Mustafa Azkara/Erhan Oral (TUR) d. Rolandos Murashka/Aistis Slajus (LTU) 6–3 6–4. **Final: Turkey d. FYR of Macedonia 3–0:** Erhan Oral (TUR) d. Dragan Jovanovski (MKD) 6–0 6–1; Efe Ustundag (TUR) d. Ognen Nikolovski (MKD) 6–1 6–2; Mustafa Azkara/Erhan Oral (TUR) d. Lazar Magdincev/Zoran Sevcenko (MKD) 7–6(4) 7–6(4). **Play-off for 3rd/4th positions: Lithuania d. Nigeria 2–1:** Tomas Petrouskas (LTU) d. Yakubu Suleiman (NGR) 3–1 ret; Jonathan Igbinovia (NGR) d. Aistis Slajus (LTU) 6–7(5) 6–4 6–1; Rolandos Murashka/Tomas Petrouskas (LTU) d. Ganiyu Adelekan/Jonathan Igbinovia (NGR) 7–6(4) 6–4.

Play-offs for 5th–8th positions: Tunisia d. Malta 2–1: Gordon Asciak (MLT) d. Issam Jallali (TUN) 6–2 6–4; Oualid Jallali (TUN) d. Christopher Gatt (MLT) 7–6(3) 6–4; Issam Jallali/Oualid Jallali (TUN) d. Gordon Asciak/Mark Schembri (MLT) 6–4 7–6(4). **Moldova d. San Marino 2–1:** Iuri Gorban (MDA) d. William Forcellini (SMR) 6–2 6–0; Domenico Vicini (SMR) d. Evgueni Plougarev (MDA) 6–3 6–7(5) 7–5; Victor Ribas/Oleg Sinic (MDA) d. Cristian Rosti/Domenico Vicini (SMR) 6–3 6–4. **Final: Tunisia d. Moldova 2–1:** Iuri Gorban (MDA) d. Issam Jallali (TUN) 6–2 7–5; Oualid Jallali (TUN) d. Evgueni Plougarev (MDA) 6–3 1–6 6–2; Issam Jallali/Oualid Jallali (TUN) d. Victor Ribas/Oleg Sinic (MDA) 6–4 7–6(7). **Play-off for 7th/8th positions: San Marino d. Malta 2–1:** Mark Schembri (MLT) d. William Forcellini (SMR) 6–3 6–1; Domenico Vicini (SMR) d. Marco Cappello (MLT) 6–3 7–5; Cristian Rosti/Domenico Vicini (SMR) d. Gordon Asciak/Mark Schembri (MLT) 7–6(5) 6–2.

Final Positions: Turkey 1, FYR of Macedonia 2, Lithuania 3, Nigeria 4, Tunisia 5, Moldova 6, San Marino 7, Malta 8.
FYR of Macedonia and Turkey were promoted to Euro/African Group II for the 1999 competition.
Malta and San Marino were relegated to Euro/African Group IV for the 1999 competition.

AMERICAN GROUP IV
St Lucia 23–29 March
Nations: Barbados, Honduras, Netherlands Antilles, OECS, St Lucia, Trinidad & Tobago, US Virgin Islands.
Honduras d. Barbados 2–1: Calton Alvarez (HON) d. James Betts (BAR) 3–6 6–2 6–3; Carlos Caceres (HON) d. Duane Williams (BAR) 6–2 6–2; Bernard Frost/Kodi Lewis (BAR) d. Carlos Caceres/Franklin Garcia (HON) 3–6 6–4 7–5. **US Virgin Islands d. Trinidad & Tobago 3–0:** Wilbur Callender Jr (ISV) d. Ronald Greaves (TRI) 7–6(3) 6–2; Eugene Highfield (ISV) d. Floyd Williams (TRI) 6–1 6–2; Eugene Highfield/Morris Brown (ISV) d. Brian Khan/Stephen George (TRI) 6–3 6–2. **Netherlands Antilles d. OECS 3–0:** Jean Julien Rojer (AHO) d. Nigel Liverpool (ECA) 6–3 7–6(5); Elmar Gerth (AHO) d. Kirsten Cable (ECA) 6–1 6–0; Elmar Gerth/Kevin Jonckheer (AHO) d. Nigel Liverpool/Peter Nanton

(ECA) 6–2 6–1. **St Lucia d. OECS 2–1:** Vernon Lewis (LCA) d. Nigel Liverpool (ECA) 6–1 6–2; Henri Sinson (LCA) d. Kirsten Cable (ECA) 6–1 6–3; Haydon Ashton/Kirsten Cable (ECA) d. Kane Easter/Glynne James (LCA) 3–6 7–5 6–4. **Netherlands Antilles d. US Virgin Islands 3–0:** Jean Julien Rojer (AHO) d. Wilbur Callender Jr (ISV) 6–3 7–5; Elmar Gerth (AHO) d. Eugene Highfield (ISV) 6–4 6–2; Elmar Gerth/Kevin Jonckheer (AHO) d. Morris Brown/George Lewis (ISV) 6–0 6–3. **Honduras d. Trinidad & Tobago 2–1:** Carlton Alvarez (HON) d. Brian Khan (TRI) 6–4 6–0; Carlos Caceres (HON) d. Stephen George (TRI) 6–0 6–3; Brian Khan/Floyd Williams (TRI) d. Carlos Caceres/Franklin Garcia (HON) 6–3 6–4. **St Lucia d. US Virgin Islands 3–0:** Kane Easter (LCA) d. Morris Brown (ISV) 6–4 7–5; Vernon Lewis (LCA) d. Eugene Highfield (ISV) 6–1 6–4; Glynne James/Henri Sinson (LCA) d. Wilbur Callender Jr/George Lewis (ISV) 6–3 6–2. **Netherlands Antilles d. Barbados 3–0:** Jean Julien Rojer (AHO) d. James Betts (BAR) 6–0 7–5; Elmar Gerth (AHO) d. Duane Williams (BAR) 6–0 6–1; Elmar Gerth/Kevin Jonckheer (AHO) d. Bernard Frost/Kodi Lewis (BAR) 6–1 6–3. **Trinidad & Tobago d. OECS 3–0:** Brian Khan (TRI) d. Nigel Liverpool (ECA) 6–3 6–2; Ronald Greaves (TRI) d. Hayden Ashton (ECA) 6–1 6–0; Brian Khan/Floyd Williams (TRI) d. Nigel Liverpool/Peter Nanton (ECA) 6–4 7–5. **Trinidad & Tobago d. St Lucia 2–1:** Ronald Greaves (TRI) d. Vernon Lewis (LCA) 7–5 6–0; Henri Sinson (LCA) d. Floyd Williams (TRI) 6–4 7–5; Ronald Greaves/Brian Khan (TRI) d. Glynne James/Henri Sinson (LCA) 6–2 6–2. **Honduras d. US Virgin Islands 2–1:** Calton Alvarez (HON) d. Wilbur Callender Jr (ISV) 6–3 1–6 6–2; Carlos Caceres (HON) d. Eugene Highfield (ISV) 6–4 7–6(3); Wilbur Callender Jr/George Lewis (ISV) d. Franklin Garcia/Humberto Rodriguez (HON) 7–6(2) 7–5. **Barbados d. OECS 2–1:** Kodi Lewis (BAR) d. Nigel Liverpool (ECA) 4–6 6–3 6–2; Bernard Frost (BAR) d. Kirsten Cable (ECA) 6–3 6–4; Haydon Ashton/Kirsten Cable (ECA) d. James Betts/Duane Williams (BAR) 3–6 6–3 6–4. **Honduras d. St Lucia 2–1:** Calton Alvarez (HON) d. Kane Easter (LCA) 6–4 7–6(4); Carlos Caceres (HON) d. Vernon Lewis (LCA) 6–1 6–4; Kane Easter/Henri Sinson (LCA) d. Calton Alvarez/Franklin Garcia (HON) 6–1 6–4. **Barbados d. US Virgin Islands 2–1:** James Betts (BAR) d. Wilbur Callender Jr (ISV) 7–6(4) 7–5; Eugene Highfield (ISV) d. Duane Williams (BAR) 6–0 6–2; James Betts/Bernard Frost (BAR) d. Eugene Highfield/George Lewis (ISV) 6–3 6–4. **Netherlands Antilles d. Trinidad & Tobago 3–0:** Jean Julien Rojer (AHO) d. Brian Khan (TRI) 6–2 6–2; Elmar Gerth (AHO) d. Ronald Greaves (TRI) 6–4 6–4; Elmar Gerth/Kevin Jonckheer (AHO) d. Ronald Greaves/Brian Khan (TRI) 6–0 6–2. **St Lucia d. Barbados 2–1:** Kane Easter (LCA) d. James Betts (BAR) 6–3 6–3; Henri Sinson (LCA) d. Bernard Frost (BAR) 6–3 6–3; Bernard Frost/Kodi Lewis (BAR) d. Glynne James/Vernon Lewis (LCA) 3–6 7–6(5) 6–4. **Netherlands Antilles d. Honduras 2–1:** Calton Alvarez (HON) d. Jean Julien Rojer (AHO) 7–6(2) 6–1; Elmar Gerth (AHO) d. Carlos Caceres (HON) 6–3 6–2; Elmar Gerth/Kevin Jonckheer (AHO) d. Calton Alvarez/Carlos Caceres (HON) 6–1 6–7(5) 6–1. **US Virgin Islands d. OECS 2–1:** Wilbur Callendar Jr (ISV) d. Kirsten Cable (ECA) 6–4 6–3; Eugene Highfield (ISV) d. Hayden Ashton (ECA) 6–1 6–4; Hayden Ashton/Kirsten Cable (ECA) d. Wilbur Callender Jr/Eugene Highfield (ISV) 6–4 3–6 10–8. **Netherlands Antilles d. St Lucia 2–1:** Vernon Lewis (LCA) d. Jean Julien Rojer (AHO) 3–6 6–1 6–2; Elmar Gerth (AHO) d. Henri Sinson (LCA) 6–2 6–2; Raul Behr/Elmar Gerth (AHO) d. Vernon Lewis/Henri Sinson (LCA) 6–3 7–5. **Trinidad & Tobago d. Barbados 2–1:** Brian Khan (TRI) d. Kodi Lewis (BAR) 6–2 6–0; Ronald Greaves (TRI) d. Bernard Frost (BAR) 6–2 4–6 7–5; James Betts/Duane Williams (BAR) d. Stephen George/Floyd Williams (TRI) 6–3 6–7(4) 6–4. **Honduras d. OECS 2–1:** Calton Alvarez (HON) d. Kirsten Cable (ECA) 6–0 6–3; Carlos Caceres (HON) d. Haydon Ashton (ECA) 6–1 2–0 ret; Kirsten Cable/Nigel Liverpool (ECA) d. Calton Alvarez/Franklin Garcia (HON) 4–6 6–3 6–3.

Final Positions: Netherlands Antilles 1, Honduras 2, Trinidad & Tobago 3, St Lucia 4, Barbados 5, US Virgin Islands 6, OECS 7.
Netherlands Antilles and Honduras were promoted to American Group III for the 1999 competition.

ASIA/OCEANIA GROUP IV

Dhaka, Bangladesh 9–15 February
Nations: Bangladesh, Oman, Bahrain, UAE, Iraq, Brunei, Jordan.
Bangladesh d. Oman 2–1: Mudrik-Nadhim Al-Rawahi (OMA) d. Dilip Passia (BAN) 7–5 3–6 6–2; Shibu Lal (BAN) d. Khalid Al-Nabhani (OMA) 6–1 6–0; Shibu Lal/Moin-ud-din Walliullah (BAN) d. Khalid Al-Nabhani/Mudrik-Nadhim Al-Rawahi (OMA) 6–3 6–2. **Iraq d. Brunei 3–0:** Mohamad Ibrahim (IRQ) d. Aki Ismasufian Bin Pj Haji Ibrahim (BRU) 6–3 6–1; Saddam Hussain Kadhim (IRQ) d. Tony Shim (BRU) 6–0 6–1; Saddam Hussain Kadhim/Hussein Ahmed Rashid (IRQ) d. Aki Ismasufian Bing Pg Haji Ibrahim/Latif Isa (BRU) 6–4 6–2. **Bahrain d. UAE 3–0:** Essam-Jaafar Ali Abdul-Aal (BRN) d. Mahmoud Nader Al-Baloushi (UAE) 6–1 6–0; Abdul-Latif Ahmed (BRN) d. Othman Al-Ulama (UAE) 6–3 6–1; Mohamed Jasim Sanad Ahmed/Abdul-Latif Ahmed (BRN) d. Mahmoud Nader Al-Baloushi/Mohammed Jamal Buschager (UAE) 6–1 6–0. **Bahrain d. Oman 3–0:** Essam-Jaafar Ali Abdul- Aal (BRN) d. Mazin Al-Shaibani (OMA) 6–0 6–0; Abdul-Latif Ahmed (BRN) d. Mudrik-Nadhim Al-Rawahi (OMA) 6–1 3–6 6–4; Essam Jaafar Ali Abdul-Aal/Mohamed Jasim Sanad Ahmed (BRN) d. Khalid Al-Nabhani/Barkat-Salim Al-Sharji 6–3 6–2. **Bangladesh d. UAE 3–0:** Dilip Passia (BAN) d. Mahmoud Nader Al-Baloushi (UAE) 6–2 6–3; Shibu Lal (BAN) d. Othman Al-Ulama (UAE) 6–0 6–1; Muammer Husain Khan/Moin-ud-din Walliullah (BAN) d. Mahmoud Nader Al-Baloushi/Mohammed-Saeed Al-Marri (UAE) 6–3 6–2. **Jordan d. Brunei 3–0:** Fares Azzouni (JOR) d. Aki Ismasufian Bin Pj Haji Ibrahim (BRU) 6–2 3–6 11–9; Ahmed Al-Hadid (JOR) d. Tony Shim (BRU) 6–0 6–0; Fares Azzouni/Laith Azzouni (JOR) d. Aki Ismasufian Bin Pj Hj Ibrahim/Latif Isa (BRU) 6–4 6–2. **Bangladesh d. Jordan 2–1:** Dilip Passia (BAN) d. Fares Azzouni (JOR) 6–0 6–3; Laith Azzouni (JOR) d. Shibu Lal (BAN) 3–6 6–3 6–2; Shibu Lal/Moin-ud-din Walliullah (BAN) d. Fares Azzouni/Laith Azzouni (JOR) 2–6 6–2 6–3. **Bahrain d. Iraq 2–1:** Essam-Jaafar Ali Abdul-Aal (BRN) d. Haider Hussain Kadhim (IRQ) 6–1 6–2; Abdul-Latif Ahmed (BRN) d. Saddam Hussain Kadhim (IRQ) 6–1 2–6 6–2; Saddan Hussain Kadhim/Hussein Ahmed Rashid (IRQ) d. Mohamed Jasim Sanad Ahmed/Essam-Jaafar Ali Abdul-Aal (BRN) 7–6(2) 6–7(3) 7–5. **UAE d. Brunei 2–1:** Aki Ismasufian Bin Pj Haji Ibrahim (BRU) d. Mohammed Jamal Buschager (UAE) 6–3 6–2; Mahmoud Nader Al-Baloushi (UAE) d. Chua Pheng How (BRU) 6–0 7–5; Mahmoud Nader Al-Baloushi/Mohammed-Saeed Al-Marri (UAE) d. Aki Ismasufian Bin Pj Haji Ibrahim/Latif Isa (BRU) 7–5 7–6(6). **Jordan d. Oman 2–1:** Mudrik-Nadhim Al-Rawahi (OMA) d. Ahmed Al-Hadid (JOR) 6–1 6–2; Laith Azzouni (JOR) d. Khalid Al-Nabhani (OMA) 6–1 6–4; Fares Azzouni/Laith Azzouni (JOR) d. Khalid Al-Nabhani/Mudrik-Nadhim Al-Rawahi (OMA) 6–4 6–0. **Bahrain d. Brunei 3–0:** Essam-Jaafar Ali Abdul-Aal (BRN) d. Chua Pheng How (BRU) 6–0 6–0; Abdul-Latif Ahmed (BRN) d. Tony Shim (BRU) 6–0 6–0; Bader-Jaafar Ali Abdul-Aal/Mohamed Jasim Sanad Ahmed (BRN) d. Aki

Ismasufian Bin Pj Haji Ibrahim/Latif Isa (BRU) 7–6(4) 7–5. **Iraq d. UAE 3–0:** Mohamad Ibrahim (IRQ) d. Mahmoud Nader Al-Baloushi (UAE) 6–1 6–1; Saddam Hussain Kadhim (IRQ) d. Othman Al-Ulama (UAE) 6–0 6–2; Saddam Hussain Kadhim/Husein Ahmed Rashid (IRQ) d. Othman Al-Ulama/Mohammed Jamal Buschager (UAE) 6–1 6–0. **Bangladesh d. Brunei 3–0:** Dilip Passia (BAN) d. Aki Ismasufian Bin Pj Haji Ibrahim (BRU) 6–4 6–4; Shibu Lal (BAN) d. Chua Pheng How (BRU) 6–0 6–0; Shibu Lal/Moin-ud-din Walliullah (BAN) d. Chua Phen How/Latif Isa (BRU) 6–4 6–0. **Iraq d. Oman 2–1:** Husein Ahmed Rashid (IRQ) d. Barkat-Salim Al-Sharji (OMA) 6–0 6–0; Mudrik-Nadhim Al-Rawahi (OMA) d. Mohamed Ibrahim (IRQ) 6–4 6–4; Saddam Hussain Kadhim/Husein Ahmed Rashid (IRQ) d. Khalid Al-Nabhani/Mudrik-Nadhim Al-Rawahi (OMA) 7–5 7–5. **Jordan d. UAE 3–0:** Ahmed Al-Hadid (JOR) d. Mahmoud Nader Al-Baloushi (UAE) 6–7(2) 6–2 6–1; Laith Azzouni (JOR) d. Othman Al-Ulama (UAE) 6–0 6–1; Fares Azzouni/Laith Azzouni (JOR) d. Mahmoud Nader Al-Baloushi/Mohammed-Saeed Al-Marri (UAE) 6–4 6–3. **Bangladesh d. Iraq 3–0:** Dilip Passia (BAN) d. Mohamed Ibrahim (IRQ) 1–6 6–3 6–2; Shibu Lal (BAN) d. Saddam Hussain Kadhim (IRQ) 6–3 1–6 6–4; Muammer Husain Khan/Moin-uid-din Walliullah (BAN) d. Haider Hussain Kadhim/Husein Ahmed Rashid (IRQ) 6–2 2–6 6–2. **Bahrain d. Jordan 2–1:** Essam-Jaafar Ali Abdul-Aal (BRN) d. Ahmed Al-Hadid (JOR) 6–1 6–1; Laith Azzouni (JOR) d. Abdul-Latif Ahmed (BRN) 6–4 6–4; Essam-Jaafar Ali Abdul-aal/Mohamed Jasim Sanad Ahmed (BRN) d. Fares Azzouni/Laith Azzouni (JOR) 6–2 6–3. **Oman d. Brunei 2–1:** Mudrik-Nadhim Al-Rawahi (OMA) d. Latif Isa (BRU) 6–1 6–0; Khalid Al-Nabhani (OMA) d. Aki Ismasufian Bin Pj Haji Ibrahim (BRU) 6–2 6–2; Aki Ismasufian Bin Pj Haji Ibrahim/Latif Isa (BRU) d. Khalid Al-Nabhani/Mudrik-Nadhim Al-Rawahi (OMA) 7–6(3) 7–5. **Bahrain d. Bangladesh 2–1:** Essam-Jaafar Ali Abdul-aal (BRN) d. Muammer Husain Khan (BAN) 6–3 6–2; Dilip Passia (BAN) d. Abdul-Latif Ahmed (BRN)1–6 6–3 6–4; Essam-Jaafar Ali Abdul-aal/Mohamed Jasim Sanad Ahmed (BRN) d. Muammer Hussain Khan/Moin-ud-din Walliullah (BAN) 3–6 6–3 6–3. **Iraq d. Jordan 3–0:** Husein Ahmed Rashid (IRQ) d. Fares Azzouni (JOR) 2–6 6–3 7–5; Saddam Hussain Kadhim (IRQ) d. Ahmed Al-Hadid (JOR) 6–2 7–5; Haider Hussain Kadhim/Husein Ahmed Rashid (IRQ) d. Laith Azzouni/Yazid Saoud Ahmad Nsairat (JOR) 1–2 (40-0) ret. **Oman d. UAE 2–1:** Mudrik-Nadhim Al-Rawahi (OMA) d. Mahmoud Nader Al-Baloushi (UAE) 6–3 6–2; Othman Al-Ulama (UAE) d. Khalid Al-Nabhani (OMA) 6–1 6–3; Khalid Al-Nabhani/Mudrik-Nadhim Al-Rawahi (OMA) d. Mahmoud Nader Al-Baloushi/Othman Al-Ulama (UAE) 7–5 6–7(5) 3–2 ret.

Final positions: Bahrain 1, Bangladesh 2, Iraq 3, Jordan 4, Oman 5, UAE 6, Brunei 7.
Bahrain and Bangladesh were promoted to Asia/Oceania Group III for the 1999 competition.

EURO/AFRICAN GROUP IV

ZONE A

Kampala, Uganda 28 January–1 February

GROUP A – Armenia, Benin, Uganda, Djibouti.
Armenia d. Uganda 2–1: Tsolak Gevorgyan (ARM) d. Charles Yokwe (UGA) 6–0 6–0; Sargius Sargsian (ARM) d. John Oduke (UGA) 6–2 6–4; John Oduke/Renato Sebbi (UGA) d. Davit Babayan/Haik Hakobyan (ARM) 6–1 6–3. **Benin d. Djibouti 3–0:** Sourou Gandonou (BEN) d. Abdou-Rahman Omar (DJI) 6–1 6–0; Christophe Pognon (BEN) d. Omar Awad Mohammed (DJI) 6–0 6–0; Jean-Marie Da Silva/Alphonse Gandonou (BEN) d. Ali Aden/Kadar Mohamed (DJI) 6–0 6–1. **Armenia d. Djibouti 2–0:** Tsolak Gevorgyan (ARM) d. Ali Aden (DJI) 6–0 6–0; Sargius Sargsian (ARM) d. Abdou-Rahman Omar (DJI) 6–0 6–0; Doubles not played due to bad weather. **Benin d. Uganda 2–0:** Sourou Gandonou (BEN) d. Renato Sebbi (UGA) 6–1 6–2; Christophe Pognon (BEN) d. John Oduke (UGA) 4–6 6–2 6–3; Doubles – not played due to bad weather. **Armenia d. Benin 2–1:** Tsolak Gevorgyan (ARM) d. Sourou Gandonou (BEN) 5–7 7–6(4) 6–2; Sargius Sargsian (ARM) d. Christophe Pognon (BEN) 6–0 6–2; Jean-Marie Da Silva/Alphonse Gandonou (BEN) d. Davit Babayan/Haik Hakobyan (ARM) 6–3 6–4. **Uganda d. Djibouti 3–0:** Robert Buyinza (UGA) d. Kadar Mohamed (DJI) 6–0 6–2; John Oduke (UGA) d. Ali Aden (DJI) 6–0 6–0; Renato Sebbi/Charles Yokwe (UGA) d. Omar-Awad Mohammed/Abdou-Rahman Omar (DJI) 6–0 6–4.

GROUP B – Botswana, Cameroun, Azerbaijan, Sudan.
Botswana d. Azerbaijan 3–0: Michael Judd (BOT) d. Dmitri Zaraubin (AZE) 6–2 6–3; Petrus Molefhe (BOT) d. Igor Borisov (AZE) 6–2 6–4; Michael Judd/Thato Kgosimore (BOT) d. Raouf Eyvazov/Eldar Kafarov (AZE) 6–3 6–2. **Cameroun d. Sudan 3–0:** Michel Ekwe (CMR) d. Mandour Abdalla (SUD) 7–6(7) 6–7(6) 1–2 1–0; Abel Lobe Tabi (CMR) d. Nour El Din Gaafar (SUD) 7–5 6–3; Maurice Fomete/Simplice Neng (CMR) d. Mogeeb Abdalla/Asim-Omer El Agraa (SUD) 6–4 6–2. **Botswana d. Sudan 2–0:** Thato Kgosimore (BOT) d. Mandour Abdalla (SUD) 4–6 7–6(5) 6–2; Petrus Molefhe (BOT) d. Nour El Din Gaafar (SUD) 6–0 6–2; Doubles – not played due to bad weather. **Cameroun d. Azerbaijan 2–0:** Michel Ekwe (CMR) d. Dmitri Zaraubin (AZE) 7–5 6–4; Abel Lobe Tabi (CMR) d. Igor Borisov (AZE) 6–4 3–6 6–3; Doubles – not played due to bad weather. **Cameroun d. Botswana 2–1:** Michel Ekwe (CMR) d. Michael Judd (BOT) 7–5 6–4; Petrus Molefhe (BOT) d. Abel Lobe Tabi (CMR) 7–6(3) 3–6 6–2; Michel Ekwe/Maurice Fomete (CMR) d. Michael Judd/Thato Kgosimore (BOT) 6–4 6–4. **Azerbaijan d. Sudan 2–1:** Raouf Eyvazov (AZE) d. Asim-Omer Abdul-Rahma El Agraa (SUD) 6–2 5–7 6–4; Mandour Abdalla (SUD) d. Dmitri Zaraubin (AZE) 6–3 7–6(2); Igor Borisov/Raouf Eyvazov (ARM) d. Mandour Abdalla/Mogeeb Abdalla (SUD) 7–6(6) 6–2.

Play-offs for 1st–4th positions: Armenia d. Botswana 2–1: Tsolak Gevorgyan (ARM) d. Michael Judd (BOT) 6–2 6–2; Sargius Sargsian (ARM) d. Petrus Molefhe (BOT) 6–2 6–3; Michael Judd/Thato Kgosimore (BOT) d. Davit Babayan/Haik Hakobyan (ARM) 4–6 7–5 8–6. **Benin d. Cameroun 2–1:** Sourou Gandonou (BEN) d. Simplice Neng (CMR) 6–3 1–0 ret. Christophe Pognon (BEN) d. Michel Ekwe (CMR) 7–6(7) 6–2; Maurice Fomete/Abel Lobi Tabi (CMR) d. Alphonse Gandonou/Sourou Gandonou (BEN) 1–6 6–2 6–2. **Final: Armenia d. Benin 3–0:** w/o. **Play-off for 3rd/4th positions: Botswana d. Cameroun 3–0:** Thato Kgosimore (BOT) d. Michel Ekwe (CMR) 6–3 6–3: Petrus Molefhe (BOT) d. Maurice Fomete (CMR) 6–1 6–4; Michael Judd/Thato Kgosimore (BOT) d. Maurice Fomete/Abel Lobe Tabi (CMR) 6–3 6–2.

Play-offs for 5th–8th positions: Uganda d. Sudan 3–0: Robert Buyinza (UGA) d. Asim-Omer El Agraa (SUD) 6–1 6–4; John Oduke (UGA) d. Nour El Din Gaafar (SUD) 6–0 6–0; Robert Buyinza/Renato Sebbi (UGA) d. Mogeeb Abdalla/Nour El Din Gaafar (SUD) 7–6(6) 5–7 8–6. **Azerbaijan d. Djibouti 3–0:** Eldar Kafarov (AZE) d. Kadar

Mohamed (DJI) 6–4 6–1; Raouf Eyvazov (AZE) d. Ali Aden (DJI) 6–1 6–0; Eldar Kafarov/Raouf Eyvazov (AZE) d. Kadar Mohamed/Abdou-Rahman Omar (DJI) 6–1 6–1. **Final: Uganda d. Azerbaijan 2–1:** Dmitri Zaraubin (AZE) d. Robert Buyinza (UGA) 6–3 6–2; John Oduke (UGA) d. Igor Borisov (AZE) 7–5 5–7 6–4; John Oduke/Renato Sebbi (UGA) d. Raouf Eyvazov/Dmitri Zaraubin (AZE) 6–3 6–4. **Play-off for 7th/8th positions: Sudan d. Djibouti 3–0:** Mandour Abdalla (SUD) d. Abdou-Rahman Omar (DJI) 6–0 6–0; Nour El Din Gaafar (SUD) d. Omar-Awad Mohammed (DJI) 6–1 6–0; Mogeeb Abdalla/Omar-Awad Mohammed (SUD) d. Ali Aden/Kadar Mohamed (DJI) 6–0 6–0.

Final Positions: Armenia 1, Benin 2, Botswana 3, Cameroun 4, Uganda 5, Azerbaijan 6, Sudan 7, Djibouti 8.
Armenia and Benin were promoted to Euro/African Group III for the 1999 competition.

ZONE B
Ndola, Zambia 4–10 May

Nations: Algeria, Ethiopia, Iceland, Liechtenstein, Zambia.
Zambia d. Ethiopia 3–0: Sidney Bwalya (ZAM) d. Yohannes Setegne (ETH) 6–3 6–3; Lighton Ndefway (ZAM) d. Samuel Gabriel (ETH) 3–6 6–1 6–2; Kachinga Sinkala/Dermot Sweeney (ZAM) d. Asfawe Michaile/Yohannes Setegne (ETH) 6–2 6–2. **Algeria d. Liechtenstein 3–0:** Nourredine Mahmoudi (ALG) d. Jurgen Tomordy (LIE) 7–6(3) 4–6 6–3; Abdelhak Hameurlaine (ALG) d. Stephan Ritter (LIE) 3–6 6–1 8–6 Sid Ali Akkal/Nourredine Mahmoudi (ALG) d. Frank Heeb/Rainer Kovac (LIE) 6–3 2–6 6–1. **Ethiopia d. Liechtenstein 2–1:** Yohannes Setegne (ETH) d. Jurgen Tomordy (LIE) 6–3 6–3; Stephan Ritter (LIE) d. Samuel Gabriel (ETH) 6–4 6–2; Asfawe Michaile/Yohannes Setegne (ETH) d. Rainer Kovac/Stephan Ritter (LIE) 6–3 1–6 6–4. **Zambia d. Iceland 3–0:** Dermot Sweeney (ZAM) d. Einar-Axel Sigurgeirsson (ISL) 4–6 6–3 6–4; Lighton Ndefway (ZAM) d. Raj Bonifacius (ISL) 6–4 6–2; Kachinga Sinkala/Dermot Sweeney (ZAM) d. Gunnar Einarsson/David Halldorsson (ISL) 4–6 6–3 6–2. **Algeria d. Ethiopia 2–1:** Mohamed Mahmoudi (ALG) d. Yohannes Setegne (ETH) 3–6 6–1 6–4; Abdelhak Hameurlaine (ALG) d. Samuel Gabriel (ETH) 6–2 6–1; Asfawe Michaile/Yohannes Setegne (ETH) d. Sid Ali Akkal/Nourredine Mahmoudi (ALG) 5–7 6–4 6–2. **Iceland d. Liechtenstein 2–1:** Einar-Axel Sigurgeirsson (ISL) d. Jurgen Tomordy (LIE) 6–0 6–1; Stephan Ritter (ISL) d. Raj Bonifacius (ISL) 6–2 4–6 6–1; Gunnar Einarsson/David Halldorsson (ISL) d. Rainer Kovac/Stephan Ritter (LIE) 7–6(4) 4–6 8–6. **Zambia d. Liechtenstein 3–0:** Sidney Bwalya (ZAM) d. Frank Heeb (LIE) 6–1 6–0; Dermot Sweeney (ZAM) d. Stephan Ritter (LIE) 6–4 6–3; Sidney Bwalya/Kachinga Sinkala (ZAM) d. Frank Heeb/Rainer Kovac (LIE) 6–2 7–6(0). **Algeria d. Iceland 3–0:** Nourredine Mahmoudi (ALG) d. Gunnar Einarsson (ISL) 7–5 4–6 6–1; Abdelhak Hameurlaine (ALG) d. Einar-Axel Sigurgeirsson (LIE) 6–7(6) 6–0 6–4; Abdelhak Hameurlaine/Mohamed Mahmoudi (ALG) d. Raj Bonifacius/David Halldorsson (ISL) 6–2 6–4. **Zambia d. Algeria 2–1:** Sidney Bwalya (ZAM) d. Mohamed Mahmoudi (ALG) 6–3 6–2; Abdelhak Hameurlaine (ALG) d. Kachinga Sinkala (ZAM) 1–6 6–3 6–4; Sidney Bwalya/Lighton Ndefway (ZAM) d. Abdelhak Hameurlaine/Mourredine Mahmoudi (ALG) 6–4 6–3. **Ethiopia d. Iceland 2–1:** Yohannes Setegne (ETH) d. Gunnar Einarsson (ISL) 6–3 7–6(1); Einar-Axel Sigurgeirsson (ISL) d Samuel Gabriel (ETH) 6–1 6–1; Asfawe Michaile/Yohannes Setegne (ETH) d. Raj Bonifacius/Einar-Axel Sigurgeirsson (ISL) 2–6 6–3 6–4.

Final Positions: Zambia 1, Algeria 2, Ethiopia 3, Iceland 4, Liechtenstein 5.
Algeria and Zambia were promoted to Euro/African Group III for the 1999 competition.

WORLD GROUP 1999 (16 nations)

	1st Round 2–4 April	2nd Round 16–18 July	Semi-finals 24–26 September	Final 3–5 December	Winner
1	SWEDEN C				
2	Slovak Republic				
3	GERMANY C				
4	Russia				
5	USA				
6	Great Britain C				
7	AUSTRALIA				
8	Zimbabwe C				
9	Netherlands				
10	FRANCE C				
11	Brazil				
12	SPAIN C				
13	Belgium C				
14	CZECH REPUBLIC				
15	Switzerland C				
16	ITALY				

Seeded nations in capital letters. C = choice of ground

Above: *Spain, the most successful of modern Fed Cup nations, celebrate their fifth 1990's win in Geneva: (l to r) Arantxa Sanchez-Vicario, Magui Serna, Virginia Ruano-Pascual, Conchita Martinez and Miguel Margets (capt.).* (Paul Zimmer)

Below: *Despite the presence of world No.1 Martina Hingis – and home advantage – the Swiss lost the deciding doubles and with it the chance of a first Fed Cup success: (l to r) Patty Schnyder, Emanuelle Gagliardi, Melanie Molitor (capt.) and Martina Hingis.* (Paul Zimmer)

KB Fed Cup

Wendy Kewley

The 1998 KB Fed Cup Final was a triumph of experience over youth when the renowned Spanish force of Conchita Martinez and Arantxa Sanchez-Vicario defeated the Swiss teenagers, Martina Hingis and Patty Schnyder 3–2 in Geneva. Sanchez-Vicario and Martinez had brought their country all five of its Fed Cup titles but their 1998 victory probably ranks as the best win of all, thought Sanchez-Vicario. 'We played one of the best teams and worked so hard to get the victory. Viva España!' said the jubilant victor.

There had been an atmosphere of high expectation in the days leading up to the September Final and tickets were sold out weeks before the tie. With the world No. 1 Martina Hingis participating alongside Patty Schnyder, plus Martinez and Arantxa Sanchez-Vicario, the Fed Cup Final was showcasing four of the top ten players in the world. The Swiss were also supported by Emmanuelle Gagliardi while Virginia Ruano-Pascual and Magui Serna completed the Spanish line-up. Sanchez-Vicario and Martinez had the benefit of 21 years of Fed Cup competition between them while Hingis and Schnyder had five. Would the new wave be capable of ousting the old guard? This was also the first time that the Swiss had reached the Fed Cup Final, further fuelling their determination to win the rose bowl trophy before their home crowd in Geneva.

On Saturday morning the Palexpo arena was buzzing with over 12,000 Swiss fans and hundreds of Spanish whose vocal support more than compensated for the difference in numbers. The spectators also included IOC President His Excellency Juan Antonio Samaranch who was attending as a special guest of ITF President Brian Tobin.

The first match featured Sanchez-Vicario against Schnyder. Three months previously, the Spaniard had won her first Grand Slam since 1994 at Roland Garros, and was still on form. Schnyder was also confident, having won five titles in 1998 which had swept her into the top ten for the first time. At one set all, the Spaniard began to exploit her opponent's increasing fatigue and she quickly secured the third set and the match. Next on court was 17-year-old Hingis, already with four Grand Slam titles to her name. She had defeated Martinez in straight sets at the Australian Open in January and at Indian Wells in March and this meeting was no different. Hingis coolly levelled the tie by winning 6–4 6–4.

On Sunday, the crowds convened to see the key encounter of the weekend between the two No. 1 players, Hingis and Sanchez-Vicario. Both athletes rose to the occasion resulting in two sets of exceptionally spectacular tennis. Hingis had won seven of their eight previous meetings and once again her skilful play gave her the edge over Sanchez Vicario, winning 7–6 6–3. The Swiss fans were ecstatic: 2–1 to Switzerland with just two matches to go.

The pressure was now on Spain as Martinez emerged to face Schnyder, knowing that only victory would suffice. The former Wimbledon champion began positively and secured the first set 6–3. Encouraged by the screams of the home fans, Schnyder seized the initiative and the second set, 6–2. The third set demanded grit and was closely fought until, at 8–7, Martinez finally broke Schnyder's serve to battle through 6–3 2–6 9–7 after three hours, 18 minutes. Two matches all.

The Spaniards were on the comeback trail. Forty-five minutes later, Hingis and Schnyder took on Sanchez-Vicario and Martinez in the deciding doubles. It was the first Fed Cup Final to go to the wire since Sanchez-Vicario and Martinez had narrowly defeated the USA in 1991. After winning their last seven Fed Cup doubles, the Spaniards were confident. Hitting everything at the tired Schnyder to bypass the sharper Hingis, Sanchez-Vicario and Martinez gave Spain a straightforward 6–0 6–2 win and, more significantly, a fifth Fed Cup title.

The Spanish victory was particularly welcome given that they nearly did not make the Final at all. In the first round, without an injured Sanchez-Vicario, they had struggled to defeat Germany away at Saarbrucken. Although a lacklustre Martinez had dropped both her singles, Magui Serna saved the tie by defeating first Andrea Glass and then Jana Kandarr. Spain's semi-final tie against traditional rivals the United States in Madrid, was also tough but produced one of the most memorable Fed Cup ties ever. In the deciding doubles, Martinez and Sanchez-

Vicario narrowly overcame Mary Joe Fernandez and Lisa Raymond 11–9 in the third set of a gripping three hour, 40 minute marathon. 'It was the most incredible Fed Cup match I've ever played,' said Sanchez-Vicario afterwards. 'We finished at 1.30 in the morning but the most amazing thing was the crowd who stayed there until the end, waiting for us to celebrate the victory and they were behind us all the time – and I think that makes the Fed Cup more special.' The United States Fed Cup captain, Billie Jean King, echoed those sentiments, adding, 'It's a great day for tennis and for Fed Cup.'

In contrast, Switzerland's route to the Final was a less rocky affair. Any fears that the Swiss harboured about meeting a Czech team led by the Wimbledon champion Jana Novotna in the first round were allayed when they won 4–1. In the semi-final, the Swiss faced the 1997 Fed Cup champion nation, France – a tie which attracted capacity crowds to the picturesque Alpine stadium at Sion. Despite brilliant play from former ITF Junior World Champion Amelie Mauresmo, who stretched both Hingis and Schnyder to three sets, the Swiss eventually came through 5–0. 'It's the first time I've played in front of 8,000 fans screaming for you. It's unbelievable how it feels,' remarked an ecstatic Schnyder.

Competition in World Group I is likely to be equally fierce in 1999. In the World Group I/World Group II Play-Off Round, Croatia, Italy, Russia and the Slovak Republic all earned promotion to World Group I for the first time since the format of the competition was changed in 1995. Able to field the likes of Anna Kournikova, Iva Majoli, Mirjana Lucic and Karina Habsudova, these newcomers are capable of giving the might of Spain, Switzerland and USA a run for their money next year.

Croatia, Russia and the Slovak Republic all enjoyed home advantage in the 1998 World Group I/World Group II Play-Off Round, while Italy had an away tie in Czech Republic. Iva Majoli and Silvija Talaja anchored Croatia to victory over the 1997 finalists, Netherlands, 3–2. Russia achieved a surprise 4–1 win against a German team spearheaded by Anke Huber. Karina Habsudova and Henrieta Nagyova steered Slovak Republic to a 4–1 victory over Belgium while Italy swept past a Czech Republic without Jana Novotna by the same scoreline.

In the World Group II/Regional Qualifying Play-Offs, Belarus will join the eight nations in World Group II for the first time after Natasha Zvereva and Olga Barabanschikova engineered a 4–1 win over Venezuela. Existing positions were maintained in World Group II after the Austrians defeated Poland 5–0 in Austria, the Australians defeated Argentina 5–0 in Australia and Japan defeated Korea 4–1 in Korea.

1998 KB FED CUP

WORLD GROUP I

Seeding: 1 = France & USA; 3 = Spain & Switzerland

FIRST ROUND (18–19 April) – France d. Belgium 3–2, Gent, BEL: Sandrine Testud (FRA) d. Sabine Appelmans (BEL) 6–3 6–2; Dominique Van Roost (BEL) d. Sarah Pitkowski (FRA) 4–6 6–4 6–2; Dominique Van Roost (BEL) d. Sandrine Testud (FRA) 7–5 7–6(7); Sarah Pitkowski (FRA) d. Sabine Appelmans (BEL) 4–6 6–3 6–1; Alexandra Fusai/Nathalie Tauziat (FRA) d. Els Callens/Laurence Courtois (BEL) 6–4 6–0. **Switzerland d. Czech Republic 4–1, Brno, CZE:** Jana Novotna (CZE) d. Patty Schnyder (SUI) 3–6 6–2 6–3; Martina Hingis (SUI) d. Adriana Gersi (CZE) 6–2 6–1; Martina Hingis (SUI) d. Jana Novotna (CZE) 4–6 6–3 6–2; Patty Schnyder (SUI) d. Adriana Gersi (CZE) 6–3 6–3; Martina Hingis/Patty Schnyder (SUI) d. Denisa Chladkova/Ludmila Richterova (CZE) 6–0 6–1. **Spain d. Germany 3–2, Saarbrucken, GER:** Magui Serna (ESP) d. Andrea Glass (GER) 6–3 6–7(3) 6–3; Jana Kandarr (GER) d. Conchita Martinez (ESP) 6–1 1–6 7–5; Andrea Glass (GER) d. Conchita Martinez (ESP) 3–6 6–3 6–2; Magui Serna (ESP) d. Jana Kandarr (GER) 6–3 6–4; Conchita Martinez/Magui Serna(ESP) d. Andrea Glass/Wiltrud Probst (GER) 6–4 7–6(5). **USA d. Netherlands 5–0, Kiawah Island, SC, USA:** Lindsay Davenport (USA) d. Amanda Hopmans (NED) 6–4 6–1; Monica Seles (USA) d. Miriam Oremans (NED) 6–1 6–2; Lindsay Davenport (USA) d. Miriam Oremans (NED) 6–1 6–2; Monica Seles (USA) d. Amanda Hopmans 6–1 6–2; Mary Joe Fernandez/Lisa Raymond (USA) d. Manon Bollegraf/Caroline Vis (NED) 6–1 ret.

SEMI-FINALS (25–26 July) – Spain d. USA 3–2, Madrid, ESP: Arantxa Sanchez-Vicario (ESP) d. Lisa Raymond (USA) 6–7(4) 6–3 6–0; Monica Seles (USA) d. Conchita Martinez (ESP) 6–3 3–6 6–1; Monica Seles (USA) d. Arantxa Sanchez-Vicario (ESP) 6–4 6–0; Conchita Martinez (ESP) d. Lisa Raymond (USA) 7–6(1) 6–4; Conchita Martinez/Arantxa Sanchez-Vicario (ESP) d. Mary Joe Fernandez/Lisa Raymond (USA) 6–4 6–7(5) 119. **Switzerland d. France 5–0, Sion, SUI:** Martina Hingis (SUI) d. Julie Halard-Decugis (FRA) 7–5 6–1; Patty Schnyder (SUI) d. Amelie Mauresmo (FRA) 7–5 2–6 6–3; Martina Hingis (SUI) d. Amelie Mauresmo (FRA) 6–7(6) 6–4 6–2; Patty Schnyder (SUI) d. Julie Halard-Decugis (FRA) 6–3 6–2; Emmanuelle Gagliardi/Patty Schnyder (SUI) d. Alexandra Fusai/Nathalie Tauziat (FRA) 2–6 6–3 6–3.

FINAL (19–20 September) – Spain d. Switzerland 3–2, Geneva, SUI: Arantxa Sanchez-Vicario (ESP) d. Patty Schnyder (SUI) 6–2 3–6 6–2; Martina Hingis (SUI) d. Conchita Martinez (ESP) 6–4 6–4; Martina Hingis (SUI) d. Arantxa Sanchez-Vicario (ESP) 7–6(5) 6–3; Conchita Martinez (ESP) d. Patty Schnyder (SUI) 6–3 2–6 9–7; Conchita Martinez/Arantxa Sanchez-Vicario (ESP) d. Martina Hingis/Patty Schnyder (SUI) 6–0 6–2.

WORLD GROUP I PLAY-OFFS (25–26 July) – Italy d. Czech Republic 4–1, Prague, CZE: Silvia Farina (ITA) d. Radka Bobkova (CZE) 6–0 6–4; Rita Grande (ITA) d. Kvetoslava Hrdlickova (CZE) 7–6(3) 4–6 6–4; Silvia Farina (ITA) d. Kvetoslava Hrdlickova (CZE) 6–2 6–1; Radka Bobkova (CZE) d. Rita Grande (ITA) 2–6 6–3 7–6(5); Francesca Lubiani/Flora Perfetti (ITA) d. Lenka Nemeckova/Michaela Pastikova (CZE) 6–2 4–6 7–5. **Russia d. Germany 4–1, Moscow, RUS:** Tatiana Panova (RUS) d. Andrea Glass (GER) 6–3 6–1; Elena Makarova (RUS) d. Anke Huber (GER) 6–1 7–6(6); Tatiana Panova (RUS) d. Anke Huber (GER) 7–5 6–3; Elena Makarova (RUS) d. Andrea Glass (GER) 6–4 6–1; Meike Babel/Jana Kandarr (GER) d. Evgenia Koulikovskaya/Ekaterina Syssoeva (RUS) 6–4 6–2. **Slovak Republic d. Belgium 4–1, Bratislava, SVK:** Henrieta Nagyova (SVK) d. Sabine Appelmans (BEL) 7–5 6–4; Karina Habsudova (SVK) d. Dominique Van Roost (BEL) 6–2 6–3; Henrieta Nagyova (SVK) d. Dominique Van Roost (BEL) 6–4 6–3; Karina Habsudova (SVK) d. Sabine Appelmans (BEL) 6–2 4–6 7–5; Els Callens/Dominique Van Roost (BEL) d. Janette Husarova/Katarina Studenikova (SVK) 7–5 6–1. **Croatia d. Netherlands 3–2, Bol, CRO:** Silvija Talaja (CRO) d. Miriam Oremans (NED) 6–3 6–3; Amanda Hopmans (NED) d. Iva Majoli (CRO) 6–1 6–0; Iva Majoli (CRO) d. Miriam Oremans (NED) 6–2 6–2; Silvija Talaja (CRO) d. Amanda Hopmans (NED) 6–2 6–3; Manon Bollegraf/Caroline Vis (NED) d. Jelena Kostanic/Silvija Talaja (CRO) 6–4 3–6 7–6(1).

Slovak Republic, Russia, Croatia and Italy qualified for World Group I for the 1999 competition.
Belgium, Germany, Netherlands and Czech Republic remained in, or were relegated to World Group II for the 1999 competition.

WORLD GROUP II

Seeding: 1 = Austria & Slovak Republic; 3 = Croatia & Russia
FIRST ROUND (18–19 April) – Italy d. Austria 3–2, Foligno, ITA: Barbara Schett (AUT) d. Francesca Lubiani (ITA) 6–1 6–3; Silvia Farina (ITA) d. Barbara Schwartz (AUT) 6–4 3–6 9–7; Silvia Farina (ITA) d. Barbara Schett (AUT) 6–7(4) 7–6(3) 6–2; Francesca Lubiani (ITA) d. Sylvia Plischke(AUT) 7–6(5) 1–6 6–1; Sylvia Plischke/Barbara Schett (AUT) d. Laura Golarsa/Francesca Lubiani (ITA) 7–6(0) 7–5. **Russia d. Australia 3–2, Perth, AUS:** Tatiana Panova (RUS) d. Kerry-Anne Guse (AUS) 4–6 6–3 6–3; Ekaterina Syssoeva (RUS) d. Rachel McQuillan (AUS) 2–6 6–4 12–10; Tatiana Panova (RUS) d. Rachel McQuillan (AUS) 7–6(0) 6–3; Kerry-Anne Guse (AUS) d. Ekaterina Syssoeva (RUS) 4–6 6–3 7–5; Annabel Ellwood/Rennae Stubbs (AUS) d. Anastasia Myskina/Tatiana Panova (RUS) 6–2 6–2. **Slovak Republic d. Argentina 4–1, Buenos Aires, ARG:** Henrieta Nagyova (SVK) d. Mariana Diaz-Oliva (ARG) 6–2 6–2; Florencia Labat (ARG) d. Karina Habsudova (SVK) 6–4 3–6 6–3; Henrieta Nagyova (SVK) d. Florencia Labat (ARG) 7–5 6–4; Karina Habsudova (SVK) d. Mariana Diaz-Oliva (ARG) 3–6 6–2 11–9; Karina Habsudova/Janette Husarova (SVK) d. Florencia Labat/Mercedes Paz (ARG) 3–6 6–1 6–4. **Croatia d. Japan 4–1, Dubrovnik, CRO:** Mirjana Lucic (CRO) d. Naoko Sawamatsu (JPN) 6–3 7–6(5); Iva Majoli (CRO) d. Yuka Yoshida (JPN) 6–2 6–2; Iva Majoli (CRO) d. Naoko Sawamatsu (JPN) 6–2 6–3; Mirjana Lucic (CRO) d. Yuka Yoshida (JPN) 6–1 6–2; Rika Hiraki/Nana Miyagi (JPN) d. Jelena Kostanic/Dora Krstulovic (CRO) 6–3 6–3.

WORLD GROUP II PLAY-OFFS (25–26 July) – Austria d. Poland 5–0, Bergheim, AUT: Sylvia Plischke (AUT) d. Magdalena Grzybowska (POL) 6–2 3–6 6–0; Barbara Schett (AUT) d. Aleksandra Olsza (POL) 4–6 6–0 6–3; Barbara Schett (AUT) d. Magdalena Feistel (POL) 6–0 6–2; Sylvia Plischke (AUT) d. Aleksandra Olsza (POL) 6–0 6–1; Sylvia Plischke/Barbara Schett (AUT) d. Magdalena Feistel/Katarzyna Teodorowicz(POL) 6–4 6–0. **Japan d. Korea 4–1, Seoul, KOR:** Miho Saeki (JPN) d. Eun-Ha Kim (KOR) 2–6 6–4 6–4; Ai Sugiyama (JPN) d. Ju-Yeon Choi (KOR) 6–1 6–1; Ai Sugiyama (JPN) d. Eun-Ha Kim (KOR) 6–4 7–5; Miho Saeki (JPN) d. Yoon-Jeong Cho (KOR) 6–4 6–3; Young-Ja Choi/Eun-Ha Kim (KOR) d. Naoko Kijimuta/Nana Miyagi (JPN) 6–2 7–6(5). **Australia d. Argentina 5–0, Bruce, ACT, AUS:** Jelena Dokic (AUS) d. Mariana Diaz Oliva (ARG) 6–2 6–2; Nicole Pratt (AUS) d. Celeste Contin (ARG) 6–2 6–4; Nicole Pratt (AUS) d. Mariana Diaz Oliva (ARG) 7–6(4) 6–1; Jelena Dokic (AUS) d. Laura Montalvo (ARG) 6–2 6–1; Kerry-Anne Guse/Rachel McQuillan (AUS) d. Erica Krauth/Laura Montalvo (ARG) 6–4 6–3. **Belarus d. Venezuela 4–1, Minsk, BLR:** Olga Barabanschikova (BLR) d. Maria Alejandra Vento (VEN) 6–2 6–2; Natasha Zvereva (BLR) d. Milagros Sequera (VEN) 6–1 6–2; Maria Alejandra Vento (VEN) d. Natasha Zvereva (BLR) 6–3 3–6 6–4; Olga Barabanschikova (BLR) d. Milagros Sequera (VEN) 6–3 6–2; Olga Barabanschikova/Nadejda Ostrovskaya (BLR) d. Milagros Sequera/Maria Alejandra Vento (VEN) 7–5 6–3.

Austria, Belarus, Australia and Japan qualified for World Group II for the 1999 competition.
Poland, Venezuela, Argentina and Korea remained in, or were relegated to Zonal Qualifying Group I for the 1999 competition.

AMERICAS GROUP I

Academia de Tenis de Brasilia, Brazil, 13–18 April

GROUP A – Paraguay, Uruguay, Canada.
Round Robin: Paraguay d. Canada 2–1: Jana Nejedly (CAN) d. Laura Bernal (PAR) 6–4 6–2; Larissa Schaerer (PAR) d. Sonja Jeyaseelan (CAN) 6–7(4) 7–5 6–1; Laura Bernal/Larissa Schaerer (PAR) d. Patricia Hy-Boulais/Rene Simpson (CAN) 6–1 6–3. **Paraguay d. Uruguay 2–1:** Laura Bernal (PAR) d. Claudia Brause (URU) 6–2 7–5; Larissa Schaerer (PAR) d. Daniela Oliviera (URU) 6–2 6–0; Claudia Brause/Elena Juricich (URU) d. Mariana Quintanilla/Valeria Rolon (PAR) 7–6(4) 6–3. **Canada d. Uruguay 2–0:** Jana Nejedly (CAN) d. Daniela Oliviera (URU) 6–2 6–1; Sonya Jeyaseelan (CAN) d. Elena Juricich (URU) 6–4 6–2; Sonya Jeyaseelan/Rene Simpson (CAN) v Claudia Brause/Cecilia Guillenea (URU) 6–4 5–5 abn.

GROUP B – Colombia, Brazil, Chile.
Round Robin: Colombia d. Brazil 2–1: Vanessa Menga (BRA) d. Mariana Mesa (COL) 6–2 6–2; Fabiola Zuluaga (COL) d. Miriam D'Agostini (BRA) 6–1 7–5; Mariana Mesa/Fabiola Zuluaga (COL) d. Miriam D'Agostini/Vanessa Menga (BRA) 6–1 2–6 6–2. **Colombia d. Chile 2–1:** Mariana Mesa (COL) d. Barbara Castro (CHI) 6–4 6–2; Fabiola Zuluaga (COL) d. Paula Cabezas (CHI) 6–1 6–2; Paula Cabezas/Barbara Castro (CHI) d. Mariana Mesa/Fabiola Zuluaga (COL) 4–6 7–6(5) 6–2. **Brazil d. Chile 2–1:** Vanessa Menga (BRA) d. Barbara Castro (CHI) 6–2 6–2; Paula Cabezas

(CHI) d. Miriam D'Agostini (BRA) 6–2 2–6 6–3; Miriam D'Agostini/Vanessa Menga (BRA) d. Paula Cabezas/Barbara Castro (CHI) 5–7 6–3 8–6.

GROUP C – Venezuela, Ecuador, Peru.
Round Robin: Venezuela d. Ecuador 3–0: Milagros Sequera (VEN) d. Maria Dolores Campana (ECU) 6–2 6–0; Maria Alejandra Vento (VEN) d. Alexandra Guzman (ECU) 6–1 6–1; Milagros Sequera/Maria Alejandra Vento (VEN) d. Maria Dolores Campana/Nuria Niemes (ECU) 6–2 6–4. **Ecuador d. Peru 2–1:** Maria Dolores Campana (ECU) d. Carla Rodriguez (PER) 6–0 6–1; Alexandra Guzman (ECU) d. Maria Eugenia Rojas (PER) 7–5 6–4; Carla Rodriguez/Maria Eugenia Rojas (PER) d. Maria Dolores Campana/Alexandra Guzman (PER) 1–6 6–4 6–4. **Venezuela d. Peru 2–1:** Milagros Sequera (VEN) d. Ariana Rojas (PER) 6–2 6–4; Maria Alejandra Vento (VEN) d. Maria Eugenia Rojas (PER) 6–0 6–1; Carla Rodriguez/Maria Eugenia Rojas (PER) d. Analia Longoni/Fabiana Taverna (VEN) 7–5 6–4.

Play-offs for 1st-3rd positions: Venezuela d. Paraguay 2–1: Milagros Sequera (VEN) d. Laura Bernal (PAR) 6–0 6–3; Larissa Schaerer (PAR) d. Maria Alejandra Vento (VEN) 6–7(3) 6–1 6–1; Milagros Sequera/Maria Alejandra Vento (VEN) d. Laura Bernal/Larissa Schaerer (PAR) 6–3 6–2. **Paraguay d. Colombia 3–0:** Laura Bernal (PAR) d. Mariana Mesa (COL) 5–7 6–3 9–7; Larissa Schaerer (PAR) d. Fabiola Zuluaga (COL) 7–5 6–4; Laura Bernal/Larissa Schaerer (PAR) d. Mariana Mesa/Fabiola Zuluaga (COL) 2–6 6–3 6–3. **Venezuela d. Colombia 2–1:** Milagros Sequera (VEN) d. Mariana Mesa (COL) 7–6(6) 6–2; Fabiola Zuluaga (COL) d. Maria Alejandra Vento (VEN) 6–7(4) 7–6(6) 6–1; Milagros Sequera/Maria Alejandra Vento (VEN) d. Mariana Mesa/Fabiola Zuluga (COL) 6–4 6–2.

Play-offs for 4th-6th positions: Canada d. Ecuador 3–0: Jana Nejedly (CAN) d. Maria Dolores Campana (ECU) 6–4 5–7 6–4; Sonya Jeyaseelan (CAN) d. Alexandra Guzman (ECU) 6–1 6–1; Sonya Jeyaseelan/Rene Simpson (CAN) d. Paola Guerrero/Nuria Niemes (ECU) 6–0 6–2. **Canada d. Brazil 3–0:** Jana Nejedly (CAN) d. Joana Cortez (BRA) 6–4 6–3; Sonya Jeyaseelan (CAN) d. Vanessa Menga (BRA) 6–1 6–2; Sonya Jeyaseelan/ Rene Simpson (CAN) d. Miriam D'Agostini/Vanessa Menga (BRA) 6–4 7–6(6). **Brazil d. Ecuador 2–0:** Vanessa Menga (BRA) d. Maria Dolores Campana (ECU) 7–5 6–3; Miriam D'Agostini (BRA) d. Alexandra Guzman (ECU) 6–4 6–2; Doubles not played.

Play-offs for 7th-9th positions: Uruguay d. Peru 2–1: Claudia Rodriguez (PER) d. Claudia Brause (URU) 6–4 6–3; Elena Juricich (URU) d. Maria Eugenia Rojas (PER) 7–5 6–3; Claudia Brause/Cecilia Guillenea (URU) d. Carla Rodriguez/Maria Eugenia Rojas (PER) 6–4 4–6 6–4. **Chile d. Uruguay 3–0:** Barbara Castro (CHI) d. Cecilia Guillenea (URU) 6–2 6–3; Paula Cabezas (CHI) d. Elena Juricich (URU) 6–3 6–2; Valentina Castro/Karem Harboe (CHI) d. Cecilia Guillenea/Daniela Oliviera (URU) 6–1 6–1. **Chile d. Peru 2–0:** Valentina Castro (CHI) d. Ariana Rojas (PER) 6–4 6–2; Paula Cabezas (CHI) d. Maria Eugenia Rojas (PER) 6–1 6–2; Doubles not played.

Final Positions: Venezuela 1, Paraguay 2, Colombia 3, Canada 4, Brazil 5, Ecuador 6, Chile 7, Uruguay 8, Peru 9.

Venezuela qualified for the World Group II play-offs.
Uruguay and Peru were relegated to Americas Group II for the 1999 competition.

ASIA/OCEANIA GROUP I

Thana City Golf and Country Club, Bangkok, Thailand, 16–21 February

Group A – Chinese Taipei, Indonesia, Uzbekistan.
Round Robin: Chinese Taipei d. Indonesia 2–1: Janet Lee (TPE) d. Wukirasih Sawondari (INA) 6–3 6–3; Shi-Ting Wang (TPE) d. Wynne Prakusya (INA) 6–3 6–2; Wukirasih Sawondari/ Eny Sulistyowati (INA) d. Julie Huang/Tzu-Ting Weng (TPE) 4–6 7–6(1) 2–1 ret. **Chinese Taipei d. Uzbekistan 3–0:** Janet Lee (TPE) d. Iroda Tulyaganova (UZB) 6–4 6–1; Shi-Ting Wang (TPE) d. Lilya Biktyakova (UZB) 6–0 6–3; Julie Hûang/Janet Lee (TPE) d. Luiza Biktyakova/Lilya Biktyakova (UZB) 6–0 6–1. **Indonesia d. Uzbekistan 3–0:** Wukirasih Sawondari (INA) d. Irona Tulyaganova (UZB) 6–2 3–1 ret; Wynne Prakusya (INA) d. Lilya Biktyakova (UZB) 6–1 4–6 6–3; Wynne Prakusya/Wukirasih Sawondari (INA) d. Lilya Biktyakova/Luiza Biktyakova (UZB) 6–1 6–2.

Group B – Korea, China PR, Hong Kong.
Round Robin: Korea d. China PR 3–0: Young-Ja Choi (KOR) d. Li Li (CHN) 6–4 6–3; Sung-Hee Park (KOR) d. Jing-Qian Yi (CHN) 6–3 6–2; Yoon-Jeong Cho/Yang-Jin Chung (KOR) d. Li Li/Jing-Qian-Yi (CHN) 6–4 4–6 6–3. **Korea d. Hong Kong 3–0:** Yang-Jin Chung (KOR) d. Ning Lin (HKG) 6–4 6–2; Yoon-Jeong Cho (KOR) d. Ka-Po Tong (HKG) 6–3 6–3; Young-Ja Choi/Sung-Hee Park (KOR) d. Karen Fisher/Min Tang (HKG) 6–1 6–3. **China PR d. Hong Kong 2–1:** Li Li (CHN) d. Min Tang (HKG) 6–1 6–1; Ka-Po Tong (HKG) d. Jing-Qian Yi (CHN) 6–3 1–6 6–3; Li Li/Jing Qian Yi (CHN) d. Min Tang/Ka-Po Tong (HKG) 7–6(3) 6–2.

Group C – Thailand, New Zealand, Philippines.
Round Robin: New Zealand d. Thailand 2–1: Leanne Baker (NZL) d. Suvimol Duangchan (THA) 4–6 6–3 8–6; Tamarine Tanasugarn (THA) d. Rewa Hudson (NZL) 6–3 6–1; Leanne Baker/Rewa Hudson (NZL) d. Benjamas Sangaram/Tamarine Tanasugarn (THA) 6–7(4) 6–4 6–1. **Thailand d. Philippines 3–0:** Suvimol Duangchan (THA) d. Pamela Floro (PHI) 7–5 7–5; Tamarine Tanasugarn (THA) d. Marisu Jacutin (PHI) 6–3 6–2; Benjamas Sangaram/Tamarine Tanasugarn (THA) d. Pamela Floro/Jennifer Saret (PHI) 6–0 6–0. **New Zealand d. Philippines 3–0:** Leanne Baker (NZL) d. Pamela Flora (PHI) 6–0 6–1; Rewa Hudson (NZL) d. Marisu Jacutin (PHI) 6–3 6–2; Shelley Stephens/Nicola Tippins (NZL) d. Pamela Floro/Jennifer Saret (PHI) 6–1 6–2.

Play-offs for 1st-3rd positions: Korea d. Chinese Taipei 2–1: Janet Lee (TPE) d. Young-Ja Choi (KOR) 7–5 6–3; Sung Hee Park (KOR) d. Shi-Ting Wang (TPE) 6–2 6–4; Young-Ja Choi/Sung Hee Park (KOR) d. Janet Lee/Shi-Ting Wang (TPE) 4–6 7–5 6–3. **Chinese Taipei d. New Zealand 2–1:** Janet Lee (TPE) d. Leanne Baker (NZL) 7–6(4) 2–6 6–4; Shi-Ting Wang (TPE) d. Rewa Hudson (NZL) 6–1 6–4; Leanne Baker/Rewa Hudson (NZL) d. Janet Lee/Shi-Ting Wang (TPE) 6–4 6–4. **Korea d. New Zealand 2–0:** Yoon-Jeong Cho (KOR) d. Leanne Baker (NZL) 6–2 6–4; Sung-Hee Park (KOR) d. Rewa Hudson (NZL) 6–2 7–5; Doubles not played.

Play-offs for 4th-6th positions: Thailand d. Indonesia 2–1: Suvimol Duangchan (THA) d. Wukirasih Sawondari (INA) 6–3 6–1; Wynne Prakusya (INA) d. Tamarine Tanasugarn (THA) 7–6(5) 7–6(5); Benjamas Sangaram/Tamarine Tanasugarn (THA) d. Wynne Prakusya/Wukirasih Sawondari (INA) 7–6(4) 6–3. **China PR d. Indonesia 2–1:** Li Li (CHN) d. Wukirasih Sawondari (INA) 6–2 6–3; Wynne Prakusya (INA) d. Jing-Qian Yi (CHN) 6–3 6–4; Li Li/Jing-Qian Yi (CHN) d. Wynne Prakusya/Wukirasih Sawondari (INA) 7–6(6) 6–4. **China PR d. Thailand 2–1:** Li Li (CHN) d. Suvimol Duangchan (THA) 6–0 6–1; Tamarine Tanasugarn (THA) d. Jing-Qian Yi (CHN) 6–7(4) 6–2 6–1; Li Li/Jing-Qian Yi (CHN) d. Suvimol Duangchan/Benjamas Sangaram (THA) 6–4 6–1.

Play-offs for 7th-9th positions: Hong Kong d. Philippines 3–0: Ning Lin (HKG) d. Jennifer Saret (PHI) 4–6 6–4 6–1; Ka-Po Tong (HKG) d. Marisu Jacutin (PHI) 6–1 6–4; Min Tang/Ka-Po Tong (HKG) d. Pamela Floro/Jennifer Saret (PHI) 6–1 6–4. **Uzbekistan d. Philippines 2–1:** Iroda Tulyaganova (UZB) d. Pamela Floro (PHI) 6–2 6–4; Lilya Biktyakova (UZB) d. Marisu Jacutin (PHI) 6–4 6–4; Pamela Floro/Marisu Jacutin (PHI) d. Luiza Biktyakova/Natelie Nikitina (UZB) 6–3 6–3. **Hong Kong d. Uzbekistan 2–1:** Iroda Tulyaganova (UZB) d. Ning Lin (HKG) 6–1 6–2; Ka-Po Tong (HKG) d. Lilya Biktyakova (UZB) 6–3 6–2; Min Tang/Ka-Po Tong (HKG) d. Lilya Biktyakova/Iroda Tulyaganova (UZB) 7–5 6–3.

Final Positions: Korea 1, Chinese Taipei 2, New Zealand 3, China PR 4, Thailand 5, Indonesia 6, Hong Kong 7, Uzbekistan 8, Philippines 9.

Korea qualified for the World Group II play-offs.
Philippines and Uzbekistan were relegated to Asia/Oceania Group II for the 1999 competition.

EURO/AFRICA GROUP I

La Manga Club Resort, Murcia, Spain, 14–18 April

GROUP A – Belarus, Slovenia, Greece, Israel.
Round Robin: Belarus d. Slovenia 3–0: Olga Barabanschikova (BLR) d. Tina Pisnik (SLO) 6–4 7–6(3); Natasha Zvereva (BLR) d. Petra Rampre (SLO) 6–2 6–2; Olga Barabanschikova/Natasha Zvereva (BLR) d. Tina Pisnik/Petra Rampre (SLO) 6–1 6–0. **Greece d. Israel 2–1:** Hila Rosen (ISR) d. Eleni Danilidou (GRE) 6–2 6–3; Christina Papadaki (GRE) d. Anna Smashnova (ISR) 6–3 5–7 6–4; Christina Papadaki/Eleni Danilidou (GRE) d. Tzipora Obziler/Hila Rosen (ISR) 7–5 6–3. **Belarus d. Israel 2–1:** Olga Barabanschikova (BLR) d. Hila Rosen (ISR) 6–3 7–5; Natasha Zvereva (BLR) d. Anna Smashnova (ISR) 6–2 6–4; Tzipora Obziler/Hila Rosen (ISR) d. Nadejda Ostrovskaya/Tatiana Poutchek (BLR) 6–3 6–1. **Greece d. Slovenia 2–1:** Tina Pisnik (SLO) d. Eleni Danilidou (GRE) 6–3 6–1; Christina Papadaki (GRE) d. Petra Rampre (SLO) 6–2 7–5; Eleni Danilidou/Christina Papadaki (GRE) d. Tina Pisnik/Maja Matevzic (SLO) 5–7 6–3 6–3. **Belarus d. Greece 2–1:** Eleni Danilidou (GRE) d. Olga Barabanschikova (BLR) 6–3 6–4; Natasha Zvereva (BLR) d. Christina Papadaki (GRE) 6–0 6–4; Olga Barabanschikova/Natasha Zvereva (BLR) d. Eleni Danilidou/Christina Papadaki (GRE) 6–2 6–1. **Slovenia d. Israel 2–1:** Tina Pisnik (SLO) d. Hila Rosen (ISR) 6–2 6–1; Anna Smashnova (ISR) d. Barbara Mulej (SLO) 4–6 6–4 6–4; Maja Matevzic/Tina Pisnik (SLO) d. Tzipora Obziler/Hila Rosen (ISR) 6–7(4) 7–6(2) 6–4.
Final Positions: Belarus 1, Greece 2, Slovenia 3, Israel 4.

GROUP B – Portugal, Great Britain, Poland, Madagascar.
Round Robin: Portugal d. Great Britain 2–1: Louise Latimer (GBR) d. Ana Nogueira (POR) 7–6(5) 7–6(6); Sofia Prazeres (POR) d. Karen Cross (GBR) 6–2 6–3; Ana Nogueira/Sofia Prazeres (POR) d. Julie Pullin/Lorna Woodroffe (GBR) 2–6 6–2 6–4. **Poland d. Madagascar 3–0:** Aleksandra Olsza (POL) d. Natacha Randriantefy (MAD) 6–2 4–6 6–1; Magdalena Grzybowska (POL) d. Aina Rafolomanantsiatosika (MAD) 6–0 6–1; Aleksandra Olsza/Katarzyna Teodorowicz (POL) d. Aina Rafolomanantsiatosika/Nirina Rajaoarisoa (MAD) 6–0 6–0. **Poland d. Great Britain 2–1:** Aleksandra Olsza (POL) d. Louise Latimer (GBR) 7–6(5) 6–0; Magdalena Grzybowska (POL) d. Karen Cross (GBR) 6–1 6–2; Julie Pullin/Lorna Woodroffe (GBR) d. Aleksandra Olsza/Sylwia Rynarzewska (POL) 7–6(7) 6–3. **Portugal d. Madagascar 2–1:** Natacha Randriantefy (MAD) d. Ana Nogueira (POR) 6–4 6–3; Sofia Prazeres (POR) d. Aina Rafolomanantsiatosika (MAD) 6–2 6–0; Ana Nogueira/Sofia Prazeres (POR) d. Nirina Rajaoarisoa/Natacha Randriantefy (MAD) 6–2 6–0. **Poland d. Portugal 2–1:** Aleksandra Olsza (POL) d. Christina Correia (POR) 6–2 3–6 6–2; Sofia Prazeres (POR) d. Magdalena Grzybowska (POL) 6–2 7–6(2); Magdalena Grzybowska/Aleksandra Olsza (POL) d. Cristina Correia/Ana Nogueira (POR) 6–1 6–2. **Great Britain d. Madagascar 3–0:** Louise Latimer (GBR) d. Natacha Randriantefy (MAD) 6–4 4–6 6–3; Karen Cross (GBR) d. Viviane Faratiana Rasoarilalao (MAD) 6–1 6–3; Louise Latimer/Julie Pullin (GBR) d. Aina Rafolomanantsiatosika/Natacha Randriantefy (MAD) 6–3 6–2.
Final Positions: Poland 1, Portugal 2, Great Britain 3, Madagascar 4.

GROUP C – South Africa, Latvia, Romania, Bulgaria.
Round Robin: South Africa d. Latvia 3–0: Jessica Steck (RSA) d. Agnese Blumberga (LAT) 6–0 5–7 6–3; Mariaan De Swardt (RSA) d. Elena Krutko (LAT) 6–0 6–3; Liezel Horn/Nannie De Villiers (RSA) d. Liga Dermeijere/Elena Krutko (LAT) 6–0 6–0. **Romania d. Bulgaria 2–1:** Alice Pirsu (ROM) d. Desislava Topalova (BUL) 6–3 6–2; Raluca Sandu (ROM) d. Magdalena Maleeva (BUL) 6–1 6–3; Filipa Gabrovska/Antoaneta Pandjerova (BUL) d. Oana-Elena Golimbioschi/Alice Pirsu (ROM) 4–6 6–4 7–6(3). **South Africa d. Bulgaria 2–1:** Antoaneta Pandjerova (BUL) d. Liezel Horn (RSA) 6–3 5–7 6–4; Mariaan De Swardt (RSA) d. Magdalena Maleeva (BUL) 6–1 7–5; Mariaan De Swardt/Nannie De Villiers (RSA) d. Filipa Gabrovska/Antoaneta Pandjerova (BUL) 6–0 6–4. **Romania d. Latvia 3–0:** Alice Pirsu (ROM) d. Liga Dermeijere (LAT) 6–4 6–4; Raluca Sandu (ROM) d. Elena Krutko (LAT) 6–1 6–2; Oana-Elena Golimbioschi/Raluca Sandu (ROM) d. Agnese Blumberga/Liga Dermeijere (LAT) 6–2 6–4. **South Africa d. Romania 3–0:** Jessica Steck (RSA) d. Alice Pirsu (ROM) 7–5 6–2; Mariaan De Swardt (RSA) d. Raluca Sandu (ROM) 3–6 6–4 8–6; Leizel Horn/Nannie De Villiers (RSA) d. Oana-Elena Golimbioschi/Alice Pirsu (ROM) 6–4 6–1. **Latvia d. Bulgaria 2–1:** Antoaneta Pandjerova (BUL) d. Agnese Blumberga (LAT) 7–6(3) 6–2; Elena Krutko (LAT) d. Magdalena Maleeva (BUL) 7–6(2) 1–6 6–1; Agnese Blumberga/Elena Krutko (LAT) d. Antoaneta Pandjerova/Desislava Topalova (BUL) 6–4 6–4.
Final Positions: South Africa 1, Romania 2, Latvia 3, Bulgaria 4.

GROUP D – Sweden, Hungary, Ukraine, Yugoslavia.
Round Robin: Sweden d. Hungary 3–0: Kristina Triska (SWE) d. Zsofia Gubacsi (HUN) 6–4 6–3; Asa Carlsson (SWE) d. Petra Gaspar (HUN) 7–6(5) 7–5; Asa Carlsson/Kristina Triska (SWE) d. Zsofia Gubacsi/Adrienn Hegedus (HUN) 6–4 6–3. **Ukraine d. Yugoslavia 3–0:** Anna Zaporozhanova (UKR) d. Tatjana Jecmenica (YUG) 4–6 6–1 6–4; Elena Tatarkova (UKR) d. Sandra Nacuk (YUG) 6–3 2–6 8–6; Elena Tatarkova/Anna Zaporozhanova (UKR) d. Sanja Jukic/Dragana Zaric (YUG) 7–5 6–7(3) 6–0. **Sweden d. Yugoslavia 2–1:** Kristina Triska (SWE) d. Dragana Zaric (YUG) 7–5 5–7 9–7; Sandra Nacuk (YUG) d. Asa Carlsson (SWE) 4–6 6–3 6–4; Asa Carlsson/Kristina Triska (SWE) d. Sandra Nacuk/Dragana Zaric (YUG) 5–7 6–1 6–1. **Ukraine d. Hungary 3–0:** Anna Zaporozhanova (UKR) d. Zsofia Gubacsi (HUN) 6–4 5–7 6–4; Elena Tatarkova (UKR) d. Petra Gaspar (HUN) 6–1 6–4; Tatiana Kovalchuk/Elena Tatarkova (UKR) d. Petra Gaspar/Adrienn Hegedus (HUN) 6–4 6–7(8) 6–3. **Sweden d. Ukraine 2–1:** Anna Zaporozhanova (UKR) d. Kristina Triska (SWE) 6–3 7–6(8); Asa Carlsson (SWE) d. Elena Tatarkova (UKR) 6–1 6–1; Asa Carlsson/Kristina Triska (SWE) d. Elena Tatarkova/Anna Zaporozhanova (UKR) 7–5 6–3. **Yugoslavia d. Hungary 2–1:** Zsofia Gubacsi (HUN) d. Dragana Zaric (YUG) 4–6 6–2 8–6; Sandra Nacuk (YUG) d. Petra Gaspar (HUN) 6–1 6–3; Tatjana Jecmenica/Dragana Zaric (YUG) d. Petra Gaspar/Zsofia Gubacsi 6–4 6–3.
Final Positions: Sweden 1, Ukraine 2, Yugoslavia 3, Hungary 4.

Semi-finals: Belarus d. Ukraine 2–1: Olga Barabanschikova (BLR) d. Anna Zaporozhanova (UKR) 6–1 6–1; Natasha Zvereva (BLR) d. Elena Tartakova (UKR) 6–2 6–4; Tatiana Kovalchuk/Olga Teplinskaya (UKR) d. Nadejda Ostrovskaya/Tatiana Poutchek (BLR) 7–6(6) 6–4. **Romania d. Sweden 2–1:** Kristina Triska (SWE) d. Alice Pirsu (ROM) 6–4 6–2; Raluca Sandu (ROM) d. Asa Carlsson (SWE) 2–6 6–1 8–6; Alice Pirsu/Raluca Sandu (ROM) d. Asa Carlsson/Kristina Triska (SWE) 6–3 3–6 6–3. **South Africa d. Portugal 3–0:** Jessica Steck (RSA) d. Cristina Correia (POR) 6–1 6–3; Mariaan De Swardt (RSA) d. Sofia Prazeres (POR) 4–6 6–2 6–3; Leizel Horn/Nannie De Villiers (RSA) d. Cristina Correia/Ana Nogueira (POR) 6–3 6–2. **Poland d. Greece 2–1:** Aleksandra Olsza (POL) d. Eleni Danilidou (GRE) 4–6 6–1 6–4; Magdalena Grzybowska (POR) d. Christina Papadaki (GRE) 6–4 6–1; Eleni Danilidou/Christina Papadaki (GRE) d. Sylwia Rynarzewska/ Katarzyna Teodorowicz 6–3 6–1.

Final: Belarus d. South Africa 2–0: Olga Barabanschikova (BLR) d. Jessica Steck (RSA) 7–6(2) 7–6(4); Natasha Zvereva (BLR) d. Mariaan De Swardt (RSA) 4–6 6–4 6–2; Doubles not played. **Poland d. Romania 2–0:** Aleksandra Olsza (POL) d. Alice Pirsu (ROM) 7–5 6–1; Magdalena Grzybowska (POR) d. Raluca Sandu (ROM) 7–5 6–1; Doubles not played.

Poland and Belarus qualified for the World Group II play-offs.
Bulgaria, Hungary, Israel and Madagascar were relegated to Europe/Africa Group II for the 1999 competition.

AMERICAS GROUP II
Chipinque Racquet Club, Monterrey, Mexico, 27 April–3 May

GROUP A: Antigua & Barbuda, Barbados, Bermuda, Costa Rica, El Salvador, Guatemala, Haiti, Mexico.
Round Robin: Mexico d. Bermuda 3–0: Karin Palme (MEX) d. Kelly Holland (BER) 6–0 6–0; Jessica Fernandez (MEX) d. Danielle Paynter (BER) 6–0 6–0; Melody Falco/Paola Palencia (MEX) d. Elizabeth Osborne/Allison Tolson (BER) 6–1 6–1. **Costa Rica d. Antigua & Barbuda 3–0:** Melissa Mendieta (CRC) d. Isoke Perry (ANT) 6–1 6–1; Melissa Golfin (CRC) d. Niki Williams (ANT) 6–0 6–0; Paola Almeida/Paula Umana (CRC) d. Francine Harvey/Cheryl Lewis (ANT) 6–0 6–1. **El Salvador d. Barbados 3–0:** Ingrid Gonzalez (ESA) d. Kim Brandford (BAR) 6–1 7–5; Claudia Castro (ESA) d. Richele LeSaldo (BAR) 7–6(4) 6–1; Claudia Castro/Ingrid Gonzalez (ESA) d. Kim Brandford/Richele LeSaldo (BAR) 6–4 7–6(7). **Haiti d. Guatemala 3–0:** Jennifer Adrien (HAI) d. Maria Fernanda Carrillo (GUA) 1–6 7–6(7) 6–4; Neyssa Etienne (HAI) d. Luisa Lopez (GUA) 6–3 6–0; Emmanuelle Duval/Neyssa Etienne (HAI) d. Karla Lehnhoff/Luisa Lopez (GUA) 7–6(3) 5–7 8–6. **Mexico d. Antigua & Barbuda 3–0:** Karin Palme (MEX) d. Cheryl Lewis (ANT) 6–0 6–0; Jessica Fernandez (MEX) d. Isoke Perry (ANT) 6–0 6–0; Melody Falco/Paola Palencia (MEX) d. Francine Harvey/Niki WIlliams (ANT) 6–0 6–0. **Guatemala d. Costa Rica 2–1:** Maria Fernanda Carrillo (GUA) d. Paula Umana (CRC) 7–6(4) 6–4; Luisa Lopez (GUA) d. Melissa Golfin (CRC) 7–5 6–4; Paola Almeida/Melissa Mendieta (CRC) d. Maria Fernanda Carrillo/Karla Lehnhoff (GUA) 7–6(3) 7–6(4). **El Salvador d. Haiti 3–0:** Ingrid Gonzalez (ESA) d. Jennifer Adrien (HAI) 6–4 6–7(6) 6–1; Claudia Castro (ESA) d. Neyssa Etienne (HAI) 6–2 6–4; Claudia Castro/Ingrid Gonzalez (ESA) d. Jennifer Adrien/Neyssa Etienne (HAI) 6–7(4) 6–2 6–3. **Barbados d. Bermuda 2–1:** Kelly Holland (BER) d. Marisa Howell (BAR) 4–6 7–6(3) 7–5; Richelle LeSaldo (BAR) d. Danielle Paynter (BER) 6–7(4) 6–1 6–4; Richelle LeSaldo/Kim Brandford (BAR) d. Danielle Paynter/Allison Tolson (BER) 3–6 6–1 8–6. **Mexico d. Barbados 3–0:** Karin Palme (MEX) d. Donna Gibbs (BAR) 6–0 6–0; Jessica Fernandez (MEX) d. Richele LeSaldo (BAR) 6–2 6–3; Melody Falco/Paola Palencia (MEX) d. Kim Brandford/Richele LeSaldo (BAR) 6–0 6–2. **Guatemala d. Antigua & Barbuda 3–0:** Karla Lehnhoff (GUA) d. Cheryl Lewis (ANT) 6–0 6–1; Maria Fernanda Carrillo (GUA) d. Niki Williams (ANT) 6–0 6–2; Maria Fernanda Carrillo/Luisa Lopez (GUA) d. Isoke Perry/Niki WIlliams (ANT) 6–0 6–1. **Haiti d. Bermuda 3–0:** Jennifer Adrien (HAI) d. Allison Tolson (BER) 6–4 6–1; Neyssa Etienne (HAI) d. Danielle Paynter (BER) 6–2 6–1; Neyssa Etienne/Emmanuelle Duval (HAI) d. Elizabeth Osborne/Allison Tolson (BER) 6–0 6–2. **El Salvador d. Costa Rica 3–0:** Ingrid Gonzalez (ESA) d. Paula Umana (CRC) 6–2 6–3; Claudia Castro (ESA) d. Melissa Mendieta (CRC) 7–5 6–2; Claudia Castro/Ingrid Gonzalez (ESA) d. Paula Almeida/Melissa Golfin (BER) 4–6 6–1 6–2. **Mexico d. Guatemala 3–0:** Karin Palme (MEX) d. Karla Lehnhoff (GUA) 6–0 6–1; Jessica Fernandez (MEX) d. Luisa Lopez (GUA) 6–0 6–0; Melody Falco/Paola Palencia (MEX) d. Maria Fernanda Carrillo/Luisa Lopez (GUA) 6–1 6–2. **Costa Rica d. Bermuda 3–0:** Melissa Mendieta (CRC) d. Elizabeth Osborne (BER) 6–3 6–0; Melissa Golfin (CRC) d. Danielle Paynter (BER) 6–1 6–0; Paola Almeida/Melissa Mendieta (CRC) d. Danielle Paynter/Allison Tolson (BER) 6–4 5–7 6–4. **Haiti d. Barbados 2–1:** Jennifer Adrien (HAI) d. Marisa Howell (BAR) 6–1 6–2; Neyssa Etienne (HAI) d. Richele LeSaldo (BAR) 6–0 6–1; Kim Brandford/Donna Gibbs (BAR) d. Jennifer Adrien/Emmanuelle Duval (HAI) 3–6 6–2 6–1. **El Salvador d. Antigua & Barbuda 3–0:** Claudia Argumedo (ESA) d. Cheryl Lewis (ANT) 6–2 6–1; Claudia Castro (ESA) d. Isoke Perry (ANT) 6–0 6–0; Claudia Argumedo/Claudia Castro (ESA) d. Cheryl Lewis/Isoke Perry (ANT) 6–2 6–0. **Mexico d. Haiti 3–0:** Karin Palme (MEX) d. Jennifer Adrien (HAI) 6–0 6–3; Jessica Fernandez (MEX) d. Neyssa Etienne (HAI) 6–4 7–6(1); Melody Falco/Paola Palencia (MEX) d. Jennifer

Adrien/Neyssa Etienne (HAI) 6–1 6–0. **Costa Rica d. Barbados 3–0:** Melissa Mendieta (CRC) d. Kim Brandford (BAR) 6–1 6–3; Melissa Golfin (CRC) d. Richele LeSaldo (BAR) 6–2 6–1; Melissa Mendieta/Paula Umana (CRC) d. Kim Brandford/Donna Gibbs (BAR) 6–7(5) 6–2 6–1. **Bermuda d. Antigua & Barbuda 2–1:** Elizabeth Osborne (BER) d. Isoke Perry (ANT) 6–0 6–4; Niki Williams (ANT) d. Kelly Holland (BER) 6–4 4–6 6–4; Kelly Holland/Allison Tolson (BER) d. Francine Harvey/Isoke Perry (ANT) 6–0 6–0. **El Salvador d. Guatemala 2–1:** Ingrid Gonzalez (ESA) d. Maria Fernanda Carrillo (GUA) 6–0 6–2; Luisa Lopez (GUA) d. Claudia Castro (ESA) 6–2 7–5; Claudia Castro/Ingrid Gonzalez (ESA) d. Maria Fernanda Carrillo/Luisa Lopez (GUA) 4–6 6–2 6–3. **Mexico d. El Salvador 3–0:** Karin Palme (MEX) d. Ingrid Gonzalez (ESA) 6–0 6–0; Jessica Fernandez (MEX) d. Claudia Castro (ESA) 7–5 6–2; Melody Falco/Paola Palencia (MEX) d. Claudia Argumedo/Ingrid Gonzalez (ESA) 6–1 6–1. **Costa Rica d. Haiti 2–1:** Melissa Mendieta (CRC) d. Jennifer Adrien (HAI) 6–4 6–4; Neyssa Etienne (HAI) d. Melissa Golfin (CRC) 6–4 7–6(1); Melissa Golfin/Paula Umana (CRC) d. Jennifer Adrien/Neyssa Etienne (HAI) 6–7(2) 6–2 7–5. **Barbados d. Antigua & Barbuda 3–0:** Donna Gibbs (BAR) d. Isoke Perry (ANT) 6–0 6–0; Richele LeSaldo (BAR) d. Niki Williams (ANT) 6–0 6–0; Kim Brandford/Marisa Howell (BAR) d. Francine Harvey/Niki Williams (ANT) 6–2 6–1. **Guatemala d. Bermuda 2–1:** Karla Lehnhoff (GUA) d. Elizabeth Osborne (BER) 6–3 6–1; Danielle Paynter (BER) d. Maria Fernanda Carrillo (GUA) 7–6(3) 6–3; Maria Fernanda Carrillo/Luisa Lopez (GUA) d. Kelly Holland/Allison Tolson (BER) 6–2 6–4. **Mexico d. Costa Rica 3–0:** Melody Falco (MEX) d. Melissa Mendieta (CRC) 7–5 6–2; Paola Palencia (MEX) d. Melissa Golfin (CRC) 6–4 6–3; Jessica Fernandez/Karin Palme (MEX) d. Melissa Mendieta/Paula Umana (CRC) 7–5 6–0. **El Salvador d. Bermuda 3–0:** Ingrid Gonzalez (ESA) d. Elizabeth Osborne (BER) 6–0 6–2; Claudia Castro (ESA) d. Danielle Paynter (BER) 6–0 6–1; Claudia Argumedo/Ingrid Gonzalez (ESA) d. Danielle Paynter/Allison Tolson (BER) 6–1 6–4. **Haiti d. Antigua & Barbuda 3–0:** Emmanuelle Duval (HAI) d. Isoke Perry (ANT) 6–7(2) 6–3 6–3; Neyssa Etienne (HAI) d. Niki Williams (ANT) 6–1 6–1; Emmanuelle Duval/Neyssa Etienne (HAI) d. Isoke Perry/Niki Williams (ANT) 6–1 6–2. **Guatemala d. Barbados 3–0:** Maria Fernanda Carrillo (GUA) d. Marisa Howell (BAR) 6–2 6–0; Luisa Lopez (GUA) d. Richele LeSaldo (BAR) 6–3 6–0; Maria Fernanda Carrillo/Luisa Lopez (GUA) d. Kim Brandford/Donna Gibbs (BAR) 6–2 6–4.

Final Positions: Mexico 1, El Salvador 2, Costa Rica and Haiti 3 tied, Guatemala 5, Barbados 6, Bermuda 7, Antigua & Barbuda 8.

GROUP B: Bahamas, Bolivia, Cuba, Dominican Republic, Jamaica, Panama, Puerto Rico, Trinidad & Tobago. Round Robin: Puerto Rico d. Jamaica 3–0: Joanna Bauza (PUR) d. Tamara Davis (JAM) 7–5 6–1; Mari Toro (PUR) d. Alexandra Chong (JAM) 6–0 6–2; Joanna Bauza/Mari Toro (PUR) d. Alexandra Chong/Tamara Davis (JAM) 6–1 6–2. **Cuba d. Bahamas 3–0:** Yamile Cordova (CUB) d. Janelle Watson (BAH) 6–1 6–1; Yoannis Montesino (CUB) d. Kim Cartwright (BAH) 6–2 6–4; Yamile Cordova/Yoannis Montesino (CUB) d. Kim Cartwright/Jodi Saunders (BAH) 6–3 6–1. **Dominican Republic d. Bolivia 2–1:** Daniela Alvarez (BOL) d. Monica Pimentel (DOM) 6–3 6–3; Joel Schad (DOM) d. Moyra Peres (BOL) 5–7 6–2 6–3; Glennys Cepeda/Joelle Schad (DOM) d. Claudia Herbas/Monica Ribero (BOL) 6–1 6–0. **Trinidad & Tobago d. Panama 2–1:** Anabelle Espinosa (PAN) d. Jeanine Baillie (TRI) 6–3 6–1; Anneliese Rose (TRI) d. Lorena Porras (PAN) 6–1 6–1; Jeanine Baillie/Anneliese Rose (TRI) d. Anabelle Espinosa/Lorena Porras (PAN) 6–0 7–6(5). **Puerto Rico d. Bahamas 3–0:** Joanna Bauza (PUR) d. Jodi Saunders (BAH) 3–6 6–3 7–5; Mari Toro (PUR) d. Kim Cartwright (BAH) 6–0 6–1; Mari Toro/Edna Vazquez (PUR) d. Kim Cartwright/Janelle Watson (BAH) 6–0 6–2. **Dominican Republic d. Trinidad & Tobago 2–1:** Glennys Cepeda (DOM) d. Jeanine Baillie (TRI) 6–3 6–0; Joelle Schad (DOM) d. Anneliese Rose (TRI) 6–4 6–3; Jeanine Baillie/Anneliese Rose (TRI) d. Monica Pimentel/Carla Prieto (DOM) 6–1 6–0. **Bolivia d. Jamaica 2–1:** Moyra Peres (BOL) d. Alexandra Chong (JAM) 7–5 6–1; Camille Walter (JAM) d. Claudia Herbas (BOL) 6–4 6–1; Daniela Alvarez/Moyra Peres (BOL) d. Alexandra Chong/Camille Walter (JAM) 6–4 2–6 6–3. **Cuba d. Panama 3–0:** Yamile Cordova (CUB) d. Anabelle Espinsoa (PAN) 6–2 6–2; Yoannis Montesino (CUB) d. Lorena Porras (PAN) 6–0 6–2; Yanelys Jimenez/Yanet Nunez (CUB) d. Anabelle Espinosa/Yvonne Lohrer (PAN) 6–4 6–3. **Puerto Rico d. Bolivia 3–0:** Joanna Bauza (PUR) d. Daniela Alvarez (BOL) 6–3 4–6 6–2; Mari Toro (PUR) d. Moira Peres (BOL) 6–2 6–2; Joanna Bauza/Mari Toro (PUR) d. Claudia Herbas/Monica Ribero (BOL) 6–1 6–3. **Panama d. Bahamas 2–1:** Anabelle Espinosa (PAN) d. Jodi Saunders (BAH) 7–6(4) 4–6 7–5; Lorena Porras (PAN) d. Janelle Watson (BAH) 6–1 6–0; Kim Cartwright/Jodi Saunders (BAH) d. Yvonne Lohrer/Lorena Porras (PAN) 6–2 6–4. **Trinidad & Tobago d. Jamaica 2–1:** Jeanne Baillie (TRI) d. Tamara Davis (JAM) 6–2 2–6 7–5; Anneliese Rose (TRI) d. Camille Walter (JAM) 6–1 6–4; Tamara Davis/Camille Walter (JAM) d. Nisha Narayansingh/Camille Sesanker (TRI) 6–1 6–1. **Cuba d. Dominican Republic 2–1:** Yamile Cordova (CUB) d. Glennys Cepeda (DOM) 6–0 6–0; Yoannis Montesino (CUB) d. Joelle Schad (DOM) 6–3 6–2; Glennys Cepeda/Karla Prieto (DOM) d. Yanelys Jimenez/Yanet Nunez (CUB) 6–3 7–6(4). **Dominican Republic d. Bahamas 2–1:** Janelle Watson (BAH) d. Monica Pimentel (DOM) 3–6 6–4 6–2; Joelle Schad (DOM) d. Kim Cartwright (BAH) 6–0 6–0; Monica Pimentel/Joelle Schad (DOM) d. Kim Cartwright/Janelle Watson (BAH) 7–5 6–4. **Puerto Rico d. Panama 2–1:** Maria Del Valle (PUR) d. Anabelle Espinosa (PAN) 6–3 7–5; Lorena Porras (PAN) d. Mari Toro (PUR) 6–4 1–6 6–4; Joanna Bauza/Mari Toro (PUR) d. Anabelle Espinosa/Lorena Porras (PAN) 7–5 6–3. **Trinidad & Tobago d. Bolivia 2–1:** Monica Ribero (BOL) d. Jeanne Baillie (TRI) 6–4 7–6(3); Anneliese Rose (TRI) d. Claudia Herbas (BOL) 6–2 6–2; Jeanne Baillie/Anneliese Rose (TRI) d. Moyra Peres/Monica Ribero (BOL) 6–2 6–4. **Cuba d. Jamaica 3–0:** Yamile Cordova (CUB) d. Tamara Davis (JAM) 6–3 6–3; Yoannis Montesino (CUB) d. Alexandra Chong (JAM) 6–1 6–2; Yanelys Jimenez/Yanet Nunez (CUB) d. Alexandra Chong/Tamara Davis (JAM) 6–0 6–4. **Dominican Republic d. Panama 2–1:** Anabelle Espinosa (PAN) d. Carla Prieto (DOM) 6–1 6–3; Jeolle Schad (DOM) d. Lorena Porras (PAN) 6–1 6–4; Glennys Cepeda/Joelle Schad (DOM) d. Anabelle Espinosa/Lorena Porras(PAN) 6–2 4–6 6–1. **Puerto Rico d. Trinidad & Tobago 3–0:** Joanna Bauza (PUR) d. Jeanne Baillie (TRI) 6–1 6–1; Mari Toro (PUR) d. Anneliese Rose (TRI) 6–2 7–6(2); Joanna Bauza/Mari Toro (PUR) d. Jeanne Baillie/Anneliese Rose (TRI) 6–3 6–2. **Jamaica d. Bahamas 3–0:** Tamara Davis (JAM) d. Jodi Saunders (BAH) 6–0 34 ret; Camille Walter (JAM) d. Janelle Watson (BAH) 6–2 6–1; Alexandra Chong/Camille Walter (JAM) d. Kim Cartwright/Janelle Watson (BAH) 6–1 6–2. **Cuba d. Bolivia 3–0:** Yamile Cordova (CUB) d. Daniela Alvarez (BOL) 6–2 6–2; Yoannis Montesino (CUB) d. Moyra Peres (BOL) 6–2 6–1; Yamile Cordova/Yoannis Montesino (CUB) d. Moyra Peres/Monica Ribero (BOL) 6–3 6–3. **Puerto Rico d. Dominican Republic 2–1:** Joanna Bauza (PUR) d. Monica Pimentel (DOM) 6–0 6–0; Mari Toro (PUR) d. Joelle Schad (DOM) 6–3 2–6 6–2; Glennys Cepeda/Carla Prieto (DOM) d. Maria Del Valle/Edna Vazquez (PUR) 6–3 7–6(5). **Cuba d. Trinidad & Tobago 3–0:** Yamile Cordova (CUB) d. Camille Sesanker (TRI) 6–0 6–1; Yoannis Montesino (CUB) d. Anneliese Rose

(TRI) 6–1 5–7 6–2; Yamile Cordova/Yanet Nunez (CUB) d. Jeanne Baillie/Nisha Narayansingh (TRI) 6–1 6–0. **Panama d. Jamaica 3–0:** Anabelle Espinosa (PAN) d. Alexandra Chong (JAM) 6–3 6–3; Lorena Porras (PAN) d. Camille Walter (JAM) 1–6 6–1 6–3; Anabelle Espinosa/Lorena Porras (PAN) d. Alexandra Chong/Tamara Davis (JAM) 6–2 6–2. **Bahamas d. Bolivia 2–1:** Daniela Alvarez (BOL) d. Janelle Watson (BAH) 6–4 7–5; Kim Cartwright (BAH) d. Moyra Peres (BOL) 1–6 6–2 6–2; Kim Cartwright/Jodi Saunders (BAH) d. Daniela Alvarez/Claudia Herbas (BOL) 6–3 6–0. **Puerto Rico d. Cuba 2–1:** Yamile Cordova (CUB) d. Joanna Bauza (PUR) 6–1 6–1; Mari Toro (PUR) d. Yoannis Montesino (CUB) 6–4 6–0; Joanna Bauza/Mari Toro (PUR) d. Yamile Cordova/Yoannis Montesino (CUB) 6–1 2–6 6–3. **Dominican Republic d. Jamaica 3–0:** Glennys Cepeda (DOM) d. Tamara Davis (JAM) 6–2 6–0; Joelle Schad (DOM) d. Camille Walter (JAM) 7–5 6–0; Glennys Cepeda/Carla Prieto (DOM) d. Alexandra Chong/Camille Walter (JAM) 7–6(9) 3–6 7–5. **Panama d. Bolivia 2–1:** Daniela Alvarez (BOL) d. Anabelle Espinosa (PAN) 6–2 6–2; Lorena Porras (PAN) d. Moyra Peres (BOL) 6–3 1–6 6–2; Annabelle Espinosa/Lorena Porras (PAN) d. Daniela Alvarez/Moyra Peres (BOL) 7–5 6–3. **Trinidad & Tobago d. Bahamas 3–0:** Jeanne Baillie (TRI) d. Janelle Watson (BAH) 6–2 6–0; Anneliese Rose (TRI) d. Kim Cartwright (BAH) 6–1 6–2; Jeanne Baillie/Anneliese Rose (TRI) d. Kim Cartwright/Jodi Saunders (BAH) 5–7 6–2 6–1.

Final Positions: Puerto Rico 1, Cuba 2, Dominican Republic 3, Trinidad & Tobago 4, Panama 5, Bolivia 6, Jamaica 7, Bahamas 8.

Mexico and Puerto Rico were promoted to Americas Group I for the 1999 competition.

ASIA/OCEANIA GROUP II

Thana City Golf and Country Club, Bangkok, Thailand, 16–21 February

Group A – India, Pakistan, Iraq.
Round Robin: India d. Pakistan 3–0: Uzma Khan (IND) d. Haleema Rahim (PAK) 6–1 6–1; Nirupama Vaidyanathan (IND) d. Nida Waseem (PAK) 6–0 6–1; Rushmi Chakravarti/Arati Ponnappa (IND) d. Haleema Rahim/Nida Waseem (PAK) 6–1 6–7(5) 6–1. **India d. Iraq 3–0:** Uzma Khan (IND) d. Mina Abdul-Rahman (IRQ) 6–0 6–0; Nirupama Vaidyanathan (IND) d. Ishraq Salman (IRQ) 6–0 6–0; Rushmi Chakravarti/Arati Ponnappa (IND) d. Mina Abdul-Rahman/Ishraq Salman (IRQ) 6–0 6–0. **Pakistan d. Iraq 3–0:** Haleema Rahim (PAK) d. Mina Abdul-Rahman (IRQ) 6–3 6–3; Nida Wassem (PAK) d. Ishraq Salman (IRQ) 6–2 6–1; Mariam Rahim/Nida Waseem (PAK) d. Mina Abdul-Rahman/Ishraq Salman (IRQ) 6–2 6–2.

Group B – Malaysia, Pacific Oceania, Singapore.
Round Robin: Pacific Oceania d. Malaysia 2–1: Paiao Short (POC) d. Lynn-Yin Tan (MAS) 6–2 6–3; Chin-Bee Khoo (MAS) d. Tagifano So'onalole (POC) 6–3 6–0; Paiao Short/ Tagifano So'onalole (POC) d. Chin-Bee Khoo/Lynn-Yin Tan (MAS) 6–3 6–3. **Malaysia d. Singapore 3–0:** Lynn-Yin Tan (MAS) d. Jil-Lin Leong (SIN) 6–4 4–6 6–1; Chin-Bee Khoo (MAS) d. Rui-Jing Wong (SIN) 6–0 6–1; Shau-Shan Liew/Lynn-Yin Tan (MAS) d. Jil-Lin Leong/Rui-Jing Wong 5–7 6–4 6–4. **Pacific Oceania d. Singapore 2–1:** Paiao Short (POC) d. Jil-Lin Leong (SIN) 6–3 7–6(6) 6–1; Tagifano So'onalole (POC) d. Rui-Jing Wong (SIN) 6–1 6–3; Jil-Lin Leong/Rui-Jing Wong (SIN) d. Davilyn Godinet/Adriana Thaggard (POC) 6–3 7–5.

Group C – Tajikistan, Syria, Kazakhstan.
Round Robin: Tajikistan d. Syria 3–0: Eugenia Silantieva (TAJ) d. Farah Dayoub (SYR) 6–1 6–0; Ioulia Roudkovskaia (TAJ) d. Sara Tawil (SYR) 6–1 6–1; Ioulia Roudkovskaia/ Eugenia Silantieva (TAJ) d. Farah Dayoub/Sara Tawil (SYR) 6–3 6–0. **Tajikistan d. Kazakhstan 2–1:** Eugenia Silantieva (TJK) d. Tatiana Babina (KAZ) 6–3 6–1; Alissa Velts (KAZ) d. Ioulia Roudkovskaia (TJK) 4–6 6–3 14–12; Ioulia Roudkovskaia /Eugenia Silantieva (TJK) d. Tatiana Babina/Alissa Velts (KAZ) 6–2 7–5. **Kazakhstan d. Syria 3–0:** Tatiana Babina (KAZ) d. Farah Dayoub (SYR) 7–6(7) 6–1; Alissa Velts (KAZ) d. Sara Tawil (SYR) 5–7 6–2 6–1; Tatiana Babina/Alissa Velts (KAZ) d. Farah Dayoub/Sara Tawil (SYR) 6–0 6–3.

Play-offs for 1st-3rd positions: India d. Tajikistan 2–1: Uzma Khan (IND) d. Eugenia Silantieva (TJK) 4–6 6–0 6–0; Nirupama Vaidyanathan (IND) d. Ioulia Roudkovskaia (TJK) 7–6(4) 6–4; Ioulia Roudkovskaia/Eugenia Silantieva (TJK) d. Rushmi Chakravarti/Arati Ponnappa (IND) 6–4 7–6(0). **India d. Pacific Oceania 2–0:** Uzma Khan (IND) d. Paiao Short (POC) 7–5 7–5; Nirupama Vaidyanathan (IND) d. Tagifano So'onalole (POC) 6–2 7–5; Doubles not played. **Pacific Oceania d. Tajikistan 2–0:** Paiao Short (POC) d. Eugenia Silantieva (TJK) 6–3 6–1; Tagifano So'onalole (POC) d. Ioulia Roudkovskaia (TJK) 6–2 6–3; Doubles not played.

Play-offs for 4th-6th positions: Malaysia d. Pakistan 3–0: Lynn-Yin Tan (MAS) d. Haleema Rahim (PAK) 6–0 6–0; Chin-Bee Khoo (MAS) d. Nida Waseem (PAK) 6–0 6–1; Shau-Shan Liew/Lynn-Yin Tan (MAS) d. Mehnish Chishti/Mariam Rahim (PAK) 6–0 6–0. **Malaysia d. Kazakhstan 2–0:** Lynn-Yin Tan (MAS) d. Tatiana Babina (KAZ) 6–3 3–6 7–5; Chin-Bee Khoo (MAS) d. Alissa Velts (KAZ) 6–3 3–6 6–3; Doubles not played. **Kazakhstan d. Pakistan 2–0:** Tatiana Babina (KAZ) d. Haleema Rahim (PAK) 6–1 6–1; Alissa Velts (KAZ) d. Nida Waseem (PAK) 7–6(5) 6–1; Doubles not played.

Play-offs for 7th-9th positions: Singapore d. Iraq 3–0: Yee-Hong Tan (SIN) d. Mina Abdul-Rahman (IRQ) 3–6 6–3 6–1; Rui-Jing Wong (SIN) d. Ishraq Salman (IRQ) 6–0 6–0; Yee-Hong Tan/Rui-Jing Wong (SIN) d. Mina Abdul-Rahman/Ishraq Salman (IRQ) 6–3 6–0. **Singapore d. Syria 2–1:** Jil-Lin Leong (SIN) d. Farah Dayoub (SYR) 6–2 6–3; Rui-Jing Wong (SIN) d. Sara Tawil (SYR) 6–3 6–1; Farah Dayoub/Sara Tawil (SYR) d. Jil-Lin Leong/Yee-Hong Tan (SIN) 6–2 6–4. **Syria d. Iraq 2–0:** Sandrella Droubi (SYR) d. Salima-Esmat Salman (IRQ) 6–1 6–2; Shaza Tinawi (SYR) d. Mina Abdul-Rahman (IRQ) 7–5 6–3; Doubles not played.

Final Positions: India 1, Pacific Oceania 2, Tajikistan 3, Malaysia 4, Kazakhstan 5, Pakistan 6, Singapore 7, Syria 8, Iraq 9.

India and Pacific Oceania were promoted to Asia/Oceania Group II for the 1999 competition.

EURO/AFRICA GROUP II

Ali Bey Club, Manavgat, Turkey, 5–9 May

GROUP A: Algeria, Cyprus, Denmark, Lithuania, Tunisia.
Round Robin: Denmark d. Lithuania 3–0: Eva Dyrberg (DEN) d. Ilona Jarkova (LIT) 6–0 6–2; Charlotte Aagaard (DEN) d. Ruta Deduraite (LIT) 6–7(2) 6–1 6–4; Eva Dyrberg/Maria Rasmussen (DEN) d. Ruta Deduraite/Edita Liachoviciute (LIT) 6–2 6–0. **Algeria d. Cyprus 3–0:** Samira Takorabt (ALG) d. Stephanie Kambery (CYP) 6–1 6–0; Lamia Hameurlaine (ALG) d. Andria Hadjioannou (CYP) 6–0 6–3; Feriel Esseghir/Lamia Hameurlaine (ALG) d. Daphne Nicolatou/Eleni Papanicolaou (CYP) 4–6 6–1 6–3. **Denmark d. Cyprus 3–0:** Eva Dyrberg (DEN) d. Daphne Nicolatou (CYP) 6–0 6–0; Charlotte Aagaard (DEN) d. Andria Hadjioannou (CYP) 6–0 6–2; Rikke Faurfelt/Maria Rasmussen (DEN) d. Stephanie Kambery/Eleni Papanicolaou (CYP) 6–2 6–0. **Tunisia d. Lithuania 2–1:** Edita Liachoviciute (LIT) d. Issem Essaies (TUN) 6–4 6–1; Selima Sfar (TUN) d. Ruta Deduraite (LIT) 6–0 6–1; Issem Essaies/Selima Sfar (TUN) d. Ruta Deduraite/Edita Liachoviciute (LIT) 6–3 6–1. **Denmark d. Algeria 3–0:** Eva Dyrberg (DEN) d. Siham-Soumeya Bennacer (ALG) 6–1 6–1; Charlotte Aagaard (DEN) d. Feriel Esseghir (ALG) 6–2 6–7(5) 6–0; Eva Dyrberg/Maria Rasmussen (DEN) d. Feriel Esseghir/Lamia Hameurlaine (ALG) 6–2 6–1. **Tunisia d. Cyprus 3–0:** Issem Essaies (TUN) d. Stephanie Kambery (CYP) 6–3 6–1; Selima Sfar (TUN) d. Daphne Nicolatou (CYP) 6–0 6–0; Issem Essaies/Selima Sfar (TUN) d. Andria Hadjioannou/Eleni Papanicolaou (CYP) 6–0 6–1. **Denmark d. Tunisia 2–1:** Maria Rasmussen (DEN) d. Nadia Kilani (TUN) 6–0 6–0; Eva Dyrberg (DEN) d. Selima Sfar (TUN) 7–6(2) 6–2; Issem Essaies/Selima Sfar (TUN) d. Rikke Faurfelt/Maria Rasmussen (DEN) 6–4 5–7 6–2. **Lithuania d. Algeria 3–0:** Ilona Jarkova (LIT) d. Samira Takorabt (ALG) 6–2 6–0; Ruta Deduraite (LIT) d. Lamia Hameurlaine (ALG) 6–0 6–2; Ruta Deduraite/Edita Liachoviciute (LIT) d. Siham-Soumeya Bennacer/Feriel Esseghir (ALG) 4–6 6–4 6–2. **Lithuania d. Cyprus 3–0:** Edita Liachoviciute (LIT) d. Stephanie Kambery (CYP) 6–1 6–0; Ruta Deduraite (LIT) d. Daphne Nicolatou (CYP) 6–0 6–1; Ilona Jarkova/Goda Kuliesyte (LIT) d. Andria Hadjioannou/Daphne Nicolatou (CYP) 6–2 6–2. **Algeria d. Tunisia 2–0:** Siham-Soumeya Bennacer (ALG) d. Nadia Kilani (TUN) 6–2 6–2; Feriel Esseghir (ALG) d. Issem Essaies (TUN) 6–1 6–2; Doubles not played.
Final Positions: Denmark 1, Lithuania 2, Tunisia 3, Algeria 4, Cyprus 5.

Group B: Botswana, Egypt, Finland, FYR Macedonia, Liechtenstein.
Round Robin: Finland d. Botswana 3–0: Kirsi Lampinen (FIN) d. Kelesitse Makgale (BOT) 6–2 6–0; Hanna-Katri Aalto (FIN) d. Mmaphala Letsatle (BOT) 6–0 6–0; Nanne Dahlman/Linda Jansson (FIN) d. Mmaphala Letsatle/Kelesitse Makgale (BOT) 6–0 6–0. **Egypt d. Liechtenstein 2–1:** Dalia El Sheikh (EGY) d. Jeannine Niedhardt (LIE) 6–2 6–3; Marwa El Wany (EGY) d. Angelika Schaedler (LIE) 7–5 7–5; Angelika Schaedler/Sidonia Wolfinger (LIE) d. Marwa El Wany/Dalia El Sheikh (EGY) 4–6 7–5 6–1. **Finland d. Egypt 3–0:** Kirsi Lampinen (FIN) d. May Emara (EGY) 6–2 6–2; Hanna-Katri Aalto (FIN) d. Dalia El Sheikh (EGY) 6–0 6–1; Nanne Dahlman/Linda Jansson (FIN) d. Dalia El Sheikh/May Emara (EGY) 6–0 6–0. **FYR Macedonia d. Liechtenstein 3–0:** Biljana Trpeska (MKD) d. Fabienne Gmeiner (LIE) 6–2 6–3; Marina Lazarovska (MKD) d. Angelika Schaedler (LIE) 6–0 6–1; Marina Lazarovska/Biljana Trpeska (MKD) d. Jeannine Niedhardt/Sidonia Wolfinger (LIE) 6–4 6–0. **Finland d. Liechtenstein 3–0:** Kirsi Lampinen (FIN) d. Sidonia Wolfinger (LIE) 6–0 6–1; Hanna-Katri Aalto (FIN) d. Fabienne Gmeiner (LIE) 6–0 6–1; Nanne Dahlman/Linda Jansson (FIN) d. Angelika Schaedler/Sidonia Wolfinger (LIE) 6–2 6–1. **FYR Macedonia d. Botswana 3–0:** Ana Buraku (MKD) d. Kelesitse Makgale (BOT) 4–6 6–1 6–3; Marina Lazarovska (MKD) d. Mmaphala Letsatle (BOT) 6–1 6–1; Marina Lazarovska/Elena Manevska (MKD) d. Mmaphala Letsatle/Razalia Phethu (BOT) 6–0 6–2. **Liechtenstein d. Botswana 3–0:** Fabienne Gmeiner (LIE) d. Kelesitse Makgale (BOT) 6–0 6–0; Angelika Schaedler (LIE) d. Mmaphala Letsatle (BOT) 6–3 6–3; Fabienne Gmeiner/Jeannine Niedhardt (LIE) d. Mmaphala Letsatle/Kelesitse Makgale (BOT) 7–5 3–6 7–5. **FYR Macedonia d. Egypt 2–1:** Biljana Trpeska (MKD) d. Dalia El Sheikh (EGY) 6–1 7–5; Marina Lazarovska (MKD) d. Marwa El Wany (EGY) 50 ret; Dalia El Sheikh/May Emara (EGY) d. Ana Buraku/Elena Manevska (MKD) 6–4 3–6 8–6. **Finland d. FYR Macedonia 2–1:** Kirsi Lampinen (FIN) d. Biljana Trpeska (MKD) 6–3 6–2; Marina Lazarovska (MKD) d. Hanna-Katri Aalto (FIN) 6–3 7–6(1); Nanne Dahlman/Linda Jansson (FIN) d. Marina Lazarovska/Biljana Trpeska (MKD)1–6 7–5 6–2. **Egypt d. Botswana 2–0:** May Emara (EGY) d. Kelesitse Makgale (BOT) 6–0 6–0; Dalia El Sheikh (EGY) d. Mmaphala Letsatle (BOT) 6–2 6–3; Doubles not played.
Final Positions: Finland 1, FYR Macedonia 2, Egypt 3, Liechtenstein 4, Botswana 5.

GROUP C: Armenia, Ethiopia, Luxembourg, Malta, Norway, Turkey.
Round Robin: Turkey d. Armenia 2–1: Ismet Duygu Aksit (TUR) d. Tereza Simonian (ARM) 6–4 6–4; Sona Saringulian (ARM) d. Gulberk Gultekin (TUR) 6–4 1–6 6–3; Ismet Duygu Aksit/Gulberk Gultekin (TUR) d. Naira Santrosian/Sona Saringulian (ARM) 6–0 4–6 7–5. **Norway d. Malta 3–0:** Caroline Tidemand (NOR) d. Lisa Camenzuli (MLT) 6–4 7–5; Karoline Borgersen (NOR) d. Carol Torreggiani (MLT) 6–0 6–2; Karoline Borgersen/Tina Samara (NOR) d. Lisa Camenzuli/Carol Torreggiani (MLT) 6–7(3) 6–2 6–2. **Luxembourg d. Ethiopia 3–0:** Claudine Schaul (LUX) d. Kefyalw Rediet (ETH) 6–0 6–0; Anne Kremer (LUX) d. Seble Woldegebrail (ETH) 6–0 6–0; Anne Kremer/Alexandra Scholer (LUX) d. Kefyalw Rediet/Seble Woldegebrail (ETH) 6–0 6–1. **Turkey d. Norway 3–0:** Ismet Duygu Aksit (TUR) d. Caroline Tidemand (NOR) 3–6 6–1 6–4; Gulberk Gultekin (TUR) d. Tina Samara (NOR) 7–6(4) 6–1; Ismet Duygu Aksit/Gulberk Gultekin (TUR) d. Karoline Borgersen/Tina Samara (NOR) 5–7 7–6(3) 6–3. **Armenia d. Ethiopia 3–0:** Tereza Simonian (ARM) d. Kefyalw Rediet (ETH) 6–0 6–1; Sona Saringulian (ARM) d. Seble Wodegebrail (ETH) 6–0 6–1; Tereza Simonian/Lilit Telumian (ARM) d. Kefyalw Rediet/Seble Woldegebrail (ETH) 6–2 6–1. **Luxembourg d. Malta 3–0:** Claudine Schaul (LUX) d. Helen Asciak (MLT) 6–4 6–1; Anne Kremer (LUX) d. Lisa Camenzuli (MLT) 6–2 6–0; Celine Francois/Anne Kremer (LUX) d. Lisa Camenzuli/Carol Toreggiani (MLT) 3–6 7–6(4) 6–3. **Turkey d. Malta 2–1:** Ismet Duygu Aksit (TUR) d. Lisa Camenzuli (MLT) 6–3 7–5; Gulberk Gultekin (TUR) d. Carol Torreggiani (MLT) 7–6(4) 7–5; Helen Asciak/Lisa Camenzuli (MLT) d. Serra Olgac/Seden Ozlu (TUR) 6–2 6–3. **Norway d. Ethiopia 3–0:** Karoline Borgersen (NOR) d. Kefyalw Rediet (ETH) 6–0 6–0; Tina Samara (NOR) d. Seble Woldegebrail (ETH) 6–0 6–1; Karoline Borgersen/Tina Samara (NOR) d. Kefyalw Rediet/Seble Woldegebrail (ETH) 6–0 6–0. **Luxembourg d. Armenia 2–1:** Claudine Schaul (LUX) d. Tereza Simonian (ARM) 6–4 6–0; Anne Kremer (LUX) d. Sona Saringulian (ARM) 3–6 6–2 6–3; Naira Santrosian/Sona Saringulian (ARM) d. Celine Francois/Claudine Schaul (LUX) 7–6(5) 5–7 7–5. **Turkey d. Ethiopia 3–0:** Serra Olgac (TUR) d. Kefyalw Rediet (ETH) 6–0 6–0; Seden Ozlu (TUR) d. Seble

Woldegebrail (ETH) 6–0 6–0; Serra Olgac/Seden Ozlu (TUR) d. Kefyalw Rediet/Seble Woldegebrail (ETH) 6–0 6–0. **Armenia d. Malta 2–1:** Naira Santrosian (ARM) d. Helen Asciak (MLT) 6–2 2–6 6–3; Sona Saringulian (ARM) d. Lisa Camenzuli (MLT) 6–3 5–7 6–2; Helen Asciak/Lisa Camenzuli (MLT) d. Tereza Simonian/Lilit Telumian (ARM) 6–3 6–2. **Luxembourg d. Norway 3–0:** Claudine Schaul (LUX) d. Caroline Tidemand (NOR) 6–4 6–3; Anne Kremer (LUX) d. Karoline Borgersen (NOR) 6–3 6–0; Celine Francois/Anne Kremer (LUX) d. Karoline Borgersen/Tina Samara (NOR) 6–1 6–1. **Luxembourg d. Turkey 2–1:** Claudine Schaul (LUX) d. Ismet Duygu Aksit (TUR) 6–2 7–5; Anne Kremer (LUX) d. Gulberk Gultekin (TUR) 6–3 6–3; Ismet Duygu Aksit/Gulberk Gultekin (TUR) d. Celine Francois/Alexandra Scholer (LUX) 6–2 6–1. **Norway d. Armenia 2–1:** Karoline Borgersen (NOR) d. Tereza Simonian (ARM) 6–4 6–1; Sona Saringulian (ARM) d. Tina Samara (NOR) 6–3 6–2; Karoline Borgersen/Tina Samara (NOR) d. Naira Santrosian/Sona Saringulian (ARM) 7–5 6–2. **Malta d. Ethiopia 2–0:** Helen Asciak (MLT) d. Temesgen Metasebeya (ETH) 6–0 6–0; Lisa Camenzuli (MLT) d. Seble Woldegebrail (ETH) 6–0 6–0; Doubles not played.
Final Positions: Luxembourg 1, Turkey 2, Norway 3, Armenia 4, Malta 5, Ethiopia 6.

GROUP D: Bosnia & Herzogovina, Estonia, Georgia, Iceland, Ireland, Moldova.
Round Robin: Estonia d. Iceland 3–0: Liina Suurvarik (EST) d. Rakel Petursdottir (ISL) 6–0 6–1; Helen Laupa (EST) d. Stefania Stefansdottir (ISL) 7–5 6–3; Maret Ani/Helen Holter (EST) d. Rakel Petursdottir/Stefania Stefansdottir (ISL) 6–1 6–2. **Bosnia & Herzogovina d. Ireland 2–1:** Mervana Jugic (BIH) d. Lesley O'Halloran (IRL) 7–6(2) 6–1; Asja Tankic (BIH) d. Gina Niland (IRL) 6–1 7–6(5); Yvonne Flynn/Aoife O'Neill (IRL) d. Harisa Delic/Adisa Salibasic (BIH) 4–6 6–4 6–2. **Georgia d. Moldova 3–0:** Margalita Chakhnashvili (GEO) d. Evghenia Ablovatchi (MOL) 6–4 6–4; Nino Louarsabishvili (GEO) d. Natalia Volcova (MOL) 7–5 0–6 6–2; Margalita Chakhnashvili/Nino Louarsabishvili (GEO) d. Evghenia Ablovatchi/Natalia Volcova (MOL) 6–2 6–4. **Ireland d. Estonia 2–1:** Lesley O'Halloran (IRL) d. Helen Holter (EST) 7–5 6–1; Gina Niland (IRL) d. Liina Suurvarik (EST) 0–6 6–2 6–2; Maret Ani/Helen Laupa (EST) d. Yvonne Flynn/Lesley O'Halloran (IRL) 6–2 6–1. **Moldova d. Iceland 3–0:** Elena Arabadji (MOL) d. Rakel Petursdottir (ISL) 6–2 6–2; Evghenia Ablovatchi (MOL) d. Stefania Stefansdottir (ISL) 6–1 6–1; Evghenia Ablovatchi/Elena Petrenco (MOL) d. Stella Kristiansdottir/Stefania Stefansdottir (ISL) 6–2 6–0. **Georgia d. Bosnia & Herzogovina 2–1:** Mervana Jugic (BIH) d. Margalita Chakhnashvili (GEO) 6–4 6–4; Nino Louarsabishvili (GEO) d. Asja Tankic (BIH) 6–0 6–2; Margalita Chakhnashvili/Nino Louarsabishvili (GEO) d. Mervana Jugic/Asja Tankic (BIH) 6–1 6–2. **Estonia d. Bosnia & Herzegovina 2–1:** Helen Holter (EST) d. Mervana Jugic (BIH) 6–4 6–1; Asja Tankic (BIH) d. Liina Suurvarik (EST) 6–2 6–7(5) 6–4; Maret Ani/Helen Laupa (EST) d. Mervana Jugic/Asja Tankic (BIH) 1–6 6–3 6–2. **Ireland d. Moldova 2–1:** Lesley O'Halloran (IRL) d. Evghenia Ablovatchi (MOL) 6–1 4–6 7–5; Gina Niland (IRL) d. Natalia Volcova (MOL) 7–5 6–2; Elena Petrenco/Natalia Volcova (MOL) d. Yvonne Flynn/Aoife O'Neill (IRL) 6–7(2) 6–4 7–5. **Georgia d. Iceland 3–0:** Margalita Chakhnashvili (GEO) d. Rakel Petursdottir (ISL) 6–1 6–0; Nino Louarsabishvili (GEO) d. Stefania Stefansdottir (ISL) 6–0 6–0; Irene Kakulia/Nino Louarsabishvili (GEO) d. Stella Kristiansdottir/Stefania Stefansdottir (ISL) 6–1 6–0. **Estonia d. Moldova 2–1:** Helen Holter (EST) d. Evghenia Ablovatchi (MOL) 6–2 6–3; Natalia Volcova (MOL) d. Helen Laupa (EST) 6–1 6–2; Maret Ani/Liina Suurvarik (EST) d. Evghenia Ablovatchi/Natalia Volcova (MOL) 6–1 6–1. **Bosnia & Herzegovina d. Iceland 3–0:** Mervana Jugic (BIH) d. Rakel Petursdottir (ISL) 6–1 6–2; Asja Tankic (BIH) d. Stefania Stefansdottir (ISL) 6–1 6–0; Harisa Delic/Adisa Salibasic (BIH) d. Stella Kristiansdottir/Stefania Stefansdottir (ISL) 6–0 6–1. **Georgia d. Ireland 3–0:** Margalita Chakhnashvili (GEO) d. Lesley O'Halloran (IRL) 6–4 6–2; Nino Louarsabishvili (GEO) d. Gina Niland (IRL) 6–3 6–1; Margalita Chakhnashvili/Nino Louarsabishvili (GEO) d. Yvonne Flynn/Aoife O'Neill (IRL) 6–3 6–1. **Georgia d. Estonia 2–1:** Margalita Chakhnashvili (GEO) d. Helen Holter (EST) 5–7 6–2 6–3; Nino Louarsabishvili (GEO) d. Liina Suurvarik (EST) 6–4 6–3; Maret Ani/Helen Laupa (EST) d. Irene Kakulia/Nino Louarsabishvili (GEO) 6–4 7–6(2). **Ireland d. Iceland 3–0:** Yvonne Flynn (IRL) d. Rakel Petursdottir (ISL) 6–1 6–1; Gina Niland (IRL) d. Stefania Stefansdottir (ISL) 6–0 6–0; Lesley O'Halloran/Aoife O'Neill (IRL) d. Stella Kristiansdottir/Stefania Stefansdottir (ISL) 6–1 6–1. **Moldova d. Bosnia & Herzegovina 2–1:** Mervana Jugic (BIH) d. Elena Petrenco (MOL) 6–3 2–6 6–1; Natalia Volcova (MOL) d. Asja Tankic (BIH) 2–6 7–6(1) 6–0; Elena Arabadji/Natalia Volcova (MOL) d. Mervana Jugic/Asja Tankic (BIH) 0–6 7–5 6–3.
Final Positions: Georgia 1, Estonia 2, Ireland 3, Bosnia & Herzegovina 4, Moldova 5, Iceland 6.

Denmark, Finland, Luxembourg and Georgia were promoted to Euro/Africa Group I for the 1999 competition.

Hyundai Hopman Cup

Barry Wood

The winners of the 10th Hyundai Hopman Cup, the Slovak Republic, were by a strange irony direct beneficiaries of the Asian financial crisis that swept through the region in the second half of 1997. It was originally intended that a play-off would be held between Asian nations to earn a qualifying spot against Romania, but the crisis put an end to those ambitions.

By coincidence, as that idea was abandoned, Miloslav Mecir, a member of the winning 1989 Czechoslovakian team, called the organisers and asked if there was any possibility of a place being found in the draw for the Slovak Republic. He was told they could play the qualifying match, which they won, and they then astonished everyone by going on to win the event.

Karol Kucera, coached by Mecir, and Karina Habsudova, lost their first tie against Spain, with Arantxa Sanchez-Vicario overcoming Habsudova 6–2 6–3 and Kucera beating Carlos Moya 7–5 6–4 before the Spaniards took the doubles 7–6 6–1. The Slovaks rebounded by beating the Swedish team of Thomas Enqvist and Asa Carlsson 3–0, and then edged past Australia 2–1 to earn a place in the final. Habsudova defeated Annabel Ellwood 6–3 6–3, and in one of the highlights of the week Patrick Rafter levelled the score at 1–1 as he battled to a three set win over Kucera. The Slovaks advanced with a 7–5 6–2 win in the doubles.

The final, against France, also went to a deciding rubber, as Mary Pierce – who along with Sanchez-Vicario and Rafter went through the week undefeated – overcame Habsudova 6–4 7–5, and Kucera defeated Cedric Pioline 7–6 6–4 in the Frenchman's only setback of the week. The Slovak Republic then claimed victory with a 6–3 6–4 win in the doubles.

France had reached the final by beating the German team of Tommy Haas and Anke Huber, the USA pairing of Chanda Rubin and Jonathan Stark, and finally the South African team of Amanda Coetzer and Wayne Ferreira, all without dropping a rubber.

In a re-match of the 1997 final, this time played in the first round, South Africa defeated the defending champions, USA, with Coetzer losing to Rubin and Ferreira getting the better of Stark before matters were settled in the doubles. Stark was a late, but higher ranked, replacement for the injured Justin Gimelstob, who had been the American hero in 1997.

Last-minute participants for a qualifying spot, Slovak Republic, represented by Karol Kucera and Karina Habsudova, won the world's Mixed Team Championship for the first time and received the trophy from Mrs Lucy Hopman. (Stephen Wake)

Attendance approached record levels, helped by the very real possibility of Australia reaching the final. Their quest was helped by some superb performances by Rafter, who was playing on home soil for the first time since winning the US Open, and some gallant back-up from the inexperienced but inspired play of Ellwood, who more than held her own in the doubles. Rafter beat Enqvist 6–3 1–6 7–5 in a tense battle against Sweden, struggled past Moya 7–5 1–6 7–6 and then won 7–6 3–6 7–6 against Kucera.

Participants in the Hyundai Hopman Cup often go on to perform exceptionally well during the remainder of the Australian circuit. On this occasion Kucera won Sydney and overcame Pete Sampras in Melbourne, and Huber reached the semi-finals of the Australian Open.

HYUNDAI HOPMAN CUP 1998

BURSWOOD DOME RESORT, PERTH, 4–10 JANUARY 1998

SEEDS: **1 Spain:** Carlos Moya/Arantxa Sanchez-Vicario. **2 France:** Cedric Pioline/Mary Pierce. **3 South Africa:** Wayne Ferreira/Amanda Coetzer. **4 Australia:** Patrick Rafter/Annabel Ellwood
UNSEEDED: **Sweden:** Thomas Enqvist/Asa Carlsson. **Slovak Republic:** Karol Kucera/Karina Habsudova. **USA:** Jonathan Stark/Chanda Rubin. **Germany:** Tommy Haas/Anke Huber. ***ALTERNATE:*** **Romania:** Dinu Pescariu/Irina Spirlea

Qualifying playoff
Slovak Republic d. Romania 2–1: K. Habsudova d. I. Spirlea 3–6 6–4 6–2; K. Kucera d. D. Pescariu 6–1 6–2; D. Pescariu/I. Spirlea d. K. Kucera/K. Habsudova 6–4 4–6 8–6 (tiebreak).

Round Robin results
Group A
Australia d. Sweden 3–0: A. Ellwood d. A. Carlsson 6–4 6–4; P. Rafter d. T. Enqvist 6–3 1–6 7–5; P. Rafter/A. Ellwood d. T. Enqvist/A. Carlsson 6–2 6–4.
Spain d. Slovak Republic 2–1: A. Sanchez-Vicario d. K. Habsudova 6–2 6–3; K. Kucera d. C. Moya 7–5 6–4; C. Moya/A. Sanchez-Vicario d. K. Kucera/K. Habsudova 7–6(3) 6–1.
Slovak Republic d. Sweden 3–0: K. Habsudova d. A. Carlsson 6–3 6–3; K. Kucera d. T. Enqvist 6–4 6–4; K. Kucera/K. Habsudova d. T. Enqvist/A. Carlsson 7–5 6–3.
Australia d. Spain 2–1: A. Sanchez-Vicario d. A. Ellwood 6–2 6–4; P. Rafter d. C. Moya 7–5 1–6 7–6(6); P. Rafter/A. Ellwood d. C. Moya/A. Sanchez-Vicario 7–5 6–2.
Slovak Republic d. Australia 2–1: K. Habsudova d. A. Ellwood 6–3 6–3; P. Rafter d. K. Kucera 7–6(3) 3–6 7–6(3); K. Kucera/K. Habsudova d. P. Rafter/A. Ellwood 7–5 6–2.
Spain d. Sweden 2–1: A. Sanchez-Vicario d. A. Carlsson 6–1 6–2; T. Enqvist d. C. Moya 6–4 6–1; C. Moya/A. Sanchez-Vicario d. T. Enqvist/A. Carlsson 6–3 6–4.
Group B
South Africa d. USA 2–1: C. Rubin d. A. Coetzer 6–4 6–3; W. Ferreira d. J. Stark 3–6 6–3 6–4; W. Ferreira/ A. Coetzer d. J. Stark/C. Rubin 6–2 5–7 6–1.
France d. Germany 3–0: M. Pierce d. A. Huber 4–6 6–4 6–3; C. Pioline d. T. Haas 6–4 6–4; C. Pioline/ M. Pierce d. T. Haas/A. Huber 2–6 6–3 7–3 (tiebreak).
South Africa d. Germany 2–1: A. Huber d. A. Coetzer 6–3 6–3; W. Ferreira d. T. Haas 6–4 3–6 6–1; W. Ferreira/A. Coetzer d. T. Haas/A. Huber 6–2 6–2.
France d. USA 3–0: M. Pierce d. C. Rubin 6–0 6–3; C. Pioline d. J. Stark 6–4 6–3; C. Pioline/M. Pierce d. J. Stark/C. Rubin 6–4 7–6(3).
USA d. Germany 2–1: A. Huber d. C. Rubin 6–3 6–1; J. Stark d. T. Haas 7–6(4) 6–7(3) 6–4; J. Stark/C. Rubin d. T. Haas/A. Huber 6–3 6–4.
France d. South Africa 3–0: M. Pierce d. A. Coetzer 6–3 6–3; C. Pioline d. W. Ferreira 7–6(6) 6–3; C. Pioline/M. Pierce d. W. Ferreira/A. Coetzer 6–4 7–6(4).

FINAL: Slovak Republic d. France 2–1: M. Pierce d. K. Habsudova 6–4 7–5; K. Kucera d. C. Pioline 7–6(7) 6–4; K. Kucera/K. Habsudova d. C. Pioline/M. Pierce 6–3 6–4.

Cedric Pioline's only singles loss was to Kucera in the final as the French were beaten 2–1. (Stephen Wake)

ITF Youth Cups

Sunshine Cup & Connolly Continental Cup

Rosie Hyde

The superb USTA National Training Center at Crandon Park, Key Biscayne this year played host to the prestigious ITF Sunshine Cup and ITF Connolly Continental Cup competitions. In its second year under the ITF/USTA umbrella, the standard of tennis displayed did not fail to impress.

With no less than five top junior boys vying for the ITF Junior World Champion title spread among the teams, competition in the boys' event always promised to be tough. It proved to be just that. The 6th and 7th seeded nations, Brazil and Sweden respectively, fell in the first round against two fearless European teams. Switzerland's convincing 3–0 win over Sweden, with world No. 4 Roger Federer at the helm, led them to a dramatic contest with the No. 1 seeds, Spain, in the quarter-finals, whilst Croatia fought hard to overcome 6th seeded Brazil in the deciding doubles after two long, arduous but evenly-matched singles rubbers.

Spain faced the sore possibility of early defeat in the quarter-finals when, in the deciding doubles against Switzerland, they just managed to clinch the second set 7–6(6) after falling in the first 4–6. Fortunes swung like a pendulum in the third set with Spain appearing certain victors at 5–2. However, Federer's awesome strength and resolution assisted the Swiss in pulling back to 5–5. The tie could have gone either way, but after a marathon struggle the Spanish came out on top taking the final set 9–7.

USA, seeded 8, kept the home crowd entertained, ousting the No. 2 seeds, Argentina, in another marathon conflict. It was a fiery confrontation which saw both singles rubbers go to three sets. With Guillermo Coria, ranked No. 6 in the world, and David Nalbandian, ranked No. 3, in the Argentine line-up and the memory of last year's tortuous semi-final doubles defeat against France still fresh in everyone's mind, it seemed inevitable that the immense stamina of Nalbandian and Edgardo Massa would result in the downfall of the 8th seeds. This was not to be. USA's Simone Amorico and David Martin were more than a match for the emotionally charged South American duo and, with home support behind them, they came through eventually to win 7–5 6–4.

In the remaining quarter-finals, 4th seeded Russia's hopes were soon dashed by Croatia who put on an impressive display to defeat them 3–0. Unfortunately, Frenchman Julien Jeanpierre, ranked No. 1 in the world, never found his form in the competition and failed to put up any real fight against Italy's Federico Luzzi who sealed the singles and the tie 6–3 2–6 6–3.

Having held on until the semi-finals, unseeded Croatia could not hold off USA whose ever-increasing confidence saw them to a 3–0 victory and a place in the final. It was third time unlucky for Lovro Zovko. In spite of overcoming opponents such as Russian No. 1 Artem Derepasko and Brazil's Ricardo Mello in earlier rounds, he could not find the strength to bring down USA's Zack Fleishman who delighted fans by securing the match and the tie 6–4 6–2.

Spain progressed comfortably to the final defeating Italy 3–0. Tommy Robredo, gold medallist in this year's NEC World Youth Cup final, proved rock solid in Spain's overall performance at the Sunshine Cup, never dropping a set in singles and playing a crucial role in all but one of the doubles rubbers. The semi-finals were no different as he saw off Francesco Aldi 6–3 6–2 thus paving the way for Juan Carlos Ferrero to claim Spain's rightful position in the finals, beating Luzzi 6–4 6–4.

In the final, the USA boys, sporting patriotic red, white and blue hair colour, as they had throughout the event, thoroughly enjoyed performing on centre stage for their enthusiastic audience. However, Spain's superiority as No. 1 seeds shone through and their 3–0 triumph confirmed them as worthy champions.

Only one seed went down in the first round of the girls' event when Croatia, 8, fell victim to the Czech Republic. The Czech girls, who had been in the running for a seeding position and just missed out, proved how fine the line really was between the two teams. After losing the first singles rubber, Czech Republic levelled the tie 1–1 with Iveta Benesova's 6–7(4) 6–2 6–1 victory over Dora Krstulovic and it was left to the deciding doubles to see them through to the quarter-finals.

In the next round, Czech Republic faced the No. 1 seeds, USA, but the might of Jackie Trail and Alexandra Stevenson was too much for them and USA took the tie 3–0.

For entertainment value, the battle between No. 2 seeds Russia, and France, 7, was the highlight of the quarter-finals. The first set of the opening singles rubber went to Stephanie Foretz 6–4, but Anastassia Myskina fought back in the second set winning it 7–6(5). However, Foretz proved just too strong for Myskina and she finally clinched the third set 8–6. Elena Dementieva looked to be in trouble after going down 1–6 in the first set against Aurelie Vedy, but her natural fighting spirit saved the day as she snatched the second set 7–6(2). By the third set, Dementieva had recaptured her form and overcame the French girl taking it 6–2. The Russians dominated the deciding doubles to win through to the semi-finals.

Germany's Mia Buric forced Argentina to a deciding doubles with a surprise victory over Erica Krauth, who at No. 4 in the ITF Junior World Rankings was the highest ranked girl in the competition. Nevertheless, Clarisa Fernandez and Maria Emilia Salerni were invincible in the doubles and the South Americans sealed the tie 2–1 to claim a semi-final slot.

With all the top seeds still intact going into the semi-finals, it was satisfying to see teams representing three different regions battling it out for the title.

The Russian girls secured their place in the Final for the second year running with a 2–1 win over Argentina. USA and Spain were on level terms going into the doubles and provided a dramatic three-setter which kept the home crowd on the edges of their seats. After taking the first set 6–1, Spain looked unbeatable, but USA's Alexandra Stevenson and Sarah Taylor reversed fortunes by taking the second 6–4. However, the persistence of Marta Marrero and Maria Jose Martinez was too much for the No. 1 seeds and Spain grasped the final set to make it an all European Final.

Myskina, who, along with Dementieva, was runner-up in the 1997 Final, looked certain of winning the opening rubber when she led by a set and 5–2 against Spain's Marta Marrero. The title then threatened to slip away as Marrero fought bravely back to win a gripping match 3–6 7–6(5) 6–2. Lourdes Dominguez made life very difficult for Dementieva and was unlucky to lose the second singles match in two tie-break sets. It was left to the doubles to decide the championship and at 3–6 6–3, the two teams seemed inseparable. But it was the might and determination of the Russians which saw them take the final set in style 6–1 and a highly deserved championship trophy.

In the third place play-offs, the Italian boys took bronze with a 2–1 win over Croatia in the deciding doubles whilst Argentina girls came through to beat USA to the medal position.

There was to be no double for Spain, but all teams were honoured to receive their respective trophies and medals in the presence of Eddie Herr, founder of the Competitions.

ITF SUNSHINE CUP 1998
Boys' 18 & Under International Team Championship

16 nations competed. Event played in Key Biscayne, Florida, USA, 7–12 December.
Quarter-finals: Spain d. Switzerland 2–1; Italy d. France 3–0; Croatia d. Russia 3–0; USA d. Argentina 2–1.
Semi-finals: Spain d. Italy 3–0; USA d. Croatia 3–0.
Final: **Spain d. USA 3–0** (T. Robredo d. D. Martin 6–3 6–3; J. C. Ferrero d. Z. Fleishman 6–4 6–3; F. Lopez/T. Robredo d. S. Amorico/D. Martin 6–4 7–5).

ITF CONNOLLY CONTINENTAL CUP 1998
Girls' 18 & Under International Team Championship

16 nations competed. Event played in Key Biscayne, Florida, USA, 7–12 December.
Quarter-finals: USA d. Czech Republic 3–0; Spain d. Slovak Republic 2–1; Argentina d. Germany 2–1; Russia d. France 2–1. ***Semi-finals:*** Spain d. USA 2–1; Russia d. Argentina 2–1.
Final: **Russia d. Spain 2–1** (A. Myskina lost to M. Marrero 6–3 6–7(5) 2–6; E. Dementieva d. L. Dominguez 7–6(1) 7–6(4); E. Dementieva/A. Myskina d. M. Marrero/M. J. Martinez 3–6 6–3 6–1).

NEC World Youth Cup

Jackie Nesbitt

A crowd of over 2,000 had plenty to cheer about on the final day of the 14th NEC World Youth Cup Competition in Cuneo, Italy as the home country's girls overturned the seeding to defeat top ranked Slovak Republic 2–1 to take the girls' title and neighbours Spain fully justified top billing and took the boys' title following a 2–1 win over Croatia.

The Spanish boys, led by Tommy Robredo, had looked odds-on favourites for the title from the outset. In practice the team of Robredo, David Ferrer and Marc Lopez had drawn admiring glances from their fellow competitors and the nature of their first two victories over Australia and Italy, had led to fears that they would overwhelm all opponents.

Russia (5) laid to rest that myth in the semi-finals when Dmitriy Vlasov took the first rubber over Ferrer. Mikhail Youzhny captured the opening set of the top singles against Robredo, but the Spaniard clawed his way to a three-set win and later teamed with Lopez to put in a superb performance in the deciding doubles.

The final produced play of the highest quality, with Italy attempting to win their first ever girls' trophy. Roko Karanusic and Lopez opened with an entertaining tussle, won eventually by the Croatian 3–6 6–3 6–3. Robredo levelled matters, but not before Mario Radic had forced him to produce a top quality performance to stem a flow of stinging winners from his opponent.

A tense opening set of the deciding doubles went the way of the Spanish, following which Lopez and Robredo were able to relax and produce some flamboyant shot-making to excite the spectators. The applause received by Robredo when he and his team mates were introduced at the Closing Ceremony was not far short of that reserved for the home girls and it was quite clear that the flair of the Spanish had been much appreciated.

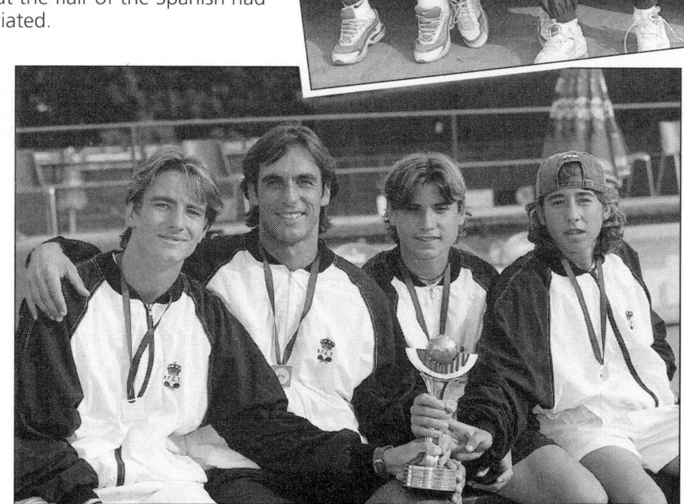

The Italian Girls (above right) and the Spanish Boys took the honours at the NEC World Youth Cup played at Cuneo in Italy. (Georgio Maiozzi)

Italy's girls may not have matched the quality of play produced by the Spanish, but for sheer entertainment value they simply could not be faulted. Opening against the Japanese, they struggled early on when Roberta Vinci lost a thrilling opening singles 8–6 in the third set. Maria Elena Camerin levelled and the scene was set for what was to become a familiar pattern for Italy throughout the week – a deciding doubles.

If the people of Cuneo were looking forward to a relaxing few hours watching tennis after work, the Italian match court was not the place to be. Vinci made up for her singles loss, teaming with Flavia Pennetta to pull off an inspired win over a very solid Japanese pair, in a match that saw the spectators agonising over every point.

The quarter-final tie against Sweden was to prove no easier, despite a more solid singles performance by Vinci over Klara Petersson. Camerin was well beaten by the athletic Jenny Lindstrom and it needed another drama filled doubles by Vinci and Pennetta to keep Italian hopes on track.

Although finishing behind Italy in qualifying, the French team had been strengthened considerably by the addition at no. 1 of Virginie Razzano, probably the best individual participant in the girls' event. She demolished Pennetta for the loss of one game to level after Vinci's win over Melinda Malouli, and surely only the incredible support of the spectators enabled Pennetta and Vinci to pull off a nail-biting 7–5 third set doubles victory.

After the celebrations following the semi-final doubles, it would have been almost cruel if Italy had not managed to claim the title. They got off to the worst possible start, however, against the Slovaks when Vinci lost another 8–6 third set marathon, this time to a determined Stanislava Hrozenska. Camerin came to the rescue with a 6–4 6–2 win over the much higher ranked Daniela Hantuchova, in a match that saw the big hitting Slovak become increasingly frustrated by some brilliant retrieving.

When Pennetta and Vinci closed out the first set of the deciding doubles, Slovak heads dropped and in the final game of the second set, neither Italian could keep a smile of expectant elation from her face.

The French teams suffered a day of mixed fortunes during the battles for third place. Razzano was once again in masterful form, dropping just the one game against Argentina's Maria Emilia Salerni, to follow Stephanie Cohen-Aloro's earlier win over Eugenia Chialvo. Their boys came close against Russia, but with Youzhny still showing the form he displayed against Robredo in the semi-finals, they succumbed in the deciding doubles.

A week of perfect weather, super matches and great spectator support was capped by a wonderful home win – nothing less than the organisers in Cuneo deserved.

NEC WORLD YOUTH CUP 1998
ITF Team Championships for 16 & Under

82 nations competed, 82 taking part in the boys' event and 69 in the girls' event. Final stages took place in Cuneo, Italy, 15–20 September.

FINAL POSITIONS – BOYS: Champion nation: Spain; runners-up: Croatia; 3rd: Russia; 4th: France; 5th: Argentina; 6th: Slovenia; 7th: USA; 8th: Italy; 9th: India; 10th: Mexico; 11th: China; 12th: Japan; 13th: Australia; 14th: Brazil; 15th: Ecuador; 16th: Egypt; **GIRLS:** Champion nation: Italy; runners-up: Slovak Republic; 3rd: France; 4th: Argentina; 5th: Australia; 6th: Czech Republic; 7th: Croatia; 8th: Sweden; 9th: USA; 10th: China; 11th: Japan; 12th: South Africa; 13th: Canada; 14th: Korea; 15th: Brazil; 16th: Chile.
BOYS' CHAMPIONSHIP – Semi-finals: Spain d. Russia 2–1: (D. Ferrer lost to D. Vlassov 2–6 3–6; T. Robredo d. M. Youzhny 3–6 6–4 6–2; M. Lopez/T. Robredo d. D. Vlassov/M. Youzhny 6–3 6–0). **Croatia d. France 2–1:** (R. Karanusic d. J. Cassaigne 7–6(4) 6–0; M. Radic lost to N. Mahut 2–6 3–6; R. Karanusic/ M. Radic d. J. Cassaigne/N. Mahut 6–4 5–7 10–8). **3rd place play-off: Russia d. France 2–1:** (D. Vlassov lost to J. Maigret 6–4 3–6 4–6; M. Youzhny d. N. Mahut 6–2 6–2; S. Pozdnev/M. Youzhny d. J. Cassaigne/ N. Mahut 7–6(5) 6–3). **Final: Spain d. Croatia 2–1:** (M. Lopez lost to R. Karanusic 6–3 3–6 3–6; T. Robredo d. M. Radic 6–4 6–4; M. Lopez/T. Robredo d. R. Karanusic/M. Radic 6–4 6–2).
GIRLS' CHAMPIONSHIP – Semi-finals: Slovak Republic d. Argentina 2–1: (S. Hrozenska d. E. Chialvo 3–6 6–1 6–4; D. Hantuchova d. M. Salerni 6–2 6–4; D. Hantuchova/S. Hrozenska lost to E. Chialvo/M. Salerni 4–6 0–6). **Italy d. France 2–1:** (R. Vinci d. M. Malouli 6–2 6–3; F. Pennetta lost to V. Razzano 0–6 1–6; F. Pennetta/R. Vinci d. M. Malouli/V. Razzano 6–3 2–6 7–5). **3rd place play-off: France d. Argentina 2–0:** (S. Cohen Aloro d. E. Chialvo 6–3 6–4; V. Razzano d. M. Salerni 6–0 6–1). **Final: Italy d. Slovak Republic 2–1:** (R. Vinci lost to S. Hrozenska 6–2 2–6 6–8; M. E. Camerin d. D. Hantuchova 6–4 6–2; F. Pennetta/R. Vinci d. D. Hantuchova/S. Hrozenska 6–4 6–1).

World Junior Tennis

Jackie Nesbitt

While Europe reigned supreme as Austria defeated Argentina to win the boys' trophy and Czech Republic edged out Russia to collect the girls' title, the 8th World Junior Tennis Final in Nagoya, Japan, also revealed the strength of talent elsewhere in the world.

With Typhoon Bonny heading towards Nagoya, weather conditions were a concern, but play was transferred indoors for one day only as the city somehow managed to avoid the rain sweeping the rest of the country.

In the boys' draw, three seeds out of eight survived the first round – eventual champion nation, Austria (7), who defeated Brazil 2–1; Argentina (8), who swept aside the host nation, Japan, 3–0; and Uruguay (4), who were fortunate to have the services of the outstanding Marcel Felder.

The Austrian campaign was spearheaded by the powerful Stefan Wiespeiner, the only player to have equalled the achievements of the highly talented Argentinian Brian Dabul on the European 14 & Under Circuit earlier this year.

Germany's boys were actually tipped to win the competition, but no sooner had they arrived in Nagoya than they were sent packing by Spain. Similarly, second favourites, France, were eliminated by South Africa. Third-seeded Russia, whose squad included Serguei Demekhine, a member of the 1997 bronze medal-winning team, completed the demise of the top teams when they fell to USA 2–1.

Indonesia (6) were dispatched by one of the dark horses of the competition, Chinese Taipei, who were to finish the event in a creditable fifth position, while fifth-seeded Mexico lost out to Italy in a very entertaining tie.

In the second round, results went more to form. Austria overturned a one match deficit against South Africa, while Argentina dashed any hopes the Spanish had of progressing further. USA proved too strong for Chinese Taipei, while Italy once again found themselves involved in the tie of the day against Uruguay. The deciding doubles was evenly balanced at one set apiece when the Italian pairing of Daniele Giorgini and Matteo Volante managed to hit each other in an attempt to return a lob. Although able to continue after treatment, their challenge faded, allowing Uruguay to advance to the semi-finals.

The strength of Austria's challenge was underlined in their semi-final 3–0 victory over USA while in the other half of the draw, Argentina also advanced 3–0 against Uruguay.

Concerns about Typhoon Bonny receded as the sun shone for the boys' final. The action began with Austria's Johannes Ager engineering a solid victory over Argentina's Juan Monaco 6–4 6–4 to give first blood to Europe. As the heat and humidity soared, Dabul came out to face Wiespeiner in a much anticipated match-up. The Argentinian began well, managing to neutralise Wiespeiner's brutal ground strokes and dictate play. Taking the first set 6–4 and serving with a break at 5–4 in the second, however, Dabul seemed to be

The Austrian boys who beat Argentina 3–0 in the final of the World Junior Tennis competition in Nagoya, Japan and the girls of the Czech Republic who beat the Russians 2–1. (Yoshio Kato)

suffering from the heat. Wiespeiner took full advantage, eventually coming through 4–6 6–4 6–1 to clinch a second World Junior Tennis title for Austria.

In contrast to the boys' event, the opening round of the girls' draw proved less harrowing for the top seeds. The 1997 champion nation, Russia, once again the favourites, despite being without the outstanding 14-year-old, Lina Krasnoroutskaia, began with a 3–0 victory over Brazil.

The second-seeded Czech Republic dismissed Japan 3–0, much to the chagrin of the home supporters, while Croatia (3) advanced against Colombia, but not without somewhat of a struggle. Argentina (4) eased past Indonesia and Slovak Republic (8) put out Great Britain.

The plight of the remaining seeds provided less comfort for the seeding committee. France (7), succumbed to Chinese Taipei, for whom Hsiao-Han Chao produced the first of several impressive performances. Mexico's Melissa Torres provided the backbone for Mexico's excellent 2–1 victory over Thailand (6). Another player who rose to the occasion was South Africa's Chanelle Scheepers, who guided her team to a surprise 2–1 win over the fifth seeded USA.

Second round matches saw Russia and Czech Republic move into the semi-finals with victories over Chinese Taipei and Slovak Republic respectively. In contrast, Croatia (3) and Argentina (4) both floundered. When Croatia's Daniela Calikusic led by a set and 5–2, a semi-final berth seemed a formality. However, Mexico's Torres turned the match around and it was Mexico who went on to earn a place in the last four. The South Africans also came back from a one match deficit against Argentina. Scheepers evened the score with a good win over the powerful Gisela Dulko, before teaming up with Maretha Van Niekerk to clinch the doubles.

In the semi-finals, play was moved indoors owing to rain and the quicker courts appeared to favour the two hard-hitting top seeded nations. The Mexicans fought well against Russia, but when Torres succumbed to Fokina in the second singles, their chance of gold had gone. Giantkillers South Africa finally met their match against Czech Republic leaving the scene set for a correctly predicted match-up in the Final.

The showdown between the top two seeds provided one of the most memorable encounters for years and fully entertained a crowd of over 1000 spectators. The contest opened with Czech Republic's Eva Birnerova disposing of Russia's Vera Zvonareva 6–3 6–4, thereby maintaining her record of not dropping a set in singles throughout the week. Fokina, probably the strongest individual competitor, levelled proceedings following a tense three-set battle against Petra Cetkovska. In the deciding doubles, Fokina and Raissa Gourevitch produced several patches of inspired tennis but could not sustain the quality. The more consistent play of Brinerova and Cetkovska finally brought Czech Republic the title.

In the third place play-offs, South Africa comfortably beat Mexico in the girls' event, while Uruguay defeated USA in the boy's draw, but needed a third-set tiebreak in the deciding doubles to do so.

WORLD JUNIOR TENNIS 1998
ITF Team Championships for 14 & Under

84 nations competed, 82 taking part in the boys' event and 68 in the girls' event. Final stages took place in Nagoya, Japan, 26–30 August.

FINAL POSITIONS – BOYS: Champion nation: Austria; runners-up: Argentina; 3rd: Uruguay; 4th: USA; 5th: Chinese Taipei; 6th: Spain; 7th: Italy; 8th: South Africa; 9th: Russia; 10th: Germany; 11th: France; 12th: Mexico; 13th: Japan; 14th: Indonesia; 15th: Brazil; 16th: India; **GIRLS:** Champion nation: Czech Republic; runners-up: Russia; 3rd: South Africa; 4th: Mexico; 5th: Argentina; 6th: Croatia; 7th: Slovak Republic; 8th: Chinese Taipei; 9th: Great Britain; 10th: Thailand; 11th: France; 12th: USA; 13th: Indonesia; 14th: Colombia; 15th: Japan; 16th: Brazil.

BOYS' CHAMPIONSHIP – Semi-finals: Argentina d. Uruguay 3–0 (J. Monaco d. M. Vilarrubi 6–1 6–1; B. Dabul d. M. Felder 6–1 6–3; B. Dabul/J. Ottaviani d. M. Felder/L. Perera 7–5 7–6(8)). **Austria d. USA 3–0** (J. Ager d. V. Banada 6–3 2–6 6–2; S. Wiespeiner d. D. Stewart 6–1 6–0; C. Polessnig/S. Wiespeiner d. D. Bauer/D. Stewart 6–1 6–3). **3rd place play-off: Uruguay d. USA 2–1** (M. Vilarrubi lost to V. Banada 4–6 2–6; M. Felder d. D. Stewart 6–4 3–0 ret; M. Felder/M. Vilarrubi d. V. Banada/D. Bauer 5–7 7–6(0) 6–3). **Final: Austria d. Argentina 3–0** (J. Ager d. J. Monaco 6–4 6–4; S. Wiespeiner d. B. Dabul 4–6 6–4 6–1; J. Ager/C. Polessnig d. B. Dabul/J. Ottaviani 6–4 7–5).

GIRLS' CHAMPIONSHIP – Semi-finals: Russia d. Mexico 3–0 (V. Zvonareva d. M. J. Lopez 6–2 6–3; G. Fokina d. M. Torres 7–5 6–1; R. Gourevitch/V. Zvonareva d. M. J. Lopez/E. Vela 6–0 6–3). **Czech Republic d. South Africa 2–0** (E. Birnerova d. M. Van Niekerk 6–3 6–3; P. Cetkovska d. C. Scheepers 6–3 6–4). **3rd place play-off: South Africa d. Mexico 3–0** (M. Van Niekerk d. M. J. Lopez 6–2 6–1; C. Scheepers d. M. Torres 6–2 6–7(4) 6–4; M. Mojzis/M. Van Niekerk d. M. Torres/E. Vela 6–0 6–1). **Final: Czech Republic d. Russia 2–1** (E. Birnerova d. V. Zvonareva 6–3 6–4; P. Cetkovska lost to G. Fokina 2–6 6–2 4–6; E. Birnerova/P. Cetkovska d. G. Fokina/ R. Gourevitch 7–5 1–6 6–3).

Slam Attack

Julian Muscat

Ask any player how best to approach a Grand Slam tournament and the response will invariably be: 'You have to survive the first week. After that, anything can happen.' Anything can and did happen in 1998, only the fourth year on record when the eight Grand Slam singles trophies were clasped by as many different pairs of hands.

This remarkable detail amplifies the virtues of tennis as it approaches the new millennium. It tells of a deeply competitive game, strong in numbers so as to make each Blue Riband event a searching test of skill, character and stamina. Yet even more exciting about 1998 was the absence of a 'lottery factor.' With the exception of Pete Sampras's Wimbledon waltz, every Grand Slam champion had telegraphed a menacing intent in advance of raising their trophies.

For instance, who could argue with Petr Korda's scissor-kicking sequence in Australia, where his defeat of Marcelo Rios marked his twelfth consecutive victory of the new season? Or with Carlos Moya's French Open romp, just weeks after the Spaniard downed three Grand Slam champions en route to the Monte Carlo title? Sampras, the grass-court master, proved the exception – although his Wimbledon triumph was his fifth in six years. But Pat Rafter reverted to type, prefacing his US Open triumph with a majestic hardcourt hat-trick in Cincinnati, Toronto and Long Island.

It was a similar story among women. Martina Hingis picked up where she had left off in 1997 by mastering Melbourne. Then a reviving Arantxa Sanchez-Vicario, exceptional on clay in advance, was crowned in Paris before Jana Novotna's Wimbledon triumph marked the culmination of a 16-match unbeaten sequence on grass. Yet perhaps the most revealing Grand Slam champion was Lindsay Davenport, who, having dominated the summer hardcourt season in her native California, journeyed east to conquer New York.

Davenport's US Open triumph exemplified the theme of intense competition in contemporary women's tennis. Here was a player who had previously flattered to deceive; one who frustrated for her failure to raise her level of fitness. In that respect, her metamorphosis was truly something to behold. It stands as a monument to dedication over the rubble of a squandered talent.

Doubtless those with long memories will question whether this diversity of Grand Slam winners is the product of a higher standard within an increasingly competitive sport. Similar conclusions were probably drawn after 1948, 1966 and 1990 – each of which heralded eight different singles champions. However, the notion that standards were so high as to militate against multiple future champions proved erroneous indeed. They were merely quirks of circumstance.

The question thus intriguing the tennis community is whether 1998 will mark that watershed. Two persuasive arguments suggest that the time may be nigh. The first concerns the timespan between the dates in question. From 1948, a gap of 18 years elapsed before there were again eight different champions in 1966. A further 24 years punctuated the next such occasion in 1990 – yet only eight years separated 1990 from this most recent occurrence. A personal opinion is that a fifth example of eight different champions will not be as long in the making.

The second argument advancing 1998 as a potential watershed revolves around the strength of Grand Slam fields as against those assembled in 1948, 1966 and 1990. The stronger the field, the lesser the prospects of a multiple Slam winner.

In post-war 1948 there were still restrictions on international travel. The sheer inconvenience of it yielded vastly different entries for the four Slams. And the exclusion of professional players from Grand Slam tournaments was still in place in 1966, when acknowledged masters like Rod Laver and Ken Rosewall where frozen out.

Even in 1990, the four men's singles champions may have benefitted from a degree of absenteeism. Ivan Lendl, the winner in Australia, missed the French Open – where he had triumphed three times previously. So, too, did Sampras, the victor at Flushing Meadows; and Andre Agassi, a finalist in both France and the US, did not compete at either Wimbledon or Melbourne.

Contrast that with 1998, when no man reached more than one final in a year when all eight finalists contested each of the four Slams. Indeed, only Sampras (Wimbledon and New York) and Moya (France and New York) reached two semi-finals due to the sheer depth of competition. The canvas was almost as varied among women: Hingis was the only dual finalist in a season when a clutch of precocious teenagers elevated standards to previously unscaled heights.

It is fair to say that Hingis did not regress in 1998. While she maintained the same level of performance, others caught up and unseated her. Yet it was not the over-fanfared 'Young Guns' who contrived to depose Hingis from her No.1 ranking. The woman with real prospects of holding the four Slam titles simultaneously was usurped by her elders.

Advancements in racket technology have added an extra dimension to women's tennis. Crisper ball-striking, coupled with more developed physiques, had led to a surge in popularity for the women's game. Interestingly, however, the old guard stole the limelight in 1998. Players like Novotna, Sanchez-Vicario, Conchita Martinez and Nathalie Tauziat spoke of their collective pique at the premature trumpeting of youth. So they raised their games – with outstanding results.

Indeed, of the four 'nouveau' teenagers advancing on the Grand Slams, only Venus Williams made any sort of impact through her semi-final appearance at Flushing Meadows – where she had been a finalist 12 months earlier. That may change in 1999, when Serena Williams, Anna Kournikova and Mirjana Lucic will be far more court-wise. Further gains in the women's standard appear inevitable in 1999 – and that is without dwelling on the possible re-entrance of a pair of once-regal champions in Steffi Graf and Monica Seles.

The respective rehabilitations of Graf and Seles are intriguing. It was Graf who dominated 1990 despite her failure to win more than one Grand Slam. She made two other finals, at Flushing Meadows and Roland Garros, where Seles' clay-court defeat of the German effec-

Left: *Richard Krajicek's late season surge in Stuttgart and St Petersburg lifted him back into the top ten but he chose to miss the ATP Tour Championship in Hannover so that he could have knee surgery in time to play in Australia.* (Stephen Wake)

Right: *Conchita Martinez started the year by reaching the final of the Australian Open and won the tournaments in Berlin and Warsaw to maintain her position among the top ten at No. 8.* (Stephen Wake)

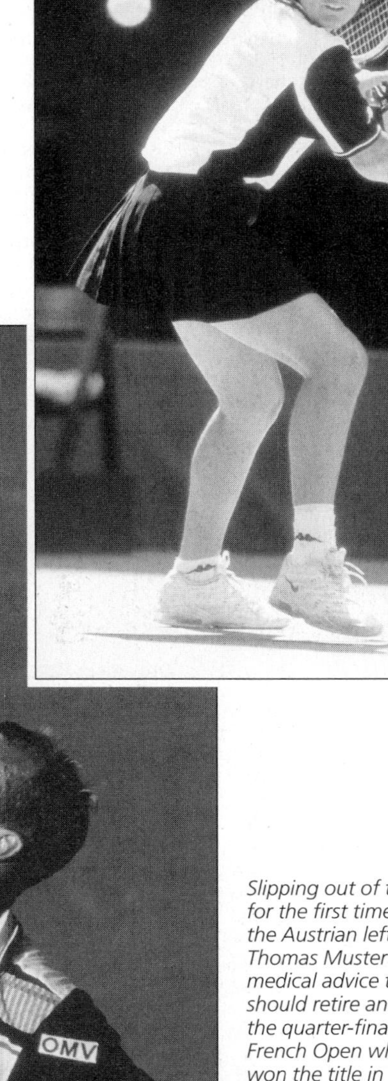

Slipping out of the top ten for the first time since 1994, the Austrian left-hander Thomas Muster ignored medical advice that he should retire and reached the quarter-finals at the French Open where he had won the title in 1995. (Stephen Wake)

tively heralded the transfer of power between them. Should Graf and Seles reach out for their former glories, the 1999 vintage will be a special one for women's tennis.

As for the men, one only need amplify Sampras's thoughts on retaining his world No.1 status for a record-breaking sixth successive year at the ATP Tour World Championships in Hannover. 'This is a record that may not be broken – ever,' Sampras ventured. It was certainly no idle boast from a man renowned for his modesty.

It is fascinating to ponder whether Sampras's narrow, rankings-race victory over Rios in 1998 signals a waning of his influence. That Sampras ultimately wrested the longevity record from Jimmy Connors was only due to the generous spirit of Boris Becker – who gifted Sampras his wild-card entry to Vienna on the latter's request. But for the 358 ranking points Sampras accrued on triumphing in Vienna, Rios would have prevailed in the race for No.1.

For all that, Sampras remains the principal men's candidate to win more than one Grand Slam title in 1999. There is no obvious heir-apparent to the game's barometer of excellence. Indeed, apart from Jim Courier's dual Slam triumph (Australia and France) in 1992, it is Sampras who has single-handedly maintained the trend for multiple Slam wins since 1990. He achieved this in 1993, '94, '95 and '97 to ensconce himself firmly in the pantheon of great champions.

Yet the odds against Sampras perpetuating his dominance are lengthening all the time. Proven grass court campaigners like Goran Ivanisevic and Sampras's nemesis, Richard Krajicek, will combine with local talents Tim Henman and Greg Rusedski to offer stiff resistance to his perennial dominance at Wimbledon. And the revived Andre Agassi, who under-performed at Grand Slam level in 1998, will be a constant threat on American hardcourts. All of which contributes to what Sampras himself maintains of contemporary Grand Slam tennis: that very few matches are won without maximum physical and mental effort.

Women's tennis is following a similar path. In every year since there were four different champions in 1990, one player has won three Slams – except in 1995 when Sanchez-Vicario won two. Hingis looked set to further that theme when she won three Slams last year, but she has been reeled in by her eager pursuers. As much as Hingis's own fallibility, the raw desire of the chasing pack has been responsible for stopping her in her tracks.

Multiple Slam winners will never quite become an extinct species – as may well be the case, within the ranks of men, for the completion of a Grand Slam in its purest sense. An increasing specialisation within the four distinct surfaces employed at Grand Slam venues militates against any man usurping Laver as the last Grand Slam winner 29 years ago. So much so that even multiple Slam winners may quickly become the exception rather than the rule. If 1998 celebrated 30 years of Open tennis, it was open tennis with a difference.

Still searching for his first Grand Slam title, 27-year-old Goran Ivanisevic won through to the Wimbledon final for the third time but found Sampras too strong. (Stephen Wake)

Grand Slam Championships

Australian Open Championships
French Open Championships
The Championships – Wimbledon
US Open Championships
Compaq Grand Slam Cup

Alex Corretja of Spain was a Grand Slam finalist for the first time in Paris and ended the year as ATP Tour World Champion and ranked No. 3. (Michael Cole)

In Melbourne Petr Korda celebrates with his famous scissor-kick as he claims a first Grand Slam title at the age of 30 – a remarkable achievement. (Stephen Wake)

Australian Open Championships

Alan Trengove

'Come to the party!' That was the joyful theme of the Australian Open, which celebrated its 10th anniversary at what was originally Flinders Park but is now Melbourne Park. 'And don't forget to bring your hat and plenty of sun-cream,' the organisers might well have added, having spent the previous nine months devising an Extreme Heat Policy as a consequence of the scorching weather that engulfed the 1997 Open.

As it transpired, the only real heat in the 1998 championships came from the outsiders who blow-torched the top seeds in the men's event. Those who attended the party welcomed the relatively mild days, and certainly had fun – especially in the first week when there were more unexpected coups on Centre Court than on the gambling tables at the spectacular Crown Casino a mile away. In fact, the Open had some of the characteristics of a crap shoot.

At long last the dice fell felicitously for the immensely gifted Petr Korda, who won his first Grand Slam singles title at the age of 30 – or at 'five minutes to twelve', as he wryly put it. The women's singles ended more predictably, with 17-year-old Martina Hingis successfully defending her first Grand Slam crown, though no-one surely would have tipped Conchita Martinez as her opponent in the final.

Public enthusiasm towards the Open has mounted every year since 1988 when the new stadium supplanted Kooyong as the venue. This year's total attendance of 434,807 was an 11 percent increase on the previous year's. No fewer than 18 of the 23 sessions smashed crowd records. The upsurge was due largely to the 1997 US Open triumph of Queenslander Patrick Rafter and his new status as a close rival to Pete Sampras.

There was keen speculation as to whether Rafter could become the first Australian to win the national title since Mark Edmondson in 1976. Sampras himself was intent on securing another Grand Slam title in his effort to surpass Roy Emerson's record bag of 12; a keen, trim Andre Agassi was making a determined attempt to resurrect his career; Mark Philippoussis was 'likely to do anything', as was another Aussie, 'boy wonder' Lleyton Hewitt, sensational winner of the Australian hardcourt title at Adelaide a week earlier. It added up to enticing box-office fare.

The women's singles was deprived of four-time champion Steffi Graf, who decided at the 11th hour that she wasn't quite ready to return to the possibly harsh summer environment Down Under. Monica Seles, another four-time champion, and Jana Novotna were also notable absentees. The fans, however, were able to focus on the exciting new generation of women players, like Hingis, Anna Kournikova, Venus and Serena Williams, and Mirjana Lucic.

In 1997 we became inured to continual upsets among the men at the major Championships, what with the unseeded Gustavo Kuerten walking off with the French title, the unseeded Cedric Pioline reaching the Wimbledon final, and Rafter and the unseeded Greg Rusedski contesting the US Open final. The pattern continued here, with nine of the seeds eliminated in the first two rounds and only four reaching the fourth round – a Grand Slam record in the Open era.

Among the first-round casualties were eighth seed Thomas Muster, who lost in straight sets to Swedish qualifier Jan Apell, and 13th seed Goran Ivanisevic, beaten by Dutchman Jan Siemerink. It was an unhappy few days for Ivanisevic: he clashed with umpire Rudi Berger, was warned for stalling, refused to attend a press conference, and ran foul of another umpire while losing his first-round doubles match. His various misdemeanours proved so costly to the Croatian that he finished in the red. Others with cause to rue included 10th seed Sergi Bruguera, who retired with blistered feet, and Yevgeny Kafelnikov and Jim Courier, who pulled out with injuries on the eve of the tournament.

Third seed Michael Chang, seventh seed Carlos Moya, 12th seed Kuerten, and 15th seed Philippoussis didn't survive the second round; and fifth seed Rusedski succumbed in the third. While it's possibly true that the Open is held too early in the year, and before some players have picked up form after their Christmas break, the depth of talent throughout the ranks of the top hundred men – and beyond – is undeniable.

A somewhat jaded Chang and an equally lacklustre Kuerten fell to Frenchmen Guillaume

Raoux and Nicolas Escude respectively. The 21-year-old Escude, ranked in the 400s less than 12 months earlier, and more accustomed to satellite and Challenger events than the heady atmosphere of a Grand Slam, proved he was no flash-in-the-pan by reaching the semi-finals. Showing remarkable stamina as well as court speed and fine attacking strokes, he recovered three times from a two-sets-to-love deficit and claimed Magnus Larsson, Richey Reneberg, Todd Woodbridge and Nicolas Kiefer as his other scalps.

According to the French press, Escude was a highly talented junior who 'lost his way' amid a surfeit of praise and public expectation. If so, he seemed to find the right track on the tennis courts that abut the Flinders Street railyards, and it will be surprising in the next few years if it doesn't lead him to somewhere near the pinnacle of the game.

Moya, an unheralded hero at the 1997 Open, was bundled out by Richard Fromberg. A year earlier the so-called Spanish Armada had wreaked havoc, but this time, with the exception of Alberto Berasategui, most of the 19 Spaniards who embarked for Melbourne were soon sunk without trace.

Philippoussis, after a promising start, lost control of his match with Hicham Arazi, the flashy left-hander from Morocco. The Australian went down in five sets after holding a match point in the fifth. His early departure was an anti-climax for local fans, as was the exit of the 16-year-old Hewitt, albeit after a stirring five-set battle with the Czech Republic's Daniel Vacek that augured well for the youngster's future.

As for Rusedski, Britain's chief hope found Woodbridge in the kind of form that took him to the semi-finals of Wimbledon. In a masterly display of all-court tennis in which he returned Rusedski's feared service effectively, volleyed beautifully and lobbed cleverly, the slightly built Australian won in straight sets. He had only a day to savour the plaudits before losing by the same margin to Escude when unsettled by the closing of the stadium roof because of rain.

The greatest shocks of all, of course, were the defeats of Rafter and Sampras. Rafter came into the tournament after two weeks of close matches at Perth and Sydney. He had worked his way into good form, but the pressure he felt in carrying a nation's hopes was much heavier than at the US Open, and shouldn't be underestimated. Rafter won a torrid five-set encounter with Jeff Tarango under lights, and then, against Todd Martin, came from a service-break down in the fifth set to survive another marathon. Both matches drained him, as much because of his intensity as the resistance of his opponents. 'It took a lot out of me physically and emotionally,' he said of the Tarango match, and added, 'I've got to learn to relax a little more.'

The draw gave Rafter no respite. Against Berasategui in a third-round night match, he again put in a grueling all-out effort. Three times he was within a point of taking a two-sets-to-love lead that might have seen him safely through. But the little Spaniard, runner-up to Bruguera at the 1994 French Open, was too solid from the back of the court, winning in four sets, three of them tie-breaks. Millions of Australians huddled round their television sets heaved a collective sigh that might have caused a stiff breeze across the Nullarbor.

Berasategui's victory looked less of a freak upset when, in the next round, he also ousted Agassi. Winner of the Australian title in 1995, Agassi had been so impressive in beating Andrea Gaudenzi and Albert Costa that many began to believe he would reach the final, and perhaps even repeat his 1994 US Open feat of triumphing when unseeded. Before yet another sell-out crowd that included his newly arrived wife Brooke Shields, Agassi took a two-sets-to-love lead, but Berasategui kept hammering his unorthodox forehand and simply wore him down.

No-one now, except possibly Korda, seemed capable of stopping Sampras from winning the title for a third time. The world champion scored three routine victories and was approaching his best form as he won a potentially awkward match against Arazi in three tight sets. This uneventful prelude made his four-set defeat by unseeded Karol Kucera in a night match so much more shocking.

Kucera admittedly had led Slovakia to victory in the Hopman Cup (with Karina Habsudova) and had won the Adidas International in Sydney, but here in dropping sets to Vacek and Fromberg he seemed well short of Sampras's class. However, he handled the Sampras serve almost with ease, covered the court with cat-like speed and anticipation, and – most surprising of all – broke down the famous Sampras forehand. We were left to wonder whether Pistol Pete was shooting himself in the foot by saying so often in TV commercials that his biggest opponent was history. Was the pressure he was imposing on himself by publicly aiming for Emerson's record becoming just too much?

In the other quarter-finals, Korda, seeded sixth, came from two-sets-to-love down to score a hugely satisfying win over the fourth seeded Bjorkman, to whom he had defaulted at the US

Open because of illness; ninth seed Marcelo Rios beat a weary Berasategui; and Escude outlasted Kiefer.

Thus, a new Grand Slam champion was inevitable. The record – and current form – suggested it would be Korda. Having won the tournament at Doha before coming to Melbourne, he was better prepared in this his 34th Grand Slam Championship than in any previous challenge. His only other appearance in a Grand Slam final was at Roland Garros in 1992, when, too nervous to do his ability justice, he was trounced by Courier. Now, a more mature and relaxed Korda reached the final by defeating his erstwhile compatriot Kucera. It was a fascinating contest between Kucera's silky touch and Korda's penetrating groundstrokes.

Rios, too, had enjoyed a recent triumph, at Auckland. He reached his first Grand Slam final by beating Escude, whose rearguard heroics, on the law of averages, had to come to an end sooner or later. Korda was the first seeded player that Rios met in seven matches, though he'd had to overcome some excellent players, including Thomas Enqvist in the first round.

This was the first Australian final between left-handers since Roscoe Tanner defeated Guillermo Vilas in January 1977. It also became one of the most one-sided. Confounding those who had doubted whether he had the temperament, strength and consistency to win a major, Korda was dominant from the start, outplaying the 22-year-old Chilean in all departments and winning 6–2 6–2 6–2.

Rios didn't play at his best, but perhaps that was because of Korda's superlative hitting. The skinny Czech, whose career has been severely interrupted by countless injuries and illness, won Australian hearts not only by his brilliance but by the way he expressed his exhilaration with scissor kicks, cartwheels, and finally a leap into the stands to embrace his wife Regina and five-year-old daughter Jessica. If this was five minutes to midnight, let's hope he can continue to turn back the clock.

While Korda was comparatively old to be joining the Grand Slam Club, Hingis achieved another first in being the youngest player – man or woman – to win back-to-back singles titles at any of the majors. She did so with the aplomb of a veteran, dropping sets only to Kournikova in the third round, and to Anke Huber in the quarter-finals. She admitted, though, that defending the title was much harder than winning for the first time. 'There were,' she said, 'so many expectations and pressures – especially from myself – which made it the toughest Grand Slam I've won so far.'

The Hingis-Kournikova match was their closest to date, and suggested that Kournikova was narrowing the gap between them. The Russian played a splendid all-court game, often dictating the terms, showing flair at the net, and thumping 34 winners. Hingis did so much running that she looked very tired in the third set. As usual, however, she produced the right shots at the right time, and it was Kournikova who faltered with a critical string of unforced errors.

The Williams sisters were equally impressive. Sixteen-year-old Serena shrugged off the hype that surrounded her first-round match with sixth seed Irina Spirlea – the player who had brushed controversially with Venus at the 1997 US Open – and won in three sets. This set up her first significant match with her older sister, a fact that may well be the subject of a Trivial Pursuit question a few years hence.

Although both were unseeded, the match understandably was scheduled for Centre Court. Venus won 7–6, 6–1; the girls hugged, raised their arms together and took a bow. Venus became a crowd favourite as she hit her way to the quarter-finals, where she lost a torrid three-set match against second seed Lindsay Davenport. Serena did not allow herself to be forgotten – after every match she interviewed her sister on court for the Channel 7 TV network.

Lucic, the Australian junior champion of 1997, had a difficult draw, clashing with fellow-Croatian and French title-holder Iva Majoli in the second round. She lost 7–5 6–4, was fined for having allegedly received coaching advice from her father in the stands, and injudiciously criticised the umpire at a press conference. Majoli, the fourth seed, was routed in her next match by Thailand's Tamarine Tanasugarn – the biggest upset of the women's event.

As the tournament evolved, the main question was whether any of the few remaining players who had beaten Hingis in 1997 could do the same in a Grand Slam Championship. Mary Pierce appeared to have the best chance. She had retained her excellent Hopman Cup form and had won two of her matches without conceding a game. But against Hingis an erratic Pierce was confined to five games.

Anke Huber scored fighting wins over Amanda Coetzer and Arantxa Sanchez-Vicario, and, after a bad start, seemed to have Hingis's measure until her confidence suddenly evaporated and she lost the third set 6–1.

Men's Singles

Holder: P. Sampras (USA)

	FIRST ROUND	SECOND ROUND	THIRD ROUND	FOURTH ROUND	QUARTER-FINALS	SEMI-FINALS	FINAL
1	**P. Sampras** (USA) (1)	**Sampras** (1) 7–5 6–4 6–2	**Sampras** (1) 6–2 6–1 6–2	**Sampras** (1) 7–5 6–3 6–4	**Sampras** (1) 7–6(9) 6–4 6–4	Kucera 6–4 6–2 6–7(5) 6–3	**Korda** (6) 6–1 6–4 1–6 6–2
2	S. Schalken (NED)						
3	A. Martin (ESP)	Sanguinetti 6–0 3–6 7–6(8) 6–3					
4	D. Sanguinetti (ITA)						
5	M. Gustafsson (SWE)	Gustafsson 6–4 6–3 6–0	Gustafsson 4–6 6–2 6–1 6–3				
6	D. Van Scheppingen (NED) (Q)						
7	S. Dosedel (CZE)	Dosedel 6–4 3–6 6–3 7–6(2)					
8	A. Boetsch (FRA)						
9	F. Clavet (ESP)	Clavet 2–6 6–2 6–3 6–4	Clavet By Walkover	Arazi 4–6 6–4 3–6 6–2 6–1			
10	L. Burgsmuller (GER) (Q)						
11	R. Vasek (CZE)	Washington 6–2 6–4 4–6 7–5					
12	M. Washington (USA)						
13	H. Dreekmann (GER)	Arazi 7–6(2) 6–3 6–2	Arazi 1–6 6–2 4–6 6–1 9–7				
14	H. Arazi (MAR)						
15	A. Calatrava (ESP)	**Philippoussis** (15) 7–6(0) 6–4 7–6(4)					
16	**M. Philippoussis** (AUS) (15)						
17	**S. Bruguera** (ESP) (10)	Kucera 3–6 7–5 6–1 RET	Kucera 7–6(4) 6–7(5) 2–6 6–0 6–1	Kucera 6–2 7–6(3) 6–1	Kucera 6–2 3–6 6–2 7–5		
18	K. Kucera (SVK)						
19	D. Vacek (CZE)	Vacek 6–2 6–4 1–6 2–6 6–3					
20	L. Hewitt (AUS) (W)						
21	G. Schaller (AUT)	Nestor 6–3 6–0 7–6(6)	Nestor 5–7 7–5 6–2 6–1				
22	D. Nestor (CAN)						
23	M. Damm (CZE)	Damm 6–4 7–6(3) 3–0 RET					
24	M. Woodforde (AUS)						
25	M. Tillstrom (SWE)	Tillstrom 6–3 6–2 6–2	Lareau (Q) 6–7(1) 6–3 6–3 4–6 6–4	Fromberg 6–0 6–2 4–6 6–3			
26	L. Paes (IND) (W)						
27	S.Lareau (CAN) (Q)	Lareau (Q) 6–4 6–7(5) 7–6(6) 6–7(4) 7–5					
28	M. Norman (SWE)						
29	R. Fromberg (AUS)	Fromberg 2–6 6–3 6–4 3–6 6–3	Fromberg 4–6 6–4 7–6(2) 6–4				
30	T. Larkham (AUS) (W)						
31	P. Tramacchi (AUS) (W)	**Moya** (7) 6–4 6–3 6–7(6) 7–6(3)					
32	**C. Moya** (ESP) (7)						
33	**J. Bjorkman** (SWE) (4)	**Bjorkman** (4) 2–6 6–1 6–1 6–1	**Bjorkman** (4) 6–7(3) 4–6 6–4 6–2 6–3	**Bjorkman** (4) 7–5 6–3 6–4	**Bjorkman** (4) 6–2 6–1 6–4	**Korda** (6) 3–6 5–7 6–3 6–4 6–2	
34	A. Belobrajdic (AUS) (W)						
35	W. Ferreira (RSA)	Ferreira 6–4 3–6 6–2 6–3					
36	J. Kroslak (SVK)						
37	N. Lapentti (ECU)	Lapentti 5–7 6–3 6–4 6–7(3) 6–1	Santoro 6–4 3–6 3–6 6–2 6–4				
38	J. A. Viloca (ESP)						
39	E. Alvarez (ESP)	Santoro 4–6 6–0 6–3 5–7 6–4					
40	F. Santoro (FRA)						
41	J. Gimelstob (USA)	Campbell (Q) 3–6 6–3 3–6 6–3 6–4	Campbell (Q) 6–4 6–3 6–4	B. Black 6–4 6–0 6–2			
42	S. Campbell (USA) (Q)						
43	J. M. Gambill (USA) (Q)	O'Brien 3–6 7–5 6–1 6–3					
44	A. O'Brien (USA)						
45	A. Clement (FRA)	Pozzi 6–4 4–6 5–7 6–2 6–4	B. Black 6–2 5–0 ret				
46	G. Pozzi (ITA)						
47	B. Black (ZIM)	B. Black 6–4 6–0 4–6 6–4					
48	**F. Mantilla** (ESP) (14)						
49	**A. Corretja** (ESP) (11)	**Corretja** (11) 6–4 7–5 2–6 6–3	**Corretja** (11) 6–4 6–3 6–0	Pioline 6–2 6–1 6–4	**Korda** (6) 6–4 6–4 3–6 6–3		
50	L. Arnold (ARG)						
51	D. Prinosil (GER)	Prinosil 3–6 6–7(2) 6–1 6–4 6–1					
52	J. Van Herck (BEL)						
53	F. Meligeni (BRA)	Pioline 6–4 1–6 6–5 RET	Pioline 6–3 7–5 3–6 6–3				
54	C. Pioline (FRA)						
55	S. Sargsian (ARM)	Burillo 6–3 6–4 1–6 3–6 9–7					
56	J. Burillo (ESP)						
57	B. MacPhie (USA) (Q)	Rosset 6–4 0–6 6–4 3–6 6–4	Spadea 6–3 4–6 6–4 6–3	**Korda** (6) 6–2 7–6(8) 6–2			
58	M. Rosset (SUI)						
59	V. Spadea (USA)	Spadea 6–7(4) 6–1 6–4 4–6 6–3					
60	J. Stasiak (AUS) (W)						
61	S. Draper (AUS)	Draper 6–4 7–5 7–5	**Korda** (6) 7–6(3) 6–3 6–3				
62	D. Hrbaty (SVK)						
63	A. Portas (ESP)	**Korda** (6) 6–3 4–6 6–1 6–4					
64	**P. Korda** (CZE) (6)						

Winner: **P. Korda** (CZE) (6)

6–2 6–2 6–2

65 **G. Rusedski** (GBR) (5)
66 D. Witt (USA) (Q)
67 J. Stark (USA)
68 C. Costa (ESP)
69 T. Woodbridge (AUS)
70 F. Dewulf (BEL)
71 C Ruud (NOR)
72 C. Van Garsse (BEL) (Q)
73 T. Johansson (SWE)
74 F. Squillari (ARG)
75 M. Ondruska (RSA)
76 R. Reneberg (USA)
77 N. Escude (FRA)
78 M Larsson (SWE)
79 J. Diaz (ESP) (Q)
80 **G. Kuerten** (BRA) (12)
81 **G. Ivanisevic** (CRO) (13)
82 J. Siemerink (NED)
83 J. Golmard (FRA) (Q)
84 T. Henman (GBR)
85 M. Craca (GER)
86 D. Wheaton (USA) (Q)
87 N. Kiefer (GER)
88 M. Draper (AUS) (Q)
89 M. Tebbutt (AUS) (W)
90 M. Filippini (URU)
91 W. Black (ZIM)
92 B. Steven (NZL)
93 G Raoux (FRA)
94 S. Stolle (AUS)
95 K. Carlsen (DEN)
96 **M. Chang** (USA) (3)
97 **T. Muster** (AUT) (8)
98 J. Apell (SWE) (Q)
99 T. Nydahl (SWE)
100 L. Roux (FRA)
101 A. Radulescu (GER)
102 K. Alami (MAR)
103 R. Furlan (ITA)
104 J. Alonso (ESP)
105 J. Stoltenberg (AUS)
106 G. Blanco (ESP)
107 A. Ilie (AUS) (Q)
108 J. Knippschild (GER)
109 T. Enqvist (SWE)
110 J. A. Marin (ESP)
111 G. Stafford (RSA)
112 **M. Rios** (CHI) (9)
113 **A. Costa** (ESP) (16)
114 T. Haas (GER)
115 M. Martelli (ITA) (Q)
116 A. Agassi (USA)
117 O. Gross (GER)
118 M.K. Goellner (GER)
119 A. Gaudenzi (ITA)
120 D. Pescariu (ROM)
121 A. Berasategui (ESP)
122 K. Braasch (GER) (Q)
123 L. Smith (AUS) (W)
124 A. Medvedev (UKR)
125 J. Sanchez (ESP)
126 T. Martin (USA)
127 J. Tarango (USA)
128 **P. Rafter** (AUS) (2)

Rusedski (5) 7–6(4) 6–3 6–4
Stark 6–3 4–1 RET
Woodbridge 7–5 6–3 7–5
Van Garsse (Q) 7–6(4) 4–6 1–6 6–4 6–3
Squillari 6–4 2–6 6–3 6–7(6) 8–6
Reneberg 6–3 6–1 6–1
Escude 5–7 4–6 7–5 6–1 10–8
Kuerten (12) 6–3 3–6 6–3 6–2
Siemerink 6–2 7–6(3) 3–6 6–4
Golmard (Q) 6–3 6–7(3) 6–2 3–6 11–9
Wheaton (Q) 6–4 3–6 6–3 6–3
Kiefer 6–4 6–4 6–0
Tebbutt (W) 7–5 7–5 6–7(5) 6–4
W. Black 6–4 6–2 6–2
Raoux 2–6 6–3 4–6 6–2 6–0
Chang (3) 6–3 7–6(2) 5–7 6–3
Apell (Q) 6–4 7–6(5) 7–5
Roux 6–3 7–6(5) 6–3
Alami 7–6(0) 5–7 6–3 6–2
Alonso 7–6(9) 6–2 2–6 6–2
Stoltenberg 6–2 ret
Ilie (Q) 6–4 6–2 6–3
Enqvist 6–3 6–4 6–3
Rios (9) 6–1 6–0 6–3
Costa (16) 7–6(5) 6–2 6–4
Agassi 3–6 7–6(3) 6–2 6–2
Gross 7–6(8) 6–4 6–2
Gaudenzi 6–2 4–6 6–2 6–2
Berasategui 3–6 6–3 6–4 6–3
Medvedev 6–2 6–0 6–2
Martin 6–1 6–4 6–1
Rafter (2) 7–6(4) 7–6(4) 6–7(4) 7–5

Rusedski (5) 6–4 6–4 1–0 RET
Woodbridge 6–4 4–6 6–3 6–4
Reneberg 6–0 6–4 1–6 4–6 6–3
Escude 5–7 6–3 6–1 7–5
Golmard (Q) 7–6(2) 7–5 6–7(5) 3–6 6–1
Kiefer 2–6 1–6 6–2 7–6(3) 6–2
W. Black 6–2 6–4 5–7 6–4
Raoux 6–4 7–6(4) 7–6(5)
Roux 6–3 6–7(5) 6–3 3–6 6–3
Alami 6–7(5) 6–3 7–6(4) 6–4
Ilie (Q) 6–3 6–2 7–6(6)
Rios (9) 6–4 7–6(4) 4–6 6–4
Agassi 6–4 6–4 2–6 7–5
Gaudenzi 4–6 6–1 6–4 6–4
Berasategui 6–4 7–6(1) 6–4
Rafter (2) 2–6 7–6(2) 6–7(4) 6–4 6–3

Woodbridge 7–6(5) 6–4 6–2
Escude 1–6 6–7(0) 6–2 7–5 6–4
Kiefer 7–5 4–0 ret
Raoux 6–3 6–2 7–5
Roux 7–6(2) 6–2 6–4
Rios (9) 6–2 6–3 6–2
Agassi 6–2 6–2 6–0
Berasategui 6–7(2) 7–6(7) 6–2 7–6(4)

Escude 7–6(4) 6–3 6–2
Kiefer 6–3 6–4 7–5
Rios (9) 6–2 4–6 6–2 6–4
Berasategui 3–6 3–6 6–2 6–3 6–3

Escude 4–6 3–6 6–4 6–1 6–2
Rios (9) 6–7(6) 6–4 6–4 6–0

Rios (9) 6–1 6–3 6–2

Bold type denotes seeded players. Numbers following player's name gives seeding order (Q) = Qualifier, (W) = Wild Card, (LL) = Lucky Loser

Women's Singles

Holder: M. Hingis (SUI)

FIRST ROUND

1 **M. Hingis** (SUI) (1)
2 W. Probst (GER)
3 B. Rittner (GER)
4 E. Tatarkova (UKR) (Q)
5 E. Callens (BEL)
6 C. Morariu (USA)
7 A. Kournikova (RUS)
8 K. Studenikova (SVK)
9 Y. Basuki (INA)
10 M. Tu (USA)
11 K. Boogert (NED)
12 R. Bobkova (CZE) (Q)
13 P. Hy-Boulais (CAN)
14 T. Snyder (USA)
15 R. Simpson (CAN)
16 **D. Van Roost** (BEL) (14)
17 **B. Schultz-McCarthy** (NED) (11)
18 M. Maruska (AUT)
19 H. Nagyova (SVK)
20 A. Wunderlich (USA)
21 M. McGrath (USA)
22 Y. Yoshida (JPN)
23 R. Reid (AUS) (W)
24 E. Likhovtseva (RUS)
25 J. Nejedly (CAN) (Q)
26 R. Chanda (USA)
27 O. Barabanschikova (BLR)
28 D. Chladkova (CZE)
29 C. Torrens-Valero (ESP)
30 O. Lugina (UKR)
31 F. Li (CHN)
32 **M. Pierce** (FRA) (5)
33 **A. Coetzer** (RSA) (3)
34 B. Paulus (AUT)
35 L. Neiland (LAT)
36 C. Barclay (AUS) (W)
37 K. Brandi (USA)
38 A. Ellwood (AUS)
39 L. Ghirardi-Rubbi (FRA) (LL)
40 N. Kijimuta (JPN)
41 A. Gavaldon (MEX)
42 J. Kruger (RSA)
43 S. Jeyaseelan (CAN)
44 S.H. Park (KOR)
45 A. Miller (USA) (Q)
46 H. Sukova (CZE)
47 S. Pitkowski (FRA)
48 **A. Huber** (GER) (10)
49 **A. Sugiyama** (JPN) (16)
50 M. A. Sanchez Lorenzo (ESP)
51 M. Endo (JPN)
52 M. Saeki (JPN)
53 M. Grzybowska (POL)
54 C. Cristea (ROM)
55 N. Vaidyanathan (IND) (W)
56 G. Pizzichini (ITA)
57 S. Kriventcheva (BUL) (Q)
58 G. Helgeson-Nielsen (USA) (Q)
59 A. Glass (GER)
60 R. Hiraki (JPN)
61 E. Makarova (RUS)
62 L. Golarsa (ITA)
63 I. Lee (TPE)

SECOND ROUND

Hingis (1) 6–1 6–2
Rittner 6–1 7–6(5)
Morariu 6–4 1–6 6–3
Kournikova 6–2 6–1
Basuki 6–7(4) 6–3 6–1
Boogert 6–3 6–2
Snyder 7–6(5) 6–4
Van Roost (14) 6–3 6–2
Schultz-McCarthy (11) 7–6(6) 7–5
Nagyova 6–3 6–1
Yoshida 6–1 6–3
Likhovtseva 6–2 6–1
Nejedly (Q) 6–2 6–4
Barabanschikova 6–3 6–3
Torrens-Valero 6–4 6–4
Pierce (5) 6–0 6–0
Coetzer (3) 6–2 6–0
Neiland 6–3 7–6(3)
Ellwood 6–4 5–7 6–3
Ghirardi-Rubbi 1–6 7–5 6–1
Kruger 6–0 2–0 RET
Jeyaseelan 6–7(2) 6–1 7–5
Miller (Q) 4–6 7–5 6–0
Huber (10) 5–7 6–0 6–0
Sugiyama (16) 4–6 6–1 6–3
Saeki 6–4 6–3
Grzybowska 6–3 6–2
Vaidyanathan (W) 5–7 6–4 6–2
Helgeson-Nielsen (Q) 6–3 7–6(7)
Hiraki 6–2 6–2
Makarova 6–4 1–6 6–4
Sanchez-Vicario (7)

THIRD ROUND

Hingis (1) 7–5 6–1
Kournikova 7–5 6–2
Basuki 5–7 6–4 6–3
Van Roost (14) 6–3 6–4
Nagyova 6–1 6–4
Likhovtseva 6–4 4–6 6–1
Barabanschikova 6–2 6–4
Pierce (5) 6–1 6–2
Coetzer (3) 2–6 6–1 6–0
Ellwood 4–6 6–4 6–1
Kruger 6–3 6–2
Huber (10) 6–4 6–0
Sugiyama (16) 6–7(4) 7–5 6–1
Grzybowska 6–2 6–1
Hiraki 7–6(6) 7–5
Sanchez-Vicario (7) 6–0 6–0

FOURTH ROUND

Hingis (1) 6–4 4–6 6–4
Basuki 6–4 6–4
Nagyova 6–7(1) 7–5 6–2
Pierce (5) 7–5 6–3
Coetzer (3) 6–3 6–1
Huber (10) 6–7(4) 6–3 6–2
Sugiyama (16) 7–6(5) 1–6 6–4
Sanchez-Vicario (7) 6–2 6–3

QUARTER-FINALS

Hingis (1) 6–0 6–0
Pierce (5) 6–0 6–0
Huber (10) 2–6 6–4 7–5
Sanchez-Vicario (7) 6–2 6–4

SEMI-FINALS

Hingis (1) 6–2 6–3
Huber (10) 7–6(7) 7–5

FINAL

Hingis (1) 6–1 2–6 6–1

Winner: **M. Hingis** (SUI) (1

6–3 6–3

Player	Round 2	Round 3	Round 4	Quarter-finals	Semi-finals	Final
65 **C. Martinez** (ESP) (8)	**Martinez** (8) 6–2 6–2	**Martinez** (8) 7–5 6–2	**Martinez** (8) 3–6 6–0 6–3	**Martinez** (8) 6–3 6–3	**Martinez** (8) 6–3 6–2	**Martinez** (8) 4–6 6–3 6–3
66 S. Kloesel (GER)						
67 K. Kunce (AUS) (W)	Oremans 7–5 6–2					
68 M. Oremans (NED)						
69 S. Kleinova (CZE)	Ruano-Pascual 7–6(2) 7–5	Sidot 6–4 6–4				
70 V. Ruano-Pascual (ESP)						
71 L. Nemeckova (CZE)	Sidot 6–4 6–3					
72 A.G. Sidot (FRA)						
73 F. Lubiani (ITA)	Panova 6–4 6–4	Schett 6–3 6–2	Schett 6–3 6–1			
74 T. Panova (RUS)						
75 M. Diaz-Oliva (ARG)	Schett 6–4 6–1					
76 B. Schett (AUT)						
77 M. Shaughnessy (USA) (Q)	Grande 6–4 6–3	Zvereva 6–4 6–4				
78 R. Grande (ITA)						
79 N. Zvereva (BLR)	Zvereva 2–6 6–2 6–3					
80 **S. Appelmans** (BEL) (12)						
81 **S. Testud** (FRA) (9)	**Testud** (9) 6–3 6–2	**Testud** (9) 6–7(6) 6–0 6–1	**Testud** (9) 6–4 6–2	**Testud** (9) 3–6 6–1 6–2		
82 G. Leon Garcia (ESP)						
83 J. Kandarr (GER)	Kandarr 6–1 6–4					
84 S. Drake Brockman (AUS) (W)						
85 J. Husarova (SVK)	Husarova 4–6 6–4 7–5	Gersi 6–2 7–5				
86 H. Inoue (JPN)						
87 M. Maleeva (BUL)	Gersi 2–6 6–2 6–2					
88 A. Gersi (CZE)						
89 T. Tanasugarn (THA)	Tanasugarn 6–1 6–3	Tanasugarn 6–4 4–6 6–4	Tanasugarn 6–0 6–2			
90 M. A. Vento (VEN)						
91 E. Wagner (GER)	Wagner 6–2 6–1					
92 J. Watanabe (USA)						
93 R. Stubbs (AUS) (W)	Lucic 7–5 6–1	**Majoli** (4) 7–5 7–4				
94 M. Lucic (CRO)						
95 N. Sawamatsu (JPN)	**Majoli** (4) 6–4 6–2					
96 **I. Majoli** (CRO) (4)						
97 **I. Spirlea** (ROM) (6)	S. Williams 6–7(5) 6–3 6–1	V. Williams 7–6(4) 6–1	V. Williams 6–1 6–4	V. Williams 6–4 6–1	**Davenport** (2) 1–6 7–5 6–3	
98 S. Williams (USA)						
99 A. Dechaume-Balleret (FRA)	V. Williams 6–3 6–0					
100 V. Williams (USA)						
101 A. Mauresmo (FRA)	Mauresmo 7–6(4) 7–5	Mauresmo 1–6 6–4 6–3				
102 S. Farina (ITA)						
103 E. Gagliardi (SUI)	Plischke 7–5 6–1					
104 S. Plischke (AUT)						
105 S.T. Wang (TPE)	Wang 6–1 4–6 6–4	Schnyder 6–3 6–4	Schnyder 2–6 6–3 8–6			
106 I. Gorrochategui (ARG)						
107 N. Dechy (FRA)	Schnyder 6–1 6–2					
108 P. Schnyder (SUI)						
109 S. Dopfer (AUT)	Miyagi 6–2 6–1	**Raymond** (13) 6–2 3–6 7–5				
110 N. Miyagi (JPN)						
111 N. Pratt (AUS)	**Raymond** (13) 6–1 2–6 6–3					
112 **L. Raymond** (USA) (13)						
113 **R. Dragomir** (ROM) (15)	**Dragomir** (15) 6–2 6–1	**Dragomir** (15) 7–6(5) 2–6 6–3	**Dragomir** (15) 6–2 7–5	**Davenport** (2) 6–0 6–0		
114 M. Babel (GER)						
115 M. Serna (ESP)	Serna 6–3 4–6 9–7					
116 R. McQuillian (AUS)						
117 K.A. Guse (AUS)	Labat 2–6 6–3 6–4	Labat 6–4 5–7 6–4				
118 F. Labat (ARG)						
119 A. Carlsson (SWE)	Carlsson 6–3 2–6 6–4					
120 E. Dominikovic (AUS) (W)						
121 T. Musgrave (AUS) (W)	Suarez 6–3 7–5	Perfetti 6–3 6–2	**Davenport** (2) 6–2 6–2			
122 P. Suarez (ARG)						
123 S. Cacic (USA)	Perfetti 5–7 6–4 8–6					
124 F. Perfetti (ITA)						
125 K. Habsudova (SVK)	Habsudova 6–3 6–4	**Davenport** (2) 2–6 6–0 9–7				
126 S. Reeves (USA) (Q)						
127 A. Cocheteux (FRA)	**Davenport** (2) 6–2 6–3					
128 **L. Davenport** (USA) (2)						

Bold type denotes seeded players. Numbers following player's name gives seeding order (Q) = Qualifier, (W) = Wild Card, (LL) = Lucky Loser

Men's Doubles

Holders: Woodbridge (AUS)/Woodforde (AUS)

FIRST ROUND

1 **Woodbridge/Woodforde** (1)
2 Keil/Middleton
3 Berasategui/Roditi
4 Doyle/Larkham (W)
5 De Jager/Koenig
6 Nijssen/Zdrazila
7 Fleurian/Nyborg
8 **B. Black/Kulti** (16)
9 **Philippoussis/Rafter** (9)
10 Albano/Corretja
11 Flach/Kinnear
12 Randall/Waite
13 Petrovic/Silcock (W)
14 Kempers/Oosting
15 Siemerink/Vacek
16 **Lobo/Sanchez** (8)
17 **O'Brien/Stark** (3)
18 Barnard/Haygarth
19 Groen/Ivanisevic
20 Kilderry/Lapentti
21 Ondruska/Van Emburgh
22 Macpherson/Wheaton
23 Alami/Van Houdt
24 **Arnold/Orsanic** (14)
25 **Galbraith/Steven** (12)
26 Noteboom/Wibier
27 Draper/Stoltenberg (W)
28 Burillo/Martin
29 Brandi/Messori
30 Sapsford/Wilkinson
31 Goellner/Prinosil
32 **Knowles/Nestor** (6)
33 **Bjorkman/Eltingh** (5)
34 Braasch/Kohlmann
35 Apell/W. Black
36 Stafford/Ullyett
37 Coupe/Rosner
38 Godwin/Haggard
39 Knippschild/Tarango
40 **Stolle/Suk** (11)
41 **Delaitre/Santoro** (13)
42 Djordjevic/Sa
43 Bowen/Cunha-Silva
44 Grabb/Reneberg
45 Bergh/Talbot
46 Kuerten/Sell
47 El Sawy/Koves
48 **E. Ferreira/Leach** (4)
49 **Lareau/Norval** (7)
50 Gimelstob/MacPhie
51 Tebbutt/Tillstrom
52 Eagle/Florent
53 Henman/Rosset
54 Dosedel/Pimek
55 Alonso/Davis
56 **Johnson/Montana** (10)
57 **Adams/Kitinov** (15)
58 Fromberg/Holmes (W)
59 Gould/Kerr (W)
60 Hewitt/Smith (W)
61 Arthurs/Kratzmann
62 Ellwood/Tramacchi (W)
63 Mirnyi/Sargsian

SECOND ROUND

Woodbridge/Woodforde (1) 6–4 6–4
Doyle/Larkham (W) 6–4 6–3
De Jager/Koenig 7–5 5–7 6–4
Fleurian/Nyborg 6–3 6–2
Albano/Corretja 6–3 3–6 7–5
Randall/Waite 7–5 6–4
Kempers/Oosting 6–3 4–6 6–3
Lobo/Sanchez (8) 6–4 6–2
O'Brien/Stark (3) 7–6(3) 7–5
Kilderry/Lapentti 6–3 6–2
Macpherson/Wheaton 6–4 6–4
Alami/Van Houdt 2–6 6–3 6–2
Galbraith/Steven (12) 6–2 6–4
Draper/Stoltenberg (W) 6–3 7–6(4)
Brandi/Messori 6–2 6–4
Goellner/Prinosil 7–5 7–5
Bjorkman/Eltingh (5) 6–3 7–5
Apell/W. Black 7–5 5–7 6–1
Godwin/Haggard 6–4 4–6 9–7
Stolle/Suk (11) 6–2 6–4
Delaitre/Santoro (13) 7–5 6–4
Grabb/Reneberg 6–7(5) 6–2 6–4
Kuerten/Sell 6–4 7–6(5)
E. Ferreira/Leach (4) 6–4 6–2
Gimelstob/MacPhie 7–6(4) 6–7(3) 6–3
Eagle/Florent 6–1 6–3
Dosedel/Pimek 6–2 6–4
Johnson/Montana (10) 6–4 3–6 6–2
Adams/Kitinov (15) 7–6(5) 6–7(6) 6–3
Hewitt/Smith (W) 6–3 6–1
Arthurs/Kratzmann 7–5 2–6 6–3
Bhupathi/Paes (2)

THIRD ROUND

Woodbridge/Woodforde (1) 6–4 6–2
De Jager/Koenig 7–5 3–6 6–4
Albano/Corretja 7–5 0–6 6–3
Lobo/Sanchez (8) 3–6 6–3 18–16
O'Brien/Stark (3) 4–6 7–6(4) 6–2
Macpherson/Wheaton 6–3 6–4
Galbraith/Steven (12) 6–2 6–3
Goellner/Prinosil 6–4 6–4
Bjorkman/Eltingh (5) 6–4 6–4
Stolle/Suk (11) 6–2 6–2
Delaitre/Santoro (13) 4–6 6–2 6–4
E. Ferreira/Leach (4) 6–3 6–4
Gimelstob/MacPhie 6–2 6–2
Johnson/Montana (10) 6–4 6–4
Hewitt/Smith (W) 6–3 6–7(4) 14–12
Bhupathi/Paes (2) 6–2 6–3

QUARTER-FINALS

Woodbridge/Woodforde (1) 6–1 6–3
Lobo/Sanchez (8) 6–4 2–6 10–8
Macpherson/Wheaton 7–6(2) 7–6(3)
Galbraith/Steven (12) 6–7(6) 6–2 6–2
Bjorkman/Eltingh (5) 6–3 3–6 6–4
E. Ferreira/Leach (4) 3–6 6–2 6–1
Gimelstob/MacPhie 6–3 3–6 6–1
Bhupathi/Paes (2) 6–0 7–6(2)

SEMI-FINALS

Woodbridge/Woodforde (1) 6–3 6–4 7–6(1)
Macpherson/Wheaton 7–6(5) 6–7(3) 3–6 7–6(6) 13–11
Bjorkman/Eltingh (5) 6–2 6–4 7–5
Bhupathi/Paes (2) 7–6(2) 6–3 6–2

FINAL

Woodbridge/Woodforde (1) 6–4 7–5 6–3
Bjorkman/Eltingh (5) 4–6 7–5 6–3 3–6 6–3

Winners: **Bjorkman** (SWE)/**Eltingh** (SWE) (5) 6–2 5–7 2–6 6–4 6–3

Women's Doubles

Holders: Hingis (SUI)/Zvereva (BLR)

Winners: **Hingis** (SUI)/**Lucic** (CRO) (W) 6–4 2–6 6–3

FIRST ROUND

1 **Davenport/Zvereva** (1)
2 Csurgo/Marosi
3 Louarsabishvili/Lugina
4 Grzybowska/Nagyova
5 Dechaume-Balleret/Testud
6 Babel/Barclay
7 Probst/Sidot
8 **Dragomir/Majoli** (10)
9 **Hiraki/Paz** (14)
10 Kschwendt/Perfetti
11 De Lone/Horn
12 Williams/Williams
13 Ghirardi-Rubbi/Pizzichini
14 Asagoe/Stoyanova
15 Martincova/Nemeckova
16 **Kijimuta/Miyagi** (7)
17 **Martinez/Tarabini** (4)
18 De Swardt/Grande
19 Jeyaseelan/Simpson
20 Schnyder/Schultz-McCarthy
21 Carlsson/Hy-Boulais
22 Kunce/Morariu
23 Adams/McGrath
24 **Coetzer/Huber** (11)
25 **Melicharova/Vildova** (16)
26 De Villiers/McShea
27 Reeves/Tu
28 Dominikovic/Drake-Brockman (W)
29 Callens/Courtois
30 Cristea/Wunderlich
31 Husarova/Tanasugarn
32 **Likhovtseva/Sugiyama** (6)
33 **Raymond/Stubbs** (8)
34 Biggs/Grahame (W)
35 Kim/Schneider
36 Bobkova/Langrova
37 Noorlander/Van Lottum
38 Dechy/Vaidyanathan
39 Park/Wang
40 **Gorrochategui/Spirlea** (13)
41 **Guse/McQuillan** (15)
42 Diaz-Oliva/Kloesel (LL)
43 Jones/Olsza
44 Golarsa/Van Roost
45 Rittner/Wagner
46 Barabanschikova/Pleming
47 Molik/Stewart (W)
48 **Basuki/Vis** (3)
49 **Rubin/Sukova** (5)
50 Musgrave/ Pullin
51 Reid/Smith
52 Kriventcheva/Tatarkova
53 Saeki/Yoshida
54 Hingis/Lucic (W)
55 Habsudova/Labat
56 **Kournikova/Neiland** (9)
57 **Appelmans/Oremans** (12)
58 Ellwood/Pratt
59 Lee/Lee
60 Dhenin/Wood
61 Ruano-Pascual/Suarez
62 Farina/Schett
63 Helgeson-Nielsen/Krizan
64 **Bollegraf/Sanchez-Vicario** (2)

SECOND ROUND

Davenport/Zvereva (1) 6–2 6–2
Grzybowska/Nagyova 6–1 1–0 ret
Dechaume-Balleret/Testud 3–6 6–0 9–7
Dragomir/Majoli (10) 6–4 6–3
Hiraki/Paz (14) 6–4 6–4
Williams/Williams 6–4 6–2
Asagoe/Stoyanova 7–6(5) 7–6(1)
Kijimuta/Miyagi (7) 6–4 6–0
Martinez/Tarabini (4) 3–6 6–3 6–4
Schnyder/Schultz-McCarthy 6–2 6–4
Kunce/Morariu 6–3 7–6(6)
Coetzer/Huber (11) 6–2 4–6 6–0
De Villiers/McShea 6–7(4) 6–2 6–1
Reeves/Tu 6–3 6–3
Cristea/Wunderlich 7–6(3) 7–5
Likhovtseva/Sugiyama (6) 6–1 6–3
Raymond/Stubbs (8) 6–2 6–1
Kim/Schneider 7–5 6–3
Noorlander/Van Lottum 7–6(2) 6–2
Park/Wang 6–4 6–3
Guse/McQuillan (15) 6–3 2–0 ret
Golarsa/Van Roost 6–4 6–1
Rittner/Wagner 7–5 6–4
Basuki/Vis (3) 6–2 6–4
Musgrave/Pullin 4–6 6–1 6–4
Kriventcheva/Tatarkova 6–1 6–2
Hingis/Lucic (W) 6–2 6–3
Kournikova/Neiland (9) 6–2 6–1
Appelmans/Oremans (12) 6–2 6–2
Lee/Lee 6–3 6–3
Ruano-Pascual/Suarez 6–4 5–7 7–5
Bollegraf/Sanchez-Vicario (2) 3–6 6–3 6–3

THIRD ROUND

Davenport/ Zvereva (1) 6–2 1–6 6–1
Dragomir/Majoli (10) 7–5 6–4
Williams/Williams 2–6 6–2 6–2
Kijimuta/Miyagi (7) 6–2 6–2
Martinez/Tarabini (4) 7–6(4) 6–3
Coetzer/Huber (11) 6–1 6–0
Reeves/Tu 6–4 6–0
Likhovtseva/Sugiyama (6) 6–2 7–5
Raymond/Stubbs (8) 6–1 6–0
Park/Wang 6–3 6–3
Guse/McQuillan (15) 6–1 7–5
Basuki/Vis (3) 6–2 6–4
Kriventcheva/Tatarkova 7–6(1) 6–4
Hingis/Lucic (W) 7–5 6–2
Appelmans/Oremans (12) 6–3 1–6 6–3
Bollegraf/Sanchez-Vicario (2) 6–1 6–1

QUARTER-FINALS

Davenport/Zvereva (1) 6–1 6–1
Kijimuta/Miyagi (7) 6–3 6–3
Martinez/Tarabini (4) 7–5 7–5
Likhovtseva/Sugiyama (6) 6–4 6–2
Raymond/Stubbs (8) 6–1 6–2
Guse/McQuillan (15) 6–3 3–0 ret
Hingis/Lucic (W) 6–1 6–3
Bollegraf/Sanchez-Vicario (2) 3–6 7–5 6–2

SEMI-FINALS

Davenport/Zvereva (1) 6–1 6–0
Martinez/Tarabini (4) 6–4 6–7(1) 6–1
Raymond/Stubbs (8) 6–4 3–6 6–3
Hingis/Lucic (W) 6–1 6–1

FINAL

Davenport/ Zvereva (1) 6–3 6–1
Hingis/Lucic (W) 4–6 6–4 6–1

Bold type denotes seeded players. Numbers following player's name gives seeding order (Q) = Qualifier, (W) = Wild Card, (LL) = Lucky Loser

Mixed Doubles

Holders: Leach (USA)/Bollegraf (NED)

FIRST ROUND	SECOND ROUND	QUARTER-FINALS	SEMI-FINALS	FINAL
1 Arthurs/Pleming (LL)	Arthurs/Pleming (LL)			
2 Roditi/Hiraki	4–6 6–3 7–5	Mirnyi/Likhovtseva		
3 Mirnyi/Likhovtseva	Mirnyi/Likhovtseva	7–5 6–4		
4 Montana/Helgeson-Nielsen	6–2 6–4		Mirnyi/Likhovtseva	
5 Florent/Zvereva	Florent/Zvereva		6–3 6–2	
6 Hewitt/S. Williams (W)	7–6(3) 6–2	Florent/Zvereva		
7 Macpherson/McQuillan	Macpherson/McQuillan	6–3 6–3		
8 **Orsanic/Tarabini** (8)	6–0 6–0			Gimelstob/V. Williams (W)
9 **Galbraith/Raymond** (3)	**Galbraith/Raymond** (3)			6–2 6–1
10 Ellwood/Ellwood (W)	6–3 6–0	**Galbraith/Raymond** (3)		
11 Nyborg/Vildova	Johnson/Boogert	7–6(3) 6–1		
12 Johnson/Boogert	6–3 6–3		Gimelstob/V. Williams (W)	
13 Lobo/Gorrochategui	Knowles/Kournikova		7–6(2) 3–6 6–2	
14 Knowles/Kournikova	6–7(4) 6–2 6–4	Gimelstob/V. Williams (W)		
15 Gimelstob/V. Williams (W)	Gimelstob/V. Williams (W)	7–5 6–2		
16 **Ferreira/K. Adams** (6)	6–3 7–5			
17 **D. Adams/Neiland** (7)	**D. Adams/Neiland** (7)			
18 Albano/Paz	6–4 7–5	Kratzmann/Guse		
19 Kratzmann/Guse	Kratzmann/Guse	2–6 6–3 6–4		
20 Lapentti/Suarez	6–2 1–0 ret		**Bhupathi/Vis** (4)	
21 Kinnear/Miyagi	Kinnear/Miyagi		4–6 7–6(7) 6–2	
22 Eagle/Stubbs	1–6 6–3 7–6(4)	**Bhupathi/Vis** (4)		
23 Pimek/Grande	**Bhupathi/Vis** (4)	4–6 6–4 7–5		
24 **Bhupathi/Vis** (4)	6–2 6–0			**Suk/Sukova** (5)
25 **Suk/Sukova** (5)	**Suk/Sukova** (5)			6–2 3–6 7–6(3)
26 Waite/McGrath	5–7 6–3 6–4	**Suk/Sukova** (5)		
27 Norval/Oremans	Talbot/Barclay (LL)	6–2 6–4		
28 Talbot/Barclay (LL)	3–6 6–1 6–3		**Suk/Sukova** (5)	
29 Arnold/Dragomir	Kitinov/Melicharova		3–6 7–6(1) 6–4	
30 Kitinov/Melicharova	6–3 5–7 6–4	Kitinov/Melicharova		
31 Grabb/Kunce	Grabb/Kunce	6–4 7–5		
32 **Leach/Bollegraf** (2)	7–5 6–1			

Winners:
Gimelstob (USA)/**V. Williams** (USA) (W)
6–2 6–1

Bold type denotes seeded players. Numbers following player's name gives seeding order (Q) = Qualifier, (W) = Wild Card, (LL) = Lucky Loser

Davenport, too, surrendered to negative feelings in her semi-final with Martinez, a player whose mixture of topspin and slice had occasionally reduced her to despair in the past. The tall American had saved a match point in her second-round match with Habsudova, but 66 unforced errors prevented her from extricating herself from her long, often tedious tangle with Martinez.

The Spaniard's performance was a reward for her increased diligence after a poor year in which she had failed to win a title. She played well enough to suggest she may yet enhance the reputation she won at Wimbledon in 1994. Although Martinez needed pain-killers for a groin injury, she made Hingis earn her second Australian title, testing the champion's patience and resilience, and keeping her on court for almost 90 minutes before losing 6–3 6–3.

The doubles events contained many surprises. Hingis retained her women's doubles title, but with a new partner, her friend Lucic. In the final they defeated Davenport and Natasha Zvereva. 'I'm used to having older partners, so it was a different experience to be the boss of the court,' said Martina with her knack of applying a humorous slant to whatever happens.

The Woodies, as usual, represented Australia's best hope of a title, but lost a five-set men's doubles final to the scratch pair of Jonas Bjorkman and Jacco Eltingh. Another scratch pair, David Macpherson and David Wheaton, put in a phenomenal quarter-final effort by saving nine match points in beating Pat Galbraith and Brett Steven 7–6 6–7 3–6 7–6 13–11 in 5 hours and 26 minutes, one of the longest matches in Grand Slam history.

The mixed doubles allowed Venus Williams to capture her first Grand Slam title when she and compatriot Justin Gimelstob overcame the Czech brother-sister combination of Cyril Suk and Helena Sukova.

JUNIOR EVENTS

BOYS' SINGLES – Final: Julien Jeanpierre (FRA) (2) d. Andreas Vinciguerra (SWE) 4–6 6–4 6–3.
GIRLS' SINGLES – Final: Jelena Kostanic (CRO) (5) d. Wynne Prakusya (INA) 6–0 7–5.
BOY'S DOUBLES – Final: Jerome Haehnel (FRA)/Julien Jeanpierre (FRA) (3) d. Mirko Pehar (CRO)/Lovro Zovko (CRO) (4) 6–3 6–3.
GIRLS' DOUBLES – Final: Evie Dominikovic (AUS)/Alicia Molik (AUS) d. Leanne Baker (NZL)/Rewa Hudson (NZL) (1) 6–3 3–6 6–2.
LEGENDS' DOUBLES – Final: Mark Edmondson (AUS)/Kim Warwick (AUS) d. John Newcombe (AUS)/Tony Roche (AUS) 6–1 7–6.
LEGENDS' MIXED DOUBLES – Final: Wally Masur (AUS)/Elizabeth Smylie (AUS) d. Stan Smith (USA)/Diane Balestrat (AUS) 6–2 6–4.

AUSTRALIAN OPEN CHAMPIONSHIPS 1998
PRIZE MONEY – AUS $10,004,000

MEN'S SINGLES – Winner $615,000; Runner-up $307,500; Semi-finalists $153,500; Quarter-finalists $78,750; Fourth-round losers $42,000; Third-round losers $24,000; Second-round losers $14,625; First-round losers $9,500. **Total: $3,340,500**
WOMEN'S SINGLES – Winner $572,000; Runner-up $286,000; Semi-finalists $142,500; Quarter-finalists $74,000; Fourth-round losers $39,000; Third-round losers $22,750; Second-round losers $13,750; First-round losers $8,625. **Total: $3,107,000**
MEN'S DOUBLES (per team) – Winners $256,000; Runners-up $128,000; Semi-finalists $63,000; Quarter-finalists $31,500; Third-round losers $18,000; Second-round losers $9,750; First-round losers $5,500. **Total: $1,112,000**
WOMEN'S DOUBLES (per team) – Winners $237,000; Runners-up $118,500; Semi-finalists $59,000; Quarter-finalists $29,500; Third-round losers $16,500; Second-round losers $9,000; First-round losers $5,250. **Total: $1,035,500**
MIXED DOUBLES (per team) – Winners $92,000; Runners-up $46,000; Semi-finalists $23,000; Quarter-finalists $10,700; Second-round losers $5,400; First-round losers $2,600. **Total $311,600**
LEGENDS DOUBLES (per player) Winners (2) $10,000. Runners-up (2) $7,500. Other players (8) $5,000. Reserves (2) $3,000. **Total: $81,000**
LEGENDS MIXED DOUBLES (per player) Winners (2) $7,500; Runners-up (2) $5,000; Other players (4) $4,000; Reserve (1) $3,000. **Total: $44,000**

MEN'S QUALIFYING (128 DRAW)
Losers in round of 32 – $5,800
Losers in round of 64 – $3,000
Losers in round of 128 – $1,550
Total: $288,000

WOMEN'S QUALIFYING (64 DRAW)
Losers in round of 16 – $5,400
Losers in round of 32 – $2,900
Losers in round of 128 – $1,400
Total: $134,400

Plus **PER DIEM** allowances of $170 per day per player, commencing on the day prior to the player's first match and including the day of the player's last match. Total $550,000 (estimated).

In the second all-Spanish final at the French Open in five years, Carlos Moya won his first major title by beating his friend and fellow Davis Cup player, Alex Corretja. (Michael Cole)

French Open Championships

Richard Evans

Not for the first time in the nineties, Stade Roland Garros was draped in the colours of Spain. With King Juan Carlos, through his on-site co-ordinator Manolo Santana, organising various members of his family to fly into Paris to support his country's players, Spain's finest ensured that the royal journeys were worthwhile. The King's sister witnessed the return of Arantxa Sanchez-Vicario to the winner's circle at a Grand Slam event for the first time since Flushing Meadows in 1994 when she beat Monica Seles, the sentimental favourite, 7–6 0–6 6–2. Then it was the turn of the King's daughter, the Infanta Cristina, to watch the crowning moment of Carlos Moya's career when he beat his friend Alex Corretja 6–3 7–5 6–3 in the second all-Spanish men's final in five years.

Throughout this momentous weekend, no one looked on with a greater sense of pride than Santana himself. This remarkable athlete with the crooked smile had single handedly ignited the tennis bushfire in Spain when he had stood on this very Centre Court, sobbing with joy on the shoulder of Italy's Nikki Pietrangeli, the man he had just beaten to win the French title in 1961. When Santana, the former ball boy from Madrid, was clasped to Franco's bosom after winning Wimbledon five years later, the average Spaniard suddenly woke up to the fact that this really was a sport that could be played outside the snob-ridden confines of a members-only country club.

But if those were personal thoughts for Spain's current Davis Cup captain, the rest of us were left to marvel at the spirit of sportsmanship that pervaded the latter rounds of a memorable Championship – a sportsmanship that showed the world that it is still possible, even in this over-hyped material age, to fight the good fight while retaining the utmost respect for one's opponent. And in doing so, the finalists were able to bring a degree of regality to the occasion that was as uplifting as it was appropriate.

Arantxa's speech on the victory podium set the tone. 'I'd like to congratulate Monica for getting to the final,' she said. 'I'm sorry that I had to beat you. I have so much respect for you. All the players are so sorry your father passed away.'

Moya and Corretja had suffered nothing so serious as the loss of a parent – Karolj Seles had died a mere two weeks before the start of the French Open – but Corretja, in private, was desolate over the loss of this tennis match. Few would have thought it had hurt him so deeply because it was he who jumped the net at the end, running to congratulate the prostrate Moya and conveying very publicly the happiness he felt for his young Davis Cup team mate. That these two leaders of the Spanish pack who now maraud the ATP Tour with such success are trusting friends was born out by the fact that umpire Bruno Rebeuh and his line judges quickly discovered, once the final got underway, that their role was, at best, peripheral. Whenever a call was close, one player would inspect the mark and signal his decision. Without a moment's hesitation, his opponent would accept it. It was a pleasure to see such chivalry. In fact the demeanour of these two Spaniards set a wonderful example that, hopefully, was noted by those many youngsters who seem to feel it is necessary to posture and pout after every close decision.

Although he was almost three years younger than Corretja, Moya's progress through the draw suggested that he was the readier of the two for the great leap forward to that exalted status of Grand Slam winner. The 21-year-old from Mallorca had, of course, already appeared in a final of one of the world's Big Four championships. But it had been as much of a shock to him as to everyone else when he had found himself facing Pete Sampras in the final of the Australian Open in January 1997. 'But here it is different,' he said after beating his compatriot Felix Mantilla in four authoritative sets in the semi-final. 'I am much more confident in myself now. Maybe to play in one Grand Slam final is a coincidence. But I don't think two times is a coincidence. I think it means I am a good player and this time I want to be the winner.'

It soon became clear that he was ready to become just that. The overall strength of his game, in which inherent clay court skills are matched by the power of a big first serve and an improving volley, suggests that he has the ability to establish himself as an enduring champion – a species that has not been seen in great abundance of late. Moya was, in fact, the fourth new

Grand Slam champion to be crowned out of the last six to be played. Some, like Gustavo Kuerten, Petr Korda and Yevgeny Kafelnikov who preceded Kuerten as French champion in 1996, have never looked like becoming repeat champions and it would do Grand Slam tennis no harm at all if Moya helped this showcase level of the game to re-discover the plot. Surprise and variety is great but substance is needed as well and, just recently, too few have suggested they have what it takes to build on fleeting success.

Nevertheless a fortnight of increasingly warm weather and vast crowds at Roland Garros produced an interesting collection of new faces as old favourites struggled to maintain their credibility. The Americans had least reason to enjoy their time in Paris. Incredibly Michael Chang, the No 11 seed, was the only American to get as far as the third round. And that was as far as the 1989 champion could go. On legs that no longer carry him as far or as fast, Chang was outmanouvred by one of the Spaniards, Francisco Clavet, and lost in four sets.

Prior to that, of course, there had been the shocking demise of Pete Sampras – shocking not so much because he lost on clay but rather that he went out in the second round in straight sets to Ramon Delgado, the best young Paraguayan we have seen since Victor Pecci. Sampras, who had looked as confident as he ever can be on clay while beating Todd Martin 6–4 6–3 6–3 in the first round, was simply outplayed by a talented performer who knew how to work the surface. Incredibly, it was Sampras who looked like the novice.

For the rest, neither the old nor the new could carry the Stars and Stripes very far. Jim Courier, who might have won this title three straight years with a bit more fortune in 1993 when he lost to Bruguera in the fifth set of a magnificent final, managed to get past Richard Fromberg in the first round but fell to Germany's Jens Knippschild in the second. Meanwhile the promising American, Jan Michael Gambill, beat the Argentine qualifyer Martin Rodriguez handily enough but was then outplayed by Daniel Vacek in the fourth set tie-break of their second round encounter.

There was certainly no sign amongst the American ranks of anyone with half the potential of the most explosive newcomer to the Championships – a ruggedly handsome Russian giant with a flashing smile and a quick wit called Marat Safin. In fact Safin is a Tartar – as raw as the steak and as tasty as the sauce. At 18-years-old, he exploded into his first Grand Slam in a manner that few have achieved since John McEnroe and Boris Becker. It is not impossible that he will end up being as successful.

If that may seem fanciful to those who did not witness his progress to the last sixteen then perhaps they would have been convinced had they seen this 6 ft 4 in athlete step up to serve for the match in the first round against Andre Agassi and hit him with an ace, a service winner and a couple of unreturnables. It was the end of a fifth set that Safin had dominated with the depth of his hitting off the ground and the consistency of his serving.

But that was just the beginning. Kuerten, the defending champion, played better than Agassi on the Centre Court but, having led by two sets to one, he could do nothing to prevent Safin pounding his way back into the match, sprinkling deft little touches like the occasional stop volley or drop shot onto the diet of unrelenting power. Again, when it came to that arm-stiffening moment when a player has to serve for the match, Safin opened up with an ace and won the game with the kind of unfussed assurance one might have expected had it been early in the first set. Vacek was the next to feel the edge of Safin's sword and it took Wimbledon finalist Cedric Pioline, roared on by his own Parisian crowd, to halt the surge towards stardom by holding steady under extreme pressure to win 6–4 in the fifth.

The other youngster to make a name for himself was Mariano Zabaleta. The former world junior champion outfought No.2 seed Petr Korda over five sets in the first round and then went on to beat Jeff Tarango in the second before falling to Hicham Arazi who mesmerised the Roland Garros crowds for the second year running with his wondrous skills. The previous year the left-handed Moroccan had beaten Marcelo Rios in a duel that had held the Suzanne Lenglen Court spellbound. Arazi did much the same against the 16th seed Alberto Berasategui this time but couldn't last the distance against the determined Pioline and lost 6–3 in the fifth.

Filip Dewulf, an unseeded semi-finalist twelve months before, suddenly re-discovered his touch in front of a travelling pack of Belgian fans and promptly knocked out Thomas Enqvist before reaching the quarter-finals at the expense of Clavet. It then required Corretja's superior tactical know how to prevent Dewulf from reaching the semis again.

All this was but a supporting act to the main theme of the tournament which centered around Moya's progress and his ultimate, title-deciding clash with Rios in the quarter-finals. You could not find an expert at Roland Garros during the first week who did not think that the

Chilean left-hander was about to re-confirm his right to be No.1 in the world by winning the Championship. Win it or not, Rios would have overtaken Sampras again had he just beaten Moya. Despite a brief renaissance in the second set, however, Rios never looked remotely capable of such an achievement.

On top of his successes at Indian Wells and the Lipton, Rios had swept imperiously through the fields at Rome and St Polten prior to the French Open. Moya, though, was something else. The weight of his shots, the ability to mix it up and get in on Rios behind his huge forehand, coupled with a serve that Marcelo found difficult to return, all added up to an amazingly one sided defeat 6–1 2–6 6–2 6–4. It was the match that virtually won Moya the title and he looked every inch a champion doing it.

Meanwhile Felix Mantilla had outlasted the ever determined Thomas Muster to set up a semi-final clash with Moya and once again the Mallorcan came through in four against a resolute baseliner who had bleached his hair blond but still could not find a style that is either interesting or varied enough to worry the class performers.

Corretja accounted for an exhausted Pioline in straight sets in the other semi-final but Alex had been put through the ringer himself in the third round when, in a match that, happily, was spread over two days, he beat Argentina's Hernan Gumy 9–7 in the fifth after five hours and thirty minutes. The records have been poorly kept but, as far as anyone could remember, this was the longest match played at Roland Garros since the advent of Open Tennis in 1968. Gumy had missed match points after leading by two sets to one and Corretja, having endured similar pain himself after losing to Sampras at Flushing Meadows in 1996, embraced Gumy at the end and offered consoling words. Few people know how to win and lose better than this impressive 24-year-old.

In the final, it soon became clear that Moya was better prepared mentally and physically, than his opponent. His superiority siphoned off any element of drama from the occasion but it was a match full of fine shot making with Moya's ability to mix power with delicacy of touch always worth watching.

In the men's doubles, Paul Haarhuis and Jacco Eltingh enhanced their reputations by outplaying the dangerous pair of Jonas Bjorkman and Patrick Rafter 6–2 6–2 in the semi-final before defeating Mark Knowles and Daniel Nestor 6–3 3–6 6–3 in the final.

The French Open provided the first serious evidence that the teenage brigade who were widely expected to take over the womens' game would not be having things all their own way in 1998. The youngsters did not disgrace themselves but neither did they win. Venus Williams proved raw power could work on clay for the women by pounding her way into the quarter-finals without the loss of a set, beating someone as accomplished as the improving Slovak, Henrieta Nagyova 6–1 6–3 along the way. Yet when she met Martina Hingis in a quarter-final rightly scheduled on the Centre Court instead of the smaller but hardly less impressive Suzanne Lenglen where women's quarter-finals are traditionally held, Venus found herself confounded by the depth and accuracy of the Swiss player's ground strokes and lost 6–3 6–4.

Martina's Fed Cup colleague, Patty Schnyder, was the other teenager to break through to the quarters after a thrilling first round victory over Amanda Coetzer, the seed in her quarter, 8–6 in the third set. Schnyder's potential has been overshadowed by Hingis' phenomenal success but not, one suspects, for much longer. She will, however, have to keep a tighter grip on her talent than she managed in the first and final sets against Sanchez-Vicario who feasted off Swiss gifts to win 6–0 in the third.

In the previous round Sanchez-Vicario had accounted for the other teenager to leave her mark on these Championships, Serena Williams. The athletic 16-year-old was playing in her first French Open but, like her sister, she was unconcerned by such things. Imbued with utter self belief by her father Richard, Serena looked as if she had been playing on red clay all her life.

Having crushed the promising American Corina Morariu 6–1 6–0, amazingly she was just as harsh on the feisty No 15 seed from Belgium, Dominique Van Roost, winning 6–1 6–1. Just what she might have accomplished had she continued to play the kind of tennis that took her to a 6–4 5–2 lead over the ultimate champion will never be known but, up to that moment, she had totally dominated the match with her power driven ground strokes.

Williams served for it at 5–3 and failed. Even then she had Sanchez-Vicario 0–30 on her serve at 5–4. Match point beckoned when Serena had a clear opening for a backhand winner at 15–30 but she fluffed it and was never quite the same player again. In familiar fashion, Arantxa chased and parried and seized such control of the match that she won five consecutive games and eleven of the last fourteen to win 4–6 7–5 6–3.

Unhappily it was not an encounter played in a friendly spirit. Sanchez-Vicario did not appreciate the crowd's fervent support for her opponent and became very fussed when Williams raced in for a drop shot as Arantxa lay prone on her back after a fall. The Spaniard was convinced Serena took the ball on the second bounce but the umpire did not agree. Words were exchanged at the net and afterwards Arantxa accused her young opponent of not showing her sufficient respect.

Jana Novotna had accounted for the most glamorous of the teenage prodigies, Anna Kournikova. In a fine fourth round struggle the Czech had battled back with great fortitude after losing the first set on a tie-break. She continued to play some clever tactical tennis against a rampant Seles in the most fascinating of the quarter-finals and fought back from 2–4 and 0–40 down in the first set to win it 6–4. Novotna's ability to slice an early backhand on the rise and get in was the perfect antidote to the power Seles was generating off the ground, However, such tactics are incredibly difficult to maintain against this class of opposition. Slowly, but with an ever increasing air of inevitability, Seles regained control by upping her tempo to a still more furious level of endeavour and came through 6–3 in the third.

Having defeated Conchita Martinez in three tough sets, the defending champion, Iva Majoli, ran into even more rugged opposition in the quarters. The crown toppled from her head as Olympic champion, Lindsay Davenport, hitting the ball with awesome power, played unstoppable tennis in the third set, to win it 6–3.

The semi-finals offered a wonderful opportunity for two veterans of the tour to re-establish their dominance. Neither wasted it. Hingis and Davenport must have come off court wondering what on earth went wrong. Both had played well below their own high standards. Against Seles, Hingis seemed strangely distracted and downbeat – possibly as a result of a tiff with her boyfriend Julian Alonso the night before – and gifted the first set with two double-faults at 3–5. In contrast Seles was concentrating like the Monica of old, narrowing her eyes as the racket came back to unleash another fizzing drive to some far corner of the court. Hingis, overwhelmed, looked like the little girl she would have been but for her talent at tennis. When a series of forehand service returns found the net she tried to dig herself out of trouble with injudicious drop shots. They didn't work either. In fact, nothing did. Seles was allowed to come through with shocking ease 6–3 6–2 to ensure that Hingis would have to wait at least one more year for the one Grand Slam title she has never owned.

In the other semi-final, Davenport was just as disappointing against Sanchez-Vicario. The American never seemed to have a clear idea of how she wanted to tackle the little dynamo on the other side of the net and compounded the problem by serving badly. In fact the American held serve only twice in ten games. Despite leading 5–3 in the second set tie-break Davenport was beaten 6–3 7–6 and had never really looked capable of preventing the Spaniard from reaching the French Open final for the sixth time.

The score in the final, 7–6 0–6 6–2, was strange but not entirely unrecognisable to Seles. In 1995, she had lost 7–6 0–6 6–3 to Steffi Graf in the US Open final and there were similarities here. When Seles was hot she sizzled and there was little her opponent could do about it. But errors cost her the chance to establish an early lead, especially when she was up 5–3 in the first set and, at 30-all, put a bounced smash into the net.

Having lost the breaker 7–5, Seles promptly launched a blitz on the second set that all but left Sanchez-Vicario as a spectator. Seles won three games at love and dropped only seven points the entire set. Dust flew, lines were hit and the crowd erupted as one Seles winner after another found its mark. But it was unsustainable. Sanchez-Vicario, as obstinate a player as ever stepped on a tennis court, dug her heels into the clay and refused to buckle – not even in the face of five break points scattered through her opening three service games of the deciding set. The Seles fire flickered and died and Sanchez-Vicario was a deserving queen of Roland Garros for the third time.

There was some consolation for Hingis in the doubles where she teamed with Novotna to win the title with a 6–1 7–6 victory over Davenport and Natasha Zvereva.

But it was the Mixed Doubles final that carried special interest. For the first time, but probably not the last, the Williams sisters met in a major final. Venus teamed with Justin Gimelstob and, despite trailing 0–3 in the first set, ensured they would claim their second Grand Slam title of the year by beating Serena and Argentina's Luis Lobo 6–4 6–4.

Martina Hingis and Jana Novotna, victors in Paris, went on to win together at Wimbledon and the US Open, a run that completed a doubles Grand Slam for Hingis who had triumphed in Melbourne with Mirjana Lucic. (Michael Cole)

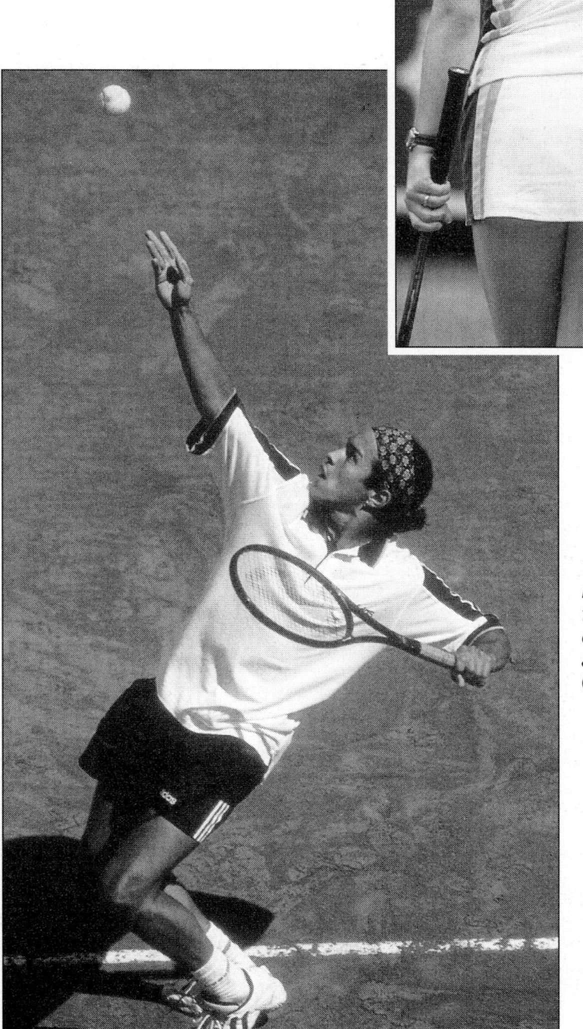

The mercurial Moroccan Hicham Arazi was a quarter-finalist in Paris but ran out of energy in the final set against Cedric Pioline. (Stephen Wake)

Men's Singles

Holder: G. Kuerten (BRA)

FIRST ROUND

1 **P. Sampras** (USA) (1)
2 T. Martin (USA)
3 R. Delgado (PAR)
4 M. Damm (CZE)
5 S. Sargsian (ARM)
6 T. Henman (GBR)
7 A. Medvedev (UKR)
8 A. Gaudenzi (ITA)
9 L. Arnold (ARG)
10 D. Sanguinetti (ITA)
11 F. Santoro (FRA)
12 J-F. Bachelot (FRA) (W)
13 A. Clement (FRA)
14 B. Black (ZIM)
15 W. Schranz (AUT) (Q)
16 **F. Mantilla** (ESP) (15)
17 **K. Kucera** (SVK) (9)
18 T. Woodbridge (AUS)
19 J. A. Marin (CRC)
20 G. Raoux (FRA)
21 V. Spadea (USA)
22 D. Nestor (CAN)
23 F. Meligeni (BRA)
24 T. Johansson (SWE)
25 T. Nydahl (SWE)
26 S. Draper (AUS)
27 M. Craca (GER)
28 C. Van Garsse (BEL) (Q)
29 N. Kiefer (GER)
30 T. Haas (GER)
31 T. Muster (AUT)
32 **J. Bjorkman** (SWE) (7)
33 **M. Rios** (CHI) (3)
34 B. Steven (NZL)
35 E. Alvarez (ESP)
36 M. Tebbutt (AUS)
37 B. Karbacher (GER) (Q)
38 M. Norman (SWE)
39 M. Sinner (GER)
40 W. Ferreira (RSA)
41 B. Ulihrach (CZE)
42 W. Black (ZIM)
43 M. Philippoussis (AUS)
44 O. Gross (GER) (LL)
45 J. Burillo (ESP)
46 M-K. Goellner (GER)
47 K. Carlsen (DEN)
48 **A. Costa** (ESP) (13)
49 **C. Moya** (ESP) (12)
50 S. Grosjean (FRA) (W)
51 J-B. Perlant (FRA) (W)
52 J.P. Imaz (ESP) (Q)
53 S. Dosedel (CZE)
54 M. Tillstrom (SWE)
55 J. Alonso (ESP)
56 A. Ilie (AUS) (Q)
57 J. Courier (USA)
58 R. Fromberg (AUS)
59 J. Knippschild (GER) (Q)
60 C. Costa (ESP)
61 J. Mas (ESP) (Q)
62 M. Sell (USA) (Q)
63 J. Van Herck (BEL)
64 **G. Rusedski** (GBR) (5)

SECOND ROUND

Sampras (1) 6–4 6–3 6–3
Delgado 6–2 0–0 Ab
Sargsian 5–2 Ab
Gaudenzi 7–6(5) 6–1 0–6 2–6 6–1
Arnold 4–6 6–4 6–1 6–4
Santoro 6–3 6–1 6–2
B. Black 6–4 6–1 6–2
Mantilla (15) 6–2 6–4 6–2
Woodbridge 1–6 6–2 6–4 6–3
Raoux 6–3 7–6(6) 7–6(2)
Spadea 5–7 5–2 Ab
Meligeni 6–4 6–2 6–4
Draper 6–3 7–6(2) 6–3
Van Garsse (Q) 6–1 6–1 6–1
Kiefer 6–1 6–2 7–6(3)
Muster 6–3 6–3 6–3
Rios (3) 7–5 6–2 3–6 6–3
Alvarez 5–7 7–5 6–7(12) 6–4 6–3
Norman 6–2 1–6 6–3 6–1
Ferreira 7–6 (4) 6–4 7–5
Ulihrach 6–1 6–7(7) 6–2 6–3
Philippoussis 6–1 7–5 6–4
Goellner 6–7(6) 6–3 6–2 6–3
Costa (13) 6–3 6–2 6–2
Moya (12) 7–5 6–1 6–4
Imaz (Q) 7–6(6) 3–6 6–3 3–6 6–1
Tillstrom 7–5 6–1 6–2
Ilie (Q) 4–6 6–3 6–3 6–2
Courier 7–6(1) 6–4 0–6 6–4
Knippschild (Q) 6–4 6–2 6–4
Mas (Q) 0–6 6–4 6–2 7–6(4)
Van Herck 6–4 6–4 6–4

THIRD ROUND

Delgado 7–6(6) 6–3 6–4
Sargsian 6–4 6–2 6–7(5) 6–4
Santoro 4–6 4–6 6–4 6–0 6–3
Mantilla (15) 6–2 6–2 7–6(2)
Woodbridge 6–4 4–6 6–3 6–0
Meligeni 7–6(5) 7–6(3) 6–3
Van Garsse (Q) 6–3 3–6 6–7(5) 7–6(2) 6–2
Muster 6–2 6–1 6–3
Rios (3) 6–4 6–2 6–2
Ferreira 6–4 6–4 6–4
Ulihrach 3–6 6–7(2) 7–5 6–4 9–7
Costa (13) 6–4 6–3 6–1
Moya (12) 6–4 7–6(14) 6–2
Ilie (Q) 6–7(9) 6–3 6–3 6–4
Knippschild (Q) 6–4 6–2 6–3
Van Herck 6–3 7–6(4) 7–5

FOURTH ROUND

Delgado 2–6 7–6(4) 6–4 7–6(7)
Mantilla (15) 4–6 6–2 6–2 7–5
Meligeni 7–5 6–3 6–2
Muster 6–2 4–6 7–6(3) 6–2
Rios (3) 6–1 6–3 Ab
Costa (13) 6–3 6–3 6–0
Moya (12) 6–2 7–6(1) 6–3
Knippschild (Q) 2–6 0–6 7–6(6) 6–4 6–2

QUARTER-FINALS

Mantilla (15) 6–2 6–2 6–4
Muster 6–4 6–7(8) 6–3 3–6 6–3
Rios (3) 4–6 6–4 6–3 6–3
Moya (12) 6–3 7–5 3–6 6–4

SEMI-FINALS

Mantilla (15) 6–4 6–2 4–6 6–3
Moya (12) 6–1 2–6 6–2 6–4

FINAL

Moya (12) 5–7 6–2 6–4 6–2

Winner: **C. Moya** (ESP) (12)

6–3 7–5 6–3

First round

65 **Y. Kafelnikov** (RUS) (6)
66 M. Navarra (ITA) (Q)
67 D. Pescariu (ROM)
68 T. Enqvist (SWE)
69 M. Martelli (ITA) (Q)
70 G. Ivanisevic (CRO)
71 F. Dewulf (BEL)
72 M. Larsson (SWE)
73 A. Di Pasquale (FRA) (W)
74 O. Delaitre (FRA) (W)
75 F. Clavet (ESP)
76 A. Chesnokov (RUS)
77 J. Van Lottum (NED) (Q)
78 J. Siemerink (NED)
79 A. Calatrava (ESP)
80 **M. Chang** (USA) (11)
81 **A. Corretja** (ESP) (14)
82 K. Alami (MAR)
83 F. Vicente (ESP)
84 M. Woodforde (AUS)
85 M. Rosset (SUI)
86 G. Pozzi (ITA)
87 H. Gumy (ARG)
88 S. Bruguera (ESP)
89 O. Mutis (FRA) (W)
90 D. Prinosil (GER)
91 M. Gustafsson (SWE)
92 A. O'Brien (USA)
93 J. Stoltenberg (AUS)
94 G. Blanco (ESP)
95 S. Lareau (CAN)
96 **P. Rafter** (AUS) (4)
97 **G. Kuerten** (BRA) (8)
98 C. Auffray (FRA) (W)
99 M. Safin (RUS) (Q)
100 A. Agassi (USA)
101 S. Schalken (NED)
102 D. Vacek (CZE)
103 M. Rodriguez (ARG) (Q)
104 J-M. Gambill (USA)
105 M. Filippini (URU)
106 C. Pioline (FRA)
107 J. Boutter (FRA) (Q)
108 C. Vinck (GER)
109 R. Gilbert (FRA) (Q)
110 A. Portas (ESP)
111 N. Lapentti (ECU)
112 **R. Krajicek** (NED) (10)
113 **A. Berasategui** (ESP) (16)
114 G. Stafford (RSA)
115 G. Solves (FRA) (W)
116 R. Reneberg (USA)
117 D. Hrbaty (SVK)
118 S. Campbell (USA)
119 J. Sanchez (ESP)
120 J. A. Viloca (ESP)
121 J. Novak (CZE)
122 H. Arazi (MAR)
123 J. Golmard (FRA)
124 N. Escude (FRA)
125 J. Tarango (USA)
126 P. Haarhuis (NED)
127 M. Zabaleta (ARG) (Q)
128 **P. Korda** (CZE) (2)

Second round

Kafelnikov (6) 6–4 4–6 6–1 6–4
Enqvist 7–6(4) 6–4 6–4
Martelli (Q) 7–6(3) 7–6(6) 7–6(2)
Dewulf 7–6(0) 7–5 7–6(5)
Delaitre (W) 2–6 7–5 7–6(4) 1–6 6–0
Clavet 6–1 6–4 6–1
Van Lottum (Q) 6–7(5) 6–3 6–2 3–6 6–2
Chang (11) 7–5 6–3 6–2
Corretja (14) 6–3 6–2 0–6 6–4
Vicente 4–6 6–4 6–2 6–1
Pozzi 6–2 6–1 4–6 6–4
Gumy 6–2 6–2 6–3
Prinosil 6–4 1–6 4–6 6–3 6–2
Gustafsson 6–2 4–6 6–2 6–2
Stoltenberg 6–2 4–6 6–0 4–6 10–8
Rafter (4) 6–7(5) 3–6 6–1 6–3 6–2
Kuerten (8) 6–0 6–2 6–2
Safin (Q) 5–7 7–5 6–2 3–6 6–2
Vacek 1–6 6–2 6–4 7–5
Gambill 6–3 6–2 6–4
Pioline 6–1 3–6 7–5 6–7(4) 6–4
Boutter (Q) 6–7(6) 6–3 6–4 7–6(5)
Gilbert (Q) 6–3 6–3 2–6 2–6 11–9
Krajicek (10) 6–4 6–4 6–7(2) 7–6(5)
Berasategui (16) 4–6 7–6(7) 6–3 6–1
Solves (W) 6–4 6–2 3–6 6–7(5) 8–6
Hrbaty 2–6 6–3 6–3 6–3
Viloca 7–6(6) 3–6 5–7 6–4 6–3
Arazi 6–0 6–2 7–6(1)
Escude 6–1 6–2 6–0
Tarango 6–4 6–1 7–6(4)
Zabaleta (Q) 6–0 6–2 3–6 4–6 6–3

Third round

Enqvist 4–6 7–6(10) 7–6(4) 6–1
Dewulf 7–6(5) 6–4 7–6(7)
Clavet 6–2 6–4 6–7(4) 6–1
Chang (11) 7–5 6–2 3–0 ret
Corretja (14) 6–3 6–2 6–3
Gumy 6–2 6–3 3–6 5–7 11–9
Gustafsson 6–4 6–3 6–7(9) 6–1
Stoltenberg 6–4 2–6 6–3 6–2
Safin (Q) 3–6 7–6(5) 3–6 6–1 6–4
Vacek 6–4 2–6 7–5 7–6(0)
Pioline 7–5 6–0 3–6 6–4
Krajicek (10) 7–5 6–4 6–1
Berasategui (16) 6–3 3–6 6–3 6–4
Hrbaty 6–3 6–3 6–3
Arazi 6–3 6–4 6–2
Zabaleta (Q) 6–0 6–2 6–2

Fourth round

Dewulf 6–3 6–2 6–3
Clavet 3–6 7–6(5) 6–2 6–4
Corretja (14) 6–1 5–7 6–7(4) 7–5 9–7
Stoltenberg 6–1 2–6 6–4 6–4
Safin (Q) 6–3 3–6 6–3 7–5
Pioline 6–3 6–2 7–5
Berasategui (16) 6–7(2) 6–3 7–5 7–5
Arazi 6–4 0–6 6–4 7–6(3)

Quarter-finals

Dewulf 7–5 6–3 6–1
Corretja (14) 6–4 6–4 6–3
Pioline 7–5 4–6 6–7(5) 6–4 6–4
Arazi 6–2 6–4 3–6 6–3

Semi-finals

Corretja (14) 7–5 6–4 6–3
Pioline 3–6 6–2 7–6(6) 4–6 6–3

Final

Corretja (14) 6–3 6–4 6–2

Bold type denotes seeded players. Numbers following player's name gives seeding order (Q) = Qualifier, (W) = Wild Card, (LL) = Lucky Loser

Women's Singles

Holder: I. Majoli (CRO)

	FIRST ROUND	SECOND ROUND	THIRD ROUND	FOURTH ROUND	QUARTER-FINALS	SEMI-FINALS	FINAL
1	**M. Hingis** (SUI) (1)	**Hingis** (1)					
2	M. A. Sanchez Lorenzo (ESP)	6–2 6–1	**Hingis** (1)				
3	M. Babel (GER)	Babel	6–1 6–2				
4	Y. Yoshida (JPN)	6–1 6–0		**Hingis** (1)			
5	N. Pratt (AUS)	Pratt		6–3 6–2			
6	I. Gorrochategui (ARG)	6–0 6–2	Habsudova				
7	K. Habsudova (SVK)	Habsudova	7–6(5) 6–2				
8	D. Chladkova (CZE)	6–4 6–0			**Hingis** (1)		
9	S. Berger (FRA) (W)	Rittner			6–1 6–2		
10	B. Rittner (GER)	6–0 6–2	Rittner				
11	N. Sawamatsu (JPN)	Sawamatsu	6–3 6–4				
12	L. Nemeckova (CZE)	6–3 2–6 7–5		Smashnova			
13	A. Smashnova (ISR)	Smashnova		1–6 6–4 6–1			
14	L. Neiland (LAT)	3–6 6–3 6–2	Smashnova				
15	E. Gagliardi (SUI)	Gagliardi	5–7 6–0 6–1				
16	**N. Tauziat** (FRA) (12)	4–6 7–5 6–4				**Hingis** (1)	
17	**I. Spirlea** (ROM) (9)	Plischke				6–3 6–4	
18	S. Plischke (AUT)	6–2 6–4	Nagyova				
19	H. Nagyova (SVK)	Nagyova	6–4 6–3				
20	R. McQuillan (AUS)	6–3 6–4		Nagyova			
21	N. Dechy (FRA)	Dechy		7–6(5) 3–6 6–1			
22	O. Barabanschikova (BLR)	6–3 1–6 6–1	Dechy				
23	A. Cocheteux (FRA)	Wunderlich	6–1 6–1				
24	A. Wunderlich (USA)	7–5 7–6(5)			**V. Williams** (8)		
25	A. Dechaume-Balleret (FRA)	Dechaume-Balleret			6–1 6–3		
26	O. Lugina (UKR)	6–1 5–7 6–2	Dechaume-Balleret				
27	B. Schett (AUT)	Gersi	6–2 5–7 6–1				
28	A. Gersi (CZE)	5–7 6–2 6–2		**V. Williams** (8)			
29	L. Golarsa (ITA)	Sugiyama		6–2 6–1			
30	A. Sugiyama (JPN)	7–5 6–3	**V. Williams** (8)				
31	T. Tanasugarn (THA)	**V. Williams** (8)	6–0 6–2				
32	**V. Williams** (USA) (8)	6–3 6–1					**Seles** (6)
33	**J. Novotna** (CZE) (3)	**Novotna** (3)					6–3 6–2
34	A. Miller (USA)	7–5 6–4	**Novotna** (3)				
35	E. Loit (FRA) (W)	Loit (W)	7–5 6–0				
36	C. Torrens-Valero (ESP)	6–4 6–3		**Novotna** (3)			
37	E. Tatarkova (UKR) (Q)	Tatarkova (Q)		6–3 7–6(5)			
38	K. Brandi (USA)	6–4 6–4	Tatarkova (Q)				
39	K. Hrdlickova (CZE)	Hrdlickova	6–4 6–1				
40	E. Bes (ESP) (Q)	6–4 3–6 6–3			**Novotna** (3)		
41	G. Nielsen (USA)	Jeyaseelan			6–7(2) 6–3 6–3		
42	S. Jeyaseelan (CAN)	6–0 0–6 12–10	Carlsson				
43	H. Inoue (JPN)	Carlsson	6–4 6–0				
44	A. Carlsson (SWE)	7–5 6–1		**Kournikova** (13)			
45	S. Kleinova (CZE)	Studenikova		6–0 6–0			
46	K. Studenikova (SVK)	6–3 6–1	**Kournikova** (13)				
47	A. Mauresmo (FRA)	**Kournikova** (13)	6–2 7–6(2)				
48	**A. Kournikova** (RUS) (13)	6–2 6–4				**Seles** (6)	
49	**L. Raymond** (USA) (16)	Panova				4–6 6–3 6–3	
50	T. Panova (RUS)	6–3 6–4	Rubin				
51	L. McNeil (USA)	Rubin	6–1 6–1				
52	C. Rubin (USA)	3–6 6–3 6–4		Rubin			
53	S. Pitkowski (FRA)	Saeki		6–3 6–4			
54	M. Saeki (JPN)	7–5 7–5	Saeki				
55	L. Andretto (FRA) (W)	Andretto (W)	6–1 7–6(5)				
56	M. A. Vento (VEN)	6–3 6–3			**Seles** (6)		
57	W. Probst (GER)	Schwartz			6–1 6–4		
58	B. Schwartz (AUT)	7–6(5) 6–1	Schwartz				
59	M. Oremans (NED)	Oremans	6–4 6–2				
60	E. Makarova (RUS)	6–1 1–6 6–3		**Seles** (6)			
61	K-A. Guse (AUS)	Maruska		6–1 7–5			
62	M. Maruska (AUT)	7–5 6–3	**Seles** (6)				
63	A. Ellwood (AUS)	**Seles** (6)	2–6 6–1 6–0				
64	**M. Seles** (USA) (6)	6–0 6–2					

Winner: **A. Sanchez-Vicario** (ESP) (4)

7–6(5) 0–6 6–2

65 **A. Coetzer** (RSA) (5)
66 P. Schnyder (SUI)
67 N. Kijimuta (JPN)
68 J. Halard-Decugis (FRA) (W)
69 A. Glass (GER)
70 J. Kruger (RSA)
71 S-T. Wang (TPE)
72 S. Farina (ITA)
73 R. Dragomir (ROM)
74 J. Husarova (SVK)
75 F. Perfetti (ITA)
76 S. Cecchini (ITA)
77 P. Hy-Boulais (CAN)
78 M. Serna (ESP)
79 S. Appelmans (BEL)
80 **M. Pierce** (FRA) (11)
81 **D. Van Roost** (BEL) (15)
82 M. Grzybowska (POL)
83 L. Ghirardi-Rubbi (FRA)
84 E. Callens (BEL) (Q)
85 C. Morariu (USA)
86 N. Schultz-McCarthy (NED)
87 J. Nejedly (CAN)
88 S. Williams (USA)
89 T. Snyder (USA)
90 E. Curutchet (FRA) (W)
91 B. Paulus (AUT)
92 A. Fusai (FRA)
93 C. Cristea (ROM)
94 M. De Swardt (RSA)
95 J. Kandarr (GER)
96 **A. Sanchez-Vicario** (ESP) (4)
97 **C. Martinez** (ESP) (7)
98 M. Lamarre (FRA) (W)
99 J. Lee (TPE)
100 R. Grande (ITA)
101 S. Kloesel (GER)
102 V. Ruano-Pascual (ESP)
103 N. Van Lottum (FRA) (W)
104 A-G. Sidot (FRA)
105 S-H. Park (KOR)
106 F. Lubiani (ITA)
107 M. Diaz-Oliva (ARG) (Q)
108 F. Li (CHN)
109 F. Labat (ARG)
110 N. Zvereva (BLR)
111 P. Stoyanova (BUL)
112 **I. Majoli** (CRO) (10)
113 **S. Testud** (FRA) (14)
114 S. Reeves (USA)
115 N. Miyagi (JPN)
116 E. Wagner (GER)
117 Y. Basuki (INA)
118 G. Leon Garcia (ESP)
119 R. Bobkova (CZE) (Q)
120 P. Suarez (ARG)
121 S. Cacic (USA)
122 E. Likhovtseva (RUS)
123 A. Alcazar (ESP) (Q)
124 C. Black (ZIM) (Q)
125 C. Dhenin (FRA) (W)
126 L. Horn (RSA) (Q)
127 K. Po (USA)
128 **L. Davenport** (USA) (2)

Schnyder 6–4 3–6 8–6
Halard-Decugis (W) 6–1 6–2
Kruger 6–3 6–4
Farina 6–2 6–1
Dragomir 6–2 4–6 6–3
Perfetti 6–4 6–3
Serna 6–1 6–1
Pierce (11) 6–2 6–3
Van Roost (15) 7–5 3–6 6–4
Callens (Q) 6–2 6–7(8) 6–3
Morariu 6–3 2–0 Ab
S. Williams 6–2 1–6 6–4
Snyder 7–5 6–1
Fusai 6–1 7–5
Cristea 6–1 6–2
Sanchez-Vicario (4) 6–2 7–5
Martinez (7) 6–1 6–1
Grande 7–6(7) 6–3
Ruano-Pascual 6–1 6–2
Sidot 2–6 6–3 6–2
Park 5–7 6–1 6–2
Diaz-Oliva (Q) 7–6(8) 6–1
Zvereva 6–1 7–5
Majoli (10) 6–3 6–1
Testud (14) 2–6 6–2 6–3
Wagner 3–6 6–0 6–1
Leon Garcia 6–3 6–2
Suarez 3–6 7–6(1) 9–7
Likhovtseva 6–4 6–3
Black 6–3 4–6 6–3
Horn (Q) 3–6 6–3 6–0
Davenport (2) 6–2 6–2

Schnyder 6–3 3–6 6–1
Farina 4–6 6–3 6–0
Dragomir 6–0 6–2
Serna 7–5 6–2
Van Roost (15) 6–3 6–0
S. Williams 6–1 6–0
Fusai 6–4 6–3
Sanchez-Vicario (4) 6–2 6–3
Martinez (7) 6–1 6–2
Ruano-Pascual 6–4 7–6(6)
Diaz-Oliva (Q) 6–2 6–2
Majoli (10) 6–3 6–4
Testud (14) 6–2 6–0
Leon Garcia 6–2 1–6 7–5
Likhovtseva 7–5 7–5
Davenport (2) 6–2 6–0

Schnyder 6–2 6–1
Serna 6–4 2–6 6–1
S. Williams 6–1 6–1
Sanchez-Vicario (4) 6–2 6–1
Martinez (7) 6–1 6–0
Majoli (10) 6–2 7–6(2)
Testud (14) 6–1 6–1
Davenport (2) 7–5 7–5

Schnyder 6–1 6–3
Sanchez-Vicario (4) 4–6 7–5 6–3
Majoli (10) 7–6(1) 6–7(3) 6–3
Davenport (2) 6–3 4–6 6–2

Sanchez-Vicario (4) 6–2 6–7(5) 6–0
Davenport (2) 6–1 5–7 6–3

Sanchez-Vicario (4) 6–3 7–6(5)

Bold type denotes seeded players. Numbers following player's name gives seeding order (Q) = Qualifier, (W) = Wild Card, (LL) = Lucky Loser

Men's Doubles

Holders: Kafelnikov (RUS) / Vacek (CZE)

FIRST ROUND	SECOND ROUND	THIRD ROUND	QUARTER-FINALS	SEMI-FINALS	FINAL
1 **Eltingh/Haarhuis** (1)	**Eltingh/Haarhuis** (1) 6–3 6–4				
2 Arthurs/Kratzmann		**Eltingh/Haarhuis** (1) 6–2 6–3			
3 Ivanisevic/Philippoussis	Olhovskiy/Prinosil 3–6 7–6(2) 6–2				
4 Olhovskiy/Prinosil			**Eltingh/Haarhuis** (1) 6–1 6–4		
5 Novak/Rikl	Novak/Rikl 1–6 7–6(6) 6–2				
6 Barnard/Haygarth		Braasch/Knippschild 7–6(7) 1–6 6–4			
7 Braasch/Knippschild	Braasch/Knippschild 6–4 6–1				
8 **Broad/Norval** (16)				**Eltingh/Haarhuis** (1) 6–3 6–2	
9 **Grabb/Macpherson** (9)	**Grabb/Macpherson** (9) 6–3 7–6(4)				
10 Boutter/Pequery		**Grabb/Macpherson** (9) 6–3 4–6 6–3			
11 Albano/Puerta	De Jager/Koenig 5–7 7–6(4) 6–3				
12 De Jager/Koenig			**Johnson/Montana** (7) 7–5 6–3		
13 Stafford/Ullyett	Stafford/Ullyett 6–4 6–2				
14 Adams/Dosedel		**Johnson/Montana** (7) 2–6 6–3 6–4			
15 Kempers/Oosting	**Johnson/Montana** (7) 6–1 6–1				
16 **Johnson/Montana** (7)					**Eltingh/Haarhuis** (1) 6–2 6–2
17 **Kafelnikov/Vacek** (4)	**Kafelnikov/Vacek** (4) 4–6 6–3 6–4				
18 Pimek/Vizner		Burillo/Goellner 6–3 6–7(0) 6–4			
19 Bowen/Roditi	Burillo/Goellner 6–4 3–6 6–1				
20 Burillo/Goellner			Kuerten/Meligeni 6–2 4–6 6–4		
21 Aerts/Sa	Kuerten/Meligeni 6–3 6–2				
22 Kuerten/Meligeni		Kuerten/Meligeni 7–6(5) 7–5			
23 Stolle/Suk	**Carbonell/Roig** (13) 6–2 6–7(3) 6–1				
24 **Carbonell/Roig** (13)				**Bjorkman/Rafter** (6) 7–6(5) 0–0 Disq	
25 **Eagle/Florent** (11)	**Eagle/Florent** (11) 4–6 6–1 6–4				
26 Gilbert/Simian (W)		**Eagle/Florent** (11) 6–4 6–4			
27 Coupe/Noteboom	Coupe/Noteboom 6–2 7–6(1)				
28 Escude/Raoux (W)			**Bjorkman/Rafter** (6) 7–5 6–7(2) 7–5		
29 Groen/Santopadre	Martin/Zdrazila 7–6(8) 6–2				
30 Martin/Zdrazila		**Bjorkman/Rafter** (6) 6–4 6–2			
31 Gimelstob/MacPhie	**Bjorkman/Rafter** (6) 3–6 7–6(1) 6–4				
32 **Bjorkman/Rafter** (6)					
33 **Ferreira/Leach** (5)	Alonso/Lapentti 7–6(2) 5–7 6–4				
34 Alonso/Lapentti		Alonso/Lapentti 6–4 6–4			
35 Sapsford/Wilkinson	Sapsford/Wilkinson 6–1 6–1				
36 Pasquale/Jeanpierre (W)			Alonso/Lapentti 6–4 6–7(3) 6–2		
37 Arnold/Orsanic	Dilucia/Keil 6–1 6–3				
38 Dilucia/Keil		**W. Black/Lareau** (12) 4–6 7–5 6–3			
39 Delaitre/Grosjean	**W. Black/Lareau** (12) 6–1 6–1				
40 **W. Black/Lareau** (12)				**Bhupathi/Paes** (3) 6–3 6–4	
41 **Lobo/J. Sanchez** (14)	**Lobo/J. Sanchez** (14) 4–6 6–3 6–2				
42 Forget/Lavergne		Bergh/Nyborg 6–2 7–6(5)			
43 Bergh/Nyborg	Bergh/Nyborg 6–0 6–7(2) 6–2				
44 Grant/Tebbutt			**Bhupathi/Paes** (3) 6–4 7–6(7)		
45 Brandi/Messori	Godwin/Ketola 6–3 6–4				
46 Godwin/Ketola		**Bhupathi/Paes** (3) 6–3 7–6(2)			
47 Randall/Van Emburgh	**Bhupathi/Paes** (3) 7–6(2) 3–6 6–3				
48 **Bhupathi/Paes** (3)					Knowles/Nestor 6–1 7–6(6)
49 **O'Brien/Stark** (8)	Hood/Prieto 6–2 6–4				
50 Hood/Prieto		Hood/Prieto 0–6 7–5 6–2			
51 Kilderry/Kinnear	Kilderry/Kinnear 7–6(4) 6–2				
52 L. Jensen/M. Jensen			**Galbraith/Steven** (10) 6–3 7–5		
53 Fleurian/Waite	Kitinov/Vanhoudt 6–3 1–6 8–6				
54 Kitinov/Vanhoudt		**Galbraith/Steven** (10) 6–2 6–4			
55 Clement/Golmard (W)	**Galbraith/Steven** (10) 3–6 6–0 7–5				
56 **Galbraith/Steven** (10)				Knowles/Nestor 6–3 6–4	
57 **Kulti/Tillstrom** (15)	Koves/Tarango 5–7 6–1 6–2				
58 Koves/Tarango		Knowles/Nestor 4–6 6–4 6–4			
59 Knowles/Nestor	Knowles/Nestor 4–6 6–4 7–5				
60 Siemerink/Wibier			Knowles/Nestor 6–4 6–2		
61 Merklein/Sell	Merklein/Sell 6–3 6–4				
62 B. Black/Reneberg		**Woodbridge/Woodforde** (2) 6–2 6–0			
63 Haggard/Rosner	**Woodbridge/Woodforde** (2) 6–4 6–3				
64 **Woodbridge/Woodforde** (2)					

Winners: **Eltingh** (NED)**/Haarhuis** (NED) (1) 6–3 3–6 6–3

Winners: **Hingis** (SUI)/**Novotna** (CZE) (2) 6–1 7–6(4)

FIRST ROUND

1 **Davenport/Zvereva** (1)
2 Pullin/Woodroffe
3 Krizan/Srebotnik
4 Jones/Schneider
5 Cristea/Montalvo
6 Jeyaseelan/Simpson
7 De Swardt/Graham
8 **Gorrochategui/McQuillan** (15)
9 **Schett/Schnyder** (14)
10 Cacic/Pierce
11 Musgrave/Olsza
12 Dechaume-Balleret/Mauresmo (W)
13 De Beer/Lee
14 Labat/Van Roost
15 Langrova/Perfetti
16 **Basuki/Vis** (5)
17 **Fusai/Tauziat** (4)
18 Bobkova/Melicharova
19 Grzybowska/Sidot
20 Carlsson/Rubin
21 Noorlander/Van Lottum
22 De Lone/Schlukebir
23 Saeki/Yoshida
24 **Likhovtseva/Sugiyama** (10)
25 **Appelmans/Oremans** (12)
26 Dechy/Ghiradi-Rubbi
27 Babel/Probst
28 Barabanschikova/Nagyova
29 Curutchet/Georges (W)
30 Singer/Vildova
31 Kamstra/Rottier
32 **Kournikova/Neiland** (8)
33 **Raymond/Stubbs** (6)
34 Dhenin/Loit (W)
35 Hy-Boulais/Rittner
36 Horn/Reeves
37 Farina/Habsudova
38 Callens/Nielsen
39 Grande/Spirlea
40 **Kijimuta/Miyagi** (11)
41 **Barclay/Guse** (13)
42 Feber/Kriventcheva
43 Halard-Decugis/Testud
44 Freye/Stoyanova
45 Park/Tanasugarn
46 McNeil/Po
47 Csurgo/Marosi
48 **Sanchez-Vicario/Sukova** (3)
49 **Adams/Bollegraf** (7)
50 Lugina/Wagner
51 De Villiers/McShea
52 Golarsa/Paz
53 Cocheteux/Pitkowski (W)
54 Kschwendt/Tatarkova
55 Dragomir/Majoli
56 **Martinez/Tarabini** (9)
57 **Ruano-Pascual/Suarez** (16)
58 Ellwood/Pratt
59 Kim/Pleming
60 Kunce/Morariu
61 Lee/Wang
62 Husarova/Medvedeva
63 Hiraki/Wunderlich
64 **Hingis/Novotna** (2)

SECOND ROUND

Davenport/Zvereva (1) 6–2 6–2
Krizan/Srebotnik 6–1 6–1
Cristea/Montalvo 6–1 6–3
De Swardt/Graham 6–4 7–6(14)
Schett/Schnyder (14) 6–7(4) 6–3 6–2
Dechaume-Balleret/Mauresmo (W) 6–2 6–2
Labat/Van Roost 3–6 6–3 6–2
Basuki/Vis (5) 6–4 7–6(3)
Fusai/Tauziat (4) 6–1 2–6 6–0
Grzybowska/Sidot 6–3 1–6 6–4
De Lone/Schlukebir 6–1 6–3
Likhovtseva/Sugiyama (10) 6–4 6–4
Appelmans/Oremans (12) 6–4 6–2
Babel/Probst 6–4 6–3
Singer/Vildova 7–6(0) 5–7 6–2
Kournikova/Neiland (8) 6–2 6–3
Dhenin/Loit (W) 7–5 7–5
Hy-Boulais/Rittner 6–4 6–1
Farina/Habsudova 6–1 6–1
Grande/Spirlea 6–4 7–6(5)
Barclay/Guse (13) 6–2 6–1
Halard-Decugis/Testud 6–4 6–1
McNeil/Po 6–2 6–3
Sanchez-Vicario/Sukova (3) 6–0 6–2
Adams/Bollegraf (7) 6–2 6–7(2) 6–2
Golarsa/Paz 7–5 7–5
Cocheteux/Pitkowski (W) 5–7 6–3 7–5
Martinez/Tarabini (9) 5–7 6–4 6–2
Ruano-Pascual/Suarez (16) 6–3 6–2
Kunce/Morariu 6–3 6–4
Lee/Wang 6–3 4–6 6–4
Hingis/Novotna (2) 6–1 6–0

THIRD ROUND

Davenport/Zvereva (1) 6–4 6–1
De Swardt/Graham 7–6(9) 6–2
Schett/Schnyder (14) 6–4 6–4
Basuki/Vis (5) 6–3 6–7(4) 6–3
Fusai/Tauziat (4) 6–4 6–1
Likhovtseva/Sugiyama (10) 6–2 6–2
Babel/Probst 6–4 7–6(5)
Kournikova/Neiland (8) 6–2 6–1
Dhenin/Loit (W) 6–1 6–2
Farina/Habsudova 5–7 7–5 8–6
Barclay/Guse (13) 6–1 6–3
Sanchez-Vicario/Sukova (3) 5–7 6–1 6–2
Adams/Bollegraf (7) 6–1 7–6(5)
Martinez/Tarabini (9) WO
Kunce/Morariu 6–4 6–2
Hingis/Novotna (2) 6–0 6–2

QUARTER-FINALS

Davenport/Zvereva (1) 6–1 6–2
Schett/Schnyder (14) 6–1 6–4
Fusai/Tauziat (4) 5–7 7–6(7) 6–4
Kournikova/Neiland (8) 6–0 6–3
Farina/Habsudova 6–2 6–7(5) 6–3
Sanchez-Vicario/Sukova (3) 6–7(6) 6–3 14–12
Martinez/Tarabini (9) 4–6 6–3 6–4
Hingis/Novotna (2) 6–0 6–1

SEMI-FINALS

Davenport/Zvereva (1) 6–4 7–5
Kournikova/Neiland (8) 7–5 6–3
Sanchez-Vicario/Sukova (3) 6–0 6–3
Hingis/Novotna (2) 6–3 6–2

FINAL

Davenport/Zvereva (1) 6–3 6–2
Hingis/Novotna (2) 7–5 7–6(2)

Bold type denotes seeded players. Numbers following player's name gives seeding order (Q) = Qualifier, (W) = Wild Card, (LL) = Lucky Loser

Mixed Doubles

Holders: Bhupathi (IND)/Hiraki (JPN)

FIRST ROUND

1 **Paes/Neiland** (1)
2 bye/
3 Vizner/Vildova
4 Lobo/S. Williams
5 Knowles/Kournikova
6 Haygarth/De Villiers
7 bye/
8 **Grabb/Nielsen** (14)
9 **Johnson/Boogert** (11)
10 bye/
11 Hood/Montalvo
12 Braasch/Rittner
13 Roditi/Labat
14 Nyborg/Horn
15 bye/
16 **Suk/Sukova** (5)
17 **Galbraith/Raymond** (4)
18 bye/
19 Keil/Cristea
20 Tebbutt/Barclay
21 Coupe/Kriventcheva
22 Vanhoudt/Husarova
23 bye/
24 **Macpherson/McQuillan** (10)
25 **Eagle/McNeil** (15)
26 bye/
27 Waite/Po
28 Koenig/K. Adams
29 Kilderry/Hiraki
30 L. Jensen/Graham
31 bye/
32 **D. Adams/Fusai** (7)
33 **Florent/Zvereva** (6)
34 bye/
35 Barnard/Singer (W)
36 Martin/Majoli (W)
37 Wibier/Medvedeva
38 Gimelstob/V. Williams
39 bye/
40 **E. Ferreira/Oremans** (9)
41 **De Jager/Vis** (16)
42 bye/
43 Kitinov/Melicharova
44 Kratzmann/Tatarkova
45 Noteboom/Schneider
46 Grosjean/Sidot (W)
47 bye/
48 **Bhupathi/Stubbs** (3)
49 **Orsanic/Tarabini** (8)
50 bye/
51 Alonso/Golarsa
52 Albano/Paz
53 Broad/De Swardt
54 Olhovskiy/Likhovtseva
55 bye/
56 **Montana/Kunce** (12)
57 **Norval/Appelmans** (13)
58 bye/
59 Kinnear/Miyagi
60 Fleurian/Dechaume-Balleret (W)
61 Golmard/Mauresmo (W)
62 Nijssen/Basuki
63 bye/
64 **Leach/Bollegraf** (2)

SECOND ROUND

Paes/Neiland (1)
Lobo/S. Williams 6–3 6–2
Knowles/Kournikova 6–2 7–6(0)
Grabb/Nielsen (14)
Johnson/Boogert (11)
Hood/Montalvo 5–7 6–2 10–8
Roditi/Labat 7–6(4) 6–2
Suk/Sukova (5)
Galbraith/Raymond (4)
Tebbutt/Barclay 7–5 7–6(5)
Coupe/Kriventcheva 6–3 3–6 6–3
Macpherson/McQuillan (10)
Eagle/McNeil (15)
Waite/Po 7–5 6–3
Kilderry/Hiraki 3–6 6–2 6–2
D. Adams/Fusai (7)
Florent/Zvereva (6)
Martin/Majoli (W) 6–3 6–2
Gimelstob/V. Williams 6–1 6–2
E. Ferreira/Oremans (9)
De Jager/Vis (16)
Kratzmann/Tatarkova 7–6(0) 6–2
Grosjean/Sidot 7–5 6–3
Bhupathi/Stubbs (3)
Orsanic/Tarabini (8)
Albano/Paz 7–5 6–2
Broad/De Swardt 6–4 6–1
Montana/Kunce (12)
Norval/Appelmans (13)
Fleurian/Dechaume-Balleret (W) 6–1 6–4
Nijssen/Basuki 5–7 6–3 6–1
Leach/Bollegraf (2)

THIRD ROUND

Lobo/S. Williams 7–6(4) 6–3
Grabb/Nielsen (14) 3–6 6–4 6–3
Johnson/Boogert (11) 6–2 7–6(6)
Suk/Sukova (5) 6–0 6–3
Galbraith/Raymond (4) 7–6(4) 7–5
Macpherson/McQuillan (10) 6–4 6–7(3) 6–1
Eagle/McNeil (15) 7–5 5–7 6–2
Kilderry/Hiraki 6–2 2–6 6–2
Martin/Majoli (W) 6–4 7–6(4)
Gimelstob/V. Williams 6–4 6–4
De Jager/Vis (16) 3–3 ret
Grosjean/Sidot 6–4 6–4
Albano/Paz 3–6 6–2 7–5
Montana/Kunce (12) 6–4 5–7 7–5
Fleurian/Dechaume-Balleret (W) 7–6(7) 6–2
Leach/Bollegraf (2) 6–3 7–6(3)

QUARTER-FINALS

Lobo/S. Williams 6–4 3–6 6–0
Johnson/Boogert (11) 6–2 6–3
Macpherson/McQuillan (10) 7–6(4) 6–3
Eagle/McNeil (15) 6–2 6–2
Gimelstob/V. Williams 6–0 7–6(4)
De Jager/Vis (16) 6–7(2) 6–2 6–3
Montana/Kunce (12) 7–6(7) 6–2
Leach/Bollegraf (2) 6–1 2–6 6–4

SEMI-FINALS

Lobo/S. Williams 6–3 7–5
Macpherson/McQuillan (10) 7–6(6) 6–1
Gimelstob/V. Williams 6–4 6–3
Montana/Kunce (12) 7–5 3–6 6–2

FINAL

Lobo/S. Williams 6–1 6–0
Gimelstob/V. Williams 6–2 6–3

Winners: **Gimelstob** (USA)/**V. Williams** (USA) 6–4 6–4

JUNIOR EVENTS

BOYS' SINGLES – Final: Fernando Gonzales (CHI) d. Juan Carlos Ferrero (ESP) 4–6 6–4 6–3
GIRLS' SINGLES – Final: Nadeida Petrova (RUS) d. Jelena Dokic (AUS) 6–3 6–3
BOYS' DOUBLES – Final: Jose de Armas (VEN)/Fernando Gonzales (CHI) d. Juan Carlos Ferrero (ESP)/ Feliciano Lopez (ESP) 6–7 7–5 6–3
GIRLS' DOUBLES – Final: Kim Clijsters (BEL)/Jelena Dokic (AUS) d. Elena Dementieva (RUS)/Nadeida Petrova (RUS) 6–4 7–6
LEGENDS OVER 35 – Final: Gene Mayer (USA)/Peter McNamara (AUS) d Mansour Bahrami (IRN)/Henri Leconte (FRA) 6–3 3–6 6–3
LEGENDS OVER 50 – Final: John Newcombe (AUS)/Tony Roche (AUS) d. Ken Rosewall (AUS)/Fred Stolle (AUS) 6–3 6–3

FRENCH OPEN CHAMPIONSHIPS

PRIZE MONEY – 60,861,400FF

MEN – Total: 29,830,400FF

MEN'S SINGLES – Winner 3,852,000. Runner-up 1,926,000. Semi-finalists 963,000. Quarter-finalists 507,800. Fourth-round losers 272,000. Third-round losers 157,600. Second-round losers 96,300. First-round losers 58,000.
Total: 21,226,400FF

MEN'S DOUBLES (per team) – Winners 1,584,000. Runners-up 792,000. Semi-finalists 396,000. Quarter-finalists 201,400. Third-round losers 114,800. Second-round losers 57,400. First-round losers 39,000.
Total: 7,058,400FF

MEN'S QUALIFYING (each): 16 × Third-round losers 31,500. 32 × Second-round losers 15,750. 64 × First-round losers 8,400.
Total: 1,545,600FF

WOMEN – Total: 24,565,000FF

WOMEN'S SINGLES – Winner 3,624,000. Runner-up 1,812,000. Semi-finalists 906,000. Quarter-finalists 453,000. Fourth-round losers 232,000. Third-round losers 129,100. Second-round losers 78,100. First-round losers 48,000.
Total: 18,552,800FF

WOMEN'S DOUBLES (per team) – Winners 1,241,500. Runners-up 620,750. Semi-finalists 310,375. Quarter-finalists 157,700. Third-round losers 80,300. Second-round losers 42,700. First-round losers 25,000.
Total: 5,239,400FF

WOMEN'S QUALIFYING (each): 8 × Third-round losers 31,500. 16 × Second-round losers 15,750. 32 × First-round losers 8,400.
Total: 772,800FF

MIXED DOUBLES (per team) – Winners 346,000. Runners-up 208,000. Semi-finalists 124,400. Quarter-finalists 76,000. Second-round losers 41,200. First-round losers 18,100.
Total: 1,726,000FF

TROPHY OF THE LEGENDS(per team) – Winners 75,000. Runners-up 60,000. Semi-finalists 50,000. First-round losers 40,000.
Total: 900,000FF

Per Diem allowances (estimated total) 3,840,000FF

Pete Sampras on his way to the net at Wimbledon where he equalled Bjorn Borg's modern record of five singles wins – though not in consecutive years like the Swede. (Tommy Hindley)

The Championships – Wimbledon

John Barrett

The grass was greener at the 112th Championship meeting, where the re-laid Centre Court played fast and true to the end. It provided a perfect stage for defending champion Pete Sampras, who won for the fifth time in six years, and for Jana Novotna who at last proved herself to be a champion after twice faltering at the final hurdle.

Sampras was superb. Despite indifferent pre-Wimbledon form the 26-year-old American lost only one set on his way to the final. There, in a heavyweight bout that spanned 2 hours and 51 minutes of relentless aggression, he held off a fierce challenge from two-time finalist Goran Ivanisevic to take his first Grand Slam title of the year 6–7 7–6 6–4 3–6 6–2. This win brought Sampras a first prize of £435,000 but he was more concerned that this 11th Grand Slam success put him level with Rod Laver and Bjorn Borg on the all-time list. He was now just one title behind Australia's Roy Emerson.

Novotna was nervous. Facing an unexpected finalist in 16th seeded Frenchwoman Nathalie Tauziat (who always seems to play well against her), the 29-year-old Czech had everything to lose. Yet to her credit Novotna, seeded three, held her nerve in the crucial moments of the second set tie-break to claim her first Grand Slam crown 6–4 7–6 in an hour and 34 minutes. This fine achievement, which earned Novotna £391,500, was ample compensation for her loss to Steffi Graf in 1993 and to Martina Hingis in 1997.

For the second year in a row rain disrupted play for much of the first week, causing problems for players and officials. The stoic British fans, though, took it all in their stride and attended The Championships in record numbers – despite competition from football's World Cup. The 13-day attendance total of 424,998 broke the comparable 1997 record of 405,327 by 19,671.

Once again the seeding committee exercised their right to stray from the ATP Tour's ranking list to recognise past performances on grass and current form, a policy broadly supported by the players themselves. Two men in the top 16, Michael Chang (14) and Albert Costa (15), were excluded and as no entry had been received from Alberto Berasategui (16) there were three lower ranked players elevated. Tim Henman (17), a quarter-finalist in 1997, came in at No.12 and responded by going through to the semi-finals, a round not reached by a Briton since Roger Taylor in 1973; Andre Agassi (19), the 1992 champion, came in at No.13 but was beaten in the second round by the young German Tommy Haas; Ivanisevic (24) became the 14th seed.

Despite doubts about the left ankle injury sustained by Greg Rusedski at the Stella Artois tournament at Queen's Club the previous week, the British No.1 was left in as the No.4 seed while the 1997 finalist Cedric Pioline (10) joined the elite at No.8. at the expense of Jonas Bjorkman (9) who went down to No.11. A minor shuffle of lower places dropped French Open finalist Alex Corretja (8) to No.10, Karol Kucera (11) to No.15 and Felix Mantilla (13) to No.16

The women's list was affected only by the late return from injury of Steffi Graf whose ranking had slipped to 75. How could you leave out someone who had won the title seven times, assuming she was fit to play? But where to place her? In the end she was given the No.4 spot so that all those players from Arantxa Sanchez-Vicario (4) onwards moved down one place. Sadly Anna Kournikova, the No.12 seed, withdrew on the first day because her right thumb, injured at Eastbourne, had not healed.

Six men's seeds lost in the first round. There were two in the top half – Yevgeny Kafelnikov (7) and Alex Corretja (10) – who had been due to meet in the fourth round. Corretja found the tearaway American giant Justin Gimelstob too hot to handle while Kafelnikov was unlucky to face Mark Philippoussis. The powerful Australian with the big game was another who must have been considered for seeding. It was Philippoussis who emerged to challenge Sampras in the quarter-finals but the 'Scud' could not fire enough missiles to repeat his spectacular 1996 Australian Open win over the favourite and lost in straight sets.

Curiously, two of the losing seeds in the bottom half – Marcelo Rios (2) and Karol Kucera (15) – were also supposed to be fourth round opponents. Rios blew hot and cold in a rain-delayed match against Spanish left-hander Francisco Clavet and bowed out in five sets. They played on

Court No.2 instead of No.1 where they had originally been scheduled, a factor that may have contributed to Rios's defeat. Kucera was surprised by the Belorussian qualifier Vladimir Voltchkov.

The unexpected beneficiary in this quarter was David Sanguinetti, a 25-year-old former Italian junior champion, ranked 65, who had spent two years at UCLA where he had earned All-American honours. After beating both Voltchkov and Clavet he was honoured throughout Italy as the first Italian to reach the last eight at Wimbledon since 1979 when Adriano Panatta had lost to Pat DuPre. Not surprisingly Sanguinetti could make no headway against the 1996 champion Richard Krajicek (9) and lost in straight sets.

The other defeated seeds were Cedric Pioline (8) who was beaten 13–11 in the final set by Marc Rosset in a match containing 66 games, the second longest of the tournament, and Greg Rusedski (4) who retired when trailing Australian qualifier Mark Draper 6–4 2–6 4–5 overnight.

Rusedski's decision to play at all with an immobile left ankle that made it impossible to move normally was at best unwise, at worst stupid. This was no time for false heroics. Clearly Rusedski could not possibly compete even to 50% of his potential. He should not have played, a view forcibly expressed by his coach Tony Pickard who could not find Rusedski the previous week when a decision had to be made about whether to withdraw. It transpired that Rusedski had flown secretly to Istanbul with his medical advisor, Rexa Daneshmand. Immediately after Rusedski's retirement Pickard called a press conference to announce that he was not prepared to continue as his coach. It was a bolt from the blue that left Rusedski in total shock.

The arrival in the quarter-finals of the unseeded Dutch left-hander, Jan Siemerink, was less of a shock. Following his splendid third round win over Bjorkman – a tense five set battle won 7–5 in the final set – Siemerink beat Sweden's Magnus Larsson in four sets. Against Ivanisevic, however, he was thwarted in three tie-break sets.

Henman's passage to the semi-final, via wins over a lacklustre Pat Rafter (6) and an injured Petr Korda (3) was perhaps a trifle fortuitous but the British No.2 had risen to the occasion splendidly in the first round when hotly challenged by Jiri Novak who had come back to win the third and fourth sets.

Nor was Henman overwhelmed in the penultimate round by Sampras. In fact Henman played on equal terms with his regular practice partner and occasional doubles partner for three sets. If, at one set all and 5–6 in the third, he had found the inspiration to hold serve, the defending champion might have been brought down. But Sampras found the right shots at the right time and survived, confidently enough in the end. 'I knew that set was the key...,' said Sampras afterwards.'...if we had gone into a tie-break anything could have happened. Once I took it I knew I'd got him.'

The other semi-final was between Krajicek and Ivanisevic. A 3 hour 21 minute battle of big serves and opportunistic returns and passes (that impressed Boris Becker in the BBC commentary box) it was, in many ways, the match of the tournament. The Croatian left-hander, poised on match point when leading 6–3 6–4 5–7 5–4 and 40–15, delivered an apparent ace. No-one heard the ball clip the net. 'Let' called the umpire, aided by the device that detects vibrations.

'I thought the match was over,' said Krajicek who was already moving forward to shake hands. Grinning, Ivanisevic resumed the battle. Krajicek, saving the match point with a volley, broke with a superb running forehand pass. With the momentum running for him he took the tie-break 7–5. After two early breaks in the fifth set, service was dominant until, at last, the tiring Croat broke again to win the deciding set 13–11.

Ultimately that 'let' serve in the fourth set, that kept him on court an extra 78 minutes, was Ivanisevic's undoing in the final. It might not have been, though, if the Croatian had taken a two sets to love lead, which he so nearly did. After winning the first set tie-break 7–2 Ivanisevic led 6–5 and 8–7 in the second breaker. On both Sampras serves he failed to get his backhand returns into court.

Battling bravely in the fifth set, the Croat's legs began to wilt. He could never reproduce the series of blistering passes that had broken the helpless Sampras in the sixth game of the fourth. Furthermore, he was now struggling to hold his own serve. After being broken to 15 in the sixth game he delivered a 20th double fault in the eighth that put him 0–30 down. It was the virtually the end.

'This is the worst moment of my life,' said the dejected loser. 'It hurts the most because this time I had the chance.'

For Sampras, who was winning his 148th Grand Slam singles match from a total of 174 he has played in 34 Championships, this fifth Wimbledon victory equalled the exploits of Bjorn

Tim Henman's arrival in the semi-finals was the first by a Briton since Roger Taylor in 1973. (Stephen Wake)

Natasha Zvereva set a frustrating record with Lindsay Davenport in 1998 by reaching every Grand Slam doubles final and winning none. (Michael Cole)

Borg (1976–1980) and Laurie Doherty (1902–1906) but still left him two short of William Renshaw's record of seven titles (1881–86, 1889).

'All Wimbledons are sweet, but five! They get better every year. It's all a bit overwhelming,' said the champion, whose win prevented Rios from overtaking him atop the ATP Tour rankings. How ridiculous it would have been if the Chilean, a first round loser, had returned to the top! Just as well perhaps that the players are ready to change the present ranking system for a yearly points race in 2000.

The women's event was a triumph for the old stagers. In a year when youth was supposed to dominate through the likes of Hingis, aged 17, Venus Williams, just 18, her sister Serena,17, and Mirjana Lucic,16, it was a 29-year-old and a 30-year-old who fought for the title. What went wrong?

For a start Kournikova, a semi-finalist in 1997, was missing. That was a pity when you remember how brilliantly she had played at Eastbourne, well enough in the opinion of her coach Pavel Slozil (who used to guide Graf), to have won her first Grand Slam title.

Then there was Hingis's delightful romance with the 20-year-old Spanish player, Julian Alonso. How refreshing that a normal teenager had got her priorities right! Despite the distraction, the defending champion seemed to be as resourceful as ever in resisting a strong challenge from Sanchez-Vicario in the quarter-finals.

One round later, though, Novotna reminded the world champion that on grass a great natural volleyer with adequate groundstrokes and the ability to get to the net behind a sliced backhand will usually beat a great baseliner who is a reluctant volleyer. Novotna's 6–4 6–4 upset was cleverly conceived with coach Hana Mandlikova and admirably executed. Chip and charge was the order of the day and the normally imperturbable Swiss Miss became rattled.

In the quarter-finals Novotna had exposed the limitations of Venus Williams on a surface that demands finesse plus an ability to adjust quickly to changing situations. As Williams discovered, hitting and hoping is not enough.

The much anticipated clash between the Williams sisters never materialised. Serena's unexpected loss to Virginia Ruano Pascual of Spain put paid to that. Afterwards Serena complained of a stiff neck but there was no evidence of inhibited movement or awkward shot making during the match.

Of the five seeds who failed to reach the fourth round the two most spectacular losers were Graf (4) and Conchita Martinez (8). Graf lost to an inspired performance from the usually casual Belorussian, Natasha Zvereva. Exploiting Graf's erratic game she swept to victory 6–4 7–5, her first win in 18 meetings against the former world No.1. Zvereva maintained a deep concentration throughout. Her consistency was a revelation.

Nor did Zvereva react following such a big win, as so many do. Two rounds later she upset a bewildered Seles (6) 7–6 6–2, her first win in five meetings against the naturalised American. Tauziat, though, posed other, harder problems in the semi-finals. The Zvereva bubble finally burst after she had taken the opening set and she went down 6–1 6–7 3–6.

Martinez found herself embroiled in a long battle against Sam Smith, Britain's lone direct entry, ranked 94, on Court No.2. In a tense finish Smith produced two moments of brilliance to break serve and then, to her credit, held firm on her own delivery to beat the 1994 champion 2–6 6–3 7–5. 'I felt really, really calm...and played some of the best tennis ever – and at the right time. I really took my chances,' said the delighted winner. Thus Smith became the first British woman to upset a former Wimbledon champion at a Grand Slam since Virginia Wade's defeat of Chris Evert in 1977. Nor had a British woman reached the fourth round since Jo Durie 13 years earlier.

Against Tauziat, however, Smith reacted. The Frenchwoman's greater all round ability made Smith look rather clumsy at times as she beat her 6–3 6–1.

It was the same in the quarter-finals against Davenport. Tauziat's natural serve-and-volley game was perfectly suited to the conditions as she dismissed the world No.2 6–3 6–3. Why Davenport persisted in trying to blast her way to victory from the baseline and ignored numerous opportunities to move forward it is hard to understand. After all, she is a respectable volleyer herself and must have the courage to develop that part of her game.

The final was not a great match but it did at least resolve all doubts about Novotna's ability to close out important matches. With a 4–4 record against Tauziat, the No.3 seed realised it would not be easy.

Not surprisingly they were both nervous. This was Tauziat's first Grand Slam final and, at the age of 30, likely to be her last. She was, after all, the lowest ranked player at No.15 to reach a

Wimbledon final in the open era. For Novotna, only one year younger, there would never be a better chance of making the career breakthrough that had eluded her for so long. But would here nerve hold? That was the question.

Having survived the shaky opening spell which put her 0–2 behind she broke back immediately and broke again in a long 7th game. It was enough to give her the set 6–4 after 43 minutes, an improvement on their last meeting in 1998, indoors in Chicago, where Tauziat had won a close first set and completed her victory 7–5 6–3.

Tauziat, the first Frenchwoman to appear in a Wimbledon singles final since the great Suzanne Lenglen in 1925, was struggling with her own game as well as being constantly pressured by Novotna's aggression and greater weight of shot. It was as if she was inhibited by the enormity of her own achievement.

Novotna's 3–1 lead in the second set became 3–3 but she broke again at once for 5–3 and two games later was serving for the match. Here was the test. Would she freeze? At 15–40 it seemed she had. The two forehand volleying errors were reminiscent of the game she played when leading 4–1 in the final set against Graf in 1993. But this time it was Tauziat, not Graf, across the net. Two French errors gave Novotna a second chance. But from deuce it was Tauziart who reasserted hersef to get her break.

Surely history was not about to repeat itself. The tie-break provided the answer. Confidence restored, Novotna raced to 5–2. Coming in on her return of Tauziat's serve she hit a winning backhand volley across the court out of reach. Four match points. Now, as Tauziat came in, Novotna hit a firm forehand pass and it was all over.

In an hour and 34 minutes Novotna had exorcised all the ghosts of Championships past. This one was hers. As she sank to her knees in the middle of the court the tears of joy overflowed. Then it was up to the box to hug Mandlikova, Cash '87 style, before renewing aquaintance with the Duchess of Kent who had been offering encouragement from the Royal Box throughout. This time Novotna needed no shoulder to cry on. 'This is what I've been working for for so many years,' she said. 'I wouldn't have made it without Hana.'

Nor was Tauziat downhearted. 'It was still one of the best days of my life,' she said with a smile. 'I think I did my best – it would have been sad to let myself down. Today Jana was just too good, too aggressive for me.'

Novotna's aggression, allied to Hingis's bubbling enthusiam, brought these two singles champions a well deserved victory in the doubles final. Their 6–3 3–6 8–6 win over the No.2 seeds Davenport and Zvereva provided some of the most entertaining tennis of the fortnight.

There was no happy ending for the Woodies. Australians Todd Woodbridge and Mark Woodforde narrowly failed in their attempt to win six doubles titles in a row. In a repeat of the 1997 final they lost a thrilling contest to Dutchmen Jacco Eltingh and Paul Haarhuis 2–6 6–4 7–6 5–7 10–8.

The newcomer from Belarus, Max Mirnyi, teamed with Serena Williams to take the mixed doubles title. Unseeded, they won their semi-final against the No.2 seeds Haarhuis and Caroline Vis of Holland, then outplayed the No.5, Mahesh Bhupathi of India and Mirjana Lucic of Croatia 6–4 6–4 in the final.

Four days after the end of the tournament Wimbledon received some sad news. After getting the show on the road for the fifteenth year, Richard Berens, who had been The Championships' Press Officer since 1984, lost his brave fight with cancer on 9 July.

Men's Singles

Holder: P. Sampras (USA)

FIRST ROUND	SECOND ROUND	THIRD ROUND	FOURTH ROUND	QUARTER-FINALS	SEMI-FINALS	FINAL
1 **P. Sampras** (USA) (1)	**Sampras** (1)					
2 D. Hrbaty (SVK)	6–3 6–3 6–2	**Sampras** (1)				
3 M. Tillstrom (SWE)	Tillstrom	6–4 6–4 7–6(5)				
4 A. Radulescu (GER) (Q)	6–4 6–7(5) 7–5 6–3		**Sampras** (1)			
5 D. Nestor (CAN)	Enqvist		6–3 7–6(4) 7–6(3)			
6 T. Enqvist (SWE)	6–7(2) 6–7(8) 6–4 6–0 6–0	Enqvist				
7 S. Draper (AUS)	Draper	6–7(5) 6–1 6–4 6–3				
8 R. Schuttler (GER)	6–3 7–5 3–6 6–3			**Sampras** (1)		
9 K. Alami (MAR)	MacPhie (Q)			6–3 6–4 6–4		
10 B. MacPhie (USA) (Q)	4–6 6–3 6–4 3–6 7–5	Grosjean (Q)				
11 M. Damm (CZE)	Grosjean (Q)	6–4 3–6 6–1 6–4				
12 S. Grosjean (FRA) (Q)	6–3 7–6(8) 6–3		Grosjean (Q)			
13 R. Vasek (CZE)	Vasek		6–0 7–6(8) 6–2			
14 O. Gross (GER)	7–6(4) 6–3 6–1	**Mantilla** (16)				
15 C. Van Garsse (BEL) (LL)	**Mantilla** (16)	7–6(4) 3–6 6–3 6–4				
16 **F. Mantilla** (ESP) (16)	6–2 6–2 1–6 4–6 6–3				**Sampras** (1)	
17 **A. Corretja** (ESP) (10)	Gimelstob				7–6(5) 6–4 6–4	
18 J. Gimelstob (USA)	7–6(3) 6–2 6–3	Woodforde				
19 J. Knippschild (GER)	Woodforde	2–6 6–1 6–4 6–4				
20 M. Woodforde (AUS)	4–6 6–3 7–6(7) 6–1		Stoltenberg			
21 P. Haarhuis (NED)	Tarango		6–1 3–6 6–3 3–6 6–3			
22 J. Tarango (USA)	1–6 6–3 6–3 6–0	Stoltenberg				
23 G. Kuerten (BRA)	Stoltenberg	6–4 2–6 6–2 6–7(3) 6–3				
24 J. Stoltenberg (AUS)	4–6 6–3 6–1 4–6 10–8			Philippoussis		
25 L. Arnold (ARG)	Ulihrach			5–7 6–1 6–3 6–3		
26 B. Ulihrach (CZE)	2–6 7–6(6) 6–3 6–3	Bracciali (Q)				
27 D. Bracciali (ITA) (Q)	Bracciali (Q)	6–4 6–4 3–6 6–2				
28 M. Lee (GBR) (W)	4–6 6–7(6) 7–6(6) 6–2 6–2		Philippoussis			
29 A. O'Brien (USA) (Q)	O'Brien (Q)		6–3 6–4 6–4			
30 K. Carlsen (DEN)	4–6 4–6 6–4 6–3 6–4	Philippoussis				
31 M. Philippoussis (AUS)	Philippoussis	6–7(3) 6–4 7–6(2) 6–3				
32 **Y. Kafelnikov** (RUS) (7)	6–7(5) 7–6(1) 6–4 6–2					**Sampras** (1)
33 **P. Korda** (CZE) (3)	**Korda** (3)					6–3 4–6 7–5 6–3
34 J. Sanchez (ESP)	6–3 6–4 6–3	**Korda** (3)				
35 S. Campbell (USA)	Dewulf	6–4 6–3 6–2				
36 F. Dewulf (BEL)	6–3 2–6 6–1 6–0		**Korda** (3)			
37 D. E. Sapsford (GBR) (W)	Golmard		4–6 7–5 7–5 7–5			
38 J. Golmard (FRA)	7–6(6) 6–2 6–3	Golmard				
39 D. Wheaton (USA) (W)	Escude	6–3 6–4 4–6 7–6(6)				
40 N. Escude (FRA)	6–1 7–6(3) 6–4			**Korda** (3)		
41 S. Lareau (CAN)	Lareau			6–3 6–4 7–6(4)		
42 R. A. Reneberg (USA)	6–4 6–3 6–3	Van Lottum				
43 J. Van Lottum (NED)	Van Lottum	6–2 5–7 6–4 6–3				
44 G.Raoux (FRA)	7–6(1) 6–3 4–6 7–6(3)		Van Lottum			
45 T. Haas (GER)	Haas		6–3 6–3 6–3			
46 R. Delgado (PAR)	6–7(4) 6–3 6–3 6–3	Haas				
47 A. Calatrava (ESP)	**Agassi** (13)	4–6 6–1 7–6(4) 6–4				
48 **A. Agassi** (USA) (13)	6–2 6–4 6–3				**Henman** (12)	
49 **T. Henman** (GBR) (12)	**Henman** (12)				6–3 6–4 6–2	
50 J. Novak (CZE)	7–6(4) 7–5 5–7 4–6 6–2	**Henman** (12)				
51 T. Ketola (FIN) (Q)	Nainkin	6–3 5–7 6–4 6–2				
52 D. Nainkin (RSA) (Q)	6–1 7–6(4) 6–4		**Henman** (12)			
53 J-M. Gambill (USA)	Gambill		6–4 6–4 3–6 7–5			
54 S. Schalken (NED)	7–6(6) 6–4 6–7(5) 4–6 8–6	B. Black				
55 B. Black (ZIM)	B. Black	7–5 6–4 7–5				
56 R. Fromberg (AUS)	7–5 3–6 3–6 7–6(7) 6–2			**Henman** (12)		
57 M. R. J. Petchey (GBR) (W)	Gustafsson			6–3 6–7(3) 6–3 6–2		
58 M. Gustafsson (SWE)	6–2 1–6 6–3 6–2	Gustafsson				
59 J. Viloca (ESP)	Chang	6–2 5–7 6–2 1–6 6–2				
60 M. Chang (USA)	6–4 6–3 3–6 3–6 6–2		**Rafter** (6)			
61 T. Nydahl (SWE)	Nydahl		6–3 6–7(7) 6–2 6–1			
62 H. Gumy (ARG)	7–5 6–2 7–6(6)	**Rafter** (6)				
63 I. Heuberger (SUI) (Q)	**Rafter** (6)	7–6(3) 6–2 7–6(3)				

Winner: **P. Sampras** (USA) (1

6–7(2) 7–6(9) 6–4 3–6 6–2

First round

65 **C. Moya** (ESP) (5)
66 M. Bhupathi (IND) (Q)
67 A. L. Richardson (GBR) (W)
68 H. Arazi (MAR)
69 S. Sargsian (ARM)
70 A. Portas (ESP)
71 M. Filippini (URU)
72 M. Larsson (SWE)
73 N. Lapentti (ECU)
74 D. Prinosil (GER)
75 J. Siemerink (NED)
76 S. Dosedel (CZE)
77 S. Pescosolido (ITA) (Q)
78 J. A. Marin (CRC)
79 D. Dilucia (USA) (Q)
80 **J. Bjorkman** (SWE) (11)
81 **G. Ivanisevic** (CRO) (14)
82 G. Stafford (RSA)
83 M. Safin (RUS) (W)
84 A. Medvedev (UKR)
85 G. Pozzi (ITA)
86 D. Vacek (CZE)
87 J. Burillo (ESP)
88 M-K. Goellner (GER)
89 T. A. Woodbridge (AUS)
90 G. Blanco (ESP)
91 W. Black (ZIM)
92 L. Paes (IND)
93 T. Martin (USA)
94 A. Sa (BRA)
95 M. Draper (AUS)(Q)
96 **G. Rusedski** (GBR) (4)
97 **C. Pioline** (FRA) (8)
98 M. Rosset (SUI)
99 M. Knowles (BAH) (Q)
100 C. Wilkinson (GBR) (W)
101 M. Norman (SWE)
102 A. Costa (ESP)
103 A. Clement (FRA)
104 W. Ferreira (RSA)
105 J. Alonso (ESP)
106 N. Kiefer (GER)
107 H. Dreekmann (GER)
108 B. Cowan (GBR)(W)
109 N. Godwin (RSA) (Q)
110 D. Pescariu (ROM)
111 B. Steven (NZL)
112 **R. Krajicek** (NED) (9)
113 **K. Kucera** (SVK) (15)
114 V. Voltchkov (BLR) (Q)
115 W. McGuire (USA) (Q)
116 M. Tebbutt (AUS)
117 M. Puerta (ARG)
118 F. Squillari (ARG)
119 D. Sanguinetti (ITA)
120 J. Van Herck (BEL)
121 A. Pavel (ROM)
122 V. Spadea (USA)
123 J. Courier (USA)
124 T. Johansson (SWE)
125 M. Sinner (GER)
126 G. Canas (ARG)
127 F. Clavet (ESP)
128 **M. Rios** (CHI) (2)

Second round

Moya (5) 6–4 4–6 6–4 2–6 6–3
Arazi 6–4 2–6 6–3 6–2
Sargsian 6–0 7–5 6–2
Larsson 7–5 6–1 6–4
Prinosil 4–6 6–3 6–4 6–3
Siemerink 6–1 6–4 7–6(3)
Pescosolido (Q) 6–2 6–1 6–1
Bjorkman (11) 6–4 3–6 6–3 6–2
Ivanisevic (14) 6–3 6–3 6–2
Medvedev 6–3 6–4 3–6 6–4
Vacek 7–6(1) 7–6(4) 6–3
Goellner 4–6 5–7 6–3 6–1 6–2
Woodbridge 6–1 6–2 6–1
W. Black 6–4 7–5 6–4
Martin 6–3 6–4 6–4
Draper (Q) 4–6 6–2 5–4 ret
Rosset 6–4 3–6 4–6 7–6(5) 13–11
Wilkinson 7–5 6–0 6–1
Costa 7–5 7–5 7–6(5)
W. Ferreira 4–6 6–3 6–4 6–2
Kiefer 6–2 6–2 6–3
Dreekmann 6–7(3) 7–6(10) 6–3 3–6 6–3
Pescariu 6–4 6–2 6–3
Krajicek (9) 6–3 7–6(7) 4–6 6–2
Voltchkov 7–6(6) 6–3 6–4
Tebbutt 6–3 6–0 7–5
Squillari 6–7(5) 6–3 7–5 6–4
Sanguinetti 6–7(0) 6–1 6–1 2–0 ret
Spadea 6–3 6–3 6–3
Johansson 6–4 7–6(6) 6–4
Canas 6–2 6–2 6–4
Clavet 6–3 3–6 7–5 3–6 6–3

Third round

Arazi 4–6 6–4 6–3 6–4
Larsson 6–3 6–7(5) 6–3 7–5
Siemerink 6–4 6–7(3) 6–4 6–2
Bjorkman (11) 4–6 6–4 6–4 6–2
Ivanisevic (14) 6–3 7–6(4) 4–6 6–0
Vacek 6–4 7–5 6–3
Woodbridge 6–1 3–6 6–3 6–2
Martin 6–3 7–5 6–2
Wilkinson 6–4 6–4 7–6(3)
W. Ferreira 3–6 7–5 6–3 6–3
Kiefer 6–4 6–3 1–6 6–4
Krajicek (9) 6–1 6–3 6–2
Voltchkov 6–4 6–3 7–6(4)
Sanguinetti 6–1 6–3 6–2
Johansson 7–5 6–1 6–3
Clavet 6–7(2) 2–6 7–6(4) 6–1 6–4

Fourth round

Larsson 6–3 6–3 6–2
Siemerink 7–6(6) 5–7 2–6 6–4 7–5
Ivanisevic (14) 6–7(6) 7–6(4) 6–3 6–4
Martin 6–4 4–6 7–6(1) 6–4
W. Ferreira 6–2 4–6 6–3 6–1
Krajicek (9) 6–4 7–6(2) 7–6(4)
Sanguinetti 3–6 6–1 5–7 6–2 6–1
Clavet 7–6(4) 6–3 6–3

Quarter-finals

Siemerink 4–6 6–3 6–3 6–2
Ivanisevic (14) 7–6(5) 6–3 3–6 7–6(2)
Krajicek (9) 6–3 6–3 7–5
Sanguinetti 7–6(3) 6–1 6–4

Semi-finals

Ivanisevic (14) 7–6(10) 7–6(5) 7–6(6)
Krajicek (9) 6–2 6–3 6–4

Final (semi-final winner)

Ivanisevic (14) 6–3 6–4 5–7 6–7(5) 15–13

Bold type denotes seeded players. Numbers following player's name gives seeding order (Q) = Qualifier, (W) = Wild Card, (LL) = Lucky Loser

Women's Singles

Holder: M. Hingis (SUI)

	FIRST ROUND	SECOND ROUND	THIRD ROUND	FOURTH ROUND	QUARTER-FINALS	SEMI-FINALS	FINAL
1	**M. Hingis** (SUI) (1)	**Hingis** (1)					
2	L. M. Raymond (USA)	7–5 6–3	**Hingis** (1)				
3	E. Makarova (RUS)	Makarova	7–6(2) 6–4				
4	S. Talaja (CRO) (Q)	6–4 6–2		**Hingis** (1)			
5	F. Perfetti (ITA)	Perfetti		6–2 6–1			
6	D. Chladkova (CZE)	6–0 6–1	Likhovtseva				
7	Y. Yoshida (JPN)	Likhovtseva	6–4 6–0				
8	E. Likhovtseva (RUS)	7–6(6) 6–2			**Hingis** (1)		
9	K. M. Cross (GBR) (W)	Cross			6–3 6–2		
10	J. Ward (GBR) (W)	6–3 6–4	Tanasugarn				
11	T. Tanasugarn (THA)	Tanasugarn	6–2 7–5				
12	K. Hrdlickova (CZE)	6–0 7–5		Tanasugarn			
13	C. Black (ZIM) (Q)	Black (Q)		6–4 6–0			
14	S. Jeyaseelan (CAN)	6–2 6–4	Black (Q)				
15	H. Sukova (CZE)	**Schnyder** (13)	6–7(3) 7–5 6–3				
16	**P. Schnyder** (SUI) (13)	3–6 6–4 6–3				**Hingis** (1)	
17	**D. Van Roost** (BEL) (15)	**Van Roost** (15)				6–3 3–6 6–3	
18	J. Kruger (RSA)	6–1 6–3	**Van Roost** (15)				
19	N. Dechy (FRA)	Miller	6–1 6–1				
20	A. Miller (USA)	7–6(3) 6–2		**Van Roost** (15)			
21	L. Latimer (GBR) (W)	Latimer		6–1 6–2			
22	J. Kandarr (GER)	6–4 6–1	Appelmans				
23	S. Appelmans (BEL)	Appelmans	6–1 6–4				
24	C. Torrens-Valero (ESP)	6–3 6–3			**Sanchez-Vicario** (5)		
25	J. Lee (TPE)	Lee			3–6 6–3 6–2		
26	L. A. Woodroffe (GBR) (W)	6–4 6–1	Plischke				
27	A. Sugiyama (JPN)	Plischke	6–2 6–0				
28	S. Plischke (AUT)	6–4 6–7(2) 6–3		**Sanchez-Vicario** (5)			
29	M. Grzybowska (POL)	Grzybowska		7–5 6–2			
30	R. Dragomir (ROM)	6–2 6–4	**Sanchez-Vicario** (5)				
31	C. Cristea (ROM)	**Sanchez-Vicario** (5)	4–6 6–4 6–3				
32	**A. Sanchez-Vicario** (ESP) (5)	5–7 6–2 6–0					**Novotna** (3)
33	**J. Novotna** (CZE) (3)	**Novotna** (3)					6–4 6–4
34	S. Kleinova (CZE)	6–2 6–2	**Novotna** (3)				
35	E. Gagliardi (SUI)	Panova	6–3 4–6 6–1				
36	T. Panova (RUS)	4–6 7–5 6–4		**Novotna** (3)			
37	P. Hy-Boulais (CAN)	Hy-Boulais		6–3 6–1			
38	M. Babel (GER)	4–6 6–2 6–3	Morariu				
39	C. Morariu (USA)	Morariu	7–5 6–0				
40	M. Maruska (AUT)	4–6 6–1 6–2			**Novotna** (3)		
41	S. De Beer (RSA) (Q)	De Beer (Q)			6–2 6–3		
42	I. Gorrochategui (ARG)	6–4 6–4	De Beer (Q)				
43	K. Brandi (USA)	Wang	6–2 4–6 6–3				
44	S-T. Wang (TPE)	7–6(4) 7–5		**Spirlea** (10)			
45	B. Rittner (GER)	Rittner		6–4 6–4			
46	A. Cocheteux (FRA)	7–6(6) 6–0	**Spirlea** (10)				
47	F. Lubiani (ITA)	**Spirlea** (10)	6–4 6–4				
48	**I. Spirlea** (ROM) (10)	7–5 6–3				**Novotna** (3)	
49	L. Osterloh (USA) (LL)	Po				7–5 7–6(2)	
50	K. Po (USA)	6–2 2–6 6–1	Ruano-Pascual				
51	A. Glass (GER)	Ruano-Pascual	6–2 6–4				
52	V. Ruano-Pascual (ESP)	6–1 6–7(4) 6–3		Ruano-Pascual			
53	L. Golarsa (ITA)	S. Williams		7–5 4–1 ret			
54	S. Williams (USA)	6–4 6–3	S. Williams				
55	A. Smashnova (ISR)	Lucic	6–3 6–0				
56	M. Lucic (CRO)	6–4 6–7(5) 6–3			**V .Williams** (7)		
57	G. Nielsen (USA)	Rubin			6–3 6–1		
58	C. Rubin (USA)	4–6 6–0 6–2	Rubin				
59	T. Snyder (USA)	Snyder	3–6 7–5 11–9				
60	L. Nemeckova (CZE)	6–3 6–0		**V. Williams** (7)			
61	B. Schett (AUT)	Schett		6–3 6–4			
62	P. Stoyanova (BUL)	6–0 6–2	**V. Williams** (7)				
63	J. Nejedly (CAN)	**V.Williams** (7)	6–1 6–2				

Winner: **J. Novotna** (CZE) (3

6–4 7–6(2)

65 **M. Seles** (USA) (6)
66 M. A. Sanchez Lorenzo (ESP)
67 A. Fusai (FRA)
68 K. Studenikova (SVK)
69 Y. Basuki (INA)
70 S. Reeves (USA)
71 A. Mauresmo (FRA)
72 M. Schnitzer (GER) (Q)
73 N. J. Pratt (AUS)
74 J. Capriati (USA) (W)
75 L. M. McNeil (USA) (W)
76 E. S. H. Callens (BEL) (Q)
77 S. Noorlander (NED)
78 O. Lugina (UKR)
79 R. P. Stubbs (AUS) (Q)
80 **S. Testud** (FRA) (14)
81 **M. Pierce** (FRA) (11)
82 E. Tatarkova (UKR)
83 B. Schwartz (AUT)
84 M. De Swardt (RSA)
85 A. Gersi (CZE)
86 A. Carlsson (SWE)
87 E. Wagner (GER)
88 M. Oremans (NED)
89 N. Miyagi (JPN)
90 J. M. Pullin (GBR) (W)
91 N. Zvereva (BLR)
92 R. McQuillan (AUS)
93 H. Nagyova (SVK)
94 A. Frazier (USA)
95 G. Leon Garcia (ESP)
96 **S. Graf** (GER) (4)
97 **C. Martinez** (ESP) (8)
98 S. Farina (ITA)
99 K. Boogert (NED)
100 M. Saeki (JPN)
101 M. Diaz Oliva (ARG)
102 P. Suarez (ARG)
103 A-G. Sidot (FRA)
104 S. Smith (GBR) (W)
105 S-H. Park (KOR)
106 J. Halard-Decugis (FRA)
107 O. Barabanschikova (BLR)
108 A. Dechaume-Balleret (FRA)
109 I. Majoli (CRO)
110 K. Habsudova (SVK)
111 H. Inoue (JPN) (Q)
112 **N. Tauziat** (FRA) (16)
113 **A. J. Coetzer** (RSA) (9)
114 K-A. Guse (AUS)
115 N. Sawamatsu (JPN)
116 B. Paulus (AUT)
117 F. Li (CHN)
118 R. Grande (ITA)
119 M. Serna (ESP)
120 R. Bobkova (CZE) (Q)
121 K. Miller (USA) (LL)
122 N. Kijimuta (JPN)
123 M. A. Vento (VEN)
124 S. Cacic (USA)
125 S. Pitkowski (FRA)
126 L. Neiland (LAT)
127 F. Labat (ARG)
128 **L. A. Davenport** (USA) (2)

Seles (6) 6–3 6–4
Fusai 6–3 6–2
Basuki 6–4 6–0
Mauresmo 6–3 6–4
Capriati (W) 6–4 3–6 6–4
McNeil 2–6 6–4 6–4
Noorlander 6–3 6–1
Testud (14) 7–6(5) 6–0
Tatarkova 7–6(4) 6–3
De Swardt 7–6(5) 6–3
Carlsson 6–1 6–1
Oremans 2–6 6–3 6–2
Miyagi 6–3 1–6 6–2
Zvereva 7–5 6–4
Nagyova 6–7(3) 6–2 6–4
Graf (4) 6–4 6–1
Martinez (8) 6–1 6–0
Boogert 3–6 6–2 6–1
Diaz Oliva 6–3 6–2
Smith (W) 6–3 4–6 6–2
Halard-Decugis 6–2 6–4
Dechaume-Balleret 6–4 6–7(5) 11–9
Majoli 6–2 6–3
Tauziat (16) 2–6 6–1 6–3
Coetzer (9) 6–2 6–2
Sawamatsu 2–6 6–3 6–2
Grande 6–1 6–4
Serna 7–5 4–6 6–1
Kijimuta 3–6 6–3 6–4
Vento 7–6(1) 4–6 6–3
Neiland 6–1 5–7 6–3
Davenport (2) 6–2 6–2

Seles (6) 6–1 6–1
Basuki 6–3 6–4
McNeil 4–6 6–4 6–2
Testud (14) 6–3 6–1
De Swardt 6–4 7–6(5)
Oremans 6–2 6–3
Zvereva 6–1 6–3
Graf (4) 6–0 6–4
Martinez (8) 7–5 7–5
Smith (W) 6–1 6–3
Halard-Decugis 6–4 7–6(6)
Tauziat (16) 6–0 6–1
Sawamatsu 3–6 6–3 6–2
Serna 6–4 6–1
Vento 6–0 7–5
Davenport (2) 6–1 7–5

Seles (6) 6–2 6–3
Testud (14) 6–3 7–6(7)
Oremans 6–4 7–5
Zvereva 6–4 7–5
Smith (W) 2–6 6–3 7–5
Tauziat (16) 7–6(5) 3–6 6–4
Serna 6–3 5–7 6–0
Davenport (2) 6–3 1–6 6–2

Seles (6) 6–3 6–2
Zvereva 6–4 6–2
Tauziat (16) 6–3 6–1
Davenport (2) 6–1 6–0

Zvereva 7–6(4) 6–2
Tauziat (16) 6–3 6–3

Tauziat (16) 1–6 7–6(1) 6–3

Bold type denotes seeded players. Numbers following player's name gives seeding order (Q) = Qualifier, (W) = Wild Card, (LL) = Lucky Loser

Men's Doubles

Holders: Woodbridge (AUS)/Woodforde (AUS)

Winners: **Eltingh** (NED)/**Haarhuis** (NED) (1) 2–6 6–4 7–6(3) 5–7 10–8

FIRST ROUND

1 **Eltingh/Haarhuis** (1)
2 Fleurian/Waite
3 Kinnear/Randall
4 Siemerink/Wibier
5 L.B. Jensen/M. Jensen
6 Flach/Van Emburgh
7 Kilderry/Nyborg
8 **Stolle/Suk** (16)
9 **Kulti/Macpherson** (10)
10 Pimek/Zdrazila
11 Adams/Dosedel
12 Kitinov/Vizner
13 Coupe/Dilucia
14 Ardinghi/Bertolini
15 Gould/Petchey (W)
16 **Kafelnikov/Vacek** (7)
17 **Bhupathi/Paes** (3)
18 Mirnyi/Olhovskiy
19 B. Black/Reneberg
20 Gimelstob/MacPhie
21 Bowen/Talbot
22 Braasch/Knippschild
23 Roditi/Sargsian
24 **Broad/Norval** (14)
25 **W. Black/Lareau** (12)
26 Matheson/Weal (Q)
27 Milligan/Parmar (W)
28 Orsanic/Ruah
29 Koves/Tarango
30 Kempers/Oosting
31 Sapsford/Wilkinson
32 **Johnson/Montana** (6)
33 **Bjorkman/Rafter** (5)
34 Novak/Rikl
35 Stafford/Ullyett
36 Nijssen/Noteboom
37 Djordjevic/Groen
38 Arthurs/Kratzmann
39 Keil/Middleton
40 **Knowles/Nestor** (11)
41 **Eagle/Florent** (13)
42 Godwin/Ketola
43 Delgado/Foster (W)
44 Haggard/Rosner
45 Hood/Prieto
46 Albano/Lapentti
47 MacLagan/Richardson (W)
48 **E. Ferreira/Leach** (4)
49 **Damm/Grabb** (8)
50 Barnard/Grant
51 Luxa/Skoch (Q)
52 Holmes/Painter (Q)
53 Brandi/Messori
54 Marques/Vanhoudt
55 Cowan/Spinks (W)
56 **Galbraith/Steven** (9)
57 **Goellner/Prinosil** (15)
58 Merklein/Sell
59 Aerts/Sa
60 De Jager/Koenig
61 Martin/O'Brien
62 Tebbutt/Tramacchi
63 Burillo/Carbonell
64 **Woodbridge/Woodforde** (2)

SECOND ROUND

Eltingh/Haarhuis (1) 6–4 7–5
Siemerink/Wibier 7–6(13) 6–4
Flach/Van Emburgh 6–1 6–3
Stolle/Suk (16) 6–3 7–6(5)
Kulti/Macpherson (10) 4–6 7–6(2) 6–1
Kitinov/Vizner 6–4 3–6 6–3
Coupe/Dilucia 6–4 6–2
Kafelnikov/Vacek (7) 6–3 6–0
Bhupathi/Paes (3) 6–4 6–3
Gimelstob/MacPhie 6–1 6–4
Braasch/Knippschild 6–3 6–7(8) 6–4
Broad/Norval (14) 6–7(3) 7–6(5) 7–5
W. Black/Lareau (12) 6–2 6–4
Milligan/Parmar (W) 1–6 7–5 8–6
Koves/Tarango 6–3 6–4
Johnson/Montana (6) 6–7(5) 6–2 6–3
Bjorkman/Rafter (5) 6–3 6–2
Stafford /Ullyett 7–6(8) 4–6 9–7
Arthurs/Kratzmann 5–7 7–6(2) 8–6
Knowles/Nestor (11) 7–6(7) 6–2
Godwin/Ketola 6–4 7–6(5)
Haggard/Rosner 6–3 6–4
Albano/Lapentti 7–6(4) 6–4
E. Ferreira/Leach (4) 6–3 6–1
Damm/Grabb (8) 2–6 6–4 6–2
Holmes/Painter (Q) 7–5 6–3
Marques/Vanhoudt 4–6 6–4 6–4
Galbraith/Steven (9) 6–3 3–6 6–3
Goellner/Prinosil (15) 6–2 6–2
De Jager/Koenig 6–3 6–4
Martin/O'Brien 7–6(3) 7–6(4)
Woodbridge/Woodforde (2) 6–1 6–4

THIRD ROUND

Eltingh/Haarhuis (1) 6–4 6–2
Stolle/Suk (16) 2–6 7–6(3) 8–6
Kulti/Macpherson (10) 7–6(8) 6–1
Kafelnikov/Vacek (7) 6–1 6–4
Gimelstob/MacPhie 4–6 7–6(4) 6–4
Broad/Norval (14) 6–3 4–6 9–7
W. Black/Lareau (12) 6–2 6–3
Johnson/Montana (6) 6–2 7–5
Bjorkman/Rafter (5) 6–3 7–5
Knowles/Nestor (11) 6–3 6–3
Haggard/Rosner 6–3 7–6(1)
E. Ferreira/Leach (4) 6–7(10) 6–3 6–3
Damm/Grabb (8) 6–4 7–6(7)
Galbraith/Steven (9) 6–3 7–5
De Jager/Koenig 7–6(4) 4–6 6–3
Woodbridge /Woodforde (2) 7–6(4) 6–3

QUARTER-FINALS

Eltingh/Haarhuis (1) 6–4 6–4
Kulti/Macpherson (10) 7–6(3) 6–3
Gimelstob/MacPhie 6–3 7–6(9)
W. Black/Lareau (12) 6–3 7–6(9)
Bjorkman/Rafter (5) 7–5 5–7 6–2
E. Ferreira/Leach (4) 7–6(4) 6–0
Galbraith/Steven (9) 7–6(5) 6–2
Woodbridge/Woodforde (2) 6–1 7–6(6)

SEMI-FINALS

Eltingh/Haarhuis (1) 6–4 5–7 7–6(2) 6–2
W. Black/Lareau (12) 6–4 6–4 7–6(4)
Bjorkman/Rafter (5) 5–7 5–7 6–3 6–4 11–9
Woodbridge/Woodforde (2) 6–0 5–7 6–4 4–6 6–3

FINAL

Eltingh/Haarhuis (1) 6–4 6–4 7–5
Woodbridge/Woodforde (2) 6–4 1–6 6–2 7–5

Bold type denotes seeded players. Numbers following player's name gives seeding order

Women's Doubles

Holders: G. Fernandez (USA)/Zvereva (BLR)

FIRST ROUND

1 **Hingis/Novotna** (1)
2 De Beer/Lee
3 Freye/Noorlander
4 Krizan/Srebotnik
5 Rippner/Steck (LL)
6 Jeyaseelan/Simpson
7 S. Williams/V. Williams
8 **Kijimuta/Miyagi** (11)
9 **Ruano-Pascual/Suarez** (16)
10 Sidot/Wagner
11 Ellwood/Pratt
12 Callens/Halard-Decugis
13 Bobkova/Schneider
14 Smith/Ward (W)
15 Black/Selyutina (Q)
16 **Basuki/Vis** (5)
17 **Sanchez-Vicario/Sukova** (3)
18 Cristea/Melicharova
19 Cross/Latimer (W)
20 Dhenin/Loit
21 Singer/Vildova
22 Kschwendt/Tatarkova
23 Pullin/Woodroffe
24 **Likhovtseva/Sugiyama** (10)
25 **Appelmans/Oremans** (13)
26 Grande/Nielsen
27 Musgrave/Olsza
28 Kim/Saeki
29 Crook/Davies (W)
30 De Villiers/McShea
31 Dechaume-Balleret/Horn
32 **Raymond/Stubbs** (7)
33 **Martinez/Tarabini** (9)
34 Barabanschikova/De Lone
35 Habsudova/Lugina
36 Coetzer/Testud
37 Husarova/Rittner
38 Grzybowska/Tanasugarn
39 Farina/Montalvo
40 **Schett/Schnyder** (12)
41 **De Swardt/Graham** (17)
42 Golarsa/Paz
43 Garbin/Serra-Zanetti (LL)
44 Lee/Wang
45 Gorrochategui/Spirlea
46 McNeil/Rubin
47 Csurgo/Yoshida
48 **Fusai/Tauziat** (4)
49 **Adams/Bollegraf** (8)
50 Jones/Po
51 Stoyanova/Van Lottum
52 Babel/Probst
53 Kunce/Morariu
54 Boogert/McQuillan
55 Cacic/Pierce
56 **Barclay/Guse** (14)
57 **Labat/Van Roost** (15)
58 Kriventcheva/Pleming
59 Cho/Park
60 Drake/Osterloh (Q)
61 Ahl/Wainwright (W)
62 Frazier/Schlukebir
63 Dragomir/Majoli
64 **Davenport/Zvereva** (2)

SECOND ROUND

Hingis/Novotna (1) 6–1 6–1
Krizan/Srebotnik 6–4 6–2
Jeyaseelan/Simpson 6–4 6–2
Kijimuta/Miyagi (11) w/o
Ruano-Pascual/Suarez (16) 6–4 4–6 6–4
Callens/Halard-Decugis 6–4 6–2
Bobkova/Schneider 6–2 7–5
Basuki/Vis (5) 6–2 5–7 7–5
Sanchez-Vicario/Sukova (3) 7–6(3) 6–2
Dhenin/Loit 7–5 7–5
Kschwendt/Tatarkova 6–4 6–2
Likhovtseva/Sugiyama (10) 6–3 6–2
Grande/Nielsen 5–7 6–1 9–7
Kim/Saeki 6–0 4–6 6–4
De Villiers/McShea 6–4 6–4
Raymond/Stubbs (7) 6–2 7–6(5)
Barabanschikova/De Lone 2–6 6–4 6–3
Coetzer/Testud 6–3 6–4
Grzybowska/Tanasugarn 6–2 7–6(1)
Farina/Montalvo 6–4 6–7(5) 6–1
De Swardt/Graham (17) 6–4 7–6(6)
Lee/Wang 7–6(2) 7–5
McNeil/Rubin 6–3 4–6 11–9
Fusai/Tauziat (4) 6–2 6–3
Adams/Bollegraf (8) 6–7(0) 6–2 8–6
Babel/Probst 6–3 6–3
Kunce/Morariu 3–6 6–1 7–5
Barclay/Guse (14) 6–7(6) 6–3 6–3
Labat/Van Roost (15) 6–1 7–5
Drake/Osterloh 6–2 7–5
Frazier/Schlukebir 6–4 6–2
Davenport/Zvereva (2) 3–1 Ret'd

THIRD ROUND

Hingis/Novotna (1) 4–6 6–1 6–2
Kijimuta/Miyagi (11) 6–4 6–3
Callens/Halard-Decugis 6–3 6–4
Basuki/Vis (5) 3–6 6–3 6–4
Sanchez-Vicario/Sukova (3) 7–6(2) 7–5
Likhovtseva/Sugiyama (10) 6–2 6–2
Grande/Nielsen 6–3 6–3
Raymond/Stubbs (7) 7–6(6) 6–3
Coetzer/Testud 6–2 7–5
Farina/Montalvo 6–1 6–2
De Swardt/Graham (17) 6–0 6–2
McNeil/Rubin 6–2 6–1
Adams/Bollegraf (8) w/o
Barclay/Guse (14) 6–2 4–6 6–3
Labat/Van Roost (15) 7–5 3–6 6–3
Davenport/Zvereva (2) 6–1 4–6 6–3

QUARTER-FINALS

Hingis/Novotna (1) 6–3 6–4
Callens/Halard-Decugis 4–6 6–4 9–7
Sanchez-Vicario/Sukova (3) 6–3 6–2
Raymond/Stubbs (7) 5–7 6–0 6–3
Farina/Montalvo 7–6(5) 6–4
De Swardt/Graham (17) 6–1 6–2
Barclay/Guse (14) 6–3 6–4
Davenport/Zvereva (2) 6–3 6–2

SEMI-FINALS

Hingis/Novotna (1) 6–1 6–4
Raymond/Stubbs (7) 4–6 6–3 6–1
De Swardt/Graham (17) 6–2 7–6(5)
Davenport/Zvereva (2) 6–4 6–2

FINAL

Hingis/Novotna (1) 6–2 6–3
Davenport/Zvereva (2) 6–3 6–0

Winners: **Hingis** (SUI)/**Novotna** (CZE) (1) 6–3 3–6 8–6

Bold type denotes seeded players. Numbers following player's name gives seeding order (Q) = Qualifier, (W) = Wild Card, (LL) = Lucky Loser

Mixed Doubles

Holders: Suk (CZE)/Sukova (CZE)

FIRST ROUND

1 **Paes/Neiland** (1)
2 Kempers/Habsudova
3 Tebbutt/Barclay
4 Ruah/Labat
5 Albano/Paz
6 Sapsford/Pullin (W)
7 Godwin/Noorlander
8 **Roditi/Suarez** (13)
9 **Norval/Morariu** (15)
10 Olhovskiy/Lugina
11 Keil/McShea
12 Pimek/Kriventcheva
13 Bowen/Hiraki
14 Noteboom/Oremans
15 Gimelstob/V. Williams
16 **Suk/Sukova** (7)
17 **Leach/Bollegraf** (3)
18 Arthurs/Guse
19 Kitinov/Melicharova
20 Ullyett/Golarsa
21 Nijssen/Basuki
22 O'Brien/Barabanschikova
23 W. Black/C. Black (W)
24 **De Jager/K. Adams** (11)
25 **Orsanic/Tarabini** (9)
26 Johnson/Jeyaseelan
27 Randall/Vildova
28 Koves/Schett
29 Braasch/Schnyder
30 L. B. Jensen/Graham
31 Dilucia/Park
32 **Bhupathi/Lucic** (5)
33 **Galbraith/Raymond** (6)
34 Stolle/Kunce
35 Middleton/McNeil
36 Kinnear/Miyagi
37 Sell/Lee
38 Vanhoudt/Van Roost
39 Eagle/De Lone
40 **Macpherson/McQuillan** (10)
41 **MacPhie/Davenport** (16)
42 Wheaton/Nielsen
43 Mirnyi/S. Williams
44 Grant/Cristea
45 Florent/Pleming
46 Kilderry/Ellwood
47 Tramacchi/Stubbs
48 **Nestor/Tauziat** (4)
49 **D. Adams/Fusai** (8)
50 Barnard/Boogert
51 Koenig/Pratt
52 Haggard/De Villiers
53 Nyborg/Horn
54 Tarango/Likhovtseva
55 Kratzmann/Tatarkova
56 **Broad/De Swardt** (12)
57 **Oosting/Appelmans** (14)
58 Waite/Po
59 Montana/Schneider
60 Delgado/Jelfs (W)
61 Wilkinson/Woodroffe (W)
62 Milligan/Moore (W)
63 Talbot/Callens
64 **Haarhuis/Vis** (2)

SECOND ROUND

Paes/Neiland (1) 6–4 6–3
Ruah/Labat 6–4 3–6 6–3
Albano/Paz 6–1 7–6(2)
Godwin/Noorlander 7–6(5) 6–4
Olhovskiy/Lugina 7–5 3–6 7–5
Keil/McShea 6–3 3–6 6–4
Bowen/Hiraki 7–5 6–4
Gimelstob/V. Williams 6–3 5–7 6–4
Arthurs/Guse 7–6(4) 6–4
Ullyett/Golarsa 6–2 6–4
O'Brien/Barabanschikova 6–3 7–6(0)
W. Black/C. Black (W) 5–7 6–2 6–4
Johnson/Jeyaseelan 6–2 6–7(7) 9–7
Koves/Schett 6–1 5–7 6–0
Braasch/Schnyder 6–1 3–0 ret
Bhupathi/Lucic (5) 7–5 3–6 6–3
Stolle/Kunce 6–0 6–4
Middleton/McNeil 7–6(7) 7–6(4)
Vanhoudt/Van Roost 6–3 6–3
Macpherson/McQuillan (10) 6–3 6–4
MacPhie/Davenport (16) 7–6(5) 6–4
Mirnyi/S. Williams 6–1 7–6(9)
Kilderry/Ellwood 3–6 6–2 6–2
Nestor/Tauziat (4) 6–3 7–5
Barnard/Boogert 6–4 3–6 6–3
Koenig/Pratt 3–6 6–3 9–7
Tarango/Likhovtseva 6–2 7–5
Kratzmann/Tatarkova 6–2 3–6 6–3
Waite/Po 6–3 6–4
Delgado/Jelfs (W) 6–3 6–4
Wilkinson/Woodroffe (W) 6–4 6–2
Haarhuis/Vis (2) 6–1 5–7 6–3

THIRD ROUND

Paes/Neiland (1) 6–1 6–4
Godwin/Noorlander 6–4 2–6 6–4
Olhovskiy/Lugina 3–6 7–5 8–6
Gimelstob/V. Williams 6–3 6–4
Arthurs/Guse 6–3 3–6 6–3
W. Black/C. Black (W) 6–2 6–2
Johnson/Jeyaseelan 6–4 6–4
Bhupathi/Lucic (5) 7–6(6) 7–5
Stolle/Kunce 7–5 6–3
Macpherson/McQuillan (10) 7–6(3) 6–4
Mirnyi/S. Williams 4–6 7–6(4) 6–2
Nestor/Tauziat (4) 4–6 7–5 6–3
Koenig/Pratt 7–5 4–6 6–2
Tarango/Likhovtseva 6–1 7–6(2)
Waite/Po 6–1 6–2
Haarhuis/Vis (2) 6–4 6–4

QUARTER-FINALS

Paes/Neiland (1) 6–3 6–4
Gimelstob/V. Williams 6–3 6–2
Arthurs/Guse 6–1 6–4
Bhupathi/Lucic (5) 7–6(1) 6–3
Stolle/Kunce 6–3 7–6(4)
Mirnyi/S. Williams 5–7 6–3 6–4
Tarango/Likhovtseva 7–6(5) 6–2
Haarhuis/Vis (2) 6–2 6–3

SEMI-FINALS

Gimelstob/V. Williams 6–3 6–4
Bhupathi/Lucic (5) 7–6(2) 3–6 6–3
Mirnyi/S. Williams 7–5 5–7 6–4
Haarhuis/Vis (2) 6–2 7–5

FINAL

Bhupathi/Lucic (5) 6–4 7–5
Mirnyi/S. Williams 4–6 6–4 7–5

Winners: **Mirnyi** (BLR)/**S. Williams** (USA) 6–4 6–4

Bold type denotes seeded players. Numbers following player's name gives seeding order (Q) = Qualifier, (W) = Wild Card, (LL) = Lucky Loser

JUNIOR EVENTS

BOYS' SINGLES – Final: Roger Federer (SUI) (5) d. Irakli Labadze (GEO) (7) 6–4 6–4
GIRLS' SINGLES – Final: Miss Katarina Srebotnik (SLO) (7) d. Miss Kim Clijsters (BEL) 7–6 6–3
BOYS' DOUBLES – Final: Roger Federer (SUI)/Olivier Rochus (BEL) d. Michael Llodra (FRA)/Andy Ram (ISR) (4) 6–4 6–4
GIRLS' DOUBLES – Final: Miss Eva Dyrberg (DEN)/Miss Jelena Kostanic (CRO) d. Miss Petra Rampre (SLO)/ Miss Iroda Tulyaganova (UZB) 6–2 7–6

SENIOR EVENTS

35 AND OVER GENTLEMEN'S INVITATION DOUBLES (Round robin in 4 groups of 4 with knock-out semi-final and final) **Final:** Gene Mayer (USA)/Tim Wilkison (USA) d. Gary Donnelly (USA)/Danie Visser (RSA) 6–4 7–5
35 AND OVER LADIES' INVITATION DOUBLES (Round robin in 2 groups of 4 with knock-out final)
Final: Miss Pam Shriver (USA)/Mrs Elizabeth Smylie (AUS) d. Miss Jo Durie (GBR)/Miss Anne Smith (USA) 3–6 6–4 6–3
45 AND OVER GENTLEMEN'S INVITATION DOUBLES (Knock-out for 16 prs.)
Final: Marty Riessen (USA)/Sherwood Stewart (USA) (4) d. Brian Gottfried (USA)/Tom Gullikson (USA) w/o

THE 1998 CHAMPIONSHIPS

TOTAL PRIZE MONEY – £6,884,952

MEN'S SINGLES – Winner £435,000. Runner-up £217,500. Semi-finalists £108.750. Quarter-finalists £56,550. Fourth-round losers £30,450. Third-round losers £17,610. Second-round losers £10,660. First-round losers £6,530.
Total: £2,380,600

WOMEN'S SINGLES – Winner £391,500. Runner-up £195,750. Semi-finalists £92,440. Quarter-finalists £48,070. Fourth-round losers £25,120. Third-round losers £13,650. Second-round losers £8,260. First-round losers £5,060.
Total: £1,971,930

MEN'S DOUBLES (per pair) – Winners £178,220. Runners-up £89,100. Semi-finalists £45,730. Quarter-finalists £23,740 Third-round losers £12,650. Second-round losers £6,870. First-round losers £4,020.
Total: £793,500

WOMEN'S DOUBLES (per pair) – Winners £154,160. Runners-up £77,070. Semi-finalists £36,580. Quarter-finalists £18,990. Third-round losers £9,490. Second-round losers £5,150. First-round losers £2,920.
Total: £632,110

MIXED DOUBLES (per pair) – Winners £75,700. Runners-up £37,850. Semi-finalists £18,920. Quarter-finalists £8,700. Third-round losers £4,350. Second-round losers £2,160. First-round losers £990.
Total: £277,230

35 AND OVER MEN'S INVITATION DOUBLES (per pair) – Winners £14,500. Runners-up £11,400. Semi-finalists £9,000. Second place in each group £7,200. Third place in each group £6,600. Fourth place in each group £6,000.
Total: £123,100

45 AND OVER MEN'S INVITATION DOUBLES (per pair) – Winners £11,400. Runners-up £9,000. Semi-finalists £7,200. Second round losers £6,000. First round losers £5,200.
Total: £100,400

35 AND OVER WOMEN'S INVITATION DOUBLES (per pair) – Winners £10,400. Runners-up £7,800. Second place in each group £6,000. Third place in each group £5,450. Fourth place in each group £4,650.
Total: £50,400

QUALIFYING – MEN (each): 16 × Third-round losers £4,140. 32 × Second-round losers £2,070. 64 × First-round losers £1,035.
Total £198,720

QUALIFYING – WOMEN (each): 8 × Third-round losers £3,210. 16 × Second-round losers £1,605. 32 × First-round losers £805.
Total: £77,120

Per Diem allowances: Championship Events: £471,520. Invitation Doubles: £87,360. Qualifying Competition: £33,600. **Total: £592,480**

Lindsay Davenport looks towards her coach Robert Van't Hof whose encouragement and understanding contributed to this first US Open title. (Stephen Wake)

US Open Championships

Bud Collins

'Waltzing Matilda,' the Australian theme song, came out of Queensland, and so did Patrick Michael Rafter, Australia's national hero, who waltzed his way to the 1998 US Open title, taking it Down Under once more.

'California Dreamin'' would fit the startling other champ, Long Lindsay Davenport who, like Rafter, restored her home territory to the Championship picture.

For years, when the American titles were fought for on the lawns of Forest Hills, Australia and California were the strengths. Melburnian Frank Sedgman started the rush up from Down Under to American silver with 1951–52 triumphs, launching a reign of terror that accounted for 15 men's singles prizes for Australians over 23 years.

Rafter, in 1997, ended the long drought, dating to 1973 champion John Newcombe, and became the first Aussie repeater since lefty Neale Fraser won in 1959–60.

Davenport, out of Newport Beach, ended a female Californian dry spell almost as parching. She succeeds one of her inspirational mentors, Billie Jean King, the last Californian to rule their country in 1974. Commencing with Helen Wills Moody in 1923, and up to Billie Jean, female Californians had won 28 of 54 US titles.

Lindsay and Patrick's victorious $700,000 slices of the $14 million cake (yes, equal prize money at the US Open since 1973) were earned during a warm, pleasant Flushing Meadow fortnight that may have reminded them of home, and concluded the majors of a wide-wide-open 1998. An extraordinary season of eight different winners of the pre-eminent singles titles, its like had been seen only three times before in 1948, 1966 and 1990.

What a dancing master Rafter was – an Astaire in sneakers cakewalking blithely across Arthur's Gulch, the year-old stadium, to extend his lease on the massive tennis palace named after America's first champion of the 'open' era 30 years before, Arthur Ashe. It takes two to tangle on a court, but the hulking 21-year-old Mark Philippoussis just couldn't keep up with Rafter, who kept his own party swinging to win 6–3 3–6 6–2 6–0. Parsimoniously tossing his compatriot five unforced errors and dropping serve only once, the champion showed no mercy to his unseeded foe, the 12th such outsider to make it all the way to a US title round.

It was an Aussies-only occasion, the sort of battle that had become commonplace at Forest Hills: 10 of 14 finals between the 1956 victory of Ken Rosewall over Lew Hoad and the 1970 victory of ageless Rosewall over Tony Roche. Both Rosewall, 63, and Roche, 53, were present, smiling in patriotic approval among the gallery of 21,447, stretching overall attendance to a record 535,155 for 25 sessions

Is a female battering ram a battering ewe? We'll leave that one to the etymologists, zoologists, feminists or whomever. There can be no doubt, however, that at the paved pasture called Flushing Meadows no defending champion has ever taken such a final round battering and ramming as No.1 Martina Hingis, floored by 6 ft 3 in Davenport – the loftiest woman to grasp a major title.

The kid champ of 1997 went down for the count of 6–3 7–5. When it looked as if she could get up, just as she had to take out a fade-out Jana Novotna in the semis (3–6 6–1 6–4, from 1–4 in the third), Hngis ran into a series of high-velocity punches – forehands and double-barreled backhands – that sent her reeling on 12 of the last 15 points. That barrage left her muttering: 'She killed me. I got ahead 5–4 in the second set, and she killed me.'

But Hingis, beginning her title defence shakily, was up to speed by the quarters, nailing ex-champ Monica Seles, 6–4 6–4. At such a tender age Martina could be proud of gracing her sixth major final over a two-season passage. She retained her usual good humour. If she did feel unlucky, she certainly didn't show it.

Perhaps the Open's luckiest were losers: Mark Rosset and Dinu Pescariu, knocked out in the first round. Deciding to stick around New York an extra day, they cancelled reservations on doomed SwissAir flight 111 to Zurich, and were not among 249 victims in a horrendous crash from which no one escaped.

Regardless of her own No. 2 ranking, and streamlined frame (down 30 lb to 175 lb), Davenport was nobody's choice to put American women back in the title business at the American Championship, a bauble that hadn't been won by a citizen since – take your pick – naturalized Martina Navratilova in 1987 or native Chris Evert in 1982.

Venus Williams, astounding unseeded finalist to Hingis in 1997, looked capable, as the 5th seed, of going all the way this time, closing thunderously in a 2–6 6–1 6–1, quarter-final removal of the French Open champ and 4th seeded Arantxa Sanchez-Vicario, Flushing ruler in 1994. But Lindsay was ready, and outslugged the 18-year-old, 6–4 6–4, completing the tournament without loss of a set.

Disappointed in singles, Hingis rebounded a day later and into the record book by completing a rare feat, a personal Grand Slam in doubles. With Novotna as her accomplice, as she had been in Paris and London, they scored a a 6–3 6–3 decision over Natasha Zvereva and Davenport.

Because Novotna avoided Australia, 17-year-old Martina had joined there with 15-year-old Mirjana Lucic to begin her run to the four titles, the youngest pair to capture a major. The achievement put her in the exalted doubles company of Brazilian Maria Bueno – a Slammer with two helpers in 1960 (Christine Truman at the Aussie and Darlene Hard for the rest) – and also with team Slammers Ken McGregor and Sedgman in 1951, and Martina Navratilova and Pam Shriver in 1984. Curiously, and unprecedentedly, Davenport and Zvereva lost all four finals – a Grand Slop?

Jacco Eltingh might have emulated Hingis had paternity not intervened. He had won Australia with Jonas Bjorkman, the French and Wimbledon in the company of countryman Paul Haarhuis with whom he hoped to conclude a Slam. But when his wife, Hellas, gave birth to a son, Lars, two weeks ahead of predictions, Jacco withdrew to be at her side, preferring a grand heir to a Grand Slam.

A unique 'Sisterly Slam' was claimed by the Williams family when 17-year-old Serena linked with a mammoth Belarus 21-year-old, 6 ft 4 in Max Mirnyi, for a 6–2 6–2, mixed victory over Lisa Raymond and Patrick Galbraith, the 1996 champs. Serena, with Max, had won Wimbledon following sibling Venus's French and Australian successes with Justin Gimelstob, thus landing all four prizes in the Williams's Florida homestead.

Two more familiar family names returned to the doubles honour roll as Aussie Sandon Stolle and Czech Cyril Suk withstood two tie-breaker match points to oust the Bahamian–Canadian coalition of Mark Knowles and Daniel Nestor, 4–6 7–6(10–8) 6–2. Sandon's father, Fred Stolle, had won the same title in 1965–66 with Roy Emerson, and in 1969 with Rosewall. They are the only father and son to take major titles. Suk is a member of a singular familial pair, too. His sister, Helena Sukova, was a US doubles victor in 1985 with Claudia Kohde-Kilsch and in 1993 with Sanchez-Vicario and together they had been Wimbledon champions in 1996 and 1997.

The one-two punch of Rafter – seemingly countryman Roy Emerson's bodyguard – in removing No. 1 Pete Sampras in the semis, 6–7(8–10) 6–4 2–6 6–4 6–3 and then seizing the title, squelched the feeling voiced by many that he was a Johnny One-note, incapable of winning another major. True, Sampras, on the trail of his 12th major singles that would have tied Emerson's 31-year-old record, did break down in the third set. Leading 4–2, he strained a quadriceps muscle in his left thigh, requiring departure from the court for treatment at 5–2. Though able to take the set, he was thereafter hampered, at times noticeably.

But, as Pete said, 'It was bad luck.' There was no guarantee that, even at full strength, he could have held off the swift, rapaciously-volleying Rafter. as he had done most impressively in his only other dangerous start, the 6–3 7–5 6–4 quarter-final win over 9th seed Karol Kucera, his conqueror at the Australian. Patrick's constant pressuring of opponents with Charge of the Light Brigade daring seemed to transform Flushing asphalt to Wimbledon grass.

Still, Patrick was fortunate himself not to be a mournful stat as the only defending champ ever to fold at the starting gate. The gifted little Moroccan lefty, Hicham Arazi, shackled him for the first two sets and longer, holding two break points at 15–40 for a 4–3 lead in the third, and another for a 2–1 lead in the fifth. Rafter's serve and backhand returns kept him breathing, and finally liberated him as No. 44 Arazi's composure drooped, the Aussie winning 4–6 4–6 6–3 6–3 6–1.

Sampras, blocked on the road to a fifth US title, did get closer than Steffi Graf to a sixth. It was a triumph for her merely to return after injuries kept her from defending in 1997. Justifiably seeded (8th) though ranked No. 26, Steffi wasn't solid enough to cope with 19-year-old Swiss left-hander, 11th Patty Schnyder, in the fourth round, 6–3 6–4. That was superconsistent Steffi's lowest New York finish since first appearing in 1984, losing her debut to Sylvia Hanika. Schnyder was then beaten by Novotna, who had roared through her first 11 sets in the tournament against all-comers before Hingis revived to overtake her.

Two other perennial high-finishers, No. 20 Michael Chang, unseeded for the first time since 1988, and 1994 champ Andre Agassi, 8th, were disappointments. Making a very un-Chang-like exit in the second round, Michael was at the edge of a restorative win, holding a two-set lead and three match points in the 10th game of the third against the serve of Carlos Moya, the French Open champ. Yet, he faltered, 3–6 1–6 7–6(7–5) 6–4 6–3.

Agassi's fourth round full-distance defeat in two acts by Kucera – 6–3 6–3 6–7(5–7) 1–6 6–3 – was delayed by a deluge as Andre led 3–0 in the fourth. Seemingly rejuvenated the next day to lead 2–0 and hold two break points for 3–0 in the fifth, Andre then was simply and sensationally outgunned.

Three left-handed principals of 1997 were gone by the first weekend. Defending finalist, 6th seeded Greg Rusedski, fell in the 15th set of his arduous three rounds. He eluded two opening round match points on second serves and a blistered toe that required mid-match lancing in beating No. 29 Wayne Ferreira, and another match point to get past No. 35 Bohdan Ulihrach in the second. But five more sets were too much against yet another lefty, No. 21 Jan Siemerink.

Australian Open champ Petr Korda, seeded 4th, did nothing reminiscent of his 1997 derailing of Sampras. At the very start he surrendered meekly to a qualifier, No. 155 Bernd Karbacher, 2–6 6–3 6–2 6–1, pleading homesickness. Moody Marcelo Rios, seeded 2nd and suspect on big occasions, came up two wins short of the quarters, his previous station. After taking a 2–1 lead, Rios could provide only token resistance to the towering No. 34 Magnus Larsson in the last two sets (6–3 6–2). But one leftist who usually does nothing right at the Meadow, 14th seed Goran Ivanisevic, played winningly well until the fourth round where Rafter tamed his power in four.

Philippoussis, like Rafter, was determined to serve-and-volley, chip-and-charge, and he did so thrillingly right to the end, removing a brace of seeds, 13th Tim Henman in the fourth round and 10th Moya in the semis, both in four sets. Moya had survived a five-set challenge by young American hope, No. 57 Jan-Michael Gambilll, and eliminated a compatriot, 7th seed Alex Corretja. Growing comfortable on tarmac, Carlos looked like the finalist – until Philippoussis's tactics kept him off balance.

However, the tourney's utmost screamer, peppered with 50 aces, was No. 22 Philippoussis's match points-dodging survival against the darkest of horses, No. 33 Tom Johansson, 4–6 6–3 6–7(3–7) 6–3 7–6(12–10). Johansson, a compact 23-year-old Swede, never this high in a major before, had evicted two seeds himself: 5th Richard Krajicek (defaulting in the second set with a gimpy knee) and the enigmatic Russian, 11th Yevgeny Kafelnikov, and was two holds from the semis. In the quarters he led the Aussie, 4–2 in the fifth. Presently he would have three match points in the conclusive tie-breaker. He, Larsson and 12th Jonas Bjorkman gave Sweden a

Serena Williams who won two of the year's Grand Slam mixed titles at Wimbledon and the US Open with the 21-year-old newcomer from Belarus, Max Mirnyi. (Stephen Wake)

Men's Singles

Holder: P. Rafter (AUS)

FIRST ROUND

1 **P. Sampras** (USA) (1)
2 M. Goellner (GER)
3 P. Goldstein (USA) (W)
4 A. Illie (AUS)
5 A. Park (USA) (W)
6 M. Tillstrom (SWE)
7 S. Dosedel (CZE)
8 F. Dewulf (BEL)
9 T. Dent (USA) (W)
10 A. Radulescu (GER) (Q)
11 M. Safin (RUS)
12 M. Gustafsson (SWE)
13 J. Gimelstob (USA)
14 W. Black (ZIM)
15 T. Muster (AUT)
16 **A. Berasategui** (ESP) (15)
17 **K. Kucera** (SLO) (9)
18 S. Campbell (USA)
19 J. Golmard (FRA)
20 J. Novak (CZE)
21 B. Bryan (USA) (W)
22 M. Ondruska (RSA)
23 A. Voinea (ROM)
24 A. Gaudenzi (ITA)
25 M. Damm (CZE)
26 S. Schalken (NED)
27 J. Sekulov (AUS) (Q)
28 D. Sanguinetti (ITA)
29 G. Raoux (FRA)
30 N. Escude (FRA)
31 S. Grosjean (FRA)
32 **A. Agassi** (USA) (8)
33 **P. Rafter** (AUS) (3)
34 H. Arazi (MAR)
35 J. A. Marin (CRC)
36 H. Gumy (ARG)
37 M. Merklein (USA) (Q)
38 D. Nainkin (RSA) (Q)
39 N. Behr (ISR) (Q)
40 G. Keurten (BRA)
41 G. Blanco (ESP)
42 G. Canas (ARG)
43 J. Alonso (ESP)
44 P. Haarhuis (NED)
45 T. Martin (USA)
46 J.Tarango (USA)
47 M. Woodforde (AUS)
48 **G. Ivanisevic** (CRO) (14)
49 **J. Bjorkman** (SWE) (12)
50 C. Pioline (FRA)
51 Y-I Yoon (KOR) (Q)
52 J. Stark (USA) (W)
53 W. Arthurs (AUS) (Q)
54 C. Costa (ESP)
55 N. Lapentti (ECU)
56 F. Santoro (FRA)
57 D. Pescariu (ROM)
58 J. Siemerink (NED)
59 M. Rosset (SUI)
60 D. Hrbaty (SVK)
61 B. Ulihrach (CZE)
62 S. Sargsian (ARM)
63 W. Ferreira (RSA)
64 **G. Rusedski** (GBR) (6)

SECOND ROUND

Sampras (1) 6–3 6–2 6–2
Goldstein (W) 6–7(7) 7–6(4) 6–4 3–0 ret
Tillstrom 7–5 6–3 6–1
Dosedel 6–4 3–6 6–3 6–4
Dent (W) 4–6 7–5 2–1 ret
Safin 6–2 3–6 6–3 7–6(4)
W. Black 3–6 7–5 2–3 ret.
Muster 7–6(1) 6–2 6–3
Kucera (9) 6–4 6–2 6–4
Golmard 6–3 6–4 7–6(5)
Bryan (W) 3–6 6–7(5) 6–1 6–4 6–4
Voinea 6–4 3–6 6–2 2–0 ret
Damm 6–3 6–3 7–5
Sanguinetti 6–4 6–4 6–2
Raoux 6–3 3–6 6–3 1–6 7–6(6)
Agassi (8) 6–4 6–1 6–4
Rafter (3) 4–6 4–6 6–3 6–3 6–1
Gumy 6–3 0–6 4–6 6–2 6–1
Nainkin (Q) 6–7(3) 6–0 6–4 6–4
Kuerten 4–6 6–4 6–3 6–3
Canas 6–3 6–0 6–2
Haarhuis 6–4 6–3 6–2
Martin 7–6(4) 6–2 7–5
Ivanisevic (14) 6–3 6–4 6–4
Bjorkman (12) 6–2 4–6 6–1 6–7(3) 6–2
Stark (W) 6–2 6–4 6–4
Arthurs (Q) 6–3 5–7 6–4 6–4
Santoro 4–6 7–5 6–3 3–6 7–6(4)
Siemerink 6–4 6–3 6–0
Hrbaty 7–6(5) 7–6(3) 7–5
Ulihrach 6–1 6–3 4–6 6–4
Rusedski (6) 4–6 7–6(2) 5–7 7–6(7) 6–4

THIRD ROUND

Sampras (1) 7–6(4) 2–6 6–3 6–3
Tillstrom 1–6 6–3 7–6(5) 3–6 6–3
Safin 6–3 6–1 7–6(2)
Muster 6–7(5) 6–4 6–3 6–0
Kucera (9) 7–5 6–3 6–0
Voinea 0–6 6–2 6–4 6–4
Sanguinetti 7–6(6) 7–6(5) 6–4
Agassi (8) 6–3 6–2 6–7(6) 3–6 6–1
Rafter (3) 6–4 6–1 6–2
Nainkin (Q) 2–6 6–4 6–3 6–4
Haarhuis 6–1 6–1 7–5
Ivanisevic (14) 1–6 7–6(5) 7–5 6–3
Bjorkman (12) 6–2 6–3 6–1
Santoro 7–6(3) 6–4 6–3
Siemerink 6–4 6–3 6–4
Rusedski (6) 4–6 6–3 4–6 6–2 7–5

FOURTH ROUND

Sampras (1) 6–2 6–3 6–1
Safin 6–4 6–4 1–6 6–3
Kucera (9) 7–5 6–3 6–2
Agassi (8) 6–2 6–3 6–0
Rafter (3) 6–1 6–1 6–1
Ivanisevic (14) 7–6(5) 6–3 6–4
Bjorkman (12) 6–3 6–1 6–2
Siemerink 4–6 6–4 5–7 6–2 6–4

QUARTER-FINALS

Sampras (1) 6–4 6–3 6–2
Kucera (9) 6–3 6–3 6–7(5) 1–6 6–3
Rafter (3) 6–3 6–4 4–6 6–1
Bjorkman (12) 6–4 2–6 6–2 6–2

SEMI-FINALS

Sampras (1) 6–3 7–5 6–4
Rafter (3) 6–2 6–3 7–5

FINAL

Rafter 6–7(8) 6–4 2–6 6–4 6–3

Winner: **P. Rafter** (AUS) (3)

6–3 3–6 6–2 6–0

First round

65 **R. Krajicek** (NED) (5)
66 A. Clement (FRA)
67 A. O'Brien (USA) (W)
68 L. Paes (IND)
69 H. Dreekmann (GER)
70 R. Fromberg (AUS)
71 T. Johansson (SWE)
72 F. Meligeni (BRA)
73 F. Clavet (ESP)
74 A. Pavel (ROM)
75 N. Keifer (GER)
76 L. Roux (FRA)
77 J. Burillo (ESP)
78 T. Haas (GER)
79 D. Van Scheppingen (NED)
80 **Y. Kafelnikov** (RUS) (11)
81 **T. Henman** (GBR) (13)
82 S. Draper (AUS)
83 F. Mantilla (ESP)
84 B. Steven (NZL)
85 T. Woodbridge (AUS)
86 M. Kohlmann (GER) (Q)
87 D. Wheaton (USA) (Q)
88 A. Di Pasquale (FRA) (Q)
89 C. Ruud (NOR)
90 M. Philippoussis (AUS)
91 S. Lareau (CAN)
92 R. Delgado (PAR)
93 K. Carlsen (DEN)
94 L. Arnold (ARG)
95 B. Karbacher (GER) (Q)
96 **P. Korda** (CZE) (4)
97 **A. Corretja** (ESP) (7)
98 G. Pozzi (ITA)
99 J-B. Perlant (FRA) (Q)
100 J. Stoltenberg (AUS)
101 V. Spadea (USA)
102 B. Black (ZIM)
103 D. Prinosil (GER)
104 F. Vicente (ESP)
105 M. Norman (SWE)
106 D. Nestor (CAN)
107 J-M. Gambill (USA)
108 K. Braasch (GER) (Q)
109 E. Erlich (ISR) (Q)
110 M. Chang (USA)
111 M. Puerta (ARG)
112 **C. Moya** (ESP) (10)
113 **A. Costa** (ESP) (16)
114 O. Gross (GER)
115 M. Rodriguez (ARG) (Q)
116 S. Bruguera (ESP)
117 A. Medvedev (UKR)
118 J. Van Lottum (NED)
119 J. Sanchez (ESP)
120 G. Grant (USA) (W)
121 M. Larsson (SWE)
122 M. Washington (USA)
123 F. Squillari (ARG)
124 M. Filippini (URU)
125 M. Russell (USA) (W)
126 G. Galimberti (ITA) (Q)
127 D. Vacek (CZE)
128 **M. Rios** (CHI) (2)

Second round

Krajicek (5) 6–3 6–1 6–1
O'Brien (W) 7–5 6–3 7–6(7)
Dreekmann 6–3 1–6 6–3 6–3
Johansson 7–6(5) 6–3 7–6(3)
Clavet 6–7(10) 6–4 7–5 6–2
Keifer 6–4 6–3 6–1
Haas 6–3 7–5 6–4
Kafelnikov (11) 6–1 6–2 6–4
Henman (13) 6–3 7–6(4) 7–6(3)
Mantilla 6–3 3–6 6–4 7–5
Kohlmann (Q) 6–7(5) 7–6(0) 4–4 ret
Di Pasquale (Q) 6–4 6–1 6–4
Philippoussis 7–5 6–4 6–3
Lareau 7–5 7–6(3) 6–3
Arnold 7–6(0) 6–4 4–6 6–1
Karbacher (Q) 2–6 6–3 6–2 6–1
Corretja (7) 2–6 6–3 7–5 7–5
Perlant (Q) 1–6 7–5 6–3 6–3
B. Black 6–4 6–1 6–2
Vicente 6–4 6–3 2–6 6–4
Norman 7–6(7) 6–7(6) 6–7(4) 6–4 6–4
Gambill 6–3 1–6 6–3 7–5
Chang 6–1 6–3 6–1
Moya (10) 6–1 7–6(4) 6–7(3) 4–4 ret
Gross 2–6 4–6 7–5 6–2 6–4
Bruguera 6–1 6–2 6–2
Medvedev 6–4 7–5 6–2
Grant (W) 6–2 7–5 4–6 6–3
Larsson 3–6 6–3 1–6 6–4 6–4
Filippini 7–6(5) 6–0 6–1
Galimberti 7–5 6–4 3–6 6–3
Rios (2) 6–4 6–2 6–3

Third round

Krajicek (5) 6–1 7–6(5) 6–2
Johansson 2–6 7–5 6–2 6–3
Kiefer 6–4 7–6(3) 6–1
Kafelnikov (11) 7–5 6–2 1–6 7–5
Henman (13) 6–3 5–7 7–5 6–4
Kohlmann (Q) 7–5 6–4 6–4
Philippoussis 6–7(3) 6–3 6–3 6–4
Arnold 7–5 3–6 6–2 6–3
Corretja (7) 6–4 5–7 6–7(8) 6–1 6–0
B. Black 7–6(4) 6–1 7–5
Gambill 6–4 6–2 6–7(8) 6–3
Moya (10) 3–6 1–6 7–6(5) 6–4 6–3
Gross 6–1 6–3 6–4
Grant (W) 4–6 6–3 7–6(4) 6–4
Larsson 6–3 6–2 6–2
Rios (2) 6–2 6–7(4) 6–2 6–2

Fourth round

Johansson 6–7(5) 5–4 ret
Kafelnikov (11) 6–4 6–0 6–2
Henman (13) 6–3 7–5 1–6 6–4
Philippoussis 7–6(5) 6–3 6–3
Corretja (7) 6–3 4–6 6–2 7–6(5)
Moya (10) 6–2 3–6 3–6 6–3 7–6(4)
Gross 7–5 6–7(5) 5–7 6–3 7–5
Larsson 6–1 6–7(3) 2–6 6–3 6–2

Quarter-finals

Johansson 3–6 6–3 6–3 7–6(6)
Philippoussis 7–5 0–6 6–4 6–1
Moya (10) 7–6(4) 7–5 6–3
Larsson 6–4 7–5 5–7 6–3

Semi-finals

Philippoussis 4–6 6–3 6–7(3) 6–3 7–6(10)
Moya (10) 6–4 6–3 6–3

Final

Philippoussis 6–1 6–4 5–7 6–4

Bold type denotes seeded players. Numbers following player's name gives seeding order (Q) = Qualifier, (W) = Wild Card, (LL) = Lucky Loser

Women's Singles

Holder: M. Hingis (SUI)

FIRST ROUND

1 **M. Hingis** (SUI) (1)
2 A. Olsza (POL) (Q)
3 A. Huber (GER)
4 I. Majoli (CRO)
5 L. Richterova (CZE) (Q)
6 A. Mauresmo (FRA)
7 J. Craybas (USA) (Q)
8 M. Saeki (JPN)
9 S-H. Park (KOR)
10 L. Nemeckova (CZE)
11 B. Paulus (AUS)
12 N. Dechy (FRA)
13 J. Lee (TAI)
14 G. Leon Garcia (ESP)
15 R. Dragomir (ROM)
16 **A. Sugiyama** (JPN) (16)
17 **D. Van Roost** (BEL) (14)
18 J. Halard-Decugis (FRA)
19 K. Studenikova (SVK)
20 M. Grzybowska (POL)
21 L. Granville (USA) (W)
22 P. Suarez (ARG)
23 K-A. Guse (AUS)
24 K. Po (USA)
25 E. Koulikovskaya (RUS) (Q)
26 S. Kleinova (CZE)
27 S. Nacuk (YUG)
28 A. Miller (USA)
29 J. Kruger (RSA)
30 B. Rittner (GER)
31 F. Labat (ARG)
32 **M. Seles** (USA) (6)
33 **J. Novotna** (CZE) (3)
34 J. Capriati (USA) (W)
35 A. Cocheteux (FRA)
36 S. Dopfer (AUT)
37 K. Hrdlickova (CZE)
38 B. Schwartz (AUT)
39 S. Testud (FRA)
40 S-T. Wang (TAI)
41 T. Tanasugarn (THA)
42 P. Stoyanova (BUL) (Q)
43 S. Williams (USA)
44 N. Pratt (AUS)
45 E. Tatarkova (UKR)
46 M. Schnitzer (GER) (Q)
47 E. Likhovtseva (RUS)
48 **I. Spirlea** (ROM) (9)
49 **P. Schnyder** (SUI) (11)
50 Y. Yoshida (JPN)
51 A. Frazier (USA)
52 B. Rippner (USA) (W)
53 M. J. Fernandez (USA)
54 T. Krizan (SLO) (Q)
55 A. Stevenson (USA) (W)
56 A. Fusai (FRA)
57 M. Lucic (CRO)
58 K. Boogert (NED)
59 N. Sawamatsu (JPN)
60 C. Torrens-Valero (ESP)
61 M. Weingartner (GER) (Q)
62 M. Shaughnessy (USA)
63 C. Morariu (USA)

SECOND ROUND

Hingis (1) 6–2 6–0
Majoli 6–3 6–3
Mauresmo 6–2 6–1
Saeki 6–1 2–6 6–3
Park 1–6 6–3 6–4
Dechy 6–2 7–5
Leon Garcia 6–4 6–7(6) 7–6(4)
Sugiyama (16) 6–1 6–2
Van Roost (14) 6–2 6–2
Grzybowska 6–0 6–1
Granville (W) 6–4 6–4
Po 6–4 6–1
Koulikovskaya (Q) 4–6 6–1 6–3
Miller 6–2 6–3
Kruger 6–1 6–3
Seles (6) 7–6(0) 6–2
Novotna (3) 6–4 6–3
Cocheteux 6–3 6–3
Hrdlickova 6–2 6–3
Testud 6–0 6–2
Stoyanova (Q) 7–6(3) 6–2
S. Williams 6–3 3–6 6–4
Schnitzer (Q) 0–6 7–6(6) 6–3
Spirlea (9) 7–6(0) 6–4
Schnyder (11) 7–6(5) 7–5
Rippner (W) 6–3 6–1
Fernandez 6–4 7–6(4)
Fusai 6–4 6–4
Lucic 6–3 6–2
Sawamatsu 4–6 7–5 6–1
Weingartner (Q) 6–4 1–6 6–2
Graf (8)

THIRD ROUND

Hingis (1) 7–6(4) 6–0
Mauresmo 6–4 6–1
Dechy 6–2 6–4
Leon Garcia 2–3 ret
Van Roost (14) 6–0 6–0
Po 6–3 6–3
Miller 6–1 4–6 6–2
Seles (6) 6–2 6–3
Novotna (3) 6–2 7–6(1)
Testud 7–6(5) 6–3
S. Williams 6–2 6–1
Spirlea (9) 6–3 6–2
Schnyder (11) 6–1 6–2
Fernandez 6–3 4–6 7–6(10)
Lucic 4–6 6–1 6–1
Graf (8) 6–0 6–1

FOURTH ROUND

Hingis (1) 4–6 6–2 6–2
Dechy 6–4 6–4
Po 6–4 6–2
Seles (6) 6–3 6–3
Novotna (3) 6–2 6–3
Spirlea (9) 6–3 0–6 7–5
Schnyder (11) 6–1 7–6(3)
Graf (8) 6–1 6–1

QUARTER-FINALS

Hingis (1) 6–4 6–4
Seles (6) 6–2 4–6 6–3
Novotna (3) 6–3 6–3
Schnyder (11) 6–3 6–4

SEMI-FINALS

Hingis (1) 6–4 6–4
Novotna (3) 6–2 6–3

FINAL

Hingis (1) 3–6 6–1 6–4

Winner: **L. Davenport** (USA) (2)

6–3 7–5

65 **V. Williams** (USA) (5)
66 E. Wagner (GER)
67 A. Kremer (LUX) (Q)
68 Y. Basuki (IND)
69 L. Courtois (BEL) (Q)
70 M. De Swardt (RSA)
71 L. Neiland (LAT)
72 T. Panova (RUS)
73 M. Serna (ESP)
74 M. A. Vento (VEN)
75 E. Gagliardi (SUI)
76 L. Golarsa (ITA)
77 V. Webb (CAN) (W)
78 C. Black (ZIM)
79 M. Babel (GER)
80 **M. Pierce** (FRA) (12)
81 **A. Kournikova** (RUS) (15)
82 L. Ghiradi (FRA)
83 J. Okada (USA) (Q)
84 R. Bobkova (CZE)
85 A. Dechaume–Balleret (FRA)
86 K. Miller (USA)
87 S. Farina (ITA)
88 A. Smashnova (ISR)
89 A. Carlsson (SWE)
90 S. Smith (GBR)
91 S. Pitkowski (FRA)
92 K. Habsudova (SLO)
93 F. Zuluaga (COL) (Q)
94 R. Grande (ITA)
95 K. Brandi (USA) (W)
96 **A. Sanchez-Vicario** (ESP) (4)
97 **C. Martinez** (ESP) (7)
98 M. Oremans (NED)
99 M. Diaz-Oliva (ARG)
100 J. Trail (USA) (Q)
101 N. Zvereva (BLR)
102 R. McQuillan (AUS)
103 M. A. Sanchez Lorenzo (ESP)
104 L. Raymond (USA)
105 M. Washington (USA) (W)
106 B. Schett (AUT)
107 N. Miyagi (JPN)
108 S. Plischke (AUT)
109 L. Horn (RSA) (Q)
110 R. Sandu (ROM) (Q)
111 S. Cacic (USA)
112 **A. Coetzer** (RSA) (13)
113 **N. Tauziat** (FRA) (10)
114 F. Perfetti (ITA)
115 O. Barabanschikova (BLR)
116 A-G. Sidot (FRA)
117 F. Li (CHN)
118 C. Rubin (USA)
119 H. Nagyova (SVK)
120 A. Gersi (CZE)
121 T. Snyder (USA)
122 A. Glass (GER)
123 V. Ruano-Pascual (ESP)
124 J. Nejedly (CAN)
125 S. Reeves (USA) (W)
126 L. McNeil (USA)
127 C. Cristea (ROM)
128 **L. Davenport** (USA) (2)

V. Williams (5) 6–1 6–0
Kremer (Q) 6–4 5–7 7–5
De Swardt 7–6(3) 6–4
Neiland 6–7(5) 6–3 6–4
Vento 6–7(2) 7–5 6–4
Golarsa 6–3 7–6(3)
Black 6–4 6–2
Pierce (12) 6–1 4–6 6–2
Kournikova (15) 6–1 6–3
Bobkova 6–2 6–2
Dechaume–Balleret 6–4 6–2
Farina 6–4 3–6 6–2
Carlsson 6–2 6–4
Pitkowski 1–6 7–5 6–3
Zuluaga (Q) 6–4 6–4
Sanchez-Vicario (4) 6–2 6–2
Martinez (7) 6–1 6–2
Trail (Q) 6–6(2) ret
Zvereva 3–6 6–3 6–4
Raymond 6–3 6–3
Schett 6–3 6–3
Plischke 3–6 7–5 6–2
Sandu (Q) 6–4 6–4
Coetzer (13) 6–1 7–6(3)
Tauziat (10) 6–3 6–2
Barabanschikova 6–1 6–7(4) 6–3
Rubin 6–3 6–2
Nagyova 6–2 6–0
Snyder 6–4 6–1
Ruano-Pascual 6–3 6–2
McNeil 4–6 6–4 6–1
Davenport (2) 6–0 6–2

V. Williams (5) 6–1 6–3
Neiland 5–7 6–0 6–2
Golarsa 6–4 3–6 6–4
Pierce (12) 6–1 6–1
Kournikova (15) 6–3 6–4
Farina 6–3 1–6 6–3
Pitkowski 6–3 6–3
Sanchez-Vicario (4) 6–3 6–2
Martinez (7) 7–6(4) 6–1
Raymond 6–2 6–2
Schett 6–1 7–6(6)
Coetzer (13) 6–0 6–2
Tauziat (10) 6–7(4) 6–2 6–3
Nagyova 7–6(3) 6–4
Ruano-Pascual 6–4 6–4
Davenport (2) 6–1 6–1

V. Williams (5) 5–0 ret
Pierce (12) 6–1 6–0
Kournikova (15) 6–4 6–1
Sanchez-Vicario (4) 6–2 6–3
Martinez (7) 6–3 3–6 6–2
Coetzer (13) 3–6 6–0 6–3
Tauziat (10) 6–1 6–1
Davenport (2) 6–2 6–1

V. Williams (5) 6–1 7–6(4)
Sanchez-Vicario (4) 7–6(5) 6–3
Coetzer (13) 6–4 4–6 6–2
Davenport (2) 6–1 6–4

V. Williams (5) 2–6 6–1 6–1
Davenport (2) 6–0 6–4

Davenport (2) 6–4 6–4

Bold type denotes seeded players. Numbers following player's name gives seeding order (Q) = Qualifier, (W) = Wild Card, (LL) = Lucky Loser

Men's Doubles

Holders: Kafelnikov (RUS)/Vacek (CZE)

FIRST ROUND

1 Rodriguez/Sa (LL)
2 Coupe/Randall
3 Macpherson/Wheaton
4 Goldstein/Grant
5 Koves/Tarango (W)
6 Kohlmann/Ruah (Q)
7 Del Rio/Djordjevic
8 **Broad/Norval** (16)
9 **Johnson/Montana** (10)
10 Arnold/Roditi
11 Goellner/Prinosil
12 De Jager/Koenig
13 Kulti/Tillstrom
14 Martin/Reneberg
15 Golmard/Santoro
16 **Kafelnikov/Vacek** (8)
17 **Bjorkman/Rafter** (3)
18 W. Ferreira/Ivanisevic
19 MacPhie/P. McEnroe (W)
20 Flach/Keil
21 Martin/Hippensteel (W)
22 Bowen/Zdrazila
23 B. Bryan/M. Bryan (W)
24 **Adams/Delaitre** (14)
25 **Eagle/Florent** (11)
26 Stafford/Ullyett
27 Bergh/Nyborg
28 Hoods/Prieto
29 Humphries/Palmer (Q)
30 Gimelstob/Stark
31 Silcock/Wakefield (Q)
32 **Knowles/Nestor** (6)
33 **E. Ferreira/Leach** (5)
34 Lobo/Sanchez
35 Kempers/Oosting
36 Carbonell/Roig
37 Haygarth/Kinnear
38 Orsanic/Siemerink
39 B. Black/O'Brien
40 **W. Black/Lareau** (12)
41 **Novak/Riki** (13)
42 Albano/Lapentti
43 Noteboom/Wibier
44 Bale/Sapsford (Q)
45 Braasch/Ondruska
46 Pimek/Talbot
47 Meligeni/Puerta
48 **Bhupathi/Paes** (4)
49 **Damm/Grabb** (7)
50 Arthurs/Tramacchi
51 Merklein/Spadea (W)
52 Dent/Russell (W)
53 L. Jensen/M. Jensen (W)
54 Mirnyi/Vizner
55 Barnard/Olhovskiy
56 **Galbraith/Steven** (9)
57 **Stolle/Suk** (15)
58 Kratzmann/Tebbutt
59 Haggard/Waite
60 Kitinov/Rosner
61 Di Lucia/Sell
62 Alonso/Conde
63 Godwin/Ketola
64 **Woodbridge/Woodforde** (2)

SECOND ROUND

Coupe/Randall 4–6 6–4 6–3
Macpherson/Wheaton 6–1 6–3
Kohlmann/Ruah (Q) 6–4 7–5
Broad/Norval (16) 6–4 7–6(4)
Arnold/Roditi 6–4 0–6 6–4
De Jager/Koenig 7–6(3) 7–6(2)
Kulti/Tillstrom 4–6 6–2 7–5
Kafelnikov/Vacek (8) 4–6 6–3 6–3
Bjorkman/Rafter (3) 6–4 7–6(7)
MacPhie/P. McEnroe (W) 6–2 6–1
Bowen/Zdrazila 6–2 6–2
Adams/Delaitre (14) 6–1 5–7 7–6(2)
Stafford/Ullyett 3–6 6–3 6–4
Bergh/Nyborg 6–3 6–7(4) 6–3
Gimelstob/Stark 7–6(4) 7–6(4)
Knowles/Nestor (6) 3–6 6–2 7–6(5)
Lobo/Sanchez 6–2 6–4
Carbonell/Roig 6–7(4) 6–4 6–4
Haygarth/Kinnear 4–6 6–4 7–6(4)
B. Black/O'Brien 6–2 6–3
Novak/Riki (13) 7–6(5) 6–4
Bale/Sapsford (Q) 6–3 6–2
Braasch/Ondruska 7–6(6) 6–3
Bhupathi/Paes (4) 7–5 7–6(5)
Damm/Grabb (7) 5–7 7–6(5) 6–3
Merklein/Spadea (W) 6–4 6–4
L. Jensen/M. Jensen (W) 6–4 6–4
Barnard/Olhovskiy 6–4 6–4
Stolle/Suk (15) 6–4 6–4
Haggard/Waite 7–6(13) 6–4
Di Lucia/Sell 6–2 6–1
Woodbridge/Woodforde (2) 6–3 3–6 6–3

THIRD ROUND

Coupe/Randall 6–3 6–4
Broad/Norval (16) 7–6(2) 4–6 6–3
De Jager/Koenig 7–5 6–3
Kulti/Tillstrom 6–4 6–4
Bjorkman/Rafter (3) 7–5 4–6 6–3
Adams/Delaitre (14) 6–3 6–2
Bergh/Nyborg 6–3 7–5
Knowles/Nestor (6) 6–1 7–6(7)
Lobo/Sanchez 6–4 6–4
B. Black/O'Brien 6–3 6–2
Bale/Sapsford (Q) 6–4 6–3
Bhupathi/Paes (4) 6–2 6–4
Damm/Grabb (7) 7–6(12) 6–0
L. Jensen/M. Jensen (W) 6–4 6–3
Stolle/Suk (15) 7–6(3) 6–4
Woodbridge/Woodforde (2) 6–3 7–5

QUARTER-FINALS

Broad/Norval (16) 6–4 6–4
De Jager/Koenig 7–6(6) 6–3
Bjorkman/Rafter (3) 6–3 6–3
Knowles/Nestor (6) 6–3 6–0
Lobo/Sanchez 6–4 2–6 6–4
Bhupathi/Paes (4) 6–0 6–2
Damm/Grabb (7) 6–4 4–6 6–2
Stolle/Suk (15) 3–6 6–3 7–5

SEMI-FINALS

De Jager/Koenig 5–7 6–4 6–2
Knowles/Nestor (6) 5–7 6–2 6–4
Bhupathi/Paes (4) 6–3 6–3
Stolle/Suk (15) 7–6(4) 6–7(5) 7–5

FINAL

Knowles/Nestor (6) 7–6(7) 6–2
Stolle/Suk (15) 6–3 7–6(4)

Winners: **Stolle** (AUS)/**Suk** (CZE) (15) 4–6 7–6(8) 6–2

Winners: **Hingis** (SUI)/**Novotna** (CZE) (1) 6–3 6–3

FIRST ROUND

1 **Hingis/Novotna** (1)
2 Stoyanova/Wagner
3 De Villiers/McShea
4 Habsudova/Tanasugarn
5 Labat/Van Roost
6 Black/Selyutina (Q)
7 Kriventcheva/Melicharova
8 **Halard-Decugis/McQuillan** (12)
9 **Schett/Schnyder** (14)
10 Boogert/Callens
11 Hiraki/Nielsen
12 Singer/Vildova
13 Cacic/Pierce
14 Lugina/Tatarkova
15 Rubin/Spirlea
16 Pullin/Woodroffe (LL)
17 **Raymond/Stubbs** (4)
18 Cenkova/Koulikovskaya (Q)
19 Jeyaseelan/Simpson
20 Lucic/Seles
21 Carlsson/Rittner
22 Babel/Paz
23 Park/Cho
24 **De Swardt/Graham** (10)
25 **Kunce/Morariu** (15)
26 Osterloh/Washington (Q)
27 Capriati/Stevenson
28 Csurgo/Kim
29 Barabanschikova/Dechaume-Balleret
30 Frazier/Schlukebir
31 Craybas/Snyder (W)
32 **Kournikova/Neiland** (6)
33 **Martinez/Tarabini** (7)
34 Lee/Wang
35 Ellwood/Musgrave
36 Courtois/Muric
37 Bradshaw/Spears (W)
38 Dhenin/Loit
39 Coetzer/Huber
40 **Kijimuta/Miyagi** (11)
41 **Ruano-Pascual/Suarez** (16)
42 Freye/Van Lottum
43 Husarova/Nagyova
44 Noorlander/Pleming
45 Kschwendt/Sidot
46 Cristea/Grzybowska
47 Drake/Lee (Q)
48 **Fusai/Tauziat** (3)
49 **Basuki/Vis** (5)
50 Bobkova/Schneider
51 Saeki/Yoshida
52 Golarsa/Horn
53 Dragomir/Majoli
54 Farina/Montalvo
55 Grande/Testud
56 **Adams/Bollegraf** (9)
57 **Barclay/Guse** (13)
58 McNeil/Po
59 Augustus/Jensen (W)
60 Fernandez/Sanchez-Vicario
61 DeLone/Pratt
62 Krizan/Srebotnik
63 Gorrochategui/Oremans
64 **Davenport/Zvereva** (2)

SECOND ROUND

Hingis/Novotna (1) 6–4 6–2
Habsudova/Tanasugarn 6–2 6–2
Labat/Van Roost 6–3 6–4
Halard-Decugis/McQuillan (12) 6–1 6–1
Schett/Schnyder (14) 6–3 4–6 6–4
Singer/Vildova 4–6 6–4 6–4
Lugina/Tatarkova 4–6 6–3 6–2
Rubin/Spirlea 6–0 6–2
Raymond/Stubbs (4) 6–4 6–3
Jeyaseelan/Simpson 3–6 7–6(5) 6–2
Babel/Paz 7–5 7–5
De Swardt/Graham (10) 7–6(4) 6–2
Osterloh/Washington 2–6 7–6(3) 6–4
Csurgo/Kim 6–1 5–7 6–2
Frazier/Schlukebir 6–1 6–2
Kournikova/Neiland (6) 6–3 6–2
Lee/Wang 4–6 6–4 6–2
Courtois/Muric 6–2 6–2
Dhenin/Loit 7–6(4) 4–6 6–4
Kijimuta/Miyagi (11) 6–2 7–5
Ruano-Pascual/Suarez (16) 6–1 6–3
Noorlander/Pleming 7–6(12) 6–4
Kschwendt/Sidot 6–4 6–3
Fusai/Tauziat (3) 6–4 6–3
Basuki/Vis (5) 6–4 6–4
Saeki/Yoshida 7–6(3) 6–4
Dragomir/Majoli 7–5 6–4
Adams/Bollegraf (9) 6–1 2–6 6–2
Barclay/Guse (13) 3–6 6–4 6–3
Fernandez/Sanchez-Vicario 6–2 6–2
DeLone/Pratt 2–6 6–3 6–3
Davenport/Zvereva (2) 6–3 6–1

THIRD ROUND

Hingis/Novotna (1) 7–6(0) 6–0
Halard-Decugis/McQuillan (12) 7–5 4–6 7–5
Schett/Schnyder (14) 6–1 7–5
Rubin/Spirlea 6–2 3–6 6–2
Raymond/Stubbs (4) 6–3 6–4
De Swardt/Graham (10) 6–1 6–2
Osterloh/Washington 6–0 6–1
Frazier/Schlukebir 6–2 4–6 6–3
Courtois/Muric 6–4 6–4
Dhenin/Loit 4–6 6–4 6–3
Ruano-Pascual/Suarez (16) 6–1 6–4
Kschwendt/Sidot 6–1 7–5
Saeki/Yoshida 4–6 7–5 6–4
Dragomir/Majoli 6–3 1–6 6–1
Fernandez/Sanchez-Vicario 6–3 6–1
Davenport/Zvereva (2) 6–3 6–3

QUARTER-FINALS

Hingis/Novotna (1) 6–1 6–0
Schett/Schnyder (14) 7–6(5) 7–6(2)
Raymond/Stubbs (4) 6–1 6–4
Frazier/Schlukebir 6–4 6–2
Dhenin/Loit 7–5 6–4
Ruano-Pascual/Suarez (16) 6–4 6–2
Saeki/Yoshida 7–6(1) 3–6 7–6(6)
Davenport/Zvereva (2) 6–4 6–3

SEMI-FINALS

Hingis/Novotna (1) 6–3 6–4
Raymond/Stubbs (4) 6–3 6–4
Ruano-Pascual/Suarez (16) 7–6(4) 6–7(4) 6–3
Davenport/Zvereva (2) 6–1 6–1

FINAL

Hingis/Novotna (1) 6–2 6–2
Davenport/Zvereva (2) 6–2 6–4

Bold type denotes seeded players. Numbers following player's name gives seeding order (Q) = Qualifier, (W) = Wild Card, (LL) = Lucky Loser

Mixed Doubles

Holders: Leach (USA)/Bollegraf (NED)

FIRST ROUND	SECOND ROUND	QUARTER-FINALS	SEMI-FINALS	FINAL
1 **Woodforde/Neiland** (1)	**Woodforde/Neiland** (1) 6–3 6–4			
2 Reneberg/Sugiyama		Macpherson/McQuillan 6–3 6–2		
3 Paes/Hiraki	Macpherson/McQuillan 4–6 6–4 6–4			
4 Macpherson/McQuillan			Stolle/Graham 7–5 7–5	
5 Koenig/Po	Stolle/Graham 7–6(6) 6–3			
6 Stolle/Graham		Stolle/Graham 6–3 6–4		
7 MacPhie/Morariu (W)	MacPhie/Morariu (W) 6–2 6–4			
8 **D. Adams/Fusai** (7)				Mirnyi/S. Williams (W) 6–7(5) 7–6(3) 6–2
9 **Leach/Bollegraf** (4)	Gambill/Davenport (W) 7–6(4) 6–1			
10 Gambill/Davenport (W)		Mirnyi/S. Williams (W) w/o		
11 Kulti/Oremans	Mirnyi/S. Williams (W) 6–1 6–3			
12 Mirnyi/S. Williams (W)			Mirnyi/S. Williams (W) 3–6 7–5 7–5	
13 Oosting/Likhovtseva	Oosting/Likhovtseva 6–4 7–6(3)			
14 Florent/K. Adams		**Bhupathi/Lucic** (5) 6–3 6–3		
15 Eagle/Huber	**Bhupathi/Lucic** (5) 3–6 6–2 7–5			
16 **Bhupathi/Lucic** (5)				
17 **Johnson/Tarabini** (6)	**Johnson/Tarabini** (6) 5–7 6–1 6–4			
18 Suk/Majoli		**Johnson/Tarabini** (6) 7–6(6) 6–2		
19 Roditi/Miyagi	Roditi/Miyagi 6–3 6–2			
20 Orsanic/Suarez			**Galbraith/Raymond** (3) 6–3 6–2	
21 De Jager/Vis	De Jager/Vis 6–7(3) 6–3 6–3			
22 Delaitre/Halard-Decugis		**Galbraith/Raymond** (3) 6–3 4–6 7–6(1)		
23 Knowles/Boogert	**Galbraith/Raymond** (3) 6–4 4–6 6–4			
24 **Galbraith/Raymond** (3)				**Galbraith/Raymond** (3) 6–3 6–4
25 **Montana/Kunce** (8)	**Montana/Kunce** (8) 6–4 7–5			
26 Nestor/Tatarkova		Gimelstob/V. Williams 6–3 6–3		
27 Kempers/Basuki	Gimelstob/V. Williams 2–6 6–3 6–3			
28 Gimelstob/V. Williams			**Grabb/Stubbs** (2) 6–2 7–6(7)	
29 Rikl/Van Roost	Kratzmann/Guse 7–6(4) 5–7 6–4			
30 Kratzmann/Guse		**Grabb/Stubbs** (2) 6–2 7–5		
31 Damm/Husarova	**Grabb/Stubbs** (2) 6–2 6–4			
32 **Grabb/Stubbs** (2)				

Winners:
Mirnyi (BLR)/**S. Williams** (USA) (W) 6–2 6–2

Bold type denotes seeded players. Numbers following player's name gives seeding order (Q) = Qualifier, (W) = Wild Card, (LL) = Lucky Loser

triumvirate in the quarters for a second time, emulating Mats Wilander, Anders Jarryd and Joakim Nystrom of 1985.

But Johansson, serving his first match point at 6–5 in the climactic overtime, went for too much, losing the point as Philippoussis attacked the second serve. He had two more, 6–7 and 8–9, but Mark crashed out with huge serves, the latter his tournament high 30th ace. The Swede created two match points himself, 7–8 and 9–10 with forehand passers, then fell to a massive forehand and a service winner.

Rafter, who had worked his socks off during a demanding American hard court campaign of seven consecutive weeks (four titles, 26–2 in matches) was jubilant in 'proving the 1997 Open wasn't a fluke.' So was Davenport, relishing a comparable summer, playing six of seven weeks (four titles, 20–1), 'proving my hard work really paid off.'

They both felt like waltzing – with Matilda, each other, or anyone else.

JUNIOR EVENTS

BOYS' SINGLES – Final: David Nalbandian (ARG) (10) d. Roger Federer (SUI) (4) 6–3 7–5
GIRLS' SINGLES – Final: Jelena Dokic (AUS) (2) d. Katarina Srebotnik (SLO) (1) 6–4 6–2
BOYS' DOUBLES – Final: K. J. Hippensteel (USA)/David Martin (USA) (5) d. Andy Ram (ISR)/Louro Zovko (CRO) (6) 6–7 7–6 6–2
GIRLS' DOUBLES – Final: Kim Clijsters/Eva Dyrberg (3) d. Jelena Dokic (AUS)/Evie Dominikovic (AUS) (8) 7–6 6–4

SENIOR EVENTS

MEN'S 35s DOUBLES MASTERS (Round Robin in two groups of 4) – Final: Scott Davis (USA)/David Pate (USA) d. John Fitzgerald (AUS)/Danie Visser (RSA) 6–4 6–2
MEN'S 45s DOUBLES MASTERS (Round Robin in four groups of 4) – Final: Vijay Amritraj (IND)/Jose Higueras (ESP) d. Tom Gullikson (USA)/ Dick Stockton (USA) 6–4 6–4
WOMEN'S DOUBLES MASTERS (Round Robin in two groups of 4) – Final: Betsy Nagelsen (USA)/Wendy Turnbull (AUS) d. Gigi Fernandez (USA)/Betty Stove (NED) 7–6 6–3
MIXED DOUBLES MASTERS (Eight teams, knock-out) – Final: Jaime Fillol (CHI)/Wendy Turnbull (AUS) d. Manuel Orantes (ESP)/Mima Jausovec 6–3 7–5

1998 US OPEN CHAMPIONSHIPS

PRIZE MONEY – Total $14,000,000

MEN'S AND WOMEN'S SINGLES – 128 draws. Winner $700,000. Runner-up $400,000. Semi-finalists $200,000. Quarter-finalists $100,000. Fourth-round losers $50,000. Third-round losers $30,000. Second-round losers $18,000. First-round losers $12,000.
Totals: MEN – $4,124,000; WOMEN – $4,124,000.

MEN'S AND WOMEN'S DOUBLES – 64 draws (per pair) – Winners $320,000. Runners-up $160,000. Semi-finalists $80,000. Quarter-finalists $40,000. Third-round losers $20,000. Second-round losers $13,000. First-round losers $8,000.
Totals: MEN $1,424,000; WOMEN $1,424,000.

MIXED DOUBLES – 32 draw (per pair) – Winners $120,000. Runners-up $60,000. Semi-finalists $30,000. Quarter-finalists $15,000. Second-round losers $10,000. First-round losers $5,000.
Total: $460,000.

MEN'S AND WOMEN'S SINGLES QUALIFYING COMPETITIONS – 128 draws.
16 × Third-round losers $7,000. 32 × Second-round losers $5,000. 64 × First-round losers $3,000.
Totals: MEN $464,000; WOMEN $464,000.

MEN'S AND WOMEN'S DOUBLES QUALIFYING COMPETITIONS – 16 draws (per pair)
4 × Second round losers $2,000; 8 × First round losers $1,500
Totals: MEN $20,000; WOMEN $20,000.

Total for senior events – $400,000. Total for per diem allowances and other fees – $1,076,000

Compaq Grand Slam Cup

John Parsons

The long overdue introduction of a women's event alongside the men's should have been enough to mark another step towards genuine acceptance for the Compaq Grand Slam Cup. Yet the new competition is blighted by the same inherent weaknesses still apparent in the men's competition – namely the lack of world rankings points and a date that is three weeks ahead of the ideal. In these circumstances some players find it impossible to find total inspiration so that it was not until the semi-finals and finals that the 1998 tournament provided matches to challenge the cynicism of its critics.

In principal there is nothing wrong with staging a tournament based on performances in the four most important tournaments of the year. In fact several of the leading women players now echo the views of their male counterparts in saying that most of their planning and preparation is geared towards reaching peak form at the Slams.

Yet, when three of the four men's Grand Slam champions are absent – Pete Sampras with an injury, Pat Rafter saying there was not sufficient time for him to fly in from a Davis Cup match in Australia and Carlos Moya already contracted to play in his home town, Majorca – officials are understandably on the defensive. Unfortunately the action they took to camouflage the problem, sound though it might have been commercially, served only to damage rather than enhance the credibility they have been striving so hard to achieve.

'Andre Agassi is not only still one of the finest players in the game but also a Grand Slam champion,' was the explanation for granting the American the wild card he had requested. USTA president Harry Marmion had reservations about the decision, feeling that it cut across what the event was supposed to be all about.

He was right. By reaching the final and competing more fiercely in his first match than on any of his three previous visits, Agassi contributed immensely to the impact of the week. Yet his most recent Grand Slam title had been in 1995 and although he competed in all four Grand Slam tournaments during the year he did not do well enough to be one of the 12 players invited to Munich. On that basis there was no justification for his presence. Given time to think about it officials seemed to feel that way too. After the 1999 competition, there will be no more wild cards.

In the event victory went to two players still dreaming of adding a Grand Slam title to their CVs, Marcelo Rios and Venus Williams. Few, though, would be surprised if either or both made their Grand Slam breakthrough in 1999. Rios, having been runner-up at the Australian Open, was one of the four seeds who had byes under the new system whereby the men's draw was reduced from 16 to 12 players.

On both the semi-finals and finals days, the vast majority of the 11,000 seats in the spectacular Olympiahalle were filled. But when Britain's Tim Henman had set proceedings in motion with a first round match against Jonas Bjorkman, both of whom had been triumphantly involved in Davis Cup matches 48 hours earlier, barely 1,000 spectators were present. The numbers more than trebled later in the afternoon but with the sun shining, the Oktoberfest was a bigger crowd puller on the day, underlining why another change of date is essential.

It was not an auspicious start – nor was Henman's lacklustre effort which prompted him, after a 7–5, 6–4 defeat, to apologise to the organisers for having 'nothing left to give' after a six weeks stint in which he had enjoyed only one completely free day at home.

Henman could do little more than go through the motions as a 5–1 lead in the first set slipped away, mainly through 27 backhand errors. He admitted that with hindsight it might have been better if he said 'thanks – but no thanks' to the $100,000 on offer just for turning up.

Felix Mantilla beat Nicolas Escude routinely enough 6–3 6–3. Nor was there much excitement as Martina Hingis, the world champion, appropriately became the first winner of a women's match when she repeated her defeat of Conchita Martinez in the Australian Open final. The score was 6–2 7–5 but with ten service breaks in the first 13 games it was hardly a classic – despite some blistering forehand winners from the Spaniard.

By no stretch of the imagination could Day Two have been called dull. Agassi's 6–0 6–0 defeat of Cedric Pioline in 34 minutes was the shortest in terms of games as well as time since

First-time winners at the Compaq Grand Slam Cup were Marcelo Rios and Venus Williams, neither of whom had won any of the main titles, though Rios was a finalist in Melbourne and Williams a semi-finalist in New York. (Stephen Wake)

the event began nine years earlier. But this ruthless execution, on a much slower court surface than in the past, was overshadowed by the American's ferocious verbal attack on his tennis president. One could only feel sorry for Pioline and Harry Marmion.

After being short-changed the crowd were soon being handsomely rewarded. Karol Kucera produced some fine tennis to win 6–4 6–4 against Hicham Arazi (an alternate for the injured Richard Krajicek); then Patty Schnyder took full advantage of another heartbreaking collapse by Jana Novotna to beat the new Wimbledon champion 2–6 7–5 7–5. Novotna double faulted at 5–4 on match point in the second set and twice served for the third. It was the old story again.

Exactly one week before she would overtake Hingis as number one in the world rankings, Lindsay Davenport could only ask 'Who knows why you suddenly play well one week and not another?' Some saw her 4–6 6–1 7–5 loss to Nathalie Tauziat as a further opportunity to whip the tournament. The carpers were given additional ammunition 24 hours later when Hingis, in her semi-final, did what she would surely never have done if rankings points had been at stake. She quit with cramp at 5–5 in the final set against her Fed Cup team-mate Schnyder. Hingis, who had missed a backhand on a match point at 5–2 won few friends when she dismissed the situation as 'a lot of money (in her case £189,000 for one match and her bonus as Australian Open champion) but no ranking.'

Yet those two losses and the manner of them did not do justice to the committed and enterprising efforts of those who beat them or to the four quarter-finals in the men's singles, three of which went to a third set and all of which produced spells of great tennis.

Mark Philippoussis, hitting out freely on serve and returns, recovered from a set and a break down to beat a tiring Bjorkman, 4–6, 7–6, 6–1; Rios was full of guile in a 7–6, 7–5 defeat of Mantilla; a rampant Agassi, took eight games in succession in beating Petr Korda after dropping the first set. He punished the Czech for serving 16 double faults, the last of them on match point to win 4–6, 6–0, 6–1; Kucera upset Goran Ivanisevic 5–7 6–4 8–6 after the most thrilling finish to date in which both of them held match points. It was hard on the Slovakian that, at the behest of television, his semi-final against Agassi 17 hours later, was played before the Rios v Philippoussis match, even though those two had had the previous day off.

Kucera, who had beaten the American in the US Open, held four match points at 5–2 in the fourth set but time was against him. Cramp was a fast-developing menace and once Agassi had escaped, with, among others, a stunning drive volley and an even more spectacular lashed forehand which landed on the line, the threat was over. Unlike Hingis, Kucera fought on bravely but was beaten 7–6 6–7 2–6 7–5 6–0. Rios came through 7–6 6–3 6–4 against Philippoussis, whose challenge never really took off.

So to the finals. Rios eventually won 6–4 2–6 7–6 5–7 6–3 after 2 hours 55 minutes but at least twice during the often bewildering first three sets the Chilean thought about quitting because of a back muscle spasm. Yet every time a premature ending seemed likely, his game suddenly became electrifying again and Agassi, whose usually potent returns made surprisingly little impact, had to settle for second place.

Williams, still 18, was a worthy winner of the women's title and won £500,000, the biggest prize in women's tennis. Having overcome Tauziat in the semi-finals, the American's extra strength, both on serve and off the ground, proved too much for 19-year-old Schnyder who went down 6–2 3–6 6–2. They played in a near empty arena because after a five-sets men's final most of the 10,000 spectators went for tea. Next year the women's final should be staged first.

COMPAQ GRAND SLAM CUP 1998

Olympiahalle, Munich, 29 September–4 October

Prize money ($6 million): MEN – Winner 1,300,000; Runner-up 650,000; Semi-finalists 325,000; Quarter-finalists 175,000; First round 100,000; (Alternates 50,000) Note: A bonus of 125,000 is paid to the winner of each Grand Slam who participates. **WOMEN** – Winner 800,000; Runner-up 400,000; Semi-finalists 200,000; Quarter-finalists 100,000 (Alternates 50,000) Note: A bonus of 100,000 is paid to the winner of each Grand Slam who participates. **MEN – *First round:*** A. Agassi (WC) d. C. Pioline 6–0 6–0: K. Kucera d. H. Arazi 6–4 6–4; J. Bjorkman d. T. Henman 7–5 6–3; F. Mantilla d. N. Escude 6–3 6–3. ***Quarter-finals:*** Agassi (WC) d. P. Korda (1) 4–6 6–0 6–1; Kucera d. G. Ivanisevic (4) 5–7 6–4 8–6; M. Philippoussis (3) d. Bjorkman 4–6 7–6 6–1; M. Rios (2) d. Mantilla 7–6 7–5. ***Semi-finals:*** Agassi (WC) d. Kucera 7–6 6–7 2–6 7–5 6–0; Rios (2) d. Philippoussis (3) 7–6 6–3 6–4. ***Final:*** Rios (2) d. Agassi (WC) 6–4 2–6 7–6 5–7 6–3 **WOMEN – *Quarter-finals:*** M. Hingis (1) d. C. Martinez 6–2 7–5; P. Schnyder d. J. Novotna (4) 2–6 7–5 7–5; V. Williams d. A. Sanchez-Vicario (3) 6–3 6–2; N. Tauziat d. L. Davenport (2) 4–6 6–1 7–5. ***Semi-finals:*** Schnyder d. Hingis (1) 5–7 7–5 5–5 ret; V. Williams d. Tauziat 6–4 6–0. ***Final:*** V. Williams d. Schnyder 6–2 3–6 6–2.

COMPAQ GRAND SLAM CUP RESULTS 1990–97 – Olympiahalle, Munich

1990 (11–16 Dec) **Prize Money ($6 million):** Winner: 2,000,000 ; Runner-up: 1,000,000 ; Semi-finalists: 450,000; Quarter-finalists: 300,000; First Round: 100,000, Alternates:50,000. ***First Round:*** M. Chang d. S. Edberg (1) 6–4 4–6 7–5; H. Leconte d. T. Muster (7) 6–3 6–4; P. Sampras (4) d. A. Cherkasov 5–7 6–2 7–5; G. Ivanisevic (5) d. K. Curren 7–6 7–6; B. Gilbert d. J. Svensson (6) 2–6 6–3 6–4; A. Krickstein d. A. Gomez (3) 6–3 6–4; D. Wheaton (8) d. Y. Noah 7–6 6–7 6–3; I. Lendl (2) d. C. Bergstrom 6–4 6–0. ***Quarter-Finals:*** Chang d. Leconte 7–6 6–3; Sampras (4) d. Ivanisevic (5) 7–6 6–7 8–6; Gilbert d. Krickstein 6–7 6–4 6–3; Wheaton (8) d. Lendl (2) 6–2 7–6. ***Semi-Finals:*** Sampras (4) d. Chang 6–3 6–4 6–4; Gilbert d. Wheaton (8) 6–3 3–6 7–6 2–6 6–4. ***Final:*** Sampras (4) d. Gilbert 6–3 6–4 6–2.

1991 (10–15 Dec) **Prize Money ($6 million)**: Winner: 2,000,000 ; Runner-up: 1,000,000 ; Semi-finalists: 450,000; Quarter-finalists: 300,000; First Round: 100,000, Alternates:50,000. ***First Round:*** T. Woodbridge d. A. Krickstein 6–3 6–3; D. Wheaton (7) d. P. Haarhuis, 1–6 6–3 6–2; M.Stich (3) d. G. Prpic 6–4 6–3; G. Forget (5) d. J. Yzaga 6–3 6–3; J. Hlasek d. J. Connors (6) 0–6 6–4 6–4; I. Lendl (4) d. C. Caratti 6–4 6–1; P. McEnroe (8) d. T. Champion 4–6 6–1 6–4; M. Chang d. J. Courier (2) 6–4 6–2. ***Quarter-Finals:*** Wheaton (7) d. Woodbridge 6–4 7–6; Stich (3) d. Forget (5) 7–6 6–4; Lendl (4) d. Hlasek 7–6 6–3; Chang d. McEnroe 6–2 6–4. ***Semi-Finals:*** Wheaton (7) d. Stich (3) 7–6 7–6 7–6; Chang d. Lendl (4) 2–6 4–6 6–4 7–6 9–7. ***Final:*** Wheaton (7) d. Chang 7–5 6–2 6–4.

1992 (8–13 Dec) **Prize Money ($6 million):** Winner: 2,000,000 ; Runner-up: 1,000,000 ; Semi-finalists: 450,000; Quarter-finalists: 300,000; First Round: 100,000, Alternates:50,000. ***First Round:*** M. Stich d. S. Edberg (1) 7–6 6–7 8–6; R. Krajicek (8) d. E. Sanchez 6–3 6–2; P. Sampras (3) d. A. Volkov 6–3 6–4; H. Leconte d. W. Ferreira (5) 3–6 6–3 6–0; P. McEnroe (6) d. N. Kulti 6–1 6–4 G. Ivanisevic (4) d. G. Forget (5) 7–5 6–4; P. Korda (7) d. W. Masur 2–6 7–5 6–4 M. Chang d. A. Agassi (2) 6–4 6–2. ***Quarter-Finals:*** Stich d. Krajicek (8) 7–6 7–5; Sampras (3) d. Leconte 7–6 6–4; Ivanisevic (4) d. McEnroe (6) 3–6– 6–4 6–2; Chang d. Korda (7); ***Semi-Finals:*** Stich d. Sampras (3) 7–6 7–6 3–6 7–6; Chang d. Ivanisevic (4). ***Final:*** Stich d. Chang 6–7 6–2 6–4 3–6 6–3.

1993 (7–12 Dec) **Prize Money ($6 million):** Winner 1,625,000; Runner-up 812. 500; Semi-finalists 431. 250; Quarter-finalists 262. 500: First round 100. 000. Alternates 50,000 **(Note:** A bonus of $250,000 is paid to the winner of each Grand Slam Championship who participates). ***First Round:*** P. Sampras (1) d. T. Muster 6–3 6–1; M. Chang d. W. Masur (8) 6–2 4–6 7–5; S. Bruguera (3) d. M. Larsson 6–3 6–4; P. Korda d. A. Volkov 6–2 6–3; M.Stich (5) d. M-V. Washington 6–3 6–1; B. Steven (ALT) d. C. Pioline (4) 6–4 7–6 (9–7); W. Ferreira d. B. Becker (7) 7–5 6–4; S. Edberg (2) d. T. Martin 6–3 6–2. ***Quarter-Finals:*** Sampras (1) d. Chang 7–6 (9–7) 6–3; Korda d. Sergi Bruguera (3) 4–6 6–0 6–4; Stich (5) d. Steven 5–7 6–4 6–4; Edberg (2) d. Ferreira 6–7 (7–5) 6–1 6–0. **Semi Finals:** Korda d. Sampras (1) 3–6 7–6 (7–3) 3–6 7–6 (12–10) 13–11; Stich (5) d. Edberg (2) 2–6 3–6 6–3 6–3 6–l. ***Final:*** Korda d. Stich (5) 2–6 6–4 7–6 2–6 11–9.

1994 (6–11 Dec) **Prize money ($6 million):** Winner 1,500,000; Runner-up 750,000; Semi-finalists 425,000; Quarter-finalists 250,000; First round 100,000. Alternates 50,000 (**Note:** A bonus of 250,000 is paid to the winner of each Grand Slam Championship who participates). ***First Round:*** P. Sampras (1) d. J. Yzaga 6–2 6–4; M. Chang (8) d. A. Berasategui 6–1 7–5; B. Becker (3) d. W. Ferreira 5–7 6–4 6–3; G. Ivanisevic (6) d. J. Bjorkman 6–4 6–2; T. Martin (5) d. K. Novacek 7–6 6–4; S. Bruguera (4) d. A. Medvedev 5–7 6–4 6–0; M. Larsson d. S. Edberg (7) 6–4 6–7 8–6; A. Agassi (2) d. T. Muster. ***Quarter-Finals:*** Sampras (1) d. Chang (8) 6–4 6–3; Ivanisevic (6) d. Becker (3) 6–4 6–1; Martin (5) d. Bruguera (4) 7–6 6–4; Larsson d. Agassi (2) 6–3 1–6 6–0. ***Semi-Finals:*** Sampras (1) d. Ivanisevic (6) 5–7 6–3 6–4 6–7 (5) 10–8; Larsson d. Martin (5) 6–4 6–1 6–1; ***Final:*** Larsson d. Sampras (1) 7–6 4–6 7–6 6–4.

1995 (5–10 Dec) **Prize money ($6 million):** Winner 1,625,000; Runner-up 812,500; Semi-finalists 431,250; Quarter-finalists 262,500; First round 100,000; (Alternates 50,000) Note: A bonus of 250,000 is paid to the winner of each Grand Slam who participates. ***First Round:*** P. Sampras (1) d. P. McEnroe 6–1 7–6; G. Ivanisevic (8) d. P. Korda 7–6 6–3; J. Eltingh d. M. Chang (4) 7–6 6–3; Y. Kafelnikov (6) d. R. Furlan 6–4 6–1; B. Black d. T. Muster (5) 7–6 2–6 6–1; B. Becker (3) d. C. Pioline 6–1 6–7 9–7; A. Medvedev (10) d. A. Krickstein 6–2 7–6; T. Martin (9) d. S. Bruguera 7–6 6–4. ***Quarter-Finals:*** Ivanisevic (8) d. Sampras (1) injured; Kafelnikov (6) d. Eltingh 3–6 6–3 6–2; Becker (3) d. Black 7–6 6–1; Martin (9) d. Medvedev (10) 6–3 1–6 4–0 ret. ***Semi-Finals:*** Ivanisevic (8) d. Kafelnikov (6) 7–6 4–6 6–3 6–4; Martin (9) d. Becker (3) 5–7 6–3 6–4; ***Final:*** Ivanisevic (8) d. Martin (9) 7–6 6–3 6–4.

1996 (3–8 Dec) **Prize money ($6 million):** Winner 1,625,000; Runner-up 812,500; Semi-finalists 431,250; Quarter-finalists 262,500; First round 100,000; (Alternates 50,000) Note: A bonus of 250,000 is paid to the winner of each Grand Slam who participates. ***First Round:*** T. Henman d. M. Stich 6–3 6–3; M-V. Washington d. R. Krajicek (7) 6–1 6–2; B. Becker (4) d. J. Stoltenberg 6–3 6–3; J. Hlasek d. C. Pioline 2–6 6–3 6–4; J. Courier d. M. Rosset 7–5 6–2; Y. Kafelnikov (3) d. A. Corretja 6–4 7–6; Woodforde d. Agassi (8) 6–3 6–4; Ivanisevic (2) d. Tillstrom 6–4 6–2. ***Quarter-Finals:*** Henman d. Washington 7–6 6–3; Becker (4) d. J. Hlasek 6–4 6–1; Kafelnikov (3) d. Courier 2–6 6–4 8–6; Ivanisevic (2) d. Woodfrode 6–4 6–4. ***Semi-Finals:*** Becker (4) d. Henman 7–6 6–3 6–1; Ivanisevic (2) d. Kafelnikov (3) 6–7 2–6 6–3 6–2 6–4. ***Final:*** Becker (4) d. Ivanisevic (2) 6–3 6–4 6–4.

1997 (23–28 Sep) **Prize money ($6 million):** Winner 1,500,000; Runner-up 750,000; Semi-finalists 425,000; Quarter-finalists 250,000; First round 100,000; (Alternates 50,000) Note: A bonus of 250,000 is paid to the winner of each Grand Slam who participates. ***First Round:*** P. Sampras (1) d. F. Mantilla 6–4 3–6 6–2; J. Bjorkman (8) d. B. Becker (WC) 6–3 6–2; G. Rusedski (4) d. T. Woodbridge 4–6 6–1 7–5; Y. Kafelnikov d. S. Bruguera (5) 6–4 6–3; C. Pioline (6) d. F. Dewulf 7–6 2–2 ret; P. Korda d. G. Kuerten (3) 6–3 5–3 ret; M. Rios (7) d. M. Woodforde (A) 6–7 6–3 6–1; P. Rafter (2) d. T. Muster 6–2 5–3; ***Quarter-Finals:*** Sampras (1) d. Bjorkman (8) 7–6 6–4; Rusedski (4) d. Kafelnikov 6–7 6–3 6–1; Korda d. Pioline (6) 7–5 6–3; Rafter (2) d. Rios (7) 6–1 7–6. ***Semi-Finals:*** Sampras (1) d. Rusedski (4) 3–6 7–6 7–6 6–2; Rafter (2) d. Korda 7–5 3–6 6–7 7–6 9–7. ***Final:*** Sampras (1) d. Rafter (2) 6–2 6–4 7–5.

GREATEST GRAND SLAM SINGLES WINNERS

Below are lists of all those players who have won five or more singles titles at the four Grand Slam Championships in Australia, France, Great Britain and the United States, the cornerstones of the sport. Listed separately are their combined doubles and mixed doubles totals at the four events to give a final overall total of Grand Slam titles won.

It is interesting that no men have totally dominated the sport during their playing spans like several of their female counterparts. That is partly because there has always been a greater strength in depth among the men and partly because from the late 1930s to the arrival of open tennis in 1968 most of the top amateur men turned professional and could not participate in the great Championships. One can only speculate how many more titles Rod Laver, for instance, might have won if he had not been barred from the Grand Slams from 1963 to 1967.

Four of the top men in the overall list are Australians who lived in an age when all the top men played doubles and many played mixed doubles too. That is not the case today. The totals for Lendl, Sampras and Becker contain only singles victories.

Furthermore, all the players in the lists who won their titles at Wimbledon, the US Championships and the Australian Championships before 1975 won them on grass courts. In 1975 the US Open became a clay court event for three years before switching to its present hard court surface, while the Australian Open changed to another type of hard court in 1988.

In comparing players of different eras it must always be remembered that before 1939 inter-continental travel meant a sea voyage. Thus only a handful of players crossed the Atlantic each year and fewer still ventured to Australia. In considering the overall totals, also remember that the opportunities for competition were fewer in the early years. Although Wimbledon's 1877 meeting was the world's first tennis tournament, there was no ladies' doubles or mixed doubles at the All England Lawn Tennis and Croquet Club until 1913.

Furthermore, the Australian men's Championship began in 1906 and the women's in 1922 while the French Championships were open only to national players until 1924. Accordingly their international records do not begin until 1925.

	MEN	*TOTAL SING*	*AUS*	*FRA*	*WIM*	*USA*	*Dbls*	*Mxd*	*TOTAL*
1	Roy Emerson (1961–67)	12	6	2	2	2	16	0	28 (1)
=2	Rod Laver (1960–69)	11	3	2	4	2	6	3	20 (5)
	Bjorn Borg (1974–81)	11	0	6	5	0	0	0	11
	Pete Sampras (1990–98)	11	2	0	5	4	0	0	11
5	William Tilden (1920–30)	10	0	0	3	7	6	5	21 (4)
=6	Fred Perry (1933–36)	8	1	1	3	3	2	4	14
	Ken Rosewall (1953–72)	8	4	2	0	2	9	1	18
	Jimmy Connors (1974–83)	8	1	0	2	5	3	0	11
	Ivan Lendl (1984–90)	8	2	3	0	3	0	0	8
=10	Richard Sears (1881–87)	7	0	0	0	7	6	0	13
	William Renshaw (1882–86)	7	0	0	7	0	5	0	12
	William Larned (1901–1911)	7	0	0	0	7	0	0	7
	Rene Lacoste (1925–28)	7	0	3	2	2	3	0	10
	Henri Cochet (1926–32)	7	0	4	2	1	5	3	15
	John Newcombe (1967–75)	7	2	0	3	2	17	2	26 (2)
	John McEnroe (1979–84)	7	0	0	3	4	9	1	17
	Mats Wilander (1982–88)	7	3	3	0	1	1	0	8
=18	Laurence Doherty (1902–06)	6	0	0	5	1	10	0	16
	Anthony Wilding (1906–1913)	6	2	0	4	0	5	0	11
	Don Budge (1937–38)	6	1	1	2	2	4	4	14
	Jack Crawford (1931–35)	6	4	1	1	0	6	5	17
	Stefan Edberg (1985–92)	6	2	0	2	2	3	0	9
	Boris Becker (1985–96)	6	2	0	3	1	0	0	6
=24	Frank Sedgman (1949–52)	5	2	0	1	2	9	8	22 (3)
	Tony Trabert (1953–55)	5	0	2	1	2	5	0	10

WOMEN	*TOTAL SING*	*AUS*	*FRA*	*WIM*	*USA*	*Dbls*	*Mxd*	*TOTAL*
1 Margaret Court (1960–75)	24	11	5	3	5	19	19	62 (1)
2 Steffi Graf (1987–1996)	21	4	5	7	5	1	0	22
3 Helen Wills Moody (1923–38)	19	0	4	8	7	9	3	31 (5)
=4 Martina Navratilova (1974–95)	18	3	2	9	4	31	7	56 (2)
Chris Evert (1974–89)	18	2	7	3	6	3	0	21
6 Billie Jean King (1961–1981)	12	1	1	6	4	16	11	39 (3)
=7 Maureen Connolly (1951–54)	9	1	2	3	3	2	1	12
Monica Seles (1990–96)	9	4	3	0	2	0	0	9
=9 Molla Bjurstedt Mallory (1915–1922)	8	0	0	0	8	2	3	13
Suzanne Lenglen (1919–1926) [1]	8	0	2	6	0	8	5	21
=11 Dorothea Lambert Chambers (1903–14)	7	0	0	7	0	0	0	7
Maria Bueno (1958–68)	7	0	0	3	4	12	1	20
Evonne Goolagong (1971–80)	7	4	1	2	0	6	1	14
=14 Blanche Bingley Hillyard (1889–1900)	6	0	0	6	0	0	0	6
Nancy Wynne-Bolton (1936–52)	6	6	0	0	0	10	4	20
Louise Brough (1942–57) *	6	1	0	4	1	17	7	30
Margaret Osborne DuPont (1941–60) **	6	0	2	1	3	16	7	29
Doris Hart (1950–55)	6	1	2	1	2	14	15	35 (4)
=19 Lottie Dod (1887–93)	5	0	0	5	0	0	0	5
Charlotte Cooper Sterry (1895–1908)	5	0	0	5	0	0	0	5
Daphne Akhurst (1924–30)	5	5	0	0	0	5	4	14
Helen Jacobs (1932–36)	5	0	0	1	4	3	1	9
Alice Marble (1936–39)	5	0	0	1	4	6	7	18
Pauline Betz (1942–46) ***	5	0	0	1	4	0	1	6
Althea Gibson (1956–58)	5	0	1	2	2	5	1	11
Doubles titles only:								
Elizabeth Ryan (1914–34)	0	0	0	0	0	17	9	26

Notes:

1 Suzanne Lenglen won another four French Championships before 1925 when the event was restricted to members of French clubs (1920–23).

2 During the war years 1940–45, no Championships were staged in France or at Wimbledon. The Australian Championships were held in 1940 and the USTA continued to hold their Championships every year. During this period:

* Louise Brough won four US doubles titles (1942–45) and one US mixed doubles title (1943).

** Margaret Osborne DuPont won five US doubles titles (1941–45) and three US mixed doubles titles (1943–45).

*** Pauline Betz won three of her four US singles titles (1942–44).

GRAND SLAM WINNERS IN THE OPEN ERA

The first figure in brackets after a player's name denotes the number of titles won at that Championship, the second figure denotes the total number of Grand Slam titles won. Several of the players winning titles in the early years of open tennis had already won some as amateurs. **GS** in bold denotes a **Grand Slam** (winning all four Championships in the same calendar year.)

YEAR	AUSTRALIAN 1968–77 (Jan) 1977–85 (Dec) 1987– (Jan)	FRENCH (May/June)	WIMBLEDON (Jun/July)	US OPEN (Aug/Sep)
1968	Bowrey (1,1) King (1,4)	Rosewall (2,5) Richey (1,2)	Laver (3,7) King (3,5)	Ashe (1,1) Wade (1,1)
1969	**Laver (2,8)** Court (8,14)	**Laver (2,9)** Court (3,15)	**Laver (4,10)** Jones (1,3)	**Laver (2,11) GS** Court (3,16)
1970	Ashe (1,2) **Court (9,17)**	Kodes (1,1) **Court (4,18)**	Newcombe (2,3) **Court (3,19)**	Rosewall (2,6) **Court (4,20) GS**
1971	Rosewall (3,7) Court (10,21)	Kodes (2,2) Goolagong(1,1)	Newcombe (3,4) Goolagong (1,2)	Smith (1,1) King (2,6)
1972	Rosewall (4,8) Wade (1,2)	Gimeno (1,1) King (1,7)	Smith (1,2) King (4,8)	Nastase (1,1) King (3,9)
1973	Newcombe (1,5) Court (11,22)	Nastase (1,2) Court (5,23)	Kodes (1,3) King (5,10)	Newcombe (1,6) Court (5,24)
1974	Connors (1,1) Goolagong (1,3)	Borg (1,1) Evert (1,1)	Connors (1,2) Evert (1,2)	Connors (1,3) King (4,11)
1975	Newcombe (2,7) Goolagong (2,4)	Borg (2,2) Evert (2,3)	Ashe (1,3) King (6,12)	Orantes (1,1) Evert (1,4)
1976	Edmondson (1,1) Cawley (3,5)	Panatta (1,1) Barker (1,1)	Borg (1,3) Evert (2,5)	Connors (2,4) Evert (2,6)
1977 Jan Dec Jan Dec	Tanner (1,1) Gerulaitis (1,1) Reid (1) Cawley (4,6)	Vilas (1,1) Jausovec (1,1)	Borg (2,4) Wade (1,3)	Vilas (1,2) Evert (3,7)
1978 Dec	Vilas (1,3) O'Neil (1,1)	Borg (3,5) Ruzici (1,1)	Borg (3,6) Navratilova (1,1)	Connors (3,5) Evert (4,8)
1979 Dec	Vilas (2,4) Jordan (1,1)	Borg (4,7) Evert Lloyd (3,9)	Borg (4,8) Navratilova (2,2)	McEnroe (1,1) Austin (1,1)
1980 Dec	Teacher (1,1) Mandlikova (1,1)	Borg (5,9) Evert Lloyd (4,10)	Borg (5,10) Cawley (2,7)	McEnroe (2,2) Evert Lloyd (5,11)
1981 Dec	Kriek (1,1) Navratilova (1,3)	Borg (6,11) Mandlikova (1,2)	McEnroe (1,3) Evert Lloyd (3,12)	McEnroe (3,4) Austin (2,2)
1982 Dec	Kriek (2,2) Evert Lloyd (1,13)	Wilander (1,1) Navratilova (1,4)	Connors (2,6) Navratilova (3,5)	Connors (4,7) Evert Lloyd (6,14)
1983 Dec	Wilander (1,2) Navratilova (2,6)	Noah (1,1) Evert Lloyd (4,15)	McEnroe (2,5) Navratilova (4,7)	Connors (5,8) Navratilova (1,8)
1984 Dec	Wilander (2,3) Evert Lloyd (2,16)	Lendl (1,1) Navratilova (2,9)	McEnroe (3,6) Navratilova (5,10)	McEnroe (4,7) Navratilova (2,11)
1985 Dec	Edberg (1,1) Navratilova (3,12)	Wilander (2,4) Evert Lloyd (5,17)	Becker (1,1) Navratilova (6,13)	Lendl (1,2) Mandlikova (1,3)
1986	Not Held	Lendl (2,3) Evert Lloyd (6,18)	Becker (2,2) Navratilova (7,14)	Lendl (2,4) Navratilova (3,15)
1987 Jan	Edberg (2,2) Mandlikova (2,4)	Lendl (3,5) Graf (1,1)	Cash (1,1) Navratilova (8,16)	Lendl (3,6) Navratilova (4,17)
1988	Wilander (3,5) **Graf (1,2)**	Wilander (3,6) **Graf (2,3)**	Edberg (1,3) **Graf (1,4)**	Wilander (1,7) **Graf (1,5) GS**

YEAR	AUSTRALIAN	FRENCH	WIMBLEDON	US OPEN
1989	Lendl (1,7) Graf (2,6)	Chang (1,1) Sanchez-Vicario (1,1)	Becker (3,3) Graf (2,7)	Becker (1,4) Graf (2,8)
1990	Lendl (2,8) Graf (3,9)	Gomez (1,1) Seles (1,1)	Edberg (2,4) Navratilova (9,18)	Sampras (1,1) Sabatini (1)
1991	Becker (1,5) Seles (1,2)	Courier (1,1) Seles (2,3)	Stich (1) Graf (3,10)	Edberg (1,5) Seles (1,4)
1992	Courier (1,2) Seles (2,5)	Courier (2,3) Seles (3,6)	Agassi (1,1) Graf (4,11)	Edberg (2,6) Seles (2,7)
1993	Courier (2,4) Seles (3,8)	Bruguera (1,1) Graf (3,12)	Sampras (1,2) Graf (5,13)	Sampras (2,3) Graf (3,14)
1994	Sampras (1,4) Graf (4,15)	Bruguera (2,2) Sanchez -Vicario (2,2)	Sampras (2,5) Martinez (1,1)	Agassi (1,2) Sanchez-Vicario (1,3)
1995	Agassi (1,3) Pierce (1,1)	Muster (1,1) Graf (4,16)	Sampras (3,6) Graf (6,17)	Sampras (3,7) Graf (4,18)
1996	Becker (2,6) Seles (4,9)	Kafelnikov (1,1) Graf (5,19)	Krajicek (1,1) Graf (7,20)	Sampras (4,8) Graf (5,21)
1997	Sampras (2,9) Hingis (1,1)	Kuerten (1,1) Majoli (1,1)	Sampras (4,10) Hingis (1,2)	Rafter (1,1) Hingis (1,3)
1998	Korda (1,1) Hingis (2,4)	Moya (1,1) Sanchez-Vicario (3,4)	Sampras (5,11) Novotna (1,1)	Rafter (2,2) Davenport (1,1)

The powerful Australian Mark Philippoussis is one who benefits from modern technology by using his aerodynamic graphite frame to smite the ball at a velocity that few opponents can handle. (Michael Cole)

Future Perfect?

John Roberts

If the tennis court did not fit neatly into a television screen, the sport's administrators would probably squeeze it until it did. Tinkering for television is the name of the game. Tennis is not alone in performing contortions for the cameras. No professional sport can survive without television revenue and exposure, and television companies, finding sport a comparatively economical way to generate ratings, are calling the shots.

Television demands a 'package', a compact presentation that does not stretch the attention span of the viewer or the patience of the sponsor. Tennis matches, which by their nature are of indeterminate length, may be about to undergo a pruning process.

Experimental rule changes were already in place before last December's Davis Cup final between Italy and Sweden highlighted television's ambivalence towards the sport. Magnus Norman, leading Italy's Andrea Gaudenzi 5–4 in the fifth set of the opening rubber, was about to serve for the match after more than four and a half hours when the Swedish terrestrial channel, SVT, cut their coverage and switched to regional news programmes.

Swedish viewers missed the most dramatic action of the tie. Gaudenzi saved a match point and broke serve for 5–5. His damaged right shoulder then gave way as he served to 6–5, forcing him to retire at 6–6 0–30, after four hours and 57 minutes.

The match was a good example of how a game of tennis can develop slowly – tediously at times – to a rousing climax, where it becomes a celebration of physical and mental endurance in harmony with the skills of the competitors. The rules were designed to make such matches possible. But the 'advantage' point, one of the cornerstones of the game, may be sacrificed as part of the streamlining for television.

Starting this year, the International Tennis Federation, has decided to experiment with a 'No-Ad' scoring system on the men's satellite circuits for a two year period. Rule 26 describes the 'No-Ad' system thus – 'If a player wins his first point, the score is called 15 for that player. On winning his second point, the score is called 30 for that player. On winning his third point, the score is called 40 for that player. And the fourth point won by a player is scored game for that player except as below:

'If both players have won three points, the score is called deuce. One deciding point shall then be played whereby the Receiver shall choose whether he wishes to receive the service from the right half of the court or the left half of the court. The player who wins the deciding point is scored the game.'

Tennis is not meant to be easy. ('That's why the net's there,' said Jimmy Connors, the epitome of skill allied to effort.) Down the years, the 'advantage' point has been an integral part of the psychological and physical duelling which makes the sport so fascinating. When the score reaches deuce, mental doors tend to open or close. One of the players, for instance, might have fought back from 0–40. Will there be a sudden shift in confidence?

'If you get into a long deuce game you have a situation where you can wear your opponent down,' observed John Newcombe, Australia's former Wimbledon champion and former world No. 1. 'The No-Ad rule was tried in college tennis in the States, and it made the tennis very mundane.'

Andre Agassi, a marvellous returner of serve who memorably defeated Goran Ivanisevic in five sets in the 1992 Wimbledon final, has spoken in favour of a 'No-Ad' system. 'If a guy is serving at 40–30, you have to win the next point and then win two in a row,' Agassi said. 'Now, if you had to win one of the next two points, there is a heck of a chance you are going to break the guy. If you are playing against Sampras and he is serving at 15–40, there is still a 60 per cent chance he is going to hold serve. A No-Ad scoring system and that drops considerably, to maybe a 23 per cent chance he is going to hold serve.'

Agassi's preoccupation with breaking Sampras's serve is understandable, but the 'No-Ad' system is a potential passion killer. The rule would have denied us, for example, the 20-minute game between Steffi Graf and Arantxa Sanchez-Vicario which transformed the 1995 Wimbledon women's singles final into one of the great matches. The marathon game, in which

Sanchez-Vicario was serving at one set all and 5–5, comprised 32 points, including 13 deuces, six break points and eight game points.

Under the 'No-Ad' system, Sanchez-Vicario would have held serve within five minutes with a forehand pass down the line after the first deuce. Instead, 25 points later, she was broken, unable to control her backhand in attempting to parry a trademark Graf forehand.

One-day club tournaments, where time is tight, sometimes adopt a 'One-Ad' sytem. If the score goes back to deuce after the first advantage, the next point wins. This compromise, while preferable to 'No-Ad', still dilutes the sport as a comprehensive test of skill, nerve and endurance.

Another possible match-shrinker under review is the introduction of tie-breaks at five games all, or even four games all, instead of at six games all. The tie-break, originated by a American, Jimmy Van Alen, was a response to television's need for shorter matches after interest in the sport soared following the advent of open tennis in 1968. A successful ITF experiment in 1970 validated the innovation. Wimbledon adopted the tie-break at eight games all in 1971 and at six games all in 1979 (although there is no tie-break in fifth sets at Wimbledon).

Four years after the tie-break was first introduced at Wimbledon to speed the game up for television, chairs were provided on the court for the players during changeovers. This blatant contradiction of the philosophy that play shall be continuous was designed to guarantee pauses in the match so that advertisements could be shown overseas on television.

The ITF is keen to reduce the amount of rest time during changeovers without denying television its commercial breaks. 'The thing that annoys me,' Brian Tobin, the ITF President, said, 'is that players come out and warm up for five minutes and the umpire calls 'Play', and they sit down.'

Either that, or they go to the bathroom, or do up their shoelaces, or have a drink. Then there is the spectacle of players sitting down and taking a break after the opening game of a match. 'Why sit down after one game?' Tobin said. 'Maybe it's only four points.'

One proposal, which has been set aside for the moment, is the abolition of the service let (where a serve is retaken if the ball touches the net before landing in court). The ITF decided that 'further research, analysis and consultation' was needed over the next 12 months. In the meantime, we shall be spared the sight of the ball tripping over the net-cord and be declared an ace (Agassi, incidentally, would like service lets to be regarded as faults).

Net-cords in open play are accepted as part of the luck of the game. Boris Becker comes to mind as a particular beneficiary, his backhand drive thudding against the top of the net and 'dying' in Ivan Lendl's court on the concluding point a a fifth set tie-break in the final of the 1988 Masters (now the ATP Tour Championship).

The difference between that kind of incident, traditionalists argue, and a serve clipping the net and dropping over for an ace, is that the opponent would not have had an opportunity to participate in the point. Pure aces, of course, represent one of the skills of the sport.

It is possible that Davis Cup ties will be reduced to three-set singles matches for the first two rounds of the World Group competition, with five-set singles matches continuing for the semi-finals and final. The doubles (the only match played on the second day) would continue to be over five sets.

'The Davis Cup Committee is looking into that proposal (for 2001),' Tobin said during last year's final in Milan. 'It's out of deference to the players to some extent, (with regard to) their schedule. It's out of deference to the time people sit, and to the television time you can get.' Tobin acknowledged that drastic change may damage the purity of the game. 'That's the fear,' he said, 'but we'd be silly if we didn't look at all sorts of options.'

Billie Jean King, winner of a record 20 Wimbledon titles (six singles, 10 doubles, four mixed doubles), and triumphant against the middle-aged Bobby Riggs in the 1973 'Battle of the Sexes' match at the Houston Astrodome, has advocated that all matches are played over three sets. 'It's boring, five sets,' King said.

Methods of making tennis more attractive are constantly given consideration. A few years ago, at the height of a debate concerning the power and speed of the men's game, the ATP Tour produced some interesting statistics comparing the 1990s with the 1970s. Research showed that the amount of time the ball was in play per hour on grass was down to 3min 55sec compared with 7min 18 sec in the 1970s. The length of points on grass had reduced from 3.8sec to 2.7sec.

Grass-court tennis presents a particular problem in the men's game. Other surfaces can be made slower or faster, but Wimbledon's lawns will always favour pace. So what is to be done?

Venus Williams is a blur as she hits one of her cannonball serves, one of which was recorded at 127 mph in Zurich – the fastest ever by a women player. (Tommy Hindley)

Raise the height of the net? Restrict players to one serve instead of two? Revive the old foot-fault rule (one foot to remain on the ground)? Use a bigger ball? In the words of Pete Sampras, 'Goran would still serve aces if you gave him a basketball'.

Although Sampras, the five times Wimbledon singles champion, is among those who have not changed the basic composition of their rackets for years, modern technology is blamed for the power game. The opportunity to ban all but wooden rackets was missed during the 1970s.

It has been suggested many times that the only way to improve the variety of tennis in the men's game at Wimbledon is to abandon the lawns in favour of medium-pace concrete courts, such as those at the United States Open and the Australian Open.

The Americans made the switch from grass in the late 1970s and the Australians followed suit in the late 1980s. It is possible that the All England Club will dig up the lawns during the next millennium. Whether they gain more than they lose is another matter. It is sometimes overlooked that Wimbledon's unique appeal owes as much to ambience as it does to tennis.

For more than a century, the sport at large has grown in people's affections. The majority who follow tennis enjoy it for what it is and like the quaint scoring system that can produce fascinating results. Deuce would not be deuce if did not mean two more to win.

Experiments are all very well as long as they do not interfere with what matters. Change for the sake of change is not a good idea. Change for the sake of television may be worse. Caution is advised. It is best if the ITF do not act in haste. Given a year or so, the choice of matches offered viewers by the advent of digital television may eliminate the need to squeeze the game out of recognition.

The ITF Foundation is comprised of international manufacturers and companies involved in the tennis industry. The ITF and the ITF Foundation work together for the development and promotion of the game:

Supporting and Sponsoring Members:

DUNLOP SLAZENGER GROUP

General Members: Asics, Babolat, Desso, Diadora, Donnay, Fischer, Gosen, GreenSet, Lacoste, Major Sports, Milliken, Nassau, Nova Sports USA, Pro Mark Sports, Sergio Tacchini, Shanghai Tennis Ball Factory, Sports and Play Contractors Association, Tex-Tech, Van der Meer Tennis University, Völkl, US Tennis Court and Track Builders Association.

Any organisation interested in joining the ITF Foundation should contact:
International Tennis Federation Bank Lane Roehampton London SW15 5XZ
tel: +44 181 878 6464 fax: +44 181 878 7799

ATP Tour

ATP Tour Year • Points Explanation and Allocation • ATP Tour Tournaments – Mercedes Super 9, Championship and World Series • ATP Tour World Championship

As he did the previous year, Russia's Yevgeny Kafelnikov earned a place in Hannover only at the last moment by winning the title in Moscow. (Michael Cole)

In a year when Jonas Bjorkman slipped 20 places in singles there was compensation in doubles when he won his first Grand Slam title at the Australian Open with Jacco Eltingh. It was their first outing together. (Stephen Wake)

ATP Tour Year

John Parsons

According to the script at the time of the ATP Championship in Hannover, for Pete Sampras to achieve the phenomenal success of ending 1998 as world number one for a record sixth consecutive year, he would probably have to beat Marcelo Rios, the man who had briefly snatched the baton from him earlier in the campaign.

Sampras had set his heart on overtaking the five-times record he shared with Jimmy Connors. Yet, going into this grand finale to 78 tournaments in six continents, only 33 points, less than half the value of one victory in the round-robin section of the showdown, separated the American from his most persistent pursuer; this despite the fact that the Chilean had not won any of the four Grand Slam titles.

So close had been the race for No. 1 for much of 1998 that after winning his first Grand Slam title a few days after his 30th birthday at the Australian Open, Petr Korda would have soared to the top of the rankings had he won either in Antwerp or at the new British tournament in London's Battersea Park. Instead he lost to Karol Kucera in the quarter-finals of Antwerp and even earlier in London. Indeed, in the end the Czech left-hander failed to make the top eight for Hannover despite a ranking cut-off of ten after the withdrawals of third ranked Pat Rafter and eighth ranked Richard Krajicek. Both had opted out to ensure that injuries healed in time for the Australian Open.

Nor was this merely a two-horse race. Rafter, too, had been tantalisingly close to assuming the cherished top place. The handsome Australian might have done so if he had been able to sustain his glorious form during the American summer circuit where he won consecutive Super 9 finals in Toronto and Cincinatti and then retained the US Open crown.

Rios, though, did knock Sampras from the top perch twice. Having started the year well, but not quite well enough, by taking only six games in a dismal performance in the Australian Open final, Rios won the Lipton Championships on 30 March and thus became the first Chilean to achieve the No.1 ranking. After four weeks Sampras regained the top spot but Rios displaced him again for two weeks in mid-August.

That March ranking list which showed Rios at number one was unique. For the first time in the 25-year history of ATP Tour rankings the top ten players were all from different countries. The countries were Chile, the United States (Sampras), the Czech Republic (Korda), Australia (Rafter), Great Britain (Greg Rusedski), Russia (Yevgeny Kafelnikov), Spain (Alex Corretja), Sweden (Jonas Bjorkman), the Netherlands (Richard Krajicek) and Brazil (Gustavo Kuerten). Although there were positional changes within the list, it would stay that way for another three weeks.

Even though Rios picked himself up after the disappointment of Melbourne to win three of the first four Super 9 titles, in Indian Wells, Lipton and Rome, his shortcomings were still apparent, especially at the other three Grand Slams. He faltered in the quarter-finals of the French, the first round at Wimbledon and the third round of the US Open. True, Rios did win six Tour tournaments, one more than anyone else, plus the Compaq Grand Slam Cup. But to have finished the year on top of the world rankings with a record that did not include at least one Grand Slam title would have intensified the debate about the credibility of the ranking system.

In the event, the climactic excitement – which would have reached fever pitch if Sampras and Rios had faced each other for the first time since the 1994 French Open – never materialised. Rios, who arrived in Hannover still fretting about a lower back problem which had forced him to retire two weeks earlier in Santiago, lost his opening round-robin match to Tim Henman. He retired altogether from the tournament minutes before he was due on court to face Greg Rusedski, a replacement for the also injured Andre Agassi.

Sampras received the news while he was sitting in his hotel room, all alone, having a bowl of pasta. If that initial moment of celebration was low key, what followed was riotous behaviour by his style. After trouncing Karol Kucera that evening 6–2 6–1 the usually reserved Sampras grabbed the bottle of champagne which was being poured over him and then did likewise to Mark Miles, chief executive officer of the ATP Tour, as well as tournament promoter Ion Tiriac, before spraying what was left over the world's media.

By his own high standards, Sampras had not had the best of years. On the way into Hannover, he had won only four tournaments, his lowest since 1991, while Rios had won seven. And on hard courts, Sampras collected one title while Rios, like Patrick Rafter, had won five. The turning point for the American had been Wimbledon. Winning there for a fifth time focussed his mind even more clearly on his determination to hold on to the number one ranking for a sixth time. 'I will do whatever it takes to bring that about,' he kept saying and proved it by choosing to play six consecutive weeks in Europe in the autumn – Basle, Vienna, Lyon, Stuttgart, Paris and Stockholm – something which would normally have been anathema to him.

Rios, Sampras, Rafter, Agassi, Moya and Corretja, in that order, were sure of places at Hannover with none of the anxiety surrounding the fight for the remaining two places, which at Stuttgart, with a month to go, had still offered the opportunity to eight others. In the event (partly thanks to Rafter's withdrawal and then Krajicek's decision not to take one of the last two places after he had earned it) three among that octet made it – Kucera, Kafelnikov and Henman. Even so the last two were not sure until the very last week of the regular circuit. But Henman did sufficient in Stockholm to clinch his place and Kafelnikov retained his title in Moscow to stay ahead of a second British candidate, Rusedski.

Sampras's semi-final defeat by Alex Corretja somewhat dimmed the American's joy over a triumph which most believe will never be surpassed – and reduced the points cushion he was able to take with him into 1999, when he will only need to retain the number one ranking for another 18 weeks to have been there longer than anyone else since Tour rankings began in 1973. Going into 1999, Sampras will have been world number one for a total of 253 weeks. Only Jimmy Connors, with 268 weeks and Ivan Lendl with 270, have been there longer.

Although Sampras only finished fifth on the list of players winning the most titles on the Tour (behind not only Rios and Rafter but also Agassi and Corretja), he became the first player since 1993 to win at least one title on all four of the game's principal surfaces. With victories on grass at Wimbledon, on indoor hard courts in Philadelphia, on carpet in Vienna and on clay at the AT&T Challenger in Atlanta Sampras underlined his versatility.

During 1997, four players had won titles on three different surfaces. In 1998 that was back down to just one – Corretja, runner-up to fellow Spaniard, Carlos Moya at the French Open, against whom he took a delighted revenge, from two sets down, in the final of Hannover. Corretja, 24, a right-hander from Barcelona, is one of the most unassuming and capable competitors in the game. His success in the year-ending Championships, an event which, it used to be said, clay court players had no chance of winning, was a significant landmark in the evolution of the game.

Under the exhortations and encouragement of their Davis Cup captain, Manuel Santana, who conquered the US Open on grass in 1965 and Wimbledon a year later, Spanish players have increasingly realised that to become acknowledged worldwide they need to show that they can win worldwide, and on a variety of surfaces. An all-Spanish indoor hard court final in Hannover was some evidence of that but Corretja's record was the most telling factor. Only one of his five titles was achieved on clay while all nine of the other titles collected by his six compatriots during the year were limited to clay.

Corretja's earlier titles were earned outdoors on hard courts in Dubai (also against a fellow Spaniard, Felix Mantilla); on clay in Gstaad when he thwarted yet another chance for Boris Becker to win a title on that surface; on outdoor hard in Indianapolis, where in successive rounds he tamed three of the power brokers – Mark Philippoussis, Greg Rusedski and Todd Martin before outlasting Agassi in the final; and on indoor carpet in Lyon, a win that underlined the all-round qualities which lifted him from 12th in the rankings to No.3.

Apart from such matters as attendance figures and television ratings, both of which almost inevitably vary according to the quality and appeal of domestic players in any particular tournament, two factors which help to provide evidence of the broad impact of tennis are the number of players who win tour titles and the number of different countries they represent, plus the number of nations who can boast at least one player among the top 100 in the world rankings.

This time there were 41 different winners of the 79 titles, representing 17 countries. That compared with 44 winners from 21 countries during 1997, while players from 33 different countries figured in the top 100 rankings at the end of the year. With the exception of an upsurge of talent in Argentina, where the number of players in this important bracket grew from one to five in the 12 months under review, the most significant difference over the year was that Spain's support crew behind top-tenners like third ranked Corretja and fifth ranked Moya, diminished appreciably.

At the end of 1997, there had been no fewer than 16 Spanish players in the top 100. Twelve months later there were ten, enough for them to remain the nation with the most players in this category – but only just. This was principally because of the continuing decline of the United States who are so dependent on Sampras and on Andre Agassi's efforts to sustain his comeback.

Nevertheless Agassi's five titles contributed to a US total of 14 tournament wins, three fewer than in 1997, though a figure that still enabled the Americans to stay joint top of that list alongside Spain, whose total also declined by one.

The United States finished the year with nine men in the top 100, one ahead of Australia, who, for the fourth consecutive year, finished with eight. France, Germany and Sweden all had seven, followed by the Czech Republic with six. Britain remained with just two, although that pays scant respect to the outstanding achievements of Tim Henman and Greg Rusedski who each won two tournaments.

Rusedski missed most of the summer after a freak ankle injury in June which forced him to retire during his first round match at Wimbledon. Yet he recovered strongly enough to become the first British player to win a Super 9 title, beating Sampras in a magnificent final at the Paris Indoors in Bercy. Henman and Rusedski finished seventh and ninth respectively to give Britain two players in the end of the year top ten rankings for the first time. Only Spain and the United States, two countries who have come to expect at least that degree of success, can match that.

A span of nine years separated the youngest from the oldest among the ten players who were first time winners in 1998. The slim, flaxen-haired Australian, Lleyton Hewitt, was only 16 years 10 months old, and ranked 550, when he beat both Agassi and his vastly more experienced fellow Australian, Jason Stoltenberg, to become the champion in Adelaide on the first week of the circuit. India's Leander Paes was 25 days past his 25th birthday when he won the first Tour singles title of his career, on the grass at Newport, Rhode Island, in July.

Persistence was also rewarded when four 24-year-olds entered the list of winners – Andrea Gaudenzi in Casablanca, Kenneth Carlsen in Hong Kong, Andrei Pavel in Tokyo and Scott Draper at Queen's Club. Others who tasted singles success for the first time were the 22-year-old Australian Andrew Ilie in Coral Springs, and three 20-year-olds, Dominik Hrbaty of Slovakia in San Marino, and the two Argentinians, Mariano Puerta in Palermo and Mariano Zabaleta in Bogota.

Although he struggled for a while to come to terms with the star status bestowed on him, Hewitt, who decided to concentrate exclusively on tennis rather than return to school, came through well enough to finish 113 in the world rankings, a 12 months improvement of 609. Indeed, but for the typhoon which prevented the singles and doubles finals being played in Hong Kong, Hewitt would have broken into the top 100 if he had beaten Daniel Nestor in the singles final.

Another Australian, Wayne Arthurs, helped by a first round upset of Kucera in Stockholm, improved his ranking even more. He climbed 964 places – from 1102 to 138 – but in a much less spectacular fashion. Leading the way among those who climbed at least 100 places and finished the year within the top 100, was Frenchman Arnaud Di Pasquale who soared from 579 to 81, an improvement of 498 places. Marat Safin, the strapping teenager from Russia, made as big an impact as any. After upsetting Agassi in the first round of the French Open with his huge serving and powerful baseline hitting, he then beat defending champion Gustavo Kuerten before losing over five sets in the fourth round to the rather more wily Frenchman, Cedric Pioline. Safin rose from 194 to 48th place.

The success of Jan-Michael Gambill in improving his ranking from 176 to 38 at least gave the United States a glimmer of hope. They needed it in a year when Italy embarrassed them at home in the Davis Cup after Sampras and Agassi had both refused to play.

Agassi, who had ended 1997 with an ignominous ranking for a player with such talent of 122, put himself back in serious contention by beating Sampras 6–2 6–4 in San Jose in February. It was his first title since August 1996 and gave a solid impression that he intended his comeback to be for real. Agassi went on to win four more finals and finished sixth in the rankings, though with the exception of Ostrava, where he did not have to meet any top ten players, all his successes came within the United States.

Once again Agassi's Grand Slam record was disappointing. Then a fall during practice on the eve of the ATP Tour Championship in Hannover forced him to withdraw after his first round-robin match. This produced an unsatisfactory end to a year which had been a mixture of encouragement and frustration for the American.

Hewitt, the only teenage title winner during the year was also the first of six wild card tournament winners. The others were Krajicek (St Peterburg), Jim Courier (Orlando), Rios (St Poelten),

Jonas Bjorkman (Nottingham) and, most signficantly of all, Sampras (Vienna). Sampras competed only through the generosity of former world number one, Boris Becker, who gave up his spot to the American. Sampras, who then won all five of his matches in straight sets was able to collect 358 priceless world ranking points.

The oldest winner of a 1998 Tour event was Sweden's Magnus Gustafsson who was 31 years 6 months old when he won in Bastad having already captured the Copenhagen title. Such has been Gustafsson's steadfastly professional approach over the years that he certainly deserved to be in a triumphant Davis Cup team. Playing in a final for the first time, Gustafsson was unlucky that his win over Andrea Gaudenzi was marred by an injury to the Italian as Sweden, the holders, finished winners for the seventh time in Milan.

If Wimbledon was the defining moment in Sampras's year, so it was to some extent in the doubles world. Whatever hopes Todd Woodbridge and Mark Woodforde held about retaining their premium status, faded after their record five-year vice-like grip on the title was wrenched free by Holland's Jacco Eltingh and Paul Haarhuis, in a classic final, 10–8 in the fifth.

From then on it became, unmistakeably, the year of the Flying Dutchmen, though ironically family responsibilities robbed both of them of the chance of a doubles Grand Slam. Haarhuis missed the Australian to be with his wife for the birth of their first child, while Eltingh was forced to withdraw on the eve of their first round match at the US Open when his wife went into labour with their first baby almost two weeks earlier than expected.

In their absence from Flushing Meadows Sandon Stolle created a little piece of tennis history. When he and the durable Cyril Suk took the title, it was the first time that the son of a former champion (Fred) had won any of the Grand Slam doubles titles.

Eltingh had won the Australian Open with Jonas Bjorkman, a thrilling triumph for a first-time partnership. It was with Haarhuis, though, that he enjoyed his finest successes in his last year before retirement from the Tour. At one stage they won 22 matches in succession, winning Philadelphia, Rotterdam, Barcelona, Monte Carlo and Roland Garros in succession. By winning Wimbledon together they became the first team in the Open era to have won all four Grand Slam doubles titles.

It is not always that the top team in the rankings wins the World Doubles Championship but in Phoenix in November, the Dutchmen wound things up in magnificent style by finishing with a 5–0 record. Having again beaten Woodbridge and Woodforde, who were appearing in the Championship for a record eighth time, one more than John McEnroe and Peter Fleming, they went on to defeat Ellis Ferreira and Rick Leach and Olivier Delaitre and Fabrice Santoro in the round-robin section. Those wins were followed by defeats of the Americans, Don Johnson and Francisco Montana in the semi-finals and then Mark Knowles and Daniel Nestor, 6–4 6–2 7–5 in the final.

'They gave us a real whipping,' said Nestor, who had also enjoyed a highly profitable year, for despite both he and his partner suffering injuries which meant they only competed together in 12 events, they finished only behind Paes and Mahesh Bhupathi, whose bid for the title in Phoenix ended when Paes was so troubled by a bone spur injury in his left heel that they had to withdraw before completing their round-robin commitments. It was a heartbreaking end to the year for the Indians, who had reached eight finals and won six titles, including Paris Bercy where they were the only team to beat Eltingh and Haarhuis in a final. They finished with an impressive 52–14 match record, compared with 41–13 in 1997.

'How can I top this?' said Eltingh after he and Haarhuis finished the year with a 46–4 record. He retired with 44 titles to his name, 39 of them with Haarhuis, which places them fifth equal on the all time list in the Open era, with Brian Gottfried and Raul Ramirez.

POINTS EXPLANATION

The tables opposite show the ranking points to be won at the four Grand Slam Championships and all tournaments on the ATP Tour – including Challengers with minimum prize money of $50,000. A player's ranking alone decides whether or not he is accepted directly into the main draw or the qualifying event at all Tour tournaments.

Identical points are awarded for singles and doubles. No points are awarded until a player has completed a match. Anyone who reaches the second round via a bye and then loses is considered to have lost in the first round and receives one point, but he does receive second round prize money. There are additional 'Bonus Points' awarded for beating players ranked between 1 and 200 in singles, or a team ranked between 2 and 400 in doubles. In addition to the points won in any tournament, a player or doubles team winning a place in the main draw via qualifying also receives half the points awarded to the second round loser in that tournament. Lucky Losers receive no qualifying points.

POINTS ALLOCATION

Category	Total Prize Money (All U.S.$)	W	F	S	Q	16	32	64	128
Grand Slams (averaged)	4.75 Million	750	537	325	163	82	41	20	1
World Championships (singles and doubles)	4 Million 3.75 million	720 710	(Points awarded to undefeated winner in Round Robin competition)						
Mercedes Super 9 (average)	2.25 Million	370	265	160	80	40	20	10	1
Championship Series	1.500 Million	320	228	135	68	34	17	1	–
	1.375 Million	310	220	130	65	33	17	1	–
	1.250 Million	300	213	125	63	32	16	1	–
	1.125 Million	290	205	120	60	30	15	1	–
	1.000 Million	280	198	115	58	29	15	1	–
	875,000	270	190	110	55	28	14	1	–
	750,000	260	183	105	53	27	14	1	–
	625,000	250	175	100	50	25	13	1	–
World Series	1.375 Million	250	183	115	58	29	15	1	
	1.250 Million	240	175	110	55	28	14	1	
	1.125 Million	230	168	105	53	27	14	1	
	1.000 Million	220	160	100	50	25	13	1	
	875,000	210	153	95	48	24	12	1	–
	750,000	200	145	90	45	23	12	1	–
	625,000	190	138	85	43	22	11	1	–
	550,000	180	130	80	40	20	10	1	–
	475,000	170	123	75	38	19	10	1	–
	400,000	160	115	70	35	18	9	1	–
	325,000	150	108	65	33	17	1	–	–
	250,000	140	100	60	30	15	1	–	–
	175,000	130	93	55	28	14	1	–	–
Challenger Series*	125,000 + Hosp.	100	73	45	23	12	1		
	125,000	90	65	40	20	10	1	–	–
	100,000	80	58	35	18	9	1	–	–
	75,000	70	50	30	15	8	1	–	–
	37,500 + Hosp.	65	47	28	14	7	1		
	50,000	60	43	25	13	7	1	–	–
Futures**	15,000 + Hosp.	20	15	10	5	1			
	15,000	16	12	8	4	1			
	10,000	12	9	6	3	1			

* Any Challenger providing hospitality will receive the points of the next highest prize money level. $25,000 + H receive points shown at $50,000. Monies shown are on-site prize amounts.

** $10,000 + Hosp. receive the same points as a $15,000 tournament. No points for first-round losers.

BONUS POINTS

(Double for all Grand Slam matches and best-of-five matches at Mercedes Super 9 tournaments. No points for a walk-over)

Singles

Ranking	Bonus Points
1	50
2-5	45
6-10	36
11-20	24
21-30	18
31-50	12
51-75	6
76-100	3
101-150	2
151-200	1

Doubles

Team Ranking	Team Bonus Points
2-3	50
4-10	45
11-20	36
21-40	24
41-60	18
61-100	12
101-150	6
151-200	3
201-300	2
301-400	1

GRAND SLAM CHAMPIONSHIPS AND ATP TOUR 1998

Date	*Venue*	*Surface*	*Singles final*	*Doubles winners*
5–11 Jan	Adelaide	Hard	L. Hewitt d. J. Stoltenberg 3–6 6–3 7–6	Eagle/Florent
5–11 Jan	Doha	Hard	P. Korda d. F. Santoro 6–0 6–3	Bhupathi/Paes
12–18 Jan	Auckland	Hard	M. Rios d. R. Fromberg 4–6 6–4 7–6	Galbraith/Steven
12–18 Jan	Sydney	Hard	K. Kucera d. T. Henman 7–5 6–4	Woodbridge/ Woodforde
19 Jan–1 Feb	**Australian Open**	**Hard**	**P. Korda d. M. Rios 6–2 6–2 6–2**	**Bjorkman/Eltingh**
2–8 Feb	Split	Carpet	G. Ivanisevic d. G. Rusedski 7–6 7–6	Damm/Novak
2–8 Feb	Marseille	Hard	T. Enqvist d. Y. Kafelnikov 6–4 6–1	Johnson/Montana
9–15 Feb	Dubai	Hard	A. Corretja d. F. Mantilla 7–6 6–1	Bhupathi/Paes
9–15 Feb	San Jose, CA	Hard	A. Agassi d. P. Sampras 6–2 6–4	Woodbridge/ Woodforde
9–15 Feb	St. Petersburg	Clay	R. Krajicek d. M. Rosset 6–4 7–6	Kulti/Tillstrom
16–22 Feb	Antwerp	Hard	G. Rusedski d. M. Rosset 7–6 3–6 6–1 6–4	W. Ferreira/Kafelnikov
16–22 Feb	Memphis, TN	Hard	M. Philippoussis d. M. Chang 6–3 6–2	Woodbridge/ Woodforde
23 Feb–1 Mar	London	Carpet	Y. Kafelnikov d. C. Pioline 7–5 6–4	Damm/Grabb
23 Feb–1 Mar	Philadelphia, PA	Hard	P. Sampras d. T. Enqvist 7–5 7–6	Eltingh/Haarhuis
2–8 Mar	Rotterdam	Clay	J. Siemerink d. T. Johansson 7–6 6–2	Eltingh/Haarhuis
2–8 Mar	Scottsdale, AZ	Hard	A. Agassi d. J. Stoltenberg 6–4 7–6	Suk/Tebbutt
9–15 Mar	Indian Wells, CA	Hard	M. Rios d. G. Rusedski 6–3 6–7 7–6 6–4	Bjorkman/Rafter
9–15 Mar	Copenhagen	Clay	M. Gustafsson d. D. Prinosil 3–6 6–1 6–1	Kempers/Oosting
19–29 Mar	Key Biscayne, FL	Hard	M. Rios d. A. Agassi 7–5 6–3 6–4	E. Ferreira/Leach
23–29 Mar	Casablanca	Clay	A. Gaudenzi d. A. Calatrava 6–4 5–7 6–4	Gaudenzi/Nargiso
6–12 Apr	Estoril	Clay	A. Berasategui d. T. Muster 3–6 6–1 6–3	Johnson/Montana
6–12 Apr	Madras	Hard	P. Rafter d. M. Tillstrom 6–3 6–4	Bhupathi/Paes
6–12 Apr	Hong Kong	Hard	K. Carlsen d. B. Black 6–2 6–0	Black/O'Brien
13–19 Apr	Tokyo	Hard	A. Pavel d. B. Black 6–3 6–4	Lareau/Nestor
13–19 Apr	Barcelona	Clay	T. Martin d. A. Berasategui 6–2 1–6 6–3 6–2	Eltingh/Haarhuis
20–26 Apr	Monte Carlo	Clay	C. Moya d. C. Pioline 6–3 6–0 7–5	Eltingh/Haarhuis
20–26 Apr	Orlando, CL	Clay	J. Courier d. M. Chang 7–5 3–6 7–5	Stafford/Ullyett
27 Apr–3 May	Munich	Clay	T. Enqvist d. A. Agassi 6–7 7–6 6–3	Woodbridge/ Woodforde
27 Apr–3 May	Prague	Clay	F. Meligeni d. C. Dosedel 6–1 6–4	Arthurs/Kratzmann
27 Apr–3 May	Atlanta, GA	Clay	P. Sampras d. J. Stoltenberg 6–7 6–3 7–6	E. Ferreira/Haygarth
4–10 May	Hamburg	Clay	A. Costa d. A. Corretja 6–2 6–0 1–0 ret	Johnson/Montana
4–10 May	Coral Springs, FL	Clay	A. Ilie d. D. Sanguinetti 7–5 6–4	Stafford/Ullyett
11–17 May	Rome	Clay	M. Rios d. A. Costa w/o	Bhupathi/Paes
18–24 May	St. Polten	Clay	M. Rios d. V. Spadea 6–2 6–0	Grabb/MacPherson
25 May–7 Jun	**Roland Garros**	**Clay**	**C. Moya d. A. Corretja 6–3 7–5 6–3**	**Eltingh/Haarhuis**
8–14 Jun	Halle	Grass	Y. Kafelnikov d. M. Larsson 6–4 6–4	E. Ferreira/Leach
8–14 Jun	Queen's	Grass	S. Draper d. L. Tieleman 7–6 6–4	Woodbridge/ Woodforde v Bjorkman/Rafter – not played
8–14 Jun	Bologna	Clay	J. Alonso d. K. Alami 6–1 6–4	Coupe/Rosner
15–21 Jun	's-Hertogenbosch	Grass	P. Rafter d. M. Damm 7–6 6–2	Raoux/Siemerink
15–21 Jun	Nottingham	Grass	J. Bjorkman d. B. Black 6–3 6–2	Gimelstob/Talbot
22 Jun–5 Jul	**Wimbledon**	**Grass**	**P. Sampras d. G. Ivanisevic 6–7 7–6 6–4 3–6 6–2**	**Eltingh/Haarhuis**
6–12 Jul	Gstaad	Clay	A. Corretja d. B. Becker 6–7 5–7 3–6	Kuerten/Meligeni
6–12 Jul	Bastad	Clay	M. Gustafsson d. A. Medvedev 6–2 6–3	Gustafsson/ Larsson
6–12 Jul	Newport, RI	Grass	L. Paes d. N. Godwin 6–3 6–2	Flach/Stolle
20–26 Jul	Stuttgart	Clay	G. Kuerten d. K. Kucera 4–6 6–2 6–4	Delaitre/Santoro
20–26 Jul	Washington, DC	Hard	A. Agassi d. S. Draper 6–2 6–0	Stafford/Ullyett
27 Jul–2 Aug	Kitzbuhel	Clay	A. Costa d. A. Gaudenzi 6–2 1–6 6–2 3–6 6–1	Kempers/Orsanic
27 Jul–2 Aug	Umag	Clay	B. Ulihrach d. M. Norman 6–3 7–6	Broad/Norval
27 Jul–2 Aug	Los Angeles, CA	Hard	A. Agassi d. T. Henman 6–4 6–4	Rafter/Stolle
3–9 Aug	Toronto	Hard	P. Rafter d. R. Krajicek 7–6 6–4	Damm/Grabb
3–9 Aug	Amsterdam	Clay	M. Norman d. R. Fromberg 6–3 6–3 2–6 6–4	Eltingh/Haarhuis
10–16 Aug	Cincinnati, OH	Hard	P. Rafter d. P. Sampras 1–6 7–6 6–4	Knowles/Nestor
10–16 Aug	San Marino	Clay	D. Hrbaty d. M. Puerta 6–2 7–5	Novak/Rikl

17–23 Aug	Indianapolis, IN	Hard	A. Corretja d. A. Agassi 2–6 6–2 6–3	Novak/Rikl
17–23 Aug	New Haven, CT	Hard	K. Kucera d. G. Ivanisevic 6–4 5–7 6–2	Arthurs/Tramacchi
24–30 Aug	Boston, MA	Hard	M. Chang d. P. Haarhuis 1–3 6–4	Eltingh/Haarhuis
24–30 Aug	Long Island, NY	Hard	P. Rafter d. F. Mantilla 7–6 6–2	Alonso/J. Sanchez
31 Aug–13 Sept	**US Open**	**Hard**	**P. Rafter d. M. Philippoussis 6–3 3–6 6–2 6–0**	**Stolle/Suk**
14–20 Sept	Bournemouth	Clay	F. Mantilla d. A. Costa 6–3 7–5	Broad/Ullyett
14–21 Sept	Bucharest	Clay	F. Clavet d. A. Di Pasquale 6–2 4–6 7–5	Pavel/Trifu
14–20 Sept	Tashkent	Hard	T. Henman d. Y. Kafelnikov 7–5 6–4	Pescosolido/Tieleman
28 Sept–4 Oct	**Grand Slam Cup**	**Carpet**	**M. Rios d. A. Agassi 6–4 2–6 7–6 5–7 6–3**	
28 Sept–4 Oct	Mallorca	Clay	G. Kuerten d. C. Moya 6–7 6–2 6–3	Albano/Orsanic
28 Sept–4 Oct	Toulouse	Hard	J. Siemerink d. G. Rusedski 6–4 6–4	Delaitre/Santoro
6–11 Oct	Basle	Carpet	T. Henman d. A. Agassi 6–4 6–3 3–6 6–4	Delaitre/Santoro
5–12 Oct	Shanghai	Hard	M. Chang d. G. Ivanisevic 4–6 6–1 6–2	Bhupathi/Paes
5–11 Oct	Palermo	Clay	M. Puerta d. F. Squillari 6–3 6–2	Johnson/Montana
12–18 Oct	Vienna	Clay	P. Sampras d. K. Kucera 6–3 7–6 6–1	Kafelnikov/Vacek
12–18 Oct	Singapore	Carpet	M. Rios d. M. Woodforde 6–4 6–2	Woodbridge/ Woodforde
19–25 Oct	Ostrava	Carpet	A. Agassi d. J. Kroslak 6–2 3–6 6–3	Kiefer/Prinosil
19–25 Oct	Lyon	Carpet	A. Corretja d. T. Haas 2–6 7–6 6–1	Delaitre/Santoro
26 Oct–1 Nov	Stuttgart	Carpet	R. Krajicek d. Y. Kafelnikov 6–4 6–3 6–3	Lareau/O'Brien
26 Oct–1 Nov	Mexico City	Clay	J. Novak d. X. Malisse 6–3 6–3	Novak/Rikl
2–8 Nov	Paris	Carpet	G. Rusedski d. P. Sampras 6–4 7–6 6–3	Bhupathi/Paes
2–8 Nov	Bogota	Clay	M. Zabaleta d. R. Delgado 6–4 6–4	Del Rio/Puerta
9–15 Nov	Moscow	Carpet	Y. Kafelnikov d. G. Ivanisevic 7–6 7–6	Palmer/Tarango
9–15 Nov	Stockholm	Hard	T. Martin d. T. Johansson 6–3 6–4 6–4	Kulti/Tillstrom
9–15 Nov	Santiago	Clay	F. Clavet d. Y. El Aynaoui 6–2 6–4	Hood/Prieto
16–22 Nov	Hartford, CT	Carpet		Eltingh/Haarhuis
23–29 Nov	Hanover	Hard	A. Corretja d. C. Moya 3–6 3–6 7–5 6–3 7–5	
4–6 Dec	**Davis Cup by NEC Final**	**Carpet**	**Sweden d. Italy 4–1**	

Nicolas Kiefer was a member of Germany's winning World Team Cup squad and maintained his place among the top 40 with another solid year. (Stephen Wake)

PLAYERS NATIONALITIES AND BIRTHDAYS (MEN)

The following players have competed in the 1998 Grand Slam Championships, the ATP Tour and Davis Cup ties. (Birthdays dd-mm-yy.)

Surname / Forename	*Nation*	*DOB*
ADAMS, David	RSA	05-01-70
AERTS, Nelson	BRA	25-04-63
AGASSI, Andre	USA	29-04-70
AGENOR, Ronald	HAI	13-11-64
AL-ALAWI, Sultan-Khalfan	QAT	16-03-77
ALAMI, Karim	MAR	24-05-73
ALBANO, Pablo	ARG	11-04-67
ALDI, Francesco	ITA	17-09-81
ALONSO-PINTOR, Julian	ESP	02-08-77
ALVAREZ, Emilio	ESP	15-11-72
ANCIC, Ivica	CRO	29-10-79
ANDERSEN, Jan-Frode	NOR	29-08-72
ANGELINI, Pietro	ITA	07-12-71
ANNACONE, Paul	USA	20-03-63
APELL, Jan	SWE	04-11-69
ARAZI, Hicham	MAR	19-10-73
ARDINGHI, Massimo	ITA	06-03-71
ARIAS, James 'Jimmy'	USA	16-08-64
ARNOLD, Lucas	ARG	12-10-74
ARNOLD, Milton	USA	15-07-74
ARRIENS, Carsten	GER	11-04-69
ARTHURS, Wayne	AUS	18-03-71
AUFFRAY, Charles	FRA	24-02-73
AUZOUX, Yann	CMR	15-05-72
BACHELOT, Jean-Francois	FRA	11-06-77
BACHERT, Boris	GER	16-04-81
BALCELLS, Juan	ESP	20-06-75
BALE, Lan	RSA	07-09-69
BARNARD, Marius	RSA	20-01-69
BARTHEZ, Lionel	FRA	18-05-67
BASTL, George	SUI	01-04-75
BECKER, Boris	GER	22-11-67
BEHR, Noam	ISR	13-10-75
BEHRENS, Wilhelm 'Bill'	USA	26-06-70
BELOBRAJDIC, Allen	AUS	18-09-76
BERASATEGUI, Alberto	ESP	28-06-73
BERGH, Fredrik	SWE	22-04-75
BERGH, Rikard	SWE	14-06-66
BERTOLINI, Massimo	ITA	30-05-74
BHUPATHI, Mahesh	IND	07-06-74
BISTRIAVICHUS, Vladimir	UZB	09-09-80
BJORKMAN, Jonas	SWE	23-03-72
BLACK, Byron	ZIM	06-10-69
BLACK, Wayne	ZIM	14-11-73
BLAKE, James	USA	28-12-79
BLAKE, Thomas	USA	29-12-76
BLANCO, Galo	ESP	08-10-76
BLUMAUER, Georg	AUT	16-07-74
BOETSCH, Arnaud	FRA	01-04-69
BOUTTER, Julien	FRA	05-04-74
BOWEN, Devin	USA	18-05-72
BRAASCH, Karsten	GER	14-07-67
BRACCIALI, Daniele	ITA	10-01-78
BRANDI, Cristian	ITA	10-06-70
BROAD, Neil	GBR	20-11-66
BROWNE, Federico	ARG	07-04-76
BRUGUERA, Sergio 'Sergi'	ESP	16-01-71
BRYAN, Mike	USA	29-04-78

Surname / Forename	*Nation*	*DOB*
BRYAN, Robert 'Bob'	USA	29-04-78
BUCHMAYER, Thomas	AUT	14-02-71
BURGSMULLER, Lars	GER	06-12-75
BURILLO, Jordi	ESP	07-12-72
BURRIEZA, Oscar	ESP	22-07-75
CABELLO, Francisco	ARG	06-12-72
CALATRAVA, Alejandro 'Alex'	ESP	14-06-73
CALDWELL, David	USA	13-06-74
CALUGARU, Marius	ROM	01-04-76
CAMPBELL, Steve	USA	22-10-70
CAMPORESE, Omar	ITA	08-05-68
CANAS, Guillermo	ARG	25-11-77
CARATTI, Cristiano	ITA	24-05-70
CARBONELL, Tomas	ESP	07-08-68
CARLSEN, Kenneth	DEN	17-04-73
CARLSSON, Marcio	BRA	24-01-75
CARRASCO, Juan-Ignacio	ESP	09-07-74
CARRETERO, Roberto	ESP	30-08-75
CASTRICHELLA, Gabrio	ITA	24-10-72
CATAR, Tomas	SVK	19-01-77
CHAEN, Tetsuya	JPN	05-11-73
CHANG, Carl	USA	13-02-69
CHANG, Michael	USA	22-02-72
CHERKASOV, Andrei	RUS	04-07-70
CHESNOKOV, Andrei	RUS	02-02-66
CHIDZIKWE, Genius	ZIM	03-08-79
CHIUDINELLI, Marco	SUI	10-09-81
CLAVET, Francisco	ESP	24-10-68
CLEMENT, Arnaud	FRA	17-12-77
COBOLLI, Stefano	ITA	02-03-77
COMMANDEUR, Malte	GER	09-02-78
CONDE, Jose-Antonio 'Pepe'	ESP	11-03-70
CORRETJA, Alex	ESP	11-04-74
CORTES, Jaime	COL	26-07-65
COSAC, Gheorghe 'George'	ROM	26-01-68
COSTA, Albert	ESP	25-06-75
COSTA, Carlos	ESP	22-04-68
COUPE, Brandon	USA	11-04-72
COURIER, James 'Jim'	USA	17-08-70
COUTO, Emanuel	POR	06-08-73
COWAN, Barry 'Baz'	GBR	25-08-74
CRACA, Marcello	GER	27-10-74
CUNHA-SILVA, Joao	POR	27-11-67
DAMM, Martin	CZE	01-08-72
DAVIDS, Hendrik-Jan	NED	30-01-69
DAVIS, Scott	USA	27-08-62
DE JAGER, John-Laffnie	RSA	17-03-73
DE WULF, Filip	BEL	15-03-72
DECKER, Chris	USA	19-06-71
DEL RIO, Diego	ARG	04-09-72
DELAITRE, Olivier	FRA	01-06-67
DELGADO, James 'Jamie'	GBR	21-03-77
DELGADO, Ramon	PAR	14-11-76
DENT, Taylor	USA	24-04-81
DEREPASKO, Artem	RUS	26-01-79
DI LUCIA, David 'Dave'	USA	15-01-70
DI PASQUALE, Arnaud	FRA	11-02-79
DIAZ, Jacobo	ESP	11-07-76

Surname / Forename	*Nation*	*DOB*
DIER, Dirk	GER	16-02-72
DINATA, Dede Suhendar	INA	14-12-69
DJORDJEVIC, Nebojsa	YUG	24-04-73
DOSEDEL, Ctislav 'Slava'	CZE	14-08-70
DOYLE, Grant	AUS	09-01-74
DRAPER, Mark	AUS	11-02-71
DRAPER, Scott	AUS	05-06-74
DREEKMANN, Hendrik	GER	29-01-75
DU PUIS, Anthony	FRA	24-02-73
DUMANIC, Josip 'Jozo'	CRO	12-12-74
DZELDE, Girts	LAT	16-07-63
EAGLE, Joshua 'Josh'	AUS	10-05-73
EL AAREJ, Mounir	MAR	16-06-77
EL AYNAOUI, Younes	MAR	12-09-71
EL SAWY, Tamer	EGY	11-02-72
ELLWOOD, Ben	AUS	12-03-76
ELTINGH, Jacco	NED	29-08-70
ENQVIST, Thomas	SWE	13-03-74
ERLICH, Eyal	ISR	01-01-77
ESCUDE, Nicolas	FRA	03-04-76
ETLIS, Gaston	ARG	04-11-74
FARCAS, Remus	ROM	11-12-71
FARRINGTON, John	BAH	26-09-58
FEDERER, Roger	SUI	08-08-81
FERREIRA, Ellis	RSA	19-02-70
FERREIRA, Wayne	RSA	15-09-71
FETTERLEIN, Frederik	DEN	11-07-70
FILIPPINI, Marcelo	URU	04-08-67
FLACH, Doug	USA	10-08-70
FLEURIAN, Jean-Philippe	FRA	11-09-65
FLORENT, Andrew	AUS	24-10-70
FLYGT, Kalle	SWE	15-06-76
FORGET, Guy	FRA	04-01-65
FOSTER, Andrew	GBR	16-03-72
FREDRIKSSON, Patrik	SWE	16-05-73
FRIEDL, Leos	CZE	01-01-77
FROMBERG, Richard	AUS	28-04-70
FURLAN, Renzo	ITA	17-05-70
GALBRAITH, Patrick	USA	16-04-67
GALIMBERTI, Giorgio	ITA	05-09-76
GAMBILL, Jan-Michael	USA	03-06-77
GAMBILL, Troy	USA	30-04-82
GAMONAL, Hermes	CHI	31-05-77
GANIEV, Timur	UZB	24-10-75
GAUDENZI, Andrea	ITA	30-07-73
GEVORGYAN, Tsolak	ARM	18-08-75
GILBERT, Rodolphe	FRA	12-12-68
GIMELSTOB, Justin	USA	26-01-77
GODWIN, Neville	RSA	31-01-75
GOELLNER, Marc	GER	22-09-70
GOLDSTEIN, Paul	USA	04-08-76
GOLMARD, Jerome	FRA	09-09-73
GOMEZ, Andres	ECU	27-02-60
GONZALEZ, Fernando	CHI	29-07-80
GOULD, Jed	AUS	19-02-79
GOULD, Nicholas 'Nick'	GBR	09-07-72
GRABB, James 'Jim'	USA	14-04-64
GRANT, Geoffrey 'Geoff'	USA	16-01-70
GREENHALGH, James	NZL	19-02-75
GROEN, Sander	NED	16-06-68
GROSJEAN, Sebastien	FRA	29-05-78
GROSS, Oliver	GER	17-06-73
GUARDIOLA, Thierry	FRA	07-08-71
GUMY, Hernan	ARG	05-03-72
GUSTAFSSON, Magnus	SWE	03-01-67
HAARHUIS, Paul	NED	19-02-66
HAAS, Thomas 'Tommy'	GER	03-04-78
HADAD, Amir	ISR	17-02-78
HADAD, Mauricio	COL	07-12-71
HAGGARD, Christopher 'Chris'	RSA	28-04-71
HAMADEH, Ali	LIB	05-09-74
HANTSCHK, Markus	GER	19-11-77
HARSANYI, Paul	USA	30-12-74
HAUSMAN, Joshua	USA	16-01-76
HAYGARTH, Brent	RSA	27-12-67
HENMAN, Tim	GBR	06-09-74
HERNANDEZ, Alejandro 'Alex'	MEX	01-10-77
HERRERA, Luis-Enrique	MEX	27-08-71
HEUBERGER, Ivo	SUI	19-02-76
HEWITT, Lleyton	AUS	24-02-81
HILPERT, Marcus	GER	01-07-71
HIPFL, Markus	AUT	26-04-78
HIPPENSTEEL, KJ	USA	08-05-80
HIPPERDINGER, Diego	ARG	17-01-77
HIRSZON, Sasa	CRO	14-07-72
HJARRAND, Lars	NOR	19-07-73
HO, Thomas 'Tommy'	USA	17-06-73
HOLMES, James 'Jamie'	AUS	04-05-73
HOOD, Mariano	ARG	14-08-73
HORNA, Luis	PER	14-09-80
HRBATY, Dominik	SVK	04-01-78
HROMEC, Martin	SVK	09-01-76
HUET, Stephane	FRA	25-04-71
HUMPHRIES, Scott	USA	26-05-76
HUNT, Alistair	NZL	11-11-72
ILIE, Andrew	AUS	18-04-76
IMAZ-RUIZ, Jose 'Pepe'	ESP	30-05-74
ISHII, Hiroki	JPN	27-07-71
ISHII, Yaoki	JPN	29-04-77
ISLAMBEGOVIC, Denan	CRO	15-10-75
IVANISEVIC, Goran	CRO	13-09-71
IVANOV-SMOLENSKY, Kerill	RUS	19-01-81
IWABUCHI, Satoshi	JPN	07-10-75
JABALI, Roberto	BRA	16-05-70
JEAN-PIERRE, Julien	FRA	10-03-80
JENSEN, Luke	USA	18-06-66
JENSEN, Murphy	USA	30-10-68
JOHANSSON, Joakim	SWE	01-07-82
JOHANSSON, Thomas	SWE	24-03-75
JOHNSON, Donald	USA	09-09-68
JONSSON, Fredrik	SWE	28-03-77
JOYCE, Michael	USA	01-02-73
KAFELNIKOV, Yevgeny	RUS	18-02-74
KANEKO, Hideki	JPN	06-03-74
KARAM, Sean	LIB	24-08-69
KARBACHER, Bernd	GER	03-04-68
KARLOVIC, Ivo	CRO	28-02-79
KATO, Jun	SUI	25-10-80
KEIL, Mark	USA	03-06-67
KEMPERS, Tom	NED	01-06-69
KERR, Jordan	AUS	26-10-79
KETOLA, Tuomas	FIN	21-02-75
KIEFER, Nicolas	GER	05-07-77
KILDERRY, Paul	AUS	11-04-73
KIM, Dong-Hyun	KOR	08-10-78
KIM, Nam-Hoon	KOR	08-03-70
KINNEAR, Kent	USA	30-11-66
KIRTANE, Sandeep	IND	27-10-73
KITINOV, Aleksandar	MKD	13-01-71
KNIPPSCHILD, Jens	GER	15-02-75

Surname / Forename	*Nation*	*DOB*
KNOWLES, Mark	BAH	04-09-71
KOENIG, Robbie	RSA	05-07-71
KOHLMANN, Michael	GER	11-01-74
KOKAVEC, Robert 'Bobby'	CAN	17-05-76
KOLL, Helge	NOR	31-05-75
KORDA, Petr	CZE	23-01-68
KOUBEK, Stefan	AUT	02-01-77
KOVACKA, Petr	CZE	23-12-71
KOVES, Gabor	HUN	01-07-70
KRAJAN, Zeljko	CRO	03-02-79
KRAJICEK, Richard	NED	06-12-71
KRALERT, Petr	CZE	20-10-79
KRATZMANN, Andrew	AUS	03-11-71
KRIEK, Johan	USA	05-04-58
KRONEMANN, Trevor	USA	03-09-68
KROSLAK, Jan	SVK	17-10-74
KRUPA, Tomas	CZE	14-11-72
KUCERA, Karol	SVK	04-03-74
KUERTEN, Gustavo	BRA	10-09-76
KULTI, Nicklas	SWE	22-04-71
KUTSENKO, Vadim	UZB	16-03-77
LAPENTTI, Giovanni	ECU	25-01-83
LAPENTTI, Nicolas	ECU	13-08-76
LAREAU, Sebastien	CAN	27-04-73
LARKHAM, Todd	AUS	13-10-74
LAROSE, Simon	CAN	28-06-78
LARSEN, Thomas	DEN	15-07-75
LARSSON, Magnus	SWE	25-03-70
LAVALLE, Leonardo	MEX	14-07-67
LAVERGNE, Regis	FRA	28-01-74
LEACH, Richard 'Rick'	USA	28-12-64
LEE, Hyung-Taik	KOR	03-01-76
LEE, Martin	GBR	13-01-78
LENHO, Tommi	FIN	17-09-75
LEVY, Harel	ISR	05-08-78
LI, Bruce	CHN	29-04-76
LIUKKO, Ville	FIN	24-05-74
LJUBICIC, Ivan	CRO	19-03-79
LOBO, Luis	ARG	09-11-70
LOPEZ, Feliciano	ESP	20-09-81
LOPEZ-MORON, Alex	ESP	28-11-70
LU, Ling	CHN	18-01-74
LUXA, Petr	CZE	03-03-72
LUZZI, Frederico	ITA	03-01-80
MACLAGAN, Miles	GBR	23-09-74
MACPHERSON, David	AUS	03-07-67
MACPHIE, Brian	USA	11-05-72
MAGGI, Fabio	ITA	30-01-75
MAKHKAMOV, Abdul-Hamid	UZB	19-04-76
MALISSE, Xavier	BEL	19-07-80
MAMIIT, Cecil	USA	27-06-76
MANDL, Gerald	AUT	12-11-70
MANKAD, Harsh	IND	10-11-79
MANTA, Lorenzo	SUI	16-09-74
MANTILLA, Felix	ESP	23-09-74
MARIN, Juan-Antonio	CRC	02-03-75
MARQUES, Nuno	POR	09-04-70
MARTELLI, Marzio	ITA	14-12-71
MARTIN, Alberto	ESP	20-08-78
MARTIN, David	USA	22-02-81
MARTIN, Todd	USA	08-07-70
MARTINEZ, Bernardo	MEX	21-08-72
MARTINEZ, Carlos	ESP	05-09-74
MARX, Guillaume	FRA	24-05-72
MAS, Jordi	ESP	31-10-71

Surname / Forename	*Nation*	*DOB*
MASSU, Nicolas	CHI	10-11-79
MASUDA, Kentaro	JPN	26-08-71
MATHESON, Ross	GBR	27-05-70
MATSUOKA, Shuzo	JPN	06-11-67
McENROE, Patrick	USA	01-07-66
McGUIRE, Wade	USA	19-08-69
MEDICA, Eduardo	ARG	10-02-76
MEDVEDEV, Andrei	UKR	31-08-74
MELIGENI, Fernando	BRA	12-04-71
MENESCHINCHERI, Marco	ITA	25-04-72
MERINGOFF, Todd	USA	07-05-74
MERINOV, Andrei	RUS	23-06-71
MERKLEIN, Mark	USA	28-06-72
MESSMER, Thomas	GER	25-11-79
MESSORI, Filippo	ITA	12-11-73
MIDDLETON, Todd 'T. J.'	USA	02-05-68
MILLIGAN, Luke	GBR	06-08-76
MIRNYI, Maxim 'Max'	BLR	06-07-77
MIYACHI, Kotaro	JPN	18-02-74
MOGGIO, Philippe	COL	23-03-73
MOLDOVAN, Ion	ROM	17-01-78
MONTANA, Francisco	USA	05-11-69
MOR, Lior	ISR	29-02-76
MOREJON, Luis	ECU	28-03-73
MORTIMER, Dentry	BAH	30-06-82
MOTA, Bernardo	POR	14-06-71
MOTEVASSEL, Oren	USA	26-08-67
MOTOMURA, Gouichi	JPN	25-12-73
MOYA, Carlos	ESP	27-08-76
MUNOZ-HERNANDEZ, Joaquin Jr.	ESP	04-01-75
MUNROE, Bjorn	BAH	13-11-78
MUSTER, Thomas	AUT	02-10-67
MUTIS, Olivier	FRA	02-02-78
NAINKIN, David	RSA	20-09-70
NARGISO, Diego	ITA	15-03-70
NATEKAR, Gaurav	IND	04-04-72
NAVARRA, Mose	ITA	18-07-74
NAVARRO, Salvador	ESP	08-01-77
NEMECEK, Libor	CZE	26-10-68
NESTOR, Daniel	CAN	04-09-72
NICOLAS, Eduardo	ESP	22-09-72
NIELSEN, Mark	NZL	08-10-77
NIEMEYER, Frederic	CAN	24-04-76
NIJSSEN, Tom	NED	01-10-64
NORMAN, Dick	BEL	01-03-71
NORMAN, Magnus	SWE	30-05-76
NORVAL, Pieter 'Piet'	RSA	07-04-70
NOTEBOOM, Stephen	NED	31-07-69
NOVAK, Jiri	CZE	22-03-75
NURMINEN, Tapio 'Tommi'	FIN	12-10-75
NYBORG, Peter	SWE	12-12-69
NYDAHL, Tomas	SWE	21-03-68
O'BRIEN, Alex	USA	07-03-70
OGORODOV, Oleg	UZB	16-07-72
OLHOVSKIY, Andrei	RUS	15-04-66
ONCINS, Jaime	BRA	16-06-70
ONDRUSKA, Marcos	RSA	18-12-72
ONODA, Michihisa	JPN	31-01-78
OOSTING, Menno	NED	17-05-64
ORSANIC, Daniel	ARG	11-06-68
ORTIZ, Oscar	MEX	09-05-73
OSORIO, Marco-Aurelio	MEX	01-04-72
PAES, Leander	IND	17-06-73
PAINTER, Andrew	AUS	18-07-75
PALA, Petr	CZE	02-10-75

Following ankle surgery, Wayne Ferreira had only the Antwerp doubles title (with Kafelnikov) to show for a lot of effort in 1998, but the South African was one of the few men to beat Pete Sampras twice. (Michael Cole)

Surname / Forename	*Nation*	*DOB*
PALMER, Jared	USA	02-07-71
PARK, Andrew	USA	02-01-80
PARMAR, Arvind	GBR	22-03-78
PARROTT, Travis	USA	16-08-80
PATE, David	USA	16-04-62
PAVEL, Andrei	ROM	27-01-74
PEQUERY, Jean-Michel	FRA	30-05-78
PERLANT, Jean-Baptiste	FRA	22-02-77
PESCARIU, Dinu	ROM	12-04-74
PESCOSOLIDO, Stefano	ITA	13-06-71
PETCHEY, Mark	GBR	01-08-70
PETERSON, Adam	USA	16-07-74
PETROVIC, Dejan	AUS	03-04-78
PHAU, Bjorn	GER	04-10-79
PHILIPPOUSSIS, Mark	AUS	07-11-76
PIMEK, Libor	BEL	03-08-63
PIOLINE, Cedric	FRA	15-06-69
PLAMBERGER, Udo	AUT	01-01-71
POLIAKOV, Dimitri	UKR	19-01-68
PORTAS, Albert	ESP	15-11-73
POZZI, Gianluca	ITA	17-06-65
PRAHLAD, Srinath	IND	10-01-73
PRETZSCH, Axel	GER	16-06-76
PRIETO, Sebastian	ARG	19-05-75
PRINOSIL, David	GER	09-03-73
PRINTZLAU, Jonathan	DEN	07-10-76
PUENTES, German	ESP	18-12-72
PUERTA, Mariano	ARG	19-09-78
PURCELL, Mel	USA	18-07-59
RADULESCU, Alexandru 'Alex'	GER	07-12-74
RAFTER, Patrick 'Pat'	AUS	28-12-72
RAN, Eyal	ISR	21-11-72
RANDALL, Dave	USA	08-05-67
RANDJELOVIC, Steven 'Steve'	AUS	21-04-75
RAOUX, Guillaume	FRA	14-02-70
RASBERGER, Emanuel	CRO	03-06-72
RASCON, Juan-Luis 'Tati'	ESP	02-03-71
RATURANDANG, Andrian	INA	29-07-76
REHMANN, Lars	GER	21-05-75
REICHEL, Alexander 'Alex'	USA	09-03-71
RENEBERG, Richard 'Richey'	USA	05-10-65
RICHARDSON, Andrew	GBR	14-03-74
RIKL, David	CZE	27-02-71
RINCON, Eduardo	COL	22-03-76
RINCON, Mario	COL	13-12-67
RIOS, Marcelo	CHI	26-12-75
ROBICHAUD, Jocelyn	CAN	08-04-78
RODITI, David	MEX	30-11-73
RODRIGUEZ, Martin	ARG	18-12-69
ROIG, Francisco	ESP	01-04-68
ROSNER, Paul	RSA	11-12-72
ROSSET, Marc	SUI	07-11-70
ROUX, Lionel	FRA	12-04-73
ROVAS, Nikos	GRE	20-09-77
ROY, Marcos	ESP	11-03-74
RUAH, Maurice	VEN	19-02-71
RUSEDSKI, Gregory 'Greg'	GBR	06-09-73
RUSSELL, Mike	USA	01-05-78
RUUD, Christian	NOR	24-08-72
RYBALKO, Andrei	UKR	05-06-72
SA, Andre	BRA	06-05-77
SABAU, Razvan	ROM	18-06-77
SAFIN, Marat	RUS	27-01-80
SALZENSTEIN, Jeff	USA	14-10-73
SAMPRAS, Pete	USA	12-08-71
SANCHEZ, David	ESP	20-04-78
SANCHEZ, Javier	ESP	01-02-68
SANCHEZ, Mariano	MEX	03-07-78

Surname / Forename	*Nation*	*DOB*
SANGUINETTI, Davide	ITA	25-09-72
SANTOPADRE, Vincenzo	ITA	11-08-71
SANTORO, Fabrice	FRA	09-12-72
SAPSFORD, Danny	GBR	03-04-69
SARGSIAN, Sargis	ARM	03-06-73
SATO, Hiroyasu	JPN	21-10-72
SAVOLT, Attila	HUN	05-02-76
SCALA, Davide	ITA	02-01-72
SCHALKEN, Sjeng	NED	08-09-76
SCHALLER, Gilbert	AUT	17-03-69
SCHIESSLING, Thomas	AUT	01-11-74
SCHLACHTER, Ricardo	BRA	07-07-77
SCHNEITER, Andres	ARG	08-04-76
SCHRANZ, Wolfgang	AUT	18-03-76
SCHUTTLER, Rainer	GER	25-04-76
SEKULOV, James	AUS	13-10-76
SELL, Michael 'Mike'	USA	23-08-72
SERRANO, Oscar	ESP	25-05-78
SHIMADA, Thomas 'Tommy'	JPN	10-02-75
SIEMERINK, Jan	NED	14-04-70
SILCOCK, Grant	AUS	21-05-75
SIMIAN, Stephane	FRA	08-06-67
SINNER, Martin	GER	07-02-68
SKOCH, David	CZE	06-11-76
SLUITER, Raemon	NED	13-04-78
SMITH, Luke	AUS	25-10-76
SMITH, Roger	BAH	20-01-64
SOLVES, Gerard	FRA	07-04-68
SPADEA, Vincent 'Vince'	USA	19-07-74
SPINKS, Tom	GBR	11-07-75
SPRENGELMEYER, Mitch	USA	09-01-75
SQUILLARI, Franco	ARG	22-08-75
SRICHAPHAN, Paradorn	THA	14-06-79
STAFFORD, Grant	RSA	27-05-71
STANOYTCHEV, Orlin	BUL	24-09-71
STARK, Jonathan	USA	03-04-71
STASIAK, Jurek 'Jerzy'	AUS	23-04-78
STAUDER, Franz	GER	28-05-77
STEPANEK, Radek	CZE	27-11-78
STEVEN, Brett	NZL	27-04-69
STOLLE, Sandon	AUS	13-07-70
STOLTENBERG, Jason	AUS	04-04-70
STRENGBERGER, Thomas	AUT	05-10-75
SUK, Cyril	CZE	29-01-67
SUSNJAK, Teo	NZL	23-07-77
SUZUKI, Takao	JPN	20-09-76
SYED, Fazaluddin	IND	18-10-74
TABARA, Michael	CZE	11-08-79
TAHIRI, Mehdi	MAR	28-07-77
TAINO, Eric	USA	18-03-75
TAKADA, Mitsuru	JPN	26-09-69
TALBOT, Byron	RSA	15-09-64
TARANGO, Jeffrey 'Jeff'	USA	20-11-68
TCHERNENKO, Artemi	RUS	04-04-78
TEBBUTT, Michael	AUS	22-12-70
THOMAS, James 'Jim'	USA	24-09-74
TIELEMAN, Laurence	ITA	14-11-72
TILLSTROM, Mikael	SWE	05-03-72
TOBON, Miguel	COL	22-06-68
TOMASHEVICH, Dmitri	UZB	06-03-74
TOWN, Andrew	AUS	04-01-72
TRAMACCHI, Peter	AUS	08-11-70
TRIBLER, Jan-Axel	DEN	10-03-78
TRIFU, Gabriel	ROM	14-04-75
TRIMMEL, Clemens	AUT	08-06-78
TSUJINO, Ryuso	JPN	24-02-69
TUDOR, Mario	CRO	13-07-78
TUREK, Jerry	CAN	02-04-75
ULIHRACH, Bohdan	CZE	23-02-75
ULLYETT, Kevin	RSA	23-05-72
UPPAL, Vishal	IND	10-11-76
URH, Borut	SLO	28-07-74
VACEK, Daniel	CZE	01-04-71
VAJDA, Ivan	CRO	04-09-78
VALERI, Massimo	ITA	13-03-72
VAN EMBURGH, Gregory 'Greg'	USA	10-05-66
VAN GARSSE, Christophe	BEL	21-06-74
VAN HERCK, Johan	BEL	24-05-74
VAN HOUDT, Tom	BEL	28-07-72
VAN LOTTUM, John	NED	10-04-76
VAN SCHEPPINGEN, Dennis	NED	05-07-75
VASEK, Radomir	CZE	23-09-72
VEGLIO, Filippo	SUI	21-03-74
VELASCO, Jairo Jr	ESP	21-01-74
VEMIC, Dusan	YUG	17-06-76
VERKERK, Martin	NED	10-10-78
VICENTE, Fernando	ESP	08-03-77
VILOCA, Joan-Albert	ESP	17-01-73
VINCIGUERRA, Andreas	SWE	19-02-81
VINCK, Christian	GER	03-09-75
VIZNER, Pavel	CZE	15-07-70
VOINEA, Adrian	ROM	06-08-74
VOLKOV, Alexander	RUS	03-03-67
VOLTCHKOV, Vladimir 'Vlad'	BLR	07-04-78
WAHLGREN, Lars-Anders	SWE	24-08-66
WAITE, Jack	USA	01-05-69
WAKEFIELD, Myles	RSA	13-06-74
WANG, Yu-Wei Jr.	CHN	19-09-75
WASHINGTON, MaliVai	USA	20-06-69
WASSEN, Rogier	NED	09-08-76
WEAL, Nicholas 'Nick'	GBR	04-09-73
WEINER, Glenn	USA	27-04-76
WELGREEN, Nir	ISR	17-12-76
WESSELS, Peter	NED	07-05-78
WHEATON, David	USA	02-06-69
WHITEHOUSE, Westley	RSA	13-03-79
WIBIER, Fernon	NED	25-02-71
WIBOWO, Sulistyo	INA	17-02-69
WIDIANTO, Feby	INA	09-02-80
WILKINSON, Chris	GBR	05-01-70
WIRYAWAN, Bonit	INA	10-02-68
WITT, David	USA	02-06-73
WONG, Wayne	HKG	21-03-81
WOODBRIDGE, Todd	AUS	02-04-71
WOODFORDE, Mark	AUS	23-09-65
WOODRUFF, Chris	USA	02-01-73
YAKIMENKO, Denis	UKR	14-06-77
YANG, Jing-Zhu	CHN	19-01-76
YOON, Yong-Il	KOR	23-09-73
ZAATINI, Jicham	LIB	17-06-76
ZABALETA, Mariano	ARG	28-02-78
ZAKHARIA, Alex	LIB	12-06-78
ZDRAZILA, Tomas	CZE	24-06-70
ZHANG, Yu	CHN	26-09-76
ZHENG, Yu	CHN	15-05-76
ZIB, Tomas	CZE	31-01-76
ZIMONJIC, Nenad	YUG	04-06-76
ZINCHENKO, Konstantin 'Kosta'	BLR	05-08-77
ZOVKO, Lovro	CRO	18-03-81

Mercedes Super 9 Tournaments

NEWSWEEK CHAMPIONS CUP ($2,200,000)

INDIAN WELLS, CA, 9–15 MARCH

MEN'S SINGLES – 1st round: P. Sampras (1) bye; T. Martin (P) d. M. Larsson 5–7 6–4 7–5; T. Muster d. C. Woodruff 6–4 6–4; C. Pioline (15) d. M. Rosset 6–3 6–4; M. Norman d. A. Corretja (9) 7–5 6–3; A. Medvedev d. G. Ivanisevic 7–6 2–6 7–6; W. Black (Q) d. T. Henman 6–3 6–4; N. Lapentti (LL) bye; Y. Kafelnikov (4) bye; B. Ulihrach d. M. Filippini 6–4 6–0; T. Enqvist d. R. Reneberg (WC) 6–3 6–1; A. Costa d. F. Mantilla (13) 4–6 6–4 6–3; K. Kucera (11) d. D. Hrbaty 6–4 1–6 7–6; C. Moya d. G. Stafford (Q) 6–4 6–3; V. Spadea (Q) d. J. Viloca (Q) 6–4 6–1; G. Rusedski (6) bye; J. Bjorkman (5) bye; J. Courier d. G. Raoux 3–6 6–4 6–3; F. Clavet d. A. Portas 6–1 6–1; J. Gambill (WC) d. M. Philippoussis (12) 7–6 5–7 7–6; S. Bruguera (14) d. J. Alonso-Pintor 7–6 6–3; A. Agassi (WC) d. T. Woodbridge 7–6 6–4; W. Ferreira d. F. Santoro 6–3 1–6 6–4; P. Rafter (3) bye; M. Rios (7) bye; H. Dreekmann (Q) d. L. Hewitt (WC) 6–4 6–4; M. Washington (WC) d. M. Woodforde 7–6 6–4; N. Kiefer d. G. Kuerten (10) 6–4 6–7 6–2; C. Dosedel d. A. Berasategui (16) 6–4 1–0 ret; T. Haas d. J. Stoltenberg 6–3 3–6 6–1; S. Draper (Q) d. A. Gaudenzi (Q) 6–4 4–6 6–4; P. Korda (2) bye.

2nd round: Sampras (1) d. Martin 6–1 7–5; Muster d. Pioline (15) 4–6 6–3 6–4; Medvedev d. Norman 6–7 6–1 6–2; Lapentti (LL) d. Black (Q) 1–6 6–3 6–0; Ulihrach d. Kafelnikov (4) 6–3 6–3; Enqvist d. Costa 6–4 6–3; Moya d. Kucera (11) 7–6 6–4; Rusedski (6) d. Spadea (Q) 4–6 6–3 6–4; Courier d. Bjorkman (5) 4–6 6–1 7–6; Gambill (WC) d. Clavet 6–3 6–4; Agassi (WC) d. Bruguera (14) 6–2 6–4; Rafter (3) d. Ferreira 7–5 5–7 6–4; Rios (7) d. Dreekmann (Q) 6–4 7–6; Kiefer d. Washington (WC) 6–3 6–4; Haas d. Dosedel 7–6 6–3; Korda (2) d. Draper (Q) 6–3 3–6 6–0.

3rd round: Muster d. Sampras (1) 7–5 6–3; Medvedev d. Lapentti (LL) 6–1 6–4; Enqvist d. Ulihrach 6–2 7–6; Rusedski (6) d. Moya 6–3 7–5; Gambill (WC) d. Courier 6–2 6–4; Agassi (WC) d. Rafter (3) 6–3 3–6 6–2; Rios (7) d. Kiefer 6–4 6–3; Korda (2) d. Haas 7–6 6–2.

Quarter-finals: Muster d. Medvedev 5–7 6–3 6–4; Rusedski (6) d. Enqvist 2–6 7–6 6–4; Gambill (WC) d. Agassi (WC) 7–6 3–6 6–3; Rios (7) d. Korda (2) 6–4 6–2.

Semi-finals: Rusedski (6) d. Muster 7–6 6–1; Rios (7) d. Gambill (WC) 7–6 6–3.

Final: Rios (7) d. Rusedski (6) 6–3 6–7 7–6 6–4.

MEN'S DOUBLES – Final: Bjorkman/Rafter (4) d. Martin/Reneberg (WC) 6–4 7–6

THE LIPTON CHAMPIONSHIPS ($2,450,000)

KEY BISCAYNE, FL, 19–29 MARCH

MEN'S SINGLES – 1st round: P. Sampras (1) bye; J. Sanchez d. W. Black 4–6 6–4 6–1; F. De Wulf d. M. Sell (LL) 1–6 6–3 6–2; W. Ferreira (32) bye; A. Berasategui (17) bye; T. Martin d. J. Golmard 4–6 7–6 7–5; S. Campbell (Q) d. O. Gross 6–4 6–2; M. Philippoussis (15) bye; S. Prieto (LL) bye; C. Vinck (Q) d. A. Clement 6–4 6–2; G. Canas (LL) d. R. Reneberg 7–5 6–3; F. Santoro (23) bye; M. Larsson (26) bye; G. Blanco d. J. Stoltenberg 7–5 6–4; J. Courier d. R. Vasek (WC) 6–1 6–0; A. Corretja (8) bye; P. Rafter (4) bye; V. Spadea d. J. Alonso-Pintor 3–6 6–4 6–4; N. Escude d. L. Hewitt (WC) 6–4 3–6 6–4; A. Agassi (29) bye; A. Costa (19) bye; S. Sargsian d. D. Norman (Q) 6–4 6–2; L. Arnold (WC) d. J. Van Herck 6–1 3–6 6–1; C. Pioline (14) bye; F. Mantilla (12) bye; P. Haarhuis d. S. Lareau (Q) 6–4 6–3; J. Tarango d. D. Prinosil 6–1 7–5; M. Norman (21) bye; J. Siemerink (28) bye; G. Pozzi d. R. Jabali (Q) 6–4 6–3; C. Dosedel d. N. Lapentti 3–6 7–6 6–4; Y. Kafelnikov (6) bye; G. Rusedski (5) bye; D. Hrbaty d. D. Vacek 6–3 6–2; M. Filippini d. I. Heuberger (Q) 1–6 6–1 6–2; M. Rosset (27) bye; T. Enqvist (22) bye; C. Costa d. D. Wheaton (Q) 6–1 6–4; G. Raoux d. J. Novak 6–4 7–6; K. Kucera (11) bye; S. Bruguera (13) bye; D. Van Scheppingen (Q) d. S. Draper 6–7 7–5 6–3; D. Nestor d. N. Godwin (Q) 6–2 7–6; G. Ivanisevic (20) bye; T. Haas (30) bye; M. Tebbutt d. S. Stolle 6–7 6–2 7–5; H. Dreekmann d. T. Nydahl 3–6 6–1 6–4; M. Rios (3) bye; J. Bjorkman (7) bye; L. Paes (LL) d. J. Salzenstein (WC) 6–4 6–3; M. Washington (WC) d. J. Viloca 6–3 6–2; N. Kiefer (25) bye; A. Medvedev (24) bye; B. MacPhie (LL) d. A. Cherkasov (Q) 2–6 6–3 6–4; F. Roig (Q) d. B. Ulihrach 7–5 2–6 6–1; G. Kuerten (10) bye; C. Moya (16) bye; M. Woodforde d. J. Gambill (WC) 6–1 6–2; G. Stafford d. E. Alvarez 7–5 6–4; T. Henman (18) bye; F. Clavet (31) bye; J. Stark d. O. Burrieza (LL) 6–3 6–3; R. Delgado (Q) d. B. Black 7–6 5–7 7–6; P. Korda (2) bye.

2nd round: Sampras (1) d. Sanchez 6–1 6–2; Ferreira (32) d. De Wulf 7–5 6–7 6–4; Martin d. Berasategui (17) 6–3 6–4; Campbell (Q) d. Philippoussis (15) 3–6 6–3 6–3; Prieto (LL) d. Vinck (Q) 3–6 6–3 6–4; Santoro (23) d. Canas (LL) 2–6 7–6 6–1; Blanco d. Larsson (26) 6–4 7–6; Corretja (8) d. Courier 7–6 6–3; Spadea d. Rafter (4) 6–3 7–5; Agassi (29) d. Escude 6–2 6–3; A. Costa (19) d. Sargsian 7–5 6–1; Pioline (14) d. Arnold (WC) 6–4 6–3; Haarhuis d. Mantilla (12) 6–7 6–4 7–6; Tarango d. Norman (21) 7–5 6–0; Siemerink (28) d. Pozzi 6–3 6–2; Kafelnikov (6) d. Dosedel 6–7 7–6 7–6; Rusedski (5) d. Hrbaty 6–3 6–1; Rosset (27) d. Filippini 4–6 6–4 6–2; Enqvist (22) d. C. Costa 6–1 5–7 6–1; Kucera (11) d. Raoux 6–4 6–2; Van Scheppingen (Q) d. Bruguera (13) 3–6 6–4 6–3; Ivanisevic (20) d. Nestor 7–6 6–4; Haas (30) d. Tebbutt 6–2 6–4; Rios (3) d. Dreekmann 6–3 6–4; Bjorkman (7) d. Paes (LL) 6–3 6–4; Kiefer (25) d. Washington (WC) 6–1 6–3; Medvedev (24) B. MacPhie (LL) 7–5 6–2; Kuerten (10) d. Roig (Q) 3–6 6–2 7–6; Moya (16) d. Woodforde 7–6 6–3; Henman (18) d. Stafford 6–4 6–2; Clavet (31) d. Stark 3–6 6–3 6–4; Korda (2) d. Delgado (Q) 6–2 7–6.

3rd round: Ferreira (32) d. Sampras (1) 0–6 7–6 6–3; Campbell (Q) d. Martin 1–6 7–5 7–6; Santoro (23) d. Prieto (LL) 6–2 6–3; Corretja (8) d. Blanco 6–3 6–1; Agassi (29) d. Spadea 6–4 7–5; A. Costa (19) d. Pioline (14) 7–6 3–6 6–3; J. Tarango d. Haarhuis 6–3 ret; Kafelnikov (6) d. Siemerink (28) 6–4 7–6; Rusedski (5) d. Rosset (27) 6–1 7–6; Enqvist

(22) d. Kucera (11) 6–3 3–6 6–3; Ivanisevic (20) d. Van Scheppingen (Q) 6–3 6–4; Rios (3) d. Haas (30) 6–4 6–3; Kiefer (25) d. Bjorkman (7) 7–6 7–6; Kuerten (10) d. Medvedev (24) 6–2 4–6 7–6; Henman (18) d. Moya (16) 6–1 6–4; Korda (2) d. Clavet (31) 6–4 4–6 6–3.
4th round: Campbell (Q) d. Ferreira (32) 6–7 6–2 7–5; Corretja (8) d. Santoro (23) 6–1 3–6 6–3; Agassi (29) d. A. Costa (19) 7–6 4–6 6–1; Tarango d. Kafelnikov (6) 3–6 6–3 6–2; Enqvist (22) d. Rusedski (5) 6–2 6–2; Rios (3) d. Ivanisevic (20) 6–2 6–3; Kuerten (10) d. Kiefer (25) 6–4 5–7 6–4; Henman (18) d. Korda (2) 6–4 6–4.
Quarter-finals: Corretja (8) d. Campbell (Q) 6–3 6–1; Agassi (29) d. Tarango 6–4 6–3; Rios (3) d. Enqvist (22) 6–3 2–0 ret; Henman (18) d. Kuerten (10) 6–2 6–4.
Semi-finals: Agassi (29) d. Corretja (8) 6–4 6–2; Rios (3) d. Henman (18) 6–2 4–6 6–0.
Final: Rios (3) d. Agassi (29) 7–5 6–3 6–4.
MEN'S DOUBLES – Final: E. Ferreira/Leach (7) d. O'Brien/Stark (8) 6–2 6–4.

MONTE CARLO OPEN '98 ($2,200,000)

MONTE CARLO, 20–26 APRIL
MEN'S SINGLES – 1st round: P. Sampras (WC) (1) bye; A. Agassi d. T. Martin 6–2 6–1; F. Santoro d. A. Clement (WC) 6–2 6–1; S. Bruguera (15) d. J. Tarango (Q) 6–1 1–6 7–5; C. Pioline (10) d. C. Costa 6–2 3–6 6–3; S. Grosjean (WC) d. N. Lapentti (Q) 6–2 6–4; F. Clavet d. A. Portas 6–2 6–1; G. Kuerten (8) bye; G. Rusedski (3) bye; B. Becker (WC) d. J. Siemerink 5–7 6–3 6–1; M. Norman d. M. Filippini 2–6 6–2 7–6; M. Philippoussis (13) d. J. Alonso-Pintor 7–6 4–6 6–4; A. Berasategui (12) d. T. Woodbridge 6–0 7–5; D. Vacek (WC) d. J. Sanchez (Q) 6–3 4–6 6–4; C. Dosedel d. R. Fromberg 7–6 6–4; J. Bjorkman (5) bye; A. Corretja (6) bye; A. Medvedev d. G. Ivanisevic 4–6 6–2 7–6; A. Gaudenzi d. B. Steven 6–3 6–1; G. Blanco (Q) d. T. Henman (11) 6–2 6–4; C. Moya (14) d. T. Muster 6–0 6–3; H. Arazi d. J. Burillo (Q) 6–4 6–0; M. Woodforde d. T. Johansson 5–7 7–6 6–3; Y. Kafelnikov (4) bye; R. Krajicek (7) bye; J. Viloca (LL) d. D. Nargiso (Q) 6–3 6–4; B. Ulihrach d. M. Rosset 6–1 3–0 ret; N. Kiefer d. F. Mantilla (9) 6–1 6–4; A. Costa (16) d. T. Enqvist 6–1 6–3; M. Gustafsson d. K. Alami (LL) 6–3 7–5; W. Ferreira d. S. Schalken (Q) 4–6 6–2 6–4; P. Korda (2) bye.
2nd round: Sampras (WC) (1) d. Agassi 6–4 7–5; Santoro d. Bruguera (15) 6–3 6–0; Pioline (10) d. Grosjean (WC) 6–1 7–6; Kuerten (8) d. Clavet 7–5 7–5; Becker (WC) d. Rusedski (3) 6–4 3–6 6–3; Philippoussis (13) d. Norman 6–4 6–3; Berasategui (12) d. Vacek (WC) 6–0 7–6; Dosedel d. Bjorkman (5) 6–1 6–0; Corretja (6) d. Medvedev 7–6 6–4; Gaudenzi d. Blanco (Q) 6–4 4–6 6–3; Moya (14) d. Arazi 6–1 6–1; Kafelnikov (4) d. Woodforde 4–6 6–2 6–2; Krajicek (7) d. Viloca (LL) 6–4 6–2; Ulihrach d. Kiefer 6–4 6–2; A. Costa (16) d. Gustafsson 6–4 6–2; Korda (2) d. Ferreira 6–1 6–3.
3rd round: Santoro (15) d. Sampras (WC) (1) 6–1 6–1; Pioline (10) d. Kuerten (8) 7–6 6–1; Becker (WC) d. Philippoussis (13) 6–1 6–1; Berasategui (12) d. Dosedel 3–6 6–3 6–3; Corretja (6) d. Gaudenzi 7–6 6–4; Moya (14) d. Kafelnikov (4) 6–2 6–3; Krajicek (7) d. Ulihrach 6–4 6–0; Korda (2) d. A. Costa (16) 5–7 6–4 6–4.
Quarter-finals: Pioline (10) d. Santoro (15) 1–6 6–2 6–4; Berasategui (12) d. Becker (WC) 6–7 7–5 6–1; Moya (14) d. Corretja (6) 6–3 6–2; Krajicek (7) d. Korda (2) 4–6 7–6 6–1.
Semi-finals: Pioline (10) d. Berasategui (12) 6–3 0–6 7–6; Moya (14) d. Krajicek (7) 4–6 6–1 6–4.
Final: Moya (14) d. Pioline (10) 6–3 6–0 7–5.
MEN'S DOUBLES – Final: Eltingh/Haarhuis (2) d. Woodbridge/Woodforde (1) 6–4 6–2

LICHER GERMAN OPEN ($2,200,000)

HAMBURG, 4–10 MAY
MEN'S SINGLES – 1st round: M. Rios (1) bye; W. Ferreira d. J. Siemerink 6–4 6–2; A. Costa d. A. Medvedev 6–3 1–6 7–6; O. Gross (WC) d. N. Kiefer (15) 3–6 6–2 6–1; T. Haas d. C. Moya (10) 6–2 7–5; F. Santoro d. C. Costa 6–3 6–3; S. Schalken d. M. Rosset 6–2 1–0 ret; R. Krajicek (WC) (7) bye; Y. Kafelnikov (3) bye; T. Muster d. A. Portas 6–2 6–0; F. De Wulf d. F. Vicente (Q) 7–5 6–4; J. Knippschild (Q) d. M. Norman (14) 6–3 6–0; M. Chang (WC) (11) d. D. Prinosil (WC) 6–4 3–6 6–1; F. Clavet d. M. Goellner 6–4 2–6 6–4; R. Fromberg d. M. Filippini 6–3 6–7 6–4; K. Kucera (6) bye; G. Kuerten (5) bye; C. Dosedel d. D. Hrbaty 6–0 6–2; H. Arazi d. A. Gaudenzi 7–5 7–5; T. Henman (12) d. J. Apell (Q) 6–3 6–2; S. Bruguera (13) d. J. Diaz (Q) 6–2 6–1; N. Escude d. J. Alonso-Pintor 6–4 7–6; K. Alami d. M. Sinner (WC) 7–5 6–2; A. Corretja (4) bye; A. Berasategui (8) bye; M. Gustafsson d. B. Becker 7–5 6–4; B. Ulihrach d. B. Karbacher (Q) 6–3 4–6 6–2; F. Mantilla (9) d. G. Raoux 6–4 ret; G. Ivanisevic (16) d. G. Blanco 4–6 6–4 6–3; N. Lapentti d. B. Steven 6–4 6–4; E. Alvarez (Q) d. M. Martelli (Q) 6–1 7–5; G. Rusedski (2) bye.
2nd round: Ferreira d. Rios (1) 3–6 6–4 6–3; Costa d. Gross (WC) 6–2 6–2; Santoro d. Haas 6–4 6–4; Krajicek (WC) (7) d. Schalken 7–6 6–2; Muster d. Kafelnikov (3) 6–4 6–2; Knippschild (Q) d. F. De Wulf 6–4 6–3; Clavet d. Chang (WC) (11) 6–3 6–7 6–2; Kucera (6) d. Fromberg 6–2 6–1; Kuerten (5) d. Dosedel 6–4 6–4; Arazi d. Henman (12) 6–3 6–3; Bruguera (13) d. Escude 6–0 6–2; Corretja (4) d. Alami 6–2 4–6 6–3; Berasategui (8) d. Gustafsson 6–3 6–3; Mantilla (9) d. Ulihrach 6–4 6–2; Ivanisevic (16) d. Lapentti 4–6 6–1 6–4; Rusedski (2) d. Alvarez (Q) 7–6 0–6 6–3.
3rd round: Costa d. Ferreira 6–3 6–3; Santoro d. Krajicek (WC) (7) 7–5 7–6; Muster d. Knippschild (Q) 6–1 6–4; Kucera (6) d. Clavet 6–2 6–2; Kuerten (5) d. Arazi 6–1 4–6 6–2; Corretja (4) d. Bruguera (13) 6–7 6–4 6–3; Mantilla (9) d. Berasategui (8) 1–6 7–6 7–6; Ivanisevic (16) d. Rusedski (2) 6–4 6–2.
Quarter-finals: Costa d. Santoro 6–3 6–4; Kucera (6) d. Muster 6–3 6–2; Corretja (4) d. Kuerten (5) 4–6 7–6 6–4; Mantilla (9) d. Ivanisevic (16) 6–0 2–0 ret.
Semi-finals: Costa d. Kucera (6) 3–0 ret; Corretja (4) d. Mantilla (9) 6–2 3–6 6–3.
Final: Costa d. Corretja (4) 6–2 6–0 1–0 ret.
MEN'S DOUBLES – Final: Johnson/Montana (4) d. Adams/Steven 6–2 7–5.

CAMPIONATI INTERNAZIONALI D'ITALIA ($2,200,000)

ROME, 11–17 MAY
MEN'S SINGLES – 1st round: P. Sampras (1) d. T. Enqvist 7–6 6–4; M. Norman d. S. Bruguera 6–3 1–0 ret; A. Clement (Q) d. J. Siemerink 6–1 6–4; M. Chang (15) d. A. Medvedev 6–2 4–6 6–3; A. Corretja (9) d. M. Woodforde 7–6 6–4; K. Alami d. A. Gaudenzi 6–3 3–6 7–5; A. Costa d. H. Gumy (Q) 6–3 6–1; F. De Wulf d. J. Bjorkman (7) 6–2

6–3; S. Schalken (LL) d. P. Rafter (4) 6–3 6–7 6–4; B. Steven d. G. Raoux 7–5 6–2; F. Clavet d. D. Vemic (Q) 6–2 6–4; C. Moya (14) d. G. Blanco 6–4 2–6 6–2; A. Berasategui (12) d. G. Galimberti (Q) 6–4 6–2; W. Ferreira d. L. Arnold (Q) 6–1 6–1; J. Golmard (Q) d. J. Tarango 6–4 6–1; B. Ulihrach d. G. Rusedski (5) 7–5 7–6; Y. Kafelnikov (6) d. T. Johansson 7–6 6–2; T. Martin d. A. Portas 5–7 7–6 6–4; N. Escude d. R. Fromberg 3–6 7–5 6–3; R. Krajicek (11) d. M. Philippoussis 5–7 7–6 6–1; F. Mantilla (13) d. J. Courier 6–2 6–3; T. Muster d. M. Filippini 6–1 6–0; T. Henman d. F. Santoro 6–1 6–0; M. Rios (3) d. M. Martelli (WC) 6–3 6–0; G. Kuerten (8) d. C. Costa 1–6 6–4 6–2; N. Lapentti (Q) d. G. Pozzi (WC) 7–6 6–4; T. Haas d. D. Nargiso (WC) 4–6 6–3 6–3; V. Santopadre (WC) d. K. Kucera (10) 6–4 6–3; C. Pioline (16) d. G. Ivanisevic 6–4 6–4; D. Sanguinetti (WC) d. J. Alonso-Pintor 6–1 6–0; F. Vicente (Q) d. M. Goellner 2–6 6–3 6–1; H. Arazi d. P. Korda (2) 6–2 6–4.
2nd round: Sampras (1) d. Norman 7–6 6–4; Chang (15) d. Clement (Q) 7–5 6–1; Alami d. Corretja (9) 3–6 7–6 6–4; A. Costa d. De Wulf 6–1 6–4; Steven d. Schalken (LL) 2–6 6–3 6–1; Moya (14) d. Clavet 6–3 7–6; Berasategui (12) d. W. Ferreira 6–3 7–6; Ulihrach d. Golmard (Q) 6–2 6–2; Kafelnikov (6) d. Martin 1–6 7–6 6–3; Krajicek (11) d. Escude 6–3 6–3; Muster d. Mantilla (13) 6–4 3–6 6–4; Rios (3) d. Henman 6–3 6–1; Kuerten (8) d. Lapentti (Q) 6–0 7–5; Haas d. Santopadre (WC) 6–2 6–1; Sanguinetti (WC) d. Pioline (16) 6–4 6–2; Vicente (Q) d. Arazi 3–6 6–3 6–2.
3rd round: Chang (15) d. Sampras (1) 6–2 7–6; A. Costa d. Alami 6–2 7–6; Steven d. Moya (14) 7–5 6–0; Berasategui (12) d. Ulihrach 7–6 4–6 6–2; Krajicek (11) d. Kafelnikov (6) 6–2 3–6 7–6; Rios (3) d. Muster 6–3 6–1; Kuerten (8) d. Haas 6–4 6–2; Vicente (Q) d. Sanguinetti (WC) 6–2 7–5.
Quarter-finals: A. Costa d. Chang (15) 6–2 6–1; Berasategui (12) d. Steven 6–4 6–2; Rios (3) d. Krajicek (11) 7–6 6–3; Kuerten (8) d. Vicente (Q) 6–3 6–4.
Semi-finals: A. Costa d. Berasategui (12) 6–3 4–6 6–3; Rios (3) d. Kuerten (8) 6–0 7–5.
Final: Rios (3) d. A. Costa w/o .
MEN'S DOUBLES – Final: Bhupathi/Paes (2) d. E. Ferreira/Leach (4) 6–4 4–6 7–6.

DU MAURIER OPEN ($2,200,000)
TORONTO, 3–9 AUGUST
MEN'S SINGLES – 1st round: P. Sampras (WC) (1) bye; G. Pozzi d. J. Tarango 7–6 4–6 6–2; T. Haas d. M. Ondruska 6–2 6–3; F. Santoro (15) d. M. Damm 6–3 6–4; G. Ivanisevic (10) d. S. Lareau (WC) 7–6 7–6; S. Sargsian d. A. Clement 3–6 6–4 7–5; G. Raoux d. T. Ketola (LL) 7–5 6–3; A. Agassi (WC) (8) bye; Y. Kafelnikov (4) bye; T. Martin d. M. Russell (Q) 6–3 6–4; R. Kokavec (WC) d. S. Campbell 6–1 6–2; M. Washington (PR) d. J. Siemerink (13) 7–6 6–3; A. O'Brien (LL) d. G. Kuerten (12) 6–3 7–6; R. Delgado d. B. MacPhie (Q) 7–6 6–7 6–1; D. Nainkin (Q) d. L. Tieleman (Q) 6–1 3–6 7–5; R. Krajicek (6) bye; J. Bjorkman (5) bye; S. Draper d. J. Courier 7–5 5–7 6–4; V. Santopadre d. F. Niemeyer (WC) 6–4 6–4; N. Kiefer (17) d. D. Nestor 6–2 7–6; M. Philippoussis (14) d. D. Flach (Q) 6–4 6–3; W. Black d. B. Black 6–4 6–0; N. Godwin (Q) d. C. Mamiit (Q) 6–4 1–6 6–4; P. Rafter (3) bye; T. Henman (7) bye; G. Canas d. G. Stafford 2–6 7–6 6–2; J. Gambill d. N. Escude 6–3 6–2; A. Costa (9) d. J. Stoltenberg 7–5 6–4; M. Tebbutt d. W. Ferreira (16) 3–2 ret.; D. Vacek d. S. Schalken 4–6 6–4 6–3; V. Spadea d. A. Ilie 6–3 6–0; P. Korda (2) bye.
2nd round: Sampras (WC) (1) d. Pozzi 6–1 6–2; Haas d. Santoro (15) 7–6 6–2; Ivanisevic (10) d. Sargsian 6–3 6–2; Agassi (WC) (8) d. Raoux 6–4 7–5; Kafelnikov (4) d. Martin 6–2 6–3; Washington (PR) d. Kokavec (WC) 6–3 6–4; O'Brien (LL) d. Delgado 6–1 4–6 7–5; Krajicek (6) d. Nainkin (Q) 6–4 6–4; Bjorkman (5) d. Draper 7–6 6–3; Kiefer (17) d. Santopadre 2–6 6–1 7–6; Philippoussis (14) d. W. Black 6–1 6–4; Rafter (3) d. Godwin (Q) 7–5 6–3; Henman (7) d. Canas 3–6 7–6 6–2; Costa (9) d. Gambill 6–4 6–2; Vacek d. Tebbutt 6–4 7–6; Spadea d. Korda (2) 5–7 6–1 6–4.
3rd round: Sampras (WC) (1) d. Haas 7–6 6–2; Agassi (WC) (8) d. Ivanisevic (10) 2–6 7–5 6–3; Kafelnikov (4) d. Washington (PR) 7–6 6–2; Krajicek (6) d. O'Brien (LL) 3–6 6–2 6–3; Bjorkman (5) d. Kiefer (17) 6–2 6–7 6–3; Rafter (3) d. Philippoussis (14) 6–3 6–3; Henman (7) d. Costa (9) 7–6 6–2; Vacek d. Spadea 4–6 6–1 6–4.
Quarter-finals: Agassi (WC) (8) d. Sampras (WC) (1) 6–7 6–1 6–2; Krajicek (6) d. Kafelnikov (4) 6–4 6–4; Rafter (3) d. Bjorkman (5) 6–3 6–2; Henman (7) d. Vacek 6–3 5–7 6–1.
Semi-finals: Krajicek (6) d. Agassi (WC) (8) 4–6 7–5 6–2; Rafter (3) d. Henman (7) 6–2 6–4.
Final: Rafter (3) d. Krajicek (6) 7–6 6–4.
MEN'S DOUBLES – Final: Damm/Grabb (6) d. E. Ferreira/Leach (3) 6–7 6–2 7–6.

GREAT AMERICAN INSURANCE ATP CHAMPIONSHIP ($2,200,000)
CINCINNATI, OH, 10–16 AUGUST
MEN'S SINGLES – 1st round: P. Sampras (1) bye; M. Damm d. M. Woodforde 6–4 3–6 6–2; J. Gambill d. O. Delaitre (Q) 6–1 6–3; C. Pioline (16) d. R. Delgado 7–6 6–3; A. Agassi (10) d. N. Kiefer 4–6 7–6 6–2; V. Spadea d. J. Gimelstob (WC) 3–6 7–6 6–2; A. Medvedev (Q) d. A. Clement (Q) 6–4 6–3; R. Krajicek (8) bye; C. Moya (4) bye; J. Golmard (Q) d. N. Escude 6–2 6–7 6–3; T. Johansson d. W. Black 7–6 7–5; J. Tarango d. A. Berasategui (13) 7–5 6–2; A. Costa (12) d. S. Grosjean (Q) 1–6 6–4 6–1; T. Haas d. J. Courier 7–6 7–6; M. Larsson d. G. Pozzi 6–4 7–5; J. Bjorkman (6) bye; P. Rafter (5) bye; G. Raoux d. W. Schranz (Q) 7–6 5–7 6–4; T. Martin d. F. Santoro 6–1 6–4; T. Muster d. T. Henman (11) 6–4 7–5; G. Ivanisevic (14) d. A. Ilie 6–4 0–6 6–4; M. Philippoussis d. B. Black 6–2 6–3; M. Ondruska (Q) d. S. Campbell (WC) 5–7 6–2 6–3; P. Korda (3) bye; Y. Kafelnikov (7) bye; M. Chang d. T. Woodbridge 6–1 3–6 6–2; S. Draper d. N. Lapentti 6–4 4–6 7–5; A. Corretja (9) d. A. O'Brien (WC) 6–3 6–7 7–6; W. Ferreira d. F. Mantilla (15) 7–6 7–5; J. Siemerink d. S. Schalken 1–6 6–1 7–6; D. Vacek d. J. Stoltenberg 6–2 3–6 7–6; M. Rios (2) bye.
2nd round: Sampras (1) d. Damm 6–4 6–2; Gambill d. Pioline (16) 6–7 7–6 6–4; Spadea d. Agassi (10) 6–2 0–6 7–6; Krajicek (8) d. Medvedev (Q) 6–3 6–7 6–3; Golmard (Q) d. Moya (4) 6–4 6–2; Johansson d. Tarango 5–7 6–2 7–6; Haas d. Costa (12) 6–1 6–3; Larsson d. Bjorkman (6) 6–7 6–2 6–3; Rafter (5) d. Raoux 6–1 6–3; Martin d. Muster 6–3 6–4; Ivanisevic (14) d. Philippoussis 6–3 6–2; Korda (3) d. Ondruska (Q) 6–2 6–3; Kafelnikov (7) d. Chang 6–3 4–6 6–4; Draper d. Corretja (9) 6–3 6–7 7–6; Siemerink d. Ferreira 7–6 6–4; Vacek d. Rios (2) 6–3 6–2.
3rd round: Sampras (1) d. Gambill 7–6 6–3; Spadea d. Krajicek (8) 6–2 6–3; Johansson d. Golmard (Q) 7–6 7–6; Larsson d. Haas 6–4 6–4; Rafter (5) d. Martin 3–6 6–3 6–2; Korda (3) d. Ivanisevic (14) 5–7 6–4 7–5; Kafelnikov (7) d. Draper 6–3 6–3; Vacek d. Siemerink 6–1 6–4.

Quarter-finals: Sampras (1) d. Spadea 6–3 6–2; Larsson d. Johansson 6–4 7–6; Rafter (5) d. Korda (3) 6–4 7–6; Kafelnikov (7) d. Vacek 6–4 6–4.
Semi-finals: Sampras (1) d. Larsson 7–5 2–6 6–1; Rafter (5) d. Kafelnikov (7) 7–5 6–0.
Final: Rafter (5) d. Sampras (1) 1–6 7–6 6–4.
MEN'S DOUBLES – Final: Knowles/Nestor d. Delaitre/Santoro 6–1 2–1 ret.

EUROCARD OPEN ($2,200,000)

STUTTGART, 26 OCTOBER–1 NOVEMBER
MEN'S SINGLES – 1st round: P. Sampras (1) bye; N. Kiefer d. B. Black 4–6 7–6 7–6; B. Ulihrach d. R. Fromberg 3–6 7–6 6–4; A. Costa (16) bye; T. Henman (9) bye; M. Woodforde (Q) d. H. Arazi 6–2 2–6 7–6; J. Gambill d. D. Vacek 6–3 4–6 6–3; A. Corretja (7) bye; C. Moya (4) bye; B. Becker (WC) d. S. Schalken (Q) 6–2 7–5; W. Ferreira d. V. Spadea 6–2 3–6 7–5; G. Ivanisevic (14) bye; R. Krajicek (11) bye; M. Norman d. M. Rosset (WC) 7–6 3–6 6–4; A. Pavel (LL) d. P. Haarhuis (Q) 7–5 6–3; A. Agassi (6) bye; P. Korda (5) bye; T. Johansson d. M. Damm (Q) 5–7 6–3 6–2; G. Pozzi (Q) d. J. Stark (LL) 7–6 6–3; J. Bjorkman (12) bye; G. Rusedski (13) bye; J. Stoltenberg d. D. Prinosil (WC) 7–6 6–1; M. Gustafsson d. O. Gross (WC) 6–0 6–3; P. Rafter (3) bye; K. Kucera (8) bye; T. Martin d. S. Lareau (LL) 6–3 6–3; M. Philippoussis d. F. Santoro 6–1 5–7 6–2; Y. Kafelnikov (10) bye; J. Siemerink (15) bye; G. Raoux d. M. Chang 7–6 6–3; T. Haas d. D. Nainkin (LL) 6–4 6–4; M. Rios (2) bye.
2nd round: Sampras (1) d. Kiefer 6–3 6–4; Ulihrach d. Costa (16) 6–2 6–2; Henman (9) d. Woodforde (Q) 7–5 6–1; Gambill d. Corretja (7) 6–2 6–4; Becker (WC) d. Moya (4) 6–7 6–4 6–4; Ivanisevic (14) d. Ferreira 6–4 7–6; Krajicek (11) d. Norman 6–4 6–1; Agassi (6) d. Pavel (LL) 6–1 6–7 6–3; Johansson d. Korda (5) 6–2 6–4; Bjorkman (12) d. Pozzi (Q) 6–4 3–6 6–2; Rusedski (13) d. Stoltenberg 7–6 6–7 7–6; Rafter (3) d. Gustafsson 6–1 6–4; Martin d. Kucera (8) 6–2 6–4; Kafelnikov (10) d. Philippoussis 4–6 6–4 7–6; Siemerink (15) d. Raoux 6–7 7–6 6–4; Rios (2) d. Haas 6–3 7–5.
3rd round: Sampras (1) d. Ulihrach 6–3 6–3; Gambill d. Henman (9) 7–6 1–6 7–6; Ivanisevic (14) d. Becker (WC) 7–6 7–6; Krajicek (11) d. Agassi (6) 6–3 6–4; Bjorkman (12) d. Johansson 2–6 6–4 6–2; Rusedski (13) d. Rafter (3) 7–6 6–7 6–4; Kafelnikov (10) d. Martin 6–4 7–5; Rios (2) d. Siemerink (15) 6–2 ret.
Quarter-finals: Sampras (1) d. Gambill 4–1 ret; Krajicek (11) d. Ivanisevic (14) 7–6 7–6; Bjorkman (12) d. Rusedski (13) 6–3 6–2; Kafelnikov (10) d. Rios (2) w/o .
Semi-finals: Krajicek (11) d. Sampras (1) 6–7 6–4 7–6; Kafelnikov (10) d. Bjorkman (12) 6–2 7–5.
Final: Krajicek (11) d. Kafelnikov (10) 6–4 6–3 6–3.
MEN'S DOUBLES – Final: Lareau/O'Brien d. Bhupathi/Paes (3) 6–3 3–6 7–5.

13eme OPEN DE PARIS ($2,300,000)

PARIS, 2–8 NOVEMBER
MEN'S SINGLES – 1st round: P. Sampras (1) bye; T. Johansson d. S. Grosjean (WC) 7–6 6–7 6–4; J. Golmard (WC) d. B. Black 7–6 6–4; A. Costa (16) bye; P. Korda (10) bye; M. Philippoussis d. D. Vacek 7–6 7–6; F. Santoro d. H. Arazi 4–6 6–4 6–1; K. Kucera (7) bye; P. Rafter (3) bye; N. Escude d. B. Becker (WC) 6–7 7–5 6–4; T. Martin d. P. Haarhuis (Q) 6–7 6–4 6–4; G. Ivanisevic (14) bye; R. Krajicek (11) bye; M. Rosset (Q) d. W. Ferreira 6–3 6–4; G. Pozzi (Q) d. T. Enqvist 6–3 6–3; A. Agassi (5) bye; A. Corretja (6) bye; T. Haas d. C. Costa 7–5 6–1; M. Gustafsson d. M. Chang 6–4 3–6 6–3; J. Bjorkman (12) bye; G. Rusedski (13) bye; N. Kiefer d. J. Kroslak (Q) 7–5 6–1; J. Stoltenberg d. G. Raoux 2–6 7–6 6–4; C. Moya (4) bye; Y. Kafelnikov (8) bye; M. Norman d. A. Clement (Q) 7–6 6–3; A. Di Pasquale (WC) d. R. Fromberg 6–3 6–4; T. Henman (9) bye; J. Siemerink (15) bye; V. Spadea d. C. Pioline 6–4 6–4; T. Woodbridge (Q) d. B. Ulihrach 6–3 2–6 7–6; M. Rios (2) bye.
2nd round: Sampras (1) d. Johansson 7–6 6–1; Golmard d. A. Costa (16) 3–6 7–5 7–5; Philippoussis d. Korda (10) 2–6 6–4 6–4; Kucera (7) d. Santoro 6–2 3–6 6–0; Rafter (3) d. Escude 6–3 6–1; Martin d. Ivanisevic (14) 4–6 6–1 7–6; Rosset (Q) d. Krajicek (11) 6–4 5–7 2–5 ret; Agassi (5) d. Pozzi (Q) 6–4 6–2; Haas d. Corretja (6) 7–6 2–6 6–3; Gustafsson d. Bjorkman (12) 6–3 6–2; Rusedski (13) d. Kiefer 6–3 6–4; Stoltenberg d. Moya (4) 2–6 6–2 6–3; Kafelnikov (8) d. Norman 3–6 6–3 6–4; Henman (9) d. Di Pasquale (WC) 6–3 6–3; Spadea d. Siemerink (15) 7–6 3–6 7–6; Rios (2) d. Woodbridge (Q) 6–0 6–4.
3rd round: Sampras (1) d. Golmard 6–7 6–4 6–4; Philippoussis d. Kucera (7) 6–4 4–6 7–5; Martin d. Rafter (3) 5–7 7–6 7–6; Agassi (5) d. Rosset (Q) 6–4 6–4; Gustafsson d. Haas 6–4 6–2; Rusedski (13) d. Stoltenberg 7–6 6–4; Kafelnikov (8) d. Henman (9) 6–3 6–7 7–6; Rios (2) d. Spadea 7–5 6–4.
Quarter-finals: Sampras (1) d. Philippoussis 6–3 6–3; Martin d. Agassi (5) 4–6 6–4 6–4; Rusedski (13) d. Gustafsson 6–3 6–2; Kafelnikov (8) d. Rios (2) 6–3 6–2.
Semi-finals: Sampras (1) d. Martin 6–4 7–6; Rusedski (13) d. Kafelnikov (8) 6–3 4–6 6–4.
Final: Rusedski (13) d. Sampras (1) 6–4 7–6 6–3.
MEN'S DOUBLES – Final: Bhupathi/Paes (3) d. Eltingh/Haarhuis (1) 6–4 6–2.

Championship Series

EUROPEAN COMMUNITY CHAMPIONSHIP ($875,000)

ANTWERP, 16–22 FEBRUARY

MEN'S SINGLES – 1st round: P. Korda (1) d. W. Ferreira 6–3 6–3; A. Portas d. D. Hrbaty 6–7 7–6 6–4; B. Ulihrach d. F. Santoro 6–2 6–4; K. Kucera (7) d. J. van Herck (WC) 6–7 6–4 6–2; T. Johansson d. J. Bjorkman (3) 6–1 6–2; M. Damm (Q) d. F. Dewulf 4–6 7–6 6–4; G. Raoux d. F. Clavet 7–6 5–7 6–2; G. Rusedski (5) d. H. Arazi 7–6 3–6 6–3; J. Siemerink (Q) d. G. Ivanisevic (WC) (6) 6–4 6–3; M. Larsson d. M. Goellner (Q) 6–2 6–1; M. Rosset d. N. Kiefer 7–6 4–6 7–6; Y. Kafelnikov (4) d. J. Novak 7–5 5–7 6–3; M. Norman d. T. Henman (8) 7–5 6–3; J. Tarango d. D. Norman (WC) 3–6 6–4 6–3; C. Pioline d. M. Gustafsson 6–4 7–6; P. Rafter (2) d. A. Boetsch (Q) 6–2 7–6.

2nd round: Korda (1) d. Portas 7–5 6–2; Kucera (7) d. Ulihrach 6–1 6–1; Johansson d. Damm (Q) 6–2 6–4; Rusedski (5) d. Raoux 7–6 3–6 7–6; Larsson d. Siemerink (Q) 6–3 6–3; Rosset d. Kafelnikov (4) 3–6 6–4 6–3; Tarango d. Norman 7–6 6–2; Rafter (2) d. Pioline 6–4 7–6.

Quarter-finals: Kucera (7) d. Korda (1) 3–6 6–4 6–2; Rusedski (5) d. Johansson 6–3 4–6 6–4; Rosset d. Larsson w/o; Rafter (2) d. Tarango 6–7 6–2 6–1.

Semi-finals: Rusedski (5) d. Kucera (7) 6–4 6–3; Rosset d. Rafter (2) 7–6 7–6.

Final: Rusedski (5) d. Rosset 7–6 3–6 6–1 6–4.

MEN'S DOUBLES – Final: W. Ferreira/Kafelnikov d. Carbonell/Roig 7–5 3–6 6–2.

KROGER ST. JUDE ($700,000)

MEMPHIS, TN, 16–22 FEBRUARY

MEN'S SINGLES – 1st round: M. Rios (1) bye; S. Campbell d. G. Doyle (Q) 7–6 6–0; V. Spadea d. A. O'Brien 6–3 6–4; J. Sanchez (16) bye; T. Haas (10) bye; G. Stafford d. A. Martin 6–3 6–0; M. Washington (WC) d. S. Sargsian 7–6 6–4; J. Alonso-Pintor (8) bye; M. Philippoussis (4) bye; W. Black d. E. Alvarez 5–7 6–3 7–5; T. Nydahl d. N. Lapentti 6–3 7–6; S. Schalken (13) bye; J. Stoltenberg (11) bye; J. Viloca d. E. Ran (Q) 4–6 7–6 6–4; P. Haarhuis d. L. Jensen (WC) 6–7 6–4 6–4; T. Enqvist (5) bye; T. Woodbridge (6) bye; T. Martin d. F. Meligeni 7–6 7–5; J. Burillo d. J. Stark 6–7 6–3 6–2; M. Woodforde (12) bye; B. Black (14) bye; J. Gambill (WC) d. S. Stolle 6–3 6–7 6–4; G. Weiner (WC) d. C. Vinck (Q) 2–6 7–5 6–3; G. Kuerten (3) bye; J. Courier (7) bye; B. MacPhie (Q) d. T. Middleton (Q) 6–3 7–5; R. Reneberg d. J. Oncins (Q) 6–2 6–4; R. Fromberg (9) bye; A. Gaudenzi (15) bye; R. Delgado d. D. Sanguinetti 3–6 7–5 6–4; D. Nestor d. M. Craca 6–4 4–6 6–3; M. Chang (2) bye.

2nd round: Rios (1) d. Campbell 6–2 6–4; Spadea d. Sanchez (16) 7–6 6–4; Stafford d. Haas (10) 6–1 6–3; Alonso-Pintor (8) d. Washington (WC) 4–6 6–3 6–3; Philippoussis (4) d. W. Black 6–1 6–2; Schalken (13) d. Nydahl 4–6 6–3 6–4; Stoltenberg (11) d. Viloca 7–6 6–4; Enqvist (5) d. Haarhuis 6–2 6–3; Martin d. Woodbridge (6) 6–2 6–4; Woodforde (12) d. Burillo 6–3 6–4; Gambill (WC) d. B. Black (14) 5–7 7–5 7–6; Kuerten (3) d. Weiner (WC) 7–6 6–3; B. MacPhie (Q) d. Courier (7) 6–2 6–3; Fromberg (9) d. Reneberg 5–7 6–2 6–3; Gaudenzi (15) d. Delgado 3–6 6–2 7–6; Chang (2) d. Nestor 6–4 6–4.

3rd round: Rios (1) d. Spadea 6–2 6–3; Stafford d. Alonso-Pintor (8) 6–1 7–5; Philippoussis (4) d. Schalken (13) 6–4 6–4; Enqvist (5) d. Stoltenberg (11) 6–3 6–1; Woodforde (12) d. Martin 7–5 6–3; Kuerten (3) d. Gambill (WC) 6–4 7–6; Fromberg (9) d. MacPhie (Q) 4–6 6–3 6–4; Chang (2) d. Gaudenzi (15) 6–3 6–3.

Quarter-finals: Rios (1) d. Stafford 6–2 6–3; Philippoussis (4) d. Enqvist (5) 3–6 6–2 7–6; Kuerten (3) d. Woodforde (12) 4–6 6–4 6–4; Chang (2) d. Fromberg (9) 6–1 6–4.

Semi-finals: Philippoussis (4) d. Rios (1) 6–4 7–6; Chang (2) d. Kuerten (3) 7–6 7–6.

Final: Philippoussis (4) d. Chang (2) 6–3 6–2.

MEN'S DOUBLES – Final: Woodbridge/Woodforde (1) d. E. Ferreira/Roditi (7) 6–3 6–4.

GUARDIAN DIRECT CUP ($689,250)

LONDON, 23 FEBRUARY–1 MARCH

MEN'S SINGLES – 1st round: P. Korda (1) d. D. Prinosil (Q) 7–6 6–7 6–4; C. Pioline d. F. Clavet 6–1 7–6; F. Dewulf d. G. Blanco 6–2 7–5; K. Kucera (7) d. G. Raoux 6–7 7–6 6–4; M. Goellner d. G. Rusedski (4) 5–7 7–5 6–4; A. Richardson (WC) d. M. Rosset 6–3 2–1 ret; B. Ulihrach d. M. Lee (WC) 6–4 7–6; J. Siemerink (WC) d. S. Bruguera (6) 6–1 7–6; T. Henman d. R. Krajicek (5) 6–7 7–6 7–5; R. Schuttler (Q) d. M. Damm 7–5 7–6; D. Vacek d. K. Alami 7–6 6–4; Y. Kafelnikov (3) d. T. Johansson 6–3 6–2; G. Ivanisevic (8) d. K. Carlsen (Q) 6–1 6–2; W. Ferreira d. C. Wilkinson (Q) 6–7 6–4 6–2; M. Gustafsson d. B. Steven 6–7 7–6 6–2; P. Rafter (2) d. H. Arazi 6–3 3–6 6–3.

2nd round:. Pioline d. Korda (1) 6–3 6–3; Kucera (7) d. Dewulf 6–3 6–4; Goellner d. Richardson (WC) 6–4 6–7 7–5; Siemerink (WC) d. Ulihrach 6–3 6–7 6–4; Henman d. Schuttler (Q) 4–6 6–3 6–4; Kafelnikov (3) d. Vacek 6–3 6–4; Ferreira d. Ivanisevic (8) 6–2 6–4; Rafter (2) d. Gustafsson 6–3 7–6.

Quarter-finals: Pioline d. Kucera (7) 6–3 4–6 6–2; Siemerink (WC) d. Goellner 6–3 6–4; Kafelnikov (3) d. Henman 4–6 6–4 6–2; Ferreira d. Rafter (2) 6–4 6–4.
Semi-finals: Pioline d. Siemerink (WC) 6–3 7–6; Kafelnikov (3) d. Ferreira 7–5 6–4.
Final: Kafelnikov (3) d. Pioline 7–5 6–4.
MEN'S DOUBLES – Final: Damm/Grabb (3) d. Kafelnikov/Vacek (1) 6–4 7–5.

ADVANTA CHAMPIONSHIPS ($589,250)

PHILADELPHIA, PA, 23 FEBRUARY–1 MARCH
MEN'S SINGLES – 1st round: P. Sampras (1) d. X. Malisse (Q) 4–6 6–3 7–5; A. Gaudenzi d. D. Sanguinetti 4–6 6–4 6–3; M. Safin (WC) d. W. Black (Q) 6–1 2–6 6–3; S. Schalken (8) d. J. Salzenstein (WC) 6–3 4–6 7–6; J. Stark (WC) d. J. Alonso-Pintor (4) 6–1 6–7 6–3; J. Tarango d. S. Stolle (Q) 7–5 6–1; F. Meligeni d. J. Viloca 7–6 6–4; T. Haas (6) d. V. Spadea 6–3 6–2; T. Martin d. B. Black (9) 6–4 7–6; R. Reneberg d. J. Burillo 6–3 6–1; M. Craca d. N. Lapentti 6–4 6–4; T. Enqvist (3) d. E. Alvarez (LL) 6–4 6–3; G. Stafford d. R. Fromberg (7) 7–6 7–6; P. Haarhuis d. J. Sanchez 6–3 6–4; S. Lareau (Q) d. T. Nydahl 6–4 6–3; J. Courier (5) d. C. Ruud 6–7 6–4 6–4.
2nd round: Sampras (1) d. Gaudenzi 7–6 6–3; Schalken (8) d. Safin (WC) 6–2 4–6 7–6; Tarango d. Stark (WC) 6–2 6–7 6–3; Haas (6) d. Meligeni 3–0 ret; Reneberg d. Martin 6–4 7–5; Enqvist (3) d. Craca 4–6 7–6 6–2; Stafford d. Haarhuis 6–3 6–4; Lareau (Q) d. Courier (5) 7–6 7–5.
Quarter-finals: Sampras (1) d. Schalken (8) 6–2 6–2; Haas (6) d. Tarango 4–6 6–4 6–4; Enqvist (3) d. Reneberg 6–4 7–6; Lareau (Q) d. Stafford 6–4 6–3.
Semi-finals: Sampras (1) d. Haas (6) 6–4 6–4; Enqvist (3) d. Lareau (Q) 6–3 3–6 6–3.
Final: Sampras (1) d. Enqvist (3) 7–5 7–6.
MEN'S DOUBLES – Final: Eltingh/Haarhuis (1) d. MacPherson/Reneberg 7–6 6–7 6–2.

JAPAN OPEN ($575,000)

TOKYO, 13–19 APRIL
MEN'S SINGLES – 1st round: P. Rafter (1) bye; B. MacPhie d. K. Flygt (Q) 7–6 6–4; R. Vasek d. S. Lareau 6–4 4–6 7–6; A. Pavel (16) d. O. Delaitre 6–3 6–0; S. Campbell (9) d. A. Richardson 6–1 7–6; I. Heuberger d. S. Matsuoka (WC) 6–3 6–3; D. di Lucia (Q) d. D. Wheaton 6–3 3–6 6–3; K. Carlsen (8) bye; T. Henman (3) bye; D. Nestor d. N. Godwin 6–2 6–2; S. Iwabuchi (WC) d. D. Sapsford 7–5 0–1 ret; J. Golmard (14) d. T. Chaen (Q) 6–2 3–6 6–1; J. Gambill (11) d. S. Pescosolido (Q) 6–3 6–2; K. Miyachi (Q) d. A. Belobrajdic 6–2 6–1; R. Schuttler d. C. Vinck 6–4 3–6 6–3; M. Damm (6) bye; V. Spadea (5) bye; S. Stolle d. T. Suzuki (WC) 6–2 6–3; G. Motomura (WC) d. C. Wilkinson 4–6 6–4 7–5; D. Vacek (12) d. V. Santopadre 6–1 6–1; M. Tillstrom (13) d. K. Masuda (Q) 4–6 6–3 6–0; A. O'Brien d. O. Burrieza 6–2 6–0; D. Prinosil d. M. Sell 6–2 6–1; T. Johansson (4) bye; G. Pozzi (7) bye; C. Caratti d. B. Ellwood (Q) 6–0 7–6; L. Burgsmuller d. S. Koubek 6–4 6–1; B. Black (10) d. J. Stark 3–6 7–6 6–4; H. Dreekmann d. A. Clement (15) 6–3 6–4; T. Ketola d. M. Tebbutt 6–4 6–4; J. van Lottum d. H. Kaneko (WC) 6–4 0–6 7–5; M. Chang (2) bye.
2nd round: MacPhie d. Rafter (1) 6–3 7–6; Pavel (16) d. Vasek 5–7 6–0 7–5; Heuberger d. Campbell (9) 6–3 7–6; di Lucia (Q) d. Carlsen (8) 4–6 6–3 6–3; Henman (3) d. Nestor 6–2 7–5; Golmard (14) d. Iwabuchi (WC) 6–4 6–4; Gambill (11) d. Miyachi (Q) 6–0 6–3; Schuttler d. Damm (6) 6–2 6–4; Stolle d. Spadea (5) 6–3 6–0; Vacek (12) d. Motomura (WC) 6–2 6–2; Tillstrom (13) d. O'Brien 5–7 6–4 6–4; Prinosil d. Johansson (4) 6–3 6–3; Caratti d. Pozzi (7) 6–3 7–6; Black (10) d. Burgsmuller 6–4 6–2; Dreekmann d. Ketola 7–6 7–6; Chang (2) d. van Lottum 6–4 6–1.
3rd round: Pavel (16) d. MacPhie 3–6 6–3 6–4; di Lucia (Q) d. Heuberger 6–3 0–6 6–3; Henman (3) d. Golmard (14) 6–4 6–1; Gambill (11) d. Schuttler 6–0 6–0; Vacek (12) d. Stolle 7–5 6–3; Prinosil d. Tillstrom (13) 6–4 7–6; Black (10) d. Caratti 6–3 6–4; Dreekmann d. Chang (2) 6–2 5–7 6–4.
Quarter-finals: Pavel (16) d. di Lucia (Q) 6–3 7–6; Gambill (11) d. Henman (3) 6–3 4–6 6–3; Vacek (12) d. Prinosil 6–4 6–1; Black (10) d. Dreekmann 6–2 6–3.
Semi-finals: Pavel (16) d. Gambill (11) 6–4 6–3; Black (10) d. Vacek (12) 6–3 7–5.
Final: Pavel (16) d. Black (10) 6–3 6–4.
MEN'S DOUBLES – Final: Lareau/Nestor (3) d. Delaitre/Pescosolido 6–3 6–4.

OPEN SEAT – GODO '98 ($825,000)

BARCELONA, 13–19 APRIL
MEN'S SINGLES – 1st round: Y. Kafelnikov (1) bye; F. Roig (WC) d. J. Alonso-Pintor 6–1 3–6 6–4; J. Munoz-Hernandez (Q) d. S. Schalken 7–6 6–3; F. Clavet (16) d. J. Sanchez 6–3 6–4; A. Costa (9) d. N. Lapentti 4–6 6–3 6–1; G. Blanco d. J. Marin 6–3 6–1; F. Meligeni d. F. Vicente (WC) 6–4 7–6; A. Berasategui (7) bye; K. Kucera (4) bye; D. Hrbaty d. D. Sanguinetti 6–3 6–3; K. Alami d. D. Pescariu 6–7 6–3 6–4; M. Gustafsson (14) d. M. Goellner 6–1 6–1; R. Carretero (Q) d. A. Medvedev (11) 7–6 7–6; B. Ulihrach d. J. Viloca 4–6 7–6 7–5; T. Carbonell (WC) d. T. Nydahl 5–7 6–3 6–3; C. Moya (6) bye; F. Mantilla (5) bye; C. Dosedel d. J. Burillo 6–3 1–6 7–6; T. Martin d. R. Fromberg 6–2 6–4; T. Muster (12) d. M. Filippini 6–3 2–6 6–2; M. Safin (WC) d. M. Larsson (13) 6–3 6–2; J. Novak d. F. Lopez (Q) 6–0 6–2; C. Costa d. D. Hipperdinger (Q) 6–2 6–2; G. Kuerten (3) bye; S. Bruguera (8) bye; E. Alvarez (LL) d. A. Portas 6–7 6–4 6–4; F. de Wulf d. H. Arazi 6–4 6–4; J. Tarango d. F. Santoro (10) 6–3 6–1; W. Ferreira (15) d. J. Rascon (Q) 6–3 6–2; A. Gaudenzi d. D. Sanchez (Q) 6–4 6–2; A. Martin (Q) d. S. Navarro (WC) 4–6 7–5 6–2; A. Corretja (2) bye.

2nd round: Kafelnikov (1) d. Roig (WC) 6–4 4–6 6–4; Munoz-Hernandez (Q) d. Clavet (16) 6–4 6–2; A. Costa (9) d. Blanco 6–3 6–4; Berasategui (7) d. Meligeni 6–2 6–1; Hrbaty d. Kucera (4) 7–6 6–2; Gustafsson (14) d. Alami 6–0 6–1; Ulihrach d. Carretero (Q) 6–4 6–4; Moya (6) d. Carbonell (WC) 3–6 6–2 6–2; Dosedel d. Mantilla (5) 6–4 7–6; Martin d. Muster (12) 6–4 7–6; Safin (WC) d. Novak 4–6 6–4 7–6; C. Costa d. Kuerten (3) 6–4 6–3; Bruguera (8) d. Alvarez (L) 7–5 6–0; de Wulf d. Tarango 6–4 7–6; Gaudenzi d. Ferreira (15) 4–6 6–1 6–2; Corretja (2) d. Martin (Q) 6–1 6–0.
3rd round: Kafelnikov (1) d. Munoz-Hernandez (Q) 7–6 3–6 6–1; Berasategui (7) d. A. Costa (9) 6–4 6–4; Hrbaty d. Gustafsson (14) 5–7 6–4 6–3; Moya (6) d. Ulihrach 6–4 7–6; Martin d. Dosedel 6–3 7–5; C. Costa d. Safin (WC) 6–4 3–6 6–2; Bruguera (8) d. de Wulf 6–3 1–6 7–5; Gaudenzi d. Corretja (2) 3–6 6–1 6–3.
Quarter-finals: Berasategui (7) d. Kafelnikov (1) 6–4 6–4; Moya (6) d. Hrbaty 4–6 6–3 6–3; Martin d. C. Costa 6–2 6–4; Gaudenzi d. Bruguera (8) 3–6 6–2 6–3.
Semi-finals: Berasategui (7) d. Moya (6) 7–6 6–4; Martin d. Gaudenzi 6–4 7–6.
Final: Martin d. Berasategui (7) 6–2 1–6 6–3 6–2.
MEN'S DOUBLES – Final: Eltingh/Haarhuis (1) d. E. Ferreira/Leach (2) 7–5 6–0.

1998 MERCEDES CUP ($915,000)
STUTTGART, 20–26 JULY
MEN'S SINGLES – 1st round: M. Rios (1) bye; J. Knippschild (WC) d. M. Kohlmann (Q) 3–6 6–3 6–3; H. Dreekmann (WC) d. M. Tillstrom 6–3 6–0; M. Larsson (15) bye; C. Pioline (9) bye; B. Becker d. A. Gaudenzi 6–1 7–5; R. Fromberg d. J. Marin (LL) 7–6 6–1; F. Mantilla (7) bye; Y. Kafelnikov (4) bye; B. Ulihrach d. S. Grosjean (Q) 7–5 6–2; G. Blanco d. M. Safin 2–6 7–6 6–2; F. Clavet (14) bye; M. Gustafsson (11) bye; T. Haas d. M. Goellner (WC) 7–6 7–5; C. Dosedel d. M. Rosset 6–3 6–4; K. Kucera (5) bye; A. Costa (6) bye; F. Squillari (Q) d. N. Lapentti 6–2 3–6 6–1; A. Portas (LL) d. T. Johansson 7–6 6–4; F. Santoro (12) bye; G. Kuerten (13) bye; F. Meligeni d. D. Prinosil (WC) 3–6 6–4 6–4; C. Costa d. R. Vasek (Q) 6–2 6–0; A. Corretja (3) bye; A. Berasategui (8) bye; G. Raoux d. D. Sanguinetti 6–2 7–6; F. Vicente (Q) d. M. Meneschincheri (Q) 6–7 7–5 4–0 ret; T. Muster (10) bye; N. Escude (16) bye; D. Hrbaty d. M. Norman 6–3 6–2; J. Alonso-Pintor d. S. Bruguera 6–4 6–2; C. Moya (2) bye.
2nd round: Rios (1) d. Knippschild (WC) 7–6 6–2; Dreekmann (WC) d. Larsson (15) 6–4 7–5; Becker d. Pioline (9) 7–6 6–1; Mantilla (7) d. Fromberg 7–6 7–5; Ulihrach d. Kafelnikov (4) 6–3 3–6 6–3; Clavet (14) d. Blanco 7–6 7–5; Gustafsson (11) d. Haas 6–3 6–1; Kucera (5) d. Dosedel 6–1 6–1; A. Costa (6) d. Squillari (Q) 6–3 6–4; Portas (LL) d. Santoro (12) 1–6 6–2 7–6; Kuerten (13) d. Meligeni 7–6 6–4; C. Costa d. Corretja (3) 7–6 6–7 7–5; Raoux d. Berasategui (8) 6–1 6–2; Vicente (Q) d. Muster (10) 6–3 6–7 7–5; Hrbaty d. Escude (16) 2–6 6–3 6–3; Moya (2) d. Alonso-Pintor 7–6 7–5.
3rd round: Rios (1) d. Dreekmann (WC) 6–3 6–4; Becker d. Mantilla (7) 7–6 7–5; Ulihrach d. Clavet (14) 7–6 6–2; Kucera (5) d. Gustafsson (11) 6–1 6–3; A. Costa (6) d. Portas (LL) 6–1 6–3; Kuerten (13) d. C. Costa 6–2 6–4; Vicente (Q) d. Raoux 6–7 6–3 6–2; Moya (2) d. Hrbaty 6–2 6–2.
Quarter-finals: Rios (1) d. Becker 6–2 6–0; Kucera (5) d. Ulihrach 6–4 6–4; Kuerten (13) d. A. Costa (6) 7–5 6–0; Moya (2) d. Vicente (Q) 3–6 6–3 6–2.
Semi-finals: Kucera (5) d. Rios (1) 6–1 6–7 6–4; Kuerten (13) d. Moya (2) 7–6 6–4.
Final: Kuerten (13) d. Kucera (5) 4–6 6–2 6–4.
MEN'S DOUBLES – Final: Delaitre/Santoro d. Eagle/Grabb (3) 6–1 3–6 6–3.

LEGG MASON TENNIS CLASSIC ($575,000)
WASHINGTON, DC, 20–26 JULY
MEN'S SINGLES – 1st round: M. Chang (1) bye; M. Sell d. R. Bryan (WC) 7–6 6–0; L. Burgsmuller d. C. Caratti 7–6 6–1; M. Damm (15) d. G. Canas 6–4 7–6; A. Ilie (10) d. I. Heuberger 6–4 5–7 6–3; J. Gimelstob d. L. Hewitt 6–3 2–6 6–2; M. Ondruska d. E. Ran (Q) 6–4 6–0; J. Courier (WC) (7) bye; B. Black (4) bye; G. Stafford d. M. Tebbutt 6–4 3–6 6–3; W. Black d. J. Van Lottum 6–3 6–3; S. Draper (14) d. A. Hernandez 6–3 3–6 6–4; G. Pozzi (11) d. O. Burrieza 4–6 6–4 6–0; A. Sa d. T. Ketola 7–6 6–4; S. Sargsian d. P. Goldstein (WC) 3–6 6–4 7–5; F. De Wulf (5) bye; V. Spadea (6) bye; D. Nainkin (Q) d. S. Stolle 6–2 7–6; D. Nargiso d. O. Motevassel (Q) 6–4 6–4; R. Schuttler d. J. Gambill (12) 4–6 6–3 6–3; D. Caldwell (Q) d. K. Carlsen (13) 3–6 6–4 7–5; R. Delgado d. S. Campbell 6–3 6–2; J. Arias (Q) d. W. McGuire (Q) 6–4 2–5 ret; W. Ferreira (3) bye; S. Schalken (8) bye; M. Ruah (Q) d. P. Harsanyi (WC) 6–0 6–7 6–2; S. Lareau d. S. Humphries (WC) 6–4 6–4; J. Tarango (9) d. J. Van Herck 6–1 6–2; D. Nestor d. D. Vacek (16) 6–4 6–4; C. Van Garsse d. M. Hadad (PR) 6–3 6–4; D. Wheaton d. P. Tramacchi 6–3 6–3; A. Agassi (2) bye.
2nd round: Chang (1) d. Sell 6–2 6–3; Damm (15) d. Burgsmuller 6–2 6–4; Gimelstob d. Ilie (10) 6–7 6–3 6–1; Courier (WC) (7) d. Ondruska 7–6 7–6; B. Black (4) d. Stafford 4–6 6–1 6–0; Draper (14) d. W. Black 4–6 6–3 7–6; Pozzi (11) d. Sa 7–6 6–1; De Wulf (5) d. Sargsian 7–6 6–1; Spadea (6) d. Nainkin (Q) 6–4 6–7 6–1; Nargiso d. Schuttler 6–4 6–4; Caldwell (Q) d. Delgado 3–6 7–6 6–2; Ferreira (3) d. Arias (Q) 6–1 6–2; Ruah (Q) d. Schalken (8) 3–6 6–4 6–3; Lareau d. Tarango (9) 7–6 6–2; Van Garsse d. Nestor 6–7 6–4 6–4; Agassi (2) d. Wheaton 6–4 6–2.
3rd round: Chang (1) d. Damm (15) 6–4 6–1; Courier (WC) (7) d. Gimelstob 6–3 6–4; Draper (14) d. B. Black (4) 6–2 6–4; De Wulf (5) d. Pozzi (11) 7–6 6–4; Spadea (6) d. Nargiso 7–6 6–4; Ferreira (3) d. Caldwell (Q) 7–5 6–3; Lareau d. Ruah (Q) 6–4 6–3; Agassi (2) d. Van Garsse 6–3 6–4.
Quarter-finals: Chang (1) d. Courier (WC) (7) 6–3 6–4; Draper (14) d. De Wulf (5) 6–3 6–2; Ferreira (3) d. Spadea (6) 6–4 6–7 6–1; Agassi (2) d. Lareau 6–1 6–2.

Semi-finals: Draper (14) d. Chang (1) w/o; Agassi (2) d. Ferreira (3) 6–1 6–0.
Final: Agassi (2) d. Draper (14) 6–2 6–0.
MEN'S DOUBLES – Final: Stafford/Ullyett (5) d. W. Ferreira/Galbraith (1) 6–2 6–4.

RCA CHAMPIONSHIPS ($745,000)

INDIANAPOLIS, IN, 17–23 AUGUST

MEN'S SINGLES – 1st round: M. Rios (1) bye; R. Bryan (WC) d. S. Campbell 6–1 0–6 6–1; B. Black d. B. Ellwood (Q) 6–2 6–2; G. Pozzi d. A. Gaudenzi (16) 7–6 6–1; C. Pioline (9) d. M. Damm 7–6 6–2; R. Delgado d. J. Golmard 6–3 6–2; B. MacPhie (WC) d. J. Burillo 6–4 6–3; A. Berasategui (8) bye; J. Bjorkman (4) bye; J. Stoltenberg d. A. Ilie 6–7 6–3 6–4; J. Novak d. X. Malisse (WC) 6–3 7–5; W. Ferreira (14) d. D. Nestor 6–4 7–6; T. Muster (12) d. P. Goldstein (Q) 6–2 6–2; W. Black d. B. Karbacher (Q) 6–1 3–6 7–6; M. Tebbutt d. M. Sell (Q) 7–5 4–6 6–3; A. Agassi (5) bye; A. Corretja (6) bye; S. Draper d. L. Tieleman (Q) 6–4 6–7 6–3; A. Voinea d. T. Ketola (LL) 6–2 6–0; M. Philippoussis (11) d. G. Stafford 6–3 6–2; F. Clavet (13) d. M. Merklein (Q) 6–3 6–2; T. Haas d. F. Vicente 7–6 6–2; M. Larsson d. S. Grosjean 2–6 7–6 6–2; G. Rusedski (3) bye; A. Costa (7) bye; D. Wheaton (WC) d. T. Dent (WC) 6–7 7–5 6–1; H. Arazi d. M. Ondruska 7–6 6–2; F. Mantilla (10) d. V. Spadea 7–5 7–6; T. Martin (15) d. W. McGuire (Q) 6–3 6–4; A. Clement d. P. Haarhuis 6–4 6–4; T. Johansson d. M. Tillstrom 6–3 6–4; C. Moya (2) bye.
2nd round: Rios (1) d. Bryan (WC) 6–4 6–4; B. Black d. Pozzi 7–6 6–4; Delgado d. Pioline (9) 7–6 6–1; MacPhie (WC) d. Berasategui (8) 6–1 6–4; Stoltenberg d. Bjorkman (4) 7–5 6–3; Ferreira (14) d. Novak 7–6 6–2; W. Black d. Muster (12) 6–3 5–7 6–4; Agassi (5) d. Tebbutt 6–1 6–0; Corretja (6) d. Draper 6–3 6–7 7–5; Philippoussis (11) d. Voinea 7–5 6–4; Clavet (13) d. Haas 6–4 6–0; Rusedski (3) d. Larsson 7–6 6–3; Wheaton (WC) d. A. Costa (7) 6–2 6–4; Arazi d. Mantilla (10) 6–2 4–6 6–4; Martin (15) d. Clement 4–6 6–1 6–4; Johansson d. Moya (2) 6–7 6–0 6–1.
3rd round: B. Black d. Rios (1) 5–7 6–1 7–5; Delgado d. MacPhie (WC) 7–5 7–5; Ferreira (14) d. Stoltenberg 3–6 7–5 7–6; Agassi (5) d. W. Black 7–6 3–6 6–1; Corretja (6) d. Philippoussis (11) 4–6 6–4 6–3; Rusedski (3) d. Clavet (13) 6–1 7–6; Arazi d. Wheaton (WC) 6–3 6–2; Martin (15) d. Johansson 6–1 7–6.
Quarter-finals: Delgado d. B. Black 6–1 2–6 6–4; Agassi (5) d. Ferreira (14) 6–2 6–1; Corretja (6) d. Rusedski (3) 6–4 6–3; Martin (15) d. Arazi (WC) 7–6 7–6.
Semi-finals: Agassi (5) d. Delgado 7–6 6–3; Corretja (6) d. Martin (15) 6–2 7–6.
Final: Corretja (6) d. Agassi (5) 2–6 6–2 6–3.
MEN'S DOUBLES – Final: Novak/Rikl d. Knowles/Nestor (5) 6–2 7–6.

PILOT PEN INTERNATIONAL TENNIS TOURNAMENT ($745,000)

NEW HAVEN, CT, 17–23 AUGUST

MEN'S SINGLES – 1st round: P. Sampras (1) bye; L. Hewitt (WC) d. S. Sargsian 6–3 6–4; S. Bruguera d. P. McEnroe (WC) 7–6 3–6 6–3; L. Paes (Q) d. M. Rosset (15) 6–3 6–0; N. Kiefer (10) d. L. Burgsmuller (Q) 6–3 6–3; M. Woodforde d. M. Safin 6–4 7–5; G. Grant (WC) d. C. Dosedel 6–2 6–3; G. Ivanisevic (8) bye; P. Korda (3) bye; A. Medvedev d. E. Erlich (Q) 7–6 6–3; K. Carlsen d. D. Prinosil 7–6 6–4; B. Ulihrach (13) d. J. Sanchez 6–1 6–1; G. Kuerten (11) d. M. Puerta 6–3 6–4; A. O'Brien (WC) d. M. Mirnyi (Q) 6–3 6–4; T. Woodbridge d. M. Goellner 3–6 6–4 6–3; Y. Kafelnikov (5) bye; T. Henman (6) bye; V. Santopadre d. A. Radulescu (LL) 6–2 6–3; D. Sanguinetti d. J. Stark (WC) 6–4 7–5; F. Santoro (12) d. L. Arnold 1–6 6–3 6–1; R. Schuttler d. N. Escude (14) 4–6 6–4 6–3; H. Levy (Q) d. G. Canas 7–5 6–3; M. Washington (PR) d. S. Lareau 6–4 6–4; R. Krajicek (4) bye; K. Kucera (7) bye; H. Gumy d. D. Vacek 5–3 ret; D. Van Scheppingen d. I. Heuberger (Q) 6–4 ret; J. Siemerink (9) d. N. Lapentti 6–4 6–3; G. Raoux (16) d. J. Gimelstob 7–6 6–4; J. Van Lottum d. J. Alonso-Pintor 6–4 6–2; J. Tarango d. L. Roux (Q) 6–2 6–2; P. Rafter (2) bye.
2nd round: Sampras (1) d. Hewitt (WC) 6–1 7–6; Paes (Q) d. Bruguera 6–1 6–2; Kiefer (10) d. Woodforde 6–0 7–5; Ivanisevic (8) d. Grant (WC) 6–3 3–6 6–3; Korda (3) d. Medvedev 6–3 3–6 6–1; Ulihrach (13) d. Carlsen 3–6 6–4 6–4; Kuerten (11) d. O'Brien (WC) 6–3 6–2; Kafelnikov (5) d. Woodbridge 6–0 6–2; Henman (6) d. Santopadre (LL) 6–2 6–3; Sanguinetti d. Santoro (12) 6–1 6–7 7–5; Levy (Q) d. Schuttler 6–3 6–3; Krajicek (4) d. Washington (P) 7–5 6–4; Kucera (7) d. Gumy 6–3 6–3; Siemerink (9) d. Van Scheppingen 6–3 6–3; Raoux (16) d. Van Lottum 6–3 6–4; Rafter (2) d. Tarango 6–2 6–1.
3rd round: Paes (Q) d. Sampras (1) 6–3 6–4; Ivanisevic (8) d. Kiefer (10) 6–3 7–5; Ulihrach (13) d. Korda (3) 7–6 6–3; Kafelnikov (5) d. Kuerten (11) 6–4 6–4; Henman (6) d. Sanguinetti 4–6 6–3 6–3; Krajicek (4) d. Levy (Q) 6–2 6–4; Kucera (7) d. Siemerink (9) 6–4 7–5; Raoux (16) d. Rafter (2) 7–6 6–3.
Quarter-finals: Ivanisevic (8) d. Paes (Q) 6–2 6–4; Kafelnikov (5) d. Ulihrach (13) 4–6 6–3 6–3; Krajicek (4) d. Henman (6) 5–7 6–2 7–6; Kucera (7) d. Raoux (16) 3–6 6–3 6–1.
Semi-finals: Ivanisevic (8) d. Kafelnikov (5) 6–3 6–4; Kucera (7) d. Krajicek (4) 7–6 6–4.
Final: Kucera (7) d. Ivanisevic (8) 6–4 5–7 6–2.
MEN'S DOUBLES – Final: Arthurs/Tramacchi d. Lareau/O'Brien (4) 7–6 1–6 6–3.

CA TENNIS TROPHY ($675,000)

VIENNA, 12–18 OCTOBER

MEN'S SINGLES – 1st round: P. Sampras (WC) (1) d. J. Kroslak (Q) 6–2 7–5; J. Tarango (Q) d. J. Stoltenberg 6–2 6–2; T. Enqvist d. W. Schranz (WC) 4–6 6–3 6–2; T. Henman (8) d. M. Gustafsson 6–3 6–4; P. Korda (4) d. F. Santoro 7–6 6–2; T. Martin d. N. Kiefer 4–6 6–3 6–4; C. Pioline d. R. Fromberg 6–3 7–6; R. Krajicek (6) d. A. Costa 6–3 6–7 6–4; K. Kucera (5) d. W. Ferreira 6–4 3–6 7–5; T. Haas d. A. Clement (Q) 6–4 1–6 6–3;

J. Bjorkman d. D. Prinosil (Q) 6–4 7–6; B. Ulihrach d. C. Moya (3) 7–6 6–4; G. Rusedski d. Y. Kafelnikov (WC) (7) 6–3 3–6 7–6; T. Muster d. J. Siemerink 6–2 6–4; M. Norman d. D. Vacek 7–5 6–4; P. Rafter (2) d. B. Black 6–3 7–6.
2nd round: Sampras (WC) (1) d. Tarango (Q) 5–7 6–1 6–3; Henman (8) d. Enqvist 6–7 6–3 6–3; Martin d. Korda (4) 6–3 7–6; Pioline d. Krajicek (6) 7–6 6–7 6–4; Kucera (5) d. Haas 7–5 6–4; Bjorkman d. Ulihrach 6–4 6–1; Rusedski d. Muster 6–4 6–3; Rafter (2) d. Norman 6–3 6–2.
Quarter-finals: Sampras (WC) (1) d. Henman (8) 6–0 6–3; Martin d. Pioline 6–4 6–4; Kucera (5) d. Bjorkman 6–3 6–2; Rusedski d. Rafter (2) 6–3 7–6.
Semi-finals: Sampras (WC) (1) d. Martin 6–3 7–6; Kucera (5) d. Rusedski 7–6 6–4.
Final: Sampras (WC) (1) d. Kucera (5) 6–3 7–6 6–1.
MEN'S DOUBLES – Final: Kafelnikov/Vacek d. Adams/De Jager 7–5 6–3.

HEINEKEN OPEN SINGAPORE ($575,000)

SINGAPORE, 12–18 OCTOBER
MEN'S SINGLES – 1st round: M. Rios (1) d. S. Lareau 6–2 6–0; A. Pavel d. D. Van Scheppingen 7–6 6–4; L. Hewitt (Q) d. L. Roux (PR) 6–2 7–6; J. Gimelstob d. R. Delgado (8) 6–4 6–4; J. Gambill (4) d. J. Stark (WC) 6–1 6–2; B. Steven d. C. Vinck (Q) 6–3 6–4; J. Courier (WC) d. D. Nestor (Q) 6–3 6–2; M. Tillstrom (6) d. M. Bhupathi (WC) 6–1 6–3; S. Schalken d. A. Ilie (5) 6–4 6–2; T. Woodbridge d. S. Sargsian 7–6 6–7 6–4; J. Van Lottum d. W. Black 7–5 6–2; M. Kohlmann (Q) d. M. Chang (3) 2–6 6–3 6–4; K. Carlsen d. P. Haarhuis (7) 0–6 6–3 6–4; M. Damm d. L. Paes 7–5 6–1; M. Woodforde d. M. Ondruska 7–6 6–2; G. Ivanisevic (2) d. S. Campbell 6–2 6–1.
2nd round: Rios (1) d. Pavel 6–2 6–4; Hewitt (Q) d. Gimelstob 6–7 6–2 7–6; Gambill (4) d. Steven w/o; Courier (WC) d. Tillstrom (WC) 6–4 2–6 7–6; Schalken d. Woodbridge 7–6 6–4; Van Lottum d. Kohlmann (Q) 6–4 6–2; Carlsen d. Damm 6–1 6–1; Woodforde d. Ivanisevic (2) 6–4 7–6.
Quarter-finals: Rios (1) d. Hewitt (Q) 5–7 6–3 6–4; Courier (WC) d. Gambill (4) 6–4 6–4; Schalken d. Van Lottum 3–6 6–3 6–4; Woodforde d. Carlsen 4–6 6–2 6–3.
Semi-finals: Rios (1) d. Courier (WC) 6–2 6–1; Woodforde d. Schalken 0–6 6–4 6–2.
Final: Rios (1) d. Woodforde 6–4 6–2.
MEN'S DOUBLES – Final: Woodbridge/Woodforde (1) d. Bhupathi/Paes (2) 6–2 6–3.

World Series

QATAR MOBIL OPEN ($975,000)

DOHA, 5–11 JANUARY

MEN'S SINGLES – Quarter-finals: F. Santoro (8) d. G. Rusedski (1) 6–2 3–6 6–3; G. Ivanisevic (4) d. B. Karbacher (WC) 7–6 6–7 6–3; P. Korda (3) d. T. Henman (5) 7–5 4–6 6–4; A. Medvedev (7) d. S. Schalken 4–6 6–4 6–4. ***Semi-finals:*** Santoro (8) d. Ivanisevic (4) 6–1 6–4; Korda (3) d. Medvedev (7) 6–3 6–4. ***Final:*** Korda (3) d. Santoro (8) 6–0 6–3.
MEN'S DOUBLES – Final: Bhupathi/Paes (1) d. Delaitre/Santoro 6–4 3–6 6–4.

AUSTRALIAN MEN'S HARDCOURT CHAMPIONSHIPS ($315,000)

ADELAIDE, 5–11 JANUARY

MEN'S SINGLES – Quarter-finals: J. Stoltenberg d. N. Escude (Q) 6–7 6–1 7–5; T. Woodbridge (5) d. J. Golmard (Q) 2–6 6–4 6–4; L. Hewitt (WC) d. V. Spadea 7–5 3–6 6–1; A. Agassi (WC) d. B. Steven 1–6 6–1 6–1. ***Semi-finals:*** Stoltenberg d. Woodbridge (5) 6–4 6–1; Hewitt (WC) d. Agassi (WC) 7–6 7–6. ***Final:*** Hewitt (WC) d. Stoltenberg 3–6 6–3 7–6.
MEN'S DOUBLES – Final: Eagle/Florent d. E. Ferreira/Leach (2) 6–4 6–7 6–3.

SYDNEY OPEN ($315,000)

SYDNEY, 12–17 JANUARY

MEN'S SINGLES – Quarter-finals: P. Rafter (1) d. T. Martin 6–4 6–7 6–1; T. Henman (6) d. T. Enqvist 3–6 7–5 6–4; K. Kucera d. J. Stoltenberg 6–3 2–6 6–4; M. Tebbutt (Q) d. A. Costa (7) 6–3 6–3. ***Semi-finals:*** Henman (6) d. Rafter (1) 7–6 7–5; Kucera d. Tebbutt (Q) 4–6 7–6 6–0. ***Final:*** Kucera d. Henman (6) 7–5 6–4.
MEN'S DOUBLES – Final: Woodbridge/Woodforde (1) d. Eltingh/Nestor (3) 6–3 7–5.

BELL SOUTH OPEN ($315,000)

AUCKLAND, 12–17 JANUARY

MEN'S SINGLES – Quarter-finals: M. Rios (1) d. K. Carlsen 5–7 6–4 6–1; B. Black d. C. Vinck (Q) 6–4 2–6 7–5; R. Fromberg d. D. Hrbaty (3) 6–2 7–6; F. Mantilla (2) d. C. Costa 6–2 6–3. ***Semi-finals:*** Rios (1) d. Black 6–1 6–3; Fromberg d. Mantilla (2) 6–3 7–6. ***Final:*** Rios (1) d. Fromberg 4–6 6–4 7–6.
MEN'S DOUBLES – Final: Galbraith/Steven (2) d. Nijssen/Tarango 6–4 6–2.

CROATIAN INDOOR CHAMPIONSHIPS ($375,000)

SPLIT, 2–8 FEBRUARY

MEN'S SINGLES – Quarter-finals: G. Rusedski (WC) (1) d. M. Damm 6–1 6–4; M. Rosset (5) d. R. Schuttler 6–2 6–2; M. Sinner d. K. Carlsen 5–7 6–3 7–6; G. Ivanisevic (2) d. J. Novak (7) 7–6 7–6. ***Semi-finals:*** Rusedski (WC) (1) d. Rosset (5) 6–7 7–6 7–6; Ivanisevic (2) d. Sinner 6–3 7–6. ***Final:*** Ivanisevic (2) d. Rusedski (WC) (1) 7–6 7–6.
MEN'S DOUBLES – Final: Damm/Novak (1) d. Bergh/Fredriksson 7–6 6–2.

MARSEILLE OPEN ($514,250)

MARSEILLE, 2–8 FEBRUARY

MEN'S SINGLES – Quarter-finals: Y. Kafelnikov (1) d. A. Clement 6–2 3–6 6–4; M. Tillstrom d. A. Boetsch 4–6 6–0 7–6; T. Enqvist (6) d. M. Gustafsson 6–2 1–6 6–3; R. Krajicek (2) d. D. Vacek 4–6 6–4 6–4. ***Semi-finals:*** Kafelnikov (1) d. Tillstrom 7–6 6–4; Enqvist (6) d. Krajicek (2) 6–3 6–7 6–3. ***Final:*** Enqvist (6) d. Kafelnikov (1) 6–4 6–1.
MEN'S DOUBLES – Final: Johnson/Montana (2) d. Keil/Middleton 6–4 3–6 6–3.

DUBAI OPEN ($1,014,250)

DUBAI, 9–15 FEBRUARY

MEN'S SINGLES – Quarter-finals: J. Bjorkman (1) d. C. Moya 7–6 6–1; A. Corretja (4) d. C. Costa (WC) 7–6 5–7 6–4; F. Mantilla (6) d. A. Berasategui 6–4 6–4; W. Ferreira d. N. Kiefer 6–3 6–2. ***Semi-finals:*** Corretja (4) d. Bjorkman (1) 6–3 6–3; Mantilla (6) d. Ferreira 7–6 4–6 6–4. ***Final:*** Corretja (4) d. Mantilla (6) 7–6 6–1.
MEN'S DOUBLES – Final: Bhupathi/Paes (1) d. Johnson/Montana (2) 6–2 7–5.

SYBASE OPEN ($315,000)
SAN JOSE, CA, 9–15 FEBRUARY
MEN'S SINGLES – Quarter-finals: P. Sampras (1) d. M. Woodforde (8) 6–0 6–2; J. van Lottum (Q) d. T. Martin 2–6 6–4 7–6; A. Agassi (WC) d. J. Gambill (Q) 7–5 7–6; M. Chang (2) d. T. Haas (7) 6–3 6–7 6–4. ***Semi-finals:*** Sampras (1) d. van Lottum (Q) 6–3 2–6 6–2; Agassi (WC) d. Chang (2) 6–4 7–6. ***Final:*** Agassi (WC) d. Sampras (1) 6–2 6–4.
MEN'S DOUBLES – Final: Woodbridge/Woodforde (1) d. Aerts/Sa 6–1 7–5.

ST. PETERSBURG OPEN ($315,000)
ST. PETERSBURG, 9–15 FEBRUARY
MEN'S SINGLES – Quarter-finals: R. Krajicek (WC) (1) d. D. Vacek (8) 7–6 6–1; T. Johansson (5) d. F. Santoro (3) 6–3 6–3; M. Rosset (4) d. D. Hrbaty (6) 6–4 6–3; C. Pioline (2) d. H. Dreekmann 4–6 6–3 7–5. ***Semi-finals:*** Krajicek (WC) (1) d. Johansson (5) 6–4 6–4; Rosset (4) d. Pioline (2) 6–1 6–4. ***Final:*** Krajicek (WC) (1) d. Rosset (4) 6–4 7–6.
MEN'S DOUBLES – Final: Kulti/Tillstrom (4) d. Barnard/Haygarth (Q) 3–6 6–3 7–6.

ABN/AMRO WORLD TENNIS TOURNAMENT ($725,000)
ROTTERDAM, 2–8 MARCH
MEN'S SINGLES – Quarter-finals: J. Siemerink d. P. Rafter (1) 6–4 6–4; R. Krajicek (5) d. G. Rusedski (3) 3–6 7–6 7–6; T. Johansson d. J. van Herck 7–6 6–2; B. Steven d. T. Carbonell (Q) 4–6 7–6 7–5. ***Semi-finals:*** Siemerink d. Krajicek (5) 6–4 4–6 6–4; Johansson d. Steven 6–3 7–5. ***Final:*** Siemerink d. Johansson 7–6 6–2.
MEN'S DOUBLES – Final: Eltingh/Haarhuis (1) d. Broad/Norval (2) 7–6 6–3.

FRANKLIN TEMPLETON TENNIS CLASSIC ($315,000)
SCOTTSDALE, AZ, 2–8 MARCH
MEN'S SINGLES – Quarter-finals: T. Haas d. S. Lareau (E) 6–4 6–1; A. Agassi (WC) d. J. Gambill (Q) 6–3 7–6; J. Stoltenberg d. A. Gaudenzi 7–5 7–6; S. Schalken d. A. Costa (2) 6–3 6–4. ***Semi-finals:*** Agassi (WC) d. Haas 6–2 6–1; Stoltenberg d. Schalken 6–3 6–3. ***Final:*** Agassi (WC) d. Stoltenberg 6–4 7–6.
MEN'S DOUBLES – Final: Suk/Tebbutt d. Kinnear/Wheaton (Q) 4–6 6–1 7–6.

COPENHAGEN OPEN ($210,000)
COPENHAGEN, 9–15 MARCH
MEN'S SINGLES – Quarter-finals: D. Prinosil d. O. Delaitre (Q) 6–3 6–3; J. Siemerink (4) d. B. Steven (6) 6–3 6–3; K. Carlsen d. G. Pozzi 6–3 3–6 6–1; M. Gustafsson (2) d. A. Pavel 6–3 4–6 6–3. ***Semi-finals:*** Prinosil d. Siemerink (4) 6–3 7–6; Gustafsson (2) d. Carlsen 6–4 5–7 6–2. ***Final:*** Gustafsson (2) d. Prinosil 3–6 6–1 6–1.
MEN'S DOUBLES – Final: Kempers/Oosting (4) d. Siemerink/Steven 6–4 7–6.

GRAND PRIX HASSAN II ($210,000)
CASABLANCA, 23–29 March
MEN'S SINGLES – Quarter-finals: A. Calatrava d. A. Portas (1) 6–2 6–4; K. Alami (3) d. F. Vicente 3–6 7–6 7–5; A. Gaudenzi (4) d. J. Marin (6) 6–7 7–5 6–2; S. Grosjean (Q) d. H. Arazi (2) 7–5 2–6 6–3. ***Semi-finals:*** Calatrava d. Alami (3) 6–3 6–7 7–6; Gaudenzi (4) d. Grosjean (Q) 6–4 6–4. ***Final:*** Gaudenzi (4) d. Calatrava 6–4 5–7 6–4.
MEN'S DOUBLES – Final: Gaudenzi/Nargiso (WC) d. Brandi/Messori (4) 6–4 7–6.

ESTORIL OPEN ($600,000)
LISBON, 6–12 APRIL
MEN'S SINGLES – Quarter-finals: K. Alami d. F. Mantilla (WC) (1) 3–6 7–5 6–1; T. Muster (6) d. A. Costa (4) 6–4 6–4; A. Berasategui (3) d. J. Marin (Q) 3–6 6–4 6–3; C. Moya (2) d. C. Costa 7–6 6–7 6–2. ***Semi-finals:*** Muster (6) d. Alami 3–6 6–2 6–4; Berasategui (3) d. Moya (2) 6–1 6–1. ***Final:*** Berasategui (3) d. Muster (6) 3–6 6–1 6–3.
MEN'S DOUBLES – Final: Johnson/Montana (1) d. Roditi/Wibier 6–1 2–6 6–1.

GOLD FLAKE OPEN ($398,940)
MADRAS, 6–12 APRIL
MEN'S SINGLES – Quarter-finals: P. Rafter (1) d. L. Burgsmuller 7–6 0–6 7–5; L. Paes d. G. Solves 6–7 6–4 7–5; M. Tillstrom (5) d. M. Woodforde (3) 6–3 2–6 7–6; T. Woodbridge (2) d. A. Pavel (8) 6–4 6–4. ***Semi-finals***: Rafter (1) d. Paes 6–3 7–6; Tillstrom (5) d. Woodbridge (2) 6–2 6–2. ***Final:*** Rafter (1) d. Tillstrom (5) 6–3 6–4.
MEN'S DOUBLES – Final: Bhupathi/Paes (2) d. Delaitre/Mirnyi (4) 6–7 6–3 6–2.

SALEM OPEN ($315,000)
HONG KONG, 6–12 APRIL
MEN'S SINGLES – Quarter-finals: B. Black d. G. Pozzi (7) 6–4 6–0; S. Lareau d. O. Burrieza 6–1 7–6; T. Johansson (3) d. S. Stolle 7–6 7–5; K. Carlsen (8) d. N. Godwin (Q) 7–5 6–1. ***Semi-finals:*** Black d. Lareau 6–7 7–5 7–6; Carlsen (8) d. Johansson (3) 6–2 6–2. ***Final:*** Carlsen (8) d. Black 6–2 6–0.
MEN'S DOUBLES – Final: Black/O'Brien (3) d. Godwin/Ketola 7–5 6–1.

US MEN'S CLAY COURT CHAMPIONSHIPS ($289,250)

ORLANDO, FL, 20–26 APRIL

MEN'S SINGLES – Quarter-finals: M. Chang (1) d. M. Carlsson (Q) 6–3 6–1; M. Tillstrom d. A. Ilie (Q) 6–3 6–3; J. Courier (3) d. M. Craca 6–0 6–3; A. Pavel d. A. Calatrava 6–4 2–6 6–4. ***Semi-finals:*** Chang (1) d. Tillstrom 6–3 6–4; Courier (3) d. Pavel 4–6 6–3 6–2. ***Final:*** Courier (3) d. Chang (1) 7–5 3–6 7–5.
MEN'S DOUBLES – Final: Stafford/Ullyett d. Tebbutt/Tillstrom (4) 4–6 6–4 7–5.

BMW OPEN 1998 ($500,000)

MUNICH, 27 APRIL–3 MAY

MEN'S SINGLES – Quarter-finals: T. Enqvist (7) d. O. Gross 6–3 6–3; M. Gustafsson d. N. Escude 6–3 6–1; G. Blanco d. T. Nydahl 7–5 5–7 7–6; A. Agassi (8) d. J. Bjorkman (2) 6–2 6–2. ***Semi-finals:*** Enqvist (7) d. Gustafsson 6–3 6–4; Agassi (8) d. Blanco 6–4 6–4. ***Final:*** Enqvist (7) d. Agassi (8) 6–7 7–6 6–3.
MEN'S DOUBLES – Final: Woodbridge/Woodforde (1) d. Eagle/Florent (2) 6–0 6–3.

PAEGAS CZECH OPEN ($340,000)

PRAGUE, 27 APRIL–3 MAY

MEN'S SINGLES – Quarter-finals: C. Dosedel d. J. Diaz 6–1 6–4; N. Lapentti d. F. Vicente 6–0 7–5; D. Pescariu d. J. Sanchez 6–7 6–3 6–3; F. Meligeni d. A. Chesnokov 6–3 6–1. ***Semi-finals:*** Dosedel d. Lapentti 3–6 6–3 6–2; Meligeni d. Pescariu 7–6 7–6. ***Final:*** Meligeni d. Dosedel 6–1 6–4.
MEN'S DOUBLES – Final: Arthurs/Kratzmann d. Bergh/Kulti 6–1 6–1.

AT&T CHALLENGE ($315,000)

ATLANTA, GA, 27 APRIL–3 MAY

MEN'S SINGLES – Quarter-finals: P. Sampras (1) d. R. Delgado 7–6 7–6; A. Calatrava (Q) d. S. Campbell 4–0 ret; A. Pavel (6) d. F. Squillari 6–1 6–2; J. Stoltenberg (2) d. R. Reneberg 6–4 6–1. ***Semi-finals:*** Sampras (1) d. Calatrava (Q) 7–6 6–3; Stoltenberg (2) d. Pavel (6) 6–2 6–4. ***Final:*** Sampras (1) d. Stoltenberg (2) 6–7 6–3 7–6.
MEN'S DOUBLES – Final: E. Ferreira/Haygarth d. O'Brien/Reneberg (1) 6–3 0–6 6–2.

AMERICA'S RED CLAY TENNIS CHAMPIONSHIP ($245,000)

CORAL SPRINGS, FL, 4–10 MAY

MEN'S SINGLES – Quarter-finals: A. Ilie (Q) d. S. Grosjean 6–3 6–7 6–3; J. Gimelstob d. X. Malisse (Q) 6–3 4–6 6–3; J. Van Herck d. M. Tebbutt 6–1 6–4; D. Sanguinetti (8) d. R. Delgado 6–4 6–4. ***Semi-finals:*** Ilie (Q) d. Gimelstob 4–6 6–1 6–4; Sanguinetti (8) d. Van Herck 6–3 6–4. ***Final:*** Ilie (Q) d. Sanguinetti (8) 7–5 6–4.
MEN'S DOUBLES – Final: Stafford/Ullyett (4) d. Merklein/Spadea (WC) 7–5 6–4.

INTERNATIONALER RAIFFEISEN GRAND PRIX ($400,000)

ST. POLTEN, 18–24 MAY

MEN'S SINGLES – Quarter-finals: M. Rios (WC) (1) d. G. Blanco (7) 6–2 6–2; A. Gaudenzi (4) d. F. Clavet (6) 6–3 6–4; M. Filippini d. T. Muster (3) 6–3 6–4; V. Spadea d. S. Schalken 7–6 6–1. ***Semi-finals:*** Rios (WC) (1) d. Gaudenzi (4) 6–4 6–3; Spadea d. Filippini 6–3 6–0. ***Final:*** Rios (WC) (1) d. Spadea 6–2 6–0.
MEN'S DOUBLES – Final: Grabb/MacPherson (1) d. Adams/W. Black (3) 6–4 6–4.

GERRY WEBER OPEN ($875,000)

HALLE, 8–14 JUNE

MEN'S SINGLES – Quarter-finals: P. Haarhuis d. G. Pozzi 6–3 7–6; M. Larsson d. R. Krajicek (3) 6–4 6–2; T. Johansson d. H. Dreekmann (WC) 3–6 6–1 6–4; Y. Kafelnikov (2) d. M. Norman (8) 7–6 6–2. ***Semi-finals:*** Larsson d. Haarhuis 7–6 6–2; Kafelnikov (2) d. Johansson 7–6 6–7 6–3. ***Final:*** Y. Kafelnikov (2) d. M. Larsson 6–4 6–4.
MEN'S DOUBLES – Final: E. Ferreira/Leach (2) d. De Jager/Goellner 4–6 6–4 7–6.

THE STELLA ARTOIS GRASS COURT CHAMPIONSHIPS ($725,000)

QUEEN'S, LONDON, 8–14 JUNE

MEN'S SINGLES – Quarter-finals: M. Woodforde (15) d. T. Enqvist (8) 6–3 1–6 6–2; S. Draper d. D. Flach (Q) 7–6 7–6; B. Black (14) d. B. MacPhie (LL) 7–5 6–1; L. Tieleman (Q) d. T. Henman (7) 2–6 7–6 6–4. ***Semi-finals:*** Draper d. Woodforde (15) 6–3 6–2; Tieleman (Q) d. Black (14) 3–6 6–3 6–2. ***Final:*** Draper d. Tieleman (Q) 7–6 6–4.
MEN'S DOUBLES – Final: Abandoned: Woodbridge/Woodforde (1) v. Bjorkman/Rafter (3).

INTERNAZIONALI DI TENNIS CARISBO ($315,000)

BOLOGNA, 8–14 JUNE

MEN'S SINGLES – Quarter-finals: J. Marin d. M. Puerta 6–1 6–3; J. Alonso-Pintor (3) d. C. Costa (WC) (5) 6–3 7–6; K. Alami (6) d. M. Martelli 6–4 6–4; D. Hrbaty (8) d. F. Squillari 7–5 6–4. ***Semi-finals:*** Alonso-Pintor (3) d. Marin 7–5 6–3; Alami (6) d. Hrbaty (8) 1–6 7–6 7–5. ***Final:*** Alonso-Pintor (3) d. Alami (6) 6–1 6–4.
MEN'S DOUBLES – Final: Coupe/Rosner (1) d. Galimberti/Valeri (WC) 7–6 6–3.

HEINEKEN TROPHY ($475,000)
DEN BOSCH, 15–21 JUNE
MEN'S SINGLES – Quarter-finals: P. Rafter (1) d. S. Schalken 6–1 6–4; D. Van Scheppingen (Q) d. R. Krajicek (4) w/o; M. Damm d. K. Kucera (3) 6–7 6–1 6–4; J. Siemerink (7) d. S. Campbell 2–6 6–1 6–3. ***Semi-finals:*** Rafter (1) d. Van Scheppingen (Q) 6–3 6–4; Damm d. Siemerink (7) 7–6 6–3. ***Final:*** Rafter (1) d. Damm 7–6 6–2.
MEN'S DOUBLES – Final: Raoux/Siemerink (WC) d. Eagle/Florent 7–6 6–2.

THE NOTTINGHAM OPEN ($315,000)
NOTTINGHAM, 15–21 JUNE
MEN'S SINGLES – Quarter-finals: B. Black (7) d. G. Pozzi 7–5 6–2; S. Sargsian d. B. Steven (6) 7–6 6–2; J. Golmard d. S. Draper 6–4 6–3; J. Bjorkman (WC) (2) d. D. Prinosil 7–6 6–3. ***Semi-finals:*** Black (7) d. Sargsian 6–4 6–2; Bjorkman (WC) (2) d. Golmard 6–3 2–6 6–3. ***Final:*** Bjorkman (WC) (2) d. Black (7) 6–3 6–2.
MEN'S DOUBLES – Final: Gimelstob/Talbot (Q) d. Lareau/Nestor (3) 7–5 6–7 6–4.

RADO SWISS OPEN ($525,000)
GSTAAD, 6–12 JULY
MEN'S SINGLES – Quarter-finals: M. Rios (1) d. F. Clavet 6–3 7–5; B. Becker d. F. Mantilla (5) 6–4 6–4; A. Corretja (3) d. A. Costa (6) 5–7 6–2 6–2; F. De Wulf d. N. Kiefer (8) 1–6 6–3 6–4. ***Semi-finals:*** Becker d. Rios (1) 6–4 7–6; Corretja (3) d. De Wulf 6–3 6–7 6–3. ***Final:*** Corretja (3) d. Becker 7–6 7–5 6–3.
MEN'S DOUBLES – Final: Kuerten/Meligeni d. Orsanic/Suk (2) 6–4 7–5.

INVESTOR SWEDISH OPEN ($315,000)
BASTAD, 6–12 JULY
MEN'S SINGLES – Quarter-finals: M. Gustafsson (1) d. J. Golmard 6–7 1–0 ret; T. Johansson (6) d. K. Alami w/o; A. Medvedev d. A. Gaudenzi (3) 6–3 6–4; D. Hrbaty (7) d. J. Novak 3–6 6–4 6–4. ***Semi-finals:*** Gustafsson (1) d. Johansson (6) 6–3 4–6 7–5; Medvedev d. Hrbaty (7) 6–3 7–6. ***Final:*** Gustafsson (1) d. Medvedev 6–2 6–3.
MEN'S DOUBLES – Final: Gustafsson/Larsson (WC) d. Bale/Norval 6–4 6–2.

MILLER LITE HALL OF FAME TENNIS CHAMPIONSHIPS ($275,000)
NEWPORT, RI, 6–12 JULY
MEN'S SINGLES – Quarter-finals: J. Stoltenberg (1) d. J. Van Lottum (7) 6–1 6–2; N. Godwin d. J. Gimelstob 6–7 7–6 6–3; L. Paes d. R. Schuttler 7–6 6–2; L. Tieleman (WC) d. M. Knowles (Q) 6–4 7–5. ***Semi-finals:*** Godwin d. Stoltenberg (1) 3–6 6–1 7–6; Paes d. Tieleman (WC) 6–3 6–4. ***Final:*** Paes d. Godwin 6–3 6–2.
MEN'S DOUBLES – Final: Flach/Stolle d. Draper/Stoltenberg (WC) 6–2 4–6 7–6.

GENERALI OPEN ($500,000)
KITZBUHEL, 27 JULY–2 AUGUST
MEN'S SINGLES – Quarter-finals: F. Squillari (16) d. R. Fromberg (8) 6–4 4–6 6–4; A. Costa (3) d. F. De Wulf (12) 2–6 6–3 6–4; F. Clavet (6) d. F. Meligeni (13) 6–3 6–1; A. Gaudenzi (7) d. N. Lapentti (15) 6–3 7–6. ***Semi-finals:*** Costa (3) d. Squillari (16) 7–5 1–6 6–3; Gaudenzi (7) d. Clavet (6) 6–2 2–6 6–2. ***Final:*** Costa (3) d. Gaudenzi (7) 6–2 1–6 6–2 3–6 6–1.
MEN'S DOUBLES – Final: Kempers/Orsanic (2) d. Eagle/Kratzmann (1) 6–3 6–4.

INTERNATIONAL CHAMPIONSHIP OF CROATIA-UMAG ($375,000)
UMAG, 27 JULY–2 AUGUST
MEN'S SINGLES – Quarter-finals: J. Marin d. P. Haarhuis 6–2 7–6; M. Norman (WC) (6) d. K. Kucera (3) 1–6 6–4 6–4; M. Puerta d. G. Kuerten (4) 6–4 1–6 7–6; B. Ulihrach (7) d. F. Mantilla (2) 6–3 3–6 7–6. ***Semi-finals:*** Norman (WC) (6) d. Marin 7–6 6–3; Ulihrach (7) d. Puerta 6–3 6–3. ***Final:*** Ulihrach (7) d. Norman (WC) (6) 6–3 7–6.
MEN'S DOUBLES – Final: Broad/Norval (1) d. Novak/Rikl (2) 6–1 3–6 6–3.

INFINITI OPEN ($315,000)
LOS ANGELES, CA, 27 JULY–2 AUGUST
MEN'S SINGLES – Quarter-finals: J. Gimelstob (WC) d. P. Rafter (1) 6–4 6–3; A. Agassi (5) d. S. Stolle (LL) 7–6 6–2; G. Raoux d. M. Joyce (Q) 6–7 6–4 7–5; T. Henman (2) d. B. Black (7) 5–7 6–1 6–4. ***Semi-finals:*** Agassi (5) d. Gimelstob (WC) 6–0 7–6; Henman (2) d. Raoux 7–5 6–3. ***Final:*** Agassi (5) d. Henman (2) 6–4 6–4.
MEN'S DOUBLES – Final: Rafter/Stolle (3) d. Tarango/Vacek 6–4 6–4.

GROLSCH OPEN ($475,000)
AMSTERDAM, 3–9 AUGUST
MEN'S SINGLES – Quarter-finals: K. Kucera (1) d. D. Hrbaty (7) 6–2 6–1; R. Fromberg (6) d. A. Voinea (Q) 6–3 6–4; M. Norman d. G. Blanco 6–2 6–4; M. Zabaleta (Q) d. C. Dosedel (8) 2–6 7–6 7–6. ***Semi-finals:*** Fromberg (6) d. Kucera (1) 6–1 6–7 6–2; Norman d. Zabaleta (Q) 7–5 6–4. ***Final:*** Norman d. Fromberg (6) 6–3 6–3 2–6 6–4.
MEN'S DOUBLES – Final: Eltingh/Haarhuis (1) d. Hrbaty/Kucera (WC) 6–3 6–2.

INTERNAZIONALI DI TENNIS DI SAN MARINO ($275,000)

SAN MARINO, 10–16 AUGUST

MEN'S SINGLES – Quarter-finals: C. Costa (7) d. A. Gaudenzi (1) 7–5 6–1; D. Hrbaty (3) d. J. Viloca 2–6 6–4 6–0; M. Puerta d. M. Zabaleta (SE) 4–6 6–3 4–0 ret; R. Fromberg (2) d. V. Santopadre 6–4 7–5. ***Semi-finals:*** Hrbaty (3) d. Costa (SE) (7) 6–0 4–6 7–6; Puerta d. Fromberg (2) 6–2 3–6 6–3. ***Final:*** Hrbaty (3) d. Puerta 6–2 7–5.

MEN'S DOUBLES – Final: Novak/Rikl (2) d. Hood/Prieto (3) 6–4 7–6.

MFS PRO TENNIS CHAMPIONSHIP ($315,000)

BOSTON, MA, 24–30 AUGUST

MEN'S SINGLES – Quarter-finals: S. Grosjean (Q) d. J. Bjorkman (1) 7–6 6–1; M. Chang (4) d. G. Pozzi 6–4 2–6 6–1; C. Pioline (WC) (3) d. T. Muster (5) 7–5 6–3; P. Haarhuis (WC) d. S. Schalken 0–6 6–4 6–3. ***Semi-finals:*** Chang (4) d. Grosjean (Q) 7–5 4–6 6–3; Haarhuis (WC) d. Pioline (WC) (3) 7–5 4–6 6–3. ***Final:*** Chang (4) d. Haarhuis (WC) 6–3 6–4.

MEN'S DOUBLES – Final: Eltingh/Haarhuis (1) d. Haggard/Waite 6–3 6–2.

THE HAMLET CUP ($315,000)

LONG ISLAND, NY, 24–30 AUGUST

MEN'S SINGLES – Quarter-finals: F. Mantilla (8) d. G. Kuerten (WC) 6–4 2–6 6–4; M. Safin d. D. Prinosil (LL) 6–1 7–6; G. Rusedski (4) d. D. Vacek 6–2 6–3; P. Rafter (2) d. N. Escude 6–3 6–2. ***Semi-finals:*** Mantilla (8) d. Safin 6–3 5–7 6–4; Rafter (2) d. Rusedski (4) 6–4 7–5. ***Final:*** Rafter (2) d. Mantilla (8) 7–6 6–2.

MEN'S DOUBLES – Final: Alonso-Pintor/J. Sanchez (2) d. Coupe/Randall 6–4 6–4.

THE SAMSUNG OPEN ($375,000)

BOURNEMOUTH, 14–20 SEPTEMBER

MEN'S SINGLES – Quarter-finals: M. Goellner d. A. Berasategui (1) 6–4 6–3; F. Mantilla (3) d. S. Koubek 6–7 6–4 6–4; V. Santopadre d. A. Lopez-Moron 6–3 6–3; A. Costa (2) d. A. Clement (8) 4–6 6–3 7–6. ***Semi-finals:*** Mantilla (3) d. Goellner 6–4 6–2; Costa (2) d. Santopadre 7–6 6–0. ***Final:*** Mantilla (3) d. Costa (2) 6–3 7–5.

MEN'S DOUBLES – Final: Broad/Ullyett (2) d. Arthurs/Berasategui (4) 7–6 6–3.

PRESIDENT'S CUP ($475,000)

TASHKENT, 14–20 SEPTEMBER

MEN'S SINGLES – Quarter-finals: Y. Kafelnikov (1) d. G. Etlis 6–3 3–6 6–1; C. Pioline (3) d. M. Safin (6) 6–7 6–2 7–6; N. Escude (4) d. K. Braasch (Q) 6–4 7–6; T. Henman (2) d. S. Pescosolido 6–4 6–4. ***Semi-finals:*** Kafelnikov (1) d. Pioline (3) 6–2 6–2; Henman (2) d. Escude (4) 3–6 6–3 6–4. ***Final:*** Henman (2) d. Kafelnikov (1) 7–5 6–4.

MEN'S DOUBLES – Final: Pescosolido/Tieleman d. Carlsen/Schalken 7–5 4–6 7–5.

OPEN ROMANIA ($315,000)

BUCHAREST, 14–21 SEPTEMBER

MEN'S SINGLES – Quarter-finals: F. Clavet (1) d. J. Alonso-Pintor (8) 7–5 6–0; A. Portas d. A. Pavel 2–6 6–3 7–5; A. Di Pasquale (Q) d. G. Blanco 7–6 2–6 6–2; A. Voinea d. E. Alvarez 6–4 6–1. ***Semi-finals:*** Clavet (1) d. Portas 3–6 6–0 6–2; Di Pasquale (Q) d. Voinea 6–3 2–6 7–5. ***Final:*** Clavet (1) d. Di Pasquale (Q) 6–2 4–6 7–5.

MEN'S DOUBLES – Final: Pavel/Trifu d. Cosac/Pescariu (WC) 7–6 4–6 7–6.

MALLORCA OPEN ($475,000)

MALLORCA, 28 SEPTEMBER–4 OCTOBER

MEN'S SINGLES – Quarter-finals: C. Moya (1) d. T. Schiessling (Q) 7–5 6–4; F. Vicente d. T. Carbonell (LL) 3–6 7–6 6–4; T. Muster (5) d. T. Haas 3–6 6–3 6–4; G. Kuerten (8) d. S. Bruguera (WC) 6–4 6–4. ***Semi-finals:*** Moya (1) d. Vicente 6–1 6–2; Kuerten (8) d. Muster (5) 7–5 7–5. ***Final:*** Kuerten (8) d. Moya (1) 6–7 6–2 6–3.

MEN'S DOUBLES – Final: Albano/Orsanic (4) d. Novak/Rikl (2) 7–6 6–3.

GRAND PRIX DE TENNIS DE TOULOUSE ($375,000)

TOULOUSE, 28 SEPTEMBER–4 OCTOBER

MEN'S SINGLES – Quarter-finals: G. Rusedski (WC) (1) d. A. Clement 6–4 6–1; N. Kiefer (4) d. M. Rosset 6–3 3–6 6–1; T. Johansson (3) d. S. Huet (Q) 3–6 6–4 7–5; J. Siemerink (2) d. R. Federer (Q) 7–6 6–2. ***Semi-finals:*** Rusedski (WC) (1) d. Kiefer (4) 6–4 6–1; Siemerink (2) d. Johansson (3) 6–3 3–6 7–5. ***Final:*** Siemerink (2) d. Rusedski (WC) (1) 6–4 6–4.

MEN'S DOUBLES – Final: Delaitre/Santoro (1) d. Haarhuis/Siemerink (3) 6–2 6–4.

CAMPIONATI INTERNAZIONALI DI SICILIA ($315,000)

PALERMO, 5–11 OCTOBER

MEN'S SINGLES – Quarter-finals: A. Corretja (WC) (1) d. N. Lapentti 7–5 6–2; M. Puerta d. F. Vicente 6–4 6–4; F. Squillari d. M. Zabaleta 5–7 6–4 6–3; G. Blanco d. A. Di Pasquale (Q) 7–6 6–2. ***Semi-finals:*** Puerta d. Corretja (WC) (1) 7–5 6–2; Squillari d. Blanco 6–1 2–6 7–6. ***Final:*** Puerta d. Squillari 6–3 6–2.

MEN'S DOUBLES – Final: Johnson/Montana (1) d. Albano/Orsanic (3) 6–4 7–6.

SHANGHAI OPEN '98 ($315,000)
SHANGHAI, 5–12 OCTOBER
MEN'S SINGLES – Quarter-finals: G. Ivanisevic (1) d. K. Carlsen (7) 6–3 7–6; R. Delgado (6) d. M. Tebbutt 6–4 6–7 6–3; P. Haarhuis (5) d. M. Woodforde 7–6 7–6; M. Chang (2) d. T. Woodbridge (8) 6–2 6–2. ***Semi-finals:*** Ivanisevic (1) d. Delgado (6) 5–7 6–3 7–5; Chang (2) d. Haarhuis (5) 7–5 6–3. ***Final:*** Chang (2) d. Ivanisevic (1) 4–6 6–1 6–2.
MEN'S DOUBLES – Final: Bhupathi/Paes (2) d. Woodbridge/Woodforde (1) 6–4 6–7 7–6.

DAVIDOFF SWISS INDOORS BASEL ($975,000)
BASLE, 6–11 OCTOBER
MEN'S SINGLES – Quarter-finals: M. Rosset d. D. Prinosil (Q) 6–3 7–6; A. Agassi (4) d. M. Gustafsson 6–3 6–3; T. Henman (6) d. N. Kiefer 6–3 6–4; T. Johansson d. F. Santoro 6–3 6–3. ***Semi-finals:*** Agassi (4) d. Rosset 6–4 6–2; Henman (6) d. Johansson 6–3 2–6 7–6. ***Final:*** Henman (6) d. Agassi (4) 6–4 6–3 3–6 6–4.
MEN'S DOUBLES – Final: Delaitre/Santoro (4) d. Norval/Ullyett 6–3 7–6.

IPB CZECH INDOOR ($975,000)
OSTRAVA, 19–25 OCTOBER
MEN'S SINGLES – Quarter-finals: T. Enqvist (7) d. N. Kulti (Q) 6–3 6–4; J. Kroslak (Q) d. A. Medvedev 6–3 6–0; W. Black (Q) d. M. Damm 7–6 6–7 6–3; A. Agassi (2) d. T. Johansson (8) 6–7 6–4 6–4. ***Semi-finals:*** Kroslak (Q) d. Enqvist (7) 4–3 ret; Agassi (2) d. Black (Q) 7–6 6–3. ***Final:*** Agassi (2) d. Kroslak (Q) 6–2 3–6 6–3.
MEN'S DOUBLES – Final: Kiefer/Prinosil (WC) d. Adams/Vizner 6–4 6–3.

GRAND PRIX DE TENNIS DE LYON ($725,000)
LYON, 19–25 OCTOBER
MEN'S SINGLES – Quarter-finals: T. Haas d. P. Sampras (1) w/o ; M. Rios (3) d. A. Di Pasquale (WC) 6–4 6–0; A. Corretja (4) d. O. Delaitre (Q) 7–6 7–5; W. Ferreira d. P. Rafter (2) 6–4 6–1. ***Semi-finals:*** Haas d. Rios (3) 6–2 1–0 ret; Corretja (4) d. Ferreira 6–3 6–2. ***Final:*** Corretja (4) d. Haas 2–6 7–6 6–1.
MEN'S DOUBLES – Final: Delaitre/Santoro (1) d. Carbonell/Roig (4) 6–2 6–2.

ABIERTO MEXICANO DE TENIS ($315,000)
MEXICO CITY, 26 OCTOBER–1 NOVEMBER
MEN'S SINGLES – Quarter-finals: X. Malisse (Q) d. J. Marin 6–3 7–5; F. Clavet (4) d. D. Sanguinetti 7–6 7–5; M. Puerta (6) d. A. Hernandez (WC) 5–7 6–1 6–4; J. Novak d. J. Burillo (Q) 6–3 3–6 6–3. ***Semi-finals:*** Malisse (Q) d. Clavet (4) 6–2 6–2; Novak d. Puerta (6) 6–3 6–7 6–3. ***Final:*** Novak d. Malisse (Q) 6–3 6–3.
MEN'S DOUBLES – Final: Novak/Rikl (2) d. Orsanic/Roditi (1) 6–4 6–2.

CERVEZA CLUB COLOMBIA OPEN ($315,000)
BOGOTA, 2–8 NOVEMBER
MEN'S SINGLES – Quarter-finals: R. Delgado d. J. Courier (WC) 6–7 6–1 7–5; S. Sargsian d. J. Balcells (Q) 7–6 7–5; M. Zabaleta d. M. Hadad (WC) 6–7 6–4 7–6; J. Novak d. D. Sanguinetti 7–5 4–6 6–4. ***Semi-finals:*** Delgado d. Sargsian 6–3 4–6 3–1 ret; Zabaleta d. Novak 6–2 6–4. ***Final:*** Zabaleta d. Delgado 6–4 6–4.
MEN'S DOUBLES – Final: Del Rio/Puerta d. Koves/Taino 6–7 6–3 6–2.

KREMLIN CUP '98 ($1,125,000)
MOSCOW, 9–15 NOVEMBER
MEN'S SINGLES – Quarter-finals: A. Clement d. S. Lareau 6–3 7–5; G. Ivanisevic (WC) (3) d. L. Burgsmuller (Q) 6–2 6–1; M. Rosset (6) d. J. Kroslak (LL) 6–2 6–4; Y. Kafelnikov (2) d. G. Raoux 6–1 6–1. ***Semi-finals:*** Ivanisevic (WC) (3) d. Clement 7–5 6–2; Kafelnikov (2) d. Rosset (6) 6–1 2–0 ret. ***Final:*** Kafelnikov (2) d. Ivanisevic (WC) (3) 7–6 7–6.
MEN'S DOUBLES – Final: Palmer/Tarango d. Kafelnikov/Vacek 6–4 6–7 6–3.

SCANIA STOCKHOLM OPEN ($800,000)
STOCKHOLM, 9–15 NOVEMBER
MEN'S SINGLES – Quarter-finals: T. Johansson (7) d. J. Stoltenberg 7–5 7–5; G. Rusedski (4) d. D. Nestor 7–6 1–6 6–3; T. Henman (3) d. M. Gustafsson 6–3 3–6 7–6; T. Martin d. T. Suzuki (Q) 6–3 6–4. ***Semi-finals:*** Johansson (7) d. Rusedski (4) 7–5 7–6; Martin d. Henman (3) 4–6 6–1 6–2. ***Final:*** Martin d. Johansson (7) 6–3 6–4 6–4.
MEN'S DOUBLES – Final: Kulti/Tillstrom d. Haggard/Nyborg 7–5 3–6 7–5.

CHEVROLET CUP ($315,000)
SANTIAGO, 9–15 NOVEMBER
MEN'S SINGLES – Quarter-finals: J. Marin d. M. Rios (1) 6–4 6–7 7–5; F. Clavet (5) d. N. Lapentti 6–4 6–4; Y. El Aynaoui d. M. Puerta (6) 6–2 1–0 ret; F. Mantilla (2) d. J. Courier (WC) 3–6 6–3 7–6. ***Semi-finals:*** Clavet (5) d. Marin 6–2 7–5; El Aynaoui d. Mantilla (2) 6–4 6–4. ***Final:*** Clavet (5) d. El Aynaoui 6–2 6–4.
MEN'S DOUBLES – Final: Hood/Prieto (3) d. Bertolini/Bowen 7–6 6–7 7–6.

ATP Tour World Championship

Barry Flatman

The toast was drunk in rioja but not, as first seemed the case, to absent friends. When Alex Corretja sank to his knees in reverent thanks before rising to romp in delight around the court, nobody could say he did not deserve every bit of glory which came from beating his friend and compatriot Carlos Moya to win the ATP Tour World Championship.

True, two of the world's top eight did not even make it to Hannover. Both Richard Krajicek and Patrick Rafter were suffering with knee injuries brought on by the relentless demands of the tennis calender. Then back injuries forced first Andre Agassi and then Marcelo Rios to catch early flights back across the Atlantic, long before the round-robin group matches were completed.

In addition, who is to say whether Pete Sampras subconsciously found things positively anti-climactic when he stepped out for the semi-final, almost 48 hours after celebrating with champagne and firework-festooned chocolate cake, the achievement of his almost obsessional quest to break Jimmy Connors' two decade old record and end the year as world No.1 for the sixth time in succession.

When the two Spaniards walked onto court for the final, the 14,000 crowd and the world of tennis at large were wondering whether this was perhaps quite the right contest to end 11 months of touring rigour. After all, the pair had conspired to produce one of the more forgettable French Open finals just six months earlier. Fractionally more than four hours later, when Moya's final forehand flew long to present Corretja a 3–6 3–6 7–5 6–3 7–5 victory (and a small matter of $1.36 million into the bargain), not one paying customer in Hannover's huge Messe Hall 13 could say they had not been given their money's worth.

Rarely in such a high profile final have fortunes turned around so dramatically. Corretja may have gone into the match as the man who had ended the Sampras run, (a 4–6 6–3 7–6 win that revealed a closing of the gap between the American and his peers), but he knew only too well that he had failed to take a single set off Moya in their three previous encounters during the year.

For two sets it looked like Roland Garros revisited, the younger of the two Spaniards seeming to have the edge with his greater variety of shots. But then deep in the recesses of Corretja's memory, a spark ignited which jump-charged an inspired fightback. As a youngster in Barcelona, his idol was always Ivan Lendl and for some reason he remembered that 1984 French final when John McEnroe was powerless to stop an emphatic two sets lead crumbling against the colossus from Ostrava.

What Corretja did not realize is that he also became the only man, other than his hero, to recover from such a deficit in the final and win the year-ending event. Lendl had achieved it in the 1981 Masters final at New York's Madison Square Garden against the late Vitas Gerulaitis.

Corretja is no Lendl in terms of physique but clearly his determination knows few bounds. Even when he broke serve early in the third set an ill-timed double fault immediately surrendered the lead but still he refused to buckle. After breaking again in the 12th game, the man who had lost that epic, gut wrenching encounter with Sampras at the 1996 US Open, proved he now knows how to win a marathon.

'It has always been my ambition to one day be a great champion,' Corretja told the thousands who applauded him long and loudly. 'It is something I have been dreaming about since I was seven years old and this has realized all my dreams.' What the crowd, including Olympic chief Juan Antonio Samaranch, did not know was that Corretja could number some pretty high profile names among his congratulation committee. One of the first to shake his hand when he left court was former French, Wimbledon and US champion Manolo Santana while Spanish president Jose Maria Aznar was soon telephoning his praise from Madrid. Earlier in the day King Juan Carlos had called both his subjects to offer his good wishes.

Yet when Corretja and Moya had arrived in Hannover a week earlier, neither was regarded as a potential winner. Even though, five weeks earlier in Lyons, Corretja had become the first Spanish male to win an indoor title for decades, neither man appeared in peak form. Indeed Moya had yet to register a solitary indoor victory in 1998 and both had turned down invitations to play in September's Grand Slam Cup, prefering instead to compete on Majorcan clay in an ATP Tour event.

Before Sunday's final, an ante-room of Hall 13 saw ATP Tour CEO Mark Miles and ITF President Brian Tobin sitting at the same table as Samaranch, showing the major factions which have made tennis so disjointed in recent years are moving towards some sort of agreement. The problem of staging two major competitions at the tail end of the calender appears to be something on their agenda and certainly the experiences of this year, with both the ATP Tour World Championship and the Grand Slam Cup having depleted fields, suggests an amalgamation can only be good for the game.

Corretja had no time to ponder such political matters as he revelled in his victory. But a couple of days later, after the immediate jubilation subsided, did he perhaps think he was lucky to survive to the semi-final stage? If the rules had been the same as in previous years he would probably have been back in Barcelona by Saturday morning.

Corretja came second in his group after beating Agassi by default when the American's back injury became too painful with the Spaniard leading 5–7 6–3 2–1. He then lost to Tim Henman 7–6 6–7 6–2, in an intense contest which lasted two and a half hours and finally pipped alternate Greg Rusedski for a place in the last four by registering an unsurprising victory over second replacement Albert Costa (who is still seeking his first win indoors after six years of trying).

Rusedski, the on-site reserve after narrowly being beaten by Yevgeny Kafelnikov for the last place in the eight, had been forced to limp away from the action after two matches 12 months earlier. Yet, but for a rule change, giving the advantage on matches played rather than sets lost, Rusedski's two straight sets wins over Costa (7–6 6–1) and British Davis Cup team-mate Henman (6–2 6–4), would have been sufficient to send him through.

Agassi's form throughout the year marked him down as a clear contender for the title but a practice session before the tournament had started effectively wrecked his chances. He slipped on the rubberized carpet surface, landed on his backside and caused such damage that it hurt even to position himself in his normal stance to return serve. For more than an hour and a half he tried bravely against Corretja, even hitting a fourth ace to move to set point before taking the lead. But with increasing regularity a grimace of pain appeared across his face and finally, when the Spaniard broke serve to go in front in the final set, Agassi decided it was time to quit.

Marcelo Rios was the next to succumb to injury. Two months earlier he had suffered intense back pain while beating Agassi in the Grand Slam Cup final and although his withdrawals in Lyons and Stuttgart were officially attributed to leg injuries, the Chilean admitted that playing on indoor courts always resulted in discomfort. On his return to Germany, Rios declared the prospect of usurping Sampras for the No.1 position was something which excited him but he, too, only lasted one match. For a set against Henman he seemed able to give of his best but that commitment soon diminished as he fell to the determined Englishman 7–5 6–1.

That was not quite the end of the Rios story. The next day he decided to undergo an MRI scan in hospital which showed no serious damage. After declaring a clean bill of health he even sprinted up a 40-step flight of stairs two at a time to escape

At the ATP World Championships Carlos Moya, the French Open champion, was pipped at the post by the man he had beaten in the Paris final, his friend and fellow Spaniard Alex Corretja. (Tommy Hindley)

any more intense questioning from the media. But literally minutes before he was due on court against Agassi's replacement Rusedski, Rios also pulled out to be substituted with Costa, thus guaranteeing Sampras that treasured sixth successive year at No.1 in the most disappointing of circumstances.

While Henman went on to top the White Group with Corretja keeping Rusedski out of second place, Sampras looked positively devastating in the Red. If he was bordering on physical exhaustion after his stint of six tournaments in six weeks, he did not show it. In fact he looked refreshed and revitalised. Kafelnikov lasted barely an hour against him before losing 6–2 6–4; a day later it was much the same story as Moya fell 6–3 6–3 and Karol Kucera could muster only 46 minutes of resistence before Sampras rounded off a 6–2 6–1 annihilation.

Nobody would have bet against the American record breaker collecting a fifth ATP Tour World Championship crown, his third in succession. But the semi-final proved everyone wrong. For a while it seemed as though the Sampras steamroller would just keep on going but Corretja is clearly made of sterner stuff. A titanic final set saw the eventual champion save three match points before winning 4–6 6–3 7–6, the tiebreak eventually being a rather one-sided 7–3 affair.

It was the first day of a memorable weekend for Spain. In the group matches Moya had solidly if unspectacularly plugged away, sandwiching his defeat by Sampras between two workmanlike wins over first Kucera and then Kafelnikov. But if those victories came from two of the more low-key matches of the week, the semi-final victory over Henman was an encounter brimful of drama.

Both men experienced highs and lows, Henman struggling painfully with a malfunctioning first serve and Moya then seeming to lose his way as the Englishman finally got his act together. Henman immediately took the upper-hand in the final set with a break of serve in the first game but Moya's huge baseline armoury saw him fight back and survive a spate of break points to win eventually 6–4 3–6 7–5 after two hours and 19 minutes.

Both Corretja and Moya could have claimed fatigue a problem in the final. Neither did as they proved indisputably that their domain extends far beyond courts of clay. As a result of his win, the first by a debutant in the event since John McEnroe 20 years earlier, Corretja ended the year no.3 in the world while Moya had to be content with fifth spot. It was Spain's first major indoor title since Manual Orantes won the 1976 Masters in Houston. It was also a final to toast after all.

ATP TOUR WORLD CHAMPIONSHIP 1998

HANNOVER, 24–29 NOVEMBER

ROUND ROBIN SECTION – Red Group: 1st P. Sampras (1) d. K. Kucera (6) 6–2 6–1; d. C. Moya (4) 6–3 6–3; d. Y. Kafelnikov (8) 6–2 6–4; 2nd Moya (4) d. Kucera (6) 6–7 7–5 6–3; d. Kafelnikov (8) 7–5 7–5; 3rd Kafelnikov (8) d. Kucera (6) 6–7 6–3 6–2; 4th Kucera (6). ***White Group*** 1st T. Henman (7) d. Rios (2) 7–5 6–1; d. A. Corretja (5) 7–6 6–7 6–2; lost to G. Rusedski (Alt1) 2–6 4–6; 2nd A. Corretja (5) d. A. Agassi (3) 5–7 6–3 2–1 ret.; d. A. Costa (Alt2) 6–2 6–4; 3rd G. Rusedski (Alt1) d. Costa (Alt2) 7–6 6–1; 4th A. Costa (Alt2); 5th A. Agassi (3); 6th M. Rios (2). (Note: Rios suffered a back injury while playing Henman and withdrew. Agassi fell during practice, also damaging his back, so that he was unable to complete his match against Corretja)
PLAY-OFFS – Semi-finals: Moya (4) d. Henman (7) 6–4 3–6 7–5; Corretja (5) d. Sampras (1) 4–6 6–3 7–6.
Final: Corretja (5) d. Moya (4) 3–6 3–6 7–5 6–3 7–5.
PRIZE MONEY (POINTS): Corretja $1,360,000 (630); Moya $660,000 (360); Sampras $415,000 (270); Henman $305,000 (180); Rusedski $260,000 (180); Kafelnikov $195,000 (90); Kucera $85,000 (0); Costa $40,000 (0); Rios $40,000 (0); Agassi $20,000 (0)

ATP TOUR WORLD DOUBLES CHAMPIONSHIP 1998

HARTFORD CT, 17–22 NOVEMBER

ROUND ROBIN SECTION – Green Group: 1st J. Eltingh/P. Haarhuis (1) d. E. Ferreira/R. Leach (5) 6–4 6–4; d. O. Delaitre/F. Santoro (7) 4–6 7–5 7–5; d. T. Woodbridge/M. Woodforde (3) 7–6 6–4; 2nd Delaitre/Santoro (7) d. Woodbridge/Woodforde (3) 6–7 6–3 6–4; d. Ferreira/Leach (5) 7–6 4–6 7–6; 3rd Ferreira/Leach (5) d. Woodbridge/Woodforde (3) 7–6 6–3; 4th Woodbridge/Woodforde (3). ***Gold Group:*** 1st M. Knowles/ D. Nestor (4) d. S. Stolle/C. Suk (6) 2–6 6–4 6–2; d. D. Johnson/F. Montana (8) 6–3 6–2; lost to J. Eagle/A. Florent (Alt) 6–7 0–6; 2nd Johnson/Montana (8) d. M. Bhupathi/L. Paes (2) 3–6 6–4 7–6; d. Stolle/Suk (6) 6–7 7–6 7–6; 3rd Stolle/Suk (6) d. Bhupathi/Paes (2) 4–6 6–3 6–4; 4th Eagle/Florent (Alt); 5th Bhupathi/Paes (2). (Note: Eagle and Florent replaced Bhupathi and Paes because of a bone spur injury suffered by Paes in his left heel).
PLAY-OFFS – Semi-finals: Eltingh/Haarhuis (1) d. Johnson/Montana (8) 7–6 6–4; Knowles/Nestor (4) d. Delaitre/Santoro (7) 6–4 6–2 6–3.
Final: Eltingh/Haarhuis (1) d. Knowles/Nestor (4) 6–4 6–2 7–5.
PRIZE MONEY (POINTS): Eltingh/Haarhuis $258,500 (720); Knowles/Nestor $129,000 (360); Delaitre/Santoro $74,000 (180); Johnson/Montana $64,000 (180); Ferreira/Leach $59,500 (90); Stolle/Suk $49,500 (90); Eagle/Florent $29,500 (90); Bhupathi/Paes $70,000 (0); Woodbridge/Woodforde $60,000 (0).

Corel WTA Tour

Corel WTA Tour Year • Points Explanation and Allocation
Corel WTA Tour Tournaments – Tiers I, II, III and IV
Corel WTA Chase Championships

With five tournament victories Switzerland's Patty Schnyder was one of the most successful women on the Corel WTA Tour and for a brief moment entered the top ten but ended the year at No. 11. (Michael Cole)

Two great past champions made welcome returns to the Tour in 1998 – Monica Seles spectacularly by reaching the final at the French Open shortly after the death of her father and coach, Karoly, and Steffi Graf more quietly at Eastbourne. By the year's end they were both well established in the top ten where they belong. (Michael Cole and Tommy Hindley)

Corel WTA Tour Year

Barry Wood

While the youngest players on the Corel WTA Tour justifiably continued to attract considerable attention, they by no means drew all the headlines. Two of the Grand Slams were claimed by veterans and a third by a player who could be considered middle-aged in this brave new world of women's tennis. But the interest generated by the teenagers not only resulted in their appearing within many non-tennis magazines, but in record crowds at most events.

Martina Hingis became the youngest woman this century to retain a Grand Slam title when she won her second consecutive Australian Open, but by that stage she had already fallen to one of her young rivals, Venus Williams in Sydney. This left her in no doubt that she would face an almost impossible task in holding on to the 12 singles titles she had won in 1997.

Indeed, the Swiss teenager failed to win another Grand Slam title, and was perhaps guilty of complacency when in the middle of the year she claimed she had no real rivals. On 12 October, her 80 weeks reign as the world number one ended when she was replaced at the top of the rankings by Lindsay Davenport, her conqueror in the US Open final. In all, Hingis had to be satisfied with just five titles – Melbourne, Indian Wells, Hamburg and Rome in the first five months of the year, and finally the Chase Championships.

Davenport, who over the past two years had dedicated herself to losing more weight than you could comfortably carry home from the supermarket, saw her efforts rewarded with a spectacular run during the American hardcourt season. She won a California Grand Slam with titles in Stanford, San Diego and Los Angeles in consecutive weeks, and climaxed that run with victory at the US Open. In the other Grand Slams she was a semi-finalist at the Australian and French Opens and went to the quarter-finals at Wimbledon. A February winner of the Pan Pacific title in Tokyo, she later added a win in Zurich and was also a runner-up at Indian Wells, Filderstadt, Philadelphia and the Chase Championships.

Those six victories were the most by any player during the year, but Davenport's total was challenged by the unexpected emergence of Patty Schnyder. Coached by Eric Van Harpen, who had guided Conchita Martinez to her 1994 Wimbledon victory, Schnyder won five events, in Hobart, Hannover, Madrid, Maria Lankowitz and Palermo. She was the runner-up at the Grand Slam Cup, first saving two match points as she beat Jana Novotna, and then defeating Hingis who retired with cramps at 5–5 in the deciding set. Schnyder was also a quarter-finalist at Roland Garros, and at the US Open where she beat Steffi Graf.

The Williams sisters continued to make an impact. Venus claimed her first career title at Oklahoma in February, and with Serena also took the doubles title, establishing them as the only sister team to win a tour event. A little over a month later Venus added the prestigious Lipton title. That earned her a place in the top 10, making her only the second player to make her top 10 debut having been ranked outside the top 100, at 110, a year previously. Only Conchita Martinez, who rose from 116 to 10 between June 1988 and June 1989, has done better. Venus also struck the fastest recorded serve in women's tennis, her 127 mph (205 kmph) delivery against Mary Pierce in the Zurich quarter-finals.

Serena, by defeating 10th ranked Irina Spirlea at Key Biscayne in only her 16th career main draw singles match, became the fastest ever player in the history of professional women's tennis to defeat five top 10 players. Serena broke the record set in 1989 by Monica Seles who had recorded her fifth career top 10 victory in her 33rd main draw match. Venus and Serena also scored a family Grand Slam in mixed doubles, winning two each.

At the beginning of the year Anna Kournikova had engaged the services of Pavel Slozil, Steffi Graf's former coach. Although a title continued to elude her she became the first woman in Tour history to defeat four top 10 players in one tournament when she beat Seles, Martinez, Davenport, and Arantxa Sanchez-Vicario at the Lipton. Ranked 25, she was also the lowest ranked player to score consecutive wins over four top 10 players.

In the Lipton final Kournikova lost to Venus Williams, but her most satisfying achievement was surely her win over Hingis in the quarter-finals of the German Open. She also defeated Graf at Eastbourne, but in doing so injured a thumb which forced her to miss Wimbledon.

The glamorous Russian teenager Anna Kournikova enjoyed a sensational run at the Lipton Championships where she became the first player to beat four top 10 players in succession – Seles, Martinez, Davenport and Sanchez-Vicario en route to her first Tour final. (Michael Cole)

Kournikova's year was also marred by difficulties with her serve. In one match she delivered 22 double-faults, and 17 on two other occasions.

Kournikova's win over Hingis in Berlin was not the most noteworthy item of the week. Amelie Mauresmo, the 1996 world junior champion, advanced all the way to the final before falling to Martinez. In doing so, Mauresmo became the first qualifier ever to reach the final of a Tier One event. Her victims included world number two Davenport and number three Novotna, making her the lowest ranked player, at 65, to defeat two of the top three players in the world in a single tournament. Her efforts resulted in her being called up by Yannick Noah for Fed Cup duty, the realisation of a dream for Mauresmo, who had been inspired to take up the game after watching Noah win the French Open.

Martinez, by beating Mauresmo in the Berlin final, ended her 18-month streak without a title. Another Spaniard, Sanchez-Vicario, also ended a title drought that had stretched to 11 months when she won the Sydney event. Having been written off by many over the last year or two, the 26-year-old then made a statement for the old guard by winning her third Roland Garros singles title and fourth Grand Slam.

While most eyes were focused on the teenagers who were threatening to take over the game, 29-year-old Novotna and 30-year-old Nathalie Tauziat contested the Wimbledon final. Novotna also won in Linz and Eastbourne (her first grass court title immediately preceding her second), as well as switching from grass to clay to win the Prague event in the week after her Wimbledon triumph. She was also a finalist in Hannover, Hamburg and New Haven.

Dominique Van Roost made a breakthrough with a solid year that saw her reach five finals, winning in Auckland and finishing as runner-up in Hobart, the Paris indoor event, Linz and Madrid. Her most successful week came in Filderstadt, where she reached the semi-finals with wins over Venus Williams and Hingis. In beating Hingis, she became only the third woman to defeat a world number one in a first career meeting since the current ranking system was established. The others are Pam Shriver, who defeated Martina Navratilova in the 1978 US Open semi-finals, and Schnyder who accomplished the feat via Hingis at the Grand Slam Cup. Van Roost's win over Hingis ended the Swiss Miss's reign as number one, and also earned the Belgian the accolade of becoming the first from her country, man or woman, to enter the world's top 10. In the final, Van Roost lost to Sandrine Testud, who had never previously won a match there in seven appearances.

Mirjana Lucic, who turned 16 on 9 March failed to join the other teenagers in the top 20, but still made an impact. She teamed with Hingis at the Australian Open, where as wild cards they became the youngest ever pairing to win a Grand Slam doubles title. By doing so, Lucic also became the first player to win the first tour event she has played in both singles and doubles. The following week in Tokyo, Hingis and Lucic were nevertheless required to qualify in doubles. Lucic also successfully defended her Bol title, the youngest player ever to score a repeat win. She also produced her first win over a top 10 opponent when she beat Mary Pierce at the Italian Open. Shortly before the US Open, Lucic announced that she and the rest of her immediate family had moved to the United States because of physical abuse by her father.

Steffi Graf had played only two events early in the year before injury intervened again, losing to Sabine Appelmans in Hannover and retiring against Davenport in the semi-finals at Indian Wells. She returned in Birmingham, reaching a semi-final that was not contested because of rain, and then lost to Kournikova at Eastbourne. But it was only a matter of time before she won again, and that came in New Haven, where she beat Davenport and Novotna. Then, unseeded for the first time in 13 years, she won Leipzig, and by defeating Davenport and Hingis to win in Philadelphia she became the first unseeded player ever to defeat the top two ranked players in the world in the same tournament.

Monica Seles, distracted by the illness of her father until his death from cancer shortly before the French Open, played a limited schedule in the early part of the year. She reached the semi-finals of Hilton Head, and then became the sentimental favourite as she reached the final at Roland Garros. Later, she won the Canadian Open and Toyota, Tokyo.

Pierce had an excellent year, also winning the Paris indoor title and Amelia Island. Then, after claiming the Moscow title, she won in Luxembourg. That event earned it's own unique place in the history books when both finals ended with a player defaulting because of injury!

The most frustrated doubles team of the year was the combination of Lindsay Davenport and Natasha Zvereva. Together they reached all four Grand Slam finals but lost every one. Hingis and Lucic beat them in Australia, and Hingis and Novotna defeated them in the other three. Hingis, therefore, won a doubles Grand Slam.

POINTS EXPLANATION

The present Corel WTA Tour ranking system, which came into effect on 26 December 1996, is based on the accumulation of points earned at the player's best 18 tournaments over a moving 52-week period. The points are no longer averaged according to the number of events played as they were in the system that had been in use since 1983. A player's ranking in singles and doubles depends upon the points won at each tournament, according to the round reached. To these are added 'quality points' which are awarded for beating players ranked in the top 500 (different for singles and doubles). The rankings determine player acceptances and seedings for all tournaments.

RANKING POINTS

Equal points are awarded for singles and doubles. The figures beneath each Tier heading indicate minimum prize money.

Category	*W*	*F*	*S/F*	*Q/F*	*R16*	*R32*	*R64*	*R128*	*QFR*	*Q3*	*Q2*	*Q1*
Grand Slams	520	364	234	130	72	44	26	2	16.5	12	6	2
Chase Chps	390	273	175	97	54	—	—	—	—	—	—	—
Tier I (16) $926,250	260	182	117	65	36	—	—	—	—	—	—	—
Tier I (32) $926,250	260	182	117	65	36	1	—	—	11	6	3	1
Tier I (64) $926,250	260	182	117	65	36	22	1	—	6	—	3	1
Tier I (128) $926,250	260	182	117	65	36	22	13	1	11	6	3	1
Tier II (16) $450,000	200	140	90	50	1	—	—	—	—	—	—	—
Tier II (32) $450,000	200	140	90	50	26	1	—	—	9	5	3	1
Tier II (64) $450,000	200	140	90	50	26	14	1	—	5	—	3	1
Tier III (16) $164,250	140	98	63	35	1	—	—	—	—	—	—	—
Tier III (32) $164,250	140	98	63	35	18	1	—	—	7	3	2	1
Tier III (64) $164,250	140	98	63	35	18	10	1	—	4	—	2	1
Tier IV (16) $107,500	80	56	36	20	1	—	—	—	—	—	—	—
Tier IV (32) $107,500	80	56	36	20	10	1	—	—	4.5	3	2	1
Tier IV (64) $107,500	80	56	36	20	10	6	1	—	2.5	—	1.5	1
Other Tournaments												
$75,000 (16)	54	38	24	14	1	—	—	—	—	—	—	—
$75,000	54	38	24	14	7	1	—	—	2.5	2	1.5	1
$50,000 (16)	36	25	16	9	1	—	—	—	—	—	—	—
$50,000	36	25	16	9	5	1	—	—	2.5	2	1.5	1
$25,000 (16)	22	15	10	6	1	—	—	—	—	—	—	—
$25,000	22	15	10	6	3	1	—	—	1.5	1	5	0.25
$10,000 (8)	10	7	5	1	—	—	—	—	—	—	—	—
$10,000 (M)	10	7	5	3	1	—	—	—	—	—	—	—
$10,000 (16)	5	4	2	1.5	1	—	—	—	—	—	—	—
$ 5,000 (8)	5	4	2	1	—	—	—	—	—	—	—	—
$ 5,000 (M)	5	4	2	1.5	1	—	—	—	—	—	—	—

POINTS ALLOCATION *(continued)*

Notes for Qualifiers

1) No points are awarded for doubles qualifying.
2) Players who qualify and then lose in the first round of the main draw receive points indicated in the QFR column on the previous page.
3) Players who qualify and lose after the first round of the main draw will receive QFR points, plus round and quality points.
4) Lucky Losers who lose in the first round of the main draw will receive round points plus any quality points earned in the qualifying.

QUALITY POINTS – SINGLES

Loser's Rank	Points	Grand Slam Points
1	100	150
2	75	113
3	66	99
4	55	83
5	50	75
6–10	43	65
11–16	35	53
17–25	23	35
26–35	15	23
36–50	10	15
51–75	8	12
76–150	4	6
151–250	2	3
251–500	1	1.5

QUALITY POINTS – DOUBLES

Loser's Rank	Points	Grand Slam Points
3–5	100	150
6–10	90	135
11–20	65	97.5
21–30	45	67.5
31–50	30	45
51–80	20	30
81–130	14	21
131–200	9	13.5
201–300	6	9
301–500	4	6
Both Ranked	2	3

GRAND SLAM CHAMPIONSHIPS AND WTA TOUR 1998

Date	*Venue*	*Surface*	*Singles final*	*Doubles winners*
4–10 Jan	Queensland	Hard	A. Sugiyama d. M. Vento 7–5 6–0	Likhovtseva/Sugiyama
5–11 Jan	Auckland	Hard	D. Van Roost d. S. Farina 4–6 7–6 7–5	Miyagi/Tanasugarn
11–17 Jan	Sydney	Hard	A. Sanchez-Vicario d. V. Williams 6–1 6–3	Hingis/Sukova
11–17 Jan	Hobart	Hard	P. Schnyder d. D. Van Roost 6–3 6–2	Ruano-Pascual/Suarez
19 Jan–1 Feb	**Australian Open**	**Hard**	**M. Hingis d. C. Martinez 6–3 6–3**	Hingis/Lucic
2–8 Feb	Tokyo	Carpet	L. Davenport d. M. Hingis 6–3 6–3	Hingis/Lucic
9–15 Feb	Paris	Carpet	M. Pierce d. D. Van Roost 6–3 7–5	Appelmans/Oremans
16–22 Feb	Hannover	Carpet	P. Schnyder d. J. Novotna 6–0 2–6 7–5	Raymond/Stubbs
16–22 Feb	Bogota	Clay	P. Suarez d. S. Jeyaseelan 6–3 6–4	Husarova/Suarez
23 Feb–1 Mar	Linz	Carpet	J. Novotna d. D. Van Roost 6–1 7–6	Fusai/Tauziat
23 Feb–1 Mar	Oklahoma City, OK	Hard	V. Williams d. J. Kruger 6–3 6–2	S. Williams/V. Williams
5–15 Mar	Indian Wells, CA	Hard	M. Hingis d. L. Davenport 6–3 6–4	Davenport/Zvereva
19–29 Mar	Key Biscayne, FL	Hard	V. Williams d. A. Kournikova 2–6 6–4 6–1	Hingis/Novotna
30 Mar–5 Apr	Hilton Head, SC	Clay	A. Coetzer d. I. Spirlea 6–3 6–4	Martinez/Tarabini
6–12 Apr	Amelia Island, FL	Clay	M. Pierce d. C. Martinez 6–7 6–0 6–2	Cacic/Pierce
13–19 Apr	Tokyo	Hard	A. Sugiyama d. C. Morariu 6–3 6–3	Kijimuta/Miyagi
13–19 Apr	Makarska	Clay	K. Hrdlickova (Q) d. F. Li 6–3 6–1	Krizan/Srebotnik
20–26 Apr	Budapest	Clay	V. Ruano-Pascual d. S. Farina 6–4 4–6 6–3	Ruano-Pascual/Suarez
27 Apr–3 May	Hamburg	Clay	M. Hingis d. J. Novotna 6–3 7–5	Schett/Schnyder
27 Apr–3 May	Bol	Clay	M. Lucic d. C. Morariu 6–2 6–4	Montalvo/Suarez
4–10 May	Rome	Clay	M. Hingis d. V. Williams 6–3 2–6 6–3	Ruano-Pascual/Suarez
11–17 May	Berlin	Clay	C. Martinez d. A. Mauresmo (Q) 6–4 6–4	Davenport/Zvereva
18–23 May	Strasbourg	Clay	I. Spirlea d. J. Halard-Decugis (WC) 7–6 6–3	Fusai/Tauziat
18–23 May	Madrid	Clay	P. Schnyder d. D. Van Roost 3–6 6–4 6–0	Labat/Van Roost
25 May–7 Jun	**Roland Garros**	**Clay**	**A. Sanchez-Vic. d. M. Seles 7–6 0–6 6–2**	**Hingis/Novotna**
8–14 Jun	Birmingham	Grass	Abandoned due to rain	Callens/ Halard-Decugis
15–20 Jun	Eastbourne	Grass	J. Novotna d. A. Sanchez-Vicario 6–1 7–5	De Swardt/Novotna
15–20 Jun	Rosmalen	Grass	J. Halard-Decugis d. M. Oremans 6–3 6–4	Appelmans/Oremans
22 Jun – 5 Jul	**Wimbledon**	**Grass**	**J. Novotna d. N. Tauziat 6–4 7–6**	**Hingis/Novotna**
6–12 Jul	Prague	Clay	J. Novotna d. S. Testud 6–3 6–0	Farina/Habsudova
6–12 Jul	Maria Lankowitz	Clay	P. Schnyder d. G. Leon-Garcia 6–2 4–6 6–3	Montalvo/Suarez
13–19 Jul	Warsaw	Clay	C. Martinez (WC) d. S Farina 6–0 6–3	Habsudova/Lugina
13–19 Jul	Palermo	Clay	P. Schnyder d. B. Schett 6–1 5–7 6–2	Stojanova/Wagner
27 Jul–2 Aug	Stanford, CA	Hard	L. Davenport d. V. Williams 6–4 5–7 6–4	Davenport/Zvereva
27 Jul–2 Aug	Sopot	Clay	H. Nagyova d. E. Wagner 6–3 5–7 6–1	Hrdlickova/Vildova
3–9 Aug	San Diego, CA	Hard	L. Davenport d. M. Pierce 6–3 6–1	Davenport/Zvereva
3–9 Aug	Istanbul	Hard	H. Nagyova d. O. Barabanschikova 6–4 3–6 7–6(9)	Babel/Courtois
10–16 Aug	Los Angeles, CA	Hard	L. Davenport d. M. Hingis 4–6 6–4 6–3	Hingis/Zvereva
10–16 Aug	Boston, MA	Hard	M. De Swardt d. B. Schett 3–6 7–6 7–5	Raymond/Stubbs
17–23 Aug	Montreal	Hard	M. Seles d. A. Sanchez-Vicario 6–3 6–2	Hingis/Novotna
24–30 Aug	New Haven, CT	Hard	S. Graf d. J. Novotna 6–4 6–1	Fusai/Tauziat
31Aug–13 Sep	**US Open**	**Hard**	**L. Davenport d. M. Hingis 6–3 7–5**	**Hingis/Novotna**
19–20 Sep	**KB Fed Cup Final**	**Hard**	**Spain d. Switzerland 3–2**	
21–27 Sep	Tokyo	Hard	M. Seles d. A. Sanchez-Vicario 4–6 6–3 6–4	Kournikova/Seles
29 Sep–4 Oct	**Grand Slam Cup**	**Carpet**	**V. Williams d. P. Schnyder 6–2 3–6 6–2**	
5–11 Oct	Filderstadt	Hard	S. Testud d. L. Davenport 7–5 6–3	Davenport/Zvereva
12–18 Oct	Zurich	Carpet	L. Davenport d. V. Williams 7–5 6–3	S. Williams/ V. Williams (WC)
19–25 Oct	Moscow	Carpet	M. Pierce d. M. Seles 7–6 6–3	Pierce/Zvereva
26 Oct–1 Nov	Quebec City	Hard	T. Snyder d. C. Rubin 4–6 6–4 7–6	McNeil/Po
26 Oct–1 Nov	Luxembourg	Carpet	M. Pierce d. S. Farina 6–0 2–0 ret.	Likhovtseva/Sugiyama
2–8 Nov	Leipzig	Carpet	S. Graf (WC) d. N. Tauziat 6–3 6–4	Likhovtseva/Sugiyama
9–15 Nov	Philadelphia, PA	Carpet	S. Graf d. L. Davenport 4–6 6–3 6–4	Likhovtseva/Sugiyama
16–22 Nov	WTA Championships	Carpet	M. Hingis d. L. Davenport 7–5 6–4 4–6 6–2	Davenport/Zvereva
16–22 Nov	Pattaya	Hard	J. Halard-Decugis d. F. Li 6–1 6–2	Callens/Halard-Decugis

Lindsay Davenport has just become the eighth different Grand Slam winner in 1998 after out-hitting the world No.1 Martina Hingis – whose mantle she will now assume – at the US Open. (Stephen Wake)

PLAYER NATIONALITIES AND BIRTHDAYS (WOMEN)

The following players have competed in the 1998 Grand Slam Championships, the WTA Tour and Fed Cup ties. (Birthdays are shown as dd-mm-yy)

Surname / Forename	*Nation*	*DOB*
ABE, Julia	GER	21-05-76
ADAMS, Katrina	USA	05-08-68
AHL, Lucie	GBR	23-07-74
AIZENBERG, Geraldine	ARG	31-01-78
ALCAZAR, Ana	ESP	08-06-79
ANDRETTO, Laurence	FRA	12-02-79
APPELMANS, Sabine	BEL	22-04-72
ASAGOE, Shinobu	JPN	28-06-76
AUGUSTUS, Amanda	USA	19-01-78
BABEL, Meike	GER	22-11-74
BAKER, Leanne	NZL	08-01-81
BARABANSCHIKOVA, Olga	BLR	02-11-79
BARCLAY, Catherine	AUS	12-06-73
BARNA, Adriana	GER	21-05-78
BASUKI, Nany 'Yayuk'	INA	30-11-70
BERGER, Segolene	FRA	25-03-78
BERNAL, Laura	PAR	27-01-78
BES, Eva	ESP	14-01-73
BIGGS, Gail	AUS	25-08-70
BIKTYAKOVA, Lilia	UZB	02-02-79
BIKTYAKOVA, Louiza	UZB	11-04-82
BLACK, Cara	ZIM	17-02-79
BLESZYNSKI, Anna	USA	21-10-76
BLUMBERGA, Agnese	LAT	09-04-71
BOBKOVA, Radka	CZE	12-02-73
BOLLEGRAF, Manon	NED	10-04-64
BOOGERT, Kristie	NED	16-12-73
BRADSHAW, Alison	USA	14-11-80
BRANDI, Kristina	USA	29-03-77
BRAUSE, Claudia	URU	29-08-70
BURIC, Mia	GER	01-01-82
CABEZAS, Paula	CHI	21-08-72
CACIC, Sandra	USA	10-09-74
CALLENS, Els	BEL	20-08-70
CAMPANA, Maria-Dolores	ECU	05-04-75
CANEPA, Alice	ITA	30-04-78
CAPRIATI, Jennifer	USA	29-03-76
CARLSSON, Asa	SWE	16-06-75
CASONI, Giulia	ITA	19-04-78
CASTRO, Barbara	CHI	08-09-75
CASTRO, Valentina	CHI	17-07-81
CECCHINI, Anna-Maria 'Sandra'	ITA	27-02-65
CENKOVA, Lenka	CZE	24-01-77
CERVANOVA, Ludmila	SVK	15-10-77
CHEN, Li	CHN	13-03-71
CHI, Jane	USA	21-06-74
CHLADKOVA, Denisa	CZE	08-02-79
CHO, Yoon-Jeong	KOR	02-04-79
CHOI, Ju-Yeon	KOR	19-11-75
CHOI, Young-Ja	KOR	30-05-75
CHUNG, Yang-Jin	KOR	06-11-78
COCHETEUX, Amelie	FRA	27-03-78
COETZER, Amanda	RSA	22-10-71
CONTIN, Maria-Celeste	ARG	17-02-78
CORREIA, Christina	POR	19-02-79
COURTOIS, Laurence	BEL	18-01-76
CRAYBAS, Jill	USA	04-07-74
CRISTEA, Catalina	ROM	02-06-75
CROOK, Helen	GBR	20-11-71
CROSS, Karen	GBR	19-02-74
CSURGO, Virag	HUN	10-11-72
CURUTCHET, Emmanuelle	FRA	19-12-78
D'AGOSTINI, Miriam	BRA	15-08-78
DANILIDOU, Eleni	GRE	19-09-82
DAVENPORT, Lindsay	USA	08-06-76
DAVIES, Victoria	GBR	07-08-72
DE BEER, Surina	RSA	28-06-78
DE LONE, Erika	USA	14-10-72
DE SWARDT, Mariaan	RSA	18-03-71
DE VILLIERS, Esme 'Nannie'	RSA	05-01-76
DECHAUME-BALLERET, Alexia	FRA	03-05-70
DECHY, Nathalie	FRA	21-02-79
DELL'ANGELO, Laura	ITA	17-05-81
DEMENTIEVA, Elena	RUS	15-10-81
DERMEIJERE, Liga	LAT	21-05-83
DHENIN, Caroline	FRA	13-06-73
DI NATALE, Germana	ITA	02-04-74
DIAZ-OLIVA, Mariana	ARG	11-03-76
DING, Ding	CHN	17-08-77
DOKIC, Jelena	AUS	12-04-83
DOMAN, Eva	HUN	17-02-79
DOMINIKOVIC, Evie	AUS	29-05-80
DOPFER, Sandra	AUT	25-05-70
DRAGOMIR, Ruxandra	ROM	24-10-72
DRAKE, Maureen	CAN	21-03-71
DRAKE-BROCKMAN, Siobhan	AUS	07-04-78
DUANGCHAN, Suvimol	THA	10-04-74
ELLWOOD, Annabel	AUS	02-02-78
ENDO, Mana	JPN	06-02-71
ESCOBAR, Marina	ESP	02-02-77
FARINA, Silvia	ITA	27-04-72
FAUTH, Evelyn	AUT	27-11-76
FEBER, Nancy	BEL	05-02-76
FEISTEL, Magdalena	POL	22-08-70
FERNANDEZ, Jessica	MEX	19-07-79
FERNANDEZ, Mary Joe	USA	19-08-71
FISHER, Karen	HKG	31-12-71
FLORO, Pamela	PHI	18-08-79
FRAZIER, Amy	USA	19-09-72
FREYE, Kirstin	GER	29-05-75
FULCO-VILLELLA, Bettina	ARG	23-10-68
FUSAI, Alexandra	FRA	22-11-73
GABROVSKA, Filipa	BUL	26-03-82
GAGLIARDI, Emmanuelle	SUI	09-07-76
GARBIN, Tathiana	ITA	30-06-77
GARCIA, Juliana	COL	21-10-80
GASPAR, Petra	HUN	13-02-77
GAVALDON, Angelica	MEX	03-10-73
GEORGES, Sophie	FRA	08-02-77
GERSI, Adriana	CZE	26-06-76
GHIRARDI-RUBBI, Lea	FRA	10-02-74
GLASS, Andrea	GER	17-07-76
GOLARSA, Laura	ITA	27-11-67
GOLIMBIOSCHI, Oana-Elena	ROM	21-05-80
GORROCHATEGUI, Ines	ARG	13-06-73
GORUR, Hande	TUR	16-06-83
GRAF, Stefanie 'Steffi'	GER	14-06-69
GRAHAM, Deborah 'Debbie'	USA	25-08-70

Surname / Forename	*Nation*	*DOB*
GRAHAME, Amanda	AUS	25-03-79
GRANDE, Rita	ITA	23-03-75
GRANVILLE, Laura	USA	12-05-81
GRZYBOWSKA, Magdalena	POL	22-11-78
GUBACSI, Zsofia	HUN	06-04-81
GUERRERO, Paulo	ECU	07-06-83
GUILLENEA, Cecilia	URU	24-01-81
GUSE, Kerry-Anne	AUS	04-12-72
GUZMAN, Alexandra	ECU	19-01-78
HAAK, Debby	NED	25-02-77
HABSUDOVA, Karina	SVK	02-08-73
HALARD-DECUGIS, Julie	FRA	10-09-70
HARBOE, Karem	CHI	23-04-79
HEGEDUS, Adrienn	HUN	26-12-77
HELGESON-NIELSEN, Ginger	USA	14-09-68
HINGIS, Martina	SUI	30-09-80
HIRAKI, Rika	JPN	06-12-71
HISAMATSU, Shiho	JPN	04-07-79
HLAVACKOVA, Jana	CZE	22-05-81
HOPMANS, Amanda	NED	11-02-76
HORN, Liezel	RSA	21-08-76
HOTTA, Tomoe	JPN	16-04-75
HRDLICKOVA, Kvetoslava	CZE	09-07-75
HUANG, Julie	TPE	05-10-77
HUBER, Anke	GER	04-12-74
HUDSON, Rewa	NZL	15-09-80
HUSAROVA, Janette	SVK	04-06-74
HY-BOULAIS, Patricia	CAN	22-08-65
INOUE, Haruka	JPN	07-06-77
INOUE, Maiko	JPN	05-02-79
IRVIN, Marissa	USA	23-06-80
JACUTIN, Marisue	PHI	14-05-79
JAGIENIAK, Karolina	FRA	04-06-79
JECMENICA, Tatjana	YUG	04-07-78
JENSEN, Amy	AUS	31-07-78
JENSEN, Rebecca	USA	19-11-72
JEON, Mi-Ra	KOR	06-02-78
JEYASEELAN, Sonya	CAN	24-04-76
JONES, Danielle	AUS	04-03-69
JUKIC, Sanja	YUG	11-09-82
JURICICH, Elena	URU	06-09-79
KAMSTRA, Petra	NED	18-03-74
KANDARR, Jana	GER	21-09-76
KEYMAN, Ceyda	TUR	06-06-83
KIJIMUTA, Naoko	JPN	26-03-72
KIM, Eun-Ha	KOR	08-03-75
KLEINOVA, Sandra	CZE	08-05-78
KLOESEL, Sandra	GER	22-06-79
KOLBOVIC, Renata	CAN	30-07-76
KONUK, Ceylan	TUR	01-01-83
KOSTANIC, Jelena	CRO	06-02-81
KOULIKOVSKAYA, Eugenia	RUS	21-12-78
KOURNIKOVA, Anna	RUS	07-06-81
KOVALCHUK, Tatiana	UKR	24-07-79
KOVES, Nora	HUN	13-06-71
KRAUTH, Erica	ARG	20-05-81
KREMER, Anne	LUX	17-10-75
KRIVENTCHEVA, Svetlana	BUL	30-12-73
KRIZAN, Tina	SLO	18-03-74
KROUPOVA, Katerina	CZE	20-02-74
KRSTULOVIC, Dora	CRO	19-06-81
KRUGER, Joannette	RSA	03-09-73
KRUTKO, Elena	LAT	17-11-76
KSCHWENDT, Karin	AUT	14-09-68
KUMBAROVA, Blanka	CZE	22-06-76
KUNCE, Kristine	AUS	03-03-70
KUTI-KIS, Rita	HUN	13-02-78
LABAT, Florencia	ARG	12-06-71
LAMARRE, Magali	FRA	24-02-78
LANDA, Maria-Fernanda	ARG	29-07-75
LANGROVA, Petra	CZE	27-06-70
LATIMER, Louise	GBR	19-01-78
LEE, Janet	TPE	22-10-76
LEE, Lindsay	USA	28-06-77
LEON-GARCIA, Gala	ESP	23-12-73
LI, Fang	CHN	01-01-73
LI, Li	CHN	03-10-76
LI, Ting	CHN	05-01-80
LIKHOVTSEVA, Elena	RUS	08-09-75
LIN, Ning	HKG	28-02-70
LOIT, Emilie	FRA	09-06-79
LOMBARDI, Alessia	ITA	24-05-76
LONGONI, Analia	VEN	29-01-82
LOUARSABISHVILI, Nino	GEO	03-02-77
LUBIANI, Francesca	ITA	12-07-77
LUCIC, Mirjana	CRO	09-03-82
LUGINA, Olga	UKR	08-01-74
MAJOLI, Iva	CRO	12-08-77
MAKAROVA, Elena	RUS	01-02-73
MALEEVA, Magdalena	BUL	01-04-75
MAROSI, Katalin	HUN	12-11-79
MARTINCOVA, Eva	CZE	04-03-75
MARTINEK, Veronika	GER	03-04-72
MARTINEZ, Conchita	ESP	16-04-72
MARTINEZ-GRANADOS, Conchita	ESP	20-01-76
MARUSKA, Marion	AUT	15-12-72
MASANTE, Luciana	ARG	04-12-78
MATEVZIC, Maja	SLO	13-06-80
MAURESMO, Amelie	FRA	05-07-79
MAZZOTTA, Melissa	USA	21-06-72
McGRATH, Meredith	USA	28-04-71
McNEIL, Lori	USA	18-12-63
McQUILLAN, Rachel	AUS	02-12-71
McSHEA, Lisa	AUS	29-10-74
MEDVEDEVA, Natalia	UKR	15-11-71
MELICHAROVA, Eva	CZE	20-02-70
MENGA, Vanessa	BRA	20-10-76
MESA, Mariana	COL	01-04-80
MIKKERS, Anne-Marie	NED	13-05-73
MILLER, Anne	USA	19-01-77
MILLER, Karin	USA	10-12-77
MIYAGI, Nana	JPN	10-04-71
MOLIK, Alicia	AUS	27-01-81
MONTALVO, Laura	ARG	29-03-76
MONTERO, Nuria	ESP	08-10-78
MORARIU, Corina	USA	26-01-78
MORIGAMI, Akiko	JPN	12-01-80
MULEJ, Barbara	SLO	29-05-74
MURIC, Maja	CRO	27-02-74
MUSGRAVE, Trudi	AUS	10-09-77
MYSKINA, Anastasia 'Nastya'	RUS	08-07-81
NACUK, Sandra	YUG	17-08-80
NAGATOMI, Keiko	JPN	22-11-74
NAGYOVA, Henrieta	SVK	15-12-78
NEILAND, Larisa	LAT	21-07-66
NEJEDLY, Jana	CAN	09-06-74
NEMECKOVA, Lenka	CZE	20-04-76
NIELSEN, Ginger	USA	14-09-68
NIEMES, Nuria	ECU	19-06-72
NIKITINA, Natalia	UZB	05-04-78

Surname / Forename	*Nation*	*DOB*
NOGUEIRA, Ana-Catarina	POR	20-09-78
NOORLANDER, Seda	NED	22-05-75
NOVOTNA, Jana	CZE	02-10-68
OBATA, Saori	JPN	23-04-78
OBZILER, Tzipora 'Tzipi'	ISR	19-04-73
OKADA, Jean	USA	07-06-74
OLIVIERA, Daniela	URU	10-12-80
OLSZA, Aleksandra	POL	08-12-77
OREMANS, Maria 'Miriam'	NED	09-09-72
ORTUNO, Alicia	ESP	02-05-76
OSTERLOH, Lilia	USA	07-04-78
OSTROVSKAYA, Nadejda	BLR	29-10-80
OTAKEYAMA, Riei	JPN	21-05-74
OTTOBONI, Romina	ARG	19-06-78
PANDJEROVA, Antoneta	BUL	22-06-77
PANOVA, Tatiana	RUS	13-08-76
PAPADAKI, Christina	GRE	24-02-73
PARK, Seon-Young	KOR	05-03-76
PARK, Sung-Hee	KOR	17-02-75
PASTIKOVA, Michaela	CZE	27-03-80
PAULUS, Barbara	AUT	01-09-70
PAZ, Mercedes	ARG	27-06-66
PELIKANOVA, Radka	CZE	03-04-77
PELLETIER, Marieve	CAN	18-05-82
PERFETTI, Flora	ITA	29-01-69
PETROVA, Nadejda 'Nadia'	RUS	08-06-82
PIERCE, Mary	FRA	15-01-75
PIRSU, Alice	ROM	16-05-79
PISKI, Andrea	HUN	05-07-77
PISNIK, Tina	SLO	19-02-81
PITKOWSKI, Sarah	FRA	13-11-75
PIZZICHINI, Gloria	ITA	24-07-75
PLEMING, Louise	AUS	22-06-67
PLISCHKE, Sylvia	AUT	20-07-77
PO, Kimberly	USA	20-10-71
POJATINA, Kristina	CRO	26-05-78
POSPISILOVA, Jana	CZE	23-03-70
POUTCHEK, Tatiana	BLR	09-01-79
PRAKUSYA, Wynne	INA	26-04-81
PRATT, Nicole	AUS	05-03-73
PRAZERES, Sofia	POR	19-06-74
PROBST, Wiltrud	GER	29-05-69
PULLIN, Julie	GBR	05-11-75
QUINTANILLA, Mariana	PAR	16-07-82
RAFOLOMANANTSIATOSIKA, Aina	MAD	27-04-81
RAJAOARISOA, Mirina	MAD	12-06-82
RAMON, Mariam	ESP	26-08-76
RAMPRE, Petra	SLO	20-01-80
RANDRIANTEFY, Natacha	MAD	14-03-78
RASOARILALAO, Faratiana	MAD	12-01-80
RAYMOND, Lisa	USA	10-08-73
REEVES, Sally	GBR	08-07-64
REEVES, Samantha	USA	17-01-79
REID, Renee	AUS	28-05-78
RICHTEROVA, Ludmila	CZE	07-03-77
RIERA, Gisela	ESP	07-05-76
RINALDI, Karina	ARG	05-06-78
RIPPNER, Aubrie 'Brie'	USA	21-01-80
RITTNER, Barbara	GER	25-04-73
RODRIGUEZ, Carla	PER	29-05-72
ROJAS, Ariana	PER	18-12-81
ROJAS, Maria-Eugenia	PER	27-12-77
ROLON, Ana-Valeria	PAR	08-01-76
ROSEN, Hila	ISR	05-09-77
ROTTIER, Stephanie	NED	22-01-74
RUANO-PASCUAL, Virginia	ESP	21-09-73
RUBIN, Chanda	USA	18-02-76
RYNARZEWSKA, Sylwia	POL	14-06-76
SAEKI, Miho	JPN	18-03-76
SALAS, Ana	ESP	12-07-72
SALVADOR, Elena	ESP	15-05-79
SANCHEZ LORENZO, Maria Antonia	ESP	07-11-77
SANCHEZ-VICARIO, Arantxa	ESP	18-12-71
SANDU, Raluca	ROM	03-02-80
SANGARAM, Benjamas	THA	11-01-75
SARET, Jennifer	PHI	12-12-74
SASANO, Yoshiko	JPN	17-10-73
SAWAMATSU, Naoko	JPN	23-03-73
SAWONDARI, Wurtraish	INA	20-11-80
SCHAERER, Larissa	PAR	15-04-75
SCHETT, Barbara	AUT	10-03-76
SCHIAVONE, Francesca	ITA	23-06-80
SCHLUKEBIR, Katrina 'Katie'	USA	29-04-75
SCHMIDLE, Syna	GER	20-11-78
SCHNEIDER, Alexandra	GER	29-04-76
SCHNEIDER, Caroline	GER	01-06-73
SCHNITZER, Miriam	GER	14-01-77
SCHNYDER, Patty	SUI	14-12-78
SCHULTZ-McCARTHY, Brenda	NED	28-12-70
SCHWARTZ, Barbara	AUT	27-01-79
SCOTT, Julie	USA	16-10-75
SELES, Monica	USA	02-12-73
SELYUTINA, Irina	KAZ	07-11-79
SEQUERA, Milagros	VEN	30-09-80
SERNA, Maria-Luisa	ESP	01-09-79
SERRA-ZANETTI, Adriana	ITA	05-03-76
SERRA-ZANETTI, Antonella	ITA	25-07-80
SHAUGHNESSY, Meghann	USA	13-04-79
SHIBATA, Kaoru	JPN	25-06-73
SIDOT, Anne-Gaelle	FRA	24-07-79
SIMPSON, Rene	CAN	14-01-66
SINGER, Christina	GER	27-07-68
SINGIAN, Tracy	USA	06-10-79
SMASHNOVA, Anna	ISR	16-07-76
SMITH, Samantha 'Sam'	GBR	27-11-71
SNYDER, Tara	USA	26-05-77
SOUKUP, Aneta	CAN	30-12-78
SPEARS, Abigail	USA	12-07-81
SPIRLEA, Irina	ROM	26-03-74
SREBOTNIK, Katarina	SLO	12-03-81
SROMOVA, Hana	CZE	10-04-78
STECK, Jessica	RSA	06-08-78
STELE, Veronica	ARG	19-11-77
STEPHENS, Shelley	NZL	29-07-78
STEVEN, Julie	USA	24-04-76
STEVENSON, Alexandra	USA	15-12-80
STEWART, Bryanne	AUS	09-12-79
STOJANOVA, Pavlina	BUL	14-07-74
STUBBS, Rennae	AUS	26-03-71
STUDENIKOVA, Katerina	SVK	02-09-72
SUAREZ, Paola	ARG	23-06-76
SUGIYAMA, Ai	JPN	05-07-75
SUKOVA, Helena	CZE	23-02-65
SULISTYOWATI, Eny	INA	14-01-80
SYSSOEVA, Ekaterina	RUS	03-06-81
TALAJA, Silvija	CRO	14-01-78
TANASUGARN, Tamarine	THA	24-05-77
TANG, Min	HKG	26-01-71

Germany's 22-year-old Jana Kandarr slipped eight places in 1998 to end the year with a singles ranking of 90. (Michael Cole)

Surname / Forename	*Nation*	*DOB*
TARABINI, Patricia	ARG	06-08-68
TATARKOVA, Elena	UKR	22-08-76
TAUZIAT, Nathalie	FRA	17-10-67
TAVERNA, Fabiana	VEN	20-04-82
TAYLOR, Sarah	USA	06-11-81
TEODOROWICZ, Katarzyna	POL	28-11-72
TEPLINSKAIA, Olga	UKR	05-01-79
TESTUD, Sandrine	FRA	03-04-72
TIPPINS, Niki	NZL	15-05-76
TONG, Ka-Po	HKG	17-03-81
TOPALOVA, Desislava	BUL	08-06-78
TORRENS-VALERO, Cristina	ESP	12-09-74
TRAIL, Jacqueline 'Jackie'	USA	26-11-80
TRISKA, Kristina	SWE	06-03-80
TU, Meilen	USA	17-01-78
TULYAGANOVA, Iroda	UZB	07-01-82
VAIDYANATHAN, Nirupama	IND	08-12-76
VAN LOTTUM, Noelle	FRA	12-07-72
VAN ROOST, Dominique	BEL	31-05-73
VASKOVA, Alena	CZE	08-11-75
VENTO, Maria-Alejandro	VEN	24-05-74
VENTO, Maria-Eugenia	VEN	17-08-70
VILDOVA, Helena	CZE	19-03-72
VIS, Caroline	NED	04-03-70
VISIC, Ivana	CRO	07-10-80

Surname / Forename	*Nation*	*DOB*
WAGNER, Elena	GER	17-05-72
WAINWRIGHT, Amanda 'Mandy'	GBR	24-03-76
WANG, Shi-Ting	TPE	19-10-73
WARD, Jo	GBR	22-06-75
WARTUSCH, Patricia	AUT	05-08-78
WASHINGTON, Mashona	USA	31-05-76
WATANABE, Jolene	USA	31-08-68
WEBB, Vanessa	CAN	24-01-76
WEINGARTNER, Marlene	GER	30-01-80
WENG, Tzu-Ting	TPE	01-07-78
WILLIAMS, Serena	USA	26-09-81
WILLIAMS, Venus	USA	17-06-80
WOHR, Jasmin	GER	21-08-80
WONGKAMALASAI, Orawan	THA	25-08-81
WOOD, Clare	GBR	08-03-68
WOODROFFE, Lorna	GBR	18-08-76
WUNDERLICH, Ann	USA	13-10-70
YI, Jing-Qian	CHN	28-02-74
YOSHIDA, Yuka	JPN	01-04-76
ZAPOROZHANOVA, Anna	UKR	09-08-79
ZARIC, Dragana	YUG	01-08-77
ZARSKA, Anna	POL	22-07-79
ZAVAGLI, Maria-Paola	ITA	04-06-77
ZULUAGA, Fabiola	COL	07-01-79
ZVEREVA, Natalia	BLR	16-04-71

Germany's Anke Huber was a semi-finalist at the Australian Open but then suffered problems with a foot which required surgery in March and kept her off court until August. (Stephen Wake)

Championship Series

Tier I and II Tournaments

SYDNEY INTERNATIONAL ($339,500)
SYDNEY, 11–17 JANUARY
WOMEN'S SINGLES – 1st round: M. Hingis (1) bye; V. Williams d. R. Dragomir 6–4 ret; M. Maleeva d. S. Appelmans 6–1 1–6 6–3; C. Rubin d. A. Huber (8) 6–2 6–3; I. Spirlea (4) bye; B. Paulus d. M. Oremans 6–0 6–2; A. Sugiyama d. F. Lubiani 6–1 7–6; C. Martinez (6) d. G. Leon-Garcia 6–2 6–3; A. Sanchez-Vicario (5) d. K. Habsudova 7–5 6–4; J. Lee d. B. Schultz-McCarthy 6–0 1–1 ret; N. Zvereva d. R. McQuillan 6–2 7–5; A. Coetzer (3) bye; S. Testud (7) d. K. Guse 6–1 6–2; S. Williams d. M. Lucic 3–6 6–4 7–5; A. Kournikova d. N. Basuki 6–4 3–0 ret; L. Davenport (2) bye.
2nd round: V. Williams d. Hingis (1) 3–6 6–4 7–5; Maleeva d. Rubin 6–3 1–6 6–4; Paulus d. Spirlea (4) 6–2 1–6 6–3; Sugiyama d. Martinez (6) 7–6 6–3; Sanchez-Vicario (5) d. Lee 6–2 3–6 6–3; Zvereva d. Coetzer (3) 6–7 6–3 7–5; S. Williams d. Testud (7) 7–6 3–0 ret; Davenport (2) d. Kournikova 6–2 6–7 6–3.
Quarter-finals: V. Williams d. Maleeva 6–2 6–2; Sugiyama d. Paulus 6–1 7–6; Sanchez-Vicario (5) d. Zvereva 6–1 6–2; S. Williams d. Davenport (2) 1–6 7–5 7–5.
Semi-finals: V. Williams d. Sugiyama 6–1 7–6; Sanchez-Vicario (5) d. S. Williams 6–2 6–1.
Final: Sanchez-Vicario (5) d. V. Williams 6–1 6–3.
WOMEN'S DOUBLES – Final: Hingis/Sukova (3) d. Adams/McGrath 6–1 6–2.

TORAY PAN PACIFIC OPEN ($926,250)
TOKYO, 3–8 FEBRUARY
WOMEN'S SINGLES – 1st round: M. Hingis (1) bye; E. Likhovtseva d. M. Lucic 6–1 6–2; R. Grande d. K. Boogert (Q) 3–6 6–1 6–4; M. Vento d. R. Dragomir (9) 6–0 6–3; I. Majoli (4) bye; F. Li (Q) d. T. Tanasugarn 6–1 6–3; M. Saeki (WC) d. M. Serna 3–6 6–3 6–3; M. Maleeva d. A. Huber (6) 3–6 7–6 6–1; A. Sugiyama (8) d. K. Guse 7–6 6–0; Y. Yoshida (WC) d. M. Grzybowska 4–6 7–6 6–4; S. Reeves (Q) d. Y. Cho (Q) 6–3 6–4; A. Coetzer (3) bye; I. Spirlea (5) d. S. Park (LL) 7–5 6–0; J. Kruger d. N. Zvereva 6–4 7–6; N. Sawamatsu d. M. Sanchez Lorenzo 6–1 6–1; L. Davenport (2) bye.
2nd round: Hingis (1) d. Likhovtseva 6–1 6–0; Grande d. Vento 1–6 6–3 6–3; Majoli (4) d. Li (Q) 6–3 3–0 ret; Saeki (WC) d. Maleeva 6–4 7–6; Sugiyama (8) d. Yoshida (WC) 6–1 7–6; Coetzer (3) d. Reeves (Q) 6–4 6–4; Spirlea (5) d. Kruger 6–1 6–2; Davenport (2) d. Sawamatsu 6–2 6–2.
Quarter-finals: Hingis (1) d. Grande 6–2 7–5; Majoli (4) d. Saeki (WC) 6–2 6–1; Coetzer (3) d. Sugiyama (8) 6–3 2–6 6–2; Davenport (2) d. Spirlea (5) 7–6 7–6.
Semi-finals: Hingis (1) d. Majoli (4) 6–0 6–2; Davenport (2) d. Coetzer (3) 6–2 6–1.
Final: Davenport (2) d. Hingis (1) 6–3 6–3.
WOMEN'S DOUBLES – Final: Hingis/Lucic (Q) d. Davenport/Zvereva (1) 7–5 6–4.

OPEN GAZ DE FRANCE ($450,000)
PARIS, 9–15 FEBRUARY
WOMEN'S SINGLES – 1st round: J. Novotna (1) bye; R. Grande d. M. Oremans 7–6 6–1; S. Farina d. D. Chladkova 2–6 6–2 6–3; B. Paulus (7) d. S. Kleinova 6–3 7–5; M. Pierce (3) bye; K. Habsudova d. J. Halard-Decugis 7–6 4–6 6–4; A. Kournikova d. A. Dechaume-Balleret (WC) 6–3 7–5; A. Huber (5) d. A. Fusai (WC) 6–1 6–1; S. Appelmans (8) d. L. Neiland (Q) 6–1 6–3; S. Pitkowski (LL) d. A. Sidot 6–4 6–0; E. Loit (Q) d. M. Maleeva 6–0 6–2; N. Tauziat (4) bye; D. Van Roost (6) d. B. Schett 6–2 4–6 6–0; W. Probst (Q) d. L. Courtois (Q) 3–6 7–5 6–4; F. Labat d. E. Likhovtseva 6–4 6–1; I. Majoli (2) bye.
2nd round: Novotna (1) d. Grande 6–1 6–4; Paulus (7) d. Farina 6–1 6–3; Pierce (3) d. Habsudova 6–1 1–6 6–1; Huber (5) d. Kournikova 6–2 1–6 6–4; Pitkowski (LL) d. Appelmans (8) 5–7 6–3 6–1; Tauziat (4) d. Loit (Q) 4–6 7–6 6–4; Van Roost (6) d. Probst (Q) 5–7 6–2 7–6; Majoli (2) d. Labat 5–7 6–2 6–4.
Quarter-finals: Novotna (1) d. Paulus (7) 6–2 1–6 6–4; Pierce (3) d. Huber (5) 1–6 6–1 6–2; Tauziat (4) d. Pitkowski (LL) 6–1 2–6 7–6; Van Roost (6) d. Majoli (2) 7–5 6–3.
Semi-finals: Pierce (3) d. Novotna (1) 6–4 2–6 6–3; Van Roost (6) d. Tauziat (4) 7–6 1–6 6–1.
Final: Pierce (3) d. Van Roost (6) 6–3 7–5.
WOMEN'S DOUBLES – Final: Appelmans/Oremans (4) d. Kournikova/Neiland (3) 1–6 6–3 7–6.

FABER GRAND PRIX ($450,000)
HANOVER, 18–22 FEBRUARY
WOMEN'S SINGLES – 1st round: J. Novotna (1) bye; D. Van Roost d. A. Cocheteux (Q) 6–2 6–0; A. Gersi (Q) d. R. Dragomir 6–1 6–7 7–6; L. Raymond (8) d. A. Fusai (Q) 7–6 6–2; W. Probst (LL) bye; A. Kournikova d. S. Farina 6–4 6–3; B. Schett d. F. Labat 7–5 6–1; A. Huber (6) d. E. Likhovtseva 6–7 6–2 6–4; N. Tauziat (7) d. M. Grzybowska 6–2 6–1; K. Habsudova d. B. Rittner (WC) 6–4 7–6; P. Schnyder d. A. Sidot 6–0 6–2; I. Majoli

(3) bye; S. Appelmans d. I. Spirlea (5) 4–1 ret; M. Maleeva d. M. Babel (Q) 6–4 6–2; A. Glass (WC) d. B. Paulus 2–6 6–3 6–0; S. Graf (2) bye.
2nd round: Novotna (1) d. Van Roost 4–6 6–4 6–3; Raymond (8) d. Gersi (Q) 6–1 6–0; Kournikova d. Probst (LL) 6–3 6–1; Huber (6) d. Schett 6–4 6–2; Tauziat (7) d. Habsudova 6–4 6–4; Schnyder d. Majoli (3) 6–1 6–3; Appelmans d. Maleeva 7–5 6–3; Graf (2) d. Glass (WC) 6–4 6–2.
Quarter-finals: Novotna (1) d. Raymond (8) 6–1 7–5; Kournikova d. Huber (6) 6–4 3–6 6–4; Schnyder d. Tauziat (7) 6–4 6–3; Appelmans d. Graf (2) 6–3 7–6.
Semi-finals: Novotna (1) d. Kournikova 6–3 6–3; Schnyder d. Appelmans 6–3 6–3.
Final: Schnyder d. Novotna (1) 6–0 2–6 7–5.
WOMEN'S DOUBLES – Final: Raymond/Stubbs (4) d. Likhovtseva/Vis (3) 6–1 6–7 6–3.

EA-GENERALI LADIES AUSTRIAN OPEN ($450,000)

LINZ, 23 FEBRUARY–1 MARCH
WOMEN'S SINGLES – 1st round: J. Novotna (1) bye; A. Mauresmo (Q) d. A. Carlsson 6–0 7–6; B. Rittner d. N. Dechy (Q) 6–3 6–3; A. Kournikova (8) d. S. Plischke (WC) 5–7 6–4 7–5; N. Tauziat (3) bye; A. Fusai d. D. Chladkova 7–5 7–5; K. Kschwendt (Q) d. K. Studenikova 6–3 2–6 6–3; S. Farina d. N. Basuki (6) 6–3 6–4; S. Appelmans (7) d. S. Kleinova 6–4 6–2; F. Labat d. M. Maruska (WC) 7–5 6–0; A. Gersi d. K. Habsudova 7–6 ret; D. Van Roost (4) bye; L. Raymond (5) d. M. Sanchez Lorenzo 6–2 6–3; M. Oremans d. A. Sidot 7–6 6–7 6–3; M. Maleeva d. A. Glass (Q) 6–1 6–0; I. Majoli (2) bye.
2nd round: Novotna (1) d. Mauresmo (Q) 6–4 6–2; Kournikova (8) d. Rittner 6–3 6–4; Tauziat (3) d. Fusai 4–6 6–2 6–2; Farina d. Kschwendt (Q) 7–5 6–4; Appelmans (7) d. Labat 6–2 6–1; Van Roost (4) d. Gersi 2–6 7–5 7–6; Raymond (5) d. Oremans 7–6 7–6; Majoli (2) d. Maleeva 6–1 6–1.
Quarter-finals: Novotna (1) d. Kournikova (8) 6–1 6–3; Farina d. Tauziat (3) 6–4 7–6; Van Roost (4) d. Appelmans (7) 6–3 7–6; Majoli (2) d. Raymond (5) 7–6 4–6 6–3.
Semi-finals: Novotna (1) d. Farina 6–4 6–1; Van Roost (4) d. Majoli (2) 5–2 ret.
Final: Novotna (1) d. Van Roost (4) 6–1 7–6.
WOMEN'S DOUBLES – Final: Fusai/Tauziat (2) d. Kournikova/Neiland (3) 6–3 3–6 6–4.

STATE FARM EVERT CUP ($1,250,000)

INDIAN WELLS, CA, 5–15 MARCH
WOMEN'S SINGLES – 1st round: M. Hingis (1) bye; S. Pitkowski d. A. Fusai 6–4 6–3; F. Labat d. L. Neiland (Q) 6–2 3–6 6–1; M. Babel d. B. Schultz-Mc Carthy (14) 6–7 6–3 7–6; A. Kournikova (16) d. A. Dechaume-Balleret (Q) 3–6 6–4 6–0; C. Rubin d. E. Likhovtseva 3–6 6–3 7–6; M. Vento d. K. Kunce (Q) 6–3 6–4; C. Martinez (5) bye; A. Coetzer (4) bye; A. Miller (Q) d. S. Taylor 6–1 6–1; B. Schett d. R. Grande 6–7 6–3 7–6; J. Kruger (17) d. R. McQuillan 6–0 1–6 7–5; D. Van Roost (10) d. C. Morariu 6–1 6–3; B. Paulus d. N. Basuki 6–4 1–6 7–5; S. Farina d. S. Kleinova 6–0 6–2; V. Williams (8) bye; I. Spirlea (6) bye; F. Li d. O. Barabanschikova 6–4 6–1; N. Sawamatsu d. M. Lucic 6–2 4–6 6–3; N. Zvereva (15) d. S. Jeyaseelan (LL) 6–2 6–4; A. Sugiyama (11) d. K. Guse (LL) 6–3 6–3; T. Snyder (Q) d. L. Osterloh (WC) 7–5 6–0; T. Tanasugarn d. M. Sanchez Lorenzo 6–1 4–6 7–5; S. Graf (3) bye; N. Tauziat (7) bye; S. Cacic d. C. Cristea (Q) 6–1 6–1; J. Halard-Decugis d. A. Carlsson 6–0 6–2; S. Testud (9) d. M. Serna 6–4 4–6 7–5; R. Dragomir (13) d. C. Black (WC) 6–3 6–3; T. Panova (Q) d. K. Boogert (Q) 1–6 6–4 6–1; A. Frazier d. F. Lubiani (LL) 6–4 6–1; L. Davenport (2) bye.
2nd round: Hingis (1) d. Pitkowski 6–2 6–1; Babel d. Labat 4–6 6–1 6–4; Kournikova (16) d. Rubin 3–6 6–2 7–6; Martinez (5) d. Vento 7–6 7–5 6–3; Coetzer (4) d. Miller (Q) 6–3 6–3; Kruger (17) d. Schett 6–4 6–3; Van Roost (10) d. Paulus 6–4 6–0; Williams (8) d. Farina 6–3 6–1; Spirlea (6) d. Li 7–5 6–2; Zvereva (15) d. Sawamatsu 6–4 6–3; Sugiyama (11) d. Snyder (Q) 6–1 4–6 6–1; Graf (3) d. Tanasugarn 6–4 6–1; Cacic d. Tauziat (7) 1–6 2–6 7–5; Testud (9) d. Halard-Decugis 6–3 6–7 7–5; Dragomir (13) d. Panova (Q) 5–7 6–0 6–0; Davenport (2) d. Frazier 6–3 6–1.
3rd round: Hingis (1) d. Babel 6–2 6–0; Martinez (5) d. Kournikova (16) 6–3 6–4; Kruger (17) d. Coetzer (4) 2–6 6–4 6–4; Williams (8) d. Van Roost (10) 6–4 6–1; N Zvereva (15) d. Spirlea (6) 6–3 7–5; Graf (3) d. Sugiyama (11) 6–0 6–1; Cacic d. Testud (9) 4–6 7–6 7–6; Davenport (2) d. Dragomir (13) 6–2 6–2.
Quarter-finals: Hingis (1) d. Martinez (5) 6–1 7–5; Williams (8) d. Kruger (17) 6–1 6–3; Graf (3) d. Zvereva (15) 6–3 6–0; Davenport (2) d. Cacic 6–1 7–5.
Semi-finals: Hingis (1) d. Williams (8) 6–0 7–6; Davenport (2) d. Graf (3) 6–4 4–6 4–2 ret.
Final: Hingis (1) d. Davenport (2) 6–3 6–4.
WOMEN'S DOUBLES – Final: Davenport/Zvereva (1) d. Fusai/Tauziat (2) 6–4 2–6 6–4.

THE LIPTON CHAMPIONSHIPS ($1,900,000)

KEY BISCAYNE, FL, 19–28 MARCH
WOMEN'S SINGLES – 1st round: M. Hingis (1) bye; C. Rubin d. T. Tanasugarn 6–3 6–3; A. Miller d. L. Ghirardi-Rubbi (Q) 6–4 6–7 6–1; J. Kruger (21) bye; B. Schett (27) bye; L. McNeil (WC) d. P. Hy-Boulais 6–0 1–6 7–5; A. Carlsson d. A. Rippner (WC) 7–6 7–5; S. Testud (13) bye; I. Spirlea (10) bye; S. Williams d. D. Chladkova 6–4 6–0; M. Saeki d. A. Gersi 6–1 6–2; B. Paulus (24) bye; P. Schnyder (17) bye; C. Torrens-Valero d. A. Stevenson (WC) 2–6 6–3 6–2; K. Habsudova d. W. Probst 6–3 4–6 6–3; T. Tanasugarn (7) bye; R. Grande (4) bye; S. Plischke d. K. Studenikova 7–6 7–5; A. Mauresmo d. L. Golarsa 7–5 6–1; N. Basuki (25) bye; S. Pitkowski (32) bye; O. Barabanschikova d. N. Dechy (Q) 7–6 2–6 6–1; T. Panova (LL) d. M. Washington (WC) 6–2 7–5; V. Williams (11) bye; A. Sugiyama (16) bye; B. Rittner d. J. Watanabe (Q) 1–6 6–3 6–2; G. Leon-

Garcia d. R. Grande 6–4 7–5; S. Farina (29) bye; N. Zvereva (19) bye; Y. Yoshida d. K. Guse 0–6 7–5 6–1; A. Dechaume-Balleret d. M. Oremans 3–6 6–3 6–2; A. Coetzer (6) bye; A. Sanchez-Vicario (8) bye; S. Wang d. F. Lubiani 6–4 6–1; T. Snyder (WC) d. E. Makarova 7–5 ret; F. Labat (31) bye; M. Vento (30) bye; L. Neiland d. S. Kleinova 6–1 3–6 6–2; E. Likhovtseva d. J. Husarova 6–3 6–2; D. Van Roost (15) bye; A. Huber (14) bye; J. Lee (Q) d. N. Kijimuta 6–1 6–4; J. Halard-Decugis d. M. Serna 3–6 7–5 6–3; S. Appelmans (18) bye; B. Schultz-McCarthy (22) bye; J. Kandarr (Q) d. A. Fusai 6–4 6–3; M. Grzybowska d. J. Capriati (WC) 6–0 7–5; J. Novotna (3) bye; M. Seles (5) bye; M. Sanchez Lorenzo d. S. Cacic 6–3 6–3; M. Lucic d. M. Diaz-Oliva (Q) 6–3 6–0; A. Kournikova (23) bye; N. Sawamatsu (28) bye; K. Brandi (WC) d. C. Morariu 6–3 5–7 6–4; A. Smashnova (Q) d. V. Ruano-Pascual 6–1 6–1; C. Martinez (9) bye; N. Tauziat (12) bye; A. Wunderlich (WC) d. A. Cecchini 7–5 6–2; M. Babel d. S. Reeves (WC) 6–3 6–2; H. Nagyova (26) bye; R. Dragomir (20) bye; F. Li d. R. McQuillan 7–6 6–2; P. Stojanova (Q) d. A. Frazier 0–6 6–3 6–4; L. Davenport (2) bye.

2nd round: Hingis (1) d. Rubin 6–1 6–0; Kruger (21) d. Miller 6–4 6–0; McNeil (WC) d. Schett (27) 6–2 6–2; Testud (13) d. Carlsson 6–1 6–2; S. Williams d. Spirlea (10) 7–6 6–0; Paulus (24) d. Saeki 7–6 6–3; Schnyder (17) d. Torrens-Valero 6–0 6–3; Tanasugarn (7) d. Habsudova 6–1 3–6 6–2; Grande (4) d. Plischke 3–6 6–3 6–2; Basuki (25) d. Mauresmo 7–5 7–6; Barabanschikova d. Pitkowski (32) 6–4 1–0 ret; V. Williams (11) d. Panova (LL) 6–3 6–3; Sugiyama (16) d. Rittner 6–2 6–3; Farina (29) d. Leon-Garcia 6–4 6–1; Zvereva (19) d. Yoshida 6–3 6–4; Coetzer (6) d. Dechaume-Balleret 5–7 6–3 6–3; Sanchez-Vicario (8) d. Wang 4–6 6–4 6–2; Labat (31) d. Snyder (WC) 7–5 6–4; Vento (30) d. Neiland 7–5 6–3; Likhovtseva d. Van Roost (15) 6–1 1–0 ret; Huber (14) d. Lee (Q) 2–6 6–4 6–4; Appelmans (18) d. Halard-Decugis 6–2 6–1; Kandarr (Q) d. Schultz-McCarthy (22) 6–1 6–4; Novotna (3) d. Grzybowska 6–1 6–1; Seles (5) d. Sanchez Lorenzo 6–4 6–7 6–3; Kournikova (23) d. Lucic 6–4 6–2; Sawamatsu (28) d. Brandi (WC) 7–5 6–3; Martinez (9) d. Smashnova (Q) 6–4 6–2; Tauziat (12) d. Wunderlich (WC) 7–5 6–4; Nagyova (26) d. Babel 6–2 6–1; Li d. Dragomir (20) 2–6 7–6 6–4; Davenport (2) d. Stojanova (Q) 6–2 6–2.

3rd round: Hingis (1) d. Kruger (21) 6–0 6–0; Testud (13) d. McNeil (WC) 6–3 6–3; S. Williams d. Paulus (24) 6–3 6–2; Schnyder (17) d. Tanasugarn (7) 6–0 6–2; Grande (4) d. Basuki (25) 6–4 3–6 6–4; V. Williams (11) d. Barabanschikova 6–2 6–1; Farina (29) d. Sugiyama (16) 6–3 7–5; Coetzer (6) d. Zvereva (19) 7–5 6–3; Sanchez-Vicario (8) d. Labat (31) 6–0 6–1; Vento (30) d. Likhovtseva 7–5 5–7 6–3; Huber (14) d. Appelmans (18) 6–7 6–4 6–4; Novotna (3) d. Kandarr (Q) 6–3 4–6 6–3; Kournikova (23) d. Seles (5) 7–5 6–4; Martinez (9) d. Sawamatsu (28) 6–2 6–2; Tauziat (12) d. Nagyova (26) 6–1 6–1; Davenport (2) d. Li 3–6 6–1 6–3.

4th round: Hingis (1) d. Testud (13) 6–3 5–7 6–2; S. Williams d. Schnyder (17) 6–0 4–6 6–3; V. Williams (11) d. Grande (4) 6–1 6–4; Farina (29) d. Coetzer (6) 6–7 6–2 6–1; Sanchez-Vicario (8) d. Vento (30) 6–2 6–1; Novotna (3) d. Huber (14) 6–2 6–2; Kournikova (23) d. Martinez (9) 6–3 6–0; Davenport (2) d. Tauziat (12) 6–1 6–2.

Quarter-finals: Hingis (1) d. S. Williams 6–3 1–6 7–6; V. Williams (11) d. Farina (29) 6–1 6–2; Sanchez-Vicario (8) d. Novotna (3) 6–2 6–1; Kournikova (23) d. Davenport (2) 6–2 5–7 6–2.

Semi-finals: V. Williams (11) d. Hingis (1) 6–2 5–7 6–2; Kournikova (23) d. Sanchez-Vicario (8) 3–6 6–1 6–3.

Final: V. Williams (11) d. Kournikova (23) 2–6 6–4 6–1.

WOMEN'S DOUBLES – Final: Hingis/Novotna (1) d. Sanchez-Vicario/Zvereva (2) 6–2 3–6 6–3.

FAMILY CIRCLE MAGAZINE CUP ($926,250)

HILTON HEAD ISLAND, SC, 30 MARCH–5 APRIL

WOMEN'S SINGLES – 1st round: L. Davenport (1) bye; C. Morariu d. C. Rubin 6–4 6–4; N. Sawamatsu d. N. Basuki 6–1 1–6 6–1; R. Dragomir d. S. Testud (11) 6–3 6–3; I. Spirlea (9) d. M. Babel 6–3 6–3; F. Labat d. W. Probst (Q) 6–1 6–1; M. Grzybowska d. T. Tanasugarn 5–7 6–4 6–4; C. Martinez (8) bye; M. Seles (3) bye; B. Paulus d. S. Cacic (Q) 3–6 6–3 6–1; B. Schultz-McCarthy d. O. Barabanschikova 6–1 7–6; N. Zvereva (16) d. G. Leon-Garcia 6–4 7–5; P. Schnyder (14) d. A. Mauresmo (Q) 6–3 7–6; L. McNeil (WC) d. J. Capriati (WC) 6–7 6–4 6–4; M. De Swardt (WC) d. D. Chladkova 5–0 ret; I. Majoli (6) bye; A. Sanchez-Vicario (7) bye; A. Glass (Q) d. C. Cristea (Q) 7–5 6–2; C. Torrens-Valero (Q) d. F. Li 7–5 6–2; A. Fusai d. A. Sugiyama (13) 2–6 7–5 6–4; N. Tauziat (10) d. M. Vento 6–4 6–1; V. Ruano-Pascual d. M. Sanchez Lorenzo 6–4 2–6 6–4; S. Farina d. O. Lugina (Q) 5–1 ret; A. Coetzer (4) bye; M. Pierce (5) bye; A. Miller (WC) d. B. Schett 6–3 2–6 6–4; R. Grande d. A. Sidot 6–3 1–6 6–4; L. Raymond (15) d. S. Wang 6–1 4–6 6–1; M. Serna d. A. Huber (12) 7–5 7–6; E. Likhovtseva d. T. Panova (Q) 3–6 6–2 6–4; S. Kleinova d. J. Kruger 7–6 6–2; J. Novotna (2) bye.

2nd round: Davenport (1) d. Morariu 6–3 6–0; Dragomir d. Sawamatsu 6–0 6–2; Spirlea (9) d. Labat 6–7 6–2 6–0; Grzybowska d. Martinez (8) 7–5 6–2; Seles (3) d. Paulus 6–2 0–1 ret; Zvereva (16) d. Schultz-McCarthy 6–2 6–2; Schnyder (14) d. McNeil (WC) 6–3 6–2; De Swardt (WC) d. Majoli (6) 6–4 7–5; Glass (Q) d. Sanchez-Vicario (7) 6–7 7–5 6–2; Fusai d. Torrens-Valero (Q) 7–6 6–7 6–4; Ruano-Pascual d. Tauziat (10) 7–5 6–1; Coetzer (4) d. Farina 6–4 6–3; Miller (WC) d. Pierce (5) 6–3 6–3; Raymond (15) d. Grande 6–1 7–6; Serna d. Likhovtseva 7–5 2–6 6–2; Novotna (2) d. Kleinova 6–4 6–3.

3rd round: Davenport (1) d. Dragomir 1–6 6–3 7–5; Spirlea (9) d. Grzybowska 6–3 6–4; Seles (3) d. Zvereva (16) 6–0 6–7 6–2; Schnyder (14) d. De Swardt (WC) 6–3 6–2; Glass (Q) d. Fusai 6–3 7–6; Coetzer (4) d. Ruano-Pascual 6–0 6–4; Raymond (15) d. Miller (WC) 1–6 6–2 6–3; Serna d. Novotna (2) 3–6 6–4 6–2.

Quarter-finals: Spirlea (9) d. Davenport (1) 6–7 6–4 7–6; Seles (3) d. Schnyder (14) 4–6 6–3 7–6; Coetzer (4) d. Glass (Q) 4–6 7–6 ret; Raymond (15) d. Serna 6–4 6–1.

Semi-finals: Spirlea (9) d. Seles (3) 6–4 1–6 7–6; Coetzer (4) d. Raymond (15) 6–4 6–1.

Final: Coetzer (4) d. Spirlea (9) 6–3 6–4.

WOMEN'S DOUBLES – Final: Martinez/Tarabini (6) d. Raymond/Stubbs (7) 3–6 6–4 6–4.

BAUSCH & LOMB CHAMPIONSHIPS ($450,000)

AMELIA ISLAND, FL, 6–12 APRIL

WOMEN'S SINGLES – 1st round: L. Davenport (1) bye; A. Dechaume-Balleret d. P. Suarez (Q) 7–6 6–1; F. Labat d. T. Tanasugarn 6–4 6–2; B. Paulus (14) d. A. Mauresmo 2–6 6–3 7–5; P. Schnyder (9) d. V. Ruano-Pascual 7–5 6–2; M. De Swardt (Q) d. A. Wunderlich (WC) 6–4 6–2; W. Probst d. K. Studenikova 6–2 6–1; A. Kournikova (8) bye; M. Pierce (4) bye; C. Cristea (Q) d. S. Kleinova 7–6 6–4; E. Gagliardi (Q) d. C. Torrens-Valero 2–6 6–2 6–4; E. Likhovtseva d. J. Kruger (12) 6–4 6–2; B. Schett (15) d. T. Panova (Q) 6–1 7–6; J. Capriati (WC) d. L. Osterloh (WC) 6–4 6–2; B. Rittner (Q) d. C. Rubin 7–6 6–1; I. Majoli (5) bye; C. Martinez (6) bye; A. Miller d. G. Leon-Garcia 6–2 6–2; L. Neiland (Q) d. C. Morariu 6–1 5–7 6–0; M. Sanchez Lorenzo d. M. Vento (16) 7–5 7–5; L. Raymond (10) d. M. Maruska (Q) 4–6 7–5 6–4; J. Kandarr (LL) d. A. Cecchini 4–6 6–4 6–4; M. Babel d. F. Li 6–2 6–2; M. Seles (3) bye; I. Spirlea (7) bye; T. Snyder (WC) d. P. Hy-Boulais 6–0 6–7 6–0; E. Makarova d. A. Sidot 7–5 6–0; R. McQuillan d. B. Schultz-McCarthy (13) 6–1 2–6 7–6; R. Dragomir (11) d. S. Cacic 6–3 6–2; A. Carlsson d. O. Barabanschikova 6–3 6–0; M. Serna d. S. Wang 6–2 6–3; A. Coetzer (2) bye.

2nd round: Davenport (1) d. Dechaume-Balleret 6–0 6–2; Paulus (14) d. Labat 6–1 6–0; Schnyder (9) d. De Swardt (Q) 6–3 6–4; Kournikova (8) d. Probst 6–1 6–2; Pierce (4) d. Cristea (Q) 6–1 6–2; Likhovtseva d. Gagliardi (Q) 6–2 7–5; Capriati (WC) d. Schett (15) 6–2 6–3; Majoli (5) d. Rittner (Q) 5–7 6–3 7–6; Martinez (6) d. Miller 6–4 6–3; Sanchez Lorenzo d. Neiland (Q) 6–3 6–7 6–3; Raymond (10) d. Kandarr (LL) 6–1 6–2; Seles (3) d. Babel 6–3 1–2 ret; Snyder (WC) d. Spirlea (7) 2–6 6–2 6–3; McQuillan d. Makarova 6–1 6–3; Dragomir (11) d. Carlsson 7–5 6–2; Coetzer (2) d. Serna 6–3 6–3.

3rd round: Davenport (1) d. Paulus (14) 7–5 6–4; Kournikova (8) d. Schnyder (9) 6–1 6–3; Pierce (4) d. Likhovtseva 6–4 6–1; Majoli (5) d. Capriati (WC) 6–4 6–1; Martinez (6) d. Sanchez Lorenzo 6–3 6–1; Raymond (10) d. Seles (3) 7–6 6–4; Snyder (WC) d. McQuillan 5–7 6–2 6–1; Coetzer (2) d. Dragomir (11) 6–4 6–7 6–0.

Quarter-finals: Davenport (1) d. Kournikova (8) 7–5 6–3; Pierce (4) d. Majoli (5) 6–3 6–2; Martinez (6) d. Raymond (10) 6–4 7–5; Coetzer (2) d. Snyder (WC) 6–4 6–4.

Semi-finals: Pierce (4) d. Davenport (1) 4–6 6–3 6–3; Martinez (6) d. Coetzer (2) 6–4 6–0.

Final: Pierce (4) d. Martinez (6) 6–7 6–0 6–2.

WOMEN'S DOUBLES – Final: Cacic/Pierce (WC) d. Schett/Schnyder 7–6 4–6 7–6.

INTERSPORT WOMEN'S GRAND PRIX ($450,000)

HAMBURG, 27 APRIL–3 MAY

WOMEN'S SINGLES – 1st round: M. Hingis (1) bye; J. Halard-Decugis d. W. Probst (WC) 6–4 6–0; J. Capriati (WC) d. F. Labat 6–2 6–4; S. Noorlander (Q) d. R. Dragomir (7) 6–2 6–2; I. Majoli (4) bye; B. Schett d. M. Babel 6–4 6–4; V. Ruano-Pascual d. R. Bobkova (Q) 6–3 6–1; E. Likhovtseva d. S. Appelmans (6) 6–0 3–6 6–0; P. Schnyder (5) d. F. Perfetti (Q) 6–1 6–0; A. Sidot d. K. Habsudova 6–3 6–3; H. Nagyova d. S. Pitkowski 6–1 5–7 6–3; A. Sanchez-Vicario (3) bye; A. Fusai d. B. Paulus (8) 6–7 6–4 6–2; J. Abe (Q) d. P. Hy-Boulais 6–1 6–3; M. Serna d. S. Kloesel (WC) 7–6 6–0; J. Novotna (2) bye.

2nd round: Hingis (1) d. Halard-Decugis 7–5 6–1; Capriati (WC) d. Noorlander (Q) 6–3 6–2; Schett d. Majoli (4) 7–5 6–2; Ruano-Pascual d. Likhovtseva 6–0 6–4; Schnyder (5) d. Sidot 3–6 6–3 6–4; Sanchez-Vicario (3) d. Nagyova 6–4 6–4; Abe (Q) d. Fusai 6–2 6–4; Novotna (2) d. Serna 6–4 6–2.

Quarter-finals: Hingis (1) d. Capriati (WC) 6–1 6–3; Schett d. Ruano-Pascual 6–0 6–0; Schnyder (5) d. Sanchez-Vicario (3) 6–3 6–0; Novotna (2) d. Abe (Q) 6–1 6–3.

Semi-finals: Hingis (1) d. Schett 6–2 6–2; Novotna (2) d. Schnyder (5) 2–6 7–5 6–3.

Final: Hingis (1) d. Novotna (2) 6–3 7–5.

WOMEN'S DOUBLES – Final: Schett/Schnyder (4) d. Hingis/Novotna (1) 7–6 3–6 6–3.

ITALIAN OPEN ($926,250)

ROME, 4–10 MAY

WOMEN'S SINGLES – 1st round: M. Hingis (1) bye; F. Li d. O. Barabanschikova 7–6 6–2; V. Ruano-Pascual d. G. Leon-Garcia 7–5 6–3; I. Spirlea (10) d. J. Halard-Decugis 6–4 6–2; A. Kournikova (14) d. V. Csurgo (Q) 6–0 6–1; B. Paulus d. M. Vento 6–2 6–3; J. Kandarr (Q) d. F. Labat 4–6 6–4 7–6; I. Majoli (8) bye; M. Pierce (4) bye; S. Pitkowski d. S. Appelmans 6–1 3–6 6–3; M. Lucic d. S. Cacic 6–1 6–7 7–6; E. Likhovtseva d. P. Schnyder (16) 4–6 6–4 6–4; S. Testud (12) d. L. Golarsa (WC) 2–6 6–4 6–2; B. Schett d. M. Grzybowska 4–6 6–3 6–2; S. Farina d. F. Lubiani (WC) 6–0 6–1; M. Seles (6) bye; A. Sanchez-Vicario (5) bye; C. Torrens-Valero (Q) d. B. Schultz-McCarthy 4–6 6–2 6–3; N. Sawamatsu d. L. Courtois 1–6 6–2 6–4; D. Van Roost (13) d. K. Habsudova 6–4 6–2; L. Raymond (15) d. A. Sidot 2–6 6–3 7–5; A. Miller (Q) d. R. Grande 6–3 6–0; R. Dragomir d. J. Capriati (WC) 6–3 6–2; A. Coetzer (3) bye; C. Martinez (7) bye; F. Perfetti (WC) d. E. Gagliardi (Q) 7–5 6–2; J. Kruger d. T. Garbin (Q) 6–7 6–4 6–1; S. Williams d. N. Tauziat (11) 7–5 6–0; V. Williams (9) d. N. Basuki 6–2 6–3; M. Sanchez Lorenzo (Q) d. M. Oremans 6–4 6–1; A. Fusai (Q) d. A. Sugiyama 7–6 6–0; J. Novotna (2) bye.

2nd round: Hingis (1) d. Li 6–3 6–0; Spirlea (10) d. Ruano-Pascual 6–3 7–6; Kournikova (14) d. Paulus 6–2 6–2; Majoli (8) d. Kandarr (Q) 4–6 6–4 6–4; Pierce (4) d. Pitkowski 6–1 6–2; Lucic d. Likhovtseva 3–6 6–2 6–2; Testud (12) d. Schett 4–6 6–2 6–3; Seles (6) d. Farina 6–2 6–1; Sanchez-Vicario (5) d. Torrens-Valero (Q) 6–3 7–5; Van Roost (13) d. Sawamatsu 6–4 6–4; Raymond (15) d. Miller (Q) 6–2 3–6 7–6; Dragomir d. Coetzer (3) 6–2 6–2; Martinez (7) d. Perfetti (WC) 6–1 4–6 6–3; S. Williams d. Kruger 5–1 ret; V. Williams (9) d. Sanchez Lorenzo (Q) 6–1 6–4; Fusai (Q) d. Novotna (2) 2–6 7–6 6–3.

3rd round: Hingis (1) d. Spirlea (10) 6–1 6–2; Kournikova (14) d. Majoli (8) 6–3 3–6 6–2; Lucic d. Pierce (4) 7–5

6–4; Testud (12) d. Seles (6) 6–2 4–6 7–5; Sanchez-Vicario (5) d. Van Roost (13) 6–1 6–2; Raymond (15) d. Dragomir 6–4 6–1; S. Williams d. Martinez (7) 6–2 6–2; V. Williams (9) d. Fusai (Q) 6–1 6–1.
Quarter-finals: Hingis (1) d. Kournikova (14) 6–2 6–4; Lucic d. Testud (12) 7–5 ret; Sanchez-Vicario (5) d. Raymond (15) 6–7 6–1 6–2; V. Williams (9) d. S. Williams 6–4 6–2.
Semi-finals: Hingis (1) d. Lucic 6–2 6–1; V. Williams (9) d. Sanchez-Vicario (5) 6–3 2–6 7–5.
Final: Hingis (1) d. V. Williams (9) 6–3 2–6 6–3.
WOMEN'S DOUBLES – Final: Ruano-Pascual/Suarez d. Coetzer/Sanchez-Vicario (6) 7–6 6–4.

GERMAN OPEN ($926,250)

BERLIN, 11–17 MAY

WOMEN'S SINGLES – 1st round: M. Hingis (1) bye; S. Farina d. N. Sawamatsu 6–3 6–2; M. Grzybowska d. S. Schmidle (WC) 4–6 7–5 6–1; I. Majoli (9) d. A. Sidot 6–3 6–2; A. Kournikova (14) d. R. Bobkova (Q) 6–2 6–1; E. Likhovtseva d. J. Lee (Q) 7–5 6–4; M. Vento d. N. Basuki 6–4 6–3; A. Sanchez-Vicario (5) bye; A. Coetzer (4) bye; A. Glass (WC) d. R. Mc Quillan (LL) 6–1 0–6 7–6; A. Fusai (Q) d. F. Perfetti (Q) 7–5 7–5; A. Sugiyama (16) d. K. Habsudova 6–0 6–2; S. Testud (11) d. N. Zvereva 4–6 6–4 7–5; J. Halard-Decugis d. R. Dragomir 2–6 6–3 7–6; M. Serna d. B. Schultz-McCarthy 6–3 6–2; C. Martinez (7) bye; I. Spirlea (8) bye; M. Shaughnessy (Q) d. J. Wohr (Q) 6–3 6–4; C. Morariu d. R. Grande 6–4 6–2; L. Raymond (15) d. J. Kandarr (WC) 6–3 6–3; M. Sanchez Lorenzo d. P. Schnyder (13) 2–6 7–6 6–3; T. Tanasugarn d. J. Capriati (Q) 6–3 6–1; B. Schett d. A. Miller 6–2 6–2; J. Novotna (3) bye; M. Pierce (6) bye; B. Paulus d. C. Rubin (WC) 6–4 6–2; F. Li d. M. Oremans 6–0 6–2; S. Cacic d. N. Tauziat (10) 7–5 6–4; A. Mauresmo (Q) d. D. Van Roost (12) 3–6 6–4 7–5; F. Labat d. K. Po 6–4 6–2; H. Nagyova d. S. Appelmans 2–6 6–3 7–5; L. Davenport (2) bye.
2nd round: Hingis (1) d. Farina 6–0 7–5; Majoli (9) d. Grzybowska 6–4 6–0; Kournikova (14) d. Likhovtseva 6–2 6–1; Sanchez-Vicario (5) d. Vento 7–5 6–4; Coetzer (4) d. Glass (WC) 6–0 4–6 6–1; Sugiyama (16) d. Fusai (Q) 6–4 6–3; Testud (11) d. Halard-Decugis 6–4 6–0; Martinez (7) d. Serna 6–2 6–2; Spirlea (8) d. Shaughnessy (Q) 6–4 6–1; Morariu d. Raymond (15) 7–5 1–6 6–2; Sanchez Lorenzo d. Tanasugarn 3–6 6–1 6–3; Novotna (3) d. Schett 1–6 7–6 7–6; Paulus d. Pierce (6) 4–6 7–6 3–1 ret; Cacic d. Li 6–4 6–4; Mauresmo (Q) d. Labat 7–5 7–5; Davenport (2) d. Nagyova 6–3 4–6 6–1.
3rd round: Hingis (1) d. Majoli (9) 6–1 6–2; Kournikova (14) d. Sanchez-Vicario (5) 6–4 6–2; Sugiyama (16) d. Coetzer (4) 4–6 6–2 6–3; Martinez (7) d. Testud (11) 4–6 7–5 6–2; Spirlea (8) Morariu w/o ; Novotna (3) d. Sanchez Lorenzo 6–4 6–4; Paulus d. Cacic 3–6 6–3 6–3; Mauresmo (Q) d. Davenport (2) 6–2 6–4.
Quarter-finals: Kournikova (14) d. Hingis (1) 6–3 7–6; Martinez (7) d. Sugiyama (16) 6–3 6–3; Novotna (3) d. Spirlea (8) 6–3 5–7 6–3; Mauresmo (Q) d. Paulus 6–4 6–2.
Semi-finals: Martinez (7) d. Kournikova (14) 6–0 6–1; Mauresmo (Q) d. Novotna (3) 7–5 5–7 6–4.
Final: Martinez (7) d. Mauresmo (Q) 6–4 6–4.
WOMEN'S DOUBLES – Final: Davenport/Zvereva (1) d. Fusai/Tauziat (2) 6–3 6–0.

DIRECT LINE INSURANCE CHAMPIONSHIPS ($450,000)

EASTBOURNE, SUSSEX, 15–20 JUNE

WOMEN'S SINGLES – 1st round: J. Novotna (1) bye; N. Dechy (Q) d. F. Li 6–4 6–4; K. Guse (Q) d. S. Pitkowski 7–5 6–3; I. Spirlea (5) d. R. Grande 6–3 4–6 6–4; V. Williams (4) bye; N. Zvereva d. M. Vento 7–5 6–3; M. Serna d. T. Panova (Q) 6–7 6–3 6–1; E. Likhovtseva d. N. Tauziat (7) 6–2 4–6 8–6; A. Sugiyama (8) d. M. Grzybowska 6–4 6–4; S. Williams (WC) d. N. Sawamatsu 6–4 7–5; T. Tanasugarn d. A. Miller 6–4 6–4; A. Sanchez-Vicario (3) bye; A. Kournikova (6) d. A. Fusai 2–6 6–1 6–3; M. De Swardt (Q) d. L. Raymond 6–0 7–6; S. Smith (WC) d. N. Basuki 6–4 3–3 ret; S. Graf (2) bye.
2nd round: Novotna (1) d. Dechy (Q) 6–2 6–2; Spirlea (5) d. Guse (Q) 6–0 7–5; Zvereva d. V. Williams (4) 6–2 6–1; Serna d. Likhovtseva 6–4 7–5; S. Williams (WC) d. Sugiyama (8) 6–2 7–5; Sanchez-Vicario (3) d. Tanasugarn 6–2 7–5; Kournikova (6) d. M. De Swardt (Q) 6–4 6–1; Graf (2) d. Smith (WC) 6–1 6–2.
Quarter-finals: Novotna (1) d. Spirlea (5) 6–4 7–5; Zvereva d. Serna 7–6 6–2; Sanchez-Vicario (3) d. S. Williams (WC) 4–6 6–4 6–4; Kournikova (6) d. Graf (2) 6–7 6–3 6–4.
Semi-finals: Novotna (1) d. Zvereva 6–2 6–1; Sanchez-Vicario (3) d. Kournikova (6) w/o .
Final: Novotna (1) d. Sanchez-Vicario (3) 6–1 7–5.
WOMEN'S DOUBLES – Final: De Swardt/Novotna d. Sanchez-Vicario/Zvereva (1) 6–1 6–3.

BANK OF THE WEST CLASSIC ($450,000)

STANFORD, CA, 27 JULY–2 AUGUST

WOMEN'S SINGLES – 1st round: L. Davenport (1) bye; K. Po d. N. Pratt 7–5 6–0; T. Tanasugarn d. Y. Yoshida 6–0 6–3; A. Stevenson (Q) d. R. Grande (8) 6–1 7–5; S. Graf (4) bye; M. Fernandez d. C. Rubin 6–4 6–4; E. Tatarkova (Q) d. S. Cacic 7–6 2–6 7–5; N. Zvereva (5) d. T. Snyder 6–2 6–4; E. Likhovtseva (7) d. M. Irvin (WC) 6–1 4–6 6–0; A. Frazier d. J. Lee (Q) 3–6 6–2 6–3; C. Morariu d. J. Capriati (Q) 6–4 3–6 6–4; V. Williams (3) bye; J. Kruger (6) d. L. Osterloh (WC) 1–6 6–2 6–4; A. Sidot d. M. Saeki 7–6 6–2 6–3; F. Li d. N. Dechy 4–6 6–4 6–3; M. Seles (2) bye.
2nd round: Davenport (1) d. Po 6–1 6–3; Tanasugarn d. Stevenson (Q) 6–2 6–0; Graf (4) d. Fernandez 6–4 6–0; Zvereva (5) d. Tatarkova (Q) 0–6 6–4 6–2; Likhovtseva (7) d. Frazier 6–1 6–4; Williams (3) d. Morariu 4–6 6–1 6–0; Sidot d. Kruger (6) 6–3 7–6; Seles (2) d. Li 2–6 6–3 6–1.
Quarter-finals: Davenport (1) d. Tanasugarn 7–6 6–1; Graf (4) d. Zvereva (5) 6–1 6–3; Williams (3) d. Likhovtseva (7) 6–2 6–4; Seles (2) d. Sidot 6–3 6–1.

Semi-finals: Davenport (1) d. Graf (4) 6–4 6–7 6–3; Williams (3) d. Seles (2) 6–3 6–4.
Final: Davenport (1) d. Williams (3) 6–4 5–7 6–4.
WOMEN'S DOUBLES – Final: Davenport/Zvereva (1) d. Neiland/Tatarkova (4) 6–4 6–4.

TOSHIBA TENNIS CLASSIC ($450,000)

SAN DIEGO, CA, 3–9 AUGUST
WOMEN'S SINGLES – 1st round: M. Hingis (1) bye; N. Zvereva d. M. Lucic (WC) 7–6 6–3; I. Majoli d. A. Fusai 7–6 6–3; J. Kruger d. I. Spirlea (7) 3–6 6–2 6–4; V. Williams (3) bye; C. Rubin d. N. Basuki 6–0 6–1; M. Pierce d. B. Paulus 6–3 7–5; C. Martinez (5) d. K. Po 6–4 6–2; S. Graf (6) d. J. Halard-Decugis 6–2 6–2; A. Sugiyama d. J. Capriati (Q) 5–7 6–2 6–2; S. Testud d. A. Stevenson (WC) 4–6 6–2 6–0; M. Seles (4) bye; N. Tauziat (8) d. S. Wang (Q) 7–5 3–6 6–1; A. Frazier (Q) d. J. Lee (Q) 7–6 6–2; L. Raymond d. E. Likhovtseva 6–2 5–1 ret; L. Davenport (2) bye.
2nd round: Hingis (1) d. Zvereva 6–3 6–2; Kruger d. Majoli 6–3 7–6; Williams (3) d. Rubin 6–3 6–2; Pierce d. Martinez (5) 6–7 6–2 6–3; Sugiyama d. Graf (6) 6–4 1–6 7–5; Seles (4) d. Testud 7–6 7–5; Tauziat (8) d. Frazier (Q) 6–2 3–6 6–1; Davenport (2) d. Raymond 6–1 6–4.
Quarter-finals: Hingis (1) d. Kruger 6–1 6–3; Pierce d. Williams (3) 2–6 7–6 4–0 ret; Seles (4) d. Sugiyama 6–4 6–3; Davenport (2) d. Tauziat (8) 6–4 6–3.
Semi-finals: Pierce d. Hingis (1) 3–6 7–6 6–2; Davenport (2) d. Seles (4) 6–4 2–6 7–5.
Final: Davenport (2) d. Pierce 6–3 6–1.
WOMEN'S DOUBLES – FINAL: Davenport/Zvereva (1) d. Fusai/Tauziat (2) 6–2 6–1.

ACURA CLASSIC ($450,000)

MANHATTAN BEACH, CA, 10–16 AUGUST
WOMEN'S SINGLES – 1st round: M. Hingis (1) bye; I. Majoli d. R. Grande 1–6 6–2 6–4; S. Williams d. L. Neiland (Q) 6–0 6–0; S. Testud (7) d. A. Serra-Zanetti (Q) 6–3 7–5; A. Sanchez-Vicario (3) bye; A. Sugiyama d. A. Sidot (WC) 6–4 6–3; E. Tatarkova (LL) d. N. Basuki 4–6 6–3 6–3; I. Spirlea (6) d. F. Li 6–0 6–2; N. Tauziat (5) d. C. Rubin (WC) 6–4 7–5; A. Fusai d. A. Stevenson (Q) 6–3 6–3; B. Paulus d. N. Sawamatsu 3–6 6–3 6–2; M. Seles (4) bye; N. Zvereva (8) d. A. Kremer (Q) 7–5 6–2; M. Serna d. T. Tanasugarn (WC) 6–7 7–5 6–2; J. Halard-Decugis d. K. Po 6–2 6–4; L. Davenport (2) bye.
2nd round: Hingis (1) d. Majoli 6–3 6–3; Williams d. Testud (7) 6–4 3–6 6–1; Sanchez-Vicario (3) d. Sugiyama 4–6 6–4 6–4; Tatarkova (LL) d. Spirlea (6) 6–2 6–2; Tauziat (5) d. Fusai 6–3 6–3; Seles (4) d. Paulus 6–1 6–2; Zvereva (8) d. Serna 6–2 6–1; Davenport (2) d. Halard-Decugis 6–0 6–4.
Quarter-finals: Hingis (1) d. Williams 6–4 6–1; Sanchez-Vicario (3) d. Tatarkova (LL) 6–3 6–3; Seles (4) d. Tauziat (5) 6–4 6–4; Davenport (2) d. Zvereva (8) 6–2 6–3.
Semi-finals: Hingis (1) d. Sanchez-Vicario (3) 6–4 6–4; Davenport (2) d. Seles (4) 6–4 6–2.
Final: Davenport (2) d. Hingis (1) 4–6 6–4 6–3.
WOMEN'S DOUBLES – Final: Hingis/Zvereva (1) d. Tanasugarn/Tatarkova 6–4 6–2.

DU MAURIER OPEN ($926,250)

MONTREAL, QUEBEC, 17–23 AUGUST
WOMEN'S SINGLES – 1st round: M. Hingis (1) bye; S. Plischke d. R. Grande 6–1 6–1; M. Vento d. A. Mauresmo 6–3 6–4; A. Sugiyama (16) d. N. Dechy (Q) 7–6 7–5; S. Testud (14) d. R. McQuillan (Q) 6–1 6–3; I. Majoli d. B. Paulus 6–3 6–1; S. Jeyaseelan (WC) d. N. Pratt (Q) 7–5 6–3; I. Spirlea (9) bye; M. Seles (5) bye; T. Snyder d. A. Miller 7–5 6–2; N. Basuki d. S. Wang (Q) 6–3 6–1; D. Van Roost (12) d. J. Nejedly (WC) 6–4 6–2; F. Labat (Q) d. P. Schnyder (10) 6–4 6–3; A. Huber d. V. Webb (WC) 6–4 6–1; F. Li d. A. Dechaume-Balleret (Q) 6–3 7–5; A. Coetzer (8) bye; C. Martinez (6) bye; A. Frazier (Q) d. J. Halard-Decugis 6–0 5–7 7–6; R. Dragomir d. A. Sidot 6–3 7–6; A. Kournikova (15) d. A. Fusai 6–2 6–4; N. Tauziat (11) d. S. Cacic (Q) 4–6 6–4 6–2; K. Po d. T. Tanasugarn 6–1 7–6; K. Habsudova d. N. Sawamatsu 6–4 6–3; A. Sanchez-Vicario (3) bye; S. Graf (7) bye; V. Ruano-Pascual d. K. Hrdlickova (LL) 5–7 6–4 6–2; M. Serna d. A. Smashnova (LL) 1–6 7–5 6–2; C. Morariu d. L. Raymond (17) 7–6 1–6 6–2; M. Fernandez d. M. Pierce (13) 6–1 6–1; S. Farina d. B. Schett 7–5 6–7 6–1; E. Likhovtseva d. M. Oremans 6–4 6–3; J. Novotna (2) bye.
2nd round: Hingis (1) d. Plischke 6–4 6–1; Sugiyama (16) d. Vento 6–4 6–0; Testud (14) d. Majoli 6–7 6–4 6–1; Spirlea (9) d. Jeyaseelan (WC) 6–7 7–6 6–0; Seles (5) d. Snyder 6–2 6–1; Basuki d. Van Roost (12) 7–5 6–3; Huber d. Labat (Q) 6–2 6–4; Coetzer (8) d. Li 6–3 6–4; Martinez (6) d. Frazier (Q) 7–6 6–4; Kournikova (15) d. Dragomir 4–6 6–2 6–4; Tauziat (11) d. Po 6–3 6–3; Sanchez-Vicario (3) d. Habsudova 0–6 7–5 6–2; Graf (7) d. Ruano-Pascual 6–0 6–1; Serna d. Morariu 7–6 6–3; Farina d. Fernandez 7–5 6–3; Novotna (2) d. Likhovtseva 7–5 6–2.
3rd round: Hingis (1) d. Sugiyama (16) 6–3 6–0; Testud (14) d. Spirlea (9) 7–6 4–6 6–1; Seles (5) d. Basuki 6–3 6–3; Huber d. Coetzer (8) 7–5 7–6; Martinez (6) d. Kournikova (15) 6–0 6–3; Sanchez-Vicario (3) d. Tauziat (11) 3–6 6–1 6–2; Serna d. Graf (7) 6–4 6–4; Novotna (2) d. Farina 6–1 6–4.
Quarter-finals: Hingis (1) d. Testud (14) 7–6 3–6 6–4; Seles (5) d. Huber 6–3 6–4; Sanchez-Vicario (3) d. Martinez (6) 6–3 6–4; Novotna (2) d. Serna 2–6 6–1 6–1.
Semi-finals: Seles (5) d. Hingis (1) 4–6 6–3 6–2; Sanchez-Vicario (3) d. Novotna (2) 4–6 7–6 6–2.
Final: Seles (5) d. Sanchez-Vicario (3) 6–3 6–2.
WOMEN'S DOUBLES – Final: Hingis/Novotna (1) d. Basuki/Vis (4) 6–3 6–4.

US WOMEN'S HARDCOURT CHAMPIONSHIPS ($450,000)

NEW HAVEN, CT, 24–30 AUGUST

WOMEN'S SINGLES – 1st round: L. Davenport (1) bye; V. Ruano-Pascual (Q) d. A. Miller (Q) 6–2 3–6 6–2; A. Huber d. S. Farina 6–2 6–3; P. Schnyder (6) d. R. Grande (Q) 6–4 6–3; S. Graf (WC) (4) bye; H. Nagyova d. M. Vento 6–3 6–2; A. Kournikova d. B. Schett 6–3 6–2; A. Coetzer (7) d. M. Serna 7–6 6–3; M. Fernandez (WC) d. D. Van Roost (8) 3–6 6–0 6–1; S. Testud d. R. Dragomir 6–4 6–1; J. Halard-Decugis d. N. Sawamatsu 3–6 6–3 7–5; A. Sanchez-Vicario (3) bye; A. Mauresmo d. N. Tauziat (5) 7–6 6–0; A. Dechaume-Balleret (Q) d. J. Kruger 6–4 3–6 7–6; C. Rubin (WC) d. E. Likhovtseva 3–6 6–3 6–1; J. Novotna (2) bye.

2nd round: Davenport (1) Ruano-Pascual (Q) w/o; Huber d. Schnyder (6) 7–5 7–6; Graf (WC) (4) d. Nagyova 6–1 6–3; Coetzer (7) d. Kournikova 1–6 6–4 7–5; Fernandez (WC) d. Testud 6–3 4–6 6–4; Halard-Decugis d. Sanchez-Vicario (3) 7–6 6–2; Mauresmo d. Dechaume-Balleret (Q) 6–4 6–1; Novotna (2) d. Rubin (WC) 6–1 7–5.

Quarter-finals: Davenport (1) d. Huber 6–3 6–3; Graf (WC) (4) d. Coetzer (7) 6–3 6–0; Halard-Decugis d. Fernandez (WC) 7–5 6–1; Novotna (2) d. Mauresmo 6–1 7–6.

Semi-finals: Graf (WC) (4) d. Davenport (1) 6–3 7–6; Novotna (2) d. Halard-Decugis 6–4 6–4.

Final: Graf (WC) (4) d. Novotna (2) 6–4 6–1.

WOMEN'S DOUBLES – Final: Fusai/Tauziat (1) d. De Swardt/Novotna (2) 6–1 6–0.

TOYOTA PRINCESS CUP ($450,000)

TOKYO, 21–27 SEPTEMBER

WOMEN'S SINGLES – 1st round: A. Sanchez-Vicario (1) bye; E. Likhovtseva d. J. Husarova (PR) 6–3 6–4; S. Wang d. H. Inoue (Q) 6–0 6–4; A. Kournikova (5) d. A. Gersi 6–2 6–1; D. Van Roost (4) bye; O. Barabanschikova d. M. Saeki (WC) 3–6 6–3 6–3; F. Li d. M. Jeon (Q) 6–2 6–0; A. Huber (7) d. N. Kijimuta (Q) 6–3 3–6 6–0; H. Nagyova (8) d. J. Lee (Q) 7–5 6–1; T. Tanasugarn d. Y. Yoshida (WC) 6–4 6–3; A. Frazier d. M. Lucic 6–2 6–3; A. Coetzer (3) bye; M. Fernandez d. L. Raymond (6) 7–6 7–5; J. Halard-Decugis d. K. Po 6–0 6–3; N. Sawamatsu d. A. Smashnova 6–1 6–2; M. Seles (2) bye.

2nd round: Sanchez-Vicario (1) d. Likhovtseva 6–0 6–4; Kournikova (5) d. Wang 6–0 6–4; Barabanschikova d. Van Roost (4) 3–6 6–3 7–5; Huber (7) d. Li 7–5 6–3; Tanasugarn d. Nagyova (8) 6–4 7–6; Frazier d. Coetzer (3) 0–6 6–3 6–2; Halard-Decugis d. Fernandez 6–1 6–3; Seles (2) d. Sawamatsu 6–3 3–6 6–3.

Quarter-finals: Sanchez-Vicario (1) d. Kournikova (5) 6–3 6–2; Huber (7) d. Barabanschikova 6–3 6–1; Tanasugarn d. Frazier 6–1 6–3; Seles (2) d. Halard-Decugis 6–2 6–1.

Semi-finals: Sanchez-Vicario (1) d. Huber (7) 6–1 3–6 6–3; Seles (2) d. T. Tanasugarn 6–1 6–4.

Final: Seles (2) d. Sanchez-Vicario (1) 4–6 6–3 6–4.

WOMEN'S DOUBLES – Final: Kournikova/Seles (4) d. Fernandez/Sanchez-Vicario 6–4 6–4.

PORSCHE TENNIS GRAND PRIX ($450,000)

FILDERSTADT, 5–11 OCTOBER

WOMEN'S SINGLES – 1st round: M. Hingis (1) bye; A. Kournikova d. B. Schett (Q) 1–6 6–4 7–6; D. Van Roost (WC) d. M. Serna 2–6 7–5 6–2; V. Williams (5) d. S. Farina 6–2 4–6 6–3; J. Novotna (3) bye; S. Williams d. K. Hrdlickova (Q) 7–6 3–6 6–0; S. Testud d. E. Likhovtseva 5–7 6–1 6–0; A. Huber d. P. Schnyder (8) 6–4 6–1; C. Martinez (WC) (6) d. I. Spirlea 3–6 6–2 6–2; L. Raymond d. R. Dragomir 3–6 6–2 6–4; A. Mauresmo (Q) d. A. Glass (WC) 6–2 6–1; A. Sanchez-Vicario (4) bye; N. Tauziat (7) d. K. Po (PR) 6–4 6–7 6–2; N. Zvereva d. J. Kandarr (Q) 6–3 6–2; M. Pierce d. A. Coetzer 6–2 6–2; L. Davenport (2) bye.

2nd round: Hingis (1) d. Kournikova 1–6 6–2 6–2; Van Roost (WC) d. V. Williams (5) 6–1 6–2; S. Williams d. Novotna (3) 2–6 6–3 2–0 ret; Testud d. Huber 6–2 4–6 6–2; Raymond d. Martinez (WC) (6) 6–4 2–6 6–2; Sanchez-Vicario (4) d. Mauresmo (Q) 6–3 6–2; Tauziat (7) d. Zvereva 6–3 6–3; Davenport (2) d. Pierce 6–1 6–3.

Quarter-finals: Van Roost (WC) d. Hingis (1) 6–3 6–7 6–4; Testud d. S. Williams 6–3 1–6 6–1; Sanchez-Vicario (4) d. Raymond 1–6 7–5 6–2; Davenport (2) d. Tauziat (7) 7–6 7–5.

Semi-finals: Testud d. Van Roost (WC) 6–2 6–0; Davenport (2) d. Sanchez-Vicario (4) 7–6 6–4.

Final: Testud d. Davenport (2) 7–5 6–3.

WOMEN'S DOUBLES – Final: Davenport/Zvereva (1) d. Kournikova/Sanchez-Vicario (4) 6–4 6–2.

EUROPEAN CHAMPIONSHIPS ($926,250)

ZURICH, 12–18 OCTOBER

WOMEN'S SINGLES – 1st round: L. Davenport (1) bye; J. Halard-Decugis (Q) d. A. Sugiyama 7–5 6–1; R. Dragomir d. A. Huber 3–6 6–4 6–4; A. Coetzer (6) d. N. Zvereva 7–5 6–4; C. Martinez (3) bye; I. Spirlea d. M. Oremans (Q) 7–6 6–2; A. Mauresmo (WC) d. S. Plischke (Q) 4–6 6–4 6–1; D. Van Roost (8) d. A. Kournikova 6–3 6–1; P. Schnyder (5) d. S. Farina 6–2 6–3; B. Schett (WC) d. K. Po (PR) 6–3 6–3; L. Raymond d. C. Cristea (LL) 6–4 6–4; N. Tauziat (4) bye; M. Pierce (7) d. C. Rubin (WC) 7–5 2–6 6–3; J. Kruger (LL) d. K. Hrdlickova (LL) 2–6 6–4 6–2; C. Morariu (Q) d. S. Testud 6–3 2–6 6–4; V. Williams (2) bye.

2nd round: Davenport (1) d. Halard-Decugis (Q) 6–4 6–2; Coetzer (6) d. Dragomir 6–3 6–1; Spirlea d. Martinez (3) 6–2 7–6; Van Roost (8) d. Mauresmo (WC) 6–3 6–4; Schett (WC) d. Schnyder (5) 6–4 1–6 7–6; Tauziat (4) d. Raymond 6–2 6–3; Pierce (7) d. Kruger (LL) 7–6 6–1; Williams (2) d. Morariu (Q) 7–5 6–3.

Quarter-finals: Davenport (1) d. Coetzer (6) 6–3 6–1; Spirlea d. Van Roost (8) 6–4 6–0; Tauziat (4) d. Schett (WC) 4–6 7–5 6–1; Williams (2) d. Pierce (7) 6–4 6–1.

Semi-finals: Davenport (1) d. Spirlea 6–2 6–3; Williams (2) d. Tauziat (4) 6–3 6–4.
Final: Davenport (1) d. Williams (2) 7–5 6–3.
WOMEN'S DOUBLES – Final: S. Williams/V. Williams (WC) d. De Swardt/Tatarkova 5–7 6–1 6–3.

KREMLIN CUP ($1,000,000)

MOSCOW, 20–25 OCTOBER

WOMEN'S SINGLES – 1st round: V. Williams (1) bye; E. Likhovtseva d. R. Dragomir 3–6 6–3 6–3; K. Studenikova (Q) d. J. Kruger 6–4 3–6 6–4; C. Rubin d. I. Spirlea (8) 6–2 6–3; P. Schnyder (4) bye; M. Serna d. L. Raymond 5–7 6–3 6–4; S. Appelmans (WC) d. E. Dementieva (Q) 6–4 6–4; M. Pierce (5) d. A. Sugiyama 5–7 6–2 6–4; S. Testud (7) d. N. Dechy (Q) 6–2 6–2; N. Zvereva d. T. Panova (WC) 6–3 6–2; N. Petrova (WC) d. I. Majoli 6–7 7–6 6–0; C. Martinez (3) bye; S. Farina d. A. Kournikova (6) 7–6 4–6 6–1; H. Nagyova d. K. Habsudova (Q) 6–2 6–3; B. Schett d. A. Huber 6–2 6–3; M. Seles (2) bye.
2nd round: Williams (1) d. Likhovtseva 6–3 6–1; Studenikova (Q) d. Rubin 6–3 7–5; Serna d. Schnyder (4) 7–6 6–4; Pierce (5) d. Appelmans (WC) 6–2 6–2; Testud (7) d. Zvereva 6–4 6–3; Martinez (3) d. Petrova (WC) 6–0 6–0; Farina d. Nagyova 6–3 6–1; Seles (2) d. Schett 6–3 6–4.
Quarter-finals: Williams (1) d. Studenikova (Q) 6–1 6–0; Pierce (5) d. Serna 7–5 6–3; Testud (7) d. Martinez (3) 7–6 7–5; Seles (2) d. Farina 6–0 6–1.
Semi-finals: Pierce (5) d. Williams (1) 2–6 6–2 6–0; Seles (2) d. Testud (7) 6–3 7–6.
Final: Pierce (5) d. Seles (2) 7–6 6–3.
WOMEN'S DOUBLES – Final: Pierce/Zvereva d. Raymond/Stubbs (1) 6–3 6–4.

SPARKASSEN CUP INTERNATIONAL GRAND PRIX ($450,000)

LEIPZIG, 2–8 NOVEMBER

WOMEN'S SINGLES – 1st round: A. Sanchez-Vicario (1) bye; A. Sidot (Q) d. A. Mauresmo 6–3 6–3; S. Graf (WC) d. R. Dragomir 6–3 6–3; A. Sugiyama (6) d. S. Kloesel (WC) 6–4 6–3; D. Van Roost (3) bye; I. Majoli d. C. Black 6–4 6–1; S. Plischke (Q) d. C. Morariu 6–2 6–2; N. Zvereva (7) d. H. Nagyova 7–5 6–3; A. Coetzer (5) d. E. Tatarkova (Q) 6–4 4–6 6–4; S. Pitkowski d. B. Rittner (WC) 6–3 6–4; M. Serna d. R. Grande (Q) 6–2 6–1; I. Spirlea (4) bye; A. Huber (8) d. S. Farina 6–4 6–2; B. Schett d. A. Fusai 6–1 6–2; E. Likhovtseva d. S. Appelmans 6–1 7–5; N. Tauziat (2) bye.
2nd round: Sidot (Q) d. Sanchez-Vicario (1) 6–1 4–6 6–2; Graf (WC) d. Sugiyama (6) 6–4 6–3; Van Roost (3) d. Majoli 6–4 6–4; Zvereva (7) d. Plischke (Q) 6–1 6–7 6–4; Pitkowski d. Coetzer (5) 6–3 7–6; Spirlea (4) d. Serna 7–6 6–3; Huber (8) d. Schett 6–3 6–3; Tauziat (2) d. Likhovtseva 7–6 6–1.
Quarter-finals: Graf (WC) d. Sidot (Q) 7–5 6–3; Van Roost (3) d. Zvereva (7) 6–3 3–6 6–2; Spirlea (4) d. Pitkowski 6–1 6–1; Tauziat (2) d. Huber (8) 6–3 6–4.
Semi-finals: Graf (WC) d. Van Roost (3) 6–1 3–6 6–0; Tauziat (2) d. Spirlea (4) 2–6 6–3 6–2.
Final: Graf (WC) d. Tauziat (2) 6–3 6–4.
WOMEN'S DOUBLES – Final: Likhovtseva/Sugiyama (4) d. Bollegraf/Spirlea 6–3 6–7 6–2.

ADVANTA CHAMPIONSHIPS ($450,000)

PHILADELPHIA, PA, 9–15 NOVEMBER

WOMEN'S SINGLES – 1st round: L. Davenport (1) bye; K. Po d. C. Morariu 6–1 6–3; A. Frazier (Q) d. I. Majoli 2–6 6–2 6–4; P. Schnyder (7) d. S. Farina (WC) 7–6 4–6 6–4; J. Novotna (3) bye; N. Zvereva d. T. Snyder (WC) 6–2 6–1; A. Sugiyama d. M. Vento 6–1 6–2; M. Seles (5) d. I. Spirlea 6–3 6–4; N. Tauziat (6) d. A. Huber 6–3 6–2; L. Raymond d. E. Callens (Q) 6–3 6–3; A. Coetzer d. S. Cacic (Q) 6–2 6–0; A. Sanchez-Vicario (4) bye; E. Likhovtseva d. S. Testud (8) 7–6 6–7 1–0 ret; S. Graf d. M. Fernandez (WC) 6–3 7–6; A. Rippner (Q) d. A. Fusai 7–6 6–2; M. Hingis (2) bye.
2nd round: Davenport (1) d. Po 6–1 6–2; Frazier (Q) d. Schnyder (7) 6–3 6–1; Zvereva d. Novotna (3) 6–4 6–4; Seles (5) d. Sugiyama 6–3 7–5; Tauziat (6) d. Raymond 6–2 7–6; Coetzer d. Sanchez-Vicario (4) 6–4 6–1; Graf d. Likhovtseva 6–7 6–2 6–4; Hingis (2) d. Rippner (Q) 6–4 6–1.
Quarter-finals: Davenport (1) d. Frazier (Q) 5–7 6–3 6–3; Seles (5) d. Zvereva 6–0 6–1; Tauziat (6) d. Coetzer 6–3 4–6 6–4; Graf d. Hingis (2) 6–2 4–6 6–0.
Semi-finals: Davenport (1) d. Seles (5) 6–3 6–3; Graf d. Tauziat (6) 6–1 6–4.
Final: Graf d. Davenport (1) 4–6 6–3 6–4.
WOMEN'S DOUBLES – Final: Likhovtseva/Sugiyama d. Seles/Zvereva 7–5 4–6 6–2.

World Series

Tier III and IV Tournaments

AUSTRALIAN WOMEN'S HARDCOURT ($164,250)
HOPE ISLAND, 4–10 JANUARY
WOMEN'S SINGLES – Quarter-finals: M. Vento d. B. Schultz-McCarthy (1) 4–0 ret; S. Plischke (Q) d. M. De Swardt 7–6 6–4; A. Sugiyama (4) d. S. Pitkowski 6–0 7–5; S-T. Wang d. R. Dragomir (2) 6–3 5–7 6–3.
Semi-finals: Vento d. Plischke (Q) 6–2 6–3; Sugiyama (4) d. Wang 6–4 7–5.
Final: Sugiyama (4) d. Vento 7–5 6–0.
WOMEN'S DOUBLES – Final: Likhovtseva/Sugiyama (2) d. Park/Wang 1–6 6–3 6–4.

ASB BANK CLASSIC ($107,500)
AUCKLAND, 5–10 JANUARY
WOMEN'S SINGLES – Quarter-finals: S. Testud (1) d. S. Cacic 6–2 6–2; S. Farina (6) d. J. Halard-Decugis (WC) 6–4 6–3; D. Van Roost (3) d. T. Tanasugarn (7) 6–0 6–3; A. Miller (Q) d. L. Raymond (2) 7–5 1–0 ret.
Semi-finals: Farina (6) d. Testud (1) 6–2 7–6; Van Roost (3) d. Miller (Q) 6–2 6–3.
Final: Van Roost (3) d. Farina (6) 4–6 7–6 7–5.
WOMEN'S DOUBLES – Final: Miyagi/Tanasugarn (2) d. Halard-Decugis/Husarova 7–6 6–4.

ANZ TASMANIAN OPEN ($107,500)
HOBART, 11–17 JANUARY
WOMEN'S SINGLES – Quarter-finals:: D. Van Roost (1) d. F. Li (Q) 7–5 6–3; M. Grzybowska d. H. Nagyova (5) 6–1 2–1 ret; J. Kruger (3) d. A. Sidot (6) 7–5 6–2; P. Schnyder (2) d. B. Schett (7) 6–4 1–6 6–3.
Semi-finals: Van Roost (1) d. Grzybowska 6–7 6–1 6–3; Schnyder (2) d. Kruger (3) 7–6 6–2.
Final: Schnyder (2) d. Van Roost (1) 6–3 6–2.
WOMEN'S DOUBLES – Final: Ruano-Pascual/Suarez d. Halard-Decugis/Husarova 7–6 6–3.

BOGOTA ($107,500)
BOGOTA, 18–22 FEBRUARY
WOMEN'S SINGLES – Quarter-finals: S. Jeyaseelan (6) d. C. Morariu (1) 4–2 ret; L. Schaerer d. J. Husarova 6–7 6–3 7–6; P. Suarez d. F. Zuluaga 5–7 6–1 6–1; C. Martinez-Granados d. L. Courtois 4–6 6–2 6–2.
Semi-finals: Jeyaseelan (6) d. Schaerer 7–5 6–2; Suarez d. Martinez-Granados 6–1 6–2.
Final: Suarez d. Jeyaseelan (6) 6–3 6–4.
WOMEN'S DOUBLES – Final: Husarova/Suarez (4) d. Mazzotta/Syssoeva 3–6 6–2 6–3

IGA TENNIS CLASSIC ($164,250)
OKLAHOMA CITY, OK, 23 FEBRUARY–1 MARCH
WOMEN'S SINGLES – Quarter-finals: L. Davenport (1) d. L. Ghirardi-Rubbi (Q) 6–1 6–4; V. Williams (7) d. F. Lubiani 7–6 6–4; J. Kruger (4) d. S. Williams (5) 6–1 6–1; S. Pitkowski (7) d. S. Testud (2) 6–3 6–4.
Semi-finals: Williams (7) d. Davenport (1) 6–7 6–2 6–3; Kruger (4) d. Pitkowski (7) 3–6 6–3 6–4.
Final: Williams (7) d. Kruger (4) 6–3 6–2.
WOMEN'S DOUBLES – Final: S. Williams/V. Williams d. Cristea/Kunce 7–5 6–2.

JAPAN OPEN ($164,250)
TOKYO, 13–19 APRIL
WOMEN'S SINGLES – Quarter-finals: A. Sugiyama (1) d. E. De Lone 4–6 6–1 6–1; S. Wang (6) d. L. McNeil 4–6 6–4 6–1; A. Frazier (4) d. N. Pratt 6–2 4–6 6–2; C. Morariu (5) d. N. Sawamatsu (2) 7–5 6–3.
Semi-finals: Sugiyama (1) d. Wang (6) 6–3 6–2; Morariu (5) d. Frazier (4) 4–6 7–6 6–4.
Final: Sugiyama (1) d. Morariu (5) 6–3 6–3.
WOMEN'S DOUBLES – Final: Kijimuta/Miyagi (1) d. Frazier/Hiraki (2) 6–3 4–6 6–4.

MAKARSKA LADIES OPEN ($107,500)
MAKARSKA, 13–19 APRIL
WOMEN'S SINGLES – Quarter-finals: F. Li (1) d. P. Suarez 6–4 6–2; G. Leon-Garcia (4) d. A. Alcazar 7–6 3–6 6–1; L. Nemeckova (9) d. S. Kloesel 7–6 4–6 6–0; K. Hrdlickova (Q) d. O. Lugina 3–6 7–5 6–4.
Semi-finals: Li (1) d. Leon-Garcia (4) 6–2 6–1; Hrdlickova (Q) d. Nemeckova (9) 6–1 6–3.
Final: Hrdlickova (Q) d. Li (1) 6–3 6–1.
WOMEN'S DOUBLES – Final: Krizan/Srebotnik d. Koulikovskaya/Kschwendt 7–6 6–1.

BUDAPEST LOTTO LADIES OPEN ($107,500)
BUDAPEST, 20–26 APRIL
WOMEN'S SINGLES – Quarter-finals: F. Li (6) d. S. Testud (1) 5–7 7–6 6–4; S. Farina (3) d. M. Sanchez Lorenzo (8) 6–1 6–2; S. Pitkowski (5) d. J. Halard-Decugis (WC) 5–7 6–3 6–2; V. Ruano-Pascual (7) d. R. Kuti-Kis (Q) 6–3 6–0.
Semi-finals: Farina (3) d. Li (6) 4–6 6–2 6–3; Ruano-Pascual (7) d. Pitkowski (5) 2–6 6–1 7–5.
Final: Ruano-Pascual (7) d. Farina (3) 6–4 4–6 6–3.
WOMEN'S DOUBLES – Final: Ruano-Pascual/Suarez (1) d. Cristea/Montalvo (2) 4–6 6–1 6–1.

CROATIAN BOL LADIES OPEN ($107,500)
BOL, 27 APRIL–3 MAY
WOMEN'S SINGLES – Quarter-finals: J. Kruger (1) d. R. Sandu (Q) 4–6 6–3 6–2; M. Lucic (4) d. M. Diaz-Oliva 6–2 6–3; S. Talaja (Q) d. L. Ghirardi-Rubbi 7–5 6–2; C. Morariu d. A. Cecchini 6–3 6–1.
Semi-finals: Lucic (4) d. Kruger (1) 6–2 6–1; Morariu d. Talaja (Q) 4–6 6–4 6–3.
Final: Lucic (4) d. Morariu 6–2 6–4.
WOMEN'S DOUBLES – Final: Montalvo/Suarez (2) d. Kruger/Lucic w/o.

INTERNATIONAUX DE STRASBOURG ($200,000)
STRASBOURG, 18–24 MAY
WOMEN'S SINGLES – Quarter-finals: J. Halard-Decugis (WC) d. A. Coetzer (1) 7–6 6–2; E. Likhovtseva d. N. Tauziat (3) 6–4 6–2; A. Fusai (WC) d. A. Sugiyama (4) 6–2 6–2; I. Spirlea (2) d. H. Nagyova (8) 6–4 6–2.
Semi-finals: Halard-Decugis (WC) d. Likhovtseva 6–3 7–6; Spirlea (2) d. Fusai (WC) 7–5 6–3.
Final: Spirlea (2) d. Halard-Decugis (WC) 7–6 6–3.
WOMEN'S DOUBLES – Final: Fusai/Tauziat (1) d. Basuki/Vis (2) 6–4 6–3.

OPEN PAGINAS AMARILLAS ($164,250)
MADRID, 18–23 MAY
WOMEN'S SINGLES – Quarter-finals: S. Testud (1) d. C. Rubin 6–4 6–3; P. Schnyder (3) d. M. Serna (7) 3–6 7–6 6–4; B. Schett (4) d. T. Snyder 6–2 6–2; D. Van Roost (2) d. K. Boogert (Q) 6–0 7–6.
Semi-finals: Schnyder (3) d. Testud (1) 6–4 7–5; Van Roost (2) d. Schett (4) 6–2 6–2.
Final: Schnyder (3) d. Van Roost (2) 3–6 6–4 6–0.
WOMEN'S DOUBLES – Final: Labat/Van Roost (2) d. McQuillan/Pratt (3) 6–3 6–1.

DFS CLASSIC ($164,250)
BIRMINGHAM, 8–14 JUNE
WOMEN'S SINGLES – Quarter-finals: S. Graf (WC) (1) d. M. Serna (8) 6–4 6–4; N. Tauziat (3) d. K. Guse 6–2 6–3; E. Likhovtseva (7) d. D. Van Roost (4) 6–3 6–4; N. Basuki (6) d. I. Spirlea (2) 6–4 5–7 7–5.
Semi-finals: Tauziat (3) led Graf (WC) 3–0; Likhovtseva (7) v Basuki (6) not played; singles tournament abandoned due to rain, doubles concluded indoors.
WOMEN'S DOUBLES – Final: Callens/Halard-Decugis (8) d. Raymond/Stubbs (1) 2–6 6–4 6–4.

HEINEKEN TROPHY ($164,250)
DEN BOSCH, 15–20 JUNE
WOMEN'S SINGLES – Quarter-finals: K. Po d. C. Rubin 6–2 6–3; M. Oremans d. K. Boogert (WC) 6–3 2–6 6–4; J. Halard-Decugis d. S. Appelmans (4) 6–7 7–6 6–3; S. Testud (2) d. G. Leon-Garcia (8) 7–6 6–4.
Semi-finals: Oremans d. Po 6–1 6–7 7–6; Halard-Decugis d. Testud (2) 6–3 6–3.
Final: Halard-Decugis d. Oremans 6–3 6–4.
WOMEN'S DOUBLES – Final: Appelmans/Oremans (1) d. Cristea/Melicharova 6–7 7–6 7–6.

SKODA CZECH OPEN ($160,000)
PRAGUE, 6–12 JULY
WOMEN'S SINGLES – Quarter-finals: J. Novotna (1) d. S. Pitkowski 6–2 6–3; H. Nagyova (5) d. M. Shaughnessy 6–1 6–2; N. Zvereva (4) d. A. Mauresmo (WC) (8) 6–3 6–2; S. Testud (2) d. S. Farina (6) 2–6 6–3 6–2.
Semi-finals: Novotna (1) d. Nagyova (5) 2–6 6–3 7–5; Testud (2) d. Zvereva (4) 6–3 4–6 6–4.
Final: Novotna (1) d. Testud (2) 6–3 6–0.
WOMEN'S DOUBLES – Final: Farina/Habsudova (2) d. Hrdlickova/Pastikova (WC) 2–6 6–1 6–2.

STYRIA OPEN MARIA LANKOWITZ ($107,500)
MARIA LANKOWITZ, 6–12 JULY
WOMEN'S SINGLES – Quarter-finals: P. Schnyder (1) d. S. Plischke (6) 6–2 6–2; E. Gagliardi (8) d. B. Schett (4) 0–6 6–2 7–6; G. Leon-Garcia (5) d. B. Paulus (3) 4–6 6–4 6–3; A. Cocheteux d. M. Babel 6–1 6–4.
Semi-finals: Schnyder (1) d. Gagliardi (8) 6–2 6–4; Leon-Garcia (5) d. Cocheteux 6–0 6–3.
Final: Schnyder (1) d. Leon-Garcia (5) 6–2 4–6 6–3.
WOMEN'S DOUBLES – Final: Montalvo/Suarez (3) d. Krizan/Srebotnik 6–1 6–2.

WARSAW CUP BY HEROS ($164,250)
WARSAW, 13–19 JULY
WOMEN'S SINGLES – Quarter-finals: C. Martinez (WC) (1) d. K. Habsudova 6–2 6–4; H. Nagyova (3) d. C. Cristea 6–0 6–1; S. Farina (4) d. A. Glass 6–3 6–2; M. Grzybowska (7) d. J. Kruger (2) 6–3 6–2.
Semi-finals: Martinez (WC) (1) d. Nagyova (3) 6–2 4–6 6–2; Farina (4) d. Grzybowska (7) 4–6 6–4 4–2 ret.
Final: Martinez (WC) (1) d. Farina (4) 6–0 6–3.
WOMEN'S DOUBLES – Final: Habsudova/Lugina (4) d. Horn/Kschwendt 7–6 7–5.

TORNEO INTERNAZIONALE ($163,000)
PALERMO, 13–19 JULY
WOMEN'S SINGLES – Quarter-finals: P. Schnyder (1) d. M. Zavagli (Q) 6–2 6–3; M. Oremans (6) d. E. Wagner 6–0 6–2; B. Schett (4) d. R. Bobkova 4–6 7–6 6–2; B. Rittner d. J. Capriati 2–6 6–4 6–2.
Semi-finals: Schnyder (1) d. Oremans (6) 6–1 6–3; Schett (4) d. Rittner 4–6 6–4 6–4.
Final: Schnyder (1) d. Schett (4) 6–1 5–7 6–2.
WOMEN'S DOUBLES – Final: Stojanova/Wagner (4) d. Schett/Schnyder (1) 6–4 6–2.

PROKOM POLISH OPEN ($107,500)
SOPOT, 27 JULY–2 AUGUST
Quarter-finals: H. Nagyova (1) d. C. Torrens-Valero 6–4 6–1; G. Leon-Garcia (5) d. B. Rittner 3–6 6–4 6–4; A. Smashnova (6) d. K. Hrdlickova (9) 6–3 7–6; E. Wagner d. M. Weingartner (Q) 6–2 7–6.
Semi-finals: Nagyova (1) d. Leon-Garcia (5) 1–6 6–4 6–1; Wagner d. Smashnova (6) 6–3 0–6 6–4.
Final: Nagyova (1) d. Wagner 6–3 5–7 6–1.
WOMEN'S DOUBLES – Final: Hrdlickova/Vildova d. Carlsson/Noorlander 6–3 6–2.

ENKA LADIES OPEN ($107,500)
ISTANBUL, 3–9 AUGUST
Quarter-finals: H. Nagyova (1) d. M. Shaughnessy 6–4 6–4; F. Labat (4) d. H. Inoue 6–3 3–6 6–4; O. Barabanschikova (7) d. F. Lubiani 6–2 6–3; L. Golarsa d. A. Smashnova (6) 3–6 6–4 6–4.
Semi-finals: Nagyova (1) d. Labat (4) 7–6 6–0; Barabanschikova (7) d. Golarsa 6–1 7–6.
Final: Nagyova (1) d. Barabanschikova (7) 6–4 3–6 7–6.
WOMEN'S DOUBLES – Final: Babel/Courtois (2) d. Carlsson/Labat 6–0 6–2.

BOSTON ($164,250)
BOSTON, MA, 10–16 AUGUST
Quarter-finals: B. Schett (7) d. A. Coetzer (1) 6–7 6–4 6–1; C. Black d. E. Likhovtseva (5) 1–6 6–1 6–2; L. Raymond (3) d. C. Morariu (8) 7–6 6–2; M. De Swardt d. A. Huber (2) 6–3 7–6.
Semi-finals: Schett (7) d. Black 6–2 2–6 6–2; De Swardt d. Raymond (3) 4–6 6–4 7–5.
Final: De Swardt d. Schett (7) 3–6 7–6 7–5.
WOMEN'S DOUBLES – Final: Raymond/Stubbs (1) d. De Swardt/ M. Fernandez 6–4 6–4.

SEAT OPEN ($164,250)
LUXEMBOURG, 26–31 OCTOBER
WOMEN'S SINGLES – Quarter-finals: N. Tauziat (1) d. A. Huber (6) 6–3 6–3; S. Farina d. I. Spirlea (3) 6–4 4–6 6–3; E. Likhovtseva d. E. Koulikovskaya (Q) 6–2 6–0; M. Pierce (2) d. A. Sugiyama (5) 6–3 6–2.
Semi-finals: Farina d. Tauziat (1) 6–2 2–6 6–3; Pierce (2) d. Likhovtseva 6–1 7–5.
Final: Pierce (2) d. Farina 6–0 2–0 ret.
WOMEN'S DOUBLES – Final: Likhovtseva/Sugiyama (3) d. Neiland/Tatarkova (2) 6–7 6–3 2–0 ret.

BELL CHALLENGE ($164,250)
QUEBEC CITY, 26 OCTOBER–1 NOVEMBER
WOMEN'S SINGLES – Quarter-finals: C. Rubin (5) d. D. Van Roost (1) 6–2 6–2; N. Dechy (8) d. A. Stevenson (Q) 6–2 7–6; T. Snyder (7) d. C. Cristea 6–4 6–4; J. Chi d. S. Testud (2) 6–4 7–5.
Semi-finals: Rubin (5) d. Dechy (8) 6–2 6–4; Snyder (7) d. Chi 1–6 6–3 7–5.
Final: Snyder (7) d. Rubin (5) 4–6 6–4 7–6.
WOMEN'S DOUBLES – Final: McNeil/Po (2) d. Rubin/Testud (3) 6–7 7–5 6–4.

VOLVO WOMEN'S OPEN ($107,500)
PATTAYA CITY, 16–22 NOVEMBER
WOMEN'S SINGLES – Quarter-finals: S. Talaja d. O. Barabanschikova (7) 6–4 6–1; F. Li (5) d. T. Tanasugarn (3) 7–6 6–4; K. Brandi d. M. Tu 6–3 6–3; J. Halard-Decugis (2) d. S. Wang (8) 5–7 6–2 6–0.
Semi-finals: Li (5) d. Talaja 6–3 6–3; Halard-Decugis (2) d. Brandi 6–0 6–1.
Final: Halard-Decugis (2) d. Li (5) 6–1 6–2.
WOMEN'S DOUBLES – Final: Callens/Halard-Decugis (1) d. Hiraki/Olsza 3–6 6–2 6–2.

Saving the best till last, Martina Hingis won the Chase Championships by beating Lindsay Davenport, the player who had taken over her role as the world's No.1. (Stephen Wake)

Corel WTA Chase Championships

Barry Wood

At the end of a week in which day sessions were introduced for the first time, Martina Hingis finished what must have been a disappointing season for her by overcoming Lindsay Davenport 7–5 6–4 4–6 6–2 in the final of the Chase Championships.

Unfortunately, the quality of play did not match the occasion, as physical and mental fatigue at the end of a long year took its toll and became a theme of the tournament. Indeed, Bart McGuire, the Chief Executive Officer of the WTA, revealed that efforts are being made to shorten the season by two or three weeks.

Neither player managed to dominate and there was plenty of carelessness with Davenport carrying the additional burden of having played six sets the day before the best-of-five-sets final. It was simply a matter of who would make fewer errors. That proved to be Hingis.

Often, a player making their debut at Madison Square Garden fails to win her opening match, but that was not the case with Dominique Van Roost. She defeated Conchita Martinez 7–6(9–7) 6–2, saving three set points at 5–4. Her forceful forehand was largely responsible for her victory, and she also showed more versatility.

The next match confirmed that Davenport would finish the year ranked as the world number one, even though she did not play on the opening night. Irina Spirlea's 7–6(8–6) 6–1 win over Arantxa Sanchez-Vicario meant that Hingis could not gather enough bonus points to overtake the American at the top of the rankings, even though she eventually won the tournament.

Both Spaniards had capitulated quite meekly in the second set, and afterwards complained of being tired after a long season. 'I give my best, but at the end of the year everybody is very tired. It is impossible to be 100 per cent for each tournament,' said Sanchez Vicario. 'By the end of the year, mostly any player you ask is either burned out or injured. It is late in the season to play an important tournament like this,' said Martinez.

On the second day, Nathalie Tauziat defeated Natasha Zvereva 6–3 6–1. The score rather flattered the Frenchwoman, but it was a good contest with Tauziat's serve perhaps being the deciding factor. Hingis then faced a re-match with fellow Swiss, Patty Schnyder, against whom she had retired at the Grand Slam Cup. This time Hingis, with only pride to play for, was again taken to three sets but eventually won quite comfortably, 4–6 6–0 6–3. It was a fine match distinguished by fierce baseline rallies, but Schnyder managed just seven points in the second set after taking the first, and ended the match with 49 unforced errors against 25 from Hingis.

Jana Novotna entered the history books on the same day, but wished she had not, as she became the first defending champion in the 27-year history of the event to lose in the opening round. Her opponent, however, was Steffi Graf, who won 6–7(5–7) 6–4 6–1. Having lost the first set, a break in the opening game of the second was enough to level the match, and Novotna suffered from cramps in the third. 'It was pretty frustrating because I think I played very well,' said Novotna, and she did.

On the third day Amanda Coetzer was overwhelmed 6–1 6–0 by Mary Pierce in 46 minutes. Pierce returned superbly and was more aggressive. She was also quick to put away the short ball. When she is on song it is difficult for anyone to compete with Pierce, and Coetzer didn't even earn a game point until 18 minutes into the match. 'I just had a good day,' said Pierce.

Next, Monica Seles tackled Anna Kournikova and won 6–4 6–3. The young Russian struck her forehand with passion and looked a class act, but she had recently lost confidence in her serve and her embarrassing total of 17 double-faults destroyed any chance of victory.

The final match of the opening round saw Davenport only narrowly avert an upset by Sandrine Testud. The American eventually won 4–6 7–6(7–4) 6–0, after leading 4–2 in the first set and then being two points from defeat at 4–5 in the second. 'It wasn't looking good the first two sets, but at the end of the second set I won the few really important points,' said Davenport.

The second round produced the best match of the tournament, and in seasoned observers' minds perhaps the best match of the year, when Graf took on Seles. Since Seles was attacked in Hamburg in 1993 the pair had met only twice, in the 1995 and 1996 US Open finals, with Graf winning both. This time Graf won again, 1–6 6–4 6–4, in a superb contest that reminded spectators of what a great rivalry they may have enjoyed had Seles' career not been so cruelly interrupted. 'Thank you for a great match,' cried a spectator in the third set. It was an appropriate assessment.

In the second set Graf twice took the lead, for 2–1 and 4–3, only to see Seles immediately break back. But when the German broke a third time to lead 5–4, she held on to take the match into a deciding set. This time Graf faced two break points in the fourth game, one when she broke a string and another when she double-faulted, but it was the German who eventually broke, to lead 5–4 and serve out for the match. She was ecstatic.

'The last two weeks have been amazing,' said Graf, who had won titles in Leipzig and Philadelphia, 'and that just tops it off. Now I hope I don't have to answer any more why I'm doing this. It speaks for itself. Seles had gone out hoping to avoid a whitewash, and was philosophical after her defeat. 'It was a great match in my mind, win or lose,' she said.

On the same evening, Spirlea served well and Van Roost didn't, with predictable consequences. By the time Van Roost settled down and began to compete on equal terms it was too late, and the Romanian won 6–2 6–3.

On the fifth day, Davenport came out far stronger than she had against Testud and despatched Tauziat 6–0 6–3 in 54 minutes. 'When you get through matches like Wednesday (against Testud) it loosens you up,' said Davenport. 'I was seeing the ball well and played really great tennis.'

Hingis became the last player to reach the semi-finals when she overcame Pierce 7–6(7–4) 6–4. Pierce is often entertaining whether she intends it or not, and she spent nearly every changeover with one ice pack on her neck, and another tucked under her skirt, and she would drop the ice pack like a chicken laying an egg every time she got up to play again. 'I wasn't feeling well,' was her only explanation.

The match was as close as the score suggests, with the Pierce forehand causing some damage while being counteracted to some extent by Hingis' dropshots. Pierce held a set point at 6–5, and in the second set she also led 40–0 on the Hingis serve at 1–1, broke for 3–2 but was broken back for 3–3. Hingis finally closed out the match by breaking again in the final game.

In the semi-finals, Davenport – and a pulled hamstring – brought Graf's run to an end. In a contest that was undistinguished, despite the outcome hanging in the balance until late in the final set, the German had her right leg strapped and lost the next three games, and the match, 6–1 2–6 6–3. Graf was the only woman to play four consecutive three-set matches in 1998, and it was only the second time she had done so in her career.

'You get days when both players don't play well. There were not a lot of great points,' said Davenport. The same observation could be made concerning Hingis' 6–2 7–6(9–7) win over Spirlea. The Romanian did impress with the quality of her returns, but lost the second set after leading 5–1 and holding three set points in the tiebreak. Still, despite a disappointing day's play, the scene was set for an appropriate season-ending showdown between the two players who had held the number one ranking during the year.

Seven players qualified to compete in both singles and doubles, a tribute to the commitment of top singles players to doubles. Hingis and Novotna, who had won three Grand Slams (Hingis had won a fourth with Mirjana Lucic) were top seeds, but lost 6–4 2–6 6–4 in the first round to Yayuk Basuki and Caroline Vis. The final was won by second seeds Davenport and Zvereva, who defeated fourth seeds Alexandra Fusai and Tauziat 6–7(6–8) 7–5 6–3.

COREL WTA CHASE CHAMPIONSHIPS 1998

MADISON SQUARE GARDEN, NY, 16–22 NOVEMBER

WOMEN'S SINGLES – 1st round: L. Davenport (1) d. S. Testud 4–6 7–6 6–0; N. Tauziat (8) d. N. Zvereva 6–3 6–1; S. Graf d. J. Novotna (3) 6–7 6–4 6–1; M. Seles (5) d. A. Kournikova 6–4 6–3; D. Van Roost d. C. Martinez (7) 7–6 6–2; I. Spirlea d. A. Sanchez-Vicario (4) 7–6 6–1; M. Pierce (6) d. A. Coetzer 6–1 6–0; M. Hingis (2) d. P. Schnyder 4–6 6–0 6–3.

Quarter-finals: Davenport (1) d. Tauziat (8) 6–0 6–3; Graf d. Seles (5) 1–6 6–4 6–4; Spirlea d. Van Roost 6–2 6–3; Hingis (2) d. Pierce (6) 7–6 6–4.

Semi-finals: Davenport (1) d. Graf 6–1 2–6 6–3; Hingis (2) d. Spirlea 6–2 7–6.

Final: Hingis (2) d. Davenport (1) 7–5 6–4 4–6 6–2.

WOMEN'S DOUBLES – Final: L. Davenport/N. Zvereva (2) d. A. Fusai/N. Tauziat (4) 6–7 7–5 6–3.

Prize Money (per team): Winners $200,000; Runners-up $100,000; Semi-finalists $50,000; First round $25,000. Total: $2,000,000.

Other Official Pro Tournaments

Men's Challenger Tournaments
ITF Men's Circuit
ITF Women's Circuit

Britain's Tim Henman finished the year at No. 7 in the world after reaching the semi-finals at Wimbledon, retaining his title in Tashkent and winning for the first time in Basle. (Stephen Wake)

Men's Challenger Tournaments

In 1998 there were 114 Challenger tournaments for men in 45 countries. Where a tournament provides hospitality for its players the event is credited another US$25,000 in terms of its ranking points level. The prize money and points levels (H = plus hospitality) were:

US$125,000H	100 points to the champion
US$125,000 (or US$100,000H)	90 points to the champion
US$100,000 (or US$75,000H)	80 points to the champion
US$75,000 (or US$50,000H)	70 points to the champion
US$35,000H	65 points to the champion
US$50,000 (or US$25,000H)	60 points to the champion

HEILBRONN (GER) (100H) 26 JANUARY–1 FEBRUARY – ***Singles:*** M. Sinner d. G. Pozzi (6) 6–0 3–6 6–3. ***Doubles:*** G. Grant/M. Merklein (1) d. S. Pescosolido/V. Santopadre 6–3 7–6.

WEST BLOOMFIELD (USA) (50H) 2–7 FEBRUARY – ***Singles:*** A. O'Brien (3) d. G. Doyle 4–6 6–3 6–4. ***Doubles:*** J. Thomas/L. Tieleman d. A. Hernandez/D. Roditi 7–6 6–4.

LIPPSTADT (GER) (25H) 2–8 FEBRUARY – ***Singles:*** D. Dier d. M. Martelli (5) 7–6 4–3 ret. ***Doubles:*** A. Richardson/M. Wakefield d. R. Sluiter/P. Wessels 4–6 7–6 6–4.

WOLFSBURG (GER) (25H) 9–15 FEBRUARY – ***Singles:*** I. Heuberger d. D. Dier 6–7 6–4 6–4. ***Doubles:*** M. Safin/D. Vemic d. J. Brandt/T. Messmer 6–4 4–6 6–2.

SINGAPORE (SIN) (50H) 16–22 FEBRUARY – ***Singles:*** F. Vicente (4) d. J. Marin (1) 6–4 6–4. ***Doubles:*** J. Thomas/L. Tieleman d. J. Holmes/A. Painter 6–3 3–6 7–6.

LUBECK (GER) (25H) 16–22 FEBRUARY – ***Singles:*** P. Wessels (Q) d. M. Kohlmann (Q) 7–6 6–3. ***Doubles:*** L. Manta/A. Richardson (Q) d. S. Simian/T. Ketola 7–6 6–2.

HO CHI MINH CITY (VIE) (50H) 23 FEBRUARY–1 MARCH – ***Singles:*** A. Sa d. J. Marin (1) 6–3 3–6 6–2. ***Doubles:*** M. Bhupathi/P. Tramacchi (1) d. M. Mirnyi/K. Ullyett (3) 6–4 6–0.

CHERBOURG (FRA) (37.5H) 23 FEBRUARY–1 MARCH – ***Singles:*** J. Golmard (2) d. G. Pozzi (1) 3–6 6–4 6–3. ***Doubles:*** M. Ardinghi/M. Bertolini d. J. Fleurian/S. Simian 6–3 2–6 6–4.

BANGKOK (THA) (50H) 2–8 MARCH – ***Singles:*** L. Paes d. G. Motomura (Q) 6–4 7–5. ***Doubles:*** P. Tramacchi/K. Ullyett d. G. Koves/A. Savolt 6–4 6–3.

MAGDEBURG (GER) (25H) 2–8 MARCH – ***Singles:*** L. Burgsmuller d. A. Pavel (3) 6–4 6–3. ***Doubles:*** E. Erlich/M. Navarra (Q) d. M. Ondruska/C. Wilkinson (2) 4–6 6–1 6–4.

SALINAS (ECU) (50H) 9–15 MARCH – ***Singles:*** A. Sa (3) d. G. Canas (6) 7–5 5–7 6–4. ***Doubles:*** D. Di Lucia/M. Sell (2) d. M. Hood/S. Prieto (1) 7–6 6–4.

KYOTO (JPN) (25H) 9–15 MARCH – ***Singles:*** M. Kohlmann (3) d. S. Campbell (1) 7–6 3–6 6–3. ***Doubles:*** T. Suzuki/K. Ullyett d. O. Ortiz/M. Ruah (1) 4–6 6–1 6–4.

BARLETTA (ITA) (25H) 30 MARCH – 5 APRIL – ***Singles***: F. Cabello (8) d. S. Navarro (LL) 6–4 6–4. ***Doubles:*** J. Balcells/J. Carrasco d. T. Strengberger/D. Vemic 7–6 6–3.

BERMUDA (BER) (100H) 6–12 APRIL – ***Singles:*** H. Gumy (5) d. L. Arnold (6) 7–6 4–6 6–2. ***Doubles:*** D. Flach/R. Reneberg (3) d. A. Cherkasov/R. Gilbert 3–6 6–4 6–2.

NAPOLI (ITA) (100H) 6–12 APRIL – ***Singles:*** D. Sanguinetti (WC) (4) d. M. Safin (WC) 6–4 6–4. ***Doubles:*** M. Bertolini/D. Bowen d. T. El Sawy/G. Koves 7–6 6–2.

SAN LUIS POTOSI (MEX) (25H) 6–12 APRIL – ***Singles:*** L. Morejon d. A. Zingman (Q) 6–1 2–6 6–4. ***Doubles:*** E. Kempes/P. Wessels (2) d. J. Frontera/R. Kokavec 7–6 4–6 7–5.

NICE (FRA) (100H) 13–19 APRIL – ***Singles:*** M. Puerta d. A. Di Pasquale (WC) 6–7 6–4 6–4. ***Doubles:*** D. Bowen/M. Hood (4) d. M. Puerta/A. Sa 7–5 3–6 6–4.

BIRMINGHAM (USA) (50H) 13–19 APRIL – ***Singles:*** C. Ruud (2) d. J. Van Herck (1) 2–6 6–1 6–1. ***Doubles:*** D. Flach/D. Witt (4) d. E. Erlich/E. Taino (2) 6–4 7–5.

VADODARA (IND) (50H) 13–19 APRIL – ***Singles***: P. Tramacchi (2) d. A. Du Puis 7–6 6–7 6–3.
Doubles: M. Wakefield/W. Whitehouse d. M. Mirnyi/P. Tramacchi (1) 7–6 7–6.

PUERTO VALLARTA (MEX) (25H) 13–19 APRIL – ***Singles:*** G. Grant (Q) (1) d. M. Sanchez (WC) 6–2 6–4.
Doubles: L. Herrera/G. Trifu d. O. Fukarek/R. Lavergne 6–3 6–4.

ESPINHO (POR) (125H) 20–26 APRIL – ***Singles:*** G. Canas (8) d. M. Puerta 6–1 2–6 6–2.
Doubles: J. Knippschild/S. Noteboom (4) d. A. Martin/T. Zdrazila 7–6 7–5.

PRAGUE (CZE) (25H) 20–26 APRIL – ***Singles:*** M. Tabara (LL) d. W. Schranz 6–2 6–1.
Doubles: J. Balcells/N. Zimonjic d. J. Novak/R. Stepanek (3) 7–6 7–6.

JERUSALEM (ISR) (50) 4–9 MAY – ***Singles:*** N. Godwin (7) d. G. Trifu 6–4 7–6. ***Doubles:*** N. Behr/E. Erlich w/o.

LJUBLJANA (SLO) (125H) 4–10 MAY – ***Singles:*** D. Pescariu (5) d. A. Voinea 7–6 2–6 6–3.
Doubles: M. Barnard/S. Noteboom (4) d. A. Martin/T. Zdrazila (3) 7–6 6–7 7–6.

KOSICE (SVK) (125H) 11–17 MAY – ***Singles:*** D. Hrbaty (WC) (1) d. F. Meligeni (2) 7–5 6–4.
Doubles: J. Novak/D. Rikl (1) d. N. Djordjevic/M. Ondruska 7–6 6–4.

DRESDEN (GER) (50H) 11–17 MAY – ***Singles:*** D. Dier (7) d. M. Hantschk (WC) 0–6 6–1 6–4.
Doubles: P. Albano/S. Groen (1) d. J. Holmes/A. Painter 6–4 6–3.

BUDAPEST (HUN) (100H) 18–24 MAY – ***Singles:*** M. Ondruska d. D. Sanguinetti (4) 4–6 7–5 7–6.
Doubles: C. Haggard/P. Rosner (3) d. D. Del Rio/G. Silcock 6–4 6–2.

KIEV (UKR) (50H) 25–31 MAY – ***Singles:*** N. Zimonjic (Q) d. J. Kroslak (4) 6–3 6–3.
Doubles: T. Buchmayer/T. Strengberger (3) d. J. Coetzee/J. Thomas (4) 6–4 7–6.

MEDELLIN (COL) (25H) 25–31 MAY – ***Singles:*** A. Ferreira (6) d. R. Wassen (Q) (3) 6–0 6–4.
Doubles: A. Ferreira/C. Testa (2) d. J. Gamboa/M. Hadad (WC) 3–6 6–1 6–2.

PROSTEJOV (CZE) (125H) 2–7 JUNE – ***Singles:*** R. Fromberg (WC) (2) d. A. Ilie 6–2 6–2.
Doubles: E. Kempes/P. Wessels d. T. Cibulec/T. Krupa (WC) 6–4 7–5.

FURTH (GER) (50H) 2–7 JUNE – ***Singles:*** C. Ruud d. J. Andersen (Q) 6–4 7–5.
Doubles: A. Lopez-Moron/A. Portas (Q) d. J. Carrasco/M. Rodriguez 6–4 6–4.

SURBITON (GBR) (50) 2–7 JUNE – ***Singles:*** G. Pozzi (1) d. K. Ullyett (Q) 6–4 6–3.
Doubles: S. Stolle/P. Tramacchi (3) d. M. Merklein/M. Sell (2) 4–6 7–6 6–4.

SPLIT (CRO) (100H) 8–14 JUNE – ***Singles:*** O. Stanoytchev d. A. Savolt 7–6 6–4.
Doubles: G. Grant/A. Savolt (4) d. A. Lopez-Moron/A. Martin (3) 4–6 6–3 6–2.

WEIDEN (GER) (25H) 8–14 JUNE – ***Singles:*** A. Calleri d. G. Etlis 6–2 6–1.
Doubles: N. Marques/N. Zimonjic (1) d. S. Aspelin/C. Tontz 6–4 3–6 6–3.

BRAUNSCHWEIG (GER) (125H) 15–21 JUNE – ***Singles:*** F. Squillari d. L. Arnold 6–2 4–6 6–1.
Doubles: T. Carbonell/F. Roig (1) d. J. Balcells/E. Couto 6–2 7–6.

ZAGREB (CRO) (100H) 15–21 JUNE – ***Singles:*** J. Novak (3) d. M. Puerta (4) 7–5 6–1.
Doubles: J. Alonso-Pintor/M. Puerta (2) d. E. Nicolas/G. Puentes 6–1 6–4.

BIELLA (ITA) (25H) 22–28 JUNE – ***Singles:*** A. Ilie (WC) (1) d. J. Perlant 6–7 6–4 6–4.
Doubles: D. Del Rio/E. Taino (1)/E. Couto/J. Cunha-Silva (2) 7–6 5–7 6–2.

EISENACH (GER) (25H) 22–28 JUNE – ***Singles:*** E. Kempes d. M. Meneschincheri (6) 7–6 6–3.
Doubles: J. Oncins/C. Testa d. R. Nicklisch/P. Sommer 6–1 6–3.

PRIBRAM (CZE) (25H) 22–28 JUNE – ***Singles:*** A. Di Pasquale (3) d. R. Stepanek 6–3 6–1.
Doubles: O. Fukarek/U. Plamberger d. P. Pala/R. Stepanek (3) 2–6 6–3 6–4.

VENICE (ITA) (100H) 30 JUNE–5 JULY – ***Singles:*** A. Voinea d. F. Squillari (8) 6–3 6–3.
Doubles: N. Djordjevic/M. Ondruska (4) d. M. Bertolini/S. Groen (3) 1–6 6–1 6–2.

ULM (GER) (50H) 30 JUNE–5 JULY – ***Singles:*** Y. El Aynaoui d. D. Pescariu (2) 6–4 6–3.
Doubles: M. Carlsson/J. Oncins d. D. Dier/M. Kohlmann (4) 6–4 6–7 6–3.

DENVER (USA) (50) 30 JUNE–5 JULY – ***Singles:*** T. Suzuki d. J. Bower 6–3 4–6 6–4.
Doubles: M. Hill/G. Weiner d. J. Bower/T. Budgen 7–6 6–4.

MONTAUBAN (FRA) (25H) 30 JUNE–5 JULY – ***Singles:*** E. Kempes d. W. Schranz 7–5 6–3.
Doubles: E. Nicolas/G. Puentes (1) d. E. Kempes/R. Wassen (2) 7–5 7–5.

OSTEND (BEL) (75H) 6–11 JULY – ***Singles:*** A. Ilie (1) d. M. Rodriguez 6–2 6–2.
Doubles: C. Brandi/F. Messori (2) d. D. Del Rio/V. Santopadre (4) 4–6 6–2 6–3.

GRANBY (CAN) (50H) 6–12 JULY – ***Singles:*** T. Suzuki d. D. Caldwell 7–6 6–3.
Doubles: G. Motomura/T. Suzuki (3) d. R. Kokavec/F. Niemeyer 7–6 6–1.

OBERSTAUFEN (GER) (25H) 6–12 JULY – ***Singles:*** W. Schranz d. R. Wassen 6–4 6–2.
Doubles: N. Marques/R. Wassen (1) d. O. Camporese/D. Vemic (4) 7–6 7–6.

BRISTOL (GBR) (50) 7–12 JULY – ***Singles***: D. Van Uffelen (Q) d. A. Ferreira 6–3 6–2.
Doubles: M. Mirnyi/V. Voltchkov d. W. Arthurs/B. Ellwood (4) 6–4 3–6 7–6.

MERANO (ITA) (125H) 13–19 JULY – ***Singles:*** C. Dosedel (WC) (2) d. C. Ruud 7–6 7–6.
Doubles: P. Albano/N. Lapentti (4) d. G. Galimberti/M. Valeri (WC) 6–1 6–1.

CONTREXEVILLE (FRA) (50H) 13–19 JULY – ***Singles:*** Y. El Aynaoui d. A. Di Pasquale (WC) 6–4 6–7 6–0.
Doubles: D. Del Rio/M. Rodriguez (4) d. A. Lopez-Moron/J. Velasco 7–6 4–6 6–4.

APTOS (USA) (50) 13–19 JULY – ***Singles:*** C. Mamiit d. T. Suzuki 6–7 6–3 6–2.
Doubles: M. Bryan/R. Bryan (WC) d. A. Peterson/C. Tontz 6–4 6–4.

MANCHESTER (GBR) (50) 13–20 JULY – ***Singles:*** C. Wilkinson (2) d. S. Pescosolido (4) 6–3 6–4.
Doubles: M. Navarra/S. Pescosolido (4) d. W. Arthurs/B. Ellwood (2) 6–1 6–7 7–6.

NEWCASTLE (GBR) (50H) 20–26 JULY – ***Singles:*** A. Calleri d. S. Navarro 6–3 6–4.
Doubles: J. Coetzee/E. Kempes (2) d. N. Djordjevic/D. Vemic (1) 1–6 7–6 6–2.

TAMPERE (FIN) (50) 20–26 JULY – ***Singles:*** T. Zib d. T. Lenho (WC) 4–6 6–2 7–6.
Doubles: T. Hildebrand/F. Loven d. J. Knowle/C. Rochus 7–6 1–6 6–0.

ISTANBUL (TUR) (100H) 27 JULY–2 AUGUST – ***Singles:*** T. Zib d. P. Luxa (6) 4–6 6–2 6–1.
Doubles: P. Luxa/E. Ran (2) d. T. Larkham/C. Wilkinson (1) 6–4 7–6.

SCHEVENINGEN (NED) (50H) 27 JULY–2 AUGUST – ***Singles:*** Y. El Aynaoui (5) d. M. Rodriguez (4) 6–3 6–1.
Doubles: A. Calleri/T. Hildebrand d. S. Prieto/M. Rodriguez (2) 6–2 3–6 6–2.

WINNETKA (USA) (50) 27 JULY–2 AUGUST – ***Singles:*** G. Grant (8) d. D. Nargiso (2) 5–7 6–3 7–5.
Doubles: G. Silcock/M. Wakefield (3) d. G. Grant/M. Merklein (2) 1–6 7–6 7–6.

POZNAN (POL) (100H) 3–9 AUGUST – ***Singles:*** C. Ruud (1) d. M. Rodriguez 1–6 6–3 6–3.
Doubles: S. Prieto/M. Rodriguez (2) d. C. Brandi/M. Carlsson 6–3 6–4.

SEGOVIA (ESP) (100H) 3–9 AUGUST – ***Singles:*** R. Stepanek d. A. Radulescu 7–5 7–5.
Doubles: R. Stepanek/T. Zib d. J. Conde/R. Fernandez 6–3 7–6.

LEXINGTON (USA) (50H) 3–9 AUGUST – ***Singles:*** P. Goldstein d. H. Lee 6–1 6–4.
Doubles: B. Ellwood/L. Hewitt d. P. Goldstein/J. Thomas 5–7 6–3 6–2.

GRAMADO (BRA) (25H) 3–9 AUGUST – ***Singles:*** A. Sa (1) d. H. Kaneko (8) 6–7 6–1 6–4.
Doubles: J. Coetzee/D. Roberts (3) d. F. Costa/G. Motomura (4) 7–5 6–4.

TIJUANA (MEX) (25H) 3–9 AUGUST – ***Singles:*** M. Hill (4) d. A. Hernandez (1) 7–5 6–1.
Doubles: M. Hill/S. Humphries d. M. Sprengelmeyer/E. Taino (2) 6–3 6–2.

BINGHAMTON (USA) (50H) 10–16 AUGUST – ***Singles:*** T. Suzuki (8) d. D. Nargiso (3) 5–2 ret.
Doubles: M. Wakefield/W. Whitehouse d. P. Luxa/B. Martinez (1) 7–5 2–6 7–5.

BELO HORIZONTE (BRA) (25H) 10–16 AUGUST – ***Singles:*** F. Costa (3) d. G. Gaudio 4–6 6–2 6–4.
Doubles: S. Iwabuchi/T. Shimada d. J. Coetzee/D. Roberts (3) 6–7 7–5 7–5.

NETTINGSDORF (AUT) (25H) 10–16 AUGUST – ***Singles:*** M. Hipfl d. C. Trimmel (WC) 6–2 6–0.
Doubles: T. Krupa/B. Urh (2) d. T. Cibulec/L. Friedl 6–1 6–4.

SOPOT (POL) (25H) 10–16 AUGUST – ***Singles:*** M. Chmela (WC) d. T. Larsen 6–2 7–6.
Doubles: J. Greenhalgh/N. Zimonjic (2) d. A. Shvec/M. Velev (LL) 6–1 6–3.

GRAZ (AUT) (100H) 17–23 AUGUST – ***Singles:*** C. Costa (WC) (1) d. A. Portas (5) 7–5 7–6.
Doubles: D. Pescariu/A. Portas d. L. Bale/N. Djordjevic 6–3 6–4.

WARSAW (POL) (50H) 17–23 AUGUST – ***Singles:*** J. Vanek d. A. Cherkasov (WC) (2) 7–6 7–5.
Doubles: J. Greenhalgh/N. Zimonjic (3) d. A. Hamadeh/J. Landsberg w/o.

BRONX, NY (USA) (50) 17–23 AUGUST – ***Singles:*** M. MacLagan (Q) d. O. Motevassel 7–6 6–2.
Doubles: J. Palmer/T. Suzuki d. O. Fukarek/G. Trifu 6–1 6–2.

GENEVA (SUI) (50H) 24–30 AUGUST – ***Singles:*** J. Viloca (6) d. Y. El Aynaoui (4) 6–3 6–4.
Doubles: R. Bergh/J. Knippschild d. M. Tabara/R. Vasek (Q) 6–2 3–6 6–4.

ALPIRSBACH (GER) (37.5H) 31 AUGUST–6 SEPTEMBER – ***Singles:*** S. Koubek (6) d. O. Stanoytchev (4) 7–6 6–4. ***Doubles:*** T. Cibulec/L. Friedl d. M. Hilpert/F. Veglio 6–1 7–6.

BELGRADE (YUG) (25H) 31 AUGUST–6 SEPTEMBER – ***Singles:*** J. Vanek (3) d. D. Moyano 6–3 6–3.
Doubles: R. Sluiter/N. Zimonjic (2) d. A. Hamadeh/J. Landsberg 6–4 6–4.

SANTA CRUZ (BOL) (25H) 31 AUGUST–6 SEPTEMBER – ***Singles:*** G. Gaudio (5) d. L. Morejon (2) 6–2 6–3. ***Doubles:*** M. Charpentier/A. Schneiter d. K. Orellana/J. Szymanski 6–2 6–3.

QUITO (ECU) (50H) 7–13 SEPTEMBER – ***Singles:*** N. Massu d. M. Sanchez 3–6 6–3 6–0. ***Doubles:*** A. Ferreira/O. Ortiz (2) d. K. Orellana/J. Szymanski 6–3 6–4.

EDINBURGH (GBR) (50) 8–13 SEPTEMBER – ***Singles:*** T. Nydahl (Q) (2) d. J. Andersen 6–4 6–1. ***Doubles:*** E. Kempes/P. Wessels (2) d. M. Ondruska/C. Wilkinson (1) 6–7 6–3 6–2.

BUDVA (YUG) (25H) 8–13 SEPTEMBER – ***Singles:*** T. Behrend d. F. Jonsson 3–6 6–3 6–2. ***Doubles:*** E. Nicolas/G. Puentes (1) d. E. Couto/J. Cunha-Silva (2) 3–6 6–1 6–3.

BRASOV (ROM) (50H) 8–14 SEPTEMBER – ***Singles:*** D. Pescariu (2) d. T. Larsen 6–3 3–6 6–2. ***Doubles:*** J. Carrasco/J. Velasco (1) d. T. Cibulec/L. Friedl (2) 6–4 3–6 6–2.

BUDAPEST II (HUN) (50H) 14–20 SEPTEMBER – ***Singles:*** R. Furlan d. C. Van Garsse (5) 6–2 6–3. ***Doubles:*** G. Koves/T. Strengberger (2) d. L. Friedl/R. Stepanek 6–4 6–4.

SKOPJE (MKD) (25H) 14–20 SEPTEMBER – ***Singles:*** J. Mas (5) d. T. Behrend (7) 6–3 6–4. ***Doubles:*** E. Nicolas/G. Puentes (1) d. A. Merinov/A. Stoliarov 7–5 3–6 7–6.

FLORIANOPOLIS (BRA) (125H) 14–21 SEPTEMBER – ***Singles:*** G. Canas (3) d. M. Carlsson (8) 6–2 7–5. ***Doubles:*** J. Oncins/A. Sa (3) d. M. Filippini/G. Rodriguez (WC) 6–0 6–1.

SEVILLE (ESP) (25H) 21–26 SEPTEMBER – ***Singles:*** A. Martin d. D. Scala 6–1 5–7 6–2. ***Doubles:*** A. Martin/S. Navarro (2) d. E. Kempes/R. Wassen (1) 2–6 7–5 6–3.

SZCZECIN (POL) (125H) 21–27 SEPTEMBER – ***Singles:*** Y. El Aynaoui (8) d. J. Knippschild 6–3 6–4. ***Doubles:*** O. Stanoytchev/R. Vasek (Q) d. M. Ardinghi/A. Lopez-Moron 7–6 3–6 6–4.

URBANA, IL (USA) (37.5H) 21–27 SEPTEMBER – ***Singles:*** D. Nestor (2) d. M. Ruah 3–6 7–6 6–3. ***Doubles:*** J. Palmer/J. Stark (2) d. D. Flach/M. Merklein (1) 6–4 7–6.

OPORTO (POR) (125H) 28 SEPTEMBER–4 OCTOBER – ***Singles:*** Y. El Aynaoui (7) d. S. Koubek 4–6 6–2 6–4. ***Doubles:*** J. Carrasco/J. Velasco d. C. Brandi/S. Noteboom (2) 7–5 6–4.

CARACAS (VEN) (100) 28 SEPTEMBER–4 OCTOBER – ***Singles:*** A. Ferreira (7) d. K. Orellana (WC) 6–1 6–4. ***Doubles:*** G. Grant/M. Ruah (1) d. G. Motomura/A. Sa (2) 4–6 6–1 6–2.

DALLAS, TX (USA) (50) 28 SEPTEMBER–4 OCTOBER – ***Singles:*** D. Nestor (2) d. C. Carratti (8) 6–1 6–2. ***Doubles:*** J. Palmer/J. Stark (3) d. M. Hill/S. Humphries 6–3 6–4.

OLBIA (ITA) (50) 28 SEPTEMBER–4 OCTOBER – ***Singles:*** D. Bracciali d. E. Ran 7–6 6–4. ***Doubles:*** T. Larkham/C. Wilkinson (1) d. T. Shimada/F. Veglio (2) 3–6 6–3 7–6.

SANTIAGO (CHI) (100) 5–11 OCTOBER – ***Singles:*** S. Prieto d. P. Wessels 7–5 6–4. ***Doubles:*** O. Fukarek/A. Savolt d. E. Kempes/P. Wessels (2) 7–6 6–4.

TEL AVIV (ISR) (50H) 5–11 OCTOBER – ***Singles:*** G. Pozzi (1) d. L. Mor 6–1 6–7 6–3. ***Doubles:*** R. Stepanek/M. Tabara d. N. Okun/N. Welgreen 7–6 6–3.

SAN ANTONIO, TX (USA) (50) 5–11 OCTOBER – ***Singles:*** G. Grant (2) d. M. Knowles (WC) 6–1 6–7 4–1 ret. ***Doubles:*** D. Di Lucia/M. Sell (1) d. M. Hill/S. Humphries 6–3 6–1.

BARCELONA (ESP) (100) 12–18 OCTOBER – ***Singles:*** F. Vicente (2) d. J. Andersen (SE) 6–3 6–3. ***Doubles:*** J. Conde/J. Sanchez d. M. Bertolini/C. Brandi 4–6 6–4 6–3.

SAO PAULO (BRA) (100) 12–18 OCTOBER – ***Singles:*** F. Meligeni (WC) (1) d. M. Filippini 6–1 6–4. ***Doubles:*** D. Del Rio/M. Rodriguez (2) d. E. Kempes/P. Wessels (1) 7–6 6–3.

SAN DIEGO, CA (USA) (50) 12–18 OCTOBER – ***Singles:*** V. Liukko (Q) d. P. Goldstein 7–5 7–6. ***Doubles:*** P. Goldstein/A. Peterson d. M. Hill/S. Humphries 6–2 7–5.

CAIRO (EGY) (100H) 19–25 OCTOBER – ***Singles:*** A. Portas (2) d. A. Martin 6–2 1–6 6–3. ***Doubles:*** A. Lopez-Moron/A. Portas d. A. Martin/S. Navarro 4–6 6–3 6–2.

MONTEVIDEO (URU) (100) 19–25 OCTOBER – ***Singles:*** E. Medica d. C. Ruud (4) 6–4 6–4. ***Doubles:*** F. Cabello/A. Calleri d. P. Taicher/C. Testa 6–4 6–4.

HONG KONG (HKG) (50H) 19–25 OCTOBER – ***Singles:*** D. Nestor (3) v. L. Hewitt (8). ***Doubles:*** B. Ellwood/L. Hewitt (3) v. J. Thomas/L. Tieleman (2). Matches not played due to typhoon.

ECKENTAL (GER) (25H) 19–25 OCTOBER – ***Singles:*** J. Palmer (SE) d. W. Schranz (8) 7–6 6–2. ***Doubles:*** T. Cibulec/R. Sluiter d. B. Cowan/F. Veglio 7–6 6–3.

SAMARKAND (UZB) (25H) 19–25 OCTOBER – ***Singles:*** F. Jonsson (6) d. O. Ogorodov 7–6 6–3. ***Doubles:*** N. Behr/E. Ran (1) d. A. Merinov/A. Stoliarov 1–6 6–4 7–6.

BREST (FRA) (100H) 26 OCTOBER–1 NOVEMBER – ***Singles:*** J. Golmard (1) d. J. Perlant (WC) 6–4 6–4. ***Doubles:*** N. Godwin/M. Ondruska d. J. Gimelstob/B. MacPhie (2) 6–4 5–7 6–4.

AACHEN (GER) (50H) 2–8 NOVEMBER – ***Singles:*** H. Dreekmann (1) d. O. Stanoytchev 7–6 6–4. ***Doubles:*** M. Oosting/P. Vizner (1) d. T. Ketola/P. Pala 7–6 6–3.

LAS VEGAS, NV (USA) (50H) 9–15 NOVEMBER – ***Singles:*** C. Mamiit (WC) d. M. Ruah 7–5 6–3. ***Doubles:*** M. Ondruska/B. Talbot (2) d. D. Di Lucia/M. Sell (1) 7–6 6–3.

BUENOS AIRES (ARG) (100) 16–22 NOVEMBER – ***Singles:*** Y. El Aynaoui (5) d. A. Martin 7–6 6–1. ***Doubles:*** G. Canas/M. Garcia (WC) d. A. Martin/S. Navarro 6–7 6–1 6–4.

ANDORRA (AND) (75H) 16–22 NOVEMBER – ***Singles:*** J. Gimelstob (7) d. G. Bastl (Q) 6–3 2–6 7–6. ***Doubles:*** J. Gimelstob/J. Waite (1) d. M. Ardinghi/V. Santopadre 2–6 6–4 6–3.

PUEBLA (MEX) (25H) 16–22 NOVEMBER – ***Singles:*** V. Voltchkov (6) d. C. Rochus 6–3 6–3. ***Doubles:*** A. Hernandez/M. Sanchez d. B. Martinez/G. Motomura (4) 7–6 7–6.

RANCHO MIRAGE, CA (USA) (25H) 16–22 NOVEMBER – ***Singles:*** C. Ruud (2) d. C. Mamiit (SE) 6–7 6–3 6–2. ***Doubles:*** W. Arthurs/P. Tramacchi (1) d. T. Larkham/G. Silcock 6–3 3–6 6–3.

LIMA (PER) (100) 23–29 NOVEMBER – ***Singles:*** S. Koubek (6) d. J. Chela (Q) 6–3 2–6 6–0. ***Doubles:*** D. Del Rio/M. Rodriguez (3) d. F. Browne/E. Medica 6–4 7–6.

BURBANK, CA (USA) (25H) 23–29 NOVEMBER – ***Singles:*** C. Mamiit (SE) d. D. Nainkin (9) 7–6 7–5. ***Doubles:*** M. Bryan/R. Bryan d. D. Di Lucia/M. Sell (2) 6–0 7–6.

PORTOROZ (SLO) (25H) 23–29 NOVEMBER – ***Singles:*** R. Schuttler (6) d. P. Wessels 6–3 6–2. ***Doubles:*** M. Mirnyi/A. Olhovskiy (2) d. A. Kitinov/T. Suzuki (3) 6–4 7–6.

TOLUCA (MEX) (25H) 23–29 NOVEMBER – ***Singles:*** R. Wassen (3) d. G. Etlis 5–7 6–1 6–4. ***Doubles:*** A. Hernandez/M. Sanchez (WC) d. E. Kempes/R. Wassen (2) 6–3 6–4.

GUADALAJARA (MEX) (100) 30 NOVEMBER–6 DECEMBER – ***Singles:*** M. Hipfl d. Y. El Aynaoui (1) 6–7 7–6 7–6. ***Doubles:*** S. Groen/A. Hamadeh d. M. Garcia/S. Prieto 6–4 6–2.

NUMBRECHT (GER) (50H) 30 NOVEMBER–6 DECEMBER – ***Singles:*** C. Vinck d. P. Wessels 6–7 6–4 6–4. ***Doubles:*** M. Mirnyi/A. Olhovskiy (3) d. S. Hirszon/A. Kitinov (4) 6–4 7–6.

PERTH (AUS) (25H) 7–13 DECEMBER – ***Singles:*** L. Hewitt (1) d. M. Draper (3) 6–4 6–4. ***Doubles:*** L. Hewitt/P. Kilderry (2) d. D. Petrovic/G. Silcock (4) 6–7 6–3 7–6.

SANTIAGO II (CHI) (25H) 7–13 DECEMBER – ***Singles:*** G. Gaudio (5) d. K. Alami (1) 6–2 3–6 6–4. ***Doubles:*** E. Artoni/F. Browne (4) d. H. Gamonal/R. Schlachter 6–2 6–4.

AHMEDEBAD (IND) (25H) 21–26 DECEMBER – ***Singles:*** A. Du Puis (2) d. O. Ogorodov (4) 6-4 6–2. ***Doubles:*** N. Okun/N. Welgreen (3) d. N. Behr/E. Ran (1) 3–6 6–0 6–4.

BOMBAY (IND) (25H) 28 DECEMBER–2 JANUARY – ***Singles:*** A. Du Puis (3) d. J. Boutter 7–5 7–6. ***Doubles:*** N. Behr/E. Ran (1) d. M. Bhupathi/G. Natekar (WC) 6–2 7–6.

ITF Men's Circuit

In 1998 there were 52 Satellite Circuits for men in 27 countries and 209 Futures tournaments for men in 52 countries. Each Satellite Circuit comprises three tournaments plus a Masters play-off at which prize money and ranking points are awarded. In 1998 single-week Futures tournaments were played for the first time, giving players more opportunities to earn ranking points and prize money.

Each Satellite Circuit and Futures tournament was organised and run by the National Association of the country in which the event took place. Below are listed the winners of each Satellite Circuit, with the ATP Tour ranking points won in brackets (based on the total number of circuit points plus bonuses during the four weeks). Futures results are listed after this; here (10) and (15) refer to prize money of US$10,000 and US$15,000 respectively.

Satellite Circuits

VALUE CIRCUIT (+ US$'000)	*START*	*SINGLES WINNERS (+PTS)*	*DOUBLES WINNERS (+PTS)*
France I (25)	05–01	S. Saoudi (FRA) (37)	G. Carraz (FRA)/J. Hanquez (FRA) (39)
Italy I (25)	05–01	R. Stepanek (CZE) (55)	M. Ardinghi (ITA)/E. Taino (USA) (45)
Spain I (25)	05–01	J. Rascon (ESP) (50)	J. Carrasco (ESP)/J. Velasco (ESP) (42)
Central America (25)	12–01	E. Kempes (NED) (50)	K. Brill (USA)/J. Palmer (USA) (52)
France II (25)	02–02	O. Malcor (FRA) (50)	G. Carraz (FRA)/J. Hanquez (FRA) (45)
Portugal I (25)	02–02	N. Marques (POR) (47)	J. Cunha-Silva (POR)/N. Marques (POR) (48)
Spain II	02–02	D. Caballero (ESP) (59)	E. Nicolas (ESP)/G. Puentes (ESP) (58)
Cuba/Mexico (25)	09–02	T. El Sawy (EGY) (47)	J. Coetzee (RSA)/J. Weir-Smith (RSA) (50)
Australia I (25H)	02–03	B. Madsen (HAI) (59)	M. Draper (AUS)/T. Mitchell (AUS) (55)
Egypt I (25)	02–03	L. Jonsson (SWE) (53)	P. Dezort (CZE)/P. Kovacka (CZE) (43)
Spain III (25)	02–03	O. Serrano (ESP) (52)	D. Salvador (ESP)/J. Velasco (ESP) (52)
France III (50H)	09–03	N. Thomann (FRA) (67)	P. Pala (CZE)/D. Skoch (CZE) (52)
Mexico I (25)	09–03	J. Palmer (USA) (50)	R. Nicklisch (GER)/P. Sommer (GER) (35)
Croatia I (25)	16–03	C. Rochus (BEL) (44)	D. Fiala (CZE)/T. Krupa (CZE) (48)
USA 1 (50)	30–03	O. Motevassel (USA) (48)	C. Mahony (AUS)/M. Sprengelmeyer (USA) (45)
Chile 1 (25)	06–04	E. Medica (ARG) (48)	F. Allgauer (ITA)/J. Jimenez-Guerra (AND) (40)
New Zealand (25)	06–04	M. Draper (AUS) (49)	J. Greenhalgh (NZL)/A. Painter (AUS) (41)
Spain 4 (25)	06–04	M. Joachim (GER) (45)	E. Nicolas (ESP)/G. Puentes (ESP) (44)
Bulgaria (25)	04–05	M. Velev (BUL) (50)	M. Pampoulov (AUT)/M. Velev (BUL) (41)
Chile 2 (25)	04–05	E. Medica (ARG) (50)	F. Ruiz (CHI)/A. Venero (PER) (49)
Croatia 2 (25)	04–05	I. Ljubicic (CRO) (50)	I. Karlovic (CRO)/Z. Krajan (CRO) (50)
Greece 1 (25)	04–05	Y. Ishii (JPN) (47)	J. Bower (RSA)/D. Roberts (RSA) (48)
Portugal 2 (25)	04–05	N. Marques (POR) (48)	J. Cunha-Silva (POR)/N. Marques (POR) (50)
Australia 2 (25)	11–05	J. Sekulov (AUS) (49)	M. Draper (AUS)/T. Mitchell (AUS) (49)
Spain 5 (25)	11–05	D. Salvador (ESP) (45)	D. Salvador (ESP)/J. Velasco (ESP) (48)
Spain 6 (25)	08–06	V. Sendin (ESP) (51)	C. Martinez (ESP)/M. Roy (ESP) (48)
Netherlands (25H)	15–06	J. Vanek (CZE) 57	M. Bartonek (CZE)/J. Vanek (CZE) (42)
Turkey 1 (25)	15–06	J. Ziv (ISR) (46)	J. Erlich (ISR)/N. Welgreen (ISR) (49)
Italy 2 (25)	29–06	G. Montenet (ITA) (40)	M. Boscatto (ITA)/N. Kischkewitz (FRA) (58)
Japan 1 (25)	29–06	K. Miyachi (JPN) (46)	H. Ishii (JPN)/A. Matsushita (JPN) (44)
Hungary (25)	20–07	Y. Schukin (RUS) (47)	F. Cermak (CZE)/P. Dezort (CZE) (48)
Great Britain (25)	27–07	M. Lee (GBR) (49)	D. Sapsford (GBR)/T. Spinks (GBR) (49)
Slovak Republic (25)	17–08	P. Kralert (CZE) (49)	V. Platenik (SVK)/M. Van Gemerden (NED) (44)
Turkey 2 (25)	17–08	J. Pequery (FRA) (46)	N. Okun (ISR)/O. Sela (ISR) (48)
Italy 3 (25)	31–08	U. Vico (ITA) (47)	T. Chaen (JPN)/K. Masuda (JPN) (44)
Switzerland 1 (25)	31–08	M. Kratochvil (SUI) (39)	M. Muller (GER) (44)/A. Fahlke (GER) (41)
Mexico 3 (25)	14–09	M. Stepanek (CZE) (48)	C. Groer (USA)/C. Singer (USA) (49)
USA 3 (50)	14–09	V. Liukko (FIN) (57)	S. Larose (CAN)/J. Robichaud (CAN) (58)
Australia 3 (25H)	21–09	J. Sirianni (AUS) (59)	A. Painter (AUS)/G. Silcock (AUS) (55)
Greece 2 (25)	28–09	R. Nicklisch (GER) (49)	R. Kokavec (CAN) (49)/Y. Doumbia (SEN) (48)
Portugal 3 (25)	05–10	G. Carraz (FRA) (51)	V. Snyman (RSA)/K. Spencer (GBR) (52)
India (25)	12–10	F. Rovai (SWE) (50)	N. Kirtane (IND)/S. Kirtane (IND) (49)

Jan-Michael Gambill soared up the world rankings to a best-ever No. 38 in 1998. (Stephen Wake)

Spain 8 (25)	19–10	G. Puentes (ESP) (52)	E. Nicolas (ESP)/G. Puentes (ESP) (48)
Switzerland 2 (25)	19–10	R. Federer (SUI) (48)	Y. Allegro (SUI)/R. Federer (SUI) (45)
USA 4 (50)	19–10	V. Liukko (FIN) (56)	C. Groer (USA)/M. Sprengelmeyer (USA) (57)
Czech Republic (25)	26–10	R. Svetlik (CZE) (48)	M. Bartonek (CZE)/P. Kovacka (CZE) (44)
Turkey 3 (25)	26–10	I. Bozic (SLO) (47)	K. Orellana (VEN)/J. Szymanski (VEN) (50)
Central Africa (25)	02–11	J. Coetzee (RSA) (51)	J. Coetzee (RSA)/D. Roberts (RSA) (51)
Israel 2 (25)	02–11	O. Sela (ISR) (49)	J. Erlich (ISR)/A. Hadad (ISR) (45)
Egypt 2 (25)	09–11	F. Messori (ITA) (49)	F. Cermak (CZE)/P. Dezort (CZE) (48)
South Africa (25)	16–11	J. Coetzee (RSA) (52)	J. Coetzee (RSA)/D. Roberts (RSA) (52)

Futures tournaments

NEW DELHI (IND) (10) 29 DECEMBER–2 JANUARY – ***Singles:*** V. Kutsenko (1) d. D. Tomashevich (5) 6–4 6–4. ***Doubles:*** J. Erlich/N. Okun (3) d. J. Delgado/L. Mor (2) 6–7 7–6 7–6.

CHANDIGARH (IND) (10) 5–9 JANUARY – ***Singles:*** S. Fazaluddin (Q) d. P. Srinath 6–4 3–6 6–4. ***Doubles:*** M. Hilpert/T. Meringoff d. A. Hamadeh/A. Rueb (1) 6–3 6–4.

INDORE (IND) (10) 12–16 JANUARY – ***Singles:*** A. Rueb (5) d. T. Meringoff 6–3 6–4. ***Doubles:*** A. Hamadeh/A. Rueb (1) d. J. Erlich/N. Okun (2) 7–6 6–4.

BERGHEIM I (AUT) (10) 2–8 FEBRUARY – ***Singles:*** B. Urh d. K. Bardoczky 6–3 6–1. ***Doubles:*** L. Friedl/M. Stepanek (3) d. M. Menzler/M. Wislsperger (4) 7–6 3–6 6–4.

BRAMHALL (GBR) (15) 4–8 FEBRUARY – ***Singles:*** M. Merry (Q) d. M. Navarra 4–6 7–6 7–6. ***Doubles:*** M. Hellstrom/F. Loven d. M. Merry/M. Navarra 7–6 6–1.

BERGHEIM II (AUT) (10) 9–15 FEBRUARY – ***Singles:*** I. Traykov (Q) d. J. Boutter (7) 6–3 6–2. ***Doubles:*** M. Menzler/M. Wislsperger d. J. Boutter/J. Pequery (4) 4–6 6–1 6–0.

ACCRA I (GHA) (10) 9–15 FEBRUARY – ***Singles:*** G. Castrichella (3) d. S. Randjelovic (1) 6–2 7–5. ***Doubles:*** N. Kischkewitz/M. MacLagan (3) d. F. Beraldo/G. Castrichella (2) w/o.

CHIGWELL (GBR) (15) 11–15 FEBRUARY – ***Singles:*** F. Loven (Q) d. R. Matheson (WC) 6–4 6–1. ***Doubles:*** B. Cowan/T. Spinks (1) d. M. Belgraver/M. Verkerk 6–4 6–4.

MONDSEELAND (AUT) (10) 16–21 FEBRUARY – ***Singles:*** R. Stepanek (5) d. I. Traykov 6–4 7–6. ***Doubles:*** P. Pala/B. Urh (1) d. I. Traykov/M. Velev 6–4 7–6.

ACCRA II (GHA) (10) 16–22 FEBRUARY – ***Singles:*** S. Randjelovic (1) d. M. MacLagan (4) 6–4 6–4. ***Doubles:*** C. Gomez-Diaz/R. Schlachter (1) d. L. Kirschner/W. Winkler 6–2 6–2.

EASTBOURNE (GBR) (15) 18–22 FEBRUARY – ***Singles:*** K. Flygt d. C. Haggard 6–3 6–2. ***Doubles:*** K. Flygt/F. Loven d. B. Cowan/T. Spinks (2) 6–7 6–4 6–4.

LOME (TOG) (10) 23 FEBRUARY–1 MARCH – ***Singles:*** C. N'Goran (7) d. S. Randjelovic (1) 7–6 6–3. ***Doubles:*** P. Madarassy/S. Randjelovic (1) d. J. Jimenez-Guerra/R. Schlachter (2) 7–6 6–4.

OBERHACHING (GER) (10) 25 FEBRUARY–1 MARCH – ***Singles:*** J. Settergren (Q) d. M. Menzler (WC) 6–3 6–3. ***Doubles:*** B. Cowan/N. Gould (2) d. J. Knowle/L. Milligan 1–6 7–6 6–4.

MANILA I (PHI) (15) 2–7 MARCH – ***Singles:*** J. Szymanski (5) d. R. Brostowicz (LL) 6–2 6–1. ***Doubles:*** C. Mamiit/E. Taino d. M. Boye/T. Guardiola 4–6 6–2 6–1.

OFFENBACH (GER) (10) 4–8 MARCH – ***Singles:*** M. Sarstrand (Q) d. N. Gould 6–0 6–3. ***Doubles:*** S. Matheu/O. Morel d. T. Lenho/A. Simoni (4) 7–5 2–6 6–3.

MANILA II (PHI) (15) 9–14 MARCH – ***Singles:*** J. Szymanski (5) d. S. Peppas (Q) 6–3 6–4. ***Doubles:*** C. Chen/H. Lee d. D. Caldwell/C. Tontz 6–1 6–4.

SEROS (GRE) (10) 16–22 MARCH – ***Singles:*** P. Fredriksson (1) d. F. Loven (Q) 6–2 6–2. ***Doubles:*** F. Bergh/J. Hermansson d. P. Fredriksson/F. Loven (2) 6–3 6–2.

JAFFA (ISR) (15) 16–22 MARCH – ***Singles***: H. Levy (WC) d. N. Behr (4) 6–3 6–2. ***Doubles:*** T. Nurminen/J. Ojala d. J. Erlich/A. Hadad 6–2 7–5.

ISHIWA (JPN) (15) 16–22 MARCH – ***Singles:*** V. Kutsenko (5) d. G. Motomura (2) 6–4 6–3. ***Doubles:*** T. Meringoff/A. Rueb d. J. Greenhalgh/A. Painter (1) 6–4 6–2.

CAGLIARI (ITA) (15) 17–22 MARCH – ***Singles:*** D. Caballero d. M. Hantschk (8) 6–1 1–6 7–6. ***Doubles:*** R. Stepanek/M. Tabara d. G. Galimberti/M. Valeri (1) 7–5 6–7 6–4.

ASHKELON (ISR) (15) 23–28 MARCH – ***Singles:*** V. Voltchkov (4) d. E. Erlich (1) 7–5 6–4. ***Doubles:*** H. Levy/L. Mor (4) d. B. Cowan/F. Veglio (1) 6–4 7–6.

KALAMATA (GRE) (10) 23–29 MARCH – ***Singles:*** P. Fredriksson (1) d. L. Manta (4) 6–2 6–1. ***Doubles:*** N. Gould/T. Spinks (3) d. J. Landsberg/K. Pettersson (4) 7–5 6–2.

SASSARI (ITA) (15) 24–29 MARCH – ***Singles:*** K. Tiilikainen (Q) d. M. Hantschk 6–3 6–2. ***Doubles:*** M. Hantschk/J. Unterberger d. J. Jimenez-Guerra/K. Tiilikainen 7–6 6–3.

SHIRAKO (JPN) (15) 25–29 MARCH – ***Singles:*** T. Chaen (5) d. K. Masuda (6) 7–6 7–5. ***Doubles:*** T. Meringoff/A. Rueb d. Y. Ishii/H.Sato 6–0 6–3.

CHALKIDA (GRE) (10) 30 MARCH–4 APRIL – ***Singles:*** J. Brandt (Q) d. F. Jonsson (2) 6–2 6–1. ***Doubles:*** D. Draper/J. Hermansson d. J. Landsberg/K. Pettersson (3) 6–4 6–7 6–1.

ROME (ITA) (10) 14–19 APRIL – ***Singles:*** M. Pastura d. J. Ferrero (Q) 6–4 7–5. ***Doubles:*** A. Calleri/O. Rodriguez d. D. Bottini/D. Caracciolo 6–3 5–7 6–4.

BUENOS AIRES (ARG) (15) 20–26 APRIL – ***Singles:*** R. Schlachter (8) d. A. Garizzio (1) 6–0 6–1.
Doubles: C. Testa/J. Zwetsch (1) d. A. Prieto/R. Schlachter 6–3 6–2.

RIEMERLING (GER) (15) 20–26 APRIL – ***Singles:*** D. Elsner (WC) d. J. Haehnel (Q) 6–0 6–3.
Doubles: T. Cibulec/P. Kovacka d. J. Brandt/T. Messmer (1) 7–5 4–6 6–3.

BOURNEMOUTH (GBR) (15) 20–26 APRIL – ***Singles:*** G. Carraz (7) d. K. Flygt 6–3 6–0.
Doubles: B. Ellwood/K. Flygt (3) d. J. Davidson/J. Fox 6–4 6–3.

ANDIGAN (UZB) (15) 20–26 APRIL – ***Singles:*** M. Mirnyi (4) d. A. Derepasko 3–6 6–0 7–6.
Doubles: M. Mirnyi/V. Voltchkov (1) d. V. Kutsenko/D. Tomashevich (2) 6–2 6–4.

ROME (ITA) (10) 20–26 APRIL – ***Singles:*** A. Calleri (1) d. P. Angelini 6–4 4–6 7–5.
Doubles: A. Calleri/I. Saric d. G. Galimberti/M. Valeri (1) 6–3 6–4.

NAMANGAN (UZB) (15) 27 APRIL–1 MAY – ***Singles:*** G. Motomura (1) d. V. Kutsenko (3) 6–4 7–5.
Doubles: M. Kogan/O. Sela (2) d. Y. Zheng/B. Zhu 6–4 6–4.

MENDOZA (ARG) (15) 27 APRIL–3 MAY – ***Singles:*** R. Schlachter (7) d. A. Aramburu (1) 7–5 6–7 6–4.
Doubles: C. Testa/J. Zwetsch (1) d. A. Prieto/R. Schlachter 6–3 6–4.

ESSLINGEN (GER) (15) 27 APRIL–3 MAY – ***Singles:*** J. Mas (6) d. J. Boutter (8) 6–2 6–2.
Doubles: F. Browne/M. Garcia (1) d. J. Boutter/J. Lisnard (3) 7–6 6–2.

FRASCATI (ITA) (10) 27 APRIL–3 MAY – ***Singles:*** A. Calleri (1) d. G. Galimberti (6) 6–1 6–2.
Doubles: G. Galimberti/M. Valeri (2) d. O. Camporese/I. Ljubicic (1) 7–6 6–1.

HATFIELD (GBR) (15) 29 APRIL–3 MAY – ***Singles:*** C.Rochus d. L. Milligan 6–4 6–7 6–1.
Doubles: J. Bower/D. Roberts (3) d. J. Davidson/J. Fox 6–1 6–2.

BEIJING (CHN) (15) 4–10 MAY – ***Singles:*** Y. Yoon (1) d. H. Kaneko (2) 6–3 7–5.
Doubles: D. Kim/R. Sluiter (1) d. H. Ishii/H. Kaneko 6–1 6–7 6–2.

SCHWABISCH-HALL (GER) (15) 4–10 MAY – ***Singles:*** M. Belgraver (8) d. T. Guardiola (Q) 6–4 6–2.
Doubles: M. Menzler/M. Wislsperger d. K. Bardoczky/T. Gyorgy 6–4 3–6 7–6.

CARDIFF (GBR) (15) 4–10 MAY – ***Singles:*** R. Cadart d. N. Gould 6–4 6–4.
Doubles: N. Gould/T. Spinks (2) d. M. Merry/J. Pequery (1) 6–2 6–0.

TIAN JIN (CHN) (15) 11–17 MAY – ***Singles:*** H. Kaneko (2) d. Y. Yoon (1) 6–4 6–7 6–0.
Doubles: H. Lee/Y. Yoon (1) d. C. Chen/A. Raturandang (3) 6–1 5–7 6–3.

NECKARAU (GER) (15) 11–17 MAY – ***Singles:*** A. Garizzio (1) d. G. Cosac (WC) 6–3 7–6.
Doubles: B. Dabrowski/J. Stasiak d. T. Cibulec/A. Simoni 6–4 6–1.

SARATOV (RUS) (15) 11–17 MAY – ***Singles:*** M. Mirnyi (2) d. A. Stoliarov (1) 6–3 6–2.
Doubles: D. Golovanov/M. Mirnyi d. A. Derepasko/K. Ivanov-Smolensky (2) 6–2 6–3.

DELRAY BEACH, FL (USA) (15) 11–17 MAY – ***Singles:*** R. Agenor d. M. Hill (9) 6–3 6–3.
Doubles: S. Aspelin/C. Tontz (2) d. M. Hill/S. Humphries 6–4 6–4.

BELGRADE (YUG) (10) 11–17 MAY – ***Singles:*** V. Roubicek (4) d. A. Musil (6) 6–1 4–6 6–4.
Doubles: M. Hromec/A. Musil (1) d. N. Gnjatovic/M. Jovanovic (4) 6–1 6–2.

AUGSBURG (GER) (15) 18–24 MAY – ***Singles:*** R. Schlachter (5) d. B. Dabrowski (Q) 1–6 6–2 6–1.
Doubles: S. Bandermann/J. Greenhalgh (3) d. M. Belgraver/M. Verkerk 6–3 6–7 6–1.

SAMARA (RUS) (15) 18–24 MAY – ***Singles:*** M. Mirnyi (2) d. K. Ivanov-Smolensky (5) 3–6 6–0 6–1.
Doubles: D. Golovanov/M. Mirnyi d. A. Derepasko/K. Ivanov-Smolensky (2) 6–4 6–4.
VERO BEACH, FL (USA) (15) 18–24 MAY – ***Singles:*** R. Agenor (12) d. N. Massu 6–3 3–6 6–3.
Doubles: S. Aspelin/C. Tontz (3) d. L. Hjarrand/R. Loel (5) 6–4 6–2.

ROME (ITA) (10) 18–24 MAY – ***Singles:*** G. Gatto (4) d. M. Valeri (7) 6–3 6–1.
Doubles: N. Kischkewitz/M. Valeri (1) d. G. Gatto/E. Grossi (2) 7–5 7–5.

BELGRADE (YUG) (10) 18–24 MAY – ***Singles:*** I Gaudi (4) d. V. Roubicek (1) 6–1 6–2.
Doubles: N. Gnjatovic/D. Petrovic (2) d. M. Boscatto/I. Gaudi (1) 6–3 3–6 6–3.

SOGWIPO (KOR) (15) 25–29 MAY – ***Singles:*** H. Lee (3) d. P. Srichaphan (5) 6–3 6–3.
Doubles: M. Han/S. Lee (Q) d. C. Chen/A. Raturandang 6–2 6–4.

BOCO RATON, FL (USA) (15) 25–31 MAY – ***Singles:*** R. Agenor (4) d. N. Massu (7) 6–1 6–2.
Doubles: T. Berkowitz/J. Gutierrez d. E. Caldas/A. Prieto (3) 6–2 6–3.

PARMA (ITA) (10H) 25–31 MAY – ***Singles:*** M. Valeri (SE) (8) d. Y. Doumbia (Q) (1) 6–4 6–2.
Doubles: G. Galimberti/M. Valeri (1) d. Y. Doumbia/A. Simoni (4) 7–5 3–6 7–5.

SCHWAIGERN (GER) (10) 25–31 MAY – ***Singles:*** O. Malcor (Q) d. D. Moyano (Q) (2) 6–1 4–6 6–4.
Doubles: T. Cibulec/P. Kovacka (3) d. T. Hildebrand/F. Loven 3–6 6–3 7–6.

BELGRADE (YUG) (10) 25–31 MAY – ***Singles:*** V. Roubicek (3) d. A. Banus-Sado 6–4 6–4.
Doubles: D. Fiala/D. Petrovic (1) d. V. Platenik/J. Sirianni (3) 6–3 5–7 6–3.

SOGWIPO (KOR) (15) 1–5 JUNE – ***Singles:*** H. Lee (3) d. N. Welgreen (2) 6–0 6–3.
Doubles: D. Kim/Y. Kim (WC) d. C. Chen/A. Raturandang (2) 6–3 7–5.

DUBLIN (IRL) (15) 1–7 JUNE – ***Singles:*** M. Hill (5) d. N. Okun 4–6 6–4 6–3.
Doubles: H. Levy/R. Weidenfeld (2) d. D. Bracciali/I. Gaudi 7–6 6–4.

TALLAHASSEE, FL (USA) (15) 1–7 JUNE – ***Singles:*** C. Mamiit (1) d. E. Caldas (13) 6–4 6–2.
Doubles: C. Mamiit/K. Spencer d. J. Robichaud/M. Russell (7) 3–6 6–2 6–1.

VILLINGEN (GER) (10H) 1–7 JUNE – ***Singles:*** D. Caballero (4) d. R. Willems 7–6 6–3.
Doubles: L. Friedl/S. Randjelovic d. A. Ferreira/C. Testa (2) 6–4 6–4.

BRESSANONE (ITA) (10) 1–7 JUNE – ***Singles:*** R. Svetlik (6) d. G. Galimberti (WC) (1) 6–1 ret.
Doubles: R. Svetlik/B. Urh (1) d. F. Allgauer/F. Luzzi (4) 6–4 3–6 6–4.

NIS (YUG) (10) 1–7 JUNE – ***Singles:*** M. Colla (5) d. Z. Tosic (WC) 6–2 6–3.
Doubles: D. Fiala/D. Petrovic (1) d. M. Pampoulov/P. Taicher (2) w/o.

DUBLIN (IRL) (15) 8–13 JUNE – ***Singles:*** J. Knowle (2) d. D. Bracciali 6–4 4–6 6–2.
Doubles: M. Hill/S. Humphries d. J. Coetzee/D. Roberts (1) 3–6 6–3 6–2.

OULU (FIN) (10) 8–14 JUNE – ***Singles:*** V. Liukko d. M. Sarstrand (2) 6–4 6–2.
Doubles: T. Hildebrand/V. Liukko (2) d. J. Landsberg/K. Pettersson (1) 7–5 6–3.

VALDENGO (ITA) (10) 8–14 JUNE – ***Singles:*** B. Urh (7) d. N. Kischkewitz (5) 6–2 6–1.
Doubles: N. Kischkewitz/G. Marx (1) d. F. Massetta/A. Schneiter (WC) 6–1 6–2.

ZAJECAR (YUG) (10) 8–14 JUNE – ***Singles:*** M. Velev (1) d. D. Petrovic (4) 6–4 7–6.
Doubles: D. Fiala/D. Petrovic (1) d. M. Jancso/G. Jaross (3) 6–1 3–6 6–3.

CORFU (GRE) (15) 15–21 JUNE – ***Singles:*** L. Mor (2) d. S. Peppas 6–1 3–6 6–3.
Doubles: G. Elseneer/W. Neefs (2) d. N. Karagiannis/A. Vasiliadis (3) 6–4 6–2

KRAKOW (POL) (15) 15–21 JUNE – ***Singles:*** A. Schneiter (1) d. B. Dabrowski (8) 7–5 6–4.
Doubles: T. Cibulec/P. Szczepanik (3) d. M. Chmela/M. Gawlowski 7–6 7–6.

LAFAYETTE, LA (USA) (15) 15–21 JUNE – ***Singles:*** C. Mamiit (1) d. N. Massu (Q) (2) 0–6 6–3 6–0.
Doubles: C. Groer/M. Sprengelmeyer (1) d. L. Dahan/R. Weidenfeld 7–6 7–5.

MISSISSAUGA (CAN) (10) 15–21 JUNE – ***Singles:*** E. Agaev d. J. Robichaud (4) 6–4 6–2.
Doubles: A. Hamadeh/T. Meringoff (1) d. J. Robichaud/M. Russell (2) 6–4 6–7 6–3.

VIERUMAKI (FIN) (10) 15–21 JUNE – ***Singles:*** T. Lenho (2) d. T. Nurminen (1) 6–1 6–3.
Doubles: J. Landsberg/K. Pettersson (1) d. J. Gisbert/A. Tattermusch 7–6 6–3.

SKOPJE (MKD) (10) 15–21 JUNE – ***Singles:*** C. Buscaglione (5) d. M. Velev (1) 4–6 6–4 6–3.
Doubles: M. Pampoulov/M. Velev (1) d. C. Buscaglione/O. Knutel (2) 3–6 6–4 6–4.

TURIN (ITA) (10) 16–21 JUNE – ***Singles:*** O. Malcor (4) d. M. El Aarej 6–3 1–0 ret.
Doubles: O. Camporese/J. Cunha-Silva (1) d. G. Gatto/U. Vico (4) 7–5 7–5.

ALBSTADT (GER) (10) 17–21 JUNE – ***Singles:*** D. Elsner (WC) d. C. Arriens (Q) 6–3 6–2.
Doubles: J. Giner/J. Vicente (3) d. C. Mahony/J. Weir-Smith (1) 2–6 6–3 6–1.

BUDAPEST (HUN) (10) 17–21 JUNE – ***Singles:*** R. Falenti (1) d. K. Bardoczky (WC) (2) 6–4 4–6 6–4.
Doubles: K. Bardoczky/M. Jancso (1) d. A. La Porte/C. Saulnier (4) 6–4 5–7 6–4.
ATHENS (GRE) (15) 22–28 JUNE – ***Singles:*** L. Mor (2) d. N. Okun (4) 6–4 6–1.
Doubles: L. Mor/W. Neefs (1) d. K. Economidis/N. Rovas 7–5 6–3.

ZABRZE (POL) (15) 22–28 JUNE – ***Singles:*** J. Hernych d. C. Gomez-Diaz (3) 6–4 6–7 6–2.
Doubles: F. Cermak/P. Dezort (3) d. P. Szczepanik/P. Taicher (4) 6–1 0–1 ret.

MONTREAL (CAN) (10) 22–28 JUNE – ***Singles:*** H. Lee (3) d. M. Russell (2) 6–0 7–5.
Doubles: S. Larose/J. Robichaud (1) d. J. Brandt/M. Russell 6–3 6–4.

VELI LOSINJ (CRO) (10) 22–28 JUNE – ***Singles:*** M. Tkalec (7) d. S. Hirszon (4) 4–1 ret.
Doubles: S. Hirszon/Z. Krajan (1) d. I. Karlovic/I. Saric (2) 7–6 6–3.

HAMEENLINNA (FIN) (10) 22–28 JUNE – ***Singles:*** T. Nurminen (1) d. J. Sirianni (2) 6–0 6–0.
Doubles: L. Ketola/J. Ojala d. J. Davidson/P. Langvardt (4) 3–6 6–3 6–2.

KOCANI (MKD) (10) 22–28 JUNE – ***Singles:*** M. Markov (8) d. A. Di Mauro (2) 7–5 4–6 6–1.
Doubles: M. Pampoulov/M. Velev (1) d. E. Csarnakovics/S. Galvani (3) 7–5 6–3.

WACO, TX (USA) (15) 23–28 JUNE – ***Singles:*** R. Bryan (7) d. M. Breen (Q) 6–4 2–6 7–5.
Doubles: M. Bryan/R. Bryan (4) d. B. Hawk/A. Peterson (1) 7–5 7–5.

BUDAPEST (HUN) (10) 24–28 JUNE – ***Singles:*** K. Bardoczky (1) d. I. Neumuller (7) 7–5 4–6 6–4.
Doubles: L. Fono/K. Keresztes (WC) d. K. Bardoczky/M. Jancso (1) 6–1 7–6.

TRIER (GER) (15) 24–28 JUNE – ***Singles:*** D. Elsner (8) d. I. Gaudi (7) 6–3 6–7 6–3.
Doubles: G. Fauser/T. Messmer d. J. Gerlach/J. Gruninger 6–4 6–4.

KOLDING (DEN) (10) 29 JUNE–4 JULY – ***Singles:*** F. Fetterlein (2) d. A. Vinciguerra (Q) 6–1 6–2.
Doubles: P. Harris/T. Perry d. J. Printzlau/J. Tribler (4) 2–6 6–3 6–4.

BOUCHERVILLE (CAN) (10) 29 JUNE–5 JULY – ***Singles:*** H. Lee (8) d. J. Sekulov (Q) (1) 4–6 6–4 6–1.
Doubles: T. Berkowitz/J. Gutierrez d. H. Lee/Y. Yoon 6–3 1–6 6–3.

MALI LOSINJ (CRO) (10) 29 JUNE–5 JULY – ***Singles:*** V. Platenik d. V. Roubicek (2) 6–1 6–0.
Doubles: L. Kutanjac/V. Platenik (3) d. G. Oresic/I. Vajda (4) w/o.

COLLEGE STATION, TX (USA) (15) 30 JUNE–5 JULY – ***Singles***: R. Sachire (Q) d. N. Todero (9) 7–6 6–3.
Doubles: B. Gabler/A. Swan d. E. Jacques/M. Mather 6–3 6–4.

KASSEL (GER) (15H) 1–5 JULY – ***Singles:*** A. Schneiter (7) d. S. Cobolli 6–0 4–6 6–4.
Doubles: E. Artoni/F. Browne (1) d. A. Aramburu/G. Gaudio 6–3 6–3.

SOPRON (HUN) (10) 1–5 JULY – ***Singles:*** G. Kisgyorgy (5) d. Z. Nagy 6–4 4–2 ret.
Doubles: G. Kisgyorgy/D. Petrovic (3) d. A. Sikanov/A. Youznyi 6–2 7–6.

ODENSE (DEN) (10) 6–11 JULY – ***Singles:*** R. De Mesa d. R. Rake 6–3 6–3.
Doubles: J. Printzlau/J. Tribler (4) d. D. Pahlsson/R. Samuelsson 7–6 6–4.

VERIA (GRE) (15) 6–12 JULY – ***Singles:*** L. Mor (2) d. H. Levy (1) 6–4 6–4.
Doubles: M. Menzler/P. Sommer (1) d. M. Kogan/A. Ram (2) 6–0 6–4.

ALBUFERETA (ESP) (15) 6–12 JULY -***Singles:*** A. Schneiter (1) d. J. Giner 6–3 6–0.
Doubles: J. Giner/J. Vicente (2) d. S. Duran/J. Perez-Vasquez 6–4 7–6.

BOURG-EN-BRESSE (FRA) (10H) 6–12 JULY – ***Singles:*** J. Haehnel d. H. Armando (5) 6–2 6–2.
Doubles: H. Armando/P. Bianchi d. J. Haehnel/M. Llodra 6–3 1–6 6–2.

MALI LOSINJ (CRO) (10) 6–12 JULY – ***Singles:*** A. Belobrajdic (1) d. I Cinkus (Q) 6–3 7–5.
Doubles: G. Prpic/K. Ritz d. B. Celiscak/V. Pest 6–0 6–3.

TULSA, OK (USA) (15) 7–12 JULY – ***Singles:*** R. Bryan (5) d. A. Peterson (4) 6–2 6–1.
Doubles: M. Bryan/R. Bryan (4) d. J. Roddick/R. Sachire (WC) 7–6 6–3.

SEEFELD (AUT) (10) 8–12 JULY – ***Singles:*** P. Dezort (8) d. T. Schiessling (Q) (4) 5–7 6–2 7–6.
Doubles: A. Musil/D. Petrovic (1) d. R. Dueller/Z. Mlynarik (2) 6–4 6–3.

LEUN (GER) (10) 8–12 JULY – ***Singles:*** T. Behrend (2) d. M. Tahiri 6–3 7–6.
Doubles: M. Huning/T. Huning (4) d. T. Behrend/F. Stauder 6–3 6–2.

AIX-EN-PROVENCE (FRA) (10) 13–18 JULY – ***Singles:*** C. Gomez-Diaz (3) d. H. Armando (4) 6–4 6–4.
Doubles: H. Armando/P. Bianchi d. S. Matheu/O. Morel (1) 6–4 7–5.

SVENDBORG (DEN) (10) 13–19 JULY – ***Singles:*** J. Settergren d. A. Pretzsch 7–5 6–1.
Doubles: L. Holland/J. Sirianni d. J. Arnedo/P. Hartveg (3) 6–1 6–1.

ATHENS (GRE) (15) 13–19 JULY – ***Singles:*** H. Levy (2) d. W. Neefs (5) 6–0 6–1.
Doubles: H. Levy/L. Mor (1) d. G. Elseneer/W. Neefs (3) 6–3 0–6 6–3.

ELCHE (ESP) (15) 13–19 JULY – ***Singles:*** G. Gaudio (3) d. D. Hipperdinger (7) 6–3 6–4.
Doubles: S. Duran/J. Perez-Vasquez d. J. Ferrero/F. Lopez 7–6 6–3.
SCHWAZ (AUT) (10) 15–19 JULY – ***Singles:*** H. Moretti (1) d. T. Schiessling 0–6 6–4 6–4.
Doubles: P. Hanley/D. Petrovic (2) d. T. Cibulec/A. Musil (1) 4–6 6–1 6–4.

KRANJ (SLO) (10) 15–19 JULY – ***Singles:*** P. Kudrnac (Q) d. B. Borgula (4) 7–6 6–4.
Doubles: L. Friedl/P. Kovacka (1) d. B. Borgula/V. Platenik (2) 6–3 6–3.

BERGHEIM (AUT) (10) 20–24 JULY – ***Singles:*** A. Peya (WC) d. G. Castrichella (2) 2–6 6–3 6–0.
Doubles: P. Sommer/M. Wislsperger (1) d. L. Rehmann/U. Seetzen (3) 6–4 6–4.

LONDRINA (BRA) (15) 20–26 JULY – ***Singles:*** S. Roitman d. P. Taicher 6–3 6–4.
Doubles: D. Furmanski/M. Garcia (1) d. A. Simoni/P. Taicher (3) 7–5 5–4 ret.

AIX-LES-BAINS (FRA) (10) 20–26 JULY – ***Singles:*** M. Boye d. M. Canovas 7–6 6–4.
Doubles: R. Alvarez/P. Bianchi d. M. Muzikant/K. Patel 6–4 6–2.

GANDIA (ESP) (10) 20–26 JULY – ***Singles:*** J. Ferrero (4) d. G. Fraile (3) 6–2 6–0.
Doubles: G. Fraile/J. Saiz d. R. Diaz/F. Sanchez 4–6 6–3 7–6.

PORTOROZ (SLO) (10) 22–26 JULY – ***Singles:*** J. Vacek (Q) (6) d. I. Gaudi (Q) (3) w/o.
Doubles: A. Kracman/B. Trupej (WC) d. L. Friedl/P. Kovacka (1) 6–4 7–6.

CAMPOS DO JORDAO (BRA) (15) 27 JULY-2 AUGUST – ***Singles:*** J. Chela d. F. Saretta (Q) 7–5 6–1. ***Doubles:*** N. Aerts/C. Testa (1) d. R. Schlachter/T. Shimada (2) 6–4 3–6 6–4.

CAIRO (EGY) (10) 27 JULY–2 AUGUST – ***Singles:*** M. Tahiri (3) d. J. Zaatini (4) 1–6 6–2 6–1. ***Doubles:*** P. Gottesleben/M. Hromec (1) d. J. Zaatini/S. Zaman (2) 6–2 7–6.

TOULON (FRA) (10) 27 JULY–2 AUGUST – ***Singles:*** I. Rodrigo-Marin d. C. Saulnier 6–2 6–3. ***Doubles:*** L. Olguin/K. Orellana (3) d. R. Alvarez/P. Bianchi (2) 6–7 6–3 6–1.

FORLI (ITA) (10) 27 JULY–2 AUGUST – ***Singles:*** G. Luddi (WC) (4) d. P. Angelini (5) 6–0 6–2. ***Doubles:*** F. Allgauer/I. Gaudi (WC) (1) d. A. Da Col/M. Gotti 4–6 7–5 6–3.

DENIA (ESP) (10) 27 JULY –2 AUGUST – ***Singles:*** J. Perez-Vasquez d. O. Martinez (3) 6–4 6–0. ***Doubles:*** P. Canovas-Garcia/J. Giner d. J. Lido/S. Ventura (4) w/o.

NEVO MESTO (SLO) (10) 29 JULY–2 AUGUST – ***Singles:*** J. Bozic (Q) d. L. Svarc 7–6 6–4. ***Doubles:*** J. Bozic/B. Trupej (WC) d. R. Chrz/J. Hernych 7–6 6–4.

LOUVAIN-LA-NEUVE (BEL) (15) 3–9 AUGUST – ***Singles:*** K. Flygt (2) d. T. Aerts 3–6 6–2 6–0. ***Doubles:*** N. Coutelot/J. Potron (3) d. C. Rochus/O. Rochus (4) 6–3 2–6 6–2.

GARDONE VAL TROMPIA (ITA) (15) 3–9 AUGUST – ***Singles:*** M. Wislsperger d. N. Kischkewitz (3) 7–5 4–6 7–6. ***Doubles:*** M. Menzler/M. Wislsperger (1) d. L. Olguin/M. Pastura (2) 7–6 5–7 6–3.

GUAYAQUIL (ECU) (10) 3–9 AUGUST – ***Singles:*** L. Horna (Q) (6) d. S. Roitman (Q) (5) 6–1 7–6. ***Doubles:*** L. Horna/R. Rake (3) d. R. Pena/S. Roitman (4) 6–4 6–1.

CAIRO (EGY) (10) 3–9 AUGUST – ***Singles:*** S. Galvani (Q) (2) d. M. El Aarej (1) 3–6 6–1 6–1. ***Doubles:*** A. Ghoneim/K. Maamoun d. P. Cannova/M. Pontarin 7–6 6–3.

PARNU (EST) (10) 3–9 AUGUST – ***Singles:*** P. Szczepanik d. J. Ojala (2) 6–7 7–5 7–5. ***Doubles:*** H. Andersson/N. Timfjord (3) d. L. Ketola/J. Ojala (4) 6–3 7–5.

XATIVA (ESP) (10) 3–9 AUGUST – ***Singles:*** J. Giner (3) d. P. Rico (WC) 6–4 3–6 6–3. ***Doubles:*** A. Banos-Florez/R. Serpa-Guinazu (2) d. C. Castellanos/A. Martin (1) 6–2 6–4.

MARIBOR (SLO) (10) 5–9 AUGUST – ***Singles:*** Z. Krajan (8) d. J. Vacek (4) 6–3 6–3. ***Doubles:*** L. Friedl/P. Kovacka (1) d. J. Hernych/J. Vacek 6–3 6–2.

CAIRO (EGY) (10) 10–14 AUGUST – ***Singles:*** M. Tahiri (3) d. T. Quahabi (Q) 6–1 6–0. ***Doubles:*** T. Maier/D. Merkert d. K. Ben Mansour/T. Quahabi 4–6 7–6 6–4.

CHARLEROI (BEL) (15) 10–15 AUGUST – ***Singles:*** F. Loven (6) d. R. Willems (1) 6–0 6–3. ***Doubles:*** A. Fontaine/W. Neefs (1) d. P. Schaul/M. Scheidweiller 7–6 5–7 6–1.

MINSK (BLR) (15) 10–16 AUGUST – ***Singles:*** D. Tomashevich (1) d. I. Kunitcin (8) 6–4 7–6. ***Doubles:*** E. Mikheev/A. Samets d. P. Szczepanik/D. Tomashevich (1) 7–6 6–2.

VARESE (ITA) (15) 10–16 AUGUST – ***Singles:*** C. Saulnier (5) d. I. Rodrigo-Marin 6–3 6–3. ***Doubles:*** M. Boscatto/S. Tarallo (3) d. L. Olguin/M. Pastura (2) 7–6 7–5.

UMAG (CRO) (10) 10–16 AUGUST – ***Singles:*** J. Herm-Zahlava d. J. Bozic (Q) 6–1 6–1. ***Doubles:*** I. Karlovic/L. Zovko d. J. Bozic/M. Por (Q) 7–5 7–6.

QUITO (ECU) (10) 10–16 AUGUST – ***Singles:*** M. Tobon (1) d. R. Valdes (3) 6–3 6–4. ***Doubles:*** P. Braga/J. Gamboa d. A. Garcia/R. Valdes (2) 3–6 6–4 6–4.

JURMALA (LAT) (10) 10–16 AUGUST – ***Singles:*** A. Popp (2) d. J. Ojala (1) 6–4 6–3. ***Doubles:*** M. Jorquera/R. Lindstedt d. G. Dzelde/A. Filimonovs 5–7 6–3 6–3.

SUBOTICA (YUG) (10) 10–16 AUGUST – ***Singles:*** J. Perez-Vasquez (8) d. I. Traykov (5) 6–4 6–1. ***Doubles:*** M. Kogan/D. Petrovic (1) d. M. Hromec/A. Musil (2) 6–3 7–5.

VILNIUS (LTU) (10) 17–22 AUGUST – ***Singles:*** J. Ortegren (LL) (1) d. A. Gietl (Q) 6–3 6–1. ***Doubles:*** V. Bruthans/J. Shortall (4) d. C. Campbell/M. Pehar (3) 2–6 6–3 7–5.

PAVIA (ITA) (15) 17–23 AUGUST – ***Singles:*** R. Willems (3) d. R. Svetlik 4–6 6–1 6–1. ***Doubles:*** E. Artoni/S. Scaiola (1) d. M. Boscatto/S. Tarallo (2) 6–2 6–2.

VIGO (ESP) (15) 17–23 AUGUST – ***Singles:*** N. Massu (2) d. T. Robredo (WC) 6–4 6–2. ***Doubles:*** P. Canovas-Garcia/T. Robredo d. I. Guezurraga/E. Velez 6–4 6–2.

IBARRA (ECU) (10) 17–23 AUGUST – ***Singles:*** M. Tobon (6) d. S. Roitman (5) 6–1 6–2. ***Doubles:*** P. Moggio/M. Tobon (2) d. D. Ayala/R. De Mesa 7–6 3–6 7–6.

NIS (YUG) (10) 17–23 AUGUST – ***Singles:*** I. Traykov (4) d. M. Pampoulov (3) 6–2 6–3. ***Doubles:*** J. Arnedo/N. Gnjatovic (2) d. M. Hromec/D. Petrovic (1) 6–4 7–6.

VIENNA (AUT) (15) 18–22 AUGUST – ***Singles:*** T. Schiessling (6) d. M. Kratochvil 6–3 6–4. ***Doubles:*** P. Dezort/P. Kovacka (1) d. W. Neefs/J. Unterberger (2) 7–6 6–4.

MOSCOW (RUS) (15) 18–22 AUGUST – ***Singles:*** P. Gottesleben (8) d. A. Gavrilov (2) 7–6 7–6. ***Doubles:*** K. Ivanov-Smolensky/D. Tomashevich (1) d. E. Mikheev/A. Samets (2) 6–7 7–5 6–2.

UMAG (CRO) (10) 18–23 AUGUST – ***Singles:*** L. Zovko (WC) d. B. Trupej 6–1 3–6 6–4. ***Doubles:*** S. Aspelin/H. Koll (1) d. I. Karlovic/L. Zovko 7–5 6–4.

IRUN (ESP) (15) 24–30 AUGUST – ***Singles:*** N. Massu (SE) (1) d. M. Boye (6) 6–4 3–6 6–3. ***Doubles:*** A. Martin/N. Massu (1) d. M. Roy/J. Saiz (3) 7–6 7–5.

NIKSIC (YUG) (10) 24–30 AUGUST – ***Singles:*** I. Traykov (3) d. J. Perez-Vasquez (5) 6–3 6–2. ***Doubles:*** N. Gnjatovic/D. Petrovic (1) d. J. Arnedo/M. Kogan (2) 6–4 5–7 6–2.

VIENNA (AUT) (15) 25–30 AUGUST – ***Singles:*** J. Vacek d. T. Catar (1) 4–6 6–4 7–6. ***Doubles:*** W. Neefs/J. Unterberger (4) d. M. Muller/P. Sommer (1) 5–7 6–3 6–1.

MANERBIO (ITA) (15) 25–30 AUGUST – ***Singles:*** R. Svetlik (SE) d. G. Luddi (WC) (5) 1–6 7–6 6–0. ***Doubles:*** F. Messori/M. Valeri d. M. Boscatto/N. Kischkewitz (2) 6–4 3–6 6–1.

UMAG (CRO) (10) 25–30 AUGUST – ***Singles:*** Z. Krajan (1) d. I. Karlovic (LL) 6–3 3–6 6–3. ***Doubles:*** J. Dumanic/K. Ritz (2) d. T. Crichton/D. McNamara 0–6 7–6 7–6.

GORLOVKA (UKR) (15) 26–30 AUGUST – ***Singles:*** D. Poliakov (WC) d. J. Ziv (Q) (3) 5–7 7–6 6–4. ***Doubles:*** M. Jorquera/C. N'Goran (1) d. A. Gavrilov/E. Mikheev 7–5 6–2.

LIMA (PER) (10) 31 AUGUST–6 SEPTEMBER – ***Singles:*** L. Horna (1) d. M. Daniel 7–6 6–4. ***Doubles:*** M. Daniel/R. Monte (4) d. L. Horna/R. Rake (2) 5–7 7–6 7–5.

SANTANDER (ESP) (15) 31 AUGUST–6 SEPTEMBER – ***Singles:*** J. Ferrero (3) d. E. Viuda (2) 6–1 6–1. ***Doubles:*** D. Pahlsson/R. Samuelsson d. J. Ferrero/F. Lopez 6–3 3–6 6–2.

GALATI (ROM) (15) 1–5 SEPTEMBER – ***Singles:*** B. Dabrowski (2) d. P. Thornadtsson (4) 7–5 ret. ***Doubles:*** J. Knowle/P. Szczepanik (1) d. F. Aniola/M. Domka (Q) 6–4 6–7 6–3.

GORLOVKA (UKR) (15) 1–6 SEPTEMBER – ***Singles:*** I. Kunitcin d. K. Ivanov-Smolensky (7) 7–6 6–3. ***Doubles:*** K. Ivanov-Smolensky/D. Tomashevich (1) d. L. Dahan/C. N'Goran 4–6 6–1 6–0.

BAGNERES DE BIGORRE (FRA) (15H) 7–13 SEPTEMBER – ***Singles:*** T. Guardiola (WC) d. M. Joachim (4) 6–2 6–3. ***Doubles:*** J. Lisnard/M. Llodra (3) d. Y. Doumbia/L. Manta (1) 3–6 6–3 7–6.

BACAU (ROM) (15) 7–13 SEPTEMBER – ***Singles:*** B. Dabrowski (2) d. M. Logarzo 6–1 6–2. ***Doubles:*** M. Jorquera/R. Lindstedt (2) d. B. Dabrowski/M. Gawlowski (1) 7–6 4–6 7–6.

OVIEDO (ESP) (15) 7–13 SEPTEMBER – ***Singles:*** R. Cadart (3) d. V. Sendin (1) 6–3 6–1. ***Doubles:*** D. Morente/A. Weber d. R. Menendez/F. Sanchez 2–6 6–0 6–3.

LIMA (PER) (10) 7–13 SEPTEMBER – ***Singles:*** L. Horna (3) d. C. Gomez-Diaz (1) 7–6 7–6. ***Doubles:*** P. Carvallo/E. Massa d. A. Prieto/P. Taicher (1) 6–3 7–6.

OSLO (NOR) (10) 14–19 SEPTEMBER – ***Singles:*** N. Timfjord (4) d. J. Hermansson (7) 4–6 6–3 7–6. ***Doubles:*** L. Hjarrand/H. Koll (2) d. B. Gabler/A. Swan 6–1 3–6 6–3.

MULHOUSE (FRA) (15H) 14–20 SEPTEMBER – ***Singles:*** L. Manta (4) d. T. Guardiola 6–7 6–0 6–2. ***Doubles:*** A. Rueb/V. Snyman (1) d. K. Spencer/L. Vosloo (4) 6–4 6–1.

LIMA (PER) (10) 14–20 SEPTEMBER – ***Singles:*** L. Horna (8) d. C. Gomez-Diaz (2) 6–2 7–6. ***Doubles:*** P. Carvallo/E. Massa d. K. Brill/J. Coetzee (1) 3–6 6–2 7–6.

PLAISIR (FRA) (15H) 21–27 SEPTEMBER – ***Singles:*** R. Gilbert (2) d. D. Bracciali (1) 6–3 6–1. ***Doubles:*** A. Rueb/V. Snyman (2) d. J. Lisnard/M. Llodra 6–4 6–2.

LA PAZ (BOL) (10) 21–27 SEPTEMBER – ***Singles:*** E. Redondi (Q) d. P. Taicher (1) 6–4 6–3. ***Doubles:*** P. Braga/V. Romero d. K. Brill/P. Taicher (1) 4–6 7–6 7–6.

GOTHENBURG (SWE) (10) 22–26 SEPTEMBER – ***Singles:*** F. Jonsson (1) d. N. Timfjord (6) 6–3 6–4. ***Doubles:*** M. Arnold/T. Meringoff (3) d. J. Christensen/R. Lindstedt 4–6 6–4 6–3.

SUNDERLAND (GBR) (10) 23–27 SEPTEMBER – ***Singles:*** M. Lee (1) d. R. Matheson (8) 4–6 7–5 6–4. ***Doubles:*** R. Matheson/T. Spinks (2) d. J. Delgado/M. Lee (3) 6–3 6–4.

GOTHENBURG (SWE) (10) 28 SEPTEMBER–2 OCTOBER – ***Singles:*** M. Hellstrom (8) d. J. Hermansson 3–6 6–1 6–4. ***Doubles:*** J. Christensen/R. Lindstedt d. M. Spottl/J. Unterberger 6–4 6–4.

NEVERS (FRA) (15) 28 SEPTEMBER–4 OCTOBER – ***Singles:*** R. Gilbert (1) d. J. Bachelot (2) 2–6 7–6 6–3. ***Doubles:*** J. Lisnard/M. Llodra (3) d. A. Rueb/V. Snyman (2) 6–3 6–7 6–3.

BELGRADE (YUG) (15) 28 SEPTEMBER–4 OCTOBER – tournament abandoned due to political situation.

COCHABAMBA (BOL) (10) 28 SEPTEMBER–4 OCTOBER – ***Singles:*** P. Carvallo (4) d. P. Braga 6–4 6–1. ***Doubles:*** J. Loglo/L. Navarro d. M. Daniel/R. Monte (3) 5–7 6–4 7–5.

FUKOUKA (JPN) (15) 30 SEPTEMBER–4 OCTOBER – ***Singles:*** O. Kwon (5) d. T. Terachi (4) 6–2 6–4. ***Doubles:*** C. Chen/B. Lin d. W. Cheng/A. Qureshi (WC) 6–3 3–6 6–1.

GLASGOW (GBR) (10) 30 SEPTEMBER–4 OCTOBER – ***Singles:*** A. Popp (6) d. A. Weber (7) 3–6 6–3 6–2. ***Doubles:*** J. Davidson/D. Sherwood d. R. Matheson/T. Spinks (1) 6–4 5–7 6–4.

FERGANA (UZB) (15) 5–10 OCTOBER – ***Singles:*** A. Stoliarov (3) d. O. Ogorodov (WC) (2) 6–2 6–1. ***Doubles:*** O. Ogorodov/D. Tomashevich (1) d. M. Nielsen/V. Platenik (2) w/o.

OULU (FIN) (10) 5–10 OCTOBER – ***Singles:*** A. Vinciguerra (6) d. O. Tauma (7) 6–3 1–0 ret. ***Doubles:*** R. Lindstedt/R. Samuelsson d. A. Fisher/A. Ford (2) 6–3 6–4.

FORBACH (FRA) (10) 5–11 OCTOBER – ***Singles:*** O. Rochus (Q) d. P. Riha 6–4 6–7 6–3. ***Doubles:*** P. Kudrnac/R. Zitko d. C. N'Goran/N. Perrein (4) 6–1 6–4.

SANTA CRUZ (BOL) (10) 5–11 OCTOBER – ***Singles:*** D. Veronelli (6) d. P. Carvallo (5) 6–2 6–3. ***Doubles:*** S. Contador/E. Rincon d. K. Brill/P. Carvallo (1) 4–6 6–3 6–2.

LEEDS (GBR) (15) 7–11 OCTOBER – ***Singles:*** A. Popp d. R. Smotlak 6–2 3–6 6–3. ***Doubles:*** I. Bates/A. Popp d. J. Lisnard/A. Naumann (3) 6–4 4–6 6–4.

MAISHIMA (JPN) (15) 7–11 OCTOBER – ***Singles:*** H. Lee (1) d. Y. Yoon (Q) (2) 7–6 2–6 6–4. ***Doubles:*** H. Lee/Y. Yoon (2) d. C. Chen/B. Lin 6–4 1–4 ret.

KARSHI (UZB) (15) 12–17 OCTOBER – ***Singles:*** O. Ogorodov (3) d. T. Nurminen (1) 6–2 6–3. ***Doubles:*** O. Ogorodov/D. Tomashevich (1) d. A. Merinov/A. Stoliarov (4) 3–6 6–2 6–3.

SAINT DIZIER (FRA) (10) 12–18 OCTOBER – ***Singles:*** S. Blanc d. J. Delinbeuf 4–6 6–1 7–5. ***Doubles:*** P. Kudrnac/R. Zitko d. G. Bergraaf/M. Van Gemerden 6–4 6–4.

SANTA FE (ARG) (10) 12–18 OCTOBER – ***Singles:*** R. Alvarez (3) d. M. Pastura (2) 7–6 1–0 ret. ***Doubles:*** I. Gonzalez-King/E. Massa d. R. Cerdera/S. Weisz 5–7 6–4 6–3.

EDINBURGH (GBR) (15) 14–18 OCTOBER – ***Singles:*** A. Popp d. M. Menzler (6) 6–2 6–3. ***Doubles:*** A. Naumann/A. Rueb (4) d. J. Davidson/D. Sherwood 6–3 6–2.

LA ROCHE SUR YON (FRA) (10H) 19–25 OCTOBER – ***Singles:*** R. Cadart (WC) (3) d. R. Lavergne (WC) (1) 6–1 6–0. ***Doubles:*** R. Lavergne/G. Marx (1) d. S. Matheu/O. Morel (3) 6–2 6–1.

RESISTENCIA-CHACO (ARG) (10) 19–25 OCTOBER – ***Singles:*** R. Alvarez (3) d. G. Coria (WC) 6–4 6–1. ***Doubles:*** M. Barman/S. Di Stefano (WC) d. I. Gonzalez-King/E. Massa 3–6 6–3 6–4.

RODEZ (FRA) (10) 26–31 OCTOBER – ***Singles:*** O. Rochus (Q) d. M. Belgraver (3) 4–6 6–3 6–1. ***Doubles:*** S. Matheu/O. Morel (2) d. J. Cuaz/W. Neefs (1) 5–7 7–6 7–5.

TUNIS (TUN) (15) 26 OCTOBER–1 NOVEMBER – ***Singles:*** R. Cadart (8) d. F. Cermak (Q) 7–6 6–3. ***Doubles:*** A. Banos-Florez/O. Burrieza (4) d. F. Cermak/P. Dezort (1) 2–6 6–4 6–3.

BEAUMARIS, VIC (AUS) (15) 28 OCTOBER–1 NOVEMBER – ***Singles:*** J. Sirianni (2) d. T. Mitchell (3) 6–2 6–4. ***Doubles:*** P. Hanley/N. Healey (4) d. T. Crichton/D. McNamara 4–6 7–5 7–6.

ANDAR SERI BEGAWAN (BRU) (10) 26–30 OCTOBER – ***Singles:*** M. Jessup (6) d. Y. Yamamoto (3) 6–4 6–3. ***Doubles:*** T. Shimada/J. Thomas (1) d. M. Jessup/M. Le 6–3 6–3.

BUENOS AIRES (ARG) (10) 26 OCTOBER–1 NOVEMBER – ***Singles:*** J. Chela (4) d. R. Alvarez 6–4 6–1. ***Doubles:*** E. Artoni/M. Pastura (2) d. H. Armando/P. Bianchi 6–4 6–0.

TUNIS (TUN) (15) 2–7 NOVEMBER – ***Singles:*** O. Burrieza (4) d. M. Tahiri 6–2 2–6 6–2. ***Doubles:*** F. Cermak/P. Dezort (1) d. A. Banos-Florez/O. Burrieza 7–6 6–0.

RECIFE (BRA) (10) 2–8 NOVEMBER – ***Singles:*** L. Silva d. A. Prieto (3) 1–6 6–3 6–4. ***Doubles:*** M. Daniel/A. Simoni (2) d. R. Gunther/P. Hartveg 6–1 6–2.

ASUNCION (PAR) (10) 2–8 NOVEMBER – ***Singles:*** J. Chela (1) d. E. Artoni (6) 6–4 6–2. ***Doubles:*** D. Furmanski/M. Garcia (1) d. R. Alvarez/J. Arnedo (2) 3–6 6–1 6–4.

BANGKOK (THA) (10) 2–8 NOVEMBER – ***Singles:*** P. Srichaphan (1) d. M. Gregorc (7) 6–7 6–1 6–3. ***Doubles:*** C. Chen/B. Lin (3) d. N. Srichaphan/P. Srichaphan (2) 6–3 3–6 6–3.

FRANKSTON, VIC (AUS) (15) 4–8 NOVEMBER – ***Singles:*** T. Mitchell (1) d. B. Ellwood (2) 3–6 6–1 7–5. ***Doubles:*** K. Goossens/T. Mitchell (1) d. L. Bourgeois/A. Painter (2) 4–6 6–1 6–2.

CALCUTTA (IND) (15) 9–14 NOVEMBER – ***Singles:*** V. Kutsenko (2) d. O. Ogorodov (1) 6–3 6–3. ***Doubles:*** V. Kutsenko/O. Ogorodov (1) d. V. Gupta/V. Uppal 6–2 7–5.

PIRACICABA (BRA) (10) 9–15 NOVEMBER – ***Singles:*** P. Taicher (2) d. A. Vasiliadis (5) 6–1 4–6 6–4. ***Doubles:*** D. Melo/A. Prieto (2) d. L. Barbosa/F. Saretta (WC) 6–2 6–3.

ASUNCION (PAR) (10) 9–15 NOVEMBER – ***Singles:*** S. Roitman (5) d. A. Aramburu (2) 6–1 6–3. ***Doubles:*** P. Carvallo/G. Rodriguez (2) d. I. Beros/I. Saric 6–2 6–4.

HO CHI MINH CITY (VIE) (10) 9–15 NOVEMBER – ***Singles***: B. Lin d. M. Jessup (2) 6–3 6–7 7–5. ***Doubles:*** C. Chen/B. Lin (2) d. M. Jessup/M. Le 6–0 6–4.

FLORIANOPOLIS (BRA) (10) 16–22 NOVEMBER – ***Singles:*** F. Dondo (5) d. A. Simoni (8) 7–6 6–3. ***Doubles:*** D. Melo/A. Prieto (1) d. P. Hartveg/T. Schiessling w/o.

SANTIAGO (CHI) (10) 16–22 NOVEMBER – ***Singles:*** G. Keymer (Q) d. H. Gamonal (2) 6–1 7–5. ***Doubles:*** F. Gonzalez/M. Tobon d. S. Cortes/F. Ruiz (1) 6–2 6–4.

ASUNCION (PAR) (10) 16–22 NOVEMBER – ***Singles:*** S. Roitman (3) d. I. Rodrigo-Marin (4) 6–2 2–6 6–3. ***Doubles:*** P. Carvallo/G. Rodriguez (3) d. R. Rake/I. Rodrigo-Marin 6–4 6–2.

ISLAMABAD (PAK) (15) 17–22 NOVEMBER – ***Singles:*** I. Vajda (6) d. O. Ogorodov (1) 2–6 6–3 6–3. ***Doubles***: V. Kutsenko/O. Ogorodov (1) d. Y. Zhang/B. Zhu (4) 6–1 6–3.

BERRI, SA (AUS) (15) 18–22 NOVEMBER – ***Singles:*** B. Ellwood (3) d. G. Knox (Q) 3–6 6–3 6–4. ***Doubles:*** P. Hanley/N. Healey (3) d. L. Pearson/J. Sirianni 5–7 7–6 6–4.

KUMAMOTO (JPN) (15) 18–22 NOVEMBER – ***Singles:*** O. Kwon (7) d. P. Gottesleben (8) 3–6 6–3 6–2. ***Doubles:*** Y. Ishii/M. Takada (2) d. A. Matsushita/H. Sato (1) 6–2 6–0.

CURITIBA (BRA) (15) 23–29 NOVEMBER – ***Singles:*** T. Schiessling (1) d. P. Taicher (3) 6–1 6–3. ***Doubles:*** D. Melo/A. Prieto (1) d. M. Daniel/A. Simoni (3) 6–1 6–4.

VINA DEL MAR (CHI) (10) 23–29 NOVEMBER – ***Singles:*** H. Gamonal (7) d. M. Rincon (Q) 6–4 6–2. ***Doubles***: S. Cortes/F. Ruiz (1) d. E. Artoni/D. Moyano (2) 6–4 2–6 7–6.

MONTEVIDEO (URU) (10) 23–29 NOVEMBER – ***Singles:*** A. Garizzio (1) d. I. Rodrigo-Marin (7) 6–4 3–6 6–3. ***Doubles:*** P. Carvallo/G. Rodriguez (2) d. J. Arnedo/P. Nieto (1) 6–1 4–6 6–2.

BARMERA, SA (AUS) (15) 25–29 NOVEMBER – ***Singles:*** A. Hunt d. T. Mitchell (1) 7–5 3–6 7–5. ***Doubles:*** J. Kerr/M. Logarzo d. A. Hunt/T. Mitchell 6–1 3–6 7–5.

SAITAMA (JPN) (15) 25–29 NOVEMBER – ***Singles:*** S. Iwabuchi (2) d. A. Matsushita (5) 6–4 6–3. ***Doubles:*** M. Jessup/M. Le d. Y. Ishii/M. Takada (2) 6–2 5–7 6–4.

TUCSON, AZ (USA) (15) 24–29 NOVEMBER – ***Singles:*** K. Orellana (3) d. A. Popp (4) 6–3 4–6 6–0. ***Doubles:*** S. Aspelin/D. Sistermans (3) d. K. Cecek/J. Unterberger 6–4 6–4.

PAYSANDU (URU) (10) 30 NOVEMBER–6 DECEMBER – ***Singles:*** A. Garizzio (2) d. E. Couto (1) 4–6 6–1 6–3. ***Doubles:*** P. Carvalho/G. Rodriguez (1) d. E. Couto/P. Pereira (3) 3–6 6–4 7–5.

POUSO ALEGRE (BRA) (15) 30 NOVEMBER–6 DECEMBER – ***Singles:*** T. Schiessling (1) d. M. Daniel (8) 6–0 7–6. ***Doubles:*** D. Melo/A. Prieto (1) d. R. Ferreiro/M. Wowk 6–3 5–7 6–0.

SANTIAGO (CHI) (10) 30 NOVEMBER–6 DECEMBER – ***Singles:*** F. Gonzalez (WC) d. E. Artoni (6) 6–1 6–2. ***Doubles:*** S. Bandermann/F. Browne (4) d. J. Arnedo/I. Rodrigo-Marin 6–3 7–5.

CLEARWATER, FL (USA) (15) 1–6 DECEMBER – ***Singles:*** J. Cunha-Silva (2) d. G. Trifu (3) 6–1 6–3. ***Doubles:*** C. Groer/M. Sprengelmeyer (4) d. T. Guardiola/M. MacLagan 6–7 6–4 7–5.

PHOENIX, AZ (USA) (15) 1–7 DECEMBER – ***Singles:*** M. Joyce (3) d. T. Blake (WC) 6–4 6–4. ***Doubles:*** M. Bryan/R. Bryan (1) d. S. Aspelin/C. Tontz (2) w/o.

GRENELEFE, FL (USA) (15) 7–13 DECEMBER – ***Singles:*** R. Bryan (2) d. T. Guardiola (8) 6–1 7–5. ***Doubles:*** M. Bryan/R. Bryan (1) d. W. Criswell/M. Pledger 6–3 6–4.

PUNTA DEL ESTE (URU) (10) 7–13 DECEMBER – ***Singles:*** E. Couto (1) d. A. Brause 6–4 7–5. ***Doubles:*** A. Olivera/M. Peyrot d. J. Margotto/F. Tazza (Alt) 5–7 6–4 7–6.

ITF Women's Circuit

Ingrid Lofdahl-Bentzer

Women's tennis has gained intense public and media interest with the rise of young players to the top of the rankings. The ITF Women's Circuit continues to provide tournaments world-wide to enable players to gain experience and ranking points for entering the COREL WTA TOUR. The ITF Women's Circuit is the vital link between Junior tennis and the Tour and Grand Slams. Prize money levels and numbers of tournaments have risen steadily over the last twelve years and in 1998, for the first time, prize money exceeded the $5 million mark with almost 290 events scheduled.

The country by country breakdown of events for 1998 shows good global representation, with significant rises in both North and South America over 1997. One of the goals of the Women's Circuit remains to provide balance in the calendar, giving players around the world the best access to tournaments upon which to build their careers. New events in the United Arab Emirates and India were welcome additions to the 1998 calendar, bringing play opportunities to previously under-represented areas.

The ITF Women's Circuit programmes continue with great success. The Junior Exempt Project, where the year-end top ten female Junior players are given places in the Main Draws of selected ITF $25,000, $50,000 and $75,000 events has now been in effect for two years. The Women's Circuit, in conjunction with the ITF Junior Department, is investigating ways of expanding the programme as it brings great benefit to the participating players in terms of gaining important experience on the senior circuit.

As well as serving the needs of its players, the Women's Circuit has an obligation to encourage the growth and development of tournaments, both through National Associations and private promoters. With this in mind, the Department is compiling a set of comprehensive guidelines to assist organisers of all levels of Women's Circuit events with the planning and preparation of an international women's tennis tournament.

The continuing aim of the ITF Women's Circuit's is to strive towards raising the profile and improving standards at all Women's Circuit events and to promote tennis in general to the benefit of all women tennis players and the National Associations.

ITF WOMEN'S CIRCUIT RESULTS 1998

ITF WOMEN'S $20,000 CIRCUITS

Reynosa, Mexico (Week 1) – February 16–22 – ***Singles:*** J. Craybas (USA) d. M. Falco (MEX) 6–0 6–1. ***Doubles:*** J. Craybas (USA)/A. E. Nefedova (RUS) d. H. Bethard (JPN)/I. Plesu (CAN) 6–0 6–3.

Matamoros, Mexico (Week 2) – February 23–March 1 – ***Singles:*** J.Craybas (USA) d. I. Plesu (CAN) 2–6 6–3 6–3. ***Doubles:*** J. Craybas (USA)/A. E. Nefedova (RUS) d. M. Falco (MEX)/G. Velez (MEX) 6–3 4–6 6–4.

CD Victoria, Mexico (Week 3) – March 2–8 – ***Singles:*** J. Craybas (USA) d. M. Falco (MEX) 6–1 6–2. ***Doubles:*** M. Falco (MEX)/G. Velez (MEX) d. C. Mucino (MEX)/L. Neuville (FRA) 7–5 6–0.

Nuevo Laredo, Mexico (Master) – March 9–15 – ***Singles:*** J. Craybas (USA) d. M. Petrovic (YUG) 6–2 6–2. ***Doubles:*** E. Juricich (URU)/M. E Rojas (PER) d. H. Bethard (JPN)/I. Plesu (CAN) 6–3 6–4.

Ahmedeasad, India (Week 1) – October 12–18 – ***Singles:*** C. Rushmi (IND) d. J. L. Sai (IND) 7–6(5) 6–3. ***Doubles:*** C. Rushmi (IND)/J. L. Sai (IND) d. W. Orawan (THA)/A. Montika (THA) 1–6 6–4 6–3.

Pune, India (Week 2) – October 18–25 – ***Singles:*** S. Jayalakshmi (IND) d. M. Anuchan (THA) 6–3 3–6 6–1. ***Doubles:*** R. Chakravarthi (IND)/S. Jayalakshmi (IND) d. A. Venkatraman (IND)/A. Venkatraman (IND) 6–2 6–4.

Indore, India (Week 3) – October 26–November 1 – ***Singles:*** S. Jayalakshmi (IND) d. R. Chakravarthi (IND) 6–0 6–2. ***Doubles:*** G. Sheethal (IND)/S. Dhawan (IND) d. S. Jayalakshmi (IND)/ R. Chakravarthi (IND) 6–4 6–4.

New Delhi, India (Master) – November 2–8 – ***Singles:*** S. Dhawan (IND) d. S. Jayalaksmi (IND) 7–5 6–3. ***Doubles:*** R. Chakravarthi (IND)/S. Jayalakshmi (IND) d. O. Wongkamalasai (THA)/M. Anuchan (THA) 7–6(4) 1–6 6–2.

Pretoria, South Africa (Week 1) – November 16–21 – ***Singles:*** A. Pillay (RSA) d. K. Coetzee (RSA) 6–4 7–6(4). ***Doubles:*** L. Gibbs (RSA)/G. Swart (RSA) d. K. Coetzee (RSA)/C. Venter (RSA) 6–2 6–3.

Johannesburg, South Africa (Week 2) – November 23–28 – ***Singles:*** A. Nefedova (RUS) d. G. Swart (RSA) 6–3 6–3. ***Doubles:*** L. Ackron (RSA)/K. Bacon (RSA) d. L. Gibbs (RSA)/G. Swart (RSA) 5–7 6–4 7–5.

Pretoria, South Africa (Week 3) – November 30–December 5 – ***Singles:*** A. Pillay (RSA) d. A. Anastasiu (RSA) 6–1 6–2. ***Doubles:*** L. Ackron (RSA)/K. Bacon (RSA) d. A. Pillay (RSA)/K. Sadaj (POL) 6–3 6–2.

Benoni, South Africa (Master) – December 7–13 – ***Singles:*** A. Pillay (RSA) d. A. Nefedova (RUS) 6–1 6–3. ***Doubles:*** L. Ackron (RSA)/K. Bacon (RSA) d. A. Pillay (RSA)/K. Sadaj (POL) 6–3 6–0.

ITF WOMEN'S $40,000 CIRCUITS

Warrambool, Australia (Week 1) – March 2–8 – ***Singles:*** A. Grahame (AUS) d. M. Beadman (AUS) 4–6 6–2 6–1. ***Doubles:*** L. McShea (AUS)/A. Molik (AUS) d. G. Biggs (AUS)/S. Stephens (AUS) 6–3 6–1.

Wodonga, Australia (Week 2) – March 9–15 – ***Singles:*** A. Molik (AUS) d. L. McShea (AUS) 6–3, 6–2. ***Doubles:*** L. McShea (AUS)/A. Molik (AUS) d. H. Crook (GBR)/V. Davies (GBR) 6–4, 6–4.

Lyneham, Australia (Week 3) – March 16–22 – ***Singles:*** A. Grahame (AUS) d. E. Krejcova (CZE) 6–3 6–4. ***Doubles:*** L. McShea (AUS)/A. Molik (AUS) d. M. Beadman (AUS)/B. Stewart (AUS) 7–6(5) 6–7(1) 7–5.

Corowa, Australia (Masters) – March 23–29 – ***Singles:*** A. Grahame (AUS) d. E. Krejcova (CZE) 6–3 6–2. ***Doubles:*** L. McShea (AUS)/A. Molik (AUS) d. T. Hotta (JPN)/M. Mastalirova (CZE) 6–0 6–0.

Ipswich, Australia (Week 1) – April 13–19 – ***Singles:*** M. L. Radu (ROM) d. A. Grahame (AUS) 5–7 7–6(7) 7–6(2). ***Doubles:*** Terminated due to rain.

Caboolture, Australia (Week 2) – April 20–26 – ***Singles:*** M. Beadman (AUS) d. M. L. Radu (ROM) 1–6 6–2 6–0. ***Doubles:*** L. McShea (AUS)/M. Mastalirova (CZE) d. M. Beadman (AUS)/B. Stewart (AUS) 2–6 7–6(9) 7–5.

Bundaberg, Australia (Week 3) – April 27–May 3 – ***Singles:*** M. Beadman (AUS) d. L. McShea (AUS) 6–4 6–2. ***Doubles:*** abandoned due to rain.

Maryborough, Australia (Masters) – May 4–10 – ***Singles:*** M. L. Radu (ROM) d. L. McShea (AUS) 6–3 6–4. ***Doubles:*** L. McShea (AUS)/M. Mastalirova (CZE) d. S. Duanoghan (THA)/M. Niroj (THA) 6–4 6–0.

Kugayama, Tokyo (Week 1) – September 7–13 – ***Singles:*** A. Molik (AUS) d. B. Stewart (AUS) 6–4 6–2. ***Doubles:*** A. Molik (AUS)/B. Stewart (AUS) d. A. Matsuda (JPN)/Y. Nishimata (JPN) 6–1 6–3.

Ibaraki, Japan (Week 2) – September 14–20 – ***Singles:*** A. Molik (AUS) d. R. Otakeyama (JPN) 6–2 6–1. ***Doubles:*** Y. Hosoki (JPN)/H. L. Hsu (TPE) d. R. Otakeyama (JPN)/Y. Sasano (JPN) 6–4 4–6 7–5.

Ibaraki, Japan (Week 3) – September 21–27 – ***Singles:*** A. Molik (AUS) d. Y. Sasano (JPN) d. R. Otakeyama (JPN) 3–6 6–0 6–1. ***Doubles:*** A. Molik (AUS)/B. Stewart (AUS) d. Y. Sasano (JPN)/R. Otakeyama (JPN) 1–6 6–3 6–3.

Kyoto, Japan (Masters) – September 28–October 4 – ***Singles:*** A. Molik (AUS) d. A. Takase (JPN) 6–2 6–3. ***Doubles:*** A. Molik (AUS)/S. Bryanne (AUS) d. S. Katsumi (JPN)/A. Takase (JPN) 3–6 6–3 6–4.

ITF WOMEN'S $10,000 TOURNAMENTS

San Antonio, TX, USA – January 5–11 – ***Singles:*** A. Sebova (SLO) d. M. Washington (USA) 7–5 6–1. ***Doubles:*** M. Washington (USA)/K. Grant (RSA) d. A. Sebova (SLO)/S. Urickova (SLO) 4–6 7–6(5) 6–2.

Delray Beach, FL, USA – January 12–18 – ***Singles:*** L. Latimer (GBR) d. M. Vavrinec (SUI) 6–2 6–0. ***Doubles:*** M. Drake (CAN)/R. Kolbovic (CAN) d. J. Okada (USA)/K. Phebus (USA) 7–6(3) 6–4.

Reykjavik, Iceland – January 12–18 – ***Singles:*** C. Jagieniak (FRA) d. G. Navratilova (CZE) 7–6(1) 6–0. ***Doubles:*** K. Kilsdonk (NED)/J. Mens (NED) d. O. Blahotova (CZE)/G. Navratilova (CZE) 6–4 5–7 7–5.

Bastad, Sweden – January 19–25 – ***Singles:*** M. Goloviznina (RUS) d. M. Wolfbrandt (SWE) 6–3 7–5. ***Doubles:*** C. Aagaard (DEN)/M. Pape (DEN) d. G. Navratilova (CZE)/M. Pastikova (CZE) 7–6(4) 6–3.

Miami, FL, USA – January 19–25 – ***Singles:*** G. Kucerova (GER) d. L. Osterloh (USA) 6–2 6–1. ***Doubles:*** L. Osterloh (USA)/Z. Valekova (SLO) d. A. Tricerri (SWE)/A. Zhidkova (RUS) 6–4 6–4.

Dinan, France – January 26–1 February – ***Singles:*** E. Loit (FRA) d. E. Le Bescond (FRA) 6–1 6–1. ***Doubles:*** C. Pin (FRA)/A. Vedy (FRA) d. T. Garbin (ITA)/O. Golimbioschi (ROM) w/o.

Orense, Spain – January 26–1 February – ***Singles:*** L. Seelen (NED) d. E. Salvador (ESP) 6–2 7–6(7). ***Doubles:*** E. Salvador (ESP)/L. Dominguez (ESP) d. S. Da Ponte (ITA)/M. Scartoni (ITA) 6–4 6–4.

Istanbul I, Turkey – February 2–8 – ***Singles:*** A. Tordoff (GBR) d. A. Hegedus (HUN) 6–3 6–3. ***Doubles:*** A. Hegedus (HUN)/G. Navratilova (CZE) d. H. Sromova (CZE)/O. Blahotova (CZE) 6–4 4–6 6–2.

Wellington, New Zealand – February 2–8 – ***Singles:*** W. Prakusya (INA) d. R. Hudson (NZL) 7–5 6–2. ***Doubles:*** K. Hazzard (AUS)/S. Stephens (NZL) d. W. Prakusya (INA)/J. Leong (SIN) 6–1 1–6 7–6(4).

Mallorca I, Spain – February 2–8 – ***Singles:*** L. Dominguez (ESP) d. J. Abe (GER) 6–2 6–3. ***Doubles:*** K Altilia (ITA)/A. Canepa (ITA) d. E. Belbl (GER)/A. Roesch (GER) 7–5 6–6(4).

Birkenhead, Great Britain – February 2–8 – ***Singles:*** P. Mandula (HUN) d. G. Casoni (ITA) 6–0 2–6 6–3. ***Doubles:*** G. Casoni (ITA)/A. Zaporozhanova (UKR) d. N. Egorova (RUS)/O. Ivanova (RUS) 6–3 6–2.

Faro, Portugal – February 9–15 – ***Singles:*** P. Hermida (ESP) d. S. Prazeres (POR) 6–4 6–4. ***Doubles:*** N. Hubnerova (CZE)/A. Paulenkova (SVK) d. S. Prazeres (POR)/A. Tordoff (GBR) 6–2 6–2.

Mallorca II, Spain – February 9–15 – ***Singles:*** G. Riera (ESP) d. R. M. Andres (ESP) 6–4 6–3. ***Doubles:*** E. Belbl (GER)/S. Frankl (GER) d. A. Canepa (ITA)/C. Martinez-Granados (ESP) 6–3 6–3.

Birmingham, Great Britain – February 9–15 – ***Singles:*** J. Pullin (GBR) d. J. Ward (GBR) 6–1 1–6 6–3. ***Doubles:*** K. Freye (GER)/J. Okada (USA) d. H. Van Aaldere (NED)/A. Van Den Hurk (NED) 6–4 6–4.

Mumbai (Bombay), India – February 23–March 1 – ***Singles:*** Q. Yang (CHN) d. D. Aldbrecht (AUT) 6–0 6–3. ***Doubles:*** Q. Yang (CHN)/J. J. Chen (CHN) d. Y. Yamagishi (JPN)/N. Urabe (JPN) 7–6(5) 6–2.

Buchen, Germany – March 2–8 – ***Singles:*** E. Dementieva (RUS) d. M. Schnitzer (GER) 6–1 6–3. ***Doubles:*** J. Ondrouchova (CZE)/A. Sebova (SVK) d. E. Dementieva (RUS)/A. Zarska (POL) 7–6(4) 6–4 6–4.

New Delhi, India – March 2–8 – ***Singles:*** D. Ding (CHN) d. Q. Yang (CHN) 6–0 6–0. ***Doubles:*** L. Ting (CHN)/D. Ding (CHN) d. Q. Yang (CHN)/M. Uchida (JPN) 6–3 6–2.

Jaffa, Israel – March 16–22 – ***Singles:*** T. Oblizier (ISR) d. N. Ostrovskaya (BLR) 6–3 6–3. ***Doubles:*** H. Reesby (GBR)/C. Wood (GBR) d. L. Gabai (ISR)/K. Warne-Holland (GBR) 7–5 7–5.

Ashlekon, Israel – March 23–29 – ***Singles:*** K. Kilsdonk (NED) d. T. Perebiynis (UKR) 6–1 3–6 6–3. ***Doubles:*** L. Gabai (ISR)/K. Warne-Holland (GBR) d. N. Ostrovskaya (BLR)/L. Steflova (CZE) 3–6 7–5 7–5.

Makarska, Croatia – March 23–29 – ***Singles:*** N. Petrova (RUS) d. Z. Valekova (SVK) 6–4 6–2. ***Doubles:*** J. Kostanic (CRO)/K. Srebotnik (SLO) d. L. Cervanova (SVK)/Z. Valekova (SVK) 6–3 6–1.

Dinan, France – March 30–April 5 – ***Singles:*** L. Bacheva (BUL) d. S. Georges (FRA) 7–5 6–0. ***Doubles:*** S. Georges (FRA)/S. Berger (FRA) d. H. Collin (GBR)/L. Perkins (GBR) 3–6 6–0 6–2.

Hvar, Croatia – March 30–April 5 – ***Singles:*** P. Kucova (CZE) d. E. Doman (HUN) 6–2 6–2. ***Doubles:*** J. Kostanic (CRO)/K. Srebotnik (SLO) d. A. Pandjerova (BUL)/H. Vildova (CZE) 7–6 6–3.

Pontevedra, Spain – March 30–April 5 – ***Singles:*** P. Hermida (ESP) d. M. Gusheva (BUL) 6–1 6–2. ***Doubles:*** J. Choudhury (GBR)/S. Sallabery (FRA) d. T. Aranda (ESP)/J. Carballal (ESP) 6–3 6–1.

Brindisi, Italy – April 6–12 – ***Singles:*** S. Sallabery (ITA) d. M. Sucha (SVK) 6–0 6–4. ***Doubles:*** F. Pennetta (ITA)/R. Vinci (ITA) d. A. Paulenkova (SVK)/R. Vinci (ITA) 6–4 7–6(5).

Dubrovnik, Croatia – April 6–12 – ***Singles:*** N. Petrova (RUS) d. K. Srebotnik (SLO) 6–4 7–5. ***Doubles:*** E. Melicharova (CZE)/H. Vildova (CZE) d. B. Kumbarova (CZE)/M. Pastikova (CZE) 5–7 6–4 6–4.

Viña del Mar, Chile – April 6–12 – ***Singles:*** C. Contin (ARG) d. P. Cabezas (CHI) 6–2 6–4.
Doubles: M. Arevalo (ARG)/D. Musculino (ARG) d. P. Cabezas (CHI)/C. Contin (ARG) 6–3 6–4.

Galatina, Italy – April 13–19 – ***Singles:*** N. Serra (ESP) d. R. Ottoboni (ROM) 6–2 4–6 6–2.
Doubles: R. M . Andres (ESP)/N. Serra (ESP) d. D. Haak (NED)/S. Urickova (SVK) 6–4 6–1.

Cagnes-Sur-Mer, France – April 13–19 – ***Singles:*** N. Feber (FRA) d. C. Bornu (FRA) 6–0 6–1.
Doubles: H. Crook (GBR)/V. Davies (GBR) d. Y. Basting (NED)/M. Zedencova (CZE) 6–3 6–3.

Bari, Italy – April 20–26 – ***Singles:*** R. Ottoboni (ARG) d. R. Andres (ESP) 2–6 6–2 7–5.
Doubles: R. Andres (ESP)/V. Stele (ARG) d. S. Da Ponte (ITA)/S. Urickova (SVK) 6–1 6–1.

Gelos, France – April 20–26 – ***Singles:*** J. Henin (FRA) d. A. Vedy (FRA) 6–0 6–0.
Doubles: Y. Basting (NED)/E. Curutchet (FRA) d. J.Henin (FRA)/A. Vedy (FRA) 0–6 6–3.

Bournemouth, Great Britain – April 20–26 – ***Singles:*** J. Ward (GBR) d. L. Ahl (GBR) 7–6(2) 6–4.
Doubles: E. Jelfs (GBR)/M. Joubert (RSA) d. L. Gabai (ISR)/K. Warne-Holland (GBR) 6–3 6–3.

San Severo, Italy – April 27–May 3 – ***Singles:*** V. Stele (ARG) d. K. Piccolini (ITA) 6–4 6–3.
Doubles: E. Maia (BRA)/R. Ottoboni (ARG) d. G. Gutierrez (COL)/V. Stele (ARG) 1–6 7–5 7–5.

Sofia, Bulgaria – April 27–May 3 – ***Singles:*** M. Gusheva (BUL) d. O. Blahtova (CZE) 4–6 6–2 6–1.
Doubles: O. Blahtova (CZE)/M. Pastikova (CZE) d. T. Nedova (BUL)/D. Topalova (BUL) 7–5 7–6(5).

Guimaraes, Portugal – April 27–May 3 – ***Singles :*** S. De Silva (USA) d. M. Ostrovskaya (BLR) 6–2 6–4.
Doubles: M. Escobar (ESP)/P. Hermida (ESP) d. B. Colosio (BRA)/C. Correia (POR) 7–6(2) 6–4.

Hatfield, Great Britain – April 27–May 3 – ***Singles:*** M. Ramon (ESP) d. E. Jelfs (GBR) 6–1 1–6 6–3.
Doubles: M. Ramon (ESP)/M. C. Contin (ARG) d. E. Jelfs (GBR)/A. Janes (GBR) 3–6 6–3 6–4.

Presov, Slovakia – May 4–10 – ***Singles:*** L. Cervanova (SVK) d. S. Hrozenska (SVK) 6–2 6–0.
Doubles: M. Zdenovcova (SVK)/J. Lubasova (CZE) d. T. Kovalchuk (UKR)/A. Zaporozhanova (UKR) 6–2 6–4.

Elvas, Portugal – May 4–10 – ***Singles:*** R. M. Andres (ESP) d. A. Salas (ESP) 6–1 6–3.
Doubles: R. M. Andres (ESP)/D. Haak (NED) d. M. Escobar (ESP)/P. Hermida (NED) w/o.

Quartu S. Elena, Italy – May 4–10 – ***Singles:*** H. Froehlich (GER) d. P Van Acker (BEL) 6–4 3–6 6–1.
Doubles: F. Pennetta (ITA)/R. Vinci (ITA) d. G. Gutierrez (COL)/G. Misuriova (LIT) 6–3 6–0.

Tortosa, Spain – May 11–17 – ***Singles:*** B. Mouthtassine (MAR) d. P. Aznar (ESP) 7–6(4) 6–2.
Doubles: n/a.

Le Touquet, France – May 11–17 – ***Singles:*** K. Nowak (POL) d. M. Koutstaall (NED) 7–6(5) 6–2.
Doubles: V. Casanova (FRA)/R. Ottoboni (ARG) d. E. Lebescond (FRA)/S. Sfar (FRA) 7–6 1–0 ret.

Nitra, Slovakia – May 11–17 – ***Singles:*** U. Markova (SVK) d. Z. Kovalchuk (UKR) 6–0 6–3.
Doubles: n/a.

Novi Sad, Yugoslavia – May 11–17 – ***Singles:*** P. Mandula (HUN) d. A. Pandjerova (BUL) 0–6 7–5 6–1.
Doubles: T. Jecmenica (YUG)/D. Zaric (YUG) d. A. Pandjerova (BUL)/D. Toplova (BUL) 6–2 7–5.

Caracas, Venezuela – May 11–17 – ***Singles:*** N. Pardo (VEN) d. K. Wong (USA) 6–3 1–6 7–6(3).
Doubles: M. Salinas (VEN)/S. Schenck (USA) d K. Wong (USA)/L. Kramer (USA) 6–4 2–6 6–3.

Poza Rica, Mexico – May 11–17 – ***Singles:*** V. Menga (BRA) d. A. Jidkova (RUS) 6–2 6–7(3) 6–1.
Doubles: P. Cabezas (CHI)/V. Menga (BRA) d. A. Jidkova (RUS)/A. Engel (USA) 3–6 6–2 6–2.

Coatzacoalcos, Mexico – May 18–24 – ***Singles:*** A. Jidkova (RUS) d. A. Engel (USA) 6–3 6–1.
Doubles: P. Cabezas (CHI)/V. Menga (BRA) d. A. Engel (USA)/A. Jidkova (RUS) 6–3 6–2.

Azemeis, Portugal – May 18–24 – ***Singles:*** P. Hermida (ESP) d. I. Selyutina (KAZ) 6–1 6–1.
Doubles: B. Colosio (BRA)/C. Correia (POR) d. K. Liggan (IRE)/I. Selyutina (KAZ) 6–2 6–4.

Modena, Italy – May 18–24 – ***Singles:*** A. Canepa (ITA) d. Y. Angeli (ITA) 4–6 6–4 6–2.
Doubles: A. Canepa (ITA)/A. Lombardi (ITA) d. K. Pojatina (CRO)/M. Kovacevic (CRO) 6–7(5) 6–3 7–5.

Zaragoza, Spain – May 18–24 – ***Singles:*** S. Sallaberry (FRA) d. V. Stele (ARG) 7–5 6–4.
Doubles: G. Riera (ESP)/A. Tricerri (SUI) d. L. Dominguez (ESP)/V. Stele (ARG) 6–4 6–1.

Rhodes, Greece – May 18–24 – ***Singles:*** M. Losey (SUI) d. I. Stavridou (GRE) 6–1 6–1.
Doubles: D. Asencio (SUI)/J. Tinnacher (GER) d. H. Puustingen (FIN)/K. Lampinen (FIN) 6–3 6–4.

San Severino, Italy – May 25–June 1 – ***Singles:*** P. Van Acker (BEL) d. M. Matevzic (SLO) 7–5 6–3.
Doubles: R. Jensen (USA)/K. Pojatina (CRO) d. M. Matevzic (SLO)/A. Skafar (SLO) w/o.

Salzburg, Austria – May 25–June 1 – ***Singles:*** A. Foldenyi (HUN) d. P. Mandula (HUN) 1–6 6–2 6–2.
Doubles: L. Steflova (CZE)/M. Zdenkova (CZE) d. K. Fitz (GER)/S. Weis (GER) 6–1 6–4.

El Paso, TX, USA – May 25–June 1 – ***Singles:*** E. Bovina (RUS) d. D. Ospina (USA) 3–6 7–6(5) 7–6(1).
Doubles: K. Ishida (JPN)/K. Nagatomi (JPN) d. K. Smashey (USA)/S. Walker (USA) 6–2 6–3.

North Little Rock, AR, USA – June 1–7 – ***Singles:*** C. Watson (AUS) d. B. K. Choi (MAS) 5–7 6–4 6–3. ***Doubles:*** K. Ishida (JPN)/K. Nagatomi (JPN) d. T. Li (CHN)/L. Li (CHN) 7–5 6–1.

Ceuta, Spain – June 1–7 – ***Singles:*** G. Riera (ESP) d. B. Mouhtassine (MAR) 7–5 2–6 6–2. ***Doubles:*** G. Riera (ESP)/A. Tricerri (SUI) d. T. Aranda (ESP)/J. Carballal(ESP) 6–3 6–3.

Antalya, Turkey – June 1–7 – ***Singles:*** S. De Silva (SRI) d. A. Tordoff (GBR) 6–4 6–3. ***Doubles:*** H. Aalto (FIN)/M. Rautajoki (FIN) d. M. Samoilenko (RUS)/A. Takase (JPN) 6–2 6–4.

Bourgas, Bulgaria – June 1–7 – ***Singles:*** C. Schuurmans (BEL) d. L. Nanusevic (YUG) 6–2 6–1. ***Doubles:*** K. Diankova (BUL)/A. Pozzi (ITA) d. F. Gabrovska (BUL)/D. Krasteviitch (BUL)1–6 6–4 6–2.

Camucia, Italy – June 8–14 – ***Singles:*** A. Lombardi (ITA) d. M. Palaversic (CRO) 6–2 6–1. ***Doubles:*** A. Lombardi (ITA)/A. Canepa (ITA) d. B. Karpenschif (FRA)/E. Pioppo (ITA) 6–3 6–2.

Lenzerheide, Switzerland – June 8–14 – ***Singles:*** M. Zdenovcova (CZE) d. P. Van Acker (BEL)1–6 7–6(2) 6–4. ***Doubles:*** L. Bao (SUI)/C. Charbonnier (SUI) d. P. Racedo (ARG)/E. Zardo (SUI) 6–4 6–0.

Kedzierzyn-Kozle, Poland – June 8–14 – ***Singles:*** Z. Ondraskova (CZE) d. M. Nekvapilova (CZE) 0–6 6–1 6–2. ***Doubles:*** K. Teodorowicz (POL)/A. Zarska (POL) d. Nekvapilova (CZE)/H. Sromova (CZE) 7–6(5) 6–1.

Hilton Head, SC, USA – June 8–14 – ***Singles:*** H. Parkinson (USA) d. R. Kolbovic (CAN) 3–6 6–4 6–4. ***Doubles:*** S. Sureephong (USA)/V. Webb (CAN) d. H. Parkinson (USA)/T. Singian (USA) 6–2 7–6(4).

Stare Splavy, Czech Republic – June 15–21 – ***Singles:*** J. Hlavackova (CZE) d. M. Nekvapilova (CZE) 3–6 6–2 6–2. ***Doubles:*** Z. Lesenarova (CZE)/L. Steflova (CZE) d. H. Sromova (CZE)/M. Nekvapilova (CZE) 6–3 5–7 6–2.

Grado, Italy – June 15–21 – ***Singles:*** E. Fauth (AUT) d. A. Vanc (ROM) 6–7(4) 6–1 6–1. ***Doubles:*** M. Kovacevic (CRO)/M. Palaversic (CRO) d. V. Casaova (FRA)/A. Vanc (ROM) 3–6 6–3 6–1.

Tallinn, Estonia – June 15–21 – ***Singles:*** A. Myskina (RUS) d. M. Rautajoki (FIN) 7–5 6–3. ***Doubles:*** H. Fremuthova (CZE)/I. Kornienko (RUS) d. M. Ani (EST)/H. Laupa (EST) 6–3 6–2.

Biel II, Switzerland – June 15–21 – ***Singles:*** S. Lohrmann (GER) d. A. Voina (GER) 6–2 6–3. ***Doubles:*** K. Freye (GER)/J. Okada (USA) d. L. Bao (SUI)/S. Schoeffel (FRA) 6–0 6–7(1) 6–1.

Springfield, MO, USA – June 22–28 – ***Singles:*** A. Cohen (USA) d. A. Grahame (USA 6–2 6–3. ***Doubles:*** A. Augustus (USA)/J. Scott (USA) d. A. Grahame (AUS)/B. Stewart (AUS) 6–0 6–0.

Sezze, Italy – June 22–28 – ***Singles:*** A. Canepa (ITA) d. S. Sfar (TUN) 7–5 6–2. ***Doubles:*** V. Casanova (ITA)/S. Sfar (TUN) d. A. Canepa (ITA)/A. Lombardi (ITA) 6–3 6–1.

Santander, Spain – June 22–28 – ***Singles:*** L. Dominguez (ESP) d. P. Aznar (ESP) 1–6 6–3 7–6(3). ***Doubles:*** L. Dominguez (ESP)/M. Escobar (ESP) d. J. Garcia (COL)/M.Mesa (COL) 6–1 7–6(1).

Bastad II, Sweden – June 22–28 – ***Singles:*** G. Navratilova (CZE) d. M. Persson (SWE) 6–2 7–6(4). ***Doubles:*** J. Lindstrom (SWE)/A. K. Svensson (SWE) d. H. Fremuthova (CZE)/G. Navratilova (CZE) 7–6(1) 6–3.

Velp, Netherlands – June 22–28 – ***Singles:*** Y. Basting (NED) d. A. Van Den Hurk (NED) 6–1 5–7 6–2. ***Doubles:*** A. Van Den Hurk (NED)/C. Reimering (NED) d. J. Mens (NED)/K. Kilsdonnk (NED) 6–3 6–1.

Orestiada, Kavla, Greece – June 22–28 – ***Singles:*** B. Pavlova (BUL) d. D. Ilic (YUG) 6–3 7–6(1). ***Doubles:*** R. Vidats (HUN)/M. Pavlidou (GRE) d. B. Bojovic (YUG)/E. Roussi (GRE) 6–1 6–1.

Montreal, Canada – June 22–28 – ***Singles:*** V. Webb (CAN) d. R. Kolbovic (CAN) 6–3 6–4. ***Doubles:*** V. Webb (CAN)/R. Kolbovic (CAN) d. M. Marios (CAN)/K. Rammo (CAN) 6–3 6–1.

Edmond, OK, USA – June 29–July 5 – ***Singles:*** C. Popescu (CAN) d. C. Watson (AUS) 3–6 6–4 6–2. ***Doubles:*** M. Beadman (AUS)/S. Drake-Brockman (AUS) d. G. Biggs (AUS)/B. Stewart (AUS) 7–6(2) 7–6(5).

Lohja, Finland – June 29–July 5 – ***Singles:*** M. Wolfbrandt (SWE) d. M. Persson (SWE) 6–3 7–5. ***Doubles:*** J. Choudhury (GBR)/A. Tricerri (SUI) d. H. Fremuthova (CZE)/I. Kornienko (RUS) 6–3 6–2.

Alkamaar, Netherlands – June 29–July 5 – ***Singles:*** D. Topalova (BUL) d. Y. Basting (NED) 7–6(3) 6–2. ***Doubles:*** Y. Basting (NED)/H. Van Aalderen (NED) d. C. Buis (NED)/A. Van Den Hurk (NED) 6–2 6–1.

Skopje, FYROM – June 29–July 5 – ***Singles:*** C. Schuurmans (BEL) d. M. Moldovan (ROM) 7–6(4) 7–6(3). ***Doubles:*** T. Nedeva (BUL)/A. Pandjerova (BUL) d. F. Gabrovska (BUL)/R. Topalova (BUL) 6–3 6–0.

Mont-De-Marsan, France – June 29–July 5 – ***Singles:*** S. Testard (FRA) d. O. Sanchez (FRA) 6–2 7–5. ***Doubles:*** M. Caiazzo (FRA)/S. Testard (FRA) d. B. Loogen (GER)/A. Stueckle (GER) 6–3 6–4.

Vigo, Spain – July 6–12 – ***Singles:*** M. Mesa (COL) d. P. Racedo (ARG) 6–1 6–4. ***Doubles:*** L. Dominguez (ESP)/E. Salvador (ESP) d. V. Menga (BRA)/P. Racedo (ARG) 6–1 4–6 6–2.

Fumicino, Italy – July 6–12 – ***Singles:*** K. Piccolini (ITA) d. A. Lombardi (ITA) 6–2 1–6 6–2. ***Doubles:*** A. Lombardi (ITA)/A. Vanc (ROM) d. A. Hegedus (HUN)/T. Hotta (JPN) 6–2 6–4.

Amersfoort, Holland – July 6–12 – ***Singles:*** no final due to rain.

Felixstowe, Great Britain – July 6–12 – ***Singles:*** M. Joubert (RSA) d. L. Ahl (GBR) 7–5 6–3. ***Doubles:*** L. McShea (AUS)/T. Musgrave (AUS) d. L. Ahl (GBR)/A. Wainwright (GBR) 6–4 7–6(4).

Easton, MD, USA – July 6–12 – ***Singles:*** T. T. Weng (TPE) d. J. Scott (USA) 6–0 4–6 7–6(6). ***Doubles:*** A. Augustus (USA)/J. Scott (USA) d. D. Buth (USA)/S. Nickitas (USA) 6–2 3–6 6–1.

Frinton, Great Britain – July 13–19 – ***Singles:*** L. Ahl (GBR) d. L. McShea (AUS) w/o. ***Doubles:*** E. Jelfs (GBR)/M. Joubert (RSA) d. L. Ahl (GBR)/A. Wainwright (GBR) 6–2 7–5.

Harkiv, Ukraine – July 13–19 – ***Singles:*** N. Ostrovskaya (BLR) d. E. Voropaeva (RUS) 7–5 6–0. ***Doubles:*** N. Ostrovskaya (BLR)/E. Kovalchuk (UKR) d. N. Nemchinova (UKR)/N. Bondarenko (UKR) 6–1 3–6 6–1.

Civitanova, Italy – July 13–19 – ***Singles:*** Z. Ondraskova (CZE) d. M. Zdenovcova (CZE) 6–2(3) 6–2. ***Doubles:*** M. Zdenovcova (CZE)/J. Lubasova (CZE) d. G. Gutierrez (COL)/J. Lubasova (CZE) 6–3 6–4.

Lido di Camaiore, Italy – July 20–26 – ***Singles:*** M. Kovacevic (CRO) d. A. Canepa (ITA) 5–7 6–4 6–2. ***Doubles:*** M. Kovacevic (CRO)/Z. Hejdova (CZE) d. G. Gutierrez (COL)/E. Maia (BRA) 6–2 6–0.

Brussels I, Belgium – July 20–26 – ***Singles:*** K. Clijsters (BEL) d. D. Sobotkova (CZE) 7–6 6–1. ***Doubles:*** K. Clijsters (BEL)/S. Deville (BEL) d. M. E. Krutko (LAT)/Boboedova (RUS) 6–1 7–5.

Torun, Poland – July 27–August 2 – ***Singles:*** J. Macurova (CZE) d. C. Grunes (GER) 3–6 6–4 6–1. ***Doubles:*** J. Macurova (CZE)/O. Blahotova (CZE) d. G. Navritilova (CZE)/P. Plackova (CZE) 7–6(2) 6–0.

Muri Antichi, Italy – July 27–August 2 – ***Singles:*** S. Mantler (AUT) d. C. Aagaard (DEN) 2–6 6–2 6–4. ***Doubles:*** A. Brianti (ITA)/C. Dalbon (ITA) d. S. Mantler (AUT)/S. Stephens (NZL) 6–3 6–4.

Horb, Germany – July 27–August 2 – ***Singles:*** A. Foldenyi (HUN) d. Z. Gubacsi (HUN) 6–3 6–0. ***Doubles:*** E. Brunn (GER)/C. Kremer (GER) d. L. Suurvarik (EST)/L. Nikoian (RUS) 6–1 7–6(2).

Ilkley, Great Britain – July 27–August 2 – ***Singles:*** M. Joubert (RSA) d. C. Lyte (GBR) 6–3 6–4. ***Doubles:*** E. Jelfs (GBR)/M. Joubert (RSA) d. H. Crook (GBR)/H. Davies (GBR) 6–3 6–4.

Rabat, Morroco – July 27–August 2 – ***Singles:*** B. Mouhtassine (MAR) d. N. Schwartz (AUT) 5–7 6–1 6–1. ***Doubles:*** S. Fillip (AUT)/B. Resch (AUT) d. N. Schwartz (AUT)/S. Haidner (AUT) 4–6 7–5 6–2.

Perigueux, France – August 3–9 – ***Singles:*** A. Goni (ESP) d. S. Foretz (FRA) 6–0 6–4. ***Doubles:*** P. Garcia (ESP)/K. Liggan (IRL) d. S. Schoeffel (FRA)/S. Testard (FRA) 3–6 6–3 7–6(3).

Rebecq, Belgium – August 3–9 – ***Singles:*** D. Van De Zande (BEL) d. L. Steinbech (GER) 6–1 6–3. ***Doubles:*** L. Masante (ARG)/D. Van De Zande (BEL) d. S. Borgions (BEL)/C. Shuurmans (BEL) 6–1 6–4.

Southsea, Great Britain – August 3–9 – ***Singles:*** E. Danilidou (GRE) d. M. Malhotra (IND) 7–6(1) 6–3. ***Doubles:*** E. Jelfs (GBR)/M. Joubert (FRA) d. E. Danilidou (GRE)/L. Wood (GBR) 6–2 6–3.

Paderborn, Germany – August 3–9 – ***Singles:*** P. Van Acker (BEL) d. M. Wolfbrandt (SWE) 6–0 6–4. ***Doubles:*** L. Faltynkova (CZE)/P. Kucova (CZE) d. E. Brunn (GER) /D. Topalova (BUL) 7–6(4) 6–3.

Umberto, Italy – August 3–9 – ***Singles:*** R. Ottoboni (ARG) d. B. Fulco- Viella (ARG) 6–4 7–6(2). ***Doubles:*** A. Brianti (ITA)/C. Dalbon (ITA) d. B. Fulco-Viella (ARG)/J. Torti (ARG) 7–5 6–4.

Saint Gaudens, France – August 10–16 – ***Singles:*** D. Caporusso (FRA) d. M. Vulpe (ROM) 3–6 7–5 6–3. ***Doubles:*** S. Sallabery (FRA)/A. Vedy (FRA) d. P. Garcia (ESP)/ K. Liggan (IRL) 6–3 7–6(5).

Koksijde, Belgium – August 10–16 – ***Singles:*** K. Clijsters (BEL) d. L. Dominguez (ESP) 6–3 6–4. ***Doubles:*** L. Masante (ARG)/M. Mastalirova (CZE) d. L. Seelen (NED)/K. Valkyova (SVK) 6–3 7–5.

Istanbul II, Turkey – August 10–16 – ***Singles:*** E. Danilidou (GRE) d. R. Otakeyama (JPN) 6–0 6–1. ***Doubles:*** N. Cahana (ISR)E. Danilidou (GRE)/D. Aksit (TUR)/G. Gultekin (TUR) 3–6 6–3 6–3.

Nicolosi, Italy – August 10–16 – ***Singles:*** L. Dell'Angelo (ITA) d. R.Takemura (JPN) 6–2 7–5. ***Doubles:*** A. Lombardi (ITA)/E. Pioppo d. L. Dell'Angelo (ITA)/M. Santangelo (ITA) 3–6 6–2 6–4.

Ibarra, Ecuador – August 17–23 – ***Singles:*** M. Arevalo (ARG) d. D. Olivera (URU) 6–4 6–1. ***Doubles:*** P. Cabezas (CHI)/J. Moore (GBR) d. E. Juricich (URU)/M. E. Rojas (PER) 6–3 6–4.

Valasske Mezirici, Czech Republic – August 17–23 – ***Singles:*** M. Sucha (SVK) d. L. Prusova (CZE) 3–6 6–3 6–1. ***Doubles:*** M. Kucerova (GER)/J. Pospisilova (CZE) d. K. Teodorowicz (POL)/A. Zarska (POL) 6–3 4–6 7–6(5).

Maribor, Slovenia – August 17–23 – ***Singles:*** A. Hegedus (HUN) d. K. Miscolczi (HUN) 7–6 6–2. ***Doubles:*** L. Faltynkova (SVK)/P. Plackova (CZE) d. J. Adlbrecht (AUT)/S. Haidner (AUT) 6–2 6–1.

Brussels II, Belgium – August 17–23 – ***Singles:*** L. Dominguez (ESP) d. E. Last (BEL) 2–6 6–3 6–2. ***Doubles:*** K. Clijsters (BEL)/C. Schuurmans (BEL) d. L. Dominguez (ESP)/L. Masante (ARG) 7–6(5) 7–5.

Carraba, Italy – August 17–23 – ***Singles:*** A. Vanc (ROM) d. M. Dittmann (AUS) 2–6 6–3 6–1. ***Doubles:*** E. Syssoeva (RUS)/A. Takase (JPN) d. M. Dittmann (AUS)/N. Dittmann (AUS) 6–2 6–0.

Plzen, Czech Republic – August 24–30 – ***Singles:*** L. Prusova (CZE) d. A. Zarska (CZE) 6–4 6–3. ***Doubles:*** O. Blahotova (CZE)/J. Macurova (CZE) d. G. Navratilova (CZE)/V. Ramirova (CZE) 1–6 6–2 6–1.

Milan, Italy – August 24–30 – ***Singles:*** M. Kucerova (GER) d. M. Kovacevic (CRO) 6–2 3–6 6–2. ***Doubles:*** H. Mochizuki (JPN)/A. Takemura (JPN) d. G. Casoni (ITA)/M. Kovacevic (CRO) 4–6 7–6(5) 6–4.

Skiathos, Greece – August 24–30 – ***Singles:*** E. Danilidou (GRE) d. T. Poutchek (BLR) 6–3 6–4. ***Doubles:*** E. Danilidou (GRE)/E. Roussi (GRE) d. T. Poutchek (BLR)/M. Lazarovska (FYR) 3–6 6–4 6–2.

Westende, Belgium – August 24–30 – ***Singles:*** L. Masante (ARG) d. P. Van Acker (BEL) 6–7 6–3 6–4. ***Doubles:*** L. Masante (ARG)/P. Markova (SVK) d. B. Bruls (NED)/C. Shuurmans (BEL) 2–6 6–3 6–3.

Guayaquil, Ecuador – August 31–September 6 – ***Singles:*** M. Arevalo (ARG) d. C. Gussoni (ARG) 3–6 6–3 6–3. ***Doubles:*** M. Arevalo (ARG)/F. Basile (ARG) d. E. Juricich (URU)/M. E. Rojas (PER) 6–2 6–2.

Xanthi, Greece – August 31–September 6 – ***Singles:*** E. Danilidou (GRE) d. E. Jelfs (GBR) 6–2 6–0. ***Doubles:*** E. Danilidou (GRE)/E. Roussi (GRE) d. L. Nanusevic (YUG)/D. Ilic (YUG) 6–0 6–3.

Vila do Conde, Portugal – August 31–September 6 – ***Singles:*** W. Fix (USA) d. K. Karner (GER) 6–2 6–2. ***Doubles:*** K. Karner (GER)/A. Briegel (GER) d. D. Hofer (GER)/M. Tulfer (NED) 6–4 6–1.

Hechingen, Germany – August 31–September 6 – ***Singles:*** A. Roesch (GER) d. O. Blahotova (CZE) 6–4 5–7 7–5. ***Doubles:*** S. Meier (GER)/J. Woehr (GER) d. L. Faltynkova (CZE)/B. Kumbar (CZE) 6–2 6–2.

México City DF, Mexico – September 7–13 – ***Singles:*** C. Papadaki (GRE) d. S. Noorlander (NED) 6–3 6–1. ***Doubles:*** C. Papadaki (GRE)/S. Noorlander d. C. Contin (ARG)/J. Fernandez (MEX) 6–3 6–1.

Fano, Italy – September 7–13 – ***Singles:*** L. Dominguez (ESP) d. L. Dell'Angelo (ITA) 6–1 6–1. ***Doubles:*** L. Dominguez (ESP)/L. Dell'Angelo (ITA) d. P. Markova (SVK)/P. Rampre (SLO) 7–6(5) 2–6 6–3.

Povoa De Varzim, Portugal – September 7–13 – ***Singles:*** M. Marrero (ESP) d. W. Fix (USA) 6–0 6–0. ***Doubles:*** M. Marrero (ESP)/A. Srndovic (SWE) d. A. Gaspar (POR)/F. Piedade (POR) 6–1 6–0.

Denain, France – September 7–13 – ***Singles:*** S. Erre (FRA) d. S. Bouilleau (FRA) 6–2 6–3. ***Doubles:*** A. Dulon (FRA)/O. Sanchez (FRA) d. L. Ackron (RSA)/K. Bacon (RSA) 5–7 7–5 6–3.

Lima, Peru – September 7–13 – ***Singles:*** M. Mesa (COL) d. S. Valenti (ARG) 6–0 7–6(5). ***Doubles:*** M. Mesa (COL)/N. Nittinger (GER) d. N. Gussoni (ARG)/S. Valenti (ARG) 6–3 7–5.

Zadar, Croatia – September 7–13 – ***Singles:*** L. Prusova (CZE) d. K. Straczy (POL) 7–5 6–0. ***Doubles:*** C. Pin (FRA)/I. Visic (CRO) d. L. Prusova (CZE)/A. Zarska (POL) 7–6(3) 7–6(4).

Constanta, Romania – September 14–20 – ***Singles:*** A. Zaporozhanova (UKR) d. A. Pirsu (ROM) 7–6(5) 6–1. ***Doubles:*** D. Haak (NED)/J. Mens (NED) d. N. Louarsabishvili (GEO)/A. Pirsu (ROM) 6–3 7–6(5).

Reggio Calabria, Italy – September 14–20 – ***Singles:*** A. Vanc (ROM) d. S. Haidner (AUT) 7–5 6–3. ***Doubles:*** K. Altilia (ITA)/M. Santangelo (ITA) d. E. Pioppo (ITA)/A. Vanc (ROM) 6–7(3) 4–6 6–4.

La Paz, Bolivia – September 14–20 – ***Singles:*** L. Bernal (PAR) d. H. Vieira (POR) 6–3 6–2. ***Doubles:*** L. Bernal (PAR)/D. Olivera (URU) d. C. Mayorga (COL)/C. Castaño (COL) 7–5 6–7 6–1.

Biograd, Croatia – September 14–20 – ***Singles:*** A. Zarska (POL) d. A. Myskina (RUS) 6–4 5–7 7–6(5). ***Doubles:*** G. Arn (GER)/L. Miholcek (CRO) d. D. Asensio (SUI)/M. Jugic-Salkic (BIH) 6–3 6–2.

Sibenik, Croatia – September 21–27 – ***Singles:*** K. Srebotnik (SLO) d. E. Molnar (HUN) 6–1 6–2. ***Doubles:*** M. Kovacevic (CRO)/K. Srebotnik (SLO) d. O. Blahotova (CZE)/B. Kumbarova (CZE) 6–3 6–1.

Sunderland, Great Britain – September 21–27 – ***Singles:*** M. Buric (GER) d. J. Lutrova (RUS) 6–2 7–6(4). ***Doubles:*** E. Jelfs (GBR)/M. Joubert (RSA) d. H. Crook (GBR)/V. Davies (GBR) 6–1 6–1.

Lecce, Italy – September 21–27 – ***Singles:*** A. Goni (ESP) d. E. Last (BEL) 4–6 6–3 7–5. ***Doubles:*** K. Altilia (ITA)/S. Haidner (AUT) d. J. Casoni (ITA)/S. Chieppa (ITA) 6–0 6–2.

Santiago, Chile – September 21–27 – ***Singles:*** P. Cabezas (CHI) d. M. Lopez Palacios (ARG) 6–4 7–5. ***Doubles:*** P. Cabezas (CHI)/A. Tricerri (SUI) d. M. Lopez Palacios (ARG)/M. A. Quezada (CHI) 6–4 6–1.

Llerida, Spain – September 28–October 4 – ***Singles:*** M. Ramon (ESP) d. J. Vakulenko (UKR) 6–1 6–3. ***Doubles:*** P. Aznar (ESP)/M. Ramon (ESP) d. C. Aagaard (DEN)/M. Rasmussen (DEN) 6–2 6–0.

Supetar, Croatia – September 28–October 4 – ***Singles:*** S. Sosnarova (SVK) d. D. Penic (CRO) 7–5 4–6 7–6(5). ***Doubles:*** O. Balhotova (CZE)/P. Kucova (CZE) d. R. Kucerova (CZE)/B. Kumbarova (CZE) 6–1 6–2.

Glasgow, Scotland – September 28–October 4 – ***Singles:*** M. Buric (GER) d. B. Bruhls (NED) 6–4 3–6 6–1. ***Doubles:*** E. Dyrberg (DEN)/L. Steinbach (GER) d. H. Crook (GBR)/V. Davies (GBR) 6–4 5–7 6–3.

Cordoba, Argentina – September 28–October 4 – ***Singles:*** E. Krauth (ARG) d. K. Marosi (HUN) 2–6 6–1 6–4. ***Doubles:*** J. Cravero (ARG)/E. Chialvo (ARG) d. C. Kremer (GER)/N. Nittinger (GER) 6–4 2–6 6–3.

Girona, Spain – October 5–11 – ***Singles:*** A. Montolio (ESP) d. M. Marrero (ESP) 6–4 6–1. ***Doubles:*** R. M. Rosa (ESP)/L. Dominguez (ESP) d. M. J. Martinez (ESP)/M. Marrero (ESP) 4–6 6–1 7–6(5).

Dalby, Australia – October 5–11 – ***Singles:*** L. McShea (AUS) d. D. Buth (USA) 7–6(7) 5–7 6–2. ***Doubles:*** L. McShea (AUS)/T. Musgrave (AUS) d. D. Buth (USA)/K. Hunt (AUS) 4–6 7–5 6–4.

Orestadia, Greece – October 5–11 – ***Singles:*** A. Pandjerova (BUL) d. J. Aldbrecht (AUT) 2–6 6–3 6–4. ***Doubles:*** J. Aldbrecht (AUT)/M. Lazarovska (FYR) d. A. Pandjerova (BUL)/M. L. Radu (ROM) 6–0 6–4.

Montevideo, Uruguay – October 5–11 – ***Singles:*** Z. Gubacsi (HUN) d. C. Fernandez (ARG) 0–6 6–3 6–4. ***Doubles:*** Z. Gubacsi (HUN)/M. Lopez Palacios (ARG) d. J. Cortez (BRA)/E. Maia (BRA) 3–6 6–3 6–4.

Asunción, Paraguay – October 12–18 – ***Singles:*** L. Schaerer (PAR) d. Z. Gubacsi (HUN) 6–1 6–4. ***Doubles:*** S. Bernal (PAR)/L. Schaerer (PAR) d. Z. Gubacsi (HUN)/A. Tricerri (SUI) 3–6 7–6(3) 6–4.

Saint Raphael, France – October 12–18 – ***Singles:*** K. Nowak (POL) d. M. Kucerova (GER) 6–1 7–6(1). ***Doubles:*** V. Henke (GER)/S. Lohrmann (GER) d. S. Trik (NED)/H. Van Aalderen (NED) 6–4 6–3.

Kooralbyn, Australia – October 12–18 – ***Singles:*** L. McShea (AUS) d. C. Watson (AUS) 6–4 5–7 7–6(4). ***Doubles:*** L. McShea (AUS)/T. Musgrave (AUS) d. G. Biggs (AUS)/S. Stephens (NZL) 6–3 7–6(5).

Nicosia, Cyprus – October 12–18 – ***Singles:*** E. Molnar (HUN) d. C. Aagaard (DEN) 6–1 6–4. ***Doubles:*** A. Zweck (GER)/E. Birnerova (CZE) d. L. Suurvarik (EST)/G. Misuriova (LIT) 6–3 6–4.

Minsk, Belarus – October 26–November 1 – ***Singles:*** N. Ostrovskaya (BLR) d. M. Stets (BLR) 6–1 6–1. ***Doubles:*** E. Panioushkina (RUS)/A. Rodionova (RUS) d. O. Glouschenko (BLR)/T. Poutchek (BLR) 7–5 5–7 6–3.

Moulins, France – November 2–8 – ***Singles:*** S. De Ville (BEL) d. B. Karpenschiff (FRA) 1–6 6–4 6–1. ***Doubles:*** D. Asensio (SUI)/I. Tulyaganova (UZB) d. D. Haak (NED)/A. Van Den Hurk (NED) 7–5 2–6 6–2.

Rungsted, Denmark – November 2–8 – ***Singles:*** E. Dyrberg (DEN) d. M. Ani (EST) 6–3 6–4. ***Doubles:*** C. Aagaard (DEN)/M. Pape (DEN) d. G. Gultekim (TUR)/K. Karner (GER) 6–4 6–2.

Le Havre, France – November 9–15 – ***Singles:*** S. Foretz (FRA) d. C. Beigbeder (FRA) 1–6 6–4 6–3. ***Doubles:*** C. Shuurmans (BEL)/I. Tulyaganova (UZB) d. C. Carlotti (FRA)/S. Foretz (FRA) 6–2 7–5.

Bossonnens, Switzerland – November 9–15 – ***Singles:*** Z. Ondraskva (CZE) d. L. Bao (SUI) 6–2 7–5. ***Doubles:*** Z. Hedjdova (CZE)/A. Vaskova (CZE) d. D. Bedanova (CZE)/Z. Ondraskova (CZE) 6–4 7–6(5).

Suzano, SP, Brazil – November 9–15 – ***Singles:*** A. Vanc (ROM) d. L. Dell'Angelo (ITA) 6–4 6–3. ***Doubles:*** A. Sebova (SVK)/S. Urickova (SVK) d. L. Dell'Angelo (ITA)/A. Serra Zanetti (ITA) 3–6 6–2 6–4.

El Salvador, San Salvador – November 9–15 – ***Singles:*** A. Ortuno (ESP) d. A. Tricerri (SUI) 6–1 6–0. ***Doubles:*** J. Moore (GBR)/A. Ortuno (ESP) d. S. Starrett (USA)/A. Tricerri (SUI) 6–3 3–6 6–1.

Sao Jose dos Campos, SP, Brazil – November 16–22 – ***Singles:*** A. Sebova (SVK) d. D. Olivera (URU) 6–4 6–4. ***Doubles:*** A. Sebova (SVK)/S. Urickova (SVK) d. T. Dabek (USA)/J. Myrna (UKR) 6–0 6–2.

Manila I, Philippines – November 16–22 – ***Singles:*** M. Fernandez (PHI) d. L. Van Rooyen (RSA) 6–2 6–0. ***Doubles:*** L. Andrtiyani (INA)/I. Iskandar (INA) d. Y. A. Chen (TPE)/H. L. Hsu (TPE) 2–6 6–3 6–3.

Biel III, Switzerland – November 16–22 – ***Singles:*** A. Vaskova (CZE) d. Z. Ondraskova (CZE) 6–2 6–1. ***Doubles:*** D. Bedanova (CZE)/L. Steinbach (GER) d. G. Arn (GER)/K. Miskolozi (HUN) 6–2 6–1.

Haibara, Japan – November 16–22 – ***Singles:*** M. Inoue (JPN) d. K. Ishida (JPN) 6–4 6–3. ***Doubles:*** K. Isida (JPN)/T. Isida (JPN) d. M. Inoue (JPN)/Y. Nishimata (JPN) 5–7 7–6(7) 6–3.

Deauville, France – November 16–22 – ***Singles:*** L. Bacheva (BUL) d. S. Sosnarova (SVK) 6–0 6–0. ***Doubles:*** E. Curutchet (FRA)/S. Schoeffel (FRA) d. L. Bacheva (BUL)/I. Tulyaganova (UZB) 6–0 6–0.

Campos, Brazil – November 23–29 – ***Singles:*** V. Sassi (ITA) d. J. Cortez (BRA) 7–6(1) 3–6 6–3. ***Doubles:*** K. Chevalier (FRA)/S. Urickova (SVK) d. L. Bernal (PAR)/P. Racedo (ARG) 6–3 7–6(7).

Culiacan, Mexico – November 23–29 – ***Singles:*** Z. Gubacsi (HUN) d, A. Tricerri (SUI) 6–0 ret. ***Doubles:*** A. Jidkova (RUS)/R. Kolbovic (CAN) d. Z. Gubasci (HUN)/A. Tricerri (SUI) 6–3 6–2.

Ioujima, Japan – November 23–29 – ***Singles:*** M. Inoue (JPN) d. R. Fujiwara (JPN) 6–1 3–6 7–6(3). ***Doubles:*** A. Gunji (JPN)/K. Ishida (JPN) d. S. Okamoto (JPN)/K. Taguchi (JPN) 6–2 6–2.

Manila II, Philippines – November 23–29 – ***Singles:*** K. P. Tong (HKG) d. L. Van Rooyen (RSA) 6–3 6–1. ***Doubles:*** K-M. Chang (KOR)/J-H. Kim (KOR) d. L. Andriyani (INA)/I. Iskandar (INA) 6–3 7–6(4).

Rio de Janeiro, Brazil – November 30–December 6 – ***Singles:*** K. Chevalier (FRA) d. S. Valentini (ARG) 6–4 0–6 6–2. ***Doubles:*** K. Chevalier (FRA)/S. Urickova (SVK) d. J. Cortez (BRA)/S. Valenti (ARG) 6–2 3–6 6–3.

Prerov, Czech Republic – November 30–December 6 – ***Singles:*** L. Prusova (CZE) d. Z. Ondraskova (CZE) 6–3 6–3. ***Doubles:*** R. Kucerova (CZE)/ L. Prusova (CZE) d. O. Blahotova (CZE)/E. Martincova (CZE) 6–7(3) 6–1 6–2.

Mallorca III, Spain – November 30–December 6 – ***Singles:*** J. Vakulenko (UKR) d. L. Pena (ESP) 6–4 6–1. ***Doubles:*** A. Nogueira (POR)/Y. Yamagishi (JPN) d. S. Sosnarova (SVK)/M. Vrba (GER) 6–4 3–6 6–1.

Cairo, Egypt – November 30–December 6 – ***Singles:*** B. Mouhtassine (MAR) d. N. Louarsabishvili (GEO) 3–6 6–3 6–2. ***Doubles:*** N. Louarsabishvili (GEO)/B. Mouhtassine (MAR) d. S. Da Ponte (ITA)/N. Vierin (ITA) 7–5 6–3.

Mallorca IV, Spain – December 7–13 – ***Singles:*** R. M. Andres (ESP) d. G. Casoni (ITA) 5–7 6–4 6–3. ***Doubles:*** K. Altilia (ITA)/G. Casoni (ITA) d. P. Garcia (ESP)/K. Liggan (IRE) 6–3 7–6.

Cairo, Egypt – December 7–13 – ***Singles:*** N. Louarsabishvili (GEO) d. G. Volekova (SVK) 1–6 6–2 7–5. ***Doubles:*** N. Louarsabishvili (GEO)/B. Mouhtassine (MAR) d. L. Nanusevic (YUG)/G. Volekova (SVK) 6–3 6–3.

ITF WOMEN'S $25,000 TOURNAMENTS

Clearwater, FL, USA – January 26–February 1 – ***Singles:*** K. Bandi (USA) d. M. Washington (USA) 6–2 6–1. ***Doubles:*** M. Drake (CAN)/R. Kolbovic (CAN) d. K. Brandi (USA)/K. Miller (USA) 4–6 6–3 6–4.

Rogaska Slatina, Slovenia – February 9–15 – ***Singles:*** K. Hrdlickova (CZE) d. M. Shaughnessy (USA) 6–2 3–6 6–4. ***Doubles:*** T. Krizan (SLO)/K. Srebotnik (SLO) d. T. Pisnik (SLO)/M. Schnitzer (GER) 6–0 6–3.

Redbridge, Great Britain – February 16–22 – ***Singles:*** S. Nacuk (YUG) d. L. Woodroffe (GBR) 6–4 6–3. ***Doubles:*** V. Csurgo (HUN)/E. Tatarkova (UKR) d. K. Freye (GER)/H. Rosen (ISR) 7–5 6–3.

Bushey, Great Britain – February 23–March 1 – ***Singles:*** E. Tatarkova (UKR) d. D. Zaric (YUG) 6–2 4–6 6–0. ***Doubles:*** T. Musgrave (AUS)/A. A. Siddall (GBR) d. K. Freye (GER)/N. Van Lottum (FRA) 7–6(2) 4–6 6–2.

Rockford, IL, USA – March 2–8 – ***Singles:*** N. Pratt (AUS) d. J. Steck (RSA) 6–2 6–3. ***Doubles:*** S. De Beer (RSA)/L. Lee (USA) d. N. Louarsabishvili (GEO)/S. Noorlander (NED) 6–2 6–4.

Biel I, Switzerland – March 9–15 – ***Singles:*** N. Feber (BEL) d. K. Hrdlickova (CZE) 6–7(8) 6–3 6–4. ***Doubles:*** K. Freye (GER)/N. Van Lottum (FRA) d. N. Feber (BEL)/T. Krizan (SLO) 6–3 3–6 7–6(4).

Noda, Japan – March 16–22 – ***Singles:*** S. Asagoe (JPN) d. H. Inoue (JPN) 6–2 6–4. ***Doubles:*** K. Ishida (JPN)/K. Nagatomi (JPN) d. K. Nagatsuka (JPN)/S. Obata (JPN) 3–6 6–2 6–3.

Reims, France – March 16–22 – ***Singles:*** L. Andretto (FRA) d. S. Valekova (SVK) 6–2 6–1. ***Doubles:*** D. Van De Zande (BEL)/A. Hopmans (NED) d. E. Bes (ESP)/C. Martinez Granados (ESP) 6–4 6–3.

The Woodlands, TX, USA – March 23–29 – ***Singles:*** E. Wagner (GER) d. A. Smashnova (ISR) 2–6 6–1 7–5. ***Doubles:*** E. Callens (BEL)/L. Horn (RSA) d. N. Dechy (FRA)/L. Ghirardi-Rubbi (FRA) 6–4 6–2.

Calvi, France – April 6–12 – ***Singles:*** G. Kucerova (GER) d. N. Feber (BEL) 7–5 6–1. ***Doubles:*** N. Feber (BEL)/J. Wohr (GER) d. E. Curutchet (FRA)/S. Georges (FRA) 6–1 ret.

Athens, Greece – April 6–12 – ***Singles:*** A. Smashnova (ISR) d. R. Kuti-Kis (HUN) 1–6 6–2 6–2. ***Doubles:*** A. Canepa (ITA)/T. Garbin (ITA) d. A. Pirsu (ROM)/A. Vanc (ROM) 5–7 6–2 6–4 .

Dubai, United Arab Emirates – April 6–12 – ***Singles:*** K. Nagy (HUN) d. W. Prakusya (INA) 6–4 6–1. ***Doubles:*** W. Prakusya (INA)/B. Sangaram (THA) d. P. Gaspar (POR)/L. Varmuza (SMR) 7–6(1) 1–6 6–3.

Burbank, CA, USA – April 13–19 – ***Singles:*** L. Lee (USA) d. J. Watanabe (USA) 6–4 6–4. ***Doubles:*** D. Graham (USA)/J. Okada (USA) d. L. Plemming (AUT)/K. Schlukebir (USA) 2–6 7–5 6–3.

Shenzhen, China – April 20–26 – ***Singles:*** E. H. Kim (KOR) d. J-Q. Yi (CHN) 6–3 6–1. ***Doubles:*** C. Barclay (AUS)/E. H. Kim (KOR) d. T. Hotta (JPM)/G. Biggs (AUS) 6–3 6–2(1).

Industry Hills, CA, USA – April 20–26 – ***Singles:*** M. Drake (CAN) d. L. Osterloh (USA) 6–4 6–4. ***Doubles:*** E. De Lone (USA)/K. Schlukebir (USA) d. K. Grant (RSA)/J. Watanabe (USA) 6–4 4–6 6–3.

Espinho, Portugal – April 20–26 – ***Singles:*** M. Ramon (ESP) d. A. Ortuno (ESP) 6–0 6–2. ***Doubles:*** K. De Weille (NED)/N. Van Lottum (FRA) d. K. Freye (GER)/S. Meier (GER) 4–6 6–3 7–5.

Seoul, Korea – May 4–10 – ***Singles:*** J-Y. Choi (KOR) d. J-Q. Yi (KOR) 6–3 7–5. ***Doubles:*** Y-J. Cho (KOR)/S-H. Park (KOR) d. D. Ding (CHN)/T. Li (CHN) 6–1 3–6 6–2.

Midlothian, VA, USA – May 4–10 – ***Singles:*** C. Papadaki (GRE) d. M. P. Zavagli (ITA) 7–5 6–4. ***Doubles:*** T. Musgrave (AUS)/B. Rippner (USA) d. M. Drake (CAN)/R. Kolbovic (CAN) 6–3 6–3.

Tampico, Mexico – May 4–10 – ***Singles:*** S. Taylor (USA) d. L. Varmuza (SMR) 4–6 6–4 4–1 ret. ***Doubles:*** A. Engel (USA)/A. Jidkova (RUS) d. P. Cabezas (CHI)/V. Menga (BRA) 7–6(2) 7–5.

Orlando, FL, USA – May 11–17 – ***Singles:*** J. Hennin (BEL) (Junior Exempt) d. J. Chi (USA) 6–2 6–3. ***Doubles:*** N. De Villiers (RSA)/J. Steck (RSA) d. M. Drake (CAN)/R. Kolbovic (CAN) 6–3 6–2.

Spartenberg, SC, USA – May 18–24 – ***Singles:*** C. Papadaki (GRE) d. T. Singian (USA) 6–3 6–0. ***Doubles:*** K. Ishida (JPN)/K. Nagatomi (JPN) d. R. Kolbovic (CAN)/J. Steck (RSA) 6–3 7–5.

Warsaw, Poland – May 25 –June 1 – ***Singles:*** M. Pastikova (CZE) d. R. M. Andres (ESP) 7–5 6–3. ***Doubles:*** O. Blahotova (CZE)/J. Ondrouchova (CZE) d. A. Canepa (ITA)/A. Lombardi (ITA) 7–6(4) 6–4.

Surbiton, Great Britain – June 1–7 – ***Singles:*** A. Cocheteux (FRA) d. S. Noorlander (NED) 6–2 6–4. ***Doubles:*** Cancelled.

Budapest, Hungary – June 1–7 – ***Singles:*** A. Foldenyi (HUN) d. S. Talaja (CRO) 6–2 6–4. ***Doubles:*** A. Foldenyi (HUN)/R. Kuti-Kis (HUN) d. P. Gaspar (HUN)/P. Mandula (HUN) 6–0 6–4.

Bytom, Poland – June 1–7 – ***Singles:*** L. Cervanova (SVK) d. S. Georges (FRA) 6–3 6–0. ***Doubles:*** R. M. Andres (ESP)/M. Ramon (ESP) d. L. Cervanova (SVK)/J. Husarova (SVK) 6–3 6–3.

Sopot, Poland – June 15–21 – ***Singles:*** A. Foldenyi (HUN) d. N. Petrova (RUS) 3–6 6–2 7–6(5). ***Doubles:*** A. Foldenyi (HUN)/R. Kuti-Kis (HUN) d. M. Kotchta (GER)/S. Schmilde (GER) 6–1 7–6(4).

Mount Pleasant, SC, USA – June 15–21 – ***Singles:*** V. Webb (CAN) d. D. Ding (CHN) 4–6 7–6(2) 6–2. ***Doubles:*** V. Webb (CAN)/K. Phebus (USA) d. A. Engel (USA)/K. Palme (MEX) 6–2 6–1.

Vaihingen, Germany – June 29–July 5 – ***Singles:*** L. Cervanova (SVK) d. S. Kloesel (GER) 6–2 7–5. ***Doubles:*** L. Courtois (BEL)/M. Muric (CRO) d. J. Abe (GER)/L. Bacheva (BUL) 6–1 6–4.

Orbetello, Italy – June 29–July 5 – ***Singles:*** F. Zuluaga (COL) d. M. Diaz-Oliva (ARG) 6–1 7–6(6). ***Doubles:*** A. Canepa (ITA)/T. Garbin (ITA) d. F. Zuluaga (COL)/M. Mazzota (USA) 6–2 6–3.

Puchheim, Germany – July 6–12 – ***Singles:*** G. Riera (ESP) d. L. Bacheva (BUL) 6–4 6–4. ***Doubles:*** V. Csurgo (HUN)/N. Koves (HUN) d. S. Meier (GER)/J. Woehr (GER) 4–6 6–0 6–3.

Qing Dao, China – July 13–19 – ***Singles:*** J-Q. Yi (CHN) d. D. Ding (CHN) 6–2 6–3. ***Doubles:*** L. Li (CHN)/J-Q Yi (CHN) d. C. B. Khoo (MAS)/S. Kurioka (JPN) 6–4 6–2.

Darmstadt, Germany – July 13–19 – ***Singles:*** P. Mandula (HUN) d. L. Bacheva (BUL) 3–6 6–4 7–5. ***Doubles:*** L. Courtois (BEL)/N. Van Lottum (FRA) d. V. Csurgo (HUN)/N. Koves (HUN) 7–5 6–2.

Gexto, Spain – July 13–19 – ***Singles:*** A. Montolio (ESP) d. K. Nagy (HUN) 7–6(4) 7–6(5). ***Doubles:*** L. Dominguez (ESP)/V. Menga (BRA) d. T. Hotta (JPN)/P. Rampre (SLO) 3–6 6–4 7–5.

Peachtree, GA, USA – July 20–26 – ***Singles:*** K. Brandi (USA) d. A. Kremer (LUX) 6–3 6–3. ***Doubles:*** J. Pulin (GBR)/L. Woodroffe (GBR) d. V. Webb (CAN)/K. Phebus (USA) 3–6 6–2 6–4.

Dublin, Ireland – July 20–26 – ***Singles:*** L. Ahl (GBR) d. P. Mandula (HUN) 7–6(11) 6–3. ***Doubles:*** K. Freye (GER)/A. Ortuno (ESP) d. L. McShea (AUS)/T. Musgrave (AUS) w/o.

Valladolid, Spain – July 20–26 – ***Singles:*** R. Sandu (ROM) d. R. Kuti-Kis (HUN) 6–3 6–3. ***Doubles:*** G. Riera (ESP)/S. Sfar (TUN) d. R. M. Andres (ESP)/E. Bes (ESP) 7–6(5) 7–6(3).

Les Contamines, France – July 27–August 2 – ***Singles:*** A. Barna (GER) d. L. Bacheva (BUL) 7–6(7) 6–1. ***Doubles:*** L. Bacheva (BUL)/J. Woehr (GER) d. C. Dhenin (FRA)/S. Geroges (FRA) 2–6 6–1 6–3.

Pamplona, Spain – July 27–August 2 – ***Singles:*** P. Rampre (SLO) d. M. Froehlich (GER) 6–2 7–6(3). ***Doubles:*** E. Bes (ESP)/A. Hopmans (NED) d. M. Froehlich (GER)/S. Sfar (TUN) w/o.

Winnipeg, Canada – July 27–August 2 – ***Singles:*** H. Rosen (ISR) d. M. Kochta (GER) 1–6 6–4 7–6(6). ***Doubles:*** K. Phebus (USA)/V. Webb (USA) d. R. Kolbovic (CAN)/J. Pullin (GBR) 4–6 6–4 7–6(2).

Lexington, KY, USA – August 3–9 – ***Singles:*** J. Pullin (GBR) d. A. Tordoff (GBR) 6–4 6–4. ***Doubles:*** A. Grahame (AUS)/B. Stewart (AUS) d. N. Vaidyanathan (IND)/J-Q. Yi (CHN) 6–4 1–6 6–3.

Bronx, NY, USA – August 17–23 – ***Singles:*** S. Pitowski (FRA) d. C. Black (ZIM) 6–2 7–5. ***Doubles:*** J. Pullin (GBR)/L. Woodroffe (GBR) d. C. Papadaki (GRE)/S. Pitowski (FRA) 6–3 6–1.

Spoleto, Italy – August 31–September 6 – ***Singles:*** R. Kuti-Kis (HUN) d. L. Cervanova (SVK) 6–1 6–2. ***Doubles:*** J. Kostanic (CRO)/M. Pastikova (CZE) d. H. Mochizuki (JPN)/R. Takemura (JPN) 6–3 6–4.

Manaus, Brazil – August 31–September 6 – ***Singles:*** V. Menga (BRA) d. D. Krstulovic (CRO) 1–6 6–1 6–2. ***Doubles:*** B. Colosio (BRA)/C. Tiene (BRA) d. M. J. Gaidano (ARG)/J. Moore (USA) 3–6 6–3 6–4.

Sofia 2, Bulgaria – August 31–September 6 – ***Singles:*** D. Topalova (BUL) d. N. Ostrovskaya (BLR) 6–4 4–6 6–2. ***Doubles:*** L. Bacheva (BUL)/M. Koutstaal (NED) d. M. Mihalache (ROM)/Z. Valekova (SVK) 6–1 7–5.

Edinburgh, Great Britain – September 7–13 – ***Singles:*** D. Chladkova (CZE) d. J. Ward (GBR) 6–3 6–2. ***Doubles:*** F. Schiavone (ITA)/S. Serra-Zanetti (ITA) d. L. Latimer (GBR)/H. Reesby (GBR) 6–3 6–3.

Otocec, Slovenia – September 14–20 – ***Singles:*** J. Kostanic (CRO) d. A. Barna (GER) 6–4 7–6(2). ***Doubles:*** K. Srebotnik (SLO)/J. Woehr (GBR) d. N. Koves (HUN)/D. Zaric (YUG) 6–2 6–3.

Bucharest, Romania – September 21–27 – ***Singles:*** A. Foldeyni (HUN) d. B. Mouthassine (MAR) 6–4 6–4. ***Doubles:*** R. M. Andres (ESP)/E. Bes (ESP) d. L. Cenkova (CZE)/K. Kschwendt (AUT) 4–6 7–6(6) 6–0.

Tucuman, Argentina – September 21–27 – ***Singles:*** L. Scharerer (PAR) d. G. Riera (ESP) 6–4 6–2. ***Doubles:*** M. Paz (ARG)/P. Tarbin (ARG) d. L. Masante (ARG)/L. Montalvo (ARG) 5–7 6–4 7–6(3).

Caracas, Venezuela (Copa Ericsson 1) – September 28–October 4 – ***Singles:*** N. Cahana (ISR) d. S. Bammer (AUT) 6–1 3–6 6–3. ***Doubles:*** M. F. Landa (ARG)/S. Noorlander (NED) d. N. De Villiers (RSA)/J. Husarova (SVK) 6–4 5–7 7–6(2)

Thessaloniki, Greece – September 28–October 4 – ***Singles:*** R. Kuti-Kis (HUN) d. D. Chladkova (CZE) 1–6 6–1 6–1. ***Doubles:*** E. Danilidou (GRE)/C. Papdaki (GRE) d. L. Cervanova (SVK)/M. Kucerova (GER)7–6(5) 4–6 7–5.

Tiblisi, Georgia – September 28–October 4 – ***Singles:*** E. Koulikovskaya (RUS) d. E. Makarova (RUS) 2–6 6–2 7–5. ***Doubles:*** O. Glouschenko (BLR)/T. Poutchek (BLR) d. M. Chakhnashvilli (GEO)/S. Mandagadze (GEO) 6–2 6–4.

Santiago, Chile (Copa Ericsson 2) – October 5–11 – ***Singles:*** P. Suarez (ARG) d. C. Martinez (ESP) 3–6 6–4 6–1. ***Doubles:*** M. F. Landa (ARG)/S. Noorlander (NED) d. N. De Villiers (RSA)/J. Husarova (SVK) 6–4 5–7 7–6(2).

Saga, Japan – October 5–11 – ***Singles:*** A. Molik (AUS) d. J. Dokic (AUS) 6–4 6–3. ***Doubles:*** C. Barclay (AUS)/A. Molik (AUS) d. E. Dominikovic (AUS)/B. Stewart (AUS) 7–6(3) 6–4.

Batumi, Georgia – October 5–11 – ***Singles:*** A. Hopmans (NED) d. A. Myskina (RUS) 6–2 7–5. ***Doubles:*** E. Koulikovskaya (RUS)/E. Syssoeva (RUS) d. A. Hopmans (NED)/M. Schnell (AUT) 6–4 3–6 6–0.

Seoul, Korea – October 12–18 – ***Singles:*** J. Y. Choi (KOR) d. S. H. Park (KOR) 6–4 6–3. ***Doubles:*** S. Asagoe (JPN)/K. Freye (GER) d. C. Barclay (AUS)/Y. J. Choi (KOR) 6–2 7–6(3).

Sao Paulo, Brazil – October 12–18 – ***Singles:*** C. Papadaki (GRE) d. F. Schiavone (ITA) 4–6 6–4 6–2. ***Doubles:*** S. Noorlander (NED)/C. Papdaki (GRE) d. A. Canepa (ITA)/A. Serra Zanetti (ITA) 6–3 6–7(4) 7–6(4).

Indian Wells, CA, USA – October 12–18 – ***Singles:*** P. Stoyanova (BUL) d. E. H. Kim (KOR) 6–3 6–4. ***Doubles:*** P. Stoyanova (BUL)/L. Lee (USA) d. E. De Lone (USA)/K. Schlukebir (USA) 6–0 6–7(4) 6–1.

Jous-les-Tours, France – October 18–25 – ***Singles:*** A. Cocheteux (FRA) d. S. Foretz (FRA) 6–1 6–1. ***Doubles:*** L. Cenkova (CZE)/E. Martincova (CZE) d. E. Loit (FRA)/ A. Cocheteux (FRA) 3–6 6–4 7–5.

Montevideo, Uruguay – October 18–25 – ***Singles:*** P. Suarez (ARG) d. A. Serra-Zanetti (ITA) 7–5 6–4. ***Doubles:*** P. Suarez (ARG)/L. Montalvo (ARG) d. E. Bes (ESP)/M. F. Landa (ARG) 6–2 6–2.

Welwyn, Great Britain – October 18–25 – ***Singles:*** E. Gagliardi (SUI) d. A. Kremer (LUX) 6–1 1–1 ret. ***Doubles:*** L. Courtois (BEL)/T. Kriznan (SLO) d. L. Plemming (AUS)/S. Smith (GBR) 7–6(2) 6–4.

Gold Coast, Australia – October 18–25 – ***Singles:*** A. Molik (AUS) d. C. Barclay (AUS) 6–4 7–6(1). ***Doubles:*** C. Barclay (AUS)/K. A. Guse (AUS) d. L. McShea (AUS)/T. Musgrave (AUS) 6–4 6–2.

Mogi das Cruzes, Brazil – November 2–8 – ***Singles:*** J. Husarova (SVK) d. P. Suarez (ARG) 6–2 2–6 6–1. ***Doubles:*** E. Bes (ESP)/M. F. Landa (ARG) d. L. Masante (ARG)/A. Ortuno (ESP) 4–6 6–2 6–2.

Hull, Great Britain – November 9–15 – ***Singles:*** B. Schwartz (AUT) d. F. Lubiani (ITA) 3–6 6–3 6–2. ***Doubles:*** B. Schwartz (AUT)/J. Woehr (GER) d. F. Lubiani (ITA)/M. P. Zavagli (ITA) 6–2 6–3.

Mount Gambier, Australia – November 9–15 – ***Singles:*** C. Watson (AUS) d. C. Barclay (AUS) 3–6 6–0 7–5. ***Doubles:*** C. Barclay (AUS)/K. A. Guse (AUS) d. D. Buth (USA)/T. Musgrave (AUS) 6–7(6) 6–3 6–1.

Ramat Hasharon, Israel – November 9–15 – ***Singles:*** J. Henin (BEL) d. P. Wartusch (AUT) 6–2 6–4. ***Doubles:*** K. Clijsters (BEL)/J. Henin (BEL) d. O. Glouschenko (BLR)/T. Poutchek (BLR) 6–2 6–0.

Caracas, Venezuela – November 16–22 – ***Singles:*** M. Drake (CAN) d. V. Menga (BRA) 6–1 6–2. ***Doubles:*** V. Menga (BRA)/A. Ortuno (ESP) d. M. Drake (CAN)/C. Schneider (GER) 6–3 5–7 6–3.

Port Pirie, Australia – November 16–22 – ***Singles:*** K. Miller (USA) d. V. Webb (CAN) 6–2 7–6(4). ***Doubles:*** C. Barclay (AUS)/T. Musgrave (AUS) d. A. Grahame (AUS)/B. Stweart (AUS) 5–7 7–5 6–2.

Buenos Aires, Argentina – November 16–22 – ***Singles:*** P. Suarez (ARG) d. A. Vanc (ROM) 4–6 6–1 6–4. ***Doubles:*** S. Noorlander (NED)/K. Srebotnik (SLO) d. E. Bes (ESP)/M. F. Landa (ARG) 7–6(5) 6–3.

Nurioopta, Australia – November 23–29 – ***Singles:*** K. Miller (USA) d. A. Grahame (AUS) 6–2 6–2. ***Doubles:*** D. Jones (AUS)/V. Webb (CAN) d. C. Barclay (AUS)/T. Musgrave (AUS) 6–3 7–5.

Lima, Peru – November 23–29 – ***Singles:*** M. Ramon (ESP) d. J. Husarova (SVK) 6–1 4–1 ret. ***Doubles:*** K. Srebotnik (SLO)/Z. Valekova (SVK) d. A. Canepa (ITA)/C. G. Martinez (ESP) 6–7(4) 7–5 6–4.

Bogota, Colombia – November 30–December 6 – ***Singles:*** F. Zuluaga (COL) d. A. Serra Zanetti (ITA) 6–3 6–2. ***Doubles:*** K. Srebotnik (SLO)/Z. Valekova (SVK) d. M. Mesa (COL)/F. Zuluaga (COL) 6–3 6–4.

Guadalajara, Mexico – November 30–December 6 – ***Singles:*** K. Marosi (HUN) d. V. Menga (BRA) 7–5 6–3. ***Doubles:*** L. Lee (USA)/M. Shaughnessy (USA) d. M. D'Agostini (BRA)/K. Marosi (HUN) 6–1 6–3.

Cali, Colombia, – December 7–13 – ***Singles:*** F. Zulaga (COL) d. A. Glass (GER) 6–1 6–1. ***Doubles:*** K. Srebotnik (SLO)/Z. Valekova (SVK) d. L. Montalvo (ARG)/A. Ortuno (ESP) 2–6 6–3 6–2.

Pruhonice, Czech Republic – December 14–20 – ***Singles:*** F. Zuluaga (COL) d. A. Glass (GER) 6–1 6–3. ***Doubles:*** E. Melchirova (CZE)/H. Vildova (CZE) d. L. Cervanova (SVK)/M. Kucerova (GER) 4–6 6–3 6–4.

ITF WOMEN'S $50,000 TOURNAMENTS

Midland, MI, USA – February 9–15 – ***Singles:*** A Stevenson (USA) d. S. Reeves (USA) 7–6(6) 6–1. ***Doubles:*** C. Barclay (AUS)/K. A. Guse (AUS) d. O. Barabanschikova (BLR)/E. De Lone (USA) 6–2 6–4.

Phoenix, AZ, USA – March 30–April 5 – ***Singles:*** K. Brandi (USA) d. L. Osterloh (USA) 6–0 6–4. ***Doubles:*** A. Olsza (POL)/K. Triska (SWE) d. A. Frazier (USA)/R. Hiraki (JPN) 6–4 7–6(5).

Gifu, Japan – April 27–May 3 – ***Singles:*** M. Miyauchi (JPN) d. S-H. Park (KOR) 6–3 6–4. ***Doubles:*** C. Barclay (AUD)/K. A. Guse (AUS) d. Y-J. Cho (KOR)/S-H. Park (KOR) 7–6(3) 6–4.

Cardiff, Great Britain – May 4–10 – ***Singles:*** K. Hrdlickova (CZE) d. A. Smashnova (ISR) 7–5 6–4. ***Doubles:*** L. Horn (RSA)/K. Srebotnik (SLO) d. N. Feber (BEL)/P. Langrova (CZE) 6–4 6–3.

Tashkent, Uzbekistan – June 1–7 – ***Singles:*** P. Wartusch (AUT) d. T. Obzilier (ISR) 6–3 6–3. ***Doubles:*** M. Mazzota (USA)/F. Zuluaga (COL) d. L. Schaerer (PAR)/M. Vavrinec (SMR) 6–2 6–1.

Sochi, Russia – June 8–14 – ***Singles:*** M. Shaughanessy (USA) d. S. Obata (JPN) 7–6(3) 6–7(0) 6–2. ***Doubles:*** S. Obata (JPN)/K. Shibata (JPN) d. N. Louarsabishvilli (GEO)/E. Tatarkova (UKR) 3–6 6–4 6–2.

Mahwah, NJ, USA – July 13–19 – ***Singles:*** A. Frazier (USA) d. F. Li (CHN) w/o. ***Doubles:*** A. Frazier (USA)/R. Hiraki (JPN) d. J. Chi (USA)/J. Okada (USA) 4–6 6–4 6–4.

Bordeaux, France – September 14–20 – ***Singles:*** L. Sanchez (ESP) d. R. Kuti-Kis (HUN) 6–1 6–4. ***Doubles:*** A. Foldenyi (HUN)/R. Kuti-Kis (HUN) d. A. Hopmans (NED)/S. Kloesel (GER) 6–2 6–3.

Seattle, WA, USA – September 21–27 – ***Singles:*** J. Nejedly (CZE) d. L. Osterloh (USA) 6–1 6–3. ***Doubles:*** E. Callens (BEL)/L. Horn (RSA) d. L. Osterloh (USA)/M. Washington (USA) 6–2 3–6 6–3.

Albuquereque, NM, USA – October 5–11 – ***Singles:*** A. Kremer (LUX) d. J. Chi (USA) 2–6 6–4 6–4. ***Doubles:*** R. McQuillan (AUS)/M. Nana (JPN) d. E. De Lone (USA)/N. Pratt (AUS) 7–6(5) 6–2.

Southampton, Great Britain – October 12–18 – ***Singles:*** A. G. Sidot (FRA) d. A. Cocheteux (FRA) 7–5 6–4. ***Doubles:*** E. Callens (BEL)/L. Courtois (FRA) d. E. Loit (DRA)/A. Cocheteux (FRA) 6–2 6–2.

Houston, TX, USA – October 18–25 – ***Singles:*** T. Snyder (USA) d. J. Craybas (USA) 6–3 6–4. ***Doubles:*** N. Miyagi (JPN)/M. Saeki (JPN) d. R. Hiraki (JPN)/E. H. Kim (KOR) 6–1 4–6 6–1.

Austin, TX, USA – October 26–November 1 – ***Singles:*** K. Brandi (USA) d. M. Tu (USA) 3–6 6–3 6–4. ***Doubles:*** L. Lee (USA)/M. Drake (CAN) d. N. De Villers (RSA)/L. Horn (RSA) 6–1 6–1.

Poitiers, France – October 26–November 1 – ***Singles:*** S. Nacuk (YUG) d. E. Makarova (RUS) 6–0 5–7 6–1. ***Doubles:*** O. Lugina (UKR)/E. Markova (RUS) d. G. Kucerova (GER)/R. Pelikanova (CZE) 6–0 6–1.

Cergy Pontoise, France – November 30–December 6 – ***Singles:*** S. Pitkowski (FRA) d. N. Dechy (FRA) 7–5 3–6 7–6(4). ***Doubles:*** K. Boogert (NED)/A. G. Sidot (FRA) d. C. Dhenin (FRA)/F. Loit (FRA) 7–5 6–2.

Bad Gogging, Germany – December 7–13 – ***Singles:*** K. Habsudova (SVK) d. M. Weingartner (GER) 7–6 6–2. ***Doubles:*** K. Hrdlickova (CZE)/H. Vildova (CZE) d. Adriana Barna (GER)/Anca Barna (GER) 6–4 6–3.

ITF WOMEN'S $75,000 TOURNAMENTS

Rochester, MN, USA – February 16–22 – ***Singles:*** L. McNeil (USA) d. A. Miller (USA) 7–6(6) 7–5. ***Doubles:*** C. Barclay (AUS)/K. A Guse (AUS) d. G. Helgeson-Nielsen (CAN)/N. De Villiers (RSA) 6–4 6–4.

Estoril, Portugal – April 6–12 – ***Singles:*** B. Schwartz (AUT) d. R. Sandu (ROM) 6–2 6–3. ***Doubles:*** E. Loit (FRA)/C. Dhenin (FRA) d. R. Bobkova (CZE)/C. Schneider (GER) 6–2 6–3.

Prostejov, Czech Republic – April 20–26 – ***Singles:*** R. Dragomir (ROM) d. A. Gersi (CZE) 6–0 6–0. ***Doubles:*** L. Cenkova (CZE)/K. Kroupova (CZE) d. O. Lugina (UKR)/E. Wagner (GER) 6–4 4–6 6–4.

Oporto, Portugal – May 11–17 – ***Singles:*** A. Smashnova (ISR) d. A. Dechaume-Balle (FRA) 6–2 6–2. ***Doubles:*** N. Feber (BEL)/K. Srebotnik (SLO) d. S. De Beer (RSA)/R. Jensen (USA) 5–7 6–1 6–4.

Salt Lake City, UT, USA – July 27–August 2 – ***Singles:*** M. De Swardt (RSA) d. K. Brandi (USA) 6–2 6–2. ***Doubles:*** M. De Swardt (RSA)/S. Smith (GBR) d. L. Horn (RSA)/K. Kschwent (AUT) 6–2 6–2.

Bratislava, Slovak Republic – August 10–16 – ***Singles:*** M. Sanchez-Lorenzo (ESP) d. R. Bobkova (CZE) 3–6 6–2 6–2. ***Doubles:*** M. Nekvapilova (CZE)/H. Sromova (CZE) d. L. Nemeckova (CZE)/K. Studenikova (SVK) 6–2 6–4.

Santa Clara, CA, USA – September 28–October 4 – ***Singles:*** A. Smashnova (ISR) d. A. Frazier (USA) 2–6 6–4 6–2. ***Doubles:*** E. Callens (BEL)/L. Horn (RSA) d. L. Osterloh (USA)/M. Washington (USA) 6–2 3–6 6–3.

New Delhi, India – November 30–December 6 – ***Singles:*** T. Garbin (ITA) d. A. Hopmans (NED) 6–3 6–2. ***Doubles:*** L. Cenkova (CZE)/A. Hopmans (NED) d. T. Krizan (SLO)/K. Kschwendt (AUT) w/o.

International Team Competitions

European Cups – Men and Women
Peugeot ATP Tour World Team Championship

Undefeated in the World Team Cup, where he was the mainstay of Germany's success, Tommy Haas climbed from 41 to 34 in the rankings after reaching the final in Lyon where he held a match point against Alex Corretja. (Stephen Wake)

European Cup

Henry Wancke

MEN

Italy, having lost to Sweden in the final of the Davis Cup, fielded their second string to claim the European equivalent. In so doing, they gained some revenge over the Scandinavians who were amongst their victims in the group matches. For Italy it was busy time. Not only did they host the Davis Cup in Milan, but also the Champions Division of the European Men's Team Championships at Montecatini. This meant delaying the European Cup by a few weeks resulting in the withdrawal of Germany and the Netherlands who, despite their non-appearance, retain their places in the top division for 1999.

Italy beat both Great Britain, the defending champions, and Sweden 2–1 to reach the final where they met Bulgaria, who topped the second group with a better win-loss record following a 3–0 victory over the Czech Republic, and a 1–2 loss to Spain.

As Paolo Bertolucci, who captained both the Italian's Davis Cup and European Cup teams, pointed out, playing the Davis Cup final in Italy a few weeks earlier had whetted the home crowd's appetite and it was their enthusiasm which helped his young team to claim a 2–0 victory over Bulgaria in the final which started with a close contest between the two second strings, Giorgio Galimberti and Ivaylo Traykov. However, once the Italian gained the upper hand with an 8–6 first-set tie-break, he ran out a confident 7–6 6–3 winner to take the pressure off Marzio Martelli who quickly disposed of Milen Velev 6–2 6–2.

Greece and Belgium gained promotion from the First Division while Romania, the Slovak Republic, Malta and Portugal drop down to be replaced from the Second Division by Switzerland, Austria, Luxembourg and Monaco.

The European Cup is still viewed as an excellent training ground for future Davis Cup players, a point reinforced by Bertolucci and Jeremy Bates, the British team captain. Bertolucci, however, would like the competition to be restricted to players of 23 and under, a point seemingly endorsed by Bates.

Champions Division (Montecatini, Italy)

Group One: **Italy d. Sweden 2–1:** Giorgio Galimberti lost to Bjoern Rehnquist 4–6 0–6; Marzio Martelli d. Fredrik Loven 6–2 6–2; Daniele Bracciali/Martelli d. Johan Landsberg/Loven 2–6 7–6(4) 6–0. **Italy d. Great Britain 2–1:** Bracciali lost to Martin Lee 3–6 0–6; Martelli d. Chris Wilkinson 6–2 7–5; Bracciali/Galimberti d. Lee/Wilkinson 7–5 7–6(4). **Great Britain d. Sweden 2–1:** Martin Lee lost to Rehnquist 4–6 6–2 1–6; Chris Wilkinson d. Loven 6–0 6–4; Lee/Wilkinson d. Landsberg/Loven 6–4 6–4.

Group Two: **Bulgaria d. Czech Republic 3–0:** Ivaylo Traykov d. Ota Fukarek 6–4 7–6(4); Milen Velev d. Radek Stepanek 6–2 7–6(6); Traykov/Velev d. Martin/Radek Stepanek 6–2 6–3. **Czech Republic d. Spain 3–0:** Fukarek d. Juan Balcells 6–2 6–1 R. Stepanek d. Alex Calatrava 6–4 6–3; M. Stepanek/R. Stepanek d. Balcells/Calatrava 6–3 7–5. **Spain d. Bulgaria 2–1:** Balcells lost to Traykov 6–7(4) 2–6; Calatrava d. Velev 7–6(4) 7–6(2); Balcells/Calatrava d. Traykov/Lukaev 3–2 ret.

Final: **Italy d. Bulgaria 2–0:** Galimberti d. Traykov 7–6(3) 6–3; Martelli d. Velev 6–2 6–2.

First Division

Blue Group (Athens, Greece)

Group 1: Israel d. Romania 3–0 Slovenia 2–1; Slovenia d. Romania 2–1.

Group 2: Greece d. Croatia 2–1 Slovak republic 3–0; Croatia d. Slovak republic 2–1.

Final: Greece d. Israel 2–0.

White Group (Marsa, Malta)

Ireland d. Denmark 3–0, Malta 3–0; Denmark d. Malta 3–0.

Final: Belgium d. Ireland 2–1.

Second Division

Group One (Reykjavik, Iceland)

Group 1: Belgium d. Poland 2–1, Portugal 3–0; Poland d. Portugal 3–0.

Group 2: Luxembourg d. Iceland 3–0, Monaco 3–0; Monaco d. Iceland 2–1.

Group Two (Reykjavik, Iceland)

Semi-Finals: Switzerland d. Belarus (1) 3–0; Austria (2) d. Turkey 3–0.

Final: Switzerland d. Austria 2–1.

WOMEN

The top seeded Czech Republic were unable to take advantage of the partisan home support provided by the Frydlant Nad Ostravici crowds as they slipped to a 3–0 defeat against Italy, the second favourites, in the final of the Women's European Team Championships.

It was the second time in four years that the Italians had upset the seedings and outplayed the home favourites to collect the top European prize. On this occasion, however, the task was made easier by Germany, the reigning champions, who were unable to defend their title due to 'technical reasons'. This was also the cause of the Netherlands' non-appearance.

For Italy it was the start of a remarkable few weeks as they followed this victory with an appearance in the Davis Cup final and then collected the Men's European Cup in mid-December.

Playing just two ties to become European Champions and collect the Honda Cup, the Italian team of Flora Perfetti, Gloria Pizzichini, Guilia Casoni and Paola Zavagli dropped just three sets in six matches. Surprisingly the team captain, Rafaella Reggi deployed Pizzichini in the second singles slot, who, despite her low ranking of 663, delivered two solid wins defeating first Spain's Marta Marrero (350) 6–4 6–1 and then the Czech Michaela Pastikova, 6–3 7–6.

In the First Division Poland and Croatia won their respective groups to gain promotion. Poland, who lost to Great Britain 1–2 when both their singles players were unable to upset the Britons in the group-match stage, gained their revenge in the Promotion match when the team captain, Katarzyna Teodorowicz replaced Anna Zarska with Aleksandra Olsza at number-one, pushing Katarzyna Straczy into the second singles. This strategy proved successful as they squeezed through 2–0 in two very tight matches.

Promotion to the First Division was gained by Slovenia, Luxembourg, Belarus and Ukraine who are replaced in a smaller Second Division for 1999, by Romania and Russia.

Champion's Division (Frydlant Nad Ostravici, Czech Republic)

***First round:* Greece d. Hungary 2–1:** Eleni Danilidou d. Petra Mandula 6–3 6–7(6) 6–2; Christina Papadaki lost to Annamaria Foldenyi 5–7 2–6; Danilidou/Papadaki d. Foldenyi/Mandula 6–1 7–6(5). **Spain d. Belgium 3–0:** Marta Marrero d. Cindy Schuurmans 7–5 6–3; Maria Antonia Sanchez Lorenzo d. Stephanie Deville 7–5 6–3; Lourdes Dominguez/Marrero d. Evy Last/Schuurmans 7–5 6–3.

***Semi-finals:* Czech Republic d. Greece 2–1:** Michaela Pastikova d. Eleni Danilidou 7–6(4) 5–7 6–0; Kvetoslava Hrdlickova lost to Christina Papadaki 3–6 6–1 6–7(5); Pastikova/Hrdlickova d. Danilidou/Papadaki 6–2 2–6 6–4. **Italy d. Spain 3–0:** Gloria Pizzichini d. Marrero 6–4 6–1; Flora Perfetti d. Sanchez Lorenzo 3–6 7–5 6–4; Giulia Casoni/Paola Zavagli d. Dominguez/Marrero 2–6 6–4 6–4.

***Final:* Italy d. Czech Republic 3–0:** Pizzichini d. Pastikova 6–3 7–6(5); Perfetti d. Hrdlickova 6–1 6–3; Casoni/ Zavagli d. Bedanova/Pastikova 6–3 5–7 7–5.

First Division:

Blue Group (Istanbul, Turkey)
Group One: Croatia d. Romania 2–1, Switzerland 3–0; Switzerland d. Romania 2–1.
Group Two: Slovak Republic d. Russia 3–0; Russia d. Turkey 2–1; Turkey d. Slovak Republic 2–1.
Final: Croatia d. Slovak Republic 2–1.
White Group (Zabrze, Poland)
Great Britain d. Denmark 2–1, Poland 2–1, Sweden 3–0; Poland d. Denmark 2–1; Sweden 2–1; Denmark d. Sweden 2–1.
Final: Poland d. Great Britain 2–0.

Second Division:

Group One (Espinho, Portugal): ***Semi-Finals:*** Slovenia (1) d. Ireland 2–1; Luxembourg d. Portugal (2) 2–1.
Final: Slovenia d. Luxembourg 2–1.
Group Two (Jurmala, Latvia): Belarus d. Latvia 3–0, Ukraine 3–0; Ukraine d. Latvia 3–0.

PEUGEOT ATP TOUR WORLD TEAM CHAMPIONSHIP 1998

DUSSELDORF, GERMANY, 18–24 MAY
Eight-team draw. Prize Money: $1,650,000. Surface: Clay

BLUE GROUP

Germany: Boris Becker, Tommy Haas, Nicolas Kiefer, David Prinosil
Slovakia: Dominik Hrbaty, Karol Kucera
Spain: Sergi Bruguera, Tomas Carbonell, Carlos Moya, Francisco Roig
France: Olivier Delaitre, Cedric Pioline, Fabrice Santoro

RED GROUP

Czech Republic: Slava Dosedel, Petr Korda, Cyril Suk, Daniel Vacek
Australia: Mark Philippoussis, Todd Woodbridge, Mark Woodforde
Sweden: Jonas Bjorkman, Magnus Norman, Mikael Tillstrom
United States: Michael Chang, Jim Courier, Richey Reneberg

TEAM STANDINGS

BLUE GROUP W–L Germany 4–0*, Slovakia 2–1, Spain 1–2, France 0–3
RED GROUP W–L Czech Republic 3–1*, Australia 2–1, Sweden 1–2, USA 0–3
**includes final*

BLUE GROUP RESULTS: ***Germany d. Slovakia 2–1:*** Haas (GER) d. Hrbaty (SVK) 7–6(4) 7–6(3); Kucera (SVK) d. Kiefer (GER) 6–4 6–2; Becker/Prinosil (GER) d. Hrbaty/Kucera 6–4 4–6 6–4 ***Spain d. France 2–1*** Moya (ESP) d Pioline (FRA) 6–1 6–1; Santoro (FRA) d. Bruguera (ESP) 6–2 1–6 6–0; Carbonell/ Roig (ESP) d. Delaitre/Santoro (FRA) 6–4 6–2. ***Slovakia d. Spain 3–0*** Kucera (SVK) d. Moya (ESP) 4–6 6–3 7–5; Hrbaty (SVK) d. Bruguera (ESP) 7–5 6–4; Kucera/Hrbaty (SVK) d. Carbonell/Roig (ESP) 6–4 6–3 ***Germany d. France 2–1*** Haas (GER) d. Santoro (FRA) 7–5 6–2; Pioline (FRA) d. Kiefer (GER) 7–6(4) 6–4; Becker/Prinosil (GER) d. Santoro/Delaitre (FRA) 6–3 6–4 ***Germany d. Spain 3–0*** Haas (GER) d. Bruguera (ESP) 6–1 6–4; Kiefer (GER) d. Moya (ESP) 6–1 6–4; Becker/Prinosil (GER) d. Roig/Carbonell (ESP) 7–5 6–3 ***Slovakia d. France 2–1*** Kucera (SVK) d. Pioline (FRA) 6–2 6–2; Santoro (FRA) d. Hrbaty (SVK] 3–6 6–3 7–6(6);Kucera/Hrbaty (SVK) d. Santoro/Delaitre (FRA) 7–5 6–0.

RED GROUP RESULTS: ***Czech Republic d. Sweden 3–0*** Korda (CZE) d. Bjorkman (SWE) 6–3 6–1; Dosedel (CZE) d. Norman (SWE) 6–0 6–4; Vacek/Suk (CZE) d. Bjorkman/Tillstrom (SWE) 7–6(5) 6–2. ***Australia d. USA 2–1*** Reneberg (USA) d. Woodbridge (AUS) 6–3 7–6(5); Philippoussis (AUS) d. Courier (USA) 6–3 6–4; Woodbridge/Mark Woodforde (AUS) d. Todd Martin/Reneberg (USA) 5–7 6–4 6–3. ***Australia d. Sweden 2–1*** Philippoussis (AUS) d. Bjorkman (SWE) 6–3 6–4; Norman (SWE) d. Woodforde (AUS) 6–2 6–3; Woodbridge/Woodforde (AUS) d. Bjorkman/Tillstrom (SWE) 6–3 2–6 6–3. ***Czech Republic d. USA 2–1*** Dosedel (CZE) d. Courier (USA) 6–3 6–1; Korda (CZE) d. Chang (USA) 7–6(6) 3–6 6–3; Martin/Reneberg (USA) d. Vacek/Suk (CZE) 6–4 6–4. ***Sweden d. USA 2–1*** Bjorkman (SWE) d. Chang (USA) 6–2 3–6 7–6(2); Norman (SWE) d. Courier (USA) 6–4 6–4; Martin/Reneberg (USA) d. Bjorkman/Tillstrom (SWE) 5–7 6–4 6–4. ***Czech Republic d. Australia 2–1*** Korda (CZE) d. Philippoussis (AUS) 6–3 3–6 6–2; Dosedel (CZE) d. Woodbridge (AUS) 6–1 6–4; Woodbridge/Woodforde (AUS) d. Suk/Vacek (CZE) 6–3 2–6 6–3

FINAL: ***Germany d. Czech Republic 3–0*** Haas (GER) d. Dosedel (CZE) 6–1 6–4; Kiefer (GER) d. Korda (CZE) 7–5 6–3; Becker/Prinosil (GER) d. Suk/Vacek (CZE) 6–4 4–6 6–2.

Australian Open Championships

Left: At the age of 30 the Czech left-hander Petr Korda captured his first Grand Slam title. *(Stephen Wake/Prosport)*

Below: Teenage doubles champions Mirjana Lucic (15) of Croatia (left) and world champion Martina Hingis (17), who also retained her singles crown. *(Stephen Wake/Prosport)*

Bottom left: Marcelo Rios of Chile, bred on clay, demonstrated his versatility by reaching his first Grand Slam final on hard courts. *(Stephen Wake/Prosport)*

(Stephen Wake/Prosport)

French Open Championships

A double for Spain in Paris when Arantxa Sanchez-Vicario *(right)* won for the third time and Carlos Moya *(below)* for the first. *(Stephen Wake/Prosport; Tommy Hindley/Prosport)*

Below right: The victory of Martina Hingis and Jana Novotna was the second leg of Hingis's doubles Grand Slam. *(Michael Cole)*

Left: An impressive start by the young Russian giant, Marat Safin, whose victims included Andre Agassi and the reigning champion, Gustavo Kuerten. *(Michael Cole)*

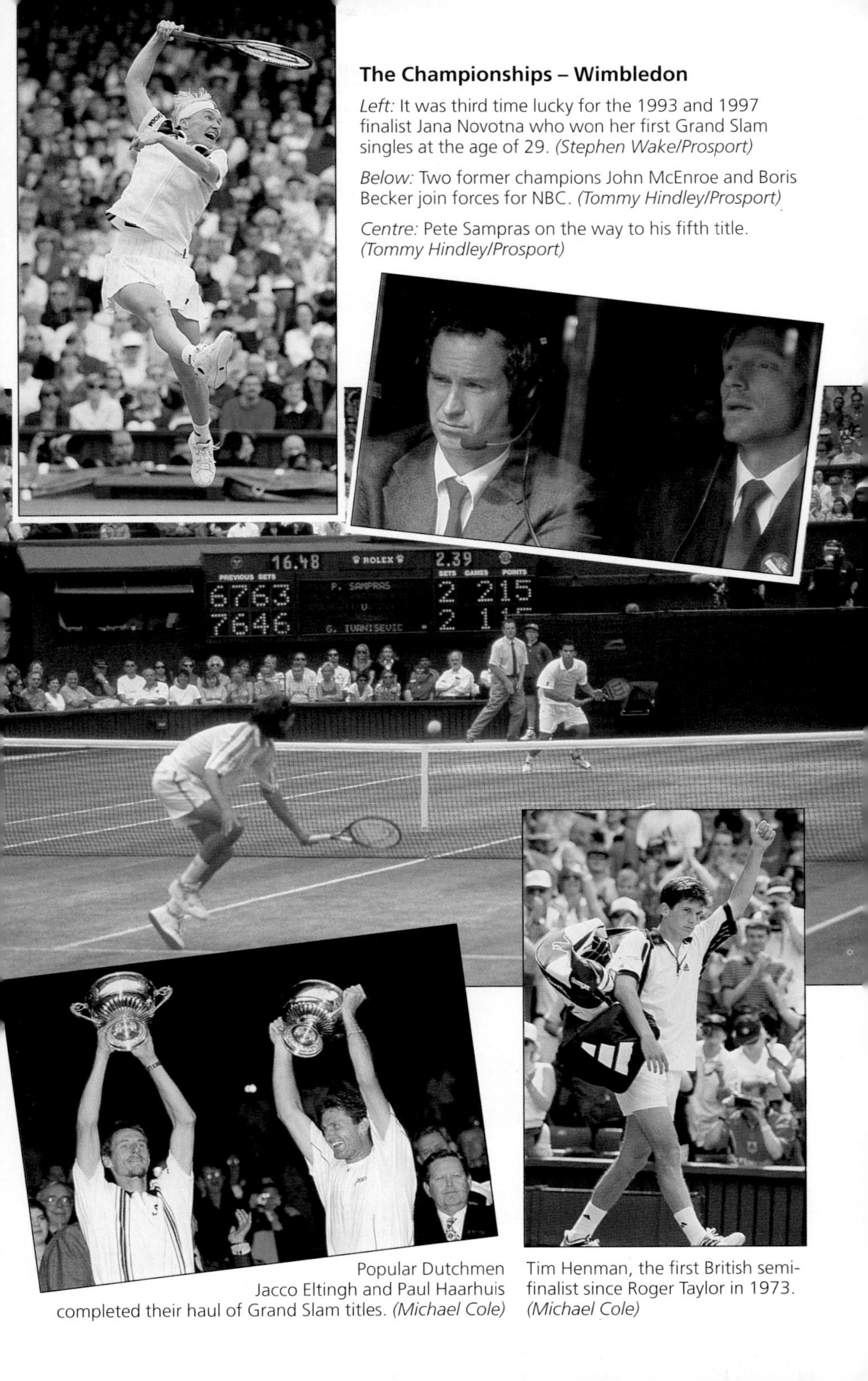

The Championships – Wimbledon

Left: It was third time lucky for the 1993 and 1997 finalist Jana Novotna who won her first Grand Slam singles at the age of 29. *(Stephen Wake/Prosport)*

Below: Two former champions John McEnroe and Boris Becker join forces for NBC. *(Tommy Hindley/Prosport)*

Centre: Pete Sampras on the way to his fifth title. *(Tommy Hindley/Prosport)*

Popular Dutchmen Jacco Eltingh and Paul Haarhuis completed their haul of Grand Slam titles. *(Michael Cole)*

Tim Henman, the first British semi-finalist since Roger Taylor in 1973. *(Michael Cole)*

US Open Championships

In the first all-Australian final since 1970, Pat Rafter *(right)* retained his tile by beating Mark Philippoussis *(below)*. *(Stephen Wake/Prosport)*

Above left: Lindsay Davenport won a first Grand Slam singles title and was the first native born US champion since Chris Evert in 1982. *(Stephen Wake/Prosport)*

A family Grand Slam in mixed doubles was completed by Serena Williams *(above centre)* who won in New York with Max Mirnyi, also her partner at Wimbledon. Sister Venus *(above right)* had won in Melbourne and Paris with Justin Gimelstob. *(Stephen Wake/Prosport)*

Rest of the year . . .

Below: A season of mixed fortunes for French No.1 Mary Pierce. *(Michael Cole)*

Left: A first Grand Slam final for 30-year-old Frenchwoman Nathalie Tauziat at Wimbledon. *(Michael Cole)*

Below: An injured thumb interrupted the season of the glamorous Russian teenager, Anna Kournikova. *(Michael Cole)*

Inset: Steffi Graf made a welcome return to the circuit in mid-season and in New Haven won her first title since May 1997. *(Michael Cole)*

Left: The Swiss No.2 Patty Schnyder, the winner of five titles in 1998, emerged at last from Hingis's shadow. *(Stephen Wake/Prosport)*

Left: Mirjana Lucic of Croatia, doubles winner in Australia. *(Stephen Wake/Prosport)*

Below left: Natasha Zvereva of Belarus, losing doubles finalist at all four Grand Slams with Davenport – a frustrating first. *(Michael Cole)*

Below right: Congratulations for Lipton winner Marcelo Rios from girlfriend Patricia Larrain. *(Michael Cole)*

Below: Richard Krajicek of Holland bends the suspect kneee that will require further surgery. *(Michael Cole)*

Right: A new blond look for Felix Mantilla of Spain, a French Open semi-finalist. *(Stephen Wake/Prosport)*

Left: French finalist Alex Corretja lost to his friend Carlos Moya in the second all-Spanish final in Paris in five years. *(Tommy Hindley/Prosport)*

Below left: Andre Agassi of the United States, firmly back in the top ten. *(Michael Cole)*

Below right: Greg Rusedski of Great Britain, the world's fastest server. *(Stephen Wake/Prosport)*

Above: Carlos Moya of Spain, down but not out in Paris. *(Tommy Hindley/ Prosport)*

Two Frenchmen who excelled at moments in 1989 – Nicolas Escude (*above left*) a semi-finalist in Melbourne and Cedric Pioline (*above right*) who reached the same stage in Paris. *(Tommy Hindley/Prosport; Stephen Wake/Prosport)*

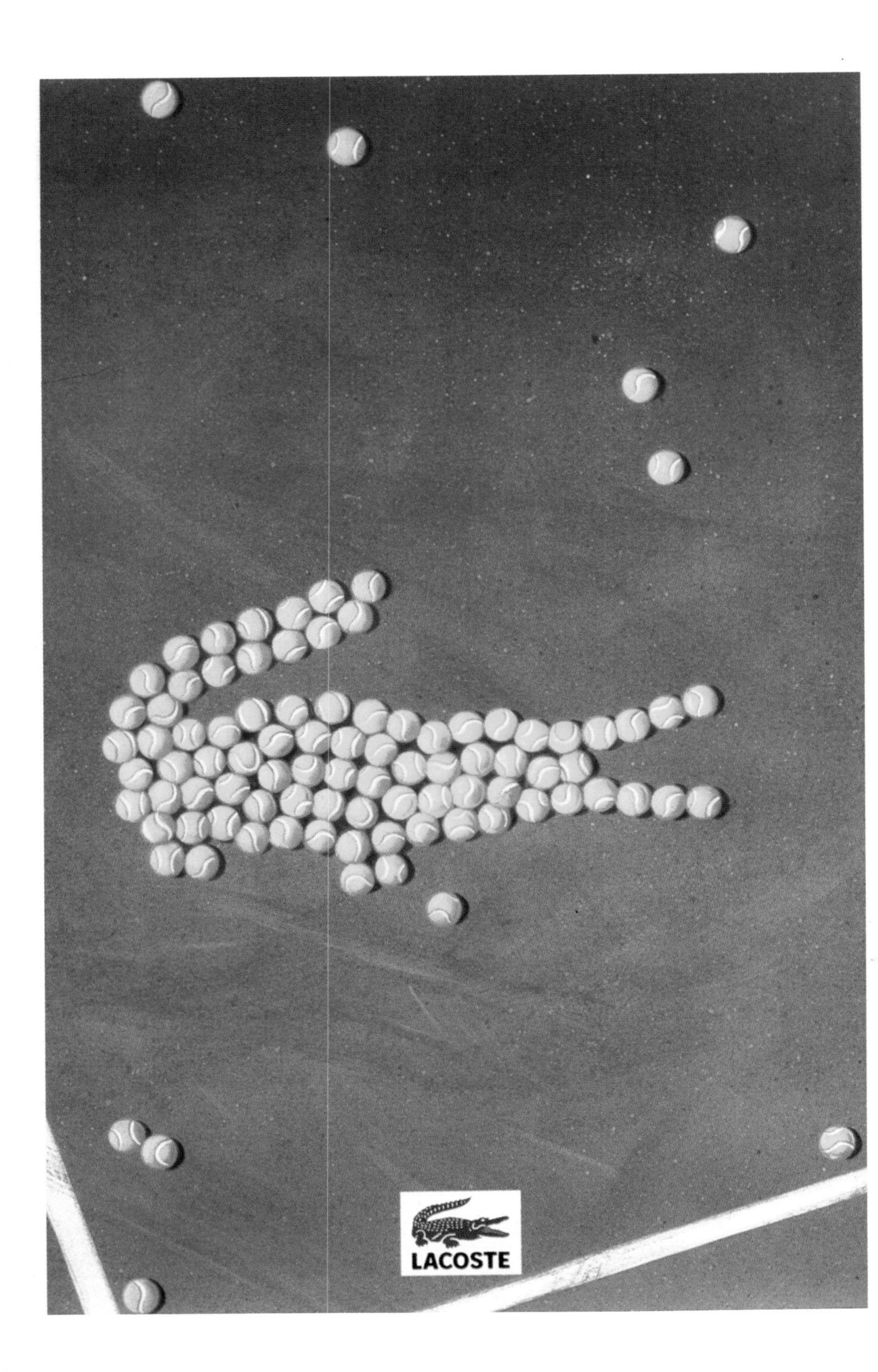
LACOSTE

Rankings

World Rankings
ATP Tour Rankings and Prize Money
History of the ATP Tour No.1 Men's Ranking
Corel WTA Tour Rankings and Prize Money
History of the WTA Tour No.1 Women's Ranking

Nicolas Escude made a spectacular start to the year by reaching the semi-finals of the Australian Open unseeded, a performance that contributed to a year-end ranking of 37, a career high. (Stephen Wake)

1998 World Rankings

John Barrett

1998 WORLD RANKINGS (last year's ranking in brackets)

1	Pete Sampras (1)	1	Lindsay Davenport (3)
2	Marcelo Rios (8)	2	Martina Hingis (1)
3	Pat Rafter (2)	3	Jana Novotna (2)
4	Carlos Moya (7)	4	Arantxa Sanchez-Vicario (8)
5	Alex Corretja (–)	5	Venus Williams (–)
6	Andre Agassi (–)	6	Monica Seles (4)
7	Tim Henman (–)	7	Mary Pierce (6)
8	Karol Kucera (–)	8	Conchita Martinez (–)
9	Greg Rusedski (5)	9	Steffi Graf (–)
=10	Petr Korda (–)	=10	Nathalie Tauziat (–)
=10	Richard Krajicek (–)	=10	Patty Schnyder (–)

After another year of mixed fortunes Pete Sampras is still the man to beat. He was lucky that no-one else could find the consistency to unseat him from his perch atop the world rankings, a position he has filled with distinction for the past six years, a modern record.

Yet others had their chances and failed to take them – none more obviously than Marcelo Rios and Petr Korda, the two who fought out the Australian Open final. Following his splendid win in Key Biscayne, Rios did for a short spell reach the summit but could not consolidate in the Grand Slams. After reaching the quarter-finals in Paris he lost in the first round at Wimbledon and the 3rd round in New York. However, his seven tournament wins, three of them Super 9s, kept the race alive until the last week of the season.

Korda was less impressive. Every time he entered a tournament with the opportunity to overtake Sampras he flopped. With poor performances in the other Grand Slams and only one other tournament win to his name he occupies equal last place with Wimbledon semi-finalist Richard Krajicek who claimed two titles during the year.

Pat Rafter's retention of his US Open title, plus the five other tournaments he won, two of them Super 9s, kept him just ahead of the new French Open champion, Carlos Moya. The Spaniard was also a semi-finalist in New York and won two other titles. If he had not lost the ATP Tour Championship final from a winning position he might have been ahead of Rafter who chose not to play there.

It was Moya's compatriot Alex Corretja who took that title. Together with his splendid run to the final of the French Open, and his five other tournament wins, Corretja comfortably fills fifth place. Behind him is Andre Agassi, rejuvenated in 1998 and the winner of five titles. What a pity this great entertainer could not find his top form in the Grand Slams.

Tim Henman just pips Karol Kucera for seventh place. The British No.1's Wimbledon semi-final matched Kucera's performance in Australia but the Slovakian was also a quarter-finalist at the US Open where Henman lost one round earlier. Like Henman, Kucera won two tournaments, one a Championship Series event, one in the World Group while Henman's were both World Group tournaments. Elsewhere, however, Henman progressed further through the rounds.

Considering his serious ankle injury, sustained in June, Greg Rusedski made an amazing recovery to finish at No. 9. If his late season charge had earned him a direct place in the ATP Tour World Championship who knows what might have happened.

Like the men, the women provided four different Grand Slam champions in 1998. To the surprise of many, last year's outstanding World Champion, Martina Hingis, lost two of her three crowns. Having retained her Australian title, the Swiss teenager saw her Wimbledon semi-final conqueror Jana Novotna take her title there.

At the US Open she fought valiantly but unavailingly against Lindsay Davenport in a superb final that gave the American a first major success. That win, along with her five other tournament victories kept Davenport's nose in front to the end, despite the loss to Hingis in the Chase

Having recovered from all the injury problems that had plagued her in 1997, Mary Pierce looked more like the champion of old as she added four more tournaments to her trophy bag – Paris Indoor, Amelia Island, Moscow and Luxembourg. (Michael Cole)

Championships. It was third time lucky for Novotna at Wimbledon and crowned a career that had always threatened to bring major honours but, until now, never did. Her three other wins – in Eastbourne, Linz and Prague – confirmed that the 29-year-old Czech player is still a major force in the game.

How delightful to see Arantxa Sanchez-Vicario back in the frame. Her performance in Paris was full of gritty determination and marvellously resourceful defence. The absorbing final against Monica Seles was one of the year's great battles.

Only Venus Williams among the much vaunted younger brigade made any real impression against older and wiser campaigners. Her wins over Hingis and Kournikova in Key Biscayne, following a career-first victory in Oklahoma City, contributed to her final placing of fifth.

Monica Seles, suffering the pain of her father's last illness, was very brave indeed – especially in Paris where she seemed to draw on a new dimension of inner strength in beating Hingis in a superb semi-final. Her wins in Tokyo and Montreal bore testimony to her resilience and she ended the year looking fit and strong for the challenges that lay ahead.

All year Mary Pierce blew hot and cold but her wins in Luxembourg, Paris, Moscow and Amelia Island revealed her continuing versatility that kept her just ahead of Conchita Martinez. It was particularly pleasing to see Steffi Graf back to something like her best at the end of another season interrupted by injury. Her wins over Novotna and Seles in the Chase Championships suggests that she will once more be a real threat in 1999.

Nathalie Tauziat of France, the surprise Wimbledon finalist, and Patty Schnyder share the last place. The Swiss No. 2 had a win over her illustrious compatriot Hingis during the year and won titles in Maria Lankowitz, Palermo, Hobart, Madrid, Quebec and Hannover.

JOHN BARRETT'S WORLD RANKINGS 1983–97

MEN

	1983		1984		1985		1986		1987
1	McEnroe	1	McEnroe	1	Lendl	1	Lendl	1	Lendl
2	Connors	2	Lendl	2	Wilander	2	Becker	2	Edberg
3	Wilander	3	Connors	3	Edberg	3	Edberg	3	Wilander
4	Lendl	4	Wilander	4	Becker	4	Leconte	4	Cash
5	Noah	5	Gomez	5	McEnroe	5	Nystrom	5	Mecir
=6	Arias	6	Cash	6	Connors	6	Mecir	6	Connors
=6	Higueras	7	Sundstrom	7	Jarryd	7	Wilander	7	Becker
8	Solomon	8	Jarryd	8	Leconte	8	Noah	8	Noah
9	Clerc	9	Nystrom	9	Nystrom	9	McEnroe	9	Mayotte
10	Teltscher	10	Arias	=10	Gunthardt	10	Gomez	10	Gomez
				=10	Noah				

	1988		1989		1990		1991		1992
1	Wilander	1	Becker	1	Edberg	1	Edberg	1	Courier
2	Edberg	2	Lendl	2	Lendl	2	Courier	2	Edberg
3	Lendl	3	Edberg	3	Agassi	3	Becker	3	Agassi
4	Becker	4	McEnroe J.	4	Sampras	4	Stich	4	Ivanisevic
5	Agassi	5	Chang	5	Becker	5	Lendl	5	Sampras
6	Mayotte	6	Gilbert	6	Gomez	6	Forget	6	Becker
7	Mecir	7	Krickstein	7	Muster	7	Agassi	7	Rossetl
8	Carlsson K.	8	Mecir	8	Ivanisovic	8	Sampras	8	Chang
9	Cash	9	Mayotte	9	Sanchez	9	Novacek	9	Korda
=10	Leconte	10	Agassi	10	McEnroe J.	10	Korda	=10	Lendl
=10	Svensson							=10	Ferreira

	1993		1994		1995		1996		1997
1	Sampras	1	Sampras	1	Sampras	1	Sampras	1	Sampras
2	Courier	2	Agassi	2	Agassi	2	Becker	2	Rafter
3	Stich	3	Bruguera	3	Muster	3	Kafelnikov	3	Chang
4	Bruguera	4	Becker	4	Becker	4	Chang	4	Bjorkman
5	Edberg	5	Martin	5	Chang	5	Krajicek	5	Rusedski
6	Medvedev	6	Ivanisevic	6	Kafelnikov	6	Agassi	6	Kafelnikov
7	Chang	7	Chang	7	Enqvist	7	Muster	7	Moya
8	Ivanisevic	8	Stich	8	Courier	8	Ivanisevic	8	Rios
9	Pioline	9	Edberg	9	Ferreira	=9	Washington	9	Kuerten
10	Muster	10	Berasategui	10	Ivanisevic	=9	Stich	=10	Bruguera
								=10	Muster

WOMEN

	1983		1984		1985		1986		1987
1	Navratilova	1	Navratilova	1	Navratilova	1	Navratilova	1	Graf
2	Evert Lloyd	2	Evert Lloyd	2	Evert Lloyd	2	Evert	2	Navratilova
3	Jaeger	3	Mandlikova	3	Mandlikova	3	Graf	3	Evert
4	Durie	4	Shriver	4	Garrison	4	Sukova	4	Mandlikova
5	Shriver	5	Bassett	5	Kohde-Kilsch	5	Mandlikova	5	Sabatini
6	Mandlikova	6	Maleeva, M.	6	Sukova	6	Sabatini	6	Shriver
7	Turnbull	7	Garrison	7	Shriver	7	Shriver	7	Sukova
8	Hanika	8	Jordan, K.	8	Graf	8	Garrison	8	Kohde-Kilsch
9	Temesvari	9	Turnbull	9	Maleeva, M.	9	Maleeva M	9	Maleeva-Frag.
10	Potter	10	Kohde-Kilsch	=10	Rinaldi	10	Rinaldi	10	McNeil
				=10	Sabatini				

	1988		1989		1990		1991		1992
1	Graf	1	Graf	1	Graf	1	Seles	1	Seles
2	Sabatini	2	Navratilova	2	Seles	2	Graf	2	Graf
3	Navratilova	3	Sanchez-Vicario	3	Sabatini	3	Sabatini	3	Sanchez-Vicario
4	Evert	4	Sabatini	4	Navratilova	4	Navratilova	4	Capriati
5	Shriver	5	Seles	5	Fernandez	5	Sanchez-Vicario	5	Sabatini
6	Sukova	6	Evert	6	Maleeva, K.	6	Fernandez	6	Fernandez
7	Zvereva	7	Garrison	7	Garrison	7	Capriati	7	Maleeva-Frag.
8	Garrison	8	Sukova	8	Sanchez-Vicario	8	Novotna	8	Navratilova
9	Maleeva-Fragniere	9	Maleeva-Fragniere	9	Maleeva-Fragniere	9	Martinez	9	Martinez
10	Kohde-Kilsch	10	Lindqvist	10	Capriati	10	Maleeva-Fragniere	10	Zvereva

	1993		1994		1995		1996		1997
1	Graf	1	Sanchez-Vicario	1	Graf	1	Graf	1	Hingis
2	Seles	2	Graf	2	Seles	2	Seles	2	Novotna
3	Sanchez-Vicario	3	Martinez	3	Sanchez-Vicario	3	Sanchez-Vicario	3	Davenport
4	Martinez	4	Pierce	4	Martinez	4	Martinez	4	Seles
5	Navratilova	5	Novotna	5	Pierce	5	Novotna	5	Majoli
6	Novotna	6	Sabatini	6	Sabatini	6	Huber	6	Pierce
7	Sabatini	7	Davenport	7	Date	7	Davenport	7	Coetzer
8	Huber	8	Navratilova	8	Fernandez	8	Hingis	8	Sanchez-Vicario
9	Fernandez	9	Date	9	Novotna	9	Date	9	Spirlea
10	Maleeva-Fragniere	10	Zvereva	10	Huber	10	Coetzer	10	Fernandez, M-J.

ATP Tour Rankings and Prize Money 1998

The following tables show the rankings of the top 300 men in singles, the top 200 in doubles and the top 250 on the prize money list, plus those players whose career earnings exceed $1 million. For the purposes of rankings and prize money, the season is deemed to have ended on 23 November rather than the 31 December. Nevertheless, points earned by players who participated in Challenger and Satellite events taking place between the November date and the end of the year still had them added to subsequent lists.

Besides the four Grand Slam Championships, all official ATP Tour tournaments, including Mercedes Super 9, Championship Series, World Series and Challenger Series events, as well as the Satellite Circuits administered by member nations of the ITF, were eligible for ranking purposes. Rankings for 1998, adjusted every week, were based on a player's best 14 results (including bonus points) during a moving twelve-month period. All players had to commit to at least 11 tournaments during the year. Somewhat controversially, in 1998, as in every year since 1991, points were also given for the season-ending ATP Tour World Championship, but have never been awarded at the Compaq Grand Slam Cup. (Statistics supplied by ATP Tour)

(The nationalities and birthdays of players can be found on pp 142–146.)

SINGLES

Rank	*Player*	*Total Points*	*Tourns Played*
1	Pete Sampras	3915	22
2	Marcelo Rios	3670	23
3	Alex Corretja	3398	24
4	Patrick Rafter	3315	26
5	Carlos Moya	3159	24
6	Andre Agassi	2879	20
7	Tim Henman	2620	29
8	Karol Kucera	2579	25
9	Greg Rusedski	2573	25
10	Richard Krajicek	2548	18
11	Yevgeny Kafelnikov	2515	31
12	Goran Ivanisevic	2137	28
13	Petr Korda	2114	21
14	Albert Costa	1823	26
15	Mark Philippoussis	1792	19
16	Todd Martin	1774	22
17	Thomas Johansson	1761	30
18	Cedric Pioline	1710	25
19	Jan Siemerink	1669	26
20	Felix Mantilla	1643	26
21	Alberto Berasategui	1556	27
22	Thomas Enqvist	1500	17
23	Gustavo Kuerten	1472	26
24	Jonas Bjorkman	1439	24
25	Thomas Muster	1344	20
26	Wayne Ferreira	1285	24
27	Jason Stoltenberg	1280	23
28	Byron Black	1259	26
29	Michael Chang	1242	18
30	Francisco Clavet	1216	28
31	Magnus Gustafsson	1187	24
32	Marc Rosset	1169	27
33	Bohdan Ulihrach	1077	30
34	Tommy Haas	1044	26
35	Nicolas Kiefer	1007	25
36	Hicham Arazi	999	27
37	Nicolas Escude	989	21
38	Jan-Michael Gambill	983	24
39	Mariano Puerta	983	27
40	Richard Fromberg	937	35
41	Fabrice Santoro	935	27
42	Vincent Spadea	935	27
43	Magnus Larsson	930	16
44	Andrea Gaudenzi	926	26
45	Dominik Hrbaty	892	30
46	Jerome Golmard	883	25
47	Davide Sanguinetti	853	30
48	Marat Safin	852	23
49	Younes El Aynaoui	850	15
50	Daniel Vacek	842	32
51	Scott Draper	819	18
52	Magnus Norman	818	31
53	Guillaume Raoux	803	27
54	Fernando Vicente	799	33
55	Filip Dewulf	789	22
56	Ramon Delgado	784	28
57	Fernando Meligeni	779	26
58	Mark Woodforde	773	25
59	Andrew Ilie	771	27
60	Franco Squillari	747	30
61	Andrei Medvedev	739	22
62	Gianluca Pozzi	730	36
63	Mariano Zabaleta	723	20
64	Slava Dosedel	723	22
65	Todd Woodbridge	722	22
66	Andrei Pavel	722	31
67	Sjeng Schalken	712	32
68	Carlos Costa	710	29
69	Boris Becker	688	11
70	Juan Antonio Marin	678	35

Rank	Player	Total Points	Tourns Played
71	Adrian Voinea	676	19
72	Jeff Tarango	675	33
73	Paul Haarhuis	674	20
74	Jiri Novak	669	27
75	Martin Damm	657	29
76	Jim Courier	635	18
77	David Prinosil	633	26
78	Karim Alami	631	25
79	Sebastien Lareau	622	22
80	Justin Gimelstob	615	19
81	Arnaud Di Pasquale	613	22
82	Galo Blanco	612	30
83	Kenneth Carlsen	606	27
84	Albert Portas	600	33
85	Mikael Tillstrom	588	23
86	Christian Ruud	584	28
87	Hendrik Dreekmann	576	22
88	Oliver Gross	570	26
89	Sebastien Grosjean	568	27
90	Jan Kroslak	563	27
91	Leander Paes	559	22
92	Nicolas Lapentti	545	31
93	Brett Steven	528	20
94	Stefan Koubek	526	27
95	Wayne Black	518	26
96	Guillermo Canas	516	28
97	Martin Rodriguez	516	30
98	Michael Kohlmann	507	30
99	John Van Lottum	502	27
100	Sargis Sargsian	499	28
101	Jens Knippschild	469	25
102	Steve Campbell	464	32
103	Dinu Pescariu	461	30
104	Julian Alonso	461	36
105	Arnaud Clement	460	31
106	Alberto Martin	455	32
107	Daniel Nestor	452	24
108	Laurence Tieleman	448	19
109	Hernan Gumy	442	20
110	Geoff Grant	439	22
111	Rainer Schuttler	434	36
112	Lucas Arnold	433	25
113	Lleyton Hewitt	428	19
114	Alex Calatrava	423	29
115	Takao Suzuki	415	19
116	Johan Van Herck	413	26
117	Bernd Karbacher	407	24
118	Marc-Kevin Goellner	403	27
119	Vincenzo Santopadre	401	27
120	Eduardo Medica	400	18
121	Dennis Van Scheppingen	394	26
122	Michael Tebbutt	393	23
123	Marcio Carlsson	393	31
124	Peter Wessels	391	24
125	Marzio Martelli	382	30
126	Andre Sa	381	27
127	Orlin Stanoytchev	377	28
128	Neville Godwin	376	19
129	Ivo Heuberger	376	34
130	Diego Nargiso	371	22
131	Lars Burgsmuller	366	29
132	Cecil Mamiit	365	22
133	Dirk Dier	364	24
134	Martin Sinner	359	26
135	Sergi Bruguera	358	24
136	Marcelo Filippini	351	27
137	David Nainkin	350	24
138	Wayne Arthurs	349	21
139	Christian Vinck	342	30
140	Tomas Zib	340	21
141	Oscar Serrano	338	23
142	Jean-Baptiste Perlant	337	23
143	Brian MacPhie	335	21
144	Renzo Furlan	324	33
145	Jacobo Diaz	323	29
146	Jan Frode Andersen	321	27
147	Alex O'Brien	320	27
148	Marcos Ondruska	318	29
149	Jordi Burillo	317	26
150	Juan Albert Viloca	314	32
151	Vladimir Voltchkov	302	19
152	Edwin Kempes	300	20
153	Richey Reneberg	298	17
154	Wolfgang Schranz	297	19
155	Luis Adrian Morejon	296	18
156	Agustin Calleri	296	21
157	Christophe Van Garsse	295	14
158	Rogier Wassen	294	22
159	Cristiano Caratti	293	29
160	Sebastian Prieto	292	25
161	Xavier Malisse	290	9
162	Grant Stafford	290	26
163	Andrei Cherkasov	290	29
164	Radek Stepanek	289	19
165	Marco Meneschincheri	289	31
166	Tomas Carbonell	288	10
167	Alex Lopez-Moron	284	27
168	Gaston Gaudio	283	16
169	Javier Sanchez	278	38
170	Gaston Etlis	277	26
171	Jiri Vanek	275	18
172	Jared Palmer	275	18
173	Alejandro Hernandez	270	24
174	Adriano Ferreira	267	20
175	Maurice Ruah	267	24
176	Malivai Washington	258	14
177	Tomas Nydahl	258	26
178	Salvador Navarro	257	21
179	Thomas Larsen	255	18
180	Mark Draper	254	18
181	Rodolphe Gilbert	254	22
182	Chris Wilkinson	251	24
183	Attila Savolt	251	27
184	Olivier Delaitre	248	19
185	David Caldwell	248	23
186	Tuomas Ketola	248	28
187	Ville Liukko	246	9
188	Nicolas Massu	246	22
189	Paul Goldstein	245	13
190	Stefano Pescosolido	244	24
191	Emilio Alvarez	244	25
192	Nenad Zimonjic	239	18
193	Razvan Sabau	237	19
194	Markus Hipfl	236	20
195	David Caballero	231	17
196	Lorenzo Manta	230	20
197	Markus Hantschk	228	30
198	Justin Bower	226	19

Rank	Player	Total Points	Tourns Played
199	Jordi Mas	225	19
200	Tomas Behrend	225	24
201	Christophe Rochus	224	24
202	Marcello Craca	224	29
203	Francisco Costa	222	25
204	Juan Ignacio Chela	221	16
205	Daniele Bracciali	221	19
206	Anthony Dupuis	221	20
207	Lior Mor	221	22
208	Radomir Vasek	221	26
209	Iztok Bozic	220	23
210	Fredrik Jonsson	215	19
211	Michal Tabara	215	19
212	Petr Luxa	215	24
213	Francisco Cabello	215	25
214	Oleg Ogorodov	215	27
215	Stephane Huet	213	19
216	Doug Flach	212	18
217	Mose Navarra	212	20
218	Alex Radulescu	210	15
219	Hideki Kaneko	207	22
220	Harel Levy	205	18
221	Quino Munoz	204	19
222	George Bastl	203	15
223	Andres Zingman	202	17
224	Pepe Imaz	199	17
225	Michael Hill	199	18
226	Goichi Motomura	199	20
227	Jaime Oncins	197	15
228	Nuno Marques	196	12
229	Eyal Ran	196	23
230	Todd Larkham	195	23
231	Kim Tiilikainen	193	21
232	Gerard Solves	193	21
233	Peter Tramacchi	192	22
234	Juan Balcells	189	12
235	David Wheaton	189	12
236	Federico Browne	185	20
237	Sandon Stolle	185	22
238	German Puentes	182	14
239	Oren Motevassel	180	24
240	Mariano Sanchez	179	15
241	Ronald Agenor	179	17
242	Karsten Braasch	177	10
243	Hector Moretti	177	17
244	Noam Behr	174	18
245	Axel Pretzsch	173	14
246	Raemon Sluiter	172	13
247	Olivier Malcor	172	14
248	Milen Velev	172	16
249	Vadim Kutsenko	171	18

Rank	Player	Total Points	Tourns Played
250	Charles Auffray	170	17
251	Grant Doyle	168	17
252	Jan Apell	160	10
253	Andrei Stoliarov	160	26
254	Gregory Carraz	158	8
255	Lionel Roux	158	15
256	Tapio Nurminen	158	21
257	Ota Fukarek	157	23
258	Andres Schneiter	155	20
259	Jeff Coetzee	152	12
260	Joao Cunha-Silva	152	14
261	Oscar Burrieza	149	28
262	Hyung-Taik Lee	148	11
263	Ricardo Schlachter	147	21
264	Max Mirnyi	146	15
265	Radovan Svetlik	145	13
266	Toby Mitchell	145	16
267	Michael Joyce	144	15
268	Jonathan Stark	144	17
269	Bob Bryan	142	11
270	Lars Jonsson	142	13
271	Dusan Vemic	142	13
272	Mark Joachim	141	9
273	Mauricio Hadad	139	8
274	Herbert Wiltschnig	139	14
275	Igor Gaudi	139	22
276	Mark Knowles	137	11
277	Ben Ellwood	137	21
278	Jimy Szymanski	136	11
279	Julien Boutter	136	15
280	Michael Sell	136	24
281	David Dilucia	134	12
282	Davide Scala	134	22
283	Gabriel Trifu	134	22
284	Ofer Sela	132	12
285	Rodolphe Cadart	130	12
286	Tomas Catar	130	19
287	Bartlomiej Dabrowski	128	13
288	Michael Russell	128	19
289	Emanuel Couto	127	12
290	Nicklas Kulti	125	7
291	Wesley Whitehouse	125	11
292	Tommi Lenho	124	14
293	Ivan Ljubicic	124	19
294	Patrik Fredriksson	123	9
295	Nir Welgreen	123	15
296	Ion Moldovan	123	22
297	Paradorn Srichaphan	122	12
298	Diego Moyano	122	13
299	Yaoki Ishii	122	16
300	Borut Urh	121	13

DOUBLES

Rank	*Player*	*Total Points*	*Tourns Played*
1	Jacco Eltingh	5143	15
2	Paul Haarhuis	4270	17
3	Mahesh Bhupathi	3816	24
4	Leander Paes	3781	21
5	Todd Woodbridge	3398	21
6	Mark Woodforde	3398	22
7	Daniel Nestor	3260	17
8	Jonas Bjorkman	3202	19
9	Mark Knowles	2967	20
10	Ellis Ferreira	2835	25
11	Cyril Suk	2450	30
12	Olivier Delaitre	2425	22
13	Rick Leach	2392	22
14	Sandon Stolle	2309	28
15	Jim Grabb	2243	27
16	Patrick Rafter	2179	15
17	Sebastien Lareau	2150	22
18	Fabrice Santoro	2136	22
19	Yevgeny Kafelnikov	2123	25
20	Alex O'Brien	2029	20
21	David Macpherson	2006	29
22	Martin Damm	1983	24
23	Joshua Eagle	1961	29
24	Donald Johnson	1927	26
24	Francisco Montana	1927	26
26	Daniel Vacek	1890	29
27	Brett Steven	1853	19
28	Patrick Galbraith	1753	23
29	Piet Norval	1718	34
30	Andrew Florent	1712	27
31	Richey Reneberg	1680	19
32	Jiri Novak	1649	27
33	John-Laffnie De Jager	1596	25
34	Neil Broad	1578	30
35	Kevin Ullyett	1566	29
36	Javier Sanchez	1545	31
37	David Adams	1534	37
38	Nicklas Kulti	1524	20
39	Luis Lobo	1469	26
40	Tomas Carbonell	1429	23
41	Francisco Roig	1409	20
42	Jonathan Stark	1386	17
43	David Rikl	1363	17
44	Robbie Koenig	1334	25
45	Daniel Orsanic	1334	33
46	Wayne Black	1278	26
47	Grant Stafford	1274	21
48	David Roditi	1273	32
49	Chris Haggard	1240	28
50	Justin Gimelstob	1225	18
51	Pablo Albano	1213	31
52	Jeff Tarango	1150	28
53	Nicolas Lapentti	1122	27
54	Tom Kempers	1122	33
55	Wayne Arthurs	1108	27
56	Brian MacPhie	1033	19
57	Mikael Tillstrom	1027	19
58	Peter Tramacchi	1027	26
59	Peter Nyborg	1018	25
60	Pavel Vizner	987	31
61	Mariano Hood	977	30
62	Menno Oosting	976	34
63	David Prinosil	973	24
64	Sebastian Prieto	971	28
65	Andrew Kratzmann	933	30
66	Wayne Ferreira	911	15
67	Marc-Kevin Goellner	893	18
68	Goran Ivanisevic	893	20
69	Marcos Ondruska	865	29
70	Byron Black	863	21
71	Michael Tebbutt	845	26
72	Diego Del Rio	845	31
73	Jack Waite	836	38
74	Brn Coupe	817	36
75	Fredrik Bergh	805	11
76	Fernando Meligeni	793	23
77	Brent Haygarth	792	24
78	Mariano Puerta	788	23
79	Julian Alonso	786	27
80	Andrei Olhovskiy	785	25
81	Devin Bowen	778	38
82	Tuomas Ketola	777	30
83	Lan Bale	767	16
84	Marius Barnard	767	30
85	Paul Rosner	766	33
86	Gabor Koves	763	34
87	Jared Palmer	733	15
88	Massimo Bertolini	730	27
89	Edwin Kempes	705	18
90	Aleksandar Kitinov	702	42
91	Michael Sell	695	23
92	Mark Merklein	685	20
93	Gustavo Kuerten	680	19
94	David Wheaton	677	7
95	Neville Godwin	677	21
96	David Dilucia	675	24
97	Nebojsa Djordjevic	666	32
98	Alberto Martin	661	29
99	Doug Flach	652	22
100	Eric Taino	641	24
101	Mark Keil	640	24
102	Paul Kilderry	635	26
103	Danny Sapsford	632	22
104	Stefano Pescosolido	629	14
105	Kent Kinnear	620	29
106	Lucas Arnold	604	18
107	Todd Martin	602	9
108	Sander Groen	602	31
109	Jan Siemerink	600	13
110	T .J. Middleton	600	18
111	Libor Pimek	596	30
112	Jens Knippschild	593	20
113	Peter Wessels	591	16
114	Tomas Zdrazila	589	29
115	Massimo Ardinghi	585	25
116	Nenad Zimonjic	581	20
117	Stephen Noteboom	579	32
118	Cristian Brandi	578	32
119	German Puentes	577	18
120	Eduardo Nicolas	575	18
121	Michael Kohlmann	571	29
122	Alex Lopez-Moron	569	19
123	Juan Balcells	562	20
124	Fernon Wibier	555	28
125	Max Mirnyi	554	25
126	Joao Cunha-Silva	553	18
127	Dave Randall	548	22
128	Martin Rodriguez	545	22
129	Byron Talbot	544	26
130	Andre Sa	527	29
131	Dinu Pescariu	525	17
132	Jairo Velasco	521	19
133	Jeff Coetzee	518	20
134	Myles Wakefield	517	30
135	Geoff Grant	516	23
136	Nicolas Kiefer	514	14

Rank	Player	Total Points	Tourns Played
137	Laurence Tieleman	511	14
138	Tom Vanhoudt	507	26
139	Vincenzo Santopadre	505	20
140	Jim Thomas	497	23
141	Nuno Marques	488	15
142	Tomas Cibulec	480	18
143	Jamie Holmes	480	23
144	Oscar Ortiz	474	32
145	Filippo Messori	469	23
146	Juan Ignacio Carrasco	464	26
147	Chris Wilkinson	460	28
148	Grant Silcock	452	31
149	Sasa Hirszon	451	12
150	Adriano Ferreira	447	19
151	Attila Savolt	445	21
152	James Greenhalgh	443	23
153	Tim Henman	426	12
154	Maurice Ruah	424	28
155	Albert Portas	423	10
156	Slava Dosedel	421	12
157	Sargis Sargsian	408	16
158	Radek Stepanek	408	19
159	Bernardo Martinez	404	29
160	Robert Kokavec	403	20
161	Takao Suzuki	402	14
162	Cristiano Testa	400	25
163	Goichi Motomura	399	18
164	Alberto Berasategui	397	15
165	Jaime Oncins	393	14
166	Filippo Veglio	392	23
167	Lleyton Hewitt	390	11
168	Scott Humphries	386	16
169	Andrea Gaudenzi	381	9
170	Todd Larkham	381	20
171	Andrei Cherkasov	378	21
172	Giorgio Galimberti	375	20
173	Mark Philippoussis	374	10
174	Bob Bryan	374	16
174	Mike Bryan	374	16
176	Emanuel Couto	373	13
177	Karsten Braasch	373	14
178	Massimo Valeri	369	18
179	Ben Ellwood	367	17
180	Gabriel Trifu	362	15
181	Petr Luxa	361	20
182	Ota Fukarek	360	26
183	Sjeng Schalken	359	7
184	Vincent Spadea	359	10
185	Salvador Navarro	358	16
186	Marco Osorio	357	18
187	Diego Nargiso	356	9
188	Damien Roberts	353	18
189	Andrew Painter	353	22
190	Petr Pala	350	20
191	Eyal Ran	348	22
192	Tomas Krupa	345	14
193	Rogier Wassen	345	21
194	Jim Courier	340	10
195	Davide Sanguinetti	338	11
196	Leos Friedl	336	14
197	Thomas Shimada	332	21
198	Murphy Jensen	325	20
199	Luke Jensen	325	21
200	Andrei Pavel	324	7

With a courageous recovery from two sets down, Alex Corretja reversed the result of the French Open final by beating his close friend Carlos Moya to become the first Spaniard to hold the year-end Championship title. (Tommy Hindley)

ATP TOUR BOARD OF DIRECTORS 1998–99 (Chief Executive Officer: Mark Miles)

Tournament Representatives
Franco Bartoni (Europe)
Sanji Arisawa (International Group)
Charlie Pasarell (North America)

Player Representatives
Harold Solomon
Brad Drewett
David Felgate

ATP TOUR PLAYER COUNCIL
President: Todd Martin **Vice President:** Marcelo Filippini
Members: (**1–10**) to be announced; (**11–25**) Tim Henman; (**26–50**) Marcelo Filippini; (**1–50 Doubles**) Jim Grabb; (**Div.2**) Jim Thomas; **Alumni:** Harold Solomon; (**At Large**) Tomas Carbonell, Robbie Koenig, Todd Martin, David Roditi; (**Tour Board**) Paul Annacone, Brad Drewett, David Felgate.

ATP TOUR TOURNAMENT COUNCIL
EUROPE: Franco Bartoni (Chairman), Jacques Hermenjat, Leo Huemer, Wim Buitendijk, Gunther Sanders
INTERNATIONAL: Sanji Arisawa, Ayman Azmy, Graham Pearce, Barry Masters
AMERICAS: Butch Buchholz, Tom Buford, Bob Kramer, Charlie Pasarell

ADDRESSES – ATP TOUR OFFICES (Web Site Address: http://www.atptour.com)

United States
200 ATP Tour Boulevard
Ponte Vedra Beach
Florida
32082, USA
Tel:1-904-285 8000
Fax:1-904-285 5966

Europe
Monte Carlo Sun
74 Boulevard D'Italie
98000, Monaco
Tel: 377-97-97-04-04
Fax: 377-97-97-04-00

International Group
Level 6
20 Alfred Street
Milsons Point
NSW, 2061, Australia
Tel: 61-2 9964 9900
Fax: 61-2 9964 9977

ANNUAL ATP TOUR AWARDS FOR 1997
For the third time in four years, the ATP TOUR Awards Gala was held at the Monte Carlo Sporting Club where, on 21 April 1998, Prince Albert of Monaco was among the star-studded list of guests to applaud those individuals who were being recognised for outstanding performances in 1997.

Player of the Year: Pete Sampras
Doubles Team of the Year: Todd Woodbridge/Mark Woodforde
Most Improved Player: Pat Rafter
Rado Player to Watch: Julian Alonso
Comeback Player of the Year: Sergi Bruguera
Stefan Edberg Sportsmanship Award: Pat Rafter
Senior Circuit Player of the Year: Jimmy Connors
Ron Bookman Media Excellence Award: John Parsons
Arthur Ashe Humanitarian Award: President Nelson Mandela
Championship Series Tournament of the Year: Indianapolis
World Series Tournament of the Year: Kitzbuhel
Milestone Awards – First-time winners: Julian Alonso, Hicham Arazi, Jonas Bjorkman, Tim Henman, Thomas Johansson, Nicolas Kiefer, Gustavo Kuerten, Magnus Norman, Fabrice Santoro, Sargis Sargisian, Mikael Tillstrom, Chris Woodruff,
Fifth titles: Francisco Clavet., Albert Costa, Marcelo Filippini, Felix Mantilla, Marcelo Rios, Greg Rusedski.
Tenth title: Magnus Gustafsson
Twentieth Title: Goran Ivanisevic
Fiftieth Title: Pete Sampras

PRIZE MONEY 1998

There was approximately $77 million to play for on the ATP Tour in 1998. Once again Pete Sampras heads the list, but only just. His 1997 total of $6 million had been more than twice the figure of his nearest challenger but one year later his $3,931,497 was 'only' half a million dollars ahead of Marcelo Rios's earnings.

Altogether six men achieved earnings above the $2 million mark, one more than in 1997, while the number above one million fell by one – from 18 to 17. Also one ahead of the previous year were the 40 men with earnings above $500,000. But lower down the increase was more dramatic. Whereas in 1997 165 men earned at least $100,000, twelve months later that figure had risen to 177.

Note: Prize money figures issued by the ATP Tour represent all earnings from official sources. They also include circuit bonuses, play-offs and team events where entry is based purely on merit. They do not include earnings from Davis Cup ties, invitation tournaments, special events or exhibitions, nor income from commercial contracts or endorsements. (Figures supplied by ATP Tour).

(The nationalities and birthdays of players can be found on pp 142–146.)

1	Pete Sampras	$3,931,497
2	Marcelo Rios	3,420,054
3	Patrick Rafter	2,867,017
4	Alex Corretja	2,702,569
5	Carlos Moya	2,572,553
6	Yevgeny Kafelnikov	2,543,077
7	Jonas Bjorkman	1,916,237
8	Greg Rusedski	1,860,437
9	Andre Agassi	1,836,233
10	Goran Ivanisevic	1,541,177
11	Tim Henman	1,448,770
12	Karol Kucera	1,402,557
13	Petr Korda	1,387,393
14	Mark Philippoussis	1,272,620
15	Richard Krajicek	1,219,624
16	Michael Chang	1,164,314
17	Albert Costa	1,013,446
18	Paul Haarhuis	930,522
19	Felix Mantilla	823,916
20	Cedric Pioline	808,688
21	Todd Martin	771,943
22	Fabrice Santoro	757,122
23	Jacco Eltingh	751,325
24	Mark Woodforde	736,370
25	Gustavo Kuerten	732,804
26	Todd Woodbridge	695,297
27	Daniel Vacek	695,083
28	Leander Paes	674,079
29	Thomas Johansson	667,858
30	Alberto Berasategui	645,760
31	Jan Siemerink	638,990
32	Nicolas Kiefer	623,573
33	Tommy Haas	618,633
34	Mahesh Bhupathi	569,960
35	Daniel Nestor	562,695
36	Wayne Ferreira	546,230
37	Byron Black	517,743
38	Thomas Enqvist	515,702
39	Sergi Bruguera	503,826
40	Martin Damm	501,390
41	Thomas Muster	488,775
42	David Prinosil	475,839
43	Marc Rosset	463,962
44	Hicham Arazi	458,735
45	Cyril Suk	449,071
46	Francisco Clavet	446,552
47	Sebastien Lareau	443,795
48	Jeff Tarango	443,009
49	Magnus Gustafsson	442,122
50	Mark Knowles	441,501
51	Nicolas Escude	437,965
52	Bohdan Ulihrach	436,216
53	Magnus Larsson	430,511
54	Sandon Stolle	415,552
55	Magnus Norman	412,839
56	Jan-Michael Gambill	393,524
57	Brett Steven	392,176
58	Boris Becker	389,470
59	Dominik Hrbaty	389,146
60	Olivier Delaitre	385,932
61	Alex O'Brien	370,615
62	Jiri Novak	369,125
63	Vincent Spadea	368,639
64	Ellis Ferreira	368,351
65	Slava Dosedel	367,257
66	Jason Stoltenberg	367,061
67	Guillaume Raoux	357,530
68	Wayne Black	351,117
69	Richard Fromberg	350,342
70	Mikael Tillstrom	349,130
71	Davide Sanguinetti	342,495
72	Sjeng Schalken	340,797
73	Rick Leach	338,236
74	Andrei Medvedev	334,620
75	Julian Alonso	328,773
76	Andrea Gaudenzi	325,060
77	Nicolas Lapentti	322,257
78	Fernando Meligeni	309,811
79	Jerome Golmard	305,834
80	Richey Reneberg	305,107
81	Javier Sanchez	304,231
82	Filip Dewulf	301,444
83	Scott Draper	300,753
84	Marc-Kevin Goellner	289,540
85	Andrei Pavel	288,351
86	Donald Johnson	282,499
87	Francisco Montana	276,699
88	Jim Grabb	273,074
89	Gianluca Pozzi	263,671
90	Mariano Puerta	262,697
91	Jim Courier	257,853
92	Arnaud Clement	252,098
93	Carlos Costa	250,941
94	Fernando Vicente	248,004
95	Karim Alami	246,591
96	Kenneth Carlsen	242,882
97	Ramon Delgado	240,820
98	Marat Safin	237,135

99	Grant Stafford	234,882
100	Galo Blanco	230,222
101	Albert Portas	228,157
102	Sebastien Grosjean	222,971
103	Steve Campbell	219,012
104	Sargis Sargsian	218,101
105	Justin Gimelstob	217,123
106	Juan Antonio Marin	216,867
107	John Van Lottum	216,034
108	Tomas Carbonell	215,856
109	Lucas Arnold	211,999
110	Jens Knippschild	210,259
111	Jonathan Stark	208,175
112	Joshua Eagle	203,678
113	Franco Squillari	200,586
114	Michael Tebbutt	197,753
115	Piet Norval	194,301
116	Jan Kroslak	192,988
117	Andrew Ilie	184,890
118	Nicklas Kulti	183,777
119	Francisco Roig	181,146
120	Oliver Gross	178,092
121	David Adams	175,880
122	Hendrik Dreekmann	173,512
123	Dinu Pescariu	173,325
124	Brian MacPhie	173,208
125	David Macpherson	173,070
126	Andrew Florent	170,466
127	Jordi Burillo	165,441
128	Guillermo Canas	162,658
129	Johan Van Herck	161,361
130	Neil Broad	157,849
131	Juan Albert Viloca	157,631
132	Marcelo Filippini	153,257
133	Patrick Galbraith	151,139
134	Kevin Ullyett	150,447
135	Mariano Zabaleta	149,122
136	Arnaud Di Pasquale	148,959
137	Adrian Voinea	147,480
138	Tomas Nydahl	142,100
139	Marcos Ondruska	141,020
140	Alex Calatrava	139,237
141	John-Laffnie De Jager	137,181
142	Martin Sinner	135,839
143	Daniel Orsanic	135,113
144	Rainer Schuttler	135,012
145	Vincenzo Santopadre	134,034
146	Laurence Tieleman	132,592
147	Lleyton Hewitt	131,180
148	Dennis Van Scheppingen	129,938
149	Neville Godwin	129,865
150	David Nainkin	129,600
151	Wayne Arthurs	128,350
152	Geoff Grant	125,806
153	Martin Rodriguez	125,303
154	Luis Lobo	124,959
155	Christian Ruud	124,572
156	Sebastian Prieto	124,497
157	Lars Burgsmuller	123,773
158	Alberto Martin	122,924
159	Hernan Gumy	122,818
160	Younes El Aynaoui	119,768
161	Peter Tramacchi	117,599
162	Michael Kohlmann	117,004
163	Ivo Heuberger	116,567
164	Andre Sa	116,376
165	David Roditi	114,973
166	Robbie Koenig	114,111
167	Tuomas Ketola	113,869
168	Pavel Vizner	111,853
169	Pablo Albano	111,260
170	David Wheaton	110,405
171	Malivai Washington	106,823
172	Chris Wilkinson	104,083
173	David Rikl	102,366
174	Stefano Pescosolido	102,303
175	Bernd Karbacher	102,158
176	Tom Kempers	101,910
177	Aleksandar Kitinov	101,107
178	Emilio Alvarez	99,130
179	Lionel Roux	98,991
180	Chris Haggard	98,538
181	Marzio Martelli	97,885
182	Doug Flach	94,826
183	Michael Sell	94,555
184	Jared Palmer	92,754
185	Christian Vinck	91,633
186	Peter Nyborg	91,071
187	Menno Oosting	88,440
188	Radomir Vasek	88,397
188	Fernon Wibier	88,397
190	Jacobo Diaz	88,082
191	Andrew Kratzmann	86,452
192	Diego Nargiso	84,900
193	Stefan Koubek	84,535
194	Andrei Olhovskiy	84,501
195	Mariano Hood	84,177
196	Takao Suzuki	83,320
197	Oscar Burrieza	83,046
198	Marcello Craca	80,651
199	Danny Sapsford	79,578
200	Marcio Carlsson	79,466
201	Vladimir Voltchkov	78,685
202	Peter Wessels	78,269
203	Karsten Braasch	77,694
204	Alex Lopez-Moron	77,217
205	Christophe Van Garsse	77,086
206	David Dilucia	76,974
207	Renzo Furlan	75,571
208	Jack Waite	73,835
209	Alex Radulescu	71,429
210	Brandon Coupe	71,170
211	Mark Merklein	70,890
212	Paul Rosner	69,576
213	Max Mirnyi	68,520
214	Petr Luxa	68,469
215	Andrei Cherkasov	68,172
216	Jean-Baptiste Perlant	67,685
217	Orlin Stanoytchev	64,005
218	Devin Bowen	62,403
219	Maurice Ruah	62,315
220	Mark Keil	61,638
221	Fredrik Bergh	59,422
222	Cristiano Caratti	58,190
223	Marius Barnard	58,108
224	Rodolphe Gilbert	57,693
225	Libor Pimek	57,690
226	Andrew Richardson	57,358
227	Gaston Etlis	56,806
228	Attila Savolt	56,787
230	Gabor Koves	55,985
231	Todd Larkham	55,401
232	Marco Meneschincheri	55,296
233	Gerard Solves	54,934
234	Raemon Sluiter	54,578
235	Paul Goldstein	54,305
236	Radek Stepanek	54,008
237	Gabriel Trifu	53,847
238	T. J. Middleton	53,547
239	Wolfgang Schranz	53,440
240	Dave Randall	53,355
241	Alejandro Hernandez	53,125

242	Brent Haygarth	52,903
243	Bob Bryan	52,850
244	Barry Cowan	52,558
245	Daniele Bracciali	52,204
246	Kent Kinnear	52,013
247	Oscar Serrano	51,950
248	Ben Ellwood	51,900
249	Giorgio Galimberti	51,880
250	Stephen Noteboom	50,563
251	Eyal Ran	50,417
252	Dirk Dier	50,087

THE MILLIONAIRES

Below is a list of players who, by the end of November 1998, had won at least US$1 million in prize money during the course of their careers. A further 19 players (marked*) became dollar millionaires from prize money alone in 1998. The totals do not include income from the Davis Cup or other team competitions, nor from special events or exhibitions.

1	Pete Sampras	$35,992,155
2	Boris Becker	24,905,117
3	Ivan Lendl	21,262,417
4	Stefan Edberg	20,630,941
5	Goran Ivanisevic	17,747,714
6	Michael Chang	17,451,053
7	Andre Agassi	15,049,896
8	Jim Courier	13,580,422
9	Michael Stich	12,628,890
10	John McEnroe	12,539,622
11	Yevgeny Kafelnikov	12,147,818
12	Thomas Muster	12,129,429
13	Sergi Bruguera	11,252,155
14	Petr Korda	10,427,102
15	Jimmy Connors	8,641,040
16	Richard Krajicek	8,054,963
17	Mats Wilander	7,976,256
18	Mark Woodforde	7,463,551
19	Patrick Rafter	7,382,729
20	Todd Woodbridge	6,865,044
21	Wayne Ferreira	6,474,974
22	Paul Haarhuis	6,448,674
23	Marcelo Rios	6,135,603
24	Jonas Bjorkman	6,134,727
25	Jakob Hlasek	5,784,225
26	Guy Forget	5,660,579
27	Todd Martin	5,596,692
28	Alex Corretja	5,547,784
29	Brad Gilbert	5,509,060
30	Anders Jarryd	5,377,067
31	Andrei Medvedev	5,376,705
32	Emilio Sanchez	5,339,394
33	David Wheaton	5,265,839
34	Magnus Larsson	5,197,394
35	Marc Rosset	5,145,512
36	Guillermo Vilas	4,923,882
37	Jacco Eltingh	4,921,578
38	Cedric Pioline	4,783,356
39	Thomas Enqvist	4,570,262
40	Greg Rusedski	4,498,251
41	Andres Gomez	4,385,040
42	Javier Sanchez	4,321,286
43	Carlos Moya	4,302,533
44	Alberto Berasategui	4,229,877
45	Richey Reneberg	4,121,675
46	Henri Leconte	3,917,596
47	Magnus Gustafsson	3,875,616
48	Daniel Vacek	3,841,450
49	Karel Novacek	3,739,175
50	Aaron Krickstein	3,710,447
51	Tomas Smid	3,699,738
52	Byron Black	3,677,784
53	Bjorn Borg	3,655,751
54	Jan Siemerink	3,607,963
55	Yannick Noah	3,440,390
56	Alexander Volkov	3,362,786
57	Tim Henman	3,277,128
58	Albert Costa	3,235,788
59	MaliVai Washington	3,231,805
60	John Fitzgerald	3,204,572
61	Jim Grabb	3,189,002
62	Wally Masur	3,134,447
63	Carlos Costa	3,123,903
64	Mark Philippoussis	3,117,457
65	Patrick McEnroe	3,115,636
66	Andrei Chesnokov	3,074,446
67	Kevin Curren	3,055,060
68	Arnaud Boetsch	3,054,574
69	Rick Leach	2,950,292
70	Grant Connell	2,911,095
71	Jonathan Stark	2,878,910
72	Jason Stoltenberg	2,864,849
73	Fabrice Santoro	2,824,028
74	Francisco Clavet	2,819,577
75	Tomas Carbonell	2,790,259
76	Brian Gottfried	2,782,514
77	Vitas Gerulaitis	2,778,748
78	Wojtek Fibak	2,725,133
79	Andrei Olhovskiy	2,720,085
80	Martin Damm	2,666,155
81	Tim Mayotte	2,663,672
82	Karol Kucera	2,637,765
83	Miloslav Mecir	2,632,538
84	Patrick Galbraith	2,524,303
85	Felix Mantilla	2,510,230
86	Nicklas Kulti	2,467,081
87	Gustavo Kuerten	2,459,442
88	Olivier Delaitre	2,454,230
89	Jonas Svensson	2,439,702
90	Jeff Tarango	2,436,067
91	Alex O'Brien	2,431,364
92	Amos Mansdorf	2,427,691
93	Brett Steven	2,384,035
94	Johan Kriek	2,382,594
95	Marc-Kevin Goellner	2,346,869
96	Carl-Uwe Steeb	2,320,082
97	Scott Davis	2,287,340
98	Cyril Suk	2,252,570
99	Jaime Yzaga	2,235,560
100	Guillaume Raoux	2,231,632
101	Renzo Furlan	2,230,486
102	Raul Ramirez	2,217,971
103	David Prinosil	2,189,154
104	Richard Fromberg	2,113,241

105	Sergio Casal	2,107,745
106	Andrei Cherkasov	2,087,408
107	Andrea Gaudenzi	2,085,404
108	Ilie Nastase	2,076,761
109	Joakim Nystrom	2,074,947
110	Ken Flach	2,061,390
111	David Pate	2,029,722
112	Eddie Dibbs	2,016,426
113	Daniel Nestor	2,016,137
114	Jose-Luis Clerc	1,987,036
115	Peter Fleming	1,986,529
116	Mark Knowles	1,969,519
117	Sandon Stolle	1,955,468
118	Pat Cash	1,946,669
119	Christo Van Rensburg	1,925,577
120	Robert Seguso	1,881,888
121	Martin Jaite	1,873,881
122	Bernd Karbacher	1,873,518
123	Marcelo Filippini	1,867,323
124	Jordi Arrese	1,846,849
125	Jimmy Arias	1,834,140
126	Slava Dosedel	1,819,425
127	Harold Solomon	1,802,769
128	Jim Pugh	1,780,455
129	Stan Smith	1,774,811
130	Sebastien Lareau	1,757,044
131	Bohdan Ulihrach	1,756,425
132	Ronald Agenor	1,739,223
133	Roscoe Tanner	1,696,108
134	Javier Frana	1,691,847
135	Henrik Holm	1,691,580
136	Guillermo Perez-Roldan	1,685,921
137	Eliot Teltscher	1,653,997
138	Paul Annacone	1,648,306
139	Patrik Kuhnen	1,646,328
140	Horst Skoff	1,644,748
141	Derrick Rostagno	1,621,535
142	Sherwood Stewart	1,602,565
143	Ken Rosewall	1,600,300
144	Marcos Ondruska	1,597,943
145	Omar Camporese	1,592,500
146	Arthur Ashe	1,584,909
147	Rod Laver	1,564,213
148	Leander Paes	1,563,994
149	Diego Nargiso	1,562,488
150	Heinz Gunthardt	1,550,007
151	Alberto Mancini	1,543,120
152	Danie Visser	1,527,930
153	David Adams	1,527,642
154	Jared Palmer	1,506,127
155	Libor Pimek	1,503,598
156	Luiz Mattar	1,493,136
157	Gianluca Pozzi	1,486,075
158	Tom Nijssen	1,470,062
159	Jiri Novak	1,459,178
160	Mark Edmondson	1,450,890
161	Slobodan Zivojinovic	1,450,384
162	David Rikl	1,449,206
163	Gary Muller	1,447,444
164	Balazs Taroczy	1,437,443
165	Bill Scanlon	1,427,007
166	Brian Teacher	1,426,244
167	Todd Witsken	1,420,910
168	Filip Dewulf	1,417,528
169	Jose Higueras	1,406,355
170	Manuel Orantes	1,398,303
171	Jan Apell	1,388,612
172	Stefano Pescosolido	1,387,856
173	Kenneth Carlsen	1,383,553
174	Gene Mayer	1,381,562
175	Mark Kratzmann	1,378,936
176	Francisco Roig	1,366,588
177	Mikael Pernfors	1,363,793
178	Thomas Johansson*	1,362,454
179	Jean-Philippe Fleurian	1,351,451
180	Darren Cahill	1,349,247
181	Jeremy Bates	1,339,964
182	Vijay Amritraj	1,330,503
183	Mikael Tillstrom*	1,321,402
184	Vincent Spadea*	1,316,514
185	Gilbert Schaller	1,310,216
186	Goran Prpic	1,303,639
187	Sjeng Schalken*	1,289,687
188	Tim Wilkison	1,287,675
189	Jan Gunnarsson	1,285,040
190	Piet Norval	1,283,038
191	Luke Jensen	1,277,587
192	Fernando Meligeni*	1,264,951
193	David Macpherson	1,264,837
194	Ramesh Krishnan	1,263,130
195	Christian Bergstrom	1,261,262
196	Tom Okker	1,257,200
197	Thierry Champion	1,253,739
198	Bryan Shelton	1,236,508
199	Horacio De La Pena	1,234,768
200	Paul Mcnamee	1,232,825
201	John Alexander	1,214,079
202	Hendrik Dreekmann	1,195,443
203	Jordi Burillo	1,191,514
204	Ellis Ferreira*	1,169,907
205	Nicolas Kiefer*	1,169,095
206	Robert Lutz	1,165,276
207	Kelly Jones	1,163,123
208	Francisco Montana*	1,139,417
209	Peter Lundgren	1,130,516
210	Magnus Norman*	1,125,483
211	Michiel Schapers	1,124,730
212	Tim Gullikson	1,121,430
213	Grant Stafford*	1,121,232
214	Karsten Braasch	1,120,983
215	Shuzo Matsuoka	1,117,362
216	Cristiano Caratti	1,111,778
217	Franco Davin	1,108,860
218	Hicham Arazi*	1,108,489
219	Karim Alami*	1,107,997
220	Eric Jelen	1,100,059
221	Steve Denton	1,084,214
222	Nicolas Pereira	1,083,441
223	Lionel Roux*	1,082,917
224	Glenn Michibata	1,081,397
225	Neil Broad*	1,076,464
226	Dick Stockton	1,063,385
227	John Newcombe	1,062,408
228	Rodolphe Gilbert*	1,062,339
229	Thierry Tulasne	1,058,412
230	Sandy Mayer	1,057,783
231	Peter McNamara	1,046,145
232	Chris Woodruff	1,046,074
233	Diego Perez	1,042,224
234	Menno Oosting*	1,029,840
235	Tommy Haas*	1,028,834
236	Alex Antonitsch	1,024,171
237	Christian Ruud*	1,017,054
238	Scott Draper*	1,005,650

History of the ATP Tour No.1 World Ranking

23 August 1973 – 10 January 1999

(Figures supplied by ATP Tour)

	Player	*Age*	*First date No.1*	*Total weeks*
1	Ivan Lendl	22.11	28 Feb 1983	270
2	Jimmy Connors	21.11	29 Jul 1974	268
3	Pete Sampras	21.8	12 Apr 1993	253
4	John McEnroe	21 (& 15 days)	2 Mar 1980	170
5	Bjorn Borg	21.2	23 Aug 1977	109
6	Stefan Edberg	24.9	13 Aug 1990	66
7	Jim Courier	21.5	10 Feb 1992	55
8	Ilie Nastase	27.1	23 Aug 1973	40
9	Andre Agassi	24.11	10 Apr 1995	30
10	Mats Wilander	24.1	12 Sep 1988	20
11	Boris Becker	23.2	28 Jan 1991	12
12	John Newcombe	30 (& 11 days)	3 Jun 1974	8
13	Thomas Muster	28.4	12 Feb 1996	6
14	Marcelo Rios	22.3	30 Mar 1998	6

HISTORY OF THE NO.1 RANKING

Ranking date	*Player*	*Weeks at No.1*
1973 23 August	**Ilie Nastase (1)**	**40**
1974 3 June	**John Newcombe (2)**	**8**
1974 29 July	**Jimmy Connors (3)**	**160**
1975		
1976		
1977 23 August	**Bjorn Borg (4)**	**1**
1977 30 August	Connors	84
1978		
1979 9 April	Borg	6
1979 21 May	Connors	7
1979 9 July	Borg	34
1980 3 March	**John McEnroe (5)**	**3**
1980 24 March	Borg	20
1980 11 August	McEnroe	1
1980 18 August	Borg	46
1981 6 July	McEnroe	2
1981 20 July	Borg	2
1981 3 August	McEnroe	58
1982 13 September	Connors	7
1982 1 November	McEnroe	1
1982 8 November	Connors	1
1982 15 November	McEnroe	11
1983 31 January	Connors	1
1983 7 February	McEnroe	1
1983 14 February	Connors	2
1983 28 February	**Ivan Lendl (6)**	**11**
1983 16 May	Connors	3
1983 6 June	McEnroe	1
1983 13 June	Connors	3
1983 4 July	McEnroe	17
1983 31 October	Lendl	6

HISTORY OF THE NO.1 RANKING (continued)

Ranking date	*Player*	*Weeks at No.1*
1983 12 December	McEnroe	4
1984 9 January	Lendl	9
1984 12 March	McEnroe	13
1984 11 June	Lendl	1
1984 18 June	McEnroe	3
1984 9 July	Lendl	5
1984 13 August	McEnroe	53
1985 19 August	Lendl	1
1985 26 August	McEnroe	2
1985 9 September	Lendl	157
1986		
1987		
1988 12 September	**Mats Wilander (7)**	**20**
1989 30 January	Lendl	80
1990 13 August	**Stefan Edberg (8)**	**24**
1991 28 January	**Boris Becker (9)**	**3**
1991 18 February	Edberg	20
1991 8 July	Becker	9
1991 9 September	Edberg	22
1992 10 February	**Jim Courier (10)**	**6**
1992 23 March	Edberg	3
1992 13 April	Courier	22
1992 14 September	Edberg	3
1992 5 October	Courier	27
1993 12 April	**Pete Sampras (11)**	**19**
1993 23 August	Courier	3
1993 13 September	Sampras	82
1994		
1995 10 April	**Andre Agassi (12)**	**30**
1995 6 November	Sampras	12
1996 29 January	Agassi	2
1996 12 February	**Thomas Muster (13)**	**1**
1996 19 February	Sampras	3
1996 11 March	Muster	5
1996 15 April	Sampras	102
1997		
1998 30 March	**Marcelo Rios (14)**	4
1998 27 April	Sampras	15
1998 10 August	Rios	2
1998 24 August	Sampras	20

Corel WTA Tour Rankings and Prize Money 1998

RANKINGS

The following tables show the season-ending rankings in singles and doubles. The rankings, updated weekly, are based on points won on the Corel WTA Tour, including the four Grand Slam Championships. (Statistics supplied by Corel WTA Tour)

(The players' birthdays and nationalities can be found on pp 174–177.)

SINGLES

Rank	Player	Tourns Played	Total Points
1	Lindsay Davenport	20	5654
2	Martina Hingis	17	5366
3	Jana Novotna	18	3734
4	Arantxa Sanchez-Vicario	19	3417
5	Venus Williams	15	3262
6	Monica Seles	15	3226
7	Mary Pierce	16	2414
8	Conchita Martinez	18	2331
9	Steffi Graf	13	2261
10	Nathalie Tauziat	24	2259
11	Patty Schnyder	23	2256
12	Dominique Van Roost	25	2073
13	Anna Kournikova	20	1971
14	Sandrine Testud	27	1898
15	Irina Spirlea	26	1830
16	Natasha Zvereva	22	1770
17	Amanda Coetzer	24	1752
18	Ai Sugiyama	23	1398
19	Silvia Farina	26	1389
20	Serena Williams	11	1301
21	Anke Huber	18	1294
22	Julie Halard-Decugis	25	1200
23	Barbara Schett	26	1157
24	Magui Serna	25	1154
25	Iva Majoli	20	1135
26	Elena Likhovtseva	30	1123
27	Lisa Raymond	21	1054
28	Henrieta Nagyova	21	1041
29	Amelie Mauresmo	23	961
30	Joannette Kruger	22	874
31	Corina Morariu	23	793
32	Virginia Ruano-Pascual	17	774
33	Tara Snyder	25	761
34	Chanda Rubin	23	756
35	Mariaan De Swardt	19	752
36	Sarah Pitkowski	25	707
37	Tamarine Tanasugarn	23	692
38	Ruxandra Dragomir	26	683
39	Alexandra Fusai	24	657
40	Fang Li	27	656
41	Sylvia Plischke	24	641
42	Amy Frazier	17	630
43	Maria Alejandra Vento	22	607
44	Cara Black	25	581
45	Barbara Paulus	19	578
46	Annie Miller	17	574
47	Elena Tatarkova	19	573
48	Nathalie Dechy	29	561
49	Sabine Appelmans	20	559
50	Anna Smashnova	25	554
51	Mirjana Lucic	12	535
52	Magdalena Grzybowska	20	530
53	Gala Leon Garcia	18	523
54	Anne-Gaelle Sidot	27	513
55	Naoko Sawamatsu	18	497
56	Yayuk Basuki	17	479
57	Kveta Hrdlickova	19	475
58	Miriam Oremans	20	473
59	Shi-Ting Wang	23	464
60	Rita Grande	28	463
61	Olga Barabanschikova	24	442
62	Kimberly Po	15	440
63	Adriana Gersi	25	427
64	Florencia Labat	23	425
65	Samantha Smith	24	424
66	Barbara Rittner	21	418
67	Catalina Cristea	30	397
68	Alex Dechaume-Balleret	25	388
69	Elena Wagner	23	378
70	Kristina Brandi	32	371
71	Maria Antonia Sanchez Lorenzo	24	371
72	Meghann Shaughnessy	32	368
73	Larisa Neiland	20	364
74	Anne Kremer	19	355
75	Jana Nejedly	24	353
76	Mary Joe Fernandez	8	350
77	Amelie Cocheteux	31	350
78	Tatiana Panova	25	349
79	Laura Golarsa	22	339
80	Sandra Cacic	21	335
81	Andrea Glass	24	333
82	Karina Habsudova	22	327
83	Jane Chi	25	322
84	Kristie Boogert	26	322
85	Paola Suarez	19	318
86	Janet Lee	25	312
87	Radka Bobkova	19	310
88	Miho Saeki	24	309
89	Silvija Talaja	14	305
90	Jana Kandarr	26	299
91	Lori Mcneil	9	292
92	Asa Carlsson	22	289
93	Pavlina Stoyanova	29	284
94	Els Callens	50	281
95	Fabiola Zuluaga	23	277
96	Mariana Diaz-Oliva	20	276
97	Cristin Torrens-Valero	24	274
98	Emilie Loit	24	271
99	Raluca Sandu	24	270
100	Evgenia Koulikovskaya	16	268
101	Jennifer Capriati	14	267
102	Meike Babel	21	266
103	Yuka Yoshida	26	257
104	Katarina Studenikova	23	256
105	Emmanuelle Gagliardi	20	250
106	Conchita Martinez-Granados	29	250
107	Brie Rippner	26	248
108	Barbara Schwartz	14	248

Rank	Player	Tourns Played	Total Points
109	Elena Makarova	20	245
110	Sonya Jeyaseelan	23	244
111	Lilia Osterloh	25	242
112	Samantha Reeves	27	241
113	Nicole Pratt	31	239
114	Lea Ghirardi	21	236
115	Magdalena Maleeva	7	235
116	Flora Perfetti	20	235
117	Nana Miyagi	24	233
118	Aleksandra Olsza	31	232
119	Karin Miller	36	228
120	Rita Kuti Kis	20	227
121	Marlene Weingartner	25	227
122	Seda Noorlander	28	227
123	Christina Papadaki	21	220
124	Laurence Courtois	21	215
125	Annabel Ellwood	23	211
126	Alexandra Stevenson	14	210
127	Ludmila Cervanova	19	208
128	Sandra Nacuk	13	205
129	Adriana Serra-Zanetti	24	205
130	Jolene Watanabe	28	205
131	Karin Kschwendt	24	201
132	Francesca Lubiani	24	199
133	Patricia Wartusch	21	199
134	Denisa Chladkova	29	197
135	Kerry-Anne Guse	24	192
136	Janette Husarova	19	192
137	Maureen Drake	25	184
138	Haruka Inoue	29	183
139	Lenka Nemeckova	25	183
140	Miriam Schnitzer	20	182
141	Tina Krizan	24	177
142	Nadejda Petrova	9	177
143	Surina De Beer	16	172
144	Marion Maruska	25	172
145	Annamaria Foldenyi	18	171
146	Julia Abe	26	170
147	Laurence Andretto	21	169
148	Liezel Horn	26	169
149	Ginger Nielsen	12	162
150	Sung-Hee Park	16	161
151	Jill Craybas	16	160
152	Tathiana Garbin	23	159
153	Julie Pullin	28	158
154	Amanda Hopmans	18	158
155	Lubomira Bacheva	19	156
156	Shinobu Asagoe	18	155
157	Catherine Barclay	23	153
158	Jo Ward	25	151
159	Eun-Ha Kim	24	150
160	Sandra Dopfer	26	150
161	Louise Latimer	26	150
162	Karen Cross	31	149
163	Olga Lugina	22	143
164	Sandra Kloesel	29	141
165	Sandra Kleinova	36	138
166	Mashona Washington	24	133
167	Gisela Riera	23	133
168	Ana Alcazar	13	132
169	Larissa Schaerer	22	132
170	Eva Bes	23	130
171	Erika De Lone	25	128
172	Alicia Molik	15	127
173	Maria Paola Zavagli	20	125
174	Nirupama Vaidyanathan	23	123
175	Alicia Ortuno	28	122
176	Wiltrud Probst	16	122
177	Rachel McQuillan	20	118
178	Rika Hiraki	24	117
179	Irina Selyutina	20	117
180	Amanda Grahame	24	117
181	Brenda Schultz-McCarthy	10	117
182	Elena Dementieva	11	116
183	Antonella Serra-Zanetti	21	116
184	Petra Mandula	19	116
185	Lindsay Lee	27	115
186	Hila Rosen	21	114
187	Svetlana Kriventcheva	23	114
188	Noelle Van Lottum	19	112
189	Evie Dominikovic	18	111
190	Katie Schlukebir	23	109
191	Radka Pelikanova	21	108
192	Jessica Steck	23	107
193	Jing-Qian Yi	14	107
194	Mariam Ramon	25	107
195	Lisa McShea	23	107
196	Sandra Cecchini	11	106
197	Cindy Watson	25	105
198	Jacqueline Trail	13	103
199	Paula Hermida	30	103
200	Nora Koves	19	102
201	Yoon Jeong Cho	14	102
202	Daphne Van De Zande	20	102
203	Lorna Woodroffe	27	101
204	Meilen Tu	9	101
205	Gabrielle Kucerova	23	99
206	Rosa M. Andres	28	99
207	Kyra Nagy	19	99
208	Sophie Georges	19	98
209	Anca Barna	16	98
210	Saori Obata	18	98
211	Tatiana Poutchek	24	96
212	Jean Okada	21	96
213	Patty Van Acker	25	95
214	Kristina Triska	20	95
215	Katalin Marosi	25	94
216	Alice Canepa	26	94
217	Martina Nejedly	24	94
218	Ludmila Richterova	18	93
219	Michaela Pastikova	18	90
220	Nancy Feber	11	89
221	Carolina Jagienak	23	88
222	Germana Di Natale	21	87
223	Petra Langrova	18	87
224	Jasmin Woehr	21	86
225	Lucie Ahl	26	86
226	Justine Henin	7	85
227	Jessica Fernandez	24	85
228	Ding Ding	13	85
229	Tracy Singian	28	85
230	Ju-Yeon Choi	6	84
231	Rennae Stubbs	11	84
232	Wynne Prakusya	15	84
233	Andreea Vanc	20	84
234	Vanessa Menga	19	84
235	Melanie Schnell	22	82
236	Jelena Kostanic	11	81
237	Marketa Kochta	21	81
238	Eva Martincova	20	81
239	Aurandrea Narvaez	32	80
240	Tzipora Obziler	17	80
241	Misumi Miyauchi	12	79
242	Petra Gaspar	19	79
243	Bahia Mouhtassine	23	79
244	Nataly Cahana	17	79
245	Sybille Bammer	22	78
246	Zuzana Valekova	20	77
247	Lino Lourdes Dominguez	16	77
248	Emmanuelle Curutchet	24	76
249	Segolene Berger	21	75
250	Meike Froehlich	15	73

DOUBLES

Rank	Player	Tourns Played	Total Points
1	Natasha Zvereva	20	4994
2	Martina Hingis	13	4816
3	Jana Novotna	15	4022
4	Lindsay Davenport	17	3945
5	Rennae Stubbs	21	2617
5	Lisa Raymond	21	2617
7	Nathalie Tauziat	22	2386
8	Alexandra Fusai	21	2386
9	Elena Likhovtseva	29	2101
10	Anna Kournikova	20	2067
11	Larisa Neiland	25	2010
12	Arantxa Sanchez-Vicario	18	1925
13	Ai Sugiyama	22	1857
14	Patricia Tarabini	24	1773
15	Caroline Vis	26	1687
16	Conchita Martinez	16	1605
17	Mariaan De Swardt	16	1525
18	Manon Bollegraf	18	1480
19	Yayuk Basuki	21	1444
20	Mirjana Lucic	9	1405
21	Julie Halard-Decugis	24	1400
22	Elena Tatarkova	23	1341
23	Paola Suarez	19	1337
24	Barbara Schett	23	1175
25	Katrina Adams	20	1102
26	Nana Miyagi	25	1098
27	Kerry-Anne Guse	24	1050
28	Virginia Ruano-Pascual	14	1026
29	Patty Schnyder	20	1022
30	Chanda Rubin	18	1007
31	Miriam Oremans	19	953
32	Dominique Van Roost	20	951
33	Irina Spirlea	22	949
34	Debbie Graham	21	933
35	Amanda Coetzer	16	901
36	Venus Williams	8	876
36	Serena Williams	8	876
38	Sabine Appelmans	17	865
39	Florencia Labat	21	863
40	Rachel McQuillan	19	862
41	Catherine Barclay	24	840
42	Helena Sukova	6	753
43	Els Callens	19	746
44	Silvia Farina	21	738
45	Laura Montalvo	19	713
46	Naoko Kijimuta	14	711
47	Catalina Cristea	28	708
48	Kristine Kunce	17	696
49	Corina Morariu	20	692
50	Lori McNeil	12	687
51	Kimberly Po	14	671
52	Karina Habsudova	18	628
53	Monica Seles	7	618
54	Shi-Ting Wang	21	615
55	Iva Majoli	18	603
56	Mary Pierce	7	591
57	Liezel Horn	28	576
58	Ruxandra Dragomir	18	562
59	Meike Babel	16	558
60	Yuka Yoshida	19	551
61	Katie Schlukebir	25	539
62	Anne-Gaelle Sidot	20	535
63	Seda Noorlander	24	535
64	Miho Saeki	17	532
65	Caroline Dhenin	16	531
66	Karin Kschwendt	22	519
67	Nicole Pratt	27	517
68	Erika De Lone	23	506
69	Emilie Loit	19	501
70	Sandrine Testud	17	500
71	Olga Lugina	20	500
72	Tamarine Tanasugarn	19	499
73	Tina Krizan	23	490
74	Nannie De Villiers	28	489
75	Amy Frazier	12	480
76	Sung-Hee Park	13	478
77	Katarina Srebotnik	18	471
78	Cara Black	20	452
79	Irina Selyutina	21	446
80	Laura Golarsa	17	434
81	Laurence Courtois	14	431
82	Anke Huber	11	431
83	Janet Lee	22	429
84	Rita Grande	19	427
85	Lisa McShea	28	422
86	Elena Wagner	18	416
87	Rika Hiraki	21	398
88	Lindsay Lee	24	389
89	Mary Joe Fernandez	7	388
90	Kristie Boogert	13	366
91	Eva Melicharova	20	354
92	Svetlana Kriventcheva	19	349
93	Pavlina Stoyanova	21	336
94	Helena Vildova	24	335
95	Eun-Ha Kim	22	334
96	Sonya Jeyaseelan	17	329
97	Olga Barabanschikova	17	328
98	Maureen Drake	22	325
99	Wiltrud Probst	15	324
100	Barbara Rittner	16	313

COREL WTA ANNUAL AWARDS FOR 1998

Presented during the week of 16th November 1998 at Madison Square Garden, NY during the Chase Championships to recognize performances in 1998.

Player of the Year:	Lindsay Davenport
Doubles Team of the Year:	Gigi Fernandez/Natasha Zvereva
Most Improved Player:	Patty Schnyder
Newcomer of the Year:	Serena Williams
Comeback Player of the Year:	Monica Seles
Ted Tinling Media Award:	To be announced
Karen Krantzcke Sportsmanship Award:	Yayuk Basuki
Player Service Award:	Joanette Kruger
Diamond Aces Award:	Lindsay Davenport
Most Exciting Player Award:	Steffi Graf
David Gray Special Service Award:	To be announced
Tournament of the Year (Tier I-II):	Canadian Open, Montreal
Tournament of the Year (Tier III-IV):	Bell Challenge, Quebec City

PRIZE MONEY (As at 23 November 1998)

The following table shows the prize money in US dollars (including bonuses) won at all recognized tournaments which adopted the WTA guidelines, where direct entry was based solely upon merit. It does not include income from Fed Cup, other team events, exhibitions, special events or commercial contracts. (Figures supplied by Corel WTA Tour)

Note: Players' nationalities and birthdays can be found on pp 174–177.

1	Martina Hingis	$3,175,631
2	Lindsay Davenport	2,697,788
3	Jana Novotna	2,039,912
4	Venus Williams	1,712,246
5	Arantxa Sanchez-Vicario	1,505,964
6	Monica Seles	1,003,514
7	Nathalie Tauziat	990,224
8	Natasha Zvereva	931,945
9	Patty Schnyder	901,828
10	Conchita Martinez	859,417
11	Mary Pierce	662,237
12	Steffi Graf	537,577
13	Amanda Coetzer	534,948
14	Irina Spirlea	530,988
15	Anna Kournikova	526,633
16	Sandrine Testud	477,795
17	Dominique Van Roost	440,324
18	Lisa Raymond	399,648
19	Ai Sugiyama	354,950
20	Elena Likhovtseva	330,918
21	Serena Williams	310,211
22	Alexandra Fusai	294,437
23	Iva Majoli	291,356
24	Silvia Farina	291,186
25	Barbara Schett	280,514
26	Mirjana Lucic	274,905
27	Anke Huber	272,442
28	Julie Halard-Decugis	262,153
29	Virginia Ruano-Pascual	248,391
30	Rennae Stubbs	222,922
31	Yayuk Basuki	220,005
32	Henrieta Nagyova	218,874
33	Mariaan De Swardt	216,011
34	Chanda Rubin	213,708
35	Magui Serna	213,650
36	Larisa Neiland	212,590
37	Ruxandra Dragomir	209,161
38	Tamarine Tanasugarn	203,941
39	Amelie Mauresmo	187,084
40	Corina Morariu	180,111
41	Paola Suarez	179,330
42	Miriam Oremans	176,599
43	Joannette Kruger	164,852
44	Rita Grande	164,399
45	Elena Tatarkova	156,515
46	Sabine Appelmans	155,489
47	Florencia Labat	153,926
48	Kimberly Po	152,372
49	Anne-Gaelle Sidot	151,068
50	Karina Habsudova	151,021
51	Kerry-Anne Guse	143,462
52	Tara Snyder	143,097
53	Miho Saeki	141,364
54	Nathalie Dechy	137,517
55	Patricia Tarabini	132,864
56	Caroline Vis	131,192
57	Magdalena Grzybowska	130,331
58	Sarah Pitkowski	129,944
59	Nana Miyagi	129,523
60	Shi-Ting Wang	129,062
61	Maria Alejandra Vento	127,801
62	Olga Barabanschikova	126,991
63	Rachel McQuillan	125,123
64	Anna Smashnova	124,658
65	Amy Frazier	123,742
66	Fang Li	123,241
67	Alexi Dechaume-Balleret	122,516
68	Catalina Cristea	120,622
69	Yuka Yoshida	118,095
70	Cara Black	116,203
71	Lori McNeil	115,147
72	Barbara Rittner	114,617
73	Naoko Sawamatsu	113,471
74	Sandra Cacic	112,793
75	Meike Babel	111,966
76	Annie Miller	111,577
77	Sylvia Plischke	111,487
78	Barbara Paulus	110,326
79	Gala Leon Garcia	110,019
80	Asa Carlsson	109,966
81	Janet Lee	107,522
82	Nicole Pratt	105,364
83	Maria Antonia Sanchez-Lorenzo	103,893
84	Laura Golarsa	103,445
85	Kveta Hrdlickova	98,316
86	Elena Wagner	97,529
87	Sung-Hee Park	95,491
88	Kristie Boogert	92,848
89	Kristina Brandi	92,573
90	Samantha Smith	92,490
91	Els Callens	90,632
92	Naoko Kijimuta	90,415
93	Sonya Jeyaseelan	89,471
94	Adriana Gersi	88,547
95	Debbie Graham	87,931
96	Pavlina Stoyanova	86,415
97	Radka Bobkova	85,909
98	Tatiana Panova	85,887
99	Amelie Cocheteux	85,181
100	Manon Bollegraf	84,019
101	Samantha Reeves	81,745
102	Flora Perfetti	81,643
103	Helena Sukova	81,574
104	Catherine Barclay	81,337
105	Andrea Glass	81,161
106	Mary Joe Fernandez	80,945
107	Emilie Loit	79,127
108	Katarina Studenikova	79,091
109	Olga Lugina	78,443
110	Sandra Kleinova	75,558
111	Mariana Diaz-Oliva	75,386
112	Kristine Kunce	75,309
113	Seda Noorlander	74,026
114	Cristina Torrens-Valero	73,363
115	Jana Nejedly	71,236
116	Barbara Schwartz	70,819
117	Annabel Ellwood	69,685
118	Rika Hiraki	68,545
119	Liezel Horn	67,470
120	Katrina Adams	67,226

121	Ginger Nielsen	67,092
122	Meghann Shaughnessy	66,827
123	Jana Kandarr	66,706
124	Lilia Osterloh	66,589
125	Jennifer Capriati	66,573
126	Lenka Nemeckova	66,469
127	Elena Makarova	65,944
128	Janette Husarova	65,918
129	Laurence Courtois	64,952
130	Emmanuelle Gagliardi	64,153
131	Denisa Chladkova	61,499
132	Caroline Dhenin	61,204
133	Wiltrud Probst	59,006
134	Francesca Lubiani	58,508
135	Karin Kschwendt	57,508
136	Lea Ghirardi	56,946
137	Aleksandra Olsza	55,382
138	Tina Krizan	54,756
139	Patricia Hy-Boulais	53,780
140	Eun-Ha Kim	53,606
141	Erika De Lone	53,137
142	Svetlana Kriventcheva	52,472
143	Haruka Inoue	51,886
144	Anne Kremer	51,777
145	Ines Gorrochategui	51,522
146	Marion Maruska	50,279
147	Katie Schlukebir	50,201
148	Brie Rippner	50,134
149	Julie Pullin	50,108
150	Lindsay Lee	49,728
151	Mashona Washington	49,726
152	Evgenia Koulikovskaya	48,742
153	Brenda Schultz-McCarthy	48,499
154	Karin Miller	46,907
155	Alexandra Stevenson	46,855
156	Surina De Beer	46,598
157	Fabiola Zuluaga	46,208
158	Raluca Sandu	45,240
159	Lisa McShea	45,153
160	Marlene Weingartner	45,056
161	Laura Montalvo	44,523
162	Noelle Van Lottum	44,036
163	Maureen Drake	43,783
164	Sandra Kloesel	42,856
165	Lorna Woodroffe	42,161
166	Karen Cross	40,208
167	Jolene Watanabe	40,099
168	Sandra Nacuk	40,088
169	Conchita Martinez-Granados	39,102
170	Sandra Dopfer	38,638
171	Magdalena Maleeva	38,573
172	Christina Papadaki	38,516
173	Ann Wunderlich	37,556
174	Irina Selyutina	36,795
175	Silvija Talaja	36,641
176	Miriam Schnitzer	35,689
177	Jane Chi	35,521
178	Nannie De Villiers	34,876
179	Shinobu Asagoe	34,798
180	Mercedes Paz	34,433
181	Trudi Musgrave	34,083
182	Christina Singer	33,954
183	Adriana Serra-Zanetti	33,348
184	Patricia Wartusch	33,244
185	Yoon Jeong Cho	33,090
186	Jo Ward	32,982
187	Eva Bes	31,328
188	Rita Kuti Kis	31,304
189	Louise Latimer	31,007
190	Katarina Srebotnik	31,002
191	Laurence Andretto	30,934
192	Virag Csurgo	30,931
193	Helena Vildova	30,827
194	Julia Abe	29,239
195	Petra Langrova	29,178
196	Nirupama Vaidyanathan	29,163
197	Caroline Schneider	28,443
198	Nadejda Petrova	28,418
199	Alicia Ortuno	28,361
200	Amanda Grahame	27,840
201	Jill Craybas	27,723
202	Tathiana Garbin	27,407
203	Rene Simpson	26,757
204	Larissa Schaerer	26,647
205	Sandra Cecchini	26,469
206	Vanessa Webb	26,400
207	Annamaria Foldenyi	25,856
208	Alicia Molik	25,669
209	Eva Melicharova	25,531
210	Louise Pleming	25,324
211	Siobhan Drake-Brockman	24,998
212	Jacqueline Trail	23,022
213	Ludmila Cervanova	23,018
214	Ludmila Richterova	22,903
215	Meilen Tu	22,369
216	Jean Okada	22,165
217	Nancy Feber	22,134
218	Evie Dominikovic	21,752
219	Alice Canepa	21,684
220	Eva Martincova	21,338
221	Amanda Hopmans	21,279
222	Saori Obata	21,239
223	Daphne Van De Zande	21,123
224	Gisela Riera	20,963
225	Emmanuelle Curutchet	20,726
226	Lenka Cenkova	20,412
227	Rosa M. Andres	20,211
228	Sophie Georges	20,080
229	Lucie Ahl	19,964
230	Ana Alcazar	19,703
231	Jasmin Woehr	19,672
232	Paula Hermida	18,897
233	Meredith McGrath	18,802
234	Martina Nejedly	18,754
235	Kirstin Freye	18,633
236	Hila Rosen	18,129
237	Mariam Ramon	18,050
238	Laura Granville	18,000
239	Elena Dementieva	17,987
240	Petra Mandula	17,880
241	Segolene Berger	17,238
242	Kyra Nagy	17,151
243	Lubomira Bacheva	17,107
244	Katalin Marosi	17,040
245	Cindy Watson	16,466
246	Misumi Miyauchi	16,406
247	Tracy Singian	16,244
248	Wynne Prakusya	16,125
249	Milena Nekvapilova	16,033
250	Maja Muric	15,655
251	Vanessa Menga	15,528
252	Jessica Steck	15,425
253	Syna Schmidle	15,088
254	Jing-Qian Yi	14,985
255	Nora Koves	14,893
256	Gabrielle Kucerova	14,717
257	Magalie Lamarre	14,614
258	Aurandrea Narvaez	14,578
259	Jessica Fernandez	14,455
260	Michaela Pastikova	14,313

261	Maria Paola Zavagli	14,292
262	Bryanne Stewart	14,291
263	Melissa Mazzotta	14,280
264	Renata Kolbovic	14,174
265	Radka Pelikanova	14,090
266	Danielle Jones	14,067
267	Mi-Ra Jeon	13,960
268	Maria Fernanda Landa	13,891
269	Tatiana Poutchek	13,886
270	Petra Rampre	13,647
271	Carolina Jagienak	13,602
272	Lourdes Dominguez Lino	13,549
273	Kristina Triska	13,512
274	Andreea Vanc	13,343
275	Petra Gaspar	13,268
276	Tzipora Obziler	13,220
277	Sarah Taylor	13,092
278	Gail Biggs	13,014
279	Patty Van Acker	12,842
280	Jelena Kostanic	12,769
281	Marketa Kochta	12,631
282	Zuzana Valekova	12,293
283	Gloria Pizzichini	12,024
284	Abigail Tordoff	12,020
285	Mira Lorelli Radu	11,996
286	Selima Sfar	11,718
287	Evelyn Fauth	11,648
288	Benjamas Sangaram	11,609
289	Justine Henin	11,574
290	Celeste Contin	11,509
291	Nadejda Ostrovskaya	11,329
292	Holly Parkinson	11,320
293	Anca Barna	11,191
294	Antonella Serra-Zanetti	11,162
295	Nataly Cahana	11,048
296	Germana Di Natale	11,029
297	Eleni Daniilidou	10,899
298	Ju-Yeon Choi	10,873
298	Keiko Nagatomi	10,873
300	Bahia Mouhtassine	10,682
301	Ding Ding	10,652
302	Ludmilla Varmuza	10,565
303	Alessia Lombardi	10,516
304	Alina Jidkova	10,313
305	Maria Goloviznina	10,068
306	Gabriela Navratilova	9,985
307	Tomoe Hotta	9,842
308	Helen Crook	9,823
309	Mana Endo	9,758
310	Petra Kamstra	9,675
311	Marina Escobar	9,466
312	Maiko Inoue	9,453
313	Romina Ottoboni	9,391
314	Renee Reid	9,363
315	Angelika Roesch	9,334
316	Nino Louarsabishvili	9,302
317	Katarzyna Nowak	9,289
318	Anna Zarska	9,257
319	Geraldine Aizenberg	9,224
320	Anastasia Myskina	9,152
321	Hana Sromova	9,137
322	Jennifer Poulos	9,090
323	Ainhoa Goni	9,065
324	Melissa Beadman	9,020
325	Keri Phebus	9,014
326	Ekaterina Syssoeva	8,996
327	Adria Engel	8,994
328	Desislava Topalova	8,963
329	Sybille Bammer	8,841
330	Meike Froehlich	8,561
331	Melanie Schnell	8,480
332	Miroslava Vavrinec	8,478
333	Maaike Koutstaal	8,446
334	Veronica Stele	8,408
335	Magdalena Zdenovcova	8,361
336	Yvette Basting	8,296
337	Marijana Kovacevic	8,255
338	Julie Scott	8,237
339	Alice Pirsu	8,222
340	Eva Krejcova	8,140
341	Alienor Tricerri	7,815
342	Sylvie Sallaberry	7,787
343	Olga Blahotova	7,741
344	Kaoru Shibata	7,690
344	Mariana Mesa	7,690
346	Stephanie Foretz	7,667
347	Veronika Martinek	7,657
348	Mareze Joubert	7,640
349	Libuse Prusova	7,618
350	Zsofia Gubacsi	7,617
351	Angeles Montolio	7,594
352	Luciana Masante	7,496
353	Elizabeth Jelfs	7,414
354	Rebecca Jensen	7,391
355	Martina Sucha	7,368
356	Giulia Casoni	7,356
357	Zuzana Ondraskova	7,336
358	Ryoko Takemura	7,311
359	Dragana Zaric	7,171
360	Magda Mihalache	7,148
361	Maria Gusheva	7,119
362	Sophie Erre	7,074
363	Young-Ja Choi	6,966
364	Victoria Davies	6,930
365	Kazue Takuma	6,901
366	Keiko Ishida	6,891
367	Julie Steven	6,879
368	Oana-Elena Golimbioschi	6,871
369	Kate Warne-Holland	6,870
370	Magdalena Kucerova	6,799
371	Jana Macurova	6,783
372	Andrea Sebova	6,749
373	Hiroko Mochizuki	6,712
374	Ana Salas	6,652
375	Elena Voropaeva	6,622
376	Kelly Liggan	6,547
377	Joanne Moore	6,541
378	Angelica Gavaldon	6,488
379	Maria Wolfbrandt	6,461
380	Stephanie De Ville	6,457
381	Rewa Hudson	6,456
382	Laura Pena	6,451
383	Shiho Hisamatsu	6,392
384	Cindy Schuurmans	6,388
385	Bettina Fulco-Villella	6,379
386	Patricia Aznar	6,369
387	Akiko Morigami	6,360
388	Amanda Augustus	6,224
389	Paula Cabezas	6,212
390	Melisa Arevalo	6,166
391	Silke Meier	6,147
392	Laura Dell'Angelo	6,139
393	Miriam D'agostini	6,134
394	Paula Racedo	6,111
395	Wendy Fix	6,100
396	Adrian Hegedus	6,087
397	Jasmine Choudhury	6,043

THE MILLIONAIRESSES

The players listed below have won at least US$1 million during the course of their careers. The totals include earnings at all official tournaments recognised by the WTA Tour, as well as official bonuses. They do not include income from Fed Cup, special events, exhibitions or commercial endorsements.
NOTE: * indicates the 14 players who appear for the first time.

1	Steffi Graf	$20,614,142
2	Martina Navratilova	20,344,061
3	Arantxa Sanchez-Vicario	14,029,452
4	Monica Seles	10,878,024
5	Jana Novotna	10,297,692
6	Chris Evert	8,896,195
7	Gabriela Sabatini	8,785,850
8	Martina Hingis	8,124,248
9	Conchita Martinez	7,737,227
10	Natasha Zvereva	7,014,631
11	Lindsay Davenport	6,390,242
12	Helena Sukova	6,390,095
13	Pam Shriver	5,460,566
14	Mary Joe Fernandez	4,984,831
15	Gigi Fernandez	4,680,456
16	Zina Garrison-Jackson	4,590,816
17	Nathalie Tauziat	4,005,088
18	Mary Pierce	3,881,746
19	Larisa Neiland	3,745,744
20	Iva Majoli	3,464,588
21	Lori McNeil	3,399,932
22	Anke Huber	3,392,342
23	Hana Mandlikova	3,340,959
24	Manuela Maleeva-Fragniere	3,244,811
25	Amanda Coetzer	3,148,276
26	Wendy Turnbull	2,769,024
27	Brenda Schultz-McCarthy	2,549,988
28	Claudia Kohde-Kilsch	2,227,116
29	Katerina Maleeva	2,220,371
30	Irina Spirlea	2,218,256
31	Venus Williams	2,210,894
32	Tracy Austin	1,992,380
33	Kimiko Date	1,974,253
34	Billie Jean King	1,966,487
35	Manon Bollegraf	1,879,949
36	Magdalena Maleeva	1,831,341
37	Lisa Raymond	1,771,818
38	Jennifer Capriati	1,755,201
39	Judith Wiesner	1,738,253
40	Amy Frazier	1,716,258
41	Julie Halard-Decugis	1,703,094
42	Rosalyn Nideffer	1,701,944
43	Elizabeth Smylie	1,701,837
44	Chanda Rubin	1,605,057
45	Sabine Appelmans	1,603,819
46	Kathy Jordan	1,592,111
47	Patty Fendick	1,574,956
48	Yayuk Basuki	1,550,645
49	Virginia Wade	1,542,278
50	Sandrine Testud	1,497,665
51	Meredith McGrath	1,448,132
52	Kathy Rinaldi-Stunkel	1,417,273
53	Evonne Goolagong	1,399,431
54	Andrea Jaeger	1,379,066
55	Barbara Potter	1,376,580
56	Rosie Casals	1,364,955
57	Karina Habsudova	1,328,130
58	Sandra Cecchini	1,319,077
59	Nicole Bradtke	1,298,972
60	Sylvia Hanika	1,296,560
61	Barbara Paulus	1,294,445
62	Katrina Adams	1,267,292
63	Jo Durie	1,224,016
64	Patty Schnyder*	1,211,277
65	Rachel McQuillan	1,195,694
66	Virginia Ruzici	1,183,728
67	Leila Meskhi	1,179,720
68	Robin White	1,174,349
69	Dominique Van Roost*	1,167,500
70	Mercedes Paz	1,163,693
71	Andrea Temesvari	1,162,635
72	Anne Smith	1,159,717
73	Kimberly Po	1,157,731
74	Elena Likhovtseva*	1,148,344
75	Dianne Balestrat	1,145,377
76	Florencia Labat*	1,141,121
77	Ann Wunderlich*	1,138,377
78	Catarina Lindqvist	1,126,665
79	Bettina Bunge	1,126,424
80	Linda Wild	1,124,733
81	Elna Reinach	1,114,668
82	Rennae Stubbs*	1,109,620
83	Naoko Sawamatsu*	1,107,264
84	Ai Sugiyama*	1,107,237
85	Ruxandra Dragomir*	1,097,570
86	Nicole Arendt	1,094,802
87	Patricia Tarabini*	1,091,970
88	Miriam Oremans*	1,084,847
89	Radka Zrubakova	1,052,517
90	Betty Stove	1,047,356
91	Marianne Werdel-Witmeyer	1,045,983
92	Barbara Rittner*	1,037,230
93	Betsy Nagelsen	1,016,519
94	Patricia Hy-Boulais*	1,011,116
95	Laura Arraya	1,005,589
96	Silvia Farina*	1,002,281

WTA TOUR

CORPORATE HEADQUARTERS: 1266 East Main Street, 4th Floor, Stamford, CT 06902-3546, USA
Tel: 1-203-978 1740; Fax: 1-203-978 1702

TOUR OPERATIONS: 133 First Street, St Petersburg, FL 33701, USA
Tel: 1-813 895 5000; Fax: 1-813 894 1982; Telex: 441761
TOUR HEADQUARTERS EUROPE: Bank Lane, Roehampton, London, SW15 5XZ, England
Tel: 44-181-392 4760; Fax: 44-181-392 4765
INTERNET ADDRESS: http://www.wtatour.com
FAXBACK NUMBER: 1-813 822 8868

On 1 January 1995, the Women's Tennis Association and the Women's Tennis Council merged to form the WTA TOUR with Ann Person Worcester, the former Managing Director of the Council, becoming the first Chief Executive Officer of the new body, a post she filled until her retirement at the end of 1997. Bart McGuire became the new CEO in January 1998.

WTA TOUR BOARD OF DIRECTORS
Bob Arrix (Tournament Class Director)
Franco Bartoni (Tournament Class Director)
Geoff Pollard (Tournament Class Director)
Dick Dell (Player Class Director)
Lisa Grattan (Player Class Director)
Ilana Kloss (Player Class Director)
Ingrid Bentzer (Federation Class Director)
Claude de Jouvencel (Outside Director)
Kay Kloplovitz (Outside Director)
Joe Shapiro (Outside Director)
Bart McGuire (Chief Executive Officer)

ALTERNATES AND OBSERVERS
Raquel Giscafre (Tournament Class Alternate)
Gunter Sanders (Tournament Class Alternate)
Toshio Noji (Tournament Class Alternate)
John Korff (Tournament Class Alternate)
Judy Levering (Grand Slam Observer)
Bill Babcock (Grand Slam Observer)
Bill Jemas (Grand Slam Observer)

WTA TOUR PLAYERS' COUNCIL

1–20 Singles:	Lindsay Davenport	Monica Seles	Anke Huber
	Arantxa Sanchez-Vicario		
21–50 Singles:	Joannette Kruger		
51–100 Singles:	Nicole Pratt		
21–100 Singles:	Mary Joe Fernandez		
101+ Singles:	Debbie Graham (non-voting)		
Business Advisors:	Dick Dell (Chairman)	Lisa Grattan	Ilana Kloss
Alternate:	John Korff		

WTA TOUR EXECUTIVE STAFF

Chief Executive Officer:	Bart McGuire
Chief Operating Officer:	Liz Garger
Senior VP of Tour Operations and Player Relations:	Peachy Kellmeyer
VP of Communications and Development:	Joe Favorito
Director of Public Relations:	Jim Fuhse
Director of Management Information Systems:	Jim Hill
Director of Marketing:	Marc Lowitz
Director of Finance:	Blair Caple
Director of Tour Operations:	Joan Mattraw
Director of Player Relations:	Jean Nachand
Director of Sports Sciences and Medicine:	Kathleen Stroia
Director of European Operations:	Georgina Clark

History of the WTA Tour No.1 World Ranking

1 November 1975 – 3 January 1999

(Figures supplied by WTA Tour)

	Player	*Age*	*First date No.1*	*Total weeks*
1	Steffi Graf (+)	18.2	17 Aug 1987	377
2	Martina Navratilova	21.9	10 Jul 1978	331
3	Chris Evert	20.11	1 Nov 1975	262
4	Monica Seles (+)	17.3	11 Mar 1991	178
5	Martina Hingis	16.6	31 Mar 1997	80
6	Tracy Austin	17.3	7 Apr 1980	22
7	Arantxa Sanchez-Vicario	23.2	6 Feb 1995	12
8	Lindsay Davenport	22.4	12 Oct 1998	12

(+) including 65 weeks as joint No.1

HISTORY OF THE NO.1 RANKING

Ranking date		*Player*	*Weeks at No.1*
1975	**1 Nov**	**Chris Evert (1)**	**140**
1978	**10 July**	**Martina Navratilova (2)**	**27**
1979	14 January	Chris Evert	2
1979	28 January	Martina Navratilova	4
1979	25 February	Chris Evert	7
1979	16 April	Martina Navratilova	10
1979	25 June	Chris Evert	11
1979	10 September	Martina Navratilova	30
1980	**7 April**	**Tracy Austin (3)***	**2**
1980	21 April	Martina Navratilova	10
1980	1 July	Tracy Austin	20
1980	18 November	Chris Evert	76
1981			
1982	3 May	Martina Navratilova	2
1982	17 May	Chris Evert	4
1982	14 June	Martina Navratilova +	156
1983			
1984			
1985	10 June	Chris Evert	18
1985	14 October	Martina Navratilova	2
1985	28 October	Chris Evert	4
1985	25 November	Martina Navratilova	90
1986			
1987	**17 August**	**Steffi Graf (4) ++**	**186**
1988			
1989			
1990			
1991	**11 March**	**Monica Seles (5)****	**21**
1991	5 August	Steffi Graf	1
1991	12 August	Monica Seles	1
1991	19 August	Steffi Graf	3
1991	9 September	Monica Seles	91
1992			
1993	7 June	Steffi Graf	87
1994			
1995	**6 Feb**	**Arantxa Sanchez-Vicario (6)**	**2**

HISTORY OF THE NO.1 RANKING (continued)

Ranking date		*Player*	*Weeks at No.1*
1995	20 February	Steffi Graf	1
1995	27 February	Arantxa Sanchez-Vicario	6
1995	10 April	Steffi Graf	5
1995	15 May	Arantxa Sanchez-Vicario	4
1995	12 June	Steffi Graf	9
1995	14 August	Steffi Graf	64
		and Monica Seles +++	64
1996	4 November	Steffi Graf	2
1996	18 November	Steffi Graf	1
		and Monica Seles +++	1
1996	25 November	Steffi Graf	18
1997	**31 March**	**Martina Hingis (7)*** **	**80**
1998	**12 October**	**Lindsay Davenport (8)**	**12**

* In April 1980 Tracy Austin is the youngest player to reach No. 1 at 17 years, 3 months, 26 days.

** In March 1991 Monica Seles becomes No.1 aged 17 years, 3 months, 19 days, 7 days younger than Austin.

*** In March 1997 Martina Hingis becomes the youngest woman ever to be ranked No.1, aged exactly 16 years and 6 months.

\+ Martina Navratilova held the No.1 position for 156 weeks consecutively.

++ Steffi Graf held the No.1 position for a record 186 weeks consecutively, more than any man or woman.

+++ Steffi Graf and Monica Seles co-ranked No. 1.

The Trouble with Doubles

John Barrett

There was a time when men's doubles was the most popular form of entertainment for the public. Spectators could easily relate to the doubles game because that is what most of them played at the local club.

In the post-war years there were some wonderful men's doubles matches at all the Grand Slams – and not just the finals – involving both the great singles players of the day – men like Jack Kramer, Frank Sedgman, Tony Trabert, Vic Seixas, Lew Hoad and Ken Rosewall – as well as the doubles specialists like Bob Hewitt, Frew McMillan, Bob Howe and Ken Fletcher.

The 1959 French final, for instance, was a beauty. The talented Italians Nicola Pietrangeli and Orlando Sirola teased Roy Emerson and Neale Fraser to death on the slow red clay. The combination of Pietrangeli's touch and guile with Sirola's great power was irresistible as they triumphed 6–3 6–2 14–12.

Four weeks later, back on more familiar grass at Wimbledon, Emerson and Fraser beat Rod Laver and Bob Mark 19–17 in the fourth set. This all-Australian final, full of all the doubles' arts – chipped or lobbed returns alternated with flashing drives to the feet, lightning interceptions at the net and delicate little angled volleys – had the fans cheering in the aisles.

In those days of wooden rackets, matches involving the leading women were less popular – especially on clay. Unable to generate the pace that the modern women enjoy with their graphite and titanium rapiers, the women of the 1950s, players like the glamorous Italians Sylvana Lazzarino and Lea Pericoli, would drive opponets…and spectators…crazy with lobbing campaigns that threatened to bring down low flying aircraft.

Today the situation is completely different. So few of the top singles players among the men bother to play doubles that the tournament directors around the world have even suggested dropping the doubles from men's tournaments. This is a serious matter. Unless marquee names like Sampras and Rios, Agassi and Henman, Moya and Kucera, Ivanisevic and Rusedski, can be persuaded to take doubles seriously the doubles game will continue to wither.

Conversely the doubles game in women's tennis has never been healthier and is part of the reason why women's tennis was more popular than most men's tennis in 1998.

Billie Jean King and Rosie Casals, the greatest American doubles pair of the 1960s and '70s were too athletic and aggressive for most of their contemporaries. (Michael Cole)

Consider the following facts. Of the ten men who headed the 1998 singles rankings none appeared among the top ten in doubles. Even as far down as the top 30 only three achieved similar success in doubles – Pat Rafter (4 in singles and 16 in doubles), Yevgeny Kafelnikov (11 and 19) and Jonas Bjorkman (24 and 8).

Compare that with the women. Four players held a top ten ranking in both singles and doubles – Lindsay Davenport (1, 4), Martina Hingis (2, 2), Jana Novotna (3, 3) and Nathalie Tauziat (10, 7). Of the top 30 singles players a total of 14 were also among the top 30 in doubles.

Even more revealing is the relative importance placed on doubles by men and women at last year's Grand Slams, as the following table shows.

TOP 30 SINGLES PLAYERS COMPETING IN DOUBLES AT THE 1998 GRAND SLAMS

	Australian Open	*French Open*	*Wimbledon*	*US Open*
Men	9	8	6	7
Women	26	24	24	22

While the women's game continues to be well balanced, offering the fans an opportunity to enjoy the skills of their top players in both codes, the men's game has divided into singles and doubles specialists. The fans are no longer being offered value for money. This is particularly serious because it is in doubles that players can relax and enjoy themselves. The sight of Hingis and Novotna laughing with one another, and with the fans, presents a much friendlier face for tennis than the scowls that all too often accompany men's singles matches.

How has this situation been allowed to develop? Lack of leadership is the prime reason. The top men have not been made aware of their responsibilites to the sport by the ATP Tour. By contrast the WTA Tour have done a good job in educating their young players to participate in doubles.

Martina Navratilova and Pam Shriver formed a superb doubles partnership that won 7 Australian, 5 French, 5 Wimbledon and 4 US titles. In 1984 they became the only pair to win a women's doubles Grand Slam. (Michael Cole)

Above: *The great Australian pair – South Australian left-hander Mark Woodforde and Sydneysider Todd Woodbridge – have won five consecutive Wimbledon doubles titles (1993–97), a modern record.* (Ray Giubilo)

Left: *A tactical discussion between two of the great women's doubles players of the 1990s, Natasha Zvereva and Arantxa Sanchez-Vicario.* (Michael Cole)

The media can share some of the blame by virtually ignoring doubles at most events and concentrating on the race to become No. 1. Yet if Sampras and the other leaders had been playing in doubles these last five years they would assuredly have commanded more attention than the present doubles champions like Todd Woodbridge and Mark Woodforde or Paul Haarhuis and Jacco Eltingh. Also, I suspect that these four would have welcomed the chance over the years to compete against the Sampras's and Agassi's of this world in doubles to prove their own worth.

On those few occasions in recent years when the top singles men have played doubles we have been treated to some exceptional tennis. Who could ever forget the excitement at Wimbledon in 1992 when John McEnroe teamed with Michael Stich and walked off with the doubles title in a dramatic third Monday finish on Court No. 1 against Jim Grabb and Richey Reneberg? That towering last set, 19–17 it was, had the standing-room-only crowd delerious with joy; or the occasion a month later when Stich and Boris Becker, making a rare appearance together, walked off with the gold medal at the Barcelona Olympics. That was a very special moment for them, for Germany and for tennis.

The men themselves will tell you that the pressure of the singles race and the points to be won every week make it impossible to concentrate on doubles. At the Grand Slams, they will say, you cannot play two best-of-five sets events when the gap between the top players and those chasing them continuies to shrink and where rain might lead to programme congestion. Yet even where the doubles has been reduced to the best-of-three-sets, as at the Australian Open until the quarter-finals and at the French and US Opens in every round, the top singles players still do not compete in doubles in any numbers.

What should be done? If you believe in tennis as entertainment – and the increasing dependence on television revenue makes that an automatic assumption – then it is imperative to restore doubles to a prominent place as we try to showcase tennis against the rival claims of other sports and leisure pursuits. After all doubles is fun. It *is* entertaining.

The only way to persuade players to take doubles seriously is to combine the two ranking lists. Surely it is time to give the fans their money's worth by rating a player's all-round performance as a tennis player. If everyone on the singles ranking list at a tournament is given automatic entry to the doubles (which would have half the singles points) – but not forced to play – then anyone not taking up his doubles place will risk sliding down the rankings.

I recognize that this solution would not be popular with the current doubles specialists, many of whom are my friends and wonderful guys. But I ask them to consider whether the game really owes them a living? With a growing emphasis on producing a streamlined sport that is at once intelligible to the fans and entertaining to watch – as well as being commercially viable – we must restore credibility to doubles.

The women are delivering value for money. Now it is up to the men.

Reference Section

Biographies • All-Time Greats
Obituaries • Championship Rolls

INDEX TO BIOGRAPHIES

The top 70 singles and leading doubles players on both the ATP and WTA tours are shown, together with senior and junior Grand Slam winners and all those who competed in the season-ending championships. Players ranked in the top 10 in singles are shown in bold. Figures following players' names indicate their singles ranking, junior ranking where applicable, and those in brackets show the doubles ranking where appropriate.

MEN

WOMEN

Biographies

Christine Forrest

Abbreviations used in this section:

f	final	1r	first round	Champ	Champion/ Championship
sf	semi-final	2s	second set		
qf	quarter-final	RH	right-handed	GP	Grand Prix
r/u	runner-up	LH	left-handed	Jun	Junior
def	defaulted	2HB	2-handed backhand	Nat	National
ret	retired	2HF	2-handed forehand	Pro	Professional
fs	final set	US CC	US Clay Court Championships	Tourn	Tournament
rr	round-robin			HC	Hard Court
bp	break-point	LIPC	Lipton International Players Championships	VS	Virginia Slims
sp	set-point			WT Cup	World Team Cup
mp	match-point	FC Cup	Family Circle Cup	D Cup	Davis Cup
tb	tie-break	GS Cup	Grand Slam Cup		

TOP TEN

Full biographical and statistical details of the top ten men and top ten women head separate men's and women's sections. Each individual's record contains personal details, followed by his or her 1998 prize money, career prize money, the number of career titles won and year-end rankings. A paragraph on style is followed by annual notes of career highlights, beginning with the tournaments won each year. A section giving principal singles results in full for 1998 includes all matches where a player has reached at least the semi-final. There follows a complete career record of every singles match played at each of the four Grand Slam Championships, at the Olympic Games and in Davis Cup or Fed Cup ties, in the Grand Slam Cup and in the season ending Tour Championships.

REMAINING BIOGRAPHIES

Within the two sections are the principal 1998 results, the annual notes and the career highlights of the next 60 ranked singles players of each sex, the leading doubles players, all Grand Slam winners and the juniors who have won Grand Slam titles. The final ranking for each year is shown in brackets following the year.

John Barrett's annual world rankings, as well as the year-end rankings published by the ATP Tour and the Corel WTA Tour, and total prize money together with lists of the men and women whose career earnings exceed $1 million, can be found in the Rankings Section (pp 225–250).

We gratefully acknowledge the assistance of the ATP Tour, especially Nathalie Durot, the Corel WTA Tour, and Nola Hendon of the WTA European office in supplying statistical information.

1 PETE SAMPRAS (USA)

Born: Washington, DC, 12 August 1971. **Lives:** Tampa, Fla. Son of Greek immigrants. **Father:** Sam. **Mother:** Georgia. **Sisters:** Stella and Marion. **Brother:** Gus (older).

Agent: Geoff Schwarz of IMG. **Coaches:** Paul Annacone; formerly the late Tim Gullikson. Coached first by Dr Pete Fischer and after they split in 1989 Robert Lansdorp coached him on forehand, Larry Easley on volley and Del Little on footwork. Went to Bollettieri Academy and worked with Joe Brandi. They parted in Dec. 1990, to be reunited briefly during 1991, and Sampras started working with Pat Etcheberry for strength.
Personal trainer: Todd Snyder. **Turned pro:** 1988.
Height: 6ft 1in (1.83m). **Weight:** 170lb (77kg).

Rankings: 1988: 97; **1989:** 81; **1990:** 5; **1991:** 6; **1992:** 3; **1993:** 1; **1994:** 1; **1995:** 1; **1996:** 1; **1997:** 1; **1998:** 1. **Highest:** 1 (12 April 1993).

1998 Prize Money: $3,931,497. **Career Earnings:** $35,992,155. **Career Titles:** 56.

Style: Right-handed, ever since changing from 2HB to 1HB in 1987 on advice of his then coach, Dr Pete Fischer. Sampras is one of the finest servers and volleyers on the tour and has flat, orthodox groundstrokes, hit on the rise with awesome power. He is vulnerable to shin splints that have affected his career at important moments, and his stamina is questionable. Latterly other injuries have affected him.

CAREER HIGHLIGHTS (year: (titles))
1988: Reached sf Schenectady and qf Detroit (d. Mayotte). **1989:** Upset Wilander en route to last 16 US Open and reached qf Adelaide. In doubles with Courier won Italian Open, and took 7th place at Masters. **1990: (4)** *US OPEN, Philadelphia, Manchester, GS Cup*. Upset Mayotte in 70-game struggle 1r Australian Open on his way to last 16, unseeded, and in Feb. won his 1st tour title at Philadelphia. In Sept. he won his 1st GS title at US Open and moved into the top 10. At 19 yrs 28 days he was the youngest champion there (the previous youngest was Oliver Campbell, who won in 1890 aged 19 yrs 6 mths). Shin splints had been troubling him since US Open, and although he was able to play ATP World Champ, he did not progress beyond rr. Won inaugural GS Cup and 1st prize $2m. Voted Most Improved Player of The Year. **1991: (4)** *Los Angeles, Indianapolis, Lyon, IBM/ATP World Champ*. Suffered a string of injuries to shin, foot and hamstring, returning to action in Feb. He finished the year in tremendous style by winning ATP World Champ in Frankfurt, the youngest since J. McEnroe in 1979. After Frankfurt sacked Brandi again and sought new coach on eve of D Cup f v France in Lyon where, in his 1st ever tie, he was humiliated by an inspired Leconte on opening day and lost decisive 3rd rubber to Forget. **1992: (5)** *Philadelphia, Kitzbuhel, Cincinnati, Indianapolis, Lyon*. Broke into top 3 after winning Philadelphia and on 5 Oct. took 2nd place ahead of Edberg. In US Open he upset Courier but lost f to Edberg in 4s. In July he won his 1st title on clay at Kitzbuhel. **1993: (8)** *WIMBLEDON, US OPEN, Sydney Outdoor, LIPC, Tokyo Japan Open, Hong Kong, Lyon, Antwerp*. Ousted Edberg from the No. 2 position after Australian Open, closed the gap behind Courier after winning LIPC and finally took over the top spot on 12 April, the 11th man to reach the top since rankings began in 1973. He lost the No. 1 position to Courier again on 22 Aug. after 19 weeks, but regained it 13 Sept. He won his 1st Wimbledon and 2nd US Open to take 8 titles across the year, including 3 in succession with LIPC, Tokyo Japan Open and Hong Kong. His 83 matches won in the year were the most since Lendl's 84 in 1985 and his 8 titles the most since Lendl's 10 in 1989. He was also r/u in IBM/ATP World Champ, where he lost to an inspired Stich, and reached sf GS Cup where Korda beat him in an exhausting 4½ hour match. He appeared in 5 other sf and was in winning US WT Cup squad. **1994: (10)** *AUSTRALIAN OPEN, WIMBLEDON, Sydney NSW Open, Indian Wells, LIPC, Osaka, Tokyo Japan Open, Italian Open, Antwerp, IBM/ATP Champ*. It was another extraordinary year in which he won 10 tourns – 3 more than anyone else – including a 1st Australian Open, 2nd Wimbledon and 2nd IBM/ATP Champ. After

Wimbledon he looked unassailable at the top of the rankings by the biggest margin ever and was the 1st man since Lendl in 1987 to remain unmoved at No.1 all year. He was also the only player in 1994 to win titles on all 4 surfaces. Yet he began surprisingly by losing to qualifier Alami in 1r Qatar, his 1st tourn of the year, but then overcame a stomach upset to retain his LIPC title over Agassi, who agreed to delay their f for 50 mins to allow Sampras to recover. He took a 4-week break from the tour in spring, returning to win Italian Open in May, his 5th consec. tourn success, and extended to 29 matches his winning streak (the longest since Lendl's 31 in 1985), which was ended by Stich at WT Cup after Sampras had held 2 mps. He then lost to Courier in qf French Open, 3 matches short of becoming the 1st man to win a GS on 4 different surfaces. Martin beat him in f Queen's, but at Wimbledon he was superb, sweeping to f, where he demolished Ivanisevic in ss to retain the title. In addition to the quality of his tennis, for which he was voted Player of the Year, his outfits attracted attention, for he wore baggy, knee-length shorts specially designed for him by Nike. By the end of Wimbledon, he had already qualified for the year-end IBM/ATP World Champ – the earliest ever. However, thereafter he was plagued by injury. He withdrew from Washington suffering from tendinitis in left ankle, was out for 6 weeks before US Open and was not fully fit there, suffering from exhaustion, dehydration and blisters as he lost to Yzaga in 5s in last 16. There was further disappointment when US lost D Cup sf to SWE after he was forced to retire v Edberg with hamstring injury, after having hurt his knee beating Larsson on the 1st day. He suffered a rare defeat at the hands of an inspired Becker in sf Stockholm in Oct. and his victory at Antwerp was his 1st since Wimbledon. He was still not invincible at IBM/ATP Champ, where Becker beat him in rr, although the tables were turned in their f. After beating Ivanisevic in magnificent 5s sf in GS Cup, he lost f to Larsson, again affected by fatigue. **1995: (5)** *WIMBLEDON, US OPEN, Indian Wells, Queen's, Paris Open*. His year was overshadowed by the illness of his coach, Tim Gullikson, who was receiving treatment throughout for 4 brain tumours. When the diagnosis was first made and Gullikson was flown back to US during the Australian Open, Sampras broke down during an emotional qf v Courier, recovering from 2 sets down to win the match, although he eventually lost the f to Agassi. It was an unsettled year for him as he flew back and forth over the Atlantic to visit Gullikson between tourns and he was coached on the spot at Wimbledon by Paul Annacone. Won his 1st title of the year at Indian Wells in March, but lost the No.1 ranking to Agassi 10 April after 82 consec. weeks. He regained the top spot on 6 Nov. after winning Paris Open, from which Agassi had withdrawn injured, and with Agassi sidelined for the rest of the year with a chest muscle injury, he finished the year at the top – the 1st since Lendl in 1987 to hold that position for 3 years in succession. Withdrew 2r Monte Carlo v Haarhuis with right ankle injury, returning at Hamburg in May. In an attempt to become only the 5th man to win all 4 GS titles, he changed his schedule to allow himself 2 months on European clay in preparation for French Open, but fell there 1r to Schaller. However, he retained his Wimbledon crown and won a 3rd US Open, taking 5 titles in all from 9 f and was named ATP Player of the Year. He was disappointing at IBM/ATP Champ, where it seemed that, once he had secured his year-end position at the top of the rankings, he lost interest, losing his 3rd rr match to W. Ferreira and capitulating tamely to Chang in ss in sf. In D Cup f, however, he played a heroic part, winning both his singles and then doubles (with Martin) as USA d. RUS 3–2 in Moscow. **1996: (8)** *US OPEN, San Jose, Memphis, Hong Kong, Tokyo Japan Open, Indianapolis, Basle, ATP Champ*. It was a year in which he was challenged for the top ranking at different times by Agassi, Muster, M. Chang and Kafelnikov, although he finished as No. 1 for the 4th time in succession and was again voted Player of the Year. On 29 Jan., after losing 3r Australian Open to Philippoussis, he dropped behind Agassi and Muster to be ranked as low as No. 3 for 1st time since Jan. 1993. He was back at No. 2 on 12 Feb. and returned to the top a week later after winning San Jose. The title at Memphis the following week consolidated his position, but he slipped again after withdrawing qf Rotterdam with a metatarsal sprain of his right ankle. Back-to-back titles at Hong Kong and Tokyo Japan Open saw him return to the top on 14 April and become the 10th man to win 40 titles. Withdrew from Italian Open after the death of his former coach, Tim Gullikson, and missed some of WT Cup with back spasms, although he was back later in the tourn, losing to Kafelnikov. He had played only 2 CC matches before French Open, where he recovered from 2 sets to 0 down v Courier, but was exhausted when losing sf to Kafelnikov again and withdrew from Queen's to recover. He was still below his best at Wimbledon, where Krajicek beat him in qf, and although he claimed to be feeling better at Indianapolis in August, where he won his 1st title since April, he was struggling again at US Open. In 5s of his 3 hr 52 min qf v Corretja, he was ill from severe dehydration, vomiting on court and leaning on his racket between points. However, he saved mp at 7–6 in 5s tb and then, hardly able to stand with stomach pains, produced an ace to take an 8–7 lead, whereupon Corretja served a double-fault. He was almost certainly saved by the US Open rule of playing 5s tb. Amazingly, he went on to beat Ivanisevic in 4s sf 2 days later and take the title over M. Chang 2 days after that. His final victory was particularly poignant, coming as it did on what would have been Tim Gullikson's 45th birthday, and he paid tribute to his former coach. He added the title at Basle, r/u Stuttgart Eurocard and sf LIPC, plus 3 qf, and was already confirmed as World Champion before ATP Champ. There his year finished in triumph as he and Becker played a magnificent f, which Sampras eventually took in 5s, in front of Becker's home crowd. Withdrew from GS Cup with bilateral peroneal tendinitis and ankle pain. **1997: (8)** *AUSTRALIAN OPEN, WIMBLEDON, San Jose, Philadelphia, Cincinnati, GS Cup, Paris Open, ATP Champ.* On 28 April he had been at No. 1 for 171 weeks, overtaking J. McEnroe to become 3rd on the all-time list (after Lendl, 270, and Connors, 268), and was still at the top at end of year – only 2nd after Connors to finish No. 1 for 5th consec. year. He won his 1st 17 matches of the year, including a 2nd Australian Open, before a 2r defeat by Ulihrach at Indian Wells heralded a relatively lean patch. He was hampered at LIPC by a wrist injury, although he refused to blame that for his sf defeat by Bruguera, and missed 2 tourns with the injury thereafter. After being beaten qf Queen's by Bjorkman, he went into Wimbledon having failed to reach f in previous 7 tourns. However, he was back on top there, winning the Championships for a 4th time. When he won his next tourn at Cincinnati, his 49th career title, he drew level with Becker at the top amongst active players, moving ahead on his own after taking a 50th at GS Cup. He finished the season with 52 titles, having won all 8 f he played. In French Open, however, he lost to M. Norman 3r while suffering from a stomach upset (although, in his usual style, he refused to make that an excuse for his defeat) and at US Open he fell in 5s tb in last 16 to Korda, who had also stretched him to 5s at Wimbledon. In his 8th consec ATP Champ, he lost 1st match to Moya, but was magnificent thereafter as he swept to his 4th title there, finishing the year head and shoulders above the rest of the pack. After leading US to f of D Cup, he was forced to retire injured v Larsson in 2nd rubber when trailing 6–3 6–7 1–2 as USA went down 5–0 to SWE. Voted ATP Player of the Year. **1998: (4)** *WIMBLEDON, Philadelphia, Atlanta, Vienna.* Having been No. 1 for 102 consecutive weeks, 3rd-longest behind Connors (160) and Lendl (157), he was displaced at the top of the rankings on 30 March by Rios. Although he returned to the top on 27 April, his position was never totally secure and he slipped down again on 10 Aug. after losing qf Toronto to Agassi in his 1st tourn back after minor surgery on his foot in July to remove a plantar's wart. He was back at the top on 31 August, but with both Moya and Rafter close behind, he found himself by Oct. needing every win he could muster to achieve a new record of finishing the year at No. 1 for 6 consec. seasons. He did manage it, but the record was not certain until the very last moment, and he owed much to Becker, who gave up his WC at Vienna to enable Sampras to play there – and win the title. By ATP Champ only Rios was threatening his position, and when the No. 2 withdrew after 1 match and Sampras won all his matches in rr, he had achieved his goal, whereupon he lost sf 7–6 fs to Corretja. He faced an increasing struggle to find motivation for anything other than GS, and even in those tourns he could not always give his best – except for Wimbledon, where he confirmed his supremacy with his 5th Championship title. Underprepared for Australian Open following the calf injury suffered in D Cup final, he fell to Kucera in qf; at French Open he lost 2r to Delgado, ranked 98 at the time; and at US Open he was leading in 3s sf v Rafter when he injured his leg, losing mobility and eventually the match. Fitness was often elusive during the year and he withdrew Hong Kong with a shoulder injury suffered at LIPC; indeed, a back injury might have prevented him from playing ATP Champ had the top ranking not been at stake. Atlanta was his 1st CC title since Rome 1994 and only 3rd of career, but his 3r loss to Santoro at Monte Carlo was his worst since Svensson defeated him at Munich in 1990. He also won Philadelphia, was r/u San Jose and Cincinnati, and reached sf Stuttgart Eurocard, plus qf Los Angeles and Lyon. Declined invitation to play D Cup.

PRINCIPAL 1998 RESULTS – won 4, r/u 3, sf 1 (detailed Grand Slam results follow)

won Wimbledon, **won** Philadelphia (d. Malisse 4–6 6–3 7–5, Gaudenzi 7–6 6–3, Schalken 6–2 6–2, Haas 6–4 6–4, Enqvist 7–5 7–6), **won** Atlanta (d. O'Brien 6–2 7–6, Sanguinetti 6–3 5–7 7–5, Delgado 7–6 7–6, Calatrava 7–6 6–3, Stoltenberg 6–7 6–3 7–6), **won** Vienna (d. Kroslak 6–2 7–5, Tarango 5–7 6–1 6–3, Henman 6–0 6–3, T. Martin 6–3 7–6, Kucera 6–3 7–6 6–1); **r/u** San Jose (d. Stark 6–3 6–4, Burillo 6–3 7–6, Woodforde 6–0 6–2, Van Lottum 6–3 2–6 6–2, lost Agassi 6–2 6–4), **r/u** Cincinnati (d. Damm 6–4 6–2, Gambill 7–6 6–3, Spadea 6–3 6–2, Larsson 7–5 2–6 6–1, lost Rafter 1–6 7–6 6–4), **r/u** Paris Open (d.

Johansson 7–6 6–1, Golmard 6–7 6–4 6–4, Philippoussis 6–3 6–3, T. Martin 6–4 7–6, lost Rusedski 6–4 7–6 6–3); **sf** Stuttgart Eurocard (d. Kiefer 6–3 6–4, Ulihrach 6–3 6–3, Gambill 4–1 ret, lost Krajicek 6–7 6–4 7–6).

CAREER GRAND SLAM RECORD

AUSTRALIAN OPEN – Played 8, won 2, r/u 1, sf 1, qf 1

1989: 1r lost Saceanu 6–4 6–4 7–6. **1990: last 16** d. Mayotte [6] 7–6 6–7 4–6 7–5 12–10, Arrese 0–6 6–2 3–6 6–1 6–3, Woodbridge 7–5 6–4 6–2, lost Noah 6–3 6–4 3–6 6–2. **1991–92:** Did not play. **1993: sf** [seed 3] d. Steeb 6–1 6–2 6–1, Larsson 6–3 3–6 6–3 6–4, Antonitsch 7–6 6–4 6–2, Washington [13] 6–3 6–4 6–4, Steven 6–3 6–2 6–3, lost Edberg [2] 7–6 6–3 7–6. **1994: won** [seed 1] d. Eagle 6–4 6–0 7–6, Kafelnikov 6–3 2–6 6–3 1–6 9–7, Simian 7–5 6–1 1–6 6–4, Lendl [15] 7–6 6–2 7–5, Gustafsson [10] 7–6 2–6 6–3 7–6, Courier 6–3 6–4 6–4, Martin 7–6 6–4 6–4). **1995: r/u** [seed 1] d. Pozzi 6–3 6–2 6–0, Kroslak 6–2 6–0 6–1, Jonsson 6–1 6–2 6–4, Larsson [15] 4–6 6–7 7–5 6–4 6–4, Courier [9] 6–7 6–7 6–3 6–4 6–3, Chang [5] 6–7 6–3 6–4 6–4, lost Agassi [2] 4–6 6–1 7–6 7–4. **1996: 3r** seed 1, lost Philippoussis 6–4 7–6 7–6. **1997: won** [seed 1] d. Pescariu 6–2 6–4 6–2, Voinea 3–6 6–2 6–3 6–2, Woodforde 6–1 6–0 6–1, Hrbaty 6–7 6–3 6–4 3–6 6–4, A. Costa [10] 6–3 6–7 6–1 3–6 6–2, Muster [5] 6–1 7–6 6–3, Moya 6–2 6–3 6–3. **1998: qf** [seed 1] d. Schalken 7–5 6–4 6–2, Sanguinetti 6–2 6–1 6–2, Gustafsson 7–5 6–3 6–4, Arazi 7–6 6–4 6–4, lost Kucera 6–4 6–2 6–7 6–3.

FRENCH OPEN – Played 9, sf 1, qf 3

1989: 2r d. Lozano 6–3 6–2 6–4, lost Chang [15] 6–1 6–1 6–1. **1991: 2r** [seed 6] d. Muster 4–6 4–6 6–4 6–1 6–4, lost Champion 6–3 6–1 6–1. **1992: qf** [seed 3] d. Rosset 7–6 4–6 6–4 3–6 6–3, Prades 7–6 6–4 7–6, R. Gilbert 6–3 6–2 6–3, Steeb 6–4 6–3 6–2, lost Agassi [11] 7–6 6–2 6–1. **1993: qf** [seed 1] d. Cherkasov 6–1 6–2 3–6 6–1, Ondruska 7–5 6–0 6–3, Svensson 6–4 6–4 6–2, Washington 6–3 7–6 6–1, lost Bruguera [10] 6–3 4–6 6–1 6–4. **1994: qf** [seed 1] d. A. Costa 6–3 6–4 6–4, Rios 7–6 7–6 6–4, Haarhuis 6–1 6–4 6–1, Tillstroem 6–4 6–4 1–6 6–4, lost Courier [7] 6–4 5–7 6–4 6–4. **1995: 1r** [seed 2] lost Schaller 7–6 4–6 6–7 6–2 6–4. **1996: sf** [seed 1] d. Gustafsson 6–1 7–5 7–6, Bruguera 6–3 6–4 6–7 2–6 6–3, Martin 3–6 6–4 7–5 4–6 6–2, Draper 6–4 7–5 6–2, Courier [7] 6–7 4–6 6–4 6–4 6–4, lost Kafelnikov [6] 7–6 6–0 6–2. **1997: 3r** [seed 1] d. Santoro 6–3 7–5 6–1, Clavet 6–1 6–2 6–2, lost M. Norman 6–2 6–4 2–6 6–4. **1998: 2r** [seed 1] d. T. Martin 6–4 6–3 6–3, lost Delgado 7–6 6–3 6–4.

WIMBLEDON – Played 10, won 5, sf 1, qf 1

1989: 1r lost Woodbridge 7–5 7–6 5–7 6–3. **1990: 1r** lost Van Rensburg 7–6 7–5 7–6. **1991: 2r** [seed 8] d. Marcellino 6–1 6–2 6–2, lost Rostagno 6–4 3–6 7–6 6–4. **1992: sf** [seed 5] d. Cherkasov 6–1 6–3 6–3, Woodbridge 7–6 7–6 6–7 6–4, S. Davis 6–1 6–0 6–2, Boetsch 6–3 7–5 7–6, Stich [3] 6–3 6–2 6–4, lost Ivanisevic [8] 6–7 7–6 6–4 6–2. **1993: won** [seed 1] d. Borwick 6–7 6–3 7–6 6–3, Morgan 6–4 7–6 6–4, Black 6–4 6–1 6–1, Foster 6–1 6–2 7–6, Agassi [8] 6–2 6–2 3–6 3–6 6–4, Becker [4] 7–6 6–4 6–4, Courier [3] 7–6 7–6 3–6 6–3. **1994: won** [seed 1] d. Palmer 7–6 7–5 6–3, Reneberg 6–3 6–4 6–2, C. Adams 6–1 6–2 6–4, Vacek 6–4 6–1 7–6, Chang [10] 6–4 6–1 6–3, Martin [6] 6–4 6–4 3–6 6–3, Ivanisevic 7–6 7–6 6–0. **1995: won** [seed 2] d. Braasch 7–6 6–7 6–4 6–1, Henman 6–2 6–3 7–6, Palmer 4–6 6–4 6–1 6–2, Rusedski 6–4 6–2 7–5, Matsuoka 6–7 6–3 6–4 6–2, Ivanisevic [4] 7–6 4–6 6–3 4–6 6–3, Becker [3] 6–7 6–2 6–4 6–2. **1996: qf** [seed 1] d. Reneberg 4–6 6–4 6–3 6–3, Philippoussis 7–6 6–4 6–4, Kucera 6–4 6–3 6–7 7–6, Pioline [16] 6–4 6–4 6–2, lost Krajicek 7–5 7–6 6–4. **1997: won** [seed 1] d. Tillstrom 6–4 6–4 6–2, Dreekmann 7–6 7–5 7–5, B. Black 6–1 6–2 6–2, Korda [16] 6–4 6–3 6–7 6–7 6–4, Becker [8] 6–1 6–7 6–1 6–4, Woodbridge 6–2 6–1 7–6, Pioline 6–4 6–2 6–4. **1998: won** [seed 1] d. Hrbaty 6–3 6–3 6–2, Tillstrom 6–4 6–4 7–6, Enqvist 6–3 7–6 7–6, Grosjean 6–3 6–4 6–4, Philippoussis 7–6 6–4 6–4, Henman [12] 6–3 4–6 7–5 6–3, Ivanisevic [14] 6–7 7–6 6–4 3–6 6–2.

US OPEN – Played 11, won 4, r/u 1, sf 1, qf 1

1988: 1r lost Yzaga 6–7 6–7 6–4 7–5 6–2. **1989: last 16** d. Moreno 6–3 5–7 6–4 6–1, Wilander [5] 5–7 6–3 1–6 6–4, Yzaga 4–6 6–4 6–3 6–2, lost Berger [11] 7–5 6–2 6–1. **1990: won** [seed 12] d. Goldie 6–1 7–5 6–1, Lundgren 6–4 6–3 6–3, Hlasek 6–3 6–4 6–1, Muster [6] 6–7 7–6 6–4 6–3, Lendl [3] 6–4 7–6 3–6 4–6 6–2, J. McEnroe 6–2 6–4 3–6 6–3, Agassi 6–4 6–3 6–2. **1991: qf** [seed 6] d. van Rensburg 6–0 6–3 6–2, Ferreira 6–1 6–2 2–2 ret'd, Simian 7–6 6–4 6–3, Wheaton [11] 3–6 6–2 6–2 6–4, lost Courier [4] 6–2 7–6 7–6. **1992: r/u** [seed 3] d. di Lucia 6–3 7–5 6–2, Damm 7–5 6–1 6–2, Martin 7–6 2–6 4–6 7–5 6–4, Forget [13] 6–3 1–6 1–6 6–4 6–3, Volkov 6–4 6–1 6–0, Courier [1] 6–1 3–6 6–2 6–2, lost Edberg [2] 3–6 6–4 7–6 6–2. **1993: won** [seed 2] d. Santoro 6–3 6–1 6–2, Vacek 6–4 5–7 6–2 7–6, Boetsch 6–4 6–4 7–6, Enqvist 6–4 6–4 7–6, M. Chang [7] 6–7 7–6 6–1 6–1, Volkov [14] 6–4 6–3 6–2, Pioline 6–4 6–4 6–3. **1994: last 16** [seed 1] d. Ullyett 6–2 6–2 6–2, Vacek 6–3 6–4 6–4, Smith 4–6 6–2 6–4 6–3, lost Yzaga 3–6 6–3 4–6 7–6 7–5. **1995: won** [seed 2] d. Meligeni 6–0 6–3 6–4, Yzaga 6–1 6–4 6–3, Philippoussis 6–7 7–5 7–5 6–3, Martin [15] 7–6 6–3 6–4, B. Black 7–6 6–4 6–0, Courier [14] 7–5 4–6 6–4 7–5, Agassi [2] 6–4 6–3 4–6 7–5. **1996: won** [seed 1] d. Szymanski 6–2 6–2 6–1, Novak 6–3 1–6 6–3 4–6 6–4, Volkov 6–3 6–4 6–2, Philippoussis 6–3 6–3 6–4, Corretja 7–6 5–7 5–7 6–4 7–6, Ivanisevic [4] 6–3 6–4 6–7 6–3, M. Chang [2] 6–3 6–2 6–2. **1997: last 16** [seed 1] d. Larkham 6–3 6–1 6–3, Baur 7–5 6–4 6–3, Radulescu 6–3 6–4 6–4, lost Korda [15] 6–7 7–5 7–6 3–6 7–6. **1998: sf** [seed 1] d. Goellner 6–3 6–3 6–2, Goldstein 7–6 2–6 6–3 6–3, Tillstrom 6–2 6–3 6–1, Safin 6–4 6–3 6–2, Kucera [9] 6–3 7–5 6–4, lost Rafter [3] 6–7 6–4 2–6 6–4 6–3.

OLYMPIC RECORD

1992: (Barcelona) last 16 [seed 3] d. Masur 6–1 7–6 6–4, Yzaga 6–3 6–0 3–6 6–1, lost Cherkasov [13] 6–7 1–6 7–5 6–0 6–3.

CAREER DAVIS CUP RECORD

1991: November – *World Group Final FRA d. USA 3–1 in FRA (Carpet)*. R2 lost H. Leconte 6–4 7–5 6–4; R4 lost G. Forget 7–6 3–6 6–3 6–4. **1992: January** – *World Group 1R USA d. ARG 5–0 in USA (Hard)*. R1 d. M. Jaite 3–6 6–4 6–2 6–4; R4 d. A. Mancini 6–4 6–1. **March** – *World Group qf USA d. TCH 3–2 in USA (Hard)*. R1 d. K. Novacek 6–3 6–4 6–2; R4 lost P. Korda 6–4 6–3 2–6 6–3. **September** – *World Group sf USA d. SWE 4–1 in USA (Clay)*. R3 (with J. McEnroe) d. S. Edberg/A. Jarryd 6–1 6–7 4–6 6–3 6–3. **December** – *World Group Final USA d. SWZ 3–1 in USA (Hard)*. R3 (with J. McEnroe) d. J. Hlasek/M. Rosset 6–7 6–7 7–5 6–1 6–2. **1994: July** – *World Group 2r USA d. NED 3–2 in NED (Hard)*. R2 d. J. Eltingh 6–2 6–2 6–0; R4 lost R. Krajicek 2–6 7–5 7–6 7–5. **September** – *World Group sf SWE d. USA 3–2 in SWE (Carpet)*. R2 d. M. Larsson 6–7 6–4 6–2 7–6; R4 lost S. Edberg 6–3 ret'd. **1995: March** – *World Group qf USA d. ITA 5–0 in ITA (Clay)*. R2 d. R. furlan 7–6 6–3 6–0; R 4 d. A. Gaudenzi 6–3 1–6 6–3. **September** – *World Group sf USA d. SWE 4–1 in USA (Hard)*. R1 d. T. Enqvist 6–3 6–4 3–6 6–3; R5 d. M. Wilander 2–6 7–6 6–3. **December** – *World Group Final USA d. RUS 3–2 in Moscow (Clay)*. R1 d. A. Chesnokov 3–6 6–4 6–3 6–7 6–4. R3 (+ T. Martin) d. Y. Kafelnikov/A. Olhovskiy) 7–5 6–4 6–3; R4 d. Kafelnikov 6–2 6–4 7–6. **1997: September** – *World Group sf USA d. AUS 4–1 in USA (Hard)*. R2 d. M. Philippoussis 6–1 6–2 7–6; R3 (with T. Martin) lost T. Woodbridge/M. Woodforde 3–6 7–6 6–2 6–4; R4 d. P. Rafter 6–7 6–1 6–1 6–4. **November** – *World Group Final SWE d. USA 5–0 in SWE (Hard)*. R2 lost M. Larsson 3–6 7–6 2–1 ret.

GRAND SLAM CUP RECORD – Played 6, won 2, r/u 2, sf 1

1990: won [seed 4] d. Cherkasov 5–7 6–2 7–5, Ivanisevic [5] 7–6 6–7 8–6, Chang 6–3 6–4 6–4, Gilbert 6–3 3–6 7–6 2–6 6–4. **1992: sf** [seed 3] d. Volkov 6–3 6–4, Leconte 7–6 6–4, lost Stich 7–6 7–6 3–6 7–6. **1993: r/u** [seed 1] d. Muster 6–3 6–1, Chang 7–6 6–3, lost Korda 3–6 7–6 3–6 7–6 13–11. **1994: r/u** [seed 1] d. Yzaga 6–2 6–4, Chang 6–4 6–3, Ivanisevic 5–7 6–3 6–4 6–7 10–8, lost Larsson 7–6 4–6 7–6 6–4. **1995: qf** [seed 1] d. P. McEnroe 6–1 7–6, lost Ivanisevic [8] def. **1997: won** [seed 1] d. Mantilla 6–4 3–6 6–2, Bjorkman [8] 7–6 6–4, Rusedski [4] 3–6 7–6 7–6 6–2, Rafter [2] 6–2 6–4 7–5.

GRAND PRIX MASTERS/ATP TOUR CHAMPIONSHIP – Played 9, won 4, r/u 1, sf 3

1990: Equal 3rd in rr lost Edberg 7–5 6–4, lost Agassi 6–4 6–2, d. E. Sanchez 6–2 6–4. **1991: won** in rr d. Stich 6–2 7–6, d. Agassi 6–3 1–6 6–3, lost Becker 6–4 6–7 6–1; sf d. Lendl 6–2 6–3; f d. Courier 3–6 7–6 6–3 6–4. **1992: sf** in rr d. Becker 7–6 7–6, d. Edberg 6–3 3–6 7–5, d. Korda 3–6 6–3 6–3; sf lost Courier 7–6 7–6. **1993: r/u** in rr d. Ivanisevic 6–3 4–6 6–2, d. Edberg 6–3 7–6, d. Bruguera 6–3 1–6 6–3; sf d. Medvedev 6–3 6–0; f lost Stich 7–6 2–6 7–6 6–2. **1994: won** in rr lost Becker 7–5 7–5, d. Edberg 4–6 6–3 7–6, d. Ivanisevic 6–3 6–4; sf d. Agassi 4–6 7–6 6–3; f d. Becker 4–6 6–3 7–5 6–4. **1995: sf** in rr d. Kafelnikov 6–3 6–3, d. Becker 6–2 7–6, lost W. Ferreira 7–6 4–6 6–3; sf lost M. Chang 6–4 6–4. **1996: won** in rr d. Agassi 6–2 6–1, lost Becker 7–6 7–6, d. Kafelnikov 6–4 6–4; sf d. Ivanisevic 6–7 7–6 7–5; f d. Becker 3–6 7–6 7–6 6–7 6–4. **1997: won** in rr lost Moya 6–3 6–7 6–2, d. Rusedski 6–4 7–5, d. Rafter 6–4 6–1; sf d. Bjorkman 6–3 6–4; f d. Kafelnikov 6–3 6–2 6–2. **1998: sf** in rr d. Moya 6–3 6–3, d. Kucera 6–2 6–1, d. Kafelnikov 6–2 6–4; sf lost Corretja 4–6 6–3 7–6.

2 MARCELO RIOS (CHI)

Born: Santiago, 26 December 1975. **Lives:** Santiago.
Father: Jorge, an engineer. **Mother:** Alicia, a teacher.
Sister: Paula.
Agent: Geoff Schwarz of IMG. **Coach:** Luis Lobo; formerly Larry Stefanki, Nick Bollettieri. **Fitness trainer:** Manuel Astorga. **Turned pro:** 1994.
Height: 5ft 9in (1.75m). **Weight:** 140lb (63kg).

Rankings: 1992: 487; **1993:** 549; **1994:** 107; **1995:** 25; **1996:** 11; **1997:** 10; **1998:** 2. **Highest:** 1 (30 March 1998).

1998 Prize Money: $3,420,054.
Career Earnings: $6,135,603. **Career Titles:** 12.

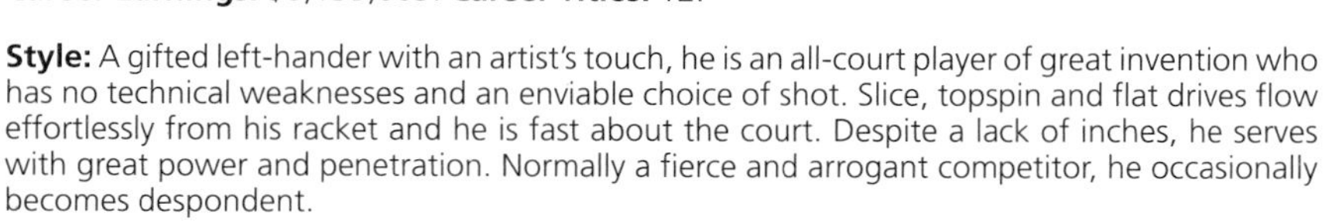

Style: A gifted left-hander with an artist's touch, he is an all-court player of great invention who has no technical weaknesses and an enviable choice of shot. Slice, topspin and flat drives flow effortlessly from his racket and he is fast about the court. Despite a lack of inches, he serves with great power and penetration. Normally a fierce and arrogant competitor, he occasionally becomes despondent.

CAREER HIGHLIGHTS (year: (titles))
1992: Won Chilean satellite aged 16. **1993:** No. 1 in ITF Jun rankings after winning US Open Jun over Downs. Joined the Chilean D Cup squad and was named his country's Athlete of the Year. **1994:** He reached sf Hilversum and qf Gstaad and at French Open, after qualifying, he kept Sampras on court more than 2½ hours in 2r. Took over the No. 1 ranking in Chile from Sergio Cortes in summer. **1995: (3)** *Bologna, Amsterdam, Kuala Lumpur.* Won his 1st tour title at Bologna and broke into the top 50, becoming the 1st Chilean to reach that level since Acuna in 1986. In July he won both singles and doubles titles at Amsterdam, having played through the qualifying after applying too late for a regular place in the draw, and in Oct. reached top 25 after winning a 3rd title in Kuala Lumpur and r/u Santiago. **1996: (1)** *St Polten.* In an impressive year he continued to shoot up the rankings, becoming in May the 1st Chilean to appear in the top 10. He won St Polten, was r/u Scottsdale, Barcelona (d. Courier and took a set off Muster) and Santiago and reached sf Indian Wells (d. W. Ferreira), Monte Carlo (d. Becker), Hamburg (d. W. Ferreira again), Toronto and Toulouse, plus 4 more qf. **1997: (1)** *Monte Carlo.* In a consistent, if not spectacular year, he maintained his ranking, finishing just inside the top 10, and narrowly missed a berth at the season-ending champ. He won Monte Carlo, was r/u Marseille (retired with leg injury), Rome, Boston and Santiago, and reached qf Australian Open (d. Enqvist), US Open (d. Bruguera and extended M. Chang to 5s), GS Cup, Auckland, Prague, Singapore and Stuttgart Eurocard (d. Kafelnikov). **1998: (7)** *Auckland, Indian Wells, LIPC, Rome, St Polten, Singapore, GS Cup.* In a spectacular year he won more titles than anyone else and for a time knocked Sampras off the top of the rankings. He began at Australian Open by becoming the 1st Chilean to reach a GS f since Ayala at French Open 38 years earlier, and the 1st in the open era, although he followed that achievement with a lacklustre performance in losing f to Korda. He confirmed his all-round ability with a successful HC season, and on 30 March, after winning his 3rd title of the year at LIPC, he became the 14th player to be ranked No. 1 – the 1st Chilean and 1st South American to reach that position. On 27 April Sampras regained his top ranking, with Korda at No. 2 and Rios 3, but Rios was back to the top on 10 Aug., dropping again 2 weeks later to 2nd place, where he finished the season. By 9 Nov. he was the only player left who could still challenge Sampras for the top year-end ranking, but his last chance to do so disappeared when he withdrew from ATP Champ with a back injury after only one match. Rome was his 3rd Super 9 title of the calendar year and on 17 Aug. he was 1st to qualify for ATP Champ – despite a relatively miserable summer, as a result of which he acrimoniously split with his coach, Stefanki. He won 7 titles in all, including GS Cup, and reached sf Memphis, Gstaad, Stuttgart Mercedes and Lyon, plus qf French Open, Stuttgart Eurocard, Paris Open and Santiago. He had his share of injury problems, being forced to retire at Lyon with a left hamstring injury and to withdraw from Barcelona and Monte Carlo with an inflammation in left elbow – possibly the result of using a larger racket this year.

PRINCIPAL 1998 RESULTS – won 7, r/u 1, sf 4 (detailed Grand Slam results follow)
won Auckland (d. Lapentti 6–3 6–3, Nielsen 7–5 6–1, Carlsen 5–7 6–4 6–1, B. Black 6–1 6–3, Fromberg 4–6 6–4 7–6), **won** Indian Wells (d. Dreekmann 6–4 7–6, Kiefer 6–4 6–3, Korda 6–4 6–2, Gambill 7–6 6–3, Rusedski 6–3 6–7 7–6 6–4), **won** LIPC (d. Dreekmann 6–3 6–4, Haas 6–4 6–3, Ivanisevic 6–2 6–2, Enqvist 6–3 2–0 ret, Henman 6–2 4–6 6–0, Agassi 7–5 6–3 6–4), **won** Rome (d. Martelli 6–3 6–0, Henman 6–3 6–1, Muster 6–3 6–1, Krajicek 7–6 6–3, Kuerten 6–0 7–5, A. Costa w.o.), **won** St Polten (d. S. Draper 6–1 6–3, Goellner 6–4 6–3, Blanco 6–2 6–2, Gaudenzi 6–4 6–3, Spadea 6–2 6–0), **won** Singapore (d. Lareau 6–2 6–0, Pavel 6–2 6–4, Hewitt 5–7 6–3 6–4, Courier 6–2 6–1, Woodforde 6–4 6–2), **won** GS Cup; **r/u** Australian Open; **sf** Memphis (d. Campbell 6–2 6–4, Spadea 6–2 6–3, Stafford 6–2 6–3, lost Philippoussis 6–4 7–6), **sf** Gstaad (d. Rosset 6–3 6–3, Arnold 6–4 6–1, Clavet 6–3 7–5, lost Becker 6–4 7–6), **sf** Stuttgart Mercedes (d. Knippschild 7–6 6–2, Dreekmann 6–3 6–4, Becker 6–2 6–0, lost Kucera 6–1 6–7 6–4), **sf** Lyon (d. Tarango 6–3 6–3, Escude 6–2 6–3, Di Pasquale 6–4 6–0, lost Haas 6–2 1–0 ret).

CAREER GRAND SLAM RECORD

AUSTRALIAN OPEN – Played 3, r/u 1, qf 1

1996: 1r lost Rafter 6–3 6–4 6–3. **1997: qf** [seed 9] d. Korda 7–6 6–3 6–3, Joyce 6–0 6–4 6–2, Schaller 4–6 7–6 6–1 6–1, Enqvist [7] 4–6 6–4 7–6 6–7 6–3, lost M. Chang [2] 7–5 6–1 6–4. **1998: r/u** [seed 9] d. Stafford 6–1 6–0 6–3, Enqvist 6–4 7–6 4–6 6–4, Ilie 6–2 6–3 6–2, Roux 6–2 4–6 6–2 6–4, Berasategui 6–7 6–4 6–4 6–0, Escude 6–1 6–3 6–2, lost Korda [6] 6–2 6–2 6–2.

FRENCH OPEN – Played 5, qf 1

1994: 2r d. Eagle 6–2 6–3 6–2, lost Sampras [1] 7–6 7–6 6–4. **1995: 2r** d. Spadea 6–4 6–4 6–7 6–3, lost Berasategui [11] 6–4 7–5 6–7 3–6 6–1. **1996: last 16** [seed 9] d. Joyce 7–6 6–1 6–4, Stoltenberg 6–4 6–3 6–3, Korda 6–3 6–3 6–2, lost Pioline 6–4 6–1 6–2. **1997: last 16** [seed 7] d. W. Black 6–4 5–7 4–6 6–2 6–1, B. Black 6–7 6–7 6–4 7–6 6–0, Boetsch 7–6 6–3 6–4, lost Arazi 6–2 6–1 5–7 7–6. **1998: qf** [seed 3] d. Steven 7–5 6–2 3–6 6–3, Alvarez 6–4 6–2 6–2, W. Ferreira 6–3 3–3 ret, A. Costa [13] 4–6 6–4 6–3 6–3, lost Moya [12] 6–1 2–6 6–2 6–4.

WIMBLEDON – Played 3

1995: 1r lost Knowles 4–6 6–3 6–4 7–6. **1997: last 16** [seed 9] d. Bhupathi 6–4 6–4 6–3, Van Scheppingen 6–2 6–3 6–7 7–6, Van Lottum 7–6 6–3 6–7 6–4, lost Becker [8] 6–2 6–2 7–6. **1998: 1r** [seed 2] lost Clavet 6–3 3–6 7–5 3–6 6–3.

US OPEN – Played 5, qf 1

1994: 2r d. Palmer 6–2 7–6 6–2, lost W. Ferreira [12] 6–2 6–2 6–4. **1995: 1r** lost Enqvist [9] 2–6 6–2 4–6 6–3 7–6. **1996: 2r** [seed 10] d. Pavel 4–6 6–1 6–4 6–2, lost Tarango 6–4 4–6 7–6 6–2. **1997: qf** [seed 10] d. Smith 6–1 6–1 6–4, Carlsen 6–4 5–7 3–6 6–1 7–6, Haas 6–4 3–6 6–3 1–6 6–1, Bruguera [7] 7–5 6–2 6–4, lost M. Chang [2] 7–5 6–2 4–6 4–6 6–3. **1998: 3r** [seed 2] d. Vacek 6–4 6–2 6–3, Galimberti 6–2 6–7 6–2 6–2, lost Larsson 6–1 6–7 2–6 6–3 6–2.

OLYMPIC RECORD

Has never competed.

CAREER DAVIS CUP RECORD

1993: February – *Zone 1 1r BAH d. CHI 3–2 in CHI (Clay).* R3 (+ G. Silberstein) lost M. Knowles/R. Smith 6–2 6–1 6–3. **1996: February** – *Zone 1 1r BRA d. CHI 3–2 in CHI (Clay).* R2 d. J. Oncins 6–3 6–2 7–5; R3 (+ M. Rebolledo) lost G. Kuerten/Oncins 7–5 6–3 4–6 6–2. R4 d. F. Meligeni 6–2 7–6 6–3. **April** – *Zone 1 Relegation CAN d. CHI 3–2 in CAN (Carpet).* R1 d. D. Nestor 6–4 7–6 6–7 3–6 14–12. R3 (+ O. Bustos) lost G. Connell/S. Lareau 6–3 6–4 7–5. **September** – *American Zone 1 Play-off CHI d. PER 5–0 in CHI (Clay).* R1 d. A. Venero 7–5 6–2 6–4; R3 (+ O. Bustos) d. L. Horna/Venero 6–4 6–3 6–7 3–6 8–6; R4 d. A. Aramburu 6–2 6–3. **1997: February** – *Zone 1 1r CHI d. ECU 4–1 in CHI (Clay).* R2 d. L. Morejon 6–1 6–3 3–6 6–2; R3 (with O. Bustos) lost P. Campana/N. Lapentti 4–6 6–4 6–0 6–3. R4 d. Lapentti 7–5 6–7 6–3 6–7 8–6. **April** – *Zone 1 2r CHI d. ARG 3–2 in CHI (Clay).* R1 d. J. Frana 6–1 6–4 7–6; R3 (with G. Silberstein) d. J. Frana/L. Lobo 3–6 7–6 4–6 6–4 6–2. R4 d. H. Gumy 6–4 7–5 6–4. **September** – *World Group Qualifying IND d. CHI 3–2 in IND (Grass).* R2 d. M. Bhupathi 6–2 3–6 6–3 6–4; R3 lost Bhupathi/L. Paes 3–6 6–3 6–4 6–7 6–3. R4 d. Paes 6–7 6–4 6–0 7–6. **1998: April** – *Zone 1 2r ARG d. CHI 4–1 in ARG (Clay).* R1 d. H. Gumy 6–4 3–6 6–3 7–5; R3 (with N. Massu) lost L. Arnold/L. Lobo 7–5 6–3 6–3. **July** – *Zone 1 Play-off CHI d. COL 5–0 in CHI (Carpet).* R1 d. P. Moggio 6–3 6–0 6–2; R4 d. M. Tobon 6–2 6–2.

GRAND SLAM CUP RECORD – Played 2, won 1, qf 1

1997: qf [seed 7] d. Woodforde 6–7 6–3 6–1, lost Rafter [2] 6–1 7–6. **1998: won** [seed 2] d. Mantilla 7–6 7–5, Philippoussis [3] 7–6 6–3 6–4, Agassi 6–4 2–6 7–6 5–7 6–3.

ATP TOUR CHAMPIONSHIP

1998: in rr lost Henman 7–5 6–1, withdrew.

3 ALEX CORRETJA (ESP)

Born: Barcelona, 11 April 1974. **Lives:** Barcelona.
Father: Luis. **Mother:** Luisa. **Brothers:** Sergio and Ivan.
Agent: ProServ. **Coach:** Javier Duarte. **Turned pro:** 1991.
Height: 5ft 11in (1.80cm). **Weight:** 155lb (70kg).

Rankings: 1991: 234; **1992:** 86; **1993:** 76; **1994:** 22; **1995:** 48; **1996:** 23; **1997:** 12; **1998:** 3. **Highest:** 3 (30 November 1998).

1998 Prize Money: $2,702,569.
Career Earnings: $5,547,784. **Career titles:** 9.

Style: A fine baseliner with heavy, topspin forehand and backhand that make him a formidable CC player. He has developed his game on other surfaces by improving his volleying technique and by adopting a more aggressive attitude. Superb fitness and the ability to concentrate over long spells make him one of the best all-rounders in the game.

CAREER HIGHLIGHTS (year: (titles))
1990: Won Orange Bowl 16s. **1991:** Began to make his mark on the satellite circuits. **1992:** Reached his 1st tour f at Guaruja in Nov. and moved into top 100. Upset E. Sanchez 1r Hamburg. **1993:** Reached sf Florence and Sao Paulo, plus qf Monte Carlo. **1994: (1)** *Buenos Aires.* His 1st tour title came at the very end of the season – at Buenos Aires, in his 3rd career f. He had scored some big upsets during the year on his way to f Palermo (where he held 2 mps v Berasategui), sf Mexico City (d. Berasategui), Barcelona (d. Courier), Madrid (d. Berasategui again), Indianapolis (d. Courier and Edberg), Athens and Santiago, as well as beating Becker at Hamburg. At French Open, he was 2-sets-to-love up v Ivanisevic 3r before letting the match slip away. **1995:** Upset W. Ferreira at French Open and at Gstaad he ended Muster's 40-match CC winning streak. He also reached sf Mexico City, Munich and Buenos Aires and in doubles won Palermo with Santoro. **1996:** He was again a dangerous opponent, as he confirmed on his way to r/u Hamburg (d. A. Costa, Rosset and Rios), Kitzbuhel and Marbella, sf Estoril (d. A. Costa and took a set off Muster) and Stuttgart Eurocard (d. Moya), plus qf Indianapolis (d. Reneberg) and Palermo. He reached the same stage at US Open, where, unseeded, he was on the verge of causing the upset of the year v Sampras: he held mp at 7–6 in fs tb, with Sampras suffering so severely from dehydration that he was hardly able to stand. However, the No. 1 drew level, served an ace for 8–7 and Corretja let the match go with a double-fault after 3 hr 52 min. Won the Stefan Edberg Sportsmanship award. **1997: (3)** *Estoril, Rome, Stuttgart Mercedes.* In his best year to date, he broke into top 10 for a while with titles at Estoril, Rome (d. Ivanisevic and Rios) and Stuttgart Mercedes. He also reached f Monte Carlo and Munich (where he won the doubles with Albano), sf Gstaad and Palermo and qf Boston. In GS he overruled an 'out' call on a crucial bp when losing to Dewulf at French Open, and withdrew 3r US Open after injuring his left thigh while warming up. **1998: (5)** *Dubai, Gstaad, Indianapolis, Lyon, ATP Champ.* He crowned an excellent year with the title at his 1st ATP Champ, earned in dramatic style: in sf he saved 3 mps v Sampras before winning 7–6 fs, then in f he pulled back from 2-sets-to-love down to d. Moya 7–5 fs in a 4-hour struggle. He became the 1st Spaniard since Orantes in 1976 to win the event and the 1st player since McEnroe in 1978 to win on his 1st appearance there. This triumph took him into the top 3, ahead of Rafter, Moya and Agassi. His 1st HC title at Dubai (d. Bjorkman) had already underlined what a complete player he was becoming, although he was no exception among the CC specialists in finding GC a puzzle. He also won Gstaad, Indianapolis (d. Agassi for his 1st title in US) and Lyon (saving mp v Haas in 2s tb in f). He reached his 1st GS f at French Open, where he met no seeded player until that stage and on the way needed 5 hr 31 min – the longest recorded GS match – to d. Gumy 3r (9–7 fs). Earlier at Hamburg another string of gruelling matches had left him too exhausted to complete his f v A. Costa, obliging him to ret 3s. In other tourns he reached sf Indian Wells and Palermo and qualified for GS Cup, although he did not take up his place.

PRINCIPAL 1998 RESULTS – won 5, r/u 2, sf 2 (detailed Grand Slam results follow)
won Dubai (d. Alonso 6–1 6–2, Sinner 6–4 6–3, C. Costa 7–6 5–7 6–4, Bjorkman 6–3 6–2, Mantilla 7–6 6–1), **won** Gstaad (d. Gross 6–4 4–6 6–1, Dosedel 6–0 7–5, A. Costa 5–7 6–2 6–2, Dewulf 6–3 6–7 6–3, Becker 7–6 7–5 6–3), **won** Indianapolis (d. S. Draper 6–3 6–7 7–6, Philippoussis 4–6 6–4 6–3, Rusedski 6–4 6–3, T. Martin 6–2 7–6, Agassi 2–6 6–2 6–3), **won** Lyon (d. Golmard 7–6 6–2, Pavel 6–4 2–6 6–3, Delaitre 7–6 7–5, W. Ferreira 6–3 6–2, Haas 2–6 7–6 6–1), **won** ATP Champ; **r/u** Hamburg (d. Alami 6–2 4–6 6–3, Bruguera 6–7 6–4 6–3, Kuerten 4–6 7–6 6–4, Mantilla 6–2 3–6 6–3, lost A. Costa 6–2 6–1 1–0 ret), **r/u** French Open; **sf** Indian Wells (d. Courier 7–6 6–3, Santoro 6–1 3–6 6–3, Campbell 6–3 6–1, lost Agassi 6–4 6–2), **sf** Palermo (d. Bruguera 6–0 2–6 6–0, Portas 6–1 6–2, Lapentti 7–5 6–2, lost Puerta 7–5 6–2).

CAREER GRAND SLAM RECORD

AUSTRALIAN OPEN – Played 3

1996: 2r d. Jonsson 6–3 6–3 6–0, lost Kafelnikov [6] 6–1 6–2 6–3. **1997: 2r** d. Mitchell 7–6 6–0 6–2, lost Schaller 4–6 6–3 6–3 4–6 6–3. **1998: 3r** [seed 11] d. Arnold 6–4 7–5 2–6 6–3, Prinosil 6–4 6–3 6–0, lost Pioline 6–2 6–1 6–4.

FRENCH OPEN – Played 7, r/u 1

1992: 1r lost Mancini 6-4 1-6 6-4 6-7 6-3. **1993: 1r** lost M. Larsson 2–6 6–3 7–6 7–6. **1994: 3r** d. Meligeni 6–3 6–1 1–6 5–7 6–3, O'Brien 6–2 4–6 6–2 6–4, lost Ivanisevic [5] 6–7 3–6 6–1 6–2 6–3. **1995: last 16** [unseeded] d. Golmard 6–4 7–5 6–0, Forget 6–2 6–3 6–3, W. Ferreira [8] 6–4 7–5 6–2, lost Kafelnikov [9] 6–3 6–2 6–2. **1996: 2r** d. Woodforde 6–3 6–4 0–6 6–4, lost Mantilla 7–6 6–2 6–4. **1997: last 16** [seed 8] d. Alami 6–3 6–4 6–1, Knippschild 4–6 6–1 6–1 7–6, Champion 6–1 3–0 ret, lost Dewulf 5–7 6–1 6–4 7–5. **1998: r/u** [seed 14] d. Alami 6–3 6–2 0–6 6–4, Vicente 6–3 6–2 6–3, Gumy 6–1 5–7 6–7 7–5 9–7, Stoltenberg 6–4 6–4 6–3, Dewulf 7–5 6–4 6–3, Pioline 6–3 6–4 6–2, lost Moya [12] 6–3 7–5 6–3.

WIMBLEDON – Played 3

1994: 2r d. Leconte 2–6 4–6 7–5 7–6 3–2 ret, lost Fromberg 6–2 7–6 7–5. **1995:** Did not play. **1996: 2r** d. Tebbutt 3–6 7–6 6–4 6–4, lost Hlasek 4–6 6–3 6–4 6–4. **1997:** Did not play. **1998: 1r** [seed 10] lost Gimelstob 7–6 6–2 6–3.

US OPEN – Played 7, qf 1

1992: 1r lost Woodbridge 6-2 6-2 6-2. **1993: 1r** lost Muster [12] 6–4 6–4 6–3. **1994: 1r** lost Enqvist 4–6 6–3 6–4 6–7 6–1. **1995: 2r** d. O'Brien 6–4 6–4 6–3, lost Agassi [1] 5–7 6–3 5–7 6–0 6–2. **1996: qf** [unseeded] d. B. Black 7–6 3–6 6–2 6–2, Veglio 6–7 6–4 6–4 6–0, Bjorkman 6–2 4–6 4–6 6–4 6–3, Forget 6–4 6–3 7–6, lost Sampras [1] 7–6 5–7 5–7 6–4 7–6. **1997: 3r** [seed 8] d. Rosset 4–6 6–3 6–2 6–2, Ulihrach 7–5 6–4 3–6 6–4, lost Krajicek w/o. **1998: last 16** [seed 7] d. Pozzi 2–6 6–3 7–5 7–5, Perlant 6–4 5–7 6–7 6–1 6–0, B. Black 6–3 4–6 6–2 7–6, lost Moya [10] 7–6 7–5 6–3.

OLYMPIC RECORD

Has never competed.

CAREER DAVIS CUP RECORD

1996: April – *Zone 1 2r ESP d. ISR 4–1 in ISR (Hard).* R3 (with E. Sanchez) lost N. Behr/E. Erlich 7–5 4–6 4–6 7–6 6–3. **September** – *World Group Qualifying ESP d. DEN 4–1 in ESP (Clay).* R3 (with T. Carbonell) d. K. Carlsen/F. Fetterlein 6–4 7–5 4–6 5–7 6–3). **1997: February** – *World Group 1r ESP d. GER 4–1 in ESP (Clay).* R3 (with C. Costa) lost M. Goellner/D. Prinosil 6–2 6–2 6–3. **1998: April** – *World Group Qualifying ESP d. BRA 3–2 in BRA (Clay).* R2 d. F. Meligeni 4–6 6–4 3–6 6–4 6–4; R3 (with J. Sanchez) lost G. Kuerten/J. Oncins 6–1 5–7 6–3 6–2; R4 d. Kuerten 6–3 7–5 4–6 6–4. **July** – *World Group qf ESP d. SUI 4–1 in ESP (Clay).* R2 d. M. Rosset 6–1 6–2 6–2; R5 d. G. Bastl 6–0 7–5. **September** – *World Group sf SWE d. ESP 4–1 in SWE (Carpet).* R1 lost J. Bjorkman 6–3 7–5 6–7 6–3.

GRAND SLAM CUP RECORD – Played 1

1996: 1r lost Kafelnikov [3] 6–4 7–6.

ATP TOUR CHAMPIONSHIP – Played 1, won 1

1998: won in rr d. Agassi 5–7 6–3 2–1 ret, lost Henman 7–6 6–7 6–2, d. A. Costa 6–2 6–4; sf d. Sampras 4–6 6–3 7–6; f d. Moya 3–6 3–6 7–5 6–3 7–5.

4 PATRICK RAFTER (AUS)

Born: Mount Isa, Queensland, 28 December 1972.
Lives: Pembroke, Bermuda.
Father: Jim. **Mother:** Jocelyn. **Siblings:** Third youngest of nine children (Stephen, Teresa, Geoff, Marie, Peter, Louise, Patrick, Michael and David).
Agent: His brother, Stephen; ProServ for marketing opportunities. **Coaches:** Has no formal coach, but is helped by Tony Roche.
Turned pro: 1991.
Height: 6ft 1in (1.85m). **Weight:** 175lb (79kg).

Rankings: 1990: 751; **1991:** 294; **1992:** 301; **1993:** 57; **1994:** 21; **1995:** 68; **1996:** 62; **1997:** 2; **1998:** 4 singles, 16 doubles. **Highest:** 2 (17 November 1997).

1998 Prize Money: $2,867,017. **Career Earnings:** $7,382,729. **Career titles:** 8.

Style: A forthright, attacking serve-and-volley right-hander, he uses his natural athletic ability to move quickly about the court, taking the ball early and moving constantly forward. Fast reflexes enable him to blanket the net, and his excellent overhead makes him a difficult man to lob. Improving groundstrokes and return of serve have lifted him into the top ten where he belongs.

CAREER HIGHLIGHTS (year: (titles))
1991: Began to make his mark on the Satellite circuits. **1993:** Emerging from the Challenger circuit, where he won Aptos, he broke into top 100 after reaching sf Indianapolis (d. Chesnokov, Ferreira and Sampras). Voted ATP Newcomer of the Year. **1994: (1)** *Manchester.* In a remarkable 18-month period he moved from 301 to 21 in the rankings. He upset Courier 1r Indian Wells, surprised Rosset and M. Chang on his way to sf LIPC, and broke into top 25 after reaching his 1st tour f at Hong Kong in April, where the match was delayed 1 hour to allow him to recover from food poisoning. He upset Muster at French Open, where he was unseeded, and after he had won his 1st title at Manchester, he played a 5-set marathon v Bruguera in 2r Wimbledon, succumbing only 13–11 after being overtaken by cramp. He also reached sf Adelaide and Sydney Indoor, 4 more qf and last 16 French Open, unseeded. Played 3 doubles f, winning Bologna with Fitzgerald. **1995:** Having achieved so much so fast, he felt somewhat drained and disillusioned, as well as being hampered during the year by a torn cartilage in his racket wrist, for which he underwent surgery on 30 Oct., missing the rest of the season. His best performances were sf Washington, qf Adelaide, Los Angeles, Ostrava and Lyon and an upset of Medvedev at Cincinnati. Played 2 doubles f, winning Adelaide with Courier. **1996:** Returning at Australian Open, he was forced to retire 2r with a recurrence of the wrist injury, and was out with that and an ankle injury until April. However, he felt more optimistic and under less pressure once Philippoussis had replaced him at the top of the Australian rankings. He did not progress beyond qf, but reached that stage at US CC (where he won the doubles with Cash), Queen's, Washington (d. Agassi) and Toronto (d. MaliVai Washington) and upset Rosset at Wimbledon, where he was unseeded. **1997: (1)** *US OPEN.* The climax of an superb season came at US Open, where, playing his 3rd f in consec. tourns and his 6th of the year, he won his 1st title of the year in tremendous style. He was the 1st Australian since Cash at Wimbledon in 1987 to win a GS title and the 1st to win US Open since Newcombe in 1973. It was his 1st title for 3 years. Hampered by a sore shoulder, he had not even been sure of competing and was grateful for his Wednesday start. His success swept him through the rankings to No. 3, the highest by an Australian since Laver was No. 2 in 1975, and at end of season he ousted M. Chang to take the No. 2 slot himself. He also performed well on clay in spring: unseeded at French Open, he upset Krajicek on his way to becoming the 1st Australian man to reach qf there since Phil Dent in 1977 and progressing to sf, unseeded. In other tourns, he was r/u Philadelphia, Hong Kong, St Polten (d. Muster on clay), New Haven, Long Island (d. M. Chang and Enqvist) and GS Cup, adding sf Tokyo Japan Open, Stuttgart Eurocard and Stockholm and qf Sydney (d. Haarhuis) and Queen's (d. Courier). Qualified for his 1st ATP Champ, where he

Rafter's Long Island victory over Felix Mantilla (above) on the eve of the US Open put the Australian in the right frame of mind for the successful defence of his title. (Tommy Hindley)

was just beaten to sf by Moya, whom he had beaten in rr. In doubles he played 5 f with 3 different partners, winning Adelaide with Shelton and Queen's with Philippoussis. When he was playing Pioline at Paris Open, a laser beam was shone in his eyes from the crowd, but he went on to save 3 mps and win the match. Voted ATP Most Improved Player. **1998: (6)** *US OPEN, Chennai, Den Bosch, Toronto, Cincinnati, Long Island.* At the beginning of the year he struggled to cope with the extra pressure after winning US Open; it seemed to crush his morale, and he found he was no longer enjoying the game – as well as being hindered by injury. He took a 4-week break and, helped by John Newcombe's advice to put less pressure on himself and to have fun, he took off again after returning at Rome. He won his 1st Super 9 tourn at Toronto, following with his 2nd at Cincinnati, where he d. Sampras in f. He beat Sampras again at US Open, returning 21 hours after their gruelling 5s sf to retain the title over Philippoussis and challenge for the top ranking. He also won titles at Chennai, Den Bosch and Long Island, reached sf Sydney and Antwerp and qf Rotterdam, Los Angeles and Vienna. Although he qualified for ATP Champ, and would still have been in with a chance of ending the year at No. 1 had he played and won, he decided to withdraw to nurse a knee injury and prepare for Australian Open. In doubles he won Los Angeles with Stolle and Indian Wells with Bjorkman, with whom he also shared Queen's.

PRINCIPAL 1998 RESULTS – won 6, sf 2 (detailed Grand Slam results follow)
won US Open, **won** Chennai (d. Stanoytchev 6–2 6–1, Heuberger 6–2 6–4, Burgsmuller 7–6 0–6 7–5, Paes 6–3 7–6, Tillstrom 6–3 6–4), **won** Den Bosch (d. Vacek 6–3 4–6 6–4, Medvedev 7–6 4–6 7–6, Schalken 6–1 6–4, Van Scheppingen 6–3 6–4, Damm 7–6 6–2), **won** Toronto (d. Godwin 7–5 6–3, Philippoussis 6–3 6–3, Bjorkman 6–3 6–2, Henman 6–2 6–4, Krajicek 4–6 7–5 6–2), **won** Cincinnati (d. Raoux 6–1 6–3, T. Martin 3–6 6–3 6–2, Korda 6–4 7–6, Kafelnikov 7–5 6–0, Sampras 1–6 7–6 6–4), **won** Long Island (d. J. Sanchez 6–2 4–6 6–4, Damm 6–4 6–3, Escude 6–3 6–2, Rusedski 6–4 7–5, Mantilla 7–6 6–2); **sf** Sydney (d. Woodbridge 6–4 6–3, Berasategui 6–3 6–4, T. Martin 6–4 6–7 6–1, lost Henman 7–6 7–5), **sf** Antwerp (d. Boetsch 6–2 7–6, Pioline 6–4 7–6, Tarango 6–7 6–2 6–1, lost Rosset 7–6 7–6). **DOUBLES:** (with Bjorkman unless stated) **won** Indian Wells (d. T. Martin/Reneberg 6–4 7–6), (with Stolle) **won** Los Angeles (d. Tarango/Vacek 6–4 6–4); **shared** Queen's with Woodbridge/Woodforde.

CAREER GRAND SLAM RECORD

AUSTRALIAN OPEN – Played 7

1992: 1r lost Grabb 3-6 6-0 7-6 6-2. **1993: 1r** lost Siemerink 4–6 2–6 6–3 6–4 6–2. **1994: 3r** d. Wekesa 6–1 3–6 6–1 6–2, Eltingh 6–4 6–4 6–4, lost Daufresne 5–7 6–2 6–1 6–4. **1995: last 16** [unseeded] d. Hlasek 6–3 1–6 5–7 7–6 6–3, Campbell 6–4 7–6 6–2, Ondruska 6–3 1–6 3–6 6–2 6–2, lost Agassi [2] 6–3 6–4 6–0. **1996: 2r** d. Rios 6–3 6–4 6–3, lost Hadad 7–6 6–4 2–2 ret'd. **1997: 1r** lost A. Costa [10] 7–5 6–2 7–5. **1998: 3r** [seed 2] d. Tarango 7–6 7–6 6–7 7–5, T. Martin 2–6 7–6 6–7 6–4 6–3, lost Berasategui 6–7 7–6 6–2 7–6.

FRENCH OPEN – Played 5, sf 1

1994: last 16 [unseeded] d. Davin 6–7 6–4 2–6 6–4 7–5, Roux 6–2 6–4 6–4, Muster [11] 6–4 5–7 6–3 6–3, lost Bruguera [6] 6–4 6–3 6–1. **1995: 1r** lost Bruguera [7] 6–3 6–1 7–6. **1996: 1r** lost Moya 6–4 7–6 6–2. **1997: sf** [unseeded] d. Gaudenzi 3–6 7–6 6–3 6–4, Fontang 6–3 6–4 6–3, Krajicek [6] 6–3 4–6 6–4 6–2, Woodforde 6–2 5–7 6–1 6–2, Blanco 6–3 7–6 6–3, lost Bruguera [16] 6–7 6–1 7–5 7–6. **1998: 2r** [seed 4] d. Lareau 6–7 3–6 6–1 6–3 6–2, lost Stoltenberg 6–4 2–6 6–3 6–2.

WIMBLEDON – Played 6

1993: 3r d. Youl 6–3 6–3 6–4, Nelson 7–6 6–4 6–2, lost Agassi [d 8] 6–1 6–7 6–0 6–3. **1994 2r** d. Morgan 6–4 5–7 6–4 7–6, lost Bruguera [8] 7–6 3–6 4–6 7–5 13-11. **1995: 1r** lost Woodforde 3–6 6–1 7–6 6–4. **1996: last 16** d. Vacek 6–2 6–4 7–6, Pozzi 6–1 7–5 6–4, Rosset [14] 4–6 6–3 4–6 6–1 6–3, lost Ivanisevic [4] 7–6 4–6 7–6 6–3. **1997: last 16** [12] d. Stafford 2–6 4–6 6–3 6–2 6–2, Knippschild 6–3 4–6 6–3 6–0, Van Garsse 7–5 6–4 4–6 6–3, lost Woodbridge 6–7 6–4 7–6 6–3. **1998: last 16** [seed 6] d. Heuberger 6–1 6–2 4–6 6–1, Nydahl 7–6 6–2 7–6, Gustafsson 6–3 6–7 6–2 6–1, lost Henman [13] 6–3 6–7 6–3 6–2.

US OPEN – Played 6, won 2

1993: 1r lost D. Flach 3–6 6–3 6–2 6–1. **1994: 3r** d. Rikl 6–4 6–1 6–4, Apell 7–5 4–6 7–6 6–3, lost Martin [9] 7–5 6–3 6–7 6–2. **1995: 2r** d. Reneberg 7–6 6–3 6–4, lost Rosset 6–4 6–4 3–6 6–3. **1996: 1r** lost Carlsen 7–6 6–3 7–6. **1997: won** [seed 13] d. Medvedev 6–3 6–4 7–5, M. Norman 6–2 6–1 6–2, Roux 6–1 6–1 6–2, Agassi 6–3 7–6 4–6 6–3, Larsson 7–6 6–4 6–2, M. Chang [2] 6–3 6–3 6–4, Rusedski 6–3 6–2 4–6 7–5. **1998: won** [seed 3] d. Arazi 4–6 4–6 6–3 6–3 6–1, Gumy 6–4 6–1 6–2, Nainkin 6–1 6–1 6–1, Ivanisevic [14] 6–3 6–4 4–6 6–1, Bjorkman [12] 6–2 6–3 7–5, Sampras [1] 6–7 6–4 2–6 6–4 6–3, Philippoussis 6–3 3–6 6–2 6–0.

OLYMPIC RECORD

Has never competed.

CAREER DAVIS CUP RECORD

1994: March – *World Group 1r RUS d. AUS 4–1 in RUS (Carpet).* R1 lost Y. Kafelnikov 6–3 6–0 6–4; R4 lost A. volkov 6–4 7–6 6–3. **September** – *World Group Qualifying AUS d. NZL 4–1 in NZL (Carpet).* R2 d. J. Greenhalgh 7–5 6–2 6–3; R4 d. B. Steven 7–5 6–4 6–1. **1995: February** – *World Group 1r RSA d. AUS 3–2 in RSA (Hard).* R1 d. M. Ondruska 6–3 6–4 2–6 6–4; R4 lost W. Ferreira 6–2 3–6 6–4 6–2. **1996: September** – *World Group Qualifying AUS d. CRO 4–1 in CRO (Clay).* R3 (with M. Woodforde) d. S. Hirszon/G. Ivanisevic 6–3 6–2 6–4. **1997: February** – *World Group 1r AUS d. FRA 4–1 in AUS (Grass).* R1 d. C. Pioline 3–6 6–7 6–4 7–5 6–4; R5 lost A. Boetsch 4–6 4–6 6–7. **April** – *World Group qf AUS d. CZE 5–0 in AUS (Grass)* R1 d. M. Damm 6–1 7–6 4–6 6–4; R5 d. D. Rikl 7–6 0–6 6–2. **September** – *World Group sf USA d. AUS 4–1 in USA (Hard).* R1 lost M. Chang 6–4 1–6 6–3 6–4; R4 lost P. Sampras 6–7 6–1 6–1 6–4. **1998: April** – *World Group 1r ZIM d. AUS 3–2 in AUS (Grass).* R2 lost B. Black 3–6 6–3 6–2 7–6. **September** – *World Group Qualifying AUS d. UZB 5–0 in AUS (Hard).* R1 d. O. Ogorodov 6–3 6–3 6–4; R4 d. D. Tomashevich 6–2 6–4.

GRAND SLAM CUP RECORD – Played 1, r/u 1

1997: r/u [seed 2] d. Muster 6–2 6–3, Rios 6–1 7–6, Korda 7–5 3–6 6–7 7–6 9–7, lost Sampras [1] 6–2 6–4 7–5.

ATP TOUR CHAMPIONSHIP – Played 1

1997: 3rd in rr d. Rusedski 4–6 6–3 6–2, d. Moya 6–4 6–2, lost Sampras 6–4 6–1.

5 CARLOS MOYA (ESP)

Born: Palma da Mallorca, 27 August 1976. **Lives:** Barcelona. **Father:** Andres. **Mother:** Pilar. **Sister:** Caroline (29).. **Brother:** Andres (27). **Girlfriend:** Raluca Sandu, who plays on women's circuit. **Agent:** IMG. **Coach:** Jose Perlas. **Turned pro:** 1995.
Height: 6ft 3in (1.90m). **Weight:** 177lb (80kg).

Rankings: 1994: 346; **1995:** 63; **1996:** 28; **1997:** 7; **1998:** 5.
Highest: 5 (8 September 1997).

1998 Prize Money: $2,572,553.
Career Earnings: $4,302,533. **Career Titles:** 5.

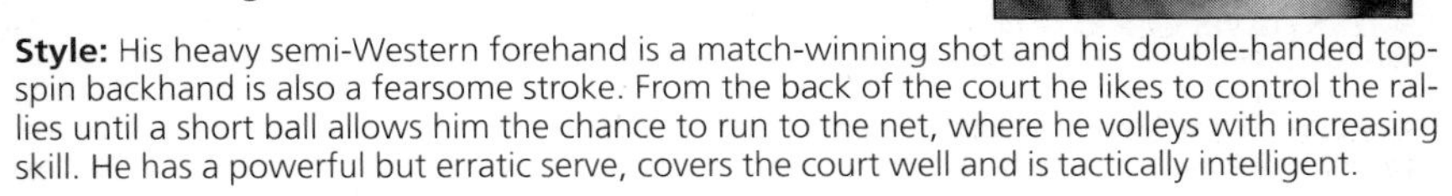

Style: His heavy semi-Western forehand is a match-winning shot and his double-handed top-spin backhand is also a fearsome stroke. From the back of the court he likes to control the rallies until a short ball allows him the chance to run to the net, where he volleys with increasing skill. He has a powerful but erratic serve, covers the court well and is tactically intelligent.

CAREER HIGHLIGHTS (year: (titles))
1994: European Jun champ in singles and doubles and played on winning Galea Cup team. A qualifier at St Polten, he upset Clavet on the way to his 1st main tour qf. **1995: (1)** *Buenos Aires.* After taking 2 Challenger titles, he finished the year in style with his 1st success on the senior tour at Buenos Aires, unseeded and without dropping a set. **1996: (1)** *Umag.* He recorded some significant upsets on his way to the title at Umag, r/u Munich (d. MaliVai Washington, Ivanisevic and Muster) and Bucharest, sf Barcelona (d. Rosset and Berasategui and took a set off Muster) and Oporto, and qf Casablanca and Amsterdam. He also surprised MaliVai Washington again at Italian Open, breaking into the top 20 in May, and removed Becker at Paris Open. **1997: (1)** *Long Island.* He began the year in style by upsetting W. Ferreira and A. Costa on the way to f Sydney, and followed with the high point of his career to date at Australian Open where, unseeded, he was r/u, upsetting Becker and M. Chang on the way. This performance took him into top 10, and he moved on up to top 5 in autumn. He became 1st Spaniard since Higueras in 1983 to win a title in US when he took Long Island in Aug., and also reached f Amsterdam, Indianapolis and Bournemouth, sf Barcelona, Monte Carlo and Umag, plus qf Scottsdale, Estoril and Munich. These results took him to his 1st ATP Champ, where he upset Sampras in rr and qualified for sf, where he lost to Kafelnikov. **1998: (2)** *FRENCH OPEN, Monte Carlo.* The climax of his year and career came at French Open, where he swept to his 1st GS title, having earlier given warning of his form by upsetting Kafelnikov, Corretja and Krajicek on the way to his 1st Super 9 title at Monte Carlo. He came close to ending his year on a similarly high note at ATP Champ, when he led Corretja by 2 sets to love at 5–all 3s in f, but his countryman fought back, leaving Moya as r/u, but still in the top 5. Already a force to be reckoned with on CC and having proved his prowess on HC in 1997, he was aiming to become a complete player on all surfaces, and played a full schedule on grass at Halle and Nottingham before Wimbledon. He was less successful there, but upset Corretja on his way to sf US Open, and reached the same stage at Estoril, Barcelona, Stuttgart Mercedes and Mallorca, plus qf Dubai.

PRINCIPAL 1998 RESULTS – won 2, r/u 1, sf 5 (detailed Grand Slam results follow)
won French Open, **won** Monte Carlo (d. Muster 6–0 6–3, Arazi 6–1 6–1, Kafelnikov 6–2 6–3, Corretja 6–3 6–2, Krajicek 4–6 6–1 6–4, Pioline 6–3 6–0 7–5); **r/u** ATP Champ; **sf** US Open, **sf** Estoril (d. Ulihrach 6–3 4–6 6–4, Goellner 6–3 6–2, C. Costa 7–6 6–7 6–2, lost Berasategui 6–1 6–1), **sf** Barcelona (d. Carbonell 3–6 6–2 6–2, Ulihrach 6–4 7–6, Hrbaty 4–6 6–3 6–3, lost Berasategui 7–6 6–4), **sf** Stuttgart Mercedes (d. Alonso 7–6 7–5, Hrbaty 6–2 6–2, Vicente 3–6 6–3 6–2, lost Kuerten 7–6 6–4), **sf** Mallorca (d. Moldovan 6–4 7–6, Dosedel 6–4 6–4, Schiessling 7–5 6–4, Vicente 6–1 6–2, lost Kuerten 6–7 6–2 6–3).

CAREER GRAND SLAM RECORD
AUSTRALIAN OPEN – Played 3, r/u 1
1996: 1r lost Medvedev 6–4 7–5 2–6 7–6. **1997: r/u** [unseeded] d. Becker [6] 5–7 7–6 3–6 6–1 6–4, McEnroe 3–6 6–0 6–3 6–1, Karbacher 6–2 6–2 6–2, Bjorkman 6–3 1–6 3–6 6–2 6–4, Mantilla 7–5 6–2 6–7 6–2, M. Chang [2] 7–5 6–2 6–4, lost Sampras [1] 6–2 6–3 6–3. **1998: 2r** [seed 7] d. Tramacchi 6–4 6–3 6–7 7–6, lost Fromberg 4–6 6–4 7–6 6–4.

FRENCH OPEN – Played 3, won 1
1996 2r d. Rafter 6–4 7–6 6–2, lost Edberg 6–2 6–2 6–1. **1997: 2r** [seed 9] d. A. Martin 6–3 6–7 5–7 6–3 6–3, lost Portas 6–4 4–6 7–5 6–3. **1998: won** [seed 12] d. Grosjean 7–5 6–1 6–4, Imaz 6–4 7–6 6–2, Ilie 6–2 7–6 6–3, Knippschild 6–3 7–5 3–6 6–4, Rios [3] 6–1 2–6 6–2 6–4, Mantilla [15] 5–7 6–2 6–4 6–2, Corretja [14] 6–3 7–5 6–3.

WIMBLEDON – Played 3
1996 1r lost Bouteyre 6–7 7–6 2–6 6–4 10–8. **1997: 2r** [seed 10] d. Bryan 7–6 6–3 4–6 6–2, lost Reneberg 6–4 6–3 6–3. **1998: 2r** [seed 5] d. Bhupathi 6–4 4–6 6–4 2–6 6–4, lost Arazi 4–6 6–4 6–3 6–4.

US OPEN – Played 3, sf 1
1996: 2r d. Humphries 6–1 6–7 6–7 6–4 6–4, lost Siemerink 7–6 6–4 6–4. **1997: 1r** [seed 8] lost Raoux 6–4 7–6 6–2. **1998: sf** [seed 10] d. Puerta 6–1 7–6 6–7 4–4 ret, M. Chang 3–6 1–6 7–6 6–4 6–3, Gambill 6–2 3–6 3–6 6–3 7–6, Corretja [7] 7–6 7–5 6–3, Larsson 6–4 6–3 6–3, lost Philippoussis 6–1 6–4 5–7 6–4.

OLYMPIC RECORD
Has never competed.

CAREER DAVIS CUP RECORD
1996: September – *World Group Qualifying ESP d. DEN 4–1 in ESP (Clay).* R2 d. K. Carlsen 6–1 6–2 6–1; R5 d. T. Larsen 6–3 6–4. **1997: February** – *World Group 1r ESP d. GER 4–1 in ESP (Clay).* R1 d. M. Goellner 6–4 6–3 6–3. R4 d. H. Dreekmann 6–4 6–4 7–5. **April** – *World Group qf ITA d. ESP 4–1 in ITA (Carpet).* R1 lost O. Camporese 6–7 6–7 6–1 6–3 6–3. R4 d. M. Martelli 7–6 4–6 6–3. **1998: April** – *World Group 1r ESP d. BRA 3–2 in BRA (Clay).* R1 lost G. Kuerten 5–7 1–6 6–4 6–4 6–4; R5 d. F. Meligeni 7–6 6–2 6–2. **July** – *World Group qf ESP d. SUI 4–1 in ESP (Clay).* R1 d. I. Heuberger 6–1 6–2 6–1; R4 d. M. Rosset 7–5 6–1 7–5. **September** – *World Group sf SWE d. ESP 4–1 in SWE (Carpet).* R2 lost T. Johansson 7–5 7–6 7–6; R4 lost J. Bjorkman 6–3 7–5.

GRAND SLAM CUP RECORD
Has never played.

ATP TOUR CHAMPIONSHIP – Played 2, r/u 1, sf 1
1997: sf in rr d. Sampras 6–3 6–7 6–2, lost Rafter 6–4 6–2, d. Muster 6–2 6–3; sf lost Kafelnikov 7–6 7–6. **1998: r/u** in rr lost Sampras 6–3 6–3, d. Kafelnikov 7–5 7–5, d. Kucera 6–7 7–5 6–3; sf d. Henman 6–4 3–6 7–5; f lost Corretja 3–6 3–6 7–5 6–3 7–5.

6 ANDRE AGASSI (USA)

Born: Las Vegas, 29 April 1970. **Lives:** Las Vegas. **Father:** Emanuel Agassian, who boxed for Iran in the 1952 Olympics, and became Mike Agassi. **Mother:** Elizabeth. **Brother:** Philip, who occasionally travels with him. **Sisters:** Tami and Rita, who was married to Pancho Gonzales. **Wife:** Brooke Shields, whose grandfather, Frank Shields, was the 1st unseeded finalist at US Open in 1930. Married 19 April 1997.
Agent: Perry Rodgers of Agassi Enterprises.
Coach: Brad Gilbert. Formerly coached by Nick Bollettieri (from age 13 until 1993). Formerly assisted by Pat Etcheberry for movement and from 1990 by Gil Reyes for strength.
Turned pro: 1986 (aged 16).
Height: 5ft 11in (1.80m). **Weight:** 165lb (75kg).

Rankings: 1985: 618; **1986:** 91; **1987:** 5; **1988:** 3; **1989:** 7; **1990:** 4; **1991:** 10; **1992:** 9; **1993:** 24; **1994:** 2; **1995:** 2; **1996:** 8; **1997:** 122; **1998:** 6. **Highest:** 1 (April 1995).

1998 Prize Money: $1,836,233. **Career Earnings:** $15,049,896. **Career Titles:** 39.

Style: A go-for-broke right-handed hitter from the back of the court with early-ball forehands and double-handed backhands that are amongst the hardest-hit strokes in tennis. A fine serve and improving volleys, added to his agility and speed about the court, make him a fearsome opponent. Inevitably he hits many unforced errors and these sometimes contribute to unexpected losses.

CAREER HIGHLIGHTS (year: (titles))
Andre is a born-again Christian who collects motor cars. As a child, he suffered from Osgood Schlatter's disease, which causes a bone in the knee to grow improperly. **1984:** Ranked 4 in US Boys' 14s and won Nat 14s. **1985:** Receiving expert counsel from brother-in-law Pancho Gonzales, he tested the waters of men's circuit. **1986:** Downed Mayotte and S. Davis on his way to qf Stratton Mountain. **1987: (1)** *Itaparica*. Reached first GP f at Seoul, won his 1st GP title at Itaparica at end of season and d. Jarryd en route to sf Basle. **1988: (6)** *Memphis, Charleston, Forest Hills, Stuttgart, Stratton Mountain, Livingston*. Began the year by winning 2nd consec. tourn at Memphis, adding 5 more during the year. After reaching 1st GS sf in Paris, he took a month's rest, missing Wimbledon. Made D Cup debut and qualified for Masters, but was restricted by a hand injury. **1989: (1)** *Orlando*. Could not maintain the high standards of 1988, having to wait until Orlando in Oct. for his 1st title for 14 months. R/u Italian Open; reached 2nd GS sf at US Open and appeared in 4 other sf to qualify for Masters, but won no match there. **1990: (4)** *San Francisco, LIPC, Washington, ATP Champ*. His year finished on a high note when he beat world No. 1, Edberg, to win ATP Tour World Champ in Nov. Reached 1st GS f at French Open, where he shocked traditionalists with his lurid outfits, which included luminous cycling shorts under black denim shorts. Did not play Wimbledon or Australian Open, but was also r/u at US Open, where he was fined $3,000 for his conduct in 3r match v Korda. In autumn was fined 20% of total earnings on ATP tour (excluding GS) for falling 2 tourns short of his commitment to the tour and was fined a further $25,000 at end of year for withdrawing from GS Cup after submitting an entry. Played in US D Cup team v AUS in f but withdrew with pulled stomach muscle in 4th rubber. **1991: (2)** *Orlando, Washington*. Reached his 3rd GS f at French Open, but in losing to Courier he again cast doubts on his ability to win a title at the highest level. Known generally for his garish outfits, he delighted both officials and crowds at Wimbledon with his pristine white attire and his enthusiasm. He reached sf there, but disappointed at US Open, falling in ss 1r to Krickstein. At ATP World Champ he reached sf but fell to Courier to finish the year with just 2 titles. Again led USA to f D Cup. **1992: (3)** *WIMBLEDON, Atlanta, Toronto*. In Jan. dropped out of top 10 for 1st time since May 1988 and reached no sf until winning Atlanta in May for his 1st title since July 1991. But everything came right for him at Wimbledon, where he removed Becker in 5s and outlasted Ivanisevic in a pulsating 5-set f to take his 1st GS title and return to top 10. Reached sf French Open and qf US Open, where he wore Wimbledon colours, and won Toronto in summer. Qualified for ATP World Champ but

was forced to withdraw with an injury to his left thigh. **1993: (2)** *San Francisco, Scottsdale*. Missed Australian Open with bronchitis and returned to play with a new commitment and discipline, winning San Francisco. However, he was forced to miss French Open with tendinitis of right wrist and returned to Wimbledon to defend his title after very little practice. He fell there to Sampras in 5s qf and surprised fans by revealing that he had trimmed his body hair 'to make him more aerodynamic'. Split with Bollettieri in July – when his former coach resigned, saying the distance between Agassi in Las Vegas and Bollettieri at his academy in Florida was too far. Joined with Pancho Segura in Aug., agreeing to work together at least through the US Open. Won Scottsdale and reached sf New Haven and Cincinnati, where he won the 1st doubles title of his career with Korda. He missed the last 3 tourns of the year with a wrist injury (dorsal capsulitis), undergoing surgery on 20 Dec. and for the 1st time since 1987 he finished outside the top 20. However, psychotherapy, which he underwent while recovering from wrist surgery at end of year, enabled him to come to terms with the harsh discipline of his upbringing, in which he was groomed for tennis from babyhood. **1994: (5)** *US OPEN, Scottsdale, Toronto, Vienna, Paris Open*. After joining forces with Brad Gilbert, who helped him restore belief in himself and his game, he enjoyed a remarkable year, the climax coming in Sept. with his 1st US Open. Ranked as low as 32 when he returned in Feb., he won Scottsdale in his 1st tourn back. Then in March he upset Becker and Edberg on his way to r/u LIPC, having agreed to delay f 50 minutes in order to let his opponent, Sampras, recover more from a stomach virus. He escaped punishment for obscene outbursts at Italian Open but at French Open, where he was not seeded, was fined $750 for an audible obscenity and $1,500 for verbal abuse. He was again a popular competitor at Wimbledon, where he lost in 5s to Martin in last 16, but his next GS outing was the highlight, when, unseeded at US Open for the 1st time since 1987, he became the 1st unseeded winner there since Fred Stolle in 1966. Playing better than ever on European carpet, where he hadn't prospered before, he upset Ivanisevic and Stich to take the title at Vienna, and beat Sampras and Bruguera in winning Paris Open – a victory that took him to a career-high ranking of No. 2. He retained that ranking at year's end, after sf showing at IBM/ATP World Champ, where he was a set up v Sampras, and was 1st man to climb to No. 2 from outside the top 20 within a year. At GS Cup he was fined $6,000 for verbal obscenity during his losing qf against ultimate winner, Larsson. **1995: (7)** *AUSTRALIAN OPEN, San Jose, LIPC, Washington, Montreal, Cincinnati, New Haven*. Startled fans by appearing at his 1st Australian Open looking rather plump and sporting a new look with his unbleached hair close-cropped and receding. He won that and 6 more titles across the year from a total of 10 f. On 10 April he replaced Sampras as No. 1, becoming the 12th player to top the rankings. He was then unexpectedly beaten by Courier in Tokyo Japan Open and the next week incurred a $5,000 fine for withdrawing from Hong Kong, owing to a lower back strain. At French Open he injured his hip when he fell in 4th game qf v Kafelnikov and lost the match. At Wimbledon he lost sf to Becker in one of the best matches of the tourn and at US Open he gained revenge in a similarly fine sf, but lost f to Sampras. In the summer he had a sequence of 4 successive titles, saving 2 mps v Krajicek at New Haven. Suffering from a chest injury incurred when he was helping USA beat SWE in D Cup in Sept., he lost 3r Essen to MaliVai Washington and was forced to withdraw from Paris Open, then IBM/ATP Champ and D Cup f. With Sampras still in action and winning in Paris, he lost the No. 1 ranking in Nov. Won the 1995 Arthur Ashe Humanitarian Award for his work with the Andre Agassi Foundation to benefit disadvantaged youth. **1996: (3)** *OLYMPICS, LIPC, Cincinnati*. Winning an Olympic gold medal was the high point of his career and an outstanding moment in a mixed year, in which he often seemed to have lost interest, concentrating too much on commercial matters and not enough on his tennis. He returned to No. 1 on 29 Jan. after Australian Open, where he appeared with his head newly shaven. The highlight there was his dramatic 5s qf win over Courier, in which he recovered from 2s down for the 1st time in his career; he came from behind in 4 of his matches there, but could not do so again v M. Chang in sf. Fell from the top spot again on 19 Feb. after losing f San Jose to Sampras, won LIPC when Ivanisevic retired in their f, but was booed off court at Monte Carlo after a sloppy performance v A. Costa 3r. He was again disappointing at French Open, where he appeared to be overweight and unfit; he let slip a 2–1 sets lead against Woodruff and was fined £2,000 for failing to appear at the press conference afterwards. He had flu just before Wimbledon – arriving there underprepared, still overweight and having played in only 4 matches since March – and was beaten by qualifier D. Flach. His subsequent fall to No. 6 on 22 July saw him ranked outside the top 5 for 1st time since Oct. 1994. Although his game eventually came good at Olympics, he struggled in the early rounds and narrowly escaped disquali-

Andre Agassi did enough last year to suggest that in 1999 he could be a serious challenger for fellow American Pete Sampras's world No. 1 ranking, a position he himself had held in 1995. (Michael Cole)

fication for an obscenity v W. Ferreira in an ill-tempered qf. He was then defaulted at Indianapolis for racket abuse and an expletive, subsequently being fined $4,000 for the misdemeanour. The umpire there had been advised by the ATP supervisor, but Agassi complained that the usual procedure of warning, point penalty, default was not followed. He reached sf US Open, where M. Chang removed him again, and qf Indian Wells and Stuttgart Eurocard. He declined to play D Cup in Prague, where USA lost to CZE. His year finished on an unsatisfactory note, when, again underprepared and suffering from a heavy cold, he put up a dismal performance v Sampras at ATP Champ, winning only 3 games, and then withdrew from the tourn. He was fined $35,000 (5% of his tour earnings, excluding GS) for failing to appear at the draw. His 1r loss at GS Cup to Woodforde did nothing to restore his reputation. **1997:** The downhill slide continued as he pulled out of Australian Open lacking motivation, fell from top 20 after his 4th consec. 1r defeat at LIPC (to Draper), and withdrew from Wimbledon, where he was unseeded, complaining of a recurring wrist injury. In his 1st year since 1986 without a title, he played 24 matches in 12 tourns, reaching sf San Jose and qf Indianapolis and extending his D Cup record to 15 consec. wins. Otherwise he seemed to have lost his way and dropped outside top 100 for 1st time since 1986, reaching a low of 141 in Nov. However, rediscovering motivation towards the end of year, he vowed to return to his previous form, and began playing in lower-level tournaments. He started with Las Vegas Challenger, where he was r/u to Vinck, and continued the upward trend with the title at Burbank Challenger. **1998: (5)** *San Jose, Scottsdale, Washington, Los Angeles, Ostrava*. As the season opened he was already showing signs of his old form, following sf finish at Adelaide with an upset of A. Costa at Australian Open, where he was unseeded. From there he simply took off, rising swiftly through the rankings to make the top 20 again on 27 April and finish the year in his old place in the top 10. When he won his 5th title of the season at Ostrava in Oct., he returned to the top 5 – and was even in contention for the No. 1 year-end ranking until his qf defeat by T. Martin at Paris Open. Still ranked low enough to be unseeded at San Jose in Feb., he removed Kuerten, M. Chang and Sampras (all in ss) to take his 1st title since August 1996, and added Scottsdale 3 weeks later. He was disappointing at both French Open and Wimbledon, but hit the HC season in style with a 3-week run in which he swept to the title at Washington, took Lost Angeles a week later and then upset Sampras again to reach sf Toronto. In other tourns he was r/u LIPC, Munich, Indianapolis, Basle and GS Cup, where he was controversially awarded a WC and lost f only in 5s to Rios. He qualified for ATP Champ, but suffered a back injury during practice the day before and was unable to complete his 1st match. He was not available for vital D Cup sf v Italy.

PRINCIPAL 1998 RESULTS – won 5, r/u 5, sf 2 (detailed Grand Slam results follow)
won San Jose (d. A. Martin 6–2 6–2, Kuerten 6–3 6–1, Gambill 7–5 7–6, M. Chang 6–4 7–6, Sampras 6–2 6–4), **won** Scottsdale (d. Portas 3–6 6–1 6–2, Lapentti 7–5 6–1, Gambill 6–3 7–6, Haas 6–2 6–1, Stoltenberg 6–4 7–6), **won** Washington (d. Wheaton 6–4 6–2, Van Garsse 6–3 6–4, Lareau 6–1 6–2, W. Ferreira 6–1 6–0, S. Draper 6–2 6–0), **won** Los Angeles (d. Bryan 6–4 6–3, Gambill 6–4 6–4, Stolle 7–6 6–2, Gimelstob 6–0 7–6, Henman 6–4 6–4), **won** Ostrava (d. Carlsen 6–4 6–4, M. Norman 6–2 7–5, Johansson 6–7 6–4 6–4, W. Black 7–6 6–3, Kroslak 6–2 3–6 6–3); **r/u** LIPC (d. Escude 6–2 6–3, Spadea 6–4 7–5, A. Costa 7–6 4–6 6–1, Tarango 6–4 6–3, Corretja 6–4 6–2, lost Rios 7–5 6–3 6–4), **r/u** Munich (d. Woodbridge 6–1 3–6 6–3, Schuttler 6–1 6–4, Bjorkman 6–2 6–2, Blanco 6–4 6–4, lost Enqvist 6–7 7–6 6–3), **r/u** Indianapolis (d. Tebbutt 6–1 6–0, W. Black 7–6 3–6 6–1, W. Ferreira 6–2 6–1, Delgado 7–6 6–3, lost Corretja 2–6 6–2 6–3), **r/u** Basle (d. Federer 6–3 6–2, Heuberger 6–2 6–2, Gustafsson 6–3 6–3, Rosset 6–4 6–2, lost Henman 6–4 6–3 3–6 6–4), **r/u** GS Cup; **sf** Adelaide (d. Sargsian 4–6 6–3 6–3, Siemerink 6–4 6–3, Steven 1–6 6–1 6–1, lost L. Hewitt 7–6 7–6), **sf** Toronto (d. Raoux 6–4 7–5, Ivanisevic 2–6 7–5 6–3, Sampras 6–7 6–1 6–2, lost Krajicek 4–6 7–5 6–2).

CAREER GRAND SLAM RECORD

AUSTRALIAN OPEN Played 3, won 1, sf 1

1987–1994: Did not play. **1995: won** [seed 2] d. Stafford 6–2 6–4 6–2, Golmard 6–2 6–3 6–1, Rusedski 6–2 6–4 6–2, Rafter 6–3 6–4 6–0, Kafelnikov [10] 6–2 7–5 6–0, Krickstein 6–4 6–4 3–0 ret'd, Sampras [1] 4–6 6–1 7–6 6–4. **1996: sf** [seed 2] d. Etlis 3–6 7–6 4–6 7–6 6–3, Spadea 6–4 6–2 6–3, Bryan 4–6 6–0 6–2 6–1, Bjorkman 4–6 6–2 4–6 6–1 6–2, Courier [8] 6–7 2–6 6–3 6–4 6–2, lost M. Chang [5] 6–1 6–4 7–6. **1997:** Did not play. **1998: last 16** [unseeded] d.Martelli 3–6 7–6 6–2 6–2, A. Costa 6–4 6–4 2–6 7–5, Gaudenzi 6–2 6–2 6–0, lost Berasategui 3–6 3–6 6–2 6–2 6–3.

FRENCH OPEN Played 10, r/u 2, sf 2, qf 1

1987: 2r d. Arraya 6–2 4–6 6–1 7–5, lost Kuchna 6–4 6–3 6–3. **1988: sf** [seed 9] d. Perez Roldan 6–2 6–2 6–4, lost Wilander 4–6 6–2 7–5 5–7 6–0. **1989: 3r** [seed 5] d. J. Carlsson 6–4 6–4 6–1, Cane 6–2 6–3 6–3, lost Courier 7–6 4–6 6–3 6–2. **1990: r/u** [seed 3] d. Wostenholme 4–6 7–6 6–0 6–1, Woodbridge 7–5 6–1 6–3, Boetsch 6–3 6–2 6–0, Courier [13] 6–7 6–1 6–4 6–0, Chang [11] 6–1 6–2 4–6 6–2, Svensson 6–1 6–4 3–6 6–3, lost Gomez [4] 6–3 2–6 6–4 6–4. **1991: r/u** [seed 4] d. Rosset 3–6 7–5 6–4 6–3, Korda 6–1 6–2 6–2, P. McEnroe 6–2 6–2 6–0, Mancini 6–3 6–3 5–7 6–1, Hlasek 6–3 6–1 6–1, Becker [2] 7–5 6–3 6–1, lost Courier [9] 3–6 6–4 2–6 6–1 6–4. **1992: sf** [seed 11] d. Frana 6–1 6–4 6–4, Pozzi 6–0 6–2 6–1, Prpic 2–6 6–4 6–1 7–6, E. Sanchez 6–0 6–4 7–6, Sampras [3] 7–6 6–2 6–1, lost Courier [1] 6–3 6–2 6–2. **1993:** Did not play. **1994: 2r** d. Wilander 6–2 7–5 6–1, lost Muster [11] 6–3 6–7 7–5 2–6 7–5. **1995: qf** [seed 1] d. Braasch 6–1 6–4 6–4, Woodbridge 7–6 6–1 6–0, Clavet 6–1 6–2 6–0, El Aynaoui 6–4 6–2 6–2, lost Kafelnikov [9] 6–4 6–3 7–5. **1996: 2r** [seed 3] d. Diaz 6–1 6–7 6–4 6–4, lost Woodruff 4–6 6–4 6–7 6–3 6–2. **1997:** Did not play. **1998: 1r** lost Safin 5–7 7–5 6–2 3–6 6–2.

WIMBLEDON – Played 8, won 1, sf 1, qf 2

1987: 1r lost Leconte [9] 6–2 6–1 6–2. **1988–90:** Did not play. **1991: qf** [seed 5] d. Connell 4–6 1–6 7–5 6–3, Prpic 7–6 3–6 6–4 6–2, Krajicek 7–6 6–3 7–6, Eltingh 6–3 6–3 6–2, lost Wheaton 6–2 0–6 3–6 7–6 6–2). **1992: won** [seed 12] d. Chesnokov 5–7 6–1 7–5 7–5, Masso 4–6 6–1 6–3 6–3, Rostagno 6–3 7–6 7–5, Saceanu 7–6 6–1 7–6, Becker [4] 4–6 6–2 6–2 4–6 6–3, J. McEnroe 6–4 6–2 6–3 Ivanisevic [8] 6–7 6–4 6–4 1–6 6–4. **1993: qf** [seed 8] d. Karbacher 7–5 6–4 6–0, Cunha-Silva 5–7 6–3 6–2 6–0, Rafter 6–1 6–7 6–0 6–3, Krajicek [9] 7–5 7–6 7–6, lost Sampras [1] 6–2 6–2 3–6 3–6 6–4). **1994: last 16** [seed 12] d. Gaudenzi 6–2 6–7 6–3 6–2, Pereira 6–7 6–3 6–4 6–7 6–4, Krickstein 6–4 6–3 7–6, lost Martin [6] 6–3 7–5 6–7 4–6 6–1. **1995: sf** [seed 1] d. Painter 6–2 6–2 6–1, P. McEnroe 6–1 6–1 6–3, Wheaton 6–2 3–6 6–4 6–2, Mronz 6–3 6–3 6–3, Eltingh 6–2 6–3 6–4, lost Becker [3] 2–6 7–6 6–4 7–6. **1996: 1r** [seed 3] lost D. Flach 2–6 7–6 6–4 7–6. **1997:** Did not play. **1998: 2r** [seed 13] d. Calatrava 6–2 6–4 6–3, lost Haas 4–6 6–1 7–6 6–4.

US OPEN – Played 13, won 1, r/u 2, sf 3, qf 1

1986: 1r lost Bates 7–6 6–3 3–6 6–4. **1987: 1r** lost Leconte [11] 6–4 7–6 4–6 6–3. **1988: sf** [seed 4] d. Chang 7–5 6–3 6–2, Connors [6] 6–2 7–6 6–1, lost Lendl [1] 4–6 6–2 6–3 6–4. **1989: sf** [seed 6] d. Weiss 6–3 7–6 6–0, Broad 6–3 6–2 6–3, Johnson 6–1 7–5 6–2, Grabb 6–1 7–5 6–3, Connors [13] 6–1 4–6 0–6 6–3 6–4, lost Lendl [1] 7–6 6–1 3–6 6–1. **1990: r/u** [seed 4] d. Connell 6–4 6–2 6–2, Korda 7–5 5–7 6–0 6–4, Davin 7–5 6–4 6–0, Berger [13] 7–5 6–0 6–2, Cherkasov 6–2 6–2 6–3, Becker [2] 6–7 6–3 6–2 6–3, lost Sampras [12] 6–4 6–3 6–2). **1991: 1r** [seed 8] lost Krickstein 7–5 7–6 6–2. **1992: qf** [seed 8] d. Pernfors 6–2 6–4 6–1, Roig 6–1 6–3 6–2, Siemerink 6–2 6–3 6–3, Costa [10] 6–4 6–3 6–2, lost Courier [1] 6–3 6–7 6–1 6–4). **1993: 1r** [seed 16] lost Enqvist 6–4 6–4 3–6 6–7 6–2. **1994: won** [unseeded] d. Eriksson 6–3 6–2 6–0, Forget 6–3 7–5 6–7 6–2, W. Ferreira 7–5 6–1 7–5, Chang [6] 6–1 6–7 6–3 3–6 6–1, Muster [13] 7–6 6–3 6–0, Martin [9] 6–3 4–6 6–2 6–3, Stich [4] 6–1 7–6 7–5). **1995: r/u** [seed 1] d. Shelton 6–2 6–2 6–2, Corretja 5–7 6–3 5–7 6–0 6–2, Edberg 6–4 6–3 6–1, Palmer 7–5 6–3 6–2, Korda 6–4 6–2 1–6 7–6, Becker [4] 7–6 7–6 4–6 6–4, lost Sampras [2] 6–4 6–3 4–6 7–5. **1996: sf** [seed 6] d. Hadad 6–3 6–3 6–2, Paes 3–6 6–4 6–1 6–0, Siemerink 6–4 6–2 7–6, Wheaton 4–6 6–2 6–3 6–4, Muster [3] 6–2 7–5 4–6 6–2, lost M. Chang [2] 6–3 6–2 6–2. **1997: last 16** [unseeded] d. Campbell 6–1 6–1 4–6 6–3, Voinea 6–0 6–2 6–2, Woodforde 6–2 6–2 6–4, lost Rafter [13] 6–3 7–6 4–6 6–3. **1998: last 16** [seed 8] d. Grosjean 6–4 6–1 6–4, Raoux 6–3 6–2 6–7 3–6 6–1, Sanguinetti 6–2 6–3 6–0, lost Kucera [9] 6–3 6–3 6–7 1–6 6–3.

OLYMPIC RECORD

1996: (Atlanta) won gold medal [seed 1] d. Bjorkman 7–6 7–6, Kucera 6–4 6–4, Gaudenzi 2–6 6–4 6–2, W. Ferreira [5] 7–5 4–6 7–5, Paes 7–6 6–3, Bruguera 6–2 6–3 6–1.

CAREER DAVIS CUP RECORD

1988: April – *Zone 1 sf USA d. PER 5–0 in PER (Clay).* R2 d. Yzaga 6–8 7–5 6–1 6–2; R5 v P. Arraya not played. **July** – *Zone 1 Final USA d. ARG 4–1 in ARG (Clay).* R2 d. M. Jaite 6–2 6–2 6–1; R4 d. G. Perez-Roldan 2–6 6–2 8–6. **1989: February** – *World Group 1r USA d. PAR 5–0 in USA (Hard).* R2 d. H. Chapacu 6–2 6–1 6–1; R5 d. F. Gonzalez 6–2 6–4. **April** – *World Group qf USA d. FRA 5–0 in USA (Carpet).* R2 d. H. Leconte 6–1 6–2 5–7 6–1; R4 d. Y. Noah 6–3 7–6. **July** – *World Group sf FRG d. USA 3–2 in FRG (Carpet).* R2 lost B. Becker 6–7 6–7 7–6 6–3 6–4; R4 lost C. Steeb 4–6 6–4 6–4 6–2. **1990: September** – *World Group sf USA d. AUT 3–2 in AUT (Clay).* R2 d. H. Skoff 7–6 6–0 6–1; R4 lost T. Muster 6–2 6–2 7–6. **December** – *World Group Final USA d. AUS 3–2 in USA (Clay).* R1 d. R. Fromberg 4–6 6–2 4–6 6–2 6–4; R4 lost D. Cahill 6–4 4–6 ret'd. **1991: September** – *World Group sf USA d. GER 3–2 in USA (Clay).* R1 d. M. Stich 6–3 6–1 6–4; R5 d. C. Steeb 6–2 6–2 6–3. **November** – *World Group Final FRA d. USA 3–1 (Carpet).* R1 d. G. Forget 6–7 6–2 6–1 6–2; R5 v H. Leconte not played. **1992: January** – *World Group 1r USA d. ARG 5–0 in USA (Hard).* R2 d. A. Mancini 6–4 6–4 6–4; R5 d. M. Jaite 7–5 6–3. **March** – *World Group qf USA d. TCH 3–2 in USA (Hard).* R2 d. P. Korda 6–2 6–4 6–1; R5 d. K. Novacek 7–5 6–0 6–0. **September** – *World Group sf USA d. SWE 4–1 in USA (Clay).* R2 d. S. Edberg 5–7 6–3 7–6 6–3; R5 d. N. Kulti 6–7 6–2 6–4. **December** – *World Group Final USA d. SUI 3–1 in USA (Hard).* R1 d. J. Hlasek 6–1 6–2 6–2; R5 v M. Rosset not played. **1993: September** – *World Group Qualifying USA d. BAH 5–0 in USA (Hard).* R1 d. R. Smith 6–2 6–2 6–3. **1995: March** – *World Group qf USA d. ITA 5–0 in ITA (Clay).* R1 d. A. Gaudenzi 6–4 6–4 6–1. **September** – *World Group sf USA d. SWE 4–1 in USA (Hard).* R2 d. M. Wilander 7–6 6–2 6–2. **1997: April** – *World Group qf USA d. NED 4–1 in USA (Hard).* R1 d. S. Schalken 7–6 6–4 7–6; R4 d. J. Siemerink 3–6 3–6 6–3 6–3 6–3. **1998: April** – *World Group 1r USA d. RUS 3–2 in USA (Hard).* R2 d. M. Safin 6–3 6–3 6–3; R4 lost Y. Kafelnikov 6–3 6–0 7–6. **July** – *World Group qf USA d. BEL 4–1 in USA (Hard).* R2 d. C. Van Garsse 6–2 6–2 6–2.

GRAND SLAM CUP RECORD – Played 4, r/u 1, qf 1

1992: 1r lost Chang 6–4 6–2. **1994: qf** [seed 2] d. Muster 6–3 7–5, lost Larsson 6–4 6–1 6–1. **1996: 1r** [seed 8] lost Woodforde 6–3 6–4. **1998: r/u** d. Pioline 6–0 6–0, Korda 4–6 6–0 6–1, Kucera 7–6 6–7 2–6 7–5 6–0, lost Rios 6–4 2–6 7–6 5–7 6–3.

GRAND PRIX MASTERS/ATP TOUR CHAMPIONSHIP (from 1990) – Played 6, won 1, sf 2

1989: 4th in rr lost Becker 6–1 6–3, lost Edberg 6–4 6–2, lost Gilbert 3–6 6–3 6–3. **1990: won** in rr d. Sampras 6–4 6–2, d. E. Sanchez 6–0 6–3, lost Edberg 7–6 4–6 7–6; sf d. Becker 6–2 6–4; f d. Edberg 5–7 7–6 7–5 6–2. **1991: sf** in rr d. Becker 6–3 7–5, lost Sampras 6–3 1–6 6–3, d. Stich 7–5 6–3; sf lost Courier 6–3 7–5. **1994: sf** in rr d. Berasategui 6–2 6–0, d. Chang 6–4 6–4, d. Bruguera 6–3 1–6 6–3; sf lost Sampras 4–6 7–6 6–3. **1996:** lost Sampras in rr 6–2 6–1, ret. **1998:** lost Corretja 5–7 6–3 2–1 ret in rr.

7 TIM HENMAN (GBR)

Born: Oxford, 6 September 1974. **Lives:** London.
Father: Anthony. **Mother:** Jane. **Brothers:** Michael and Richard (both older).
Agent: Jan Felgate of IMG. **Coach:** David Felgate.
Physical Trainer: Tim Newenham. **Turned pro:** 1993.
Height: 6ft 1in (1.85cm). **Weight:** 155lb (70kg).

Rankings: 1992: 771; **1993:** 434; **1994:** 161; **1995:** 99; **1996:** 29; **1997:** 17; **1998:** 7. **Highest:** 7 (30 November 1998).

1998 Prize Money: $1,448,770.
Career Earnings: $3,277,128. **Career titles:** 4.

Style: One of the best serve-volleyers in the game, whose instinct is to attack from the net at every opportunity. His chip-and-charge tactics and excellent touch on the volley, together with speedy court coverage (much improved through tough physical training regime) make him an attractive player to watch. His powerful but erratic first serve is backed up by a much improved kicking second delivery. His naturally strong backhand is a match-winner, but the forehand is erratic.

CAREER HIGHLIGHTS (year: (titles))
Great-grandson of Ellen Stawell-Brown, the 1st woman to serve overarm in the ladies' singles at Wimbledon, and grandson of Henry Billington, who played at Wimbledon in 1940s and 1950s. Girlfriend Lucy Heald. **1992:** Nat Jun champ in singles and doubles. **1994:** Began to make an impact on the satellite circuits and made his D Cup debut, but in September he broke his leg in 3 places and was out 5 months. **1995:** A mixed year finished on a high note when he broke into the top 100 after winning both singles and doubles at Seoul Challenger in Oct., following with Nat Champs and singles title at Reunion Challenger. On the main tour he reached his 1st qf at Nottingham, but hit a low point at Wimbledon, where he was disqualified and fined $3,000 after a ball he hit in frustration during a doubles match accidentally hit a ball-girl on the head. **1996:** In contrast to the previous year, Wimbledon provided the highlight of his career to date. Against Kafelnikov in 1r, he squandered a 2-set lead and stood 2 mps down at 3–5 fs, but served 2 aces before going on to win 7–5. He further thrilled his home crowds by progressing to qf, unseeded, a performance which took him into top 50 1st time. He went on to take an Olympic silver medal in doubles with Broad – Britain's 1st in tennis since 1924 – and at US Open he avenged his Wimbledon defeat by T. Martin en route to last 16, again unseeded. He also reached sf Shanghai, Rotterdam (d. Siemerink and Moya), Copenhagen, Seoul, Lyon (d. Siemerink again), Ostrava (d. W. Ferreira) and GS Cup (as alternate) and qf Nottingham (d. MaliVai Washington), moving into top 25 in Oct., although he slipped down again as he struggled at end of year. He took over No. 1 British ranking from Rusedski on 29 April and confirmed his position by winning Nat Champ in Nov. Won Most Improved Player award. **1997: (2)** *Sydney, Tashkent.* He began the year in style with his 1st f on the main tour at Qatar, following the next week with his 1st title at Sydney (d. Ivanisevic) and then a 3rd consec. f at Antwerp. After Qatar he became 1st GBR player since Mottram in 1983 to reach the top 20, progressing to No. 14 after Antwerp. However, he was restricted at LIPC by an elbow injury, which required arthroscopic surgery on 26 March to remove pieces of bone from the elbow joint, causing him to miss D Cup tie v Zimbabwe. At Wimbledon he reached qf again, inspired by the middle-Sunday home crowd as he d. Haarhuis 14–12 5s before upsetting Krajicek. After that, he hit a low point in losing 1r Montreal to LeBlanc, ranked more than 800 places below him, was brilliant in beating Muster 1r US Open, but dreadful in losing to W. Ferreira 2r. Avoiding clay at home at Bournemouth, he then opted instead to play in Tashkent, where he won his 2nd title of the year. By then, though, Rusedski had overtaken him as No. 1 in GBR and confirmed his dominance by winning their sf at Vienna. He reached the same stage at Nottingham and Basle (where he won the doubles with Rosset) and qf New Haven and Stockholm. Played 1 match at ATP Champ (d. Kafelnikov, who had already qualified for sf) as alternate when Bruguera withdrew after playing 2. **1998: (2)** *Tashkent, Basle.* Working with physical trainer Tim Newenham,

he gained bulk without losing agility and enjoyed his best year yet, although consistency was still a problem. He broke into top 10 1st time on 17 Aug., and although he wobbled in and out of the top ranks during the rest of the year, he finished the season there and as the No. 1 British player. His 1st 2 GS tourns were disappointing as Golmard removed him 11–9 fs 1r Australian Open and he was forced to retire 1r French Open with a back injury, suffered in practice the day before and believed to be the result of having played 33 tourns in 12 months. However, he came into his own again at Wimbledon, playing the tennis of his life to upset Rafter and Korda en route to sf, where he became the 1st player of the tourn to take a set off Sampras, with whom he practises. His 1st title of the year was Tashkent in Sept., followed 3 weeks later by Basle (d. Agassi). He was r/u Sydney (d. Rafter) and Los Angeles, reached sf LIPC (d. Moya, Korda and Kuerten), Toronto and Stockholm, as well as Wimbledon, and played qf Qatar, Tokyo Japan Open, Queen's, New Haven and Vienna. His 1st official berth at ATP Champ was clinched only at the last minute when he reached sf Stockholm, and because Krajicek and Rafter, who were ahead of him, had withdrawn. There he reached sf before losing 7–5 fs to Moya; had he won that match he could have finished the year in the top 5. GBR qualified for WT Cup 1st time in 20 years, but he declined to play, thus depriving Rusedski of the chance to compete and further straining relations between the top 2 GBR players. However, it looked likely that both would be playing in the tourn in 1999. Led GBR into World Group of D Cup with 2 key wins v IND.

PRINCIPAL 1998 RESULTS – won 2, r/u 2, sf 4 (detailed Grand Slam results follow)
won Tashkent (d. Welgreen 6–1 6–4, Ran 6–4 6–1, Pescosolido 6–4 6–4, Escude 3–6 6–3 6–4, Kafelnikov 7–5 6–4), **won** Basle (d. Stoltenberg 2–6 6–3 6–4, Arazi 6–4 7–6, Kiefer 6–3 6–4, Johansson 6–3 2–6 7–6, Agassi 6–4 6–3 3–6 6–4); **r/u** Sydney (d. Woodforde 6–2 3–6 6–4, Portas 7–6 6–4, Enqvist 3–6 7–5 6–4, Rafter 7–6 7–5, lost Kucera 7–5 6–4), **r/u** Los Angeles (d. Stafford 6–3 6–0, Tarango 7–6 7–5, B. Black 5–7 6–1 6–4, Raoux 7–5 6–3, lost Agassi 6–4 6–4); **sf** LIPC (d. Stafford 6–4 6–2, Moya 6–1 6–4, Korda 6–4 6–4, Kuerten 6–2 6–4, lost Rios 6–2 4–6 6–0), **sf** Wimbledon, **sf** Toronto (d. Canas 3–6 7–6 6–2, A. Costa 7–6 6–2, Vacek 6–3 5–7 6–1, lost Rafter 6–2 6–4), **sf** Stockholm (d. Tillstrom 6–3 6–1, W. Ferreira 7–6 6–3, Gustafsson 6–3 3–6 7–6, lost T. Martin 4–6 6–1 6–2).

CAREER GRAND SLAM RECORD
AUSTRALIAN OPEN – Played 3
1996: 2r d. Korda 5–7 7–6 6–3 6–4, lost Bjorkman 6–1 6–3 6–2. **1997: 3r** d. Pavel 7–5 6–4 6–2, Raoux 6–3 6–3 6–4, lost M. Chang [2] 6–1 7–6 6–3. **1998: 1r** lost Golmard 6–3 6–7 6–2 3–6 11–9.
FRENCH OPEN – Played 3
1996: 1r lost Goossens 6–4 6–4 7–5. **1997: 1r** [seed 14] lost Delaitre 6–2 2–6 1–6 6–2 6–4. **1998: 1r** lost Sargsian 5–2 ret.
WIMBLEDON – Played 5, sf 1, qf 2
1994: 1r lost Prinosil 4–6 6–3 6–2 6–2. **1995: 2r** d. Wekesa 7–6 6–0 6–4, lost Sampras [2] 6–2 6–3 7–6. **1996: qf** [unseeded] d. Kafelnikov [5] 7–6 6–3 6–7 4–6 7–5, Sapsford 6–1 6–7 6–0 6–1, Milligan 6–1 6–3 6–4, Gustafsson 7–6 6–4 7–6, lost Martin 7–6 7–6 6–4; **1997: qf** [seed 14] d. Nestor 7–6 6–1 6–4, Golmard 7–6 6–3 6–3, Haarhuis 6–7 6–3 6–2 4–6 14–12, Krajicek [4] 7–6 6–7 7–6 6–4, lost Stich 6–3 6–2 6–4. **1998: sf** [seed 12] d. Novak 7–6 7–5 5–7 4–6 6–2, Nainkin 6–3 5–7 6–4 6–2, B. Black 6–4 6–4 3–6 7–5, Rafter [6] 6–3 6–7 6–3 6–2, Korda [3] 6–3 6–4 6–2, lost Sampras [1] 6–3 4–6 7–5 6–3.
US OPEN – Played 4
1995: 2r d. Viloca 6–3 4–6 6–3 6–2, lost Palmer 6–4 6–7 6–3 6–1. **1996: last 16** [unseeded] d. Jabali 6–2 6–3 6–4, D. Flach 6–3 6–4 6–2, Martin [12] 6–2 7–6 6–4, lost Edberg 6–7 7–6 6–4 6–4. **1997: 2r** d. Muster [5] 6–3 7–6 4–6 6–4, lost W. Ferreira 6–3 6–2 6–4. **1998: last 16** [seed 13] d. S. Draper 6–3 7–6 7–6, Mantilla 6–3 5–7 7–5 6–4, Kohlman 6–3 7–5 1–6 6–4, lost Philippoussis 7–5 0–6 6–4 6–1.

OLYMPIC RECORD
1996: (Atlanta) 2r d. Matsuoka 7–6 6–3, lost Woodbridge 7–6 7–6. **DOUBLES:** (with Broad) **r/u silver medal** lost Woodbridge/Woodforde 6–4 6–4 6–2.

CAREER DAVIS CUP RECORD
1994: July – *Zone 1 Relegation ROM d. GBR 3–2 in GBR (Grass).* R3 (with J. Bates) d. G. Cosac/D. Pescariu 6–2 6–7 5–7 6–2 6–1. **1995: April** – *Zone 2 1r SVK d. GBR 5–0 in SVK (Clay).* R1 lost J. Kroslak 7–5 6–3 4–6 6–3; R3 (with N. Broad) lost Kroslka/K. Kucera 3–6 6–4 6–4 2–6 6–2; R4 lost Kucera 6–4 6–2. **July** – *Zone 2 Relegation GBR d. MON 5–0 in GBR (Grass).* R2 d. S. Graeff 6–0 6–3 6–2; R5 d. C. Boggetti 6–1 6–4. **1996: July** – *Zone 2 2r GBR d. GHA 5–0 in GHA (Hard)* R1 d. I. Donkor 6–2 6–0 6–2; R4 d. D. Omaboe 6–3 4–6 6–0. **September** – *Zone 2 sf GBR d. EGY 5–0 in EGY (Grass).* R2 d. A. Ghoneim 6–0 6–4 7–5; R4 d. T. El Sawy 6–7 6–2 6–2). **1997: July** – *Zone 1 Relegation GBR d. UKR 3–2 in UKR (Clay).* R1 d. A. Rybalko 2–6 6–4 6–3 4–6 6–4; R3 (with G. Rusedski) d. A. Medvedev/A. Poliakov 6–1 6–4 7–6; R4 lost Medvedev 6–7 6–3 6–4 6–4.

The world's No. 7 Tim Henman, who will be joined by No. 11 Greg Rusedski on Davis Cup duty in 1999, with real prospects of a first British success since the 1930s. (Stephen Wake)

1998: April – *Zone 1 2r GBR d. UKR 5–0 in GBR (Carpet).* R2 d. A. Medvedev 6–2 6–7 6–4 1–6 6–1; R3 (with G. Rusedski) d. Medvedev/A. Rybalko 6–4 7–5 7–6; R5 d. Rybalko 6–1 2–6 6–2. **September** – *World Group Qualifying GBR d. IND 3–2 in GBR (Hard).* R2 d. M. Bhupathi 4–6 6–3 6–3 6–3; R3 (with N. Broad) lost Bhupathi/L. Paes 7–6 6–3 7–6; R4 d. Paes 7–6 6–2 7–6.

GRAND SLAM CUP RECORD – Played 2, sf 1

1996: sf d. Stich [11] 6–3 6–3, MaliVai Washington 7–6 6–3, lost Becker [4] 7–6 6–3 6–1. **1998: 1r** lost Bjorkman 7–5 6–3.

ATP TOUR CHAMPIONSHIP – Played 2, sf 1

1997: as alt d. Kafelnikov 6–4 6–4. **1998: sf** in rr d. Corretja 7–6 6–7 6–2, Rios 7–5 6–1, lost Rusedski 6–2 6–4; sf lost Moya 6–4 3–6 7–5.

8 KAROL KUCERA (SVK)

Born: Bratislava, 4 March 1974. **Lives:** London, England. **Father:** Karol. **Mother:** Kristina. **Sister:** Karin. **Agent:** Ken Myerson of MS Consulting. **Coach:** Miloslav Mecir, for whom he was once a ball boy; formerly Vladimir Zednik and Branislav Stankovic. **Turned pro:** 1992. **Height:** 6ft 2in (1.88m). **Weight:** 165lb (75kg). **Rankings: 1990:** 862; **1991:** 351; **1992:** 214; **1993:** 181; **1994:** 57; **1995:** 74; **1996:** 63; **1997:** 24; **1998:** 8. **Highest:** 8 (1998).

1998 Prize Money: $1,402,557.
Career Earnings: $2,637,765. **Career Titles:** 4.

Style: One of the best and most consistent returners of serve, whose deceptive, early-ball groundstrokes carry the same sort of disguise that his coach, Miloslav Mecir, used to display. A talented all-rounder, whose tactical awareness makes him a fearsome competitor, he is physically strong and plays well in long matches. His serve and forehand are match-winning strokes, and his excellent volleys allow him to perform well on all surfaces.

CAREER HIGHLIGHTS (year: (titles))
1991: Member of Czech Galea Cup team for 1st of 2 years. **1992:** Won Prague Challenger. **1993:** Enjoyed some success on the Challenger circuit, although he won no title. **1994:** After winning 2 Challenger titles, he reached his 1st main tour qf at St Polten, following with his 1st f at Umag, unseeded. Upset Dosedel en route to qf Bucharest and surprised Bruguera at Moscow. **1995: (1)** *Rosmalen.* Never before having won a match on grass, he won his 1st title on the main tour at Rosmalen, as well as reaching sf Copenhagen, qf Marseille and Toulouse and upsetting Siemerink at Moscow. **1996:** He upset W. Ferreira at Australian Open, surprised M. Chang on the way to sf Long Island, took a set off Sampras at Wimbledon and reached qf Lyon. **1997: (1)** *Ostrava.* Won Ostrava, where his opponents in both sf and f ret after 1s, and was r/u Nottingham (d. Henman) and Stuttgart Mercedes (d. Medvedev, Rios and Bruguera). He also reached sf Copenhagen and Bastad, qf Adelaide (d. Woodforde), Milan, Vienna (d. Kafelnikov) and Stockholm (d. Muster) and upset Ivanisevic at Basle. **1998: (2)** *Sydney, New Haven.* Consistent rather than spectacular, he quietly slipped into the upper echelons with no great fanfare. He began on a positive note by taking the Hopman Cup for SVK with Habsudova and winning Sydney over Henman, unseeded; then at Australian Open, again unseeded, he caused the upset of the tournament by removing Sampras on his way to sf. He followed with the title at New Haven (d. Krajicek and Ivanisevic), which took him into the top 10 1st time. In other tourns he was r/u Stuttgart Mercedes and Vienna, reached sf Antwerp (d. Korda), Hamburg (ret with a badly blistered big toe), Amsterdam (where he was r/u doubles with Hrbaty) and GS Cup, plus qf US Open (d. Agassi) and Umag. He qualified for his 1st ATP Champ, but won no match there.

PRINCIPAL 1998 RESULTS – won 2, r/u 2, sf 5 (detailed Grand Slam results follow)
won Sydney (d. Schalken 6–2 6–2, Kiefer 5–2 ret, Stoltenberg 6–3 2–6 6–4, Tebbutt 4–6 7–6 6–0, Henman 7–5 6–4), **won** New Haven (d. Gumy 6–3 6–3, Siemerink 6–4 7–5, Raoux 3–6 6–3 6–1, Krajicek 7–6 6–4, Ivanisevic 6–4 5–7 6–2); **r/u** Stuttgart Mercedes (d. Dosedel 6–1 6–1, Gustafsson 6–1 6–3, Ulihrach 6–4 6–4, Rios 6–1 6–7 6–4, lost Kuerten 4–6 6–2 6–4), **r/u** Vienna (d. W. Ferreira 6–4 3–6 7–5, Haas 7–5 6–4, Bjorkman 6–3 6–2, Rusedski 7–6 6–4, lost Sampras 6–3 7–6 6–1); **sf** Australian Open, **sf** Antwerp (d. Van Herck 6–7 6–4 6–2, Ulihrach 6–1 6–1, Korda 3–6 6–4 6–2, lost Rusedski 6–4 6–3), **sf** Hamburg (d. Fromberg 6–2 6–1, Clavet 6–2 6–2, Muster 6–3 6–2, lost A. Costa 3–0 ret), **sf** Amsterdam (d. Safin 6–2 3–6 7–6, Larsen 7–5 6–3, Hrbaty 6–2 6–1, lost Fromberg 6–1 6–7 6–2), **sf** GS Cup (d. Arazi 6–4 6–4, Ivanisevic 5–7 6–4 8–6, lost Agassi 7–6 6–7 2–6 7–5 6–0). **DOUBLES:** (with Hrbaty) **r/u** Amsterdam (lost Eltingh/Haarhuis 6–3 6–2).

CAREER GRAND SLAM RECORD
AUSTRALIAN OPEN – Played 4, sf 1
1995: 1r lost Fleurian 3–6 6–3 5–7 7–6 6–2. **1996: 3r** d. D. Adams 7–5 6–0 6–6, W. Ferreira [9] 6–1 6–3 6–0, lost Ondruska 6–2 4–6 6–3 6–0. **1997: 2r** d. Haarhuis 6–1 3–6 6–3 4–6 6–4, lost Ivanisevic 6–4 6–2 6–2. **1998: sf** [unseeded] d. Bruguera [10] 3–6 7–6 6–1, Vacek 7–6 6–7 2–6 6–0 6–1, Nestor 6–2 7–6 6–1, Fromberg 6–2 3–6 6–2 7–5, Sampras [1] 6–4 6–2 6–7 6–3, lost Korda [6] 6–1 6–4 1–6 6–2.

FRENCH OPEN – Played 6

1993: 1r lost Kafelnikov 6–3 6–4 6–4. **1994: 2r** d. Ruah 6–2 6–3 6–1, lost Boetsch 6–2 6–2 6–3. **1995: 1r** lost Voinea 6–2 6–2 6–3. **1996: 3r** d. Carretero 3–6 7–6 6–4 6–2 6–2, M. Norman 7–6 6–4 6–7 4–6 6–2, lost Courier [7] 6–7 7–5 6–4 5–4 ret. **1997: 1r** lost Boetsch 6–1 6–1 6–4. **1998: 1r** [seed 9] lost Woodbridge 1–6 6–2 6–4 6–3.

WIMBLEDON – Played 5

1994: 1r lost B. Gilbert 6–3 7–6 4–6 6–2. **1995: 2r** d. Ondruska 6–1 6–4 7–5, lost Krickstein 6–0 7–6 7–6. **1996: 3r** d. Alami 6–3 6–3 6–3, B. Black 4–6 6–1 5–7 6–3 6–3, lost Sampras [1] 6–4 6–1 6–7 7–6. **1997: 1r** lost Rosset 7–5 6–3 6–2. **1998: 1r** [seed 15] lost Voltchkov 7–6 6–3 6–4.

US OPEN – Played 5, qf 1

1994: 1r lost Petchey 6–4 7–6 6–3. **1995: 1r** lost Arriens 6–4 7–6 6–2. **1996: 1r** lost Bjorkman 6–2 5–7 7–6 7–5. **1997: 1r** lost M. Norman 6–7 6–4 6–2 6–3. **1998: qf** [seed 9] d. Campbell 6–4 6–2 6–4, Golmard 7–5 6–3 6–0, Voinea 7–5 6–3 6–2, Agassi [8] 6–3 6–3 6–7 1–6 6–3, lost Sampras [1] 6–3 7–5 6–4.

OLYMPIC RECORD

1996: (Atlanta) 2r d. Tomaschevich 6–3 2–6 6–0, lost Agassi [1] 6–4 6–4.

CAREER DAVIS CUP RECORD

1994: May – *Zone 3 Round-robin SVK d. MLT 3–0 in SVK (Clay).* R2 d. S. Schranz 6–3 6–0. *Zone 3 Round-robin SVK d. SUD 3–0 in SVK (Clay).* R2 d. M. Badalla 6–1 6–1. *Zone 3 Round-robin SVK d. TUR 3–0 in SVK (Clay).* R2 d. A. Karagoz 6–3 6–2; R3 (with B. Stankovic) d. B. Albayrak/M. Azkara 6–3 6–0. *Zone 3 Round-robin SVK d. TUN 3–0 in SVK (Clay).* R2 d. A. Nabli 6–0 6–0). **1995: April** – *Zone 2 1r SVK d. GBR 5–0 in SVK (Clay).* R2 d. M. MacLagan 6–3 6–2 4–6 7–5; R3 (with J. Kroslak) d. N. Broad/T. Henman 3–6 6–4 6–4 2–6 6–2; R4 d. Henman 6–4 6–2. **July** – *Zone 2 2r EGY d. SVK 3–2 in EGY (Clay).* R1 d. A. Ghoneim 4–6 2–6 6–1 6–2 6–3; R3 (with B. Galik) lost T. El Sawy/H. Hemeda 7–6 1–6 6–4 1–6 6–4; R4 lost El Sawy 5–7 6–2 7–5 6–4. **1996: May** – *Zone 2 1r SVK d. YUG 4–1 in YUG (Clay).* R1 d. N. Djordjevic 6–1 6–3 7–5; R3 (with J. Kroslak) lost D. Vemic/N. Zimonjic 7–5 6–4 2–6 2–6 6–3; R4 d. B. Vujic 7–5 6–1 6–4. **July** – *Zone 2 2r SVK d. POR 5–0 in SVK (Carpet).* R2 d. N. Marques 7–6 2–6 6–4 6–4; R3 (with Kroslak) d. E. Couto/B. Mota 6–3 6–2 6–2; R5 d. Couto 6–4 6–1. **September** – *Zone 2 sf SVK d. POL 4–1 in POL (Carpet).* R2 d. A. Skrzypczak 6–1 6–1 6–1; R3 (with Kroslak) d. M. Chmela/M. Gawlowski 6–1 6–4 6–7 6–0; R4 d. B. Dabrowski 6–7 6–3 6–4. **1997: April** – *Zone 1 2r SVK d. ISR 3–1 in SVK (Clay).* R2 d. N. Behr 6–1 6–3 6–0; R3 (with D. Hrbaty) lost Behr/E. Ehrlich 6–4 3–6 6–3 7–6; R4 d. E. Ran 6–2 6–3 6–2. **September** – *World Group Qualifying SVK d. CAN 4–1 in CAN (Carpet).* R1 d. D. Nestor 6–3 6–3 7–6; R4 d. S. Lareau 5–7 6–2 6–4 6–3. **1998: May** – *World Group 1r SWE d. SVK 3–2 in SVK (Clay).* R2 d. M. Tillstrom 1–6 6–1 6–2 6–4; R4 lost M. Norman 6–3 4–6 6–3 3–6 6–3. **September** – *World Group Qualifying SVK d. ARG 3–2 in ARG (Clay).* R2 lost H. Gumy 6–1 6–1 6–4; R3 (with D. Hrbaty) lost L. Arnold/L. Lobo 6–3 6–4 6–4; R4 d. F. Squillari 6–3 6–3 3–6 6–7 6–4.

GRAND SLAM CUP RECORD – Played 1, sf 1

1998: sf [unseeded] d. Arazi 6–4 6–4, Ivanisevic [4] 5–7 6–4 8–6, lost Agassi 7–6 6–7 2–6 7–5 6–0.

ATP TOUR CHAMPIONSHIP – Played 1

1998: 4th in rr lost Kafelnikov 6–7 6–3 6–2, lost Sampras 6–2 6–1, lost Moya 6–7 7–5 6–3.

9 GREG RUSEDSKI (GBR)

Born: Montreal, Canada, 6 September 1973. **Lives:** London.
Father: Tom. **Mother:** Helen.
Agent: ProServ. **Coaches:** Sven Groeneveld. Formerly coached by Brad Schultz, Keith Diepraam, Louis Cayer, Scott Brooke, Brian Teacher and Tony Pickard; also works with sports psychologist Wayne Halliwell.
Fitness trainer: Pat Etcheberry. **Turned pro:** 1991.
Height: 6ft 4in (1.93m). **Weight:** 190lb (86kg).

Rankings: 1989: 1103; **1990:** 679; **1991:** 603; **1992:** 158; **1993:** 48; **1994:** 117; **1995:** 38; **1996:** 48; **1997:** 6; **1998:** 9.
Highest: 4 (6 October 1997).

1998 Prize Money: $1,860,437. **Career Earnings:** $4,498,251. **Career Titles:** 7.

Style: Featuring the fastest timed serve in the world (149 mph at Indian Wells in 1998), his game is built around this fierce left-handed delivery in which he has tremendous confidence. Confidence is also growing in his improving groundstrokes. The forehand is his main attacking weapon while topspin backhand drives and returns of serve have been added to his natural slice on that wing. For a tall man he moves well and is refining his net game, which now combines subtlety with power.

CAREER HIGHLIGHTS (year: (titles))
A British passport-holder, he switched to play for Great Britain in May 1995, qualifying through his English mother and having satisfied residency qualifications. He had not played D Cup for Canada: although he was named in the squad in 1992, he was injured, and by 1993 had decided he wanted to qualify to play for GBR. Girlfriend Lucy Connor. Canadian Under-14 and Under-18 Champ and won 6 Nat Jun titles. **1991:** Won Wimbledon Jun doubles with Alami and began to make his mark on the Challenger circuit. **1992:** Won Newcastle Challenger. **1993: (1)** *Newport.* Burst into prominence on the main tour when he reached qf Osaka after qualifying, then won his 1st tour title at Newport, unseeded. He was also r/u Beijing and appeared in sf Tokyo Seiko (d. W. Ferreira, Krajicek and M. Chang back-to-back) and shot up the rankings from 130 to 55 in 2 weeks in Oct. **1994:** Although he could not maintain the standards of the previous year, he reached qf Hong Kong and Manchester and upset Muster at Indianapolis. **1995: (1)** *Seoul.* A month after being accepted to play for Great Britain, he upset Forget at Wimbledon, where he was unseeded. Won Seoul (d. Volkov), r/u Coral Springs and reached sf Basle, qf Jakarta, San Jose and Memphis (d. Krickstein) and upset Krajicek at Cincinnati. **1996: (1)** *Beijing.* At Beijing in Oct. he won his 1st singles title since switching his allegiance to GBR. He extended Becker to 5s 1r Australian Open, upset Gustafsson at Olympics, and on his way to sf Sydney upset Krajicek 1r and beat Arriens 6–0 6–0 in 29 mins 2r. He reached the same stage Nottingham (d. A. Costa) and Singapore, as well as qf Adelaide, San Jose, Seoul, Stockholm (d. W. Ferreira) and Bournemouth, where he won the doubles with Goellner. At Wimbledon, however, he was restricted by a hip injury, which caused him to withdraw from D Cup tie v NIGH. **1997: (2)** *Nottingham, Basle.* The highlight of an extraordinary year came at US Open, where he had never before won a match, but now became the 1st British player since Fred Perry in 1936 to reach f there. A throat infection had prevented him from practising the day before his sf v Bjorkman, in which he recovered from 2–1 sets down to win on his 24th birthday. On 15 Sept. he became the 1st ever British player to break into the top 10 since rankings began, and on 6 Oct., after winning Basle, he rose to No. 4. On 27 Jan. he had fallen as low as 56, but immediately upset Siemerink and Enqvist en route to f Zagreb, where he extended Ivanisevic to fs tb. At San Jose a week later, he upset M. Chang and Agassi and took a set off Sampras in f, before retiring 0–5 down in 2s with a wrist injury, which kept him out of LIPC. Played a 20-minute tb against Ivanisevic sf Queen's, eventually losing 18–16. At Wimbledon he upset Philippoussis before winning a 5s encounter v Stark 11–9, going on to reach qf, unseeded. These results, plus the title at Nottingham, a 6th f at Vienna (where the loss of 3s tb saw him squander a 2-sets-to-0 lead v Ivanisevic), sf GS Cup, Queen's, New Haven (d. A. Costa and Krajicek), Bournemouth and Stockholm and qf Boston and Paris Open, took him past Henman as No. 1 GBR. Despite

crediting his then coach Brian Teacher for much of his success – especially improved return of serve and more relaxed attitude on court – he split with him end Sept. and began working with Tony Pickard, Edberg's former coach. He became the 1st GBR player to qualify for the season-ending champs, but his heavy schedule took its toll and, after losing his 1st 2 rr matches, he pulled out with a hamstring injury. **1998: (2)** *Antwerp, Paris Open.* The high point of a see-saw year was a superb week in autumn when he won Paris Open, taking the title with a 1st defeat of Sampras, in which he played the best tennis of his life. The low point had come in summer as he split acrimoniously with Pickard over a breakdown in communication just before Wimbledon, when Rusedski disappeared to Turkey to seek physiotherapy and holistic treatment for an ankle injury suffered at Queen's. Against the advice of Pickard and trainer Steve Green, he attempted to play Wimbledon still carrying the injury, but succeeded only in causing further damage, which forced him to retire during his 1st match. He was sidelined for 8 weeks, dropping out of the top 10, but returned to action in time for US Open. There he showed great courage in a 5s battle v W. Ferreira, twice surviving mp, although he eventually lost his 3rd 5s battle of that tourn to Siemerink. The effects of his work with Sven Groeneveld, a confidant as much as a coach, were apparent in his added self-belief, and he enjoyed an impressive autumn. Despite his heroics at Paris Open, though, when Gustafsson beat him sf Stockholm and Kafelnikov moved ahead by winning Moscow, he looked likely to have narrowly missed out on both a year-end place in the top 10 and a berth at ATP Champ. However, as 1st alternate at ATP Champ he made the most of his opportunity when Agassi withdrew injured after one match – and took himself back into the top 10 by beating both A. Costa, himself an alternate, and Henman, who had already qualified for sf. Elsewhere, Antwerp was his 1st title of the year, and he was r/u Split, Indian Wells (d. Moya) and Toulouse, as well as reaching sf Long Island, Vienna (d. Kafelnikov, Muster and Rafter) and Stockholm, plus qf Qatar, Rotterdam, Indianapolis and Stuttgart Eurocard (d. Rafter). He was bitterly disappointed that when Britain qualified for WT Cup for 1st time in 20 years, Henman's refusal to play denied him the rare chance to compete, although both players were expected to be available in 1999. In D Cup his 1st-day win v Paes was a vital part of GBR win over IND that lifted them back into World Group.

PRINCIPAL 1998 RESULTS – won 2, r/u 3, sf 3 (detailed Grand Slam results follow)
won Antwerp (d. Arazi 7–6 3–6 6–3, Raoux 7–6 3–6 7–6, Johansson 6–3 4–6 6–4, Kucera 6–4 6–3, Rosset 7–6 3–6 6–1 6–4), **won** Paris Open (d. Kiefer 6–3 6–4, Stoltenberg 7–6 6–4, Gustafsson 6–3 6–2, Kafelnikov 6–3 4–6 6–4, Sampras 6–4 7–6 6–3); **r/u** Split (d. Pozzi 6–3 6–4, Kroslak 6–4 6–3, Damm 6–1 6–4, Rosset 6–7 7–6 7–6, lost Ivanisevic 7–6 7–6), **r/u** Indian Wells (d. Spadea 4–6 6–3 6–4, Moya 6–3 7–5, Enqvist 2–6 7–6 6–4, Muster 7–6 6–1, lost Rios 6–3 6–7 7–6 6–4), **r/u** Toulouse (d. Goellner 7–6 7–6, Medvedev 6–4 6–3, Clement 6–4 6–1, Kiefer 6–4 6–1, lost Siemerink 6–4 6–4); **sf** Long Island (d. M. Norman 6–3 6–4, Meligeni 6–2 7–6, Vacek 6–2 6–3, lost Rafter 6–4 7–5), **sf** Vienna (d. Kafelnikov 6–3 3–6 7–6, Muster 6–4 6–3, Rafter 6–3 7–6, lost Kucera 7–6 6–4), **sf** Stockholm (d. Haas 6–1 6–4, Spadea 6–1 6–4, Nestor 7–6 1–6 6–3, lost Johansson 7–5 7–6).

CAREER GRAND SLAM RECORD
AUSTRALIAN OPEN – Played 5
1994: 1r lost Lendl [15] 6–4 7–6 7–5. **1995: 3r** d. Volkov 6–4 6–2 6–3, Kulti 7–6 4–6 2–6 6–2 6–3, lost Agassi [2] 6–2 6–4 6–2. **1996: 1r** lost Becker [4] 6–4 3–6 4–6 6–3 6–3. **1997: 1r** lost Mantilla [14] 6–4 5–7 7–5 6–2. **1998: 3r** [seed 5] (d. Witt 7–6 6–3 6–4, Stark 6–4 6–4 1–0 ret, lost Woodbridge 7–6 6–4 6–2.
FRENCH OPEN – Played 4
1994: 3r d. Goellner 7–6 6–3 7–6, Volkov 7–5 6–3 2–6 6–3, lost Medvedev [4] 2–6 6–3 6–4 3–6 6–2. **1995:** Did not play. **1996: 2r** d. Doyle 6–2 1–6 7–5 2–6 7–5, lost Stich [15] 6–3 7–5 6–3. **1997: 1r** lost M. Norman 6–3 6–2 3–6 4–6 9–7. **1998: 1r** [seed 5] lost Van Herck 6–4 6–4 6–4.
WIMBLEDON – Played 6, qf 1
1993: 1r lost Edberg [2] 7–6 6–4 6–7 7–6. **1994: 2r** d. Kulti 6–3 6–4 6–2, lost Bergstrom 6–4 6–4 5–7 7–6. **1995: last 16** [unseeded] d. Simian 6–3 6–3 6–3, Forget [16] 1–6 7–6 7–6 7–5, Delaitre 6–7 6–4 6–4 7–6, lost Sampras [2] 6–4 6–2 7–5. **1996: 2r** d. Nestor 7–6 7–6 6–2, lost Steven 7–6 4–6 7–6 6–2. **1997: qf** [unseeded] d. Philippoussis [7] 7–6 7–6 6–3, Stark 4–6 6–7 6–4 6–3 11–9, Richardson 6–3 6–4 6–4, Reneberg 7–6 6–4 7–6, lost Pioline 6–4 4–6 6–4 6–3. **1998: 1r** [seed 4] lost M. Draper 4–6 6–2 5–4 ret.
US OPEN – Played 5, r/u 1
1994: 1r lost Holm 6–3 6–2 3–6 7–5. **1995: 1r** lost Winnink 7–6 6–4 6–7 6–1. **1996: 1r** lost Dreekmann 6–2 6–4 6–2. **1997: r/u** [unseeded] d. Wheaton 6–2 6–3 6–3, Ondruska 7–6 6–4 6–1, Knippschild 7–6 6–3 6–1, Vacek 7–6 6–2 6–2, Krajicek 7–5 7–6 7–6, Bjorkman 6–1 3–6 3–6 6–3 7–5, lost Rafter [13] 6–3 6–2 4–6 7–5. **1998: 3r** [seed 6] d. W. Ferreira 4–6 7–6 5–7 7–6 6–4, Ulihrach 4–6 6–3 4–6 6–2 7–5, lost Siemerink 1–6 6–4 5–7 6–2 6–4.

OLYMPIC RECORD
1996: (Atlanta) 3r d. Frana 4–6 7–5 6–3, Gustafsson [13] 6–7 7–6 6–3, lost Bruguera 7–6 6–3.

CAREER DAVIS CUP RECORD
1995: July – *Zone 2 Relegation GBR d. MON 5–0 in GBR (Grass).* R1 d. Ch. Boggetti 6–2 6–2 7–6; R4 d. S. Graeff 6–0 6–1. **1996: May** – *Zone 2 1r GBR d. SLO 4–1 in GBR (Carpet).* R1 d. Borut Urh 6–1 6–4 6–7 6–3; R3 (with N. Broad) d. G. Krusic/Urh 7–6 6–2 6–3. R4 d. I. Bozic 6–1 6–2 6–2. **September** – *Zone 2 sf GBR d. EGY 5–0 in GBR (Grass).* R1 d. T. El Sawy 6–2 6–4 7–5; R5 d. A. E. S. Ghoneim 6–4 6–2. **1997: July** – *Zone 1 Relegation GBR d. UKR 3–2 in UKR (Clay).* R2 lost A. Medvedev 6–1 6–1 2–6 6–2; R3 (with T. Henman) d. Medvedev/D. Poliakov 6–1 6–4 7–6; R5 d. A. Rybalko 7–5 6–3 6–3. **1998: April** – *Zone 1 2r GBR d. UKR 5–0 in GBR (Carpet).* R1 d. A. Rybalko 6–4 6–0 6–4; R3 (with T. Henman) d. A. Medvedev/Rybalko 6–4 7–5 7–6; R4 d. Medvedev 6–1 6–4. **September** – *World Group Qualifying GBR d. IND 3–2 in GBR (Hard).* R1 d. L. Paes 2–6 6–3 3–6 6–2 11–9.

GRAND SLAM CUP RECORD – Played 1, sf 1
1997: sf [seed 4] d. Woodbridge 4–6 6–1 7–5, Kafelnikov 6–7 6–3 6–1, lost Sampras [1] 3–6 7–6 7–6 6–2.

ATP TOUR CHAMPIONSHIP – Played 2
1997: 4th in rr lost Rafter 4–6 6–3 6–4, lost Sampras 6–4 7–5, withdrew. **1998: as alt** in rr d. A. Costa 7–6 6–1, Henman 6–2 6–4.

The tall Swiss No.1 Marc Rosset was Greg Rusedski's victim in the final at Antwerp, the first of two tournament successes in 1998 for the world's fastest server. (Stephen Wake)

10 RICHARD KRAJICEK (NED)

Born: Rotterdam, 6 December 1971. **Lives:** Monte Carlo, Monaco. **Father and Mother:** Were Czech immigrants. **Girlfriend:** Daphne Deckers. **Daughter:** Emma (born 26 March 1998).
Agent: Advantage International. **Coach:** Rohan Goetzke.
Turned pro: 1989.
Height: 6ft 5in (1.96m). **Weight:** 190lb (85kg).

Rankings: 1989: 392; **1990:** 129; **1991:** 40; **1992:** 10; **1993:** 15; **1994:** 17; **1995:** 11; **1996:** 7; **1997:** 11; **1998:** 10.
Highest: 7 (25 November 1996).

1998 Prize Money: $1,219,624.
Career Earnings: $8,054,963. **Career Titles:** 13.

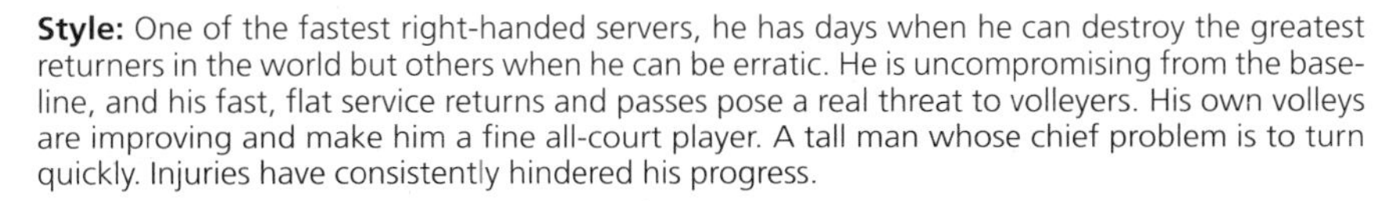

Style: One of the fastest right-handed servers, he has days when he can destroy the greatest returners in the world but others when he can be erratic. He is uncompromising from the baseline, and his fast, flat service returns and passes pose a real threat to volleyers. His own volleys are improving and make him a fine all-court player. A tall man whose chief problem is to turn quickly. Injuries have consistently hindered his progress.

CAREER HIGHLIGHTS (year: (titles))
He twice won Dutch Nat 12s and 14s. His career suddenly took off after he decided to change from two-handed to one-handed backhand at age 12. **1990:** Won Verona and Casablanca Challengers. **1991: (1)** *Hong Kong*. Reached last 16 Australian Open, unseeded, then at Hong Kong in April he won his 1st tour title in his 1st f. At New Haven he upset Edberg en route to qf (where he retired) and Hlasek and J. McEnroe in reaching sf Toulouse. At US Open held 2 mps v Lendl 1r before losing in 5s, and in doubles reached 2 f with Siemerink, winning Hilversum. **1992: (2)** *Los Angeles, Antwerp*. Upset Lendl 1r Sydney NSW Open, then made a tremendous impact at Australian Open where, unseeded, he surprised Chang and Stich before being forced to def sf v Courier with tendinitis of right shoulder. He followed by winning Los Angeles and Antwerp (d. Courier), r/u Tokyo Suntory (d. Stich and Edberg) and sf Sydney Indoor (d. Lendl again). These performances saw him become the 1st Dutchman in the top 20 since Tom Okker in 1976 and at end of year he broke into the top 10. His late surge at Antwerp gained him the last place at his 1st ATP Champ when Agassi and Lendl were forced to withdraw, but he won only 1 match there (v Chang). **1993: (1)** *Los Angeles*. At French Open he outlasted 3 opponents in consec. 5s encounters before falling to Courier in 4s, and at US Open he saved 2 mps in 3s v Martin in a match lasting 5 hr 10 min. Won Los Angeles, r/u Stuttgart Eurocard (d. Becker) and upset Agassi en route to qf LIPC, where he won the doubles with Siemerink. Out of action from Nov. with tendinitis in both knees. **1994: (3)** *Barcelona, Rosmalen, Sydney Indoor*. He returned from injury to play doubles only at Estoril in March; then in his 1st singles tourn at Barcelona in April, he won his 1st ever CC title, upsetting Bruguera on the way. Won 1st GC title at Rosmalen in June and in Sept. won Sydney Indoor for his 3rd title on a different surface during the year. This last success and sf finish at Los Angeles took him back to the top 20. **1995: (2)** *Stuttgart Eurocard, Rotterdam*. Upset W. Ferreira and Stich on his way to the title at Stuttgart Eurocard, took Rotterdam the following week, and upset Kafelnikov and Becker to reach f New Haven. He also reached sf Adelaide and 7 more qf, including Essen, where he upset Becker again. Won Rosmalen doubles with Siemerink. **1996: (1)** *WIMBLEDON*. The climax of his career came at Wimbledon, where, unseeded owing to his previous disappointing performances there and record of injury, he became the 1st Dutchman to win a GS title. He upset Stich and Sampras and lost only one set along the way, returning to top 10. The rest of the year was less spectacular, with no other title, but r/u showings at Italian Open (unseeded, d. W. Ferreira) and Los Angeles, sf ATP Champ and qf appearances at French Open, Antwerp, Hong Kong, Tokyo Japan Open, Rosmalen, New Haven and Singapore. He also upset Bruguera at LIPC and was the only player to take a set off Kafelnikov at French Open. After he withdrew 3r Australian Open with a back injury, Agassi remarked that every time Krajicek thought about tennis, he was mys-

teriously injured; thereafter he changed his attitude, became less worried about getting injured and thus relieved the pressure on himself. However, it was not all plain sailing and he retired from qf Singapore in Oct. with a right knee injury and pulled out of Stockholm with recurring knee problems. At GS Cup he lost tamely 1r to MaliVai Washington, his victim in Wimbledon f, and immediately sought a solution to his knee problem, undergoing surgery to repair torn meniscus on 9 Dec. **1997: (3)** *Rotterdam, Tokyo Japan Open, Rosmalen.* After returning in Feb., he was in fine form, winning Rotterdam (d. Enqvist), Tokyo Japan Open and Rosmalen (d. Chang). A lean patch followed, though, and by US Open, where he d. Mantilla on his way to qf, he had slipped far enough down the rankings to be unseeded. But he picked up again, upsetting Sampras in ss en route to f Stuttgart Eurocard and returning to top 10 for a while. He also reached sf Vienna and qf Dubai, Monte Carlo, Los Angeles, Montreal, New Haven and Paris Open, where he withdrew with a knee injury – the 10th time in his career he'd pulled out mid-tourn. **1998: (2)** *Stuttgart Eurocard, St Petersburg.* His best performance came in Oct. at Stuttgart Eurocard, where he put together an amazing run to d. Agassi, Ivanisevic, Sampras and Kafelnikov and return to the top 10 for season's end. One of the few players to have the measure of Sampras, he beat the No. 1 there for a 5th time in 7 meetings, seriously denting Sampras' hopes of finishing the year at No. 1 for a record 6th successive season. Once again the highlight in GS was at Wimbledon, where he recovered from 2 sets to love down v Ivanisevic in sf only to lose the match 15–13 5s. In the process he aggravated a knee injury, which then caused him to withdraw from US Open and miss GS Cup, and it became obvious that he would require surgery for a torn cartilage. Having unexpectedly qualified for ATP Champ after Stuttgart, he had been undecided whether to delay the surgery in order to play there, but eventually the decision was made for him when he was forced to retire yet again 5–2 up fs v Rosset at Paris Open and he had surgery the following week. In other tourns across the year he won St Petersburg, was r/u Toronto (d. Kafelnikov and Agassi) and reached sf Marseille, Rotterdam, Monte Carlo (d. Korda), New Haven and qf Rome (d. Kafelnikov) and Den Bosch (withdrew with knee injury). He had missed Australian Open for personal reasons, rather than because of injury, and was hoping to recover in time to play there in 1999.

PRINCIPAL 1998 RESULTS – won 2, r/u 1, sf 5 (detailed Grand Slam results follow)
won St Petersburg (d. Kroslak 6–1 4–6 6–3, Prinosil 6–7 6–4 6–2, Vacek 7–6 6–1, Johansson 6–4 6–4 Rosset 6–4 7–6), **won** Stuttgart Eurocard (d. M. Norman 6–4 6–1, Agassi 6–3 6–4, Ivanisevic 7–6 7–6, Sampras 6–7 6–4 7–6, Kafelnikov 6–4 6–3 6–3); **r/u** Toronto (d. Nainkin 6–4 6–4, O'Brien 3–6 6–2 6–3, Kafelnikov 6–4 6–4, Agassi 4–6 7–5 6–2, lost Rafter 7–6 6–4); **sf** Marseille (d. Alami 6–4 6–3, Grosjean 6–3 5–5 ret, Vacek 4–6 6–4 6–4, lost Enqvist 6–3 6–7 6–3), **sf** Rotterdam (d. Van Scheppingen 7–5 6–4, Voinea 6–2 6–2, Rusedski 3–6 7–6 7–6, lost Siemerink 6–4 4–6 6–4), **sf** Monte Carlo (d. Viloca 6–4 6–2, Ulihrach 6–4 6–0, Korda 4–6 7–6 6–1, lost Moya 4–6 6–1 6–4), **sf** Wimbledon, **sf** New Haven (d. M. Washington 7–5 6–4, Levy 6–2 6–4, Henman 5–7 6–2 7–6, lost Kucera 7–6 6–4).

CAREER GRAND SLAM RECORD

AUSTRALIAN OPEN – Played 5, sf 1

1991: last 16 [unseeded] d. Santoro 2–6 6–1 6–2 6–3, Korda 4–6 7–6 6–3 6–4, Cahill 6–7 6–3 6–3 7–6, lost Caratti 6–3 6–4 6–7 3–6 6–4. **1992: sf** [unseeded] d. Saceanu 6–3 6–3 6–3, Grabb 6–2 7–6 6–1, Chang [14] 6–4 6–1 5–7 1–6 6–3, Bergstrom 7–5 7–6 6–3, Stich [4] 5–7 7–6 6–7 6–4 6–4, lost Courier def. **1993: 2r** [seed 9] d. Wahlgren 6–1 6–2 6–1, lost Witsken 6–4 1–6 6–1 6–4. **1994:** Did not play. **1995: 2r** [seed 16] d. Marsh 6–1 6–1 6–1, lost Ondruska 7–6 6–4 6–3. **1996: 3r** [seed 11] d. Stoltenberg 6–1 6–3 6–2, Fetterlein 6–2 6–4 6–4, lost Fleurian 4–6 6–3 2–2 ret'd. **1997–98:** Did not play.

FRENCH OPEN – Played 8, sf 1, qf 1

1991: 2r d. Altur 6–0 6–4 6–1, lost Stich 6–7 7–6 6–3 6–2. **1992: 3r** [seed 12] d. Clavet 7–6 6–7 6–3 7–6, Gustafsson 6–3 6–4 4–6 6–1, lost Perez 6–4 6–1 6–1. **1993: sf** [seed 12] d. Bergstrom 7–5 6–3 7–5, Rosset 6–2 6–3 6–1, Arrese 2–6 6–2 6–2 6–7 6–2, C. Costa 7–5 3–6 6–3 5–7 10-8, Novacek [13] 3–6 6–3 3–6 6–3 6–4, lost Courier 6–1 6–7 7–5 6–2. **1994: 3r** [seed 16] d. Novacek 6–1 7–5 7–5, Champion 6–3 6–3 4–6 6–2. **1995: 2r** [seed 15] d. Sinner 6–4 6–3 6–3, lost Ilie 3–6 6–3 6–4 2–6 6–4. **1996: qf** [seed 13] d. Noszaly 4–6 6–4 6–4 7–6, Carbonell 6–2 4–6 7–6 6–2, Woodbridge 7–5 6–2 6–2, Bjorkman 6–3 6–2 6–4, lost Kafelnikov [6] 6–3 6–4 6–7 6–2. **1997: 3r** [seed 6] d. Draper 7–6 6–2 6–1, Ulihrach 6–2 3–6 6–2 6–3, lost Rafter 6–3 4–6 6–4 6–2. **1998: 3r** [seed 10] d. Lapentti 6–4 6–4 6–7 7–6, Gilbert 7–5 6–4 6–1, lost Pioline 6–3 6–2 7–5.

WIMBLEDON – Played 8, won 1, sf 1

1991: 3r d. Ruah 5–7 6–1 3–6 6–3 6–4, Larsson 6–3 6–4 6–3, lost Agassi [5] 7–6 6–3 7–6. **1992: 3r** [seed 11] d. de Jager 7–5 6–1 6–2, Haarhuis 7–6 6–3 6–1, lost Boetsch 4–6 7–6 3–6 7–6 6–2. **1993: last 16** [seed 9] d. Kulti 6–4 6–3 6–4, Eltingh 6–4 6–4 6–4, Tieleman 6–2 7–5 5–7 6–2, lost Agassi [8] 7–5 7–6 7–6. **1994: 1r** lost Cahill 6–3 6–2 5–7 7–6. **1995: 1r** [seed 12] lost Shelton 7–6 6–3 6–3. **1996: won** [unseeded] d. J.

Sanchez 6–4 6–3 6–4, Rostagno 6–4 6–3 6–3, Steven 7–6 6–7 6–4 6–2, Stich [10] 6–4 7–6 6–4, Sampras [1] 7–5 7–6 6–4, Stoltenberg 7–5 6–2 6–1, MaliVai Washington 6–3 6–4 6–3. **1997: last 16** [seed 4] d. Craca 7–5 6–2 6–4, Pavel 3–6 6–4 6–7 6–3 6–3, Rikl 6–4 6–3 7–5, lost Henman [14] 7–6 6–7 7–5 6–4. **1998: sf** [seed 9] d. Steven 6–3 7–6 4–6 6–2, Pescariu 6–1 6–3 6–2, Kiefer 6–4 7–6 7–6, W. Ferreira 6–3 6–3 7–5, Sanguinetti 6–2 6–3 6–4, lost Ivanisevic [14] 6–3 6–4 5–7 6–7 15–13.

US OPEN – Played 8, qf 1

1991: 1r lost Lendl [5] 3–6 2–6 6–4 7–6 6–0. **1992: last 16** [seed 15] 7–6 6–7 6–3 6–4, Markus 4–6 2–6 7–6 6–3 6–1, Woodforde 6–1 6–3 6–2, lost Edberg [2] 6–4 6–7 6–3 3–6 6–4. **1993: last 16** [seed 10] d. Rikl 6–3 6–3 6–1, Berasategui 6–1 6–2 6–4, Martin 6–7 4–6 7–6 6–4 6–4, lost Medvedev [8] 6–4 3–6 6–1 7–6). **1994: 2r** d. Siemerink 7–6 6–4 6–7 6–7 6–4, lost C. Costa 4–6 7–6 6–3 1–6 7–6. **1995: 3r** [seed 12] d. Novacek 6–3 6–4 6–4, Gimelstob 6–4 6–2 6–4, lost Tebbutt 6–3 3–6 6–7 7–6 7–6. **1996: 1r** [seed 5] lost Edberg 6–3 6–3 6–3. **1997: qf** [unseeded] d. W. Black 6–4 6–2 6–2, Filippini 7–6 6–2 7–5, Corretja [6] w/o, Mantilla [12] 7–5 6–3 6–4, lost Rusedski 7–5 7–6 7–6. **1998: 3r** [seed 5] d. Clement 6–3 6–1 6–1, O'Brien 6–1 7–6 6–2, lost Johansson 6–7 5–4 ret.

OLYMPIC RECORD

Has never competed.

CAREER DAVIS CUP RECORD

1991: December – *World Group Qualifying NED d. MEX 5–0 in MEX (Clay).* R3 (+ J. Siemerink) d. L. Lavalle/ J. Lozano 6–2 6–3 6–4). **1992: September** – *World Group Qualifying NED d. URU 4–1 in NED (Carpet).* R 1 d. D. Perez 6–2 6–4 7–6; R4 d. M. Filippini 7–5 7–6 6–3. **1993: July** – *World Group qf SWE d. NED 4–1 in NED (Clay).* R2 lost M. Larsson 6–3 6–4 6–4; R4 lost M. Gustafsson 6–4 7–5. **1994: July** – *World Group qf USA d. NED 3–2 in NED (Hard).* R1 lost J. Courier 6–4 6–3 6–3; R4 d. Sampras 2–6 7–5 7–6 7–5. **1995: February** – *World Group 1r NED d. SUI 4–1 in SUI (Clay).* R2 lost J. Hlasek 4–6 6–1 6–3 6–4; R4 d. L. Manta 6–4 6–4 6–2. **March** – *World Group qf GER d. NED 4–1 in NED (Hard).* R2 lost M. Stich 3–6 6–4 6–4 6–4; R4 lost B. Becker 6–3 6–4 3–6 6–1. **September** – *World Group Qualifying NED d. NZL 4–1 in NED (Hard).* R2 lost A. Hunt 7–6 3–6 4–6 4–1 ret.

GRAND SLAM CUP RECORD – Played 2, qf 1

1992: qf [seed 8] d. E. Sanchez 6–3 6–2, lost Stich 7–6 7–5. **1996: 1r** [seed 7] lost MaliVai Washington 6–1 6–2.

ATP TOUR CHAMPIONSHIP – Played 2, sf 1

1992: 3rd in rr lost Courier 6–7 7–6 7–5, d. Chang 2–6 6–3 7–6, lost Ivanisevic 6–4 6–3. **1996: sf** in rr d. M. Chang 6–4 6–4, lost Ivanisevic 6–4 6–7 7–6, d. Muster 7–6 6–7 6–3; sf lost Becker 6–7 7–6 6–3.

REMAINING MEN'S BIOGRAPHIES

The following biographies show the players' progress each year in the four Grand Slam Championships. It is shown thus: A (Australian Open), F (French Open), W (Wimbledon), US (US Open), followed by the round reached, or '–' if a player did not compete.

HICHAM ARAZI (MAR)

Born Casablanca, 19 October 1973; lives Monte Carlo, Monaco; LH; 5ft 9in; 143lb; turned pro 1993; career singles titles 1; final 1998 ATP ranking 36; 1998 prize money $458,735; career prize money $1,108,489.

Coached by Alberto Castellani. Moved to France at age 2. **1991:** (1093). **1992:** (533). **1993:** (340) Began to make his mark on the satellite circuits. **1994:** (185). **1995:** (148) A –, F –, W –, US 1. Reached 3 f on the Challenger circuit. **1996:** (78) A –, F –, W 2, US 1. Won 2 Challenger titles and on the main tour reached qf Palermo and Toulouse, breaking into the top 100. **1997:** (38) A 1, F qf, W 1, US 1. He began the year with his 1st sf at Qatar, then delighted the home crowds at Casablanca by winning his 1st career singles title there. At French Open he upset Rios to reach qf, unseeded, and reached the same stage Zagreb, Hamburg (d. Muster), Bologna and Tashkent. Played 2 doubles f, but won no title. **1998:** A 4, F qf, W 3, US 1. He made his mark in GS again (unseeded each time) with upsets of Philippoussis at Australian Open, Berasategui en route to qf French Open, where he extended Pioline to 5s, and Moya at Wimbledon. He also reached qf Casablanca and Indianapolis (d. Mantilla) as well as upsetting Kafelnikov at Dubai, Korda at Rome and Ivanisevic at Long Island. He played GS Cup, but lost 1r to Kucera. **1998 HIGHLIGHTS – SINGLES: Australian Open last 16** [unseeded] (d. Dreekmann, 7–6 6–3 6–2, Philippoussis [seed 15] 1–6 6–2 4–6 6–1 9–7, Clavet 4–6 6–4 3–6 6–2 6–1, lost Sampras [seed 1] 7–6 6–4 6–4), **French Open qf** [unseeded] (d. Novak 6–0 6–2 7–6, Escude 6–3 6–4 6–2, Zabaleta 6–4 0–6 6–4 7–6, Berasategui [seed 16] 6–2 6–4 3–6 6–3, lost Pioline 3–6 6–2 7–6 4–6 6–3), **Wimbledon 3r** (d. Richardson 6–4 2–6 6–3 6–2, Moya [seed 5] 4–6 6–4 6–3 6–4, lost Larsson 6–3 6–3 6–2), **US Open 1r** (lost Rafter [seed 3] 4–6 4–6 6–3 6–3 6–1). **CAREER HIGHLIGHTS – SINGLES: French Open – qf 1997** (d. Dreekmann 6–3 6–4 6–2, Woodbridge 6–4 7–5 6–2, Larsson 6–2 6–3 7–5, Rios 6–2 6–1 5–7 7–6, lost Bruguera 4–6 6–3 6–2 6–2), **qf 1998.**

BORIS BECKER (GER)

Born Leimen, 22 November 1967; lives Munich; RH; 6ft 3in; 187lb; turned pro 1984; career singles titles 49; final 1998 ATP ranking 69; 1998 prize money $389,470; career prize money $24,905,117.

Wife Barbara Feltus (married 17 December 1993); son Noah Gabriel (born 18 January 1994). Played both tennis and soccer as a boy, giving up soccer for tennis at the age of 12. **1982:** Won first of three consecutive German Nat Jun Champs. **1983:** (563) R/u Orange Bowl 16s. **1984:** (65) A qf, F –, W 3, US –. R/u US Open Jun and in the men's game made a surprise appearance in qf Australian Open. **1985:** (6) A 2, F 2, W won, US 4. Won Queen's and then Wimbledon, at 17 yrs 7 mths becoming youngest men's titlist, the first German, and the first unseeded player to capture the world's most prestigious event. He also won Cincinnati and closed the year with D Cup wins over Edberg and Wilander in f as FRG lost 3–2 to SWE. Won inaugural Young Masters, was r/u to Lendl in ATP Masters and was voted ATP Most Improved Player. **1986:** (2) A –, F qf, W won, US sf. Won Wimbledon again in even more convincing fashion, dismissing Lendl in f without loss of a set and still younger than any other champ. Through the year he also won Chicago, Toronto, Sydney Indoor, Tokyo Indoor and Paris Open, closing the year with streak of 3 straight tourns and 21 matches in a row before losing Masters f to Lendl. Won Young Masters in Jan. and Dec. **1987:** (4) A 4, F sf, W 2, US 4. Split with coach Gunther Bosch Jan. At end of year Bob Brett became coach and Frank Dick his trainer. Missed LIPC suffering from a form of typhus which seemed to weaken him and restrict his performance for several weeks, and he was further restricted by tendinitis of left knee for last 5 months of year. Won only 3 titles all year and, going for his 3rd consec. Wimbledon singles title, fell 2r to Doohan. After US Open took time off in Germany with his family, returning refreshed in Oct. and qualified for Masters, where he extended Lendl to 3s, but lost his Young Masters title. **1988:** (4) A –, F 4, W r/u, US 2. He was again plagued by injury problems, withdrawing from Toronto and the Olympics and playing Masters only 10 days after his foot had been removed from plaster following injury in Stockholm sf. However, he still won titles at Indian Wells, WCT Dallas, Queen's, Indianapolis, Tokyo Indoor, Stockholm and finished the year by taking his 1st Masters title in a thrilling f v Lendl, as well as leading FRG to victory over SWE in D Cup f. **1989:** (2) A 4, F sf, W won, US won. The high spot of his year was a convincing third title at Wimbledon where he beat Lendl in a stirring sf and Edberg in f. This was followed by his first triumph at US Open, where he d. Lendl in f, and r/u spot at Masters to Edberg. He won in Milan and on clay reached f Monte Carlo and sf French Open. He also won Philadelphia and Paris Open, as well as leading FRG to victory in WT Cup and D Cup. Voted ATP Player of the Year. **1990:** (2) A qf, F 1, W r/u, US sf. His 1r loss to Ivanisevic at French Open was his 1st at that stage in GS. From 9 f he won Brussels, Stuttgart Indoor, Indianapolis, Sydney Indoor and Stockholm, strongly challenging Edberg for the No. 1 spot at end of year. He gave a stunning performance at Stockholm, beating the Swede in f and taking his indoor match record since 1988 to 77–5. However, in f Paris Open he had to withdraw v the same player with a pulled left thigh, which was still undergoing treatment when he began play on 2nd day of ATP World

Champ, where he fell to Agassi in sf. **1991:** (3) A won, F sf, W r/u, US 3. Reached No. 1 for the 1st time on 28 Jan. after winning his 1st Australian Open; his 5 hr 22 min match in 3r with Camporese was the longest ever played there and lasted only 1 min less than the marathon at Wimbledon in 1969 between Gonzales and Pasarell. He was overtaken again by Edberg on 18 Feb., after retiring v Cherkasov at Brussels with a right thigh strain, but returned to the top after his appearance in f Wimbledon, where he lost in ss to countryman Stich. His disappointing 3r loss to Haarhuis at US Open saw him slip again to No. 2, and by year's end he had fallen to 3 behind Courier, having narrowly failed to qualify for sf ATP World Champ in Frankfurt. However, he played his best ever CC season, although he again failed to win his 1st title on that surface, losing f Monte Carlo to Bruguera, who had also beaten him at Barcelona. Withdrew from Italian Open with back trouble, but played French Open, where he reached sf for 3rd time. He outlasted Edberg in 5s f Stockholm in Oct. for only his 2nd title of the year; also reached f Indianapolis and sf Brussels and Cincinnati. **1992:** (5) A 3, F –, W qf, US 4. In Jan. he dropped out of top 3 1st time since April 1989, and in losing 3r Australian Open to J. McEnroe, he fell from top 5 for 1st time since 1988, eventually slipping as low as 9 in Nov. However, working since Sept. with Gunther Bresnik, he found his best form again and finished the year in tremendous style by taking ATP World Champ, surviving a close sf v Ivanisevic and sweeping Courier aside in f. Missed French Open to avoid aggravating a thigh strain and lost qf Wimbledon to Agassi. His titles at Brussels, Rotterdam, Basle, Paris Open and ATP Champ were all indoors and he also reached sf Hamburg and Indianapolis. In doubles he won an Olympic gold medal and Monte Carlo with Stich, plus Brussels with J. McEnroe. **1993:** (11) A 1, F 2, W sf, US 4. After winning singles and doubles at Qatar (d. Edberg and Ivanisevic), he put behind him 1r loss at Australian Open to Jarryd and took Milan, but was then forced to withdraw from sf Stuttgart Eurocard with a viral infection which kept him out 2 months. He suffered a disastrous CC season and split with Bresnik a week before French Open. He took the title at Indianapolis and also reached sf Antwerp, but failed to qualify for IBM/ATP World Champ for 1st time since 1985 and dropped out of the top 10 for the 1st time in 8 years. By then his mind was on the expected birth of his child in Jan. Playing the GS Cup 1st time he lost 1r to W. Ferreira and then announced that, having split from his boyhood friend and practice partner, Eric Jelen, he had appointed Nick Bollettieri as his coach. **1994:** (3) A –, F –, W sf, US 1. Inspired by the birth of his son in Jan. and giving Bollettieri much of the credit for putting the enjoyment back in his game, he moved up the rankings again. When he successfully defended his title at Milan in Feb., he ended his longest spell without a title (21 tourns), then upset Stich at Stuttgart Eurocard. He returned to the top 10 after enjoying unusual success on clay at Italian Open, where he beat Ivanisevic before falling tamely in f to Sampras. He was surrounded by controversy at Wimbledon, where he illegally received physiotherapy during a toilet break and was frequently accused of unacceptable gamesmanship on his way to sf, where he fell to Ivanisevic. At Los Angeles he won his 1st title in US for four years, and at Stockholm he was superb, becoming the only player all year to beat the current top 3 in 1 tourn (Stich, Sampras and Ivanisevic), to qualify for IBM/ATP World Champ. He seemed in peak form there, unbeaten in rr and beating Sampras in ss for 2nd time in a fortnight, but when they met in f, Sampras had the better of him in 4s. However, Becker's performance that week took him past Ivanisevic and Bruguera to the No. 3 spot. Refused to play D Cup sf v RUS, in which GER were defeated, but had stated his willingness to play in f. In GS Cup he beat W. Ferreira, his conqueror of 1993, but was thrashed by Ivanisevic. **1995:** (4) A 1, F 3, W r/u, US –. In summer he split with Bollettieri, who left to concentrate on his tennis academy. Until he finished the year on a high note by winning IBM/ATP Champ, his only title had been Marseille, although he was r/u 3 times. He reached that stage at Milan, then, still looking for a 1st CC title, he failed to capitalise on a 2-set lead over Muster at Monte Carlo. He continued to excite at Wimbledon, where he beat Pioline only 9–7 5s in qf, recovered from a set down v Agassi to upset the top seed, and took 1s in f v Sampras before letting the match slip away. Suffered back problems at Essen, but recovered in time to progress to f Paris Open the following week and also appeared in sf US Open, Stuttgart Eurocard, Indian Wells, Queen's and Basle, reaching qf or better in 11 of 16 tourns across the year. Thrilled the German crowds on his way to victory at IBM/ATP Champ, with a few scares along the way: having lost to Sampras in rr, he needed to beat Kafelnikov in ss to go through to the knockout rounds, and several times looked to have failed. **1996:** (6) A won, F –, W 3, US –. At Australian Open, where he took his 1st GS title since 1991, he was stretched to 5s in 1r by Rusedski and in 2r by Johansson, against whom he recovered from 2 sets down. He missed French Open after suffering a torn thigh muscle in WT Cup rr v Rosset, but was back in action at Queen's, where he lost no set and won his 100th GC match on the way to his 7th GC title. However, disaster struck again at Wimbledon, where, executing a late and awkward return of serve v Godwin, he suffered a badly sprained tendon in his right wrist and was forced to withdraw, also missing US Open and having already declined to play Olympics. Returning in Sept., he withdrew 1r Bucharest with a recurrence of the injury, but later in the month at Basle was encouraged to survive uninjured through a 3s match v Ulihrach, although he lost 2r to Novak. Then in Oct. he won his 2nd title of the year at Vienna, surviving 4s in f against Siemerink, and at the end of the month he beat Sampras in 5s to take the title at Stuttgart Eurocard – surprised and delighted to have made such a rapid recovery. Sampras was again his opponent in a truly memorable match in f ATP Champ, when both men were at their glorious best and Becker was eventually beaten 6–4 5s after a match of 3 tbs. Earlier he had beaten Sampras in another close encounter in their rr match. He also reached sf Antwerp and Munich and moved back into the top 3 after Stuttgart. The year ended on a high note when he beat the holder Ivanisevic in f GS Cup on home soil in Munich – his first success there. **1997:** (63) A 1, F –, W qf, US –. He was restricted all year by injury, withdrawing from Qatar with an ankle injury and being plagued throughout by recurring wrist problems. After losing qf Wimbledon to Sampras, he announced that that would be his last Wimbledon, although he would continue to play ATP tour. He withdrew US Open following the death of his manager, Axel Meyer-Wolden, so Wimbledon turned out to be his last GS tourn of all. Sf Halle marked his best performance and he dropped out of the top 10 for 1st time since 1994. By end of year, he had dropped out of top 50 for 1st time since 1984 and was intending to play only very occasionally on ATP tour. He was appointed GER D Cup manager for 1998, and became actively involved in development of younger German players, including Kiefer, who had replaced him in Oct. as No. 1 in GER. **1998:** A –, F –, W –, US –. Playing only a handful of tourns (and doubles in D Cup), he dropped out of top 100 on 6 July for 1st time since December 1984, but returned the following week after upsetting Pioline, Mantilla and Rios on his way to f Gstaad. He also reached qf Monte Carlo (d. Rusedski and Philippoussis) and Stuttgart Mercedes (d. Pioline and Mantilla) and upset Moya at Stuttgart Eurocard. He played doubles with Prinosil in winning GER WT Cup team, winning all their matches. **1998 HIGHLIGHTS – SINGLES: r/u** Gstaad (d. Bastl 6–4 6–7 7–5, Pioline 7–6 7–5, Mantilla 6–4 6–4, Rios 6–4 7–6, lost Corretja 7–6 7–5 6–3). **CAREER HIGHLIGHTS – SINGLES: Australian Open – won 1991** (d. Bates 6–4 6–2 6–3, Vajda 6–4 6–1 6–3, Camporese 7–6 7–6 0–6 4–6 14–12, Ferreira 6–4 7–6 6–4, Forget 6–2 7–6 6–3, P. McEnroe 7–6 6–3 4–6 4–6 6–2, Lendl 1–6 6–4 6–4 6–4), **won 1996** (d. Rusedski 6–4 3–6 4–6 6–3 6–3, Johansson 4–6 3–6 6–2 6–1 6–4, Larsson 7–6 6–3 6–3, Steven 1–6 6–4 6–3 6–2, Kafelnikov 6–4 7–6 6–1, Woodforde 6–4 6–2 6–0, M. Chang 6–2 6–4 2–6 6–2); **Wimbledon – won 1985** [unseeded] (d. Pfister 4–6 6–3 6–2 6–4, Anger 6–0 6–1 6–3, Nystrom 3–6 7–6 6–1 4–6 9–7, Mayotte 6–3 4–6 6–7 7–6 6–2, Leconte 7–6 3–6 6–3 6–4, Jarryd 2–6 7–6 6–3 6–3, Curren 6–3 6–7 7–6 6–4), **won 1986** (d. Bengoechea 6–4 6–2 6–1, Tom Gullikson 6–4 6–3 6–2, McNamee 6–4 6–4 4–6 6–4, Pernfors 6–3 7–6 6–2, Mecir 6–4 6–2 7–6, Leconte 6–2 6–4 6–7 6–3, Lendl 6–4 6–3 7–5), **won 1989** (d. Shelton 6–1 6–4 7–6, Matuszewski 6–3 7–5 6–4, Gunnarsson 7–5 7–6 6–3, Krickstein 6–4 6–4 7–5, Chamberlin 6–1 6–2 6–0, Lendl 7–6 6–7 2–6 6–4 6–3, Edberg 6–0 7–6 6–4), **r/u 1988** (d. Frawley 6–3 6–1 6–2, Novacek 6–3 6–4 6–4, Giammalva 7–6 6–4 6–4, Annacone 6–3 6–4 6–4, Cash 6–4 6–3 6–4, Lendl 6–4 6–3 6–7 6–4, lost Edberg 4–6 7–6 6–4 6–2), **r/u 1990** (d. Herrera 7–6 7–6 7–5, Masur 6–7 6–2 6–3 6–2, Goldie 6–3 6–4 4–6 7–5, Cash 7–6 6–1 6–4, Gilbert 6–4 6–4 6–1, Ivanisevic 4–6 7–6 6–0 7–6, lost Edberg 6–2 6–2 3–6 3–6 6–4), **r/u 1991** (d. Steeb 6–4 6–2 6–4, Lundgren 7–6 7–5 7–5, Olhovskiy 6–1 6–4 3–6 6–3, Bergstrom 6–4 6–7 6–1 7–6, Forget 6–7 7–6 6–2 7–6, Wheaton 6–4 7–6 6–5, lost Stich 6–4 7–6 6–4), **r/u 1995** (d. Alvarez 6–3 6–3 6–4, Apell 6–3 3–6 6–1 6–2, Siemerink 2–6 6–2 6–2 6–4, D. Norman 7–6 6–3 6–4, Pioline 6–3 6–1 6–7 6–7 9–7, Agassi 2–6 7–6 6–4 7–6, lost Sampras 6–7 6–2 6–4 6–2), **sf 1993** (d. Goellner 4–6 6–3 6–2 6–4, Volkov 7–6 6–1 6–3, Hlasek 6–3 3–6 6–2 6–3, Leconte 6–4 6–4 3–6 6–3, Stich 7–5 6–7 6–7 6–2 6–4, lost Sampras 7–6 6–4 6–4), **sf 1994** (d. Wheaton 6–2 6–4 6–3, Thoms 7–6 6–2 6–4, Frana 7–6 6–4 1–6 6–3, Medvedev 6–7 7–5 7–6 6–7 7–5, Bergstrom 7–6 6–4 6–3, lost Ivanisevic 6–2 7–6 6–4); **US Open – won 1989** (d. Pate 6–1 6–3 6–1, Rostagno 1–6 6–7 6–3 7–6 6–3, Mecir 6–4 3–6 6–4 6–3, Pernfors 5–7 6–3 6–2 6–1, Noah 6–3 6–3 6–2, Krickstein 6–4 6–3 6–4, Lendl 7–6 1–6 6–3 7–6), **sf 1986** (d. Michibata 6–2 5–7 6–4 6–2, Motta 6–3 6–0 6–2, Casal 7–5 6–4 6–2, Donnelly 6–4 6–3 6–7 6–4, Srejber 6–3 6–2 6–1, lost Mecir 4–6 6–3 6–4 3–6 6–3), **sf 1990** (d. Aguilera 7–5 6–3 6–2, Noah 6–4 6–2 7–6, Carbonell 6–4 6–2 6–2, Cahill 2–6 6–2 6–3 3–6 6–4, Krickstein 3–6 6–3 6–3 6–3, lost Agassi 6–7 6–3 6–2 6–3), **sf 1995** (d. Lopez–Moron 6–1 6–0 6–3, Arriens 6–1 6–3 7–5, Stoltenberg 6–2 4–6 6–0 6–4, Rosset 7–6 6–3 6–3, P. McEnroe 6–4 7–6 6–7 7–6, lost Agassi 7–6 7–6 4–6 6–4); **ATP Champ – won 1988** (d. Wilander 7–6 6–7 6–1, Leconte 6–0 1–0 ret, lost Edberg 7–6 3–6 6–4 in rr, d. Hlasek 7–6 7–6, Lendl 5–7 7–6 3–6 6–2 7–6), **won 1992** (d. Korda 6–4 6–2, Edberg 6–4 6–0, lost Sampras 7–6 7–6 in rr, d. Ivanisevic 4–6 6–4 7–6, Courier 6–4 6–3 7–5), **won 1995** (d. W. Ferreira 4–6 6–2 7–6, lost Sampras 6–2 7–6, d. Kafelnikov 6–4 7–5 in rr, d. Enqvist 6–4 6–7 7–5, d. M. Chang 7–6 6–0 7–6), **r/u 1985** (d. Annacone 3–6 6–3 6–2, Wilander 6–4 4–6 6–3, Jarryd 6–3 6–4, lost Lendl 6–2 7–6 6–3), **r/u 1986** (d. Nystrom 6–1 6–3, Leconte 0–6 6–1 6–1, Wilander 6–3 3–6 6–3 in rr, d. Edberg 6–4 6–4, lost Lendl 6–4 6–4 6–4), **r/u 1989** (d. Gilbert 2–6 6–3 6–4, Agassi 6–1 6–3, Edberg 6–1 6–4 in rr, d. J. McEnroe 6–4 6–4, lost Edberg 2–6 7–6 6–3 6–1), **r/u 1994** (d. Ivanisevic 6–3 3–6 7–6, Sampras 7–5 7–5, Edberg 6–7 6–4 7–5 in rr, d. Bruguera 6–7 6–4 6–1, lost Sampras 4–6 6–3 7–5 6–4), **r/u 1996** (d. Kafelnikov 6–4 7–5, Sampras 7–6 7–6, lost Enqvist 6–3 7–6 in rr, d. Krajicek 6–7 7–6 6–3, lost Sampras 3–6 7–6 7–6 6–7 6–4), **sf 1990** (d. Gomez 4–6 6–3 6–3, Muster 7–5 6–4, Lendl 1–6 7–6 6–4 in rr, lost Agassi 6–2 6–4); **French Open – sf 1987** (d. Perez 6–0 6–1 7–5, Buckley 6–1 4–6 6–3 6–2, Sundstrom 6–1 3–6 6–3 6–1, Arias 5–7 6–3 6–2 6–0, Connors 6–3 6–3 7–5, lost Wilander 6–4 6–1 6–2), **sf 1989** (d. Pugh 6–4 6–2 6–3, Winogradsky 7–6 7–5 6–3, Bates 7–5 6–1 6–2, Perez Roldan 3–6 6–4 6–2 4–6 7–5, Berger 6–3 6–4 6–1, lost Edberg 6–3 6–4 5–7 3–6 6–2), **sf 1991** (d. Arrese 6–2 7–5 6–2, Woodbridge 5–7 1–6 6–4 6–4 6–4, Masur 6–3 6–3 6–2, Clavet 7–6 6–4 6–3, Chang 6–4 6–4 6–2, lost Agassi 7–5 6–3 3–6 6–1). **CAREER HIGHLIGHTS – DOUBLES:** (with Stich) **Olympics – won gold medal 1992** (d. Ferreira/Norval 7–6 4–6 7–6 6–3).

ALBERTO BERASATEGUI (ESP)

Born Bilbao, 28 June 1973; lives Andorra; RH; 5ft 8in; 145lb; turned pro 1991; career singles titles 14; final 1998 ATP ranking 21; 1998 prize money $645,760; career prize money $4,229,877.
Coached by Javier Duarte. Attended school in US and trained at the Harry Hopman Academy in Saddlebrook, Fla., from age 13 to 16. **1990:** (495) Began playing the Spanish satellite circuit. **1991:** (301) European Jun champ and a member of winning Sunshine Cup and Galea Cup teams, he enjoyed some success on the Spanish satellite circuit and tested the waters on the Challenger circuit. **1992:** (115) A –, F 1, W –, US –. Reached sf Casablanca after qualifying. **1993:** (36) A –, F 2, W –, US 2. Broke into top 50 after r/u appearance at Umag (d. Gustafsson), followed with same stage Athens and then in Nov. took his 1st tour title at Sao Paulo and appeared in f Buenos Aires the next week. He reached 3 more qf and upset Bruguera at Stuttgart

Mercedes. **1994:** (8) A –, F r/u, W –, US 1. Upset Edberg and Courier on his way to the title at Nice and moved into the top 20 in May. The climax of his year came when, unseeded, he swept to f French Open without dropping a set, although Bruguera was too much for him at that stage. He broke into the top 10 in Aug. after winning Stuttgart Mercedes, and then in autumn, concentrating on CC tourns to give himself the best chance of earning a berth in his 1st IBM/ATP Champ, he won 4 more consec. titles. That took his tally of titles in the year to 7, second only to the 10 won by Sampras. However, they all came on clay – he won only 2 matches all year on surfaces other than clay – and his dismal showing at IBM/ATP Champ, where he won only 8 games in 3 matches in the weakest group, called into question the true ability of a player who can play effectively on only one surface. **1995:** (33) A –, F 3, W –, US –. He could not maintain his standards on his favourite surface in the European CC season, failing to pass 2r in 9 tourns, and had dropped out of the top 10 in May before another disappointing performance at French Open. At Oporto in June he won his 1st title since Oct. 1994, and reached f Montevideo at end of year, but otherwise his best showings were 7 qf. **1996:** (19) A –, F 3, W –, US 2. He returned to top 20 with the titles at Bologna, Kitzbuhel and Bucharest, as well as sf finishes at Scottsdale, Casablanca, Stuttgart and Santiago, qf Barcelona and Gstaad and an upset of Krajicek at Paris Open. At Casablanca v Filippini, he played and won the longest known singles game in ATP history – it lasted 20 minutes and included 28 deuces. **1997:** (23) A 3, F 1, W –, US 1. Palermo was his only title on the main tour, with Zagreb and Cairo on the Challenger circuit. At Marbella he was r/u both singles and doubles, and he also reached sf Barcelona (where he won the doubles with Burillo) and Rome (d. Rafter and Kafelnikov), plus qf Indian Wells, Estoril, Hamburg (d. Rios), Bologna, Gstaad and Stuttgart Mercedes. **1998:** A qf, F 4, W –, US 1. He began the year in style, upsetting Rafter at Australian Open, where he was unseeded, taking the title at Estoril and removing Kafelnikov on the way to his 2nd f of year at Barcelona. He followed with sf Monte Carlo and Rome, and also reached qf Dubai and Bournemouth (where he was r/u doubles with Arthurs), but once the European CC season was over, he faded away again. **1998 HIGHLIGHTS – SINGLES: Australian Open qf** [unseeded] (d. Braasch 3–6 6–3 6–4 6–3, Medvedev 6–4 7–6 6–4, Rafter [seed 2] 6–7 7–6 6–2 7–6, Agassi 3–6 3–6 6–2 6–3 6–3, lost Rios [seed 9] 6–7 6–4 6–4 6–0), **French Open last 16** [seed 16] (d. Stafford, 4–6 7–6 6–3 6–1, Solves 6–3 3–6 6–3 6–4, Hrbaty 6–7 6–3 7–5 7–5, lost Arazi 6–2 6–4 3–6 6–3), **US Open 1r** [seed 15] (lost Muster 7–6 6–2 6–3); **won** Estoril (d. Munoz 6–4 6–4, Dewulf 6–4 5–7 7–5, Marin 3–6 6–4 6–3, Moya 6–1 6–1, Muster 3–6 6–1 6–3); **r/u** Barcelona (d. Meligeni 6–2 6–1, A. Costa 6–4 6–4, Kafelnikov 6–4 6–4, Moya 7–6 6–4, lost T. Martin 6–2 1–6 6–3 6–2); **sf** Monte Carlo (d. Woodbridge 6–0 7–5, Vacek 6–0 7–6, Dosedel 3–6 6–3 6–3, Becker 6–7 7–5 6–1, lost Pioline 6–3 0–6 7–6), **sf** Rome (d. Galimberti 6–4 6–2, W. Ferreira 6–3 7–6, Ulihrach 7–6 4–6 6–2, Steven 6–4 6–2, lost A. Costa 6–3 4–6 6–3). **1998 HIGHLIGHTS – DOUBLES:** (with Arthurs) **r/u** Bournemouth (lost Broad/Ulyett 7–6 6–3). **CAREER HIGHLIGHTS – SINGLES: French Open – r/u 1994** [unseeded] (d. W. Ferreira 6–3 ret, Pioline 6–4 7–5 6–3, Kafelnikov 6–3 6–2 6–2, Frana 6–2 6–0 ret, Ivanisevic 6–4 6–3 6–3, Larsson 6–3 6–4 6–1, lost Bruguera 6–3 7–5 2–6 6–1).

MAHESH BHUPATHI (IND)

Born Madras, 7 June 1974; lives Bangalore; RH; 6ft 1in; 183lb; turned pro 1995; career singles titles 0; final 1998 ATP ranking 372 singles, 3 doubles; 1998 prize money $569,960.

Coached by Bob Carmichael. **1992:** (944). **1993:** (532). **1994:** (284). **1995:** (350) A –, F –, W –, US 1. All-American in both singles and doubles at Univ. of Mississippi, where he was No. 3 in singles and No. 1 in doubles, winning NCAA Champ with Hamadeh. Joined IND D Cup squad. **1996:** (418). **1997:** (228) A –, F –, W 1, US –. He formed a successful doubles partnership with Paes, winning the 6 f they played together and qualifying for a first World Doubles Champ. There they squeaked past Lareau/O'Brien in sf before denting their record of f won by losing to Leach/Stark. In mixed, he won French Open with Hiraki. **1998:** A –, F –, W 1, US –. His partnership with Paes continued to flourish as they won 5 of 7 f played to qualify for World Doubles Champ. There, however, a bone spur injury to Paes' hand forced them to withdraw after losing 2 matches, but they still finished the year as No. 2 pairing behind Eltingh/Haarhuis and ahead of Woodbridge/Woodforde. In mixed doubles he was r/u Wimbledon with V. Williams. **1998 HIGHLIGHTS – SINGLES: Wimbledon 1r** (lost Moya [seed 5] 6–4 4–6 6–4 2–6 6–3). **1998 HIGHLIGHTS – DOUBLES:** (with Paes) **won** Qatar (d. Delaitre/Santoro 6–4 3–6 6–4), **won** Dubai (d. Johnson/Montana 6–2 7–5), **won** Chennai (d. Delaitre/Mirnyi 6–7 6–3 6–2), **won** Rome (d. E. Ferreira/Leach 6–4 4–6 7–6), **won** Shanghai (d. Woodbridge/Woodforde 6–4 6–7 7–6); **r/u** Singapore (lost Woodbridge/Woodforde 6–2 6–3). **MIXED DOUBLES:** (with V. Williams) **r/u** Wimbledon (lost Mirnyi/S. Williams 6–4 6–4). **CAREER HIGHLIGHTS – DOUBLES:** (with Paes) **World Doubles – r/u 1997** (lost Leach/Stark 6–3 6–4 7–6). **CAREER HIGHLIGHTS – MIXED DOUBLES:** (with Hiraki) **French Open – won 1997** (d. Galbraith/Raymond 6–4 6–1).

JONAS BJORKMAN (SWE)

Born Vaxjo, 23 March 1972; lives Monte Carlo, Monaco; RH; 2HB; 6ft; 166lb; turned pro 1991; career singles titles 4; final 1998 ATP ranking 24 singles, 8 doubles; 1998 prize money $1,916,237; career prize money $6,134,727.

Coached by Fredrik Rosengren. Former Nat Jun champ. **1991:** (691). **1992:** (331) Began to make his mark on the satellite circuits. **1993:** (95) A –, F –, W –, US 2. Reached qf Kuala Lumpur Salem Open and won 3 Challenger titles, which took him into the top 100. **1994:** (50) A 2, F 3, W 4, US qf. Unseeded at Wimbledon, he took advantage of the removal of Edberg by Carlsen and the Dane's retirement during their encounter next day to reach last 16, and at US Open he upset Edberg himself on his way to qf, again unseeded. Reached sf Schenectady (d. Bruguera) plus qf Marseille, Tel Aviv and Antwerp. In doubles he appeared in his 1st GS f at French Open with Apell and with various partners he won 8 titles from 11 other f. He and Apell won 6 titles on 4 different surfaces during the year, including their 1st World Doubles Champ. Member of victorious SWE D Cup team, winning doubles with Apell. **1995:** (30) A 3, F 1, W 2, US 3. In singles he broke into top 25 after reaching his 1st f at Hong Kong. He also reached sf LIPC and Vienna, plus 4 more qf, and played on winning SWE WT Cup team. He played 5 doubles f, winning 1 with regular partner Apell and 1 each with De Jager and Frana after Apell underwent shoulder surgery in Sept. **1996:** (69) A 4, F 4, W 1, US 3. Although it was a less impressive year in singles, he reached sf Rosmalen (d. Siemerink) and qf US CC and Los Angeles. At Australian Open, where he was unseeded, he upset Martin and extended Agassi to 5s. Played 7 doubles f with 3 different partners, winning Antwerp and New Delhi with Kulti, with whom he qualified for World Doubles Champ, although they did not pass rr. **1997:** (4) In by far his best year to date, he won his 1st career singles title at Auckland and broke into the top 20 after taking his 2nd at Indianapolis. He moved into the top 5 in Oct., progressing to a career-high No. 4 after winning Stockholm. He was consistent through the year with r/u Coral Springs and Paris Open, sf Memphis (d. Haarhuis), Scottsdale (d. Rafter and A. Costa), Indian Wells, Queen's (d. Sampras), Rosmalen, Stuttgart Eurocard, US Open (unseeded, extended Rusedski to 7–5 fs), plus qf Adelaide (losing 15–17 on tb v Tarango), LIPC (d. Rios) and GS Cup (d. Becker). Qualifying for his 1st ATP Champ, he reached sf before losing in ss to Sampras, and finished the year in triumph on winning SWE D Cup team. From 4 doubles f he won Atlanta and was r/u US Open, both with Kulti. **1998:** A qf, F 1, W 3, US qf. Although it was a less spectacular year, he remained consistent, winning his 1st GC title at Nottingham and reaching sf Dubai and Stuttgart Eurocard, plus qf Australian Open, US Open, Munich, Toronto, Boston, GS Cup and Vienna. In doubles he won his 1st GS title at Australian Open with Eltingh and with Rafter won Indian Wells. In D Cup f won doubles with Kulti to give SWE 3–0 win v ITA. **1998 HIGHLIGHTS – SINGLES: Australian Open qf** [seed 4] (d. Beldbradjic 2–6 6–1 6–1 6–1, W. Ferreira 6–7 4–6 6–4 6–2 6–3, Santoro 7–5 6–3 6–4, B. Black 6–2 6–1 6–4, lost Korda [seed 6] 3–6 6–7 6–3 6–4 6–2), **French Open 1r** [seed 7] (lost Muster 6–3 6–3 6–3), **Wimbledon 3r** [seed 11] (d. Dilucia 6–4 3–6 6–3 6–2, Pescosolido 4–6 6–4 6–4 6–2, lost Siemerink 7–6 5–7 2–6 6–4 7–5), **US Open qf** [seed 12] (d. Pioline 6–2 4–6 6–1 6–7 6–2, Stark 6–2 6–3 6–1, Santoro 6–3 6–1 6–2, Siemerink 6–4 2–6 6–2 6–2, lost Rafter [seed 3] 6–2 6–3 7–5); **won** Nottingham (d. Goellner 6–4 6–4, Stafford 6–2 6–3, Prinosil 7–6 6–3, Golmard 6–3 2–6 6–3, B. Black 6–3 6–2); **sf** Dubai (d. Nainkin 6–1 6–3, M. Norman 7–6 6–2, Moya 7–6 6–1, lost Corretja 6–3 6–3), **sf** Stuttgart Eurocard (d. Pozzi 6–4 3–6 6–2, Johansson 2–6 6–4 6–2, Rusedski 6–3 6–2, lost Kafelnikov 6–2 7–5). **1998 HIGHLIGHTS – DOUBLES:** (with Rafter unless stated) (with Eltingh) **won Australian Open** (d. Woodbridge/Woodforde 6–2 5–7 2–6 6–4 6–3); **won** Indian Wells (d. T. Martin/Reneberg 6–4 7–6); **shared** Queen's with Woodbridge/Woodforde. **CAREER HIGHLIGHTS – SINGLES: US Open – sf 1997** (d. Clavet 6–2 6–4 6–4, T. Martin 7–5 6–4 6–0, Kuerten 6–3 6–1 7–5, Draper 6–3 6–3 1–6 7–6, Korda 7–6 6–2 1–0 ret, lost Rusedski 6–1 3–6 3–6 6–3 7–5), **qf 1994** [unseeded] (d. Stark 6–2 6–2 7–5, O'Brien 6–2 6–3 6–4, Edberg [seed 5] 6–4 6–4 6–3, Renzenbrink 3–6 6–3 6–2 6–7 6–3, lost Stich [seed 4] 6–4 6–4 6–7 6–3), **qf 1998**; **ATP Champ – sf 1997** (lost Kafelnikov 6–3 7–6, d. Bruguera 6–3 6–1, d. M. Chang 6–4 7–5 in rr, lost Sampras 6–3 6–4); **Australian Open – qf 1998**. **CAREER HIGHLIGHTS – DOUBLES:** (with Apell unless stated) **World Doubles Champ – won 1994** (d. Woodbridge/Woodforde 6–4 4–6 4–6 7–6 7–6); **Australian Open –** (with Eltingh) **won 1998; French Open – r/u 1994** (lost B. Black/Stark 6–4 7–6); **US Open –** (with Kulti) **r/u 1997** (lost Kafelnikov/Vacek 7–6 6–3).

BYRON BLACK (ZIM)

Born Harare, 6 October 1969, and lives there; RH; 2HF; 2HB; 5ft 10in; 155lb; turned pro 1991; career singles titles 1; final 1998 ATP ranking 28; 1998 prize money $517,743; career prize money $3,677,784.

Coached by Brett Stephens. Wife Fiona (married 14 December 1996). Brother Wayne also plays and they competed together in Olympic doubles. Sister Cara is a prominent junior and has begun to play the women's circuit. Learned to play tennis barefoot on his father's avocado plantation. Won All-African Jun Champs aged 15 and was 1st beneficiary of GS Development Fund to qualify for GS Cup. **1988:** Gold medallist in singles and doubles at All-Africa Games. **1989:** Won NCAA doubles title with Amend. **1990:** (453) Won Arthur Ashe Sportsmanship award. **1991:** (122) An All-American 3 times in singles and 4 times in doubles, he helped USC to nat team title over Georgia. On the Challenger circuit he won Winnetka and Madeira and was voted Newcomer of the Year. **1992:** (143) A 1, F 1, W 2, US 1. Upset Krajicek 1r Singapore. **1993:** (81) A 3, F –, W 3, US 3. In singles he reached sf New Haven, upset Lendl at Queen's and surprised Washington on his way to qf Vienna, as well as winning Wellington Challenger. In doubles he reached 8 f with 5 different partners, winning 6 titles. **1994:** (67) A 1, F 1, W 1, US 3. Reached sf Washington (d. W. Ferreira) and Newport, qf Antwerp (d. Yzaga) and upset Martin at LIPC. In doubles with Stark he won French Open, was r/u Australian Open and won 2 more titles from a total of 9 f with him and 1 with D. Adams. Qualified with Stark for his 1st World Doubles Champ and teamed with his brother Wayne to beat Hlasek/Rosset in D Cup. **1995:** (40) A 1, F 2, W 2, US qf. He made his mark at US Open where, unseeded, he upset Enqvist and Stich on his way to qf. Reached sf Johannesburg, Nottingham and Newport, qf Tokyo Seiko (d. Bruguera) and Moscow and won Bombay Challenger. Played 4 doubles f with different partners, winning Bologna with Stark and Moscow with Palmer. **1996:** (44) A 2, F 1, W 2, US 1. He began the year with his 1st career singles f at Adelaide and followed in April with his 1st title at Seoul. He was also r/u New Delhi and reached sf Beijing and qf

Philadelphia, Newport and Moscow (d. Rosset). From 7 doubles f, he won 4 with Connell, with whom he was also r/u Wimbledon. They qualified together for World Doubles Champ, where they were the only pairing to win all their rr matches, but lost sf to Woodbridge/Woodforde. **1997:** (77) A 1, F 2, W 3, US 1. Although he did not pass qf all year, he reached that stage at Sydney, Philadelphia, Scottsdale (d. Rios), Indian Wells (d. A. Costa), Orlando, Los Angeles and Beijing. **1998:** A 4, F 2, W 3, US 3. He moved back into top 30 with r/u Hong Kong Salem Open (where he won the doubles with O'Brien), Tokyo Japan Open and Nottingham, sf Auckland and Queen's (d. Bjorkman), and qf Los Angeles and Indianapolis. Other notable upsets included Mantilla at Australian Open, where he was unseeded, and Rafter at St Polten. **1998 HIGHLIGHTS – SINGLES: Australian Open last 16** [unseeded] (d. Mantilla [seed 14] 6–4 6–0 4–6 6–4, Pozzi 6–2 5–0 ret, Campbell 6–4 6–0 6–2, lost Bjorkman [seed 4] 6–2 6–1 6–4), **French Open 2r** (d. Clement 6–4 6–1 6–2, lost Mantilla [seed 15] 6–2 6–2 7–6), **Wimbledon 3r** (d. Fromberg 7–5 3–6 3–6 7–6 6–2, Gambill 7–5 6–4 7–5, lost Henman [seed 13] 6–4 6–4 3–6 7–5), **US Open 3r** (d. Spadea 6–4 6–1 6–2, Vicente 7–6 6–1 7–5, lost Corretja [seed 7] 6–3 4–6 6–2 7–6); **r/u** Hong Kong Salem Open (d. Dreekmann 6–7 7–5 6–2, Vinck 6–1 6–2, Pozzi 6–4 6–0, Lareau 6–7 7–5 7–6, lost Carlsen 6–2 6–0), **r/u** Tokyo Japan Open (d. Stark 3–6 7–6 6–4, Burgsmuller 6–4 6–2, Caratti 6–3 6–4, Dreekmann 6–2 6–3, Vacek 6–3 7–5, lost Pavel 6–3 6–4), **r/u** Nottingham (d. Lapentti 6–0 6–2, Canas 7–6 6–4, Pozzi 7–5 6–2, Sargsian 6–4 6–2, lost Bjorkman 6–3 6–2); **sf** Auckland (d. Gaudenzi 6–1 6–3, MaliVai Washington 6–0 6–4, Vinck 6–4 2–6 7–5, lost Rios 6–1 6–3), **sf** Queen's (d. Canas 6–2 5–7 6–3, Gambill 5–7 6–4 6–4, Bjorkman 6–3 4–6 6–3, Macphie 7–5 6–1, lost Tieleman 3–6 6–3 6–2). **1998 HIGHLIGHTS – DOUBLES:** (with O'Brien) **won** Hong Kong Salem Open (d. Godwin/Ketola 7–5 6–1). **CAREER HIGHLIGHTS – SINGLES: US Open – qf 1995** unseeded (d. Boetsch 7–6 6–3 6–3, Enqvist 6–4 6–4 3–6 6–3, Bjorkman 6–3 7–6 6–1, Stich 6–4 6–4 3–6 2–6 6–3, lost Sampras 7–6 6–4 6–0). **CAREER HIGHLIGHTS – DOUBLES:** (with Stark unless stated) **French Open – won 1994** (d. Apell/ Bjorkman 6–4 7–6); **Australian Open – r/u 1994** (lost Eltingh/Haarhuis 6–7 6–3 6–4 6–3); (with Connell) **Wimbledon – r/u 1996** (lost Woodbridge/Woodforde 4–6 6–4 6–3 6–2).

MICHAEL CHANG (USA)

Born Hoboken, NJ, 22 February 1972; lives Henderson, Nev.; RH; 2HB; 5ft 8in; 145lb; turned pro 1988; career singles titles 33; final 1998 ATP ranking 29; 1998 prize money $1,164,314; career prize money $17,451,053.

Coached by his brother, Carl. **1987:** (163) A –, F –, W –, US 2. At 15 yrs 6 mths he was the youngest player to compete in men's singles at US Open since 1918, and was the youngest ever to win a match in GS tourn, having been granted a wild card after winning US 18s at Kalamazoo. At 15 yrs 7 mths was youngest to win a pro tourn at Las Vegas Challenger and was the youngest ever GP semi-finalist at Scottsdale. **1988:** ((30) A –, F 3, W 2, US 4. At 16 yrs 4 mths was the youngest for 60 years to win a match in Wimbledon main draw, and when he won his 1st title at San Francisco at 16 yrs 7 mths, he was youngest to win a SS event and second-youngest after Krickstein to win a GP title. **1989:** (5) A –, F won, W 4, US 4. At the French Open aged 17 yrs 3 mths, he became the youngest male winner of a GS tourn and the 1st American since Trabert in 1955 to win that title. In 5s of his 4r match v Lendl, he was so badly affected with cramp that he had to serve underarm. He also won Wembley and was r/u Los Angeles, qualifying for Masters 1st time, although he failed to win a match there. Became the youngest to play D Cup for USA, making his debut v PAR, and the youngest to break into top 5. **1990:** (15) A –, F qf, W 4, US 3. Out until March with stress fracture of cup of left hip suffered Dec. 1989. He did not reach the heights of the previous year, but won his 1st HC title at Canadian Open, was r/u Los Angeles and Wembley and reached sf Washington and GS Cup, as well as playing in winning US D Cup team. **1991:** (15) A –, F qf, W 1, US 4. Although he reached sf Memphis, Tokyo Suntory and Paris Open (d. Edberg) and played 7 more qf, he had to wait until Nov. before winning his 1st title of the year at Birmingham, following with r/u to Wheaton in GS Cup. **1992:** (6) A 3, F 3, W 1, US sf. Returned to top 10 1st time since July 1991 after winning Indian Wells, following with LIPC (d. Sampras and Courier) and San Francisco (d. Courier again). Was also r/u Hong Kong and appeared in sf Tokyo Suntory (losing both times to Courier) and reached same stage Cincinnati, Long Island, Tokyo Seiko (losing all 3 to Lendl) and US Open. There he survived 5s matches v Washington and W. Ferreira, but lost a 3rd over the same length v Edberg. Qualified for ATP World Champ, but won no match there. Wore spectacles on court 1st time at Gstaad in July, switching from contact lenses after suffering build-up problems. **1993:** (8) A 2, F 2, W 3, US qf. He beat Agassi and Edberg back-to-back to win Cincinnati in Aug., but enjoyed his greatest success in Asia, where he won Jakarta, Osaka, Kuala Lumpur Salem Open and Beijing. A member of the winning US World Team Cup squad, he was r/u Los Angeles and Long Island (d. Edberg) and reached 4 more sf to qualify for IBM/ATP World Champ where he won only match 1 (v Courier) in rr. **1994:** (6) A –, F 3, W qf, US 4. After winning Jakarta in Jan., he took a 3-month break, missing Australian Open, to work on fitness and strength. He returned to take 5 more titles at Philadelphia, Hong Kong, Atlanta, Cincinnati and Beijing – his 7th title in Asia. He was r/u both Tokyo tourns and San Jose, and at Antwerp beat Ivanisevic for the 1st time. However, he disappointed again at IBM/ATP World Champ, where he beat only Berasategui. **1995:** (5) A sf, F r/u, W 2, US qf. Continued his success in Asia, winning Hong Kong, Tokyo Seiko and Beijing, with his 4th title of year coming at Atlanta. He played during the year with a slightly longer-handled racket, and, working on his serve to make it more of a weapon, he rediscovered his CC form in reaching f French Open – his best performance since he won in 1989. He also reached f San Jose, Philadelphia and Cincinnati, sf Australian Open and Tokyo Japan Open and 4 more qf. His year finished on a high note when he upset Sampras in sf IBM/ATP Champ and finished r/u to Becker, never before having progressed beyond rr. **1996:** (2) A r/u, F 3, W 1, US r/u. At

Australian Open he defied a stomach injury to beat Agassi in ss and extend Becker to 4s in f, then upset Agassi again on his way to the title at Indian Wells. However, at French Open he could not overcome a pulled abdominal muscle as he lost to an inspired Edberg in 3r, and at Wimbledon A. Costa beat him 1r. Things looked up again after that as he reached the top 3 1st time after winning Washington. He then won his next tourn at Los Angeles and reached f the following week at Cincinnati. At US Open, where he was controversially seeded 2 ahead of Muster, who was ranked above him, he upset Agassi again and was r/u to Sampras. This result took him to the No. 2 slot, and had he beaten Sampras, he would have passed him at the top of the rankings. Although his results in Asia were less impressive than before, he was r/u Hong Kong and Singapore, and also reached sf San Jose, Memphis, Atlanta and Stuttgart Eurocard, plus 3 more qf. His season tailed off in disappointment at ATP Champ, where he won only 1 rr match, and he missed GS Cup 1st time after withdrawing with tendinitis in ankle. **1997:** (3) A sf, F 4, W 1, US sf. Although he never looked likely to displace Sampras at the top of the rankings, he held on to his 2nd position until the last week of the season. He won all 5 f he played, taking Memphis, Indian Wells, Hong Kong (his 11th title in Asia), Orlando and Washington. He also appeared in sf Australian Open, US Open, Rosmalen, Montreal and Cincinnati, plus qf San Jose and Long Island. Yet again he was disappointing at ATP Champ, winning only 1 match, and lost his No. 2 ranking to Rafter. **1998:** A 2, F 3, W 2, US 2. Seeming only a shadow of his former self, he dropped out of the top 10 after LIPC and by June had slipped so far down the rankings that he was unseeded at Wimbledon and US Open. On the positive side, Boston in Aug. was his 1st title for 13 months and Shanghai his 12th in total in Asia. He also reached f Memphis and Orlando, sf San Jose and Washington, and qf Rome (d. Sampras). Injury again featured in his year: he was out of action for 6 weeks from mid-Feb. following the partial tear of a ligament in his knee, and returned at Hong Kong wearing a brace, then at Washington it was tendinitis in the left wrist that caused him to retire. **1998 HIGHLIGHTS – SINGLES: Australian Open 2r** [seed 3] (d. Carlsen 6–3 7–6 5–7 6–3, lost Raoux 6–4 7–6 7–6), **French Open 3r** [seed 11] (d. Calatrava 7–5 6–3 6–2, Van Lottum 7–5 6–2 3–0 ret, lost Clavet 3–6 7–6 6–2 6–4), **Wimbledon 2r** (d. Viloca 6–4 6–3 3–6 3–6 6–2, lost Gustafsson 6–2 5–7 6–2 1–6 6–2), **US Open 2r** (d. Erlich 6–1 6–3 6–1, lost Moya [seed 10] 3–6 1–6 7–6 6–4 6–3); **won** Boston (d. Pavel 7–5 6–2, Carlsen 7–5 6–2, Pozzi 6–4 2–6 6–1, Grosjean 7–5 4–6 6–3, Haarhuis 6–3 6–4), **won** Shanghai (d. Lareau 6–3 7–6, Tieleman 6–3 6–3, Woodbridge 6–2 6–2, Haarhuis 7–5 6–3, Ivanisevic 4–6 6–1 6–2); **r/u** Memphis (d. Nestor 6–4 6–4, Gaudenzi 6–3 6–3, Fromberg 6–1 6–4, Kuerten 7–6 7–6, lost Philippoussis 6–3 6–2), **r/u** Orlando (d. Delgado 6–4 3–6 7–6, Squillari 7–6 6–4, Carlsson 6–3 6–1, Tillstrom 6–3 6–4, lost Courier 7–5 3–6 7–5); **sf** San Jose (d. Craca 6–2 6–4, Bastl 7–5 6–3, Haas 6–3 6–7 6–4, lost Agassi 6–4 7–6), **sf** Washington (d. Sell 6–2 6–3, Damm 6–4 6–1, Courier 6–3 6–4, lost S. Draper w/o). **CAREER HIGHLIGHTS – SINGLES: French Open – won 1989** (d. Masso 6–7 6–3 6–0 6–3, Sampras 6–1 6–1 6–1, Roig 6–0 7–5 6–3, Lendl 4–6 4–6 6–3 6–3 6–3, Agenor 6–4 2–6 6–4 7–6, Chesnokov 6–1 5–7 7–6 7–5, Edberg 6–1 2–6 4–6 6–4 6–2), **r/u 1995** (d. Nargiso 6–3 6–4 6–1, Vacek 6–3 5–7 6–4 6–4, Carbonell 6–1 6–2 7–6, Stich 1–6 6–0 6–2 6–3, Voinea 7–5 6–0 6–1, Bruguera 6–4 7–6 7–6, lost Muster 7–5 6–2 6–4); **Australian Open – r/u 1996** (d. Rikl 6–2 6–1 6–2, Hlasek 6–1 6–3 6–3, Raoux 6–2 6–2 7–6, Fleurian 6–3 6–3 6–4, Tillstrom 6–0 6–2 6–4, Agassi 6–1 6–4 7–6, lost Becker 6–2 6–4 2–6 6–2), **sf 1995** (d. Kilderry 6–2 6–4 5–7 6–2, Alami 6–3 6–4 6–1, Damm 6–3 7–5 6–3, Delaitre 6–3 6–2 6–4, Medvedev 7–6 7–5 6–3, lost Sampras 6–7 6–3 6–4 6–4), **sf 1997** (d. Goossens 6–0 6–3 6–1, Reneberg 6–3 7–5 6–1, Henman 6–1 7–6 6–3, Medvedev 4–6 6–2 6–2 6–1, Rios 7–5 6–1 6–4, lost Moya 7–5 6–2 6–4); **US Open – r/u 1996** (d. Oncins 3–6 6–1 6–0 7–6, Godwin 6–1 6–3 6–1, Spadea 6–4 5–7 2–6 7–5 6–3, Hlasek 6–3 6–4 6–2, J. Sanchez 7–5 6–3 6–7 6–3, Agassi 6–3 6–2 6–2, lost Sampras 6–1 6–4 7–6), **sf 1992** (d. E. Ferreira 6–3 6–4 7–6, P. McEnroe 6–3 6–3 6–4, Boetsch 6–3 6–3 6–1, Washington 6–2 2–6 3–6 6–3 6–1, W. Ferreira 7–5 2–6 6–3 6–7 6–1, lost Edberg 6–7 7–5 7–6 5–7 6–4), **sf 1997** (d. Fredriksson 6–3 6–4 6–2, Salzenstein 4–6 6–2 6–3 6–4, Pioline 6–3 0–6 5–7 7–5 6–1, Rios 7–5 6–2 4–6 4–6 6–3, lost Rafter 6–3 6–3 6–4); **ATP Champ – r/u 1995** (d. Muster 4–6 6–2 6–3, lost Enqvist 6–1 6–4, d. Courier 6–2 7–5 in rr, d. Sampras 6–4 6–4, lost Becker 7–6 6–0 7–6); **GS Cup – r/u 1991** (d. Courier 6–4 6–2, P. McEnroe 6–2 6–4, Lendl 2–6 4–6 6–4 7–6 9–7, lost Wheaton 7–5 6–2 6–4), **r/u 1992** (d. Agassi 6–4 6–2, Korda 6–3 6–4, Ivanisevic 6–7 6–2 6–4 3–6 6–3, lost Stich 6–2 6–3 6–2), **sf 1990** (d. Edberg 6–4 4–6 7–5, Leconte 7–6 6–3, lost Sampras 6–3 6–4 6–4).

FRANCISCO CLAVET (ESP)

Born Aranjuez, 24 October 1968; lives Madrid; LH; 6ft; 156lb; turned pro 1988; career singles titles 7; final 1998 ATP ranking 30; 1998 prize money $446,552; career prize money $2,819,577.

Coached by Jose Miguel Morales (formerly by his older brother Pepo (Jose), who used to play the circuit). **1986:** (870). **1987:** (638). **1988:** (290). **1989:** (188) Qf Kitzbuhel. **1990:** (90) A –, F 1, W –, US –. Won his 1st tour title at Hilversum as a lucky loser, upsetting Jaite on the way. **1991:** (30) A 2, F 4, W 1, US 3. Reached sf Stuttgart Mercedes (d. Muster and Gomez), Kitzbuhel, Schenectady, Athens and Sao Paulo, plus 3 more qf and last 16 French Open, unseeded. **1992:** (22) A 2, F 1, W 1, US 1. Enjoying another consistent year, he was r/u Gstaad and San Marino and reached sf Philadelphia, Indian Wells, Madrid, Athens and Palermo. **1993:** (99) A –, F 2, W –, US 1. In a less successful year, his best showing was sf Genova, plus qf Hilversum, Bucharest and Sao Paulo (d. Yzaga) and an upset of Novacek at Buenos Aires. **1994:** (38) A –, F 2, W –, US 2. On the main tour he was r/u Santiago and Montevideo (losing both to Berasategui) and reached sf Athens and Buenos Aires (d. Berasategui on clay), plus qf Pinehurst, Florence, St Polten and Palermo. He also won 2 titles on the Challenger circuit. **1995:** (49) A –, F 3, W –, US 3. At Palermo he won his 1st title since 1990, as well as reaching sf Mexico City, Oporto, Umag and Montevideo. **1996:** (34) A 3, F 4, W 1, US 1. In another productive year, he won Amsterdam and appeared in sf Mexico City and Bologna, plus qf Antwerp, Estoril, St

Polten, Gstaad (d. MaliVai Washington), Stuttgart Eurocard, Bucharest and Palermo. Upset A. Costa at French Open, where he was unseeded. **1997:** (33) A –, F 2, W 2, US 1. His best performances came in Oct., when he won Mexico City and Bogota back-to-back, having earlier reached f Estoril (d. Kuerten, Moya and Mantilla), sf Tashkent and Bucharest, and qf Antwerp (d. Enqvist), Rosmalen, Amsterdam and Palermo. **1998:** A 3, F 4, W 4, US 2. Again he performed best later in the season, winning Bucharest in Sept. and Santiago in Nov. In other tourns he reached sf Kitzbuhel and Mexico City, qf St Polten and Gstaad (d. Berasategui), and in GS, unseeded each time, he upset M. Chang at French Open and Rios at Wimbledon. **1998 HIGHLIGHTS – SINGLES: Australian Open 3r** (d. Burgsmuller 2–6 6–2 6–3 6–4, MaliVai Washington w/o, lost Arazi 4–6 6–4 3–6 6–2 6–1), **French Open last 16** [unseeded] (d. Chesnokov 6–1 6–4 6–1, Delaitre 6–2 6–4 6–7 6–1, M. Chang [seed 11] 3–6 7–6 6–2 6–4, lost Dewulf 7–5 6–3 6–1), **Wimbledon last 16** [unseeded] (d. Rios [seed 2] 6–3 3–6 7–5 3–6 6–3, Canas 6–7 2–6 7–6 6–1 6–4, Johansson 7–6 6–3 6–3, lost Sanguinetti 7–6 6–1 6–4), **US Open 2r** (d. Pavel 6–7 6–4 7–5 6–2, lost Kiefer 6–4 7–6 6–1); **won** Bucharest (d. Vinck 6–2 7–6, Pescariu 3–6 7–5 6–2, Alonso 7–5 6–0, Portas 3–6 6–0 6–2, Di Pasquale 6–4 2–6 7–5), **won** Santiago (d. Delgado 6–4 6–4, Alonso 6–1 7–6, Lapentti 6–4 6–4, Marin 6–2 7–6, El Aynaoui 6–2 6–4); **sf** Kitzbuhel (d. Vinck 6–3 6–3, Hipfl 6–4 6–1, Meligeni 6–3 6–1, lost Gaudenzi 6–2 2–6 6–2), **sf** Mexico City (d. Rodrigues 4–6 6–3 6–2, El Aynaoui 3–6 6–0 6–4, Sanguinetti 7–6 7–5, lost Malisse 6–2 6–2).

ALBERT COSTA (ESP)

Born Lerida, 25 June 1975; lives Barcelona; RH; 5ft 11in; 163lb; turned pro 1993; career singles titles 8; final 1998 ATP ranking 14; 1998 prize money $1,013,446; career prize money $3,235,788.

Coached by Lorenzo Fargas. A Catalan, he prefers to be known as Albert, rather than Alberto. No relation to Carlos Costa. **1991:** On winning ESP World Youth Cup team. **1993:** Ranked No. 4 in ITF Jun rankings, he won Orange Bowl and was r/u French Open Jun to Carretero. In the senior game he reached qf Santiago (d. Berasategui) after qualifying. **1994:** (52) A –, F 1, W 1, US 1. He was voted Newcomer of the Year, in which he reached sf Estoril, Prague (d. Chesnokov) and Bucharest (d. Gaudenzi), and won 2 Challenger titles. **1995:** (24) A –, F qf, W –, US –. Unseeded at French Open, he upset Courier and was the only player to take a set off Muster, whom he extended to 5s. At Casablanca he reached his 1st f on the main tour, following with the same stage Estoril (d. Medvedev) and in Aug. won his 1st title at Kitzbuhel, upsetting Muster on clay. He also reached sf Nice and Santiago, plus 2 qf, to break into top 25. **1996:** (13) A 2, F 2, W 2, US 1. He continued his march through the rankings with the titles at Gstaad (d. Kafelnikov), San Marino and Bournemouth. He removed Agassi on the way to f Monte Carlo, where he extended Muster to 5s, reached his 1st HC f at Dubai and upset M. Chang at Wimbledon in only his 4th tourn on grass as he developed his skills on surfaces other than clay. He also appeared in sf Italian Open and Tel Aviv, plus qf Scottsdale and Umag. **1997:** (19) A qf, F 3, W –, US 1. Broke into top 10 after winning Barcelona and consolidated with the title at Marbella, although he was unable to maintain that position, despite reaching sf Sydney, Stuttgart Mercedes (d. Kafelnikov), Cincinnati (d. Corretja) and Boston, and qf Australian Open (extended Sampras to 5s), Scottsdale and Hamburg. Played in winning ESP WT Cup team. **1998:** A 2, F 4, W 2, US 1. He won Hamburg (where both his sf and f opponents were forced to retire) and Kitzbuhel, r/u Rome (d. M. Chang but withdrew before f with wrist injury) and Bournemouth, and played qf Sydney, Scottsdale, Gstaad and Stuttgart Mercedes. Coming into ATP Champ as 2nd alternate when Rios withdrew, he lost both his matches there. **1998 HIGHLIGHTS – SINGLES: Australian Open 2r** (d. Haas 7–6 6–2 6–4, lost Agassi 6–4 6–4 2–6 7–5), **French Open last 16** [seed 13] (d. Carlsen 6–3 6–2 6–2, Goellner 6–4 6–3 6–1, Ulihrach 6–3 6–3 6–0, lost Rios [seed 3] 4–6 6–4 6–3 6–3), **Wimbledon 2r** (d. M. Norman 7–5 7–5 7–6, lost W. Ferreira 3–6 7–5 6–3 6–3), **US Open 1r** [seed 16] (lost Gross 2–6 4–6 7–5 6–2 6–4); **won** Hamburg (d. Medvedev 6–3 1–6 7–6, Gross 6–2 6–2, W. Ferreira 6–3 6–3, Santoro 6–3 6–4, Kucera 3–0 ret, Corretja 6–2 6–0 1–0 ret), **won** Kitzbuhel (d. Schuttler 6–1 6–3, Huet 6–4 3–6 6–3, Dewulf 2–6 6–3 6–4, Squillari 7–5 1–6 6–3, Gaudenzi 6–2 1–6 6–2 3–6 6–1); **r/u** Rome (d. Gumy 6–3 6–1, Dewulf 6–1 6–4, Alami 6–2 7–6, M. Chang 6–2 6–1, Berasategui 6–3 4–6 6–3, lost Rios w/o), **r/u** Bournemouth (d. Craca 6–3 6–3, Van Scheppingen 6–3 6–2, Clement 4–6 6–3 7–6, Santopadre 7–6 6–0, lost Mantilla 6–3 7–5). **CAREER HIGHLIGHTS – SINGLES: Australian Open – qf 1997** (d. Rafter 7–5 6–2 7–5, Kroslak 6–1 7–6 7–6, Draper 6–4 6–2 7–5, W. Ferreira 6–3 6–2 3–2 ret, lost Sampras 6–3 6–7 6–1 3–6 6–2); **French Open – qf 1995** unseeded (d. Renzenbrink 6–3 6–4 6–0, Raoux 6–4 6–4 6–4, Karbacher 7–5 6–2 6–2, Courier 6–4 1–6 7–6 6–4, lost Muster 6–2 3–6 6–7 7–5 6–2).

CARLOS COSTA (ESP)

Born Barcelona, 22 April 1968; lives Andorra; RH; 6ft; 175lb; turned pro 1988; career singles titles 6; final 1998 ATP ranking 68; 1998 prize money $250,941; career prize money $3,123,903.

Coached by Jose Perlas. No relation to Albert. Wife Itziar (married 2 December 1994). **1986:** (870) Nat Jun champ. **1988:** (243). **1989:** (201) Won Madrid doubles with Carbonell. **1990:** (151) A –, F –, W 1, US –. Won Zaragoza Challenger; upset Korda and Cherkasov at Barcelona. **1991:** (55) A –, F 3, W –, US –. Reached sf Florence and sf Guaruja Bliss; won Venice and Siracusa Challengers. Played 2 doubles f, winning San Marino with Arrese. Won Nat Champ for 1st of 2 straight years. **1992:** (14) A –, F 4, W 2, US 4. Really came into his own during the year and broke into top 20 after upsetting E. Sanchez and Bruguera en route to his first tour title at Lisbon and following with Barcelona in April. R/u Madrid and Italian Open; sf Hamburg (d. Agassi). **1993:** (26) A 3, F 4, W 2, US 3. He made his mark in GS: unseeded at French Open, he upset Ivanisevic and extended Krajicek to 10–8 5s in last 16; at Wimbledon he extended W. Ferreira to 8–6 5s 2r and at US Open he upset Ivanisevic again. Won Hilversum and Buenos Aires (where he also took the doubles with Carbonell), r/u Mexico City and reached sf Schenectady, as well as upsetting Sampras 2r Stockholm. **1994:** (27) A –, F 2, W 2, US 3. Won Estoril and San Marino, r/u Barcelona and reached 4 more qf. **1995:** (31) A –, F 3, W –, US –. R/u Oporto and Umag (d. Berasategui and held 3 mps v Muster before letting the title slip away), reached sf Bastad and Amsterdam and won Graz Challenger. Upset Eltingh at Stuttgart Mercedes. **1996:** (61) A 2, F 1, W 1, US 1. It was a less productive year in which he slipped out of the top 50, despite appearances in f Bologna, sf Bastad and qf Indian Wells (d. Becker), Estoril and Monte Carlo (d. M. Chang). **1997:** (56) A –, F 2, W –, US 1. His best performances were sf Bastad and San Marino, plus qf Monte Carlo (d. W. Ferreira), Bucharest (d. Moya) and Bogota. On the Challenger circuit he won Barletta and Barcelona. **1998:** A 1, F 1, W –, US 1. He reached sf San Marino and qf Auckland, Dubai, Barcelona (d. Kuerten) and Bologna, as well as upsetting Bruguera at Qatar and Corretja at Stuttgart Mercedes. Although he reached no f on the main tour, he won Graz Challenger. **1998 HIGHLIGHTS – SINGLES: Australian Open 1r** (lost Stark 6–3 4–1 ret), **French Open 1r** (lost Knippschild 6–4 6–2 6–4), **US Open 1r** (lost Arthurs 6–3 5–7 6–4 6–4); **won** Graz Challenger (d. Portas 7–5 7–6); **sf** San Marino (d. Calatrava 6–4 6–2, Hood 6–4 7–5, Gaudenzi 7–5 6–1, lost Hrbaty 6–0 4–6 7–6).

JOSE DE ARMAS (VEN)

Born Florida, USA, 25 March 1981; lives Caracas; RH; 6ft; 105lb; career singles titles 0; final 1998 ATP ranking 1273; 1998 prize money $1,405.

Coached by Victor Perez. **1997:** (1122) Won French Open Jun doubles with Horna. **1998:** Won French Open Jun doubles with Gonzales.

OLIVIER DELAITRE (FRA)

Born Metz, 1 June 1967; lives Suresnes; RH; 5ft 7in; 150lb; turned pro 1986; career singles titles 0; final 1998 ATP ranking 184 singles, 12 doubles; 1998 prize money $385,932; career prize money $2,454,230.

Wife Emmanuelle Willay (married 12 October 1991); daughters Elena (born 6 April 1992) and Julia (born 31 May 1993). **1984:** (494). **1985:** (558). **1986:** (177) F 1, W –, US –. **1987:** (298) A –, F 1, W –, US –. **1988:** (129) A –, F –, W–, US –. Enjoyed some success on the satellite circuits. **1989:** (111) A 2, F 1, W –, US 2. Reached 1st GP sf at Sydney (upsetting Svensson), and appeared in qf Nancy and Basle, breaking into top 100 in Jan. **1990:** (152) A 3, F 1, W 2, US 1. Qf Hilversum, won Brasilia Challenger and extended Ivanisevic to 5s 2r Wimbledon. **1991:** (41) A –, F 3, W –, US –. Returning to the top 100, he broke into the top 50 with his 1st GP r/u showings at Bordeaux and Lyon (d. Forget and Bruguera), sf Long Island and 2 Challenger titles. Member of winning French D Cup team v USA in Lyon, but did not play. **1992:** (76) A 2, F 1, W 2, US 1. Appeared in sf Bolzano, qf Adelaide and upset Korda at Hamburg. **1993:** (80) A 1, F 2, W 2, US 1. R/u Kuala Lumpur Malaysian Open (d. Haarhuis), reached sf Bolzano, upset Muster 1r Wimbledon and Becker at Lyon. **1994:** (49) A 2, F 4, W 2, US 1. At French Open, unseeded, he made his 1st appearance in GS last 16, having recovered from 2-sets-to-love down against Santoro in 3r. Having reached no qf all year, he progressed to f Indianapolis in Aug. and followed with qf Bordeaux before finishing the year with sf showing at Antwerp (d. Krajicek). From 4 doubles f won 3 titles with Forget and 1 with Simian. **1995:** (102) A 4, F 1, W 3, US 1. In singles he reached sf Marseille, qf Milan and Bordeaux, and in doubles won Washington with Tarango. **1996:** (219) A 1, F 1, W –, US –. Qf Basle (d. Enqvist) was his best showing in singles and in doubles he played 2 f but won no title. **1997:** (139) A –, F 2, W –, US –. Reached qf St Petersburg and Lyon and upset Henman at French Open. From 3 doubles f he won Antwerp with D. Adams. **1998:** A –, F 2, W –, US –. He was a major force in doubles, playing 8 f with 3 different partners. His 4 titles were all won in partnership with Santoro, with whom he qualified for a 1st World Doubles Champ, reaching sf before bowing to Knowles/Nestor. **1998 HIGHLIGHTS – SINGLES: French Open 2r** (d. De Pasquale 2–6 7–5 7–6 1–6 6–0, lost Clavet 6–2 6–4 6–7 6–1). **1998 HIGHLIGHTS – DOUBLES:** (with Santoro unless stated) **won** Stuttgart Mercedes (d. Eagle/Grabb 6–1 3–6 6–3), **won** Toulouse (d. Haarhuis/Siemerink 6–2 6–4), **won** Basle (d. Norval/Ullyett 6–3 7–6), **won** Lyon (d. Carbonell/Roig 6–2 6–2); **r/u** Qatar (lost Bhupathi/Paes 6–4 3–6 6–4), (with Mirnyi) **r/u** Chennai (lost Bhupathi/Paes 6–7 6–3 6–2), (with Pescosolido) **r/u** Tokyo Japan Open (lost Lareau/Nestor 6–3 6–4), **r/u** Cincinnati (lost Knowles/Nestor 6–1 2–1 ret).

RAMON DELGADO (PAR)

Born Asuncion, 14 November 1976, and lives there; RH; 6ft 1in; 168lb; turned pro 1995; career singles titles 0; final 1998 ATP ranking 56; 1998 prize money $240,820.

Coached by Raul Viver. **1994:** (693). **1995:** (410) Began to make an impression on the S American satellite circuits. **1996:** (245) Reached qf Bogota. **1997:** (118) A –, F 2, W 1, US –. Won Cali Challenger. **1998:** A –, F 4, W 1, US 1. He sprang to prominence at French Open, where, unseeded, he caused the upset of the tournament by removing Sampras 2r. He upset Pioline en route to sf Indianapolis, following with same stage Shanghai, then went one better at Bogota where he played his 1st career f. In other tourns he reached qf Atlanta and Coral Springs. **1998 HIGHLIGHTS – SINGLES: French Open last 16** [unseeded] (d. Damm 6–2 0–0 ret, Sampras [seed 1] 7–6 6–3 6–4, Sargsian 2–6 7–6 6–4 7–6, lost Mantilla [seed 15] 6–2 6–2 6–4), **Wimbledon 1r** (lost Haas 6–7 6–3 6–3 6–3), **US Open 1r** (lost Lareau 7–5 7–6 6–3); **r/u** Bogota (d. Hrbaty 6–4 6–3, Meligeni 6–3 6–4, Courier 6–7 6–1 7–5, Sargsian 6–3 4–6 3–1 ret, lost Zabaleta 6–4 6–4); **sf** Indianapolis (d. Golmard

6–3 6–2, Pioline 7–6 6–1, Macphie 7–5 7–5, B. Black 6–1 2–6 6–4, lost Agassi 7–6 6–3), **sf** Shanghai (d. Nestor 6–4 3–6 6–2, Paes 2–6 6–3 7–5, Tebbutt 6–4 6–7 6–3, lost Ivanisevic 5–7 6–3 7–5).

FILIP DEWULF (BEL)

Born Mol, 15 March 1972; lives Leopoldsburg; RH; 6ft 2in; 176lb; turned pro 1990; career singles titles 2; final 1998 ATP ranking 55; 1998 prize money $301,444; career prize money $1,417,528.

Coached by Gabriel Gonzales. **1990:** (517). **1991:** (277) Won Nat Champ and joined Belgian D Cup squad. **1992:** (164) Enjoyed some success on the Challenger circuit. **1993:** (164) Reached his 1st qf on main tour at Florence. **1994:** (134) Took over his country's top ranking. **1995:** (67) A , F –, W 1, US –. The highlight of his year came at Vienna in Oct. when, after qualifying, he went on to win the title, upsetting Muster in f and breaking into the top 100. He was only the 2nd Belgian to win a title on the main tour and the 1st since Bernard Mignot at Dusseldorf in 1975. Earlier he had reached his 1st sf at San Marino and qf Oporto and Toulouse. **1996:** (96) A 2, F 1, W 2, US 1. Although it was a less spectacular year, he performed steadily, reaching sf St Petersburg and qf Zagreb (d. Gaudenzi), Marseille, Copenhagen and Kitzbuhel, as well as upsetting Haarhuis 1r Australian Open. **1997:** (40) A 2, F sf, W 1, US 1. At French Open he became the 1st Belgian man in the open era to reach GS sf and was the 1st qualifier for 20 years to reach sf at any GS. This result, which included an upset of Corretja, shot him through the rankings from 122 to 58. He continued his progress with the title at Kitzbuhel (d. Kafelnikov), without dropping a set, but his only other qf was at Antwerp (as LL), and although he qualified for GS Cup, he ret 1r v Korda with left ankle sprain. **1998:** A 1, F qf, W 2, US 1. Although he could not reach the heights of the previous year, he made his mark again at French Open, removing Enqvist and Clavet on his way to qf, unseeded. In other tourns he reached sf Gstaad and qf Kitzbuhel and upset Bjorkman at Rome. **1998 HIGHLIGHTS – SINGLES: Australian Open 1r** (lost Woodbridge 7–5 6–3 7–5), **French Open qf** [unseeded] (d. Larsson 7–6 7–5 7–6, Martelli 7–6 6–4 7–6, Enqvist 6–3 6–2 6–3, Clavet 7–5 6–3 6–1, lost Corretja [seed 14] 7–5 6–4 6–3), **Wimbledon 2r** (d. Campbell 6–3 2–6 6–1 6–0, lost Korda [seed 3] 6–4 6–3 6–2), **US Open 1r** (lost Dosedel 6–4 3–6 6–3 6–4); **sf** Gstaad (d. Portas 3–6 7–6 6–2, Meligeni 3–6 7–5 6–3, Kiefer 1–6 6–3 6–4, lost Corretja 6–3 6–7 6–3). **CAREER HIGHLIGHTS – SINGLES: French Open – sf 1997** (d. Caratti 6–3 6–3 6–1, Meligeni 6–4 6–2 3–6 1–6 6–3, Portas 6–3 7–6 4–6 6–7 8–6, Corretja 5–7 6–1 6–4 7–5, M. Norman 6–2 6–7 6–4 6–3, lost Kuerten 6–1 3–6 6–1 7–6), **qf 1998.**

SLAVA DOSEDEL (CZE)

Born Prerov, 14 August 1970; lives Monte Carlo, Monaco; RH; 6ft; 168lb; turned pro 1989; career singles titles 3; final 1998 ATP ranking 64; 1998 prize money $367,257; career prize money $1,819,425.

Formerly named Ctislav, but is now known as Slava, which is a more easily pronounced version of the same name. Coached by Petr Hutka. Wife Jana (married 14 November 1998). Former Nat 18s champ. **1988:** (561). **1989:** (265) Won Yugoslav satellite. **1990:** (146) Won Bangkok Challenger. **1991:** (202) A 2, F 2, W –, US –. **1992:** (170) A –, F –, W – , US 1. Qf Bologna and won Poznan Challenger. **1993:** (75) A –, F 4, W 1, US 1. Finished the year in style with his 1st main tour f at Sao Paulo, having never before passed qf. He reached that stage at Dubai, Bologna and San Marino and made an unexpected appearance in last 16 French Open. **1994:** (29) A –, F 2, W 2, US –. Broke into the top 50 with sf showings at Nice, Italian Open (d. Medvedev and Courier), Bologna, St Polten, Prague, Palermo and Santiago, plus 3 qf. **1995:** (62) A –, F 2, W 2, US –. Returning in Oct. after a 6-week absence with a shoulder injury, he ended the year on a high note with his 1st title at Santiago. Earlier he had reached sf St Polten, plus qf Milan (d. Berasategui), Bologna and San Marino. **1996:** (66) A –, F 2, W –, US –. He proved to be a dangerous opponent, recording some useful upsets on his way to f Munich (unseeded, d. Becker), sf St Polten (d. Edberg) and Umag (d. A. Costa), qf Amsterdam (d. C. Costa) and San Marino, as well as surprising Kafelnikov at Marseille and Pioline at Hamburg. In doubles he won St Polten with Vizner. **1997:** (44) A 2, F 1, W 1, US 1. Won Amsterdam, upset Berasategui on his way to sf Munich and removed Muster and Filippini en route to the same stage Kitzbuhel. Out of action from mid-Oct. with right elbow injury. **1998:** A 2, F 1, W 1, US 2. He continued to cause notable upsets, removing Mantilla at Barcelona, Bjorkman at Monte Carlo, and Korda on his way to f Prague. He also reached qf Amsterdam and won Merano on the Challenger circuit. **1998 HIGHLIGHTS – SINGLES: Australian Open 2r** (d. Boetsch 6–4 3–6 6–3 7–6, lost Gustafsson 4–6 6–2 6–1 6–3), **French Open 1r** (lost Tillstrom 7–5 6–1 6–2), **Wimbledon 1r** (lost Siemerink 6–1 6–4 7–6), **US Open 2r** (d. Dewulf 6–4 3–6 6–3 6–4, lost Tillstrom 1–6 6–3 7–6 3–6 6–3); **won** Merano Challenger (d. Ruud 7–6 7–6); **r/u** Prague (d. Schalken 2–6 7–6 6–1, Korda 6–3 6–2, Diaz 6–1 6–4, Lapentti 3–6 6–3 6–2, lost Meligeni 6–1 6–4).

SCOTT DRAPER (AUS)

Born Brisbane, 5 June 1974; lives there and Orlando, Fla; LH; 5ft 10in; 170lb; turned pro 1994; career singles titles 1; final 1998 ATP ranking 51; 1998 prize money $300,753.

Trained by Mark Waters. Brother of Mark, who also plays the men's tour. **1992:** (1098) Won Wimbledon Jun doubles with Baldas. **1993:** (882). **1994:** (420) Made his mark on the satellite circuits in both singles and doubles. **1995:** (81) A 1, F 4, W 1, US 3. He sprang to prominence at French Open, where he was a qualifier; he was a wild card at Australian Open, lucky loser at Wimbledon and gained direct acceptance at US Open.

Reached his 1st qf on the main tour at Tokyo Japan Open, following with the same stage at Beijing and Moscow, and won Nagoya Challenger. **1996:** (94) A 1, F 4, W 1, US 2. Reached qf Sydney, Los Angeles (d. Stich), Beijing and Tel Aviv. He was again prominent at French Open, where he was unseeded. **1997:** (59) A 3, F 1, W 1, US 4. Reached his 1st career f at Adelaide, having almost withdrawn before the tourn with wrist problems. He also appeared in qf Rome (d. Muster), Nottingham and Washington, upset Agassi at LIPC and M. Chang at Queen's, and extended W. Ferreira to 7–5 5s at Wimbledon. **1998:** A 2, F 2, W 2, US 1. The highlight of his year came at Queen's, where he upset Rafter on the way to his 1st tour title. He added r/u Washington, qf Nottingham and an upset of Corretja at Cincinnati, breaking into the top 50. **1998 HIGHLIGHTS – SINGLES: Australian Open 2r** (d. Hrbaty 6–4 7–5 7–5, lost Korda [seed 6] 7–6 6–3 6–3), **French Open 2r** (d. Nydahl 6–3 7–6 6–3, lost Van Garsse 6–3 3–6 6–7 7–6 6–2), **Wimbledon 2r** (d. Schuttler 6–3 7–5 3–6 6–3, lost Enqvist 6–7 6–1 6–4 6–3), **US Open 1r** (lost Henman [seed 13] 6–3 7–6 7–6); **won** Queen's (d. Tebbutt 6–4 2–6 6–4, Rafter 4–6 7–5 6–4, Steven 7–6 7–6, Flach 7–6 7–6, Woodforde 6–3 6–2, Tieleman 7–6 6–4); **r/u** Washington (d. Hernandez 6–3 3–6 6–4, W. Black 4–6 6–3 7–6, B. Black 6–4 6–2, Dewulf 6–3 6–2, M. Chang w/o, lost Agassi 6–2 6–0). **1998 HIGHLIGHTS – DOUBLES:** (with Stoltenberg) **r/u** Newport (lost Flach/Stolle 6–2 4–6 7–6).

YOUNES EL AYNAOUI (MAR)

Born Rabat, 12 September 1971, and lives there; RH; 6ft 4in; 185lb; turned pro 1990; career singles titles 0; final 1998 ATP ranking 49; 1998 prize money $119,768.

Coached by Eduardo Infantino and trains every winter at Bollettieri Academy in Florida. Wife Anne Sophie Rocher; son Ewen Marwan (born 11 August 1997). A three-times winner of nat champs, he has been ranked No. 1 in Morocco since 1990. **1992:** (307) Upset Muster on his way to qf Casablanca. **1993:** (51) Was a finalist at Casablanca and won Oporto Challenger, a result which took him into the top 100. Also reached qf Kitzbuhel (d. E. Sanchez), San Marino, Toulouse (d. Bruguera), Sao Paulo and Buenos Aires. **1994:** (115) A 2, F 1, W 1, US 1. Although he broke into the top 50 in March, he had slipped out of the top 100 by the end of a year in which his best performances were sf Jakarta and Casablanca, qf Schenectady and the Challenger title at Agadir. **1995:** (112) A 1, F 4, W –, US –. Although he reached no qf on the main tour, he won Challenger titles at Geneva and Siracusa. **1996:** A –, F 1, W 1, US 1. He began the year in style with r/u Qatar (d. Enqvist and Muster before losing to Korda in 3s tb) and following the next week with the same stage Jakarta (d. Haarhuis), unseeded both times. Then followed a slump in which he won only 1 match in 12 tourns until, again unseeded, he played his 3rd f of the year at Amsterdam, upsetting A. Costa on the way. **1997:** (237) A –, F –, W –, US –. Qf Casablanca was his best showing. **1998:** A –, F –, W –, US –. He won 6 Challenger titles across the year, including Szczecin and Oporto back-to-back in autumn, and burst back on to the main tour in Nov. to take r/u slot at Santiago, upsetting Berasategui, Puerta and Mantilla on the way. **1998 HIGHLIGHTS – SINGLES: won** Ulm Challenger (d. Pescariu 6–4 6–3), **won** Contrexville Challenger (d. Di Pasquale 6–4 6–7 6–0), **won** Scheveningen Challenger (d. Rodriguez 6–3 6–1), **won** Szczecin Challenger (d. Knippschild 6–3 6–4), **won** Oporto Challenger (d. Koubek 4–6 6–2 6–4), **won** Buenos Aires Challenger (d. A. Martin 7–6 6–1); **r/u** Santiago (d. Alami 6–3 6–4, Berasategui 7–6 6–1, Puerta 6–2 1–0 ret, Mantilla 6–4 6–4, lost Clavet 6–2 6–4).

JACCO ELTINGH (NED)

Born Heerde, 29 August 1970; lives Epe; RH; 6ft 2in; 180lb; turned pro 1989; career singles titles 4; final 1998 ATP ranking – singles, 1 doubles; 1998 prize money $751,325; career prize money $4,921,578.

Coached by Alex Reynders. Wife Hellas Ter Riet, who used to play on the women's tour (married 11 July 1997); son Lars (born 2 September 1998). **1988:** (439) European 18s Champ and won Orange Bowl doubles with Siemerink. **1989:** (286). **1990:** (128) Reached first ATP tour sf at Sao Paulo. **1991:** (110) A 3, F 1, W 4, US 1. In singles he reached qf Madrid and Newport and made an unexpected appearance in last 16 Wimbledon, where he took a set off Agassi. In doubles won 4 titles with 4 different partners. **1992:** (78) A 2, F 1, W 1, US 1. Scored some big upsets during the year, surprising Wheaton and Washington en route to his 1st tour title at Manchester, Svensson in reaching qf Copenhagen, Novacek 1r Auckland and Agassi at Barcelona. In doubles he won Schenectady with Haarhuis and was r/u Wimbledon mixed with Oremans. **1993:** (62) A 2, F 1, W 2, US 2. Continued his record of big upsets, surprising Sampras on the way to his 1st title on clay at Atlanta and removing Courier on the way to qf Kuala Lumpur Salem Open. He reached the same stage at US CC and Manchester. Played 10 doubles f, winning 1 with Davis and 6 with Haarhuis, including ATP World Doubles when they beat Woodbridge/Woodforde. **1994:** (23) A 2, F 4, W 2, US 1. In singles he won his 1st HC title at Schenectady, unseeded, and at Kuala Lumpur won both singles and doubles. He also appeared in sf Tokyo Seiko and Moscow (d. Korda), 6 more qf, upsetting Sampras at Philadelphia and Chang at Italian Open, and last 16 French Open, unseeded. Played 12 doubles f with Haarhuis, being voted Doubles Team of the Year. They won Australian Open, US Open and 6 others to qualify for World Doubles Champ as top pairing, although they lost sf to Woodbridge/Woodforde. **1995:** (43) A qf, F 3, W qf, US 2. Unseeded at all GS, he upset Muster at Australian Open and Stich and W. Ferreira at Wimbledon. He reached sf Halle and qf Kuala Lumpur in singles, and in doubles with Haarhuis won French Open and 6 more titles to qualify for World Doubles Champ. There they advanced to f without dropping a set, but were then surprisingly beaten by Connell/Galbraith. **1996:** (305) A 1, F –, W 1, US –. In D Cup v IND, he injured his knee v Bhupathi in the last match and was forced to retire in 4s, giving the tie to IND. He was out for much of the year with recurring tendinitis in both knees and played only a restricted schedule. However, he and Haarhuis made the most of their appearances together, winning 2 of 5 doubles f, r/u US Open, and qualifying for World Doubles Champ. **1997:** (604) A 1, F –, W –, US –. Announced in June that he would play doubles only, owing to recurring knee problems, and won 6 titles from 8 f with Haarhuis, with whom he qualified for World Doubles Champ again. There they were the only partnership to win all their rr matches, but lost sf to Leach/Stark. However, they still finished the year as the season's 2nd pairing. Aiming to add Wimbledon to their career collection of GS titles, they lost f in 4s to Woodbridge/Woodforde. **1998:** A –, F –, W –, US –. His knees having become so painful that he was unable to train, he announced that he would retire at end of season. He went out in tremendous style: he won Australian Open with Bjorkman (partnering each other for the 1st time) and 9 other doubles titles with Haarhuis, including French Open and a 1st Wimbledon. They clinched f there 10–8 fs over Woodbridge/Woodforde, whom they thus overtook as top doubles pairing, and became the only team in the open era to have won all 4 GS titles in their careers. He missed out on the chance of a calendar year GS in doubles when he left US Open early to fly home for the birth of his son (11 days earlier than expected), but finished his career with a flourish at World Doubles Champ, where he and Haarhuis won all their matches to take the title. They finished as top doubles pairing, having won all 9 f they contested, and Eltingh himself, as the year-end No. 1 doubles player, bowed out at the very peak. **1998 HIGHLIGHTS – DOUBLES:** (with Haarhuis unless stated) (with Bjorkman) **won Australian Open** (d. Woodbridge/Woodforde 6–2 5–7 2–6 6–4 6–3), **won French Open** (d. Knowles/Nestor 6–3 3–6 6–3), **won Wimbledon** (d. Woodbridge/Woodforde 2–6 6–4 7–6 5–7 10–8); **won** Philadelphia (d. Macpherson/Reneberg 7–6 6–7 6–2), **won** Rotterdam (d. Broad/Norval 7–6 6–3), **won** Barcelona (d. E. Ferreira/Leach 7–5 6–0), **won** Monte Carlo (d. Woodbridge/Woodforde 6–4 6–2), **won** Amsterdam (d. Hrbaty/Kucera 6–3 6–2), **won** Boston (d. Haggard/Waite 6–3 6–2), **won** World Doubles Champ (d. Knowles/Nestor 6–4 6–2 7–5); (with Nestor) **r/u** Sydney (lost Woodbridge/Woodforde 6–3 7–5). **CAREER HIGHLIGHTS – SINGLES: Australian Open – qf 1995** [unseeded] (d. Wilander 6–3 7–6 6–4, Lareau 7–6 5–7 7–6 7–5, Muster 6–3 6–2 2–6 7–5, P. McEnroe 6–4 6–4 6–7 5–7 6–4, lost Krickstein 7–6 6–4 5–7 6–4); **Wimbledon – qf 1995** [unseeded] (d. Stich 6–4 7–6 6–1, Olhovskiy 5–7 6–3 6–4 7–6, Wilander 7–5 6–3 7–6, W. Ferreira 6–4 4–6 7–6 6–3, lost Agassi 6–2 6–3 6–4). **CAREER HIGHLIGHTS – DOUBLES:** (with Haarhuis unless stated) **Australian Open – won 1994** (d. B. Black/Stark 6–7 6–3 6–4 6–3), (with Bjorkman) **won 1998**; **French Open – won 1995** (d. Kulti/Larsson 6–7 6–4 6–1), **won 1998**; **Wimbledon – won 1998, r/u 1997** (lost Woodbridge/Woodforde 7–6 7–6 5–7 6–3); **US Open – won 1994** (d. Woodbridge/Woodforde 6–3 7–6), **r/u 1996** (lost Woodbridge/Woodforde 4–6 7–6 7–6); **ATP World Doubles Champ – won 1993** (d. Woodbridge/Woodforde 7–6 7–6 6–4), **won 1998, r/u 1995** (lost Connell/Galbraith 7–6 7–6 3–6 7–6).

THOMAS ENQVIST (SWE)

Born Stockholm, 13 March 1974; lives Monte Carlo, Monaco; RH; 6ft 3in; 187lb; turned pro 1991; career singles titles 13; final 1998 ATP ranking 22; 1998 prize money $515,702; career prize money $4,570,262.

Coached by Mikael Stripple. Won Donald Duck Cup in 1985, 1987 and 1988. **1988:** Won European 14s. **1989:** (1103). **1990:** (472) R/u French Open Jun to Gaudenzi. **1991:** (229) In Jun singles won Australian Open over Gleeson, Wimbledon over Joyce and was r/u French Open to Medvedev to finish the year at No. 1 in the ITF Jun singles rankings. In Jun doubles won French Open with Martinelle. **1992:** (63) A 2, F –, W –, US –. Made his mark in the senior game right from the start of the year at Australian Open, where he was the only player apart from Edberg to take a set off Courier. Reached qf Adelaide, Bastad and Indianapolis and in autumn won his 1st tour title at Bolzano. **1993:** (87) A 1, F 1, W 1, US 4. Having failed to pass 2r all year to date, he won Schenectady in Aug., upsetting Lendl on the way, and followed with sf Vienna (d. Volkov) and qf Bordeaux. At US Open he upset Agassi 1r en route to last 16, unseeded. **1994:** (60) A 2, F 1, W –, US 3. Reached sf Auckland, qf Memphis (d. MaliVai Washington), Toronto (d. Korda and Yzaga), Washington (d. Yzaga again), Indianapolis and Schenectady; upset Korda 1r Australian Open and Kafelnikov at Cincinnati. **1995:** (7) A 3, F 1, W 1, US 2. Continuing to cause some big upsets, he beat Volkov on his way to the title at Auckland, Agassi and M. Chang to take Philadelphia, Ivanisevic and M. Chang at Montreal (where he lost sf to Sampras only 7–6 fs), and surprised Ivanisevic three times more on his way to f Los Angeles, sf Cincinnati and then the title at Indianapolis. That last result took him into the top 10 and ahead of Larsson to the No. 1 slot in Sweden. He also won US CC and reached 6 more qf, being voted ATP Most Improved Player of the Year. **1996:** (9) A qf, F 1, W 2, US 4. After taking the title at New Delhi in April, without losing a set, he was less consistent and dropped out of the top 10 in July. However, he found form again later in the year, upsetting Sampras on his way to sf Cincinnati and removing Kafelnikov on the way to his 1st Mercedes Super 9 title at Paris Open in Nov., which saw him back in the top 10. He also appeared in sf Lyon and qf Australian Open, Dubai, Memphis, Tokyo Japan Open, Indianapolis and Toronto. **1997:** (28) A 4, F –, W –, US –. Hampered during the year by infected blisters, an arm injury and flu, he played only Australian Open of GS and slipped out of the top 25. However, he won both singles and doubles at Marseille (with Larsson), reached f Los Angeles and sf Zagreb, Rotterdam and Paris Open, plus qf Montreal, Basle and Lyon. **1998:** A 2, F 3, W 3, US –. Returning to form after a 4-month absence with various injuries, he upset Kafelnikov and Krajicek on his way to the title at Marseille, following with a defeat of Agassi to win Munich. He was also r/u Philadelphia, and reached sf Ostrava, qf Sydney (d. Moya), Memphis, Indian Wells, LIPC (d. Kucera and Rusedski) and Queen's. **1998 HIGHLIGHTS – SINGLES: Australian Open 2r** (d. Marin 6–3 6–4 6–3, lost Rios [seed 9] 6–4 7–6 4–6 6–4), **French Open 3r** (d. Pescariu 7–6 6–4 6–4, Kafelnikov [seed 6] 4–6 7–6 7–6 6–1),

Wimbledon 3r (d. Nestor 6–7 6–7 6–4 6–0 6–0, S. Draper 6–7 6–1 6–4 6–3, lost Sampras [seed 1] 6–3 7–6 7–6); **won** Marseille (d. Burillo 6–4 6–3, Roig 6–2 6–3, Gustafsson 6–2 1–6 6–3, Krajicek 6–3 6–7 6–3, Kafelnikov 6–4 6–1), **won** Munich (d. M. Norman 7–5 6–3, Rosset 6–2 6–3, Gross 6–3 6–3, Gustafsson 6–3 6–4, Agassi 6–7 7–6 6–3); **r/u** Philadelphia (d. Alvarez 6–4 6–3, Craca 4–6 7–6 6–2, Reneberg 6–4 7–6, Lareau 6–3 3–6 6–3, lost Sampras 7–5 7–6); **sf** Ostrava (d. Haarhuis 3–6 6–4 6–2, Ulihrach 6–7 6–2 6–4, Kulti 6–3 6–4, lost Kroslak 4–3 ret). **CAREER HIGHLIGHTS – SINGLES: Australian Open – qf 1996** (d. Goellner 6–3 6–2 6–4, Voinea 6–4 6–4 6–1, Gumy 6–2 7–6 3–6 6–1, Furlan 7–5 6–0 6–3, lost Woodforde 6–4 6–4 6–4).

NICOLAS ESCUDE (FRA)

Born Chartres, 3 April 1976; lives Pau; RH; 6ft 1in; 153lb; turned pro 1995; career singles titles 0; final 1998 ATP ranking 37; 1998 prize money $437,965.

Coached by Tarik Benhabiles. **1993:** (617) A –, F 1, W –, US –. Began to play the satellite circuits. **1994:** (646) A –, F –, W –, US –. **1995:** (193) A –, F –, W –, US –. Won Morocco satellite. **1996:** (406) A –, F –, W –, US –. He was restricted for most of the season by a herniated disk. **1997:** (93) A –, F 3, W –, US 2. Success on the satellites and main-tour upsets of Berasategui and Kuerten at Paris Indoor took him into the top 100 1st time. **1998:** A sf, F 2, W 2, US 1. A change of racket in an attempt to ease arm/shoulder problems reduced his injuries but restricted his form, so he changed back to the old racket and put up with the aches and pains. He sprang to prominence at Australian Open, where he survived 3 5s matches, becoming the 1st player to recover from 2s down 3 times in GS, and removed Kuerten on his way to sf, unseeded. He reached the same stage at Tashkent, plus qf Adelaide, Munich (d. Philippoussis) and Long island, and upset Corretja at Halle. He qualified for GS Cup 1st time, but lost 1r to Mantilla. **1998 HIGHLIGHTS – SINGLES: Australian Open sf** [unseeded] (d. Larsson 5–7 4–6 7–5 6–1 10—8, Kuerten [seed 12] 5–7 6–3 6–1 7–5, Reneberg 1–6 6–7 6–2 7–5 6–4, Woodbridge 7–6 6–3 6–2, Kiefer 4–6 3–6 6–4 6–1 6–2, lost Rios [seed 9] 6–1 6–3 6–2), **French Open 2r** (d. Golmard 6–1 6–2 6–0, lost Arazi 6–3 6–4 6–2), **Wimbledon 2r** (d. Wheaton 6–1 7–6 6–4, lost golmard 6–3 6–4 4–6 7–6), **US Open 1r** (lost Raoux 6–3 3–6 6–3 1–6 7–6); **sf** Tashkent (d. Tamoshevich 6–3 6–3, Schalken 6–4 7–6, Braasch 6–4 7–6, lost Henman 3–6 6–3 6–4). **CAREER HIGHLIGHTS – SINGLES: Australian Open – sf 1998.**

ROGER FEDERER (SUI)

Born Basle, 8 August 1981; lives Munchenstein; RH; 6ft 1in; 176lb; career singles titles 0; final 1998 ATP ranking 302; 1998 prize money $27,305.

Coached by Peter Carter. **1998:** At Wimbledon he won both Jun singles (over Labadze) and doubles (with Rochus), and at US Open was r/u singles to Nalbandian. In the senior game he reached qf Toulouse (d. Raoux and Fromberg) after qualifying.

ELLIS FERREIRA (RSA)

Born Pretoria 19 February 1970; lives Atlanta, Ga.; LH; 6ft 2in; 185lb; turned pro 1992; career singles titles 0; final 1998 ATP ranking – singles, 10 doubles; 1998 prize money $368,351; career prize money $1,169,907.

Wife Ashley (married 19 September 1992); daughter Camden Lanier (born 24 July 1997). No relation to Wayne Ferreira. **1991:** (503) All-American in doubles for 3rd year at Univ. of Alabama. **1992:** (387) A –, F –, W –, US 1 . **1993:** (362) A –, F –, W –, US –. **1994:** (240) A –, F –, W 1, US 2. R/u Sun City doubles with Stafford. **1995:** (519) A –, F –, W –, US –. In doubles with Siemerink won Vienna and r/u Stuttgart Mercedes. **1996:** (–) A –, F –, W –, US –. Played 3 doubles f, winning Sydney and Monte Carlo with Siemerink. **1997:** (–) A –, F –, W –, US –. Won 5 doubles titles from 7 f with Galbraith, with whom he qualified for his 1st World Doubles Champ, where they won only 1 match. **1998:** A –, F –, W –, US –. From 8 doubles f with 3 different partners, he won 2 with Leach and 1 with Haygarth. It was with Leach that he qualified for World Doubles Champ, but they did not progress beyond rr. **1998 HIGHLIGHTS – DOUBLES:** (with Leach unless stated) **won** LIPC (d. O'Brien/Stark 6–2 6–4), (with Haygarth) **won** Atlanta (d. O'Brien/Reneberg 6–3 0–6 6–2), **won** Halle (d. De Jager/Goellner 4–6 6–4 7–6); **r/u** Adelaide (lost Eagle/Florent 6–4 6–7 6–3), (with Rodøti) **r/u** Memphis (lost Woodbridge/Woodforde 6–3 6–4), **r/u** Barcelona (lost Eltingh/Haarhuis 7–5 6–0), **r/u** Rome (lost Bhupathi/Paes 6–4 4–6 7–6), **r/u** Toronto (lost Damm/Grabb 6–7 6–2 7–6).

WAYNE FERREIRA (RSA)

Born Johannesburg, 15 September 1971, and lives there; RH; 2HB: 6ft 1in; 172lb; turned pro 1989; career singles titles 7; final 1998 ATP ranking 26; 1998 prize money $546,230; career prize money $6,474,974.

Coached by Danie Visser; physical trainer Walt Landers. Wife Liesl (married 16 Dec. 1994). No relation to Ellis Ferreira. Has represented Transvaal at cricket, football and badminton. **1989:** (229) Finished the year No. 1 doubles player in ITF Jun Rankings, having won US Open Jun with Stafford and r/u Wimbledon Jun with De Jager. **1990:** (173) A –, F –, W 2, US –. Upset Noah 1r Wimbledon. **1991:** (50) A 4, F 2, W 2, US 2. In singles reached last 16 Australian Open after qualifying and qf Sydney Indoor (d. Lendl), Brisbane and Birmingham. In doubles won LIPC with Norval and Adelaide with Kruger. **1992:** (12) A sf, F 3, W 4, US qf. Having never before progressed beyond qf on the main tour, he put in a tremendous performance at Australian Open, where he upset Wheaton and Novacek en route to sf, unseeded. Took his 1st tour title at Queen's in June and broke into top 20, progressing to top 10 in Sept. after reaching qf US Open. Won a second title at Schenectady, r/u Memphis and Stuttgart and sf Johannesburg. Played 4 doubles f, winning Olympic silver medal with Norval and taking Auckland with Grabb. **1993:** (22) A 4, F 2, W 4, US 4. It was a less spectacular year in which he slipped out of the top 20 and was unseeded at US Open, where he survived 3 5s matches. He won no title but was r/u Indian Wells and Queen's and reached sf Durban and Sydney Indoor. **1994:** (12) A 4, F 1, W qf, US 3. Won Hawaii, Indianapolis, Bordeaux, Basle, Tel Aviv; r/u Rotterdam (d. Ivanisevic), Manchester; sf Dubai and Toronto. Unseeded at Wimbledon, he upset Rosset on his way to qf, where he took Martin to 7–5 5s. **1995:** (9) A 2, F 3, W 4, US 1. Returned to top 10 after winning his 1st CC title at Munich in May, although he slipped out again later in year. Was asked to try a different racket, but did not get on with it and lost 1r or 2r of 5 tourns before returning to his old type, whereupon he won Ostrava 2 weeks later, following the next week with Lyon, where he beat Sampras in f. He also won Dubai and reached sf Tokyo Japan Open, Italian Open and Paris Open, plus 4 qf. **1996:** (10) A 2, F 4, W 3, US 1. He edged up the rankings in what was a solid, if not spectacular, year. Although his GS performances were disappointing, he won the titles at Scottsdale and Toronto, was r/u Washington and reached sf Italian Open, Queen's and New Haven, as well as qf Dubai, Indian Wells, Hamburg, Cincinnati, Ostrava and Olympics. **1997:** (43) A –, F 3, W 3, US 4. He began the year by winning Hopman Cup singles and followed with sf Gstaad and Indianapolis and qf Dubai. However, restricted by a thigh strain, he missed Australian Open, then withdrew during French Open and struggled for much of the year before undergoing ankle surgery. **1998:** A 2, F 3, W 4, US 1. Although he did not achieve his aim of making it back into the top 10 during the year, he scored some significant upsets in reaching sf London (d. Ivanisevic and Rafter), Dubai, Washington and Lyon (d. Rafter and Pioline) and qf Indianapolis. Other important scalps included Sampras twice – at LIPC and Basle – and Rios at Hamburg, while at US Open he twice had mps v Rusedski before losing in 5s. From 2 doubles f he won Antwerp with Kafelnikov. **1998 HIGHLIGHTS – SINGLES: Australian Open 2r** (d. Kroslak 6–4 3–6 6–2 6–3, lost Bjorkman [seed 4] 6–7 4–6 6–4 6–2 6–3), **French Open 3r** (d. Sinner 7–6 6–4 7–5, M. Norman 6–4 6–4 6–4, lost Rios [seed 3] 6–1 3–3 ret), **Wimbledon last 16** [unseeded] (d. Clement 4–6 6–3 6–4 6–2, A. Costa 3–6 7–5 6–3 6–3, Wilkinson 6–2 4–6 6–3 6–1, lost Krajicek [seed 9] 6–3 6–3 7–5), **US Open 1r** (lost Rusedski [seed 6] 4–6 7–6 5–7 7–6 6–4); **sf** Dubai (d. J. Sanchez 6–7 6–3 7–5, Steven 2–6 6–4 6–3, Kiefer 6–3 6–2, lost Mantilla 7–6 4–6 6–4), **sf** London (d. Wilkinson 6–7 6–4 6–2, Ivanisevic 6–2 6–4, Rafter 6–4 6–4, lost Kafelnikov 7–5 6–4), **sf** Washington (d. Arias 6–1 6–2, Caldwell 7–5 6–3, Spadea 6–4 6–7 6–1, lost Agassi 6–1 6–0), **sf** Lyon (d. Sapsford 6–2 3–6 6–4, Pioline 7–6 6–2, Rafter 6–4 6–1, lost Corretja 6–3 6–2). **1998 HIGHLIGHTS – DOUBLES:** (with Kafelnikov) **won** Antwerp (d. Carbonell/Roig 7–5 3–6 6–2); (with Galbraith) **r/u** Washington (lost Stafford/Ulyett 6–2 6–4). **CAREER HIGHLIGHTS – SINGLES: Australian Open – sf 1992** (d. Lavalle 6–2 6–4 1–6 6–3, Novacek 3–6 6–3 7–6 7–6, Woodforde 4–6 6–3 6–2 6–2, Wheaton 6–7 6–4 6–2 6–2, J. McEnroe 6–4 6–4 6–4, lost Edberg 7–6 6–1 6–2), **Wimbledon – qf 1994** (d. Hadad 6–4 3–6 7–5 6–3, Rosset [14] 6–7 6–3 6–4 6–4, Wilkinson 6–2 6–2 6–3, Bjorkman 6–3 6–7 6–4 6–3, lost Martin 6–3 6–2 3–6 5–7 7–5), **US Open – qf 1992** (d. Arrese 3–6 7–5 6–3 6–3, Bruguera 6–7 6–2 3–6 6–1 6–2, Masur 6–4 6–4 6–2, E. Sanchez 6–2 6–4 2–6 6–4, lost Chang 7–5 2–6 6–3 6–7 6–1).

RICHARD FROMBERG (AUS)

Born Ulvestone, Tas., 28 April 1970; lives Newtown, Tas.; RH; 6ft 5in; 195lb; turned pro 1988; career singles titles 4; final 1998 ATP ranking 40; 1998 prize money $350,342; career prize money $2,113,241.

Played in winning World Youth Cup team in 1985 and 1986. Coached by Ray Ruffels and working with David Tunbridge. **1987:** R/u Australian Open Jun singles and doubles (with Anderson). **1988:** (103) A 2, F –, W –, US –. Qf Brisbane and r/u Australian Open Jun doubles with J. Anderson. **1989:** (126) A 1, F 1, W –, US –. Won Bahia Challenger. **1990:** (32) A 1, F 1, W 2, US 1. Reached f Singapore then won 1st tour title at Bologna, following with Bastad. Joined AUS D Cup squad for f v USA, where he took Agassi to 5s in 1st rubber and beat Chang in dead 5th rubber. **1991:** (93) A 2, F 1, W 1, US 1. Began the year in style by winning Wellington, followed by qf showing at Italian Open. Sidelined for 5 weeks in July/August with rotator cuff tendinitis, he returned to reach qf Indianapolis and Brisbane. **1992:** (83) A 1, F 2, W 1, US 3. Won 2 Challenger titles and appeared in qf US CC (d. Rostagno), Prague and Schenectady. **1993:** (40) A 4, F 3, W 1, US 3. Was r/u Tampa and reached sf Adelaide, Hilversum (d. Haarhuis) and Lyon. In GS he upset C. Costa to reach last 16 Australian Open, unseeded, and on the Challenger circuit he won Turin. Won Australia's only rubber (v Goellner) in D Cup final as AUS lost 4–1 to GER. **1994:** (59) A 2, F 2, W 3, US 3. After suffering problems with rotator cuff muscle in right shoulder during 1st 3 months of year, he reached f Florence and Hilversum (d. Berasategui) plus sf Bastad. **1995:** (93) A 2, F 1, W –, US –. Upset Rosset on his way to f Sydney and reached qf Nice, Oporto and Valencia. Out of action June to Sept. after breaking his left wrist. **1996:** (82) A 1, F 2, W 1, US –. He did not advance beyond qf, although he reached that stage at Sydney, Casablanca, Estoril, Coral Springs (d. Woodforde) and Oporto, where he also won the Challenger title. **1997:** (70) A 2, F 1, W 1, US 2. Having reached only one qf all year – at Prague – he came good in autumn, winning Bucharest for his 1st title since 1991, and also took Szczecin Challenger. **1998:** A 4, F 1, W 1, US 1. Unseeded at Auckland he upset Mantilla to reach f, where he extended Rios to fs tb, and followed with an upset of Moya at Australian Open, where he was unseeded. He added r/u Amsterdam (d. Kucera), sf San Marino and qf Memphis and Kitzbuhel, as well as the title at Prostejov Challenger. **1998 HIGHLIGHTS – SINGLES: Australian Open last 16** [unseeded] (d. Larkham 2–6 6–3 6–4 3–6 6–3, Moya [seed 7] 4–6 6–4 7–6 6–4,

Lareau 6–0 6–2 4–6 6–3, lost Kucera 6–2 3–6 6–2 7–5), **French Open 1r** (lost Courier 7–6 6–4 0–6 6–4), **Wimbledon 1r** (lost B. Black 7–5 3–6 3–6 7–6 6–2), **US Open 1r** (lost Dreekmann 6–3 1–6 6–3 6–3); **won** Prostejov Challenger (d. Ilie 6–2 6–2); **r/u** Auckland (d. Alami 3–0 ret, Steven 7–6 6–3, Hrbaty 6–2 7–6, Mantilla 6–3 7–6, lost Rios 4–6 6–4 7–6), **r/u** Amsterdam (d. Pavel 6–3 6–4, Van Scheppingen 6–3 6–4, Voinea 6–3 6–4, Kucera 6–1 6–7 6–2, lost M. Norman 6–3 6–3 2–6 6–4); **sf** San Marino (d. Pescariu 6–4 6–0, J. Sanchez 6–2 6–3, Santopadre 6–4 7–5, lost Puerta 6–2 3–6 6–3).

JAN-MICHAEL GAMBILL (USA)

Born Spokane, Wash., 3 June 1977; lives Colbert, Wash.; RH; 6ft 2in; 172lb; turned pro 1996; career singles titles 0; final 1998 ATP ranking 38; 1998 prize money $393,524.

1994: (1192). **1995:** (554). **1996:** (474). **1997:** (176) A –, F –, W –, US 1. Won Aptos Challenger and on the main tour reached qf Auckland. **1998:** A 1, F 2, W 2, US 3. He caused some significant upsets in reaching his 1st sf at Indian Wells (d. Philippoussis and Agassi) and following with the same stage Tokyo Japan Open (d. Henman), plus qf Singapore and Stuttgart Eurocard (d. Corretja and Henman). He also surprised Pioline at Cincinnati, and at US Open extended Moya to 5s tb. **1998 HIGHLIGHTS – SINGLES: Australian Open 1r** (lost O'Brien 3–6 7–5 6–1 6–3), **French Open 2r** (d. Rodriguez 6–3 6–2 6–4, lost Vacek 6–4 2–6 7–5 7–6), **Wimbledon 2r** (d. Schalken 7–6 6–4 6–7 4–6 8–6, lost B. Black 7–5 6–4 7–5), **US Open 3r** (d. Braasch 6–3 1–6 6–3 7–5, M. Norman 6–4 6–2 6–7 6–3, lost Moya [seed 10] 6–2 3–6 3–6 6–3 7–6); **sf** Indian Wells (d. Philippoussis 7–6 5–7 7–6, Clavet 6–3 6–4, Courier 6–2 6–4, Agassi 7–6 3–6 6–3, lost Rios 7–6 6–3), **sf** Tokyo Japan Open (d. Pescosolido 6–3 6–2, Miyachi 6–0 6–3, Schuttler 6–0 6–0, Henman 6–3 4–6 6–3, lost Pavel 6–4 6–3).

ANDREA GAUDENZI (ITA)

Born Faenza, 30 July 1973; lives Monte Carlo, Monaco; RH; 2HB; 6ft; 183lb; turned pro 1990; career singles titles 1; final 1998 ATP ranking 44; 1998 prize money $325,060; career prize money $2,085,404.

Coached by Leonardo Caperchi. **1990:** (861) No. 1 in ITF Jun rankings after winning French Open Jun over Enqvist and US Open Jun over Tillstrom. **1991:** (620) Restricted by torn ligaments in left ankle. **1992:** (258) Was again hampered by a string of injuries, but enjoyed some success on the satellite circuits. **1993:** (60) Having won 2 Challenger titles, he reached his 1st main tour sf at San Marino, following with the same stage at Bucharest and Palermo and upset B. Gilbert at Athens. **1994:** (24) A 2, F 4, W 1, US 3. He scored some big upsets during the year in reaching his 1st tour f at Stuttgart Mercedes (d. Stich and Chesnokov), plus sf Gstaad (d. Pioline), qf Estoril (d. Kafelnikov), Barcelona (d. Muster), Bologna, Italian Open (d. Muster again) and Vienna. Unseeded in GS, he upset Korda 1r French Open and Courier 2r US Open. **1995:** (22) A 2, F 1, W 1, US 1. Upset Rosset 1r Australian Open and Ivanisevic on his way to f Dubai, a result which took him into the top 20. He was also r/u San Marino as well as reaching sf Sydney, Monte Carlo (d. Kafelnikov and Bruguera), Umag, plus 4 qf. **1996:** (55) A 1, F 2, W –, US 2. A finalist at Estoril, he also reached sf St Polten and qf Mexico City and Italian Open (d. Enqvist). He upset Muster 1r Milan, where he won the doubles with Ivanisevic, and at Olympics upset C. Costa and took a set off Agassi. Underwent arthroscopic surgery on his shoulder on 17 Oct., expecting to be out 3 months. **1997:** (57) A 1, F 1, W –, US –. Still looking for his 1st title on the main tour, he played his 5th f at Bucharest, as well as reaching qf Munich (d. Enqvist), Bologna and Marbella and winning Geneva Challenger. **1998:** A 3, F 2, W –, US 1. He captured that elusive 1st title at Casablanca, where he also took the doubles, and moved back into the top 50. He was r/u Kitzbuhel (d. A. Costa) and reached sf St Polten and Barcelona (unseeded, d. W. Ferreira, Corretja and Bruguera), and qf Scottsdale, Bastad and San Marino. Underwent arthroscopic surgery on his shoulder 2 Oct., returning in time to play D Cup f v SWE. However, in opening rubber v M. Norman, he had to ret at 6–6 fs as ITA lost to SWE 1–4. **1998 HIGHLIGHTS – SINGLES: Australian Open 3r** (d. Pescariu 6–2 4–6 6–2 6–2, Gross 4–6 6–1 6–4 6–4, lost Agassi 6–2 6–2 6–3), **French Open 2r** (d. Medvedev 7–6 6–1 0–6 2–6 6–1, lost Sargsian 6–4 6–2 6–7 6–4), **US Open 1r** (lost Voinea 6–4 3–6 6–2 2–0 ret); **won** Casablanca (d. Ravel 6–7 7–5 6–3, Di Pasquale 6–2 6–3, Marin 6–7 7–5 6–2, Grosjean 6–4 6–4, Calatrava 6–4 5–7 6–4); **r/u** Kitzbuhel (d. Rehmann 7–6 6–2, Alonso 5–7 6–2 6–4, Lapentti 6–3 7–6, Clavet 6–2 2–6 6–2, lost A. Costa 6–2 1–6 6–2 3–6 6–1); **sf** Barcelona (d. D. Sanchez 6–4 6–2, W. Ferreira 4–6 6–1 6–2, Corretja 3–6 6–1 6–3, Bruguera 3–6 6–2 6–3, lost T. Martin 6–4 7–6), **sf** St Polten (d. Gambill 6–3 7–5, Nargiso 6–2 4–6 6–3, Clavet 6–3 6–4, lost Rios 6–4 6–3). **1998 HIGHLIGHTS – DOUBLES:** (with Nargiso) **won** Casablanca (d. Brandi/Messori 6–4 7–6).

JUSTIN GIMELSTOB (USA)

Born Livingston, NJ, 26 January 1977; lives Morristown, NJ, and Key Biscayne, Fla; RH; 6ft 5in; 190lb; turned pro 1996; career singles titles 0; final 1998 ATP ranking 80 singles, 50 doubles; 1998 prize money $217,123.

Coached by Nick Saviano. **1991:** Ranked No. 1 in Nat 14s. **1993:** No. 1 in Nat 16s. **1994:** (1150). **1995:** (572) A –, F –, W –, US 1. Won Nat 18s and played in winning US Sunshine Cup team. **1996:** (155) A –, F –, W –, US –. Reached qf Scottsdale and won Urbana and Andorra Challengers. An All-American at UCLA in singles and doubles, he won NCAA doubles with Muskatirovic. **1997:** (102) A 1, F –, W 2, US 3. In Hopman Cup he was r/u singles and won mixed doubles with Rubin. In singles he reached qf Hong Kong and Toulouse (d. Siemerink) and upset Kuerten at Wimbledon. Played 2 doubles f, winning Newport with Steven. **1998:** A 1,

F –, W 2, US –. Reached sf Coral Springs and Los Angeles (d. Rafter), as well as upsetting Stoltenberg at Orlando and Mantilla at Wimbledon. In doubles he won Nottingham with Talbot and in mixed won his 1st 2 GS titles, both with V. Williams, at Australian and French Opens. On the Challenger circuit he finished the season by taking both singles and doubles at Andorra. **1998 HIGHLIGHTS – SINGLES: Australian Open 1r** (lost Campbell 3–6 6–3 3–6 6–3 6–4), **Wimbledon 2r** (d. Mantilla [seed 10] 7–6 6–2 6–3, lost Woodforde 2–6 6–1 6–4 6–4); **won** Andorra Challenger (d. Bastl 6–3 2–6 7–6); **sf** Coral Springs (d. Stafford 6–2 6–4, W. Black 6–1 6–2, Malisse 6–3 4–6 6–3, lost Ilie 4–6 6–1 6–4), **sf** Los Angeles (d. Vacek 6–4 6–0, Spadea 6–3 3–0 ret, Rafter 6–4 6–3, lost Agassi 6–0 7–6). **1998 HIGHLIGHTS – DOUBLES:** (with Talbot) **won** Nottingham (d. Lareau/Nestor 7–5 6–7 6–4). **MIXED DOUBLES:** (with V. Williams) **won Australian Open** (d. Suk/Sukova 6–2 6–1), **won French Open** (d. Lobo/S. Williams 6–4 6–4).

JEROME GOLMARD (FRA)

Born Dijon, 9 September 1973, and lives there; LH; 6ft 2in; 170lb; turned pro 1993; career singles titles 0; final 1998 ATP ranking 46; 1998 prize money $305,834.

1993: (425). **1994:** (205) Won Campinas Challenger. **1995:** (90) A 2, F 1, W –, US 2. Qf Indianapolis (d. Courier), upset W. Ferreira 1r US Open and won 2 Challenger titles. Out of action from Oct. with stress fracture of left femur. **1996:** (142) A –, F 1, W 1, US –. Returning to action in March, he reached qf New Delhi a month later and won Segovia Challenger. **1997:** (117) A –, F 2, W 2, US 2. He reached qf Shanghai, Scottsdale (d. W. Ferreira) and Queen's (d. Rosset). **1998:** A 3, F 1, W 3, US 2. His 1st sf appearance on the main tour came at Nottingham, and he also reached qf Adelaide (d. M. Norman) and Bastad, as well as winning 2 Challenger titles. These results, plus upsets of Moya at Cincinnati and A. Costa at Paris Open, took him back into the top 100. **1998 HIGHLIGHTS – SINGLES: Australian Open 3r** (d. Henman 6–3 6–7 6–2 3–6 11–9, Siemerink 7–6 7–5 6–7 3–6 6–1, lost Kiefer 7–5 4–0 ret), **French Open 1r** (lost Escude 6–1 6–2 6–0), **Wimbledon 3r** (d. Sapsford 7–6 6–2 6–3, Escude 6–3 6–4 4–6 7–6, lost Korda [seed 3] 4–6 7–5 7–5 7–6), **US Open 2r** (d. Novak 6–3 6–4 7–6, lost Kucera 7–5 6–3 6–0); **won** Cherbourg Challenger (d. Pozzi 3–6 6–4 6–3), **won** Brest Challenger (d. Perlant 6–4 6–4); **sf** Nottingham (d. Larsson 6–2 7–6, W. Black 6–1 6–3, S. Draper 6–4 6–3, lost Bjorkman 6–2 2–6 6–3).

MAGNUS GUSTAFSSON (SWE)

Born Lund, 3 January 1967; lives Monte Carlo, Monaco; RH; 6ft 1in; 172lb; turned pro 1986; career singles titles 12; final 1998 ATP ranking 31; 1998 prize money $442,122; career prize money $3,875,616.

Coached by Stefan Simonsson from 1996. **1986:** (273) Nat 18 Champ. **1987:** (53) Reached 1st GP sf at Stockholm, won Tampere Challenger and broke into top 50. **1988:** (51) A 3, F 4, W 2, US –. Upset Mayotte to reach last 16 French Open; sf Hilversum and Barcelona (d. Jaite and Leconte). **1989:** (34) A 4, F 1, W 1, US 1. Played his 1st GP f at Gstaad, then in autumn upset Wilander and Agassi en route to 1st SS f at Stockholm. **1990:** (31) A 2, F 4, W –, US –. Took a break in March, suffering from shin splints. Reached sf Brussels and Stuttgart (d. E. Sanchez and took Lendl to 3s) and upset Agassi at Hamburg. Forced to default last 16 French Open to Gomez owing to a knee injury. **1991:** (12) A 3, F 3, W 2, US –. Won 1st GP title at Munich, upsetting Lendl on the way, and followed with Bastad and Hilversum to break into the top 10 in July. R/u Hamburg, Kitzbuhel and Prague; sf Sydney NSW and reached 2 doubles f. Withdrew from US Open with chronic inflammation of the right elbow. **1992:** (47) A 2, F 2, W –, US 1. Won Bastad and was r/u Barcelona as well as reaching sf Florence and 2 more qf, but was plagued by injuries and slipped down the rankings. **1993:** (14) A 1, F 1, W 1, US 1. In a more successful year on the circuit, he returned to the top 20, winning Stuttgart Mercedes and reaching f Antwerp (d. Stich and Becker back-to-back), f Genova and Hilversum, plus sf Estoril, Barcelona, Prague and Umag. Upset Courier at Paris Open. **1994:** (33) A qf, F 2, W –, US –. After taking up transcendental meditation at the start of the year, he won his 1st career HC title at Auckland in Jan., following 3 weeks later with Dubai (d. Bruguera in f), which took him back to the top 10 for the 1st time since Aug. 1991. He also reached qf Stuttgart Eurocard, Copenhagen, Munich, Hamburg, but in Oct. he underwent surgery to his right shoulder to remove bone aggravating the tendon and was expected to be out for 8 months. **1995:** (88) A –, F 2, W –, US –. Back in action slightly ahead of schedule in May, he reached qf Stuttgart Mercedes, Umag and Valencia, and won Braunschweig Challenger. Threatened with foot surgery in Sept., he avoided it after trying a new sole on his shoe. **1996:** (17) A –, F 1, W 4, US 2. Returning to form, he won St Petersburg (d. Kafelnikov) and Bastad (d. Edberg) on the main tour and took Hamburg on the Challenger circuit. He also reached sf Coral Springs and Paris Open (d. Agassi, W. Ferreira and Rosset), qf Copenhagen, Monte Carlo (d. Ivanisevic), Halle, Lyon and Stuttgart Eurocard, and upset W. Ferreira at Wimbledon, where he was unseeded. These performances took him back to the top 20 in Nov. **1997:** (37) A 2, F 2, W 2, US 2. Underwent arthroscopic surgery on his right shoulder immediately after exiting Australian Open and was out 3 months. He went on to win Singapore and was r/u San Marino and Beijing, but the only other qf he played was at Qatar. His 2 biggest upsets were Ivanisevic 1r French Open and M. Chang at Paris Open. **1998:** A 3, F 3, W 3, US. Discouraged by the length of time taken for his injured shoulder to heal, he had intended to retire at end 1998, but by March he had gained a new lease of life. During a productive year he won both singles and doubles at Bastad, won Copenhagen, reached sf Munich, qf Marseille (d. Bruguera), Basle, Paris Open (d. Bjorkman) and Stockholm (d. Bjorkman) and upset M. Chang at Wimbledon. Contributed 2 singles wins in D Cup f as SWE d. ITA 4–1 in Milan. **1998 HIGHLIGHTS – SINGLES: Australian Open 3r** (d. Van Scheppingen 6–4 6–3 6–0, Dosedel 4–6 6–2 6–1 6–3, lost Sampras [seed 1] 7–5 6–3 6–4),

French Open 3r (d. O'Brien 6–2 4–6 6–2 6–2, Prinosil 6–4 6–3 6–7 6–1, lost Stoltenberg 6–1 2–6 6–4 6–4), **Wimbledon 3r** (d. Petchey 6–2 1–6 6–3 6–2, M. Chang 6–2 5–7 6–2 1–6 6–2, lost Rafter [seed 6] 6–3 6–7 6–2 6–1); **won** Copenhagen (d. Kroslak 6–1 7–6, Furlan 6–2 6–2, Pavel 6–4 4–6 6–3, Carlsen 6–4 5–7 6–2, Prinosil 3–6 6–1 6–1), **won** Bastad (d. Jonsson 6–1 6–3, Hipfl 2–6 6–1 6–2, Golmard 6–7 1–0 ret, Johansson 6–3 4–6 7–5, Medvedev 6–2 6–3); **sf** Munich (d. Grosjean 6–3 6–1, Kuerten 7–6 6–3, Escude 6–3 6–1, lost Enqvist 6–3 6–4). **1998 HIGHLIGHTS – DOUBLES:** (with Larsson) **won** Bastad (d. Bale/Norval 6–4 6–2). **CAREER HIGHLIGHTS – SINGLES: Australian Open – qf 1994** (d. Smith 3–6 7–5 6–2 2–6 6–2, Steven 7–6 6–2 4–6 6–2, Renzenbrink 6–2 6–2 6–2, Damm 2–6 6–3 6–1 6–1, lost Sampras 7–6 2–6 6–3 7–6).

PAUL HAARHUIS (NED)

Born Eindhoven, 19 February 1966; lives Monte Carlo, Monaco; RH; 2HB; 6ft 2in; 177lb; turned pro 1989; career singles titles 1; final 1998 ATP ranking 73 singles, 2 doubles; 1998 prize money $930,522; career prize money $6,448,674.

Coached by Alex Reynders. Wife Anja (married 12 September 1996); son Daan (born 3 February 1998). **1987:** (397) Finished 2nd on Dutch satellite circuit. **1988:** (462) Graduated from Florida State Univ. **1989:** (57) A –, F 3, W –, US 4. After winning Lagos Challenger, he qualified for French Open, where he upset Zivojinovic 1r, and again as a qualifier upset J. McEnroe at US Open. Qf Hilversum (d. K. Carlsson) and Itaparica. **1990:** (54) A 1, F 3, W 3, US 1. Qf Philadelphia (d. Gilbert and took Gomez to 3s) and Estoril. Reached 4 f in doubles with various partners, winning Moscow. **1991:** (37) A 2, F 3, W 1, US qf. He again excelled at US Open, upsetting top seed Becker en route to qf, unseeded. Reached sf Rotterdam, won Lagos Challenger and scored some other big upsets – E. Sanchez at Estoril and Ivanisevic at Italian Open and French Open. In doubles reached 5 f, winning 3 with different partners, and was r/u French Open mixed with Vis. **1992:** (39) A 2, F 1, W 2, US 2. Scored some useful upsets during the year on his way to f Singapore, sf Rotterdam (d. Lendl) and qf Wellington, Memphis (d. Wheaton), Philadelphia (d. Wheaton again), Hamburg (d. Muster and Chang), Schenectady and Sydney Indoor. Reached 4 doubles f, winning Hilversum with Koevermans and Schenectady with Eltingh. **1993:** (42) A 1, F 4, W 1, US 2. He was still a dangerous opponent, surprising W. Ferreira at French Open, where he was unseeded, and removing Ivanisevic and Medvedev on his way to sf Tokyo Seiko. He reached the same stage at Kuala Lumpur Malaysian Open and Jakarta, plus qf at Prague, Hilversum (d. Bruguera) and Moscow and upset Volkov at LIPC. In doubles he reached 11 f, winning 1 with Koevermans and 6 with Eltingh, including IBM/ATP World Doubles where they beat Woodbridge/Woodforde in ss. **1994:** (37) A 3, F 3, W 1, US 1. In singles r/u Qatar (d. Ivanisevic) and Philadelphia and reached sf Rotterdam (d. Becker and Volkov). Voted Doubles Team of the Year with Eltingh: their partnership flourished as they won their 1st GS title at Australian Open, following with US Open, and won a total of 8 titles from 12 f to qualify for World Doubles Champ as top pairing, but lost to Woodbridge/Woodforde. **1995:** (19) A 1, F 1, W 2, US 2. Won his 1st career singles title at Jakarta, r/u Memphis and Rotterdam (d. Kafelnikov) and reached sf Philadelphia (d. Sampras) and Halle (d. Kafelnikov again), plus 2 qf. Then after upsetting Ivanisevic at Paris Open in Nov., he broke into the top 20. In doubles with Eltingh, he won French Open and all 6 other f they played to qualify for World Doubles Champ. There they advanced to f without dropping a set before being surprisingly beaten by Connell/Galbraith. **1996:** (26) A 1, F 3, W 4, US 3. R/u Indian Wells (d. Enqvist, Sampras and Ivanisevic), sf Jakarta, Estoril and Rosmalen (d. Krajicek) and qf Washington and Paris Open (d. Ivanisevic and Martin). Other upsets across the year included Boetsch at French Open and Enqvist again at Halle. His regular doubles partner, Eltingh, was restricted for much of the year by tendinitis in both knees, but they still won 2 of 5 doubles f, were r/u US Open and qualified for World Doubles Champ. He took a 3rd title with Galbraith. **1997:** (71) A 1, F 1, W 3, US 2. Reached sf Halle (d. Medvedev) and qf Memphis and Umag, as well as upsetting A. Costa at Toulouse and Muster at Stuttgart Eurocard. In 3r Wimbledon he served for the match v Henman at 5–4 40–30 5s, but double-faulted, going on to lose 12–14. He played 9 doubles f in all, 8 of them with Eltingh, with whom he won 5 titles – but not the 1st Wimbledon title they needed to complete their collection of GS, losing f there in 4s to Woodbridge/Woodforde. They qualified for World Doubles Champ again, and were the only duo to win all their rr matches, but lost sf to Leach/Stark. However, they still finished the year as the season's 2nd pairing. **1998:** A –, F 2, W 1, US 3. He missed 1st 6 weeks of year to be with his wife for the birth of their 1st child, and was out again for 2 weeks after Monte Carlo with inflamed tendon in wrist. By missing Australian Open, he broke his sequence of 33 consec. GS tourns – the longest amongst active players. In singles he was r/u Boston and reached sf Halle and Shanghai, plus qf Umag (d. Moya), as well as upsetting Mantilla at LIPC and Korda at Halle. He won 9 doubles titles with Eltingh, including French Open and their 1st Wimbledon – winning f 10–8 fs over Woodbridge/Woodforde, whom they thus overtook as top doubles pairing – to become the only team in the open era to have won all 4 GS titles in their careers. They missed the chance of a calendar year GS when Eltingh left US Open early to be with his wife for the birth of their son. However, their season finished in triumph at World Doubles Champ, where they won all their matches to take the title and finish the year well ahead as top pairing. **1998 HIGHLIGHTS – SINGLES: French Open 1r** (lost Tarango 6–4 6–1 7–6), **Wimbledon 1r** (lost Tarango 1–6 6–3 6–3 6–0), **US Open 3r** (d. Alonso 6–4 6–3 6–2, Canas 6–1 6–1 7–5, lost Ivanisevic [seed 14] 7–6 6–3 6–4); **r/u** Boston (d. Arnold 6–1 6–3, Novak 6–1 4–6 7–5, Schalken 0–6 6–4 6–3, Pioline 7–5 4–6 6–3, lost M. Chang 6–3 6–4); **sf** Halle (d. Vinck 2–6 6–1 6–2, Korda 7–6 6–4, Pozzi 6–3 7–6, lost Larsson 7–6 6–2), **sf** Shanghai (d. Burrieza 6–3 6–4, Braasch 6–0 6–3, Woodforde 7–6 7–6, lost M. Chang 7–5 6–3). **1998 HIGHLIGHTS – DOUBLES:** (with Eltingh unless stated) **won French Open** (d. Knowles/Nestor 6–3 3–6 6–3), **won Wimbledon** (d. Woodbridge/Woodforde 2–6 6–4 7–6 5–7 10–8); **won** Philadelphia (d. Macpherson/Reneberg 7–6 6–7),

won Rotterdam (d. Broad/Norval 7–6 6–3), **won** Barcelona (d. E. Ferreira/Leach 7–5 6–0), **won** Monte Carlo (d. Woodbridge/Woodforde 6–4 6–2), **won** Amsterdam (d. Hrbaty/Kucera 6–3 6–2), **won** Boston (d. Haggard/Waite 6–3 6–2), **won** World Doubles Champ (d. Knowles/Nestor 6–4 6–2 7–5); (with Siemerink) **r/u** Toulouse (lost Delaitre/Santoro 6–2 6–4). **CAREER HIGHLIGHTS – SINGLES: US Open – qf 1991** [unseeded] (d. Jelen 2–6 6–2 6–1 3–6 6–2, Chesnokov 6–1 4–6 6–2 7–6, Becker 6–3 6–4 6–2, Steeb 6–2 6–3 6–4, lost Connors 4–6 7–6 6–4 6–2). **CAREER HIGHLIGHTS – DOUBLES:** (with Eltingh) **Australian Open – won 1994** (d. B. Black/ Stark 6–7 6–3 6–4 6–3), **won 1998**; **French Open – won 1995** (d. Kulti/Larsson 6–7 6–4 6–1), **won 1998**; **Wimbledon – won 1998, r/u 1997** (lost Woodbridge/Woodforde 7–6 7–6 5–7 6–3); **US Open – won 1994** (d. Woodbridge/Woodforde 6–3 7–6), **r/u 1996** (lost Woodbridge/ Woodforde 4–6 7–6 7–6); **IBM/ATP World Doubles Champ – won 1993** (d. Woodbridge/Woodforde 7–6 7–6 6–4), **won 1998, r/u 1995** (lost Connell/Galbraith 7–6 7–6 3–6 7–6).

TOMMY HAAS (GER)

Born Hamburg, 3 April 1978; lives Bradenton, Fla.; RH; 6ft 2in; 182lb; turned pro 1996; career singles titles 0; final 1998 ATP ranking 34; 1998 prize money $618,633; career prize money $1,028,834.

Coached by Nick Bollettieri. **1993:** (1072). **1994:** (1192). **1995:** (–) R/u Orange Bowl to Zabaleta. Broke his right ankle in Dec. **1996:** (196) A –, F –, W –, US 1. Upset Furlan and Woodforde en route to qf Indianapolis and extended Stich to 4s at US Open. He finished the season in the same way as the previous year, with a broken ankle – the left this time, and as before requiring surgery. **1997:** (41) A –, F –, W 2, US 3. Played his 1st career sf at Hamburg (d. Moya and Berasategui) and followed in Oct. at Lyon with his 1st f (unseeded, d. Enqvist and Kafelnikov), breaking into top 50. His other qf appearances came at Washington and Toulouse. **1998:** A 1, F 1, W 3, US 2. At Lyon, where he reached f by virtue of w/o Sampras and Rios ret), he held mp in 2s tb v Corretja before letting the match and title slip away. He also appeared in sf Philadelphia and Scottsdale (d. Philippoussis) and qf San Jose and Mallorca (d. Berasategui), as well as upsetting Agassi 2r Wimbledon, A. Costa at Cincinnati and Corretja at Paris Open. Played in victorious GER WT Cup team, winning all his matches. **1998 HIGHLIGHTS – SINGLES: Australian Open 1r** (lost A. Costa 7–6 6–2 6–4), **French Open 1r** (lost Kiefer 6–1 6–2 7–6), **Wimbledon 3r** (d. Delgado 6–7 6–3 6–3 6–3, Agassi [seed 13] 6–7 6–3 6–3 6–3, lost Van Lottum 6–3 6–3 6–3), **US Open 2r** (d. Burillo 6–3 7–5 6–4, lost Kafelnikov [seed 11] 7–5 6–2 1–6 7–5); **r/u** Lyon (d. Clement 6–2 6–7 6–4, Santoro 2–6 6–3 7–5, Sampras w/o, Rios 6–2 1–0 ret, lost Corretja 2–6 7–6 6–1); **sf** Philadelphia (d. Spadea 6–3 6–2, Meligeni 3–0 ret, Tarango 4–6 6–4 6–4, lost Sampras 6–4 6–4), **sf** Scottsdale (d. Joyce 6–2 6–2, Philippoussis 5–7 6–2 6–0, Lareau 6–4 6–1, lost Agassi 6–2 6–1).

JEROME HAEHNEL (FRA)

Born Mulhouse, 14 July 1980; lives Heidwiller; RH; 2HB; 6ft 1in; 163lb; career singles titles 0; final 1998 ATP ranking 546; 1998 prize money $6,377.

Coached by Thierry Tulasne. **1996:** In winning FRA World Youth Cup team. **1998:** Won Australian Open Jun doubles with Jeanpierre.

K J HIPPENSTEEL (USA)

Born Roanoake, 8 May 1980, and lives there; LH; 2HB; 6ft 8in; 183lb; career singles titles 0; final 1998 ATP ranking – singles, 1388 doubles; 1998 prize money $4,096.

Coached by Dennis and Pat Van Der Meer. Nat Jun champ in doubles. **1998:** Won US Open Jun doubles with D. Martin.

DOMINIK HRBATY (SVK)

Born Bratislava, 4 January 1978; lives Monte Carlo, Monaco; RH; 6ft; 165lb; turned pro 1996; career singles titles 1; final 1998 ATP ranking 45; 1998 prize money $389,146.

Coached by Marian Vajda. **1994:** (1024). **1995:** (364) Enjoyed some success on the satellite circuits. **1996:** (77) Joined his country's D Cup squad and was voted Player to Watch after winning 2 Challenger titles from 6 f. **1997:** (42) A 4, F 1, W 1, US 1. In May, he upset Kafelnikov as he swept to his 1st sf on the main tour at St Polten, following in Oct. with an upset of Corretja to reach his 1st f. Other highlights were sf San Marino and Marbella, and qf Umag, as well as the title at Kosice Challenger. At Australian Open, unseeded in his 1st GS, he led 4–2 and 15–40 on Sampras's serve in 5s last 16. **1998:** A 1, F 3, W 1, US 2. His 1st tour title came at San Marino, and he also appeared in sf Bologna and Bastad, plus qf Auckland, St Petersburg, Barcelona (d. Kucera and Gustafsson) and Amsterdam, where he was r/u doubles with Kucera. On the Challenger circuit he won the title at Kosice. **1998 HIGHLIGHTS – SINGLES: Australian Open 1r** (lost S. Draper 6–4 7–5 7–5), **French Open 3r** (d. Campbell 2–6 6–3 6–3 6–3, Viloca 6–3 6–3 6–3, lost Berasategui [seed 16] 6–7 6–3 7–5 7–5), **Wimbledon 1r** (lost Sampras [seed 1] 6–3 6–3 6–2), **US Open 2r** (d. Rosset 7–6 7–6 7–5); **won** San Marino (d. Scala 6–3 6–4, Novak 7–6 7–6, Viloca 2–6 6–4 6–0, C. Costa 6–0 4–6 7–6, Puerta 6–2 7–5), **won** Kosice Challenger (d. Meligeni 7–5 6–4); **sf** Bologna (d. J. Sanchez 6–4 4–6 6–3, Diaz 7–6 6–1, Squillari 7–5 6–4, lost Alami 1–6 7–6 7–5), **sf** Bastad (d. Burillo 6–3 1–1 ret, Safin 3–6 6–2 6–1, Novak 3–6 6–4 6–4, lost Medvedev 6–3 7–6). **1998 HIGHLIGHTS – DOUBLES:** (with Kucera) **r/u** Amsterdam (lost Eltingh/Haarhuis 6–3 6–2).

ANDREW ILIE (AUS)

Born Bucharest, Romania, 18 April 1996; lives Melbourne; RH; 5ft 11in; 170lb; turned pro 1994; career singles titles 1; final 1998 ATP ranking 59; 1998 prize money $184,890.

Coached by Bill Bowrey. Emigrated from Romania to Australia in 1988. **1992:** (913). **1993:** (917). **1994:** (303) R/u Australian Jun singles to Ellwood. **1995:** (165) A 1, F 3, W –, US –. Upset Krajicek 2r French Open after qualifying and won Lillehammer Challenger. **1996:** (346) A 1, F –, W 1, US –. Hampered by back problems, he was out completely from July 1996 to Dec. 1997. **1997:** (–) A –, F –, W –, US –. He was out of action all year. **1998:** A 3, F 3, W –, US 1. Returning to action, he reached his 1st qf on the main tour at Orlando, then at Coral Springs, after qualifying, he upset Stoltenberg en route to his 1st career title in his 1st f. He added Biella Challenger and broke into top 100. **1998 HIGHLIGHTS – SINGLES: Australian Open 3r** (d. Knippschild 6–4 6–2 6–3, Stoltenberg 6–3 6–2 7–6, lost Rios [seed 9] 6–2 6–3 6–2), **French Open 3r** (d. Alonso 4–6 6–3 6–3 6–2, Tillstrom 6–7 6–3 6–3 6–4, lost Moya [seed 12] 6–2 7–6 6–3), **US Open 1r** (lost Goldstein 6–7 7–6 6–4 3–0 ret); **won** Coral Springs (d. Stoltenberg 6–4 7–5, Agenor 3–6 6–4 6–1, Grosjean 6–3 6–7 6–3, Gimelstob 4–6 6–1 6–4, Sanguinetti 7–5 6–4), **won** Biella Challenger (d. Perlant 6–7 6–4 6–4).

GORAN IVANISEVIC (CRO)

Born Split, 13 September 1971; lives there and Monte Carlo, Monaco; LH; 6ft 4in; 180lb; turned pro 1988; career singles titles 21; final 1998 ATP ranking 12; 1998 prize money $1,541,177; career prize money $17,747,714.

Coached by Vedran Martic; trained by Bosko Savka. **1987:** (954) Won US Open Jun doubles with Nargiso. **1988:** (371) A –, F –, W 1, US –. Joined Yugoslav D Cup squad. R/u French Open Jun doubles with Caratti and was No. 3 in ITF Jun singles rankings. **1989:** (40) A qf, F 4, W 2, US 2. Qf Australian Open after qualifying and last 16 French Open, unseeded. Upset Leconte en route to 1st GP sf at Nice, following with 2nd at Palermo and then 1st f at Florence. **1990:** (9) A 1, F qf W sf, US 3. Helped his country to win WT Cup in May, then upset Becker 1r French Open en route to qf, following with sf appearance at Wimbledon, both unseeded. Won his 1st career title at Stuttgart, reached 2r GS Cup and broke into the top 10. R/u French Open doubles with Korda. **1991:** (16) A 3, F 2, W 2, US 4. After a good year in 1990, his game fell apart at the beginning of 1991, and he withdrew from LIPC with compact fracture of left index finger. But then he played through the qualifying to gain a place at Manchester, where he won both singles and doubles. Did not play for YUG in D Cup and, with Prpic, announced in Tokyo in October that henceforth he wanted to be known as a Croatian. **1992:** (4) A 2, F qf, W r/u US 3. In his best year to date, he won Adelaide, Stuttgart, Sydney Indoor and Stockholm, qualifying 1st time for ATP World Champ, where he lost a close sf to Becker. At Wimbledon he upset Edberg on his way to a thrilling f v Agassi, which he lost in 5s. At Olympics, where he won 4 consec. 5s matches, he won a bronze medal in both singles and doubles (with Prpic). Withdrew from Monte Carlo with arrythmia heartbeat and also missed Munich. **1993:** (7) A –, F 3, W 3, US 2. Missed Australian Open with a stress fracture of the foot which kept him out 7 weeks early in year and had to wait until Sept. before winning his 1st title of the year at Bucharest. He followed with Vienna and Paris Open, where he upset Edberg and Sampras, and also upset Sampras at Italian Open. He was r/u Qatar, Italian Open and Stockholm and reached 3 more sf, including IBM/ATP World Champ. He squeezed in there, taking the last place after Sampras d. Pioline at Antwerp, but this time the No. 1 turned the tables, inflicting his only defeat in rr before the Croat was removed in sf by Stich. His GS record was disappointing; he lost 3r French Open and 2r US Open – to C. Costa both times – and bowed out in 3r Wimbledon, after all three of his encounters had gone to 5s. **1994:** (5) A qf, F qf, W r/u, US 1. He reached his 2nd Wimbledon f for the loss of only 1 set (to Volkov), but was then overpowered by Sampras. His performance and Stich's 1r defeat saw the Croat overtake the German for the 2nd slot in the rankings, behind Sampras, although he slipped back to 5th behind Agassi, Bruguera and Becker by the end of the season. During his qf v Forget, he delivered a serve at 136 mph, the fastest ever recorded, and during the year he served a record 1,241 aces, a new record which easily beat his own 1992 record of 1,066. He was r/u Stuttgart Eurocard, Bucharest and Stockholm, reached sf Qatar, Rotterdam, Italian Open and Vienna, and played 4 more qf, including Australian Open. In French Open, where he was fined (£333) for racket abuse, he lost in last 16 to Berasategui, and at US Open Zoecke removed him 1r. He qualified for IBM/ATP World Champ, but failed to win a match. Another fine there for his outbursts earned him an 8-week suspension for accumulating fines of more than $10,000 (for the 2nd year). However, as GS Cup and Australian Open were not included in the ban, he was inconvenienced only in missing Sydney in Jan. Lost thrilling 5s sf to Sampras at GS Cup. **1995:** (10) A 1, F 1, W sf, US 1. In a difficult year he won no title and reached only one f – at Hamburg – although he appeared in sf Wimbledon, Milan, Barcelona, Monte Carlo, Italian Open, Los Angeles and Indianapolis and 4 more qf. He was plagued by injury during the year, undergoing surgery on 23 Feb. after aggravating a knee injury at Stuttgart Eurocard and returning to action at Barcelona in April. Was forced to retire 1r US Open after badly spraining his ankle and did not qualify for IBM/ATP Champ. After Bob Brett left him end Oct., unable to cope with the Croatian's wild ways, he hired Vedran Martic, a fellow-Croatian whom he'd known since he was 9. Took a complete break for a week before GS Cup, returning refreshed and in better control of his head. **1996:** (4) A 3, F 4, W qf, US sf. Under the calming influence of Martic, and travelling with Father Joe, his personal priest, masseur and trainer, he felt more relaxed, working harder off court and trying to stay cooler on it. He began the year in tremendous style, with 4 wins from 5 f in consec. tourns from 29 Jan. to 10 March, taking the inaugural Croatian Indoors at Zagreb and Dubai in consec. weeks and then winning Milan and Rotterdam back-to-back to add to Hopman Cup – which he won with Majoli – and r/u finishes at Sydney and Antwerp. At LIPC, where he played his 7th f in 9 tourns, he was saved by rain from 2–6 0–1 down in sf v Sampras, but a stiff neck forced him to retire in f v Agassi. Thereafter he was less impressive, his only other f being at Indianapolis, until winning Moscow over Kafelnikov in Nov. At ATP Champ, he took advantage of the fast surface to reach sf, where he lost to Sampras only 7–5 fs. He also reached sf US Open and Indian Wells and qf Wimbledon, Munich, Cincinnati, Vienna and Stuttgart Eurocard, and broke his world record for aces. **1997:** (15) A qf, F 1, W 2, US 1. Again his best results came in early season, when he delighted home crowds by winning both singles and doubles (with Hirszon) at Zagreb in Feb., following next week with r/u Dubai, where he won the doubles with Groen. He took Milan 3 weeks later, but his only other title came in Oct. at Vienna, where he recovered from 2-sets-to-0 down in f v Rusedski, taking 3s tb and finally the match. He withdrew Antwerp in April after breaking the middle finger on his right hand, returning 3 weeks later to reach sf Rome. He was r/u Queen's and appeared in sf Sydney, Rotterdam, Los Angeles and Ostrava (where he retired with an arm injury), plus qf Australian Open, LIPC and Long Island. His GS performances were disappointing, with qf Australian Open his best showing. In 2r Wimbledon he served a record 46 aces v M. Norman but lost 14–12 fs and stalked out, being fined for missing the press conference. **1998:** A 1, F 1, W r/u, US 4. His best performance came at Wimbledon where, having scraped past Krajicek 15–13 fs in sf, he extended Sampras to 5s in f, but still could not go the extra distance to take his elusive 1st GS title in his 3rd f there. This failure severely dented his confidence and he struggled for some time afterwards. In other tourns he won Split, was r/u New Haven, Shanghai and Moscow (having squandered sp in 1s v Kafelnikov, strongly supported by a partisan crowd) and reached sf Qatar and qf Hamburg, Stuttgart Eurocard and GS Cup. **1998 HIGHLIGHTS – SINGLES: Australian Open 1r** [seed 13] (lost Siemerink 6–2 7–5 3–6 6–4), **French Open 1r** (lost Martelli 7–6 7–6 7–6), **r/u Wimbledon** [seed 14] (d. Stafford 6–3 6–3 6–2, Medvedev 6–3 7–6 4–6 6–0, Vacek 6–7 7–6 6–3 6–4, T. Martin 7–6 6–3 3–6 7–6, Siemerink 7–6 7–6 7–6, Krajicek [seed 9] 6–3 6–4 5–7 6–7 15–13, lost Sampras [seed 1] 6–7 7–6 6–4 3–6 6–2), **US Open last 16** [seed 14] (d. Woodforde 6–3 6–4 6–4, T. Martin 1–6 7–6 7–5 6–3, Haarhuis 7–6 6–3 6–4, lost Rafter [seed 3] 6–3 6–4 4–6 6–1); **won** Split (d. Prinosil 7–6 6–4, Becker 7–6 6–7 6–4, Novak 7–6 7–6, Sinner 6–3 7–6, Rusedski 7–6 7–6); **r/u** New Haven (d. Grant 6–3 3–6 6–3, Kiefer 6–3 7–5, Paes 6–2 6–4, Kafelnikov 6–3 6–4, lost Kucera 6–4 5–7 6–2), **r/u** Shanghai (d. Steven 6–4 7–6, Gimelstob 6–1 6–4, Carlsen 6–3 7–6, Delgado 5–7 6–3 7–5, lost M. Chang 4–6 6–1 6–2), **r/u** Moscow (d. Arriens 7–6 7–6, Golmard 6–3 3–2 ret, Burgsmuller 6–2 6–1, Clement 7–5 6–2, lost Kafelnikov 7–6 7–6); **sf** Qatar (d. Arazi 6–2 6–3, Rosset 6–7 7–5 7–5, Karbacher 7–6 6–7 6–3, lost Santoro 6–1 6–4). **CAREER HIGHLIGHTS – SINGLES: GS Cup – won 1995** (d. Korda 7–6 6–3, Sampras w/o, Kafelnikov 7–6 4–6 6–3 6–4, Martin 7–6 6–3 6–4), **r/u 1996** (d. Tillstrom 6–4 6–2, Woodforde 6–4 6–4, Kafelnikov 6–7 2–6 6–3 6–2 6–4, lost Becker 6–3 6–4 6–4), **sf 1992** (d. Forget 7–5 6–4, J. McEnroe 3–6 6–4 6–2, lost Chang 6–7 6–2 6–4 3–6 6–3), **sf 1994** (d. Bjorkman 6–4 6–2, Becker 6–4 6–1, lost Sampras 5–7 6–3 6–4 6–7 10–8), **Wimbledon – r/u 1992** (d. Koslowski 6–2 6–2 6–3, Woodforde 6–4 6–4 6–7 6–3, Rosset 7–6 6–4 6–4, Lendl 6–7 6–1 6–4 1–0 ret, Edberg 6–7 7–5 6–1 3–6 6–3, Sampras 6–7 7–6 6–4 6–2, lost Agassi 6–7 6–4 6–4 1–6 6–4), **r/u 1994** (d. Meligeni 6–1 6–3 6–4, Mronz 6–2 7–6 6–1, Mansdorf 6–3 7–5 6–4, Volkov 7–6 7–6 4–6 6–2, Forget 7–6 7–6 6–4, Becker 6–2 7–6 6–4, lost Sampras 7–6 7–6 6–0), **r/u 1998, sf 1990** (d. Leach 6–4 6–0 6–4, Delaitre 6–2 6–0 4–6 6–7 6–3, Rostagno 6–2 6–2, 6–4, Koevermans 4–6 6–3 6–4 7–6, Curren 4–6 6–4 6–4 6–7 6–3, lost Becker 4–6 7–6 6–0 7–6), **sf 1995** (d. Lareau 6–2 6–4 6–4, Stark 6–4 6–2 7–5, Boetsch 6–4 6–4 6–4, Martin 6–4 7–6 6–7 7–6, Kafelnikov 7–5 7–6 6–3, lost Sampras 7–6 4–6 6–3 4–6 6–3); **US Open – sf 1996** (d. Chesnokov 1–6 6–2 6–4 6–4, Draper 6–7 6–3 6–4 6–4, Dreekmann 6–3 6–2 7–6, Medvedev 6–4 3–6 6–3 7–6, Edberg 6–3 6–4 7–6, lost Sampras 6–3 6–4 6–7 6–3); **Olympics – sf bronze medal 1992** (d. Mota 6–2 6–2 6–7 4–6 6–3, Haarhuis 6–7 6–2 1–6 6–3 6–2, Hlasek 3–6 6–0 4–6 7–6 6–7, Santoro 6–7 6–7 6–4 6–4 8–6, lost Rosset 6–3 7–5 6–2); **ATP Champ – sf 1992** (d. M. Chang 7–6 6–2, Courier 6–3 6–3, Krajicek 6–4 6–3 in rr, lost Becker 6–4 6–4 7–6), **sf 1993** (d. Bruguera 6–4 7–6, Edberg 7–6 6–7 6–3, lost Sampras 6–3 4–6 6–2 in rr, lost Stich 7–6 7–6), **sf 1996** (d. Muster 6–4 6–4, Krajicek 7–6 6–7 6–3, lost M. Chang 6–4 6–3in rr, lost Sampras 6–7 7–6 7–5).

JULIEN JEANPIERRE (FRA)

Born Remiremont, 10 March 1980; lives Paris; RH; 6ft; 160lb; career singles titles 0; final 1998 ATP ranking 1244; 1998 prize money $6,530.

1996: Led FRA to victory in World Youth Cup. **1997:** Played in winning FRA teams in Vasco Valerio Cup and Sunshine Cup. **1998:** Won Australian Open Jun (over Vinciguerra) and took the doubles there with Haehnel.

THOMAS JOHANSSON (SWE)

Born Linkoping, 24 March 1975, and lives there; RH; 5ft 11in; 165lb; turned pro 1994; career singles titles 2; final 1998 ATP ranking 17; 1998 prize money $667,858; career prize money $1,362,454.

Coached by Magnus Tideman. **1989:** European 14s champ in singles and doubles (with M. Norman). **1991:** R/u Orange Bowl 16s to Corrales. **1992:** Underwent surgery in Oct. and did not play for rest of year. **1993:** (418) Unranked at the time, he upset Novacek en route to qf Bolzano in his 1st ATP tourn. **1994:** (485) A 1, F –, W –, US –. **1995:** (126) A –, F 1, W –, US –. Won Jerusalem and Napoli on the Challenger circuit. **1996:** (60) A 2, F 2, W 4, US 2. He attracted attention at Australian Open, where he led Becker 2-sets-to-love 2r, before letting the match slip from his grasp, and at Wimbledon, where he was unseeded, he removed Eltingh in 5s before taking a set off Martin. Moved into top 100 with sf finishes at Singapore, Beijing and Moscow (d. Haarhuis), and qf Gstaad and Long Island, looking ready to crack the top 50 in 1997. **1997:** (39) A 2, F 1,

W 2, US 1. His best performances came in spring, beginning with his 1st singles title at Copenhagen, in his 1st f. He followed the next week with St Petersburg, upsetting Stich on the way, and reached sf of his next 2 tourns at Hong Kong and Tokyo Japan Open. After a quieter summer, he appeared in 2 more Asian sf at Beijing and Singapore. **1998:** A 1, A 1, W 3, US qf. In another impressive year he moved into the top 25 with r/u Rotterdam (d. Kafelnikov) and Stockholm (d. Rusedski); sf St Petersburg, Hong Kong Salem Open, Den Bosch, Toulouse, Bastad and Basle; qf Cincinnati, Antwerp (d. Bjorkman) and Ostrava. He upset Moya at Indianapolis, Korda at Stuttgart Eurocard; and at US Open, where he was unseeded, he upset Kafelnikov and extended eventual finalist Philippoussis to 5s tb. **1998 HIGHLIGHTS – SINGLES: Australian Open 1r** (lost Squillari 6–4 2–6 6–3 6–7 8–6), **French Open 1r** (lost Meligeni 6–4 6–2 6–4), **Wimbledon 3r** (d. Courier 6–4 7–6 6–4, Spadea 7–5 6–1 6–3, lost Clavet 7–6 6–3 6–3), **US Open qf** [unseeded] (d. Meligeni 7–6 6–3 7–6, Dreekmann 2–6 7–5 6–2 6–3, Krajicek [seed 5] 6–7 5–4 ret, Kafelnikov [seed 11] 3–6 6–3 6–3 7–6, lost Philippoussis 4–6 6–3 6–7 6–3 7–6); **r/u** Rotterdam (d. Kafelnikov 7–6 6–2, Carlsen 6–3 6–7 7–6, Van Herck 7–6 6–2, Steven 6–3 7–5, lost Siemerink 7–6 6–2), **r/u** Stockholm (d. Santoro 6–4 7–6, Grant 6–1 6–4, Stoltenberg 7–5 7–5, Rusedski 7–5 7–6, lost T. Martin 6–3 6–4 6–4); **sf** St Petersburg (d. Pozzi 7–6 6–2, Sanguinetti 6–2 6–2, Santoro 6–3 6–3, lost Krajicek 6–4 6–4), **sf** Hong Kong Salem Open (d. Campbell 6–7 6–0 6–3, Wheaton 6–3 3–6 6–1, Stolle 7–6 7–5, lost Carlsen 6–2 6–2), **sf** Den Bosch (d. Tarango 6–4 6–7 7–5, Escude w/o, Dreekmann 3–6 6–1 6–4, lost Kafelnikov 7–6 6–7 6–3), **sf** Toulouse (d. De Pasquale 7–6 7–5, Vacek 6–4 6–3, Huet 3–6 6–4 7–5, lost Siemerink 6–3 3–6 7–5), **sf** Bastad (d. Clement 7–5 6–1, Sanguinetti 6–7 6–3 7–6, Alami w/o, lost Gustafsson 6–3 4–6 7–5), **sf** Basle (d. Becker 6–3 6–2, B. Black 6–7 6–4 7–5, Santoro 6–3 6–3, lost Henman 6–3 2–6 7–6).

DONALD JOHNSON (USA)

Born Bethlehem, Pa, 9 September 1968; lives Chapel Hill, NC; LH; 6ft 3in; 185lb; turned pro 1992; career singles titles 0; final 1998 ATP ranking 545 singles, 24= doubles; 1998 prize money $282,499.

Coached by Sam Paul. Wife Krista (married 21 May 1995). **1989:** (943). **1990:** (–). **1991:** (518). **1992:** (295) Won his 1st doubles titles on the Challenger circuit. **1993:** (415) Won 3 more Challenger doubles titles. **1994:** (320). **1995:** (199) A –, F 2, W –, US –. Spent his honeymoon playing through qualifying at French Open. **1996:** (460) A –, F –, W –, US –. Emerging from the satellite circuits, he extended Sampras to 3s 1r Indianapolis. Won his 1st doubles title on the main tour when he took Mexico City with Montana, following with Amsterdam – and 5 more on the Challenger circuit. **1997:** (517) A –, F –, W –, US –. Appeared in 3 doubles f with Montana, winning Monte Carlo. They played as alternates at World Doubles Champ when Kafelnikov/Vacek withdrew, but lost all 3 rr matches. **1998:** A –, F –, W –, US –. Missed 1st part of season with torn tendon in left wrist, but returned to win 4 out of 5 doubles f played with Montana, with whom he qualified 1st time for World Doubles Champ, where they reached sf before bowing to Eltingh/Haarhuis. **1998 HIGHLIGHTS – DOUBLES:** (with Montana) **won** Marseille (d. Keil/Middleton 6–4 3–6 6–3), **won** Estoril (d. Roditi/Wibier 6–1 2–6 6–1), **won** Hamburg (d. D. Adams/Steven 6–2 7–5), **won** Palermo (d. Albano/Orsanic 6–4 7–6); **r/u** Dubai (lost Bhupathi/Paes 6–2 7–5).

YEVGENY KAFELNIKOV (RUS)

Born Sochi, 18 February, 1974, and lives there; RH; 2HB; 6ft 3in; 173lb; turned pro 1992; career singles titles 17; final 1998 ATP ranking 11 singles, 19 doubles; 1998 prize money $2,543,077; career singles $12,147,818.

Coached by Anatoli Lepeshin. Fitness trainer Igor Andreev. Wife Mascha (married 11 July 1998). Daughter Aleysa (born 23 October 1998). **1990:** In winning USSR World Youth Cup team. **1992:** (314) Began to make his mark on the Eastern European satellite circuits. **1993:** (104) A –, F 2, W –, US –. Upset Stich on his way to qf Barcelona in spring and again at Lyon in autumn. **1994:** (11) A 2, F 3, W 3, US 4. He sprang to prominence and the top 100 by winning his 1st tour title in his 1st f at Adelaide on HC. In 2r Australian Open he took Sampras to 9–7 5s, followed with the title at Copenhagen on carpet in Feb. and was ranked as high as 36 by March. In April he upset Agassi and Stich to reach sf Monte Carlo; in May he upset Ivanisevic and Stich on his way to f Hamburg, moving into the top 20, and in June he surprised Courier to reach sf Halle. He continued his winning ways by upsetting M. Chang on his way to the title at Long Island in Aug., upset Muster en route to sf Gstaad, Edberg and Bruguera to reach sf Stockholm and appeared in the same stage New Haven, plus 5 more qf across the year, to finish the year poised just outside the top 10. He was also a successful doubles player, winning 4 titles from 6 f with various partners. Led RUS to their first ever D Cup f and was voted Most Improved Player of the Year. **1995:** (6) A qf, F sf, W qf, US 3. Broke into the top 10 after his qf appearance at Australian Open. Upset Agassi, who was injured, at French Open and removed both Ivanisevic and Becker on his way to the title at Milan, going on to win St Petersburg, Gstaad and Long Island. He was r/u Nice, and reached sf Rotterdam, Barcelona, Gstaad, New Haven and Lyon, plus 6 more qf. In doubles played 6 f with various partners, winning 3, and was the 1st player since E. Sanchez in 1990 to end the year in top 10 both singles and doubles. In D Cup with Olhovskiy saved 5 mps to upset Becker and Stich, although he won only 1 of his 3 matches in f as RUS lost 3–2 to USA. **1996:** (3) A qf, F won, W 1, US –. The high point of his career came with a magnificent performance at French Open, where he won both singles and doubles (with Vacek, in only their 3rd tourn together). He became 1st Russian since Metreveli in 1973 to reach GS f and 1st player since Rosewall in 1968 to win both singles and doubles there. He played a heavy schedule, winning Adelaide,

Prague and Lyon, as well as r/u Rotterdam, St Petersburg, Halle, Stuttgart, Paris Open and Moscow, plus sf Milan, Hamburg, Gstaad, Basle and GS Cup (lost in 5s to Ivanisevic), and 4 qf, including Australian Open. Upset Sampras at both WT Cup and French Open (although the No. 1 was below his best on both occasions) and had hoped to overtake him at the top of the rankings by the end of HC season. However, he threw away an outside chance of achieving that when he withdrew from US Open, offended at being seeded lower than his ranking and using a slight injury as a legitimate excuse. He might still have been in with a chance had he not lost f Paris Open to Enqvist, although he reached career-high No. 3 on 4 Nov. The only man to qualify for end-of-season champs in both singles and doubles (with Vacek), he decided not to compete in the doubles, which were played in US the week before the singles in Hannover. There, in a tough group, he won only 1 match in rr. He and Vacek played 7 f together, winning 4, and he also took a 5th with Olhovskiy. **1997:** (5) A –, F qf, W 4, US 2. Broke a finger on right hand in gym the week before Australian Open and was out 3 months, returning at end April – still not fully fit but missing the game and keen to play again. He was back to form by June, when he won his 1st GC title at Halle, following with New Haven and Moscow to qualify for ATP Champ, where he was r/u to Sampras. Across the year he also reached sf Hamburg, Montreal, Tashkent, Lyon and Paris Open, plus qf French Open, Stuttgart Mercedes, Kitzbuhel, Cincinnati, Basle and GS Cup, although he was generally disappointing in GS singles. In doubles with Vacek, he won all 3 f he played – at French Open, US Open and Gstaad – and was again the only man to qualify for the season-ending champs in both singles and doubles, although injury prevented him from taking up his doubles place. **1998:** A –, F 2, W 1, US 4. Having missed Australian Open with a sprained knee, he struggled for motivation for much of the year, in which he won London, Halle and Moscow, was r/u Marseille, Tashkent and Stuttgart Eurocard, and reached sf Cincinnati, New Haven and Paris Open, plus qf Barcelona and Toronto. He squeezed into ATP Champ, taking the last place ahead of Rusedski only by virtue of his victory at Moscow and the absence of the injured Krajicek and Rafter. However, he won only 1 match there and, having managed all year to hold on to his top 10 ranking, he finished the season just outside. He played 4 doubles f, winning Antwerp with W. Ferreira and Vienna with Vacek. **1998:** A –, F 2, W 1, US 4. **1998 HIGHLIGHTS – SINGLES: French Open 2r** [seed 6] (d. Navarra 6–4 4–6 6–1 6–4, lost Enqvist 4–6 7–6 7–6 6–1), **Wimbledon 1r** [seed 7] (lost Philippoussis 6–7 7–6 6–4 6–2), **US Open last 16** [seed 11] (d. Van Scheppingen 6–1 6–2 6–4, Haas 7–5 6–2 1–6 7–5, Kiefer 6–4 6–0 6–2, lost Johansson 3–6 6–3 6–3 7–6); **won** London (d. Johansson 6–3 6–2, Vacek 6–3 6–4, Henman 4–6 6–4 6–2, W. Ferreira 7–5 6–4, Pioline 7–5 6–4), **won** Halle (d. Medvedev 1–6 7–5 6–1, Prinosil 6–4 6–3, M. Norman 7–6 6–2, Johansson 7–6 6–7 6–3, Larsson 6–4 6–4), **won** Moscow (d. Cherkasov 6–3 6–4, Grosjean 2–6 6–3 6–2, Raoux 6–1 6–1, Rosset 6–1 2–0 ret, Ivanisevic 7–6 7–6); **r/u** Marseille (d. Viloca 6–4 6–3, Voinea 6–1 3–6 6–4, Clement 6–2 3–6 6–4, Tillstrom 7–6 6–4, lost Enqvist 6–4 6–1), **r/u** Tashkent (d. Sinner 6–4 6–2, Nainkin 6–3 6–0, Etlis 6–3 3–6 6–1, Pioline 6–2 6–2, lost Henman 7–5 6–4); **sf** Cincinnati (d. M. Chang 6–3 4–6 6–4, S. Draper 6–3 6–3, Vacek 6–4 6–4, lost Rafter 7–5 6–0), **sf** New Haven (d. Woodbridge 6–0 6–2, Kuerten 6–4 6–4, Ulihrach 4–6 6–3 6–3, lost Ivanisevic 6–3 6–4), **sf** Paris Open (d. M. Norman 3–6 6–3 6–4, Henman 6–3 6–7 7–6, Rios 6–3 6–2, lost Rusedski 6–3 4–6 6–4). **1998 HIGHLIGHTS – DOUBLES:** (with Vacek unless stated) (with W. Ferreira) **won** Antwerp (d. Carbonell/Roig 7–5 3–6 6–2), **won** Vienna (d. Adams/De Jager 7–5 6–3); **r/u** London (lost Damm/Grabb 6–4 7–5), **r/u** Moscow (lost Palmer/Tarango 6–4 6–7 6–2). **CAREER HIGHLIGHTS – SINGLES: French Open – won 1996** (d. Blanco 6–1 6–3 6–3, Johansson 6–2 7–5 6–3, Mantilla 6–4 6–2 6–2, Clavet 6–4 6–3 6–3, Krajicek 6–3 6–4 6–7 6–2, Sampras 7–6 6–0 6–2, Stich 7–6 7–5 7–6), **sf 1995** (d. Siemerink 6–1 6–2 6–7 6–3, Gustafsson 6–3 6–7 6–1 7–5, Wheaton 6–2 6–1 4–6 6–3, Corretja 6–3 6–2 6–2, Agassi 6–4 6–3 7–5, lost Muster 6–4 6–0 6–4), **qf 1997** (d. Damm 6–2 6–4 6–4, Raoux 7–5 6–3 6–4, Pioline 7–5 6–4 6–7 1–6 6–4, Philippoussis 6–2 6–3 7–5, lost Kuerten 6–2 5–7 2–6 6–0 6–4); **ATP Champ – r/u 1997** (in rr d. Bjorkman 6–3 7–6, d. M. Chang 6–3 6–0, lost Henman 6–4 6–4; sf d. Moya 7–6 7–6; f lost Sampras 6–3 6–2 6–2); **GS Cup – sf 1995** (d. Furlan 6–4 6–1, Eltingh 3–6 6–3 6–2, lost Ivanisevic 7–6 4–6 6–3 6–4), **sf 1996** (d. Corretja 6–4 7–6, d. Courier 2–6 6–4 8–6, lost Ivanisevic 6–7 2–6 6–3 6–2 6–4), **qf 1997** (d. Bruguera 6–4 6–3, lost Rusedski 6–7 6–3 6–1); **Australian Open – qf 1995** (d. Larkham 6–3 6–0 6–1, Carlsen 4–6 6–3 6–1 6–3, Bjorkman 4–6 6–1 6–2 7–6, Martin 6–1 6–4 6–2, lost Agassi 6–2 7–5 6–0), **qf 1996** (d. Santoro 6–1 6–1 7–5, Corretja 6–1 6–2 6–3, Tebbutt 7–5 5–7 6–4 6–2, MaliVai Washington 6–3 6–2 6–4, lost Becker 6–4 7–6 6–1); **Wimbledon – qf 1995** (d. Dewulf 6–3 7–5 6–3, Karbacher 6–4 6–4 7–5, Volkov 7–6 6–2 6–4, Krickstein 6–3 6–3 6–2, lost Ivanisevic 7–5 7–6 6–3). **CAREER HIGHLIGHTS – DOUBLES:** (with Vacek unless stated) **French Open – won 1996** (d. Forget/Hlasek 6–3 6–3), **won 1997** (d. Woodbridge/Woodforde 7–6 4–6 6–3); **US Open – won 1997** (d. Bjorkman/Kulti 7–6 6–3).

NICOLAS KIEFER (GER)

Born Holzminden, 5 July 1977; lives Sievershansen; RH; 5ft 11in; 160lb; turned pro 1995; career singles titles 1; final 1998 ATP ranking 35; 1998 prize money $623,573; career prize money $1,169,095.

Coached by Klaus Hofsaess. **1993:** Won Nat Jun. **1994:** (1212). **1995:** (202) No. 2 in ITF Jun rankings after winning Australian Open over J. Lee, US Open over Seetzen, and r/u Wimbledon to Mutis. In the senior game he followed the title at Garmisch Challenger with qf St Petersburg on the main tour. **1996:** (127) A 1, F –, W –, US –. Qf Kitzbuhel. **1997:** (32) A –, F 1, W qf, US –. Reached his 1st sf at Milan, then upset Medvedev and Kafelnikov back-to-back on his way to qf Wimbledon, unseeded. A severe ankle injury suffered at Stuttgart Mercedes in July kept him out until Sept., but 2 weeks after his return he upset Henman and Philippoussis to take his 1st tour title in his 1st f at Toulouse, following with f Singapore (d. Rios). He also played qf Gstaad and Stuttgart Eurocard (d. Rusedski) and overtook Becker as No. 1 in GER. **1998:** A qf, F 2, W 3, US 3. Although he reached no f, he appeared in sf Toulouse and qf Australian Open (unseeded), Gstaad and Basle (d. Korda). Frequently a dangerous opponent, he upset Bruguera at Sydney, Muster at Dubai, Kuerten at Indian Wells and Bjorkman at LIPC. He also won Ostrava doubles with Prinosil and played in the winning GER WT Cup team. **1998 HIGHLIGHTS – SINGLES: Australian Open qf** [unseeded] (d. M. Draper 6–4 6–4 6–0, Wheaton 2–6 1–6 6–2 7–6 6–2, Golmard 7–5 4–0 ret, Raoux 6–3 6–4 7–5, lost Escude 4–6 3–6 6–4 6–1 6–2), **French Open 2r** (d. Haas 6–1 6–2 7–6, lost Muster 6–2 6–1 6–3), **Wimbledon 3r** (d. Alonso 6–2 6–3 6–3, Dreekmann 6–4 6–3 1–6 6–4, lost Krajicek [seed 9] 6–4 7–6 7–6), **US Open 3r** (d. Roux 6–4 6–3 6–1, Clavet 6–4 7–6 6–1, lost Kafelnikov [seed 11] 6–4 6–0 6–2); **sf** Toulouse (d. Boutter 6–1 6–2, Barthez 4–6 6–3 6–1, Rosset 6–3 3–6 6–1, lost Rusedski 6–4 6–1). **1998 HIGHLIGHTS – DOUBLES:** (with Prinosil) **won** Ostrava (d. Adams/Vizner 6–4 6–3). **CAREER HIGHLIGHTS – SINGLES: Australian Open – qf 1998; Wimbledon – qf 1997** (d. Volkov 6–4 6–4 6–2, Baur 7–5 7–6 6–1, Medvedev 6–4 6–2 6–7 6–4, Kafelnikov 6–2 7–5 2–6 6–1, lost Woodbridge 7–6 2–6 6–0 6–4).

MARK KNOWLES (BAH)

Born Nassau, 4 September 1971, and lives there; RH; 6ft 3in; 185lb; turned pro 1992; career singles titles 0; final 1998 ATP ranking 276 singles, 9 doubles; 1998 prize money $441,501; career prize money $1,969,519.

Coached by Glenn Michibata. **1986:** Nat 16s champ. **1987:** (918). **1988:** (728). **1989:** (430) Joined his country's D Cup squad. **1990:** (–). **1991:** (293) Won All-American honours in singles and doubles at UCLA. **1992:** (255) A –, F –, W 2, US –. **1993:** (175) A –, F –, W –, US –. Upset Volkov at Washington and won Montreal doubles with Courier. **1994:** (255) A 1, F –, W 2, US –. In doubles he won Bogota with Nestor and r/u LIPC with Palmer. **1995:** (147) A –, F –, W 2, US 1. In singles he won 2 Challenger titles but reached no qf on the main tour. Continued to make his mark in doubles, joining with Nestor to upset Woodbridge/Woodforde on their way to a 1st GS f at Australian Open. They played 2 more f together, winning Indianapolis and qualifying for World Doubles Champ – although they won no match there – and he also won Japan Open with Stark. **1996:** (126) A –, F 2, W 2, US 2. The highlight of his year came at Shanghai, where he became the 1st Bahamian to reach a singles f and won the doubles with Smith. He played 6 other doubles f, winning Qatar, Memphis, Hamburg and Cincinnati with Nestor, with whom he qualified for World Doubles Champ. However, they withdrew after 2 rr matches when Nestor suffered a rib injury. **1997:** (259) A 1, F –, W –, US –. He was out of action for 3 months, suffering from a stress fracture of the 7th rib, which continued to plague him. Played 4 f with Nestor, winning Indian Wells and Rome and taking the last berth at World Doubles Champ, where they lost 2 matches before an aggravation of the rib injury forced them to withdraw. **1998:** A –, F –, W 1, US –. Although rib injuries to both himself and Nestor restricted their appearances together to 13, they won Cincinnati and played 4 other f, including French Open, US Open and World Doubles Champ. **1998 HIGHLIGHTS – SINGLES: Wimbledon 1r** (lost Wilkinson 7–6 6–0 6–1). **1998 HIGHLIGHTS – DOUBLES:** (with Nestor) **r/u French Open** (lost Eltingh/Haarhuis 6–3 3–6 6–3), **r/u US Open** (lost Stolle/Suk 4–6 7–6 6–2); **won** Cincinnati (d. Delaitre/Santoro 6–1 2–1 ret); **r/u** Indianapolis (lost Novak/Rikl 6–2 7–6), **r/u** World Doubles Champ (lost Eltingh/Haarhuis 6–4 6–2 7–5). **CAREER HIGHLIGHTS – DOUBLES:** (with Nestor) **Australian Open – r/u 1995** (lost Palmer/ Reneberg 6–3 3–6 6–3 6–2); **French Open – r/u 1998; US Open – r/u 1998**; **World Doubles Champ – r/u 1998**.

PETR KORDA (CZE)

Born Prague, 23 January 1968; lives Monte Carlo, Monaco; LH; 6ft 3in; 160lb; turned pro 1987; career singles titles 10; final 1998 ATP ranking 13; 1998 prize money $1,387,393; career prize money $10,427,102.

Coached by Ivo Werner; trained by Mark Vseticek. Wife former circuit player, Regina Rajchrtova (married 19 September 1992); daughters Jessica Regina (born 27 February 1993) and Nelly Ann (born 28 July 1998). Family life is very important to him. He was unable to compete on the tour in his early 20s because of the communist regime in TCH, defections by 3 others having made the authorities reluctant to let him go abroad. **1984:** Won Nat 18s at age 16. **1985:** In Jun doubles with Suk won French Open, r/u Australian Open and Wimbledon and was joint No. 1 in ITF rankings. **1986:** (511) Won Wimbledon Jun doubles with Carbonell. **1987:** (87) Won Budapest Challenger and on the senior tour upset Srejber on his way to his 1st qf showing at Prague. **1988:** (188) A –, F 2, W 3, US 1. Broke into top 100 in May and upset E. Sanchez in his 1st tourn on grass at Wimbledon. In doubles won Gstaad and Prague. Out of action with shoulder and ankle injuries following a car accident. **1989:** (59) A –, F –, W –, US –. Reached his 1st GP f at Frankfurt in autumn after sf showing at Vienna. In doubles won Stuttgart and reached 3 other f. **1990:** (38) A 2, F 2, W 1, US 2. Reached sf Philadelphia, Munich (d. Chang) and Moscow, and upset Gomez at Toronto World Tennis. In doubles r/u French Open with Ivanisevic and reached 3 more f, winning Monte Carlo with Smid. **1991:** (9) A 2, F 2, W 1, US 1. Made tremendous strides as he moved into the top 10 in autumn. Won his 1st tour singles title at New Haven, following with Berlin and also winning the doubles at both tourns. R/u Tampa, Washington (d. B. Gilbert), Montreal (d. Agassi and Courier); sf Umag and Vienna, and upset Lendl en route to qf Stockholm. **1992:** (7) A 1, F r/u, W 2, US 1. Having never before passed 3r GS singles, he was r/u French Open to Courier, who was the 1st seeded player he encountered in the tourn. Won Washington, Long Island (d. Edberg and

Lendl) and Vienna, moving into top 5 in Oct. He was also r/u Munich, Toulouse and Basle, reached sf Italian Open and Stuttgart and qualified for ATP World Champ but won no match there. **1993:** (12) A qf, F 2, W 4, US 1. In the spring he suffered from a viral infection, which caused inflammation of the heart and build-up of fluids. Although he dropped out of the top 10, he finished the year spectacularly by winning GS Cup, beating Bruguera, Sampras and Stich back-to-back. He was also r/u Sydney Indoor and New Haven and reached sf Milan, LIPC (upset Edberg), Halle, Montreal and Vienna, plus 5 more qf. In doubles he won 3 titles with 3 different partners. **1994:** (18) A 1, F 1, W 2, US –. R/u Milan (d. Ivanisevic and Bruguera), Indian Wells (where he extended Sampras to 5s) and Munich (where he won doubles with Becker) and reached sf Sydney NSW Open. Upset Edberg on his way to qf Paris Open at end of season. He was out of action 2 months to Oct. with groin and hip problems which had hampered him since French Open. **1995:** (41) A 3, F 1, W 4, US qf. In singles he reached sf Dubai and Milan, plus qf Basle and US Open, being unseeded both there and at Wimbledon, where he upset M. Chang. Reached 2 doubles f but won no title. Underwent a hernia operation on 13 Oct., having suffered groin problems (amongst other ailments) since May 1994 and considered retiring. **1996:** (24) A 1, F 3, W –, US 3. Having been talked out of retirement by his wife and friends, he was back in style at Qatar, where, unseeded and feeling better than for a long time, he won his 1st singles title since GS Cup in December 1993. He upset Ivanisevic at Ostrava, where he was r/u, played through the qualifying to reach sf Paris Open (d. Rios), and appeared in qf Basle and Moscow. He won all his matches at WT Cup, although CZE lost f to SUI, and in doubles with Edberg he won a 1st GS title at Australian Open. **1997:** (13) A 1, F 4, W 4, US qf. Free from pain and enjoying the game more than ever, he aimed to return to top 20 for 1st time since Feb. 1995. He achieved that goal after reaching f Halle (d. Muster) and Washington, and progressed to top 10 again after winning Stuttgart Eurocard in Oct., consolidating his position with r/u Moscow. The only player to take a set off Sampras at Wimbledon, he extended the eventual champion to 5s in last 16. At US Open, he went one better, removing the top seed in 5s tb, but was forced to retire in qf against Bjorkman, suffering from a cold and breathing difficulties. In another thrilling 5s match, he lost sf GS Cup to Rafter 9–7 fs. He also reached sf Antwerp, New Haven and Basle, plus qf Qatar, Milan, Rotterdam, Prague and Atlanta. **1998:** A won, F 1, W qf, US 1. Despite his observation at the beginning of the year that his career clock had reached five to midnight, he enjoyed a terrific start to the season. The highlight came at Australian Open, where he won his 1st GS singles title, a result which took him to No. 2 in the rankings. Rios, overtaking Sampras at the top, pushed him down to No. 3, but he was back in second place on 27 April – and could have been No. 1 had he reached f Monte Carlo. As it was, he lost qf to Krajicek. He had begun the year with the title at Qatar and during the course of it added qf appearances at Antwerp, Indian Wells (d. Rafter), Monte Carlo, Cincinnati and GS Cup, his best results coming in the 1st half of the season. Suffered a badly stretched Achilles tendon in last 16 Wimbledon, but insisted he could continue to play qf v Henman, although he lost that match in ss. He had expected to retire at end of season, but, despite having fallen from the heights of the beginning of the year, he was still enjoying playing so much that he decided to continue. **1998 HIGHLIGHTS – SINGLES: won Australian Open** [seed 6] (d. Portas 6–3 4–6 6–1 6–4, S. Draper 7–6 6–3 6–3, Spadea 6–2 7–6 6–2, Pioline 6–4 6–4 3–6 6–3, Bjorkman [seed 4] 3–6 5–7 6–3 6–4 6–2, Kucera 6–1 6–4 1–6 6–2, Rios [seed 9] 6–2 6–2 6–2), **French Open 1r** [seed 2] (lost Zabaleta 6–0 6–2 3–6 4–6 6–3), **Wimbledon qf** [seed 3] (d. J. Sanchez 6–3 6–4 6–3, Dewulf 6–4 6–3 6–2, Golmard 4–6 7–5 7–5 7–5, Van Lottum 6–3 6–4 7–6, lost Henman [seed 12] 6–3 6–4 6–2), **US Open 1r** (lost Karbacher 2–6 6–3 6–2 6–1); **won** Qatar (d. Delaitre 7–5 6–1, Burgsmuller 6–3 6–2, Henman 7–5 4–6 6–4, Medvedev 6–3 6–4, Santoro 6–0 6–3) **CAREER HIGHLIGHTS – SINGLES: Australian Open – won 1998, qf 1993** (d. C. Adams 6–3 3–6 6–3 6–3, Eltingh 7–6 6–2 6–3, Medvedev 6–4 4–6 6–3 7–6, Garner 7–5 6–3 6–1, lost Courier 6–1 6–0 6–4); **French Open – r/u 1992** (d. Bergstrom 6–4 6–2 6–2, Matsuoka 1–6 4–6 6–4 6–4 6–4, Schapers 6–4 6–2 3–6 6–1, Oncins 6–4 6–3 6–3, Cherkasov 6–4 6–7 6–2 6–4, Leconte 6–2 7–5 6–3, lost Courier 7–5 6–2 6–1); **Wimbledon – qf 1998; US Open – qf 1995** [unseeded] (d. Matsuoka 7–6 6–7 6–7 6–5 ret, Eltingh 6–2 6–4 3–6 6–1, Ondruska 6–3 6–2 7–5, Spadea 6–2 7–5 6–4, lost Agassi 6–4 6–2 1–6 7–5), **qf 1997** (d. Spadea 2–6 7–5 7–6 6–4, Martelli 6–3 7–6 7–6, Damm 4–6 6–3 6–4 7–5, Sampras 6–7 7–5 7–6 3–6 7–6, lost Bjorkman 7–6 6–2 1–0 ret); **GS Cup – won 1993** (d. Volkov 6–2 6–3, Bruguera 4–6 6–0 6–4, Sampras 3–6 7–6 3–6 7–6 13–11, Stich 2–6 6–4 7–6 2–6 11–9), **sf 1997** (d. Kuerten 6–3 5–3 ret, Pioline 7–5 6–3, lost Rafter 7–5 3–6 6–7 7–6 9–7). **CAREER HIGHLIGHTS – DOUBLES:** (with Edberg) **Australian Open – won 1996** (d. Lareau/O'Brien 7–5 7–5 4–6 6–1); (with Ivanisevic) **French Open – r/u 1990** (lost Casal/E. Sanchez 7–5 6–3).

GUSTAVO KUERTEN (BRA)

Born Florianapolis, 10 September 1976, and lives there; RH; 6ft 3in; 165lb; turned pro 1995; career singles titles 3; final 1998 ATP ranking 23; 1998 prize money $732,804; career prize money $2,459,442.

Coached by Larri Passos. **1993:** (665). **1994:** (421) Won French Open Jun doubles with Lapentti, to whom he was r/u Orange Bowl 18s. **1995:** (197) Made an impact on the satellite circuits. **1996:** (88) A –, F 1, W –, US –. Reached qf Umag (d. Berasategui) and Beijing and finished the season by winning Campinas Challenger. In doubles he won Santiago with Meligeni. **1997:** (14) A 2, F won, W 1, US 3. The title at Curitiba Challenger restored his confidence after a poor start to the year, which gave no hint of what was to come at French Open. There he upset CC specialists Muster, Medvedev, Kafelnikov and Bruguera to win his 1st title, having never before passed qf. He was the 1st Brazilian to win a GS title (or even to pass qf in GS), 3rd unseeded player to win French Open, and 1st since Wilander in 1982 to win his 1st career title in GS. Only Mark Edmondson, winning Australian Open in 1976 from a ranking of 212, had won a GS ranked lower than his

66. However, that triumph saw him become the 1st Brazilian to break into top 20 at No. 15, and after r/u showing at Montreal (d. M. Chang), he moved into top 10. He also reached f Bologna (d. Berasategui) and qf Cincinnati, as well as recording other useful upsets during the year, including Agassi at Memphis and W. Ferreira at Indian Wells. In doubles with Meligeni, he played and won 3 f. **1998:** A 2, F 2, W 1, US 2. Emerging from a slump, he won his 2nd career title at Stuttgart Mercedes in July, and followed with Mallorca (d. Moya), as well as reaching sf Memphis and Rome, plus qf LIPC, Hamburg, Umag and Long Island (d. Rios). In doubles with Meligeni he won Gstaad, but was involved in an unsavoury incident at French Open: in an argument over a call on serve, he threw his racket at umpire Bruno Rebeuh, who ducked, and the racket hit a spectator. The match was awarded to their opponents, Bjorkman/Rafter, Kuerten being disqualified and fined for unsportsmanlike behaviour. **1998 HIGHLIGHTS – SINGLES: Australian Open 2r** [seed 12] (d. Diaz 6–3 3–6 6–3 6–2, lost Escude 5–7 6–3 6–1 7–5), **French Open 2r** [seed 8] (d. Auffray 6–0 6–2 6–2, lost Safin 3–6 7–6 3–6 6–1 6–4), **Wimbledon 1r** (lost Stoltenberg 4–6 6–3 6–1 4–6 10–8), **US Open 2r** (d. Behr 4–6 6–4 6–3 6–4, lost nainkin 2–6 6–4 6–3 6–4); **won** Stuttgart Mercedes (d. Meligeni 7–6 6–4, C. Costa 6–2 6–4, A. Costa 7–5 6–0, Moya 7–6 6–4, Kucera 4–6 6–2 6–4), **won** Mallorca (d. Van Herck 7–6 1–0 ret, Serrano 6–1 6–1, Bruguera 6–4 6–4, Muster 7–5 7–5, Moya 6–7 6–2 6–3); **sf** Memphis (d. Weiner 7–6 6–3, Gambill 6–4 7–6, Woodforde 4–6 6–4 6–4, lost M. Chang 7–6 7–6), **sf** Rome (d. C. Costa 1–6 6–4 6–2, Lapentti 6–0 7–5, Haas 6–4 6–2, Vicente 6–3 6–4, lost Rios 6–0 7–5). **1998 HIGHLIGHTS – DOUBLES:** (with Meligeni) **won** Gstaad (d. Orsanic/Suk 6–4 7–5). **CAREER HIGHLIGHTS – SINGLES: French Open – won 1997** (d. Dosedel 6–0 7–5 6–1, Bjorkman 6–4 6–2 4–6 7–5, Muster 6–7 6–1 6–3 3–6 6–4, Medvedev 5–7 6–1 6–2 1–6 7–5, Kafelnikov 6–2 5–7 2–6 6–0 6–4, Dewulf 6–1 3–6 6–1 7–6, Bruguera 6–3 6–4 6–2).

IRAKLI LABADZE (GEO)

Born Tbilisi, 9 June 1981, and lives there; LH; 2HB; 6ft 1in; 170lb; career singles titles 0; final 1998 ATP ranking 506; 1998 prize money $1,282.

Coached by Roberto Bogina. Nat Jun champ. **1998:** R/u Wimbledon Jun to Federer.

NICOLAS LAPENTTI (ECU)

Born Guyaquil, 13 August 1976, and lives there; RH; 6ft 2in; 180lb; turned pro 1995; career singles titles 1; final 1998 ATP ranking 69; 1998 prize money $322,257.

Coached by Raul Viver. **1991:** (922). **1992:** (–) Joined his country's D Cup squad. **1993:** (323). **1994:** (632) Won Orange Bowl 18s over Kuerten; in Jun doubles won French Open with him and US Open with Ellwood, finishing No. 2 in ITF Jun rankings in both singles and doubles. **1995:** (125) On the satellite circuits he won all his singles matches in 4 weeks on the Colombia satellite, following with the 1st 2 on the Ecuador circuit. Five days later he qualified for his 1st main tour event at Bogota and won the title. He then rounded off his season by winning Santiago Challenger. **1996:** (121) A 1, F 1, W 2, US 1. R/u Bogota in both singles and doubles (with Campana). **1997:** (64) A –, F 2, W 1, US 2. Bogota again saw him at his best: he was r/u there, having reached sf Mexico City the week before and qf Bologna and Bucharest (d. Berasategui) earlier in year. Played 3 doubles f with different partners, winning Amsterdam with Kilderry and Mexico City with Orsanic. **1998:** A 2, F 1, W 1, US 1. His best showing was sf Prague, and he also reached qf Kitzbuhel (d. Kafelnikov), Palermo and Santiago (d. Kuerten). **1998 HIGHLIGHTS – SINGLES: Australian Open 2r** (d. Viloca 5–7 6–3 6–4 5–7 6–1, lost Santoro 6–4 3–6 3–6 6–2 6–4), **French Open 1r** (lost Krajicek [seed 10] 6–4 6–4 6–7 7–6), **Wimbledon 1r** (lost Prinosil 4–6 6–3 6–4 6–3), **US Open 1r** (lost Santoro 4–6 7–5 6–3 3–6 7–6); **sf** Prague (d. Ulihrach 6–4 6–4, Sinner 6–2 6–0, Vicente 6–0 7–5, lost Dosedel 3–6 6–3 6–2).

MAGNUS LARSSON (SWE)

Born Olofstrom, 25 March 1970; lives Vaxjo; RH; 6ft 4in; 194lb; turned pro 1989; career singles titles 6; final 1998 ATP ranking 43; 1998 prize money $430,511; career prize money $5,197,394.

Coached by Carl Axel Hageskog and Stefan Simonsson. **1986:** Won European Jun doubles with Kulti. **1988:** (381) R/u French Open Jun to Pereira. **1989:** (145) A 1, F –, W –, US –. Won Geneva Challenger. **1990:** (56) A 2, F –, W 1, US –. Won Florence after qualifying, r/u Bastad and won Ljubliana Challenger. **1991:** (61) A 1, F 3, W 2, US 3. He sprung some big upsets during the year, surprising Becker en route to sf Adelaide, Edberg at Monte Carlo, Gomez at US Open and Cherkasov on his way to qf Bastad. He reached the same stage at Prague and Florence and extended Courier to 5s French Open, at one stage being 2 sets to 1 ahead. **1992:** (34) A 1, F 3, W 3, US 2. Won both singles and doubles at Copenhagen, following with the singles title at Munich (d. Stich and Korda). He also made an unexpected appearance in last 16 Olympics (d. Forget) and reached 3 qf. **1993:** (39) A 2, F 3, W 2, US qf. Usually a CC specialist, he was playing only his 6th HC tourn at US Open, where he upset Becker to reach qf, unseeded. He also appeared in sf Copenhagen and Bastad plus 4 more qf. Qualified for GS Cup but lost 1r Bruguera. **1994:** (19) A 1, F sf, W 1, US 1. At French Open he continued his unexpected success in GS when, unseeded, he upset Martin and saved 6 mps v Dreekmann to reach sf. Again rising to the big occasion, he won the dramatic final rubber in D Cup sf v US, beating Martin to take SWE to f. He finished the year in triumph, winning both his matches as SWE won D Cup over RUS in Moscow, and took his first GS Cup by beating Sampras in f. He also won Zaragoza and Toulouse, was r/u Halle and Antwerp and upset Chang at Stockholm, breaking into top 20 1st time after Antwerp. **1995:** (17) A 4, F 4, W –, US –. Upset Stich on the way to f Qatar, where he won the doubles, and removed Ivanisevic to reach f Barcelona. Extended Sampras to 5s Australian Open and Agassi to fs tb in sf LIPC, reaching the same stage at Atlanta and US CC, plus 3 more qf, and broke into top 10 in April. However, he broke a bone in 2 places in his right foot playing an exhibition match in June and was out 5 months, missing Wimbledon and US Open. Played on winning SWE team in WT Cup and reached his 1st GS f in doubles with Kulti at French Open. **1996:** (46) A 3, F 1, W 2, US 1. He struggled to regain his form, with his best performances being r/u Toulouse (d. Rios) and qf Qatar, Barcelona (d. Bruguera), Hamburg, Halle and Bastad. **1997:** (25) A 2, F 3, W –, US qf. He was always a dangerous opponent and the only player to upset Sampras twice in 1997. Although he did not progress beyond qf, he was consistent in reaching that stage at US Open, Qatar (d. Enqvist), Marseille (d. Clavet), Monte Carlo (d. Sampras), Bastad, Indianapolis (d. Sampras), Vienna (d. Enqvist), Stuttgart Eurocard (d. Corretja) and Stockholm (d. Enqvist), adding upsets of Kafelnikov at Barcelona, Rios at Indian Wells and Mantilla at French Open. Played 2 doubles f, winning Marseille with Enqvist. **1998:** A 1, F 1, W 4, US qf. He upset Muster and Krajicek on his way to f Halle, surprised Bjorkman en route to sf Cincinnati, where he took a set off Sampras, and removed Rios at US Open, where he reached qf, unseeded. He also appeared in same stage Antwerp and won Bastad doubles with Gustafsson. **1998 HIGHLIGHTS – SINGLES: Australian Open 1r** (lost Escude 5–7 4–6 7–5 6–1 10–8), **French Open 1r** (lost Dewulf 7–6 7–5 7–6), **Wimbledon last 16** [unseeded] (d. Filippini 7–5 6–1 6–4, Sargsian 6–3 6–7 6–3 7–5, Arazi 6–3 6–3 6–2, lost Siemerink 4–6 6–3 6–3 6–2), **US Open qf** [unseeded] (d. MaliVai Washington 3–6 6–3 1–6 6–4 6–4, Filippini 6–3 6–2 6–2, Rios [seed 2] 6–1 6–7 2–6 6–3 6–2, Gross 6–4 7–5 5–7 6–2, lost Moya [seed 10] 6–4 6–3 6–3); **r/u** Halle (d. Muster 6–3 6–2, Campbell 6–0 6–3, Krajicek 6–4 6–2, Haarhuis 7–6 6–2, lost Kafelnikov 6–4 6–4); **sf** Cincinnati (d. Pozzi 6–4 7–5, Bjorkman 6–7 6–2 6–3, Haas 6–4 6–4, Johansson 6–4 7–6, lost Sampras 7–5 2–6 6–1). **1998 HIGHLIGHTS – DOUBLES:** (with Gustafsson) **won** Bastad (d. Bale/Norval 6–4 6–2). **CAREER HIGHLIGHTS – SINGLES: GS Cup – won 1994** [unseeded] (d. Edberg 6–4 6–7 8–6, Agassi 6–3 1–6 6–0, Martin 6–4 6–1 6–1, Sampras 7–6 4–6 7–6 6–4); **French Open – sf 1994** [unseeded] (d. Steven 6–2 6–2 6–2, Tarango 6–2 6–4 6–3, Martin 6–7 6–3 6–0 1–6 6–3, Yzaga 6–3 6–2 6–2, Dreekmann 3–6 6–7 7–6 6–0 6–1, lost Berasategui 6–3 6–4 6–1); **US Open – qf 1993** (d. Raoux 6–2 6–4 7–6, Borwick 6–4 6–4 6–4, Fromberg 6–2 7–5 7–6, Becker 6–2 6–3 3–6 7–5, lost Masur 6–2 7–5 7–5), **qf 1997** (d. Siemerink 6–4 6–2 6–3, Escude 6–4 6–2 7–6, Meligeni 6–2 6–4 6–3, W. Ferreira 6–3 7–6 6–3, lost Rafter 7–6 6–4 6–2), **qf 1998**. **CAREER HIGHLIGHTS – DOUBLES:** (with Kulti) **French Open – r/u 1995 Open** (lost Eltingh/Haarhuis 6–7 6–4 6–1).

RICK LEACH (USA)

Born Arcadia, Cal., 28 December 1964; lives Laguna Beach, Cal.; LH; 6ft 2in; 175lb; turned pro 1987; career singles titles 0; final 1998 ATP ranking – singles, 13 doubles; 1998 prize money $338,236; career prize money $2,950,292.

Wife Christi Bondra (married 26 December 1992); daughter Paulina Christine (born 23 February 1994). Won 19 nat jun titles. **1986:** (201) Coached by his father, Dick, at USC, where he was an All-American. Won NCAA doubles with Pawsat and took 3 singles titles on USTA circuit. **1987:** (148) A –, F –, W –, US 2. Won NCAA doubles again (with Melville) and won 2 GP doubles titles. **1988:** (258) A 2, F –, W –, US 2. In doubles with Pugh won Australian Open and Masters doubles on 1st appearance there but, suffering from flu and food poisoning, was forced to default US Open doubles f. Won 6 other titles (1 with Goldie). **1989:** (195) A 1, F –, W –, US 2. In doubles with Pugh won Australian Open, r/u Wimbledon and took 4 other titles to qualify for Masters, where they surprisingly took only 6th place. **1990:** (279) A –, F –, W 1, US 2. In doubles with Pugh won a 1st Wimbledon title, plus LIPC and Philadelphia, to qualify for IBM/ATP World Doubles, where they failed to reach sf, and played together in winning US D Cup team. In mixed doubles with Garrison won Wimbledon and r/u US Open. **1991:** (402) A –, F –, W –, US 1. Won 2 doubles titles with Pugh and r/u French Open. **1992:** (429) A –, F –, W 1, US –. In doubles with Jones was r/u Australian Open and US Open, won Tokyo Suntory and New Haven and qualified for World Doubles final. **1993:** (632) A –, F –, W –, US –. Teamed with K. Flach to win his 1st US Open doubles. They won another 2 titles together, just missing IBM/ATP World Doubles, and he had a 4th win with Black. **1994:** (536) A –, F –, W –, US –. Won 2 doubles titles with different partners. **1995:** (–) A –, F –, W –, US –. Won New Haven doubles with Melville, with whom he qualified for World Doubles Champ, although they did not progress beyond rr. In mixed he took Australian Open with Zvereva. **1996:** (–) A –, F –, W –, US –. In men's doubles he won 4 of 5 f, each with a different partner, and in mixed he was r/u US Open with Bollegraf. **1997:** (–) A –, F –, W –, US –. Until the World Doubles f he had won no doubles title, although he had played 7 f – 5 with Stark and 1 each with Bjorkman and Bhupathi. However, playing his 7th season-ending champ in 10 years and with his 5th different partner (Stark), he won the title for the 2nd time. It was a triumphant end for the partnership, for he and Stark had decided in Aug. to part company at end of year. He also collected 2 mixed doubles titles, taking Australian Open and US Open with Bollegraf. **1998:** A –, F –, W –, US –. He played 6 doubles f with E. Ferreira, winning LIPC and Halle to extend to 12 his run of consec. seasons with at least 1 title to his name. Ferreira became the 6th different partner with whom he qualified for World Doubles Champ, but they did not progress beyond rr. **1998 HIGHLIGHTS – DOUBLES:** (with E. Ferreira) **won** LIPC (d. O'Brien/Stark 6–2 6–4), **won** Halle (d. De Jager/Goellner 4–6 6–4 7–6); **r/u** Adelaide (lost Eagle/Florent 6–4 6–7 6–3), **r/u** Barcelona (lost Eltingh/Haarhuis 7–5 6–0), **r/u** Rome (lost Bhupathi/Paes 6–4 4–6 7–6), **r/u** Toronto (lost Damm/Grabb 6–7 6–2 7–6). **CAREER HIGHLIGHTS – DOUBLES:** (with Pugh unless stated) **Australian Open – won 1988** (d. Bates/Lundgren 6–3 6–2 6–3), **won 1989** (d. Cahill/Kratzmann 6–4 6–4 6–4), [Jones] **r/u 1992** (lost Woodbridge/Woodforde 6–4 6–3 6–4);

Wimbledon – won 1990 (d. Aldrich/Visser 7–6 7–6 7–6), **r/u 1989** (lost Fitzgerald/Jarryd 3–6 7–6 6–4 7–6); **US Open** – (with Flach) **won 1993** (d. Damm/Novacek 6–7 6–4 6–2), **r/u 1988** (lost Casal/E. Sanchez def), (with Jones) **r/u 1992** (lost Grabb/Reneberg 3–6 7–6 6–3 6–3); **Masters/World Doubles Champ – won 1988** (d. Casal/E. Sanchez 6-4 6-3 2-6 6-0), (with Stark) **won 1997** (d. Bhupathi/Paes 6–3 6–4 7–6); **French Open – r/u 1991** (lost Fitzgerald/Jarryd 6–0 7–6). **MIXED DOUBLES:** (with Bollegraf unless stated) **Australian Open –** (with Zvereva) **won 1995** (d. Suk/G. Fernandez 7–6 6–7 6–4), **won 1997** (d. de Jager/Neiland 6–3 6–7 7–5)**; Wimbledon –** (with Garrison) **won 1990** (d. Smylie/Fitzgerald 7–5 6–2), **US Open – won 1997** (d. Albano/Paz 3–6 7–5 7–6).

DAVID MACPHERSON (AUS)

Born Launceston, Tas., 3 July 1967; lives Sarasota, Fla.; LH; 5ft 9in; 140lb; turned pro 1985; career singles titles 0; final 1998 ATP ranking – singles, 21 doubles; 1998 prize money $173,070; career prize money $1,264,837.

Wife Charlene (married 24 March 1990); daughter Alexandra Grace (born 20 November 1993). Won Nat Jun doubles with Custer in 14s, 16s and 18s (3 times). **1983:** (480) A 1, F –, W –, US –. **1984:** (552) A –, F –, W –, US –. **1985:** (389) A 1, F –, W –, US –. R/u US Open Jun doubles with Flynn. **1986:** (505) A –, F –, W –, US –. **1987:** (436) A 2, F –, W –, US –. **1988:** (509) A –, F –, W –, US –. Won Raleigh Challenger doubles with Youl. **1989:** (352) A –, F –, W –, US –. Won 3 doubles titles on the Challenger circuit and took both singles and doubles on Australian satellite circuit. **1990:** (521) A 1, F –, W –, US –. Won Toronto doubles with Galbraith. **1991:** (811) A –, F –, W –, US –. Won Rotterdam and Lyon doubles with DeVries. **1992:** (–) A –, F –, W –, US –. Won doubles titles in Milan, Indian Wells, Atlanta, US CC, Manchester and Brisbane with 3 different partners, qualifying for World Doubles Final with DeVries. **1993:** (1186) A –, F –, W –, US –. In doubles won Nice with Warder and reached 2 more f with DeVries. **1994:** (–) Won 2 Challenger doubles titles with Kronemann. **1995:** (–) Developing his doubles partnership with Kronemann, he won Scottsdale, Barcelona, Munich and r/u Sydney. **1996:** (–) It had been a less successful year, in which he and Kronemann won San Jose from only 2 f. However, they played World Doubles Champ as alternates after Forget/Hlasek and Kafelnikov/Vacek withdrew and reached sf before falling to Lareau/O'Brien. **1997:** (–) In doubles with Kronemann he played 2 f, but won no title. However, they played as alternates again at World Doubles Champ, losing their only match after Knowles/Nestor withdrew after 2 matches. **1998:** From 2 doubles f, he won St Polten with Grabb. **1998 HIGHLIGHTS – DOUBLES:** (with Grabb) **won** St Polten (d. D. Adams/W. Black 6–4 6–4); (with Reneberg) **r/u** Philadelphia (lost Eltingh/Haarhuis 7–6 6–7 6–2).

FELIX MANTILLA (ESP)

Born Barcelona, 23 September 1974, and lives there; RH; 5ft 10in; 162lb; turned pro 1993; career singles titles 7; final 1998 ATP ranking 20; 1998 prize money $823,916; career prize money $2,510,230.

Coached by Jordi Vilaro. **1992:** (680) Member of the winning Spanish Sunshine Cup team. **1993:** (432). **1994:** (301) Enjoyed some success on the satellite circuits. **1995:** (84) A –, F –, W –, US –. Broke into the top 100 at end of year, following his 1st r/u showing on the main tour at Buenos Aires. He had played through the qualifying there, as he had before reaching sf Valencia and qf Casablanca. **1996:** (18) A –, F 3, W 1, US –. He shot up into the top 20 with his 1st title on the main tour at Oporto (unseeded, d. Moya), r/u St Polten, Gstaad, San Marino and Umag, sf Marbella and Santiago, plus qf Monte Carlo (d. Bruguera), Stuttgart and Amsterdam. He also won 3 Challenger titles and upset Enqvist at Prague. **1997:** (16) A qf, F 2, W –, US 4. In an 8-week period in summer, he won Bologna, Gstaad, Umag and San Marino, reaching qf Stuttgart Mercedes in the middle of that sequence. He followed with a 5th title at Bournemouth a month later to add to f Hamburg (d. Becker), sf Estoril and qf Australian Open and Lyon. Won all his matches in winning ESP WT Cup team. He felt he should have been called ahead of Henman as alternate for last rr match ATP Champ when Bruguera withdrew, and did not accept claims by the organisers that they had been unable to contact him. **1998:** A 1, F sf, W 3, US 2. Although Bournemouth was his only title in a less spectacular year, he was r/u Dubai and Long Island, and reached sf Auckland, Hamburg, Santiago and French Open (where he faced no seeded player until losing to Moya), plus qf Gstaad, Umag and GS Cup. **1998 HIGHLIGHTS – SINGLES: Australian Open 1r** [seed 14] (lost B. Black 6–4 6–0 4–6 6–4), **French Open sf** [seed 15] (d. Schranz 6–2 6–4 6–2, B. Black 6–2 6–2 7–6, Santoro 4–6 6–2 6–2 7–6, Delgado 6–2 6–2 6–4, Muster 6–4 6–2 4–6 6–3, lost Moya [seed 12] 5–7 6–2 6–4 6–2), **Wimbledon 3r** [seed 16] (d. Van Garsse 6–2 6–2 1–6 4–6 6–3, Vasek 7–6 3–6 6–3 6–4, lost Grosjean 6–0 7–6 6–2), **US Open 2r** (d. Steven 6–3 3–6 6–4 7–5, lost Henman [seed 13] 6–3 5–7 7–5 6–4); **won** Bournemouth (d. Browne 6–4 6–2, Burillo 7–5 6–2, Koubek 6–7 6–4 6–4, Goellner 6–4 6–2, A. Costa 6–3 7–5); **r/u** Dubai (d. Alami 6–4 6–2, Becker w/o, Berasategui 6–4 6–4, W. Ferreira 7–6 4–6 6–4, lost Corretja 7–6 6–1), **r/u** Long Island (d. Bruguera 6–4 6–4, Ulihrach 7–6 6–3, Kuerten 6–4 2–6 6–4, Safin 6–3 5–7 6–4, lost Rafter 7–6 6–2); **sf** Auckland (d. Van Herck 7–6 6–3, Sell 6–3 7–6, C. Costa 6–2 6–3, lost Fromberg 6–3 7–6), **sf** Hamburg (d. Raoux 6–4 ret, Ulihrach 6–4 6–2, Berasategui 1–6 7–6 7–6, Ivanisevic 6–0 2–0 ret, lost Corretja 6–2 3–6 6–3), **sf** Santiago (d. Zabaleta 6–2 6–3, Medica 6–0 6–1, Courier 3–6 6–3 7–6, lost El Aynaoui 6–4 6–4). **CAREER HIGHLIGHTS – SINGLES: French Open – sf 1998; Australian Open – qf 1997** (d. Rusedski 6–4 5–7 7–5 6–2, Meligeni 6–2 6–4 6–1, Boetsch 6–3 1–6 7–6 6–4, MaliVai Washington 7–5 6–2 6–1, lost Moya 7–5 6–2 6–7 6–2).

JUAN ANTONIO MARIN (ESP)

Born San Jose, Costa Rica, 2 March 1975; lives Barcelona and Murcia; RH; 5ft 9in; 162lb; turned pro 1996; career singles titles 0; final 1998 ATP ranking 70; 1998 prize money $216,867.

Coached by Alex Mas. Moved to Spain from Costa Rica at age 14. Former Costa Rican nat 14s champ. **1993:** (906). **1994:** (547). **1995:** (250) Enjoyed some success on the Spanish satellite circuit. **1996:** (218) Won Samarkand Challenger. **1997:** (86) A –, F –, W 1, US 1. Broke into top 100 after appearing in his 1st career f at Bastad (d. Kucera), reached qf Mexico City and upset Filippini at Bucharest. **1998:** A 1, F 1, W 1, US 1. His best performance came in Nov. when he upset Rios en route to sf Santiago, having earlier reached the same stage at Bologna and Umag, plus qf Casablanca and Mexico City. **1998 HIGHLIGHTS – SINGLES: Australian Open 1r** (lost Enqvist 6–3 6–4 6–3), **French Open 1r** (lost Raoux 6–3 7–6 7–6), **Wimbledon 1r** (lost Pescosolido 6–2 6–1 6–1), **US Open 1r** (lost Gumy 6–3 0–6 4–6 6–2 6–1); **sf** Bologna (d. Ketola 6–4 7–6, Gumy 6–4 6–2, Puerta 6–1 6–3, lost Alonso 7–6 6–3), **sf** Umag (d. Furlan 4–6 6–3 6–4, Sanguinetti 7–6 3–6 6–3, Haarhuis 6–2 7–6, lost M. Norman 7–6 6–3), **sf** Santiago (d. Pozzi 3–6 6–1 6–3, Squillari 6–4 4–6 6–4, Rios 6–4 6–7 7–5, lost Clavet 6–2 7–5).

DAVID MARTIN (USA)

Born Oklahoma, 22 February 1981, and lives there; LH; 5ft 11in; 165lb; career singles titles 0; final 1998 ATP ranking 1067; 1998 prize money $4,589.

Coached by Doug Boswell. **1998:** Won US Open Jun doubles with Hippensteel.

TODD MARTIN (USA)

Born Hinsdale, Ill., 8 July 1970; lives Ponte Vedra Beach, Fla.; RH; 6ft 6in; 190lb; turned pro 1990; career singles titles 7; final 1998 ATP ranking 16; 1998 prize money $771,943; career prize money $5,596,692.

Coached by Dean Goldfine. **1989:** (257) Won New Haven Challenger. **1990:** (269) A –, F –, W –, US 1. All-American at Northwestern (Illinois) Univ. **1991:** (133) A –, F 4, W –, US 3. Won no match all year until winning 7 in a row through qualifying to last 16 French Open and followed with upset of Lundgren en route to 1st tour sf at Newport. **1992:** (87) A –, F –, W 2, US 3. Extended Sampras to 5s 3r US Open and reached sf Indianapolis, breaking into top 100. **1993:** (13) A 1, F 1, W qf, US 3. He burst into the top 20 with some impressive performances and some stunning upsets. He surprised Agassi and M. Chang back-to-back on his way to f Memphis, where he took a set off Courier and extended him to 2 tb, then in May won his 1st career singles title at Coral Springs. He was also r/u Washington, Montreal (d. Becker and Agassi), Tokyo Seiko (d. Edberg) and reached sf US CC and Queen's. In GS he upset Ivanisevic on his way to qf Wimbledon, unseeded, and at US Open held 2 mps v Krajicek before losing in 5 hr 10 min. **1994:** (10) A r/u, F 3, W sf, US sf. Broke into the top 10 after his 1st appearance in GS f at Australian Open, upsetting Edberg on the way. He won Memphis in Feb. and at Queen's took his 1st GC title, surprising Edberg in qf and Sampras in f. He made his mark at Wimbledon, where he played 4 5s matches, removed Agassi and was the only player to take a set off Sampras. This result took him briefly into top 5. He was also r/u Atlanta and Pinehurst and reached sf Sydney NSW Open. He made his D Cup debut in March and upset Edberg in his 2nd tie in Sept. Won Adidas Sportsmanship Award for 2nd successive year. **1995:** (18) A 4, F 3, W 4, US 4. Although it was a less spectacular year, he finished in style as r/u to Ivanisevic at GS Cup. Earlier he upset Sampras on his way to the title at Memphis and reached sf Scottsdale, Atlanta, Washington and Lyon, plus qf Indian Wells. In doubles he won 2 titles from 4 f with different partners and in D Cup f partnered Sampras to key victory over Kafelnikov/Olhovskiy as USA d. RUS 3–2 in Moscow. **1996:** (12) A 3, F 3, W sf, US 3. Aiming to return to the top 10 in 1996, he began well with the title at Sydney over Ivanisevic, following during the year with r/u Memphis and Stockholm, sf Wimbledon, Indianapolis, Toronto and Vienna (d. Ivanisevic again), plus 4 qf. He extended Sampras to 5s at French Open and came close to his 2nd GS f at Wimbledon, where, serving for the sf at 5–1 fs v MaliVai Washington, he missed his chance and eventually lost 10–8. He played US Open with his right arm heavily strapped, although he refused to blame that for his 3r defeat by Henman. **1997:** (81) A –, F –, W –, US 2. Missed Australian Open with tendinitis in right knee, and was restricted all year. Up to US Open, he had played only 2 tourns, reaching sf both San Jose and Memphis, then added qf Vienna (d. Muster) and Stuttgart Eurocard (d. Moya) in autumn, as well as winning Delray Beach Challenger. **1998:** A 2, F 1, W 4, US 2. Unseeded at Barcelona, he upset Muster and Berasategui on the way to his first title for more than 2 years, and in Nov., again unseeded, he won Stockholm (d. Henman). It was an excellent end to the season for him, following his performance the previous week at Paris Open, where he upset Ivanisevic, Rafter and Agassi to reach sf and regain his old place in the top 20. He also reached sf Indianapolis and Vienna (d. Korda), and played qf Sydney (d. Pioline) and San Jose (d. Woodbridge). In other tourns he upset Kucera at Stuttgart Eurocard and extended Rafter to 5s at Australian Open. **1998 HIGHLIGHTS – SINGLES: Australian Open 2r** (d. J. Sanchez 6–1 6–4 6–1, lost Rafter [seed 2] 2–6 7–6 6–7 6–4 6–3), **French Open 1r** (lost Sampras [seed 1] 6–4 6–3 6–3), **Wimbledon last 16** [unseeded] (d. Sa 6–3 6–4 6–4, M. Draper 6–3 7–6 6–2, Woodbridge 6–4 4–6 7–6 6–4, lost Ivanisevic [seed 14] 7–6 6–3 3–6 7–6), **US Open 2r** (d. Tarango 7–6 6–2 7–5, lost Ivanisevic [seed 14] 1–6 7–6 7–5 6–3); **won** Barcelona (d. Fromberg 6–2 6–4, Muster 6–4 7–6, Dosedel 6–3 7–5, C. Costa 6–2 6–4, Gaudenzi 6–4 7–6, Berasategui 6–2 1–6 6–3 6–2), **won** Stockholm (d. Heuberger 6–1 6–2, Arthurs 6–4 6–3, Suzuki 6–3 6–4, Henman 4–6 6–1 6–2, Johansson 6–3 6–4 6–4); **sf** Indianapolis (d. McGuire 6–3 6–4, Clement 4–6 6–1 6–4, Johansson 6–1 7–6, Arazi 7–6 7–6, lost Corretja 6–2 7–6), **sf** Vienna (d. Kiefer 4–6 6–3 6–4, Korda 6–3 7–6, Pioline 6–4 6–3, lost Sampras 6–3 7–6), **sf** Paris Open (d. Haarhuis 6–7 6–4 6–4, Ivanisevic 4–6 6–1 7–6, Rafter 5–7 7–6 7–6, Agassi 4–6 6–4 6–4, lost Sampras 6–4 7–6). **1998 HIGHLIGHTS – DOUBLES:** (with Reneberg) **r/u** Indian Wells (lost Bjorkman/Rafter 6–4 7–6). **CAREER HIGHLIGHTS – SINGLES: Australian Open – r/u 1994** (d. Yzaga 6–3 7–6 6–2, Bjorkman 6–3 6–4 6–0, Svensson 6–1 5–7 6–2 6–2, Daufresne 6–7 7–6 6–3 6–3, MaliVai Washington 6–2 7–6 7–6, Edberg 3–6 7–6 7–6 7–6, lost Sampras 7–6 6–4 6–4); **GS Cup – r/u 1995** (d. Bruguera 7–6 6–4, Medvedev 6–3 1–6 4–0 ret, Becker 5–7 6–3 6–4 7–6, lost Ivanisevic 7–6 6–3 6–4); **Wimbledon – sf 1994** (d. Stafford 6–4 6–2 6–7 6–7 6–1, Kuhnen 6–2 6–2 6–4, Damm 6–2 6–7 4–6 6–3 11–9, Agassi 6–3 7–5 6–7 4–6 6–1, W. Ferreira 6–3 6–2 3–6 5–7 7–5, lost Sampras 6–4 6–4 3–6 6–3), **sf 1996** (d. Ondruska 6–3 6–4 6–3, Grabb 6–2 6–4 7–6, Furlan 7–6 6–4 6–2, Johansson 3–6 6–3 7–6 6–2, Henman 7–6 7–6 6–4, lost MaliVai Washington 5–7 6–4 6–7 6–3 10–8); **US Open – sf 1994** (d. Raoux 6–7 4–6 6–3 6–4 7–6, Chesnokov 6–3 6–2 7–5, Rafter 7–5 6–3 6–7 6–2, Reneberg 3–6 3–0 ret, Karbacher 6–2 4–6 6–3 6–2, lost Agassi 6–3 4–6 6–2 6–3).

ANDREI MEDVEDEV (UKR)

Born Kiev, 31 August 1974, and lives there; RH; 6ft 4in; 192lb; turned pro 1991; career singles titles 11; final 1998 ATP ranking 61; 1998 prize money $334,6200; career prize money $5,376,705.

Coached by Bob Brett, formerly Boris Breskvar. Brother of Natalia Medvedeva, who plays on the women's tour. Soviet Union Jun champ in 14s, 16s and 18s. **1990:** (1007) Won Orange Bowl over Fernandez and won Sunshine Cup and World Youth Cup for USSR. **1991:** (226) Won French Open Jun over Enqvist. **1992:** (24) A –, F 4, W –, US –. His run of success began at French Open, where he played through the qualifying and on to the last 16, upsetting Hlasek on the way. Unable to obtain a visa to play the Wimbledon qualifying, he accepted a wild card for Genova and won his 1st tour title there, breaking into the top 100. He followed with the title in Stuttgart, after qualifying and upsetting 5 seeds (including Edberg), and continued to sweep up the rankings. His 3rd title, at Bordeaux, took him into the top 25, where he finished the year and was voted ATP Newcomer of the Year. **1993:** (6) A 3, F sf, W 2, US qf. The title at Estoril took him into the top 20 in April and, following that immediately with Barcelona (d. Lendl, Muster and Bruguera) and then sf appearance at French Open (d. Edberg), he moved on to the top 10. Working on developing an all-court game, he won his 1st HC title at New Haven (d. Agassi), was r/u Halle and Paris Open and appeared in sf Stuttgart and Kitzbuhel, as well as his 1st IBM/ATP World Champ. **1994:** (15) A –, F qf, W 4, US 2. In Jan. he underwent arthroscopic surgery for tendinitis and bone chips in his knee, returning in March to reach f Estoril, and then won Monte Carlo in his 3rd tourn of year, despite suffering from a fever. Won Hamburg, playing his 3rd f in 5 tourns to date, but at Italian Open he suffered pain again, having done too much too soon. In GS he reached qf French Open and extended Becker to 7–5 5s in last 16 Wimbledon, but at US Open he fell 2r to Novacek. He was also r/u Prague and reached sf Lyon. In May he parted company with his coach, Dolgopolov, who needed to spend more time with his increasing family, and started working with Brad Stine. **1995:** (16) A qf, F 4, W 2, US 2. Split with Stine early in the year, worked with Marco Dulis from end Feb. and in May began working with his friend Boris Breskvar. He lost confidence after a poor run following a broken wrist suffered at Australian Open, but returned to form in May with the title at Hamburg, where he beat Sampras and Ivanisevic back-to-back, and an upset of Berasategui at French Open. He also reached sf Nice, qf Rotterdam, LIPC, Estoril, Indianapolis and Ostrava. **1996:** (35) A 2, F 2, W 1, US 4. Although it was a less impressive year, he won Long Island, r/u Bastad, and reached sf Antwerp (d. Kafelnikov), plus qf Milan and Italian Open (d. Kafelnikov again). **1997:** (27) A 4, F 4, W 3, US 1. His best performance came at Hamburg, where he upset Krajicek, Bruguera and Kafelnikov on his way to the title, unseeded, and returned for a while to the top 20. His only other qf showings were at LIPC and Barcelona, although he upset Stich at Australian Open and Berasategui at French Open, unseeded both times. **1998:** A 2, F 1, W 2, US 2. He was r/u Bastad and reached sf Qatar, qf Indian Wells and Ostrava (d. Kucera), but otherwise he had a poor year and tumbled down the rankings. **1998 HIGHLIGHTS – SINGLES: Australian Open 2r** (d. Smith 6–2 6–0 6–2, lost Berasategui 6–4 7–6 6–4, **French Open 1r** (lost Gaudenzi 7–6 6–1 0–6 2–6 6–1), **Wimbledon 2r** (d. Safin 6–3 6–4 3–6 6–4, lost Ivanisevic [seed 14] 6–3 7–6 4–6 6–0), **US Open 2r** (d. Van Lottum 6–4 7–5 6–2, lost Grant 4–6 6–3 7–6 6–4); **r/u** Bastad (d. Karbacher 6–2 6–1, Fromberg 6–7 7–5 7–6, Gaudenzi 6–3 6–4, Hrbaty 6–3 7–6, lost Gustafsson 6–2 6–3); **sf** Qatar (d. Vacek 6–3 6–4, Tarango 6–2 2–6 7–5, Schalken 4–6 6–4 6–4, lost Korda 6–3 6–4). **CAREER HIGHLIGHTS – SINGLES: French Open – sf 1993** (d. Perez-Roldan 6–7 4–6 6–4 6–3 6–4, Furlan 6–3 6–3 6–4, Markus 7–6 3–6 7–5 6–4, Goellner 6–4 6–4 4–6 6–3, Edberg 6–0 6–7 7–5 6–4, lost Bruguera 6–0 6–4 6–2), **qf 1994** (d. Masur 6–2 6–4 6–2, Kulti 6–4 7–6 4–6 7–5, Rusedski 2–6 6–3 6–4 3–6 6–2, Eltingh 6–4 3–6 6–4 6–1, lost Bruguera 6–3 6–2 7–5); **Australian Open – qf 1995** (d. Paes 6–1 7–5 7–6, Rehmann 7–5 6–4 6–1, Pescosolido 6–4 6–3 6–3, Wheaton 3–6 6–3 6–4 6–7 10–8, lost M. Chang [seed 5] 7–6 7–5 6–3); **US Open – qf 1993** (d. Meligeni 6–2 6–2 4–6 6–1, Reneberg 4–6 7–6 6–4 6–3, Braasch 6–1 6–4 7–6, Krajicek 6–4 3–6 6–1 7–6, lost Pioline 6–3 6–1 3–6 6–2).

FERNANDO MELIGENI (BRA)

Born Buenos Aires, Argentina, 12 April 1971; lives Sao Paulo; LH; 5ft 11in; 142lb; turned pro 1990; career singles titles 3; final 1998 ATP ranking 57; 1998 prize money $309,811; career prize money $1,264,951.

Coached by Ricardo Acioly. Born in Argentina but plays D Cup for Brazil, where he lives. **1989:** (615) Won Orange Bowl over Lopez and was No. 3 in ITF Jun rankings. **1990:** (391). **1991:** (203). **1992:** (167) A –, F –,

W –, US 1. Reached his 1st tour qf at Maceio. **1993:** (98) A –, F 4, W –, US 1. Won 3 Challenger titles, reached qf Sao Paulo on the main tour and appeared in last 16 French Open after qualifying. **1994:** (92) A 1, F 1, W 1, US 1. He reached sf Coral Springs, qf Kitzbuhel, Bogota and Santiago (d. Novacek) and played 3 Challenger f, winning Ribeiro Preto. **1995:** (66) A –, F 3, W –, US 1. His 1st tour f at Mexico City in Feb., was followed 5 months later by his 1st title at Bastad. He also appeared in sf Bogota, qf US CC and Montevideo and upset Rosset at French Open. **1996:** (93) A 1, F 1, W –, US –. Came from behind in 3 matches on his way to the US CC title, unseeded. At Olympics, again unseeded, he upset A. Costa on the way to sf, losing the bronze medal contest to Paes. He reached the same stage Mexico City, plus qf Atlanta and Santiago, where he won the doubles with Kuerten, and on the Challenger circuit won Cairo. **1997:** (68) A –, F 2, W –, US 3. In singles he reached sf Mexico City again and qf Barcelona, Orlando, Atlanta (d. M. Chang), Bogota and Santiago. Played 4 doubles f, winning 3 with Kuerten and 1 with Lobo. **1998:** A 1, F 4, W –, US 1. Upset Kafelnikov on his way to the title at Prague and again 1r Gstaad, where he won the doubles with Kuerten. His only other qf on the main tour was Kitzbuhel, although he won Sao Paulo Challenger and extended Muster to 5s at French Open, where he was unseeded. **1998 HIGHLIGHTS – SINGLES: Australian Open 1r** (lost Pioline 6–4 1–6 5–5 ret), **French Open last 16** [unseeded] (d. Johansson 6–4 6–2 6–4, Spadea 7–6 7–6 6–3, Woodbridge 7–5 6–3 6–2, lost Muster 6–4 6–7 6–3 3–6 6–3), **US Open 1r** (lost Johansson 7–6 6–3 7–6); **won** Prague (d. Cherkasov 6–4 6–3, Kafelnikov 6–4 6–4, Chesnokov 6–3 6–1, Pescariu 7–6 7–6, Dosedel 6–1 6–4), **won** Sao Paulo Challenger (d. Filippini 6–1 6–4). **1998 HIGHLIGHTS – DOUBLES:** (with Kuerten) **won** Gstaad (d. Orsanic/Suk 6–4 7–5). **CAREER HIGHLIGHTS – SINGLES: Olympics – sf 1996** [unseeded] (d. Pescosolido 6–4 6–2, A. Costa 7–6 6–4, Philippoussis 7–6 4–6 8–6, Olhovskiy 6–7 7–5 6–3, lost Bruguera 7–6 6–2, lost Paes 3–6 6–2 6–4).

MAX MIRNYI (BLR)

Born Minsk, 6 July 1977, and lives there; RH; 6ft 4in; 182lb; turned pro 1996; career singles titles 0; final 1998 ATP ranking 264 singles, 125 doubles; 1998 prize money $68,520.

1993: (1186). **1994:** (1212). **1995:** (399). **1996:** (310). **1997:** (491) From 2 doubles f he won Shanghai with Ullyett. **1998:** A –, F –, W –, US –. In mixed doubles with S. Williams he won Wimbledon and US Open. **1998 HIGHLIGHTS – DOUBLES:** (with Delaitre) **r/u** Chennai (lost Bhupathi/Paes 6–7 6–3 6–2). **MIXED DOUBLES:** (with S. Williams) **won** Wimbledon (d. Bhupathi/V. Williams 6–4 6–4), **won US Open** (d. Raymond/Galbraith 6–2 6–2).

FRANCISCO MONTANA (USA)

Born Miami, Fla, 5 November 1969, and lives there; RH; 6ft; 163lb; turned pro 1990; career singles titles 0; final 1998 ATP ranking – singles, 24 doubles; 1998 prize money $276,699; career prize money $1,139,417.

Coached by his father, Francisco. Wife Isabel (married 29 November 1997). Won 10 nat jun titles. **1987:** (745). **1988:** (–). **1989:** (643) All-American at Univ. of Georgia. **1990:** (239). **1991:** (137) A –, F –, W –, US 1. **1992:** (117) A –, F –, W 1, US 1. Reached his 1st qf on the main tour at San Marino and broke into top 100 1st time in May. Played 2 doubles f, winning Long Island with Van Emburgh. **1993:** (179) A 1, F –, W –, US –. Reached sf Mexico City singles and r/u doubles there with Shelton. **1994:** (280) A –, F –, W –, US –. Won Mexico City with Shelton and r/u Atlanta with Pugh. **1995:** (326) A –, F –, W –, US –. In doubles he won Kitzbuhel with Van Emburgh and r/u Santiago with Cannon. **1996:** (296) A –, F 1, W –, US –. Won Mexico City and Amsterdam doubles with Johnson. **1997:** (739) A –, F –, W –, US –. Appeared in 3 doubles f with Johnson, winning Monte Carlo. They played at World Doubles Champ as alternates when Kafelnikov and Vacek withdrew, but lost all 3 matches. **1998:** A –, F –, W –, US –. Won 4 doubles titles from 5 f with Johnson and qualified 1st time for World Doubles Champ. Despite suffering from torn meniscus of right knee, he was determined to play on and they reached sf, where they lost to Eltingh/Haarhuis. **1998 HIGHLIGHTS – DOUBLES:** (with Johnson) **won** Marseille (d. Keil/Middleton 6–4 3–6 6–3), **won** Estoril (d. Roditi/Wibier 6–1 2–6 6–1), **won** Hamburg (d. D. Adams/Steven 6–2 7–5), **won** Palermo (d. Albano/Orsanic 6–4 7–6); **r/u** Dubai (lost Bhupathi/Paes 6–2 7–5).

THOMAS MUSTER (AUT)

Born Leibnitz, 2 October 1967; lives Monte Carlo, Monaco, and Noosa Heads, Australia; LH; 5ft 11in; 165lb; turned pro 1985; career singles titles 44; final 1998 ATP ranking 25; 1998 prize money $488,775; career prize money $12,129,429.

Coached by Ronnie Leitgeb. **1984:** (309). **1985:** (98) A –, F 1, W –, US –. Won Banana Bowl and r/u French Open Jun to Yzaga. Joined the Austrian D Cup squad and made progress on the Austrian satellite circuit. **1986:** (47) A –, F 2, W –, US 1. Won his first GP title at Hilversum. **1987:** (56) A –, F 3, W 1, US 3. Won Young Masters and upset E. Sanchez en route to sf Vienna. **1988:** (16) A 1, F 3, W –, US 1. In the space of 5 weeks won Boston, Bordeaux and Prague, following with Bari later in year. **1989:** (21) A sf, F –, W –, US –. Reached 1st GS sf at Australian Open. On 1 April, 2 hours after beating Noah to reach f LIPC, which took him into top 10 for 1st time, he was knocked down by a drunken driver in Miami and suffered 2 torn ligaments and torn cartilage in his left knee, requiring reconstructive surgery. In plaster 14 months and was expected to be out of action for about 10 months, but in May he was already practising in a specially designed wheelchair. In Sept., after only 4 months' rehabilitation, he played doubles at Geneva then reached qf Barcelona in singles, following with sf Vienna. **1990:** (7) A 3, F sf, W –, US 4. At Adelaide in Jan. won 1st tour title since injury 10 months earlier, following with Casablanca in March, Italian Open in May and reaching sf French Open to regain his place in the top 10. R/u Monte Carlo and Munich; sf Vienna; qualified for ATP World Champ but failed to reach sf and fell 1r GS Cup to Leconte. Still in pain and advised by doctors to concentrate on CC tourns in 1990. Suspended 5 weeks from 22 Oct. and fined $15,000 (reduced on appeal from a ten-week suspension from US Open plus $25,000 fine) by ATP for 'violation of best efforts and unsportsmanlike conduct' – after accepting guarantee to play at Prague he pulled out after just 1 game, having previously expressed his intention to do so. Voted Comeback Player of the Year. **1991:** (35) A –, F 1, W –, US –. Underwent arthroscopic surgery on his left knee in March and won no match in his 1st 6 tourns until Italian Open, where he reached 3r, following with qf Bologna. Having dropped out of top 100 for the 1st time since April 1986, he returned after taking the title at Florence, following with Geneva and beating Skoff in f both times. He also reached sf Genova, Prague and Athens. **1992:** (18) A 3, F 2, W 1, US –. He returned to the top 20 with the titles in Monte Carlo, Florence and Umag, plus sf showings at Stuttgart, Kitzbuhel and Tel Aviv. **1993:** (9) A 2, F 4, W 1, US qf. In a particularly productive year he won 7 titles; only Sampras with 8 won more in 1993. Florence and Genova came in successive weeks in spring and he repeated the double in summer with his 1st title in Austria at Kitzbuhel, followed the next week with San Marino – and then Umag 2 weeks after that. He also won Mexico City and Palermo, and became the 1st since Wilander in 1983 to win 6 titles on clay in one year, although he was disappointed on carpet in Vienna in Oct., when he lost f in 4s tb to Ivanisevic. He was also r/u Sydney Outdoor and reached 5 more sf, but his GS record was disappointing, with qf US Open his best showing. In Oct. he returned to top 10 for 1st time since March 1991, but just failed to qualify for IBM/ATP Champ. **1994:** (16) A qf, F 4, W 1, US qf. Won Mexico City, Madrid and St Polten and reached sf Kitzbuhel, Tel Aviv and Vienna, plus 8 more qf – including Australian Open and US Open (d. Bruguera) – but this was not enough to keep his place in the top 10. **1995:** (3) A 3, F won, W –, US qf. He returned to the top in style with 12 titles – the most since McEnroe's 13 in 1984. His 86 victories across the year were the most since Lendl's 106 in 1982. The climax came when he won his 1st GS title at French Open, becoming the 1st Austrian ever to win a GS. He put together a winning streak of 40 CC matches from Oct. 1994 until Corretja beat him 1r Gstaad in July; it was the 3rd-best run in the Open era, behind Vilas (53) and Borg (44). He declined to compete at Wimbledon and withdrew after 1r Amsterdam with a cyst on his right big toe, connected with a fracture he had not been aware of. At Kitzbuhel after that he lost his 1st CC f since Munich 1990, but at Umag he returned to his winning ways after saving 3 mps in f v C. Costa. Earlier in the year he had recovered from 2 sets down v Becker to win Monte Carlo. By Nov., after he'd won the 1st indoor title of his career at Essen over Sampras and with Agassi injured, he was beginning to look a contender for the No. 1 spot. Going into IBM/ATP Champ, he had an outside chance of overtaking Sampras at the top, but lost all his rr matches and finished the year behind both Sampras and Agassi. **1996:** (5) A 4, F 4, W –, US qf. Moved to No. 2 behind Agassi after Australian Open and to No. 1 for 1st time on 12 Feb., becoming the 13th man to top the rankings. However, Sampras overtook him a week later and it became a see-saw event as Muster regained the top spot on 11 March, Sampras took it back on 21 April, M. Chang overtook him as No. 2 after US Open, and he slipped further down to No. 5. To complete his record and aiming to remove any doubts as to the justification of his top ranking, he aimed to play well on surfaces other than clay – especially grass, on which he won his 1st senior match in D Cup v Ondruska in Johannesburg in Jan. and reached sf Queen's in June. Playing a heavy schedule to maintain his ranking in the top 10, he won seven titles – surpassed only by Sampras – at Mexico City, followed by Estoril, Barcelona and Monte Carlo back-to-back, Italian Open, Stuttgart and Bogota. Having taken his 7th successive CC title at Monte Carlo, he suffered a surprise defeat at Munich at the hands of Moya, and Alvarez beat him qf Kitzbuhel. He also reached sf Qatar, Munich and Cincinnati, but was again disappointing at ATP Champ, where the fast court did not suit his game and he beat only M. Chang. He withdrew qf St Polten with a minor injury, and injured a thigh at Queen's, aggravating the injury at Halle and withdrawing from Wimbledon. He was irritated at being seeded only 7 there, despite his No. 2 ranking, and that at US Open he was seeded behind M. Chang, contrary to the rankings. Declined to play Olympics and in D Cup tie v BRA in Sept., he walked off court, complaining of behaviour of Brazilian spectators and forfeiting the match. AUT forfeited the rest of the tie and were fined $58,760, while Muster was fined $2,000 for a visible obscenity and $6,000 for leaving the court and refusing to play. He suffered a recurrence of an old injury to his left hip, which forced him to retire 2r Stuttgart Eurocard, and he was conscious that most of his injuries resulted from playing on hard surfaces. Did not take up his place in GS Cup. **1997:** (9) A sf, F 3, W –, US 1. He returned to No. 2 in Feb. after sf finish at Australian Open (d. Ivanisevic), but it was not to be one of his better years and he dropped out of the top 10 for a while in autumn. Developing his game on surfaces other than clay, on which he struggled (by his standards), he won HC titles at Dubai and then LIPC (d. Courier 1st time since 1990). This title was particularly poignant, coming as it did 8 years almost to the day after he last reached f there, only to suffer the accident that almost ended his career. His only other f of year was also HC at Cincinnati (d. M. Chang), although he added sf Indian Wells and Ostrava, plus qf Qatar, St Polten, Halle and Paris Open. He withdrew from Wimbledon with a hip injury and lost to Henman 1r US Open, where he could have been distracted by unsubstantiated reports of his having tested positive for drugs – a rumour condemned by ATP. Played (and lost to Moya) 1 match at ATP Champ as alternate when Rusedski withdrew after 2 matches. **1998:** A 1, F qf, W –, US –. Early in the year he was strongly advised by his D Cup doctor to retire, but kept going, albeit at less than his previous peak. He was r/u Estoril and reached sf Indian Wells (d. Sampras) and Mallorca, qf Hamburg (d. Kafelnikov), St Polten, Boston and French Open – where he was unseeded, so far had he slipped down the rankings. **1998**

HIGHLIGHTS – SINGLES: Australian Open 1r [seed 8] (lost Apell 6–4 7–6 7–5), **French Open qf** [unseeded] (d. Bjorkman [seed 7] 6–3 6–3 6–3, Kiefer 6–2 6–1 6–3, Van Garsse 6–2 4–6 7–6 6–2, Meligeni 6–4 6–7 6–3 3–6 6–3, lost Mantilla [seed 15] 6–4 6–2 4–6 6–3); **r/u** Estoril (d. Pescariu 7–5 6–1, Meligeni 7–5 6–3, A. Costa 6–4 6–4, Alami 3–6 6–2 6–4, lost Berasategui 3–6 6–1 6–3); **sf** Indian Wells (d. Woodruff 6–4 6–4, Pioline 4–6 6–3 6–4, Sampras 7–5 6–3, Medvedev 5–7 6–3 6–4, lost Rusedski 7–6 6–1), **sf** Mallorca (d. Blanco 6–4 6–2, Marin 6–3 6–2, Haas 3–6 6–3 6–4, lost Kuerten 7–5 7–5). **CAREER HIGHLIGHTS – SINGLES: Australian Open – sf 1989** (d. Rive 6–4 6–2 6–4, Wekesa 4–6 7–6 6–2 6–3, Visser 6–7 6–3 3–6 6–3 1–9, Gustafsson 6–3 6–2 7–5, Edberg w/o, lost Lendl 6–2 6–4 5–7 7–5), **sf 1997** (d. Grant 6–3 6–4 6–2, Stafford 6–3 6–2 6–2, Knippschild 6–4 7–6 6–3, Courier 6–2 3–6 7–6 6–3, Ivanisevic 6–4 6–2 6–3, lost Sampras 6–1 7–6 6–3), **qf 1994** (d. Weiss 6–3 6–3, Carlsen 6–4 6–4 6–2, Raoux 6–3 6–3 6–2, Volkov 6–3 6–3 6–2, lost Edberg 6–2 6–3 6–4); **French Open – won 1995** (d. Solves 3–6 6–4 6–2 6–1, Pioline 6–1 6–3 6–3, C. Costa 6–3 7–5 6–2, Medvedev 6–3 6–3 6–0, A. Costa 6–2 3–6 6–7 7–5 6–2, Kafelnikov 6–4 6–0 6–4, Chang 7–5 6–2 6–4), **sf 1990** (d. Jonsson 7–5 6–3 6–2, Winogradsky 6–2 6–3 6–1, Haarhuis 3–6 7–5 6–2 7–6, Jaite 7–6 6–3 6–2, Ivanisevic 6–2 4–6 6–4 6–3, lost Gomez 7–6 6–1 7–5), **qf 1998**; **US Open – qf 1993** (d. Corretja 6–4 6–4 6–3, Krickstein 6–4 6–0 6–3, McEnroe 6–2 7–5 6–7 6–2, B. Gilbert 6–2 7–5 6–7 6–2, lost Volkov 7–6 6–3 3–6 2–6 7–5), **qf 1994** (d. Musa 6–3 6–2 6–0, Ruah 6–4 4–6 6–4 6–2, Enqvist 6–0 6–4 6–2, Bruguera 6–4 7–6 6–4, lost Agassi 7–6 6–3 6–0), **qf 1996** (d. Frana 6–1 7–6 6–2, Dier 6–3 6–2 6–4, Bruguera 6–2 6–4 6–3, Enqvist 7–6 6–2 4–6 6–1, lost Agassi 6–2 7–5 4–6 6–2).

DAVID NALBANDIAN (ARG)

Born Cordoba 1 January 1982, and lives there; RH; 5ft 10in; 158lb; career singles titles 0; final 1998 ATP ranking 1342; 1998 prize money $1,411.

Coached by his brother, Javier, and Horatio De La Pena. **1996:** In winning ARG World Jun Tennis team. **1998:** Won US Open Jun over Federer.

DANIEL NESTOR (CAN)

Born Belgrade, Yugoslavia, 4 September 1972; lives Willowdale, Ontario; LH; 6ft 2in; 170lb; turned pro 1991; career singles titles 0; final 1998 ATP ranking 107 singles, 7 doubles; 1998 prize money $562,695; career prize money $2,016,137.

Coached by Brian Teacher. Moved to Canada in 1976. **1989:** (823). **1990:** (741). **1991:** (247) Won Nat doubles with Pridham. **1992:** (239) A 1, F –, W –, US –. Upset Edberg in D Cup and began to make his mark on the satellite circuit. **1993:** (186) A –, F –, W –, US 1. Out of action April to July with tendinitis of left wrist. R/u Nat singles and won doubles with Lareau. **1994:** (169) A –, F –, W –, US –. Upset Volkov at Toronto and reached qf Bogota, where he won the doubles with Knowles. **1995:** (180) A 2, F –, W 2, US 2. In singles he won Aptos Challenger but reached no qf on the main tour. In partnership with Knowles, upset Woodbridge/Woodforde on the way to a 1st GS f at Australian Open and won Indianapolis from 2 more f to qualify for World Doubles Champ, although they won no match there. **1996:** (114) A 1, F –, W 1, US –. Reached sf Newport and upset Muster at Toronto. In doubles he played 6 f, winning Qatar, Memphis, Hamburg and Cincinnati with Knowles. They qualified for World Doubles Champ, but were forced to withdraw after 2 rr matches when Nestor suffered a rib injury. **1997:** (112) A 1, F 1, W 1, US 1. In singles he reached sf Moscow, upset Enqvist at LIPC, and won San Antonio Challenger. From 4 doubles f with Knowles, he won Indian Wells and Rome to take the last berth at World Doubles Champ. There they lost their 1st 2 matches and were forced to withdraw when Knowles aggravated a rib injury. **1998:** A 3, F 1, W 1, US 1. In autumn he won 2 Challenger singles titles back-to-back and upset Pioline to reach qf Stockholm. Despite being hampered by a rib injury during the year, he played 7 doubles f with 3 different partners, winning Tokyo Japan Open with Lareau and Cincinnati with Knowles, with whom he was also r/u French Open, US Open and World Doubles Champ. **1998 HIGHLIGHTS – SINGLES: Australian Open 3r** (d. Schaller 6–3 6–0 7–6, Damm 5–7 7–5 6–2 6–1, lost Kucera 6–2 7–6 6–1), **French Open 1r** (lost Spadea 5–7 5–2 ret), **Wimbledon 1r** (lost Enqvist 6–7 6–7 6–4 6–0 6–0), **US Open 1r** (lost M. Norman 7–6 6–7 6–7 6–4 6–4); **won** Urbana Challenger (d. Ruah 3–6 7–6 6–3, **won** Dallas Challenger (d. Caratti 6–1 6–2). **1998 HIGHLIGHTS – DOUBLES:** (with Knowles unless stated) **r/u French Open** (lost Eltingh/Haarhuis 6–3 3–6 6–3), **r/u US Open** (lost Stolle/Suk 4–6 7–6 6–2); (with Lareau) **won** Tokyo Japan Open (d. Delaitre/Pescosolido 6–3 6–4), **won** Cincinnati (d. Delaitre/Santoro 6–1 2–1 ret); (with Eltingh) **r/u** Sydney (lost Woodbridge/Woodforde 6–3 7–5), **r/u** Indianapolis (lost Novak/Rikl 6–2 7–6), **r/u** World Doubles Champ (lost Eltingh/Haarhuis 6–4 6–2 7–5). **CAREER HIGHLIGHTS – DOUBLES:** (with Knowles) **Australian Open – r/u 1995** (lost Palmer/Reneberg 6–3 3–6 6–3 6–2), **French Open – r/u 1998; US Open – r/u 1998; World Doubles Champ – r/u 1998.**

MAGNUS NORMAN (SWE)

Born Filipstad, 30 May 1976, and lives there; RH; 6ft 2in; 165lb; turned pro 1995; career singles titles 2; final 1998 ATP ranking 52; 1998 prize money $412,839; career prize money $1,125,483.

Coached by Thomas Hogstedt. **1992:** (679). **1993:** (733). **1994:** (686). **1995:** (174) Qf Bastad and upset Berasategui at Palermo, as well as making his mark on the satellite circuits. **1996:** (86) A 1, F 2, W –, US –. Reached sf Bournemouth and Stockholm, qf Casablanca and won 2 Challenger titles. **1997:** (22) A 1, F qf,

W 3, US 2. Caused one of the upsets of the year at French Open when he removed Sampras 3r, following with Rosset to reach qf, unseeded. He upset Agassi and Korda en route to sf Atlanta, then at Wimbledon surprised Ivanisevic in an epic 2r battle, prevailing 14–12 5s. He followed with his 1st tour title at Bastad, having saved mp when 1–5 down 3s 2r v Voinea. He continued to challenge top players by upsetting Bruguera and Muster on his way to f Ostrava, where he was forced to retire with a thigh injury that also kept him out of Stuttgart. He reached sf St Polten and Amsterdam, plus qf St Petersburg, Chennai and Basle (d. Bjorkman), finishing the year in top 25. During his long fs v Ivanisevic at Wimbledon, he suffered irregular heartbeat for 3rd time in his career, although this time it lasted only 30 sec. (as opposed to 40 min. before), and he was able to continue after receiving treatment on court. The condition is not believed to be dangerous. **1998:** A 1, F 2, W 1, US 2. In a less spectacular year he won Amsterdam and was r/u Umag, but his only other qf appearance was at Halle (d. Siemerink).In D Cup f won vital opening rubber when Gaudenzi ret at 6–6 fs as SWE d. ITA 4–1. **1998 HIGHLIGHTS – SINGLES: Australian Open 1r** (lost Lareau 6–4 6–7 7–6 6–7 7–5), **French Open 2r** (d. Karbacher 6–2 1–6 6–3 6–1, lost W. Ferreira 6–4 6–4 6–4), **Wimbledon 1r** (lost A. Costa 7–5 7–5 7–6), **US Open 2r** (d. Nestor 7–6 6–7 6–7 6–4 6–4, lost Gambill 6–4 6–2 6–7 6–3); **won** Amsterdam (d. Arazi 6–7 5–1 ret, Novak 6–1 6–3, Blanco 6–2 6–4, Zabaleta 7–5 6–4, Fromberg 6–3 6–3 3–6 6–4); **r/u** Umag (d. Ljubicic 7–6 4–6 6–3, Cobolli 7–6 3–6 6–2, Kucera 1–6 6–4 6–4, Marin 7–6 6–3, lost Ulihrach 6–3 7–6). **CAREER HIGHLIGHTS – SINGLES: French Open – qf 1997** (d. Rusedski 6–3 6–2 3–6 4–6 9–7, Paes 6–3 6–2 3–6 6–3, Sampras 6–2 6–4 2–6 6–4, Rosset 4–6 6–3 7–6 6–3, lost Dewulf 6–2 6–7 6–4 6–3).

JIRI NOVAK (CZE)

Born Zlin, 22 March 1975; lives Prostejov; RH; 6ft 3in; 176lb; turned pro 1993; career singles titles 2; final 1998 ATP ranking 74; 1998 prize money $369,125; career prize money $1,459,178.

Coached by Daniel Traunicek. **1993:** (280) R/u in singles and won doubles in European Jun Champs. **1994:** (218) Won Prague Challenger. **1995:** (55) A –, F –, W –, US 1. He reached his 1st sf on the main tour at Buenos Aires, upset Korda at Ostrava and won 2 doubles titles from 4 f with Rikl. On the Challenger circuit he took 3 singles titles from 7 f. **1996:** (52) A 1, F 2, W 2, US 2. Playing his 1st career singles f on the main tour, he won the title at Auckland and broke into top 50. He followed with r/u Mexico City, sf Basle (d. Becker), qf Memphis, Casablanca, Bucharest and Ostrava, and upset Rios at Gstaad. From 4 doubles f with 3 different partners, he won Casablanca with Rikl and Gstaad with Vizner. **1997:** (48) A 2, F –, W 1, US 2. At Dubai, he upset Moya and Krajicek before extending Ivanisevic to 3s in sf, having earlier reached same stage Auckland. He also appeared in qf Indianapolis (d. Enqvist) and Ostrava (d. Moya and won doubles with Rikl), and finished the year with an upset of Bruguera at Moscow. **1998:** A –, F 1, W 1, US 1. Until Nov. his best performance had been qf Bastad and Split (where he won the doubles with Damm) and the Challenger title at Zagreb. But then his year turned around as he won both singles and doubles (with Rikl) at Mexico City, unseeded, following the next week with sf Bogota (d. Berasategui). In doubles he played 6 doubles f in all, winning 3 with Rikl and 1 with Damm. **1998 HIGHLIGHTS – SINGLES: French Open 1r** (lost Arazi 6–0 6–2 7–6), **Wimbledon 1r** (lost Henman [seed 13] 7–6 7–5 5–7 4–6 6–2), **US Open 1r** (lost Golmard 6–3 6–4 7–6); **won** Mexico City (d. Delgado 6–4 6–7 7–6, Lavalle 6–3 7–6, Burillo 6–3 3–6 6–3, Puerta 6–3 6–7 6–3, Malisse 6–3 6–3), **won** Zagreb Challenger (d. Puerta 7–5 6–1); **sf** Bogota (d. Berasategui 6–2 6–2, Morejon 6–3 6–2, Sanguinetti 7–5 4–6 6–4, lost Zabaleta 6–2 6–4). **1998 HIGHLIGHTS – DOUBLES:** (with Rikl unless stated) (with Damm) **won** Split (d. F. Bergh/Fredriksson 7–6 6–2), **won** San Marino (d. Hood/Prieto 6–4 7–6), **won** Indianapolis (d. Knowles/Nestor 6–2 7–6), **won** Mexico City (d. Orsanic/Roditi 6–4 6–2); **r/u** Umag (lost Broad/Norval 6–1 3–6 6–3), **r/u** Mallorca (lost Albano/Orsanic 7–6 6–3).

LEANDER PAES (IND)

Born Calcutta, 17 June 1973; lives there and Orlando, Fla.; RH; 5ft 10in; 171lb; turned pro 1991; career singles titles 1; final 1998 ATP ranking 91 singles, 4 doubles; 1998 prize money $674,079; career prize money $1,563,994.

Coached by Bob Carmichael; trained by Sanjay Singh. **1990:** Won Wimbledon Jun and finished the year at No. 2 in ITF Jun rankings, as well as making his D Cup debut. **1991:** (275). **1992:** (273) Won Guangzhoa Challenger. **1993:** (178). **1994:** (133) Won Challenger titles at Bombay and Binghampton and reached his 1st qf on the main tour at Kuala Lumpur. Upset W. Ferreira in D Cup tie. **1995:** (132) A 1, F –, W –, US –. Reached qf Beijing on the main tour, won Brasilia Challenger, and made his mark in D Cup again, upsetting Ivanisevic as IND d. CRO 3–2. **1996:** (128) A –, F –, W 1, US 2. The highlight of his year was winning a bronze medal at the Olympics – India's 1st for 16 years – upsetting Enqvist and Furlan on the way. It was particularly satisfying, as his father had been in that bronze-winning hockey team in 1972 and his mother had captained India's Olympic basketball team the same year. He also reached sf Newport (d. B. Black) and qf Rosmalen and won Mauritius Challenger. **1997:** (114) A 2, F 2, W 1, US 3. In singles he reached sf Shanghai and Newport and in doubles he developed a formidable partnership with Bhupathi. They won all 6 f they played through the year to qualify for a 1st World Doubles Champ, where they progressed to a 7th f before losing to Leach/Stark. **1998:** A 1, F –, W 1, US 1. At Newport, in his 1st f on the main tour, he won his 1st title and the 1st by an Indian since Krishnan in 1990. Other highlights were his appearance in sf Chennai, a defeat of Sampras en route to qf New Haven and the Challenger title at Bangkok. In doubles he and Bhupathi won 5 of the 7 f they played to qualify again for World Doubles Champ. There, though, he suffered a bone spur injury to his hand

and they were forced to withdraw after losing 2 matches, but still finished the year as No. 2 pairing behind Eltingh/Haarhuis and ahead of Woodbridge/Woodforde. **1998 HIGHLIGHTS – SINGLES: Australian Open 1r** (lost Tillstrom 6–3 6–2 6–2), **Wimbledon 1r** (lost W. Black 6–4 7–5 6–4), **US Open 1r** (lost O'Brien 7–5 6–3 7–6); **won** Newport (d. Dilucia 3–6 6–3 6–4, Draper 7–5 6–4, Schuttler 7–6 6–2, Tieleman 6–3 6–4, Godwin 6–3 6–2), **won** Bangkok Challenger (d. Motomura 6–4 7–5); **sf** Chennai (d. Phau 6–2 6–2, Golmard 7–6 2–6 3–1 ret, Solves 6–7 6–4 7–5, lost Rafter 6–1 7–6). **1998 HIGHLIGHTS – DOUBLES:** (with Bhupathi) **won** Qatar (d. Delaitre/Santoro 6–4 3–6 6–4), **won** Dubai (d. Johnson/Montana 6–2 7–5), **won** Chennai (d. Delaitre/Mirnyi 6–7 6–3 6–2), **won** Rome (d. E. Ferreira/Leach 6–4 4–6 7–6), **won** Shanghai (d. Woodbridge/Woodforde 6–4 6–7 7–6); **r/u** Singapore (lost Woodbridge/Woodforde 6–2 6–3), **r/u** Stuttgart Eurocard (lost Lareau/O'Brien 6–3 3–6 7–5). **CAREER HIGHLIGHTS – SINGLES: Olympics – bronze medal 1996** [unseeded] (d. Reneberg [seed 11] 6–7 7–6 1–0 ret, Pereira 6–2 6–3, Enqvist [seed 3] 7–5 7–6, Furlan [seed 14] 6–1 7–5, lost Agassi [seed 1] 7–6 6–3, d. Meligeni 3–6 6–2 6–4). **CAREER HIGHLIGHTS – DOUBLES:** (with Bhupathi) **World Doubles Champ – r/u 1997** (lost Leach/Stark 6–3 6–4 7–6).

ANDREI PAVEL (ROM)

Born Constanta, 27 January 1974; lives Borgholzhausen, Germany; RH; 6ft; 185lb; turned pro 1993; career singles titles 1; final 1998 ATP ranking 66; 1998 prize money $288,351.

Coached by Robert Suevich. Wife Simone (married 19 August 1994). Moved to Germany at age 16, but plays D Cup for Romania. **1990:** (460) Won European 16s (d. Enqvist) and in the senior game won Romanian satellite. **1991:** (536). **1992:** (493) Won French Open Jun over Navarra. **1993:** (307). **1994:** (406). **1995:** (213) Continued to make his mark on the satellite circuits. **1996:** (140) Emerging from the satellite circuit he reached his 1st sf on the main tour at Bucharest (d. Novak), and on the Challenger circuit he won Montauban. **1997:** (109) A 1, F 2, W 2, US 1. During the year in which he broke into top 100 1st time he upset Krajicek en route to sf Chennai, Berasategui on his way to qf San Marino, and Kafelnikov in D Cup. **1998:** A –, F –, W 1, US 1. After winning Magdeburg Challenger, he went on to take his 1st title on the main tour at Tokyo Japan Open, becoming the 1st Romanian to win a pro title at that level since Nastase in 1978. He added sf Atlanta and qf Bucharest, where he won the doubles with Trifu. **1998 HIGHLIGHTS – SINGLES: Wimbledon 1r** (lost Spadea 6–3 6–3 6–3), **US Open 1r** (lost Clavet 6–7 6–4 7–5 6–2); **won** Tokyo Japan Open (d. Delaitre 6–3 6–0, Vasek 5–7 6–0 7–5, Macphie 3–6 6–3 6–4, Dilucia 6–3 7–6, Gambill 6–4 6–3, B. Black 6–3 6–4); **sf** Atlanta (d. Sargsian 6–4 6–4, Van Lottum 6–1 6–2, Squillari 6–1 6–2, lost Stoltenberg 6–2 6–4). **1998 HIGHLIGHTS – DOUBLES:** (with Trifu) **won** Bucharest (d. Cosac/Pescariu 7–6 4–6 7–6).

MARK PHILIPPOUSSIS (AUS)

Born Melbourne, 7 November 1976; lives there and Monte Carlo, Monaco; RH; 6ft 4in; 202lb; turned pro 1994; career singles titles 5; final 1998 ATP ranking 15; 1998 prize money $1,272,620; career prize money $3,117,457.

Coached by his father, Nick, and Gavin Hopper; advised by Pat Cash; works on fitness with Todd Viney. Speaks fluent Greek but has been to Greece only once – as a baby. **1993:** (1072) Won Victorian satellite. **1994:** (304) A 1, F –, W –, US –. R/u Wimbledon Jun singles to Humphries and in Jun doubles won Australian Open and Wimbledon with Ellwood. **1995:** (32) A 1, F –, W –, US 3. After qualifying and having never before reached qf, he upset Martin on his way to f Scottsdale in only his 5th main tour event. Upset Haarhuis on his way to f Kuala Lumpur, following the next week with f Tokyo Seiko (d. Edberg), and also reached sf Bologna. Missed Wimbledon because he did not get the wild card he had requested and his father would not let him try to qualify. Won 2 doubles titles with different partners and was voted Player to Watch. **1996:** (30) A 4, F 2, W 2, US 4. Played near-perfect tennis to beat Sampras in ss at Australian Open and upset Pioline at US Open, unseeded both times. He won his 1st ATP tour title at Toulouse in the week his manager, Brad Robinson, died of lymphoma; reached sf Memphis (d. Haarhuis) and New Haven (d. Courier and Rosset); qf Olympics (d. Haarhuis again) Munich and Toronto (d. Rosset). **1997:** (18) A –, F 4, W 1, US 3. Missed Australian Open with tendinitis in right arm, returning to win Scottsdale, unseeded. At Munich he played and won his 1st CC f, and followed with his 1st GC title at Queen's, where he also won the doubles with Rafter. It was an anticlimax when he drew, and lost to, Rusedski 1r Wimbledon. He reached f Toulouse and Basle (d. Kafelnikov), sf Lyon and qf Indian Wells (d. Agassi and Moya), Los Angeles and Montreal. **1998:** A 2, F 2, W qf, US r/u. His year began badly when he announced that he would not be available for D Cup until qf and was dropped from the squad by captain Newcombe. He won Memphis (d. Rios and M. Chang) but otherwise struggled for motivation and consistency until, as summer began, he asked Cash to help him sort out his mind. Cash turned out to be a major force in his revival, and the subsequent improvement was already noticeable at Wimbledon, where, unseeded, he upset Kafelnikov on his way to qf. He then went on to achieve new heights at US Open, where he was r/u, unseeded, with upsets of Henman and Moya. He followed with sf GS Cup, losing to Rios, and qf Paris Open (d. Korda and Kucera). **1998 HIGHLIGHTS – SINGLES: Australian Open 2r** [seed 15] (d. Calatrava 7–6 6–4 7–6, lost Arazi 1–6 6–2 4–6 6–1 9–7), **French Open 2r** (d. Gross 6–1 7–5 6–4, lost Ulihrach 3–6 6–7 7–6 6–4 9–7), **Wimbledon qf** [unseeded] (d. Kafelnikov [seed 7] 6–7 7–6 6–4 6–2, O'Brien 6–7 6–4 7–6 6–3, Bracciali 6–3 6–4 6–4, Stoltenberg 5–7 6–1 6–3 6–3, lost Sampras [seed 1] 7–6 6–4 6–4), **r/u US Open** [unseeded] (d. Ruud 7–5 6–4 6–3, Lareau 6–7 6–3 6–3 6–4, Arnold 7–6 6–3 6–3, Henman [seed 13] 7–5 0–6 6–4 6–1, Johansson 4–6 6–3 6–7 6–3 7–6, Moya [seed 10] 6–1 6–4 5–7 6–4, lost Rafter [seed 3] 6–3 3–6 6–2 6–0); **won** Memphis (d. W. Black 6–1 6–2,

Schalken 6–4 6–4, Enqvist 3–6 6–2 7–6, Rios 6–4 7–6, M. Chang 6–3 6–2); **sf** GS Cup (d. Bjorkman 4–6 7–6 6–1, lost Rios 7–6 6–3 6–4). **CAREER HIGHLIGHTS – SINGLES: US Open – r/u 1998; GS Cup – sf 1998; Wimbledon – qf 1998.**

CEDRIC PIOLINE (FRA)

Born Neuilly-sur-Seine, 15 June 1969; lives Paris; RH; 6ft 2in; 175lb; turned pro 1989; career singles titles 2; final 1998 ATP ranking 18; 1998 prize money $808,688; career prize money $4,783,356.

Coached by Pierre Cherret; physical trainer Luc Pausicles. Wife Mireille Bercot; son Andrea (born 14 March 1993). His mother was a member of Romania's World Championship volleyball squad, and he might have concentrated on that sport, but took up tennis instead after undergoing surgery to shorten one leg to match the other. **1987:** (954) R/u Nat Jun Champ. **1988:** (461). **1989:** (202) A –, F 1, W –, US –. Enjoyed some success on the Challenger circuit. **1990:** (118) A 1, F 1, W –, US –. Won his 1st pro title at Brest Challenger. **1991:** (51) A 1, F 2, W 2, US 1. Broke into top 100 after reaching sf Nice (d. Volkov and Leconte back-to-back). **1992:** (33) A 2, F 4, W 2, US 3. He reached his 1st tour f at Lyon (d. Forget) and upset B. Gilbert on his way to last 16 French Open, unseeded. **1993:** (10) A 2, F 2, W qf, US r/u. The highlight of his career came at US Open, where he swept aside Courier and Medvedev to become the 1st Frenchman since Cochet in 1932 to reach f there, eventually losing to Sampras. R/u Monte Carlo (d. Edberg), Toulouse, Bolzano and Lyon; sf Munich and Antwerp (d. Ivanisevic); upset Medvedev en route to qf Wimbledon, unseeded. He broke into top 10 in Oct., becoming only 2nd player after Pernfors to reach top 10 without a title. **1994:** (51) A 1, F 2, W 1, US 3. That 1st title still evaded him as he slipped out of the top 50. He was a finalist at Long Island, but otherwise reached qf only in Milan and Bordeaux. **1995:** (56) A 1, F 2, W qf, US 2. His best showing was sf Toulouse, plus qf Auckland, Nice, Long Island, Lyon and Wimbledon, where, unseeded, he upset Courier and recovered from 2s down to extend Becker to 9–7 5s. **1996:** (21) A –, F qf, W 4, US 3. After reaching f Zagreb and Marseille, he had played 9 f without winning that elusive 1st title: it came at last at Copenhagen in March, in his 10th f. He also appeared in sf Monte Carlo (d. Kafelnikov) and qf Rotterdam (d. Krajicek), Toulouse and French Open (d. Rios), where he was unseeded. Member of winning FRA D Cup team v SWE, he d. an injured Edberg in 1st rubber and served for the tie at 5–3 in 5s 4th, but lost to Enqvist 9–7. **1997:** (20) A –, F 3, W r/u, US 4. The highlight of his year came at Wimbledon, where, ranked 44 and unseeded, he became the 1st French finalist there since Petra in 1946. He had missed Australian Open with a back injury and in other GS lost only in 5s to both Kafelnikov at French Open and M. Chang at US Open. He won his 2nd career title at Prague, but otherwise did not pass qf, although he reached that stage at Indian Wells, Barcelona (d. Muster), GS Cup, Ostrava and Stockholm, and upset M. Chang at Stuttgart Eurocard. **1998:** A 4, F sf, W 1, US 1. He began the year with an upset of Corretja at Australian Open, where he was unseeded, and followed with r/u London (d. Korda) and Monte Carlo. He withdrew from Rome with back problems, but returned at French Open, again unseeded, to upset Krajicek and survive 3 5s matches before bowing out to Corretja in sf. He also reached sf St Petersburg, Boston and Tashkent and qf Vienna (d. Krajicek). He qualified for GS Cup, but could not salvage a single game v Agassi. **1998 HIGHLIGHTS – SINGLES: Australian Open last 16** [unseeded] (d. Meligeni 6–4 1–6 5–5 ret, Burillo 6–3 7–5 3–6 6–3, Corretja [seed 11] 6–2 6–1 6–4, lost Korda [seed 6] 6–4 6–4 3–6 6–3), **French Open sf** [unseeded] (d. Filippini 6–1 3–6 7–5 6–7 6–4, Boutter 7–5 6–0 3–6 6–4, Krajicek [seed 10] 6–3 6–2 7–5, Safin 7–5 4–6 6–7 6–4 6–4, Arazi 3–6 6–2 7–6 4–6 6–3, lost Corretja [seed 14] 6–3 6–4 6–2), **Wimbledon 1r** [seed 6] (d. Rosset 6–4 3–6 4–6 7–6 13–11), **US Open 1r** (lost Bjorkman [seed 12] 6–2 4–6 6–1 6–7 6–2); **r/u** London (d. Clavet 6–1 7–6, Korda 6–3 6–3, Kucera 6–3 4–6 6–2, Siemerink 6–3 7–6, lost Kafelnikov 7–5 6–4), **r/u** Monte Carlo (d. C. Costa 6–2 3–6 6–3, Grosjean 6–1 7–6, Kuerten 7–6 6–1, Santoro 1–6 6–2 6–4, Berasategui 6–3 0–6 7–6, lost Moya 6–3 6–0 7–5); **sf** St Petersburg (d. Ondruska 7–5 6–2, Van Herck 6–3 6–4, Dreekmann 4–6 6–3 7–5, lost Rosset 6–1 6–4), **sf** Boston (d. Voinea 6–4 6–0, Ilie 6–4 6–2, Muster 7–5 6–3, lost Haarhuis 7–5 4–6 6–3), **sf** Tashkent (d. Kutsenko 6–3 6–3, Tieleman 4–6 7–6 6–4, Safin 6–7 6–2 7–6, lost Kafelnikov 6–2 6–2). **CAREER HIGHLIGHTS – SINGLES: Wimbledon – r/u 1997** (d. Charpentier 5–7 6–3 7–5 6–2, Frana w/o, W. Ferreira [seed 15] 6–4 6–3 6–3, Steven 3–6 6–3 6–4 7–5, Rusedski 6–4 4–6 6–4 6–3, Stich 6–7 6–2 6–1 5–7 6–4, lost Sampras [seed 1] 6–4 6–2 6–4)**, qf 1993** (d. Damm 6–4 7–5 3–6 7–5, Medvedev 6–7 7–6 6–3 6–4, Carlsen 6–4 6–4 6–3, Masur 6–3 6–2 3–6 6–7 8–6, lost Edberg 7–5 7–5 6–3), **qf 1995** (d. Lopez-Moron 6–1 6–2 6–4, Courier [seed 11] 6–4 6–4 6–4, Baur 6–4 6–4 6–3, Korda 7–6 6–3 6–2, lost Becker [seed 3] 6–3 6–1 6–7 6–7 9–7); **US Open – r/u 1993** (d. Prinosil 6–7 7–5 6–4 3–6 6–1, Palmer 6–4 3–6 5–7 7–5 6–1, Wilander 6–4 6–4 6–4, Courier 7–5 6–7 6–4 6–4, Medvedev 6–3 6–1 3–6 6–2, Masur 6–1 6–7 7–6 6–1, lost Sampras 6–4 6–4 6–3); **French Open – sf 1998, qf 1996** [unseeded] (d. Frana 6–1 6–3 6–2, Reneberg 7–5 6–2 6–3, Berasategui 4–6 6–1 6–4 6–0, Rios [seed 9] 6–4 6–1 6–2, lost Stich [seed 15] 6–4 4–6 6–3 6–2).

GIANLUCA POZZI (ITA)

Born Bari, 17 June 1965, and lives there; LH; 5ft 11in; 176lb; turned pro 1984; career singles titles 1; final 1998 ATP ranking 62; 1998 prize money $263,671; career prize money $1,486,075.

Wife Cristina (married 29 November 1997). **1982:** (831). **1984:** (355). **1985:** (330). **1986:** (277) Began to play the satellite circuits. **1987:** (153) A –, F –, W –, US 2. Took his 1st Challenger title at Dublin. **1988:** (165) A 2, F –, W –, US 2. **1989:** (179) A 2, F –, W –, US 1. **1990:** (185) A 1, F –, W –, US –. **1991:** (72) A –, F –, W 2, US

–. Captured his 1st main-tour title at Brisbane and took Newport doubles with Steven. **1992:** (68) A 2, F 2, W 1, US 2. R/u Vienna (d. Bruguera and Chesnokov) as a qualifier, having entered the draw only because Cairo Challenger, where he had intended to play, was cancelled. Also reached sf Seoul, qf Milan and Los Angeles. **1993:** (114) A 1, F 1, W 1, US 1. He reached qf Qatar, Marseille (d. Lendl), Rosmalen (d. Medvedev) and Washington (d. Holm) and won Kuala Lumpur Challenger. **1994:** (84) A 1, F –, W 1, US 4. On the main tour he played qf Zaragoza and Kuala Lumpur and on the Challenger circuit he won Taipei. **1995:** (143) A 1, F 1, W 2, US 1. He won Cherbourg Challenger, but Beijing was his only qf appearance on the main tour. **1996:** (106) A –, F –, W 2, US 1. He reached qf Seoul, upset Gaudenzi at Queen's and won 2 Challenger titles. Underwent surgery on 2 Dec. for removal of a small tumour on the bone of his leg. **1997:** (96) A –, F –, W –, US –. He returned to the top 100 with qf Beijing on the main tour and 3 Challenger titles across the year, including 2 from 4 f in 5 consec. tourns. **1998:** A 2, F 2, W 1, US 1. Although he did not pass qf all year, he reached that stage at Hong Kong Salem Open, Halle, Nottingham (d. Rios) and Boston, upset Siemerink at Lyon and collected 2 more Challenger titles. Member of ITA team that lost D Cup f 4–1 SWE, but played only dead rubber v Gustafsson in place of the injured Gaudenzi. **1998 HIGHLIGHTS – SINGLES: Australian Open 2r** (d. Clement 6–4 4–6 5–7 6–2 6–4, lost B. Black 6–2 5–0 ret), **French Open 2r** (d. Rosset 6–2 6–1 4–6 6–4, lost Gumy 6–2 6–3 3–6 5–7 11–9), **Wimbledon 1r** (lost Vacek 7–6 7–6 6–3), **US Open 1r** (lost Corretja [seed 7] 2–6 6–3 7–5 7–5); **won** Surbiton Challenger (d. Ulyett 6–4 6–3), **won** Tel Aviv Challenger (d. Mor 6–1 6–7 6–3).

MARIANO PUERTA (ARG)

Born Buenos Aires, 19 September 1978, and lives there; LH; 5ft 10in; 165lb; turned pro 1995; career singles titles 1; final 1998 ATP ranking 39; 1998 prize money $262,697.

Coached by his father, Ruben, and Pablo Martin. **1995:** (756) R/u French Open Jun to Zabaleta and won South American Champs. **1996:** (419) Began to make an impression on the satellite circuits. **1997:** (147) Moving on to the Challenger circuit, he won Quito, then finished the year with qf Santiago in his 1st main tour event. **1998:** A –, F –, W 1, US 1. He upset Kuerten on his way to sf Umag, following with r/u spot at San Marino in only his 6th tourn, and then his 1st title at Palermo (d. Corretja), bursting into the top 50. He also reached sf Mexico City, qf Bologna and Santiago, won Bogota doubles with Del Rio and took the Challenger title in Nice. **1998 HIGHLIGHTS – SINGLES: Wimbledon 1r** (lost Squillari 6–7 6–3 7–5 6–4), **US Open 1r** (lost Moya [seed 10] 6–1 7–6 6–7 4–4 ret); **won** Palermo (d. Marin 7–6 6–1, Clavet 6–4 4–6 6–3, Vicente 6–4 6–4, Corretja 7–5 6–2, Squillari 6–3 6–2), **won** Nice Challenger (d. De Pasquale 6–7 6–4 6–4); **r/u** San Marino (d. Arnold 6–4 4–6 6–3, Blanco 4–6 6–3 6–1, Zabaleta 4–6 6–3 4–0 ret, Fromberg 6–2 3–6 6–3, lost Hrbaty 6–2 7–5); **sf** Umag (d. Hrbaty 6–3 2–6 6–4, J. Sanchez 6–4 4–6 6–4, Kuerten 6–4 1–6 7–6, lost Ulihrach 6–3 6–3), **sf** Mexico City (d. Alami 6–4 6–4, Arnold 6–1 6–2, Hernandez 5–7 6–1 6–4, lost Novak 6–3 6–7 6–3). **1998 HIGHLIGHTS – DOUBLES:** (with Del Rio) **won** Bogota (d. Koves/Taino 6–7 6–3 6–2).

GUILLAUME RAOUX (FRA)

Born Bagnol-sur-Cèze, 14 February 1970; lives Boca Raton, Fla; RH; 5ft 11in; 170lb; turned pro 1989; career singles titles 1; final 1998 ATP ranking 53; 1998 prize money $357,530; career prize money $2,231,632.

Coached by Thierry Tulasne. Wife Caroline (married 1 August 1992); son Romain (born 15 July 1993). **1986:** (870). **1987:** (938). **1988:** (448) A –, F 1, W –, US –. R/u Wimbledon Jun to Pereira and was ranked 2 on ITF Jun list. Won Nat 18s. **1989:** (220) A 1, F 1, W –, US –. Won Guadeloupe Challenger. **1990:** (84) A –, F 1, W 2, US –. Upset Sampras en route to qf Paris Open and won Martinique and Dijon Challengers. **1991:** (104) A 1, F 1, W 1, US 2. Reached his 1st f on the main tour at Birmingham. **1992:** (93) A 1, F 1, W 1, US 1. Won his 1st primary circuit title at Brisbane in autumn after winning Segovia Challenger earlier in year; qf Seoul, Queen's and Washington (d. Krickstein). **1993:** (82) A 3, F 1, W 1, US 1. He reached qf Copenhagen, Osaka and Manchester, upset Muster en route to last 16 LIPC, and won Jakarta doubles with Nargiso. **1994:** (118) A 3, F 1, W 1, US 1. His best performances were qf Adelaide, Osaka and Bordeaux. **1995:** (83) A 1, F 2, W 1, US 1. Reached f in 2 consec. tourns at St Petersburg and Johannesburg (here he d. Berasategui and won the doubles with R. Gilbert), appeared in qf Jakarta and Bordeaux and won Nantes Challenger. **1996:** (73) A 3, F 1, W 2, US 2. Upset Rosset on his way to sf Rotterdam, as well as reaching qf Qatar, Jakarta and Zagreb (d. Boetsch). From 2 doubles f, he won Marseille with Fleurian. **1997:** (47) A 2, F 2, W 3, US 2. He returned to the top 50 with r/u Rosmalen (d. Bjorkman), sf Los Angeles (d. Rafter and Philippoussis), qf Copenhagen, Toulouse and Paris Open (d. Bruguera) and an upset of Moya 1r US Open. **1998:** A 4, F 2, W 1, US 2. He reached sf Los Angeles (d. Ivanisevic) and qf New Haven (d. Rafter) and Moscow, as well as upsetting M. Chang at Australian Open, where he was unseeded, and extending Agassi to 5s at US Open. In doubles he won Den Bosch with Siemerink. **1998 HIGHLIGHTS – SINGLES: Australian Open last 16** [unseeded] (d. Stolle 2–6 6–3 4–6 6–2 6–0, M. Chang [seed 3] 6–4 7–6 7–6, W. Black 6–3 6–2 7–5, lost Kiefer 6–3 6–4 7–5), **French Open 2r** (d. Marin 6–3 7–6 7–6, lost Woodbridge 6–4 4–6 6–3 6–0), **Wimbledon 1r** (lost Van Lottum 7–6 6–3 4–6 7–6), **US Open 2r** (d. Escude 6–3 3–6 6–3 1–6 7–6, lost Agassi [seed 8] 6–3 6–2 6–7 3–6 6–1); **sf** Los Angeles (d. Ivanisevic 6–4 6–4, Carlsen 7–6 6–7 7–6, Joyce 6–7 6–4 7–6, lost Henman 7–5 6–3). **1998 HIGHLIGHTS – DOUBLES:** (with Siemerink) **won** Den Bosch (d. Eagle/Florent 7–6 6–2).

OLIVIER ROCHUS (BEL)

Born Namur, 18 January 1981; lives Auvelais; RH; 5ft 4in; 122lb; career singles titles 0; final 1998 ATP ranking 642; 1998 prize money $4,045.

Coach Eduardo Masso. **1994:** In r/u BEL World Jun Tennis squad. **1996:** Played in winning BEL team in Jean Borotra Cup. **1998:** Won Wimbledon Jun doubles with Federer.

MARC ROSSET (SUI)

Born Geneva, 7 November 1970; lives Monte Carlo, Monaco; RH; 2HB; 6ft 7in; 194lb; turned pro 1988; career singles titles 12; final 1998 ATP ranking 32; 1998 prize money $463,962; career prize money $5,145,512.

Coached by Stephane Oberer. **1988:** (474) Won Orange Bowl and was No. 4 on ITF Jun Rankings. **1989:** (45) Progressing from the Challenger circuit, on which he won 2 titles and reached qf or better in 8 more tourns, he won his 1st main tour title at Geneva and cracked the top 100 in Sept. **1990:** (22) A 1, F 2, W 3, US 1. Broke into the top 25 in autumn, following some big upsets during the year. Won Lyon (d. Wilander); r/u Madrid (d. E. Sanchez) and Bologna; sf Nice (d. Noah), Gstaad (d. E. Sanchez) and Geneva. **1991:** (60) A 1, F 1, W 1, US 1. Sf New Haven (d. Lendl and Chang back-to-back); qf Brussels, LIPC and Hilversum. **1992:** (35) A 4, F 1, W 3, US 1. The highlight of his career came in August when he won an Olympic gold medal, unseeded, upsetting Courier (in ss), E. Sanchez and Ivanisevic. He also won Moscow in Nov., reached last 16 Australian Open, unseeded (d. Gustafsson), sf Basle and qf Adelaide, Scottsdale (d. Agassi) and Madrid (d. E. Sanchez). In partnership with Hlasek won his 1st GS title at French Open, plus Italian Open and Lyon, and took Adelaide with Ivanisevic. Played in D Cup squad as SUI reached f, upsetting FRA in qf. **1993:** (16) A –, F 2, W 1, US 1. Began the year slowly, suffering from tonsillitis, and struggled to find his best form until Feb. when he won Marseille, following with Long Island (d. Ivanisevic and M. Chang) and then Moscow at end of year. He reached sf Bordeaux, Basle and Stockholm (d. Courier), and upset Agassi at Indian Wells, Becker at Monte Carlo and Muster at Italian Open. **1994:** (14) A 3, F 1, W 2, US 3. Still a dangerous opponent, he scored some big upsets during the year as he won Marseille (d. Stich) and Lyon (d. Courier), r/u New Haven (d. Lendl and Medvedev) and Paris Open (d. Becker and Chang) and reached sf Nice, Bordeaux and Moscow (d. Kafelnikov). **1995:** (15) A 1, F 2, W 1, US 4. Out 2 months early in year after fracturing a bone in his right foot in D Cup tie v NED in Feb. He returned to win Nice in his 1st tourn back, following with Halle (saving 7 mps v Stich), and sf Gstaad, Long Island, Toulouse and Moscow and 3 more qf. Broke into top 10 1st time in July but could not maintain his position. **1996:** (22) A –, F sf, W 3, US 1. At French Open, where he recovered from 2s down v Karbacher to win their qf, he became 1st Swiss to reach sf any GS. In WT Cup, he was undefeated in winning Swiss squad, having never before won any of his 9 matches in the competition. In other tourns he upset Kafelnikov en route to f Milan and reached qf Antwerp, Rotterdam, New Haven, Vienna (d. W. Ferreira) and Paris Open (d. Sampras in ss). At Hopman Cup in Jan. he injured his hand in a gesture of frustration after he and Hingis wasted 4 champ points in mixed doubles and was forced to def after playing 2 more points. **1997:** (31) A 2, F 4, W 2, US 1. He recorded some notable upsets on his way to winning Antwerp (d. Korda), r/u Tashkent (d. Kafelnikov), sf Munich (d. Moya) and qf Marseille and Gstaad (d. Kafelnikov). In doubles he won Basle with Henman. **1998:** A 2, F 1, W 2, US 1. He was r/u St Petersburg and Antwerp (d. Kafelnikov and Rafter), reached sf Split (extended Rusedski to 7–6 fs), Basle and Moscow and qf Toulouse and upset Pioline at Wimbledon (13–11 fs). **1998 HIGHLIGHTS – SINGLES: Australian Open 2r** (d. Macphie 6–4 0–6 6–4 3–6 6–4, lost Spadea 6–3 4–6 6–4 6–3), **French Open 1r** (lost Pozzi 6–2 6–1 4–6 6–4), **Wimbledon 2r** (d. Pioline [seed 8] 6–4 3–6 4–6 7–6 13–11, lost Wilkinson 6–4 6–4 7–6), **US Open 1r** (lost Hrbaty 7–6 7–6 7–5); **r/u** St Petersburg (d. Tchernenko 6–2 6–3, Delaitre 6–4 6–3, Hrbaty 6–4 6–3, Pioline 6–1 6–4, lost Krajicek 6–4 7–6), **r/u** Antwerp (d. Kiefer 7–6 4–6 7–6, Kafelnikov 6–3 6–3, Larsson w/o, Rafter 7–6 7–6, lost Rusedski 7–6 3–6 6–1 6–4); **sf** Split (d. Furlan 3–6 6–2 6–3, Vasek 6–3 6–1, Schuttler 6–2 6–2, lost Rusedski 6–7 7–6 7–6), **sf** Basle (d. Haas 7–6 4–6 7–6, W. Ferreira 6–4 6–0, Prinosil 6–3 7–6, lost Agassi 6–4 6–2), **sf** Moscow (d. Tarango 6–4 6–4, Pavel 6–4 6–2, Kroslak 6–2 6–4, lost Kafelnikov 6–1 2–0 ret). **CAREER HIGHLIGHTS – SINGLES: Olympics – gold medal 1992** [unseeded] (d. Alami 6–2 4–6 2–1 ret, W. Ferreira 6–4 6–0 6–2, Courier 6–4 6–2 6–1, E. Sanchez 6–4 7–6 3–6 7–6, Ivanisevic 6–3 7–5 6–2, Arrese 7–6 6–3 3–6 4–6 8–6); **French Open – sf 1996** (d. Steeb 6–4 6–4 6–0, Novak 6–2 6–4 6–3, Hlasek 6–4 6–4 6–1, Edberg 7–6 6–3 6–3, Karbacher 4–6 4–6 6–3 7–5 6–0, lost Stich 6–3 6–4 6–2). **CAREER HIGHLIGHTS – DOUBLES:** (with Hlasek) **French Open – won 1992** (d. D. Adams/Olhovskiy 7–6 6–7 7–5).

MARAT SAFIN (RUS)

Born Moscow, 27 January 1980, and lives there; RH; 6ft 4in; 180lb; turned pro 1997; career singles titles 0; final 1998 ATP ranking 48; 1998 prize money $237,135.

Coached by Rafael Mansua and trains in Valencia, Spain. **1996:** (441). **1997:** (194) Won Espinho Challenger. **1998:** A –, F 4, W 1, US 4. The 4 years he spent working on Spanish clay in Valencia paid off as he sprang to prominence at French Open. There, a qualifier, he upset Agassi and Kuerten – the 1st time in the open era that a defending champion had lost to a qualifier – and bowed out only after extending Pioline to 5s. These results took him into the top 100. Having won Napoli Challenger in April, he reached his 1st sf on the main tour at Long Island (d. Berasategui) in August, as well as reaching qf Tashkent and recording upsets of Korda at Ostrava and Larsson at Barcelona. **1998 HIGHLIGHTS – SINGLES: French Open last 16** [unseeded] (d. Agassi 5–7 7–5 6–3 3–6 6–2, Kuerten [seed 8] 3–6 7–6 3–6 6–1 6–4, Vacek 6–3 3–6 6–3 7–5, lost Pioline 7–5 4–6 6–7 6–4 6–4), **Wimbledon 1r** (lost Medvedev 6–3 6–4 3–6 6–4), **US Open last 16** [unseeded] (d.

Gustafsson 6–2 3–6 6–3 7–6, Dent 6–3 6–1 7–6, Muster 6–4 6–4 1–6 6–3, lost Sampras 6–4 6–3 6–2); **sf** Long Island (d. Berasategui 6–3 6–2, Dewulf 7–6 6–1, Prinosil 6–1 7–6, lost Mantilla 6–3 5–7 6–4).

DAVIDE SANGUINETTI (ITA)

Born Viareggio, 25 September 1972; lives Ortonovo; RH; 6ft 2in; 175lb; turned pro 1993; career singles titles 0; final 1998 ATP ranking 47; 1998 prize money $342,495.

Coached by Gianpaolo Coppo; formerly trained at Harry Hopman Academy. **1990:** (941) Won nat 18s. **1991:** (1115). **1992:** (537).**1993:** (246) All-American at UCLA and enjoyed some success on Italian satellite circuit. **1994:** (181) Began to make his presence felt on the Challenger circuit. **1995:** (262). **1996:** (282) Concentrating mainly on the satellites, he had his best results in Italy. **1997:** (92) After winning Oberstaufen Challenger, he reached his 1st sf on the main tour at Bogota, and broke into top 100. In doubles he won Umag with Pescariu. **1998:** A 2, F 1, W qf, US 3. He reached his 1st career f at Coral Springs, then at Wimbledon, where he was unseeded, he became 1st Italian quarter-finalist there since Panatta 19 years earlier. He reached the same stage Mexico City and Bogota and won Napoli Challenger. In D Cup f in Milan v SWE he lost both singles and doubles (with Nargiso) as ITA went down 4–1. **1998 HIGHLIGHTS – SINGLES: Australian Open 2r** (d. A. Martin 6–0 3–6 7–6 6–3, lost Sampras [seed 1] 6–2 6–1 6–2), **French Open 1r** (lost Arnold 4–6 6–4 6–1 6–4), **Wimbledon qf** [unseeded] (d. Van Herck 6–7 6–1 6–1 2–0 ret, Squillari 6–1 6–3 6–2, Voltchkov 3–6 6–1 5–7 6–2 6–1, Clavet 7–6 6–1 6–4, lost Krajicek [seed 9] 6–2 6–3 6–4), **US Open 3r** (d. Sekulov 6–4 6–4 6–2, Damm 7–6 7–6 6–4, lost Agassi [seed 8] 6–2 6–3 6–0); **won** Napoli Challenger (d. Safin 6–4 6–4); **r/u** Coral Springs (d. Sargsian 3–6 6–3 7–5, McEnroe 6–3 6–3, Delgado 6–4 6–4, Van Herck 6–3 6–4, lost Ilie 7–5 6–4).

FABRICE SANTORO (FRA)

Born Tahiti, 7 December 1972; lives Paris; RH; 5ft 10in; 160lb; turned pro 1989; career singles titles 1; final 1998 ATP ranking 41 singles, 18 doubles; 1998 prize money $757,122; career prize money $2,824,028.

Coached by his father, Marcel. Nat champ in 12s, 14s and 16s. **1988:** (571) Won Orange Bowl 16s. **1989:** (235) A –, F 1, W –, US –. Won French Open Jun over Palmer and was No. 2 in ITF Jun rankings. Upset Gomez at Stuttgart. **1990:** (62) A –, F 2, W 1, US 3. After winning Telford Challenger, he upset Gomez again en route to his 1st tour f at Toulouse. Qf Nice (d. Chesnokov) and Bordeaux. Voted Newcomer of the Year. **1991:** (43) A 1, F 4, W –, US 1. Won Barcelona (d. Bruguera) and Brest Challenger; qf Adelaide, Sydney, Italian Open, Florence, Indianapolis and Bordeaux; last 16 French Open, unseeded. **1992:** (43) A –, F 1, W –, US 1. Made his mark at the Olympics, where he upset Becker and extended Ivanisevic to 8–6 fs in qf. Scored other big upsets during the year as he moved to sf Nice (d. Chesnokov), Gstaad (d. Novacek), Hilversum and New Haven (d. Korda). **1993:** (55) A 2, F 1, W –, US 1. Upset Volkov on his way to f Dubai and appeared in sf Nice (d. Krickstein) plus 3 more qf, including Indian Wells, where he upset Stich. Out 4 months from May to Aug. with a serious thumb injury. **1994:** (47) A 3, F 3, W –, US –. His best performance came at Kitzbuhel, where he upset Gaudenzi and Muster and extended Ivanisevic to 5s in f. He also won Venice Challenger and reached sf Tel Aviv, plus qf Pinehurst, Bordeaux and Montevideo. **1995:** (104) A 2, F 1, W 1, US 1. Reached sf Estoril and qf Palermo, where he won the doubles with Corretja, as well as upsetting Edberg 1r Monte Carlo and Sampras 1r Italian Open. Military service left him with limited opportunities for training and practice. **1996:** (118) A 1, F –, W –, US –. Military service again restricted his schedule. **1997:** (29) A –, F 1, W 1, US 1. After winning Newcastle Challenger, he went on in Oct. to take his 1st title on the main tour at Lyon, unseeded and upsetting Krajicek, Mantilla and Philippoussis. He scored other big upsets on his way to sf Marseille (d. Korda), Monte Carlo (d. Muster and Bruguera), Prague (d. Kuerten and Rios), qf Estoril and Montreal (d. Muster) and removed Bruguera at Stuttgart Eurocard. In doubles he played 2 f with Delaitre and 1 with D. Adams, but won no title. **1998:** A 3, F 3, W –, US 3. He began the year in style at Qatar, where he upset Rusedski and Ivanisevic en route to f, unseeded. Although he did not pass qf again, he reached that stage at St Petersburg, Monte Carlo (d. Sampras 6–1 6–1), Hamburg (d. Krajicek) and Basle. He became a force in doubles with Delaitre, winning 4 titles from 6 f and qualifying for a 1st World Doubles Champ, where they reached sf before bowing to Knowles/Nestor. **1998 HIGHLIGHTS – SINGLES: Australian Open 3r** (d. Alvarez 4–6 6–0 6–3 5–7 6–4, Lapentti 6–4 3–6 3–6 6–2 6–4, lost Bjorkman [seed 4] 7–6 6–3 6–4), **French Open 3r** (d. Bachelot 6–3 6–1 6–2, Arnold 4–6 4–6 6–4 6–0 6–3, lost Mantilla [seed 15] 4–6 6–2 6–2 7–5), **US Open 3r** (d. Lapentti 4–6 7–5 6–3 3–6 7–6, Arthurs 7–6 6–4 6–3, lost Bjorkman [seed 12] 6–3 6–1 6–2); **r/u** Qatar (d. Gustafsson 6–7 6–4 6–4, Sinner 6–3 6–4, Rusedski 6–2 3–6 6–3, Ivanisevic 6–1 6–4, lost Korda 6–0 6–3). **1998 HIGHLIGHTS – DOUBLES:** (with Delaitre) **won** Stuttgart Mercedes (d. Eagle/Grabb 6–1 3–6 6–3), **won** Toulouse (d. Haarhuis/Siemerink 6–2 6–4), **won** Basle (d. Norval/Ullyett 6–3 7–6), **won** Lyon (d. Carbonell/Roig 6–2 6–2); **r/u** Qatar (lost Bhupathi/Paes 6–4 3–6 6–4), **r/u** Cincinnati (lost Knowles/Nestor 6–1 2–1 ret).

SJENG SCHALKEN (NED)

Born Weert, 8 September 1976; lives Monte Carlo, Monaco; RH; 6ft 3in; 178lb; turned pro 1994; career singles titles 3; final 1998 ATP ranking 67; 1998 prize money $340,797; career prize money $1,289,687.

Coached by Henk van Hulst and Alex Reynders. Won Nat 14s, 16s and 18s. **1994:** (187) Won US Open Jun over Tahiri. In the men's game he won Guayaquil Challenger and upset Vacek at Rosmalen. **1995:** (54) A –, F –, W 1, US 1. Upset Berasategui at Valencia on the way to his 1st title from his 1st f on the senior tour;

reached sf Casablanca, qf Rotterdam (as LL), Munich (d. Korda), Palermo (d. Gaudenzi) and Santiago and won Monte Carlo Challenger. In doubles he won Amsterdam with Rios. **1996:** (65) A 1, F 2, W 1, US 3. Won Jakarta and reached qf Monte Carlo (d. Enqvist), Bogota, Beijing and Moscow (d. Courier). **1997:** (60) A 1, F 1, W 1, US 2. A qualifier at Philadelphia, he upset Stoltenberg and took a set off Sampras in sf. Then at Boston in Aug., unseeded and defying a knee injury that had almost caused him to withdraw, he upset Corretja, A. Costa and Rios back-to-back to win the title. In other tourns he reached qf St Polten (d. Henman) and Rosmalen and extended Courier to 8–6 5s at Australian Open. **1998:** A 1, F 1, W 1, US 1. Although he won no title, he reached sf Scottsdale (d. A. Costa) and Singapore, qf Qatar, Philadelphia, St Polten and Boston, and upset Rafter at Rome as LL. **1998 HIGHLIGHTS – SINGLES: Australian Open 1r** (lost Sampras [seed 1] 7–5 6–4 6–2), **French Open 1r** (lost Vacek 1–6 6–2 6–4 7–5), **Wimbledon 1r** (lost Gambill 7–6 6–4 6–7 4–6 8–6), **US Open 1r** (lost Damm 6–3 6–3 7–5); **sf** Scottsdale (d. Blanco 6–3 7–6, Fromberg 4–6 7–6 7–6, A. Costa 6–3 6–4, lost Stoltenberg 6–3 6–3), **sf** Singapore (d. Ilie 6–4 6–2, Woodbridge 7–6 6–4, Van Lottum 3–6 6–3 6–4, lost Woodforde 0–6 6–4 6–2). **1998 HIGHLIGHTS – DOUBLES:** (with Carlsen) **r/u** Tashkent (lost Pescosolido/Tieleman 7–5 4–6 7–5).

JAN SIEMERINK (NED)

Born Rijnsburg, 14 April 1970; lives Monte Carlo, Monaco; LH; 6ft; 162lb; turned pro 1989; career singles titles 4; final 1998 ATP ranking 19; 1998 prize money $638,990; career prize money $3,607,963.

Coached by Tjerk Bogstra. **1988:** Nat 18s Champ and won Orange Bowl doubles with Eltingh. **1989:** (477). **1990:** (135) Appeared in his 1st GP sf at Singapore after qualifying. **1991:** (26) A 4, F 1, W 1, US 3. Moved into the top 100 after Australian Open, where he was unseeded, then shot through the rankings with his 1st GP title in his 1st f at Singapore in April and r/u placing at Vienna in Oct. (d. Hlasek and Skoff). In addition, he upset Forget at US Open, reached sf Stuttgart Eurocard and won Telford Challenger. From 3 doubles f he won Hilversum with Krajicek. **1992:** (57) A 2, F 1, W 1, US 3. It was a less spectacular year, but he scored some more significant upsets in reaching sf Toulouse (d. Steeb) and Vienna (d. B. Gilbert), plus qf Stuttgart (d. Becker), Rotterdam (d. Edberg), Hong Kong and Hilversum. **1993:** (53) A 3, F 1, W 1, US 2. A finalist at Marseille, he also reached qf Kitzbuhel and Vienna, as well as upsetting Washington at Italian Open and Cincinnati and Lendl at Basle. In doubles he won LIPC with Krajicek. **1994:** (82) A 2, F –, W –, US 1. Upset Lendl at LIPC, Rosset at Italian Open and Agassi at New Haven. Reached sf Seoul, qf Ostrava and Vienna (served for the match v Stich, but lost 7–5 fs) and won Aachen Challenger. In doubles he took 2 titles with different partners. **1995:** (21) A 2, F 1, W 3, US 1. In singles he was r/u Amsterdam, Long Island (d. W. Ferreira) and Basle (d. Enqvist and extended Courier to 7–5 5s); reached qf Qatar, Auckland (d. W. Ferreira), Stuttgart Eurocard and Copenhagen, as well as upsetting M. Chang at LIPC and Becker at Cincinnati. Played 4 doubles f with different partners, winning Rosmalen with Krajicek and Vienna with E. Ferreira. **1996:** (15) A 3, F 2, W 1, US 3. His 2nd career singles title, at Nottingham, was his 1st for 5 years. He was r/u New Haven (d. Krajicek and W. Ferreira), Vienna (unseeded, d. Enqvist and extended Becker to 4s), reached sf Hong Kong (took a set off Sampras) and Stuttgart Eurocard (d. Kafelnikov and Ivanisevic) and qf Rosmalen. In doubles with E. Ferreira he won Sydney and Monte Carlo. **1997:** (78) A 1, F 3, W 1, US 1. He made a poor start to the year, in which he dropped out of the top 100, and had to wait until Aug. for his 1st qf appearance at Cincinnati (d. Korda and Ivanisevic). However, he finished the year in tremendous style with r/u Stockholm, upsetting Becker, Pioline and Rusedski. **1998:** A 2, F 1, W qf, US 4. He continued his fine form into the next season, upsetting Ivanisevic at Australian Open, Antwerp (Feb.) and Rotterdam (March), where he also surprised Rafter and Krajicek on his way to the title. At Wimbledon, where he was unseeded, he upset Bjorkman before Ivanisevic took his revenge in 3 tb sets in qf. He added a 2nd title at Toulouse (d. Rusedski), reached sf London, Copenhagen and Den Bosch, and upset Rusedski again at US Open (unseeded). These results saw him return to his old place in the top 15. He played 3 doubles f, each with a different partner, winning Den Bosch with Raoux. **1998 HIGHLIGHTS – SINGLES: Australian Open 2r** (d. Ivanisevic [seed 13] 6–2 7–5 3–6 6–4, lost Golmard 7–6 7–5 6–7 3–6 6–1), **French Open 1r** (lost Van Lottum 6–7 6–3 6–2 3–6 6–2), **Wimbledon qf** [unseeded] (d. Dosedel 6–1 6–4 7–6, Prinosil 6–4 6–7 6–4 6–2, Bjorkman [seed 11] 7–6 5–7 2–6 6–4 7–5, Larsson 4–6 6–3 6–3 6–2, lost Ivanisevic [seed 14] 7–6 7–6 7–6), **US Open last 16** [unseeded] (d. Pescariu 6–4 6–3 6–0, Hrbaty 6–4 6–3 6–4, Rusedski [seed 6] 1–6 6–4 5–7 6–2 6–4, lost Bjorkman [seed 12] 6–4 2–6 6–2 6–2); **won** Rotterdam (d. Ivanisevic 5–7 7–6 6–3, Raoux 6–7 6–2 6–2, Rafter 6–4 6–4, Krajicek 6–4 4–6 6–4, Johansson 7–6 6–2), **won** Toulouse (d. Canas 6–3 6–4, Golmard 3–6 6–3 6–4, Federer 7–6 6–2, Johansson 6–3 3–6 7–5, Rusedski 6–4 6–4); **sf** London (d. Bruguera 6–1 7–6, Ulihrach 6–3 6–7 6–4, Goellner 6–3 6–4, lost Pioline 6–3 7–6), **sf** Copenhagen (d. Clement 6–1 6–3, Nargiso 6–4 4–6 6–3, Steven 6–3 6–3, lost Prinosil 6–3 7–6), **sf** Den Bosch (d. Rosset 6–3 7–5, Dewulf 6–2 6–1, Campbell 2–6 6–1 6–3, lost Damm 7–6 6–3). **1998 HIGHLIGHTS – DOUBLES:** (with Raoux) **won** Den Bosch (d. Eagle/Florent 7–6 6–2); (with Steven) **r/u** Copenhagen (lost Kempers/Oosting 6–4 7–6), (with Haarhuis) **r/u** Toulouse (lost Delaitre/Santoro 6–2 6–4).

VINCE SPADEA (USA)

Born Chicago, Ill., 19 July 1974; lives Boca Raton, Fla.; RH; 2HB; 6ft; 170lb; turned pro 1993; career singles titles 0; final 1998 ATP ranking 42; 1998 prize money $368,639; career prize money $1,316,514.

Coached by his father, Vince snr. **1988:** Won Orange Bowl and Easter Bowl 14s and 6 nat titles. **1991:** (1052). **1992:** (644) Won Orange Bowl 18s and r/u to Dunn at USTA Nat 18s. **1993:** (284) A –, F –, W –, US 1. Won all 4 tourns on Caribbean Satellite circuit. **1994:** (80) A –, F –, W –, US 2. Emerging from the Challenger circuit, on which he won 3 titles, he reached qf Pinehurst and upset Haarhuis at New Haven and Corretja at Montevideo. **1995:** (79) A 3, F 1, W 1, US 4. Reached sf Auckland (d. Siemerink) and Bermuda, upset Kafelnikov at US Open, where he was unseeded, and surprised C. Costa 1r Italian Open. He won his 1st tour title when he took the doubles at Buenos Aires with Van Rensburg after qualifying. **1996:** (54) A 2, F 1, W 1, US 3. Although he could not progress beyond qf on the main tour, he reached that stage at San Jose, LIPC (d. Enqvist and Krajicek), Bermuda, Atlanta, US CC, Coral Springs, Nottingham and Stockholm (d. Siemerink), and won Aruba Challenger. At US Open v M. Chang he served for the match at 5–4 4s, but could not see it through. **1997:** (87) A –, F 1, W 1, US 1. He appeared in sf Toulouse and Bogota, reached qf Washington and Tashkent, and upset Enqvist at Cincinnati. In doubles he won Orlando with Merklein and Tashkent with Santopadre. **1998:** A 3, F 2, W 2, US 1. In a year that saw him break into top 50 1st time, his best performance came at St Polten, where he was r/u. In other tourns he scored some notable upsets en route to qf Adelaide (d. Kiefer), Washington and Cincinnati (d. Agassi and Krajicek) as well as removing Philippoussis at San Jose, Rafter at LIPC, Korda at Toronto and Siemerink at Paris Open. **1998 HIGHLIGHTS – SINGLES: Australian Open 3r** (d. Stasiak 6–7 6–1 6–4 4–6 6–3, Rosset 6–3 4–6 6–4 6–3, lost Korda [seed 6] 6–2 7–6 6–2), **French Open 2r** (d. Nestor 5–7 5–2 ret, lost Meligeni 7–6 7–6 6–3), **Wimbledon 2r** (d. Pavel 6–3 6–3 6–3, lost Johansson 7–5 6–1 6–3), **US Open 1r** (lost B. Black 6–4 6–1 6–2); **r/u** St Polten (d. Carlsen 7–5 7–5, Fromberg 4–6 6–3 6–3, Schalken 7–6 6–1, Filippini 6–3 6–0, lost Rios 6–2 6–0). **1998 HIGHLIGHTS – DOUBLES:** (with Merklein) **r/u** Coral Springs (lost Stafford/Ulyett 7–5 6–4).

FRANCO SQUILLARI (ARG)

Born Buenos Aires, 22 August 1975, and lives there; LH; 6ft; 168lb; turned pro 1994; career singles titles 0; final 1998 ATP ranking 60; 1998 prize money $200,586.

1992: (944). **1993:** (391) Won South American Jun Champs. **1994:** (305). **1995:** (433) Began to make an impression on ARG satellite circuits. **1996:** (137) A –, F 2, W –, US –. Upset Moya on the way to qf Kitzbuhel after qualifying. **1997:** (106) A –, F 1, W –, US –. His 1st f on the main tour at Casablanca and his 1st Challenger title at Puerto Rico took him into the top 100 1st time. **1998:** A 2, F –, W 2, US 1. He moved into the top 50 with r/u Palermo, sf Kitzbuhel, qf Atlanta and Bologna (d. Clavet) and the Braunschweig Challenger title. **1998 HIGHLIGHTS – SINGLES: Australian Open 2r** (d. Johansson 6–4 2–6 6–3 6–7 8–6, lost Reneberg 6–0 6–4 1–6 4–6 6–3), **Wimbledon 2r** (d. Puerta 6–7 6–3 7–5 6–4, lost Sanguinetti 6–1 6–3 6–2), **US Open 1r** (lost Filippini 7–6 6–0 6–1); **won** Braunschweig Challenger (d. Arnold 6–2 4–6 6–1); **r/u** Palermo (d. Luzzi 6–2 6–3, Hrbaty 6–4 2–6 6–4, Zabaleta 5–7 6–4 6–3, Blanco 6–1 2–6 7–6, lost Puerta 6–3 6–2); **sf** Kitzbuhel (d. Ruud 6–4 6–3, Arthurs 7–6 6–7 6–4, Fromberg 6–4 4–6 6–4, lost A. Costa 7–5 1–6 6–3).

SANDON STOLLE (AUS)

Born Sydney, 13 July 1970; lives there and Miami Beach, Fla.; RH; 6ft 4in; 175lb; turned pro 1991; career singles titles 0; final 1998 ATP ranking 237 singles, 14 doubles; 1998 prize money $415,552; career prize money $1,955,468.

Fitness coach Brett Stevens. Son of Fred Stolle. Studied under Harry Hopman in his freshman year of high school; also helped by TCU coach 'Tut' Bartzen. **1989:** (813). **1990:** (228) All-American in doubles with Ruette at Texas Christian Univ. **1991:** (169) A 1, F –, W 2, US –. Qf Brasilia. **1992:** A 2, F –, W 3, US 2. Broke into top 100 May after winning Kuala Lumpur and Taipei Challengers, going on to reach sf Los Angeles on the main tour. **1993:** (199) A 1, F 1, W 2, US –. Won Sydney Outdoor doubles with Stoltenberg, but reached no singles qf all year. **1994:** (182) A2, F –, W –, US –. His strength was again in doubles, in which he won 3 titles with different partners. **1995:** (182) A 1, F –, W 1, US –. Reached qf Queen's (d. Bjorkman) and upset Edberg at Cincinnati. Played 4 doubles f, including his 1st GS at US Open with O'Brien, but won no title. **1996:** (58) A 2, F 1, W 3, US 1. It was a stronger year in singles, in which he reached his 1st f on the main tour at Nottingham and appeared in sf Scottsdale (d. Edberg) and Los Angeles (d. Siemerink), plus qf Dubai (d. Muster), New Delhi and Coral Springs. From 4 doubles f with 3 different partners, he won Ostrava with Suk. **1997:** (84) A 1, F 2, W 3, US –. In singles he reached sf Nottingham, qf Sydney, Philadelphia, Atlanta (d. Bjorkman) and Newport, and in doubles played 3 f with Suk but won no title. **1998:** A 1, F –, W –, US –. He won his 1st GS title in partnership with Suk at US Open, as well at taking Newport with Flach and Los Angeles with Rafter. It was with Suk that he qualified for his 1st World Doubles Champ, although they did not pass rr. In singles his best showings were qf Hong Kong Salem Open and Los Angeles. **1998 HIGHLIGHTS – SINGLES: Australian Open 1r** (lost Raoux 2–6 6–3 4–6 6–2 6–0). **1998 HIGHLIGHTS – DOUBLES:** (with Suk) **won US Open** (d. Knowles/Nestor 4–6 7–6 6–2); (with Flach) **won** Newport (d. S. Draper/Stoltenberg 6–2 4–6 7–6), (with Rafter) **won** Los Angeles.(d. Tarango/Vacek 6–4 6–4). **CAREER HIGHLIGHTS – DOUBLES: US Open –** (with Suk) **won 1998,** (with O'Brien) **r/u 1995** (lost Woodbridge/ Woodforde 6–3 6–3).

JASON STOLTENBERG (AUS)

Born Narrabri, NSW, 4 April 1970; lives Newcastle, NSW, and Orlando, Fla.; RH; 6ft 1in; 177lb; turned pro 1987; career singles titles 4; final 1998 ATP ranking 27; 1998 prize money $367,061; career prize money $2,864,849.

Coached by Bob Carmichael; trained by Ludvik Wolf. Wife Andrea (married 17 November 1995); son Matthew Jason (born 21 July 1997). **1986:** In winning AUS World Youth Cup squad for 2nd straight year.

1987: (413) A 1, F –, W –, US –. 1st to become ITF Jun Champ in both singles and doubles in the same year. Won Australian Open Jun singles and Australian and Wimbledon Jun doubles (with Woodbridge); r/u French Open and Wimbledon Jun singles. **1988:** (70) A 4, F –, W 2, US 3. In Jun doubles won Australian Open, French Open and Wimbledon, all with Woodbridge. In the senior game reached last 16 Australian Open, unseeded, and qf Rye Brook and Brisbane. **1989:** (84) A 3, F 1, W 3, US 1. Upset Chang en route to his 1st GP f at Livingston. **1990:** (108) A –, F 2, W 2, US 2. In singles reached qf Orlando and Los Angeles. In doubles won 2 titles with Kratzmann and 1 with Woodbridge. **1991:** (75) A 2, F 2, W 1, US 2. Sf Singapore and Brisbane singles and took San Francisco doubles with Masur. **1992:** (166) A 1, F 1, W 1, US –. Reached qf Queen's (d. Forget), but missed the last 4 months of year with rotator cuff injury and dropped down the rankings. **1993:** (44) A 3, F –, W 3, US 1. After taking 2 Challenger titles he followed with his 1st main tour singles title at Manchester, as well as reaching qf Cincinnati (d. Courier) and Gstaad. In GS he extended Stich to 5s Australian Open and in doubles played 2 f with Stolle, winning Sydney Outdoor. **1994:** (20) A 2, F 1, W 3, US 1. In his best year to date, he won his 1st title on clay at Birmingham, was r/u Washington (d. Rosset) and Toronto (d. Rosset and Courier), and reached sf Manchester and Los Angeles (d. Agassi), moving into top 20 in Nov. **1995:** (82) A 1, F 1, W 2, US 3. He could not maintain the high standards of the previous year, with his best showings sf Bordeaux and qf Bermuda, Queen's, Washington, Basle (d. Kafelnikov) and Tel Aviv. **1996:** (31) A 1, F 2, W sf, US 3. He hit his best form in the middle of the year, when he won Coral Springs, upset Ivanisevic en route to sf Wimbledon, unseeded, and reached the same stage US CC and Bournemouth. He also reached qf Sydney, San Jose and Philadelphia (d. W. Ferreira) and won Indian Wells Challenger as he returned to his old place in the rankings. In D Cup, he upset Ivanisevic again as AUS d. CRO. **1997:** (79) A –, F 2, W 3, US 1. He missed Australian Open with a wrist injury, but returned to enjoy a successful CC season in US, progressing from sf Orlando to r/u Atlanta and then the title at Coral Springs. He also reached qf Nottingham (d. Courier) and upset Ivanisevic at Indianapolis. **1998:** A 2, F 4, W 4, US 1. Although he won no title, he was r/u Adelaide, Scottsdale and Atlanta (where he extended Sampras to fs tb) and reached sf Newport and qf Sydney and Stockholm (upsetting Sampras 1r, when the world No. 1 was struggling to retain his top ranking for a record 6th successive season). Other significant upsets included Bjorkman at Indianapolis and Moya at Paris Open, while in GS, unseeded, he removed Rafter at French Open, and survived 3 5s matches at Wimbledon. **1998 HIGHLIGHTS – SINGLES: Australian Open 2r** (d. Blanco 6–2 ret, lost Ilie 6–3 6–2 7–6), **French Open last 16** [unseeded] (d. Blanco 6–2 4–6 6–0 4–6 10–8, Rafter [seed 4] 6–4 2–6 6–3 6–2, Gustafsson 6–1 2–6 6–4 6–4, lost Corretja [seed 14] 6–4 6–4 6–3), **Wimbledon last 16** [unseeded] (d. Kuerten 4–6 6–3 6–1 4–6 10–8, Tarango 6–4 2–6 6–2 6–7 6–3, Woodforde 6–1 3–6 6–3 3–6 6–3, lost Philippoussis 5–7 6–1 6–3 6–3), **US Open 1r** (lost Perlant 1–6 7–5 6–3 6–3); **r/u** Adelaide (d. Marin 6–4 6–1, Bjorkman 7–5 6–1, Escude 6–7 6–1 7–5, Woodbridge 6–4 6–1, lost L. Hewitt 3–6 6–3 7–6), **r/u** Scottsdale (d. Ruud 6–3 6–7 6–3, C. Costa 6–3 2–6 6–4, Gaudenzi 7–5 7–6, Schalken 6–3 6–3, lost Agassi 6–4 7–6), **r/u** Atlanta (d. Horna 6–3 6–4, MaliVai Washington 6–2 6–4, Reneberg 6–4 6–1, Pavel 6–2 6–4, lost Sampras 6–7 6–3 7–6); **sf** Newport (d. Pescosolido 1–6 6–1 7–5, Hewitt 6–1 6–3, Van Lottum 6–1 6–2, lost Godwin 3–6 6–1 7–6). **1998 HIGHLIGHTS – DOUBLES:** (with S. Draper) **r/u** Newport (lost Flach/Stolle 6–2 4–6 7–6). **CAREER HIGHLIGHTS – SINGLES: Wimbledon – sf 1996** [unseeded] (d. Voinea 4–6 6–4 5–7 6–2 6–0, Novak 7–6 6–1 6–1, Navarra 6–2 6–2 6–2, Hlasek 6–2 7–6 6–2, Ivanisevic 6–3 7–6 6–7 7–6, lost Krajicek 7–5 6–2 6–1).

CYRIL SUK (CZE)

Born Prague, 29 January 1967; lives Monte Carlo, Monaco; RH; 5ft 11in; 158lb; turned pro 1988; career singles titles 0; final 1998 ATP ranking – singles, 11 doubles; 1998 prize money $449,071; career prize money $2,252,570.

Coached by Zdenek Zofka; trained by Ivan Machytka. Brother of Helena Sukova; son of the 1962 Wimbledon finalist, the late Vera Sukova, and Cyril Suk, former President of Czech Tennis Federation. Wife Lenka (married 26 March 1991); son Cyril IV (born 21 October 1992); daughter Natalie Mia (born 8 May 1996). **1985:** No. 1 in Jun doubles rankings with Korda. **1988:** (184). **1989:** (231) A 1, F –, W –, US –. Won St Vincent doubles with Cihak. **1990:** (288) A 1, F –, W –, US –. **1991:** (532) A –, F –, W –, US –. Reached 6 doubles f, winning Prague with Flegl and Toulouse and Lyon with Nijssen, with whom he qualified for ATP Doubles Champ. In mixed doubles won French Open with his sister, Helena. **1992:** (723) A –, F –, W –, US –. Won Stuttgart and Basle doubles with Nijssen, qualifying for World Doubles Final, and in mixed won Wimbledon with Savchenko-Neiland. **1993:** (–) A –, F –, W –, US –. Appeared in 5 doubles f, winning Halle with Korda, New Haven with Vacek and Stuttgart Mercedes with Nijssen, with whom he qualified again for World Doubles Finals. **1994:** (653) A –, F –, W –, US –. Won 2 doubles titles with Nijssen, qualifying for World Doubles Champ for 4th straight year. **1995:** (–) A –, F –, W –, US –. Played 8 men's doubles f, winning 4 with Vacek, with whom he qualified for World Doubles Champ. He won a match there for the 1st time in 5 appearances, winning 2 in rr before losing sf to Eltingh/Haarhuis. In mixed with G. Fernandez was r/u Australian Open, Wimbledon and US Open. **1996:** (–) In men's doubles he appeared in 4 f with 3 different partners, winning Ostrava with Stolle, and in mixed he won Wimbledon with his sister, Helena. **1997:** (–) A –, F –, W –, US –. Won Moscow doubles with Damm and was r/u 3 other tourns with Stolle, as well as retaining his Wimbledon mixed doubles title with his sister, Helena. **1998:** A –, F –, W –, US –. He won his 1st GS men's doubles title at US Open with Stolle, and from 2 other f won Scottsdale with Tebbutt. Stolle was the 3rd different partner with whom he had qualified for World Doubles Champ, where they did not progress beyond rr. In mixed he and Helena were r/u Australian Open. **1998 HIGHLIGHTS – DOUBLES:** (with Stolle)

won US Open (d. Knowles/Nestor 4–6 7–6 6–2); (with Tebbutt) **won** Scottsdale (d. Kinnear/Wheaton 4–6 6–1 7–6); (with Orsanic) **r/u** Gstaad (lost Kuerten/Meligeni 6–4 7–5). **MIXED DOUBLES:** (with Sukova) **r/u Australian Open** (lost Gimelstob/V. Williams 6–2 6–1). **CAREER HIGHLIGHTS – DOUBLES:** (with Stolle) **US Open – won 1998. MIXED DOUBLES:** (with Sukova unless stated) **French Open – won 1991** (d. Haarhuis/Vis 3–6 6–4 6–1); **Wimbledon** – (with Savchenko-Neiland) **won 1992** (d. Eltingh/Oremans 7–6 6–2), **won 1996** (d. Woodforde/Neiland 1–6 6–3 6–2), **won 1997** (d. Olhovskiy/Neiland 4–6 6–3 6–4).

BOHDAN ULIHRACH (CZE)

Born Kolin, 23 February 1975; lives Prague and Monte Carlo, Monaco; RH; 6ft 2in; 170lb; turned pro 1993; career singles titles 2; final 1998 ATP ranking 33; 1998 prize money $436,216; career prize money $1,756,425.

Coached by Tomas Petera; trained by Roman Bart. **1992:** 1098. **1993:** (462). **1994:** (150) Made his mark on the Challenger circuit, winning Oberstaufen. **1995:** (28) A –, F 2, W 1, US 2. Never before having reached qf on main tour, he was r/u St Polten, then in Aug. won his 1st title at Prague, breaking into top 50, and followed in Nov. with Montevideo, where he upset Berasategui in f. He also won Birmingham Challenger, reached qf Amsterdam and upset Kafelnikov at Ostrava. **1996:** (41) A 2, F 3, W 3, US 2. In another solid year he was r/u Prague and reached sf Bologna, Gstaad (d. Pioline) and Indianapolis, as well as upsetting Becker at Milan and A. Costa at US Open. **1997:** (34) A 1, F 2, W –, US 2. At Indian Wells, unseeded, he upset Sampras in ss 2r and took a set off M. Chang in f. He reached the same stage Prague, plus qf Vienna (d. Kuerten) and Ostrava (d. Rosset), and upset Moya at Monte Carlo. **1998:** A –, F 3, W 2, US 2. He continued to be a dangerous opponent, causing some significant upsets on his way to f Umag (d. Mantilla) and qf Stuttgart Mercedes (d. Kafelnikov and Clavet) and New Haven (d. Korda). In other tourns he surprised Philippoussis at French Open, Kafelnikov at Indian Wells, Rusedski at Rome, Moya 1r Vienna and A. Costa at Stuttgart Eurocard, while Rusedski survived only 7–5 5s at US Open. **1998 HIGHLIGHTS – SINGLES: French Open 3r** (d. W. Black 6–1 6–7 6–2 6–3, Philippoussis 3–6 6–7 7–5 6–4 9–7), lost A. Costa [seed 13] 6–3 6–3 6–0), **Wimbledon 2r** (d. Arnold 2–6 7–6 6–3 6–3, lost Bracciali 6–4 6–4 3–6 6–2), **US Open 2r** (d. Sargsian 6–1 6–3 4–6 6–4, lost Rusedski [seed 6] 4–6 6–3 4–6 6–2 7–5); **won** Umag (d. Pescariu 7–6 6–4, Diaz 7–6 3–6 6–4, Mantilla 6–3 3–6 7–6, Puerta 6–3 6–3, M. Norman 6–3 7–6).

DANIEL VACEK (CZE)

Born Prague, 1 April 1971; lives Bradenton, Fla.; RH; 6ft 3in; 179lb; turned pro 1990; career singles titles 0; final 1998 ATP ranking 50; 1998 prize money $695,083; career prize money $3,841,450.

Coached by Vojtech Flegl; trains at Nick Bollettieri's Academy. **1989:** (711). **1990:** (607) Won doubles titles at Umag, Prague and San Marino. **1991:** (464) A 1, F –, W –, US –. Reached 2 doubles f with different partners. **1992:** (113) A –, F –, W –, US –. Won Caracas and Munich Challengers. **1993:** (113) A 2, F 1, W 1, US 2. Upset Edberg in ss at New Haven and won the doubles there with Suk. **1994:** (46) A 3, F 3, W 4, US 2. In March he reached his 1st tour f at Copenhagen, then surprised Kafelnikov at Wimbledon, where he was unseeded. He also upset Muster twice in reaching qf Sydney NSW Open and Moscow and won Rennes Challenger. In doubles he played 4 f, winning Marseille with Siemerink and Toulouse with Oosting. **1995:** (27) A 1, F 2, W 1, US 4. Upset Kafelnikov on his way to f both Marseille and Moscow (where he also beat Volkov), removed Bruguera at US Open, where he was unseeded, and surprised M. Chang at Essen, as well as reaching qf Toulouse and Paris Open. In doubles he played 7 f with Suk, winning 4 and qualifying for World Doubles Champ, where they reached sf before losing to Eltingh/Haarhuis. **1996:** (72) A 1, F 1, W 1, US 1. In singles he reached sf Halle, plus qf Adelaide, Milan (d. Krajicek), St Petersburg, Prague and New Haven (d. Rios). Formed an effective doubles partnership with Kafelnikov, winning French Open and 3 other titles from 6 f to qualify for World Doubles Champ. However, with Kafelnikov qualifying also for ATP Champ in Hannover the following week, they did not take up their place. **1997:** (53) A 1, F 1, W 1, US 4. Upset Siemerink and Ivanisevic en route to f Rotterdam, appeared in qf Milan and Moscow, and removed Philippoussis at US Open, where he was unseeded. Playing 6 doubles f with 3 different partners, he won French Open, US Open and Gstaad with Kafelnikov – with whom he qualified for World Doubles Champ – plus Hong Kong and Tokyo Japan Open with Damm. With Kafelnikov injured after a gruelling week at ATP Champ, they were again unable to take up their place at World Doubles Champ. **1998:** A 2, F 3, W 3, US 1. He reached sf Tokyo Japan Open, qf Marseille, St Petersburg, Toronto, Cincinnati (d. Rios) and Long Island (d. Siemerink), and upset Rafter at Basle. It was a quieter year in doubles, in which Vienna with Kafelnikov was his only title from 4 f. **1998 HIGHLIGHTS – SINGLES: Australian Open 2r** (d. L. Hewitt 6–2 6–4 1–6 2–6 6–3, lost Kucera 7–6 6–7 2–6 6–0 6–1), **French Open 3r** (d. Schalken 1–6 6–2 6–4 7–5, Gambill 6–4 2–6 7–5 7–6, lost Safin 6–3 3–6 6–3 7–5), **Wimbledon 3r** (d. Pozzi 7–6 7–6 6–3, Goellner 6–4 7–5 6–3, lost Ivanisevic [seed 14] 6–7 7–6 6–3 6–4), **US Open 1r** (lost Rios [seed 2] 6–4 6–2 6–3); **sf** Tokyo Japan Open (d. Santopadre 6–1 6–4, Motomura 6–2 6–2, Stolle 7–5 6–3, Prinosil 6–4 6–1, lost B. Black 6–3 7–5). **1998 HIGHLIGHTS – DOUBLES:** (with Kafelnikov unless stated) **won** Vienna (d. Adams/De jager 7–5 6–3); **r/u** London (lost Damm/Grabb 6–4 7–5), (with Tarango) **r/u** Los Angeles (lost Rafter/Stolle 6–4 6–4), **r/u** Moscow (lost Palmer/Tarango 6–4 6–7 6–2). **CAREER HIGHLIGHTS – DOUBLES:** (with Kafelnikov) **French Open – won 1996** (d. Forget/Hlasek 6–2 6–3), **won 1997** (d. Woodbridge/Woodforde 7–6 4–6 6–3); **US Open – won 1997** (d. Bjorkman/Kulti 7–6 6–3).

FERNANDO VICENTE (ESP)

Born Benicarlo, 2 March 1977; lives Splugas de Llobegrat; RH; 5ft 11in; 167lb; turned pro 1996; career singles titles 0; final 1998 ATP ranking 54; 1998 prize money $248,004.

Coached by Alvaro Margets. His twin brother, Jose Maria, also plays the circuit. **1994:** (391) Began to compete on the Spanish satellites. **1995:** (589). **1996:** (151) Reached his 1st qf on the main tour at Marbella. **1997:** (121) Appeared in qf Casablanca, upset Siemerink at Barcelona and broke into top 100 1st time in Aug. **1998:** A –, F 2, W –, US 2. In a productive year he reached his 1st sf at Mallorca (d. A. Costa), played qf Casablanca, Prague, Rome (after qualifying), Stuttgart Mercedes (d. Muster) and Palermo (d. Kuerten), and won 2 Challenger titles. **1998 HIGHLIGHTS – SINGLES: French Open 2r** (d. Woodforde 4–6 6–4 6–2 6–1, lost Corretja [seed 14] 6–3 6–2 6–3), **US Open 2r** (d. Prinosil 6–4 6–3 2–6 6–4, lost B. Black 7–6 6–1 7–5); **won** Singapore Challenger (d. Marin 6–4 6–4), **won** Barcelona Challenger (d. Andersen 6–3 6–3); **sf** Mallorca (d. Alonso 6–1 1–1 ret, A. Costa 7–6 4–6 6–3, Carbonell 3–6 7–6 6–4, lost Moya 6–1 6–2).

ANDREAS VINCIGUERRA (SWE)

Born Malmo, 19 February 1981, and lives there; LH; 2HB; 5ft 10in; 145lb; career singles titles 0; final 1998 ATP ranking 637; 1998 prize money $14,297.

Coached by Anders Henricsson. **1998:** R/u Australian Open Jun to Jeanpierre and won European Jun Champ. In the senior game he won Oulu Futures.

TODD WOODBRIDGE (AUS)

Born Sydney, 2 April 1971; lives there and Orlando, Fla; RH; 5ft 10in; 158lb; turned pro 1988; career singles titles 2; final 1998 ATP ranking 65 singles, 5 doubles; 1998 prize money $695,297; career prize money $6,865,044.

Coached by Ray Ruffels; trained by Mark Waters. Wife Natasha Provis (sister of Nicole Bradtke who plays women's tour; married 8 April 1995). **1987:** (420) R/u Australian Open Jun to Stoltenberg, with whom he won the doubles there and at Wimbledon, and in winning AUS World Youth Cup team for 2nd straight year. **1988:** (213) A 2, F 1, W 1, US –. Won Tasmania and in Jun doubles with Stoltenberg won Australian Open, French Open and Wimbledon. **1989:** (131) A 2, F –, W 2, US –. Won Brisbane Challenger, upset Fitzgerald en route to sf GP event there and finished the year by winning Hobart Challenger. In Jun doubles won Australian and French Open with J. Anderson and in Jun singles was r/u Wimbledon to Kulti. **1990:** (50) A 2, F 2, W 1, US 1. Upset Chang on the way to his 1st tour f at New Haven and Gilbert en route to sf Sydney Indoor. In doubles with various partners he reached 4 f, winning 2, and took US Open mixed with Smylie. **1991:** (77) A 4, F 2, W 3, US 3. Upset Svensson at Australian Open, where he was unseeded, and at French Open extended Becker to 5s. In doubles won 6 titles, 4 with Woodforde, with whom he qualified for ATP Doubles Champ. **1992:** (54) A 1, F 3, W 2, US 2. R/u Seoul (d. Chang), sf Hong Kong, qf Tokyo Suntory and upset Stich at Sydney NSW Open. In doubles with Woodforde won a 1st men's GS title at Australian Open, World Doubles Final and 6 other titles, winning every f they played to finish the year as the top-ranked pairing and were voted ATP Doubles Team of year. In mixed doubles with Sanchez-Vicario won French Open and r/u Australian Open. **1993:** (107) A 3, F 2, W 2, US 2. Was r/u Seoul and reached qf Tokyo Japan Open (d. M. Chang) in singles and continued to excel in doubles. Won his 1st Wimbledon and 4 other titles with Woodforde, took Hong Kong with Wheaton and qualified for ATP World Doubles with Woodforde. They were beaten there in f by Eltingh/Haarhuis, thus ending their record of having won all 17 finals they played since Feb. 1991, equalling McEnroe/Fleming's string in 1979–80. This defeat also ended Woodbridge's personal sequence of winning 21 consec. doubles f, which overtook J. McEnroe's record of 19. Their year ended on another disappointing note when they lost their match in 4–1 D Cup defeat by GER. In mixed doubles he won Australian Open with Sanchez-Vicario and US Open with Sukova. **1994:** (91) A 2, F –, W –, US 3. In singles he was r/u Newport, reached sf Kuala Lumpur and won Wellington Challenger. His year began badly, with a slide down the singles rankings and a lacklustre performance in doubles with Woodforde, notably when they were defeated in D Cup 1r v RUS as AUS were eliminated. However, they regained form to win Wimbledon and finished the year with a total of 5 titles and r/u US Open to qualify for World Doubles Champ where they were r/u. In mixed doubles with Sukova he won Wimbledon and was r/u Australian Open. **1995:** (34) A 1, F 2, W 3, US 3. Won his 1st tour singles title at Coral Springs, where he also took the doubles; was r/u Nottingham and reached sf Vienna, plus 3 more qf. In doubles with Woodforde he won a 3rd Wimbledon, 1st US Open and 5 other titles to qualify for World Doubles Champ, where they lost sf to Connell/Galbraith, although they retained their position as top-ranked pairing and were named Doubles Team of the Year. **1996:** (36) A 3, F 3, W 2, US 1. In singles he was r/u Toronto (d. Rios), reached sf Sydney, Philadelphia, Hong Kong (d. Krajicek) and Nottingham, and upset Siemerink at Olympics, breaking into top 25 in March. He enjoyed another spectacular year in doubles with Woodforde, with whom he was named Doubles Team of the Year again. Despite missing that elusive 1st French Open, they won a 4th consec. Wimbledon, and after winning US Open, they tied with Newcombe/Roche and Fleming/J. McEnroe on a record 7 GS titles as a pairing. They crowned their year with Olympic gold, surviving some close matches along the way and playing an Olympic record 34-game 3rd set v Goellner/Prinosil. Their record of 12 titles from 13 f during the year was the most since Fleming/McEnroe's 15 in 1979 and included a 2nd World Doubles Champ. **1997:** (26) A 3, F 2, W sf, US 2. A good year in singles brought him a 2nd career title at Adelaide, r/u Memphis, sf Wimbledon and qf Hong Kong and Tokyo Japan Open, with an upset of Moya at Paris

Open. Wimbledon saw him in superb form as he upset M. Chang (8–6 fs) and Rafter in the singles, unseeded, and won the doubles with Woodforde. They were again the season's top doubles pairing, overtaking Fleming/McEnroe and Newcombe/Roche when they won their 8th GS title at Australian Open. A 1st French Open title still eluded them, despite their 1st f there, but their 5th consec. Wimbledon equalled the record of the Dohertys in 1897–1901 and their 9th GS title as a pairing was a record in the open era. With 5 titles across the year, they overtook Casal/E. Sanchez on the all-time list and finished the year with 50 titles, in 3rd place behind Fleming/McEnroe and Hewitt/McMillan on 57. At World Doubles Champ, they needed only to win 1s v Leach/Stark in their last rr match to qualify for sf, but lost in ss. However, they were still clearly the season's top doubles team and were voted ATP Doubles Team of the Year for the 3rd consec. season. **1998:** A 4, F 3, W 3, US 1. In a less profitable year, his best performances in singles were sf Adelaide and Chennai, qf Shanghai, and upsets of Rusedski at Australian Open (where he was unseeded) and Kucera at French Open. He and Woodforde reached 10 doubles f, winning 5 and sharing 1, but taking no GS, although they were r/u Australian Open and Wimbledon. They slipped behind Eltingh/Haarhuis as the top doubles pairing and by end of year Bhupathi/Paes pushed them into 3rd place. However, they continued to set records by becoming the 1st pairing to qualify for the season-ending champ for 8 consec. years, although surprisingly they won no match there. **1998 HIGHLIGHTS – SINGLES: Australian Open last 16** [unseeded] (d. Dewulf 7–5 6–3 7–5, Van Garsse 6–4 4–6 6–3 6–4, Rusedski 7–6 6–4 6–2, lost Escude 7–6 6–3 6–2), **French Open 3r** (d. Kucera [seed 9] 1–6 6–2 6–4 6–3, Raoux 6–4 4–6 6–3 6–0, lost Meligeni 7–6 6–3 6–2), **Wimbledon 3r** (d. Blanco 6–1 6–2 6–1, W. Black 6–1 3–6 6–3 6–2, lost T. Martin 6–4 4–6 7–6 6–4), **US Open 1r** (lost Kohlmann 6–7 7–6 4–4 ret); **sf** Adelaide (d. Damm 7–5 4–6 6–3, Knippschild 6–7 6–2 6–4, Golmard 2–6 6–4 6–4, lost Stoltenberg 6–4 6–1), **sf** Chennai (d. Bhupathi 3–6 6–4 6–4, Caratti 6–0 6–7 6–2, Pavel 6–4 6–4, lost Tillstrom 6–2 6–2). **1998 HIGHLIGHTS – DOUBLES:** (with Woodforde) **r/u Australian Open** (lost Bjorkman/Eltingh 6–2 5–7 2–6 6–4 6–3), **r/u Wimbledon** (lost Eltingh/Haarhuis 2–6 6–4 7–6 5–7 10–8); **won** Sydney (d. Eltingh/Nestor 6–3 7–5), **won** San Jose (d. Aerts/Sa 6–1 7–5), **won** Memphis (d. E. Ferreira/Rodoti 6–3 6–4), **won** Munich (d. Eagle/Florent 6–0 6–3), **won** Singapore (d. Bhupathi/Paes 6–2 6–3); **shared** Queen's with Bjorkman/Rafter; **r/u** Monte Carlo (lost Eltingh/Haarhuis 6–4 6–2), **r/u** Shanghai (lost Bhupathi/Paes 6–4 6–7 7–6). **CAREER HIGHLIGHTS – DOUBLES:** (with Woodforde) **Australian Open – won 1992** (d. Jones/Leach 6–4 6–3 6–4), **won 1997** (d. Lareau/O'Brien 4–6 7–5 7–5 6–3), **r/u 1998**; **Wimbledon – won 1993** (d. Connell/Galbraith 6–3 6–4 6–4), **won 1994** (d. Connell/Galbraith 7–6 6–3 6–1), **won 1995** (d. Leach/Melville 7–5 7–6 7–6), **won 1996** (d. B. Black/Connell 4–6 6–4 6–3 6–2), **won 1997** (d. Eltingh/Haarhuis 7–6 7–6 5–7 6–3), **r/u 1998**; **US Open – won 1995** (d. O'Brien/Stolle 6–3 6–3), **won 1996** (d. Eltingh/Haarhuis 4–6 7–6 7–6), **r/u 1994** (lost Eltingh/Haarhuis 6–3 7–6); **Olympics – won 1996** (d. Broad/Henman 6–4 6–4 6–2); **World Doubles Final – won 1992** (d. Fitzgerald/Jarryd 6–2 7–6 5–7 3–6 6–3), **won 1996** (d. Lareau/O'Brien 6–4 5–7 6–2 7–6), **r/u 1993** (lost Eltingh/Haarhuis 7–6 7–6 6–4), **r/u 1994** (lost Apell/Bjorkman 6–4 4–6 4–6 7–6 7–6); **French Open – r/u 1997** (lost Kafelnikov/Vacek 7–6 4–6 6–3). **CAREER HIGHLIGHTS – MIXED DOUBLES:** (with Sanchez-Vicario unless stated) **Australian Open – won 1993** (d. Leach/Garrison-Jackson 7–5 6–4); **French Open – won 1992** (d. Shelton/McNeil 6–2 6–3); **Wimbledon** – (with Sukova) **won 1994** (d. Middleton/McNeil 3–6 7–5 6–3); **US Open** – (with Smylie) **won 1990** (d. Pugh/Zvereva 6–4 6–2), (with Sukova) **won 1993** (d. Woodforde/Navratilova 7–5 6–3).

MARK WOODFORDE (AUS)

Born Adelaide, 23 September 1965; lives there and Monte Carlo, Monaco; LH; 2HB; 6ft 1½in; 172lb; turned pro 1984; career singles titles 4; final 1998 ATP ranking 58 singles, 6 doubles; 1998 prize money $736,370; career prize money $7,463,551.

Coached by Ray Ruffels; trained by Mark Waters. **1984:** (385). **1985:** (127) A 3, F –, W –, US –. **1986:** (181) A –, F 1, W 1, US 1. Won 1st pro title at Auckland and reached sf Bristol. **1987:** (67) A 2, F –, W 2, US 4. Upset Mayotte on his way to last 16 US Open after qualifying. **1988:** (42) A 2, F 2, W 4, US 4. Enjoyed a remarkable year, with success on all surfaces, in which he extended Lendl to 5 close sets in 4 hr 46 min match at Wimbledon, conceding only 10–8 in 5s, upset Edberg and J. McEnroe to reach sf Toronto and beat McEnroe again at US Open, where he was unseeded. Formed a useful doubles partnership with J. McEnroe in autumn. **1989:** (75) A 3, F 3, W 1, US 2. In singles won Adelaide and r/u Brisbane. In doubles won US Open with J. McEnroe and Monte Carlo with Smid. **1990:** (101) A 3, F –, W 4, US –. Upset Chesnokov 2r Australian Open, but was forced to retire in 3r v Wheaton when he tore 2 ligaments in his ankle, requiring surgery. Out of action until June, when he progressed to last 16 Wimbledon, unseeded and a wild card, and in Aug. reached sf New Haven. **1991:** (101) A 4, F 1, W 1, US 1. Upset E. Sanchez at Australian Open (unseeded), Chesnokov in reaching qf Copenhagen and Korda 1r Moscow. Won 4 doubles titles with Woodbridge to qualify for ATP Doubles Champ. **1992:** (40) A 3, F 1, W 2, US 3. In singles he was r/u Los Angeles and Antwerp (d. Lendl and Chang) and reached qf Singapore, Tampa and US CC. With Woodbridge took Australian Open doubles, World Doubles Final and 6 other titles, winning every f they played to finish the year as the top pairing and voted ATP Doubles Team of year. In mixed doubles with Provis, he won Australian Open and US Open. **1993:** (28) A 2, F 3, W 2, US 1. Won Philadelphia singles, beating Clavet and M. Chang on his way to f, where Lendl was forced to retire, and followed with an upset of Washington en route to sf Scottsdale. He also appeared in qf Sydney (d. Medvedev), LIPC (d. Courier), New Haven and Paris Open and broke into the top 25. At Wimbledon he won a 2nd men's doubles GS title with Woodbridge and took mixed with Navratilova.

After Stockholm he and Woodbridge had won all 17 finals they played since Feb. 1991, equalling McEnroe/Fleming's string in 1979–80, but their run was ended by Eltingh/Haarhuis in f ATP World Doubles. Further disappointment followed when they lost in D Cup f as GER beat AUS 4–1. **1994:** (43) A 1, F 3, W 2, US 1. Upset Krajicek en route to f Los Angeles, Costa at LIPC, Lendl on his way to sf Coral Springs, Muster at Cincinnati, Ivanisevic at Indianapolis, and Courier at Paris Open, as well as reaching sf Pinehurst and Sydney Indoor. In doubles he and Woodbridge made a poor start to the year with failure again in D Cup as AUS lost to RUS, but they went on to win Wimbledon and r/u US Open. With various partners, he won 7 titles from 10 f, qualifying with Woodbridge for World Doubles Champ, where they were r/u. **1995:** (51) A 3, F 2, W 3, US 2. In singles he reached sf Adelaide (d. Kafelnikov), Coral Springs and Nottingham, played 3 more qf and upset Courier at LIPC. In doubles with Woodbridge he won Wimbledon, US Open and 5 other titles to qualify for World Doubles Champ, where they lost sf to Connell/Galbraith, although they still finished the year as top-ranked pairing and were named Doubles Team of the Year. When he won French Open mixed with Neiland, he had won a mixed title at all 4 GS tourns. **1996:** (27) A sf, F 1, W 1, US 1. The highlight of his singles year came at Australian Open where, unseeded, he took advantage of Sampras's removal from his half of the draw to sweep to sf, upsetting Enqvist on the way. He reached the same stage Philadelphia, Tokyo Japan Open (d. Enqvist again) and Toulouse, plus qf Sydney, Memphis and Queen's and made a 1st appearance in the top 20 on 22 April. In doubles with Woodbridge won a record 4th consec. Wimbledon and, after winning US Open, they tied with Newcombe/Roche and Fleming/J. McEnroe on a record 7 GS titles as a pairing. They also won Olympic gold, surviving some close matches along the way and playing an Olympic record 34-game 3rd set v Goellner/Prinosil. They finished a superb season with the World Doubles title, taking to 12 their titles from 13 f during the year – the most since Fleming/McEnroe's 15 in 1979 – and were voted Doubles Team of the Year again. In mixed doubles with Neiland he won Australian Open (where he and Woodbridge were surprisingly beaten 1r) and was r/u Wimbledon. **1997:** (46) A 3, F 4, W 4, US 3. Although it was a quieter year in singles, he reached sf Indianapolis (d. Rios and Agassi), qf Tokyo Japan Open (d. Rosset), Coral Springs and Newport, as well as upsetting A. Costa at French Open and Kafelnikov at US Open. He and Woodbridge were again the season's top duo with 5 titles across the year, which took them to 50, ahead of Casal/E. Sanchez and into 3rd place on the all-time list behind Fleming/McEnroe and Hewitt/McMillan on 57. Their 8th GS title at Australian Open took them ahead of Fleming/McEnroe and Newcombe/Roche in GS titles, and their 5th consec. Wimbledon, equalled the record of the Dohertys in 1897–1901. This 9th GS title as a pairing was a record in the open era, but they were still unable to add an elusive 1st French Open title, despite reaching f there 1st time. At World Doubles Champ they needed only to take a set off Leach/Stark in their last rr match to qualify for sf, but they were beaten in ss. However, they still finished the season head and shoulders above any other pairing and were voted ATP Doubles Team of the Year for the 3rd consec. season. **1998:** A 1, F 1, W 3, US 1. At Singapore in Oct. he reached his 1st singles f since 1994 (d. Ivanisevic and won the doubles). He also upset Sampras en route to sf Queen's, and appeared in qf San Jose, Memphis, Chennai and Shanghai. He and Woodbridge played 10 doubles f, winning 5 and sharing 1, but they did not add to their collection of GS, although they were r/u Australian Open and Wimbledon. They were displaced as top pairing by Eltingh/Haarhuis, and then Bhupathi/Paes pushed them down to 3rd place. However, they continued to set records as the 1st pair to qualify for the season-ending champs for 8 consec. years, although surprisingly they won no match there. **1998 HIGHLIGHTS – SINGLES: Australian Open 1r** (lost Damm 6–4 7–6 6–0 ret), **French Open 1r** (lost Vicente 4–6 6–4 6–2 6–1), **Wimbledon 3r** (d. Knippschild 4–6 6–3 7–6 6–1, Gimelstob 2–6 6–1 6–4 6–4, lost Stoltenberg 6–1 3–6 6–3 3–6 6–3), **US Open 1r** (lost Ivanisevic [seed 14] 6–3 6–4 6–4); **r/u** Singapore (d. Ondruska 7–6 6–2, Ivanisevic 6–4 7–6, Carlsen 4–6 6–2 6–3, Schalken 0–6 6–4 6–2, lost Rios 6–4 6–2); **sf** Queen's (d. Gimelstob 5–7 6–3 6–2, Wilkinson 6–2 7–6, Sampras 6–3 6–2, Enqvist 6–3 1–6 6–2, lost S. Draper 6–3 6–2). **1998 HIGHLIGHTS – DOUBLES:** (with Woodbridge) **r/u Australian Open** (lost Bjorkman/Eltingh 6–2 5–7 2–6 6–4 6–3), **r/u Wimbledon** (lost Eltingh/Haarhuis 2–6 6–4 7–6 5–7 10–8); **won** Sydney (d. Eltingh/Nestor 6–3 7–5), **won** San Jose (d. Aerts/Sa 6–1 7–5), **won** Memphis (d. E. Ferreira/Rodoti 6–3 6–4), **won** Munich (d. Eagle/Florent 6–0 6–3), **won** Singapore (d. Bhupathi/Paes 6–2 6–3); **shared** Queen's with Bjorkman/Rafter; **r/u** Monte Carlo (lost Eltingh/Haarhuis 6–4 6–2), **r/u** Shanghai (lost Bhupathi/Paes 6–4 6–7 7–6). **CAREER HIGHLIGHTS – SINGLES: Australian Open – sf 1996** [unseeded] (d. Matsuoka 2–1 ret, Sinner 6–4 6–1 6–4, Clavet 4–6 7–6 6–2 6–4, Philippoussis 6–2 6–2 6–2, Enqvist 6–4 6–4 6–4, lost Becker 6–4 6–2 6–0), **CAREER HIGHLIGHTS – DOUBLES:** (with Woodbridge unless stated) **Australian Open – won 1992** (d. Jones/Leach 6–4 6–3 6–4), **won 1997** (d. Lareau/O'Brien 4–6 7–5 7–5 6–3), **r/u 1998**; **Wimbledon – won 1993** (d. Connell/Galbraith 6–3 6–4 6–4), **won 1994** (d. Connell/Galbraith 7–6 6–3 6–1), **won 1995** (d. Leach/Melville 7–5 7–6 7–6), **won 1996** (d. B. Black/Connell 4–6 6–4 6–3 6–2), **won 1997** (d. Eltingh/Haarhuis 7–6 7–6 5–7 6–3), **r/u 1998**; **US Open** – (with J. McEnroe) **won 1989** (d. Flach/Seguso 6–4 4–6 6–3 6–3), **won 1995** (d. O'Brien/Stolle 6–3 6–3), **won 1996** (d. Eltingh/Haarhuis 4–6 7–6 7–6), **r/u 1994** (lost Eltingh/Haarhuis 6–3 7–6); **Olympics – won 1996** (d. Broad/Henman 6–4 6–4 6–2); **World Doubles Final – won 1992** (d. Fitzgerald/Jarryd 6–2 7–6 5–7 3–6 6–3), **won 1996** (d. Lareau/O'Brien 6–4 5–7 6–2 7–6), **r/u 1993** (lost Eltingh/Haarhuis 7–6 7–6 6–4), **r/u 1994** (lost Apell/Bjorkman 6–4 4–6 4–6 7–6 7–6); **French Open – r/u 1997** (lost Kafelnikov/Vacek 7–6 4–6 6–3). **CAREER HIGHLIGHTS – MIXED DOUBLES:** (with Provis unless stated) **Australian Open – won 1992** (d. Woodbridge/Sanchez-Vicario 6–3 4–6 11–9), (with Neiland) **won 1996** (d. L. Jensen/Arendt 4–6 7–5 6–0); **French Open** – (with Neiland) **won 1995** (d. de Jager/Hetherington 7–6 7–6); **Wimbledon** – (with Navratilova) **won 1993** (d. Nijssen/Bollegraf 6–3 6–4); **US Open – won 1992** (d. Nijssen/Sukova 4–6 6–3 6–3).

MARIANO ZABALETA (ARG)

Born Buenos Aires, 28 February 1978; lives Tandil; RH; 5ft 8in; 150lb; turned pro 1996; career singles titles 1; final 1998 ATP ranking 63; 1998 prize money $149,122.

Coached by Eduardo Infiniti. **1993:** (1186). **1994:** (588). **1995:** (381) He finished the year at No. 1 on ITF Jun rankings after winning French Open Jun over Puerta and Orange Bowl 18s over Haas. In the senior game he reached qf Prague after qualifying. **1996:** (103) He reached his 1st sf on the main tour at Bermuda (again as a qualifier), upset Mantilla on his way to qf Bournemouth and won Birmingham Challenger to finish the year poised just outside the top 100. **1997:** (252) A –, F 1, W –, US –. R/u Guayaquil Challenger was his best performance. **1998:** A –, F 3, W –, US –. His season ended on a high note with his 1st tour title from his 1st tour f at Bogota, where he was unseeded. Earlier in the year he had upset Mantilla en route to sf Amsterdam (still as a qualifier) and reached qf San Marino and Palermo, as well as upsetting Korda 1r French Open after qualifying. **1998 HIGHLIGHTS – SINGLES: French Open 3r** (d. Korda [seed 2] 6–0 6–2 3–6 4–6 6–3, Tarango 6–0 6–2 6–2, lost Arazi 6–4 0–6 6–4 7–6); **won** Bogota (d. Vicente 6–4 6–4, Puerta 3–6 6–3 6–4, Hadad 6–7 6–4 7–6, Novak 6–2 6–4, Delgado 6–4 6–4); **sf** Amsterdam (d. Mantilla 7–6 6–2, Marin 6–1 7–6, Dosedel 2–6 7–6 7–6, lost M. Norman 7–5 6–4).

1 LINDSAY DAVENPORT (USA)

Born: Palos Verdes, CA, 8 June 1976. **Lives:** Newport Beach, Cal. **Father:** Wink, a former Olympic volleyball player. **Mother:** Ann. **Sisters:** Shannon and Leiann (both older). **Agent:** ProServ. **Coaches:** Robert Van't Hof since Jan. 1996. Formerly Lynn Rolley and Craig Kardon.
Turned pro: 22 February 1993.
Height: 6ft 2in (1.88m). **Weight:** 175lb (79kg).

Rankings: 1991: 339; **1992:** 159; **1993:** 20; **1994:** 6; **1995:** 12; **1996:** 9; **1997:** 3; **1998:** 1 singles, 4 doubles. **Highest:** 1 (12 October 1998).

1998 Prize Money: $2,697,788.
Career Earnings: $6,390,242. **Career Titles:** 19.

Style: With a powerful, match-winning forehand, a double-handed backhand of almost equal ferocity and an intimidating serve, she likes to dominate from the baseline. Her agility is much improved, now that she has shed excess pounds, and thanks to the influence of Billie Jean King, who encouraged her to work and train harder. She has also improved her volleying, and her serve has become a potent weapon. Altogether more confident as a result of getting to more balls in time to make forceful shots.

CAREER HIGHLIGHTS (year: (titles))
1991: Won USTA 18s singles and doubles. **1992:** Ranked No. 1 in Nat 18s, in Jun tennis she won US Open over Steven, was r/u Australian Open to Limmer and won Australian Open and US Open doubles with London. **1993: (1)** *Lucerne*. She burst into prominence on the senior tour and swept up the rankings, improving by more than 100 places to 25 in May when she won her 1st title at Lucerne, and breaking into top 20 by autumn. She reached sf Oakland, where she took a set off Navratilova, plus qf VS Florida (d. Sabatini), Indian Wells (d. Schultz) and Tokyo Nicherei. At US Open, unseeded, she upset Coetzer on her way to last 16, where she extended Sabatini to 3s. Made her Fed Cup debut. **1994: (2)** *Brisbane, Lucerne*. In the year in which she graduated from high school, she established herself as one of the top women players. She broke into the top 20 in Jan. after winning Brisbane and moved into top 10 in spring, winning Lucerne in May. At Australian Open she upset M. J. Fernandez to reach qf and reached the same stage Wimbledon, removing Sabatini and taking a set off eventual champ Martinez. She also appeared in sf Indian Wells, LIPC (d. Sabatini), Amelia Island (d. Martinez) and Oakland, plus 4 more qf. These results took her to her 1st VS Champs, where she removed Novotna and Pierce before Sabatini demolished her in f. In doubles she was r/u French Open and won Indian Wells with Raymond, with whom she qualified for VS Champs, and took Oakland with Sanchez-Vicario. **1995: (1)** *Strasbourg*. She won both singles and doubles titles at Strasbourg, and achieved r/u finish at Sydney and Tokyo Pan Pacific, sf Oakland and qf Indian Wells, Manhattan Beach and Tokyo Nicherei. Qualified for VS Champs, but lost 1r to Sabatini. In doubles she played 5 f, winning 2 with M. J. Fernandez and 1 each with Novotna and Raymond. Injury restricted her towards the end of the year: she withdrew from San Diego with a tendon injury in her left leg and from Oakland with back problems, and dropped out of the top 10. **1996: (3)** *OLYMPICS, Strasbourg, Los Angeles*. She enjoyed the performance of her life at the Olympics, where she upset Huber, Majoli, M. J. Fernandez and Sanchez-Vicario – for the 1st time in 6 meetings – to take the gold medal, never before having progressed beyond qf in GS. Yet, discouraged by injury, illness and lack of self-belief, she had come close to quitting towards the end of the previous year, before being talked out of it by M. J. Fernandez. Her rehabilitation and motivation were completed by Billie Jean King in her role as coach to the US Fed Cup and Olympic squads. Fitter and 20lb lighter, she learned how to use her size and strength to advantage, playing with renewed dedication after her split with Craig Kardon. She began the year on a high note at Sydney, where she upset Date and came near to doing the same to Seles in f (letting slip mp in 2s), as well as winning the doubles with M. J. Fernandez. At Indian Wells in March she extended Graf to 2 tb in sf before losing in 3s, following with the title at Strasbourg. Then at LA, where she won both singles and doubles (with Zvereva), she became the 1st player

since 1994 to d. Graf in ss. She also reached sf LIPC and Filderstadt, plus qf French Open, Tokyo Toray, Leipzig and Chicago. In other doubles tourns, she and M. J. Fernandez won French Open (upsetting Novotna/Sanchez-Vicario and G. Fernandez/Zvereva on the way), Sydney and Oakland and were r/u Australian Open. Her year ended less dramatically in singles, as she fell to Wild at US Open and Graf 2r Chase Champs, but she finished on a high note by taking the doubles there with M. J. Fernandez. **1997: (6)** *Oklahoma City, Indian Wells, Amelia Island, Atlanta, Zurich, Chicago.* After winning Oklahoma City in Feb., she followed the next week by taking both singles and doubles at Indian Wells, coming from 1–4 and 5–6 behind in 3s qf v V. Williams. A month later she won both singles and doubles at Amelia Island, adding singles titles at Atlanta, Zurich (d. Novotna) and Chicago. Only Hingis won more tournaments across the year. She was always a dangerous opponent: at Los Angeles she became the 2nd of only 5 players all year to beat Hingis, before extending Seles to 3s in f; at French Open she was 7–5 4–0 up v Majoli, before letting the match slip away; and at US Open she upset Novotna to reach sf. She seriously challenged Hingis again at Philadelphia, losing their f only 7–5 6–7 7–6. She had upset Novotna a 3rd time there and immediately replaced her as No. 2 in the rankings on 17 Nov. However, at Chase Champs the following week, Novotna's triumph and Davenport's 1r defeat by M. J. Fernandez reversed their positions again. She had also reached sf Sydney and Stanford (where she extended Hingis to 3s) and 3 more qf, as well as being a major force in doubles. When M. J. Fernandez talked of retiring at end 1996, Davenport established a new doubles partnership with Novotna, causing some bad feeling for a while between the former best friends. During the year she reached 12 f in all with 5 different partners, winning 3 with Novotna (including US Open), 2 with Zvereva and 1 with Hingis, as well as being r/u Australian Open with Raymond. She qualified for Chase Champs in both singles and doubles, falling 1r singles to M. J. Fernandez but winning the doubles with Novotna. **1998: (6)** *US OPEN, Tokyo Pan Pacific, Stanford, San Diego, Los Angeles, Zurich.* An amazing season saw her win her 1st GS at US Open, where she was magnificent, sweeping to the title without dropping a set and for the loss of only 32 games. That triumph was followed on 12 Oct. by her arrival at the top of the rankings as she overtook Hingis and became the 8th woman to take the No. 1 spot. She had enjoyed a remarkable summer, in which she won both singles and doubles at Stanford and San Diego back-to-back, following the next week with Los Angeles (where she did not play doubles). In winning these 3 HC events in Aug., she became the 1st player since Navratilova in 1988 to win 3 titles in a month and the 1st since Graf in 1994 to win 3 consec. events. Her US Open triumph then silenced any critics who doubted her ability to go all the way in GS, having fallen sf Australian Open and French Open and qf Wimbledon, and she finished the year still at the very top. She did not manage to crown her year with the singles title at Chase Champs, losing a lacklustre f to Hingis – unsurprisingly she was drained by winning her long sf v Graf and then a long doubles f the day before – but she did hold on to her top ranking and was voted WTA Player of the Year. In other tourns she won Tokyo Japan Open and Zurich, was r/u Indian Wells, Filderstadt and Philadelphia, and reached sf Oklahoma City, Amelia Island and New Haven, plus qf Sydney (in which she served at 6–1 5–2 v S. Williams before losing the match), LIPC and FC Cup. She excelled again in doubles, too, pairing with Zvereva to win 6 titles, including Chase Champs, and being r/u 5 times, including all 4 GS.

PRINCIPAL 1998 RESULTS – won 6, r/u 4, sf 5 (detailed Grand Slam results follow)
won Tokyo Pan Pacific (d. Sawamatsu 6–2 6–2, Spirlea 7–6 7–6, Coetzer 6–2 6–1, Hingis 6–3 6–3), **won** Stanford (d. Po 6–1 6–3, Tanasugarn 7–6 6–1, Graf 6–4 6–7 6–3, V. Williams 6–4 5–7 6–4), **won** San Diego (d. Raymond 6–1 6–4, Tauziat 6–4 6–3, Seles 6–4 2–6 7–5, Pierce 6–3 6–1), **won** Los Angeles (d. Halard-Decugis 6–0 6–4, Zvereva 6–2 6–3, Seles 6–4 6–2, Hingis 4–6 6–4 6–3), **won** US Open, **won** Zurich (d. Halard-Decugis 6–4 6–2, Coetzer 6–3 6–1, Spirlea 6–2 6–3, V,. Williams 7–5 6–3); **r/u** Indian Wells (d. Frazier 6–3 6–1, Dragomir 6–2 6–2, Cacic 6–1 7–5, Graf 6–4 4–6 4–2 ret, lost Hingis 6–3 6–4), **r/u** Filderstadt (d. Pierce 6–1 6–3, Tauziat 7–6 7–5, Sanchez-Vicario 7–6 6–4, lost Testud 7–5 6–3), **r/u** Philadelphia (d. Po 6–1 6–2, Frazier 5–7 6–3 6–3, Seles 6–3 6–3, lost Graf 4–6 6–3 6–4), **r/u** Chase Champs; **sf** Australian Open, **sf** Oklahoma City (d. Halard-Decugis 6–3 6–3, Ghirardi-Rubbi 6–1 6–4 lost V. Williams 6–7 6–2 6–3), **sf** Amelia Island (d. Dechaume-Balleret 6–0 6–2, Paulus 7–5 6–4, Kournikova 7–5 6–3, lost Pierce 4–6 6–3 6–3), **sf** French Open, **sf** New Haven (d. Ruano-Pascual w/o, Huber 6–3 6–3, lost Graf 6–3 7–6). **DOUBLES:** (with Zvereva) **r/u Australian Open** (lost Hingis/Lucic 6–4 2–6 6–3), **r/u French Open** (lost Hingis/Novotna 6–1 7–6), **r/u Wimbledon** (lost Hingis/Novotna 6–3 3–6 8–6), **r/u US Open** (lost Hingis/Novotna 6–3 6–3); **won** Indian Wells (d. Fusai/Tauziat 6–4 2–6 6–4), **won** Berlin (d. Fusai/Tauziat 6–3 6–0), **won** Stanford (d. Neiland/Tatarkova 6–4 6–4), **won** San Diego (d. Fusai/Tauziat 6–2 6–1), **won** Filderstadt (d. Kournikova/Sanchez-Vicario 6–4 6–2), **won** Chase Champs (d. Fusai/Tauziat 6–7 7–5 6–3); **r/u** Tokyo Pan Pacific (lost Hingis/Lucic 7–5 6–4).

CAREER GRAND SLAM RECORD

AUSTRALIAN OPEN – Played 6, sf 1, qf 2

1993: 3r d. Fusai 7–5 6–1, Kiene 7–5 6–4, lost Pierce [10] 6–3 6–0. **1994: qf** [seed 16] d. Hy 3–6 6–2 7–5, Probst 6–1 7–5, Makarova 6–1 6–2, M. J. Fernandez [6] 6–2 6–7 6–2, lost Graf [1] 6–3 6–2. **1995: qf** [seed 6] d. Graham 4–6 6–3 6–2, Probst 6–2 6–2, Testud 6–3 6–4, Schultz 6–2 3–6 6–2, lost Martinez [2] 6–3 4–6 6–3. **1996: last 16** [seed 10] d. Singer 6–1 6–2, Stubbs 7–6 6–3, N. Dahlman 6–4 7–5, lost Martinez [2] 6–3 6–1. **1997: last 16** [seed 7] d. Dechy 4–6 6–1 6–1, Perfetti 6–2 7–5, Tanasugarn 6–1 6–0, lost Po 7–6 6–4. **1998: sf** [seed 2] d. Cocheteux 6–2 6–3, Habsudova 2–6 6–0 5–7, Perfetti 6–2 6–2, Dragomir 6–0 6–0, V. Williams 1–6 7–5 6–3, lost Martinez [8] 4–6 6–3 6–3.

FRENCH OPEN – Played 6, sf 1, qf 1

1993: 1r lost Wiesner 6–3 6–1. **1994: 3r** [seed 9] d. Rubin 6–7 6–4 6–3, Nowak 6–4 6–2, lost Halard 6–4 6–2. **1995: last 16** [seed 7] d. Tang 7–6 6–0, Testud 6–3 7–5, Hingis 4–6 6–2 6–2, lost Date [9] 6–4 6–3. **1996: qf** [seed 10] d. Perfetti 6–4 6–1, Park 6–1 6–2, Basuki 6–3 6–2, Date [7] 3–6 6–4 8–6, lost Martinez [3] 6–1 6–3). **1997 last 16** [seed 5] d. Kruger 6–2 6–3, Makarova 6–1 6–1, Schnyder 4–6 6–3 9–7, lost Majoli [9] 5–7 6–4 6–2. **1998: sf** [seed 2] d. Po 6–2 6–2, Horn 6–2 6–0, Likhovtseva 7–5 7–5, Testud 6–3 4–6 6–2, Majoli [10] 6–1 5–7 6–3, lost Sanchez-Vicario [4] 6–3 7–6.

WIMBLEDON – Played 6, qf 2

1993: 3r d. Martinek 6–0 4–6 7–5, Rittner 6–0 7–6, lost Tauziat [16] 6–3 7–6. **1994: qf** [seed 9] d. Halard 6–1 6–4, Price 6–4 6–2, Rittner 6–4 3–6 6–1, Sabatini [10] 6–1 6–3, lost Martinez [3] 6–2 6–7 6–3. **1995: last 16** [seed 7] d. G. Fernandez 6–2 4–6 7–5, Labat 6–1 6–1, Singer 6–7 6–3 6–2, lost M. J. Fernandez [seed] 7–6 6–1. **1996: 2r** [seed 8] d. Schnell 6–4 6–1, lost Neiland 6–3 6–2. **1997: 2r** [seed 5] d. Whitlinger-Jones 5–7 6–2 6–2, lost Chladkova 7–5 6–2. **1998: qf** [seed 2] d. Labat 6–2 6–2, Neiland 6–1 7–5, Vento 6–3 1–6 6–2, Serna 6–1 6–0, lost Tauziat [16] 6–3 6–3.

US OPEN – Played 8, won 1, sf 1

1991: 1r lost Graham 6–3 6–2. **1992: 2r** d. Basuki 6–4 6–4, lost Sanchez-Vicario [5] 6–1 6–3). **1993: last 16** [unseeded] d. Probst 6–4 6–2, Hy 6–4 6–2, Coetzer [15] 6–1 6–2, lost Sabatini [5] 6–7 6–4 6–4. **1994: 3r** [seed 6] d. Grossi 6–1 6–1, Shriver 6–1 6–2, lost Endo 6–3 7–6. **1995: 2r** [seed 10] d. Kamstra 6–2 6–2, lost Garrison-Jackson 6–1 6–3. **1996: last 16** [seed 8] d. Serra-Zanetti 6–2 6–1, Nagyova 6–0 6–4, Sidot 6–0 6–3, lost Wild 6–2 3–6 6–0. **1997 sf** [seed 6] d. McNeil 6–2 7–6, Probst 6–2 6–3, Schnyder 1–6 6–1 6–4, Serna 6–0 6–3, Novotna [3] 6–2 4–6 7–6, lost Hingis [1] 6–2 6–4. **1998: won** [seed 2] d. Cristea 6–0 6–2, McNeil 6–1 6–1, Ruano-Pascual 6–2 6–1, Tauziat [10] 6–1 6–4, Coetzer [13] 6–0 6–4, V. Williams 6–4 6–4, Hingis [1] 6–3 7–5.

OLYMPIC RECORD

1996: (Atlanta) won gold medal [seed 9] d. Kremer 6–2 6–1, Sawamatsu 6–2 6–2, Huber [5] 6–1 3–6 6–3, Majoli [4] 7–5 6–3, M. J. Fernandez [7] 6–2 7–6, Sanchez-Vicario [2] 7–6 6–2.

CAREER FED CUP RECORD

1993 (in GER, Clay): *1r USA d. SUI 3–0.* R1 d. C. Fauche 6–4 6–3. *2r USA d. CHN 2–1.* R1 d. Y. Bi 6–1 6–3; R3 (+ L. McNeil) d. L. Chen/F. Li 6–3 6–0. *Qf ARG d. USA 2–1.* R1 lost I. Gorrochategui 7–6 5–7 5–7. **1994 (in GER, Clay):** *1r USA d. CZE 3–0.* R2 d. L. Richterova 4–6 6–1 6–4. *2r USA d. CAN 3–0.* R2 d. P. Hy 6–2 6–4. *Qf USA d. AUT 3–0.* R2 d. J. Wiesner 2–6 6–2 6–2. *Sf USA d. FRA 3–0.* R2 d. M. Pierce 5–7 6–2 6–2. *Final ESP d. USA 3–0.* R2 lost A. Sanchez-Vicario 6–2 6–1. **1995: July** – *USA d. FRA 3–2 in USA (Carpet).* R2 d. J. Halard-Decugis 7–6 7–5; R3 d. M. Pierce 6–3 4–6 6–0; R5 (+ G. Fernandez) d. Halard-Decugis/N. Tauziat 6–1 7–6. **November** – *World Group Final ESP d. USA 3–2 in ESP (Clay).* (+ G. Fernandez) R5 D. Ruano-Pascual/ M. Sanchez Lorenzo 6–3 7–6. **1996: July** – *World Group I sf USA d. JPN 5–0 in JPN (Carpet).* R1 d. K. Date 6–2 6–1; R4 d. A. Sugiyama 7–6 7–5; R5 (+ L. Wild) d. K. Nagatsuka/A. Sugiyama 6–2 6–1. **September** – *World Group I final USA d. ESP 5–0 in USA (Carpet).* R2 d. A. Sanchez-Vicario 7–5 6–1; R4 d. G. Leon-Garcia 7–5 6–2. **1997: July** – *World Group play-off USA d. JPN 5–0 in USA (Hard).* R2 d. N. Sawamatsu 6–1 6–3; R3 d. A. Sugiyama 6–4 7–6; R5 (with L. Raymond) d. N. Kijimuta/N. Miyagi 6–4 6–4. **1998: April** – *World Group qf USA d. NED 5–0 in USA (Clay).* R1 d. A. Hopmans 6–4 6–1; R3 d. M. Oremans 6–1 6–2.

GRAND SLAM CUP RECORD – Played 1

1998: 1r lost Tauziat 4–6 6–1 7–5.

SEASON ENDING CHAMPIONSHIPS – Played 5, r/u 2

(1983–94 Virginia Slims, 1995 Corel, 1996–98 Chase)

1994: r/u d. Huber 6–2 6–3, Novotna 6–2 6–2, Pierce 6–3 6–2, lost Sabatini 6–3 6–2 6–4. **1995: 1r** lost Sabatini 6–4 6–3. **1996: 2r** d. Paulus 6–3 6–2, lost Graf 6–4 7–6. **1997: 1r** lost M. J. Fernandez 2–6 6–4 7–6. **1998: r/u** d. Testud 4–6 7–6 6–0, Tauziat 6–0 6–3, Graf 6–1 2–6 6–3, lost Hingis 7–5 6–4 4–6 6–2.

2 MARTINA HINGIS (SUI)

Born: Kosice, Czechoslovakia, 30 September 1980.
Lives: Trubbach (moved to Switzerland at age 7).
Father: Karol. **Mother:** Melanie Molitor, a former Czech champion, who named her daughter after Martina Navratilova.
Agent: IMG. **Coach:** Her mother, Melanie Molitor.
Turned pro: 1994.
Height: 5ft 7in (1.70m). **Weight:** 130lb (59kg).

Rankings: 1994: 87; **1995:** 16; **1996:** 4; **1997:** 1; **1998:** 2 singles, 2 doubles. **Highest:** 1 (31 March 1997).

1998 Prize Money: $3,175,631.
Career Earnings: $8,124,248. **Career Titles:** 19.

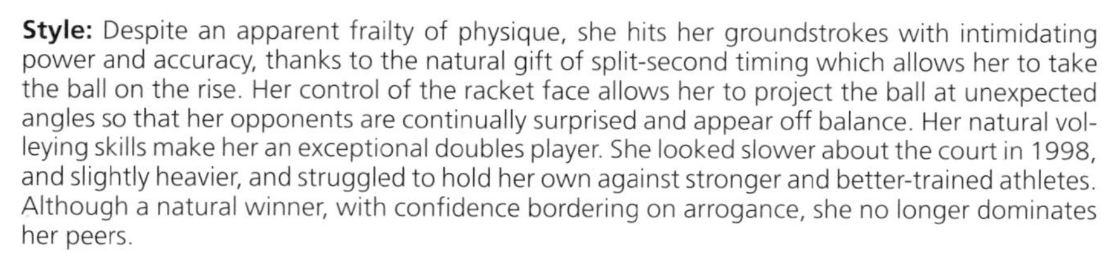

Style: Despite an apparent frailty of physique, she hits her groundstrokes with intimidating power and accuracy, thanks to the natural gift of split-second timing which allows her to take the ball on the rise. Her control of the racket face allows her to project the ball at unexpected angles so that her opponents are continually surprised and appear off balance. Her natural volleying skills make her an exceptional doubles player. She looked slower about the court in 1998, and slightly heavier, and struggled to hold her own against stronger and better-trained athletes. Although a natural winner, with confidence bordering on arrogance, she no longer dominates her peers.

CAREER HIGHLIGHTS (year: (titles))
1993: Won French Open Jun over Courtois, becoming, at age 12, the youngest to win a Jun GS title. Won the title at Langentha in her 1st Futures event. **1994:** Ranked No. 1 in ITF Jun singles after she won French Open over Jeyaseelan and Wimbledon over Jeon (becoming the youngest Jun champ there at 13 years 276 days), was r/u US Open to Tu and won European Champs; in Jun doubles, she won French Open with Nagyova. Having played 3 satellite events, she made her debut on the senior tour earlier than expected in Oct., in order to beat the new eligibility rules coming into effect in Jan. 1995. She was allowed to play only 3 tourns before returning to her private school. Her 1st appearance was at Zurich, where she beat Fendick (becoming, at 14 years 3 months 17 days, the youngest player to win a singles match in Open era) before losing to Pierce. She followed with qf at both Filderstadt and Essen where she beat Hack. **1995:** In a year in which she was voted Most Impressive Newcomer, she reached her 1st tour f at Hamburg, upsetting Novotna and Huber, surprised M. Maleeva at US Open and broke into top 20 in June, only 8 months after joining the tour. She also reached qf Paris Open (d. Halard) and played 2 doubles f, winning Hamburg with G. Fernandez. When she beat Watanabe at Australian Open, she became the youngest to win a singles match there in the Open era. **1996: (2)** *Filderstadt, Oakland.* At 15 years 3 months 22 days and unseeded, she became the youngest to reach qf Australian Open, upsetting Schultz-McCarthy on the way, and followed in May with one of the major upsets of the year when she removed Graf on her way to f Italian Open. At Wimbledon, aged 15 years 282 days, she became the youngest to win a title there when she and Sukova took the doubles – being 3 days younger than Lottie Dod when she won the singles in 1887 – and was the 1st Swiss woman to win a title at Wimbledon. She broke into the top 10 on 7 Oct., took her 1st title on the main tour at Filderstadt a week later (upsetting Sanchez-Vicario, Davenport and Huber back-to-back), and played her next f the week after that, losing in Zurich to Novotna. Her 2nd title came in tremendous style at Oakland, where she upset Seles 6–2 6–0 in f, inflicting the most lop-sided defeat of the former No. 1's career. After qualifying for her 1st Chase Champs in both singles and doubles (with Sukova), she extended Graf to 5s in f, but was virtually immobilised towards the end by cramp and was unable to take advantage of Graf's back and knee injuries. She also reached sf Tokyo Toray (d. Sabatini), following with the same stage at US Open (d. Sanchez-Vicario and Novotna) and Chicago (d. Davenport), plus qf Hamburg and the title at Prostejov Futures. At 16 years 1 month and 11 days, she became the youngest player, male or female, to pass $1m in earnings in a season. Voted Most Improved Player of the Year. **1997: (12)** *AUSTRALIAN OPEN, WIMBLEDON, US*

OPEN, Sydney, Tokyo Pan Pacific, Paris Open, LIPC, FC Cup, Stanford, San Diego, Filderstadt, Philadelphia. Her remarkable year began in tremendous style at Australian Open, where she became the youngest GS winner this century, losing no set on her way to the title, and was the 1st to win both singles and doubles there since Navratilova in 1985. On 31 March, she overtook the injured Graf at the top of the rankings, becoming the 7th woman to be ranked No. 1, and the youngest of all, aged 16 years 6 months and 1 day. At LIPC she d. Seles in f in 44 mins, becoming the 1st woman to have earned $1m by end March. She beat Seles again in f FC Cup, coming from 2–5 down in 3s tb having earlier led 5–2 fs. In April she fell from a horse and suffered a slight tear of the posterior cruciate ligament in her left knee, for which she underwent arthroscopic surgery on 21 April. She was back in action at French Open, where Majoli inflicted her 1st defeat of the year in f. She interrupted their match with a 5-minute bathroom break and later incurred a code violation for slamming down her racket. This ended her winning streak of 37 matches, but by end of French Open she had already qualified for Chase Champs. At Wimbledon she became the youngest singles champion there this century and youngest GS singles winner in the Open era. Until Chase Champs, she had failed to reach sf only at Zurich in Oct., when Raymond beat her in qf, and through the year she had been beaten only by Majoli, Davenport, Coetzer and Raymond. However, towards the end of the year, she was showing signs of tiring both physically and mentally, missing Chicago with an injury to her right heel and being extended to 3s in all 4 matches at Philadelphia. At Chase Champs, Schultz-McCarthy stretched her before retiring and Pierce was eventually too much for her, winning their qf 7–5 3s. So Hingis finished an extraordinary year firmly at the top of the rankings, but looking less invincible than she had in the summer. In addition to her singles triumphs, she was also a considerable force in doubles. She had been approached by Navratilova, who suggested that they might play GS doubles together, but she turned down the invitation from her former idol, wanting to pair with someone with whom she could play more often, although in fact she played with 6 different partners in reaching 9 doubles f. She won both singles and doubles at Australian Open (with Zvereva), Paris Open (Novotna), FC Cup (M. J. Fernandez), Stanford (Davenport), plus San Diego and Filderstadt (both with Sanchez-Vicario), and also took doubles titles at Leipzig (with Novotna) and Zurich (with Sanchez-Vicario). It was with Sanchez-Vicario that she qualified for Chase Champs, but they fared little better than she had in the singles, losing 1r to finish the year on a surprisingly downbeat note. **1998: (5)** *AUSTRALIAN OPEN, Indian Wells, Hamburg, Rome, Chase Champs.* She began the year at Sydney sporting a new look, with her hair darkened and browning contact lenses, seeming flat and lacking joie de vivre as she lost 2r to V. Williams. At Australian Open, though, she was more her old self as she became the youngest to retain a GS title, taking the doubles as well with Lucic. And that was much the pattern of her year, with ups and downs, but rarely reaching the heights of the previous year. The ups saw her qualify for the season-ending champs after only 23 weeks – the fastest ever – and her part in taking SUI to 1st ever Fed Cup f. The downs included the loss of her No. 1 ranking on 12 Oct. to Davenport and failure to add any more to her collection of GS singles titles, losing French Open sf to Seles, Wimbledon same stage to Novotna and US Open f to Davenport. However, her season ended on another high note when she added a 1st Chase Champs title to her collection, defeating Davenport in a lacklustre f to finish her year in triumph, albeit at No. 2 in the rankings. Her other titles all came in the first half of the year, and in the second half she seemed more vulnerable, as well as being affected by injury – she ret with leg cramps at 5–5 fs v Schnyder at GS Cup and missed Zurich with an ankle strain. However, she remained firmly at No. 2 with her 5 titles; r/u Tokyo Pan Pacific and Los Angeles; sf LIPC, San Diego, Montreal and GS Cup; qf Berlin, Filderstadt and Philadelphia. She had another terrific year in doubles, winning 9 of 10 f with 4 different partners and collecting a calendar year GS as she took Australian Open with Lucic and added French Open, Wimbledon and US Open with Novotna, with whom she was voted Doubles Team of the Year. They qualified together for Chase Champs, but disappointingly lost 1r to Basuki/Vis.

PRINCIPAL 1998 RESULTS – won 5, r/u 3, sf 6 (detailed Grand Slam results follow)
won Australian Open, **won** Indian Wells (d. Pitkowski 6–2 6–1, Babel 6–2 6–0, Martinez 6–1 7–5, V. Williams 6–0 7–6, Davenport 6–3 6–4), **won** Hamburg (d. Probst 7–5 6–1, Capriati 6–1 6–3, Schett 6–2 6–2, Novotna 6–3 7–5), **won** Rome (d. Li 6–3 6–0, Spirlea 6–1 6–2, Kournikova 6–2 6–4, Lucic 6–2 6–1, V. Williams 6–3 2–6 6–3), **won** Chase Champs; **r/u** Tokyo Pan Pacific (d. Likhovtseva 6–1 6–0, Grande 6–2 7–5, Majoli 6–0 6–2, lost Davenport 6–3 6–3), **r/u** Los Angeles (d. Majoli 6–3 6–3, S. Williams 6–4 6–1, Sanchez-Vicario 6–4 6–3, lost Davenport 4–6 6–4 6–3), **r/u** US Open; **sf** LIPC (d. Rubin 6–1 6–0, Kruger 6–0 6–0, Testud 6–3 5–7 6–2, S. Williams 6–3 1–6 7–6, lost V. Williams 6–2 5–7 6–2), **sf** French Open, **sf** Wimbledon, **sf** San Diego (d.

Zvereva 6–3 6–2, Kruger 6–1 6–3, lost Pierce 3–6 7–6 6–2), **sf** Montreal (d. Plischke 6–4 6–1, Sugiyama 6–3 6–0, Testud 7–6 3–6 6–4, lost Seles 4–6 6–3 6–2), **sf** GS Cup. **DOUBLES:** (with Novotna unless stated) (with Lucic) **won Australian Open** (d. Davenport/Zvereva 6–4 2–6 6–3), **won French Open** (d. Davenport/ Novotna 6–1 7–6), **won Wimbledon** (d. Davenport/Zvereva 6–3 3–6 8–6), **won US Open** (d. Davenport/ Zvereva 6–3 6–3); (with Sukova) **won** Sydney (d. Adams/McGrath 6–1 6–2), (with Lucic) **won** Tokyo Pan Pacific (d. Davenport/Zvereva 7–5 6–4), **won** LIPC (d. Sanchez-Vicario/Zvereva 6–2 3–6 6–3), (with Zvereva) **won** Los Angeles (d. Tanasugarn/Tatarkova 6–4 6–2), **won** Montreal (d. Basuki/Vis 6–3 6–4); **r/u** Hamburg (lost Schett/Schnyder 7–6 3–6 6–3).

CAREER GRAND SLAM RECORD

AUSTRALIAN OPEN – Played 4, won 2, qf 1

1995: 2r d. Watanabe 6–0 7–6, lost Nagatsuka 6–3 6–4. **1996: qf** [unseeded] d. Nejedly 6–1 6–1, Paulus 6–1 6–4, Endo 6–1 6–4, Schultz-McCarthy [11] 6–1 6–4, lost Coetzer [16] 7–5 4–6 6–1. **1997: won** [seed 4] d. Rittner 6–1 7–5, Raymond 6–4 6–2, Schett 6–2 6–1, Dragomir 7–6 6–1, Spirlea [8] 7–5 6–2, M. J. Fernandez [14] 6–1 6–3, Pierce 6–2 6–2. **1998: won** [seed 1] d. Probst 6–1 6–2, Rittner 7–5 6–1, Kournikova 6–4 4–6 6–4, Basuki 6–0 6–0, Pierce [5] 6–2 6–3, Huber [10] 6–1 2–6 6–1, Martinez [8] 6–2 6–3.

FRENCH OPEN – Played 4, r/u 1, sf 1

1995: 3r d. Wiesner 2–6 6–3 7–5, De Swardt 6–1 6–7 6–2, lost Davenport [7] 4–6 6–2 6–2. **1996: 3r** [seed 15] d. Schett 6–3 6–0, Begerow 7–5 7–5, lost Habsudova 4–6 7–5 6–4. **1997: r/u** [seed 1] (d. Nagyova 6–0 6–2, Pizzichini 3–6 6–4 6–1, Kournikova 6–1 6–3, Paulus [16] 6–3 0–6 6–0, Sanchez-Vicario [6] 6–2 6–2, Seles [3] 6–7 7–5 6–4, lost Majoli [6] 6–4 6–2. **1998: sf** [seed 1] d. Sanchez Lorenzo 6–2 6–1, Babel 6–1 6–2, Habsudova 6–3 6–2, Smashnova 6–1 6–2, V. Williams 6–3 6–4, lost Seles [6] 6–3 6–2.

WIMBLEDON – Played 4, won 1, sf 1

1995: 1r lost Graf [1] 6–3 6–1. **1996: last 16** [seed 16] d. Nejedly 6–2 6–2, Viollet 6–1 6–1, Wild 6–3 2–6 6–1, lost Graf [1] 6–1 6–4. **1997: won** [seed 1] d. Kremer 6–4 6–4, Barabanschikova 6–2 6–2, Arendt 6–1 6–3, Appelmans 6–1 6–3, Chladkova 6–3 6–2, Kournikova 6–3 6–2, Novotna [3] 2–6 6–3 6–3. **1998: sf** [seed 1] d. Raymond 7–5 6–3, Makarova 7–6 6–4, Likhovtseva 6–2 6–1, Tanasugarn 6–3 6–2, Sanchez-Vicario [5] 6–3 3–6 6–3, lost Novotna [3] 6–4 6–4.

US OPEN – Played 4, won 1, r/u 1, sf 1

1995: last 16 [unseeded] d. Feber 6–2 6–3, M. Maleeva [8] 4–6 6–4 6–2, Hy-Boulais 4–6 6–1 6–4, lost Sabatini [9] 6–2 6–4. **1996: sf** [seed 16] d. Montolio 6–1 6–0, Oremans 6–4 6–4, Kijimuta 6–2 6–2, Sanchez-Vicario [3] 6–1 3–6 6–4, Novotna [7] 7–6 6–4, lost Graf [1] 7–5 6–3. **1997: won** [seed 1] d. Whitlinger-Jones 6–0 6–1, Chladkova 6–1 6–2, Likhovtseva 7–5 6–2, Labat 6–0 6–2, Sanchez-Vicario [10] 6–3 6–2, Davenport [6] 6–2 6–4, V. Williams 6–0 6–4. **1998: r/u** [seed 1] d. Olsza 6–2 6–0, Majoli 7–6 6–0, Mauresmo 4–6 6–2 6–2, Dechy 6–4 6–4, Po 6–4 6–4, Novotna [3], lost Davenport [2] 6–3 7–5.

OLYMPIC RECORD

1996: (Atlanta) 2r [seed 15] d. Schad 6–0 6–1, lost Sugiyama 6–4 6–4.

CAREER FED CUP RECORD

1995: April *(Euro/Africa Group 1 in ESP, Clay): Round-robin LAT d. SUI 2–1.* R2 d. L. Neiland 6–1 6–2; R3 (with G. Dondit) lost A. Blumberga/Neiland 7–5 5–7 7–5. *Round-robin SUI d. FIN 3–0.* R2 d. N. Dahlman 6–1 7–6; R3 (with J. Manta) d. H. Aalto/Dahlman 6–1 6–1. *Round-robin BLR d. SUI 2–1.* R2 lost N. Zvereva 6–3 3–6 6–3; R3 (with Manta) d. M. Stets/V. Zhukovets 6–1 6–1. **1996: April** *(Euro/Africa Group 1 in ESP, Clay): Round-robin SUI d. YUG 3–0.* R2 d. B. Ivanovic 6–2 6–1; R3 (with A. Burgis) d. S. Nacuk/D. Zaric 6–1 6–3. *Round-robin SUI d. GEO 3–0.* R2 d. N. Louarsabishvili 6–1 6–1. *Round-robin SUI d. CRO 2–1.* R2 d. I. Majoli 5–7 6–1 6–1; R3 (with Burgis) d. M. Lucic/Majoli 6–1 7–5. *Qf SUI d. HUN 2–1.* R2 d. A. Temesvari 6–0 6–3. *Final SUI d. RUS 2–1.* R2 d. E. Likhovtseva 6–3 6–0. **July** – *Group 1 play-off SUI d. INA 3–2 in INA (Hard).* R2 d. L. Andriyani 6–0 6–0; R3 lost Y. Basuki 5–7 6–3 6–1; R5 (with P. Schnyder) d. Basuki/Tedjakusuma 6–3 6–2. **1997: March** – *Group I qf SUI d. SVK 3–2 in SVK (Carpet).* R1 d. K. Studenikova 6–1 6–3; R3 d. K. Habsudova 6–2 6–0. R5 (with P. Schnyder) d. Habsudova/R. Zrubakova 6–0 6–1. **July** – *World Group play-off SUI d. ARG 5–0 in SUI (Carpet).* R1 d. M. Gaidano 6–1 6–2; R3 d. F. Labat 6–2 6–1. R5 (with E. Gagliardi) d. L. Montalvo/M. Paz 6–3 6–4. **1998: April** – *World Group qf SUI d. CZE 4–1 in CZE (Carpet).* R2 d. A. Gersi 6–2 6–1; R3 d. J. Novotna 4–6 6–3 6–2; R5 d. D. Chladkova/L. Richterova 6–0 6–1. **July** – *World Group sf SUI d. FRA 5–0 in SUI (Clay).* R1 d. Halard-Decugis 7–5 6–1; R3 d. A. Mauresmo 6–7 6–4 6–2. **September** – *World Group Final ESP d. SUI 3–2 in SUI (Hard).* R2. d. C. Martinez 6–4 6–4; R3 d. A. Sanchez-Vicario 7–6 6–3; R5 (with P. Schnyder) lost Martinez/Sanchez-Vicario 6–0 6–2)

GRAND SLAM CUP RECORD – Played 1, sf 1

1998: sf d. Martinez 6–2 7–5, lost Schnyder 5–7 7–5 5–5 ret.

SEASON ENDING CHAMPIONSHIPS – Played 3, won 1, r/u 1, qf 1

(1996–98 Chase)

1996: r/u d. Spirlea 6–1 6–2, Date 6–1 6–2, Majoli 6–2 4–6 6–1, lost Graf 6–3 4–6 6–0 4–6 6–0. **1997: qf** d. Schultz-McCarthy 7–6 5–2 ret, lost Pierce 6–3 2–6 7–5. **1998: won** d. Schnyder 4–6 6–0 6–3, Pierce 7–6 6–4, Spirlea 6–2 7–6, Davenport 7–5 6–4 4–6 6–2.

3 JANA NOVOTNA (CZE)

Born: Brno, 2 October 1968. **Lives:** Antwerp, Belgium. **Father:** Frank. **Mother:** Libuse. **Brother:** Paul (older). **Agent:** Advantage International. **Coach:** Hana Mandlikova since 1990; formerly Mike Estep. **Turned pro:** 1987. **Height:** 5ft 9in (1.75m). **Weight:** 139lb (63kg).

Rankings: 1985: 305; **1986:** 172; **1987:** 49; **1988:** 45; **1989:** 11; **1990:** 13; **1991:** 7; **1992:** 10; **1993:** 6; **1994:** 4; **1995:** 11; **1996:** 3; **1997:** 2; **1998:** 3 singles, 3 doubles. **Highest:** 2 (July 1997).

1998 Prize Money: $2,039,912.
Career Earnings: $10,297,692. **Career Titles:** 23.

Style: A right-handed natural volleyer with good touch who is equally at home on the singles or doubles court. The high toss on her serve sometimes gives timing problems but she can serve-and-volley with the best. She has a large swing on the sometimes erratic forehand and can hit her backhand with slice or topspin.

CAREER HIGHLIGHTS (year: (titles))
1986: Won US Open Jun doubles with Zrubakova. **1987:** Reached last 16 Wimbledon and US Open, plus qf VS Kansas. In doubles she developed a formidable partnership with Suire, qualifying for VS Champs and taking a set off Navratilova/Shriver. **1988: (1)** *Adelaide*. Won her 1st title on the main tour at Adelaide, r/u Brisbane and upset Sabatini 1r Filderstadt. In doubles won Olympic silver medal with Sukova and took 5 doubles titles with 3 different partners. In mixed, with Pugh, won Australian and US Opens. **1989: (1)** *Strasbourg*. Was r/u Hamburg and Zurich and reached 4 more sf, as well as qf French Open, to qualify for VS Champs in both singles (lost Graf 1r) and doubles for 1st time. In doubles won 6 women's titles, including Wimbledon and LIPC with Sukova, plus Australian Open and Wimbledon mixed with Pugh. Won WTA Most Improved Player award. **1990: (1)** *Albuquerque*. She continued her successful doubles partnership with Sukova, with whom she won 8 of her 9 titles across the year. The duo were unbeaten until US Open, where, having won Australian Open, French Open and Wimbledon, they failed in their bid for a GS when they lost f to Navratilova/G. Fernandez. They were also disappointed at VS Champs, where they fell 1r to Medvedeva/Meskhi. In singles she upset Sabatini and K. Maleeva **en route** to her 1st GS sf at French Open and followed with qf Wimbledon and US Open. Extended Navratilova to 3s in sf Eastbourne. Qualified for VS Champs in both singles and doubles. **1991: (2)** *Sydney, Oklahoma*. Showing the benefits of her partnership with new coach, Mandlikova, she made a tremendous start to the year, upsetting Garrison, Graf and Sanchez-Vicario back-to-back in ss to reach her 1st GS singles f at Australian Open, where she took the 1st set off Seles. R/u Leipzig, reached sf Berlin and VS Champs, upsetting Graf on the way, and appeared in qf French Open. Was voted WTA Doubles Team of the Year with G. Fernandez, with whom she won French Open and was r/u Australian Open, Wimbledon and VS Champs. She completed a full hand of GS doubles f, being r/u US Open with Savchenko, and appeared in 14 f altogether, winning 3 with Fernandez, 3 with Savchenko and 1 with Navratilova. **1992:** Upset Graf en route to f VS Chicago and extended her to 3s in f both Leipzig and Brighton and sf Zurich, losing twice only on tb. She reached 4 more qf and qualified again for VS Champs, where she took a set off Seles in qf singles and was r/u doubles with Savchenko-Neiland. This new pairing was as successful as her previous partnerships and brought 7 titles, plus r/u Wimbledon and US Open. **1993: (2)** *Osaka, Brighton*. The high point of her year came at Wimbledon, where she beat Navratilova for the first time and, playing an all-out aggressive game, was on the brink of upsetting Graf in f before losing faith in herself and letting the match slip away. At Osaka she won her 1st singles title for 2 years and followed in autumn with Brighton, as well as reaching f Leipzig and sf 5 other tourns. She reached last 16 US Open, but, hampered by an ankle injury, fell to Date. Qualified for VS Champs in both singles and doubles, reaching qf singles and r/u doubles with Neiland. It was the 6th time they'd lost to G. Fernandez/Zvereva during the year, including f French Open and Wimbledon. In all she reached 12 doubles f, winning 3 with Neiland and 1 each with Strnadova and Sanchez-

Vicario. **1994: (3)** *Leipzig, Brighton, Essen*. She played her best tennis in autumn, when she won 3 consec. tourns, with Brighton the 1st time she had retained a title or won 2 in succession and her victory at Essen the following week extending the run to 3. In GS her best performance was sf US Open, for she fell qf Australian Open to Sabatini and lost 1r French Open to Smashnova, whereupon she withdrew from doubles with Sanchez-Vicario, complaining of muscle strain in right shoulder. She also withdrew from Eastbourne, suffering with a painful bicep, but played Wimbledon, where she progressed to qf. There she again demonstrated her inability to cope with the big situation and tendency to 'choke' with a match apparently within her grasp when she won 1s v Navratilova, but then submitted tamely for the addition of only 1 more game. She also reached sf Hamburg and Berlin, plus 3 more qf, including VS Champs. In doubles with Sanchez-Vicario she won US Open and was r/u Wimbledon and VS Champs; together they played 9 f, winning 5, and she also reached 2 more f with different partners. In mixed doubles, she was r/u US Open with Woodbridge. **1995: (1)** *Linz*. In 3r French Open v Rubin she choked again, letting a 5–0 40–0 fs lead slip away, although she claimed afterwards simply to have been upset by the rain and cramp in both legs, and at Wimbledon she allowed Graf to recover from a set down in sf. She won the only f she reached – at Linz – and also appeared in sf Paris Open, LIPC and Toronto, plus 2 qf. In doubles she won Australian Open and Wimbledon plus 2 other titles with Sanchez-Vicario and took a 5th with M. J. Fernandez. Qualified for WTA Champs in both singles and doubles, falling 1r singles to Date but winning doubles with Sanchez-Vicario. **1996: (4)** *Madrid, Zurich, Chicago, Philadelphia*. Victory in both singles and doubles (with Sanchez-Vicario) at Madrid in May took her back into the top 10 and by end of year she had climbed to a career-high No. 3. She won 3 more singles titles in consec. tourns in autumn at Zurich, Chicago and Philadelphia (when Graf retired), was r/u Essen, and reached sf French Open, Olympics, FC Cup, Eastbourne and San Diego. In a major upset at French Open, she removed a below-par Seles in ss in qf: serving for the match at 5–3, she overcame her tendency to choke, although she slipped to 15–40 before taking the game and match. She repeated the feat on her way to a bronze medal at the Olympics, becoming the first player to beat Seles twice since her comeback the previous year. Coming into Chase Champs after her 3 consec. titles, she upset Sanchez-Vicario 1st time in 5 years but lost sf to Graf, again failing to capitalise on a strong lead. In doubles, she played 9 f, winning 4 and being r/u US Open and Chase Champs with Sanchez-Vicario, winning one each with Boogert and Arendt, and taking Olympic silver with Sukova. Voted Doubles Team of Year with Sanchez-Vicario. **1997: (4)** *Madrid, Leipzig, Moscow, Chase Champs*. Beat Sanchez-Vicario and Seles back-to-back to take the title at Madrid, winning 8 successive games in f to recover from 3–5 down v Seles. She also won Leipzig (both singles and doubles) and Moscow and shared Eastbourne with Sanchez-Vicario after f was abandoned. She moved ahead of Graf to No. 2 in the rankings after Wimbledon, where she reached her 2nd f. She was superb there in 1s v Hingis before an abdominal muscle injury began to trouble her, although she refused to make that an excuse for her eventual defeat. She had already withdrawn from the doubles and pulled out of Prague afterwards. In singles she also reached sf Linz, Paris Open, LIPC, Berlin and Zurich, plus qf US Open, Atlanta, Chicago and Philadelphia. On 17 Nov. she was briefly overtaken in the rankings by Davenport, and slipped to No. 3. However, she was back at No. 2 the following week after a magnificent performance to win Chase Champs over Pierce, where she held her nerve to take her first major title. She completed her triumph by winning the doubles with Davenport. She played a total of 9 doubles f across the year, winning 4, including US Open, with Davenport, and 2 with Hingis. **1998: (4)** *WIMBLEDON, Linz, Eastbourne, Prague*. The highlight of her career came when she won Wimbledon – her 1st GS title and the one she wanted most of all – beating Tauziat in her 3rd f. She crowned that triumph by joining with Hingis (whom she had upset in singles) to become the 1st woman since Graf in 1988 to take both singles and doubles there, winning 8–6 fs over Davenport/Zvereva. She had preceded that with the titles at Linz in March and Eastbourne (her 1st on grass) the week before. When she followed Wimbledon with Prague, she had won 3 titles in a row and overtaken Davenport at No. 2. Perhaps it was unsurprising that she then withdrew from Fed Cup, suffering from exhaustion. She was restricted in autumn by back problems, which kept her out of action for a while, and fell 1r GS Cup to Schnyder 7–5 fs. In other tourns she was r/u Hannover, Hamburg and New Haven, and reached sf Paris Open, Berlin, Montreal and US Open (where she extended Hingis to 3s), plus qf LIPC and French Open. In doubles she won 6 of the 8 f she played, taking French Open, Wimbledon, US Open, LIPC and Montreal with Hingis (with whom she did not contest Australian Open) and Eastbourne with De Swardt. Voted WTA Doubles Team of the Year with Hingis, with whom she qualified for Chase Champs. Returning from a back injury, she was affected in the singles by cramp, losing 1r to Graf, fresh from a long break and 2 successive titles, and in doubles she and Hingis fell 1r to Basuki/Vis.

PRINCIPAL 1998 RESULTS – won 4, r/u 3, sf 4 (detailed Grand Slam results follow)
won Wimbledon, **won** Linz (d. Mauresmo 6–4 6–2, Kournikova 6–1 6–3, Farina 6–4 6–1, Van Roost 6–1 7–6), **won** Eastbourne (d. Dechy 6–2 6–2, Spirlea 6–4 7–5, Zvereva 6–2 6–1, Sanchez-Vicario 6–1 7–5), **won** Prague (d. Husarova 6–2 7–6, Bobkova 6–2 7–6, Pitkowski 6–2 6–3, Nagyova 2–6 6–3 7–5, Testud 6–3 6–0); **r/u** Hannover (d. Van Roost 4–6 6–4 6–3, Raymond 6–1 7–5, Kournikova 6–3 6–3, lost Schnyder 6–0 2–6 7–5), **r/u** Hamburg (d. Serna 6–4 6–2, Abe 6–1 6–3, Schnyder 2–6 7–5 6–3, lost Hingis 6–3 7–5), **r/u** New Haven (d. Rubin 6–1 7–5, Mauresmo 6–1 7–6, Halard-Decugis 6–4 6–4, lost Graf 6–4 6–1); **sf** Paris Open (d. Grande 6–2 6–4, Paulus 6–2 1–6 6–4, lost Pierce 6–4 2–6 6–3), **sf** Berlin (d. Schett 1–6 7–6 7–6, Sanchez Lorenzo 6–4 6–4, Spirlea 6–3 5–7 6–3, lost Mauresmo 7–5 5–7 6–4), **sf** Montreal (d. Likhovtseva 7–5 6–2, Farina 6–1 6–4, Serna 2–6 6–1 6–1, lost Sanchez-Vicario 4–6 7–6 6–2), **sf** US Open. **DOUBLES:** (with Hingis unless stated) **won French Open** (d. Davenport/Zvereva 6–1 7–6), **won Wimbledon** (d. Davenport/Zvereva 6–3 3–6 8–6), **won US Open** (d. Davenport/Zvereva 6–3 6–3); **won** LIPC (d. Sanchez-Vicario/Zvereva 6–2 3–6 6–3), (with De Swardt) **won** Eastbourne (d. Sanchez-Vicario/Zvereva 6–1 6–3), **won** Montreal (d. Basuki/Vis 6–3 6–4); **r/u** Hamburg (lost Schett/Schnyder 7–6 3–6 6–3), (with De Swardt) **r/u** New Haven (lost Fusai/Tauziat 6–1 6–0).

CAREER GRAND SLAM RECORD
AUSTRALIAN OPEN – Played 8, r/u 1, qf 1
1988: 1r lost Inoue 7–6 6–4. **1989: 3r** d. Ingram 7–5 7–5, Cunningham 6–2 6–2, lost Navratilova [2] 6–2 6–2. **1990: 3r** [seed 5] d. Martin 6–7 6–0 6–0, Temesvari 6–1 6–1, lost Fendick 1–6 7–6 6–4. **1991: r/u** [10] d. A.Minter 7–6 6–2, Quentrec 6–2 6–2, Stafford 6–7 6–1 8–6, Garrison [7] 7–6 6–4, Graf [1] 5–7 6–4 8–6, Sanchez-Vicario [6] 6–2 6–4, lost Seles [2] 5–7 6–3 6–1. **1992: last 16** [seed 6] d. Zrubakova 7–6 6–3, Alter 6–3 6–2, Li 6–3 6–1, lost Huber [12] 5–7 7–6 6–4. **1993: 2r** [seed 8] d. Testud 6–2 6–4, lost R. White 4–6 7–5 6–2. **1994: qf** [seed 5] d. Li 6–1 6–3, Kelesi 6–3 6–1, Taylor 6–4 6–2, Zardo 6–2 7–5, lost Sabatini [4] 6–3 6–4. **1995: last 16** [seed 3] d. Hy-Boulais 6–2 3–6 6–0, Sukova 3–6 6–3 6–2, Raymond 6–3 3–6 9–7, lost Gavaldon 7–5 6–0. **1996–98:** Did not play.
FRENCH OPEN – Played 13, sf 2, qf 4
1986: 1r lost Drescher 6–2 6–3. **1987: 3r** d. Durie 6–3 6–1, Zrubakova 6–3 4–6 6–4, lost Graf [2] 6–0 6–1. **1988: 1r** lost Tarabini 1–6 6–3 6–2. **1989: qf** [seed 11] d. Halard 6–3 6–2, Porwik 6–3 7–5, Simpson 6–1 6–0, Hanika 6–1 6–4, lost Sanchez-Vicario [7] 6–2 6–2. **1990: sf** [seed 11] d. Demongeot 6–0 6–7 10–8, Schultz 6–3 6–1, Sviglerova 7–5 6–2, Sabatini [4] 6–4 7–5, K. Maleeva [8] 4–6 6–2 6–4, lost Graf [1] 6–1 6–2. **1991: qf** [seed 6] d. Farina 7–5 6–2, Hy 6–2 6–1, Brioukhovets 7–6 6–2, Meskhi [14] 6–0 7–6, lost Sabatini [3] 5–7 7–6 6–0. **1992: last 16** [seed 10] d. Graham 6–3 6–2, Medvedeva 6–4 6–1, Schultz 6–3 6–4, lost Graf [2] 6–1 6–4. **1993: qf** [seed 7] d. Porwik 6–3 6–3, Papadaki 3–6 6–2 6–2, Kroupova 2–6 6–2 6–3, Zvereva 6–3 6–3, lost Sanchez-Vicario [2] 6–2 7–5. **1994: 1r** [seed 6] lost Smashnova 6–4 6–2. **1995: 3r** [seed 5] d. Dopfer 6–1 2–6 6–1, Schwarz-Ritter 6–4 6–3, lost Rubin 7–6 4–6 8–6. **1996: sf** [seed 10] d. Richterova 6–0 6–2, Wang 6–4 6–3, Makarova 6–1 7–5, Spirlea 6–1 7–5, Seles [1] 7–6 6–3, lost Sanchez-Vicario 6–3 7–5. **1997: 3r** [seed 4] d. Torrens-Valero 6–3 6–2, Kandarr 6–4 6–0, lost Arendt 3–6 6–4 6–4. **1998: qf** [seed 3] d. A. Miller 7–5 6–4, Loit 7–5 6–0, Tatarkova 6–3 7–6, Kournikova [13] 6–7 6–3 6–3, lost Seles [6] 4–6 6–3 6–3.
WIMBLEDON – Played 13, won 1, r/u 2, sf 1, qf 3
1986: 1r lost Mascarin 3–6 7–6 7–2. **1987: last 16** d. Reis 6–3 3–6 8–6, Hu Na 6–2 6–3, Walsh-Pete 6–2 4–6 6–4, lost Graf [2] 6–4 6–3. **1988: 2r** d. Scheuer-Larsen 6–3 7–5, lost Sukova [6] 6–2 6–2. **1989: last 16** [seed 10] d. Simpson 6–2 6–1, Burgin 6–4 3–6 6–2, K. Adams 6–4 6–1, lost Golarsa 7–6 2–6 6–4. **1990: qf** [seed 13] d. Golarsa 3–6 7–6 6–2, Cunningham 6–2 6–1, Faull 6–2 6–1, Fendick 6–2 6–4, lost Graf [1] 7–5 6–2. **1991: 2r** [seed 6] d. Pratt 6–3 6–0, lost Schultz 4–6 7–6 6–4. **1992: 3r** [seed 11] d. Monami 6–1 6–2, Lindqvist 6–3 6–2, lost Fendick 6–3 6–3. **1993: r/u** [seed 8] d. Zardo 6–1 6–3, Gorrochategui 6–0 7–5, Werdel 6–3 6–1, Oremans 7–5 4–6 6–4, Sabatini [4] 6–4 6–3, Navratilova [2] 6–4 6–4, lost Graf [1] 7–6 1–6 6–4. **1994: qf** [seed 5] d. Oremans 6–4 4–6 6–4, Probst 6–2 6–1, Monami 6–0 4–6 6–0, Sawamatsu 6–3 6–3, lost Navratilova [4] 5–7 6–0 6–1. **1995: sf** [seed 4] d. Kschwendt 6–4 6–4, Durie 6–2 6–2, Wiesner 7–5 6–4, Bradtke 6–0 5–7 6–4, Date [6] 6–2 6–3, lost Graf [1] 5–7 6–4 6–2. **1996: qf** [seed 6] (d. Martinek 6–4 6–0, Courtois 7–6 6–3, Dragomir 6–3 6–1, Hy-Boulais 6–3 6–1, lost Graf [1] 6–3 6–2). **1997: r/u** [seed 3] d. Probst 6–4 4–6 6–0, Likhovtseva 6–1 4–6 6–4, Leon-Garcia 6–4 6–2, M. J. Fernandez [11] 5–7 6–4 7–5, Basuki 6–3 6–3, Sanchez-Vicario [8] 6–4 6–2, lost Hingis 2–6 6–3 6–3. **1998: won** [seed 3] d. Kleinova 6–2 6–2, Panova 6–3 4–6 6–1, Morariu 6–3 6–1, Spirlea [10] 6–2 6–3, V. Williams [7] 7–5 7–6, Hingis [1] 6–4 6–4, Tauziat [16] 6–4 7–6.
US OPEN – Played 12, sf 2, qf 4
1987: last 16 d. Parkhomenko 6–1 7–6, Turnbull [16] 6–2 6–4, Halard 6–4 6–0, lost Shriver [5] 6–3 7–6. **1988: 1r** lost Wiesner 6–2 6–3. **1989: 2r** [seed 11] d. McGrath 7–5 6–2, lost Paulus 3–6 6–3 6–2. **1990: qf** [seed 12] d. Lapi 6–3 6–1, Rinaldi 6–4 6–3, Gildemeister 6–3 6–1, K. Maleeva [7] 6–4 6–2, lost Graf [1] 6–3 6–1. **1991: last 16** [seed 9] d. Grossman 6–3 4–6 6–1, Harper 6–2 6–3, Monami 6–1 6–2, lost Sabatini [3] 6–4 7–6. **1992: 1r** [seed 10] lost Fairbank-Nideffer 6–3 7–6. **1993: last 16** [seed 8] d. Gavaldon 6–2 6–4,

Majoli 6–3 6–0, Golarsa 6–4 6–3, lost Date 6–4 6–4. **1994: sf** [seed 7] d. Makarova 7–5 7–5, Habsudova 6–2 6–3, Hy 6–1 6–2, Mag. Maleeva [15] 6–0 6–4, Pierce [4] 6–4 6–0, lost Graf [1] 6–3 7–5. **1995: qf** [seed 5] d. Cecchini 6–2. 6–0, Carlsson 6–1 6–2, Testud 6–4 7–5, Studenikova 6–4 6–3, lost Seles [2] 7–6 6–2. **1996: qf** [seed 7] d. Lubiani 6–1 7–5, Labat 6–2 4–6 6–2, Whitlinger-Jones 6–2 6–3, Habsudova 6–2 6–0, lost Hingis [16] 7–6 6–4. **1997: qf** [seed 3] d. Ruano-Pascual 6–0 6–4, Basuki 6–4 6–2, Lucic 6–2 6–7 6–3, M. J. Fernandez [12] 7–5 6–4, lost Davenport [6] 6–2 4–6 7–6. **1998: sf** [seed 3] d. Capriati 6–4 6–3, Cocheteux 6–2 7–5, Testud 6–2 6–3, S. Williams 6–3 6–3, Schnyder [11] 6–2 6–3, lost Hingis [1] 3–6 6–1 6–3.

OLYMPIC RECORD

1988: (Seoul) 2r d. Demongeot 6–4 6–3, lost Paulus 6–4 6–3. **1992: (Barcelona) 1r** [seed 9] lost Zvereva 6–1 6–0. **1996: (Atlanta) sf bronze medal** [seed 6] d. Dragomir 6–4 4–4 ret, Wiesner 6–4 3–6 6–3, Sugiyama 6–3 6–4, Seles [1] 7–5 3–6 8–6, lost Sanchez-Vicario [3] 6–4 1–6 6–3; bronze medal play-off d. M. J. Fernandez [7] 7–5 6–4.

CAREER FED CUP RECORD

1987 (in CAN, Hard): *1r TCH d. SWE 3–0.* R3 (with H. Mandlikova) d. C. Lindqvist/M. Lindstrom 6–3 6–2. *2r TCH d. YUG 3–0.* R3 (with R. Rajchrtova) d. S. Goles/R. Sasak 6–4 5–7 6–4. **1988 (in AUS, Hard):** *1r TCH d. BRA 3–0.* R3 (with J. Pospisilova) d. N. Dias/L. Tella 6–3 6–2. *2r TCH d. NZL 3–0.* R3 (with Pospisilova) d. B. Cordwell/J. Richardson 7–6 7–6. *Qf TCH d. DEN 3–0.* R3 (with Pospisilova) d. H. Kjaer-Nielsen/T. Scheuer-Larsen 6–3 6–2. *Sf TCH d. CAN 3–0.* R3 (with Pospisilova) d. H. Kelesi/R. Simpson 7–6 6–2. *Final TCH d. URS 2–1.* R3 (with Pospisilova) lost L. Savchenko/N. Zvereva (URS) 7–6 7–5. **1989 (in JPN, Hard):** *1r TCH d. BEL 3–0.* R1 d. C. Van Reneterghem 6–0 6–2. *2r TCH d. HUN 2–1.* R1 d. A. Noszaly 6–3 6–3. *Qf TCH d. FRG 2–1.* R1 d. C. Kohde-Kilsch 6–3 6–3; R3 (with H. Sukova) d. S. Graf/Kohde-Kilsch 6–2 6–2. *Final USA d. TCH 2–0.* R1 lost C. Evert 6–2 6–3. **1990 (in USA, Hard):** *1r TCH d. KOR 3–0.* R2 d. S. Im 6–0 6–1. *2r TCH d. AUS 2–1.* R2 d. R. McQuillan 6–4 6–4. *Qf USA d. TCH 2–1.* R2 d. Z. Garrison 6–3 6–3; R3 (with R. Rajchrtova) lost G. Fernandez/Garrison 7–6 6–4. **1991 (in GBR, Hard):** *1r TCH d. SWE 2–0.* R2 d. C. Dahlman 7–6 6–2. *2r TCH d. URS 2–1.* R2 d. N. Zvereva 6–4 6–1. *Qf TCH d. SUI 2–1.* R2 d. M. Maleeva-Fragniere 6–4 6–4. *Sf USA d. TCH 3–0.* R2 lost M. J. Fernandez 6–4 0–6 9–7. **1992 (in GER, Clay):** *1r TCH d. HUN 3–0.* R2 d. A. Temesvari-Trunkos 6–2 6–1; R2 (with A. Strnadova) d. V. Csurgo/Temesvari-Trunkos 1–6 7–5 7–5. *2r TCH d. KOR 3–0.* R2 d. S. Park 4–6 6–2 6–3; R3 (with Strnadova) d. I. Kim/J. Lee 6–3 6–3. *Qf AUS d. TCH 2–1.* R2 lost N. Provis 7–5 6–0; R3 (with Strnadova) lost Provis/R. Stubbs 6–3 6–3. **1993 (in GER, Clay):** *1r TCH d. RSA 2–1.* R2 d. A. Coetzer 6–1 6–4. *2r TCH d. ITA 2–1.* R2 lost S. Cecchini 0–6 6–2 6–3; R3 (with H. Sukova) d. Cecchini/ S. Farina 6–2 6–2. *Qf FRA d. TCH 3–0.* R2 lost Tauziat 6–1 0–6 6–3. **1995: April (in ESP, Clay)** *EA1 round-robin CZE d. POL 3–0.* R2 d. K. Nowak 6–4 6–3. Round-robin CZE d. GBR 3–0. R2 d. C. Wood 6–2 6–2; R3 (with H. Sukova) d. J. Durie/Wood 6–7 6–1 6–2. *Round-robin SLO d. CZE 2–1.* R2 lost T. Krizan 0–6 6–3 6–3. *EA1 qf CZE d. SLO 3–0.* R2 d. Krizan 6–0 7–5. *EA1 sf CZE d. BLR 3–0.* R2 d. N. Zvereva 0–6 7–6 6–3. **1996: April** – *Group 1 qf CZE d. CAN 3–0 in CAN (Hard).* R1 d. J. Nejedly 6–1 6–1; R3 d. P. Hy-Boulais 6–7 6–0 6–1. **July** – *World Group play-off CZE d. ARG 3–1 in CZE (Carpet).* R2 d. M. Paz 6–1 6–2. **1997: July** – *World Group sf NED d. CZE 3–2 in CZE (Clay).* R2 d. M. Oremans 6–3 6–0; R3 d. B. Schultz-McCarthy 7–6 6–3; R5 (with E. Martincova) lost M. Bollegraf/Oremans 6–4 7–6. **1998: April** – *World Group qf SUI d. CZE 4–1 in CZE (Carpet).* R1 d. P. Schnyder 3–6 6–2 6–3; R3 lost M. Hingis 4–6 6–3 6–2.

GRAND SLAM CUP RECORD – Played 1

1998: 1r [seed 4] lost Schnyder 2–6 7–5 7–5.

SEASON ENDING CHAMPIONSHIPS – Played 9, won 1, sf 2, qf 3

(1983–94 Virginia Slims, 1995 Corel, 1996–98 Chase)

1990: 1r lost Sabatini 6–1 5–7 7–6. **1991: sf** d. Maleeva-Fragniere 6–0 3–6 6–3, Graf 6–3 3–6 6–1, lost Navratilova 6–1 6–4. **1992: qf** d. Fernandez 7–6 6–2, lost Seles 3–6 6–4 6–1. **1993: qf** d. Garrison-Jackson 6–4 6–7 6–3, lost Sanchez-Vicario 6–7 7–6 6–4. **1994: qf** d. Majoli 6–3 3–6 6–1, lost Davenport 6–2 6–2. **1995: 1r** lost Date 5–7 6–3 6–4. **1996: sf** d. Coetzer 6–4 6–1, Sanchez-Vicario 6–0 6–3, lost Graf 4–6 6–4 6–3. **1997: won** d. Martinez 6–4 6–4, Sanchez-Vicario 6–3 3–6 6–1, Spirlea 7–6 6–2, Pierce 7–6 6–2 6–3. **1998: 1r** lost Graf 6–7 6–4 6–1.

4 ARANTXA SANCHEZ-VICARIO (ESP)

Born: Barcelona, 18 December 1971. **Lives:** Andorra.
Father: Emilio. **Mother:** Marisa, whose maiden name, Vicario, she added to her own, travels with her.
Sister: Marisa (older). **Brothers:** Emilio and Javier (both older) who compete on the men's tour.
Agent: IMG. **Coach:** Angel Gimenez; formerly her brother Emilio, Gabriel Urpi, Mervyn Rose, Carlos Kirmayr, Juan Nunez, Mike Estep, Eduardo Osta, Sven Groeneveld and David De Migues.
Turned pro: 1986. **Height:** 5ft 6½in (1.69m).
Weight: 124lb (56kg).

Rankings: 1986: 124; **1987:** 47; **1988:** 18; **1989:** 5; **1990:** 7; **1991:** 5; **1992:** 4; **1993:** 2; **1994:** 2; **1995:** 3; **1996:** 2 (jointly with Seles); **1997:** 9; **1998:** 4 singles, 12 doubles. **Highest:** 1 (February 1995).

1998 Prize Money: $1,505,964. **Career Earnings:** $14,029,452. **Career Titles:** 26.

Style: One of the fastest movers on a tennis court whose attacking, all-round game and cheerful demeanour have created an enormous following round the world. A right-hander with a good forehand, accurate double-handed backhand and excellent touch on the volley, Arantxa has enjoyed outstanding success both in singles and doubles.

CAREER HIGHLIGHTS (year: (titles))
1986: Emerging from the satellite circuits, she reached sf Spanish Open and played Fed Cup. **1987:** Qf French Open in 1st GS appearance. **1988: (1)** *Brussels*. Upset Evert (suffering from a foot injury) at French Open en route to qf again and reached last 16 US Open. Won her 1st pro singles title at Brussels and was r/u Tampa. **1989: (2)** *FRENCH OPEN, Barcelona*. At 17 yrs 6 mths became the youngest woman and the 1st Spaniard to win French Open women's title. Qf Wimbledon and US Open, won Barcelona and was r/u Italian Open and Canadian Open, qualifying for 1st VS Champs, where she reached sf. Voted WTA Most Improved Player for 2nd year running. **1990: (2)** *Barcelona, Newport*. In some disappointing performances she fell to Harvey-Wild 1r VS Chicago, to Paz 2r French Open and to Nagelsen 1r Wimbledon. Won 2 titles, r/u Tokyo Toray, VS Houston, Amelia Island, Leipzig and Hamburg, where she d. Navratilova and took Graf to 3s. She lost 1r VS Champs to K. Maleeva and in GS her best showing was sf US Open, but she won French Open mixed doubles with Lozano. In women's doubles won 1 title with Navratilova and 3 with Paz, with whom she was r/u VS Champs. **1991: (1)** *Washington*. Upset Sabatini en route to sf Australian Open and Graf on her way to f French Open, inflicting on the former No. 1 her worst defeat and 1st love set since 1984. In other GS lost qf Wimbledon to M. J. Fernandez and same round US Open to Navratilova, who also stopped her at that stage VS Champs. Had to wait until late Aug. to win her 1st title of the year at VS Washington, although she had reached qf or better in all 13 tourns until then. R/u Sydney, Berlin, Eastbourne, VS Philadelphia and appeared in 6 more sf. Played in the victorious Spanish Fed Cup team, winning all her matches. In doubles won Barcelona with Navratilova and took Sydney and Amelia Island with Sukova, with whom she qualified for VS Champs. In mixed doubles r/u US Open with her brother, Emilio. **1992: (2)** *LIPC, Montreal*. Again she was remarkably consistent if not spectacular. She upset Graf qf US Open on her way to f, where she lost to Seles, whom she had beaten 3 weeks earlier at Montreal – one of only 5 defeats the No. 1 suffered all year. Reached sf Australian Open and French Open and won an Olympic bronze medal; took 2 titles and was r/u Sydney, Barcelona, Hamburg, Berlin and Philadelphia, reaching 4 more sf and losing qf VS Champs to Navratilova. She enjoyed a terrific year in doubles, winning Australian Open, VS Champs and 4 more titles with Sukova; r/u French Open, Olympic silver medal and 1 title with Martinez; plus 3 more titles with other partners. In mixed with Woodbridge won French Open and r/u Australian Open. **1993: (4)** *LIPC, Amelia Island, Barcelona, Hamburg*. Following a heavy schedule which left her exhausted and struggling to finish her f v Graf at VS Champs, she moved up to No. 2 in the rankings. She beat Graf twice during the year in winning LIPC and Hamburg (ending the German's unbeaten record there),

and also won Amelia Island and Barcelona. She was r/u VS Florida, FC Cup, San Diego, VS Los Angeles and VS Champs and appeared in 4 more sf. In GS she reached sf Australian Open, French Open and US Open and played in winning Spanish Fed Cup team, unbeaten in all her matches. She also played 7 women's doubles f, winning US Open and two others with Sukova, with whom she reached sf VS Champs, and one each with Martinez and Novotna. In mixed, she took Australian Open with Woodbridge. **1994: (8)** *FRENCH OPEN, US OPEN, Amelia Island, Barcelona, Hamburg, Montreal, Tokyo Nicherei, Oakland*. In a great year for her and for Spanish tennis, she won French Open and a 1st US Open and, with new Wimbledon champion Martinez, took ESP to victory in Fed Cup. Graf was the only player to beat her 3 times, including f Australian Open, although she beat the German in Hamburg and Montreal, both matches being decided in 3s tb, and in 3s at US Open. She was r/u VS Florida, Stratton Mountain and San Diego, but her Wimbledon singles bid ended at last 16 stage, when she lost to Garrison-Jackson, and at VS Champs she surprisingly fell 1r to Halard. She played 16 doubles f with various partners, winning 11 – including US Open with Novotna, with whom she was also r/u Wimbledon and VS Champs – and 7 times she won both singles and doubles titles at same tourn, most notably at US Open. The only woman to earn more than $2m prize money in 1994, she won almost $3m. **1995: (2)** *Barcelona, Berlin*. Took over the No. 1 ranking for the 1st time on 6 Feb., becoming the 1st Spanish player and only the 6th woman to hold that position since rankings began, and on 13 Feb. she became the 1st since Navratilova in August 1987 to top both singles and doubles rankings. However, Graf deposed her again a week later, and when she regained the top singles spot on 27 Feb., Zvereva had replaced her at the top of the doubles. She topped both rankings again twice more, on 27 March and 1 May, but Graf took over the top singles spot after French Open and by Oct. she had slipped to No. 3 behind Martinez, although she finished the year No. 1 in doubles. She had to wait until 30 April before winning her 1st title of year at Barcelona, where she also won the doubles, and Berlin was her only other singles title, although she was r/u Australian Open, French Open, Wimbledon, Italian Open and Tokyo Nicherei and reached 2 more sf. The outcome of her memorable f v Graf at Wimbledon hung on the result of a remarkable game on her serve at 5–5 fs, which covered 32 points and 20 min. For the 1st time in her 10-year career she was restricted by illness and injury, suffering a stomach virus at French Open, withdrawing qf FC Cup with a badly sprained right ankle and tenderness to the fibula and taking a break in autumn, suffering from fatigue. She still seemed below her best at WTA Champs, where she lost 1r singles to Zvereva, although she and Novotna won the doubles. Also with Novotna she won Australian Open and Wimbledon, was r/u French Open and took 2 more titles, plus a 5th with Neiland. Contributed 1 singles win as ESP d. USA 3–2 in f Fed Cup. **1996: (2)** *FC Cup, Hamburg*. Between April and August, her ranking fluctuated with that of Martinez between No. 2 and No. 3, before she settled at No. 2 on 5 Aug. after taking a silver medal at the Olympics, and was co-ranked in that spot with Seles from 4 Nov. She won both singles and doubles in 2 tourns – at FC Cup (with Novotna) and Hamburg (with Schultz-McCarthy). At French Open, she lost f to Graf only 10–8 fs in what was probably the match of the year. Earlier, though, she had been booed off the court after a disappointing display of gamesmanship in qf v Habsudova; after missing 2 mps at 5–4 in 2s, she lost tb and played dolly-shots in 3s, which she eventually won 10–8. Apparently forgetting the need to entertain, she claimed she was simply doing her job by winning. In contrast to their French Open f, her Wimbledon f defeat by Graf was disappointingly one-sided. She was also r/u Tokyo Toray, Montreal, San Diego and Tokyo Nicherei, reaching 2 more sf and 5 more qf, including Chase Champs, where she lost in ss to Novotna. In qf Australian Open v Rubin, she played (and lost) the longest women's match in the history of the tourn; it lasted 3 hours 33 min, comprising the most games in a set (30) and most in a woman's match (48) and being the 6th-longest on the WTA tour. The pair then joined together to win the doubles. Retaining her top doubles ranking, she took 9 titles from 12 f, winning a total of 4 with Novotna – with whom she was also r/u US Open and Chase Champs – 2 with Rubin and 1 each with Schultz-McCarthy, Spirlea and Neiland, as well as an Olympic bronze medal with Martinez. Her Fed Cup record suffered a setback as she won only one singles and one doubles match, losing to players she would normally expect to beat. She was restricted in the spring by a shoulder injury, caused by playing too much tennis, and in autumn took a 3-week break, feeling physically and mentally exhausted by the game. **1997:** It was another generally disappointing year in which she dropped out of the top 10 for a while and was seeded as low as 10 at US Open. She won no title, although she shared Eastbourne (where f was rained off) with Novotna and in f Tokyo Nicherei was 3–1 up in 3s v Seles before letting the match slip away. In November, she showed her old form again at

Belgium's Dominique Van Roost's amazing run to the semi-finals at Wimbledon was ended by Arantxa Sanchez-Vicario, but not without a fight. (Stephen Wake)

Philadelphia, where she upset Coetzer in ss and was on the point of doing the same to Hingis in sf before losing 2s tb and eventually the match. Then at Chase Champs, where she qualified in both singles and doubles, she upset Seles before losing qf in 3s to her former doubles partner Novotna, and, in partnership with Hingis, fell 1r doubles to Fusai/Tauziat. Her best GS performance was sf Wimbledon, and she reached the same stage Indian Wells, Madrid and Philadelphia, as well as qf French Open, US Open, Amelia Island, Los Angeles, Filderstadt and Moscow. In doubles she played and won 7 f, taking 3 titles with Hingis, 2 with Zvereva and 1 each with G. Fernandez and M. J. Fernandez. **1998: (2)** *FRENCH OPEN, Sydney.* Back to something like her old form again, she began the year in style at Sydney by winning her 1st title for more than a year. The climax of her season came in May when she won her 3rd French Open crown over Davenport and Seles. Although she did not win another title, she was r/u Eastbourne, Montreal and Tokyo Toyota, reached sf LIPC, Rome, Los Angeles and Filderstadt, qf Australian Open, Hamburg, Wimbledon and US Open, and played in the victorious ESP Fed Cup team. Her season tailed off rather as she was beaten 1r GS Cup by V. Williams and fell 1r Chase Champs to Spirlea, although she finished comfortably back in the top 5. In doubles she played 5 f with 4 different partners, but won no title.

PRINCIPAL 1998 RESULTS – won 2, r/u 3, sf 4 (detailed Grand Slam results follow)
won Sydney (d. Habsudova 7–5 6–4, J. Lee 6–2 3–6 6–3, Zvereva 6–1 6–2, S. Williams 6–2 6–1, V. Williams 6–1 6–3), **won** French Open; **r/u** Eastbourne (d. Tanasugarn 6–2 7–5, S. Williams 4–6 6–4 6–4, Kournikova w/o, lost Novotna 6–1 7–5), **r/u** Montreal (d. Habsudova 0–6 7–5 6–2, Tauziat 3–6 6–1 6–2, Martinez 6–3 6–4, Novotna 4–6 7–6 6–2, lost Seles 6–3 6–2), **r/u** Tokyo Toyota (d. Likhovtseva 6–0 6–4, Kournikova 6–3 6–2, Huber 6–1 3–6 6–3, lost Seles 4–6 6–3 6–4); **sf** LIPC (d. Wang 4–6 6–4 6–2, Labat 6–0 6–1, Vento 6–2 6–1, Novotna 6–1 6–1, lost Kournikova 3–6 6–1 6–3), **sf** Rome (d. Torrens-Valero 6–3 7–5, Van Roost 6–1

6–2, Raymond 6–7 6–1 6–2, lost V. Williams 6–3 2–6 7–5), **sf** Los Angeles (d. Sugiyama 4–6 6–4 6–4, Tatarkova 6–3 6–3, lost Hingis 6–4 6–3), **sf** Filderstadt (d. Mauresmo 6–3 6–2, Raymond 1–6 7–5 6–2, lost Davenport 7–6 6–4). **DOUBLES:** (with Zvereva) **r/u** LIPC (lost Hingis/Novotna 6–2 3–6 6–3), (with Coetzer) **r/u** Rome (lost Ruano-Pascual/Suarez 7–6 6–4), (with Zvereva) **r/u** Eastbourne (lost De Swardt/Novotna 6–1 6–3), (with Fernandez) **r/u** Tokyo Toyota (lost Kournikova/Seles 6–4 6–4), (with Kournikova) **r/u** Filderstadt (lost Davenport/Zvereva 6–4 6–2).

CAREER GRAND SLAM RECORD

AUSTRALIAN OPEN – Played 8, r/u 2, sf 3, qf 2

1991: sf [seed 6] d. Medvedeva 6–0 6–2, Javer 4–6 6–4 6–2, McNeil 6–4 3–6 6–0, Frazier [13] 6–3 6–2, Sabatini [4] 6–1 6–3, lost Novotna 6–2 6–4. **1992: sf** [seed 4] d. Provis 6–2 6–1, Testud 6–1 6–1, Strnadova 1–6 6–0 6–3, Savchenko-Neiland 6–1 7–6, Maleeva-Fragniere def, lost Seles [1] 6–2 6–2. **1993: sf** [seed 4] d. Van Lottum 6–2 6–3, Arraya 6–0 6–1, Zrubakova 6–1 6–3, Huber [11] 7–5 6–2, M. J. Fernandez [5] 7–5 6–4, lost Graf [2] 7–5 6–4. **1994: r/u** [seed 2] d. Habsudova 6–1 6–3, Wang 6–2 6–4, Grossman 6–2 6–3, Mag. Maleeva [14] 4–6 6–1 6–3, Maleeva-Fragniere [8] 7–6 6–4, Sabatini [4] 6–1 6–2, lost Graf [1] 6–0 6–2. **1995: r/u** [seed 1] d. Li 6–2 6–0, Whitlinger-Jones 6–2 6–1, Garrison-Jackson 6–1 6–3, Habsudova 7–5 6–0, Sawamatsu 6–4 7–6, Werdel-Witmeyer 6–4 6–1, lost Pierce [4] 6–3 6–2. **1996: qf** [seed 3] d. Reinstadler 6–2 6–2, Rittner 6–3 6–2, Cacic 6–3 6–3, M. J. Fernandez [9] 6–3 6–3, lost Rubin [13] 6–4 2–6 16–14. **1997: 3r** [seed 2] d. Pizzichini 6–4 6–4, De Ville 1–0 ret, lost Van Roost 1–6 6–4 8–6. **1998: qf** [seed 7] d. J. Lee 6–0 6–4, Makarova 6–0 6–0, Hiraki 6–2 6–3, Sugiyama [16] 6–2 6–4, lost Huber [10] 7–6 7–5.

FRENCH OPEN – Played 12, won 3, r/u 3, sf 2, qf 3

1987: qf d. Burgin 7–5 6–3, Dinu 6–0 6–2, Paulus 6–4 6–2, Karlsson 6–1 6–4, lost Sabatini [7] 6–4 6–0. **1988: qf** d. Kuczynska 6–2 6–0, Meier 7–5 6–0, Evert [3] 6–1 7–6, Tanvier 6–2 6–0, lost Provis 7–5 3–6 6–4. **1989: won** [seed 7] d. Rajchrtova 6–2 6–1, Demongeot 6–4 6–4, Medvedeva 6–0 3–6 6–2, Coetzer 6–3 6–2, Novotna [11] 6–2 6–2, M. J. Fernandez [15] 6–2 6–2, Graf [1] 7–6 3–6 7–5. **1990: 2r** [seed 3] d. Van Lottum 6–1 6–3, lost Paz 7–5 3–6 6–1, **1991: r/u** [seed 5] d. McNeil 6–2 6–2, Godridge 6–1 6–2, Fulco 6–1 6–1, Tami Whitlinger 6–2 6–1, M. J. Fernandez [4] 6–3 6–2, Graf [2] 6–0 6–2, lost Seles [1] 6–3 6–4. **1992: sf** [seed 4] d. Oeljeklaus 6–0 6–2, Zardo 6–3 6–2, Wiesner 6–3 6–1, Date [14] 6–1 6–2, Bollegraf 6–2 6–3, lost Graf [2] 0–6 6–2 6–2. **1993: sf** [seed 2] d. Kiene 6–3 7–6, Sawamatsu 6–0 6–0, Meskhi 6–3 6–0, Dragomir 6–0 6–1, Novotna [7] 6–2 7–5, lost M. J. Fernandez [5] 6–2 6–2. **1994: won** [seed 2] d. Labat 6–4 6–1, Van Lottum 6–1 6–0, Rittner 6–4 6–2, Huber [11] 6–3 6–2, Halard 6–1 7–6, Martinez [3] 6–3 6–1, Pierce [12] 6–4 6–4. **1995: r/u** [seed 1] d. Park 6–1 6–0, Pitkowski 6–3 6–0, Reinstadler 6–3 6–1, Smashnova 6–4 6–0, Rubin 6–3 6–1, Date [9] 7–5 6–2, lost Graf [2] 7–5 4–6 6–0. **1996: r/u** [seed 4] d. Glass 6–2 6–3, Martinek 6–0 6–1, Likhovtseva 6–0 6–0, Rittner 6–3 6–4, Habsudova 6–2 6–7 10–8, Novotna [10] 6–3 7–5, lost Graf [1] 6–3 6–7 10–8. **1997: qf** [seed 6] d. Jagieniak 6–0 6–2, Sugiyama 6–3 6–1, Van Roost 6–0 6–3, Zvereva 6–4 6–2, lost Hingis [1] 6–2 6–2. **1998: won** [seed 4] d. Kandarr 6–2 7–5, Cristea 6–2 6–3, Fusai 6–2 6–1, S. Williams 4–6 7–5 6–3, Schnyder 6–2 6–7 6–0, Davenport [2] 6–3 7–6, Seles [6] 7–6 0–6 6–2.

WIMBLEDON – Played 12, r/u 2, sf 1, qf 3

1987: 1r lost Cordwell 6–1 2–6 6–4. **1988: 1r** lost Okamoto 6–3 6–4. **1989: qf** [seed 7] d. Pospisilova 6–2 7–5, Halard 6–4 6–3, Reggi 4–6 6–3 7–5, McNeil [15] 6–3 2–6 6–1, lost Graf [1] 7–5 6–1. **1990: 1r** [seed 6] lost Nagelsen 1–6 7–6 9–7. **1991: qf** [seed 3] d. Rittner 6–1 6–2, Coetzer 6–4 6–1, McNeil 6–2 6–4, A. Minter 7–5 3–6 6–1, lost M. J. Fernandez [6] 6–2 7–5. **1992: 2r** [seed 5] d. Meskhi 6–3 7–6, lost Halard 6–3 2–6 6–3). **1993: last 16** [seed 3] d. Zrubakova 6–1 6–1, Neiland 7–6 6–0, Fendick 6–3 6–2, lost Sukova [15] 6–3 6–4. **1994: last 16** [seed 2] d. K. Maleeva 6–1 6–2, Gaidano 6–2 6–1, Feber 6–2 6–1, lost Garrison-Jackson [13] 7–5 4–6 6–3. **1995: r/u** [seed 2] d. Studenikova 6–2 6–1, Endo 7–5 6–2, Garrison-Jackson 6–1 6–2, Huber [9] 7–5 6–4, Schultz-McCarthy [15] 6–4 7–6, Martinez [4] 6–3 6–7 6–1, lost Graf [1] 4–6 6–1 7–5. **1996: r/u** [seed 4] d. Serra-Zanetti 6–3 6–4, Oremans 7–6 6–3, Sawamatsu 6–4 6–1, Appelmans 3–6 6–2 6–1, Wiesner 6–4 6–0, McGrath 6–2 6–1, lost Graf [1] 6–3 7–5. **1997: sf** [seed 8] d. Wood 6–0 6–0 Gagliardi 6–4 6–2, Labat 6–1 6–2, Pierce [9] 6–1 6–3, Tauziat 6–2 7–5, lost Novotna [3] 6–4 6–2. **1998: qf** [seed 5] d. Cristea 5–7 6–2 6–0, Grzybowska 4–6 6–4 6–3, Plischke 7–5 6–2, Van Roost 3–6 6–3 6–2, lost Hingis [1] 6–3 3–6 6–3.

US OPEN – Played 12, won 1, r/u 1, sf 2, qf 2

1987: 1r lost Dias 6–4 6–2. **1988: last 16** d. Keil 6–3 6–0, Steinmetz 6–2 6–2, Sloane 6–3 6–3, lost Garrison [11] 4–6 7–5 6–2. **1989: qf** [seed 6] d. Faull 6–3 6–1, Cammy Macgregor 6–1 6–3, Wasserman 6–1 2–6 6–4, Paulus 6–2 6–2, lost Sabatini [3] 3–6 6–4 6–1. **1990: sf** [seed 6] d. Provis 6–0 6–3, Kuhlman 6–1 6–2, Fendick 6–2 6–1, Paulus [16] 6–4 6–3, Garrison [4] 6–2 6–2, lost Graf [1] 6–1 6–2. **1991: qf** [seed 4] d. Piccolini 6–0 6–1, Godridge 6–1 6–1, Herreman 6–2 6–2, Zvereva 6–3 7–6, lost Navratilova [6] 7–6 6–7 6–4. **1992: r/u** [seed 5] d. Savchenko-Neiland 5–7 6–2 6–2, Davenport 6–2 6–1, Sawamatsu 6–1 6–3, Garrison [14] 6–0 6–1, Graf [2] 7–6 6–3, Maleeva-Fragniere [9] 6–2 6–1, lost Seles 6–3 6–3. **1993: sf** [seed 2] d. Labat 6–4 6–3, Harvey-Wild 6–2 6–2, Rubin 6–0 6–0–1, Tauziat 6–4 6–3, Zvereva 3–0 ret, lost Sukova [12] 6–7 7–5 6–2. **1994: won** [seed 2] d. Ferrando 7–5 6–1, Tauziat 6–2 7–6, Cecchini 6–2 6–1, Grossman 6–2 6–0, Date [5] 6–3 6–0, Sabatini [8] 6–1 7–6, Graf [1] 1–6 7–6 6–4. **1995: last 16** [seed 3] d. Cristea 6–1 6–1, Kruger 6–4 6–3, Gaidano 6–3 6–0, lost M. J. Fernandez [14] 1–6 6–4 6–4. **1996: last 16** [seed 3] d. Poruri 6–2 6–1, Arendt 6–2 6–2, Likhovtseva 6–1 6–0, lost Hingis 6–1 3–6 6–4. **1997: qf** [seed 10] d. Guse 6–2 6–4, Tu 6–2 5–7 6–2, Fusai 6–2 6–1, McQuillan 6–1 6–2, lost Hingis [seed 1] 6–3 6–2. **1998: qf** [seed 4] d. Brandi 6–2 6–3, Zuluaga 6–3 6–2, Pitkowski 6–2 6–3, Kournikova [15] 7–6 6–3, lost V. Williams [5] 2–6 6–1 6–1.

OLYMPIC RECORD

SINGLES: 1988: (Seoul) 1r lost Goles 6–4 6–2. **1992: (Barcelona) sf bronze medal** [seed 2] d. Spirlea 6–1 6–3, Endo 6–0 6–1, Rittner 4–6 6–3 6–1, Martinez [5] 6–4 6–4, lost Capriati [3] 6–3 3–6 6–1. **1996: (Atlanta) r/u silver medal** [seed 3] d. Van Roost 6–1 7–5, Farina 6–1 6–3, Schultz-McCarthy [11] 6–4 7–6, Date [8] 4–6 6–3 10–8, Novotna [6] 6–4 1–6 6–3, lost Davenport [9] 7–6 6–2). **DOUBLES:** (with Martinez): **1992: (Barcelona) r/u silver medal** d. McQuillan/Provis 6–3 6–3, lost G. Fernandez/M. J. Fernandez 7–5 2–6 6–2. **1996: (Atlanta) sf bronze medal** lost Novotna/Sukova; bronze medal play-off d. Bollegraf/Schultz-McCarthy 6–1 6–3.

CAREER FED CUP RECORD

1986 (in TCH, Clay): *1r ESP d. INA 2–1.* R2 d. S. Anggarkusuma 7–6 6–3. R3 (with A. Almansa) d. Anggarkusuma/Y. Basuki 7–5 6–4. *2r USA d. ESP 3–0.* R2 lost M. Navratilova 6–3 6–0. **1987 (in CAN, Hard):** *1r ESP d. JAM 3–0.* R2 d. J. Van Ryck De Groot 6–3 6–1; R3 (with M. J. Llorca) d. H. Harris/van Ryck De Groot 7–6 6–2. *2r AUS d. ESP 2–1.* R2 lost E. Smylie 6–1 4–6 6–1; R3 (with Llorca) lost Smylie/W. Turnbull 6–1 6–2. **1988 (in AUS, Hard):** *1r ESP d. NED 3–0.* R2 d. B. Schultz 6–2 7–6; R3 (with C. Martinez) d. M. Bollegraf/C. Vis 5–7 6–4 6–4. *2r ESP d. INA 3–0.* R2 d. Y. Basuki 6–1 6–1; R3 (with Martinez) d. S. Anggarkusuma/Basuki 6–0 5–7 6–2. *Qf URS d. ESP 2–1.* R2 d. N. Zvereva 7–6 6–1; R3 (with Martinez) lost L. Savchenko/Zvereva 4–6 6–4 6–4. **1989 (in JPN, Hard):** *1r ESP d. FRA 2–0.* R2 d. N. Tauziat 6–4 6–2. *2r ESP d. NED 2–0.* R2 d. B. Schultz 2–6 6–4 10–8. *Qf ESP d. URS 2–1.* R2 d. N. Zvereva 7–5 6–3; R3 (with C. Martinez) lost L. Savchenko/Zvereva 6–4 2–6 6–1. *Sf ESP d. AUS 2–0.* R2 d. A. Minter 6–1 4–6 6–2. *Final USA d. ESP 3–0.* R2 lost M. Navratilova (USA) 0–6 6–3 6–4; R3 (with Martinez) lost Z. Garrison/P. Shriver 7–5 6–1. **1990 (in USA, Hard):** *1r ESP d. CAN 2–1.* R2 d. H. Kelesi 6–3 6–2. *2r ESP d. ISR 3–0.* R2 d. Y. Segal 6–0 6–0; R3 (with C. Martinez) d. I. Berger/L. Zaltz 6–3 6–4. *Qf ESP d. FRA 3–0.* R2 d. N. Tauziat 7–6 6–1; R3 (with Martinez) d. I. Demongeot/M. Pierce 6–4 6–4. *Sf URS d. ESP 2–1.* R2 lost N. Zvereva 6–4 2–0 ret. **1991 (in GBR, Hard):** *1r ESP d. BEL 2–0.* R2 d. S. Appelmans 7–6 6–3. *2r ESP d. AUS 3–0.* R2 d. R. McQuillan 6–1 3–6 6–2; R3 (with C. Martinez) d. K. Godridge/E. Smylie 6–3 6–4. *Qf ESP d. INA 2–0.* R2 d. Y. Basuki 4–6 7–5 6–4. *Sf ESP d. GER 3–0.* R2 d. A. Huber 6–1 2–6 6–2; R3 (with Martinez) d. B. Rittner/Huber 6–1 6–1. *Final ESP d. USA 2–1.* R2 d. M. J. Fernandez 6–3 6–4; R3 (with Martinez) d. Z. Garrison/G. Fernandez 3–6 6–1 6–1. **1992 (in GER, Clay):** *1r ESP d. BEL 2–1.* R2 d. S. Appelmans 6–1 6–2; R3 (with N. Perez) lost D. Monami/S. Wasserman 7–5 6–4. *2r ESP d. CAN 2–1.* R2 d. P. Hy 6–4 6–2; R3 (with C. Martinez) d. J. Hetherington/Hy 6–4 6–0. *Qf ESP d. ARG 2–1.* R2 d. M. Paz 6–2 6–1. *Sf ESP d. AUS 3–0.* R2 d. N. Provis 6–2 6–0; R3 (with V. Ruano-Pascual) d. J. Byrne/R. Stubbs 6–3 6–3. *Final GER d. ESP 2–1.* R2 lost S. Graf 6–4 6–2; R3 (with Martinez) d. A. Huber/B. Rittner 6–1 6–2. **1993 (in GER, Clay):** *1r ESP d. GBR 3–0.* R2 d. C. Wood 6–3 6–0; R3 (with C. Martinez) d. J. Durie/Wood 6–1 4–6 6–1. *2r ESP d. INA 3–0.* R2 d. N. Basuki 6–1 6–2. *Qf ESP d. NED 3–0.* R2 d. M. Oremans 7–6 6–0. *Sf ESP d. FRA 2–1.* R2 d. N. Tauziat 6–1 6–4. *Final ESP d. AUS 3–0.* R2 d. N. Provis 6–2 6–3; R3 (with Martinez) d. E. Smylie/R. Stubbs 3–6 6–1 6–3. **1994 (in GER, Clay):** *1r ESP d. CHI 3–0.* R2 d. P. Cabezas 6–1 6–0; R3 (with C. Martinez) d. Cabezas/Castro 6–0 6–1. *2r ESP d. ARG 3–0.* R2 d. F. Labat 6–1 6–4. *Qf ESP d. JPN 3–0.* R2 d. K. Date 6–3 2–6 8–6. *Sf ESP d. GER 2–1.* R2 d. A. Huber 4–6 6–0 7–5; R3 (with Martinez) d. B. Rittner/C. Singer 7–5 6–1. *Final ESP d. USA 3–0.* R2 d. L. Davenport 6–2 6–1; R3 (with Martinez) d. G./ M. J. Fernandez 6–3 6–4. **1995: April** – *World Group qf ESP d. BUL 3–2 in BUL (Carpet).* R1 d. K. Maleeva 6–3 6–3; R2 lost M. Maleeva 6–3 6–3). **July** – *World Group sf ESP d. GER 3–2 in ESP (Clay).* R2 lost S. Hack 6–4 6–2; R3 d. A. Huber 6–3 1–6 6–2. **November** – *World Group Final ESP d. USA 3–2 in ESP (Clay).* R2 d. M. J. Fernandez 6–3 6–2; R4 lost C. Rubin 1–6 6–4 6–4. **1996: April** – *World Group sf ESP d. RSA 3–2 in ESP (Clay).* R1 d. J. Kruger 6–3 6–1; R3 lost A. Coetzer 6–4 6–1. **July** – *World Group sf ESP d. FRA 3–2 in FRA (Carpet).* R2 lost M. Pierce 6–3 6–4; R4 lost J. Halard-Decugis 2–6 6–4 7–5; R5 (with C. Martinez) d. Halard-Decugis/N. Tauziat 6–4 2–1. **September** – *World Group Final USA d. ESP 5–0 in USA (Carpet).* R2 lost L. Davenport 7–5 6–1; R3 lost M. Seles 3–6 6–3 6–1. **1997: March** – *World Group qf BEL d. ESP 5–0 in BEL (Hard).* R1 lost E. Callens 6–3 7–6; R3 lost S. Appelmans 6–3 2–6 8–6. **July** – *World Group play-off ESP d. AUS 3–2 in AUS (Hard).* R1 d. R. McQuillan 6–2 6–1; R3 d. A. Ellwood 6–2 6–0. **1998: July** – *World Group sf ESP d. USA 3–2 in ESP (Clay).* R1 d. L. Raymond 6–7 6–3 6–0; R3 lost M. Seles 6–4 6–0; R5 (with C. Martinez) d. M. J. Fernandez/Raymond 6–4 6–7 11–9. **September** – *World Group Final ESP d. SUI 3–2 in SUI (Hard).* R1 d. P. Schnyder 6–2 3–6 6–2; R3 lost M. Hingis 7–6 6–3; R5 (with Martinez) d. Hingis/Schnyder 6–0 6–2.

GRAND SLAM CUP RECORD – Played 1

1998: 1r lost V. Williams 6–3 6–2.

SEASON ENDING CHAMPIONSHIPS – Played 10, r/u 1, sf 1, qf 5

(1983–94 Virginia Slims, 1995 Corel, 1996–98 Chase)

1989: sf d. Man. Maleeva 7–5 7–6, lost Navratilova 6–2 6–2. **1990: qf** d. Zvereva 6–2 7–5, lost Seles 5–7 7–6 6–4. **1991: qf** d. Garrison 4–6 6–1 6–0, lost Navratilova 1–6 6–4 6–2. **1992: qf** d. Garrison-Jackson 7–6 6–1, lost Navratilova 6–1 2–6 6–2. **1993: r/u** d. Sukova 7–5 6–2, Novotna 6–7 7–6 6–4, Pierce 6–2 5–7 6–2, lost Graf 6–1 6–4 3–6 6–1. **1994: 1r** lost Halard 6–2 1–6 7–6. **1995: 1r** lost Zvereva 4–6 6–4 6–4. **1996: qf** d. Schultz-McCarthy 6–4 7–6, lost Novotna 6–0 6–3. **1997: qf** d. Seles 3–6 6–4 6–4, lost Novotna 6–3 3–6 6–1. **1998: 1r** lost Spirlea 7–6 6–1.

5 VENUS WILLIAMS (USA)

Born: Lynwood, Cal., 17 June 1980. **Lives:** Palm Beach Gardens, Fla. **Father:** Richard. **Mother:** Oracene. **Sisters:** Isha, Lyndrea, Yelunde (older) and Serena (younger). **Agent:** Keven Davis Esq., Garvey, Schubert and Barer. **Coach:** Her parents, Richard and Oracene; formerly Rick Macci. **Turned pro:** 1994. **Height:** 6ft 1½in (1.86m). **Weight:** 168lb (76kg).

Rankings: 1995: 204; **1996:** 204; **1997:** 22; **1998:** 5. **Highest:** 5 (1998).

1998 Prize Money: $1,712,246. **Career Earnings:** $2,210,894. **Career Titles:** 3.

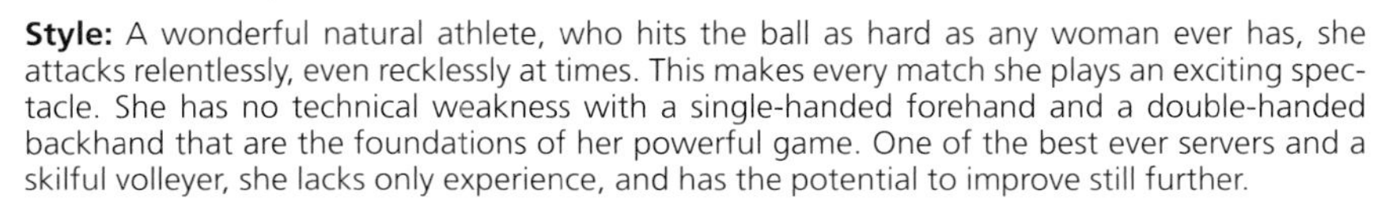

Style: A wonderful natural athlete, who hits the ball as hard as any woman ever has, she attacks relentlessly, even recklessly at times. This makes every match she plays an exciting spectacle. She has no technical weakness with a single-handed forehand and a double-handed backhand that are the foundations of her powerful game. One of the best ever servers and a skilful volleyer, she lacks only experience, and has the potential to improve still further.

CAREER HIGHLIGHTS (year: (titles))
In her 1st year as a pro, her father allowed her to play only 4 tourns to prevent burnout and to concentrate on education, which he considers very important. **1995:** Reached her 1st qf at Oakland (d. Frazier) and joined US Fed Cup squad. **1996:** Upset Wild at Los Angeles. **1997:** She produced an extraordinary performance to reach f US Open, upsetting Huber and Spirlea (saving 2 mps in 3s tb) along the way to become the 1st unseeded women's finalist there since Darlene Hard in 1958. Until then her best performance had been at Indian Wells, where she qualified, upset Majoli and was 4–1 and 6–5 up in 3s qf v Davenport before losing their tb. After US Open, she failed to qualify at Filderstadt, but reached qf Zurich (as a qualifier) the next week and followed with the same stage Moscow. She was voted Most Impressive Newcomer in her 1st full year on the circuit. **1998: (3)** *Oklahoma City, LIPC, GS Cup.* Having vowed to avenge her one-sided defeat by Hingis at US Open at their next meeting, she did just that on her way to f Sydney in Jan. Then at end Feb. she upset Davenport on the way to her 1st tour title at Oklahoma City, where she also won the doubles with her sister, Serena. She followed with the title at LIPC (beating Hingis again in sf), a result which took her into the top 10. However, she was bothered all year with knee problems: it was patella tendinitis of the left knee that kept her out for a month in spring; in summer she was given a diagnosis of chronic patellofemoral syndrome of the right knee; and it was the left knee again that kept her out of Chase Champs. She was back to play US Open and outlasted Schnyder to win the inaugural women's GS Cup, but was unable to play Chase Champs. In other tourns she was r/u Rome (d. Sanchez-Vicario), Stanford (d. Seles) and Zurich (where she won a 2nd doubles title with Serena) and reached sf Indian Wells, Moscow and US Open, plus qf Australian Open (unseeded), French Open and San Diego. Her 125 mph serve to Schett at Wimbledon was the fastest recorded by a woman until her 127 mph serve v Davenport at Zurich. In mixed doubles she won Australian Open and French Open with Gimelstob and was r/u Wimbledon with Bhupathi.

PRINCIPAL 1998 RESULTS – won 3, r/u 4, sf 3 (detailed Grand Slam results follow)
won Oklahoma City (d. Miyagi 6–3 6–2, De Swardt 6–1 6–3, Lubiani 7–6 6–4, Davenport 6–7 6–2 6–3, Kruger 6–3 6–2), **won** LIPC (d. Panova 6–3 6–3, Barabanschikova 6–2 6–1, Grande 6–1 6–4, Farina 6–1 6–2, Hingis 6–2 5–7 6–2, Kournikova 2–6 6–4 6–1), **won** GS Cup; **r/u** Sydney (d. Dragomir 6–4 ret, Hingis 3–6 6–4 7–5, Maleeva 6–2 6–2, Sugiyama 6–1 7–6, lost Sanchez-Vicario 6–1 6–3), **r/u** Rome (d. Basuki 6–2 6–3, Sanchez Lorenzo 6–1 6–4, Fusai 6–1 6–1, S. Williams 6–4 6–2, Sanchez-Vicario 6–3 2–6 7–5, lost Hingis 6–3 2–6 6–3), **r/u** Stanford (d. Morariu 4–6 6–1 6–0, Likhovtseva 6–2 6–4, Seles 6–3 6–4, lost Davenport 6–4 5–7 6–4), **r/u** Zurich (d. Morariu 7–5 6–3, Pierce 6–4 6–1, Tauziat 6–3 6–4, lost Davenport 7–5 6–3); **sf** Indian Wells (d. Farina 6–3 6–1, Van Roost 6–4 6–1, Kruger 6–1 6–3, lost Hingis 6–0 7–6), **sf** Moscow (d. Likhovtseva 6–3 6–1, Studenikova 6–1 6–0, lost Pierce 2–6 6–2 6–0), **sf** US Open. **DOUBLES:** (with S. Williams) **won** Oklahoma City (d. Cristea/Kunce 7–5 6–2), **won** Zurich (d. De Swardt/Tatarkova 5–7 6–1 6–3). **MIXED DOUBLES:** (with Gimelstob) **won Australian Open** (d. Suk/Sukova 6–2 6–1); **won French Open** (d. S. Williams/Lobo 6–4 6–4); (with Bhupathi) **r/u Wimbledon** (lost Mirnyi/S. Williams 6–4 6–4)

CAREER GRAND SLAM RECORD

AUSTRALIAN OPEN – Played 1, qf 1

1998: qf [unseeded] d. Dechaume-Balleret 6–3 6–0, S. Williams 7–6 6–1, Mauresmo 6–1 6–4, Schnyder 6–4 6–1, lost Davenport [2] 1–6 7–5 6–3.

FRENCH OPEN – Played 2, qf 1

1997: 2r d. Sawamatsu 6–2 6–7 7–5, lost Tauziat 5–7 6–3 7–5. **1998: qf** [seed 8] d. Tanasugarn 6–3 6–1, Sugiyama 6–0 6–2, Dechaume-Balleret 6–2 6–1, Nagyova 6–1 6–3, lost Hingis [1] 6–3 6–4

WIMBLEDON – Played 2, qf 1

1997: 1r lost Grzybowska 4–6 6–2 6–4. **1998: qf** [seed 7] d. Nejedly 6–3 6–3, Schett 6–1 6–2, Rubin 6–3 6–4, Ruano-Pascual 6–3 6–1, lost Novotna [3] 7–5 7–6.

US OPEN – Played 2, r/u 1, sf 1

1997: r/u [unseeded] d. Neiland 5–7 6–0 6–1, Leon-Garcia 6–0 6–1, Huber [8] 6–3 6–4, Kruger 6–2 6–3, Testud 7–5 7–5, Spirlea [11] 7–6 4–6 7–6, lost Hingis [1] 6–0 6–4. **1998: sf** [seed 5] d. Wagner 6–1 6–0, Kremer 6–1 6–3, Neiland 5–0 ret, Pierce [12] 6–1 7–6, Sanchez-Vicario [4] 2–6 6–1 6–1, lost Davenport [2] 6–4 6–4.

OLYMPIC RECORD

Has never competed.

CAREER FED CUP RECORD

Has never played.

CAREER GRAND SLAM CUP RECORD – Played 1, won 1

1998: won [unseeded] d. Sanchez-Vicario [3] 6–3 6–2, Tauziat 6–4 6–0, Schnyder 6–3 3–6 6–2.

America's Venus Williams who, with her sister Serena, won a family Grand Slam in mixed doubles, securing the titles in Melbourne and Paris while Serena was successful at Wimbledon and Flushing Meadows. (Stephen Wake)

6 MONICA SELES (USA)

Born: Novi Sad, 2 December 1973. **Lives:** Laurel Oak Estates and Country Club, Sarasota, Fla. **Father:** The late Karolj was cartoonist and TV director. **Mother:** Esther. **Brother:** Zoltan (older), who helps to train her. Discovered at 1985 Orange Bowl by Nick Bollettieri, who moved her family to USA from Yugoslavia in 1986.
Agent: IMG. **Coach:** Gavin Hopper from March–December 1998; formerly her father, Karolj. **Turned pro:** 1989.
Height: 5ft 10in (1.79m). **Weight:** 155lb (70kg).

Rankings: 1988: 86; **1989:** 6; **1990:** 2; **1991:** 1; **1992:** 1; **1993:** 8; **1994:** Not ranked; **1995:** 1 (jointly with Graf); **1996:** 2 (jointly with Sanchez-Vicario); **1997:** 5; **1998:** 6. **Highest:** 1 (March 1991).

1998 Prize Money: $1,003,514. **Career Earnings:** $10,878,024. **Career Titles:** 43.

Style: A naturally competitive left-hander who hits with two hands on both forehand and backhand. Her ability to hit a rising ball with perfect timing allows her to project thunderous drives on both wings that have destroyed all opposition. An improving serve that is now the equal of most women, plus a greater willingness to volley, allied to an acute tactical awareness, make her arguably among the finest match players of all time. Since her return in 1995, she has lost some of her speed of shot and of movement.

Ranking: Her ranking was protected when she returned in 1995, an arrangement set to last until she had played 14 tourns or after 18 months. During that time, she was co-ranked with the player whose average was immediately below hers (calculated by dividing points total by tourns played in past 52 weeks, but a minimum of 6).

CAREER HIGHLIGHTS (year: (titles))
Became a US citizen 16 March 1994. **1983:** At age 9, reached last 16 Sport Goofy singles. **1984:** Won Sport Goofy singles. **1985:** Won Sport Goofy singles and doubles. **1988:** Upset Kelesi at VS Florida in 1st pro match, took Sabatini to 1s tb 1r LIPC and upset Magers and McNeil to reach sf New Orleans. **1989: (1)** *Houston*. Won Houston over Evert and was r/u Dallas and Brighton. Unseeded at French Open, she upset Garrison and Manuela Maleeva before extending Graf to 3s sf. **1990: (9)** *FRENCH OPEN, Berlin, Los Angeles, Oakland, VS Champs, LIPC, San Antonio, Tampa, Italian Open*. Following her acrimonious split in March with Bollettieri, who she considered was spending too much time coaching Agassi, she was coached only by her father. At 16 years 6 months became the youngest French Open women's champion and second-youngest GS champion (after Lottie Dod, who was 15 years 10 months when she won Wimbledon in 1897). She went into the French Open having won 5 consec. tourns without dropping a set, but her unbeaten run of 36 matches was ended by Garrison in qf Wimbledon. She in turn had ended Graf's 66-match unbeaten run at Berlin. Her season finished in triumph when she beat Sabatini in 5s in f VS Champs to finish with 9 titles. She beat Graf twice and Navratilova 3 times and by year's end had displaced Navratilova to finish ranked 2. Won WTA Most Improved Player award. **1991: (10)** *AUSTRALIAN OPEN, FRENCH OPEN, US OPEN, VS Champs, LIPC, Houston, Los Angeles, Tokyo Nicherei, Milan, Philadelphia*. Enjoyed a spectacular year in which she reached f in all 16 tourns she entered. At 17 years 2 months she became the youngest to take the Australian Open, being 4 months younger than Margaret Smith in 1960, and in March she ousted Graf from the top ranking to become the youngest (17 years 3 months) to reach that spot (Tracy Austin had been 1 month older). Although Graf overtook her again briefly on and off during the summer, Seles finished the year firmly fixed at the top, was voted WTA Singles Player of the Year and was the youngest to be named Official World Champion. She pulled out of Wimbledon 72 hours before the start, losing her chance of completing a GS. She first said she had suffered 'a minor accident' but eventually she claimed she had panicked after being given conflicting advice that the shin splints from which she was suffering might keep her out of the game for 6 months or a year. She was fined $6,000 for with-

drawing and $20,000 for subsequently appearing in an exhibition tournament. She also missed Fed Cup, claiming injury, although she played an exhibition tournament at the same time. **1992: (10)** *AUSTRALIAN OPEN, FRENCH OPEN, US OPEN, VS Champs, Essen, Indian Wells, Houston, Barcelona, Tokyo Nicherei, Oakland*. After she had won Australian Open and become the 1st woman since Hilde Sperling in 1937 to win 3 consec French Opens, she seemed on course for a GS. But Graf, who had stretched her to 10–8 fs in Paris, demolished her in Wimbledon f and thereafter she seemed less invincible, although she won her 3rd GS title of the year at US Open and finished the season with ss win over Navratilova in f of VS Champs. She was beaten all year only 5 times – by Capriati at LIPC (the only tourn she entered in which she failed to reach the f), by Sabatini at Italian Open, Graf at Wimbledon, Navratilova at Los Angeles and by Sanchez-Vicario at Montreal. She took a total of 10 titles, including Houston for the loss of only 8 games, and when she won Barcelona at 18 years 4 months, she beat Tracy Austin's record of 18 years 8 months as youngest to achieve 25 singles titles. Controversy was never far away, and in 1992 it was her grunting which was the main subject. She played the Wimbledon final almost silently (refusing to make that an excuse for her defeat) and for the rest of the year made an attempt to control the noise, which players and spectators alike found distasteful and disturbing. She was voted Player of Year for the second straight year and set a new record for prize money won in one season, beating Edberg's record $2,363,575 in 1991. **1993: (2)** *AUSTRALIAN OPEN, VS Chicago*. She suffered a nightmare year, at the end of which there was still some question whether she would return to competitive play. Having taken a 2-month break, she returned to win Australian Open but was then sidelined for 2 months with a viral infection, missing LIPC. She returned to action at Hamburg where, on 30 April, during a changeover after she had recovered from 0–3 down to 4–3 v Magdalena Maleeva, she was stabbed in the back by Gunther Parche, a German who wanted to put her out of action to enable Steffi Graf to return to the No. 1 position. She and the rest of the world were horrified when Parche was given only a two-year suspended sentence in autumn, while Seles was sidelined for more than 2 years as the injury, which required only 2 stitches, was worse than first thought – and the psychological damage was considerable, requiring more than 100 hours of therapy. In the other 2 tourns she played, she won VS Chicago and was r/u Paris Open to Navratilova. **1994:** She did not play at all and dropped off the rankings on 14 Feb., a month before becoming a US citizen. **1995: (1)** *Toronto*. She returned to the public arena in a much-publicised exhibition match v Navratilova at Atlantic City on 29 July, which she won 6–3 6–2. Two inches taller, 10lb heavier and with some new one-handed strokes in her repertoire, she was co-ranked No. 1 with Graf when she returned to the tour, a position it was agreed she should hold for her 1st 6 matches. Despite her extra weight and suffering from tendinitis in her left knee, she was still head and shoulders above anyone else apart from Graf, sweeping to the title at her 1st tourn back at Toronto, where she dropped only 14 games in 5 matches. She then moved as convincingly to f US Open, losing no set until Graf beat her there, and was given a special invitation to play in WTA Champs. However, when her knee and ankle problems flared up again, despite a rest until end Oct., she was forced to withdraw first from Oakland and then from WTA Champs. Voted Comeback Player of the Year and Most Exciting Player. **1996: (5)** *AUSTRALIAN OPEN, Sydney, Eastbourne, Montreal, Tokyo Nicherei*. Having won her 1st 2 tourns of year at Sydney and Australian Open, she suffered only the 2nd defeat since her return when Majoli upset her in qf Tokyo Toray. At Australian Open she had recovered from 2–5 down in 3s sf v Rubin and maintained her record of never having lost a match at the event. However, she suffered tendinitis and a small tear to the lining of the shoulder socket, which may in the long term require surgery and in the short term caused her to withdraw from Indian Wells, LIPC, FC Cup and before sf Madrid. That was her 1st tourn on European red clay since her stabbing on that surface in Hamburg, and although not fully fit, she had wanted to overcome the mental barrier of returning to Europe before French Open. She was determined to play in Paris, regardless of her injury, and was magnificent in beating M. Maleeva, whom she had been playing when stabbed, but was below par (particularly her serve) when losing to Novotna. It ended her run of 25 consec. match wins there since 1989, and was only her 5th defeat on clay. Still receiving 2 hours' treatment a day on her shoulder, she won her 1st title on grass at Eastbourne, but her timing deserted her at Wimbledon and she fell 2r to Studenikova. Novotna inflicted a second defeat in qf Olympics and Graf beat her again in f US Open, but she won Montreal and Tokyo Nicherei and was in the winning USA Fed Cup team that d. ESP 5–0 in f, after making her debut in Japan in July. In Oct. she began a rehabilitation programme for her shoulder in the hope of avoiding surgery, returning at the end of the month at Chicago, where she lost sf to

Capriati. On 4 Nov. she slipped from the top to No. 2, co-ranked with Sanchez-Vicario, and at Oakland suffered the most one-sided defeat of her career at the hands of Hingis. Losing 6–2 6–0, she recorded her 1st set lost to love since Nov. 1990 and only the 4th of her pro career. The year ended in further disappointment when her shoulder injury forced her to retire v Date 1r Chase Champs, and she was left seriously considering surgery. That, however, would necessitate an absence of several months from the tour and another setback in her psychological rehabilitation. Then in Dec., warming up for an exhibition match, she broke a finger on her right hand. **1997: (3)** *Los Angeles, Toronto, Tokyo Nicherei.* Having missed 4 tourns, including Australian Open, she returned in March at LIPC, where she appeared overwhelmed both physically and mentally by Hingis in f, losing in 44 mins. She lost to the same player in 3s tb in f FC Cup, having recovered from 2–5 down in 3s, and withdrew from Amelia Island with bronchitis. She was further distracted by the absence of her father, fighting in US against stomach cancer and unable to be with her for French Open, where she lost sf in 3s to Hingis, and Wimbledon, where she was beaten 3r by Testud. From 21 July, however, she played 7 tourns in 9 weeks, winning her 1st title of the year at Los Angeles in Aug. She followed with Toronto the next week and then Tokyo Nicherei, where she also took the doubles with Sugiyama (the 5th doubles title of her career – each won with a different partner). She was also r/u Madrid and San Diego, and played qf Eastbourne, Stanford, Atlanta, Chicago and Philadelphia, qualifying for Chase Champs by end Sept. At US Open, she held mp in 2s tb v Spirlea, but went on to lose the match. She was encouraged by having played through 4 months without injury, and although she withdrew Moscow in Oct. with a shoulder injury, she was back in action the following week at Chicago, where she was r/u doubles with Davenport. At the start of Chase Champs, where she fell 1r to Sanchez-Vicario, she had slipped to No. 5 in the rankings. **1998: (2)** *Montreal, Tokyo Toyota.* Preferring to be with her father as much as possible, she played only sporadically at start of year, LIPC in March being her 1st tourn in 4 months. For 2 years she had been hampered by lack of practice and her concentration interrupted by thoughts of her dying father, but after his death on 14 May, she returned looking leaner and fully committed. At French Open, putting her grief behind her for a while, she upset Hingis in ss to reach her 1st GS f since 1996. Her 1st title of the year came at Montreal, where she upset Hingis and Sanchez-Vicario to take her 4th straight title there, and she followed with both singles and doubles (with Kournikova) at Tokyo Toyota. In other tourns she was r/u Moscow and reached sf FC Cup, Stanford, San Diego, Los Angeles and Philadelphia, plus qf Wimbledon and US Open. By then she had regained some of the excess weight lost when she returned after the death of her father, and injury was still a threat as she suffered back and shoulder problems during the year, in which she was voted WTA Comeback Player of the Year. At Chase Champs, despite being debilitated by a virus, she d. Kournikova before losing a thrilling qf v Graf. In doubles she played 2 f, winning Tokyo Toyota with Kournikova.

PRINCIPAL 1998 RESULTS – won 2, r/u 2, sf 5 (detailed Grand Slam results follow)
won Montreal (d. Snyder 6–2 6–1, Basuki 6–3 6–3, Huber 6–3 6–4, Sanchez-Vicario 6–3 6–2), **won** Tokyo Toyota (d. Sawamatsu 6–3 3–6 6–3, Halard-Decugis 6–2 6–1, Tanasugarn 6–1 6–4, Sanchez-Vicario 4–6 6–3 6–4); **r/u** French Open, **r/u** Moscow (d. Huber 6–3 6–4, Farina 6–0 6–1, Testud 6–3 7–6, lost Pierce 7–6 6–3); **sf** FC Cup (d. Paulus 6–2 0–1 ret, Zvereva 6–0 6–7 6–2, Schnyder 4–6 6–3 7–6, lost Spirlea 6–4 1–6 7–6), **sf** Stanford (d. Li 2–6 6–2 6–1, Sidot 6–3 6–1, lost V. Williams 6–3 6–4), **sf** San Diego (d. Testud 7–6 7–5, Sugiyama 6–4 6–3, lost Davenport 6–4 2–6 7–5), **sf** Los Angeles (d. Paulus 6–1 6–2, Tauziat 6–4 6–4, lost Davenport 6–4 6–2), **sf** Philadelphia (d. Sugiyama 6–3 7–5, Zvereva 6–0 6–1, lost Davenport 6–3 6–3). **DOUBLES:** (with Kournikova) **won** Tokyo Toyota (d. Fernandez/Sanchez-Vicario 6–4 6–4); (with Zvereva) **r/u** Philadelphia (lost Likhovtseva/Sugiyama 7–5 4–6 6–2).

CAREER GRAND SLAM RECORD
AUSTRALIAN OPEN – Played 4, won 4
1991: won [seed 2] d. Hack 6–0 6–0, Caverzasio 6–1 6–0, Kschwendt 6–3 6–1, Tanvier 6–2 6–1, Huber 6–3 6–1, Fernandez [3] 6–3 0–6 9–7, Novotna [10] 5–7 6–3 6–1. **1992: won** [seed 1] d. Kijimuta 6–2 6–0, Date 6–2 7–5, Basuki 6–1 6–1, Meskhi [13] 6–4 4–6 6–2, Huber [12] 7–5 6–3, Sanchez-Vicario [4] 6–2 6–2, M. J. Fernandez [7] 6–2 6–3. **1993: won** [seed 1] d. Pizzichini 6–1 6–2, Strandlund 6–2 6–0, Fendick 6–1 6–0, Tauziat [13] 6–2 6–0, Halard 6–2 6–7 6–0, Sabatini [3] 6–1 6–2, Graf [2] 4–6 6–3 6–2. **1994–95:** Did not play. **1996: won** [seed 1] d. J. Lee 6–3 6–0, Studenikova 6–1 6–1, Halard-Decugis 7–5 6–0, Sawamatsu 6–1 6–3, Majoli [7] 6–1 6–2, Rubin [13] 6–7 6–1 7–5, Huber [8] 6–4 6–1. **1997–98:** Did not play.
FRENCH OPEN – Played 7, won 3, r/u 1, sf 2, qf 1
1989: sf d. Reis 6–4 6–1, Martin 6–0 6–2, Garrison [4] 6–3 6–2, Faull 6–3 6–2, M. Maleeva [6] 6–3 7–5, lost Graf [1] 6–3 3–6 6–3. **1990: won** [seed 2] d. Piccolini 6–0 6–0, Kelesi 4–6 6–4 6–4, Meskhi 7–6 7–6,

Gildemeister [16] 6–4 6–0, Maleeva-Fragniere [6] 3–6 6–1 7–5, Capriati 6–2 6–2, Graf [1] 7–6 6–4. **1991: won** [seed 1] d. Zrubakova 6–3 6–0, De Swardt 6–0 6–2, Quentrec 6–1 6–2, Cecchini 3–6 6–3 6–0, Martinez [7] 6–0 7–5, Sabatini [3] 6–4 6–1, Sanchez-Vicario [5] 6–3 6–4. **1992: won** [seed 1] d. Mothes 6–1 6–0, Kschwendt 6–2 6–2, McNeil 6–0 6–1, Kijimuta 6–1 3–6 6–4, Capriati [5] 6–2 6–2, Sabatini [3] 6–3 4–6 6–4, Graf [2] 6–2 3–6 10–8. **1993–95:** Did not play. **1996: qf** [seed 1] d. Chenin 6–1 6–1, Sawamatsu 7–6 6–2, Appelmans 6–2 7–5, M. Maleeva [13] 6–1 6–1, lost Novotna [10] 7–6 6–3. **1997: sf** [seed 3] d. Saeki 6–0 6–3, Pitkowski 6–3 7–5, Tauziat 6–0 6–1, Pierce [10] 6–4 7–5, M. J. Fernandez [12] 3–6 6–2 7–5, lost Hingis [1] 6–7 7–5 6–4. **1998: r/u** [seed 8] d. Ellwood 6–0 6–2, Maruska 2–6 6–1 6–0, Schwartz 6–1 7–5, Rubin 6–1 6–4, Novotna [3] 4–6 6–3 6–3, Hingis [1] 6–3 6–2, lost Sanchez-Vicario [4] 7–6 0–6 6–2.

WIMBLEDON – Played 6, r/u 1, qf 2

1989: last 16 [seed 11] d. Schultz 7–6 1–6 6–4, Porwik 6–2 6–4, Sviglerova 6–4 6–3, lost Graf [1] 6–0 6–1. **1990: qf** [seed 3] d. Strandlund 6–2 6–0, Benjamin 6–3 7–5, A. Minter 6–3 6–3, Henricksson 6–1 6–0, lost Garrison [5] 6–3 3–6 6–4. **1991:** Did not play. **1992: r/u** [seed 1] d. Byrne 6–2 6–2, Appelmans 6–3 6–2, Gildemeister 6–4 6–1, G. Fernandez 6–4 6–2, Tauziat [14] 6–1 6–3, Navratilova [4] 6–2 6–7 6–4, lost Graf 6–2 6–1. **1993–95:** Did not play. **1996: 2r** [seed 2] d. Grossman 6–1 6–2, lost Studenikova 7–5 6–7 6–4. **1997: 3r** [seed 2] d. McQuillan 6–0 6–2, Brandi 5–7 6–3 6–3, lost Testud 0–6 6–4 8–6. **1998: qf** [seed 6] d. Sanchez Lorenzo 6–3 6–4, Fusai 6–1 6–1, Basuki 6–2 6–3, Testud 6–2 6–2. lost Zvereva 7–6 6–2.

US OPEN – Played 8, won 2, r/u 2, qf 2

1989: last 16 [seed 12] d. Henricksson 4–6 6–2 6–2, A. Smith 7–5 6–2, Stafford 7–6 6–2, lost Evert [4] 6–0 6–2. **1990: 3r** [seed 3] d. Pampoulova 6–0 6–0, Fairbank-Nideffer 6–2 6–2, lost Ferrando 1–6 6–1 7–6. **1991: won** [seed 2] d. Arendt 6–2 6–0, Zardo 7–5 6–1, Gomer 6–1 6–4, Rajchrtova 6–1 6–1, G. Fernandez 6–2 6–2, Capriati [7] 6–3 3–6 7–6, Navratilova [6] 7–6 6–1. **1992: won** [seed 1] d. Keller 6–1 6–0, Raymond 7–5 6–0, Porwik 6–4 6–0, G. Fernandez 6–1 6–2, Hy 6–1 6–2, M. J. Fernandez [7], Sanchez-Vicario [5] 6–3 6–3. **1993–94:** Did not play. **1995: r/u** [seed 2] d. Dragomir 6–3 6–1, De Lone 6–2 6–1, Kamio 6–1 6–1, Huber [11] 6–1 6–4, Novotna [seed 5] 7–6 6–2, Martinez [4] 6–2 6–2, lost Graf [1] 7–6 0–6 6–3. **1996: r/u** [seed 2] d. Miller 6–0 6–1, Courtois w/o, Randriantefy 6–0 6–2, Testud 7–5 6–0, Coetzer 6–0 6–3, Martinez [4] 6–4 6–3, lost Graf [1] 7–5 6–4. **1997: qf** [seed 2] d. Boogert 6–1 6–2, Snyder 6–2 6–3, Oremans 6–1 6–1, Pierce [9] 1–6 6–2 6–2, lost Spirlea [seed 11] 6–7 7–6 6–3. **1998: qf** [seed 6] d. Labat 7–6 6–2, Kruger 6–2 6–3, A. Miller 6–3 6–3, Po 6–2 4–6 6–3, lost Hingis [1] 6–4 6–4.

OLYMPIC RECORD

1996: (Atlanta) qf [seed 1] d. Chen 6–0 6–4, Hy-Boulais 6–3 6–2, Sabatini 6–3 6–3, lost Novotna [6] 7–5 3–6 8–6).

CAREER FED CUP RECORD

1996: July – *World Group sf USA d. JPN 5–0 in JPN (Carpet).* R2 d. A. Sugiyama 6–2 6–2; R3 d. K. Date 6–0 6–2. **September** – *World Group Final USA d. ESP 5–0 in USA (Carpet).* R1 d. C. Martinez 6–2 6–4; R3 d. A. Sanchez-Vicario 3–6 6–3 6–1. **1998: April** – *World Group qf USA d. NED 5–0 in USA (Clay).* R2 d. M. Oremans 6–1 6–2; R4 d. A. Hopmans 6–1 6–2. **July** – *World Group sf ESP d. USA 3–2 in ESP (Clay).* R2 d. C. Martinez 6–3 3–6 6–1; R3 d. A. Sanchez-Vicario 6–4 6–0.

SEASON ENDING CHAMPIONSHIPS – Played 7, won 3, qf 1

(1983–94 Virginia Slims, 1995 Corel, 1996–97 Chase)

1989: qf lost Navratilova 6–3 5–7 7–5. **1990: won** d. Paulus 6–2 6–2, Sanchez-Vicario 5–7 7–6 6–4, M. J. Fernandez 6–3 6–4, Sabatini 6–4 5–7 3–6 6–4 6–2. **1991: won** d. Halard 6–1 6–0, M. J. Fernandez 6–3 6–2, Sabatini 6–1 6–1, Navratilova 6–4 3–6 7–5 6–0. **1992: won** d. Tauziat 6–1 6–2, Novotna 3–6 6–4 6–1, Sabatini 7–6 6–1, Navratilova 7–5 6–3 6–1. **1993–95:** Did not play. **1996: 1r** lost Date 5–4 ret. **1997: 1r** lost Sanchez-Vicario 3–6 6–4 6–4. **1998: qf** d. Kournikova 6–4 6–3, lost Graf 1–6 6–4 6–4.

7 MARY PIERCE (FRA)

Born: Montreal, Canada, 15 January 1975. **Lives:** Paris and Bradenton, Fla., USA. **Father:** Jim. **Mother:** Yannick, who is French. **Brother:** David (younger).
Agent: IMG. **Coach:** Craig Wildey; formerly her father, then Nick Bollettieri, Sven Groeneveld, Joe Giuliano, Brad Gilbert, Craig Kardon and Michael De Jongh. **Trainer:** Jose Rincon.
Turned pro: March 1989.
Height: 5ft 10in (1.80m). **Weight:** 143lb (65kg).

Rankings: 1989: 236; **1990:** 106; **1991:** 26; **1992:** 13; **1993:** 12; **1994:** 5; **1995:** 5; **1996:** 20; **1997:** 7; **1998:** 7. **Highest:** 3 (February 1995).

1998 Prize Money: $662,237. **Career Earnings:** $3,881,746. **Career Titles:** 11.

Style: An exciting, forceful baseliner with uncompromising attitude whose forehand rivals Graf's for pace. Her two-handed backhand is also powerful, though somewhat erratic. Not a natural volleyer. Has improved her movement and also her awareness of when to take risks.

CAREER HIGHLIGHTS (year: (titles))
Decided to play for France, her mother's country, when the USTA, put off by her father's aggressive manner, were not interested in supporting her. He was banned indefinitely from all her tournaments from French Open 1993 – mainly as a consequence of his disruptive behaviour, but also after bruises on her arms and shoulders, which he had inflicted, were noticed. Free from his dominance, she gained in confidence and was advised until Feb. 1996 by Nick Bollettieri. **1989:** At 14 yrs 2 mths at Hilton Head, she was the youngest to make her pro debut – a record broken the following year by Capriati. Won York on the USTA satellite circuit. **1990:** Reached sf Athens and moved to France, representing that country in Fed Cup. **1991: (1)** *Palermo.* At Palermo she won both singles and doubles for her 1st career title, which took her into the top 50. Upset Fairbank-Nideffer en route to last 16 LIPC and appeared in sf Puerto Rico. **1992: (3)** *Cesena, Palermo, Puerto Rico.* Broke into the top 20 after winning Cesena and followed with Palermo and Puerto Rico, plus sf Essen. Reached last 16 French Open and US Open, but was forced to withdraw from LIPC with leg and back strains. **1993: (1)** *Filderstadt.* She won Filderstadt, was r/u Palermo and reached sf Brighton plus 6 more qf, including Australian Open, where she extended Sabatini to 3s. From May onwards, once her aggressive father was excluded from her affairs, she was noticeably more relaxed in her game. She confirmed this improvement and crowned her year by upsetting Sabatini and Navratilova (her 1st victories over top 10 players) on her way to sf VS Champs, for which she qualified 1st time. **1994:** The highlight of her career came at French Open, where she swept to f with the loss of only 10 games – 4 in her sf v Graf, whom she demolished, having managed to win only one game against the same opponent in 1993 US Open. Her loss of only 6 games to qf was a modern-day record. Playing Under-21 at Eastbourne to get used to grass (which she finds difficult to play on), she lost 1r and then announced her withdrawal from Wimbledon 'for reasons beyond my control', later claiming that she could not face the threat that her father might appear there, brought over by a British tabloid newspaper. Although she won no title, she was r/u Houston, Leipzig, Filderstadt, Philadelphia and reached sf FC Cup (upsetting Sanchez-Vicario) and Montreal. At VS Champs she again made her mark, upsetting Graf before falling to Davenport in sf. **1995: (2)** *AUSTRALIAN OPEN, Tokyo Nicherei.* She began the year in tremendous style at Australian Open when she took her 1st GS title without losing a set. However, things went downhill thereafter as she was restricted by a series of illness and injury problems. She suffered a groin pull in Feb., then a bad reaction to antibiotics for a kidney infection caused her to withdraw 2r Hamburg, so that the French Open was only her 7th tourn of the year. Despite complaining of shoulder and groin injuries after her defeat in last 16 there, she did appear at Wimbledon for 1st time, although Tauziat beat her 2r. She upset Sanchez-Vicario to win Tokyo Nicherei and appeared in f Paris Open and Zurich, as well as sf Italian Open and San Diego, plus 4 more qf. She moved as high as No. 3 behind Sanchez-Vicario in Feb., although she had slipped back to No. 6 by Nov. Qualified for WTA Champs but lost 1r to Huber. **1996:** She seemed to have lost

her way in what turned out to be a disappointing year in which she was affected by injuries. She began the year badly when she became the 1st defending Australian Open champ in the Open era to lose before qf. Her 2r loss saw her fall from the top 10 for 1st time since June 1994, and Nick Bollettieri resigned as her coach in an acrimonious split. She was booed off the court after her defeat at the hands of Rittner 3r French Open and departed without waiting for her opponent after a display of stalling and gamesmanship. Her best performances were at Amelia Island, where she upset Martinez en route to f, and Hamburg, where she upset Hingis to reach sf. Otherwise her only qf appearances were at Tokyo Nicherei and at Wimbledon, where, on her least favourite surface, she performed better than expected. On that occasion, she wore a demure white outfit, in contrast to the low-cut black number that aroused such interest at the French Open. She withdrew from Filderstadt, Zurich and Oakland to rest her right shoulder, which had been troubling her for much of the year. **1997:** Returning after 3 months' absence, she had slipped so far down the rankings that she was unseeded at Australian Open, where she upset Huber and Coetzer on her way to f. Then she withdrew Indian Wells with a right calf strain suffered at Fed Cup and was out for another 5 weeks. On her return, she upset Sanchez-Vicario and Majoli on her way to f Amelia Island and surprised Majoli again to reach the same stage Berlin. She also reached sf San Diego and qf Paris Open, Hamburg and Rosmalen, and played in winning FRA Fed Cup team in Oct., although an elbow injury had kept her out of sf in July. After missing another 3 tourns in autumn with a kidney infection, she was beaten by S. Williams at Chicago on her return and withdrew from Philadelphia to recover and prepare for Chase Champs. She obviously did that to good effect, for in qf she became only the 5th player all year to beat Hingis. In her 1st f there, she seriously challenged Novotna for 1s, but went on to lose in ss. Played 2 doubles f, winning Hamburg with Huber. **1998: (4)** *Paris Open, Amelia Island, Moscow, Luxembourg.* Her 1st title in France came at Paris Open (d. Novotna) and was followed by Amelia Island, where she upset Davenport and also won the doubles with Cacic. She upset V. Williams and Seles back-to-back to take Moscow (again adding the doubles – with Zvereva), and won Luxembourg the following week. Martinez and Hingis were her victims at San Diego, where she was hampered in f by a leg injury, and she also appeared in qf Australian Open, Zurich and Chase Champs. She generally lost French support as her regular home is not in France and she is apparently not committed to Fed Cup, although it was captain Noah who dropped her from the squad after her Amelia Island triumphs, saying he felt that she hadn't played enough in the year and would not have time to adapt to the faster surface.

PRINCIPAL 1998 RESULTS – won 4, r/u 1 (detailed Grand Slam results follow)
won Paris Open (d. Habsudova 6–1 1–6 6–1, Huber 1–6 6–1 6–2, Novotna 6–4 2–6 6–3, Van Roost 6–3 7–5), **won** Amelia Island (d. Cristea 6–1 6–2, Likhovtseva 6–4 6–1, Majoli 6–3 6–2, Davenport 4–6 6–3 6–3, Martinez 6–7 6–0 6–2), **won** Moscow (d. Sugiyama 5–7 6–2 6–4, Appelmans 6–2 6–2, Serna 7–5 6–3, V. Williams 2–6 6–2 6–0, Seles 7–6 6–3), **won** Luxembourg (d. Pitkowski 4–6 6–2 6–3, Sugiyama 6–3 6–2, Likhovtseva 6–1 7–5, Farina 6–0 2–0 ret); **r/u** San Diego (d. Paulus 6–3 7–5, Martinez 6–7 6–2 6–3, V. Williams 2–6 7–6 4–0 ret, Hingis 3–6 7–6 6–2, lost Davenport 6–3 6–1). **DOUBLES:** (with Cacic) **won** Amelia Island (d. Schett/Schnyder 7–6 4–6 7–6), (with Zvereva) **won** Moscow (d. Raymond/Stubbs 6–3 6–4)

CAREER GRAND SLAM RECORD
AUSTRALIAN OPEN – Played 6, won 1, r/u 1, qf 2
1993: qf [seed 10] d. Byrne 6–2 6–2, Date 6–1 6–1, Davenport 6–3 6–0, G. Fernandez 6–0 6–0, lost Sabatini [3] 4–6 7–6 6–0). **1994: last 16** [seed 9] d. Baudone 6–2 6–1, Harvey-Wild 6–7 7–5 6–3, Appelmans 6–3 6–2, lost Sabatini [4] 6–3 6–3. **1995: won** [seed 4] d. Krizan 6–1 6–0, Reinach 6–1 6–2, Randriantefy 6–3 6–3, Huber [10] 6–2 6–4, Zvereva [8] 6–1 6–4, Martinez [2] 6–3 6–1, Sanchez-Vicario 6–3 6–2. **1996: 2r** [seed 4] d. Schwarz 6–3 6–1, lost Likhovtseva 7–6 4–6 7–5. **1997: r/u** [unseeded] d. Likhovtseva 3–6 6–2 6–4, Medvedeva 6–2 6–2, Kochta 6–0 6–2, Huber [5] 6–2 6–3, Appelmans 1–6 6–4 6–4, Coetzer [12] 7–5 6–1, lost Hingis [4] 6–2 6–2. **1998: qf** [seed 5] d. Li 6–0 6–0, Torrens-Valero 6–1 6–2, Barabanschikova 7–5 6–3, Nagyova 6–0 6–0, lost Hingis [1] 6–2 6–3.
FRENCH OPEN – Played 9, r/u 1
1990: 2r d. Fulco 6–0 6–1, lost M. J. Fernandez [7] 6–4 6–4. **1991: 3r** d. Dahlman 7–6 6–0, Martinek 6–3 6–0, lost Sabatini [3] 6–2 6–1. **1992: last 16** [seed 13] d. Rajchrtova 6–1 6–1, Savchenko Neiland 6–2 6–3, Strnadova 7–6 6–4, lost Capriati [5] 6–4 6–3. **1993: last 16** [seed 12] d. Mothes 6–0 6–0, McQuillan 6–4 6–0, Po 6–7 6–3 6–3, lost Capriati [6] 6–4 7–6. **1994: r/u** [seed 12] d. Provis 6–1 6–0, Bentivoglio 6–0 6–1, McNeil 6–0 6–0, Coetzer 6–1 6–1, Ritter 6–0 6–2, Graf [1] 6–2 6–2, lost Sanchez-Vicario [2] 6–4 6–4). **1995: last 16** [seed 3] d. Bradtke 6–1 6–3, Singer 7–5 6–0, Labat 6–2 6–2, lost Majoli [12] 6–2 6–3. **1996: 3r** [seed 12] d. Schnell 7–5 6–2, Randriantefy 6–3 2–6 6–2, lost Rittner 6–4 6–2. **1997: last 16** [seed 10] d. Panova 6–2 4–6 6–4, Hy-Boulais 6–1 6–3, Testud 6–1 6–3, lost Seles [3] 6–4 7–5. **1998: 2r** [seed 11] d. Appelmans 6–2 6–3, lost Serna 7–5 6–2.

WIMBLEDON – Played 4, qf 1

1995: 2r [seed 5] d. Dopfer 6–1 6–2, lost Tauziat 6–4 3–6 6–1. **1996: qf** [seed 13] d. Schnyder 6–3 6–2, Taylor 6–4 6–2, Medvedeva 6–4 6–1, Likhovtseva 6–2 6–3, lost Date [12] 3–6 6–3 6–1. **1997: last 16** [seed 9] d. Van Roost 6–3 6–4, Ruano-Pascual 6–0 2–6 6–3, Serna 6–4 6–3, lost Sanchez-Vicario [8] 6–1 6–3. **1998: 1r** [seed 11] lost Tatarkova 7–6 6–3.

US OPEN – Played 7, qf 1

1991: 3r d. Garrone 4–6 6–0 7–6, McNeil 6–3 3–6 7–6, lost Maleeva-Fragniere [10] 4–6 5–1 ret. **1992: last 16** [seed 16] d. Vento 6–2 6–2, L. Ferrando 7–5 6–4, R. White 6–2 6–1, lost M. J. Fernandez [7] 6–0 6–4. **1993: last 16** [seed 13] d. Baudone 6–0 6–7 7–6, Arendt 6–2 6–4, Schultz 7–5 7–6, lost Graf [1] 6–1 6–0. **1994: qf** [seed 4] d. Temesvari 6–3 6–2, Studenikova 6–3 2–6 6–4, Wiesner 6–2 6–4, Majoli 6–1 6–2, lost Novotna [7] 6–4 6–0. **1995: 3r** [seed 6] d. De Swardt 6–4 6–1, Jecmenica 6–3 6–0, lost Frazier 6–3 7–6. **1996:** Did not play. **1997: last 16** [seed 9] d. G. Fernandez 6–1 6–2, Farina 6–2 3–0 ret, Zvereva 7–6 6–1, lost Seles [2] 1–6 6–2 6–2. **1998: last 16** [seed 12] d. Babel 6–1 4–6 6–2, Black 6–1 6–1, Golarsa 6–1 6–0, lost V. Williams [5] 6–1 7–6.

OLYMPIC RECORD

1996: (Atlanta) 2r [seed 12] d. Barabanschikova 6–3 7–6, lost Gorrochategui 6–4 1–6 7–5.

CAREER FED CUP RECORD

1990 (in USA, Hard): *1r FRA d. TPE 3–0.* R3 (with I. Demongeot) d. S. Lai/Y. Lin 6–2 6–2. *2r FRA d. NZL 3–0.* R3 (with Demongeot) d. B. Cordwell/J. Richardson 6–3 6–4. *Qf ESP d. FRA 3–0.* R3 (with Demongeot) lost C. Martinez/A. Sanchez-Vicario 6–4 6–4. **1991 (in GBR, Hard):** *1r POL d. FRA 2–1.* R1 d. M. Mroz 6–4 6–2; R3 (with N. Tauziat) lost Mroz/K. Teodorowicz 6–4 6–4. *Play-off FRA d. YUG 2–0.* R1 d. L. Pavlov 6–0 6–1. **1992 (in GER, Clay):** *1r FRA d. CHN 2–1.* R1 d. L. Chen 6–2 6–2. *2r FRA d. RUS 3–0.* R1 d. E. Makarova 6–1 6–2. *Qf USA d. FRA 2–1.* R1 lost G. Fernandez 6–1 6–4. **1994 (in GER, Clay):** *1r FRA d. KOR 3–0.* R2 d. S. Park 6–3 6–1. *2r FRA d. ITA 3–0.* R2 d. S. Cecchini 6–0 6–3. *Qf FRA d. BUL 2–1.* R2 lost Mag. Maleeva 6–7 6–4 6–4. *Sf USA d. FRA 3–0.* R2 lost Davenport 5–7 6–2 6–2. **1995: April** – *World Group qf FRA d. RSA 3–2 in FRA (Clay).* R2 d. J. Kruger 6–4 6–3; R3 lost A. Coetzer 6–4 6–3. **July** – *World Group sf USA d. FRA 3–2 in USA (Carpet).* R1 d. M. J. Fernandez 7–6 6–3; R3 lost L. Davenport 6–3 4–6 6–0. **1996: July** – *World Group sf ESP d. FRA 3–2 in FRA (Carpet).* R2 d. A. Sanchez-Vicario 6–3 6–4; R3 lost C. Martinez 7–5 2–1. **1997: March** – *World Group qf FRA d. JPN 4–1 in JPN (Hard).* R1 d. N. Sawamatsu 6–0 7–6; R3 lost A. Sugiyama 7–5 6–7 6–4. **October** – *World Group Final FRA d. NED 4–1 in NED (Carpet).* R2 d. M. Oremans 6–4 6–1; R3 lost B. Schultz-McCarthy 4–6 6–3 6–4.

SEASON ENDING CHAMPIONSHIPS – Played 5, r/u 1, sf 2, qf 1

(1983–94 Virginia Slims, 1995 Corel, 1996–98 Chase)

1993: sf d. Sabatini 7–6 6–3, Navratilova 6–1 3–6 6–4, lost Sanchez-Vicario 6–2 5–7 6–3. **1994: sf** d. Coetzer 5–7 6–3 6–3, Graf 6–4 6–4, lost Davenport 6–3 6–2. **1995: 1r** lost Huber 6–2 6–3. **1996:** Did not play. **1997: r/u** d. Appelmans 6–3 6–4, Hingis 6–3 2–6 7–5, Tauziat 6–2 5–7 6–4, lost Novotna 7–6 6–2 6–3. **1998: qf** d. Coetzer 6–1 6–0, lost Hingis 7–6 6–4.

8 CONCHITA MARTINEZ (ESP)

Born: Monzon, 16 April 1972. **Lives:** Barcelona and San Diego, Cal. **Father:** Cecilio. **Mother:** Conchita. **Brothers:** Fernando and Roberto (both older). **Agent:** Advantage International; Elvira Vazquez. **Coach:** Gabriel Urpi from July 1997; formerly Eric Van Harpen and Carlos Kirmayr. **Trainer:** Miguel Mir. **Turned pro:** 1988.
Height: 5ft 7in (1.70m). **Weight:** 132lb (59kg).

Rankings: 1988: 40; **1989:** 7; **1990:** 11; **1991:** 9; **1992:** 8; **1993:** 4; **1994:** 3; **1995:** 2; **1996:** 5; **1997:** 12; **1998:** 8 singles, 16 doubles. **Highest:** 2 (30 October 1995).

1998 Prize Money: $859,417.
Career Earnings: $7,737,227. **Career Titles:** 30.

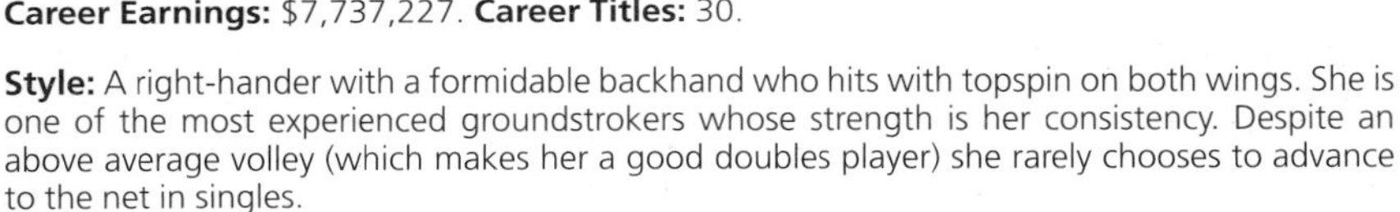

Style: A right-hander with a formidable backhand who hits with topspin on both wings. She is one of the most experienced groundstrokers whose strength is her consistency. Despite an above average volley (which makes her a good doubles player) she rarely chooses to advance to the net in singles.

CAREER HIGHLIGHTS (year: (titles))
1988: (1) *Sofia.* Upset McNeil en route to last 16 French Open after qualifying and won 1st pro title in both singles and doubles (with Paulus) at Sofia. Won Nat Champs over Sanchez and played Fed Cup. **1989: (3)** *Wellington, Tampa, VS Arizona.* Beat Sabatini on her way to the title at VS Arizona; r/u Geneva and Bayonne; qf French Open and qualified for 1st VS Champs. Voted WTA Most Impressive Newcomer. **1990: (3)** *Clarins, Scottsdale, Indianapolis.* Reached sf LIPC (d. Sabatini again), Tampa and Leipzig and appeared in qf French Open again. **1991: (3)** *Barcelona, Kitzbuhel, Clarins.* She again won 3 titles, upset Navratilova on her way to sf Italian Open, and reached the same stage Geneva, San Diego and Milan. Played in the successful Spanish Fed Cup team and qualified for VS Champs, where she fell 1r to Graf. In GS reached qf French Open again and US Open. **1992: (1)** *Kitzbuhel.* Although Kitzbuhel was her only title, she was r/u Indian Wells, VS Florida, FC Cup and San Diego and appeared in sf Amelia Island and Barcelona. She extended Sabatini to 3s in her 4th French Open qf and reached the same stage at Olympics. Qualified for VS Champs, where she beat K. Maleeva but lost qf to McNeil. In doubles with Sanchez-Vicario she was r/u French Open and Olympic Games (silver medal) and won Barcelona, reaching 4 more f with various partners. **1993: (5)** *Brisbane, VS Houston, Italian Open, Stratton Mountain, VS Philadelphia.* When she won Italian Open, with defeats of Navratilova and Sabatini, she became the 1st Spanish woman to win the title since 1930. She also won Brisbane, VS Houston (d. Sabatini), Stratton Mountain and VS Philadelphia (ending Graf's 9-match winning streak against her), was r/u Linz, Barcelona and Essen and reached 4 more sf. Qualified for VS Champs, where she fell qf to Huber and played in winning Spanish Fed Cup team. In doubles she won 2 titles from 4 f with 3 different partners. **1994: (4)** *WIMBLEDON, FC Cup, Italian Open, Stratton Mountain.* The highlight of an excellent year came when she won her first GS title at Wimbledon, ending Navratilova's dream of a 10th title in a thrilling f, where the Spaniard overcame a leg injury to play superb tennis. She was the 1st Spaniard to reach Wimbledon f since De Alvarez lost to Wills-Moody in 1928. She won 3 more titles and reached sf French Open, VS Houston and San Diego, plus qf Australian Open and same stage at 6 other tourns. One of these was Brighton, where she was accused of throwing the match v Neiland, the day before she was due to attend her coach's wedding in Switzerland. Played on the victorious Spanish Fed Cup team for the third time, and qualified for VS Champs, where she lost qf to Date. **1995: (6)** *FC Cup, Amelia Island, Hamburg, Italian Open, San Diego, Manhattan Beach.* After splitting with Van Harpen, who left 'for family reasons', she was coached by Carlos Kirmayr from March 1995, whereupon her fortunes changed and she won FC Cup, Amelia Island, Hamburg and Italian Open (d. Pierce and Sanchez-Vicario) back-to-back, following with San Diego and Manhattan Beach. She was also r/u Delray Beach and reached sf of all 4 GS tourns. She had slipped down the rankings behind Pierce, but after beating her again at San Diego, she regained the No. 3 position and at end Oct. overtook Sanchez-Vicario to take 2nd

place (behind Graf and Seles jointly). Qualified for WTA Champs in both singles and doubles (with Tarabini), but was restricted by a neck injury, losing qf singles to Schultz-McCarthy and 1r doubles to Novotna/Sanchez-Vicario. Contributed two singles wins as Spain d. USA 3–2 in f Fed Cup. **1996: (2)** *Italian Open, Moscow.* She became the 1st to win 4 consec. Italian Open titles, following in autumn with Moscow, and was r/u Indian Wells and Hamburg, as well as reaching sf French Open, US Open, Tokyo Toray, FC Cup and San Diego. Her ranking fluctuated for much of the year between 2nd and 3rd spot: on 15 April she slipped to No. 3 behind Sanchez-Vicario again, returned to No. 2 for 1 week on 29 April, but dropped back again after letting slip a 4–1 lead in 2s to lose f Hamburg to her countrywoman. She returned briefly to 2nd spot in Aug., before settling back at No. 3 then dropping to No. 5 in Nov. She finished the year on a sour note, losing to Majoli in a 2r encounter in which she received a warning for racket abuse and a point penalty for a visible obscenity. In doubles, she took an Olympic bronze medal with Sanchez-Vicario and won San Diego with G. Fernandez. **1997:** She struggled to hold on to her top 10 ranking, slipping in and out of the elite before finishing the season just outside after another disappointing performance at Chase Champs, where Novotna beat her 1r. A highlight was at Stanford, where she was r/u, upsetting Seles (1st time in 12 meetings) and Coetzer. She reached no other f, but appeared in sf FC Cup, Toronto and Moscow, as well as qf Tokyo Pan Pacific, Oklahoma City, Amelia Island, Hamburg, San Diego and Tokyo Nicherei. She also qualified for Chase Champs in doubles with Tarabini, despite having reached no f all year. **1998: (2)** *Berlin, Warsaw.* Looking fitter and more enthusiastic than for some time, she began the year on a high note with r/u slot at Australian Open, upsetting Davenport on the way and returning to the top 10. She followed in May with her 1st title for 18 months at Berlin, adding Warsaw in July. She was also r/u Amelia Island, reached qf Indian Wells, Montreal and Moscow, and played in winning ESP Fed Cup team. When she d. Perfetti 2r Rome, she became 16th woman in pro tennis to win 500 singles matches, but the later part of the year was disappointing as she lost 1r GS Cup to Hingis and fell at the same stage to Van Roost at Chase Champs. In doubles she won FC Cup with Tarabini, with whom she qualified again for Chase Champs, although they lost 1r to Raymond/Stubbs.

PRINCIPAL 1998 RESULTS – won 2, r/u 2 (detailed Grand Slam results follow)
won Berlin (d. Serna 6–2 6–2, Testud 4–6 7–5 6–2, Sugiyama 6–3 6–3, Kournikova 6–0 6–1, Mauresmo 6–4 6–4), **won** Warsaw (d. Hrdlickova 6–1 4–6 7–5, Habsudova 6–2 6–4, Nagyova 6–2 4–6 6–2, Farina 6–0 6–3); **r/u** Australian Open, **r/u** Amelia Island (d. A. Miller 6–4 6–3, Sanchez Lorenzo 6–3 6–1, Raymond 6–4 7–5, Coetzer 6–4 6–0, lost Pierce 4–6 6–3 6–3). **DOUBLES:** (with Tarabini) **won** FC Cup (d. Raymond/Stubbs 3–6 6–4 6–4).

CAREER GRAND SLAM RECORD
AUSTRALIAN OPEN – Played 8, r/u 1, sf 1, qf 2
1989: 2r d. Sviglerova 6–0 6–0, lost Sabatini [3] 3–6 6–1 6–2. **1992 last 16** [seed 8] d. Stafford 6–3 6–1, Rehe 6–1 6–2, R. White 7–5 6–0, lost Maleeva-Fragniere [9] 6–4 2–6 6–2. **1993: last 16** [seed 6] d. Rottier 2–6 6–4 6–1, Javer 7–5 6–1, Oremans 6–3 4–6 6–4, lost Halard 6–4 6–3. **1994: qf** [seed 3] d. Zvereva 5–7 6–4 6–3, Fendick 6–7 6–1 6–4, Frazier 6–3 6–0, Rubin 7–6 6–3, lost Date [10] 6–2 4–6 6–3. **1995: sf** [seed 2] d. Rittner 6–3 6–2, Martinek 6–1 6–3, Boogert 6–3 2–6 6–3, Spirlea 6–2 6–7 6–2, Davenport [6] 6–3 4–6 6–3, lost Pierce [4] 6–3 6–1. **1996: qf** [seed 2] d. Wood 6–4 6–1, Labat 6–2 6–4, Kandarr 6–3 6–0, Davenport [10] lost Huber [8] 4–6 6–2 6–1. **1997: last 16** [seed 3] d. Oremans 6–0 6–2, Gersi 6–2 7–6, Carlsson 6–0 6–1, lost Appelmans [16] 2–6 7–5 6–1. **1998: r/u** [seed 8] d. Kloesel 6–2 6–2, Oremans 7–5 6–2, Sidot 3–6 6–0 6–3, Schett 6–3 6–3, Testud [9] 6–3 6–2, Davenport [2] 4–6 6–3 6–3, lost Hingis [1] 6–3 6–3.
FRENCH OPEN – Played 11, sf 3, qf 5
1988: last 16 d. Dechaume 6–0 6–2, Scheuer Larsen 6–2 6–0, McNeil [9] 1–6 6–3 6–1, lost Fulco 6–2 6–4. **1989: qf** [seed 8] d. Herr 6–3 6–2, Pospisilova 6–0 6–4, Amiach 6–3 6–3, K. Maleeva [9] 6–0 6–1, lost Graf [1] 6–0 6–4. **1990: qf** [seed 9] d. Thompson 7–5 6–1, Etchemendy 7–6 6–3, Zrubakova 6–1 6–3, Probst 6–3 6–3, lost Graf [1] 6–1 6–3. **1991: qf** [seed 7] d. Wiesner 6–4 6–3, Rehe 6–1 7–6, Cunningham, 6–1 6–4, Capriati [10] 6–3 6–3, lost Seles [1] 6–0 7–5. **1992: qf** [seed 7] d. Gildemeister 6–2 7–6, Martinek 6–2 6–0, Grossman 6–2 6–2, Meskhi [15] 6–4 7–5, lost Sabatini [3] 3–6 6–3 6–2. **1993: qf** [seed 4] d. Ghirardi 7–5 3–6 6–4, Helgeson 7–5 6–2, Baudone 6–0 7–5, Wiesner 6–3 6–3, lost Huber [8] 6–7 6–4 6–4. **1994: sf** [seed 3] d. Neiland 6–2 6–3, Helgeson 6–2 6–3, Schultz 7–5 6–3, Dechaume-Balleret 6–1 6–2, Hack [16] 2–6 6–0 6–2, lost Sanchez-Vicario [2] 6–3 6–1). **1995: sf** [seed 4] d. Hack 6–0 6–0, Oremans 6–2 6–3, Halard 6–1 6–2, Serra-Zanetti 6–0 6–1, Ruano-Pascual 2–6 6–0 6–3, lost Graf [2] 7–5 6–3. **1996: sf** [seed 3] d. Callens 6–1 6–1, Zrubakova 6–3 7–5, Grossman 6–2 6–1, Coetzer 6–2 6–3, Davenport [9] 6–1 6–3, lost Graf [1] 6–3 6–1). **1997: last 16** [seed 7] d. Loic 4–6 6–2 6–3, Rubin 6–3 6–0, Dhenin 6–2 6–1, lost Coetzer [11] 6–7 6–4 6–3. **1998: last 16** [seed 7] d. Lamarre 6–1 6–1, Grande 6–1 6–2, Ruano-Pascual 6–1 6–0, lost Majoli [10] 7–6 6–7 6–3.

WIMBLEDON – Played 7, won 1, sf 2

1992: 2r [seed 8] d. Daniels 6–1 6–0, lost Zvereva 6–3 5–7 6–4. **1993: sf** [seed 6] d. Helgeson 7–5 6–3, Wiesner 6–1 4–6 6–1, Paradis-Mangon 7–5 6–0, Basuki 3–6 6–2 6–2, Sukova [15] 6–1 6–4, lost Graf [1] 7–6 6–3. **1994: won** [seed 3] d. Simpson-Alter 6–1 6–3, Miyagi 6–1 7–6, Tauziat 6–1 6–3, Radford 3–6 6–3 6–4, Davenport [9] 6–2 6–7 6–3, McNeil 3–6 6–2 10–8, Navratilova [4] 6–4 3–6 6–3. **1995: sf** [seed 4] d. Carlsson 6–1 6–1, Kandarr 6–4 6–3, Stafford 6–1 6–1, Kamstra 6–2 6–3, Sabatini [8] 7–5 7–6, lost Sanchez-Vicario [2] 6–3 6–7 6–1. **1996: last 16** [seed 3] d. Farina 6–0 6–0, Raymond 7–5 7–5, McNeil 7–5 7–6, lost Date [12] 6–7 7–6 6–3. **1997: 3r** [seed 10] d. Habsudova 6–1 6–2, Yoshida 6–0 6–0, lost Sukova 6–4 6–2. **1998: 3r** [seed 8] d. Farina 6–1 6–0, Boogert 7–5 7–5, lost Smith 3–6 6–3 7–5.

US OPEN – Played 11, sf 2, qf 1

1988: 1r lost Evert [3] 6–4 6–1. **1989: last 16** [seed 15] d. Birch 6–3 6–2, Amiach 6–3 6–4, Hanika 7–5 6–1, lost Sabatini [3] 6–1 6–1. **1990: 3r** [seed 10] d. Werdel 2–6 7–5 6–2, Bartos 6–4 4–6–6–4, lost Tauziat 6–2 6–1. **1991: qf** [seed 8] d. Dahlman 6–1 6–1, Basuki 6–3 6–4, Fendick 7–5 6–3, Garrison, [12] 6–4 6–4, lost Graf [1] 6–1 6–3. **1992: 1r** [seed 8] lost Grossman 6–3 2–6 6–4. **1993: last 16** [seed 4] d. Testud 6–2 6–3, Frazier 6–1 6–0, Muns-Jagerman 6–3 6–1, lost Maleeva-Fragniere [11] 1–6 6–0 6–2. **1994: 3r** [seed 3] d. Martinek 6–1 6–0, Arendt 6–3 6–3, lost Helgeson 3–6 6–4 6–1. **1995: sf** [seed 4] d. Rinaldi-Stunkel 6–2 6–2, Po 6–1 6–4, Sawamatsu 6–1 6–2, Garrison-Jackson 7–6 7–5, Schultz-McCarthy [16] 3–6 7–6 6–2, lost Seles [2] 6–2 6–2. **1996: sf** [seed 4] d. Dragomir 6–2 6–0, Tauziat 6–1 6–3, Sukova 6–4 6–3, Carlsson 6–2 6–1, Wild 7–6 6–0, lost Seles [2] 6–4 6–3. **1997: 3r** [seed 7] d. Capriati 6–1 6–2, Smith 6–1 6–0, lost McQuillan 6–2 7–5. **1998: last 16** [seed 7] d. Oremans 6–1 6–2, Trail 7–6 6–1, Raymond 6–3 3–6 6–2, lost Coetzer [13] 6–4 4–6 6–2.

OLYMPIC RECORD

1992: (Barcelona) qf [seed 5] d. Wiesner 4–6 6–1 6–2, Cecchini 6–4 6–3, Coetzer 6–4 6–3, lost Sanchez-Vicario [2] 6–4 6–4. **1996: (Atlanta) qf** [seed 2] d. Schnyder 6–1 6–2, Zrubakova 6–1 6–4, Zvereva 6–2 7–5, lost M. J. Fernandez [7] 3–6 6–2 6–3. **DOUBLES:** (with Sanchez-Vicario) **1992: (Barcelona) r/u silver medal** d. McQuillan/ Provis 6–3 6–3, lost G./M. J. Fernandez 7–5 2–6 6–2. **1996: (Atlanta) sf bronze medal** lost Novotna/Sukova; bronze medal play-off d. Bollegraf/Schultz-McCarthy 6–1 6–3.

CAREER FEDERATION CUP RECORD

1988 (in AUS, Hard): *1r ESP d. NED 3–0.* R1 d. M. Bollegraf 6–2 6–4; R3 (with A. Sanchez-Vicario) d. Bollegraf/C. Vis 5–7 6–4 6–4. *2r ESP d. INA 3–0.* R1 d. W. Walalangi 6–0 6–1; R3 (with Sanchez-Vicario) d. S. Anggarkusuma/N. Basuki 6–0 5–7 6–2. *Qf URS d. ESP 2–1.* R1 lost L. Savchenko 7–6 6–2; R3 (with Sanchez-Vicario) lost Savchenko/N. Zvereva 4–6 6–4 6–4. **1989 (in JPN, Hard):** *1r ESP d. FRA 2–0.* d. I. Demongeot 6–7 7–6 6–4. *2r ESP d. NED 2–0.* R1 d. N. Jagerman 6–4 7–5. *Qf ESP d. URS 2–1.* R1 d. L. Savchenko 6–1 6–1; R3 (with A. Sanchez-Vicario) lost Savchenko/N. Zvereva 6–4 2–6 6–1. *Sf ESP d. AUS 2–0.* R1 d. E. Smylie 6–3 6–2. *Final USA d. ESP 3–0.* R1 lost C. Evert 6–3 6–2; R3 (with Sanchez-Vicario) lost Z. Garrison/P. Shriver (USA) 7–5 6–1. **1990 (in USA, Hard):** *1r ESP d. CAN 2–1.* R1 d. J. Hetherington 6–1 6–4; R3 (with P. Perez) lost J. Hetherington/R. Simpson 7–5 2–6 6–2. *2r ESP d. ISR 3–0.* R1 (d. I. Berger 6–3 6–2; (with A. Sanchez-Vicario) d. Berger/L. Zaltz 6–3 6–4. *Qf ESP d. FRA 3–0.* R1 d. J. Halard 6–0 6–3; R3 (with Sanchez-Vicario) d. I. Demongeot/M. Pierce 6–4 6–4. *Sf ESP d. URS 2–1.* R1 d. L. Meskhi 6–3 7–5; R3 (with Perez) lost L. Savchenko/N. Zvereva 6–2 6–3. **1991 (in GBR, Hard):** *1r ESP d. BEL 2–0.* 1R d. D. Monami 6–3 6–1. *2r ESP d. AUS 3–0.* R1 d. N. Provis 6–0 2–6 7–5; R3 (with A. Sanchez-Vicario) d. K. Godridge/E. Smylie 6–3 6–4. *Qf ESP d. INA 2–0.* R1 d. S. Wibowo 6–2 6–0. *Sf ESP d. GER 3–0.* R1 d. B. Rittner 6–4 6–1; R3 (with Sanchez-Vicario) d. Rittner/A. Huber 6–1 6–1. *Final ESP d. USA 2–1.* R1 lost J. Capriati 4–6 7–6 6–1; R3 (with Sanchez-Vicario) d. Z. Garrison/G. Fernandez 3–6 6–1 6–1. **1992 (in GER, Clay):** *1r ESP d. BEL 2–1.* R1 d. D. Monami 6–1 6–4. *2r ESP d. CAN 2–1.* R1 lost H. Kelesi 7–6 6–2; R3 (with A. Sanchez-Vicario) d. J. Hetherington/P. Hy 6–4 6–0. *Qf ESP d. ARG 2–1.* R1 d. F. Labat 6–0 6–1. *Sf ESP d. AUS 3–0.* R1 d. R. McQuillan 6–1 6–4. *Final GER d. ESP 2–1.* R1 lost A. Huber 6–3 6–7 6–1; R3 (with Sanchez-Vicario) d. Huber/B. Rittner 6–1 6–2. **1993 (in GER, Clay):** *1r ESP d. GBR 3–0.* R1 d. J. Durie 6–2 6–1; (with A. Sanchez-Vicario) d. Durie/C. Wood 6–1 4–6 6–1). *2r ESP d. INA 3–0.* R1 d. R. Tedjakusuma 6–1 6–1. *Qf ESP d. NED 3–0.* R1 d. S. Rottier 7–6 6–3. *Sf ESP d. FRA 2–1.* R1 d. J. Halard 6–1 3–6 6–3. *Final ESP d. AUS 3–0.* R1 d. M. Jaggard-Lai 6–0 6–2; R3 (with Sanchez-Vicario) d. E. Smylie/R. Stubbs 3–6 6–1 6–3). **1994 (in GER, Clay):** *1r ESP d. CHI 3–0.* R1 d. M. Quezada 6–1 6–0; R3 (with A. Sanchez-Vicario) d. P. Cabezas/B. Castro 6–0 6–1. *2r ESP d. ARG 3–0.* R1 d. P. Tarabini 6–3 6–7 6–2). *Qf ESP d. JPN 3–0.* R1 d. N. Sawamatsu 6–3 6–4. *Sf ESP d. GER 2–1.* R1 lost S. Hack 2–6 7–5 6–4; R3 (with Sanchez-Vicario) d. B. Rittner/C. Singer 7–5 6–1. *Final ESP d. USA 3–0.* R1 d. M. J. Fernandez 6–2 6–2; R3 (with Sanchez-Vicario) d. G./M. J. Fernandez 6–3 6–4. **1995: April –** *World Group qf ESP d. BUL 3–2 in BUL (Carpet).* R2 d. M. Maleeva 6–2 6–4; R4 d. K. Maleeva 6–2 6–1. **July –** *World Group sf ESP d. GER 3–2 in ESP (Clay).* R1 d. A Huber 6–2 2–6 6–0; R4 d. S. Hack 6–0 6–0. **November –** *World Group Final ESP d. USA 3–2 in ESP (Clay).* R1 d. C. Rubin 7–5 7–6; R3 d. M. J. Fernandez 6–3 6–4. **1996: April –** *World Group qf ESP d. RSA 3–2 in ESP (Clay).* R2 d. A. Coetzer 7–5 6–3; R4 d. M. De Swardt 6–2 6–3. **July –** *World Group sf ESP d. FRA 3–2 in FRA (Carpet).* R1 d. J. Halard-Decugis 1–6 6–4 6–2; R3 d. M. Pierce 7–5 6–1; R5 (with A. Sanchez-Vicario) d. Halard-Decugis/N. Tauziat 6–4 6–1). **September –** *World Group Final USA d. ESP 5–0 in USA (Carpet).* R1 lost M. Seles 6–2 6–4. **1998: April –** *World Group qf ESP d. GER 3–2 in GER (Carpet).* R2 lost J. Kandarr 6–1 1–6 7–5; R3 lost A. Glass 3–6 6–3 6–2; R5 (with M. Serna) d. Glass/W.

Probst 6–4 7–6). **July** – *World Group sf ESP d. USA 3–2 in ESP (Clay).* R2 lost M. Seles 6–3 3–6 6–1; R4 d. L. Raymond 7–6 6–4; R5 (with A. Sanchez-Vicario) d. M. J. Fernandez/Raymond 6–4 6–7 11–9. **September** – *World Group Final ESP d. SUI 3–2 in SUI (Hard).* R2 lost M. Hingis 6–4 6–4; R4 d. P. Schnyder 6–3 2–6 9–7; R5 (with Sanchez-Vicario) d. Hingis/Schnyder 6–0 6–2.

GRAND SLAM CUP RECORD – Played 1

1998: 1r lost Hingis [1] 6–2 7–5.

SEASON ENDING CHAMPIONSHIPS – Played 9, qf 4

(1983–94 Virginia Slims, 1995 Corel, 1996-98 Chase)
1990: 1r lost Garrison 6–3 6–0. **1991: 1r** lost Graf 6–0 6–3. **1992: qf** d. K. Maleeva 6–4 6–3, lost McNeil 3–6 6–3 6–2. **1993: qf** d. Maleeva-Fragniere 7–5 6–2, lost Huber 6–3 6–3. **1994: qf** d. Zvereva 2–6 6–2 6–4, lost Date 2–6 6–4 7–6. **1995: qf** d. Majoli 1–6 7–5 6–0, lost Schultz-McCarthy 7–5 6–2. **1996: 2r** d. Wiesner 6–1 3–6 6–4, lost Majoli 7–6 7–6. **1997: 1r** lost Novotna 6–4 6–4. **1998: 1r** lost Van Roost 7–6 6–2.

9 STEFFI GRAF (GER)

Born: Neckarau, 14 June 1969. **Lives:** Bruhl and New York.
Father: Peter. **Mother:** Heidi. **Brother.** Michael (younger).
Boyfriend: Racing driver Michael Bartels.
Agent: Advantage International. **Coach:** Heinz Gunthardt.
Manager: Assisted by Ion Tiriac in the absence of her father.
Turned pro: 1982.
Height: 5ft 9in (1.75m). **Weight:** 132lb (59kg).

Rankings: 1982: 214; **1983:** 98; **1984:** 22; **1985:** 6; **1986:** 3; **1987:** 1; **1988:** 1; **1989:** 1; **1990:** 1; **1991:** 2; **1992:** 2; **1993:** 1; **1994:** 1; **1995:** 1 (jointly with Seles); **1996:** 1; **1997:** 28; **1998:** 9. **Highest:** 1 (August 1987).

1998 Prize Money: $537,577. **Career Earnings:** $20,614,142. **Career Titles:** 107.

Style: A right-hander with the most powerful single-handed forehand in the game and a natural sliced backhand that she uses to open up the court for forehand winners. She also has one of the best serves in women's tennis with an excessively high toss that gives trouble in the wind. A born athlete and graceful mover who is the fastest woman about a tennis court of modern times. Although she can volley, she is reluctant to leave the familiar territory of the baseline from where she can dominate all players except Seles, who can out-drive her. Suffers from chronic back injury caused by bone spurs in her back, for which she could have surgery, but feels she's too young yet. She requires constant manipulative treatment and must always be aware of the danger of other injuries being caused by compensating for her back injury. Unable to play 3 consec. tourns, she has to pace herself carefully.

CAREER HIGHLIGHTS (year: (titles))
1982: The youngest at the time to receive a WTA ranking at 13 years 4 months; won European 14s and European circuit Masters. **1983:** Reached her 1st tour sf at Freiburg. **1984: (1)** *Olympics*. Won Olympic demonstration event in Los Angeles and reached last 16 Wimbledon. **1985:** Reached sf US Open and LIPC, plus last 16 French Open and Wimbledon. **1986: (8)** *German Open, Amelia Island, Hilton Head, US CC, Tokyo Pan Pacific, Zurich, Brighton, Mahwah*. Won 8 of her last 11 tourns and 52 of her last 55 matches. Won her 1st pro tourn by beating Evert-Lloyd in Hilton Head f, then beat Navratilova in German Open f and had 3 mps in memorable US Open sf loss to Navratilova. Won 4 straight tourns and 23 consec. matches in spring. A virus infection affected her performance in Paris and kept her out of Wimbledon, and a freak accident in Prague (a heavy umbrella stand blew over and broke a toe) prevented her from playing in Fed Cup. **1987: (11)** *FRENCH OPEN, VS Florida, LIPC, FC Cup, Amelia Island, Italian Open, Berlin, VS Los Angeles, Hamburg, Zurich, VS Champs*. After a 2-month break Dec–Jan., missing Australian Open, she took over No. 2 ranking from Evert-Lloyd end Feb. and No. 1 from Navratilova 16 Aug. Won her 1st GS title at French Open, becoming, at 17 years 11 months and 23 days, the youngest-ever winner of the women's singles there. Unbeaten from 23 Nov. 1986 (VS Champs) until Wimbledon f, where she fell to Navratilova, losing to her again in f US Open when suffering from flu. She won 75 of 77 matches to take 11 titles, confirming her No. 1 ranking by taking VS Champs and being named Official World Champion by virtue of her position at head of VS points table. She became only the 2nd player after Navratilova to earn more than $1 million in prize money in a year. **1988: (11)** *AUSTRALIAN OPEN, FRENCH OPEN, WIMBLEDON, US OPEN, Olympics, LIPC, US HC, Berlin, Hamburg, Mahwah, Brighton*. At the age of 19 she achieved a unique 'Golden Slam', becoming only the 3rd woman, after Connolly and Court, to achieve the traditional GS and topping her exceptional year with a gold medal at the Olympics in Seoul. She won 8 other titles and 71 of 74 matches, losing only to Sabatini – at VS Florida (following a 6-week break) and at Amelia Island – and to Shriver (when suffering from flu) at VS Champs, ending run of 46 winning results. Became the 2nd German woman to win Wimbledon after Cilly Aussem in 1931. In doubles won Wimbledon and LIPC with Sabatini, but was forced to default qf VS Champs. **1989: (14)** *AUSTRALIAN OPEN, WIMBLEDON, US OPEN, LIPC, US HC, VS Washington, VS Florida, Hamburg, San Diego, Mahwah, Zurich, Brighton, FC Cup, VS Champs*. A second consec. GS slipped from her grasp when, feel-

ing unwell after suffering from food poisoning, she lost f French Open to Sanchez-Vicario. However, she retained her titles at Australian Open, Wimbledon and US Open, won VS Champs and took 10 other singles titles. With a record of 82 wins and 2 defeats, losing just 12 sets all year, she was beaten only by Sanchez-Vicario at French Open and Sabatini at Amelia Island in spring. In doubles was r/u French Open with Sabatini. **1990: (10)** *AUSTRALIAN OPEN, Tokyo Toray, Amelia Island, Hamburg, Canadian Open, San Diego, Leipzig, Brighton, VS New England, Zurich*. Began the year in her usual style by winning Australian Open and recorded a 66-match winning streak (the 2nd-highest in women's tennis), which was broken when she lost to Seles in f Berlin. She lost f French Open (her 13th consec. GS f) to the same player, Garrison upset her in sf Wimbledon and Sabatini beat her in f US Open and sf VS Champs. These were the only players to beat her in a year in which she won 10 titles. She was out of action from Feb. to April after breaking her thumb ski-ing, and was hampered through the year by allegations concerning her father and by sinus problems, which caused her to withdraw from the Fed Cup team and required an operation after Wimbledon. On 13 Aug. went into her 157th consec. week at No. 1 (starting 17 Aug. 1987), overtaking Navratilova's women's record of 156 (14 June 1982–9 June 1985); 3 weeks later she passed Jimmy Connors's all-time record of 159 weeks. **1991: (7)** *WIMBLEDON, San Antonio, Hamburg, Berlin, Leipzig, Zurich, Brighton*. Her loss to Novotna in qf Australian Open was her 1st so early in GS since French Open 1986, and until she beat Seles to take San Antonio in April, she had gone 5 tourns since Nov. 1990 without winning a title. She went on to take Hamburg, Berlin, Leipzig, Zurich and Brighton and was r/u VS Florida and Amelia Island. However, she lost her No. 1 ranking to Seles in March, having held that position for a record 186 consec. weeks, regained it briefly after winning her 3rd Wimbledon in a thrilling f over Sabatini, but lost it again in Aug. In sf French Open Sanchez-Vicario inflicted her worst defeat (6–0 6–2) and 1st love set since 1984, Navratilova beat her in sf US Open and Novotna removed her in qf VS Champs. When she d. Wiesner 2r Leipzig, she notched up her 500th career win, the youngest to reach that landmark, being 6 months younger than Evert, although Evert needed only 545 matches to Graf's 568. Split with Slozil in Nov., preferring to work on her own. **1992: (8)** *WIMBLEDON, VS Florida, Hamburg, Berlin, Leipzig, Zurich, Brighton, Philadelphia*. Misfortune continued to dog her as she was forced to withdraw at the last minute from Australian Open with German measles. When she returned, at VS Chicago in Feb., she fell sf to Novotna after winning the 1st set to love, but returned to the winner's circle in March when she won VS Florida. She followed with Hamburg, which took her past Evert's $8,827,034 career prize money to $8,907,534 in second place behind Navratilova. At French Open, with the crowd behind her, she saved 5 mps v Seles in f before losing 8–10 fs and at Wimbledon she ended the No. 1's chance of a GS by allowing her only 3 games in the final, for her 4th title there. She won an Olympic silver medal, losing to Capriati, and finished the year with 8 titles, but ended on a disappointing note when she fell 1r VS Champs to McNeil. Led GER to Fed Cup victory over ESP in f. **1993: (10)** *FRENCH OPEN, WIMBLEDON, US OPEN, VS Florida, FC Cup, Berlin, San Diego, Toronto, Leipzig, VS Champs*. Her 10 titles across the year took her career total to 80, 4th in the Open era behind Navratilova, Evert and Goolagong-Cawley. Was considerably upset when a fanatical supporter stabbed Seles, aiming to sideline her so that Graf could regain the No. 1 ranking. She did so on 7 June after winning French Open, delighting in her victory there but admitting that it was something of a hollow achievement without Seles on the scene. Played and won Wimbledon carrying a foot injury, which would have kept her out of any other tourn, and by end of US Open had reached qf or better in 29 GS from 1985, 2nd to Evert's Open era record 34 from 1971–1983. Underwent surgery 4 Oct. to remove bone splinters from her right foot, returning 8 Nov. at VS Philadelphia, where her winning sequence of 6 straight tourns ended when she lost f to Martinez. She won 10 titles across the year and reached 4 more f, including Australian Open, where she lost in 3s to Seles. She also lost once to Navratilova and twice to Sanchez-Vicario, who inflicted her 1st-ever defeat at Hamburg, where she'd won 32 matches. She was voted WTA Player of the Year and won VS Champs, despite needing painkillers for a back injury, finishing the year well and truly at the top of the rankings, although in the continued absence of Seles there was something of a question mark over the achievement. **1994: (7)** *AUSTRALIAN OPEN, Tokyo Toray, Indian Wells, VS Florida, LIPC, Berlin, San Diego*. She completed another non-calender GS at Australian Open, having won all 4 GS tourns during Seles's absence, and was still the only player, male or female, to win all 4 titles in the 1990s. When she won Berlin in May, she had reached 20 consec. f and until losing f Hamburg to Sanchez-Vicario, she had won 36 consec. matches since Philadelphia in Nov. However, she was unable to maintain the impetus. At French Open she was swept away in sf by Pierce and later announced that she was pulling out of Fed Cup, saying she was too tired and needed 'a long period of rest'. Then at Wimbledon, having played no match since French Open, she suffered a shock defeat in 1r at the hands of McNeil – the player who had inflicted her only previous 1r defeat in her adult life at VS Champs in 1992. It was the 1st time for 9 years that she'd lost successive matches on tour, the 1st time for 32 years that the reigning champion at Wimbledon had been beaten in her 1st match and the 1st time ever that the reigning champion had lost 1r (Margaret Smith having received a bye before her 2r defeat). She played US Open, despite suffering stress fracture of back, and in f v Sanchez-Vicario, a set up and 3–2 in 2s tb, she looked a likely winner, but by then her back was seriously bothering her and the match slipped from her grasp. At VS Champs she lost qf to Pierce, and although she refused to blame her back problems, it looked increasingly likely that she would require surgery, with the possibility that she might miss 1995 Australian Open. **1995: (9)** *FRENCH OPEN, WIMBLEDON, US OPEN, Paris Open, Delray Beach, LIPC, Houston, Philadelphia, WTA Champs*. She refused to undergo back surgery yet, and it was a strain to her right calf muscle that caused her to withdraw from Australian Open. For the 1st time since 1987 she held none of the 4 GS titles, although that soon changed when she went on to win French Open, Wimbledon and US Open, becoming the 1st woman to win all 4 GS titles at least 4 times each. When she won LIPC, her 89th title, she passed Cawley to take 3rd place in the list of title-winners after Navratilova (167) and Evert (157). Her US Open title was her 18th GS in singles, equalling the record shared by Navratilova and Evert. However, she ended her 9-year record of having won at least 50 matches per year with 47 won and 2 lost across the year. She lost the No. 1 ranking to Sanchez-Vicario 6 Feb., regained it 20 Feb., and the top position passed between them until her triumph at French Open. Her victory there was remarkable, for she had been out of action 6 weeks beforehand with flu and a recurrence of her back problems and was unable to practise until 8 days before the tourn started. She caught a virus in the 2nd week there and required drops in her eyes twice during the final – yet still she won. In her Wimbledon f v Sanchez-Vicario, which will be remembered as one of the great matches, she played a game at 5–5 fs which involved 32 points and 20 mins. Graf rated it the greatest game she had ever played. Then came the 1st of only 2 defeats all year – at the hands of Coetzer 1r Toronto – ending a 32-match winning streak, and only her 3rd at that stage since 1985. Although she would make no excuses, she was hampered by her back injury and concern over her father (who had claimed to have suffered a heart attack while being held in prison over tax evasion charges) and struggled to beat the same player in her next match – 1r US Open. Further injury plagued her there and, suffering problems with her left foot, she had to go to hospital on the eve of the f to check that it was not a stress fracture. Her opponent there was Seles, ranked equal No. 1 with Graf for her 1st 6 tourns, who was beaten in the long-awaited 1st encounter between the two since the 1993 Australian Open f. She then lost 1r Brighton to De Swardt – at 54 the lowest-ranked player to have beaten her for 10 years – and although she generously gave credit to De Swardt, she played badly and was obviously seriously distracted by her father's situation, legal investigations into her finances and her back injury. She regained her winning habit at Philadelphia, although not without dropping a set each to Frazier and McNeil, and finished the year in triumph at WTA Champs, where Huber extended her to 5s f. On 15 Dec. she underwent surgery to remove bone splinters from her left foot. **1996: (7)** *FRENCH OPEN, WIMBLEDON, US OPEN, Indian Wells, LIPC, Berlin, Chase Champs*. After missing Australian Open, she returned to action in March to win Indian Wells. When, in her next tourn, she took LIPC for a record 5th time, she became the 1st player, male or female, to win it 3 times in a row. In Fed Cup qf v Date, played on HC, she looked weary and lost 12–10 fs, also losing the doubles with Huber. Then, short of practice on clay, she was surprisingly beaten by Hingis in qf Italian Open – she claimed that her foot and back were as good as they ever are, but that she couldn't get her brain round it, undoubtedly distracted by her father having been charged on 17 April with evading $13 million taxes by failing to report $28m of Graf's earnings between 1989 and 1993. She was back in the winner's circle the following week in Berlin and was in fine form at French Open, losing no set on her way to f, where she played the longest ever f there, taking 3 hr 3 min to defeat Sanchez-Vicario. Withdrew from Eastbourne with a minor inflammation of the patella tendon of her left knee, wanting to rest it before Wimbledon. Her 7th Wimbledon title took her past Wills-Moody with 20 GS titles, 2nd behind Court's 24 – and it was also her 100th career title (30 on clay, 7 on grass, 28 indoors and 35 on HC), achieved despite the handicap of a heavy cold and continuing knee problems. She looked in danger only in sf v Date, when she surrendered 6 consec. games to lose 2nd set before play was halted for the night. However, she took fs next morning and was not troubled by Sanchez-Vicario in a disappointing f. In sf Los Angeles in Aug., Davenport inflicted her 1st ss defeat since 1994, but at US Open she managed to overcome the distraction of her father's trial in Germany for tax evasion (as well as calf and knee problems), moving smoothly to f, where she again d. Seles. On 13 May, she had passed Navratilova's record of 331 weeks in total at No. 1 and on 4 Nov., after Seles dropped to co-ranked No. 2, she regained the solo spot at the top of the rankings for the 8th time in all and 1st time since Aug. 1995, when Seles returned to the tour. Injuries plagued her throughout the year, for although her back problems were eased by her no longer having to compensate for her injured foot, her sacroiliac joint moves out of place and she still has to restrict her schedule, travelling with her personal masseur and chiropractor. A recurrence of the patella tendon injury in her left knee forced her to withdraw from sf Leipzig – the 1st time in her career that she'd withdrawn mid-tourn. She was a doubtful starter at Philadelphia in Nov. after the injury flared up yet again, but in the event it was a recurrence of her back injury that forced her to retire during her f v Novotna, soon after her father was released on bail. However, in typical fashion she lifted herself above the pain of both back and knee injuries for the big occasion at VS Champs, which she won for a 5th time after 5s f v Hingis. **1997: (1)** *Strasbourg.* At Australian Open, suffering from an infected toe and the heat, and distracted again by an imminent court verdict concerning her father, she ended her run of 45 consec. GS matches. Her defeat there by Coetzer was only the 2nd time in 12 years that she'd lost before qf in GS. When Hingis overtook her at the top of the rankings on 31 March, she had been No. 1 for a total of 364 weeks – an all-time record. She withdrew f Tokyo Pan Pacific with a severely aggravated infection of the tip of the patella tendon of left knee, suffered in sf, and was out for 3½ months, the longest break of her career to date. Returning to action at Berlin, below her best and lacking in confidence, she managed to win only one game in 57-min qf v Coetzer, suffering the worst defeat of her career. The same player extended her to fs tb in sf Strasbourg, but this time she made it back to the winner's circle for the 1st time in 1997, despite still being below her best. It was Coetzer yet again who ended her challenge at French Open, where she fell in ss qf and slipped to No. 3 in the rankings behind Seles. On 10 June she underwent surgery to repair a fracture of cartilage and shortening and partial rupture of the patellar tendon of her left knee, an injury first suffered at Wimbledon a year earlier. She was out for the rest of the year. **1998: (3)** *New Haven, Leipzig, Philadelphia.* She struggled all year for fitness and on 8 June, having played only 2 tourns in 12 months (and therefore not making the basic qualification of 3), she dropped out of the rankings for the 1st time since 17 Jan. 1983. Her 1st match of the year was at Hannover, where she looked tentative in losing to Appelmans. She was generally tense and emotional – aware that she might never have played again and now giving it one last try to get and stay fit enough to play and practise regularly – and appeared to be hampered by psychological problems at Eastbourne, where she was uncharacteristically petulant. It had been a long struggle, as first a calf strain suffered in training delayed her scheduled comeback; a hamstring injury kept her out of LIPC; and she pulled out of Rome, Berlin and French Open with an ankle injury suffered during training. At Wimbledon she lost to Zvereva 3r and then, demoralised by her early loss to Serna in Montreal, she had intended to rest and review the season, but on the spur of the moment took a WC entry at New Haven. There she d. Davenport and Novotna to take her 1st title since May 1997. However, at US Open the following week, she still had to work hard for each of her 4 victories, no longer winning on autopilot, and was out of action again following minor surgery on her right hand to correct an injury suffered there. Returning again at Leipzig in Nov., having lost her protected ranking for seeding purposes and therefore unseeded for the 1st time in 13 years, she was surprised and elated to win the tourn. The result took her back into the top 20, and the prize money she earned took her past Navratilova's record of $20,344,061 career prize money in women's tennis. The following week at Philadelphia, still unseeded, she beat Hingis and Davenport to take her 2nd consec. title, delighted at having come so far so soon and at having survived three 3s matches. So she went into Chase Champs full of confidence, and, upsetting Novotna and Seles, extended to 12 her run of consec. matches won since her return. But injury struck yet again – a hamstring this time – when she was 3–2 ahead in sf v Davenport and she won no more games. However, her progress was enough to launch her back into the top 10 and she was voted WTA Most Exciting Player of the Year. During the relatively short time in which she had been able to play, she had collected 3 titles as well as reaching sf Indian Wells, Birmingham (tourn cancelled at that stage), Stanford and Chase Champs and qf Eastbourne.

PRINCIPAL 1998 RESULTS – won 3, sf 4 (detailed Grand Slam results follow)
won New Haven (d. Nagyova 6–1 6–3, Coetzer 6–3 6–0, Davenport 6–3 7–6, Novotna 6–4 6–4), **won** Leipzig (d. Dragomir 6–3 6–3, Sugiyama 6–4 6–3, Sidot 7–5 6–3, Van Roost 6–1 3–6 6–0, Tauziat 6–3 6–4), **won** Philadelphia (d. Likhovtseva 6–7 6–2 6–4, Hingis 6–2 4–6 6–0, Tauziat 6–1 6–4, Davenport 4–6 6–3 6–4); **sf** Indian Wells (d. Tanasugarn 6–4 6–1, Sugiyama 6–0 6–1, Zvereva 6–3 6–0, lost Davenport 6–4 4–6 4–2 ret), **sf** Birmingham (d. Stubbs 5–7 6–2 6–4, Boogert 6–2 6–4, Serna 6–4 6–4, tourn cancelled), **sf** Stanford (d. Fernandez 6–4 6–0, Zvereva 6–1 6–3, lost Davenport 6–4 6–7 6–3), **sf** Chase Champs.

CAREER GRAND SLAM RECORD

AUSTRALIAN OPEN – Played 9, won 4, r/u 1, sf 1, qf 1

1983: 1r lost Sayers 7–6 6–1. **1984: 3r** d. Collins 6–2 6–4, Antonoplis 2–6 6–1 6–0, lost Turnbull [4] 6–4 6–4. **1985–87:** Did not play. **1988: won** [seed 1] d. Jonsson 6–3 6–1, Thompson 6–0 6–1, Cammy MacGregor 6–1 6–2, Lindqvist [13] 6–0 7–5, Mandlikova [5] 6–2 6–2, Kohde-Kilsch [8] 6–2 6–3, Evert [3] 6–1 7–6. **1989: won** [seed 1] d. Guse 6–2 6–1, Simpson 6–0 6–0, Werdel 6–0 6–1, Provis [16] 6–4 6–0, Kohde-Kilsch [8] 6–2 6–3, Sabatini [3] 6–3 6–0, Sukova [5] 6–4 6–4. **1990: won** [seed 1] d. Cunningham 6–2 7–5, De Lone 6–1 6–2, Meskhi 6–4 6–1, Reggi [13] 6–2 6–3, Fendick 6–3 7–5, Sukova [4] 6–3 3–6 6–4, M. J. Fernandez [6] 6–4 6–4. **1991: qf** [seed 1] d. Santrock 6–3 6–0, Kidowaki 6–1 6–0, Provis 6–4 6–2, Habsudova 6–0 6–1, lost Novotna [10] 5–7 6–4 8–6. **1992:** Did not play. **1993: r/u** [seed 2] d. Herreman 6–2 6–1, Santrock 6–1 6–1, Porwik 6–1 ret, Mag. Maleeva [15] 6–3 6–3, Capriati [7] 7–5 6–2, Sanchez-Vicario [4] 7–5 6–4, lost Seles 4–6 6–3 6–2. **1994: won** [seed 1] d. Po 6–1 2–0 ret, Provis 6–1 6–4, Rittner 6–2 6–4, Testud 6–1 6–2, Davenport [16] 6–3 6–2, Date [10] 6–3 6–3, Sanchez-Vicario [2] 6–0 6–2. **1995–96** Did not play. **1997: last 16** [seed 1] d. Husarova 5–1 ret, Neiland 7–5 6–2, Gorrochategui 7–5 6–3, lost Coetzer [12] 6–2 7–5. **1998:** Did not play.

FRENCH OPEN – Played 15, won 5, r/u 3, sf 2, qf 2

1983: 2r d. Karlsson 6–4 6–1, lost Mould 6–0 7–6. **1984: 3r** d. Longo 6–2 7–6, Solomon 6–2 6–1, lost Kohde-Kilsch 6–2 2–6 6–1. **1985: last 16** [seed 11] d. Okagawa 7–5 3–6 6–3, Kim 6–0 6–4, Bunge 6–1 7–6, lost Evert Lloyd [2] 6–2 6–3. **1986: qf** [seed 3] d. Betzner 6–1 6–0, Rush 6–1 6–1, Mesker 6–2 6–1, Casale 6–1 6–3, lost Mandlikova [5] 2–6 7–6 6–1 (held 1 mp at 5–2 2nd set). **1987: won** [seed 2] d. Bartos Cserepy 6–1 6–1, Budarova 6–1 6–1, Novotna 6–0 67–1, Kelesi 7–6 6–2, M. Maleeva [6] 6–4 6–1, Sabatini [7] 6–4 4–6 7–5, Navratilova [1] 6–4 4–6 8–6. **1988: won** [seed 1] (d. Guerree 6–0 6–4, Reis 6–1 6–0, Sloane 6–0 6–1, Tauziat 6–1 6–3, Fulco 6–0 6–1, Sabatini [4] 6–3 7–6, Zvereva [13] 6–0 6–0. **1989: r/u** [seed 1] d. Benjamin 6–1 6–1, Fulco 6–0 6–1, Jagerman 6–1 6–2, La Fratta 6–2 6–1, Martinez [8] 6–0 6–4, Seles 6–3 3–6 6–3, lost Sanchez 7–6 3–6 7–5. **1990: r/u** [seed 1] d. Paradis 6–0 6–2, Santrock 6–1 6–2, Cecchini 6–2 6–3, Tauziat [15] 6–1 6–4, Martinez [9] 6–1 6–3, Novotna [11] 6–1 6–2, lost Seles [2] 7–6 6–4. **1991: sf** [seed 2] d. Mag. Maleeva 6–3 7–6, Langrova 6–0 6–1, Stafford 6–0 6–1, Appelmans 6–2 6–2, Tauziat [13] 6–3 6–2, lost Sanchez-Vicario [5] 6–0 6–2. **1992: r/u** [seed 2] d. Simpson-Alter 6–3 6–1, Housset 6–2 6–1, Coetzer 6–2 6–1, Novotna [10] 6–1 6–4, Zvereva 6–3 6–7 6–3, Sanchez-Vicario [4] 0–6 6–2 6–2, lost Seles [1] 6–2 3–6 10–8. **1993: won** [seed 1] d. C. Dahlman 7–6 6–1, Strnadova 6–1 6–1, Arraya 6–2 6–2, Majoli 6–4 7–6, Capriati [6] 6–3 7–5, Huber [8] 6–1 6–1, M. J. Fernandez [5] 4–6 6–2 6–4. **1994: sf** [seed 1] d. Studenikova 6–2 6–2, Rottier 7–5 6–3, Kruger 6–0 4–6 6–2, Spirlea 6–0 6–1, Gorrochategui 6–4 6–1, lost Pierce [12] 6–2 6–2. **1995: won** [seed 2] d. Gorrochategui 6–1 7–5, Begerow 6–4 6–3, Baudone 6–2 6–1, Huber [11] 6–0 6–3, Sabatini [8] 6–1 6–0, Martinez [4] 6–3 6–7 6–3, Sanchez-Vicario [1] 7–5 4–6 6–0. **1996: won** [seed 1] d. Neiland 6–3 6–2, Bradtke 6–2 6–2, Langrova 6–0 1–0 ret, M. J. Fernandez [11] 6–1 7–6, Majoli [5] 6–3 6–1, Martinez [3] 6–3 6–1, Sanchez-Vicario [4] 6–3 6–7 10–8. **1997: qf** [seed 2] d. Suarez 6–1 6–4, Mauresmo 6–3 6–3, Serna 7–6 6–1, Spirlea [13] 6–7 6–2 6–2, lost Coetzer [11] 6–1 6–4. **1998:** Did not play.

WIMBLEDON – Played 13, won 7, r/u 1, sf 1

1984: last 16 d. Mascarin 6–4 5–7 10–8, Barker 7–6 6–3, Bunge 7–5 6–3, lost Durie [10] 2–6 6–3 9–7. **1985: last 16** [seed 11] d. Spain-Short 6–7 6–4 6–2, Temesvari 6–3 7–6, Rehe 6–3 6–2, lost Shriver [5] 3–6 6–2 6–4. **1986:** Did not play. **1987: r/u** [seed 2] d. Villagran 6–09 6–2, Scheuer-Larsen 6–0 6–0, Gildemeister, 6–2 6–1, Novotna 6–4 6–3, Sabatini [6] 4–6 6–1 6–1, Shriver [5] 6–0 6–2, lost Navratilova [1] 7–5 6–3. **1988: won** [seed 1] d. Na 6–0 6–0, Quentrec 6–2 6–0, Phelps 6–3 6–1, M. J. Fernandez [16] 6–2 6–2, Paradis 6–3 6–1, Shriver [4] 6–1 6–2, Navratilova [2] 5–7 6–2 6–1. **1989: won** [seed 1] d. Salmon 6–1 6–2, Kessaris 6–2 6–1, A.Minter 6–1 6–3, Seles [11] 6–4 6–3, Sanchez [7] 7–5 6–1, Evert [4] 6–2 6–1, Navratilova [2] 6–2 6–7 6–1. **1990: sf** [seed 1] d. Porwik 6–1 6–2, McGrath 6–3 6–0, Kohde-Kilsch 6–0 6–4, Capriati [12] 6–2 6–4, Novotna [13] 7–5 6–2, lost Garrison [5] 6–3 3–6 6–4. **1991: won** [seed 1] d. Appelmans 6–2 6–2, Louie-Harper 6–0 6–1, Basuki 6–2 6–3, Frazier [15] 6–2 6–1, Garrison [8] 6–1 6–3, M. J. Fernandez [6] 6–2 7–5, Sabatini [2] 6–4 3–6 8–6. **1992: won** [seed 2] d. Van Lottum 6–1 6–0, Werdel 6–1 6–1, De Swardt 5–7 6–0 7–5, Fendick 4–6 6–3 6–2, Zvereva 6–3 6–1, Sabatini [3] 6–3 6–3, Seles [1] 6–2 6–1. **1993: won** [seed 1] d. Sharpe 6–0 6–0, Wood 6–2 6–1, Kelesi 6–0 6–0, McGrath 6–1 6–4, Capriati [7] 7–6 6–1, Martinez [6] 7–6 6–3, Novotna 7–6 1–6 6–4. **1994: 1r** [seed 1] lost McNeil 7–5 7–6. **1995: won** [seed 1] d. Hingis 6–3 6–1, Coetzer 6–3 7–5, Boogert 6–1 6–0, Gorrochategui 6–0 6–1, M. J. Fernandez [13] 6–3 6–0, Novotna [4] 5–7 6–4 6–2, Sanchez-Vicario [2] 4–6 6–1 7–5. **1996: won** [seed 1] d. Richterova 6–4 6–1, Baudone 7–5 6–3, Arendt 6–2 6–1, Hingis [16] 6–1 6–4, Novotna [6] 6–3 6–2, Date [12] 6–2 2–6 6–3, Sanchez-Vicario [4] 6–3 7–5. **1997:** Did not play. **1998: 3r** [seed 4] d. Leon-Garcia 6–4 6–1, Nagyova 6–0 6–4, lost Zvereva 6–4 7–5.

US OPEN – Played 14, won 5, r/u 3, sf 3, qf 1

1984: 1r lost Hanika 6–4 6–2. **1985: sf** [seed 11] d. Fendick 4–6 6–1 7–5, A. Minter 6–3 7–6, A. White 6–4 6–2, M. Maleeva 6–4 6–2, Shriver [4] 7–6 6–7 7–6, lost Navratilova [2] 6–2 6–3. **1986: sf** [seed 3] d. Mascarin

6–0 6–1, Temesvari 6–1 6–0, Bowes 6–1 1–0 ret, Reggi 6–1 3–6 6–0, Gadusek 6–3 6–1, lost Navratilova [1] 6–1 6–7 7–6. **1987: r/u** [seed 1] d. Fulco 6–0 6–3, Huber 6–2 6–3, Tarabini 6–2 6–0, Hanika [13] 7–54 6–2, Shriver [5] 6–4 6–3, McNeil [11] 4–6 6–2 6–4, lost Navratilova [2] 7–6 6–1. **1988: won** [seed 1] d. E. Minter 6–1 6–1, Bollegraf 6–1 6–0, Herreman 6–0 6–1, Fendick 6–4 6–2, K. Maleeva [14] 6–3 6–0, Evert [3] w/o, Sabatini [5] 6–3 3 6–6–1. **1989: won** [seed 1] d. Inoue 6–3 6–2, Herreman 6–2 6–1, Phelps 6–1 6–1, Fairbank 6–4 6–0, Sukova [8] 6–1 6–1, Sabatini [3] 3–6 6–4 6–2, Navratilova [2] 3–6 7–5 6–1. **1990: r/u** [seed 1] d. Drake 6–1 6–1, McQuillan 6–1 6–3, Reinach 6–4 3–6 6–1, Capriati [13] 6–1 6–2, Novotna [12] 6–3 6–1, Sanchez-Vicario [6] 6–1 6–2, lost Sabatini [5] 6–2 7–6. **1991: sf** [seed 1] d. Temesvari 6–1 6–2, Mothes 6–0 6–0, Sviglerova 6–4 7–5, Wiesner 7–5 6–4, Martinez [8] 6–1 6–3, lost Navratilova [6] 7–6 6–7 6–4. **1992: qf** [seed 2] d. Cioffi 6–0 6–2, Shriver 7–5 6–3, N. Dahlman 6–4 6–2, Labat 6–2 6–2, lost Sanchez-Vicario [5] 7–6 6–3. **1993: won** [seed 1] d. White 6–3 6–0, McGrath 6–3 6–1, Wiesner def., Pierce [13] 6–1 6–0, Sabatini [5] 6–2 5–7 6–1, Maleeva-Fragniere [11] 4–6 6–1 6–0, Sukova [12] 6–3 6–3. **1994: r/u** [seed 1] d. Mall 6–2 6–1, Cacic 6–0 6–2, Bobkova 6–2 6–3, Garrison-Jackson [10] 6–1 6–2, Coetzer [11] 6–0 6–2, Novotna [7] 6–3 7–5, lost Sanchez-Vicario [2] 1–6 7–6 6–4. **1995: won** [seed 1] d. Coetzer 6–7 6–1 6–4, Grande 6–1 6–3, Tauziat 6–3 6–3, Rubin 6–2 6–2, Frazier 6–2 6–3, Sabatini [9] 6–4 7–6, Seles [2] 7–6 0–6 6–3. **1996: won** [seed 1] d. Basuki 6–3 7–6, Kschwendt 6–2 6–1, Zvereva 6–4 6–2, Kournikova 6–2 6–1, Wiesner 7–5 6–3, Hingis [16] 7–5 6–3, Seles [2] 7–5 6–3. **1997:** Did not play. **1998: last 16** [seed 8] d. Morariu 6–2 3–6 6–1, Weingartner 6–0 6–1, Lucic 6–1 6–1, lost Schnyder [11] 6–3 6–4.

OLYMPIC RECORD

1984: (Los Angeles) won Demonstration event (under 21) d. Goles 1–6 6–3 6–4 in final. **1988: (Seoul) won gold medal** [seed 1] bye, d. Meskhi 7–5 6–1, Suire 6–3 6–0, Savchenko [11] 6–2 4–6 6–3, Garrison-Jackson [8] 6–2 6–0, Sabatini [3] 6–3 6–3. **1992: (Barcelona) r/u silver medal** [seed 1] d. Novelo 6–1 6–1, Schultz 6–1 6–0, Mag. Maleeva 6–3 6–4, Appelmans [16] 6–1 6–0, M. J. Fernandez [4] 6–4 6–2, lost Capriati [3] 3–6 6–3 6–4.

CAREER FEDERATION CUP RECORD

1986 (in TCH, Clay): *1r FRG d. BEL 3–0.* R2 d. A. Devries 6–3 6–1; R3 (+ C. Kohde-Kilsch) d. Devries/ S. Wasserman 6–1 7–5. *2r FRG d. BRA 2–1.* R2 d. P. Medrado 6–0 6–2; R3 (+ B. Bunge) d. N. Dias/Medrado 6–2 6–1. **1987 (in CAN, Hard):** *1r FRG d. HKG 3–0.* R2 d. P. Hy 6–7 6–2 6–4. *2r FRG d. KOR 3–0.* R2 d. I. Kim 6–1 6–1; R3 (+ C. Kohde-Kilsch) d. Kim/J. Lee 6–1 6–0. *Qf FRG d. ARG 2–1.* R2 d. G. Sabatini 6–4 6–4. *Sf FRG d. TCH 2–1.* R2 d. H. Mandlikova 6–4 6–1; R3 (+ Kohde-Kilsch) d. Mandlikova/H. Sukova 7–5 6–2. *Final FRG d. USA 2–1.* R2 d. C. Evert 6–2 6–1; R3 (+ Kohde-Kilsch) d. Evert/P. Shriver 1–6 7–5 6–4. **1989 (in JPN, Hard):** *1r FRG d. FIN 3–0.* R2 d. A. Aallonen 6–0 6–1. *2r FRG d. JPN 3–0.* R2 d. A. Kijimuta 6–4 6–1; R3 (+ C. Kohde-Kilsch) d. K. Date/E. Inoue 6–4 5–7 6–2. *Qf TCH d. FRG 2–1.* R2 d. H. Sukova 6–2 6–1; R3 (+ Kohde-Kilsch) lost J. Novotna/Sukova 6–2 6–2. **1991 (in GBR, Hard):** *1r GER d. GRE 3–0.* R2 d. A. Kanellopoulou 6–1 6–2; R3 (+ B. Rittner) d. Kanellopoulou/C. Papadaki 6–3 6–0. *2r GER d. CAN 2–1.* R2 d. P. Hy 6–3 3–6 6–2. **1992 (in GER, Clay):** *1r GER d. NZL 3–0.* R2 d. C. Toleafoa 6–2 6–1. *2r GER d. NED 2–1.* R2 d. B. Schultz 6–3 7–6. *Qf GER d. POL 3–0.* R2 d. K. Nowak 6–0 6–0; R3 (+ A. Huber) d. M. Mroz/ K. Teodorowicz 6–4 7–5. *Sf GER d. USA 2–1.* R2 d. L. McNeil 6–0 6–3. *Final GER d. ESP 2–1.* R2 d. A. Sanchez-Vicario 6–4 6–2. **1993 (in GER, Clay):** *1r AUS d. GER 2–1.* R2 lost N. Provis 6–4 1–6 6–1. **1996: April** – *World Group qf JPN d. GER 3–2 in JPN (Hard).* R2 d. N. Sawamatsu 6–1 6–3; R3 lost K. Date 7–6 3–6 12–10; R5 (+ A. Huber) lost K. Nagatsuka/A. Sugiyama 4–6 6–3 6–3. **July** – *World Group play-off GER d. AUT 4–1 in AUT (Clay).* R2 d. J. Wiesner 6–1 3–6 6–2; R3 d. B. Schett 6–3 6–2.

SEASON ENDING CHAMPIONSHIPS – Played 13, won 5, r/u 1, sf 4, qf 2

(1983–94 Virginia Slims, 1995 Corel, 1996-98 Chase)

1986 (March): sf d. Sabatini 1–6 6–4 6–3, Shriver 4–6 7–6 6–3, lost Navratilova 6–3 6–2. **1986 (November): r/u** d. McNeil 7–5 4–6 6–2, Man. Maleeva 6–3 3–6 7–5, Sukova 7–6 3–6 6–1, lost Navratilova 7–6–6–3 6–2. **1987: won** d. Sukova 6–2 2–0 ret, Hanika 6–1 6–4, Sabatini 4–6 6–4 6–0 6–4. **1988: sf** d. Man. Maleeva 6–1 6–2, lost Shriver 6–3 7–6. **1989: won** d. Sukova 6–2 6–1, Sabatini 6–3 5–7 6–1, Navratilova 6–4 7–5 2–6 6–2. **1990: sf** d. Capriati 6–3 5–7 6–3, K. Maleeva 6–3 6–0, lost Sabatini 6–4 6–4. **1991: qf** d. Martinez 6–0 6–3, lost Novotna 6–3 3–6 6–1. **1992: 1r** lost McNeil 7–6 6–4. **1993: won** d. Zvereva 6–2 6–4, Coetzer, 6–1 6–2, Huber 6–2 3–6 6–3, Sanchez-Vicario 6–1 6–4 3–6 6–1. **1994: qf** d. Schultz 7–5 6–3, lost Pierce 6–4 6–4. **1995: won** d. Coetzer 6–2 6–2, M. J. Fernandez 6–3 6–4, Zvereva 6–4 6–3, Huber 6–1 2–6 6–1 4–6 6–3. **1996: won** d. Habsudova 6–1 6–4, Davenport 6–4 7–6, Novotna 4–6 6–4 6–3, Hingis 6–3 4–6 6–0 4–6 6–0. **1997:** Did not play. **1998: sf** d. Novotna 6–7 6–4 6–1, Seles 1–6 6–4 6–4, lost Davenport 6–1 2–6 6–3.

10 NATHALIE TAUZIAT (FRA)

Born: Bangul, Central African Republic, 17 October 1967.
Lives: Bayonne. **Father:** Bernard. **Mother:** Regine.
Brother: Eric.
Agent: Benoite Lardy. **Coach:** Regis DeCamaret.
Turned pro: 1984.
Height: 5ft 5in (1.65m). **Weight:** 120lb (54kg).

Rankings: 1984: 296; **1985:** 112; **1986:** 67; **1987:** 25; **1988:** 27; **1989;** 25; **1990:** 18; **1991:** 13; **1992:** 14; **1993:** 18; **1994:** 35; **1995;** 27; **1996:** 30; **1997:** 11; **1998:** 10 singles, 7 doubles. **Highest:** 8 (17 August 1998).

1998 Prize Money: $990,224.
Career Earnings: $4,005,008. **Career Titles:** 4.

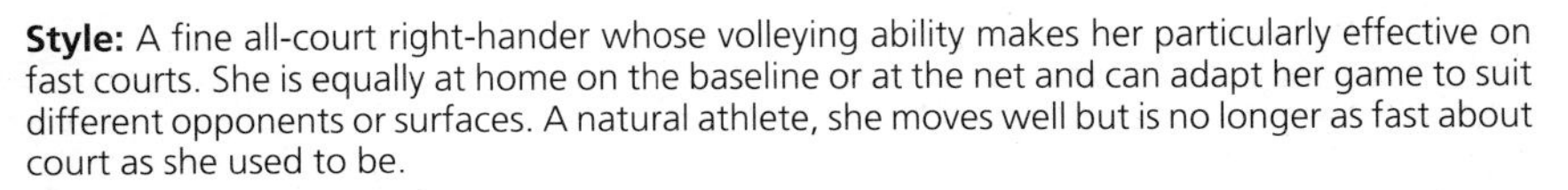

Style: A fine all-court right-hander whose volleying ability makes her particularly effective on fast courts. She is equally at home on the baseline or at the net and can adapt her game to suit different opponents or surfaces. A natural athlete, she moves well but is no longer as fast about court as she used to be.

CAREER HIGHLIGHTS (year: (titles))
1985: Upset Casale at French Open and played Fed Cup. **1986:** Qf Hilversum. **1987:** Reached sf Strasbourg, San Diego and Zurich, last 16 French Open (unseeded) and d. Rinaldi to reach qf LIPC. **1988:** R/u Nice, upset Zvereva and K. Maleeva en route to f Mahwah. In doubles with Demongeot upset Kohde-Kilsch/Sukova to win both Berlin and Zurich and qualified for VS Champs. **1989:** Sf Italian Open (d. Man. Maleeva) and San Diego. **1990: (1)** *Bayonne.* Won her 1st primary circuit title at Bayonne; r/u Wichita and reached sf LIPC, Birmingham and Canadian Open (d. Maleeva-Fragniere) to qualify for VS Champs, where she fell 1r to M. J. Fernandez. In GS she reached last 16 in all 3 tourns she entered, unseeded at both Wimbledon and US Open. **1991:** She scored some major upsets in reaching f Zurich (d. Sabatini), sf VS Palm Springs, VS Florida (d. M. J. Fernandez), Barcelona (d. Navratilova), San Diego and Bayonne and was close to beating Capriati at VS Champs, eventually losing their 1r match in 3s tb. She also reached her 1st GS qf at French Open. Played 3 doubles f, winning Bayonne with Tarabini. **1992:** R/u San Antonio and Bayonne and reached 9 more qf, including Wimbledon. Qualified for VS Champs, but lost 1r to Seles. **1993: (1)** *Quebec City.* Won Quebec City in Nov., having earlier appeared in sf Schenectady and Filderstadt plus 8 more qf, upsetting Maleeva-Fragniere at Tokyo Pan Pacific. Qualified for VS Champs but fell 1r again – to Navratilova. **1994:** Although she did not progress beyond sf, she reached that stage at Birmingham, Schenectady and Quebec City, plus qf Italian Open and Brighton (d. Huber), and upset Martinez 1r Philadelphia. From 3 doubles f she won Quebec City with Reinach and Los Angeles with Halard, with whom she qualified for VS Champs. **1995: (1)** *Eastbourne.* Upset Zvereva on her way to the title at Eastbourne, surprised M. Maleeva at French Open and Pierce at Wimbledon and reached qf Barcelona. In doubles she won Linz with McGrath. **1996:** Confirming her liking for grass, she was r/u Birmingham, reached sf Eastbourne and upset M. Maleeva at Wimbledon. Otherwise she could not pass qf, although she reached that stage at Indian Wells (d. M. J. Fernandez), Italian Open, Berlin, Strasbourg and San Diego. In doubles she played 6 f with 4 different partners, winning Leipzig and Luxembourg with Boogert. **1997: (1)** *Birmingham.* She excelled at Birmingham again, winning the title. Her 2nd f of year came at Zurich and she was r/u again at Chicago, where she upset Novotna and Majoli back-to-back and took the doubles. Her only other sf was a big one, as she upset Coetzer and Majoli to reach that stage at Chase Champs, where she extended Pierce to 3s. She also reached qf Linz, Paris Open, Indian Wells, Eastbourne (d. M. J. Fernandez), Los Angeles and Wimbledon, where she was unseeded. She enjoyed a lucky escape in last 16 there, trailing 4–5 15–40 on Testud's serve in 3s when rain interrupted play: on the resumption 75 minutes later, she took 10 points in a row and finally won 10–12 fs. A member of the winning FRA Fed Cup team, she d. Sawamatsu 7–5 4–6 17–15 in that competition, playing the longest singles set and equalling the longest rubber (Baldovonis d. Connor 6–4 11–13 11–9 in 1974). She played 6 doubles f with 3 different partners, winning Linz and Chicago with Fusai. She qualified for Chase

Champs in both singles and doubles, joining with Fusai to upset Hingis/Sanchez-Vicario in ss and extend Davenport/Novotna to 3s in f. **1998:** The highlight of her career came at Wimbledon, where she was r/u, playing her 1st GS f and becoming the 1st Frenchwoman for 73 years and at 15 the lowest-ranked woman in the open era to reach f Wimbledon. She had removed Davenport in ss on the way and upset her again en route to sf GS Cup. She broke into the top 10 1st time in Jan., slipped out again for a while in spring, but returned after Wimbledon, moving up to a career-high 8 in Aug. Although she won no title, she was consistent in progressing to qf or better in 15 tourns with a 2nd f of year at Leipzig (d. Spirlea) and reaching sf Paris Open, Birmingham (tourn cancelled at that stage), GS Cup, Zurich, Luxembourg and Philadelphia, as well as qf Hannover, Linz, Strasbourg, San Diego, Los Angeles, Filderstadt and Chase Champs. Her partnership with Fusai continued to flourish, bringing 3 titles and a berth at Chase Champs, where they narrowly lost to Davenport/Zvereva in their 7th f of season.

PRINCIPAL 1998 RESULTS – r/u 2, sf 6 (detailed Grand Slam results follow)
r/u Wimbledon, **r/u** Leipzig (d. Likhovtseva 7–6 6–1, Huber 6–3 6–4, Spirlea 2–6 6–3 6–2, lost Graf 6–3 6–4); **sf** Paris Open (d. Loit 4–6 7–6 6–4, Pitkowski 6–1 2–6 7–6, lost Van Roost 7–6 1–6 6–1), **sf** Birmingham (d. Black 2–6 6–2 6–1, Grande 6–3 6–0, Guse 6–2 6–3, tourn cancelled), **sf** GS Cup, **sf** Zurich (d. Raymond 6–2 6–3, Schett 4–6 7–5 6–1, lost V. Williams 6–3 6–4), **sf** Luxembourg (d. Plischke 6–2 6–4, Huber 6–3 6–3, lost Farina 6–2 2–6 6–3), **sf** Philadelphia (d. Raymond 6–2 7–6, Coetzer 6–3 4–6 6–4, lost Graf 6–1 6–4). **1998 HIGHLIGHTS – DOUBLES:** (with Fusai) **won** Linz (d. Kournikova/Neiland 6–3 3–6 6–4), **won** Strasbourg (d. Basuki/Vis 6–4 6–3), **won** New Haven (d. De Swardt/Novotna 6–1 6–0); **r/u** Indian Wells (lost Davenport/Zvereva 6–4 2–6 6–4), **r/u** Berlin (lost Davenport/Zvereva 6–3 6–0), **r/u** San Diego (lost Davenport/Zvereva 6–2 6–1), **r/u** Chase Champs (lost Davenport/Zvereva 6–7 7–5 6–3.

CAREER GRAND SLAM RECORD
AUSTRALIAN OPEN – Played 2
1993: last 16 [seed 13] d. Meskhi 5–7 6–4 6–4, Probst 6–2 4–6 6–2, N. Dahlman 6–2 6–1, lost Seles [1] 6–2 6–0. **1994: 1r** [seed 15] lost Basuki 6–4 7–6). **1995-98:** Did not play.
FRENCH OPEN – Played 15, qf 1
1984: 1r lost Navratilova [1] 6–1 6–2. **1985: 3r** d. W. White 6–0 6–7 6–2, Casale [16] 6–7 7–6 6–2, lost Phelps 6–3 1–6 6–2. **1986: 2r** d. Niox-Chateau 5–7 6–3 9–7, lost A. Smith 1–6 6–2 6–2. **1987: last 16** [unseeded] d. Byrne 7–5 3–6 6–3, Cueto 6–2 0–6 6–3, Rinaldi 6–1 6–3, lost Kohde-Kilsch [8] 6–1 3–6 6–0. **1988: last 16** [unseeded] d. Bollegraf 6–3 6–2, Corsato 6–3 6–0, Byrne 7–5 6–2, lost Graf [1] 6–1 6–3. **1989: 1r** lost McNeil [12] 6–4 6–4. **1990: last 16** [seed 15] d. Godridge 6–3 7–5, Hack 6–2 3–6 6–3, Lapi 6–1 2–6 6–1, lost Graf [1] 6–1 6–4. **1991: qf** [seed 13] d. Etchemendy 6–3 6–1, Guerree 6–2 6–1, Jagerman 6–4 6–0, Sawamatsu 7–5 2–6 12–10, lost Graf [2] 6–3 6–2. **1992: last 16** [seed 12] d. Gorrochategui 7-5 6-1, Helgeson 3-6 6-1 6-3, Wasserman 6-4 6-2, lost Bollegraf 6-4 1-6 6-2. **1993: 3r** [seed 13] d. Grossi 6–4 5–7 6–1, Boogert 6–3 1–6 6–4, lost Wiesner 6–3 7–6. **1994: 2r** d. Reinstadler 7–5 6–2, lost Ritter 6–3 6–1. **1995: 3r** d. Kamio 6–1 6–2, M. Maleeva [6] 4–6 6–4 7–5, lost Ruano-Pascual 6–2 7–6. **1996: 2r** d. A. Miller 6–1 6–1, lost Habsudova 6–2 4–6 8–6. **1997: 3r** d. Simpson 6–3 6–2, V. Williams 5–7 6–3 7–5, lost Seles [3] 6–0 6–1. **1998: 1r** [seed 12] lost Gagliardi 4–6 7–5 6–4.
WIMBLEDON – Played 13, r/u 1, qf 2
1986: 2r d. Nelson-Dunbar 6–1 6–2, lost K. Maleeva 6–4 6–2. **1987: 2r** d. Paulus 2–6 6–1 6–1, lost Henricksson 6–4 6–4. **1988: 2r** d. Devries 6–2 6–4, lost K. Adams 2–6 6–4 6–4. **1989: 1r** lost Kohde-Kilsch 6–4 6–2. **1990: last 16** [unseeded] d. Field 6–1 6–1, Pfaff 6–2 6–1, Frazier 3–6 6–2 7–5, lost Sabatini [4] 6–2 7–6. **1991: last 16** [seed 12] d. Rajchrtova 6–4 7–5, Kijimuta 3–6 6–2 6–2, L. Ferrando 6–1 6–1, lost Sabatini [2] 7–6 6–3. **1992: qf** [seed 14] d. Schultz 6-4 6-0, Medvedeva 7-5 2-6 6-3, Provis 4-6 7-5 6-3, Frazier 6-0 6-3, lost Seles [1] 6-1 6-3. **1993: last 16** [seed 16] d. Stubbs 7–5 6–4, Javer 6–1 6–2, Davenport 6–3 7–6, lost Navratilova [2] 6–1 6–3. **1994: 3r** d. Carlsson 6–2 6–1, Reinach 6–3 6–7 6–2, lost Martinez [3] 6–1 6–3. **1995: 3r** d. Vento 6–1 4–6 7–5, Pierce [seed 5] 6–4 3–6 6–1, lost Basuki 6–7 6–3 6–4. **1996: 3r** d. Kamstra 6–2 3–6 6–1, M. Maleeva [10] 7–6 3–6 9–7, lost Hy-Boulais 6–3 3–6 6–4. **1997: qf** [unseeded] d. Miyagi 6–3 6–4, Guse 6–0 6–3, Wiesner 3–6 6–3 6–2, Testud 4–6 7–5 12–10, lost Sanchez-Vicario [8] 6–2 7–5. **1998: r/u** [seed 16] d. Inoue 2–6 6–1 6–3, Majoli 6–0 6–1, Halard-Decugis 7–6 3–6 6–4, Smith 6–3 6–1, Davenport [2] 6–3 6–3, Zvereva 1–6 7–6 6–3, lost Novotna 6–4 7–6.
US OPEN – Played 13
1986: 1r lost Sabatini [11] 6–3 6–2. **1987: 2r** d. Ludloff 6–4 6–2, lost M. Maleeva 6–1 6–3. **1988: 2r** d. Louie-Harper 1–6 7–6 6–1, lost M. J. Fernandez 6–4 6–4. **1989: 3r** d. Farley 6–1 6–3, Rinaldi 6–2 6–1, lost Man. Maleeva [7] 6–1 6–3. **1990: last 16** [unseeded] d. Dahlman 7–5 6–2, Zardo 6–4 4–6 6–2, Martinez [seed 10] 6–2 6–1, lost Garrison [4] 6–1 7–5. **1991: 1r** [seed 14] lost Labat 7–5 6–4. **1992: 2r** [seed 12] d. Ercegovic 6-3 6-2, Coetzer 6-0 6-0. **1993: last 16** [seed 14] d. Brioukhovets 1–6 6–4 6–1, Boogert 6–1 6–4, Singer 6–3 6–2, lost Sanchez-Vicario [2] 6–4 6–3. **1994: 2r** d. Rottier 7–5 2–6 7–5, lost Sanchez-Vicario [2] 6–2 7–6. **1995: 3r** d. Bradtke 6–3 6–1, Shriver 6–4 6–3, lost Graf [1] 6–3 6–3. **1996: 2r** d. Gavaldon 7–6 6–2, lost Martinez [4] 6–1 6–3. **1997: 1r** lost Habsudova 7–5 7–6. **1998: last 16** [seed 10] d. Perfetti 6–3 6–2, Barabanschikova 6–7 6–2 6–3, Nagyova 6–1 6–1, lost Davenport [2] 6–1 6–4.

OLYMPIC RECORD

1992: (Barcelona) 2r [seed 10] d. Zrubakova 6-3 6-2, lost Rittner 6-3 6-2. **1996: (Atlanta) 1r** lost Sabatini [13] 7–5 6–2.

CAREER FED CUP RECORD

1985: October (in JPN, Hard): *World Group 1r NZL d. FRA 2–1.* R1 d. J. Richardson 3–6 6–3 6–2; R3 (with I. Demongeot) lost B. Cordwell/Richardson 6–0 7–5. *Consolation Plate 2r FRA d. URU 3–0.* R3 (with Demongeot) d. M. Clavijo/L. Rodriguez 6–1 6–0. *Consolation Plate qf RUS d. FRA 2–1.* R1 d. N. Bykova 5–7 6–4 6–4; R3 (with Demongeot) lost S. Cherneva/L. Savchenko 6–3 6–1. **1986: July (in TCH, Clay):** *World Group 1r FRA d. SWE 3–0.* R3 (with P. Paradis) d. H. Dahlstrom/M. Lundqvist 6–3 5–7 6–2). *World Group 2r BUL d. FRA 2–1.* R1 lost K. Maleeva 7–6 7–6. **1987: August (in CAN, Hard):** *World Group 1r FRA d. AUT 3–0.* R2 d. J. Wiesner 6–3 7–5. *World Group 2r USA d. FRA 3–0.* R2 lost C. Evert 6–1 6–0. **1989: October (in JPN, Hard):** *World Group 1r ESP d. FRA 2–0.* R2 lost A. Sanchez-Vicario 6–4 6–2. **1990: July (in USA, Hard):** *World Group 1r FRA d. TPE 3–0.* R2 d. S. Wang 6–3 6–2. *World Group 2r FRA d. NZL 3–0.* R2 d. B. Cordwell 6–1 6–2. *World Group qf ESP d. FRA 3–0.* R2 lost A. Sanchez-Vicario 7–6 6–1. **1991: July (in GBR, Hard):** *World Group 1r POL d. FRA 2–1.* R2 lost K. Nowak 4–6 6–4 6–4; R3 (with M. Pierce) lost M. Mroz/K. Teodorowicz 6–4 6–4). *World Group Play-off FRA d. YUG 2–0.* R2 d. N. Ercegovic 6–2 5–7 6–2. **1992: July (in GER, Clay):** *World Group 1r FRA d. CHN 2–1.* R2 lost F. Li 6–1 6–7 6–3; R3 (with I. Demongeot) d. Li/M. Tang 6–3 7–6). *World Group 2r FRA d. RUS 3–0.* R2 d. E. Maniokova 6–1 6–3; R3 (with Demongeot) d. E. Makarova/E. Pogorelova 6–3 6–3. *World Group qf USA d. FRA 2–1.* R2 d. L. McNeil 6–4 7–5; R3 (with Demongeot) lost G. Fernandez/P. Shriver 6–4 6–2. **1993: July (in GER, Clay):** *World Group 1r FRA d. CAN 2–1.* R2 d. P. Hy 6–4 6–1; R3 (with J. Halard) d. J. Hetherington/Hy 7–5 7–6. *World Group 2r FRA d. SWE 3–0.* R2 d. C. Dahlman 6–1 7–6; R3 (with Halard) d. M. Lindstrom/M. Strandlund 6–2 6–3. *World Group qf FRA d. TCH 3–0.* R2. d. J. Novotna 6–1 0–6 6–3. *World Group sf ESP d. FRA 2–1.* R2 lost A. Sanchez-Vicario 6–1 6–4. **1994: July (in GER, Clay):** *World Group 1r FRA d. KOR 3–0.* R3 (with A. Fusai) d. J. Choi/S. Park 6–4 6–4. *World Group 2r FRA d. ITA 3–0.* R3 (with J. Halard) d. R. Grande/M. Grossi 6–4 6–1. *World Group qf FRA d. BUL 2–1.* R3 (with Halard) d. K./M. Maleeva 6–2 3–6 6–2. *World Group sf USA d. FRA 3–0.* R3 (with Halard) lost G. Fernandez/Z. Garrison 3–6 6–1 6–2. **1995: April** – *World Group qf FRA d. RSA 3–2 in FRA (Clay).* R5 (with J. Halard) d. M. De Swardt/E. Rainach 7–5 6–2. **July** – *World Group sf USA d. FRA 3–2 in USA (Carpet).* R5 (with Halard) lost L. Davenport/G. Fernandez 6–1 7–6. **1996: April** – *World Group qf FRA d. ARG 3–2 in FRA (Clay).* R1 lost F. Labat 6–3 6–4; R4 lost P. Suarez 7–6 6–1; R5 (with J. Halard-Decugis) d. Labat/P. Tarabini 6–2 6–4. **July:** – *World Group sf ESP d. FRA 3–2 in FRA (Carpet).* R5 (with Halard-Decugis) lost C. Martinez/A. Sanchez-Vicario 6–4 2–1 ret. **1997: March** – *World Group qf FRA d. JPN 4–1 in JPN (Hard).* R2 d. A. Sugiyama 4–6 7–5 6–4; R4 d. N. Sawamatsu 7–5 4–6 17–15. **July** – *World Group sf FRA d. BEL 3–2 in BEL (Clay).* R5 (with A. Fusai) d. E. Callens/D. Van Roost 3–6 6–2 7–5. **October** – *World Group final FRA d. NED 4–1 in NED (Carpet).* R5 (with Fusai) d. M. bollegraf/C. Vis 6–3 6–4. **1998: April** – *World Group qf FRA d. BEL 3–2 in BEL (Hard).* R5 (with A. Fusai) d. E. Callens/L. Courtois 6–4 6–0. **July** – *World Group sf SUI d. FRA 5–0 in SUI (Clay).* R5 (with Fusai) lost E. Gagliardi/P. Schnyder 2–6 6–3 6–3.

GRAND SLAM CUP RECORD – Played 1, sf 1

1998: sf d. Davenport 4–6 6–1 7–5, lost V. Williams 6–4 6–0.

SEASON ENDING CHAMPIONSHIPS – Played 6, sf 1, qf 1

(1983-94 Virginia Slims, 1995 Corel, 1996-98 Chase)

1990: 1r lost M. J. Fernandez 6–1 7–6. **1991: 1r** lost Capriati 5–7 6–0 7–6. **1992: 1r** lost Seles 6–1 6–2. **1993: 1r** lost Navratilova 6–4 6–4. **1994-96:** Did not play. **1997: sf** d. Coetzer 6–3 6–3, Majoli 7–6 7–6, lost Pierce 6–2 5–7 6–4. **1998: qf** d. Zvereva 6–3 6–1, lost Davenport 6–0 6–3.

REMAINING WOMEN'S BIOGRAPHIES

The following biographies show the players' progress each year in the four Grand Slam Championships. It is shown thus: A (Australian Open), F (French Open), W (Wimbledon), US (US Open), followed by the round reached, or '–' if a player did not compete.

SABINE APPELMANS (BEL)

Born Aalst, 22 April 1972; lives Asse; LH; 2HB; 5ft 6in; 127lb; turned pro 1989; career singles titles 7; final 1998 WTA ranking 49; 1998 prize money $155,489; career prize money $1,603,819.

Coached by Steve Martens. Husband Serge Habourdin (married 20 September 1996). She is naturally right-handed, but chose to join a left-handed group when learning to play tennis in order to be with a friend. **1987:** (283). **1988:** (215) A –, F 2, W –, US –. Enjoyed some success on the European satellite circuits and upset Burgin 1r French Open. **1989:** (149) A –, F –, W –, US –. Reached her 1st primary circuit qf at Taipei. **1990:** (22) A 3, F 1, W –, US 3. R/u Auckland (d. Cordwell) and reached sf Wellington and Singapore, breaking into top 100 and finishing the year in the top 25. **1991:** (18) A 4, F 4, W 1, US 1. Won her 1st singles title at Phoenix, following with VS Nashville; was r/u Tokyo Suntory, reached sf Oslo and Puerto Rico and appeared in 3 doubles f. Voted Belgian Sports Celebrity of the Year. **1992:** (26) A 1, F 2, W 2, US 4. Won Pattaya City and r/u Tokyo Suntory, as well as reaching qf Olympics, Essen, Berlin and Leipzig. In GS upset Huber en route to last 16 US Open, unseeded. **1993:** (36) A 1, F 2, W 3, US 2. Having won Porto Challenger but reached no qf on the main tour, she was r/u Budapest (d. Wiesner) in Oct. and followed the next week with sf Essen (d. Maleeva-Fragniere). **1994:** (27) A 3, F 2, W 1, US 1. Won Linz (d. Huber) and Pattaya City and reached sf Tokyo Japan Open, Los Angeles (d. Novotna) and Moscow. Ranked No. 1 in Belgium, she reached her highest world ranking of 17 in May, before slipping back out of the top 20. **1995:** (31) A 3, F 3, W 1, US 3. Won Zagreb and reached qf Paris Open, Linz, Strasbourg (d. Frazier) and Tokyo Nicherei. **1996:** (21) A 4, F 3, W 4, US 1. Upset Novotna, Sukova and Halard-Decugis on her way to the title at Linz and reached sf Moscow, plus qf Jakarta, Zurich (d. Martinez) and Luxembourg. She made her mark in GS: at French Open she was 5–2 up in 2s v Seles, but won no more games, and at Wimbledon, where she was unseeded, she scraped past Schultz-McCarthy 12–10 fs before extending Sanchez-Vicario to 3s. In doubles she reached 2 f with Oremans, but won no title. **1997:** (16) A qf, F 1, W 4, US 1. She was r/u Budapest, and although she reached no other f, she appeared in qf Australian Open, Gold Coast, Berlin, Strasbourg, Rosmalen, Leipzig, Zurich (d. Schultz-McCarthy and Majoli) and Luxembourg. Once again she impressed in GS, removing Martinez at Australian Open and Schultz-McCarthy at Wimbledon, where she was unseeded. Upset M. J. Fernandez at Chicago and surprised Sanchez-Vicario in Fed Cup as BEL d. ESP. Qualified for Chase Champs 1st time, but fell 1r to Pierce at her best. **1998:** A 1, F 1, W 3, US –. Her best singles performances were an upset of Graf (returning from injury) en route to sf Hannover, and qf appearance at Linz. In doubles she won Paris Open and Hertogenbosch with Oremans. **1998 HIGHLIGHTS – SINGLES: Australian Open 1r** [seed 12] (lost Zvereva 2–6 6–2 6–3), **French Open 1r** (lost Pierce [seed 11] 6–2 6–3), **Wimbledon 3r** (d. Torrens-Valero 6–3 6–3, Latimer 6–1 6–4, lost Van Roost 6–1 6–4); **sf** Hannover (d. Spirlea 4–1 ret, Maleeva 7–5 6–3, Graf 6–3 7–6, lost Schnyder 6–3 6–3). **1998 HIGHLIGHTS – DOUBLES:** (with Oremans) **won** Paris Open (d. Kournikova/Neiland 1–6 6–3 7–6), **won** Hertogenbosch (d. Cristea/Melicharova 6–7 7–6 7–6). **CAREER HIGHLIGHTS – Australian Open – qf 1997** (d. Sukova 6–2 6–2, Grossman 6–4 6–1, Boogert 6–1 3–0 ret, Martinez 2–6 7–5 6–1, lost Pierce 1–6 6–4 6–4).

OLGA BARABANSCHIKOVA (BRS)

Born Minsk, 2 November 1979; lives London, England; RH; 5ft 8in; 124lb; career singles titles 0; final 1998 WTA ranking 61; 1998 prize money $126,991.

Coached by Victor Archutowski. Has lived in Ealing since age 12. **1994:** Won Nat Jun Champs. **1995:** Won Astrid Bowl and took her 1st pro title on the French satellite circuit. **1996:** (152) Won Wimbledon Jun doubles with Mauresmo and was a member of the Belarus Olympic Team. **1997:** (59) A –, F 1, W 2, US 3. Moving on to the women's tour, she upset Schultz-McCarthy at US Open and won Bushey Futures, before finishing the year on a high note with sf Pattaya. **1998:** A 3, F 1, W 1, US 2. She reached her 1st tour f at Istanbul, appeared in qf Pattaya and upset Van Roost at Tokyo Toyota. **1998 HIGHLIGHTS – SINGLES: Australian Open 3r** (d. Chladkova 6–3 6–3, Nejedly 6–2 6–4, lost Pierce [seed 5] 7–5 6–3), **French Open 1r** (lost Dechy 6–3 1–6 6–1), **Wimbledon 1r** (lost Dechaume-Balleret 6–4 6–7 11–9), **US Open 2r** (d. Sidot 6–1 6–7 6–3, lost Tauziat [seed 10] 6–7 6–2 6–3); **r/u** Istanbul (d. Dechaume-Balleret 6–0 6–3, Nemeckova 7–6 7–5, Lubiani 6–2 6–3, Golarsa 6–1 7–6, lost Nagyova 6–4 3–6 7–6).

YAYUK BASUKI (INA)

Born Yogyakarta, 30 November 1970; lives Jakarta; RH; 5ft 4½in; 125lb; turned pro 1990; career singles titles 6; final 1998 WTA ranking 56 singles, 19 doubles; 1998 prize money $220,005; career prize money $1,550,645.

Coached by her husband, Hary Suharyadi (married 31 January 1994). Ranked No. 1 in Indonesia. **1986:** Joined her country's Fed Cup team. **1988:** (284). **1989:** (377) Made her mark on the satellite circuits, winning Jakarta. **1990:** (266) Continued to enjoy success on the satellite circuits. **1991:** (35) A –, F 1, W 3, US 2. At Pattaya City, she became 1st native Indonesian to win a primary circuit title and was voted Indonesian Athlete of the Year. Upset Kohde-Kilsch en route to qf Eastbourne and reached the same stage at VS Nashville. **1992:** (48) A 3, F –, W 4, US 1. Upset Huber at Wimbledon and Pierce at Olympics, making an unexpected appearance in last 16 both times. Won Kuala Lumpur and reached sf Pattaya City. **1993:** (43) A 1, F 2, W 4, US 1. Won Pattaya City (d. Probst and Fendick) and Jakarta and reached qf Kuala Lumpur. Unseeded at Wimbledon, she upset Mag. Maleeva and extended Martinez to 3s. In doubles with Basuki won Sapporo and Taipei back-to-back in autumn. **1994:** (29) A 2, F –, W 4, US 1. Won Beijing and Jakarta and reached sf Eastbourne (d. Sukova). She also upset Tauziat 1r Australian Open and surprised Mag. Maleeva at Wimbledon. In doubles she reached 3 f, winning Hong Kong with Tedjakusuma. **1995:** (24) A 3, F 1, W 4, US 1. Sf Jakarta and Manhattan Beach (d. M. J. Fernandez, Tauziat and Davenport); reached qf Eastbourne; and upset Sabatini in Fed Cup. **1996:** (26) A 1, F 3, W 1, US 1. Reached f Jakarta, but withdrew with a cold. Upset Majoli and Frazier on her way to sf Montreal before reaching same stage Philadelphia, and appeared in qf Eastbourne (d. Davenport) and Beijing. In doubles she won Hobart with Nagatsuka and Strasbourg with Bradtke, although it was with Vis that she played Chase Champs. Won Karen Krantzcke Sportsmanship Award. **1997:** (21) A 2, F 2, W qf, US 2. She proved to be a dangerous opponent on her way to f Birmingham (d. Spirlea), sf Tokyo Nicherei, and qf Wimbledon (unseeded), Sydney (d. Pierce), Paris Open (d. Schultz-McCarthy), San Diego (d. Huber) and Chicago (d. Schultz-McCarthy). In doubles she played 4 f and won Los Angeles and Toronto back-to-back with Vis, with whom she qualified for Chase Champs again. Was hampered in the spring by injuries – tendinitis in right foot, ankle and calf. **1998:** A 4, F 1, W 3, US 1. Upset Van Roost at Australian Open (unseeded) and Montreal, while Spirlea was her victim at Birmingham, where she reached sf before the tourn was cancelled. She and Vis played 2 doubles f, and although they won no title they qualified for Chase Champs, where they upset Hingis/Novotna 1r. She won the Karen Krantzcke Sportsmanship award again. **1998 HIGHLIGHTS – SINGLES: Australian Open last 16** [unseeded] (d. Tu 6–7 6–3 6–1, Boogert 5–7 6–4 6–3, Van Roost [seed 14] 6–4 6–4, lost Hingis [seed 1] 6–0 6–0), **French Open 1r** (lost Leon-Garcia 6–3 6–2), **Wimbledon 3r** (d. Reeves 6–4 6–0, Mauresmo 6–3 6–4, lost Seles [seed 6] 6–2 6–3), **US Open 1r** (lost Kremer 6–4 5–7 7–5); **sf** Birmingham (d. Dechy 1–6 6–3 6–3, Smith 3–6 6–1 6–2, Spirlea 6–4 5–7 7–5, tourn cancelled). **1998 HIGHLIGHTS – DOUBLES:** (with Vis) **r/u** Strasbourg (lost Fusai/Tauziat 6–4 6–3), **r/u** Montreal (lost Hingis/Novotna 6–3 6–4). **CAREER HIGHLIGHTS – SINGLES: Wimbledon – qf 1997** (d. Sugiyama 6–3 6–0, Gorrochategui 6–2 6–0, Kijimuta 6–3 6–2, Hy-Boulais 6–0 7–6, lost Novotna 6–3 6–3).

CARA BLACK (ZIM)

Born Harare, 17 February 1979, and lives there; RH; 2HB; 5ft 4in; 120lb; career singles titles 0; final 1998 WTA ranking 44; 1998 prize money $116,203.

Coached by her father, Don Black, a former pro player, and Daria Kopsic-Segal. Her brothers, Byron and Wayne, play the men's circuit. **1992:** All-Africa champ. **1994:** Won Nat Jun Champ in singles and doubles. **1995:** (489) Won Wimbledon Jun doubles with Olsza and Nat Jun Champ in singles and doubles again. In the women's game won 2 Futures singles titles, being r/u in both doubles. **1996:** (337) Played Fed Cup and won Nitra Futures. **1997:** (189) Missed Australian Open Jun, but in other Jun GS was r/u French Open to Henin, won Wimbledon over Rippner and US Open over Chevalier, as well as taking French Open and Wimbledon doubles with Selyutina. These results placed her at No. 1 in ITF Jun rankings at year's end in both singles and doubles. In the women's game, she won Futures titles at Dinard and Mission. **1998:** A –, F 2, W 3, US 2. Playing her 1st full year on the main circuit, she broke into the top 50 with an upset of Schnyder 2r Wimbledon and her 1st career sf at Boston (d. Farina and Likhovtseva). **1998 HIGHLIGHTS – SINGLES: French Open 2r** (d. Alcazar 6–3 4–6 6–3, lost Likhovtseva 7–5 7–5), **Wimbledon 3r** (d. Jeyaseelan 6–2 6–4, Schnyder [seed 13] 6–7 7–5 6–3, lost Tanasugarn 6–4 6–0), **US Open 2r** (d. Webb 6–4 6–2, lost Pierce [seed 12] 6–1 6–1); **sf** Boston (d. Plischke 7–6 3–6 6–1, Farina 4–6 6–4 6–2, Likhovtseva 1–6 6–1 6–2, lost Schett 6–2 2–6 6–2).

MANON BOLLEGRAF (NED)

Born Den Bosch, 10 April 1964; lives Ermelo; RH; 2HB; 5ft 8in; 150lb; turned pro 1985; career singles titles 1; final 1998 WTA ranking – singles, 18 doubles; 1998 prize money $84,019; career prize money $1,879,949.

Coached by Ron Timmermans and at tournaments by Charlton Eagle. **1986:** (148) Qf Singapore. **1987:** (120) A 2, F 2, W –, US –. Qf Little Rock and took over the No. 1 ranking in her country. **1988:** (117) A 2, F 1, W 2, US 2. Qf Brisbane. **1989:** (38) A 3, F 3, W 1, US 2. In singles won 1st primary circuit title at Oklahoma (unseeded), reached sf Brussels and Nashville and upset McNeil 2r French Open. In doubles won 4 women's titles plus French Open mixed with Nijssen. **1990:** (32) A 2, F 1, W 1, US 2. In singles r/u VS Oklahoma and reached sf Strasbourg. Appeared in 5 doubles f with various partners, winning Wichita with McGrath and Zurich with Pfaff. **1991:** (49) A 1, F 1, W 3, US 1. R/u Colorado and sf Oklahoma in singles, won Leipzig with Demongeot in doubles and took US Open mixed with Nijssen. **1992:** (44) A 1, F qf, W 2, US –. In singles she upset Maleeva-Fragniere and Tauziat in reaching qf French Open, unseeded, and reached sf VS Oklahoma and qf Chicago. In doubles she reached 4 f with different partners, winning Waregem with Vis. Missed Olympics and US Open after tearing several ligaments at Frankfurt, for which she underwent surgery, and was out for rest of year. **1993:** (161) A 1, F 1, W 1, US 1. At US Open she extended eventual finalist Sukova to 3s tb 1r, but it was in doubles that she excelled. In mixed she was r/u French Open with Nijssen and in partnership with Adams she played 5 women's f, winning 3 and qualifying for VS Champs, where they failed to pass 1r. **1994:**

(109) A 1, F 1, W 1, US 1. She upset Garrison-Jackson at FC Cup, but reached no qf in singles. Again her strength lay in doubles, in which she appeared in 10 f with various partners, winning 1 with Neiland and 2 with Navratilova, with whom she qualified for VS Champs, where they reached sf. **1995:** (158) A 2, F –, W –, US 2. Played 9 doubles f with various partners, winning 4 with Arendt, with whom she qualified for WTA Champs, and 1 with Stubbs. **1996:** (–) A –, F –, W –, US –. In doubles she won Linz with McGrath and Edinburgh with Arendt; in mixed was r/u US Open with Leach. Underwent arthroscopic surgery on her left knee at end Sept., which prevented her playing at Chase Champs, for which she qualified in doubles. **1997:** (–) A –, F –, W –, US –. Returning in time for Australian Open, she won the mixed doubles there with Leach, adding US Open later in year. In women's doubles with Arendt, she was r/u Wimbledon and from 6 other f won 3 titles and shared another, qualifying for Chase Champs. There, however, they were forced to retire sf v Fusai/Tauziat. **1998:** A –, F –, W –, US –. Playing doubles only, she was r/u Leipzig with Spirlea. **1998 HIGHLIGHTS – DOUBLES:** (with Spirlea) **r/u** Leipzig (lost Likhovtseva/Sugiyama 6–3 6–7 6–1). **CAREER HIGHLIGHTS – SINGLES: French Open – qf 1992** [unseeded] (d. Maniokova 6–2 6–3, Thoren 6–2 4–6 7–5, Maleeva-Fragniere 7–5 6–2, Tauziat 6–4 1–6 6–2, lost Sanchez-Vicario 6–2 6–3). **CAREER HIGHLIGHTS – DOUBLES:** (with Arendt) **Wimbledon – r/u 1997** (lost G. Fernandez/Zvereva 7–6 6–4). **CAREER HIGHLIGHTS – MIXED DOUBLES:** (with Nijssen unless stated) **Australian Open –** (with Leach) **won 1997** (d. De Jager/Neiland 6–3 6–7 7–5), **French Open – won 1989** (d. De La Pena/Sanchez-Vicario 3–6 6–7 6–2); **US Open – won 1991** (d. E. Sanchez/Sanchez-Vicario 6–2 7–6), (with Leach) **won 1997** (d. Albano/Paz 3–6 7–5 7–6).

KRISTINA BRANDI (USA)

Born San Juan, Puerto Rico, 29 March 1977; lives Tampa, Fla; RH; 2HB; turned pro 1995; career singles titles 0; final 1998 WTA ranking 70; 1998 prize money $92,573.

Coached by her father, Joe, who formerly coached Sampras. Won Nat CC 14s. **1992:** (559). **1993:** (558). **1994:** (268) Won Indianapolis Futures. **1995:** (191). **1996:** (148) A –, F –, W –, US 2. **1997:** (78) A 3, F 1, W 2, US 1. Took a set off Seles at Wimbledon. **1998:** A 1, F 1, W 1, US 1. Emerging from the ITF circuit, where she won Peachtree $25,000 and Austin $50,000, she finished the year in style with her 1st sf on the main tour at Pattaya. **1998 HIGHLIGHTS – SINGLES: Australian Open 1r** (lost Ellwood 6–4 5–7 6–3), **French Open 1r** (lost Tatarkova 6–4 6–4), **Wimbledon 1r** (lost Wang 7–6 7–5), **US Open 1r** (lost Sanchez-Vicario [seed 4] 6–2 6–2); **won** Peachtree ITF (d. Kremer 6–3 6–3), **won** Austin ITF (d. Tu 3–6 6–3 6–4); **sf** Pattaya (d. Callens 6–4 4–6 6–2, Courtois 5–7 6–4 6–2, Tu 6–3 6–3, lost Halard-Decugis 6–0 6–1).

KIM CLIJSTERS (BEL)

Born Bilzen, 8 June 1983, and lives there; RH; 2HB; 5ft 8in; 132lb; career singles titles 0; final 1998 WTA ranking 409.

Coached by Carl Maes. **1996:** Played in winning BEL Europa Cup squad with her sister, Elke. **1998:** In Jun tennis she was r/u Wimbledon singles to Srebotnik, won French Open doubles with Dokic and US Open doubles with Dyrberg. In the women's game, on the ITF $10,000 circuit, she won both singles and doubles at Brussels I and took Koksijde singles. **1998 HIGHLIGHTS – SINGLES: won** Brussels I ITF (d. Sobotkova 7–6 6–1), **won** Koksijde ITF (d. Dominguez 6–3 6–4).

AMANDA COETZER (RSA)

Born Hoopstad, 22 October 1971, and lives there and Hilton Head, SC; RH; 2HB; 5ft 2in; 120lb; turned pro 1988; career singles titles 6; final 1998 WTA ranking 17; 1998 prize money $534,948; career prize money $3,148,276..

Coached by Nigel Sears; boyfriend and hitting partner is Mike Newell. Shares a great-grandmother with Elna Reinach. **1987:** (442). **1988:** (153) Won 4 titles on the satellite circuits. **1989:** (63) A –, F 4, W 1, US 1. Made an unexpected appearance in last 16 French Open and reached sf VS Arizona. **1990:** (75) A –, F 1, W 2, US 1. Qf VS Florida, Geneva and VS Albuquerque. **1991:** (67) A –, F 2, W 2, US 1. Upset K. Maleeva at Berlin and G. Fernandez on the way to her 1st primary circuit f at Puerto Rico. **1992:** (17) A –, F 3, W –, US 3. Scored some big upsets during the year, surprising Garrison on her way to last 16 Olympics, unseeded, Wiesner and Sabatini en route to sf VS Florida, Capriati and Zvereva in reaching the same stage Italian Open and Tauziat at US Open. She also appeared in sf Kitzbuhel and Taipei, plus 5 more qf. In doubles she played 4 f with different partners, winning Taranto with Gorrochategui and Puerto Rico with Reinach. **1993:** (15) A 1, F 2, W 2, US 3. Won her 1st Kraft tour title at Melbourne Open, following in autumn with Tokyo Nicherei (d. Sanchez-Vicario). She was r/u Indian Wells, where she extended M. J. Fernandez to 3s tb and reached sf VS Florida, Amelia Island (d. Capriati) and Barcelona. In doubles she was r/u US Open with Gorrochategui and reached 3 other f. Qualified for VS Champs 1st time in both singles, where she upset M. J. Fernandez before falling qf to Graf, and doubles, in which she and Gorrochategui lost 1r. **1994:** (18) A 2, F 4, W 4, US qf. Won both singles and doubles (with Harvey-Wild) at Prague in May, was r/u Indian Wells (d. M. J. Fernandez and Davenport) and reached sf Stratton Mountain and Schenectady. Unseeded at French Open, she upset Date as she embarked on her best year yet in GS. She qualified for VS Champs singles, but fell 1r to Pierce. **1995:** (19) A 3, F 2, W 2, US 1. Her best moments came at Toronto, where she was unseeded: after becoming the 1st of only 2 players all year to beat Graf, ending her 32-match winning streak 1r, she went on to upset Pierce and Novotna before losing f to Seles, who was playing in her 1st tourn for 2½ years. She met Graf again 1r US Open, where she held 7 mps before taking 1s tb, but lost the next 2 sets. She was also r/u Brighton (d. M. Maleeva), reached sf Barcelona and Tokyo Nicherei plus 2 more qf, upset Pierce in Fed Cup and qualified for WTA Champs, where she lost 1r to Graf. In doubles she played 3 f, winning 2 with Gorrochategui. She won the Karen Krantzcke Sportsmanship Award. **1996:** (17) A sf, F 4, W 2, US qf. She made her mark in GS, at Australian Open becoming the 1st South African in the open era to reach that stage in GS, and upsetting Huber at US Open, where she was unseeded. In other tourns she was r/u Oklahoma and appeared in qf Indian Wells, Madrid, Los Angeles and Tokyo Nicherei to qualify for Chase Champs, where Novotna removed her 1r. **1997:** (4) A sf, F sf, W 2, US 4. In her best year to date, she became only the 2nd South African woman to crack the top 10, after Greer Stevens in 1979, and in Nov. overtook Seles to reach a career-high No. 4. She continued to cause many significant upsets on her way to the titles at Budapest (singles and doubles, with Fusai) and Luxembourg, r/u Leipzig and sf Australian Open, French Open, Amelia Island, Bol, Berlin, Strasbourg, Stanford, San Diego, Atlanta and Filderstadt, plus qf Tokyo Pan Pacific, Oklahoma City, FC Cup (d. Sanchez-Vicario), Toronto and Philadelphia. At Australian Open she ended Graf's run of 25 GS matches won, she beat her again at Berlin 6–0 6–1 (inflicting the worst defeat of her career in 57 mins on the former No. 1, who was returning from injury), and upset her a third time at French Open, before extending Majoli to 7–5 3s in their sf. At Leipzig she became only the 3rd of 5 players all year to beat Hingis, and other upsets included Novotna at Amelia Island and Atlanta, M. J. Fernandez at Amelia Island, Martinez at French Open and Sanchez-Vicario at FC Cup. At Chase Champs, however, she was unexpectedly beaten 1r by Tauziat. **1998:** A 4, F 1, W 2, US qf. Although she could not reach the heights of the previous season, she won her 1st Tier I singles title at FC Cup, as well as reaching sf Tokyo Pan Pacific and Amelia Island, plus qf Indian Wells, Strasbourg, Boston, New Haven, Zurich, Philadelphia (d. Sanchez-Vicario) and US Open (d. Martinez). These results took her to Chase Champs, where she fell 1r again – to Pierce. She had 3 coaches during the year: Gavin Hopper left to coach Seles and Philippoussis; she was briefly with Michael De Jongh until he moved to coach Pierce; and she finished the year with Nigel Sears. **1998 HIGHLIGHTS – SINGLES: Australian Open last 16** [seed 3] (d. Paulus 6–2 6–0, Neiland 2–6 6–1 6–0, Ellwood 6–3 6–1, lost Huber [seed 10] 2–6 6–4 7–5), **French Open 1r** [seed 5] (lost Schnyder 6–4 3–6 8–6), **Wimbledon 2r** [seed 9] (d. Guse 6–2 6–2, lost Sawamatsu 3–6 6–3 6–2), **US Open qf** [seed 15] (d. Cacic 6–1 7–6, Sandu 6–0 6–2, Schett 3–6 6–0 6–3, Martinez [seed 7] 6–4 4–6 6–2, lost Davenport [seed 2] 6–0 6–4); **won** FC Cup (d. Farina 6–4 6–3, Ruano-Pascual 6–0 6–4, Glass 4–6 7–6, Raymond 6–4 6–1, Spirlea 6–4 6–3); **sf** Tokyo Pan Pacific (d. Reeves 6–4 6–4, Sugiyama 6–3 2–6 6–2, lost Davenport 6–2 6–1), **sf** Amelia Island (d. Serna 6–3 6–3, Dragomir 6–4 6–7 6–0, Snyder 6–4 6–4, lost Martinez 6–4 6–0). **1998 HIGHLIGHTS – DOUBLES:** (with Sanchez-Vicario) **r/u** Rome (lost Ruano-Pascual/Suarez 7–6 6–4). **CAREER HIGHLIGHTS – SINGLES: Australian Open – sf 1996** (d. Schnell 6–2 6–2, Hack 6–1 6–1, Hiraki 6–3 6–3, Likhovtseva 6–3 6–3, Hingis 7–5 4–6 6–1, lost Huber 4–6 6–4 6–2), **sf 1997** (d. Kournikova 6–2 6–2, Kandarr 6–2 7–6, Serna 6–3 6–2, Graf 6–2 7–5, Po 6–4 6–1, lost Pierce 7–5 6–1); **French Open – sf 1997** (d. Grande 6–4 6–0, Frazier 7–6 6–4, Babel 6–4 6–2, Martinez 6–7 6–4 6–3, Graf 6–1 6–4, lost Majoli 6–3 4–6 7–5); **US Open – qf 1994** (d. Ritter 6–1 7–6, Maniokova 6–2 6–0, De Swardt 6–1 6–3, Endo 6–3 6–0, lost Graf 6–0 6–2), **qf 1996** (d. Huber 6–1 2–6 6–2, De Swardt 6–2 7–5, Spirlea 7–6 7–5, Raymond 6–4 6–1, lost Seles 6–0 6–3), **qf 1998. CAREER HIGHLIGHTS – DOUBLES:** (with Gorrochategui) **US Open – r/u 1993** (lost Sanchez-Vicario/Sukova 6–4 6–2).

CATALINA CRISTEA (ROM)

Born Bucharest, 2 July 1975, and lives there; RH; 2HB; 5ft 8in; 125lb; turned pro 1992; career singles titles 0; final 1998 WTA ranking 67; 1998 prize money $120,622.

Coached by Cosmescu Constantin. **1990:** (806). **1991:** (504) R/u US Open Jun doubles with Carlsson. **1992:** (429). **1993:** (127) R/u Australian Open Jun doubles with Carlsson. On the senior tour she reached her 1st qf at Puerto Rico (d. Quentrec), following in Oct. with her 1st sf at Taipei. **1994:** (191) A 2, F 1, W –, US –. **1995:** (103) A –, F 3, W –, US 1. Upset Zvereva 1r French Open and joined her country's Fed Cup team. **1996:** (125) A 1, F 1, W 1, US –. Qf Warsaw was her best showing on the main tour, and on the ITF circuit she won Bucharest. **1997:** (73) A 1, F 2, W 1, US 1. She appeared in sf Prague, but reached no other qf on the main tour. **1998:** A 1, F 2, W 1, US 1. Her best singles performances were qf Warsaw (d. Appelmans) and Quebec City, and an upset of Van Roost 1r Budapest. In doubles she played 3 doubles f with different partners, but won no title. **1998 HIGHLIGHTS – SINGLES: Australian Open 1r** (lost Grzybowska 6–3 6–2), **French Open 2r** (d. De Swardt 6–1 6–2, lost Sanchez-Vicario [seed 4] 6–2 6–3), **Wimbledon 1r** (lost Sanchez-Vicario [seed 5] 5–7 6–2 6–0), **US Open 1r** (lost Davenport [seed 2] 6–0 6–2). **1998 HIGHLIGHTS – DOUBLES:** (with Kunce) **r/u** Oklahoma City (lost S./V. Williams 7–5 6–2), (with Montalvo) **r/u** Budapest (lost Ruano-Pascual/Suarez 4–6 6–1 6–1), (with Melicharova) **r/u** Hertogenbosch (lost Appelmans/Oremans 6–7 7–6 7–6).

ALEXIA DECHAUME-BALLERET (FRA)

Born La Rochelle, 3 May 1970; lives St Laurent; RH; 2HB; 5ft 5in; 132lb; turned pro 1985; career singles titles 0; final 1998 WTA ranking 68; 1998 prize money $122,516.

Coached by her husband Bernard Balleret (married 13 November 1993) and on the road by Philippe Duxin. **1986:** (225) A –, F 2, W –, US –. **1987:** (127) A –, F 1, W –, US –. Appeared in her 1st VS qf at Athens. **1988:** (127) A –, F 1, W 1, US 1. Reached qf Taranto on the main tour and won Bayonne on the French satellite circuit, breaking into top 100 in June. **1989:** (173) A 2, F 2, W –, US –. **1990:** (84) Reached her 1st primary circuit f at Taranto and returned to the top 100 in Sept. **1991:** (72) A 3, F 1, W 1, US 1. In singles her best showing was qf Barcelona; in doubles she reached 2 f, winning Taranto with Labat. **1992:** (54) A 3, F 1, W 2, US 1. In singles she reached sf San Marino, plus 3 more qf, and upset Wiesner at Australian Open. In partnership with Labat she won Kitzbuhel and San Marino back-to-back in July, followed by Schenectady in Aug. **1993:** (–) A –, F –, W –, US –. Withdrew Sydney with a wrist injury that kept her out all year. Married her coach, Bernard Balleret, at end of year. **1994:** (65) A –, F 4, W 2, US 3. Returned to action at Auckland in Feb. and received a wild-card at French Open, where she reached last 16. Otherwise her best showing was qf Beijing. **1995:** (132) A 1, F 1, W 1, US 1. Qf Puerto Rico and played 1 doubles f with Testud. **1996:** (95) A 2, F 1, W 1, US 1. Qf Strasbourg and reached Bol doubles with Fusai. **1997:** (65) A 1, F 1, W 1, US 2. She reached her 1st career f at Cardiff and sf Jakarta, as well as qf Auckland and Prague (d. Schultz-McCarthy). In doubles she won Tokyo Japan Open with Hiraki. **1998:** A 1, F 3, W 2, US 2. In a quieter year she reached no qf on the main tour. **1998 HIGHLIGHTS – SINGLES: Australian Open 1r** (lost V. Williams 6–3 6–0), **French Open 3r** (d. Lugina 6–1 5–7 6–2, Gersi 6–2 5–7 6–1, lost V. Williams [seed 8] 6–2 6–1), **Wimbledon 2r** (d. Barabanschikova 6–4 6–7 11–9, lost Halard-Decugis 6–4 7–6), **US Open 2r** (d. K. Miller 6–4 6–2, lost Farina 6–3 1–6 6–3).

NATHALIE DECHY (FRA)

Born Abimes, Guadeloupe, 21 February 1979; lives Villeneuf d'Ascq; RH; 2HB; 5ft 9in; 132lb; career singles titles 0; final 1998 WTA ranking 48; 1998 prize money $137,517.

Coached by Nicolas Kelaidis. Won Orange Bowl 16s and Nat 16s in singles and doubles. **1994:** (586) Enjoyed some success on the satellite circuits. **1995:** (294) A –, F 1, W –, US –. **1996:** (102) A –, F 2, W 1, US 2. R/u Australian Open Jun to Grzybowska and won Eastbourne Under-21. In the senior game, she reached qf Paris Open (d. Tauziat) after qualifying and appeared at same stage Surabaya. **1997:** (90) A 1, F 1, W 2, US 2. Upset V. Williams 1r Toronto and broke into top 100. **1998:** A 1, F 3, W 1, US 4. She moved into the top 50 with her 1st sf on the main tour at Quebec City and an upset of Paulus at US Open, where she was unseeded. **1998 HIGHLIGHTS – SINGLES: Australian Open 1r** (lost Schnyder 6–1 6–2), **French Open 3r** (d. Barabanschikova 6–3 1–6 6–1, Wunderlich 6–1 6–1, lost Nagyova 7–6 3–6 6–1), **Wimbledon 1r** (lost A. Miller 7–6 6–3), **US Open last 16** [unseeded] (d. Paulus 6–2 7–5, Park 6–2 6–4, Leon-Garcia 6–4 6–4, lost Hingis [seed 1] 6–4 6–4); **sf** Quebec City (d. Gagliardi 5–7 6–2 6–1, Callens w/o, Stevenson 6–2 7–6, lost Rubin 6–2 6–4).

MARIAAN DE SWARDT (RSA)

Born Johannesburg, 18 March 1971, and lives there; RH; 5ft 8in; 149lb; turned pro 1988; career singles titles 1; final 1998 WTA ranking 35 singles, 17 doubles; 1998 prize money $216,011.

1987: (418). **1988:** (167) Won Vereeniging on the South African satellite circuit for the second year. **1989:** (306). **1990:** (158) Won 3 titles on the satellite circuits. **1991:** (53) A –, F 2, W 2, US 2. Upset McGrath en route to qf Birmingham and won Oporto Challenger. **1992:** (94) A –, F 2, W 3, US 1. Extended Graf to 7–5 3s at Wimbledon and upset Date on her way to sf Strasbourg. Joined her country's Fed Cup team. Underwent surgery on her right shoulder to relieve arthritis. **1993:** (–) A –, F –, W –, US –. **1994:** (98) A –, F –, W –, US 3. Won San Luis Potosi Futures in both singles and doubles. **1995:** (33) A 1, F 2, W 4, US 1. Sf Zurich (as a qualifier) was her best performance in a year in which she scored some big upsets and broke into the top 50. At Brighton, where she reached qf after qualifying, she removed Graf 1r – although the No. 1 was distracted by her father's imprisonment on remand, she paid tribute to the quality of her opponent's tennis for a set and a half. She also upset Huber at Zurich, Grossman at Auckland and extended Date to 3s in last 16 Wimbledon, where she was unseeded. Played 2 doubles f, winning Bournemouth with Dragomir. **1996:** (83) A 1, F 1, W 1, US 2. In singles her best showings were qf Sydney (d. Frazier) and Cardiff, while in doubles she played 2 f, winning Cardiff with Adams. Suffering with rotator cuff tendinitis, she underwent 2nd shoulder surgery in Dec. **1997:** (161) A –, F –, W –, US –. Out 3 months at beginning of year and returned to play only a limited schedule. **1998:** A –, F 1, W 3, US 2. She upset Huber and Raymond on the way to her 1st tour title at Boston, unseeded, recovering from 1–5 down in 3s f v Schett. She also reached qf Gold Coast, upset Majoli at FC Cup, and in doubles played 4 f with 3 different partners, winning Eastbourne with Novotna. On the ITF $75,000 circuit she won both singles and doubles at Salt Lake City. **1998 HIGHLIGHTS – SINGLES: French Open 1r** (lost Cristea 6–1 6–2), **Wimbledon 3r** (d. Schwartz 7–6 6–3, Tatarkova 6–4 7–6, lost Oremans 6–4 7–5), **US Open 2r** (d. Courtois 7–6 6–4, lost Neiland 6–7 6–3 6–4); **won** Boston (d. Smith 2–6 6–3 6–2, Dechy 6–1 7–6, Huber 6–3 7–6, Raymond 4–6 6–4 7–5, Schett 3–6 7–6 7–5); **won** Salt Lake City ITF (d. Brandi 6–2 6–2). **1998 HIGHLIGHTS – DOUBLES:** (with Novotna unless stated) **won** Eastbourne (d. Sanchez-Vicario/Zvereva 6–1 6–3); (with Fernandez) **r/u** Boston (lost Raymond/Stubbs 6–4 6–4), **r/u** New Haven (lost Fusai/Tauziat 6–1 6–0), (with Tatarkova) **r/u** Zurich (lost S./V. Williams 5–7 6–1 6–3).

JELENA DOKIC (AUS)

Born Yugoslavia, 12 April 1983; lives New South Wales; RH; 2HB; 5ft 8in; 131lb; career singles titles 0; final 1998 WTA ranking 341.

Coached by Lesley Bowrey. **1998:** At French Open Jun she was r/u singles to Petrova and won doubles with Clijsters; then at US Open Jun she won singles over Srebotnik and was r/u doubles with Dominikovic.

EVIE DOMINIKOVIC (AUS)

Born Sydney, 29 May 1980, and lives there; RH; 2HB; 5ft 9in; 137lb; career singles titles 0; final 1998 WTA ranking 189.

Coached by Craig Miller. **1998:** A 1, F –, W –, US –. In Jun doubles won Australian Open with Molik and r/u US Open with Dokic. **1998 HIGHLIGHTS – SINGLES: Australian Open 1r** (lost Carlsson 6–3 2–6 6–4).

RUXANDRA DRAGOMIR (ROM)

Born Pitesti, 24 October 1972; lives Bucharest; RH; 2HB; 5ft 6in; 127lb; career singles titles 4; final 1998 WTA ranking 38; 1998 prize money $209,161; career prize money $1,097,570.

Coached by Emilian Negoita. **1990:** (294) Won 3 titles on the Futures circuits and took French Open Jun doubles with Spirlea. **1991:** (322) Won Supetar Challenger and joined her country's Fed Cup squad. **1992:** (175) Won Klagenfurt and Le Havre Challengers. **1993:** (74) A –, F 4, W 2, US 1. Upset Date on her way to an unexpected appearance in last 16 French Open and reached sf Curitiba. **1994:** (82) A 1, F 4, W 2, US 2. Upset Mag. Maleeva at French Open, where she was unseeded, and reached qf Prague. **1995:** (54) A 2, F 4, W 1, US 1. Still unseeded at French Open, she again made her mark and upset Sawamatsu. Reached her 1st f on the main tour at Styrian Open, appeared in qf Barcelona and won Bournemouth doubles with De Swardt. **1996:** (25) A 2, F 2, W 3, US 1. Won her 1st title on the main tour at Budapest (d. Halard-Decugis), followed in Sept. with Karlovy Vary at her 2nd tourn back after a hamstring injury suffered 1r Olympics, and finished the year on a high note with the title at Pattaya. She also reached sf Rosmalen and qf Hamburg and Moscow, breaking into top 25 1st time by end of year. **1997:** (19) A 4, F qf, W 1, US 1. She moved into the top 20 with the title at Rosmalen, r/u Hamburg, sf Warsaw and Pattaya, as well as upsets of Wiesner at Australian Open and Habsudova at French Open, unseeded both times. In doubles she reached 4 f with different partners, winning Prague with Habsudova and Warsaw with Gorrochategui. **1998:** A 4, F 3, W 1, US 1. Although her only qf appearance was at Gold Coast, she upset Testud at FC Cup and Coetzer at Rome, and won Prostejov on the ITF $75,000 circuit. **1998 HIGHLIGHTS – SINGLES: Australian Open last 16** [seed 15] (d. Babel 6–2 6–1, Serna 7–6 2–6 6–3, Labat 6–2 7–5, lost Davenport [seed 2] 6–0 6–0), **French Open 3r** (d. Husarova 6–2 4–6 6–3, Perfetti 6–0 6–2, lost Serna 6–4 2–6 6–1), **Wimbledon 1r** (lost Grzybowska 6–2 6–4), **US Open 1r** (lost Sugiyama [seed 16] 6–1 6–2); **won** Prostejov ITF (d. Gersi 6–0 6–0). **CAREER HIGHLIGHTS – French Open – qf 1997** (d. Jeyaseelan 6–3 6–2, Basuki 7–5 4–6 8–6, Habsudova 6–3 6–2, Arendt 6–1 6–1, lost Majoli 6–3 5–7 6–2).

EVA DYRBERG (DEN)

Born Copenhagen, 17 February 1980, and lives there; RH; 2HB; 5ft 7½in; 142lb; career singles titles 0; final 1998 WTA ranking 621.

Coached by Tine Scheuer-Larsen. **1998:** In Jun doubles she won Wimbledon with Kostanic and US Open with Clijsters; in singles she won European Jun Champ. On the ITF circuit she won the $10,000 Rungsted tourn. **1998 HIGHLIGHTS – SINGLES: won** ITF Rungsted (d. Ani 6–3 6–4).

SILVIA FARINA (ITA)

Born Milan, 27 April 1972, and lives there; RH; 5ft 8in; 138lb; career singles titles 0; final 1998 WTA ranking 19; 1998 prize money $291,186; career prize money $1,002,281.

Coached by Leonardo Lerda. **1989:** (165) Qf Taranto. **1990:** (192). **1991:** (68) A –, F 1, W –, US –. Upset Reggi en route to her 1st primary circuit f at San Marino and reached sf Taranto. **1992:** (167) A –, F 1, W 1, US –. Upset Gildemeister at LIPC and Paz on her way to sf Palermo. **1993:** (85) A –, F –, W 2, US 1. Reached qf Taranto (d. Zrubakova) and won Limoges Challenger. **1994:** (52) A 1, F 2, W 1, US 2. Reached sf Styria and qf Hobart (d. Wang), Eastbourne (d. Date and Fendick) and Moscow. Upset Sabatini at French Open, having failed to take a single game from her in their two previous meetings. **1995:** (53) A 2, F 1, W 2, US 1. Upset McNeil en route to sf FC Cup, reaching same stage Auckland, as well as qf Puerto Rico, Palermo and Styrian Open, where she won the doubles with Temesvari. **1996:** (40) A 2, F 2, W 1, US 1. She reached sf Paris Open (d. Hingis) and Palermo, plus qf Hobart (d. Basuki), Warsaw and Zurich (after qualifying). During the year she also upset Sukova at LIPC and Tauziat at Los Angeles. Withdrew 2r French Open with recurrence of a right ankle ligament sprain suffered at FC Cup. **1997:** (43) A 3, F 3, W 1, US 2. Once again Palermo saw her at her best, reaching qf singles and winning the doubles with Schett. Other highlights were upsets of Likhovtseva at FC Cup and Appelmans at Moscow. **1998:** A 1, F 3, W 1, US 3. Some impressive results and notable upsets took her into top 20 1st time. Although she won no title, she was r/u 4 times, beginning with Auckland, where she upset Testud and extended Van Roost to 7–5 fs. She followed with the same stage Budapest, Warsaw and Luxembourg, where she d. Spirlea and Tauziat before being forced to ret v Pierce with a groin strain. Basuki and Tauziat were her victims en route to sf Linz, and she also reached qf LIPC (d. Sugiyama and Coetzer), Prague (where she won the doubles with Habsudova) and Moscow (d. Kournikova). **1998 HIGHLIGHTS – SINGLES: Australian Open 1r** (lost Mauresmo 7–6 7–5), **French Open 3r** (d. Wang 6–2 6–1, Kruger 4–6 6–3 6–0, lost Schnyder 6–2 6–1), **Wimbledon 1r** (lost Martinez [seed 8] 6–1 6–0), **US Open 3r** (d. Smashnova 6–4 3–6 6–2, Dechaume-Balleret 6–3 1–6 6–3, lost Kournikova [seed 15] 6–4 6–1); **r/u** Auckland (d. Dechaume-Balleret 1–6 6–2 6–2, Schwartz 3–6 6–3 6–1, Halard-Decugis 6–4 6–3, Testud 6–2

7–6, lost Van Roost 4–6 7–6 7–5), **r/u** Budapest (d. Kriventcheva 7–6 6–3, Torrens-Valero 6–2 6–2, Sanchez Lorenzo 6–1 6–2, Li 4–6 6–2 6–3, lost Ruano-Pascual 6–4 4–6 6–3), **r/u** Warsaw (d. Carlsson 6–4 6–3, Lugina 6–1 7–6, Glass 6–3 6–2, Grzybowska 4–6 6–4 4–2 ret, lost Martinez 6–0 6–3), **r/u** Luxembourg (d. Nagyova 6–3 6–3, Kremer 6–4 6–2, Spirlea 6–4 4–6 6–3, Tauziat 6–2 2–6 6–3, lost Pierce 6–0 2–0 ret); **sf** Linz (d. Basuki 6–3 6–4, Kschwendt 7–5 6–4, Tauziat 6–4 7–6, lost Novotna 6–4 6–1). **1998 HIGHLIGHTS – DOUBLES:** (with Habsudova) **won** Prague (d. Hrdlickova/Pastikova 2–6 6–1 6–1).

AMY FRAZIER (USA)

Born St Louis, Mo., 19 September 1972; lives Rochester Hills, Mich.; RH; 2HB; 5ft 8in; 140lb; turned pro 1990; career singles titles 5; final 1998 WTA ranking 42; 1998 prize money $123,742; career prize money $1,716,258.

Coached by John Cook and John Austin. Won 7 Nat Jun titles. **1986:** (331). **1987:** (202) A –, F –, W –, US 1. Won Kona on USTA circuit. **1988:** (55) A 1, F 1, W 1, US 3. Appeared in sf Guaruja, plus qf LA (d. Shriver and Magers), Kansas and Indianapolis (d. Kelesi). **1989:** (33) A 3, F 1, W 2, US 1. Won 1st primary circuit singles title at VS Kansas as well as reaching sf Albuquerque (d. Maleeva-Fragniere) and VS Indianapolis. **1990:** (16) A 1, F –, W 3, US 1. Won VS Oklahoma and was r/u Tokyo Nicherei, where she beat Seles and K. Maleeva back-to-back and extended M. J. Fernandez to 3s. In other tourns reached sf Indian Wells and Sydney, where she upset Novotna and took Zvereva to 3s, and upset Fairbank-Nideffer at Wimbledon. **1991:** (28) A 4, F –, W 4, US 2. Although she won no title, she reached sf Tokyo Nicherei and qf VS Chicago, Tokyo Suntory, Toronto and VS California. **1992:** (19) A qf, F 2, W 4, US 1. Taking advantage of Graf's withdrawal from her part of the draw, she made an unexpected appearance in qf Australian Open, and, again unseeded, upset M. J. Fernandez at Wimbledon. Won both singles and doubles titles at Lucerne and also took the doubles at Tokyo Suntory. She reached sf singles there, as well as at VS Oklahoma and San Antonio, and qualified for VS Champs 1st time, losing 1r to Sabatini. **1993:** (39) A 1, F –, W –, US 2. Out of action for 6 months from Feb. with a chronic form of flu, she had a quieter year, in which her best showings were sf Sydney and VS Philadelphia (d. Pierce and Sabatini) and qf Tokyo Nicherei (d. K. Maleeva). **1994:** (16) A 3, F 1, W 1, US 2. At Tokyo Japan Open she reached her 1st f for 2 years, a result which took her back to the top 20. She upset Huber and Martinez on her way to the title at Los Angeles, surprised Sabatini again en route to f Tokyo Nicherei and reached sf Oklahoma and Lucerne. **1995:** (18) A 3, F 3, W 2, US qf. She was still a dangerous opponent, upsetting Pierce and Zvereva back-to-back at US Open, where she was unseeded, and removing Date to take the title at Tokyo Japan Open. She also reached sf Oklahoma, qf Chicago and Tokyo Nicherei. **1996:** (29) A 1, F 1, W 4, US 2. R/u Tokyo Japan Open and reached qf Oklahoma, Montreal (d. Pierce) and Los Angeles. Played 3 doubles f with Po, but won no title. **1997:** (37) A 1, F 2, W 2, US 1. She began the year with an upset of Sanchez-Vicario to reach qf Sydney, following with r/u Tokyo Japan Open and sf Los Angeles (d. Coetzer and Sanchez-Vicario again). **1998:** A –, F –, W 1, US 1. Her best performances came at Tokyo: at Japan Open she reached sf singles and was r/u doubles with Hiraki, and at the Toyota tourn she rallied from love set down to upset Coetzer en route to qf. Schnyder was her victim on her way to the same stage Philadelphia, and on the ITF $50,000 circuit she won both singles and doubles at Mahwah. **1998 HIGHLIGHTS – SINGLES: Wimbledon 1r** (lost Nagyova 6–7 6–2 6–4), **US Open 1r** (lost Rippner 6–3 6–1); **won** Mahwah ITF (d. Li w/o); **sf** Tokyo Japan Open (d. Choi 6–4 6–2, Endo 6–0 6–1, Pratt 6–2 4–6 6–2, lost Morariu 4–6 7–6 6–4). **1998 HIGHLIGHTS – DOUBLES:** (with Hiraki) **r/u** Tokyo Japan Open (lost Kijimuta/Miyagi 6–3 4–6 6–4). **CAREER HIGHLIGHTS – SINGLES: Australian Open – qf 1992** [unseeded] (d. Cunningham 6–3 7–5, De Vries 6–1 7–6, Hack 6–1 3–6 6–2, Monami 6–3 6–4, lost M. J. Fernandez 6–4 7–6); **US Open – qf 1995** [unseeded] (d. Rottier 6–0 6–0, Phebus 6–2 6–1, Pierce 6–3 7–6, Zvereva 6–4 4–6 6–3, lost Graf 6–2 6–3).

ALEXANDRA FUSAI (FRA)

Born St Cloud, 22 November 1973; lives Nantes; RH; 2HB; 5ft 9in; 132lb; turned pro 1991; career singles titles 0; final 1998 WTA ranking 39 singles, 8 doubles; 1998 prize money $294,437.

Coached by Regis De Camaret. **1990:** (297) Won Sezze and Cherbourg Futures. **1991:** (184) A –, F 1, W –, US –. Won European Jun Champs and in the senior game won Limoges Futures. **1992:** (141) A –, F 1, W –, US 1. Won 2 Futures titles in Australia. **1993:** (77) A 1, F 2, W 1, US 2. In her best year to date, she reached sf Taranto and upset Probst on her way to the same stage Liege, as well as reaching qf Melbourne Open and Taipei. **1994:** (92) A –, F 3, W 1, US 2. She could advance no further than qf Taranto (d. Wiesner) and Prague. **1995:** (104) A 1, F 1, W 1, US –. She reached sf Warsaw on the main tour and won Szczeciu Futures. **1996:** (72) A 3, A 2, W 2, US 2. In singles qf Cardiff was her best showing, while in doubles she played 4 f with different partners, winning Surabaya with Guse. **1997:** (51) A 2, F 2, W 1, US 3. She reached qf Budapest, upset Habsudova at FC Cup and played in winning FRA Fed Cup team. In doubles, she played 6 f with 3 different partners, winning Budapest with Coetzer and Linz and Chicago with Tauziat. At their 1st Chase Champs, she and Tauziat upset Hingis/Sanchez-Vicario en route to f, where they extended Davenport/Novotna to 3s. **1998:** A –, F 3, W 2, US 2. Notable upsets during the year included Novotna at Rome, Sugiyama en route to sf Strasbourg and Paulus at French Open. Her doubles partnership with Tauziat continued to flourish, bringing 3 titles and a berth at Chase Champs, where they narrowly lost to Davenport/Zvereva in their 7th f of season. **1998 HIGHLIGHTS – SINGLES: French Open 3r** (d. Paulus 6–1 7–5, Snyder 6–4 6–3, lost Sanchez-Vicario [seed 4] 6–2 6–1), **Wimbledon 2r** (d. Studenikova 6–3 6–2, lost Seles [seed 6] 6–1 6–1), **US Open 2r** (d. Stevenson 6–4 6–4, lost Fernandez 6–3 4–6 7–6); **sf** Strasbourg (d. Maruska 3–6 6–4 7–5, Reeves 6–3 7–6, Sugiyama 6–2

6–2, lost Spirlea 7–5 6–3). **1998 HIGHLIGHTS – DOUBLES:** (with Tauziat) **won** Linz (d. Kournikova/Neiland 6–3 3–6 6–4), **won** Strasbourg (d. Basuki/Vis 6–4 6–3), **won** New Haven (d. De Swardt/Novotna 6–1 6–0); **r/u** Indian Wells (lost Davenport/Zvereva 6–4 2–6 6–4), **r/u** Berlin (lost Davenport/Zvereva 6–3 6–0), **r/u** San Diego (lost Davenport/Zvereva 6–2 6–1), **r/u** Chase Champs (lost Davenport/Zvereva 6–7 7–5 6–3).

ADRIANA GERSI (CZE)

Born Sternberk, 26 June 1976; lives Olomouc; RH; 2HB; 5ft 5in; 118lb; turned pro 1994; career singles titles 0; final 1998 WTA ranking 63; 1998 prize money $88,547.

Coached by Pavel Gerla. **1994:** (310) Won Burg, Bratislava and Burgdorf back-to-back on the ITF circuit. **1995:** (213). **1996:** (108) Reached her 1st main tour sf at Surabaya (d. Testud and Richterova). **1997:** (94) A 2, F 1, W 1, US 1. She won both her singles matches on Fed Cup debut as CZE d. GER 3–2, upset Paulus at Berlin and broke into top 50 in June. **1998:** A 3, F 2, W 1, US 1. Although she reached no qf on the main tour, she moved back up the rankings and upset Maleeva at Australian Open. **1998 HIGHLIGHTS – SINGLES: Australian Open 3r** (d. Maleeva 2–6 6–2 6–2, Husarova 6–2 7–5, lost Testud [seed 9] 6–4 6–2), **French Open 2r** (d. Schett 5–7 6–2 6–2, lost Dechaume-Balleret 6–2 5–7 6–1), **Wimbledon 1r** (lost Carlsson 6–1 6–1), **US Open 1r** (lost Nagyova 6–2 6–0).

RITA GRANDE (ITA)

Born Napoli, 23 March 1975; lives Rivoli; RH; 5ft 10in; 146lb; career singles titles 0; final 1998 WTA ranking 60; 1998 prize money $164,399.

Coached by Antonella Canapi and Pino Carnovale. **1990** (406). **1991:** (364). **1992:** (443). **1993:** (183) R/u Wimbledon Jun to Feber and in the women's game won Vilamoura Futures. **1994:** (140) She finished the year on a high note by reaching her 1st sf on the senior tour at Taipei. **1995:** (74) A –, F –, W–, US 2. Reached sf Pattaya City and qf Tokyo Japan Open (d. Werdel-Witmeyer). **1996:** (65) A 3, F 2, W 1, US 4. Qf Auckland was her best performance. **1997:** (44) A 2, F 1, W 1, US 2. Reached sf Jakarta and Cardiff, plus qf Toronto (d. Pierce). **1998:** A 2, F 2, W 2, US 1. She upset Dragomir on the way to her only qf of year at Tokyo Pan Pacific. **1998 HIGHLIGHTS – SINGLES: Australian Open 2r** (d. Shaughnessy 6–4 6–3, lost Zvereva 6–4 6–4), **French Open 2r** (d. J. Lee 7–6 6–3, lost Martinez [seed 7] 6–1 6–2), **Wimbledon 2r** (d. Li 6–1 6–4, lost Serna 6–4 6–1), **US Open 1r** (lost Zuluaga 6–4 6–4).

MAGDALENA GRZYBOWSKA (POL)

Born Poznan, 22 November 1978; lives Krakow; RH; 2HB; 6ft 0½in; 147lb; turned pro 1995; career singles titles 0; final 1998 WTA ranking 52; 1998 prize money $130,331.

Coached by Iwona Kuczynska. **1994:** (441) Won Szezecin Futures in only her 3rd pro event, having been r/u in her 1st at Olsztyn Futures. **1995:** (73) Upset Hack on her way to sf Warsaw after qualifying, won Bratislava Futures and joined her country's Fed Cup squad. **1996:** (130) A 2, F 1, W 1, US 1. Won Australian Open Jun over Dechy. **1997:** (40) A 3, F 1, W 3, US 1. Won 2 titles on the Futures circuit and on the main tour she reached qf Leipzig (d. Paulus) and Quebec City. **1998:** A 3, F 1, W 2, US 2. She extended Van Roost to 3s sf Hobart, upset Kruger US Open en route to the same stage Warsaw and surprised Martinez at FC Cup. **1998 HIGHLIGHTS – SINGLES: Australian Open 3r** (d. Cristea 6–3 6–2, Vaidyanathan 6–2 6–1, lost Sugiyama [seed 16] 7–6 1–6 6–4), **French Open 1r** (lost Van Roost [seed 15] 7–5 3–6 6–4), **Wimbledon 2r** (d. Dragomir 6–2 6–4, lost Sanchez-Vicario [seed 5] 4–6 6–4 6–3), **US Open 2r** (d. Studenikova 6–0 6–1, lost Van Roost [seed 14] 6–0 6–0); **sf** Hobart (d. Dechy 6–2 6–2, Sawamatsu 4–6 7–6 7–5, Nagyova 6–1 2–1 ret, lost Van Roost 6–7 6–1 6–3), **sf** Warsaw (d. Noorlander 6–3 6–2, Cervanova 6–2 6–0, Kruger 6–3 6–2, lost Farina 4–6 6–4 4–2 ret).

JULIE HALARD-DECUGIS (FRA)

Born Versailles, 10 September 1970; lives La Baule; RH; 2HB; 5ft 8in; 125lb; turned pro 1986; career singles titles 8; final 1998 WTA ranking 22 singles, 21 doubles; 1998 prize money $262,153; career prize money $1,703,094.

Married her coach, Arnaud Decugis, a distant relative of 8-times French champion Max Decugis, 22 September 1995. **1986:** Won French Open Jun. **1987:** (62) A –, F 2, W –, US 3. R/u Wimbledon Jun to Zvereva and reached f Athens. **1988:** (75) A 2, F 2, W 1, US 1. Won French Open Jun over Farley. **1989:** (119) A 1, F 1, W 2, US 2. Upset Shriver en route to qf Moscow. **1990:** (41) A 3, F 3, W 2, US 2. Sf Clarins, qf Sydney and Barcelona, and upset Garrison on her way to last 16 LIPC. **1991:** (20) A 2, F 2, W 2, US 2. Won her 1st primary circuit title at Puerto Rico; r/u VS Albuquerque; sf San Antonio, Clarins and Phoenix; and upset M. J. Fernandez at Berlin. Qualified for her 1st VS Champs, but fell 1r to Seles. **1992:** (27) A 1, F 3, W 4 US 2. Won Taranto, reached sf Clarins and upset Sanchez-Vicario en route to last 16 Wimbledon, unseeded. **1993:** (29) A qf, F 3, W 1, US 2. At Australian Open, unseeded, she upset Garrison-Jackson and Martinez before extending Seles to 3s in qf. She followed with appearances at the same stage Paris Open and Toronto (d. Sabatini), then in autumn progressed to sf Tokyo Nicherei and Budapest. **1994:** (21) A 2, F qf, W 1, US 2. It was another solid year in which she won Taranto, was r/u Paris Open (d. K. Maleeva) and reached sf Auckland, Los Angeles and Brighton, plus 3 more qf. In GS she thrilled her home crowds at French Open by upsetting Davenport and Zvereva on her way to qf. Qualified for VS Champs in both singles and doubles, upsetting Sanchez-Vicario in singles and taking a set off Sabatini in qf. In doubles she played 3 f, winning Los Angeles with Tauziat, with whom she qualified for VS Champs, and Tokyo Nicherei with Sanchez-Vicario. **1995:** (51) A 1, F 3, W 1, US 2. Although she moved to a career-high ranking of 15 in Jan., it turned out to be a quieter year in which she won Prague, but otherwise reached qf only at Auckland and Quebec City. **1996:** (15) A 3, F 2, W –, US –. She returned to the top 20 with her best year yet. Unseeded both times, she won Hobart in Jan. and Paris Open in Feb. (d. Sukova, Huber and Majoli) – the 1st time she'd won 2 tourns in a year. Linz at beginning of March was her 3rd f from 5 tourns and she also reached sf Hamburg (d. Schultz-McCarthy), plus qf Auckland (d. Spirlea) and Budapest. Upset Sanchez-Vicario in sf Fed Cup, but was forced to abandon the deciding doubles (with Tauziat) when she tore a ligament in her right wrist. The same injury kept her out of Wimbledon and US Open. In doubles, she played 3 f, winning Auckland with Callens. **1997:** (–) A –, F –, W –, US –. It was an injury-plagued year in which she was restricted by knee, shoulder and wrist injuries and a strained abdominal muscle. **1998:** A –, F 2, W –, US 1. Her year ended on a high note at Pattaya, where she won both singles and doubles titles. Earlier she had returned to action and the top 25 with some useful upsets on her way to her 1st title for 2 years at Hertogenbosch, r/u Strasbourg (d. Coetzer), sf New Haven (d. Sanchez-Vicario) and qf Auckland, Budapest and Tokyo Toyota. In doubles she won Birmingham and Pattaya with Callens and reached 2 other f with Husarova. **1998 HIGHLIGHTS – SINGLES: French Open 2r** (d. Kijimuta 6–1 6–2, lost Schnyder 6–3 3–6 6–1), **US Open 1r** (lost Van Roost [seed 14] 6–2 6–2); **won** Hertogenbosch (d. Dragomir 7–6 6–3, Snyder 6–2 6–0, Appelmans 6–7 7–6 6–3, Testud 6–3 6–3, Oremans 6–1 6–7 7–6), **won** Pattaya (d. Dokic 7–6 4–6 6–3, Pratt 6–1 7–5, Wang 5–7 6–2 6–0, Brandi 6–0 6–1, Li 6–1 6–2); **r/u** Strasbourg (d. Tanasugarn 6–4 6–2, Cocheteux 6–2 6–1, Coetzer 7–6 6–2, Likhovtseva 6–3 7–6, lost Spirlea 7–6 6–3); **sf** New Haven (d. Sawamatsu 3–6 6–3 7–5, Sanchez-Vicario 7–6 6–2, Fernandez 7–5 6–1, lost Novotna 6–4 6–4). **1998 HIGHLIGHTS – DOUBLES:** (with Husarova unless stated) (with Callens) **won** Birmingham (d. Raymond/Stubbs 2–6 6–4 6–4); **r/u** Auckland (lost Miyagi/Tanasugarn 7–6 6–4), **r/u** Hobart (lost Ruano-Pascual/Suarez 7–6 6–3). **CAREER HIGHLIGHTS – SINGLES: Australian Open – qf 1993** [unseeded] (d. Kidowaki 6–0 6–0, Kschwendt 6–4 1–6 6–4, Garrison-Jackson 6–4 7–5, Martinez 6–4 6–3, lost Seles 6–2 6–7 6–0); **French Open – qf 1994** [unseeded] (d. Tarabini 6–3 6–2, Begerow 7–5 4–6 6–4, Davenport 6–4 6–2, Zvereva 7–6 7–5, lost Sanchez-Vicario 6–1 7–6).

KVETA HRDLICKOVA (CZE)

Born Bilovec, 9 July 1975, and lives there; RH; 2HB; 5ft 5in; 127lb; career singles titles 1; final 1998 WTA ranking 57; 1998 prize money $98,316.

Named Kvetoslava but known as Kveta. Coached by Torsten Peschke. R/u European Jun 18s. **1992:** Won ITF Lyss. **1993:** Won ITF Vitkovice. **1996:** On the ITF circuit she won Vitkovice and Prarov back-to-back. **1998:** A –, F 2, W 1, US 2. Emerging from the satellite circuits, she broke into top 100 in April after winning her 1st career title at Makarska as a qualifier; it was her 1st career f and she was playing in her 1st WTA tourn for 4 years. She also reached qf Sopot, where she won the doubles with Vildova, and joined her country's Fed Cup squad. On the ITF circuit she won Rogaska and the $50,000 event at Cardiff. **1998 HIGHLIGHTS – SINGLES: French Open 2r** (d. Bes 6–4 3–6 6–3, lost Tatarkova 6–4 6–1), **Wimbledon 1r** (lost Tanasugarn 6–0 7–5), **US Open 2r** (d. Schwartz 6–2 6–3, lost Testud 7–6 6–3); **won** Makarska (d. Csurgo 2–6 6–2 7–5, Lucic 6–4 7–6, Lugina 3–6 7–5 6–4, Nemeckova 6–1 6–2, Li 6–3 6–1), **won** Cardiff ITF (d. Smashnova 7–5 6–4). **1998 HIGHLIGHTS – DOUBLES:** (with Vildova) **won** Sopot (d. Carlsson/Noorlander 6–3 6–2); (with Pastikova) **r/u** Prague (lost Farina/Habsudova 2–6 6–1 6–1).

ANKE HUBER (GER)

Born Bruchsal, 4 December 1974; lives Going, Austria; RH; 2HB; 5ft 8in; 128lb; turned pro 1989; career singles titles 10; final 1998 WTA ranking 21; 1998 prize money $272,442; career prize money $3,392,342.

Coached by Gerald Mild **1986:** Won Nat 12s. **1987:** Won Nat 14s. **1988:** Won Nat 16s. **1989:** (203) Won European Jun Champs and played in winning FRG World Youth Cup team. **1990:** (34) A 3, F –, W 2, US 1. She showed great fighting spirit in extending Sabatini to 2s tb in their 2r encounter at Wimbledon. At end Aug. won her 1st tour title at Schenectady after qualifying and followed with r/u Bayonne, upsetting Garrison and breaking into top 100, then shooting up to top 50 by Oct. Voted WTA Most Impressive Newcomer. **1991:** (14) A qf, F 3, W 4, US 2. Upset Maleeva-Fragniere and Zvereva en route to qf Australian Open, unseeded, reached last 16 Wimbledon and ended Sabatini's winning run as she reached qf Berlin. The high spot of her year, though, came at Filderstadt in autumn, where she upset Garrison, Sukova and Navratilova in fs tb to take the title. It was the 1st time for 8 years that Navratilova had been beaten by an unseeded player. **1992:** (11) A qf, F2, W 3, US 1. Upset Novotna en route to qf Australian Open and appeared at same stage Olympics; reached sf Sydney, Hamburg, San Diego, Brighton and Oakland and was a member of winning German Fed Cup team. **1993:** (10) A 4, F sf, W 4, US 3. Won a 3rd career title at Kitzbuhel, was r/u Sydney (d. Sanchez-Vicario) and Brighton and reached sf VS Florida and VS Champs plus 4 more qf. **1994:** (12) A 3, F 4, W 2, US 2. Restricted early in year by injury, she did not pass qf until reaching sf Berlin in May. However, having split with coach Boris Breskvar after Wimbledon, she won Styria and Filderstadt (d. Navratilova and Pierce) before finishing the season with a flourish at Philadelphia, where she upset Sabatini and Pierce again to take the title. She also appeared in sf Leipzig and 4 more qf, but at VS Champs fell 1r to Davenport. **1995:** (10) A 4, F 4, W 4, US 4. Won Leipzig and reached sf Delray Beach, Hamburg, Filderstadt and Philadelphia (d. Sabatini), as well as qf Tokyo Pan Pacific, LIPC, Manhattan Beach and Toronto. However, she saved her best for the end, upsetting Pierce and Date on her way to f WTA Champs, where she extended Graf to 5s. **1996:** (6) A r/u, F 4, W 3, US 1. Her fine form continued into the new season, which she began on a high note by upsetting Martinez on the way to her 1st GS f at Australian Open, a performance that took her into top 5 1st time. Her 1st title on grass came at Rosmalen, followed by two indoors at Leipzig and Luxembourg. She also appeared in f Los Angeles and Filderstadt (d. Martinez again), sf Essen and Zurich, and qf Paris Open, LIPC, Berlin and Strasbourg. Her performance at Chase Champs was an anticlimax, though, as she lost 1r to Majoli. **1997:** (19) A 4, F 1, W 3, US 3. Although she won no title and was disappointing in the major tourns, she was r/u Paris Open (d. Novotna) and Toronto, reached sf Tokyo Pan Pacific, Rosmalen and Leipzig (d. Majoli), plus qf Auckland, FC Cup, Los Angeles and Philadelphia (d. Majoli). She twice extended Hingis to 3s during her unbeaten run at start of year, and qualified for Chase Champs, although she lost 1r to Majoli and finished the year outside the top 10. In doubles she won Hamburg with Pierce. **1998:** A sf, F –, W –, US 1. Her best performance came at Australian Open, where she upset Coetzer and Sanchez-Vicario before extending Hingis to 3s. Her season was curtailed in March, when she underwent foot surgery, which kept her out until Aug. By then she had slipped far enough down the rankings to be unseeded at US Open, where Majoli beat her. Although she reached no f during the year, she was consistent in reaching sf Australian Open and Tokyo Toyota and qf Paris Open, Hannover, Boston, Montreal (d. Coetzer), New Haven (d. Schnyder), Luxembourg and Leipzig. **1998 HIGHLIGHTS – SINGLES: Australian Open sf** [seed 10] (d. Pitkowski 5–7 6–0 6–0, A. Miller 6–4 6–0, Kruger 6–7 6–3 6–2, Coetzer [seed 3] 2–6 6–4 7–5, Sanchez-Vicario [seed 7] 7–6 7–5, lost Hingis [seed 1] 6–1 2–6 6–1), **US Open 1r** (lost Majoli 6–3 6–3); **sf** Tokyo Toyota (d. Kijimuta 6–3 3–6 6–0, Li 7–5 6–3, Barabanschikova 6–3 6–1, lost Sanchez-Vicario 6–1 3–6 6–3). **CAREER HIGHLIGHTS – SINGLES: Australian Open – r/u 1996** (d. Kleinova 6–1 6–4, Carlsson 6–1 6–2, Richterova 6–2 6–1, Schett 6–3 6–2, Martinez 4–6 6–2 6–1, Coetzer 4–6 6–4 6–2, lost Seles 6–4 6–1), **sf 1998; qf 1991** (d. Richardson 6–4 6–1, Maleeva-Fragniere 6–4 6–4, Shriver 6–3 7–5, Zvereva 6–3 6–4, lost Seles 6–3 6–1), **qf 1992** (d. Zivec-Skulj 2–6 6–3 6–1, Jaggard-Lai 6–0 6–1, Fairbank-Nideffer 6–0 7–5, Novotna 5–7 7–6 6–4, lost Seles 7–5 6–3); **WTA Champs – r/u 1995** (d. Pierce 6–2 6–3, Date 3–6 6–2 6–1, Schultz-McCarthy 6–3 6–3, lost Graf 6–1 2–6 6–1 4–6 6–3), **sf 1993** (d. Mag. Maleeva 6–4 1–6 7–6, Martinez 6–3 6–3, lost Graf 6–2 3–6 6–3); **Olympics – qf 1992** (d. Sawamatsu 6–0 4–6 6–2, Paulus 6–4 6–1, Muns-Jagerman 7–5 7–6, lost Capriati 6–3 7–6).

JELENA KOSTANIC (CRO)

Born Split, 6 July 1981, and lives there; LH; 2HB; 5ft 6in; 117lb; career singles titles 0; final 1998 WTA ranking 236.

Coached by Ivo Zavoreo, Peter Buyevic and Josko Vlasic. **1998:** Won Australian Open Jun singles over Prakusya and took Wimbledon Jun doubles with Dyrberg. In the women's game she won Otocec on the $25,000 ITF circuit. **1998 HIGHLIGHTS – SINGLES: won** Otocec ITF (d. Barna 6–4 7–6).

ANNA KOURNIKOVA (RUS)

Born Moscow, 7 June 1981; lives Bradenton, Fla; RH; 2HB; 5ft 8in; 123lb; turned pro 1995; career singles titles 0; final 1998 WTA ranking 13 singles, 10 doubles; 1998 prize money $526,633.

Coached by Pavel Slozil since beginning of year. **1995:** (281) No. 1 in ITF Jun rankings after winning Orange Bowl and European Champs. **1996:** (57) A –, F –, W –, US 4. At US Open, having played through the qualifying in only her 2nd main draw event, she upset Paulus to reach last 16. She surprised Coetzer at Zurich and won 2 titles on the Futures circuit. Aged 14, she became the youngest to win a Fed Cup match when she helped RUS d. SWE 3–0. Voted Most Impressive Newcomer. **1997:** (32) A 1, F 3, W sf, US 2. Playing the compulsorily restricted schedule according to her age, she found it hard to maintain her form. None the less, she upset Coetzer at LIPC and Sanchez-Vicario on her way to qf Berlin, before impressing at Wimbledon, where, unseeded, she upset Huber and Majoli on her way to sf. **1998:** A 3, F 4, W –, US 4. She gave the performance of her life at LIPC, where she became the first to beat 4 top 10 players in succession (Seles, Martinez, Davenport, Sanchez-Vicario) on the way to her 1st career f, in which she was a set up v V. Williams before losing. She followed in May with upsets of Sanchez-Vicario and Hingis to reach sf Berlin, and removed Graf to reach the same stage Eastbourne, but was forced to withdraw with a torn ligament in her thumb, which kept her out 8 weeks, missing Wimbledon. These results were enough to take her into the top 10 on 22 June, although she slipped out again during her absence from the game and, with her serve falling apart in autumn, she could not regain her place. In other tourns she reached sf Hannover (d. Huber) and qf Linz, Amelia Island, Rome (d. Majoli) and Tokyo Toyota, qualifying for her 1st Chase Champs in both singles and doubles, falling 1r in both. She played 4 doubles f with 3 different partners, winning Tokyo Toyota with Seles, although it was Neiland with whom she qualified for Chase Champs. **1998 HIGHLIGHTS – SINGLES: Australian Open 3r** (d. Studenikova 6–2 6–1, Morariu 7–5 6–2, lost Hingis [seed 1] 6–4 4–6 6–4), **French Open last 16** [seed 13] (d. Mauresmo 6–2 6–4, Studenikova 6–2 7–6, Carlsson 6–0 6–0, lost Novotna [seed 3] 6–7 6–3 6–3), **US Open last 16** [seed 15] (d. Ghirardi 6–1 6–3, Bobkova 6–3 6–4, Farina 6–4 6–1, lost Sanchez-Vicario [seed 4] 7–6 6–3); **r/u** LIPC (d. Lucic 6–4 6–2, Seles 7–5 6–4, Martinez 6–3 6–0, Davenport 6–4 2–6 6–2, Sanchez-Vicario 3–6 6–1 6–3, lost V. Williams 2–6 6–4 6–1); **sf** Hannover (d. Farina 6–4 6–3, Probst 6–3 6–1, Huber 6–4 3–6 6–4, lost Novotna 6–3 6–3), **sf** Berlin (d. Bobkova 6–2 6–1, Likhovtseva 6–2 6–1, Sanchez-Vicario 6–4 6–2, Hingis 6–3 7–6, lost Martinez 6–0 6–1), **sf** Eastbourne (d. Fusai 2–6 6–1 6–3, De Swardt 6–4 6–1, Graf 6–7 6–3 6–4, lost Sanchez-Vicario w/o). **1998 HIGHLIGHTS – DOUBLES:** (with Neiland unless stated) (with Seles)

won Tokyo Toyota (d. Fernandez/Sanchez-Vicario 6–4 6–4); **r/u** Paris Open (lost Appelmans/Oremans 1–6 6–3 7–6), **r/u** Linz (lost Fusai/Tauziat 6–3 3–6 6–4), (with Sanchez-Vicario) **r/u** Filderstadt (lost Davenport/Zvereva 6–4 6–2). **CAREER HIGHLIGHTS – SINGLES: Wimbledon – sf 1997** (d. Rubin 6–1 6–1, Rittner 4–6 7–6 6–3, Huber 3–6 6–4 6–4, Sukova 2–6 6–2 6–3, Majoli 7–6 6–4, lost Hingis 6–3 6–2).

JOANNETTE KRUGER (RSA)

Born Johannesburg, 3 September 1973; lives Benoni; RH; 2HB; 5ft 10½in; 130lb; career singles titles 2; final 1998 WTA ranking 30; 1998 prize money $164,852.

Coached by her mother, Petro Kruger. **1989:** (519). **1990:** (357) Won Bournemouth Futures. **1991:** (274). **1992:** (105) Won 3 titles on the Futures circuit and played Fed Cup. **1993:** (128) A 1, F 1, W 1, US –. Appeared in her 1st sf on the senior tour at San Marino. **1994:** (79) A 1, F 3, W 1, US 1. Reached qf Birmingham and took a set off Novotna at Brighton. **1995:** (30) A 2, F 2, W 1, US 2. Won her 1st main tour title in her 1st f at Puerto Rico, unseeded, and broke into the top 50 in April. She recorded some useful upsets on her way to qf Houston (d. Garrison-Jackson), Italian Open (d. Huber), Leipzig (d. Davenport) and Zurich (d. Sukova). **1996:** (112) A 2, F –, W 1, US 1. She reached qf Oklahoma and Bol. After passing out with heat stroke at Indian Wells, she underwent neurological tests both in US and at home, required anti-seizure medication, and missed French Open. **1997:** (27) A 2, F 1, W 2, US 4. She won Prague and reached qf Budapest (d. Davenport), Warsaw (d. Habsudova) and Luxembourg, as well as upsetting Habsudova at Maria Lankowitz and Paulus at US Open, where she was unseeded. **1998:** A 3, F 2, W 1, US 2. Her fine form continued, taking her into top 25 in Feb. Although she won no title, she was r/u Oklahoma City and reached sf Hobart and Bol (where she was r/u doubles with Lucic), plus qf Indian Wells (d. Coetzer), Warsaw and San Diego (d. Spirlea), and received the WTA Player Service award. **1998 HIGHLIGHTS – SINGLES: Australian Open 3r** (d. Gavaldon 6–0 2–0 ret, Jeyaseelan 6–3 6–2, lost Huber [seed 10] 6–7 6–3 6–2), **French Open 2r** (d. Glass 6–3 6–4, lost Farina 4–6 6–3 6–0, **Wimbledon 1r** (lost Van Roost 6–1 6–3), **US Open 2r** (d. Rittner 6–1 6–3, lost Seles [seed 6] 6–2 6–3); **r/u** Oklahoma City (d. McQuillan 3–6 6–2 7–5, McGrath w/o, S. Williams 6–1 6–1, Pitkowski 3–6 6–3 6–4, lost V. Williams 6–3 6–2); **sf** Hobart (d. Pitkowski 6–3 7–6, Ruano-Pascual 6–4 6–3, Sidot 7–5 6–2, lost Schnyder 7–6 6–2), **sf** Bol (d. Selyutina 6–3 6–4, Mauresmo 6–4 6–1, Sandu 4–6 6–3 6–2, lost Lucic 6–2 6–1). **1998 HIGHLIGHTS – DOUBLES:** (with Lucic) **r/u** Bol (lost Montalvo/Suarez w/o).

FLORENCIA LABAT (ARG)

Born Buenos Aires, 12 June 1971, and lives there; LH; 5ft 7in; 135lb; turned pro 1989; career singles titles 0; final 1998 WTA ranking 64; 1998 prize money $153,926; career prize money $1,141,121.

Coached by Jorge Gerosi. **1987:** Won S American Jun Champs and Orange Bowl 16s singles and doubles. **1988:** (389) No. 3 in ITF Jun rankings. **1989:** (70) A –, F –, W –, US 2. No. 1 in ITF Jun rankings. Won S American Jun Champs again. On the pro tour she reached qf Arcachon and VS Arizona as well as upsetting Lindqvist 1r US Open and winning 2 titles on the Futures circuit. **1990:** (118) A –, F 1, W 1, US 1. Qf Strasbourg and Puerto Rico and joined her country's Fed Cup team. **1991:** (56) A –, F 2, W –, US 3. Reached her 1st sf on the main tour at Sao Paulo, appeared in qf Taranto, Kitzbuhel (d. Kelesi) and Schenectady and upset Tauziat at US Open. In doubles won Taranto with Dechaume and Puerto Rico with Hiraki. **1992:** (51) A 1, F 1, W 1, US 4. Upset Wiesner en route to sf Kitzbuhel and Medvedeva and Zrubakova on her way to same stage Schenectady. In doubles with Dechaume she won both those tourns plus San Marino. Made an unexpected appearance in last 16 US Open. **1993:** (51) A 2, F 3, W 3, US 1. At end of year she played her 1st Kraft tour f at Curitiba, having earlier reached qf Brisbane (d. Zrubakova), Strasbourg, Kitzbuhel and San Marino. In GS she extended Capriati to 3s at Australian Open and again at French Open. Played 2 doubles f with Rittner but won no title. **1994:** (38) A 2, F 1, W 4, US 1. It was a good year for her, in which she reached f Brisbane (d. Mag. Maleeva), Singapore and Jakarta as well as sf Pattaya City and qf Tokyo Japan Open. In GS she upset Hack 1r Wimbledon, where she was unseeded. **1995:** (56) A 1, F 3, W 2, US 3. Reached sf Puerto Rico, qf Delray Beach and upset Sawamatsu at Berlin. **1996:** (43) A 2, F 1, W 3, US 2. Upset Kruger and Hack on her way to sf Auckland, followed with the same stage at Hobart the next week and played qf Montreal, Quebec City and Pattaya. **1997:** (39) A 2, F 2, W 3, US 4. Her best performance came at Madrid, where she upset Spirlea and extended Seles to 3s in sf. She reached no other qf in singles, but played – and lost – 3 doubles f with different partners. **1998:** A 3, F 1, W 1, US 1. She appeared in sf Istanbul and upset Schnyder at Montreal, while from 2 doubles f she won Madrid with Van Roost. **1998 HIGHLIGHTS – SINGLES: Australian Open 3r** (d. Guse 2–6 6–3 6–4, Carlsson 6–4 5–7 6–4, lost Dragomir [seed 15] 6–2 7–5), **French Open 1r** (lost Zvereva 6–1 7–5), **Wimbledon 1r** (lost Davenport [seed 2] 6–2 6–2), **US Open 1r** (lost Seles [seed 6] 7–6 6–2); **sf** Istanbul (d. Lugina 6–4 4–6 6–4, Sandu 6–3 6–1, Inoue 6–3 3–6 6–4, lost Nagyova 7–6 6–0). **1998 HIGHLIGHTS – DOUBLES:** (with Van Roost) **won** Madrid (d. McQuillan/Pratt 6–3 6–1); (with Carlsson) **r/u** Istanbul (lost Babel/Courtois 6–0 6–2).

GALA LEON-GARCIA (ESP)

Born Madrid, 23 December 1973; lives Barcelona; LH; 5ft 4in; 124lb; career singles titles 0; final 1998 WTA ranking 53; 1998 prize money $110,019.

Coached by Gabriel Urpi; trained by Jordi Llacer. **1991:** (694). **1992:** (481). **1993:** (289). **1994:** (329). **1995:** (134) On the Futures circuit she won 3 singles and 2 doubles titles. **1996:** (85) A –, F 4, W 1, US 1. Broke into top 100 after reaching last 16 French Open as a qualifier (d. Paulus). Played in ESP Fed Cup team r/u to USA.

1997: (58) A 1, F 1, W 3, US 2. Reached her 1st qf on the main tour at Madrid, following with same stage Warsaw and Maria Lankowitz, and won Budapest Futures. **1998:** A 1, F 3, W 1, US 3. She moved into the top 50 after upsetting Basuki at French Open and surprising Paulus en route to her 1st career f at Maria Lankowitz, where she extended Schnyder to 3s. She also reached sf Makarska and Sopot, plus qf Hertogenbosch. **1998 HIGHLIGHTS – SINGLES: Australian Open 1r** (lost Testud [seed 9] 6–3 6–2), **French Open 3r** (d. Basuki 6–3 6–2, Suarez 6–2 1–6 7–5, lost Testud [seed 14] 6–1 6–1), **Wimbledon 1r** (lost Graf [seed 4] 6–4 6–1), **US Open 3r** (d. J. Lee 6–4 6–7 7–6, Sugiyama 2–3 ret, lost Dechy 6–4 6–4); **r/u** Maria Lankowitz (d. Talaja 6–1 1–6 7–5, Wagner 5–7 6–2 6–3, Paulus 4–6 6–4 6–3, Cocheteux 6–0 6–3, lost Schnyder 6–2 4–6 6–3); **sf** Makarska (d. Kschwendt 6–1 4–6 6–4, Kostanic 6–4 7–6, Alcazar 7–6 3–6 6–1, lost Li 6–2 6–1), **sf** Sopot (d. Jagienak 6–2 6–2, Shaughnessy 6–3 6–2, Rittner 3–6 6–4 6–4, lost Nagyova 1–6 6–4 6–1).

FANG LI (CHN)

Born Hunan, 1 January 1973, and lives there; RH; 2HB; 5ft 5½in; 138lb; turned pro 1990; career singles titles 0; final 1998 WTA ranking 40; 1998 prize money $123,241.

Coached by Jiang Hongwei and Xie Fengsen. Ranked No. 1 in China. **1990:** (350) Won Murcia and Fayetteville Futures. **1991:** (153) A 3, F –, W –, US –. Won 9 Futures events. **1992:** (119) A 1, F 1, W 1, US 2. Emerging from the satellite circuits, she reached her 1st qf on main tour at Kuala Lumpur. **1993:** (132) A 1, F –, W 1, US 1. Upset Probst at Melbourne and played 2 doubles f, winning Kitzbuhel with Monami. **1994:** (66) A 1, F 2, W 2, US 1. Reached her 1st main tour sf at Singapore and appeared in qf Palermo and Beijing, where she won the doubles with Chen. **1995:** (95) A 1, F –, W –, US 1. At Hobart she upset Wiesner to reach her 1st f on the main tour and played qf Auckland and Surabaya. **1996:** (194) A –, F –, W –, US –. Reached sf Auckland after qualifying. **1997:** (68) A –, F –, W –, US 1. Although qf Tokyo Nicherei was her best showing on the senior tour, she won Phoenix, Queen's, Wichita and Salt Lake City on the ITF circuit. **1998:** A 1, F 1, W 1, US 1. She returned to the top 50 with r/u showings at Makarska and Pattaya, plus sf Budapest (d. Testud) and qf Hobart, and took a set off Seles at Stanford. **1998 HIGHLIGHTS – SINGLES: Australian Open 1r** (lost Pierce [seed 5] 6–0 6–0), **French Open 1r** (lost Diaz-Oliva 7–6 6–1), **Wimbledon 1r** (lost Grande 6–1 6–4), **US Open 1r** (lost Rubin 6–3 6–2); **r/u** Makarska (d. Stoyanova 6–1 6–1, Serra-Zanetti 7–5 5–7 7–6, Suarez 6–4 6–2, Leon-Garcia 6–2 6–1, lost Hrdlickova 6–2 6–1), **r/u** Pattaya (d. Olsza 6–1 6–3, Saeki 6–2 6–0, Tanasugarn 7–6 6–4, Talaja 6–3 6–3, lost Halard-Decugis 6–1 6–2); **sf** Budapest (d. Probst 6–1 6–0, Golarsa 6–2 6–4, Testud 5–7 7–6 6–4, lost Farina 4–6 6–2 6–3).

ELENA LIKHOVTSEVA (KAZ)

Born Alma-Ata, 8 September 1975; lives Moscow, Russia; RH; 2HB; 5ft 8½in; 128lb; turned pro 1992; career singles titles 2; final 1998 WTA ranking 26 singles, 9 doubles; 1998 prize money $330,918; career prize money $1,148,344.

Coached by Dmitriy Degtiarev. **1991:** Won Orange Bowl 18s. **1992:** (353) Won Vilamoura Futures. **1993:** A –, F –, W –, US 1. Won her 1st tour title at Montpellier and reached qf San Diego (d. Medvedeva). **1994:** A 3, F –, W 1, US 4. After upsetting Sukova at Indian Wells and reaching qf Moscow, she reached last 16 US Open, unseeded. **1995:** (45) A 1, F 2, W 1, US 1. Upset Raymond and Frazier on her way to f Oklahoma and reached qf Hobart, Indian Wells (d. Frazier), Delray Beach, Moscow and Leipzig (d. Sukova). **1996:** (23) A 4, F 3, W 4, US 3. After removing defending champion Pierce at Australian Open, where she was unseeded, she went on to reach sf Oklahoma (d. Frazier), Berlin (d. Sanchez-Vicario) and Quebec City, plus qf Oakland (d. M. J. Fernandez). **1997:** (31) A 1, F 2, W 2, US 3. Her year began on a high note with the title at Gold Coast (d. Schultz-McCarthy). Although she did not maintain that level, she reached qf Hannover and Stanford (d. Raymond), upset Basuki at Luxembourg and extended Novotna to 3s at Wimbledon. **1998:** A 3, F 3, W 3, US 1. She continued to be a dangerous opponent, removing Basuki and Tauziat on her way to sf Strasbourg and upsetting Van Roost both at LIPC and to reach sf Birmingham (at which point tourn was cancelled). She reached the same stage at Luxembourg, and appeared in qf Stanford and Boston. In doubles she won 4 titles with Sugiyama to qualify for Chase Champs, where they did not pass 1r. **1998 HIGHLIGHTS – SINGLES: Australian Open 3r** (d. Reid 6–2 6–1, Yoshida 6–4 4–6 6–1, lost Nagyova 6–7 7–5 6–2), **French Open 3r** (d. Cacic 6–4 6–3, Black 7–5 7–5, lost Davenport [seed 2] 7–5 7–5), **Wimbledon 3r** (d. Yoshida 7–6 6–2, Perfetti 6–4 6–0, lost Hingis [seed 1 6–2 6–1), **US Open 1r** (lost Spirlea [seed 9] 7–6 6–4); **sf** Strasbourg (d. Basuki 6–1 7–6, Cristea 3–6 6–0 6–3, Tauziat 6–4 6–2, lost Halard-Decugis 6–3 7–6), **sf** Birmingham (d. Barabanschikova 3–6 6–1 6–4, Neiland 6–7 6–1 3–0 ret, Van Roost 6–3 6–4, tourn cancelled), **sf** Luxembourg (d. Grande 6–1 6–1, Tatarkova 6–2 6–1, Koulikovskaya 6–2 6–0, lost Pierce 6–1 7–5). **1998 HIGHLIGHTS – DOUBLES:** (with Sugiyama unless stated) **won** Gold Coast (d. Park/Wang 1–6 6–3 6–4), **won** Luxembourg (d. Neiland/Tatarkova 6–7 6–3 2–0 ret), **won** Leipzig (d. Bollegraf/Spirlea 6–3 6–7 6–1), **won** Philadelphia (d. Seles/Zvereva 7–5 4–6 6–2); (with Vis) **r/u** Hannover (lost Raymond/Stubbs 6–1 6–7 6–3)

MIRJANA LUCIC (CRO)

Born Dortmund, Germany, 9 March 1982; lives Bradenton, Fla; RH; 2HB; 5ft 11in; 145lb; turned pro 1997; career singles titles 2; 1998 WTA ranking 51 singles, 20 doubles; 1998 prize money $274,905.

Coached by Goran Prpic and Glen Schaap. **1996:** Won US Open Jun over Weingartner. **1997:** (52) A –, F –, W –, US 3. Played Fed Cup for CRO at age 14 as CRO d. AUS 4–1. Then at 15 years 1 month 25 days, she became the youngest since Capriati in 1990 to take a title when, unranked and a qualifier, she delighted home crowds by winning Bol in her 1st ever tourn on the main tour. She followed by reaching f of her second after qualifying at Strasbourg (d. Tauziat), took the title at ITF Makarska and came into the rankings at No. 69. A hard-hitter who plays with a maturity beyond her years, she extended Novotna to 3s at US Open, having been permitted by the tourn organisers to play there, although French Open and Wimbledon had excluded her from the women's tourn as being too young, and she was restricted to 8 tourns during the year. In the Jun game, she won Australian Open over Weingartner and took the doubles there with Wohr. **1998:** A 2, F –, W 2, US 3. She became, at 15 yrs 11 mths, the youngest title-holder at Australian Open after taking the women's doubles with Hingis, who had been 2 months younger when she set a similar record at Wimbledon in 1996. They followed with Tokyo Pan Pacific at next tourn and she was r/u Bol with Kruger. She won the singles there again, becoming the youngest ever to retain a singles title, and upset Pierce on her way to sf Rome, but missed French Open with chicken pox. After Wimbledon she and her mother moved to US following claims that her father, Marinko, a former Olympic decathlon athlete who used to travel with her, had beaten her and taken some of her prize money. Although she and Hingis qualified together for Chase Champs, she could not take up her place as Hingis had also qualified (with more points) with Novotna. **1998 HIGHLIGHTS – SINGLES: Australian Open 2r** (d. Stubbs 7–5 6–1, lost Majoli [seed 4] 7–5 6–4), **Wimbledon 2r** (d. Smashnova 6–4 6–7 6–3, lost S. Williams 6–3 6–0), **US Open 3r** (d. Boogert 6–3 6–2, Sawamatsu 4–6 6–1 6–1, lost Graf [seed 8] 6–1 6–1); **won** Bol (d. Brandi 6–2 3–6 7–5, Black 6–2 6–0, Diaz-Oliva 6–2 6–3, Kruger 6–2 6–1, Morariu 6–2 6–4); **sf** Rome (d. Cacic 6–1 6–7 7–6, Likhovtseva 3–6 6–2 6–2, Pierce 7–5 6–4, Testud 7–5 ret, lost Hingis 6–2 6–1). **1998 HIGHLIGHTS – DOUBLES:** (with Hingis) **won Australian Open** (d. Davenport/Zvereva 6–4 2–6 6–3); **won** Tokyo Pan Pacific (d. Davenport/Zvereva 7–5 6–4); (with Kruger) **r/u** Bol (lost Montalvo/Suarez w/o).

IVA MAJOLI (CRO)

Born Zagreb, 12 August 1977, and lives there; RH; 2HB; 5ft 8in; 136lb; turned pro 1991; career singles titles 7; final 1998 WTA ranking 25; 1998 prize money $291,356; career prize money $3,464,588.

Coached by her father, Stanko, and brother, Drago. At 12, she moved with her father and brother to USA to attend Bollettieri Tennis Academy, where they were joined later by her sister and mother. However, missing the rest of her family and friends, she returned home. **1991:** (798). **1992:** (50) A –, F – W –, US 2. Reached qf VS Houston (d. McNeil), Oakland (d. McNeil again) and Indianapolis (d. Tauziat) to break into top 50. Won St Simons and Evansville Challengers back-to-back. **1993:** (46) A –, F 4, W –, US 2. Reached qf VS Chicago and Oakland. Unseeded at French Open, she upset Hack on her way to last 16, where she extended Graf to 2s tb. Voted WTA Most Impressive Newcomer. **1994:** (13) A –, F 4, W 1, US 4. She proved to be a dangerous opponent and recorded some big upsets during the year as she moved into the top 20. Reached her 1st tour f at Osaka, following with the same stage Barcelona (d. Martinez and Mag. Maleeva) and Essen (d. Huber), sf Indian Wells (d. Zvereva), FC Cup (d. Sabatini and Davenport) and Stratton Mountain (d. M. J. Fernandez) and 3 more qf. In GS she made an unexpected appearance in last 16 French and US Opens and qualified for VS Champs 1st time, losing 1r to Novotna. **1995:** (9) A –, F qf, W 1, US 1. She continued her upsetting ways in spring when she surprised Pierce at French Open and took a set off Sanchez-Vicario in f Barcelona. She went on to win her 1st title at Zurich in Oct. (d. Pierce again and Novotna) and broke into the top 10 after following with Filderstadt next week (d. Pierce a 3rd time and Sabatini). She also appeared in sf Tokyo Pan Pacific and Paris Open, plus qf FC Cup, Italian Open and Toronto to qualify for VS Champs, where she lost 1r to Martinez. **1996:** (7) A qf, F qf, W –, US 1. At Tokyo Toray in Jan. she became only the 2nd player (after Graf) to beat Seles since her comeback, going on to upset Sanchez-Vicario for the title and following in Feb. with Essen over Novotna. She was playing her 3rd consec. singles f, having appeared at that stage at Paris Open in between. She was also r/u Leipzig and reached sf Italian Open, Berlin and Zurich, plus qf Australian Open, French Open, Olympics, FC Cup, Rosmalen and Filderstadt, as well as winning the Hopman Cup with Ivanisevic. At Chase Champs she upset Huber and Martinez (overcoming a displaced rib during that match) before extending Hingis to 3s sf. **1997:** (6) A 1, F won, W qf, US 2. The high point of her career came at French Open, where she won her 1st GS title and ended Hingis's unbeaten run in 1997 of 37 matches. In 4r she recovered from 5–7 0–4 down v Davenport, and in sf had to overcome the debilitating effect of a virus. Earlier, she had won Hannover over Novotna and retained her record in Germany with the title at Hamburg, where she was r/u doubles with Dragomir. She also reached sf Paris Open, Amelia Island, Atlanta and Chicago, plus qf Sydney, Tokyo Pan Pacific, LIPC, Leipzig and Chase Champs. **1998:** A 3, F qf, W 2, US 2. She was never able to regain the heights of the previous year and dropped out of the top 10 on 8 June, slipping so far down the rankings that she was unseeded at both Wimbledon and US Open. Her best performances, all in the first half of the season, were sf Tokyo Pan Pacific and Linz and qf Paris Open, Amelia Island and French Open (where she d. Martinez and extended Davenport to 3s). She was out of action for a while in autumn with a shoulder injury. **1998 HIGHLIGHTS – SINGLES: Australian Open 3r** [seed 4] (d. Sawamatsu 6–4 6–2, Lucic 7–6 6–4, lost Tanasugarn 6–0 6–2), **French Open qf** [seed 10] (d. Stoyanova 6–3 6–1, Zvereva 6–3 6–4, Diaz-Oliva 6–2 7–6, Martinez [seed 7] 7–6 6–7 6–3, lost Davenport [seed 2] 6–1 5–7 6–3), **Wimbledon 2r** (d. Habsudova 6–2 6–3, lost Tauziat [seed 16] 6–0 6–1), **US Open 2r** (d. Huber 6–3 6–3, lost Hingis [seed 1] 7–6 6–0); **sf** Tokyo Pan Pacific (d. Li 6–3 3–0 ret, Saeki 6–2 6–1, lost Hingis 6–0 6–2), **sf** Linz (d. Maleeva 6–1 6–1, Raymond 7–6 4–6 6–3, lost Van Roost 6–2 ret). **CAREER HIGHLIGHTS – SINGLES: French Open – won 1997** (d. Kleinova 7–5 6–4, Fusai 6–2 6–3, Grossman 6–1 4–6 6–1, Davenport 5–7 6–4

6–2, Dragomir 6–3 5–7 6–2, Coetzer 6–3 4–6 7–5, Hingis 6–4 6–2), **qf 1995** (d. Endo 6–3 6–3, Gaidano 6–1 6–0, Wang 7–5 6–2, Pierce 6–2 6–3, lost Date 7–5 6–1), **qf 1996** (d. Meier 6–3 6–4, Grande 6–3 7–6, Testud 4–6 7–5 6–4, Leon-Garcia 6–3 6–1, lost Graf 6–3 6–1), **qf 1998**; **Australian Open – qf 1996** (d. Makarova 6–4 6–2, McNeil 6–3 6–2, Fusai 6–2 6–1, Appelmans 6–2 6–2, lost Seles 6–1 6–2).

AMELIE MAURESMO (FRA)

Born St Germain en Laye, 5 July 1979; lives Bornel; RH; 5ft 9in; 142lb; career singles titles 0; final 1998 WTA ranking 29; 1998 prize money $187,084.

Coached by Warwick Bashford. **1994:** (827). **1995:** (290) A –, F 1, W –, US –. Played in winning FRA World Youth Cup team, and in the women's game won her 1st satellite event at St Raphael. **1996:** (159) A –, F 2, W –, US –. Finished the year at No. 1 in ITF Jun singles rankings after winning French Open over Shaughnessy and Wimbledon over Serna, as well as taking the doubles there with Barabanschikova. **1997:** (109) A –, F 2, W –, US –. Won Thessaloniki Futures and played in winning FRA team in HM Queen Sofia Cup. **1998:** A 3, F 1, W 2, US 3. The highlight of her career to date came at Berlin, where she played through the qualifying then upset Van Roost, Davenport, Paulus and Novotna to reach her 1st career f, becoming the 1st qualifier ever to reach that stage in a Tier I tourn. Although she did not reach those heights again, she appeared in qf Prague and New Haven (d. Tauziat). Joining her country's Fed Cup team, she extended Hingis to 3s in that competition and again at US Open. **1998 HIGHLIGHTS – SINGLES: Australian Open 3r** (d. Farina 7–6 7–5, Plischke 1–6 6–4 6–3, lost V. Williams 6–1 6–4), **French Open 1r** (lost Kournikova [seed 13] 6–2 6–4), **Wimbledon 2r** (d. Schnitzer 6–3 6–4, lost Basuki 6–3 6–4), **US Open 3r** (d. Richterova 6–2 6–1, Saeki 6–4 6–1, lost Hingis [seed 1] 4–6 6–2 6–2); **r/u** Berlin (d. Van Roost 3–6 6–4 7–5, Labat 7–5 7–5, Davenport 6–2 6–4, Paulus 6–4 6–2, Novotna 7–5 5–7 6–4, lost Martinez 6–4 6–4).

ANNE MILLER (USA)

Born Midland, Mich., 19 January 1977, and lives there; RH; 2HB; 5ft 6in; 135lb; turned pro 1995; career singles titles 0; final 1998 WTA ranking 46; 1998 prize money $111,577.

1991: USTA 16s champ and r/u Easter Bowl 18s. **1992:** (426) Won Easter Bowl 18s. **1993:** (264) Began to make her mark on the Challenger circuits. **1994:** (236). **1995:** (123) A 1, F –, W –, US 2. On the ITF circuit she won Peachtree and Darmstadt. **1996:** (54) A –, F 1, W 2, US 1. Reached qf Strasbourg (d. Date) and Philadelphia (d. Davenport) and won Indian Wells Futures. **1997:** (118) A 1, F –, W –, US 1. Broke into top 50 in March before slipping out of the top 100 again. **1998:** A 2, F 1, W 2, US 3. She moved back up the rankings with sf finish at Auckland and an upset of Pierce at FC Cup. **1998 HIGHLIGHTS – SINGLES: Australian Open 2r** (d. Sukova 4–6 7–5 6–3, lost Huber [seed 10] 6–4 6–0), **French Open 1r** (lost Novotna [seed 3] 7–5 6–4), **Wimbledon 2r** (d. Dechy 7–6 6–2, lost Van Roost 6–1 6–1), **US Open 3r** (d. Nacuk 6–2 6–3, Koulikovskaya 6–1 4–6 6–2, lost Seles [seed 6] 6–3 6–3); **sf** Auckland (d. Saeki 6–4 6–4, Torrens-Valero 7–5 7–5, Raymond 7–5 1–0 ret, lost Van Roost 6–2 6–3).

ALICIA MOLIK (AUS)

Born Adelaide, 27 January 1981, and lives there; RH; 6ft; 155lb; career singles titles 0; final 1998 WTA ranking 172.

Coached by Roger Tyzzer. **1998:** Won Australian Open Jun doubles with Dominikovic. In the women's game she made an impact on the ITF circuit: in Japan she won 5 tourns back-to-back, also taking the doubles in 4, and followed a week later in Australia with Gold Coast. **1998 HIGHLIGHTS – SINGLES: won** Kugayama ITF (d. Stewart 6–4 6–2), **won** Ibaraki ITF (Week 2) (d. Otakeyama 6–2 6–1), **won** Ibaraki ITF (Week 3) (d. Sasano 3–6 6–0 6–1), **won** Kyoto ITF (d. Takase 6–2 6–3), **won** Saga ITF (d. Dokic 6–4 6–3), **won** ITF Gold Coast (d. Barclay 6–4 7–6)

CORINA MORARIU (USA)

Born Detroit, Mich., 26 January 1978; lives Boca Raton, Fla; RH; 5ft 8in; 130lb; career singles titles 0; final 1998 WTA ranking 31; 1998 prize money $180,111.

Coached by Andrew Turcinovich. **1994:** (622) Won Australian Open Jun doubles with Varmuzova. **1995:** (246) In Jun doubles with Varmuzova she won Australian Open, French Open and US Open, finishing No. 2 on the ITF Jun doubles rankings. In the senior game, she won 3 singles and 4 doubles titles on the Futures circuit. **1996:** (122) A –, F –, W 1, US 1. Reached qf Tokyo Japan Open after qualifying. **1997:** (60) A 1, F –, W 2, US 2. Broke into top 100 at beginning of May after playing her 1st f on the main tour at Bol, having gained direct entry via the feed-up system. She also reached qf Luxembourg, Tokyo Japan Open (r/u doubles with Guse) and Pattaya (won doubles with Kunce) and took Bogota Futures. **1998:** A 2, F 2, W 3, US 1. Bol and Tokyo Japan Open were highlights again as she reached f of both. Other qf appearances came at Bogota and Boston, and she extended Graf to 3s 1r US Open. **1998 HIGHLIGHTS – SINGLES: Australian Open 2r** (d. Callens 6–4 1–6 6–0, lost Kournikova 7–5 6–2), **French Open 2r** (d. Schultz-McCarthy 6–3 2–0 ret, lost S. Williams 6–1 6–0), **Wimbledon 3r** (d. Maruska 4–6 6–1 6–2, Hy-Boulais 7–5 6–0, lost Novotna [seed 3] 6–3 6–1), **US Open 1r** (lost Graf [seed 8] 6–2 3–6 6–1); **r/u** Tokyo Japan Open (d. Park 6–4 6–2, Shaughnessy 6–3 6–2, Sawamatsu 7–5 6–3, Frazier 4–6 7–6 6–4, lost Sugiyama 6–3 6–3), **r/u** Bol (d. Torrens-Valero 6–4 6–4, Yoshida 6–2 6–4, Cecchini 6–3 6–1, Talaja 4–6 6–4 6–3, lost Lucic 6–2 6–4).

HENRIETA NAGYOVA (SVK)

Born Nove Zamky, 15 December 1978, and lives there; RH; 2HB; 5ft 10in; 134lb; turned pro 1994; career singles titles 4; final 1998 WTA ranking 28; 1998 prize money $218,874.

Coached by Lubomir Kurhajec. **1994:** (379) Won French Open Jun doubles with Hingis and on the women's satellite circuit won Olsztyn and Porec back-to-back. **1995:** (137) Continuing to make her mark on the satellite circuit, she won Bordeaux and Athens, where she also took the doubles. **1996:** (42) A –, F 2, W 1, US 2. She broke into the top 100 in Feb., after winning Cali and later Bratislava on the Futures circuit. On the main tour, unseeded at Warsaw, she upset Paulus to take her 1st title in her 1st f at that level, upset Appelmans on her way to sf Cardiff, and reached same stage Pattaya, as well as qf Palermo, Karlovy Vary and Luxembourg (d. Coetzer). **1997:** (35) A 3, F 1, W 1, US 2. The highlight of her year came at Pattaya, in the last tourn, when she upset Dragomir and Van Roost to take the title. Earlier she had upset Dragomir on her way to f Warsaw, and reached the same stage Maria Lankowitz, plus sf Budapest and qf Luxembourg. She won Bol doubles with Montalvo and took both singles and doubles at Bratislava Futures. **1998:** A 4, F 4, W 2, US 3. She upset Schultz-McCarthy at Australian Open, where she was unseeded, and broke into top 25 on 8 June after French Open (unseeded again). In Aug. she won Sopot and Istanbul back-to-back, and during the year appeared in sf Prague (extended Novotna to 3s) and Warsaw (extended Martinez to 3s), plus qf Hobart and Strasbourg. **1998 HIGHLIGHTS – SINGLES: Australian Open last 16** [unseeded] (d. Wunderlich 6–3 6–1, Schultz-McCarthy [seed 11] 6–1 6–4, Likhovtseva 6–7 7–5 6–2, lost Pierce [seed 5] 6–0 6–0), **French Open last 16** [unseeded] (d. McQuillan 6–3 6–4, Plischke 6–4 6–3, Dechy 7–6 3–6 6–1, lost V. Williams [seed 8] 6–1 6–3), **Wimbledon 2r** (d. Frazier 6–7 6–2 6–4, lost Graf [seed 4] 6–0 6–4), **US Open 3r** (d. Gersi 6–2 6–0, Rubin 7–6 6–4, lost Tauziat [seed 10] 6–1 6–1); **won** Sopot (d. Noorlander 6–2 6–2, Husarova 6–0 6–4, Torrens-Valero 6–4 6–1, Leon-Garcia 1–6 6–4 6–1, Wagner 6–3 5–7 6–1), **won** Istanbul (d. Courtois 6–2 6–3, Chladkova 6–3 6–1, Shaughnessy 6–4 6–4, Labat 7–6 6–0, Barabanschikova 6–4 3–6 7–6); **sf** Prague (d. Panova 6–2 6–4, Smashnova 7–5 4–6 6–4, Shaughnessy 6–1 6–2, lost Novotna 2–6 6–3 7–5), **sf** Warsaw (d. Torrens-Valero 6–3 6–0, Martincova 6–3 6–1, Cristea 6–0 6–1, lost Martinez 6–2 4–6 6–2).

LARISA NEILAND (LAT)

Born Lvov, Ukraine, 21 July 1966; lives Yurmala; RH; 5ft 6½in; 134lb; turned pro 1988; career singles titles 2; final 1998 WTA ranking 73 singles, 11 doubles; 1998 prize money $212,590; career prize money $3,745,744.

Husband Alex Neiland (married 21 December 1989). Maiden name Savchenko. 1983: A –, F –, W –, US 1. Ranked 10 on ITF Jun list. **1984:** (138) A 1, F 3, W 1, US –. Won 2 titles on satellite circuit. **1985:** (55) A –, F 1, W 3, US –. Reached sf VS Denver and joined Fed Cup team. **1986:** (35) F 2, W 2, US –. Showed affinity for grass courts, reaching sf Birmingham, qf Eastbourne, and upsetting Rehe at Wimbledon. Qualified with Parkhomenko for VS Champ doubles March and Nov. **1987:** (24) A –, F –, W 2, US 2. Won 4 doubles titles with Parkhomenko and ousted Navratilova/Shriver en route to sf Wimbledon. **1988:** (16) A –, F –, W 4, US qf. R/u VS California (d. Mandlikova and Sabatini), sf Pan Pacific Open (d. Zvereva) and qf Eastbourne (d. Kohde-Kilsch), US Open and Olympics. In doubles with Zvereva r/u Wimbledon and VS Champs, for which she qualified in both singles and doubles. **1989:** (20) A –, F 3, W 1, US 4. Upset Navratilova en route to f VS California but then, frustrated by her poor form in singles, she talked of retiring after US Open. However, there she reached last 16, upsetting Shriver, and followed up with sf Moscow and r/u VS Chicago. In doubles won French Open and r/u Wimbledon and VS Champs with Zvereva, reaching 9 more f and winning 4. **1990:** (87) A 1, F 2, W 2, US 3. In singles qf Tokyo Toray and Birmingham. In doubles r/u French Open and won 3 titles with Zvereva, taking another with K. Jordan. Qualified for VS Champs with Zvereva but lost 1r to Adams/McNeil. **1991:** (48) A 2, F 2, W 2, US 1. Won her 1st singles title at St Petersburg and reached sf Brisbane, upsetting Novotna. In doubles played 8 f with Zvereva, winning Wimbledon plus 5 others and r/u French Open to qualify for VS Champs; reached another 4 f with Novotna, winning 3 and r/u US Open; and won Auckland with Fendick. **1992:** (59) A 4, F 2, W 1, US 1. In singles reached sf Auckland and last 16 Australian Open, unseeded. In doubles with Novotna won 7 titles and was r/u Wimbledon and US Open to qualify for VS Champs, where they were r/u to Sanchez-Vicario/Sukova. She won 1 more title each with Zvereva and Sanchez-Vicario and in mixed won Wimbledon with Suk. **1993:** (32) A 1, F 1, W 2, US 1. Won her 2nd career singles title at Schenectady, was r/u Tokyo Pan Pacific (upset McNeil and Novotna) and reached sf Birmingham. She continued to excel in doubles, playing 13 f, of which she won 1 with Martinez and 3 with regular partner Novotna, with whom she was r/u French Open and Wimbledon. They qualified together for VS Champs, where they were runners-up to G. Fernandez/Zvereva – as they were on 5 other occasions. **1994:** (41) A 1, F 1, W qf, US 1. It was a less spectacular year in singles, although she was r/u Schenectady and upset Martinez en route to sf Brighton. The highlight, however, came at Wimbledon, where, unseeded, she upset Date and Coetzer on her way to qf. In doubles she played 8 f, winning 6 titles with 5 different partners and in mixed with Olhovskiy won Australian and r/u French Open. **1995:** (97) A 1, F 1, W 2, US 2. Qf FC Cup was her best performance in singles. In doubles she played 13 f with various partners – winning 5 with McGrath, with whom she qualified for VS Champs, and 1 with Sanchez-Vicario – and took French Open mixed with Woodforde. **1996:** (62) A 1, F 1, W 3, US 1. She reached qf Birmingham and Rosmalen (d. Schultz-McCarthy), and upset Sawamatsu at Indian Wells and Davenport at Wimbledon. In women's doubles she played 9 f, winning Essen and Berlin with McGrath, with whom she was r/u Wimbledon and qualified for Chase Champs, as well as taking Rosmalen with Schultz-McCarthy, Montreal with Sanchez-Vicario and Moscow with

Medvedeva. In mixed, with Woodforde, she won Australian Open and was r/u Wimbledon. **1997:** (85) A 2, F 2, W 1, US 1. From 5 women's doubles f with 3 different partners, she won Birmingham with Adams and Luxembourg with Sukova, with whom she qualified for Chase Champs. There they upset G. Fernandez/Zvereva in Fernandez's farewell tourn, but lost sf to Davenport/Novotna. In mixed she was r/u Australian Open with De Jager and Wimbledon with Olhovskiy. **1998:** A 2, F 1, W 2, US 3. In singles she upset Fusai at Birmingham and in doubles played 4 f – 2 each with Kournikova and Tatarkova – but won no title. It was with Kournikova that she qualified for Chase Champs, where they lost 1r to Davenport/Zvereva. **1998 HIGHLIGHTS – SINGLES: Australian Open 2r** (d. Barclay 6–3 7–6, lost Coetzer [seed 3] 2–6 6–1 6–0), **French Open 1r** (lost Smashnova 3–6 6–3 6–2), **Wimbledon 2r** (d. Pitkowski 6–1 5–7 6–3, lost Davenport [seed 2] 6–1 7–5), **US Open 3r** (d. Panova 6–7 6–3 6–4, De Swardt 6–7 6–0 6–2, lost V. Williams [seed 5] 5–0 ret). **1998 HIGHLIGHTS – DOUBLES:** (with Kournikova unless stated) **r/u** Paris Open (lost Appelmans/Oremans 1–6 6–3 7–6), **r/u** Linz (lost Fusai/Tauziat 6–3 3–6 6–4), (with Tatarkova) **r/u** Stanford (lost Davenport/Zvereva 6–4 6–4), (with Tatarkova) **r/u** Luxembourg (lost Likhovtseva/Sugiyama 6–7 6–3 2–0 ret). **CAREER HIGHLIGHTS – SINGLES: Wimbledon – qf 1994** [unseeded] (d. Adams 6–4 6–3, Smashnova 6–3 6–4, Date 6–3 6–2, Coetzer 1–6 6–3 6–4, lost McNeil 6–3 6–4); **US Open – qf 1988** (d. Golarsa 7–6 6–2, Burgin 5–7 7–5 6–4, Bassett-Seguso 6–4 6–3, Phelps 6–3 6–1, lost Sabatini 4–6 6–4 6–2). **CAREER HIGHLIGHTS – DOUBLES:** (with Zvereva unless stated) **French Open – won 1989** (d. Graf/Sabatini 6–4 6–4), **r/u 1990** (lost Novotna/Sukova 6–4 7–5), **r/u 1991** (lost G. Fernandez/Novotna 6–4 6–0), (with Novotna) **r/u 1993** (lost G. Fernandez/Zvereva 6–3 7–5); **Wimbledon – won 1991** (d. G. Fernandez/Novotna 6–4 3–6 6–4), **r/u 1988** (lost Graf/Sabatini 6–3 1–6 12–10), **r/u 1989** (lost Novotna/Sukova 6–1 6–2), (with Novotna) **r/u 1993** (lost G. Fernandez/Zvereva 6–4 6–7 6–4), (with McGrath) **r/u 1996** (lost Hingis/Sukova 5–7 7–5 6–1); **US Open** – (with Novotna) **r/u 1991** (lost Shriver/Zvereva 6–4 4–6 7–6); **VS Champs – r/u 1988** (lost Navratilova/Shriver 6–3 6–4), **r/u 1989** (lost Navratilova/ Shriver 6–3 6–2), (with Novotna) **r/u 1993** (lost G. Fernandez/Zvereva 6–3 7–5). **MIXED DOUBLES: Australian Open** – (with Woodforde unless stated) (with Olhovskiy) **won 1994** (d. Woodbridge/Sukova 7–5 6–7 6–2), **won 1996** (d. L. Jensen/Arendt 6–2 6–4), **French Open** – **won 1995** (d. De Jager/Hetherington 7–6 7–6).

MIRIAM OREMANS (NED)

Born Berlicum, 9 September 1972, and lives there; RH; 5ft 6½in; 143lb; turned pro 1989; career singles titles 0; final 1998 WTA ranking 58; 1998 prize money $176,599; career prize money $1,084,847.

Coached by Hugo Ekker. At age 12 chose a career in tennis rather than competitive horse-riding, at which she also excelled. **1989:** (–) Won Nat 18s singles and European Jun doubles. In the women's game won 2 titles on the Israeli satellite circuit. **1990:** (191) A –, F –, W –, US 2. **1991:** (148) A 1, F –, W 1, US –. Upset Sawamatsu 1r Tokyo Suntory. **1992:** (132) A –, F –, W 1, US –. Upset Zardo 2r Brisbane, won Linz doubles with Kiene and r/u Wimbledon mixed with Eltingh. **1993:** (31) A 3, F 2, W 4, US 1. She showed she could be a dangerous opponent and swept into the top 50 with some useful upsets across the year. At Eastbourne she surprised Sukova and McNeil en route to f, where she took a set off Navratilova on grass; then, unseeded at Wimbledon, she extended Novotna to 3s in last 16. She also appeared in qf Indian Wells (d. Hy), Tokyo Japan Open and Zurich (d. Wiesner), as well as upsetting Huber at LIPC and Halard at Berlin. **1994:** (47) A 1, F 3, W 1, US 1. Restricted by a thigh strain in 1st part of year, she came into her own at French Open, where she upset Navratilova 1r, inflicting her 1st loss at that stage in GS since 1976. Reached sf Zurich (d. Pierce) and took a set off Novotna 1r Wimbledon. **1995:** (42) A 2, F 2, W 3, US 1. Although she reached qf Sydney (d. Frazier), Strasbourg (where she was r/u doubles with Appelmans) and Brighton (d. Novotna), she could progress no further. **1996:** (51) A 1, F 3, W 2, US 2. She reached sf Birmingham, plus qf Cardiff and Paris Open, where she upset Wiesner in a match that lasted more than 3 hours and ran to 3 tbs. Played 2 doubles f with Appelmans, but won no title. **1997:** (47) A 1, F 1, W 1, US 3. She was r/u Rosmalen (d. Habsudova), reached qf Hannover (d. Huber) and Luxembourg, and upset M. J. Fernandez in Fed Cup as NED d. USA. **1998:** A 2, F 2, W 4, US 1. Her best performance came at Hertogenbosch, where she was r/u singles, upsetting Van Roost along the way, and won the doubles with Appelmans, with whom she also won Paris Open. Other highlights were sf appearance at Palermo and the removal of De Swardt at Wimbledon, where she was unseeded. **1998 HIGHLIGHTS – SINGLES: Australian Open 2r** (d. Kunce 7–5 6–2, lost Martinez [seed 8] 7–5 6–2), **French Open 2r** (d. Makarova 6–1 1–6 6–3, lost Schwartz 6–4 6–2), **Wimbledon last 16** [unseeded] (d. Wagner 2–6 6–3 6–2, Carlsson 6–2 6–3, De Swardt 6–4 7–5, lost Zvereva 6–4 6–2), **US Open 1r** (lost Martinez [seed 7] 6–1 6–2); **r/u** Hertogenbosch (d. Van Roost 6–3 7–6, Dechaume-Balleret 7–6 6–7 6–2, Boogert 6–3 2–6 6–4, Po 6–1 6–7 7–6, lost Halard-Decugis 6–3 6–4); **sf** Palermo (d. Bes 6–4 6–3, Nejedly 6–1 7–6, Wagner 6–0 6–2, lost Schnyder 6–1 6–3). **1998 HIGHLIGHTS – DOUBLES:** (with Appelmans) **won** Paris Open (d. Kournikova/Neiland 1–6 6–3 7–6), **won** Hertogenbosch (d. Cristea/Melicharova 6–7 7–6 7–6).

BARBARA PAULUS (AUT)

Born Vienna, 1 September 1970; lives Hinterbruehl; RH; 5ft 9½in; 138lb; turned pro 1986; career singles titles 6; final 1998 WTA ranking 45; 1998 prize money $110,326; career prize money $1,294,445.

Coached by Peter Eipeldauer. **1982:** Won Nat 12 for 2nd year. **1985:** Won Nat 18s. **1986:** (187) Won Nat Indoor and Outdoor, reached qf Bregenz and played Fed Cup. **1987:** (96) A –, F 3, W 1, US –. Appeared in qf Guaruja and won Wels on the Futures circuit. **1988:** (25) A –, F 3, W –, US –. Won her 1st primary circuit title at Geneva over McNeil, r/u Sofia and upset Kohde-Kilsch 1r Filderstadt. **1989:** (24) A –, F 2, W –, US 4. R/u Arcachon, sf Geneva (d. Evert) and surprised Novotna at US Open, where she was unseeded. **1990:** (15) A 4, F –, W 1, US 4. In her best year she won Geneva, was r/u Sydney, Palermo and Filderstadt (d. Garrison and Sabatini) and reached sf San Diego and Leipzig. **1991:** (25) A 2, F –, W –, US 2. Reached sf Sydney (d. Maleeva-Fragniere), Leipzig (d. K. Maleeva) and Brighton, where she was forced to def ill. **1992:** (205) A 1, F –, W –, US 1. Out of action March to May following knee surgery and suffering from a wrist injury and out again from Oct. with recurring wrist problems. **1993:** (259) A –, F –, W –, US –. **1994:** (108) A –, F –, W –, US –. Reached qf Pattaya City (d. Harvey-Wild) and won Maribor Futures. **1995:** (23) A 4, F 1, W 2, US 2. Having won no title on the main tour for 5 years, she returned to her old place in the rankings with the titles at Warsaw and Pattaya City, r/u finish at Brighton, sf showing at Styrian Open and an upset of Majoli at US Open. **1996:** (10) A 2, F 3, W –, US 3. She returned to the top 20 and moved on into top 10 1st time in Nov. after winning Styria, r/u Auckland, FC Cup (unseeded, upsetting M. Maleeva and Martinez), Strasbourg, Warsaw and Moscow, as well as sf Luxembourg and qf Berlin and Philadelphia. She qualified for her 1st Chase Champs, but fell 1r to Davenport. **1997:** (24) A –, F 4, W 2, US –. An injured thumb kept her out at the beginning of the year, but she returned to reach sf Hannover, following with the same stage LIPC and Palermo, then progressing to the title at Warsaw the following week. She reached a 2nd f at Luxembourg, where she extended Coetzer to 7–5 3s, reached qf Maria Lankowitz (but withdrew with tendinitis of right elbow), and took a set off Hingis at French Open. **1998:** A 1, F 1, W 1, US 1. Although she did not pass qf, she reached that stage at Sydney (d. Spirlea), Paris Open, Berlin and Maria Lankowitz. **1998 HIGHLIGHTS – SINGLES: Australian Open 1r** (lost Coetzer [seed 3] 6–2 6–0), **French Open 1r** (lost Fusai 6–1 7–5), **Wimbledon 1r** (lost Sawamatsu 2–6 6–3 6–2), **US Open 1r** (lost Dechy 6–2 7–5).

NADEJDA PETROVA (RUS)

Born Krackow, Poland, 8 June 1982; lives Moscow; RH; 2HB; 5ft 10in; 142lb; career singles titles 0; final 1998 WTA ranking 142.

Coached by Witold Meres. **1998:** Won French Open Jun over Dokic, then in only her 2nd main tour event she upset Majoli at Moscow.

SARAH PITKOWSKI (FRA)

Born Seclin, 13 November 1975; lives Paris; RH; 5ft 2½in; 103lb; turned pro 1993; career singles titles 0; final 1998 WTA ranking 36; 1998 prize money $129,944.

Coached by Ferrante Rocchi. **1991:** (885). **1992:** (215) Won Nat 18s and took Futures titles in Swindon and Madeira. **1993:** (151) A –, F 1, W –, US –. In Jun tennis won European 18s and was a member of French team that won Annie Soisbault Cup. On the women's tour she took Caserta Futures. **1994:** (111) A –, F –, W –, US –. Won 2 Futures titles. **1995:** (107) A 2, F 2, W 1, US 1. Appeared in her 1st qf on the main tour at Surabaya and won 2 Futures titles again. **1996:** (87) A 1, F 3, W –, US 2. Reached qf Palermo and Surabaya. **1997:** (56) A 1, F 2, W 2, US 2. Progressed to her 1st sf on the main tour at Cardiff, as well as qf Bol and Surabaya, and won Reims Futures. **1998:** A 1, F 1, W 1, US 3. She showed she could be a dangerous opponent on her way to sf Oklahoma City (d. Testud), qf Gold Coast, Prague (d. Dragomir), Leipzig (d. Coetzer) and Paris Open (upset Appelmans and extended Tauziat to 7–6 fs after qualifying). She made her Fed Cup debut in March and won the $25,000 ITF Bronx tourn. **1998 HIGHLIGHTS – SINGLES: Australian Open 1r** (lost Huber [seed 10] 5–7 6–0 6–0), **French Open 1r** (lost Saeki 7–5 7–5), **Wimbledon 1r** (lost Neiland 6–1 5–7 6–1), **US Open 3r** (d. Habsudova 1–6 7–5 6–3, Carlsson 6–3 6–3, lost Sanchez-Vicario [seed 4] 6–2 6–3); **won** Bronx ITF (d. Black 6–2 7–5); **sf** Oklahoma City (d. Dechaume-Balleret 7–6 7–6, Snyder 6–3 6–4, Testud 6–3 6–4, lost Kruger 3–6 6–3 6–4), **sf** Budapest (d. Gubacsi 6–3 6–4, Makarova 2–6 7–5 6–3, Halard-Decugis 5–7 6–3 6–2, lost Ruano-Pascual 2–6 6–1 7–5).

SYLVIA PLISCHKE (AUT)

Born Plzen, Czechoslovakia, 20 July 1977; lives Innsbruck; RH; 2HB; 5ft 10in; 145lb; career singles titles 0; final 1998 WTA ranking 41; 1998 prize money $111,487.

Coached by Eric Van Harpen and by her brother, Robert; trains with her father, Lubomir, and mother, Alena, a former Czech Olympic high-jumper. Moved with her family to Innsbruck in 1983. Nat 14s and 16s champ. **1992:** (692). **1993:** (248) Won ITF Zagreb. **1994:** (227) Won ITF Limoges. **1995:** (220). **1996:** (193). **1997:** (114). **1998:** A 2, F 2, W 3, US 2. Emerging from the satellite circuits, she removed Schnyder on the way to her 1st career sf at Gold Coast after qualifying, reached qf Maria Lankowitz and surprised Spirlea 1r French Open. **1998 HIGHLIGHTS – SINGLES: Australian Open 2r** (d. Gagliardi 7–5 6–1, lost Mauresmo 1–6 6–4 6–3), **French Open 2r** (d. Spirlea [seed 9] 6–2 6–4), **Wimbledon 3r** (d. Sugiyama 6–4 6–7 6–3, Lee 6–2 6–0, lost Sanchez-Vicario [seed 5] 7–5 6–2), **US Open 2r** (d. Miyagi 3–6 7–5 6–2, lost Schett 6–1 7–6); **sf** Gold Coast (d. Kunce 6–3 6–2, Schnyder 6–7 6–4 6–4, De Swardt 7–6 6–4, lost Vento 6–2 6–3).

KIMBERLY PO (USA)

Born Los Angeles, Cal., 20 October 1971; lives Rolling Hills, Cal.; RH; 2HB; 5ft 3in; 120lb; turned pro 1991; career singles titles 0; final 1998 WTA ranking 62 singles; 1998 prize money $152,372; career prize money $1,157,731.

Coached by Donnie Young. **1988:** (541) Member of US National team. **1989:** (241) Won Fayetteville on the USTA circuit. **1990:** (459). **1991:** (103) A –, F –. W –, US 3. Reached qf Phoenix on the main tour and won

Evansville Challenger. **1992:** (70) A 3, F 1, W 2, US 3. Extended Navratilova to 3s 2r Wimbledon and reached qf VS Los Angeles. **1993:** (42) A 3, F 3, W 1, US 3. She finished the year on a high note, upsetting Sukova on her way to sf VS Philadelphia. Reached qf Los Angeles again and upset Fendick at Oakland, as well as taking sets off Pierce at French Open and Magdalena Maleeva at US Open. **1994:** (71) A 1, F 2, W 2, US 1. She salvaged her season again at Philadelphia, where she reached her only qf on the main tour. Won the Karen Krantzcke Sportsmanship Award. **1995:** (164) A –, F 1, W 1, US 2. She reached no qf all year, and slipped down the rankings. **1996:** (28) A –, F –, W 2, US 3. Working more on strategies with her new coach, Donnie Young, she moved back into the top 50. Upset Huber and M. J. Fernandez on her way to sf Montreal, removed Pierce to reach same stage Tokyo Nicherei and surprised Date 1r US Open. She also reached qf Tokyo Japan Open (after qualifying), Quebec City and Oakland (d. M. Maleeva). In doubles with Frazier played 3 f but won no title. **1997:** (23) A qf, F 3, W 1, US 3. She broke into the top 20 1st time with sf Oklahoma City and Tokyo Japan Open, qf Australian Open (unseeded), Stanford and Tokyo Nicherei, and the Midland Futures title. Her biggest upsets during the year were Davenport at Australian Open and Huber at French Open. **1998:** A –, F 1, W 2, US 4. Surgery to her right shoulder the previous November kept her out of action until May. The following month she upset Coetzer on her way to sf Hertogenbosch, and made her presence felt at US Open, where, unseeded, she upset Van Roost and took a set off Seles. In partnership with McNeil, she won Quebec City doubles. **1998 HIGHLIGHTS – SINGLES: French Open 1r** (lost Davenport [seed 2] 6–2 6–2), **Wimbledon 2r** (d. Osterloh 6–2 2–6 6–1, lost Ruano-Pascual 6–2 6–4), **US Open last 16** [unseeded] (d. Guse 6–4 6–1, Granville 6–3 6–3, Van Roost [seed 14] 6–4 6–2, lost Seles [seed 6] 6–2 4–6 6–3); **sf** Hertogenbosch (d. Glass 7–5 7–6, Coetzer 6–4 6–2, Rubin 6–2 6–3, lost Oremans 6–1 6–7 7–6). **1998 HIGHLIGHTS – DOUBLES:** (with McNeil) **won** Quebec City (d. Rubin/Testud 6–7 7–5 6–4). **CAREER HIGHLIGHTS – SINGLES: Australian Open – qf 1997** (d. Leon Garcia 4–6 7–6 6–2, Sugiyama 6–0 4–6 6–3, Hiraki 6–2 6–2, Davenport 7–6 6–4, lost Coetzer 6–4 6–1).

WYNNE PRAKUSYA (INA)

Born Solo, 26 April 1981; lives Jakarta; RH; 2HB; 5ft 3in; 118lb; career singles titles 0; final 1998 WTA ranking 232.

Coached by Deddy Tejdamukti. **1998:** R/u Australian Open Jun to Kostanic, unseeded.

LISA RAYMOND (USA)

Born Norristown, Pa, 10 Aug 1973; lives Wayne, Pa; RH; 5ft 5in; 122lb; turned pro 1993; career singles titles 1; final 1998 WTA ranking 27 singles, 5= doubles; 1998 prize money $399,648; career prize money $1,771,818.

Coached by Jim Dempsey. Won 5 Nat Jun Champs. **1988:** R/u USTA 18s GC. **1989:** (438) A –, F –, W –, US 1. No. 2 in USTA 18s. **1990:** (327) A –, F –, W –, US 1. R/u US Open Jun doubles with De Lone and was ranked No. 1 in USTA 18s. **1991:** (251) A –, F –, W –, US –. Qf Westchester. **1992:** (76) A –, F –, W –, US 2. A freshman at Univ. of Florida, she won NCAA Champs over McCarthy. In the women's game she reached qf Puerto Rico and Philadelphia. **1993:** (54) A –, F –, W 4, US 2. Took Nat Collegiate title 2nd straight year, winning all 34 of her matches. Turned pro at end of college year and at Wimbledon, unseeded and in only her 2nd tourn as pro, she took Capriati to 8–6 3s in last 16, breaking into top 50. At end of year she reached sf Sapporo and won Tokyo Nicherei doubles with Rubin. **1994:** (44) A 2, F 1, W 1, US 3. In singles she reached f Lucerne, unseeded (d. Mag. Maleeva and Frazier), and appeared in qf Eastbourne. In doubles with Davenport was r/u French Open, won Indian Wells and qualified for VS Champs. **1995:** (20) A 3, F –, W 4, US 2. Upset Zvereva, Frazier and Garrison-Jackson on her way to f Chicago (unseeded) and reached same stage San Diego, plus qf Oklahoma. Played 2 doubles f, winning Indian Wells with Davenport. **1996:** (33) A 1, F 1, W 2, US 4. Having failed to pass qf in singles all year, she upset Schultz-McCarthy on the way to her 1st main tour title at Quebec City in Oct. She also reached qf Oklahoma, Eastbourne and Philadelphia (d. Martinez) and extended M. Maleeva to 12–10 fs 1r French Open. In doubles she won Chicago and Philadelphia with Stubbs, with whom she qualified for Chase Champs, and took a 1st GS title at US Open mixed with Galbraith. **1997:** (17) A 2, F 4, W 2, US 2. An impressive 10-day period in Oct., with 4 major upsets, saw her move into the top 15 1st time. She upset Novotna and Spirlea on her way to f Filderstadt, where she lost to Hingis, then at Zurich the following week she removed Coetzer before becoming one of just 5 players all year to beat Hingis – only to lose sf to Tauziat. She was also r/u Oklahoma City, reached sf Quebec City and qf Chicago, and upset Dragomir at US Open. She played 5 women's doubles f, winning Luxembourg and Philadelphia with Stubbs, r/u Australian Open with Davenport and r/u French Open with G. Fernandez. In mixed she was r/u Australian Open with Galbraith. **1998:** A 3, F 1, W 1, US 3. She was consistent, if less spectacular, reaching sf FC Cup and Boston, plus qf Auckland, Hannover, Linz, Amelia Island (d. Seles), Rome and Filderstadt. In doubles with Stubbs she won Hannover and Boston from 5 f and qualified for Chase Champs, where they lost sf to Davenport/Zvereva. **1998 HIGHLIGHTS – SINGLES: Australian Open 3r** [seed 13] (d. Pratt 6–1 2–6 6–3, Miyagi 6–2 3–6 7–5, lost Schnyder 2–6 6–3 8–6), **French Open 1r** [seed 16] (lost Panova 6–3 6–4), **Wimbledon 1r** (lost Hingis [seed 1] 7–5 6–3), **US Open 3r** (d. Sanchez Lorenzo 6–3 6–3, Zvereva 6–2 6–2, lost Martinez [seed 7] 6–3 3–6 6–2); **sf** FC Cup (d. Wang 6–1 4–6 6–1, Grande 6–1 7–6, A. Miller 1–6 6–2 6–3, Serna 6–4 6–1, lost Coetzer 6–3 6–4), **sf** Boston (d. Frazier 6–4 6–2, Dragomir 6–3 6–3, Morariu 7–6 6–2, lost De Swardt 4–6 6–4 7–5). **1998 HIGHLIGHTS – DOUBLES:** (with Stubbs) **won** Hannover (d. Likhovtseva/Vis 6–1 6–7 6–3), **won** Boston (d. De Swardt/Fernandez 6–3 5–7 6–4); **r/u** FC Cup (lost

Martinez/Tarabini 3–6 6–4 6–4), **r/u** Birmingham (lost Callens/Halard-Decugis 2–6 6–4 6–4), **r/u** Moscow (lost Pierce/Zvereva 6–3 6–4). **CAREER HIGHLIGHTS – DOUBLES:** (with Davenport unless stated) **Australian Open – r/u 1997** (lost Hingis/Zvereva 6–2 6–2); **French Open – r/u 1994** (lost G. Fernandez/Zvereva 6–2 6–2), (with G. Fernandez) **r/u 1997** (lost G. Fernandez/Zvereva 6–2 6–3). **MIXED DOUBLES:** (with Galbraith) **US Open – won 1996** (d. Leach/Bollegraf 7–6 7–6).

BARBARA RITTNER (GER)

Born Krefeld, 25 April 1973; lives Cologne; RH; 2HB; 5ft 8in; 145lb; turned pro 1989; career singles titles 1; final 1998 WTA ranking 66; 1998 prize money $114,617; career prize money $1,037,230.

Coached by Karsten Saniter. **1989:** (349) Won Nat Jun Champs **1990:** (107) Enjoyed some success on the satellite circuits. **1991:** (43) A 2, F 1, W 1, US 3. Won Wimbledon Jun over Makarova and Australian Open Jun doubles with Habsudova. In the senior game she reached her 1st tour f at St Petersburg and appeared in qf Wellington, Puerto Rico and Leipzig. **1992:** (32) A 2, F 2, W 3, US 1. A member of the winning German Fed Cup team, she won her 1st primary circuit title at Schenectady and upset Tauziat on her way to last 16 Olympics, unseeded. She also surprised Zrubakova at Sydney and Cecchini en route to sf Essen. **1993:** (34) A 3, F 3, W 2, US 2. R/u San Marino and reached qf Sydney (d. Sukova), VS Florida (d. Zvereva), Leipzig and Filderstadt as well as appearing in 2 doubles f with Labat. **1994:** (40) A 3, F 3, W 3, US 3. Out for a month following an appendectomy in Feb. She did not advance beyond qf all year, but reached that stage at Brisbane, Sydney (d. Wiesner), Hamburg, Styria, Schenectady (d. Hack) and Zurich (d. Appelmans). **1995:** (52) A 1, F 1, W –, US 1. Upset Majoli on her way to f Linz, where she took a set off Novotna, and reached qf Delray Beach, Zagreb and Hamburg. **1996:** (52) A 2, F 4, W 1, US 3. Removed Pierce at French Open, where she was unseeded; incensed by Pierce's gamesmanship, she began to retaliate in an ill-humoured match, after which Pierce was booed off the court. Upset Schultz-McCarthy at US Open and Appelmans on her way to qf Essen. From 2 doubles f, she won Luxembourg with Van Roost. **1997:** (76) A 1, F 1, W 2, US 1. Upset Appelmans en route to qf Linz. **1998:** A 2, F 3, W 2, US 1. Her best showings were sf Palermo and qf Sopot (d. Pitkowski). **1998 HIGHLIGHTS – SINGLES: Australian Open 2r** (d. Tatarkova 6–1 7–6), **French Open 3r** (d. Berger 6–0 6–2, Sawamatsu 6–3 6–4, lost Smashnova 1–6 6–4 6–1), **Wimbledon 2r** (d. Cocheteux 7–6 6–0, lost Spirlea [seed 10] 6–4 6–4), **US Open 1r** (lost Kruger 6–1 6–3); **sf** Palermo (d. Testud 4–6 5–6 ret, Stoyanova 6–4 6–3, Capriati 2–6 6–4 6–2, lost Schett 4–6 6–4 6–4).

VIRGINIA RUANO-PASCUAL (ESP)

Born Madrid, 21 September 1973; lives Valencia; RH; 5ft 6½in; 134lb; turned pro 1992; career singles titles 2; final 1998 WTA ranking 32; 1998 prize money $248,391.

1989: (496). **1990:** (309). **1991:** (261). **1992:** (123) A –, F –, W –, US 1. Qf Sao Paulo (d. F. Bonsignori) and won Bilbao Futures. **1993:** (125) A –, F –, W –, US 1. Reached qf Liege (d. Zardo) and Kitzbuhel (d. Rittner) and played on winning Spanish Fed Cup team. **1994:** (161) A 1, F –, W –, US –. **1995:** (64) A –, F qf, W 1, US 1. Having stretched Sanchez-Vicario to 3s in Rome, she made an impact at French Open, where she was unseeded. On the Futures circuit she won Zaragoza. **1996:** (98) A 1, F 1, W 1, US 1. Reached qf Hobart (d. Hack) and won Bronx Futures. Played in ESP Fed Cup team r/u to USA. **1997:** (54) A 2, F 3, W 2, US 1. Won her 1st title on the main tour at Cardiff, unseeded, and reached sf Warsaw, plus qf Madrid (d. Frazier) and Palermo. **1998:** A 2, F 3, W 4, US 3. The highlight of her year came at Budapest, where she upset Pitkowski and Farina on her way to the singles title and won the doubles with Suarez. She also reached qf Hamburg (d. Likhovtseva), upset Kruger at Prague, and joined with Suarez in 2 other f to win Hobart and Rome. **1998 HIGHLIGHTS – SINGLES: Australian Open 2r** (d. Kleinova 7–6 7–5, lost Sidot 6–4 6–4), **French Open 3r** (d. Kloesel 6–1 6–2, Sidot 6–4 7–6, lost Martinez [seed 7] 6–1 6–0), **Wimbledon last 16** [unseeded] (d. Glass 6–1 6–7 6–3, Po 6–2 6–4, S. Williams 7–5 4–1 ret, lost V. Williams 6–3 6–1), **US Open 3r** (d. Nejedly 6–3 6–2, Snyder 6–4 6–4, lost Davenport [seed 2] 6–2 6–1); **won** Budapest (d. Nacuk 2–6 6–1 6–2, Lubiani 6–0 4–6 7–6, Kuti-Kis 6–3 6–0, Pitkowski 2–6 6–1 7–5, Farina 4–6 6–2 6–3). **1998 HIGHLIGHTS – DOUBLES:** (with Suarez) **won** Hobart (d. Halard-Decugis/Husarova 7–6 6–3), **won** Budapest (d. Cristea/Montalvo 6–2 2–6 6–1), **won** Rome (d. Coetzer/Sanchez-Vicario 7–6 6–4). **CAREER HIGHLIGHTS – SINGLES: French Open – qf 1995** [unseeded] (d. Demongeot 7–6 6–2, Fendick 7–5 6–1, Tauziat 6–2 7–6, Dragomir 2–6 6–0 6–3, lost Martinez 6–0 6–4).

CHANDA RUBIN (USA)

Born Lafayette, La, 18 February 1976, and lives there; RH; 2HB; 5ft 6in; 128lb; turned pro 1991; career singles titles 1; final 1998 WTA ranking 34; 1998 prize money $213,708; career prize money $1,605,057.

Coached by Ashley Rhoney. Did not attend a tennis academy, as her parents put an academic background before tennis. **1988:** Won Nat 12s and Orange Bowl in same age group. **1989:** Won Nat 14s. **1990:** (522) A –, F –, W –, US 1. **1991:** (83) A –, F –, W –, US 2. She announced her presence on the senior tour by upsetting Bollegraf at LIPC in spring, and at end of year broke into the top 100 after reaching her 1st tour f at Phoenix. **1992:** (68) A 1, F 1, W 1, US 4. Surprised K. Maleeva at US Open, where she was unseeded, and upset Zvereva VS Florida. In the Jun game won Wimbledon over Courtois. **1993:** (69) A 1, F –, W 2, US 3. Reached her 1st main tour sf at Birmingham (d. Coetzer) and appeared in qf FC Cup. In doubles won Tokyo

Nicherei with Raymond. **1994:** (25) A 4, F 1, W 1, US 1. Broke into top 50 after a fine start to the year, in which she followed sf appearance at Hobart with upsets of K. Maleeva and Coetzer at Australian Open. She went on to reach f Chicago (d. Mag. Maleeva) and sf VS Florida (d. Coetzer), Lucerne (d. Sukova) and Quebec City. Played 2 doubles f with Harvey-Wild, winning Hobart. **1995:** (15) A 2, F qf, W 3, US 4. She broke into the top 20 after reaching f Eastbourne (d. Date), and surprised Sabatini and Sanchez-Vicario on her way to the same stage Manhattan Beach, where she took a set off Martinez. She also reached sf Zurich and Filderstadt (d. Davenport and Zvereva and extended Majoli to fs tb), plus 3 more qf, being voted WTA Most Improved Player. She made her mark in GS: unseeded at French Open, she upset Novotna – 0–5 0–40 down in fs, she was aiming simply to win just 1 game in the set, but Novotna let the game slip away as Rubin saved 9 mps. In 2r Wimbledon she beat Hy-Boulais 7–6 6–7 17–15, breaking the Championship records for the longest women's singles match (beating by 4 games the previous record of 54 by A. Weiwers and O. Anderson in 1948) and the longest set (their 32 games being 6 more than the previous record of 26, achieved 6 times since 1919). Then she upset Sukova at US Open, where she was unseeded, and beat Sanchez-Vicario in Fed Cup f. She also won Midland Futures in both singles and doubles and from 2 doubles f on the main tour won Prague with Harvey-Wild. Qualified for her 1st WTA Champs, but lost 1r to M. J. Fernandez. **1996:** (12) A sf, F –, W –, US –. It was a frustrating year for her. She broke into top 10 1st time after reaching her 1st GS sf at Australian Open, with upsets of Sabatini and then Sanchez-Vicario 6–4 2–6 16–14 in qf. Continuing her record of lengthy matches, it was the longest women's match in the history of the tourn – lasting 3 hours 33 min, comprising the most games in a set (30) and most in a woman's match (48) – and being the 6th-longest on the WTA tour. In sf against Seles, she let slip a lead of 5–2 in 3s and at 5–3 30–15 served a double fault to let Seles back into the match, but was the only player to take a set off the eventual winner. She and Sanchez-Vicario were on court together again, upsetting G. Fernandez and Zvereva on their way to the doubles title. LIPC was her 1st major singles f, but it was at that tourn that she suffered a fracture of the hook of the hamate bone of her right hand. She missed Fed Cup and French Open with recurring tendinitis of the wrist, which caused her to retire during her 1st match at Eastbourne and withdraw from Wimbledon and then the Olympics and US Open. Underwent surgery in Sept. to remove hook of hamate bone in right wrist and was out until Nov., when she lost 1r Oakland to Wild, before upsetting Majoli on her way to qf Philadelphia. During the year she also reached sf Oklahoma, plus qf Sydney and Indian Wells. In doubles she teamed with Schultz-McCarthy to win Oklahoma and Indian Wells and with Sanchez-Vicario to add Amelia Island to their Australian title. **1997:** (30) A 4, F 2, W 1, US 1. She began the year by winning Hopman Cup with Gimelstob and made a stunning come-back at Linz, upsetting Novotna and Habsudova on the way to her 1st career title. Thereafter, though, she struggled to recapture her best form and reached no other qf until Quebec City, where she advanced to sf. **1998:** A 1, F 4, W 3, US 2. She was still struggling for form and fitness in a difficult year. She upset Spirlea at Moscow, and at Quebec City she was r/u both singles (d. Van Roost) and doubles (with Testud), but her only other qf appearances were at Madrid and Hertogenbosch. **1998 HIGHLIGHTS – SINGLES: Australian Open 1r** (lost Nejedly 6–2 6–4), **French Open last 16** [unseeded] (d. McNeil 3–6 6–3 6–4, Panova 6–1 6–1, Saeki 6–3 6–4, lost Seles [seed 6] 6–1 6–4), **Wimbledon 3r** (d. Helgeson-Nielsen 4–6 6–0 6–2, Snyder 3–6 7–5 11–9, lost V. Williams [seed 7] 6–3 6–4), **US Open 2r** (d. Li 6–3 6–2, lost Nagyova 7–6 6–4); **r/u** Quebec City (d. Lee 6–4 6–1, Washington 4–6 7–6 6–4, Van Roost 6–2 6–2, Dechy 6–2 6–4, lost Snyder 4–6 6–4 7–6). **1998 HIGHLIGHTS – DOUBLES:** (with Testud) **r/u** Quebec City (lost McNeil/Po 6–7 7–5 6–4). **CAREER HIGHLIGHTS – SINGLES: Australian Open – sf 1996** (d. McQuillan 4–6 6–3 6–2, Krizan 6–7 6–2 6–3, Courtois 6–0 6–2, Sabatini 6–2 6–4, Sanchez-Vicario [seed 3] 6–4 2–6 16–14, lost Seles 6–7 6–1 7–5); **French Open – qf 1995** [unseeded] (d. Makarova 7–6 6–3, Babel 6–3 6–2, Novotna 7–6 4–6 8–6, Sugiyama 6–2 1–6 6–2, lost Sanchez-Vicario 6–3 6–1). **CAREER HIGHLIGHTS – DOUBLES:** (with Sanchez-Vicario) **Australian Open – won 1996** (d. Davenport/M. J. Fernandez 6–4 2–6 6–2).

NAOKO SAWAMATSU (JPN)

Born Nishinomiya, 23 March 1973; lives Tokyo; RH; 2HB; 5ft 6in; 127lb; turned pro 1991; career singles titles 4; final 1998 WTA ranking 55; 1998 prize money $113,471; career prize money $1,107,264.

Coached by Ricky Brown. Her mother, Junko, played pro tennis, appearing at Wimbledon in 1970 with her sister, Kazuko Sawamatsu, who went on to win the title there in 1975 with Kiyomura. **1988:** Won nat champ. **1989:** (256) Won Nagasaki on satellite circuit. **1990:** (31) A –, F 2, W 1, US 2. Won Moulins Challenger, then, a wild-card entry, she beat 3 seeded players to win Singapore, having reached sf Tokyo Suntory 2 weeks earlier. These results saw her break into the top 100 and then top 50 in April. **1991:** (33) A 3, F 4, W 2, US 2. Unseeded at French Open, she upset Garrison 1r and took Tauziat to 12–10 fs in last 16; r/u Pattaya City and reached sf Strasbourg. **1992:** (24) A –, F 1, W 4, US 3. At Wimbledon, where she was unseeded, she upset Wiesner and took a set off Capriati. She was also r/u Strasbourg and reached sf Tokyo Suntory. **1993:** (28) A 3, F 2, W 3, US 1. Won Strasbourg, r/u Melbourne Open and upset Maleeva-Fragniere 2r Wimbledon. **1994:** (26) A 2, F 2, W 4, US 1. Won Singapore and reached sf Tokyo Japan Open, plus qf Italian Open and Strasbourg. She upset M. J. Fernandez at Wimbledon, where she was unseeded, and surprised Coetzer at Sydney. **1995:** (17) A qf, F 3, W 3, US 3. When news of the Japanese earthquake came through before her 1st match at Australian Open, she learned that her home had been destroyed. Determined to give people from her region some good news, she played the tennis of her life, reaching her 1st GS qf, unseeded, and upsetting Date. Fired with the same determination, she moved on to a career high of 14, upsetting

Davenport to reach sf Indian Wells and appearing in qf Tokyo Pan Pacific (d. Zvereva) and Tokyo Nicherei. **1996:** (34) A 4, F 2, W 3, US 2. In a less impressive year, her best performances came in Tokyo, where she reached qf both tourns, upsetting Date at Tokyo Toray. **1997:** (34) A 1, F 1, W 2, US 2. Her 1st title since 1994 came at Jakarta in April. She also reached sf Tokyo Nicherei (d. Martinez), qf Sydney, Tokyo Japan Open and Filderstadt, and upset Majoli at Toronto. In losing to Tauziat 7–5 4–6 17–15 in Fed Cup, she played the longest singles set and equalled the longest rubber (Baldovonis d. Connor 6–4 11-13 11-9 in 1974). **1998:** A 1, F 2, W 3, US 2. Feeling she had lost her desire to play and compete, she announced her retirement from the tour after Tokyo Toyota in Sept. Earlier she had reached qf Tokyo Japan Open and upset Coetzer at Wimbledon. **1998 HIGHLIGHTS – SINGLES: Australian Open 1r** (lost Majoli [seed 4] 6–4 6–2), **French Open 2r** (d. Nemeckova 6–2 2–6 7–5, lost rittner 6–3 6–4), **Wimbledon 3r** (d. Paulus 2–6 6–3 6–2, Coetzer [seed 9] 3–6 6–3 6–2, lost Serna 6–3 5–7 6–0), **US Open 2r** (d. Torrens-Valero 4–6 7–5 6–1, lost Lucic 4–6 6–1 6–1). **CAREER HIGHLIGHTS – SINGLES: Australian Open** – **qf 1995** [unseeded] (d. Sugiyama 6–3 6–3, Courtois 6–0 6–4, Date 3–6 6–3 6–3, M. J. Fernandez 6–4 7–6, lost Sanchez-Vicario 6–1 6–3).

BARBARA SCHETT (AUT)

Born Innsbruck, 10 March 1976, and lives there; RH; 2HB; 5ft 9½in; 149lb; turned pro 1992; career singles titles 2; final 1998 WTA ranking 23 singles, 24 doubles; 1998 prize money $280,514.

Coached by Thomas Prerovsky. **1991:** (753). **1992:** (299) Won Zaragoza Futures. **1993:** (136) Upset K. Maleeva after qualifying for her 1st event on the main tour at Kitzbuhel and reached same stage Montpellier. **1994:** (100) A –, F 1, W 1, US 1. In jun tennis she was r/u Australian Open Jun to Musgrave. She made her mark in the senior game with another upset of K. Maleeva on her way to sf Linz, as well as reaching qf Tokyo Japan Open and Prague to move into the top 100. **1995:** (83) A 1, F 1, W –, US 1. Upset McNeil LIPC and Cecchini on her way to sf Palermo and appeared in qf Prague. **1996:** (38) A 4, F 1, W 2, US 2. The high point of her year came at Palermo, where she won her 1st main tour singles and doubles titles (with Husarova). She reached sf Moscow, upset Frazier at Australian Open, where she was unseeded, surprised M. Maleeva on her way to qf Amelia Island and held 5 mps v Seles at Madrid, although she could not close out the match. **1997:** (38) A 3, F 1, W 2, US 2. At Maria Lankowitz she upset Wiesner on the way to her 2nd career title and 1st in her own country. She also reached sf Palermo, where she took the doubles with Farina, and upset Huber en route to qf Hamburg. **1998:** A 4, F 1, W 2, US 3. She upset Coetzer on her way to f Boston, where, serving for the title at 5–1 3s v De Swardt, she let the match slip away. She reached the same stage Palermo, sf Hamburg (d. Majoli) and Madrid, plus qf Hobart, Maria Lankowitz and Zurich (d. Schnyder). Played 3 doubles f with Schnyder, winning Hamburg. **1998 HIGHLIGHTS – SINGLES: Australian Open last 16** [unseeded] (d. Diaz-Oliva 6–4 6–1, Panova 6–3 6–2, Zvereva 6–3 6–1, lost Martinez [seed 8] 6–3 6–3), **French Open 1r** (lost Gersi 5–7 6–2 6–2), **Wimbledon 2r** (d. Stoyanova 6–0 6–2, lost V. Williams [seed 7] 6–1 6–2), **US Open 3r** (d. Washington 6–3 6–3, Plischke 6–1 7–6, lost Coetzer [seed 13] 3–6 6–0 6–3); **r/u** Palermo (d. Gagliardi 6–0 6–3, Studenikova 6–0 6–2, Bobkova 4–6 7–6 6–2, Rittner 4–6 6–4 6–4, lost Schnyder 6–1 5–7 6–2), **r/u** Boston (d. Brandi, Cristea 6–0 7–6, Coetzer 6–7 6–4 6–4, Black 6–2 2–6 6–2, lost De Swardt 3–6 7–6 7–5); **sf** Hamburg (d. Babel 6–4 6–4, Majoli 7–5 6–2, Ruano-Pascual 6–0 6–0, lost Hingis 6–2 6–2), **sf** Madrid (d. Makarova 6–3 6–1, Kandarr 6–2 7–6, Snyder 6–2 6–2, lost Van Roost 6–2 6–2). **1998 HIGHLIGHTS – DOUBLES:** (with Schnyder) **won** Hamburg (d. Hingis/Novotna 7–6 3–6 6–3); **r/u** Amelia Island (lost Cacic/ Pierce 7–6 4–6 7–6), **r/u** Palermo (lost Stoyanova/Wagner 6–4 6–2).

PATTY SCHNYDER (SUI)

Born Basel, 14 December 1978; lives Bottmingen; LH; 2HB; 5ft 6½in; 125lb; turned pro 1994; career singles titles 5; final 1998 WTA ranking 11; 1998 prize money $901,828; career prize money $1,211,277.

Coached by Eric Van Harpen. **1994:** (786) Nat Jun champ for 2nd year. **1995:** (152) On the Futures circuit she won Nitra and Presov back-to-back, following with Cureglia, and on the main tour upset Spirlea 1r Zurich. **1996:** (58) A –, F 1, W 1, US –. She reached her 1st f on the main tour at Karlovy Vary, removing Paulus on the way, and joined the Swiss Fed Cup squad. **1997:** (26) A 4, F 3, W 1, US 3. She upset Majoli at Australian Open, where she was unseeded, surprised Raymond at Madrid, and extended Davenport to 9–7 fs at French Open, taking her to 3s again at US Open. Although she did not progress beyond qf all year, she reached that stage at Maria Lankowitz and Filderstadt (d. Sukova and Majoli after qualifying). **1998:** A 4, F qf, W 2, US 4. She began an impressive year by winning her 1st career title at Hobart and following with her 2nd at Hannover in Feb. (d. Majoli, Tauziat and Novotna). By end July, having added Madrid (d. Testud and Van Roost), Maria Lankowitz and Palermo, she had won more titles than anyone else all season to date, and by mid Aug. was a member of the top 10. After that, though, her best performance was r/u GS Cup (unseeded, d. Novotna) and she finished the season just outside the elite. She also reached sf Hamburg (d. Sanchez-Vicario), qf FC Cup and French Open (unseeded, d. Coetzer); upset Raymond at Australian Open (unseeded) and Graf at US Open. She qualified for her 1st Chase Champs, where she extended Hingis to 3s 1r, and was voted WTA Most Improved Player of the Year. In doubles she won Hamburg from 3 f with Schett. Helped take SUI to 1st ever f in Fed Cup, but there lost all her matches as SUI went down 3–2 to ESP. **1998 HIGHLIGHTS – SINGLES: Australian Open last 16** [unseeded] (d. Dechy 6–1 6–2, Wang 6–3 6–4, Raymond [seed 13] 2–6 6–3 8–6, lost V. Williams 6–4 6–1), **French Open qf** [unseeded] (d. Coetzer [seed 5] 6–4 3–6 8–6, Halard-

Decugis 6–3 3–6 6–1, Farina 6–2 6–1, Serna 6–1 6–3, lost Sanchez-Vicario [seed 4] 6–2 6–7 6–0), **Wimbledon 2r** [seed 13] (d. Sukova 3–6 6–4 6–3, lost Black 6–7 7–5 6–3), **US Open last 16** [seed 11] (d. Yoshida 7–6 7–5, Rippner 6–1 6–2, Fernandez 6–1 7–6, Graf [seed 8] 6–3 6–4, lost Novotna [seed 3] 6–2 6–3); **won** Hobart (d. Ellwood 4–6 7–6 6–1, Gersi 6–3 6–3 Schett 6–4 1–6 6–3, Kruger 7–6 6–2, Van Roost 6–3 6–2), **won** Hannover (d. Majoli 6–1 6–3, Tauziat 6–4 6–3, Appelmans 6–3 6–3, Novotna 6–0 2–6 7–5), **won** Madrid (d. Brandi 6–0 ret, Babel 4–6 6–0 6–2, Serna 3–6 7–6 6–4, Testud 6–4 7–5, Van Roost 3–6 6–4 6–0), **won** Maria Lankowitz (d. Nejedly 6–4 6–1, Maruska 6–0 6–1, Plischke 6–2 6–2, Gagliardi 6–2 6–4, Leon-Garcia 6–2 4–6 6–3), **won** Palermo (d. Boogert 6–1 3–1 ret, Dechaume-Balleret 5–7 6–4 6–0, Zavagli 6–2 6–3, Oremans 6–1 6–3, Schett 6–1 5–7 6–2); **r/u** GS Cup (d. Novotna 2–6 7–5 7–5, Hingis 5–7 7–5 5–5 ret, lost V. Williams 6–3 3–6 6–2); **sf** Hamburg (d. Perfetti 6–1 6–0, Sidot 3–6 6–3 6–4, Sanchez-Vicario 6–3 6–0, lost Novotna 2–6 7–5 6–3). **1998 HIGHLIGHTS – DOUBLES:** (with Schett) **won** Hamburg (d. Hingis/Novotna 7–6 3–6 6–3); **r/u** Amelia Island (lost Cacic/Pierce 7–6 4–6 7–6), **r/u** Palermo (lost Stoyanova/Wagner 6–4 6–2).

MAGUI SERNA (ESP)

Born Las Palmas, 1 March 1979; lives Barcelona; LH; 5ft 6in; 142lb; turned pro 1993; career singles titles 0; final WTA ranking 24; 1998 prize money $213,650.

Coached by Lorenzo Fargas. Named Maria Luisa, she is known as Magui. Formerly nat champ in 12s and 14s. **1994:** (342) Won 2 Futures tourns back-to-back. **1995:** (357) Continued to make her mark on the satellite circuit with the title at Mallorca. **1996:** (138) R/u Wimbledon Jun to Mauresmo and in the senior game she won 3 Futures titles in the space of four weeks. **1997:** (41) A 3, F 3, W 3, US 4. Reached qf Gold Coast after qualifying (d. Dragomir) and upset Po at US Open, where she was unseeded. **1998:** A 2, F 4, W 4, US 1. She was consistent through the year, reaching qf FC Cup (d. Huber and Novotna), Madrid, Birmingham, Eastbourne (d. Likhovtseva), Montreal (d. Graf) and Moscow (d. Schnyder). Other notable upsets included Pierce at French Open, where she was unseeded, and Schultz-McCarthy at Berlin, and she broke into top 25 1st time in July. **1998 HIGHLIGHTS – SINGLES: Australian Open 2r** (d. McQuillan 6–3 4–6 9–7, lost Dragomir [seed 15] 7–6 2–6 6–3), **French Open last 16** [unseeded] (d. Hy-Boulais 6–1 6–1, Pierce [seed 11] 7–5 6–2, Dragomir 6–4 2–6 6–1, lost Schnyder 6–1 6–3), **Wimbledon last 16** [unseeded] (d. Bobkova 7–5 4–6 6–1, Grande 6–4 6–1, Sawamatsu 6–3 5–7 7–0, lost Davenport [seed 2] 6–1 6–0), **US Open 1r** (lost Vento 6–7 7–5 6–4).

ANNE-GAELLE SIDOT (FRA)

Born Enghien-les-Bains, 24 July 1979; lives Montlignon; LH; 5ft 8in; 124lb; turned pro 1994; career singles titles 0; final 1998 WTA ranking 54; 1998 prize money $151,0068.

Coached by Bruno Dadillon. **1995:** (163) A –, F 1, W –, US –. Won Flensburg Futures. **1996:** (55) A –, F 1, W 2, US 3. After winning Wurzburg Futures, she extended Date to 3s 2r Wimbledon and upset Halard-Decugis en route to her 1st sf on the main tour at Luxembourg, before closing her season with the title at Cardiff Futures. **1997:** (33) A 2, F 1, W 1, US 1. She recorded some useful upsets on her way to sf Gold Coast, Hamburg (d. Schultz-McCarthy) and Luxembourg (d. Habsudova, whom she had earlier beaten at Zurich), qf Hobart (d. Hack) and Hannover (d. Appelmans). **1998:** A 3, F 2, W 1, US 1. Although her year was restricted by a stress fracture of the foot, suffered in Feb., she reached qf Hobart, Stanford (d. Kruger) and Leipzig (d. Sanchez-Vicario), and on the ITF circuit won the $50,000 Southampton tourn. **1998 HIGHLIGHTS – SINGLES: Australian Open 3r** (d. Nemeckova 6–4 6–3, Ruano-Pascual 6–4 6–4, lost Martinez [seed 8] 3–6 6–0 6–3), **French Open 2r** (d. Van Lottum 2–6 6–3 6–2, lost Ruano-Pascual 6–4 7–6), **Wimbledon 1r** (lost Smith 6–3 4–6 6–2), **US Open 1r** (lost Barabanschikova 6–1 6–7 6–3); **won** Southampton ITF (d. Cocheteux 7–5 6–4).

ANNA SMASHNOVA (ISR)

Born Minsk, Russia, 16 July 1976; lives Herzelia; RH; 5ft 2in; 120lb; turned pro 1991; career singles titles 0; final 1998 WTA ranking 50; 1998 prize money $124,658.

Coached by David Cody. Emigrated to Israel from USSR with her parents in 1990. Completed a mandatory year's service in Israeli army after graduating from High School in July 1995, although her basic 2-week training was delayed to allow her to compete in Wimbledon and US Open that year. **1990:** No. 1 Jun in USSR from age 11. **1991:** (347) Won French Open Jun over Gorrochategui. **1992:** (213) Joined the Israeli Fed Cup team. **1993:** (147) Won Erlangen Futures. **1994:** (48) A 2, F 2, W 2, US 3. Reached her 1st main tour qf at Auckland in Jan. and made her mark in GS with upsets of Novotna 1r French Open and McNeil 1r US Open. **1995:** (68) A 3, F 4, W 1, US 1. Upset Garrison-Jackson FC Cup and Frazier at French Open, where she was unseeded, but reached no qf all year. **1996:** (149) A 2, F 1, W 1, US –. Upset Zvereva 1r Australian Open. **1997:** (140) A –, F –, W –, US –. At Jaffa on the ITF circuit she won her 1st pro title for 4 years. **1998:** A –, F 4, W 1, US 1. She moved back into the top 50 with sf finish at Sopot and qf Istanbul, as well as the titles at Oporto and Santa Clara on the $75,000 ITF circuit. **1998 HIGHLIGHTS – SINGLES: French Open last 16** [unseeded] (d. Neiland 3–6 6–3 6–2, Gagliardi 5–7 6–0 6–1, Rittner 1–6 6–4 6–1, lost Hingis [seed 1] 6–1 6–2), **Wimbledon 1r** (lost Lucic 6–4 6–7 6–3), **US Open 1r** (lost Farina 6–4 3–6 6–2); **won** Oporto ITF (d. Dechaume-Balleret 6–2 6–2), **won** Santa Clara ITF (d. Frazier 2–6 6–4 6–2); **sf** Sopot (d. Vaskova 7–6 6–3, Kriventcheva 6–4 6–2, Hrdlickova 6–3 7–6, lost Wagner 6–3 0–6 6–4).

SAM SMITH (GBR)

Born Epping, 27 November 1971; lives Loughton; RH; 5ft 8½in; 138lb; turned pro 1990; career singles titles 0; final 1998 WTA ranking 65; 1998 prize money $92,490.

Coached by Ian Barclay. Won 4 nat titles. **1988:** (281). **1989:** (271) No. 1 Jun in GBR. **1990:** (131) A –, F –, W 1, US –. Reached her 1st qf on the main tour at Guaruja. **1991:** (120) A –, F –, W 1, US 1. **1992:** (–) A 1, F –, W –, US –. She retired from the circuit for 3 years to attend Exeter University. **1995:** (363) A –, F –, W –, US –. Returning to the circuit with a more complete game, she won ITF Nottingham in only her 2nd tourn. back. **1996:** (141) A –, F –, W 1, US –. Took over No. 1 GBR ranking. **1997:** (126) Broke into top 100 1st time in Sept. **1998:** A –, F –, W 4, US 1. The highlight of her year came at Wimbledon where, unseeded, she upset Martinez to become the 1st GBR woman for 13 years to reach last 16 there. She also upset Pitkowski at Birmingham, but reached no qf during the year. **1998 HIGHLIGHTS – SINGLES: Wimbledon last 16** [unseeded] (d. Sidot 6–3 4–6 6–2, Diaz-Oliva 6–1 6–3, Martinez [seed 8] 2–6 6–3 7–5, lost Tauziat [seed 16] 6–3 6–1).

TARA SNYDER (USA)

Born Wichita, Kan., 26 May 1977; lives there and Houston, Tex.; RH; 2HB; 5ft 9in; 130lb; turned pro 1995; career singles titles 1; final 1998 WTA ranking 33; 1998 prize money $143,097.

Coached by Keith Christman. **1994:** (842) No. 2 in nat 18s. **1995:** (203) Won US Open Jun over Ellwood and finished No. 5 in ITF Jun rankings. **1996:** (258). **1997:** (113) Won her 1st pro title at Delray Beach ITF. **1998:** A 2, F 2, W 2, US 2. Moving onto the main tour, she won her 1st title at that level at Quebec City, reached qf Amelia Island (d. Spirlea) and Madrid (d. Labat), and broke into the top 50. On the ITF circuit she won the $50,000 tourn at Houston. **1998 HIGHLIGHTS – SINGLES: Australian Open 2r** (d. Hy-Boulais 7–6 6–4, lost Van Roost [seed 14] 6–3 6–4), **French Open 2r** (d. Curutchet 7–5 6–1, lost Fusai 6–4 6–3), **Wimbledon 2r** (d. Nemeckova 6–3 6–0, lost Rubin 3–6 7–5 11–9), **US Open 2r** (d. Glass 6–4 6–1, lost Ruano-Pascual 6–4 6–4); **won** Quebec City (d. Pratt 6–4 6–2, Rittner 6–0 6–3, Cristea 6–4 6–4, Chi 1–6 6–3 7–5, Rubin 4–6 6–4 7–6), **won** Houston ITF (d. Craybas 6–3 6–4).

IRINA SPIRLEA (ROM)

Born Bucharest, 26 March 1974, and lives there; RH; 5ft 9in; 150lb; turned pro 1990; career singles titles 1; final 1998 WTA ranking 15; 1998 prize money $530,988; career prize money $2,218,256.

Coached by Max Pace. **1990:** (310) Won French Open Jun doubles with Dragomir. **1991:** (208) Won her 1st title on the satellite circuit at Milan. **1992:** (165) A –, F 1, W –, US –. Won Jakarta on the Futures circuit. **1993:** (63) A –, F –, W –, US –. Qf Palermo on the main tour and the Challenger title at Brindisi were her best showings until Oct., when she upset Coetzer and Endo to reach her 1st main tour f at Sapporo and followed with sf Curitiba. **1994:** (43) A 1, F 4, W 2, US 1. She enjoyed her greatest success in Italy. In April she appeared in both singles and doubles f at Taranto, winning the doubles with Van Lottum but losing the singles to Halard, and the following week she upset Sabatini on her way to sf Italian Open. Then in July she won her 1st main tour title at Palermo, upsetting Schultz. She also surprised M. J. Fernandez to reach last 16 French Open, unseeded, and broke into the top 50. Voted WTA Most Impressive Newcomer. **1995:** (21) A 4, F 3, W 3, US 1. She began the year in style with r/u showing at Jakarta, where she won the doubles with Porwik, and then, unseeded at Australian Open, she upset Halard and took a set off Martinez in last 16. Continuing her progress, she won Palermo again, upset Coetzer and M. J. Fernandez before taking a set off Sanchez-Vicario in sf Berlin and reached the same stage at Zagreb, as well as upsetting Frazier at Wimbledon and Zvereva at Philadelphia. **1996:** (11) A 2, F 4, W 2, US 3. The year began badly as she failed to pass 2r in her 1st 4 tourns. In her next 3, though, she reached qf LIPC and FC Cup (d. Sabatini), then upset Sanchez-Vicario and Pierce at Amelia Island to take her 1st title in America and move into the top 20. She followed with another upset of Sanchez-Vicario to reach sf Italian Open, appeared in same stage Oakland, surprised Schultz-McCarthy at French Open, where she was unseeded, and upset Pierce again at Eastbourne, as well as reaching qf Madrid, Los Angeles and Chicago (d. M. J. Fernandez). These results took her to her 1st Chase Champs, where she lost 1r to Hingis. In doubles, she played 3 f, winning Italian Open with Sanchez-Vicario. She was fined $10,000 and defaulted for abusive language v De Ville in 2r Palermo when the score stood at 15–15 3s. **1997:** (8) A qf, F 4, W 4, US sf. She broke into the top 10 in March after reaching f Indian Wells (d. Sanchez-Vicario). She was always a tough opponent in GS, extending Graf to 3s at French Open, losing to Majoli at Wimbledon only 9–7 fs and at US Open she upset Coetzer and then saved mp in 2s tb v Seles, going on to win the match before losing sf in 3s tb to V. Williams. She also reached sf Birmingham, Philadelphia (d. Seles) and Chase Champs, plus qf Australian Open, Paris Open, LIPC, Madrid, Eastbourne and Moscow. **1998:** A 1, F 1, W 4, US 4. Although she could not maintain her top 10 ranking, she found herself back in the winner's circle again at Strasbourg in May. She upset Davenport and Seles on her way to f FC Cup, removed Martinez and Van Roost to reach sf Zurich, and appeared at same stage Leipzig, where she was r/u doubles with Bollegraf. Her other qf appearances were at Tokyo Pan Pacific, Berlin, Birmingham, Eastbourne and Luxembourg. Gaining a place at Chase Champs only when V. Williams withdrew injured, she made the most of it, upsetting Sanchez-Vicario on her way to sf. **1998 HIGHLIGHTS – SINGLES: Australian Open 1r** [seed 6] (lost S. Williams 6–7 6–3 6–1), **French Open 1r** [seed 9] (lost Plischke 6–2 6–4), **Wimbledon last 16** [seed 10] (d. Lubiani 7–5 6–3, Rittner 6–4 6–4, De Beer 6–4 6–4, lost Novotna [seed 3] 6–2 6–3), **US Open last 16** [seed 9] (d. Likhovtseva 7–5 6–4, Schnitzer 6–3 6–2, S. Williams 6–3 0–6 7–5, lost Novotna [seed 3] 6–3 6–3); **won** Strasbourg (d. Gersi 6–2 6–1, Nagyova 6–4 6–2, Fusai 7–5 6–3, Halard-Decugis 7–6 6–3); **r/u** FC Cup (d. Labat 6–7 6–2 6–1, Grzybowska 6–3 6–4, Davenport 6–7 6–4 7–6, Seles 6–4 1–6 7–6, lost Coetzer 6–3 6–4); **sf** Zurich (d. Oremans 7–6 6–2, Martinez 6–2 7–6, Van Roost 6–4 6–0, lost Davenport 6–2 6–3), **sf** Leipzig (d. Serna 7–6 6–3, Pitkowski 6–1 6–1, lost Tauziat 2–6 6–3 6–2), **sf** Chase Champs (d. Sanchez-Vicario 7–6 6–1, Van Roost 6–2 6–3, lost Hingis 6–2 7–6). **1998 HIGHLIGHTS – DOUBLES:** (with Bollegraf) **r/u** Leipzig (lost Likhovtseva/Sugiyama 6–3 6–7 6–1). **CAREER HIGHLIGHTS – SINGLES: US Open – sf 1997** (d. Frazier 6–1 6–1, Kournikova 6–1 3–6 6–3, Osterloh 6–2 7–5, Coetzer 7–6 6–4, Seles 6–7 7–6 6–3, lost V. Williams 7–6 4–6 7–6); **Chase Champs – sf 1997** (d. Testud 6–3 5–7 6–4, M. J. Fernandez 5–7 6–2 7–5, lost Novotna 7–6 6–2), **sf 1998**; **Australian Open – qf 1997** (d. Kijimuta 6–2 6–4, Kruger 6–1 6–1, Farina 6–4 6–3, Habsudova 6–4 6–4, lost Hingis 7–5 6–2).

KATARINA SREBOTNIK (SLO)

Born Slovenj Gradec, 12 March 1981; lives Velenje; RH; 2HB; 5ft 10in; 129lb; career singles titles 0; final 1998 WTA ranking 337.

Coached by Richard Neugebauer and Jaroslav Vratislav. **1995:** Played in winning SLO team in World Jun Tennis and Europa Cup. **1996:** Played in winning SLO World Youth Cup team and was r/u Orange Bowl 18s to Alcazar. **1997:** Led SLO team to victory in Connolly Continental Cup. **1998:** Won Wimbledon Jun over Clijsters and was r/u US Open Jun to Dokic. In the women's game she played 2 doubles f on the main tour with Krizan, winning Makarska, and on the $10,000 ITF circuit won both singles and doubles at Sibenik. **1998 HIGHLIGHTS – SINGLES: won** Sibenik ITF (d. Molnar 6–1 6–2). **1998 HIGHLIGHTS – DOUBLES:** (with Krizan) **won** Makarska (d. Koulikovskaya/Kschwendt 7–6 6–1); **r/u** Maria Lankowitz (lost Montalvo/Suarez 6–1 6–2).

RENNAE STUBBS (AUS)

Born Sydney, 26 March 1971; lives there and Orlando, Fla.; RH; 5ft 10in; 143lb; career singles titles 0; final 1998 WTA ranking 231 singles, 5= doubles; 1998 prize money $222,922; career prize money $1,109,620.

Coached by Ray Ruffels. **1988:** (352) Won 6 doubles titles on the satellite circuits. **1989:** (225) A 2, F –, W –, US –. Continued to make her mark in doubles on the satellite circuits. **1990:** (232) A 1, F –, W 1, US –. Won her 1st pro singles title at Perth on the satellite circuit. **1991:** (239) A 1, F –, W 1, US –. Won Mildura on the Australian satellite circuit. **1992:** (85) A 2, F 1, W 2, US –. Burst on to the main tour with an upset of Zvereva at Tokyo Pan Pacific and qf appearance at Eastbourne. In doubles won 2 titles with McNeil and 1 each with Sukova and Graf, qualifying for VS Champs with McNeil. **1993:** (170) A 1, F – W 1, US –. Reached 5 doubles f with 4 different partners, winning Indian Wells with Sukova, Hamburg with Graf, and qualifying for VS Champs with McNeil. **1994:** A 1, F –, W –, US –. In a quieter year she won Osaka with Neiland and Strasbourg with McNeil. **1995:** (90) A –, F –, W 2, US 1. Upset Raymond on her way to sf Quebec City. Played 6 doubles f with 4 different partners, winning Birmingham with Bollegraf and reaching her 1st GS f at US Open with Schultz-McCarthy. **1996:** (106) A 2, F 1, W 1, US 1. In singles she reached qf Essen and upset Habsudova at Montreal. In doubles she won Chicago and Philadelphia with Raymond, with whom she qualified for Chase Champs, and was r/u Linz with Sukova. **1997:** (–) A –, F –, W –, US –. She was out for much of the season with tendinitis of the right wrist, returning in autumn to win Luxembourg and Philadelphia doubles with Raymond. **1998:** A 1, F –, W 1, US –. Her doubles partnership with Raymond continued to flourish, bringing 2 titles from 5 f and a place at Chase Champs, where Davenport/Zvereva beat them in sf. **1998 HIGHLIGHTS – SINGLES: Australian Open 1r** (lost Lucic 7–5 6–1), **Wimbledon 1r** (lost Testud [seed 14] 7–6 6–0). **1998 HIGHLIGHTS – DOUBLES:** (with Raymond) **won** Hannover (d. Likhovtseva/Vis 6–1 6–7 6–3), **won** Boston (d. De Swardt/Fernandez 6–3 5–7 6–4); **r/u** FC Cup (lost Martinez/Tarabini 3–6 6–4 6–4), **r/u** Birmingham (lost Callens/Halard-Decugis 2–6 6–4 6–4), **r/u** Moscow (lost Pierce/Zvereva 6–3 6–4). **CAREER HIGHLIGHTS – DOUBLES:** (with Schultz-McCarthy) **US Open** – **r/u 1995** (lost G. Fernandez/Zvereva 7–5 6–3).

AI SUGIYAMA (JPN)

Born Tokyo, 5 July 1975; lives Kanagawa; RH; 5ft 4in; 115lb; turned pro 1992; career singles titles 3; final 1998 WTA ranking 18 singles, 13 doubles; 1998 prize money $354,950; career prize money $1,107,237.

Coached by Junichi Maruyama. **1991:** (568) No. 2 in ITF Jun Rankings singles. **1992:** (180) Won Roanoke Futures. **1993:** (142) A –, F –, W 1, US –. **1994:** (72) A –, F –, W 1, US 1. Reached f both singles and doubles at Surabaya, but was forced to retire in singles and def doubles with heat exhaustion. She also reached sf Osaka and qf Tokyo Nicherei (d. Sawamatsu). **1995:** (46) A 1, F 4, W 1, US 2. R/u Oakland (d. Spirlea and Garrison-Jackson), upset Sukova at French Open, where she was unseeded, and surprised Coetzer at San Diego, as well as reaching qf Zagreb. Played 2 doubles f with Nagatsuka, winning Hobart. **1996:** (32) A 3, F 1, W 4, US 2. She reached sf Tokyo Japan Open and qf Hobart, as well as scoring some big upsets across the year. At Wimbledon, where she was unseeded, she removed Huber before extending M. J. Fernandez to 3s, upset Wiesner at Auckland, Novotna at LIPC and Hingis at Olympics. In doubles she won Tokyo Japan Open with Date and joined with Nagatsuka to beat Graf/Huber as JPN d. GER in qf Fed Cup. **1997:** (20) A 2, F 2, W 1, US 2. Won her 1st ever singles title on the main tour at Tokyo Japan Open and was r/u Gold Coast and Moscow (d. Schultz-McCarthy and Sanchez-Vicario), as well as reaching qf Eastbourne and breaking into top

20 1st time in Nov. In doubles she won Tokyo Nicherei with Seles and r/u Strasbourg with Likhovtseva. **1998:** A 4, F 2, W 1, US 2. She began the year in style by winning both singles and doubles at Gold Coast and followed in April with Tokyo Japan Open. At Sydney she upset Martinez en route to sf, and in other tourns reached qf Tokyo Pan Pacific, Berlin (d. Coetzer), Strasbourg, San Diego (d. Graf) and Luxembourg. She was restricted in autumn by an ankle injury, which forced her retirement at US Open. In doubles with Likhovtseva, she won all 4 f played and qualified for her 1st Chase Champs, although they did not pass 1r. **1998 HIGHLIGHTS – SINGLES: Australian Open last 16** [seed 16] (d. Sanchez Lorenzo 4–6 6–1 6–3, Saeki 6–7 7–5 6–1, Grzybowska 7–6 1–6 6–4, lost Sanchez-Vicario [seed 7] 6–2 6–4), **French Open 2r** (d. Golarsa 7–5 6–3, lost V. Williams [seed 8] 6–0 6–2), **Wimbledon 1r** (lost Plischke 6–4 6–7 6–3), **US Open 2r** [seed 16] (d. Dragomir 6–1 6–2, lost Leon-Garcia 2–3 ret); **won** Gold Coast (d. Maleeva 7–5 6–2, Barclay 7–6 6–1, Pitkowski 6–0 7–5, Wang 6–4 7–5, Vento 7–5 6–0), **won** Tokyo Japan Open (d. Miyagi 6–3 6–2, De Lone 4–6 6–1 6–1, Wang 6–3 6–2, Morariu 6–3 6–3); **sf** Sydney (d. Lubiani 6–1 7–6, Martinez 7–6 6–3, Paulus 6–1 7–6, lost V. Williams 6–1 7–6). **1998 HIGHLIGHTS – DOUBLES:** (with Likhovtseva) **won** Gold Coast (d. Park/Wang 1–6 6–3 6–4), **won** Luxembourg (d. Neiland/Tatarkova 6–7 6–3 2–0 ret), **won** Leipzig (d. Bollegraf/Spirlea 6–3 6–7 6–1), **won** Philadelphia (d. Seles/Zvereva 7–5 4–6 6–2).

TAMARINE TANASUGARN (THA)

Born Los Angeles, USA, 24 May 1977; lives Bangkok; RH; 2HB; 5ft 5in; 140lb; turned pro 1994; career singles titles 0; final 1998 WTA ranking 37; 1998 prize money $203,941.

Coached by father, Virachai Tanasugarn. Ranked No. 1 in Thailand, and also holds US citizenship. **1992:** (654). **1993:** (494). **1994:** (249). **1995:** (209) R/u Wimbledon Jun to Olsza. **1996:** (79) Upset Wild on the way to her 1st main tour sf at Beijing, then crowned her year with r/u Pattaya. On the satellite circuits, she won 2 titles from 4 f in 4 weeks in Australia and singles and doubles at Saga. **1997:** (46) A 3, F 2, W 3, US 3. She reached sf Auckland, won Surbiton Futures and upset Dragomir at Toronto. **1998:** A 4, F 1, W 4, US 1. Played sf Tokyo Toyota and qf Auckland (where she won the doubles with Miyagi), Stanford and Pattaya. At Australian Open (unseeded) she upset Majoli and took a set off Testud. **1998 HIGHLIGHTS – SINGLES: Australian Open last 16** [unseeded] (d. Vento 6–1 6–3, Wagner 6–4 4–6 6–4, Majoli [seed 4] 6–0 6–2, lost Testud [seed 9] 3–6 6–1 6–3), **French Open 1r** (lost V. Williams [seed 8] 6–3 6–1), **Wimbledon last 16** [unseeded] (d. Hrdlickova 6–0 7–5, Cross 6–2 7–5, Black 6–4 6–0, lost Hingis [seed 1] 6–3 6–2), **US Open 1r** (lost Stoyanova 7–6 6–2); **sf** Tokyo Toyota (d. Yoshida 6–4 6–3, Nagyova 6–4 7–6, Frazier 6–1 6–3, lost Seles 6–1 6–4. **1998 HIGHLIGHTS – DOUBLES:** (with Miyagi) **won** Auckland (d. Halard-Decugis/Husarova 7–6); (with Tatarkova) **r/u** Los Angeles (lost Hingis/Zvereva 6–4 6–2).

PATRICIA TARABINI (ARG)

Born La Plata, 6 August 1968; lives Tandil; RH; 5ft 5in; 135lb; turned pro 1986; career singles titles 0; final 1998 WTA ranking – singles, 14 doubles; 1998 prize money $132,864; career prize money $1,091,970.

Coached by Jorge Todero. **1981:** Won Nat Jun Champs. **1983:** Beat Sabatini in Argentine Nat. **1984:** R/u Orange Bowl 16s. **1985:** (305) In Jun singles r/u Orange Bowl; in Jun doubles with Perez-Roldan won French Open and Orange Bowl and r/u US Open, to finish ranked No. 1 in ITF Jun doubles rankings and No. 3 singles. **1986:** (125) F 2, W –, US –. Won French Open Jun, Orange Bowl and took Argentine Nat Jun for 4th straight year. In the senior game reached sf Bregenz and won 2 titles on the Italian satellite circuit. **1987:** (69) A –, F 1, W 1, US 3. Sf Berlin, qf Argentine Open and Athens. **1988:** (34) A –, F 2, W –, US –. Upset Man. Maleeva en route to sf Tampa and reached qf at Houston and Nice. Underwent ankle surgery, following an injury suffered at Aix-en-Provence, and was out for last 5 months of year. **1989:** (75) A –, F 1, W –, US 3. In singles reached f Strasbourg and Guaruja plus sf Estoril; in doubles with Cecchini won Arcachon, Athens and Paris Open. **1990:** (55) A –, F 3, W –, US 1. R/u Clarins and sf Estoril; reached 4 doubles f with various partners, winning 2 titles. **1991:** (116) Won Bayonne doubles with Tauziat. **1992:** (97) A 1, F 1, W 1, US –. Qf Sao Paulo and San Marino in singles and won Clarins doubles with Cecchini. Fractured her right ankle practising at Houston in April. **1993:** (60) A 1, F 2, W 1, US 1. In singles she reached sf Palermo and Prague and upset Maleeva-Fragniere en route to qf VS Houston. From 3 doubles f she won Prague with Gorrochategui and San Marino with Cecchini. **1994:** (104) A 2, F 1, W 2, US 1. Qf Barcelona (d. Tauziat) was her best showing in singles, and in doubles she won Styria with Cecchini. **1995:** (324) A 2, F 1, W –, US –. Played 2 doubles f with Martinez to qualify for WTA Champs. **1996:** A –, F –, W –, US –. Won a 1st GS title at French Open mixed with Frana, unseeded. **1997:** (–) A –, F –, W –, US –. Although she played only 1 doubles f, she reached 4 sf and qualified for Chase Champs with Martinez. **1998:** A –, F –, W –, US –. Won FC Cup doubles with Martinez, with whom she qualified again for Chase Champs, but did not pass 1r. **1998 HIGHLIGHTS – DOUBLES:** (with Martinez) **won** FC Cup (d. Raymond/Stubbs 3–6 6–4 6–4). **CAREER HIGHLIGHTS – MIXED DOUBLES:** (with Frana) **French Open – won 1996** (d. L. Jensen/Arendt 6–2 6–2).

ELENA TATARKOVA (UKR)

Born Bushanabe, 22 August 1976; lives Kiev; LH; 2HB; 5ft 7in; 146lb; turned pro 1993; career singles titles 0; final 1998 WTA ranking 47 singles, 22 doubles; 1998 prize money $156,515.

Coached by Svetlana Medvedeva. **1993:** (316) Won both singles and doubles at Jurmala ITF. **1994:** (221). **1995:** (192) Upset Monami en route to her 1st qf on the main tour at Beijing after qualifying and removed

Grossman at Surabaya. **1996:** (191) Again as a qualifier, she reached qf Moscow. **1997:** (136). **1998:** A 1, F 3, W 2, US 1. In singles she upset Spirlea on her way to qf Los Angeles, removed Pierce 1r Wimbledon and Coetzer at Luxembourg, and broke into top 100. She played 4 doubles f with 3 different partners, but won no title. **1998 HIGHLIGHTS – SINGLES: Australian Open 1r** (lost Rittner 6–1 7–6), **French Open 3r** (d. Brandi 6–4 6–4, Hrdlickova 6–4 6–1, lost Novotna [seed 3] 6–3 7–6), **Wimbledon 2r** (d. Pierce [seed 11] 7–6 6–3, lost De Swardt 6–4 7–6), **US Open 1r** (lost Schnitzer 0–6 7–6 6–3). **1998 HIGHLIGHTS – DOUBLES:** (with Neiland unless stated) **r/u** Stanford (lost Davenport/Zvereva 6–4 6–4), (with Tanasugarn) **r/u** Los Angeles (lost Hingis/Zvereva 6–4 6–2), (with De Swardt) **r/u** Zurich (lost S./V. Williams 5–7 6–1 6–3), **r/u** Luxembourg (lost Likhovtseva/Sugiyama 6–7 6–3 2–0 ret).

SANDRINE TESTUD (FRA)

Born Lyon, 3 April 1972, and lives there; RH; 5ft 9½in; 150lb; career singles titles 2; final 1998 WTA ranking 14; 1998 prize money $477,795; career prize money $1,497,665.

Coached by Philippe Duxin. Husband Vittorio Magnelli (married 13 June 1998). **1989:** (279) Won Nat Jun 18s and in the senior game won her 1st Futures title at Limoges. **1990:** (185) A –, F 1, W –, US –. Won Futures titles at Eastbourne, Caltagirone and Swindon. **1991:** (118) A –, F 1, W –, US –. Reached sf Bol, plus qf Albuquerque and St Petersburg. **1992:** (108) A 2, F 2, W 1, US 2. Qf Strasbourg. **1993:** (98) A 1, F 1, W 1, US 1. Upset McNeil on her way to sf Strasbourg and Strnadova to reach qf Pattaya City. **1994:** (81) A 4, F 1, W 1, US 2. Upset Sukova at Australian Open, where she was unseeded, but reached no qf on the main tour. **1995:** (41) A 3, F 2, W 2, US 3. Broke into the top 50 after appearances in sf Strasbourg (d. M. J. Fernandez) and San Diego (d. Zvereva), plus qf Puerto Rico (d. Halard) and Quebec City. **1996:** (39) A 1, F 3, W 2, US 4. Her best performances were sf Beijing and qf San Diego (d. Sugiyama). **1997:** (13) A 2, F 3, W 4, US qf. She won her 1st career singles title at Palermo and upset Habsudova and Majoli on her way to f Atlanta, unseeded. She played no other sf, but moved into top 15 with qf US Open (unseeded, d. Majoli), Hannover (d. Schultz-McCarthy), Indian Wells (d. Raymond), LIPC (d. Sanchez-Vicario), Strasbourg, San Diego (d. Sanchez-Vicario again) and Moscow, and removed Davenport at Berlin. Having upset Seles 3r Wimbledon, again unseeded, she suffered a cruel reverse v Tauziat in her next match: 5–4 and 40–15 up in 3s when rain interrupted play for 75 minutes, she dropped the next 10 points, going on to lose the set 10–12. Won her 2 crucial singles matches in Fed Cup f as FRA d. NED and qualified 1st time for Chase Champs, where she extended Spirlea to 3s 1r. **1998:** A qf, F 4, W 4, US 3. At Filderstadt, where she was unseeded, she upset Van Roost and Davenport on the way to the title. She was consistent through the year in reaching f Prague, sf Auckland, Madrid, Hertogenbosch and Moscow (d. Martinez), and qf Australian Open, Oklahoma City, Budapest, Rome (d. Seles), Montreal (d. Spirlea) and Quebec City, where she was r/u doubles with Rubin. She qualified for Chase Champs, where, despite a leg injury, she looked set to upset Davenport 1r before losing momentum. **1998 HIGHLIGHTS – SINGLES: Australian Open qf** [seed 9] (d. Leon-Garcia 6–3 6–2, Kandarr 6–7 6–0 6–1, Gersi 6–4 6–2, Tanasugarn 3–6 6–1 6–2, lost Martinez [seed 8] 6–3 6–2), **French Open last 16** [seed 14] (d. Reeves 2–6 6–2 6–3, Wagner 6–2 6–0, Leon Garcia 6–1 6–1, lost Davenport [seed 2] 6–3 4–6 6–2), **Wimbledon last 16** [seed 14] (d. Stubbs 7–6 6–0, Noorlander 6–3 6–1, McNeil 6–3 7–6, lost Seles [seed 6] 6–3 6–2), **US Open 3r** (d. Wang 6–0 6–2, Hrdlickova 7–6 6–3, lost Novotna [[seed 3] 6–2 6–3); **won** Filderstadt (d. Likhovtseva 5–7 6–1 6–0, Huber 6–2 4–6 6–2, S. Williams 6–3 1–6 6–1, Van Roost 6–2 6–0, Davenport 7–5 6–3); **r/u** Prague (d. Gersi 1–0 ret, Chladkova 7–6 7–5, Farina 2–6 6–3 6–2, Zvereva 6–3 4–6 6–4, lost Novotna 6–3 6–0); **sf** Auckland (d. Tu 7–5 2–6 6–1, Husarova 6–2 6–0, Cacic 6–2 6–2, lost Farina 6–2 7–6), **sf** Madrid (d. Sanchez Lorenzo 6–4 6–4, Rubin 6–4 6–3, lost Schnyder 6–4 7–5), **sf** Hertogenbosch (d. Golarsa 6–3 6–4, Leon-Garcia 7–6 6–4, lost Halard-Decugis 6–3 6–3), **sf** Moscow (d. Dechy 6–2 6–2, Zvereva 6–4 6–3, Martinez 7–6 7–5, lost Seles 6–3 7–6). **1998 HIGHLIGHTS – DOUBLES:** (with Rubin) **r/u** Quebec City (lost McNeil/Po 6–7 7–5 6–4). **CAREER HIGHLIGHTS – SINGLES: Australian Open – qf 1998; US Open – qf 1997** (d. Sanchez Lorenzo 6–3 6–3, Majoli 6–4 2–6 6–1, Wagner 6–1 6–3, Habsudova 6–3 4–6 7–6, lost V. Williams 7–5 7–5).

DOMINIQUE VAN ROOST (BEL)

Born Verviers, 3 May 1973; lives Leuven; RH; 5ft 7in; 122lb; turned pro 1991; career singles titles 4; final 1998 WTA ranking 12; 1998 prize money $440,324; career prize money $1,167,500

Coached by Alfonso Gonzalez. Husband Bart Van Roost (married 1995); maiden name Monami. **1989:** (695). **1990:** (272) Won 5 consec. Futures titles on the European circuit. **1991:** (129) A –, F –, W –, US 1. Upset Golarsa at Linz. **1992:** (101) A 4, F 1, W 1, US 2. Surprised Sukova at Australian Open, where she was unseeded, and reached qf Linz and Bayonne. **1993:** (59) A 2, F 1, W 1, US 2. In singles she reached her 1st tour f at Montpellier and appeared in qf Palermo and Sapporo (d. Wang). From 3 doubles f she won Kitzbuhel with Li. **1994:** (133) A 1, F 1, W 3, US 1. In a quieter year she reached only qf Taipei and took a set off Novotna at Wimbledon. **1995:** (43) A –, F 2, W 2, US 2. Returned to the top 100 with r/u showing at Quebec City, where she upset Gorrochategui and Coetzer, and won both singles and doubles at Southampton Futures. **1996:** (46) A 1, F 1, W 3, US 1. Won her 1st singles title on the main tour at Cardiff and reached qf Rosmalen (d. Appelmans). On the Futures circuit, she won Limoges. **1997:** (18) A qf, F 3, W 1, US 1. Her best year yet saw her breaking into top 20 by end of year. She began it in style with an upset of Wild on her way to the title at Hobart, where she was r/u doubles with Rittner, and finished it with a flourish at Pattaya, where she was r/u both singles and doubles (with Labat). Unseeded at Australian Open, she upset Sanchez-Vicario and Rubin, before being forced to retire qf with an abdominal injury. She added the title at Surabaya, r/u Quebec City (d. Raymond), sf Moscow (d. Huber and Spirlea) and reached qf Cardiff, Birmingham, Rosmalen and Atlanta (d. Dragomir). **1998:** A 3, F 3, W 4, US 3. Improving still further, she broke into top 10 1st time, although by end of year she had slipped just outside again. She began in Jan. with the title at Auckland, following the next week with r/u Hobart. By end May she had also reached the same stage Paris Open (d. Majoli and Tauziat), Linz and Madrid (where she won the doubles with Labat), but could not add further to her tally of singles titles. She upset V. Williams and Hingis back-to-back en route to sf Filderstadt, removed Majoli on her way to the same stage Leipzig and played qf Birmingham, Zurich and Quebec City. She qualified for her 1st Chase Champs, where she upset Martinez but fell qf to Spirlea. **1998 HIGHLIGHTS – SINGLES: Australian Open 3r** [seed 14] (d. Simpson 6–3 6–2, Snyder 6–3 6–4, lost Basuki 6–4 6–4), **French Open 3r** [seed 15] (d. Grzybowska 7–5 3–6 6–4, Callens 6–3 6–0, lost S. Williams 6–1 6–1), **Wimbledon last 16** [seed 15] (d. Kruger 6–1 6–3, A. Miller 6–1 6–1, Appelmans 6–1 6–2, lost Sanchez-Vicario [seed 5] 3–6 6–3 6–2), **US Open 3r** [seed 14] (d. Halard-Decugis 6–2 6–2, Grzybowska 6–0 6–0, lost Po 6–4 6–2); **won** Auckland (d. Lubiani 6–3 6–3, Nemeckova 6–0 6–4, Tanasugarn 6–0 6–3, A. Miller 6–2 6–3, Farina 6–2 7–6 7–5); **r/u** Hobart (d. Tanasugarn 6–2 6–2, Courtois 6–0 6–4, Li 7–5 6–3, Grzybowska 6–7 6–1 6–3, lost Schnyder 6–7 6–1 6–3), **r/u** Paris Open (d. Schett 6–2 4–6 6–0, Probst 5–7 6–2 7–6, Majoli 7–5 6–3, Tauziat 7–6 1–6 6–1, lost Pierce 6–3 7–5), **r/u** Linz (d. Gersi 2–6 7–5 7–6, Appelmans 6–3 7–5, Majoli 6–2 ret, lost Novotna 6–1 7–6), **r/u** Madrid (d. Leon-Garcia 7–5 6–1, Boogert 6–0 7–6, Schett 6–2 6–2, lost Schnyder 6–2 6–2); **sf** Filderstadt (d. Serna 2–6 7–5 6–2, V. Williams 6–1 6–2, Hingis 6–3 6–7 6–4, lost Testud 6–2 6–0), **sf** Leipzig (d. Majoli 6–4 6–4, Zvereva 6–3 3–6 6–2, lost Graf 6–1 3–6 6–0). **1998 HIGHLIGHTS – DOUBLES:** (with Labat) **won** Madrid (d. McQuillan/Pratt 6–3 6–1). **CAREER HIGHLIGHTS – SINGLES: Australian Open – qf 1997** (d. Fulco-Villella 6–0 6–3, Yoshida 4–6 7–5 6–3, Sanchez-Vicario 1–6 6–4 8–6, Rubin 7–5 6–4, lost M. J. Fernandez 7–5 4–0 ret).

MARIA ALEJANDRA VENTO (VEN)

Born Caracas, 24 May 1974; lives there and Miami, Fla.; RH; 2HB; 5ft 6in; 130lb; turned pro 1994; career singles titles 0; final 1998 WTA ranking 43; 1998 prize money $127,801.

Coached by George Paris. **1988:** (530). **1989:** (412) Won Guadalajara Futures. **1990:** (414) Won Aguascalientes Futures and joined VEN Fed Cup squad. **1991:** (515). **1992:** (549) A –, F –, W –, US 1. **1993:** (207) A –, F –, W –, US –. Won 4 Futures titles in USA, including 3 in consec. tourns. **1994:** (165) A –, F –, W –, US –. **1995:** (87) A –, F –, W 1, US 1. Reached her 1st qf on the main tour at Pattaya and won Brasilia Futures. **1996:** (170) A 1, F –, W –, US –. **1997:** (48) A –, F –, W 4, US 2. She upset Wang on her way to sf Surabaya, Tauziat to reach qf Quebec City, and Maleeva en route to last 16 Wimbledon, after qualifying. On the Futures circuit she won Peachtree. **1998:** A 1, F 1, W 3, US 2. She played her 1st career f at Gold Coast, but reached no other qf. **1998 HIGHLIGHTS – SINGLES: Australian Open 1r** (lost Tanasugarn 6–1 6–3), **French Open 1r** (lost Andretto 6–3 6–3), **Wimbledon 3r** (d. Cacic 7–6 4–6 6–3, K. Miller 6–0 7–5, lost Davenport [seed 2] 6–3 1–6 6–2), **US Open 2r** (d. Serna 6–7 7–5 6–4, lost Golarsa 6–4 3–6 6–4); **r/u** Gold Coast (d. Serna 6–3 6–4, Likhovtseva 7–5 6–4, Schultz-McCarthy 4–0 ret, Plischke 6–2 6–3, lost Sugiyama 7–5 6–0).

CAROLINE VIS (NED)

Born Vlaardingen, 4 March 1970, and lives there; RH; 5ft 11in; 158lb; turned pro 1989; career singles titles 0; final 1998 WTA ranking – singles, 15 doubles; 1998 prize money $131,192.

Coached by Auke Dykstra. **1989:** (253). **1990:** (209) Upset Savchenko at VS Nashville and r/u doubles there with Schultz. Joined her country's Fed Cup squad. **1991:** (417) R/u French Open mixed doubles with Haarhuis and in women's doubles reached f VS Nashville with Basuki. **1992:** (333) Won Waregem doubles with Bollegraf. **1993:** (208) Won Budapest doubles with Gorrochategui and r/u Prague with Golarsa. **1994:** (117) A –, F 1, W 1, US –. Upset Pierce en route to qf Paris Open and reached 3 doubles f with different partners. **1995:** (206) A 1, F –, W –, US –. In doubles played 3 f with different partners. **1996:** (313) A –, F –, W –, US –. Although she reached no doubles f, she was a regular in qf with various partners, qualifying for Chase Champs with Basuki. **1997:** (–) A –, F –, W –, US –. In doubles she won Los Angeles and Toronto back-to-back in Aug. with Basuki and qualified for Chase Champs. **1998:** A –, F –, W –, US –. Although she won no title, she played 3 doubles f – 1 with Likhovtseva and 2 with Basuki, with whom she qualified for Chase Champs, where they upset Hingis/Novotna 1r. **1998 HIGHLIGHTS – DOUBLES:** (with Likhovtseva) **r/u** Hannover (lost Raymond/Stubbs 6–1 6–7 6–3), (with Basuki) **r/u** Strasbourg (lost Fusai/Tauziat 6–4 6–3), (with Basuki) **r/u** Montreal (lost Hingis/Novotna 6–3 6–4).

ELENA WAGNER (BUL)

Born Sofia, 17 May 1972; lives Nussloch-Heidelberg, Germany; RH; 2HB; 5ft 5in; 115lb; career singles titles 1; final 1998 WTA ranking 69; 1998 prize money $97,529.

Coached by her parents, Emil and Lubka. Married the late Axel Wagner 8 June 1991; maiden name Pampoulova. Her father and uncle played D Cup and her mother played Fed Cup. **1988:** (353) Won European Jun Champ and in the women's game she won 2 Futures titles. **1989:** (122) Qf Paris Open and won 3 titles on the satellite circuits. **1990:** (98) Reached sf Bastad and qf Strasbourg (d. Tarabini). **1991:** (134) Joined the Bulgarian Fed Cup team. **1992:** (235) Played for Bulgaria in the Olympics. **1993:** (163) Concentrated on the satellite circuits, but won no singles title. **1994:** (70) After qualifying for Hamburg, she extended Sanchez-Vicario to 7-6 3s 1r. She finished the season in style by winning her 1st main tour title at Hong Kong and moved into top

100. **1995:** (221) A 1, F 1, W 1, US 1. **1996:** (75) A –, F 1, W 1, US 1. Reached sf Budapest and on the ITF circuit she won Redbridge, Southampton and Murcia, returning to the top 100. Played 2 doubles f, winning Warsaw with Lugina. **1997:** (100) A 1, F 1, W –, US 3. She reached sf Auckland and qf Budapest, but her year ended tragically when her husband died in autumn after a short illness. **1998:** A 2, F 2, W 1, US 1. Returning to the tour, she reached f Sopot, unseeded, but her only other qf appearance was at Palermo, where she won the doubles with Stoyanova. **1998 HIGHLIGHTS – SINGLES: Australian Open 2r** (d. Watanabe 6–2 6–1, lost Tanasugarn 6–4 4–6 6–4), **French Open 2r** (d. Miyagi 3–6 6–0 6–1. lost Testud [seed 14] 6–2 6–0), **Wimbledon 1r** (lost Oremans 2–6 6–3 6–2), **US Open 1r** (lost V. Williams [seed 5] 6–1 6–0); **r/u** Sopot (d. Sromova 6–2 6–1, Boogert 4–6 6–1 6–4, Weingartner 6–2 7–6, Smashnova 6–3 0–6 6–4, lost Nagyova 6–3 5–7 6–1). **1998 HIGHLIGHTS – DOUBLES:** (with Stoyanova) **won** Palermo (d. Schett/Schnyder 6–4 6–2).

SHI-TING WANG (TPE)

Born Tainan, 19 October 1973, and lives there; RH; 2HB; 5ft 7in; 128lb; turned pro 1991; career singles titles 6; final 1998 WTA ranking 59; 1998 prize money $129,062.

Prefers to be known as Stephanie, the English version of her name. Coached by her father, Wen-Chih Wang. Ranked No. 1 in Taipei. **1989:** Won French Open Jun doubles with Pratt. **1991:** (185) Won 5 titles on the Challenger circuit, including 4 in Taipei. **1992:** (55) A –, F 1, W –, US 1. Upset Huber in reaching her 1st senior tour sf at Indianapolis, appeared in qf Pattaya City and Taipei and upset Basuki at Tokyo Suntory. **1993:** (30) A 2, F –, W –, US 2. Won her 1st title on the main tour at Hong Kong, following 3 weeks later with Taipei. Upset Halard on her way to sf Brisbane and reached qf Osaka. **1994:** (42) A 2, F 3, W –, US 3. She finished the year in style when she retained her title at Taipei, having earlier appeared in sf Brisbane and Jakarta and qf Schenectady. **1995:** (44) A 1, F 3, W –, US –. Won Surabaya and was r/u Beijing in both singles and doubles, as well as reaching qf Jakarta. **1996:** (35) A 2, F 2, W –, US 2. Won Surabaya and Beijing back-to-back in Oct., having begun the year with an upset of Wiesner on her way to sf Hobart and reached qf Tokyo Nicherei, where she was r/u doubles with Park. **1997:** (67) A 3, F 2, W 2, US –. She could not pass qf, but reached that stage at Hobart, Tokyo Japan Open and Jakarta, where she also won the Futures title. **1998:** A 2, F 1, W 2, US 1. Her best showings were sf Tokyo Japan Open and Gold Coast (where she was r/u doubles with Park) and qf Pattaya at end of year. **1998 HIGHLIGHTS – SINGLES: Australian Open 2r** (d. Gorrochategui 6–1 4–6 6–4, lost Schnyder 6–3 6–4), **French Open 1r** (lost Farina 6–2 6–1), **Wimbledon 2r** (d. Brandi 7–6 7–5, lost De Beer 6–2 4–6 6–3), **US Open 1r** (lost Testud 6–0 6–2); **sf** Gold Coast (d. Sidot 3–6 6–3 6–3, McQuillan 1–6 6–4 6–4, Dragomir 6–3 5–7 6–3), **sf** Tokyo Japan Open (d. Asagoe 3–6 6–3 6–1, Hiraki 6–3 6–2, McNeil 4–6 6–4 6–1, lost Sugiyama 6–3 6–2). **1998 HIGHLIGHTS – DOUBLES:** (with Park) **r/u** Gold Coast (lost Likhovtseva/Sugiyama 1–6 6–3 6–4).

SERENA WILLIAMS (USA)

Born Saginaw, Mich, 26 September 1981; lives Palm Beach Gardens, Fla.; RH; 2HB; 5ft 10in; 145lb; career singles titles 0; final 1998 WTA ranking 20; 1998 prize money $310,211.

Coached by her parents, Richard and Oracene Williams. Younger sister of Venus. **1997:** (99) She burst into prominence at Chicago, where, in only her 2nd tourn, she upset Pierce and Seles back-to-back on her way to sf. **1998:** A 2, F 4, W 3, US 3. Aiming for the top 10 by year's end, she began by upsetting Spirlea at Australian Open and again at LIPC, where she went on to extend Hingis to 7–6 fs. These results took her into the top 50, and she cracked the top 20 after French Open where, unseeded, she upset Van Roost and extended Sanchez-Vicario to 3s, as well as being r/u mixed doubles with Lobo. At Wimbledon she withdrew from singles with a calf injury when losing to Ruano-Pascual, but continued to play mixed doubles and went on to win the title with Mirnyi, with whom she also won US Open mixed. Although she did not quite reach the heights she had hoped for, she was always a threat to the top players and caused more significant upsets on her way to sf Sydney (d. Davenport) and qf Oklahoma City, LIPC (d. Spirlea and Schnyder), Rome (d. Tauziat and Martinez), Eastbourne (d. Sugiyama), Los Angeles (d. Testud) and Filderstadt (d. Novotna). In women's doubles she won Oklahoma City and Zurich with her sister, Venus, and was voted WTA Newcomer of the Year. **1998 HIGHLIGHTS – SINGLES: Australian Open 2r** (d. Spirlea [seed 6] 6–7 6–3 6–1, lost V. Williams 7–6 6–1), **French Open last 16** [unseeded] (d. Nejedly 6–2 1–6 6–4, Morariu 6–1 6–0, Van Roost 6–1 6–1, lost Sanchez-Vicario [seed 4] 4–6 7–5 6–3), **Wimbledon 3r** (d. Golarsa 6–4 6–3, Lucic 6–3 6–0, lost Ruano-Pascual 7–5 4–1 ret), **US Open 3r** (d. Pratt 6–3 3–6 6–4, Stoyanova 6–2 6–1, lost Spirlea [seed 9] 6–3 0–6 7–5); **sf** Sydney (d. Lucic 3–6 6–4 7–5, Testud 7–6 3–0 ret, Davenport 1–6 7–5 7–5, lost Sanchez-Vicario 6–2 6–1). **1998 HIGHLIGHTS – DOUBLES:** (with V. Williams) **won** Oklahoma City (d. Cristea/Kunce 7–5 6–2), **won** Zurich (d. De Swardt/Tatarkova 5–7 6–1 6–3). **1998 HIGHLIGHTS – MIXED DOUBLES:** (with Mirnyi unless stated) (with Lobo) **r/u French Open** (lost Gimelstob/V. Williams 6–4 6–4), **won Wimbledon** (d. Bhupathi/V. Williams 6–4 6–4), **won US Open** (d. Galbraith/Raymond 6–2 6–2).

NATASHA ZVEREVA (BRS)

Born Minsk, 16 April 1971, and lives there; RH; 2HB; 5ft 8in; 138lb; turned pro 1988; career singles titles 3; final 1998 WTA ranking 16 singles, 1 doubles; 1998 prize money $931,945; career prize money $7,014,631.

Named Natalia, but prefers to be called Natasha. She is advised by her father, Marat Zverev, but has no formal coach as she finds it hard to cope with anyone telling her what to do, and hires a local hitting partner at each tournament. **1985:** Won Bethesda on USTA circuit and World Jun Champs. **1986:** (92) In singles won Soviet

Nat Champs (d. Savchenko), won Wimbledon Jun singles, USTA Bethesda, and was r/u to Rinaldi at VS Arkansas after qualifying, becoming at 15 years 7 months the youngest player to reach f of VS Series event. In doubles won French Open Jun and r/u Wimbledon Jun with Meskhi. **1987:** (19) A –, F 3, W 4, US 3. Futures Jun Champ; won Nat Champ, Jun singles at French Open, Wimbledon and US Open and Jun doubles at French Open and Wimbledon with Medvedeva. Did not compete in Australian Open Jun. At Wimbledon she beat McNeil and extended Sabatini to 3s; won Taranto on Italian satellite and reached f Arkansas and Chicago in consecutive weeks. **1988:** (7) A –, F r/u, W 4, US 1. Played her best tennis to upset Navratilova last 16 French Open, but disappointed in her 1st GS f there, being totally outclassed 6–0 6–0 in 32 minutes by Graf. Reached qf Olympics. In doubles with Savchenko r/u Wimbledon and won 2 titles. At VS Champs reached qf in singles and r/u in doubles. Voted WTA Newcomer of the Year. **1989:** (27) A –, F 1, W 3, US 4. Was less successful in singles, winning no title, although she reached f FC Cup (d. Navratilova) and Moscow plus 3 more sf. However, in doubles with Savchenko she won French Open, was r/u Wimbledon and VS Champs and reached 7 other f, winning 4. **1990:** (12) A 2, F 4, W qf, US 2. Won 1st senior singles title at Brisbane (upset Sukova qf), following with Sydney the next week. In doubles with Savchenko r/u French Open and won 3 titles; in mixed with Pugh won Australian Open and r/u US Open. Qualified for VS Champs in singles and doubles, losing 1r singles to Sanchez-Vicario and 1r doubles to Adams/McNeil. **1991:** (21) A 4, F 2, W 2, US 4. In singles r/u Birmingham, sf FC Cup and reached last 16 Australian Open and US Open. In doubles GS won Wimbledon and r/u French Open with Savchenko and teamed with Shriver 1st time to win US Open. She also won VS Florida, Berlin, Eastbourne, Toronto and Los Angeles with Savchenko, Brighton with Shriver and FC Cup with Kohde-Kilsch, as well as reaching 4 more f with various partners, qualifying for VS Champs with Savchenko. In mixed doubles, r/u Wimbledon with Pugh. **1992:** (23) A 2, F qf, W qf, US 3. Unseeded in all the major tourns, she always made her mark. At French Open she upset Appelmans to reach qf, where she took a set off Graf; she reached the same stage at Wimbledon, upsetting Martinez and Garrison; at US Open she extended Sabatini to 3s and at Olympics she upset Novotna on her way to last 16. She also upset Navratilova at FC Cup, reaching qf there as well as at Italian Open, Oakland and Philadelphia. Yet it was in doubles where she really excelled, reaching 13 f, from which she won French Open, Wimbledon, US Open plus 2 others with G. Fernandez, 2 with Sanchez-Vicario, 1 with Savchenko-Neiland and 1 with Sukova. In addition she won an Olympic bronze medal with Meskhi and qualified for VS Champs with G. Fernandez, losing sf to Novotna/Savchenko-Neiland. **1993:** (19) A 3, F 4, W qf, US qf. In singles she had passed no qf all year until Oct., when she stunned Navratilova on her way to f Filderstadt. Otherwise, again unseeded in all GS, her best performances came at Wimbledon, where she reached qf (d. K. Maleeva), at US Open, where she retired at same stage v Sanchez-Vicario, and French Open, where she reached last 16 (d. Coetzer). In doubles with G. Fernandez, with whom she had never been beaten in GS f, won Australian Open, French Open and Wimbledon, extending to 6 their run of GS titles, 2nd only to Navratilova/Shriver's record 8 in the Open era. However, the string was broken at US Open, where, with Zvereva suffering from flu, they lost sf to Sanchez-Vicario/Sukova. They won 7 other titles together, being r/u twice, and were voted WTA Doubles Team of Year. Qualified for VS Champs in both singles, in which she lost to Graf 1r, and doubles, which she and Fernandez won. **1994:** (10) A 1, F 4, W 1, US –. At Chicago she won both singles and doubles for only her 3rd singles title and her 1st since 1990. In singles she also reached f LIPC (d. Novotna and took a set off Graf), FC Cup (d. Pierce) and Zurich, as well as appearing in sf Eastbourne and Philadelphia. After qualifying for VS Champs in both singles and doubles again, she fell 1r singles to Martinez, but retained the doubles title with G. Fernandez. They excelled again as a partnership through the year: at Australian Open they won 7th of 8 consec. GS doubles tourns, following with French Open and Wimbledon, but again they missed the chance of a GS when they unexpectedly lost to K. Maleeva/White in sf US Open. In all they won a total of 11 titles from 13 f. **1995:** (14) A qf, F 1, W 3, US 4. In singles she reached f Indian Wells (d. Sanchez-Vicario), sf FC Cup, Berlin and Eastbourne, and played qf Australian Open, LIPC, Manhattan Beach and Filderstadt. Her doubles partnership with G. Fernandez continued to flourish as they played all GS f, winning French and US Opens, and took 7 titles from 12 f. In mixed, she won Australian Open with Leach. Qualifying for VS Champs in both singles and doubles, she upset Sanchez-Vicario and Sabatini (for the 1st time in 9 meetings) to reach sf singles and was r/u doubles with G. Fernandez, with whom she was voted Doubles Team of the Year. **1996:** (53) A 1, F 3, W 2, US 3. She withdrew from Indian Wells with a stress fracture of the ribcage (right side) and was out for 14 weeks. She went into French Open having played (and lost) only 3 matches all year and her only qf showing in singles was at Luxembourg in Oct. In doubles she won US Open and was r/u French Open with G. Fernandez, also taking Tokyo Toray with her and Los Angeles with Davenport. Qualified for Chase Champs with G. Fernandez, but lost sf to Davenport/M. J. Fernandez. **1997:** (25) A 3, F 4, W 1, US 3. In singles she reached sf Eastbourne (d. Majoli and extended Novotna to 7–5 3s) and qf Strasbourg (d. Davenport), Birmingham, San Diego (d. Spirlea), Los Angeles and Tokyo Nicherei. She also upset Habsudova at LIPC, Schultz-McCarthy at French Open (unseeded), and Martinez at Filderstadt, where she extended Hingis to 3s. She continued to excel in doubles and finished the year at the top of the rankings after appearing in 11 f, including all 4 GS – of which she won Australian Open with Hingis, French Open and Wimbledon with G. Fernandez, with whom she was also r/u US Open. They qualified together for Chase Champs, but there, in Fernandez's last tourn before retiring, they disappointingly lost 1r to Neiland/Sukova. Zvereva had also won 2 titles each with Davenport and Sanchez-Vicario and 1 with Sukova. **1998:** A 3, F 2, W sf, US 2. Her best singles performances were on grass, on which she began by upsetting V. Williams on the way to sf Eastbourne. Then at Wimbledon, unseeded, she pulled off ss upsets of Graf and Seles to reach sf, where she came close to defeating Tauziat before letting the match and a place in the final slip away. It was the 1st time she had d. Graf in 19 meetings. She reached sf again at Prague the following week and appeared in qf Sydney (d. Coetzer), Indian Wells (d. Spirlea), Stanford, Los Angeles, Leipzig and Philadelphia (d. Novotna) to return to the top 20. She was the year's No. 1 doubles player, reaching 16 f, of which she won 6 with regular partner Davenport and 1 each with Hingis and Pierce. She and Davenport were r/u in all 4 GS, and although each of those titles eluded them, they finished the year in triumph by winning Chase Champs. She qualified there in singles, too, but lost 1r to Tauziat. **1998 HIGHLIGHTS – SINGLES: Australian Open 3r** (d. Appelmans [seed 12] 2–6 6–2 6–3, Grande 6–4 6–4, lost Schett 6–3 6–1), **French Open 2r** (d. Labat 6–1 7–5, lost Majoli [seed 10] 6–3 6–4), **Wimbledon sf** [unseeded] (d. McQuillan 7–5 6–4, Miyagi 6–1 6–3, Graf [seed 4] 6–4 7–5, Oremans 6–4 6–2, Seles [seed 6] 7–6 6–2, lost Tauziat [seed 16] 1–6 7–6 6–3), **US Open 2r** (d. McQuillan 3–6 6–3 ret, lost Raymond 6–2 6–2); **sf** Eastbourne (d. Vento 7–5 6–3, V. Williams 6–2 6–1, Serna 7–6 6–2, lost Novotna 6–2 6–1), **sf** Prague (d. Sanchez Lorenzo 6–4 6–2, Pastikova 7–5 3–6 6–1, Mauresmo 6–3 6–2, lost Testud 6–3 4–6 6–4). **1998 HIGHLIGHTS – DOUBLES:** (with Davenport unless stated) **r/u Australian Open** (lost Hingis/Lucic 6–4 2–6 6–3), **r/u French Open** (lost Hingis/Novotna 6–1 7–6), **r/u Wimbledon** (lost Hingis/Novotna 6–3 3–6 8–6), **r/u US Open** (lost Hingis/Novotna 6–3 6–3); **won** Indian Wells (d. Fusai/Tauziat 6–4 2–6 6–4), **won** Berlin (d. Fusai/Tauziat 6–3 6–0), **won** Stanford (d. Neiland/Tatarkova 6–4 6–4), **won** San Diego (d. Fusai/Tauziat 6–2 6–1), (with Hingis) **won** Los Angeles (d. Tanasugarn/Tatarkova 6–4 6–2), **won** Filderstadt (d. Kournikova/Sanchez-Vicario 6–4 6–2), (with Pierce) **won** Moscow (d. Raymond/Stubbs 6–3 6–4), **won** Chase Champs (d. Fusai/Tauziat 6–7 7–5 6–3); **r/u** Tokyo Pan Pacific (lost Hingis/Lucic 7–5 6–4), (with Sanchez-Vicario) **r/u** LIPC (lost Hingis/Novotna 6–2 3–6 6–3), (with Sanchez-Vicario) **r/u** Eastbourne (lost De Swardt/Novotna 6–1 6–3), (with Seles) **r/u** Philadelphia (lost Likhovtseva/Sugiyama 7–5 4–6 6–2). **CAREER HIGHLIGHTS – SINGLES: French Open – r/u 1988** (d. Golarsa, Field, Gurney, Navratilova 6–3 7–6, Sukova 6–2 6–3, Provis 6–3 6–7 7–5, lost Graf 6–0 6–0), **qf 1992** [unseeded] (d. Kohde-Kilsch, Appelmans 6–1 7–6, Mag. Maleeva, Hack, lost Graf 6–3 6–7 6–3); **Wimbledon – sf 1998, qf 1990** (d. Harper, G. Fernandez, Magers 2–6 6–2 6–4, Schultz 6–2 6–2, lost Sabatini 6–2 2–6 8–6), **qf 1992** [unseeded] (d. Herreman, Martinez [seed 8] 6–3 5–7 6–4, McNeil, Garrison 6–2 3–6 6–1, lost Graf 6–3 6–1), **qf 1993** [unseeded] (d. K. Maleeva 7–5 4–6 6–3, Strnadova 6–3 6–2, Appelmans 6–3 6–4, Garrison-Jackson 7–5 6–2, lost Navratilova 6–3 6–1); **Australian Open – qf 1995** (d. Fusai 6–4 6–0, Farina 6–4 6–2, Wiesner 4–6 7–6 6–4, Nagatsuka 3–6 6–3 6–1, lost Pierce 6–1 6–4); **US Open – qf 1993** [unseeded] (d. Smylie 6–3 6–2, Raymond 6–4 6–1, Garrison-Jackson 6–4 6–3, Gaidano 6–0 6–2, lost Sanchez-Vicario 3–0 ret). **CAREER HIGHLIGHTS – DOUBLES:** (with G. Fernandez unless stated) **Australian Open – won 1993** (d. Shriver/Smylie 6–4 6–3), **won 1994** (d. Fendick/McGrath 6–3 4–6 6–4), (with Hingis) **won 1997** (d. Davenport/Raymond 6–2 6–2), **r/u 1995** (lost Novotna/Sanchez-Vicario 6–3 6–7 6–4), (with Davenport) **r/u 1998**; **French Open** – (with Savchenko-Neiland) **won 1989** (d. Graf/Sabatini 6–4 6–4), **won 1992** (d. Martinez/Sanchez-Vicario 6–3 6–2), **won 1993** (d. Neiland/Novotna 6–3 7–5), **won 1994** (d. Davenport/Raymond 6–2 6–2), **won 1995** (d. Novotna/Sanchez-Vicario 6–7 6–4 7–5), **won 1997** (d. M. J. Fernandez/Raymond 6–2 6–3), (with Savchenko-Neiland) **r/u 1990** (lost Novotna/Sukova 6–4 7–5), (with Savchenko-Neiland) **r/u 1991** (lost G. Fernandez/Novotna 6–4 6–0), **r/u 1996** (lost Davenport/M. J. Fernandez 6–2 6–1), (with Davenport) **r/u 1998**; **Wimbledon** – (with Savchenko-Neiland) **won 1991** (d. G. Fernandez/Novotna 6–4 3–6 6–4), **won 1992** (d. Novotna/Savchenko-Neiland 6–4 6–1), **won 1993** (d. Neiland/ Novotna 6–4 6–7 6–4), **won 1994** (d. Novotna/Sanchez-Vicario 6–4 6–1), **won 1997** (d. Arendt/Bollegraf 7–6 6–4), (with Savchenko-Neiland) **r/u 1988** (lost Graf/Sabatini 6–3 1–6 12–10), (with Savchenko-Neiland) **r/u 1989** (lost Novotna/Sukova 6–1 6–2), **r/u 1995** (lost Novotna/Sanchez-Vicario 5–7 7–5 6–4), (with Davenport) **r/u 1998; US Open** – (with Shriver) **won 1991** (d. Savchenko/Novotna 6–4 4–6 7–6), **won 1992** (d. Novotna/ Savchenko-Neiland 7–6 6–1), **won 1995** (d. Schultz/McCarthy 7–5 6–3), **won 1996** (d. Novotna/Sanchez-Vicario 1–6 6–1 6–4), **r/u 1997** (lost Davenport/Novotna 6–3 6–4), (with Davenport) **r/u 1998**; **VS/Chase Champs – won 1993** (d. Neiland/Novotna 6–3 7–5), **won 1994** (d. Novotna/Sanchez-Vicario 6–3 6–7 6–3), (with Davenport) **won 1998,** (with Savchenko-Neiland) **r/u 1988** (lost Navratilova/Shriver 6–3 6–4), (with Savchenko-Neiland) **r/u 1989** (lost Navratilova/Shriver 6–3 6–2). **MIXED DOUBLES: Australian Open** – (with Pugh) **won 1990** (d. R. Leach/Garrison 4–6 6–2 6–3), (with Leach) **won 1995** (d. Suk/G. Fernandez 7–6 6–7 6–4).

All-Time Greats

David Gray and John Barrett

DAPHNE JESSIE **AKHURST** (Australia)
Born 22/4/03. Died 10/1/33. Became Mrs.R.S.Cozens (1930). The first of Australia's great women champions, she won five Australian singles titles (***1925/26/28/29/30***), five doubles titles with four different partners – S.Lance (***1924***), R.Harper (***1925***), Esna Boyd (***1928***) and L.M. Bickerton (***1929/31***), plus four mixed with three partners – J.Willard (***1924/25***), Jean Borotra (***1928***) and E.F. Moon (***1929***). She first travelled to Europe in ***1925*** and got to the quarter-finals at Wimbledon. Three years later she returned and reached the semi-finals after being a quarter-finalist in Paris, results which earned her an unofficial world ranking of No.3 that year. JB

WILMER LAWSON **ALLISON** (USA)
Born 8/12/04. Died 20/4/77. One of the greatest and most spectacular of American doubles specialists, he also gained some notable singles successes. Possessing a fierce smash, a serve with the 'kick of a Texas mustang', considerable power on the volley, and a fine backhand drive, he found an ideal doubles partner in John Van Ryn. They won at Wimbledon in ***1929–30*** and were runners-up in ***1935***. They took the US title in ***1931*** and ***1935*** and reached the final in ***1930/32/34/36***. His singles form was less consistent, but on his day could play brilliantly. He defeated Perry to win the US title in ***1935***, and in ***1930***, after beating Cochet, he was runner-up to Tilden at Wimbledon. Between ***1929–35*** he played in 45 D Cup rubbers, winning 18 out of 29 singles and 14 of his 16 doubles.

JOSEPH ASBOTH (Hungary)
Born 18/9/17. A stylish right-hander whose victory in the ***1947*** French singles, when he beat Petra, Tom Brown and Sturgess, was Hungary's most important tennis success before their victory in the Saab King's Cup in 1976; 7 times nat champ; 6 times winner of the Hungarian int title; he played 1st at Wimbledon in ***1939*** and impressed those who saw him against Austin in 1r. Lost to Bromwich in the ***1948*** sfs. From ***1938–57*** he played 41 D Cup rubbers in 16 ties, winning 18 of his 30 singles and 6 of 11 doubles.

ARTHUR ROBERT **ASHE** (USA)
Born 10/7/43. Died 13/2/93. A cool, thoughtful, dogged competitor, he was the first black American to win the Wimbledon men's singles title and, in ***1968***, playing as an amateur, he became the first US Open champion. Always happier on fast courts, he tried hard to succeed on clay but endured regular disappointments in Paris and never progressed further than the semi-finals (***1971***) in Rome. He was a semi-finalist at Wimbledon ***1968–69*** before surprising Connors in the ***1975*** final. He defeated Okker to win the US title in ***1968*** but in ***1972*** lost to Nastase after leading by two sets to one and 4–2 in the final. He won Australian singles ***1970*** and the WCT title ***1975***. Refused a visa to South Africa in ***1970***, he broke through apartheid laws to play in Johannesburg ***1973***, losing to Connors in the final and winning the doubles with Okker. After missing most of the ***1977*** season, he regained his place among the leaders of the circuit in ***1978*** and reached match-point against McEnroe in the Masters final. Between ***1963–78***, he appeared in 18 D Cup ties, winning 27 out of 32 singles and one of two doubles. US D Cup captain ***1980–85***, following his retirement from active play owing to a heart condition that had necessitated triple by-pass surgery. Started Arthur Ashe Foundation for the defeat of Aids, the sickness that claimed his life following a transfusion of contaminated blood during his heart operations.

CILLY AUSSEM (Germany)
Born 4/1/09. Died 22/3/63. Later the Contessa della Corta Brae (1936). The first German to win the women's singles at Wimbledon. Her strokes were not strong but she was a model of steadiness and persistence. 'Quite small and more of a girl in appearance with round brown eyes and a cherub face', wrote Helen Wills. 'Her agility on court and the distance that she covers in spite of her shortness are really astonishing.' ***1931*** – when the Californian did not compete – was her best year. She beat Betty Nuthall in the French f and then defeated Hilde Krahwinkel in Wimbledon's only all-German final. That was a disappointing match, because both women were handicapped by blistered feet. Her victory compensated for an unlucky failure in ***1930***. Then she slipped and sprained an ankle at 4–4 in the fs of her sf against Elizabeth Ryan and had to be carried from the court.

HENRY WILFRED ('**BUNNY**') **AUSTIN** (Great Britain)
Born 26/8/06. Bunny Austin's Wimbledon record was remarkable (and unlucky), but his most important contribution to British tennis was in the D Cup. The possessor of elegant groundstrokes, which compensated for a lack of power in his serving and smashing, he played many of the crucial singles, alongside Perry, in Britain's successful campaigns in the ***1930s***. A former Cambridge Univ captain, he played in 24 ties between ***1929–37***, winning 36 of his 48 rubbers, all singles. He won 8 rubbers out of 12 and 5 out of 8 'live' rubbers in his 6

Challenge Rounds. At Wimbledon he failed only once to reach the qf or go further between ***1929–39***. R/u to Vines ***1932*** and Budge ***1938***, in sf ***1929*** and ***1936/37***, and r/u to Henkel in ***1937*** French singles.

TRACY ANN **AUSTIN** (USA)
Born 12/12/62. Now Mrs. Scott Holt (married on 17th April 1993). An infant prodigy with 25 national age group titles to her name from the 12s to 18s, her meteoric rise under the coaching of Robert Lansdorp inspired a whole generation of teenage wonders. The youngest member of a keen tennis playing family, whose sister Pam and three brothers, Jeff, John and Doug were all tournament players, Tracy defeated Chris Evert for the US Open title in ***1979*** to become, at 16 years 9 months, the youngest ever champion there. The following year her relentless baseline driving, single-handed on the forehand, two-handed on the backhand, plus her excellent court coverage, earned her the No.1 ranking on the WTA computer, ending the four year reign of Evert and Martina Navratilova. In ***1981*** she won a second US Open title at the expense of Navratilova and, with 29 titles to her name, seemed destined to rule the game. But a series of back and neck injuries curtailed her appearances in ***1983*** and she retired from the game in February ***1984***, the victim of physical burn-out. She returned to the Tour in doubles during ***1988*** and had just started to play singles again in ***1989*** when she broke a leg in a motor accident, an injury that required surgery. This delayed her return until ***1993*** when she competed in a few tournaments and played Team Tennis for Raleigh Edge. JB

WILFRED BADDELEY (Great Britain)
Born 11/1/1872. Died 24/1/1929. Youngest winner – at 19 years, 5 months and 23 days – of Wimbledon singles in ***1891*** until Becker in ***1985***. Also won singles in ***1892/95***, and doubles (with twin brother Herbert) ***1891/94/95/96***.

MARCEL BERNARD (France)
Born 18/ 5/14. Died 28/4/94. Shrewd and stylish, a canny left-hander with considerable touch, he is one of only two French players to have won in Paris since the days of the 'Musketeers' (the other is Noah, ***1983***); demonstrated his promise early, reaching the French singles sf and, with Boussus, the doubles in ***1932***, still in sufficient form to be chosen for the French D Cup team in ***1956***. In ***1946*** he won 5 set matches against Petra in the sf and Drobny in the final to take the French title; in sf on 3 other occasions; won the doubles with Borotra (***1936***) and with Petra (***1946***) and the mixed with Lollette Payot (***1935***) and Billie Yorke (***1936***). Between ***1935–56*** he played 42 D Cup rubbers in 25 ties (singles 13–8, doubles 16–5) and he also served as President of the French Tennis Federation.

PAULINE MAY **BETZ** (USA)
Born 6/8/19. Now Mrs Addie (1949). An agile, athletic competitor, who might have gained many more titles if the war had not interrupted international competition. She was ranked eighth in the US in ***1939*** and was the most successful player in wartime competitions there, winning the national title from ***1942–44***. She won Wimbledon at a cost of only 20 games in ***1946***, defeating Louise Brough 6–2 6–4 in the final. She and Miss Hart were runners-up to Miss Brough and Miss Osborne in the doubles and, if she was disappointed in Paris, where Miss Osborne beat her 1–6 8–6 7–5 in the final, after saving two match-points with drop-shots at 5–6 in the second set, she asserted her supremacy again at Forest Hills by defeating Doris Hart 11–9 6–3 in the final. Soon afterwards she turned professional.

BLANCHE BINGLEY (Great Britain)
Born 3/11/1863. Died 6/8/1946. Became Mrs Hillyard (1887). One of the determined pioneers of women's tennis. She competed in the first women's tournament at Wimbledon in ***1884*** and lost to Maud Watson, the eventual champion, in sfs. The following year Miss Watson defeated her in f, but she avenged those failures by beating the champion in the Challenge Round in ***1886***. That was the first of her six victories. Further successes followed in ***1889/94/97/99*** and ***1900***. Only Lottie Dod, who retired in ***1893***, troubled her until Mrs Sterry ended her supremacy in ***1901***. Like many early players, her game was founded on a powerful forehand and strict command of length. A reluctant volleyer who invariably ran round her backhand, she was so quick and so fit that she was difficult to outmanoeuvre. She wore white gloves to give her a better grip and her follow-through on the forehand was said to have been 'so complete that her left shoulder was often a mass of bruises from the impact of the racket'. She married Commander G. W. Hillyard, secretary of the All England Club from ***1907–24***; altogether she competed in the Championships 24 times.

PENELOPE **DORA** HARVEY **BOOTHBY** (Great Britain)
Born 2/8/1881. Died 22/2/1970. Became Mrs Geen (1914). One of the group of players from the county of Middlesex who dominated the early years of women's tennis at Wimbledon. In ***1909*** she won one of the most exciting of the pre-***1914*** f, defeating Miss A. M. Morton 6–4 4–6 8–6 'Few closer or more interesting struggles have ever been witnessed on the famous old court', wrote G. W. Hillyard. She lost the most dismal contest in the history of the Championships to Mrs Lambert Chambers, who beat her 6–0 6–0, in the ***1911*** Challenge Round. Mrs Lambert Chambers had beaten her by the same score at the Beckenham tournament two weeks earlier and had allowed her only four games in the Challenge Round in ***1910***. Somewhat fortunately she and Mrs McNair became Wimbledon's first women's doubles champions in 1913. They were down 2–6 2–4 to Mrs Lambert Chambers and Mrs Sterry in the final when Mrs Sterry fell and retired with a torn tendon. She and Mrs McNair were also semi-finalists in 1922.

BJORN RUNE **BORG** (Sweden)
Born 6/6/56. One of the coolest match players the game has ever known, he matured early, winning his first important title, the ***1974*** Italian Open, shortly before his 18th birthday and the first of his six French Championships just after it. With fierce topspin on both his forehand and his double-handed backhand, a powerful serve and speedy court coverage plus an indomitable will to win, he was virtually invincible on European clay between ***1974–81*** adding the French Open in ***1975/78/79/80/81*** and a second Italian title in ***1978*** as well as the US Pro Champion-ship on US clay in ***1974/75/76***. Never an instinctive volleyer, he confounded those observers who thought his game was unsuited to grass by setting a modern record at Wimbledon where he won five successive titles between ***1976–80***. Only William Renshaw, in the days of the Challenge Round, won more (***1881–86***). He learned to win indoors, taking the WCT title in ***1976*** and the Masters twice (***1979/80***) and leading Sweden to their first D Cup success, a 3–2 victory over Czechoslovakia in Stockholm in ***1975***. But he never solved the problems of the high, fast bounce and positive foothold of US hard courts. Four times he was beaten in the US Open final, twice by Connors (***1976/78***) and twice by McEnroe (***1980/81***), the last three being on asphalt at Flushing Meadows. By the autumn of ***1981*** he felt burnt out and virtually retired from the mainstream, playing only exhibitions and special events. Although he attempted two comebacks, in ***1982/84*** (coincidentally, he lost both times to Henri Leconte, in Monte Carlo and Stuttgart), he could no longer make the total commitment and turned to other interests. Seven years later he again attempted a return but fell in his first match to Jordi Arrese in Monte Carlo and competed no more in ***1991***. His legacy to Swedish tennis is immeasurable for he sparked the flame that has burned so brightly ever since through Wilander, Sundstrom, Jarryd, Nystrom and Edberg. His style of errorless, counter-attacking topspin inspired a whole generation of players around the world. JB

JEAN ROBERT **BOROTRA** (France)
Born 13/8/1898. Died 17/7/94. A brilliantly agile volleyer and a shrewd player. One of the 'Four Musketeers' who won the D Cup for France from ***1927–32***. Enthusiastic and popular, he continued to play competitive lawn tennis long past his 90th year. He represented France in every International Club match against Britain from the first in ***1929*** to his 116th and last in ***1993***. Won Wimbledon singles ***1924/26*** and doubles (with R. Lacoste) ***1925*** and (with J. Brugnon) ***1932/33***. French singles ***1924/31***, and the doubles 6 times – (with Lacoste) ***1924/25/29***, (with Brugnon) ***1928/34***, (with Bernard) ***1936***. Won Australian singles and doubles (with Brugnon) ***1928***. Had long and spectacular covered court record, winning French singles title 12 times, British 11, and US 4. Played 54 D Cup rubbers ***1922–47***, winning 19 of 31 singles and 17 of 23 doubles rubbers in 32 ties.

JOHN EDWARD **BROMWICH** (Australia)
Born 14/11/18. A gracefully unorthodox player whose career might have been even more successful if it had not been interrupted by World War II. Ambidextrous but using both hands on the forehand, he used a very light, softly strung racket to control the ball with great subtlety. He won the Australian singles in ***1939*** and regained the title from Quist in ***1946***. Those were his only major singles victories, although he was agonisingly close to success in f of ***1948*** Wimbledon when he lost to Falkenburg after leading 5–2 in the fs and holding three match-points. But it was in doubles, mostly with Quist or Sedgman, that he earned most honours. He won at Wimbledon in ***1948*** (with Sedgman) ***1950*** (with Quist), took the US title three times, and he and Quist ruled in Australia from ***1938–40*** and ***1946–50***. Won the Wimbledon mixed with Louise Brough, ***1947/48***, and played in 51 D Cup rubbers between ***1937–50***, winning 19 of his 30 singles and 20 of his 21 doubles in 23 ties.

NORMAN EVERARD **BROOKES** (Australia)
Born 14/11/1877. Died 28/9/1968. The first overseas winner of men's singles at Wimbledon. Left-handed and a notable volleyer, he lost to H. L. Doherty in Challenge Round on first visit to Wimbledon ***1905***. Won singles and doubles (with A. F. Wilding) ***1907*** and ***1914*** and Australian singles in ***1911*** and doubles in ***1924*** with J. O. Anderson. With Wilding won the D Cup for Australasia in ***1907***. Between ***1905–20*** he played 39 rubbers and was 6 times a member of a side which won the Challenge Round. Returned to Wimbledon in ***1924*** at 46 and reached the 4r. Nicknamed 'The Wizard' he received the French Legion of Honour for his services as a captain in the British Army in World War One, and in ***1939*** he was knighted.

ALTHEA **LOUISE BROUGH** (USA)
Born 11/3/23. Now Mrs Clapp (1958). An aggressive server and volleyer, she played a major part in establishing American domination of women's tennis immediately after World War II. Won Wimbledon singles ***1948/49/50*** and again in ***1955*** after the retirement of Maureen Connolly (who beat her in ***1952*** and ***1954*** f), She also won US in ***1947***, and Australian, ***1950***. She and Margaret Osborne du Pont formed a redoubtable doubles partnership, winning 5 times at Wimbledon (***1946/48/49/50/54***) and 3 times in Paris, (***1946/47/49***) and holding the US title 12 times from ***1942–50*** and ***1955–57***. She was mixed doubles champ at Wimbledon with Tom Brown (***1946***), Bromwich (***1947/48***) and Sturgess (***1950***) and took all 3 titles in ***1948*** and ***1950***. She played 22 W Cup rubbers between ***1946–57*** and was never beaten.

JACQUES (**'TOTO'**) **BRUGNON** (France)
Born 11/5/1895. Died 20/3/1978. The doubles specialist of the 'Four Musketeers', he gained most of his early success with Cochet and then formed a partnership with Borotra, which was still capable of reaching the

1939 French f, when he was 44 and Borotra 40, and coming three times within a point of the title. He and Borotra returned to Wimbledon and reached the 3r in ***1948***. Won Wimbledon doubles with Cochet (***1926/28***) and Borotra (***1932/33***). Between ***1927–34*** won French doubles 3 times with Cochet (***1927/30/32***) and twice with Borotra (***1928/34***). Also Australian doubles with Borotra (***1928***). Reached singles sf at Wimbledon, ***1926***. Played 31 D Cup doubles (winning 22) and 6 singles (winning 4) in 31 ties ***1921–34***.

JOHN DONALD ('**DON**') **BUDGE** (USA)
Born 13/6/15. The first player to bring off the Grand Slam of the 4 historic singles titles in one year – ***1938*** – after which he immediately turned professional. A relentless competitor with a majestic backhand he won all 3 titles at Wimbledon in ***1937*** and ***1938***, the doubles with G. Mako and mixed with Alice Marble. Won US singles ***1937/38*** and doubles with Mako ***1936/38***. plus French and Australian singles ***1938*** and won 19 out of 21 singles and 6 out of 8 doubles rubbers in 11 D Cup ties from ***1935*** to ***1938***.

MARIA ESTHER ANDION **BUENO** (Brazil)
Born 11/10/39. The most gracefully artistic of post-war women's champions. For nearly a decade her rivalry with Margaret Court provided the principal excitement of the women's game, but at the end she was plagued by injury. Won Wimbledon singles ***1959/60/64***, and doubles (with Althea Gibson) ***1958***, (with Darlene Hard) ***1960/63***, (with Billie Jean King) ***1965***, and (with Nancy Gunter) ***1966***. US singles ***1959/63/64/66*** and doubles (with Darlene Hard) ***1960/62***, (with Nancy Gunter) ***1966***, and (with Margaret Court) ***1968***. French doubles (with Darlene Hard) ***1960***. Australian doubles (with Christine Truman) ***1960***. Italian singles, ***1958/61/65***.

DOROTHEA KATHERINE **CHAMBERS** (Great Britain)
Born 3/9/1878. Died 7/1/1960. Nee Douglass. Married Robert Lambert Chambers in 1907. The most successful British woman player before 1914, she won Wimbledon singles 7 times and lost dramatically to Suzanne Lenglen in 1919 Challenge Round after holding 2 match-points. Played in 1926 W Cup – 23 years after first success at Wimbledon. The daughter of an Ealing vicar, she became a coach in 1928. Won Wimbledon singles ***1903/04/06/10/11/13/14***, the first mother to do so, and reached f of ladies' doubles in ***1913***, its first year.

HENRI JEAN **COCHET** (France)
Born 14/12/01. Died 1/4/87. The great instinctive genius of lawn tennis, swift and imagin-ative, a master of the volley and half-volley, whose play could rise to dizzy heights and sometimes slip to unexpected disaster. Won Wimbledon singles ***1927/29*** and doubles (with J. Brugnon) ***1926/28***. US singles ***1928***. French singles ***1922/26/28/30/32*** and doubles (with Brugnon) ***1927/30/32***. With the other 'Musketeers', he played successfully in 6 Challenge Rounds. Between ***1922*** and ***1933***, when he turned professional, he won 34 of 42 D Cup singles rubbers and 10 out of 16 doubles from 26 ties. After the war reinstated as an amateur.

MAUREEN ('LITTLE MO') CATHERINE **CONNOLLY** (USA)
Born 17/9/34. Died 21/6/69. Became Mrs. Norman Brinker (1955). The most determined and concentrated of post-war women's champions she hit her groundstrokes with remorseless accuracy. Won US singles in ***1951*** at the age of 16 and thereafter lost only 4 matches – 2 to Doris Hart, one to Shirley Fry, and another to Beverley Fleitz – before she broke her leg in a riding accident in ***1954*** and retired. She was never beaten in singles at Wimbledon, winning ***1952/53/54***. She won US singles ***1951/52/53*** French singles ***1953/54*** and (with Mrs H. C. Hopman) doubles ***1954***. Australian singles and doubles (with Julie Sampson) ***1953*** Italian singles ***1954***. She won all 9 of her W Cup rubbers and in ***1953*** she was the first woman to bring off the Grand Slam of the 4 major singles titles in the same year.

JAMES ('**JIMMY**') SCOTT **CONNORS** (USA)
Born 2/9/52. One of the most durable of champions and a natural entertainer, he grew up in Bellville, Illinois where his mother Gloria, herself a fine player, and his grandmother, instilled the never-say-die attitude that was to make him one of the most competitive players of all time. Moving to California as a teenager, he was guided by the two Pancho's – Gonzales and Segura – and in ***1971*** won the NCAA Championships as a freshman at UCLA. A year later in Jacksonville, shrewdly guided by his manager Bill Riordan, he won his first professional title. Seventeen years later, in Tel Aviv, he won his last. It was his 109th tournament success – a record for men. Altogether he had spent 268 weeks as the world's No.1 ranked player (second only to Lendl's 270). His 160 consecutive weeks at the top from 29/7/74 to 23/8/77 was a world record. An aggressive left-hander with a lethal double-handed backhand, he was a natural 'street fighter', whose early vulgarity (which diminished with age), was ignored by his fans and forgiven by those who recognised his extraordinary ability as a fearless match player. The first Grand Slam title he won was the ***1973*** Wimbledon doubles, with Ilie Nastase, who also partnered him to victory in the ***1975*** US Open doubles. His service returns and passing shots were among the greatest ever seen and brought him one Australian (***1974***), two Wimbledon (***1974***,***1982***) and five US Open (***1974***,***1976***,***1978***,***1982***,***1983***) singles titles. He is the only man to have won the US title on all three surfaces – grass, clay and hard courts. His failure to win a major international title on clay was the only blemish on an otherwise brilliant career. JB

ASHLEY JOHN **COOPER** (Australia)
Born 15/9/36. A strong and determined competitor who maintained Australia's command of the international game after Hoad and Rosewall turned professional. After being overwhelmed by Hoad in the ***1957*** f at Wimbledon, he returned to beat Fraser in a stern test of endurance in 1958. He was US champion **1958** and won Australian ***1957–58***. His doubles victories included Australia ***1958***, France ***1957–58*** and US **1958**. He played singles when Australia successfully defended the D Cup in ***1957*** and in ***1958*** when Australia lost to the USA in Brisbane, winning one rubber in each match. He beat Seixas and lost to Mackay ***1957*** and beat Mackay and lost to Olmedo ***1958***.

CHARLOTTE REINAGLE **COOPER** (Great Britain)
Born 22/9/1870. Died 10/10/1966. Became Mrs Sterry (1901). One of the first successful women volleyers, she won at Wimbledon ***1895/96/98/1901/08***. Overshadowed at first by Mrs Hillyard – her first three victories were gained in years when the older player did not compete – she defeated her at last in ***1901***, the year of her marriage, after losing to Mrs Hillyard in four previous matches at the Championships. In ***1902*** she lost in the famous re-played Challenge Round to Muriel Robb (they stopped at 4–6 13–11 on the first evening, then began again and Miss Robb won 7–5 6–1) and then regained the title in ***1908*** after beating Mrs Lambert Chambers in the quarter-finals. She reached the All-Comers' final in ***1912*** and took Mrs McNair to 9–7 in the third set of a qf in ***1913***. Her attacking spirit delighted her contemporaries. 'Her smiling good temper and sportsmanship made her as popular a player as ever went on to the Centre Court', wrote Burrow. 'She had a constitution like the proverbial ostrich. She never knew what it was to be tired and was never sick or sorry', said Hillyard.

THELMA DOROTHY **COYNE** (Australia)
Born 14/10/18 Became Mrs.M.N. Long (30/1/41). A great all-rounder whose career coincided with that of Nancy Bolton who became a great friend and rival. She first reached the Australian final in ***1940*** where Bolton beat her, as she did again in ***1951***. The following year (***1952***) she won the first of two Australian titles (the other was in ***1954***). Ten of her twelve Australian doubles titles were won with Bolton (***1936/37/38/39/40/47/48/49/51/52***) and the other two with Mary Hawton (***1956/58***). Her four mixed titles were won with George Worthington (***1951/52/55***) and Rex Hartwig (***1954***). Her lone success outside Australia came in ***1956*** when she combined with Chile's Luis Ayala to win the French mixed title. JB

JOHN ('**JACK**') HERBERT **CRAWFORD** (Australia)
Born 22/3/08. Died 10/9/91. Classic stylist, he beat H. E. Vines in ***1933*** in one of the greatest of all Wimbledon f. Won Wimbledon doubles (with A. K. Quist) ***1935***. French singles ***1933*** and doubles (with Quist) ***1935***, Australian singles ***1931/33*** and doubles (with H. C. Hopman) ***1929/30***, (with E. F. Moon) ***1932***, and (with V. B. McGrath) ***1935***. Won 36 out of 58 D Cup rubbers (23–16 singles, 13–5 doubles) between ***1928–37***.

DWIGHT FILLEY **DAVIS** (USA)
Born 5/7/1879. Died 28/11/1945. The donor of the D Cup, the trophy at stake in the International Team Championship. A Harvard undergraduate, he played against the British Isles in the first two matches of that competition, winning a single and partnering Holcombe Ward successfully in the doubles in ***1900*** and, with H. Ward again, losing to the Dohertys in the doubles in ***1902***. A left-hander, he won the US doubles with H. Ward from ***1899–1901***, retiring undefeated, and also the All-Comers' final at Wimbledon with Ward in ***1901***, only to fall to the Dohertys in the Challenge Round. He was President of the US LTA in ***1923***, US Secretary of War ***1925–29*** and later Governor-General of the Philippines.

MAXIME ('**MAX**') OMER **DECUGIS** (France)
Born 24/9/1882. Died 6/9/1978. The first great French player. He spent his schooldays in England and won his first tournaments there. Short, quick, and wiry, he was an aggressive competitor, whom Laurie Doherty described as 'the most promising young player in the world'. He dominated French tennis from ***1903***, when he won in Paris for the first time, to the outbreak of World War I, winning the singles ***1903/04/07/09/12/14***, and the doubles from ***1902–14*** and again in ***1920*** when the Champs were resumed. He was still playing well enough to reach the singles final in ***1923*** when he was 41. By that time the age of the 'Musketeers' was dawning. Although he competed regularly at Wimbledon, he never progressed beyond the singles sf (***1911/12***) but, with Gobert, he gained France's first title by winning the doubles in ***1911***.

CHARLOTTE ('**LOTTIE**') **DOD** (Great Britain)
Born 24/9/1871. Died 27/6/1960. The first lawn tennis prodigy. Won the first of 5 Wimbledon titles in ***1887*** from a field of 5 challengers at the age of 15 years and 10 months. When she retired, she became an international golfer and hockey player. Nicknamed the 'Little Wonder', she won Wimbledon singles ***1887/88/91/92/93*** in years when there were never more than 9 players in the All-Comers' draw.

HUGH **LAURENCE DOHERTY** (Great Britain)
Born London, 8/10/1875. Died 21/8/1919. Learnt game with elder brother, Reginald Frank ('Reggie'), at Westminster School. Played for Cambridge Univ against Oxford in ***1896–98*** and developed into one of the most spectacular, aggressive, stylish, and successful of British players. 'Laurie' Doherty was celebrated for smashing and volleying, and for speed about the court. With his brother, formed one of the greatest doubles

partnerships in the history of the game. Won All-Comers' singles at Wimbledon, ***1898***, and singles champ ***1902–06***. Doubles champ (with R. F. Doherty) ***1897–1901***, ***1903–05***. First overseas player to win US singles, ***1903***, and doubles, ***1902/03***. In 5 D Cup Challenge Rounds, ***1902–06***, he was never beaten, winning 7 singles rubbers and 5 doubles.

REGINALD FRANK **DOHERTY** (Great Britain)
Born London, 14/10/1872. Died 29/12/1910. The senior partner of the great Doherty combination and the most notable stylist of early lawn tennis. Contemporary observers called his backhand, produced with back swing, full follow-through and remarkable touch, 'a model of perfection'. Was Wimbledon singles champ ***1897–1900*** and doubles champ ***1897–1901*** and ***1903–05***. Reached the doubles Challenge Round at Wimbledon for first time with H. A. Nisbet in ***1896***. Thereafter he and his brother, H. L. Doherty, were beaten only by S. H. Smith and F. L. Riseley at Wimbledon. They lost to this pair in ***1902***, then beat them in the next three Challenge Rounds before falling to them again in ***1906***. The Dohertys won the US doubles in ***1902/03***. Won South African singles and doubles ***1909***.

JAROSLAV DROBNY (Great Britain)
Born 12/10/21. Exiled himself from Czechoslovakia in ***1949***, became Egyptian subject in ***1950*** and a naturalised Briton in ***1960***. One of the great post-war clay court competitors with tremendous left-hand serve and smash, and delicate touch, he played in some of Wimbledon's most dramatic and emotional matches and eventually won the singles in ***1954*** at the age of 33. In ***1946*** he beat Kramer, the favourite in 4 r and lost to Geoff Brown (AUS) in sf; he lost to Schroeder in the ***1949*** f; in ***1950*** he let a two-set lead slip against Sedgman; Mottram surprised him in **1951**; he fell to Sedgman again in the ***1952*** f; and in ***1953*** he never recovered from beating Patty 8–6 16–18 3–6 8–6 12–10 in Wimbledon's second longest singles. The following year, when his chance seemed to be slipping away, he beat Rosewall, then 19, in f. He won in Paris in ***1951/52*** (after another series of dramatic failures), Italy ***1950/51/53*** and Germany ***1950***. Between ***1946–49*** he won 37 of his 43 D Cup rubbers in 15 ties, (24–4 singles, 13–2 doubles).

FRANCOISE DURR (France)
Born 25/12/42. Now Mrs Browning (1975). The outstanding French woman player of the 1960s and 1970s. Shrewd and unorthodox, particularly in her serve and on the backhand, she excelled in doubles. She gained her major singles successes in ***1967*** when she won the French and German titles and reached the US semi-finals, but in doubles won a host of titles with a variety of partners, including five successive French victories – with Gail Sheriff (later Mrs Chanfreau and now Mrs Lovera) ***1967*** and ***1970/71***, and with Ann Jones, ***1968/69***. Won US doubles ***1972*** with Betty Stove, and Italian and South African titles ***1969*** with Jones. She failed, however, in six Wimbledon doubles finals between ***1965–75***. Won Wimbledon mixed doubles with Tony Roche ***1976*** and the French with Jean-Claude Barclay in ***1968/71/73***.

STEFAN EDBERG (Sweden)
Born 19/1/96 in Vastervik, Sweden. One of the greatest of modern serve-and-volley players, he broke the Swedish double-handed mould created by Bjorn Borg when his first coach, Percy Rosberg (who had also coached Borg) advised him to change to a single-handed stroke because of his natural volleying ability. It was sound advice. In ***1983***, at the end of an outstanding junior career, he won the junior Grand Slam, the only time the feat has been achieved since the four major tournaments became Championship events in ***1975***. (Butch Buchholz had won all four in ***1958*** when they were invitation tournaments). Major honours soon followed. Revelling in the fast conditions of Australian grass he won the last two Opens played at Kooyong in December ***1985*** and January ***1987*** (no Championship was held in 1996 to accommodate a return to the traditional January date). A year later (***1988***) he won the first of his two Wimbledon titles, beating his great rival Boris Becker in the final, a success he would repeat in ***1990*** after losing to the German in the ***1989*** final. On 13th August ***1990*** he became the No.1 player in the world, a position he would hold for a total of 66 weeks in three spells until finally displaced by Jim Courier on 5 October ***1992***. In ***1991*** he won the first of two US Opens with a blistering display of attacking tennis against Courier that Edberg himself believed was his best ever performance. His second US win in ***1992***, against Pete Sampras, was his last major success in a career that brought him 41 titles altogether from the 77 singles finals he contested and 18 doubles titles from 29 finals. His three Grand Slam doubles success came ten years apart – the first two (with Jarryd) were in ***1987*** at the Australian and US Opens, the last (with Korda) at the ***1997*** Australian Open in his farewell year. His only major disappointment was the loss to Chang in the French Open final of ***1989***. In Davis Cup he was a member of Sweden's successful teams in ***1984***, ***1985*** and ***1994*** winning 35 of his 50 singles rubbers and 12 of his 20 doubles rubbers in 35 ties between ***1983*** and ***1997***. At the Olympic Games he won the ***1984*** demonstration event in Los Angeles and won bronze medals in singles and doubles at the Seoul Games in ***1988***. In Barcelona(***1992***) he carried the Swedish flag in the opening ceremony. In a long and distinguished career that earned him prize money alone totalling $20.6 million, he was respected as much for his impeccable manners and his chivalry in victory and defeat as for his beautiful backhand, fluid court coverage and wonderfully quick reflexes. It was no surprise when his peers named the annual ATP Tour Sportsmanship Award after him. JB

MARK RONALD **EDMONDSON** (Australia)
Born 28/6/54. On two golden afternoons on the fast grass at Kooyong, this burly battler from Gosford, NSW. beat first Ken Rosewall, then defending champion John Newcombe, to capture the ***1976*** Australian

Championships. Between ***1980*** and ***1984*** he won the Australian doubles title four times with three different partners (***1980***, ***1981*** with Warwick, ***1983*** with McNamee, ***1984*** with Stewart). Warwick was again his partner when he won the ***1985*** French doubles, his only other Grand Slam success. JB

ROY STANLEY **EMERSON** (Australia)
Born 3/11/36. A remarkable athlete, lean, keen, and 'trained to the last ounce', who led Australia's international challenge for five years after Laver turned professional in ***1962***. A Queenslander, his 28 Grand Slam titles (12 singles, 16 doubles) are a record for men. The only man to win singles and doubles at all four major championships, he won Wimbledon singles ***1964/65*** but injury in ***1966*** spoilt his chance of equalling Perry's record of three successive titles. Won the doubles with Fraser ***1959/61***, US singles ***1961/64*** and doubles ***1959/60*** (with Fraser) and ***1965/66*** (with Stolle), Australian singles ***1961*** and ***1963/64/65/66/67*** and doubles ***1962*** (with Fraser), ***1966*** (with Stolle) and ***1969*** (with Laver). On clay courts won the French singles ***1963/67***, Italian ***1959/61/66*** and German ***1967*** and his most interesting doubles achievement was to take the French title from ***1960–65*** with five different partners, Fraser ***1960/62***, Laver ***1961***, Santana ***1963***, Fletcher ***1964***, and Stolle ***1965***. He won 34 of his 38 D Cup rubbers (21–2 singles, 13–2 doubles) in 18 ties and played in 9 successive Challenge Rounds between ***1959–67***.

CHRISTINE ('**CHRIS**') MARIE **EVERT** (USA)
Born Fort Lauderdale, Fl., 21/12/54. Now Mrs Andy Mill (married 30 July 1988). Coached by father Jimmy in Fort Lauderdale to become the most consistent back-court player of her generation: she won at least one Grand Slam singles title every year from ***1974*** to ***1986*** during which period her friendly rivalry with Martina Navratilova dominated the women's game. When she and Jimmy Connors (who were engaged at the time) won the two Wimbledon singles titles in ***1974*** with their double-handed backhands they legitimised the stroke and set a fashion that became a world trend. Her metronomic consistency, unshakeable concentration and fearless resolve to go for her shots were legendary and earned her more professional titles (157) than any other player, male or female, during the Open era until Martina Navratilova passed that total in ***1992***, plus a fortune in prize money ($8,896,195). She competed for 19 consecutive years at the US Open and reached 9 finals, 8 semi-finals and was twice beaten in the quarter-finals, including her last year ***1989*** when she won her 101st match at these Championships, a record. As a sixteen-year-old, in ***1971***, she reached the first of four consecutive semi-finals on grass at Forest Hills. In ***1975/76/77*** she won the title there on US clay and repeated that success on hard courts at Flushing Meadows in ***1978/80/82***, by which time her first husband, John Lloyd (married 17 April 1979, divorced April 1987) had helped her to become a much better volleyer. In 13 challenges in Paris between ***1973*** and ***1988*** she won seven of the nine finals she contested (***1974/75/79/80/83/85/86***) and only in her last year failed to reach the semi-final, losing in the third round to Arantxa Sanchez Vicario. She competed at Wimbledon every year from ***1972–89*** and only in ***1983*** (when she was ill and lost to Kathy Jordan) did she fail to reach the semi-finals. She was the champion 3 times (***1974/76/81***), a finalist 7 times (***1973/78/79/80/82/84/85***) and a semi-finalist 7 times (***1972/75/77/86/87/88/89***). She competed in the Australian Open six times between ***1974–88***, winning the title in ***1982*** and ***1984*** and reaching the final in ***1974/81/85/88***. Her 18 Grand Slam singles titles place her equal fourth with Martina Navratilova behind Margaret Court (24), Steffi Graf (21) and Helen Wills Moody (19) on the list of great champions. Her streak of 125 consecutive wins on clay courts ***August 1973–May 1979*** is an all-time record and her prodigious achievement in reaching the semi-finals or better at 52 of her last 56 Grand Slams is unlikely ever to be equalled. She represented the United States eight times in the Fed Cup and won all but two of her 42 singles rubbers and 16 of 18 doubles rubbers in 42 ties between ***1977–89***. She was unbeaten in 26 W Cup singles rubbers and won 8 of the 12 doubles rubbers she contested in 13 ties between ***1971– 85***. JB

ROBERT ('**BOB**') **FALKENBURG** (USA)
Born 29/1/26. Won the US Junior Championship in ***1943–44*** and came to Europe in ***1947*** with the reputation of possessing the fastest service in the US. He won at Queen's Club, but lost to Pails in qf at Wimbledon and then won the doubles with Kramer, defeating Mottram and Sidwell in f. The following year ***1948*** he won one of Wimbledon's most dramatic f, defeating Bromwich 7–5 0–6 6–2 3–6 7–5 after saving three match-points as 3–5 in 5s. He was born in New York, learnt most of his tennis in Los Angeles and moved to Brazil, for whom he played in the D Cup on a residential qualification.

NEALE ANDREW **FRASER** (Australia)
Born 3/10/33. A consistently aggressive left-hander, with a plain, direct serve-and-volley game, he was trained by Harry Hopman, winning 18 of 21 D Cup rubbers (11–1 singles, 7–2 doubles) in 11 ties between ***1958*** and ***1963***, and later captained the Australian team which recaptured the trophy at Cleveland in ***1973*** and at Sydney in ***1977*** and Melbourne in ***1986***. Fraser started his Wimbledon career in the qualifying competition and ended by winning the singles in ***1960*** after a remarkable escape in the qf. when Butch Buchholz, who had held 5 match-points against him, retired with cramp. He won the doubles with Emerson ***1959/61*** and mixed with du Pont in ***1962*** – the year in which he and his brother, John, a Melbourne doctor, both reached the singles sf. Neither got through to the f. He won the US singles ***1959/60*** and doubles in ***1957*** (with Cooper) and ***1959/60*** (with Emerson), the French doubles in ***1958*** (with Cooper) and ***1960/62*** (with Emerson) and Australian doubles, in ***1957*** (with Hoad), ***1958*** (with Cooper) and ***1962*** (with Emerson).

Roy Emerson, from Black Butt, Queensland was the fittest of all the Australians trained by Davis Cup captain Harry Hopman and won 12 Grand Slam singles titles in the 1960s, a record on which Pete Sampras has set his sights.

SHIRLEY JUNE **FRY** (USA)
Born 30/6/27. Now Mrs Irvin (1957). A persistent competitor, whose most notable performances were in doubles. She was first ranked in the top ten in the US in ***1944***, but she did not gain her two major singles successes until ***1956*** when she won both Wimbledon and Forest Hills. Until then she had always been thwarted by fellow-Americans. She won the Wimbledon doubles from ***1951–53*** with Doris Hart, losing only four games in capturing the title in ***1953*** and beat Helen Fletcher and Jean Quertier 6–0 6–0 in sf and Julie Sampson and Maureen Connolly by the same score in f. They won the US title ***1951–54***. Her other successes included the Wimbledon mixed, with Seixas, ***1956***, the Australian singles and doubles, with Althea Gibson, ***1957***, and the French singles, ***1951***, and doubles, with Hart, ***1950–53***. She played in six W Cup contests, winning 10 rubbers and losing twice.

VITAS KEVIN **GERULAITIS** (USA)
Born 26/7/54. Died 18/9/94. Ranked among the world's top ten from ***1977–1982*** when he won 27 titles from 55 finals, this popular American, the son of Lithuanian immigrants, reached three Grand Slam finals on three different surfaces, thanks to a fine all-court game that lacked only a really decisive winning weapon. He won the Australian Open (***1977***), lost to John McEnroe in the US Open final (***1979***), and to his great friend Bjorn Borg in the French final (***1980***). Borg had also beaten him in the Wimbledon semi-final of ***1977***. This five set match of brilliant rallies contained few losers and was one of the greatest Centre Court battles of modern times. Two years earlier he had won the doubles at Wimbledon (***1975***) with Sandy Mayer, unseeded. He also reached two Masters finals. In ***1979*** Borg was simply too good for him but in ***1981*** he won the first two sets against Ivan Lendl and held a match point in the third but lost in five. He first represented the United States in the Davis Cup in ***1977*** and won 11 of the 14 rubbers he played, all in singles, in 7 ties. After retiring from the mainstream at the end of ***1985*** he played a lot of golf, became an excellent colour commentator on television, and played the guitar alongside John McEnroe to raise funds to help underprivileged kids in the New York area. In ***1994***, still a lively 40-year-old, he had started competing again on the seniors tour. Tragically, he died of carbon monoxide poisoning while watching TV at the poolside home of a friend in Southampton, Long Island, where the heater proved to be faulty. JB

ALTHEA GIBSON (USA)
Born 25/8/27. Became Mrs W A Darben (1965) and Mrs S Llewellyn (1983). The first black player to dominate international lawn tennis, relying on fierce serving and considerable strength and reach. Won Wimbledon singles ***1957/58*** and (doubles (with Angela Buxton) ***1957*** and (with Maria Bueno) ***/58***. US singles ***1957/58***. French singles and doubles (with Angela Buxton) ***1956***. Australian doubles (with Shirley Fry) ***1957***. Italian singles ***1956***. W Cup ***1957/58***, turned professional ***1958*** and for a brief spell competed on the women's golf tour.

ANDRE HENRI **GOBERT** (France)
Born 30/9/1890. Died 6/12/1951. Wallis Myers described him as 'perhaps the greatest indoor player of all time'. With Decugis, he gained France's first Wimbledon title by defeating the holders, Ritchie and Wilding, in ***1911***. Although they were beaten by Dixon and Roper Barrett the following year, the brilliant Gobert's compensation was a place in the All-Comers' singles f in which he lost to the experienced A. W. Gore. He won the French covered court title from ***1911–13*** and again in ***1920*** and the British covered court event in ***1911–12*** and again from ***1920–22***. He first played in the D Cup in ***1912*** and won 2 of his 7 singles and one of his 3 doubles rubbers in 5 ties He also won two Olympic gold medals in ***1912***.

RICHARD ALONZO ('**PANCHO**') **GONZALES** (USA)
Born 9/5/28. Died 3/7/95. A dramatic and spectacular competitor, who was undoubtedly the best player in the world for most of the 1950s. He turned pro in ***1949*** after winning the US singles in ***1948/49***, taking the US Clay Court title ***1948/49***, the US indoor title ***1949***, and winning the doubles in Paris and at Wimbledon – in his only amateur appearances there – in ***1949*** with Parker. Thereafter he played his brilliant, angry tennis away from the main arenas of the game until, at last, open competition was allowed. By then he was 40, but he played one last great match for the Wimbledon crowd. In ***1969*** he beat Pasarell 22–24 1–6 16–14 6–3 11–9 in 5hr 12min – the longest singles seen at Wimbledon. His only D Cup appearance was in the ***1949*** Challenge Round v. Australia when he beat both Sedgman and Sidwell as the USA retained the trophy.

EVONNE FAY **GOOLAGONG** (Australia)
Born 31/7/51. Now Mrs Roger Cawley (married in 1975). One of the most naturally gifted of champions, she was the first of her Aborigine race to excel at the game. Suddenly in ***1971*** at the age of 19, 3 years before her coach Vic Edwards had forecast she would, she swept through both the French Championships and Wimbledon on a cloud of inspiration to win her first major titles. Although she reached the Wimbledon final again the following year and twice more, in ***1975*** and ***1976***, it was not until ***1980*** that she won again – four years after the birth of her daughter, Kelly. This was the first win by a mother since Dorothea Lambert Chambers's success in ***1914***. The nine-year gap between her championships was also the greatest since Bill Tilden's wins in ***1921*** and ***1930***. She was always more at home on faster surfaces where her beautifully instinctive volleying paid handsome dividends and she won her native Australian Open on that surface four times – ***1974/75/76/78***. She was always a competent player on clay but tended to be rather erratic as her famous 'walkabouts' led to extravagant errors. Nevertheless, besides the French Open in ***1971*** she also won the Italian title in ***1973***. The other highlights of her singles career were the victories in the South African Championships (***1972***) and the Virginia Slims Champs (***1974/76***). She was a good doubles player and won once at Wimbledon (***1974***), four times in Melbourne (***1971/74/75/ 76***) and twice in Johannesburg (***1971/72***). In seven years of Fed Cup duty for Australia from ***1971–82*** she won 33 of the 38 rubbers she contested in 24 ties. JB

ARTHUR WILLIAM CHARLES (WENTWORTH) **GORE** (Great Britain)
Born 2/1/1868. Died 1/12/1928. Wimbledon's oldest champ and probably the most persistent and industrious competitor in the history of the Champs. He played there for the first time in ***1888*** and although the Dohertys, Brookes, and Wilding were among his contemporaries, won the singles 3 times ***1901*** and ***1908/09*** and, at the age of 44 years and 6 months, won the right to challenge Wilding for the title in ***1912***. That was his sev-

enth appearance in the Challenge Round in 13 years. He was almost entirely a forehand player, hitting the ball flat with the racket in a dead line with his outstretched arm. His lightness of foot enabled him to protect his backhand which was no more than a safe push. He competed at every Wimbledon between ***1888–1927*** and captained the first British D Cup team at Boston in ***1900***, reaching sf at the US Champs on that trip.

KAREN JANICE **HANTZE** (USA)

Born 11/12/42. Now Mrs Susman (1961). One of the new generation of aggressive Californians who arrived on the international scene at the start of the 1960s, she won the doubles at Wimbledon with the 17-year-old Billie Jean Moffitt in ***1961*** and then defeated Vera Sukova in the ***1962*** singles final. Marriage and motherhood restricted her tennis, but she won US doubles (again with Moffitt) ***1964***. She played W Cup ***1960–62*** and ***1965***, winning six of her nine matches, and Fed Cup ***1965***, when she played only in doubles and won all 4 rubbers.

DARLENE RUTH **HARD** (USA)

Born 6/1/36. An energetic volleyer, a shrewd tactician, and one of the best doubles players of her generation, she won the US singles in ***1960/61*** and the French singles ***1960***, but she failed in both her Wimbledon finals, losing to Althea Gibson in ***1957*** and Maria Bueno ***1960***. She won the Wimbledon doubles, with Gibson (***1957***), Jeanne Arth (***1959***), and twice with Bueno (***1960/63***) and the mixed in ***1957*** (with Rose), ***1959–60*** (with Laver). She won the US doubles six times – with Arth (***1958/59***), Bueno (***1960/62***), Turner (***1961***) and Durr (***1969***) and the French doubles three times – with Fleitz (***1955***), Bloomer (***1957***) and Buero (***1960***). Perhaps her most surprising American success came in ***1969***, some years after she had retired from regular competition, when she and Francoise Durr defeated Margaret Court and Virginia Wade 0–6 6–3 6–4 in f.

DORIS JANE **HART** (USA)

Born 20/6/25. In spite of childhood illness which impeded her movement, she became one of the subtlest and most graceful of post-war competitors. Won Wimbledon singles ***1951***, doubles (with Pat Todd) ***1947*** and (with Shirley Fry) ***1951/52/53***. US singles ***1954/55*** and doubles (with Shirley Fry) ***1951/52/53/54***. French singles ***1950/52*** and doubles (with Pat Todd) ***1948*** and (with Shirley Fry) ***1950/51/53***. Australian singles ***1949*** and doubles (with Louise Brough) ***1950***. Italian singles ***1951/53*** and South African singles ***1952***. Also won many mixed titles, notably with E. V. Seixas at Wimbledon ***1953/54/55***. Turned professional ***1955***.

ADRIANNE ('**ANN**') SHIRLEY **HAYDON** (Great Britain)

Born 17/10/38. Married Philip (Pip) Jones in 1962. A shrewd, persistent left-hander, who reached sf at Wimbledon 7 times in 10 years, she captured the title at last in ***1969*** after beating Margaret Court in sf and Billie Jean King, to whom she had been r/u in ***1967***, in f. She achieved international fame as a table tennis player, but decided to concentrate on lawn tennis after being r/u in three events in the ***1957*** World Table Tennis Champs. She won the French title in ***1961/66***, Rome in ***1966*** and was twice r/u at Forest Hills ***1961/67***. She took the French doubles (with Francoise Durr) in ***1968/69*** and won the Wimbledon mixed with Stolle in ***1969***. Her W Cup record – 15 successful rubbers out of 32 in 12 matches – is another remarkable illustration of her tenacity and consistency.

ROBERT ('**BOB**') ANTHONY JOHN **HEWITT** (South Africa)

Born in Sydney, Australia, 12/1/40. He moved to South Africa in the early ***1960s*** and started to represent that country when his residential qualification matured in ***1967***. A big brooding volcano of a man, he had a deceptively fine touch and became one of the greatest right-court returners of the serve of modern times. He enjoyed two careers – first with fellow-Australian Fred Stolle and then with South Africa's Frew McMillan. With Stolle he won Wimbledon twice (***1962/64***) the Australian Championship twice (***1963/64***) and the Italian twice (***1963/64***) and with McMillan he added three more Wimbledon crowns (***1967/72/78***), two German (***1967/70***), one French (***1972***), one US (***1977***), one Masters (***1977***) and one WCT (***1974***) title as well as the Italian in ***1967*** and four at home in South Africa (***1967/70/72/74***). He registered five major mixed doubles successes with four different partners, winning in Australia with Jan Lehane in ***1961***, in Paris with Billie Jean King in ***1970*** and with Wendy Turnbull in ***1979***, and twice at Wimbledon with his pupil, Greer Stevens, in ***1977/79***. He represented South Africa in D Cup ***1967–74*** and was a member of the successful team of ***1974*** that won by default from India. JB

LEWIS ('**LEW**') ALAN **HOAD** (Australia)

Born 23/11/34. Died 3/7/94. Capable of generating fierce power with great ease, he was one of the 'boy wonders' Harry Hopman produced to beat the US in the ***1953*** D Cup final. The other was Rosewall, 21 days Hoad's senior, who was to thwart his attempt on the Grand Slam in ***1956*** by beating him at Forest Hills. That year Hoad had won the Australian and French titles, and had beaten Rosewall at Wimbledon. In ***1957*** he defeated Ashley Cooper in one of the most devastating Wimbledon f ever and then turned professional, but constant back trouble spoilt his pro career and also ended his attempt to return to the circuit when the game was opened to the pros. He won the Wimbledon doubles with Rosewall (***1953/56***) and Hartwig (***1955***), the US doubles (***1956***) and the French doubles (***1953***) both with Rosewall, and the Australian doubles with Rosewall (***1953/56***) and Fraser (***1957***). He won 17 rubbers out of 21 in 9 D. Cup duties between ***1953–56*** (10–2 singles, 7–2 doubles).

HENRY ('**HARRY**') CHRISTIAN **HOPMAN** (Australia)

Born 12/8/06. Died 27/12/85. Small in stature, he was a giant as Australia's Davis Cup captain, winning 16 Challenge Rounds between ***1939*** and ***1967*** and motivating some of the finest talent that has ever emerged from any country. The list of his teams reads like a who's who of post war tennis legends and includes Sedgman, McGregor, Hoad, Rosewall, Rose, Hartwig, Emerson, Stolle, Cooper, Anderson, Newcombe, Roche and Alexander. A fine player himself, especially in men's doubles and mixed, he reached three successive Australian singles finals (***1930/31/32***), losing the last two to Jack Crawford, his partner in winning the doubles in ***1929/30***. His four mixed wins, all achieved with his wife Nell (nee Hall, they married in March 1934) came in ***1930/36/37/39***. His own Davis Cup playing record was modest. He took part in 8 ties between ***1928*** and ***1939***, winning 4 of his 9 singles and four of seven doubles. JB

HAZEL VIRGINIA **HOTCHKISS** (USA)

Born 20/12/1886. Died 5/12/1974. Became Mrs G. W. Wightman (1912). One of the most remarkable and enthusiastic competitors that the game has known. She was the donor of the W Cup and a considerable influence in American tennis for more than 60 years. She gained the first of her four US singles titles (***1909/10/11/19***) in ***1909*** and won the US indoor doubles for the 10th (***1919/21/24 /27/28/29/30/31/33/43***) and last time in ***1943***. A remarkable volleyer with great speed about the court, she and Helen Wills were never beaten in doubles. They won the Wimbledon doubles in ***1924*** and the US doubles in ***1924/28***. Her four other US doubles wins came with E. E. Rotch (***1909/10***) and E. Sears (***1911/15***). She captained the first US W Cup team in ***1923*** and between ***1923–31*** won 3 doubles rubbers in 5 matches.

HELEN HULL **JACOBS** (USA)

Born 6/8/08. Died 2/6/97. A tenacious competitor, notable for duels with fellow-Californian, Helen Wills Moody, 5 times a Wimbledon finalist between ***1929–39*** but won only in ***1936***. Won US singles ***1932/33/34/35*** and doubles (with Sarah Palfrey Fabyan) ***1930/34/35*** and mixed with George Lott ***1934***. Also won Italian singles ***1934***.

WILLIAM M. **JOHNSTON** (USA)

Born 2/11/1894. Died 1/5/1946. 'Little Bill', a Californian, small in physique but a brilliant volleyer and the possessor of a formidable topspin forehand, was 'Big Bill' Tilden's principal rival at home in the first half of the ***1920s***. He defeated McLoughlin to win the US singles in ***1915***, the first year at Forest Hills, lost to Williams in the ***1916*** final and then regained the title by beating Tilden in straight sets in ***1919***. Tilden gained his revenge the following year and, although Johnston reached the final five times between ***1920*** and ***1925***, Tilden always frustrated him. He beat Hunter in the ***1923*** Wimbledon final, losing only one set in the tournament. He won the US doubles with Griffin ***1915/16*** and ***1920*** and played in eight D Cup challenge rounds, winning 18 of his 21 D Cup rubbers (14–3 singles, 4–0 doubles) in 10 ties from ***1920–1927***.

BILLIE JEAN MOFFITT **KING** (USA)

Born 22/11/43. Perhaps the most important single figure in the history of women's tennis, as player, stateswoman, innovator and entrepreneur (usually with lawyer husband Larry King, whom she married in ***1965***), she has worked tirelessly to gain recognition and respect for the women's game. One of the founders of the women's pro tour in ***1970***, twice President of the Women's Tennis Association, and the prime mover behind Team Tennis, she has been involved in most aspects of the game. As a player her natural exuberance and bubbling personality suited her attacking serve-and-volley game and made her a fearsome opponent. She will best be remembered for her 'Battle of the Sexes' against Bobby Riggs at the Houston Astrodome on 20 September, ***1973*** where the world's largest-ever crowd of 30,492 and some 50 million more around the world on TV, saw her win 6–4 6–3 6–3. In ***1979*** she achieved her 20th Wimbledon title to pass the record she had shared with fellow-Californian Elizabeth Ryan who, ironically, had died on the eve of that unique achievement. Her unparalleled record comprises 6 singles – ***1966/67/68/72/73/75***; 10 women's doubles between ***1961*** and ***1979*** – with Hantze-Susman (***1961/62***) Bueno (***1965***), Casals (***1967/68/70/71/73***), Stove (***1972***) and Navratilova (***1979***); 4 mixed doubles with Owen Davidson (***1967/71/ 73/74***). She first played at Wimbledon in ***1961*** and won the doubles with Karen Hantze. At her last appearance in ***1983*** she was competing for the 22nd year (she had not entered in ***1981***) and reached the mixed doubles final with Steve Denton when she played her 265th and last match at Wimbledon. It was also her 29th final and, as they lost to John Lloyd and Wendy Turnbull 7–5 in the final set, she was losing at that stage for only the 9th time. She was almost as successful in her own US Championships where she won 13 titles, 4 in singles – ***1967/71/72/74***, five in doubles – with Susman (***1964***), Casals (***1967/74***) and Navratilova (***1978/80***) and four in mixed – with Davidson (***1967/71/73***) and Phil Dent (***1976***) and, in addition she became the only woman to win US National titles on all four surfaces – grass, clay, hard and indoor – a feat she repeated in doubles – with Rosie Casals. She won the French Open singles and doubles with Stove in ***1972*** and the mixed – with Davidson (***1967***) and Hewitt (***1970***) and was successful in singles and mixed at the Australian Open in ***1968*** (with Crealy), the first year of open tennis. Her 39 Grand Slam titles put her third behind Margaret Court who won 62 and Navratilova who won 56. She was also the singles and doubles champion of Italy (***1970***) and of Germany (***1971***) and won the South African title 3 times ***1966/67/69***). With 21 winning rubbers from 26 played in 9 W Cup matches between ***1961–78***, plus 52 wins from 58 rubbers (26–3 singles, 26–1 doubles) in 6 years of Fed Cup play from ***1963–79*** she contributed hugely to American dominance in those team competitions. JB

JAN KODES (Czechoslovakia)
Born 1/3/46. A dogged, industrious player with great strength and determination. He won his first major victories on clay, winning the French singles ***1970/71*** and reaching the Italian final ***1970/71/72***, but he won the Wimbledon singles in the boycott year of ***1973*** (when he won the first tie-break used in a Wimbledon final) and was runner-up in the US Champs ***1971/73***. Having served his apprenticeship in European junior team competitions (he was on a winning Galea Cup team), he first represented Czechoslovakia in D Cup in ***1966***, took them to the final in ***1975*** and was a member of their winning team in ***1980***. Altogether, in 39 ties over 15 years he won 39 of his 59 singles and 21 of his 36 doubles rubbers. For six years (***1982–87***) he was Davis Cup captain and for 5 years (***1994–98***) President of the Czech Federation.

HILDE KRAHWINKEL (West Germany)
Born 26/3/08. Died 7/3/81. Became Mrs Sperling (1933). A tall German, later Danish by marriage, whose dogged ability to retrieve from the back of the court turned her matches into long tests of endurance. She won the German indoor title in ***1929*** and then, emerging rapidly as an international player, lost to Cilly Aussem in the only all-German women's f at Wimbledon in ***1931***. She reached the final again in ***1936***, losing 6–2 4–6 7–5 to Helen Jacobs, and altogether she was in qf (or better) 8 times. She won the French singles ***1935–37***, defeating Mrs Mathieu in each of the three f, the Italian title ***1935*** and she was German singles champ ***1933/35/37/39***. (There was no competition in 1936.) Her last important victory was in the Scandinavian indoor final in ***1950***.

JOHN ('**JACK**') ALBERT **KRAMER** (USA)
Born 1/8/21. A methodical and powerful exponent of the serve-and-volley game. Played for the US in the last pre-war D Cup Challenge Round against Australia and returned to the competition in **1946** and **1947** as USA regained, then retained the trophy v Australia. His brief D Cup record produced 7 wins from 9 rubbers (6–0 singles 1–2 doubles) in 4 ties. Won Wimbledon singles title in ***1947*** after losing dramatically to the then unknown Jaroslav Drobny in **1946**. Won doubles ***1946*** (with T. Brown) and ***1947*** (with Falkenburg). Won US singles ***1946/47*** and doubles ***1940/41/47*** (with Schroeder) and ***1943*** (with Parker). Turned pro ***1947*** and then controlled pro tennis for 15 years. He was the first executive director of ATP Sept. 1972–April 1975.

JOHAN KRIEK(USA)
Born 5/4/58. This speedy South African shot to prominence at the end of ***1981*** by winning the Australian Open after saving a match point in his semi-final against McNamee. In April that year he had already given notice of his improvement by reaching the WCT final in Dallas where McEnroe had beaten him. In ***1982***, now an American citizen, he retained his Australian title by beating the same opponent as in the previous year's final, the tall American with the cannonball serve, Steve Denton. JB

JEAN **RENE LACOSTE** (France)
Born 2/7/04. Died 12/10/96. In spite of ill health, he became the best groundstroke player and most astute tactician of pre-war lawn tennis. Won Wimbledon singles ***1925/28*** and doubles (with J. Borotra) ***1925***. Won US singles ***1926/27***, French singles ***1925/27/29*** and French doubles (with Borotra) ***1924/25/29***. Won 40 of his 51 D Cup rubbers in 26 ties between ***1923–28*** (32–8 singles, 8–3 doubles) and won the crucial rubbers of the ***1927*** challenge round which brought France the trophy for the first time, when he beat Tilden and Johnston in the singles. Retiring from the mainstream in ***1929*** he built up his Chemise Lacoste clothing business until it became one of the world's best known brands with its crocodile emblem.

WILLIAM ('**BILL**') AUGUSTUS **LARNED** (USA)
Born 30/12/1872. Committed suicide on 16/12/1926. Coming late to tennis, Larned won the first of his seven US Championships in ***1901*** at the age of 28 with his heavy groundstrokes, hit with considerable top-spin on the forehand. He added the titles of ***1902/07/08/09/10/11*** and was 38 when he won for the last time, making him the oldest male champion. Ranked in the US Top Ten 19 times, he was the US No.1 eight times, a total second only to Tilden's 10. He played in 8 D Cup ties from ***1902***, winning 9 of his 14 singles. JB

ARTHUR ('**ART**') DAVID ('TAPPY') **LARSEN** (USA)
Born 6/4/25. A graceful, elegant left-hander with exquisite touch and some notable eccentricities, he was famous for his dressing-room superstitions, his physical twitches and his rituals on court. He was known as Tappy because he would have a lucky number for the day and would always tap the baseline, the umpire's chair – even his own toe – with his racket the required number of times before continuing. He won US singles ***1950***, US Clay Courts ***1952*** and US Indoor ***1953***. A motor scooter accident in which he suffered severe head injuries ended his career in ***1957***.

RODNEY ('**ROD**') GEORGE **LAVER** (Australia)
Born 9/8/38. Arguably the greatest of all male champions, he became the first player to achieve the Grand Slam twice and the master of the old professional circuit, with Rosewall as his great rival, in its last days. A left-hander, red-haired like Budge, with a spectacularly aggressive style, he brought off the slam of the four major singles titles, as an amateur, in ***1962*** and then, as a professional, in ***1969***. Disciplined, unassuming, quick and light in movement, he could produce sudden bombardments of shots, heavy with spin, which totally disconcerted his opponents. Born at Rockhampton, Queensland, 'Rocket' was a perfect nickname for the first tennis millionaire. If he had not turned professional in **1963**, he would have won many more of the traditional titles. As

it was, he won the singles at Wimbledon ***1961/62*** and ***1968/69***, the doubles with Emerson ***1971*** and the mixed, with Darlene Hard, ***1959/60***. He took the US singles and French singles ***1962*** and ***1969***, also winning the French doubles with Emerson and the mixed with Hard in ***1961***. His Australian singles victories came in ***1960/62/69***, with doubles ***1959/61*** (Mark) and ***1969*** (Emerson). He was Italian singles champion ***1962*** and ***1971***, German champion ***1961/62*** and a member of the undefeated D Cup team from ***1959–62***. He returned to D Cup in ***1973***, collecting three more rubbers in Australia's 5–0 victory over the US in the final at Cleveland. Altogether, he won 20 of his 24 rubbers in 11 ties between ***1959–73***, (16–4 singles, 4–0 doubles).

IVAN LENDL (USA)
Born 7/3/60. Grew up in Ostrava, Czechoslovakia, but went to live in Greenwich, Connecticut in ***1984*** and became an American citizen on 7th July **1992**. This 6'2" 175lb right-hander was blessed with a fine physique and abundant talent, based on a lethal match-winning forehand, a reliable backhand that he would develop into a second winning weapon, and a heavy serve – plus superb fitness and deep concentration. He was nurtured from an early age by his lawyer father Jiri, himself a ranked player, and by his mother Olga, a former Czech No.3. The Orange Bowl 18's champion in ***1977***, Lendl became the first ITF World Junior Champion in ***1978*** after winning the Wimbledon, French and Italian junior titles. Turning pro the same year, he made rapid strides in the men's game and in ***1980*** won the first six of the 94 singles titles he would amass before his retirement at the end of ***1994***, successes that earned him $21,262,417 in prize money alone. (Only Jimmy Connors, with 109 titles, has won more tournaments in modern times though Tilden won 138 titles in the ***1920's***.) During those 15 years he reached 19 Grand Slam singles finals, winning 8 of them. After failing once in Paris (***1981***), twice in New York (**1982/83**) and once in Melbourne (***1983***) some observers wrote him off, saying he did not have the belief of a true champion. Over the next seven years, guided by his Australian coach, Tony Roche, he proved his critics spectacularly wrong by claiming the French Open three times (***1984/86/87***), the US Open three times (***1985/86/87***), and the Australian Open twice (***1989/90***) as well as The Masters five times (***1981/82/85/86/87***) from a record nine consective appearances in the final between ***1980*** and ***1988***. At Wimbledon he was unlucky to face inspired opponents in two consecutive finals; in ***1986*** 18-year-old Boris Becker successfully defended his title and in ***1987*** Pat Cash proved irresistible. Lendl first headed the world rankings on 28th February ***1983*** and altogether occupied the No.1 spot for a record 270 weeks, a span that inluded 157 consecutive weeks between ***9/9/85*** and ***12/9/88***. In a relatively short Davis Cup career (***1978–1985***) Lendl won 22 of the 37 rubbers he contested, including 18 of his 29 singles matches. JB

SUZANNE RACHEL FLORE **LENGLEN** (France)
Born 24/5/1899. Died 4/7/1938. The most exciting, and successful of women players. She survived 2 match-points to win at Wimbledon in ***1919*** against Mrs Lambert Chambers and thereafter lost only in a controversial match to Molla Mallory (US) in ***1921*** US Champs until her retirement in ***1926***. Quarrelled with the Wimbledon referee in ***1926*** and turned pro. Won Wimbledon singles and doubles (with Elizabeth Ryan) ***1919/20/21/22/23/25***. French singles and doubles (with various partners) ***1920/21/22/23***, while the Championships were closed to foreigners, and again in ***1925*** and ***1926*** (doubles with D. Vlasto) when they became international.

GEORGE MARTIN **LOTT** (USA)
Born 16/10/06. Died 2/12/91. A fine, natural doubles player, he was five times the US doubles champion – in ***1928*** (with John Hennessey), ***1929*** and ***1930*** (with John Doeg), ***1933*** and ***1934*** (with Lester Stoefen). Two Wimbledon titles – in ***1931*** (with John Van Ryn) and ***1934*** (with Stoefen), plus one French in ***1931*** (with Van Ryn). In six years of Davis Cup competition from ***1928*** he won 18 of his 22 rubbers (7–4 in singles, 1–0 in doubles) then, in ***1934***, he turned professional. JB

JOHN PATRICK **McENROE** (USA)
Born 16/2/59. A left-hander with immense talent and exquisite touch, he caused a sensation at Wimbledon in ***1977*** by reaching the semi-final from the qualifying competition, thus winning a record eight matches. He was to be the centre of many other sensations throughout a turbulent career during which his perfectionist attitude made it impossible for him to accept the incompetence (as he saw it) of court officials, many of whom were subjected to a torrent of intimidating verbal abuse. Fined for his behaviour on several occasions, he was finally defaulted at the Australian Open in ***1990*** during his fourth round match against Michael Pernfors. In between these outbursts he could produce tennis of a sublime quality. His deceptive serve, delivered from a closed stance, was difficult to read and there has never been a better close volleyer. His ability to take his service returns and passing shots early and project them to unlikely angles made him a very difficult opponent. His singles successes included four US Open titles (***1979,1980,1981,1984***) and three at Wimbledon (***1981,1983,1984***) where his two heroic battles against Bjorn Borg in the ***1980*** and ***1981*** finals reached epic proportions. Among his 77 career titles the three Masters successes (***1979, 1983,1984***) and five WCT victories (***1979,1981,1983,1984,1989***) were outstanding. He was never successful in Paris, where Lendl beat him in the ***1984*** final, or in Australia, where he lost to Wilander in the ***1983*** semi-final. His lightning-fast reflexes and an instinctive positional sense made him an outstanding doubles player, arguably the best there has ever been. The ***1977*** French Open mixed, won with Mary Carillo, his neighbour from Douglaston, N.Y., was his first Grand Slam success. At Wimbledon he won four times with Peter Fleming (***1979,1981,1983,1984***) and once with Michael Stich (***1992***). At the US Open Fleming helped him to three titles (***1979,1981,1983***) His

seven consecutive Masters wins with Fleming (***1978–1984***) constitute a record that, surely, will never be broken. Always proud to represent his country, he had an outstanding D Cup record for the United States. In 12 years from ***1978*** he won 41 of his 49 singles rubbers and 18 of his 20 doubles rubbers in 30 ties. JB

KENNETH ('**KEN**') BRUCE **McGREGOR** (Australia)
Born 2/6/29. Tall, athletic and a natural competitor, this modest South Australian possessed one of the biggest serves in post war tennis. He at last became the Australian champion in ***1952*** by beating in the final his great friend and doubles partner, Frank Sedgman, who had thwarted him in the ***1950*** final. In between McGregor had lost the ***1951*** final to America's Dick Savitt who would also win their Wimbledon final six months later. With his height of 6'3", his long reach, his fast reactions and his fine touch on the volley, McGregor excelled in doubles. His short partnership with Sedgman was particularly fruitful. Together they became the Australian, French and Wimbledon champions in ***1951*** and ***1952***, and the US champions in ***1951***. Thus, in ***1951*** they became the first pair (and so far the only pair) to win the Grand Slam of men's doubles. With Margaret DuPont he also won the US mixed doubles of ***1950*** and in three years of Davis Cup play (***1950–1952***) he won four of his seven singles rubbers and both doubles rubbers in 5 ties, three of them Challenge Rounds. In ***1953*** he was lost to the amateur game when he and Sedgman signed professional forms for Jack Kramer. JB

KATHLEEN ('**KITTY**') **McKANE** (Great Britain)
Born 7/5/1896. Died 19/6/92. Became Mrs Godfree (**1926**). A fine match-player with a quick, aggressive game, she achieved the notable distinction of winning the Wimbledon singles twice – even though she was a contemporary of Suzanne Lenglen and Helen Wills. In Lenglen's absence, she beat the Californian (a feat which no other player achieved in the next 14 years at Wimbledon) in the ***1924*** final after trailing by a set and 1–4, and in ***1926*** she regained the title after being within a point of 1–4 in the third set against Lili d'Alvarez. She won the Wimbledon mixed (with Gilbert) in ***1924*** and in ***1926*** (with her husband, Leslie Godfree, the only married couple ever to do so). She was r/u to Miss Wills at Forest Hills in **1925** after beating Elizabeth Ryan and Molla Mallory, and she won the US doubles in ***1923*** (with Mrs Covell) ***1927*** (with Miss Harvey). She won 7 rubbers out of 17 in 7 W Cup matches between ***1923–34***.

CHARLES ('**CHUCK**') ROBERT **McKINLEY** (USA)
Born 5/1/41. Died 11/8/86. An energetic and athletic match-player, who won the Wimbledon singles title in ***1963*** without meeting another seeded player in the course of the tournament. He was runner-up to Laver in ***1961***, a disappointing competitor in ***1962*** but in ***1963*** bounced back to take the title. In the US Championships he never progressed further than the semi-finals, failing three times at that stage, but, with Ralston, he won the doubles in ***1961*** and ***1963–64***. Played in 16 D Cup ties between ***1960–65*** and won 29 of his 38 rubbers (16–6 singles, 13–3 doubles).

MAURICE EVANS **McLOUGHLIN** (USA)
Born 18/11/1890. Died 10/12/1957. 'The Californian Comet' was the first notable exponent of the cannonball service. Fiercely effective with volley and smash, he was US champ in***1912–13*** and his appearance at Wimbledon was, as a contemporary remarked, a sign of the way the modern game was developing. His spectacular style had considerable appeal. When he met Wilding for the title in ***1913***, there was such an indecent crush round the barriers of the Centre Court that, to avoid serious injury, several ladies had to be lifted over by policemen into the security of the arena. Wilding beat him 8–6 6–3 10–8, but McLoughlin had the consolation of winning 2 rubbers in the American capture of the D Cup from Britain at Wimbledon. In the ***1914*** D Cup Challenge Round at Forest Hills he beat both Brookes and Wilding, but Australasia took the trophy. He did not play after the war. His aggressive style was said to have burnt him out.

FREW DONALD **McMILLAN** (South Africa)
Born 20/5/42 in Springs, a small Transvaal town. A gifted and unusual doubles player who invariably wore a peaked white cloth cap and held the racket with two hands on both sides to produce just the right blend of disguise, finesse and power. His partnership with expatriate Australian Bob Hewitt was particularly fruitful and they became one of the three greatest pairs of the post-Second World War years. Together they won their native South African title four times (***1967/70/72/74***) and succeeded at Wimbledon three times (***1967/72/78***). They won once each the French (***1972***), the US (***1977***), the Masters (***1977***) played in Jan '78), the WCT (***1974***) and the Italian (***1967***) titles and won the German twice (***1967/70***). But it was in mixed doubles that he won his first and last major championships. In ***1966*** he partnered Annette Van Zyl to the French title and in ***1981*** he captured the Wimbledon mixed for the second time with Betty Stove, with whom he had been successful in ***1978*** – the same year they won a second US Open together (***1977/ 78***). He played D Cup from ***1965–76*** and was a member of the only team ever to win the famous trophy by default – from India in ***1974***. In 28 ties he played 30 rubbers, winning both singles and 23 of his 28 doubles. JB

HANA MANDLIKOVA (Australia)
Born 19/2/62. Became Mrs J. Sadlek (1986). This Czech-born right-hander, who helped her country win the Federation Cup in ***1985***, became an Australian citizen on 1 January ***1988***. A talented athlete who won four Grand Slam singles titles and might have won more had her career not coincided with two truly outstanding champions – Evert and Navratilova. She first shot to prominence in Australia where, on the grass of Kooyong

which ideally suited her natural serve-and-volley game, she won the ***1980*** title aged 18. When she took the ***1981*** French Open and 4 weeks later reached the Wimbledon final it seemed she might dislodge Evert and Navratilova from their dominant positions atop the world rankings. It was not to be. Another final round appearance, this time at the US Open of ***1981***, flattered to deceive. But in ***1985*** she did annexe that title and the following year reached the Wimbledon final for the second time. Sadly this was not the breakthrough to the summit all her supporters had hoped for. Her fourth Grand Slam success came in Melbourne in ***1987***, the last time the Australian Open was played on grass. Her lone Grand Slam doubles success came at the ***1989*** US Open in partnership with Navratilova. JB

ALICE MARBLE (USA)
Born 28/9/13. Died 13/12/90. The first brilliant server and volleyer in women's tennis whose career was interrupted by ill health and the war. Won Wimbledon singles ***1939*** and doubles (with Sarah Palfrey Fabyan) ***1938/39***. Won US singles ***1936/38/39/40*** and doubles (with Sarah Palfrey Fabyan) ***1937/38/39/40***. Turned pro ***1941***.

SIMONE MATHIEU (France)
Born 31/1/08. Died 7/1/80. Née Passemard, had married Rene Mathieu in Oct. 1925, before her tennis career had begun. A formidable clay court player, she succeeded Lenglen as the leader of the women's game in France. She was junior champ – as a married woman – at 18, and 3 years later reached the French f, losing 6–3 6–4 to Wills. She was r/u again in ***1933/36/37*** before she won at last in ***1938***, defeating Landry, and then retained her title ***1939*** against Jedrzejowska. She won the French doubles 6 times, twice with Ryan, (***1933/34***) three times with Yorke (***1936/37/38***) and once with Jedrzejowska (***1939***), and the Wimbledon doubles twice with Ryan (***1933/34***) and once with Yorke (***1937***.) Her soundness from the baseline carried her 4 times to the singles sf (***1930/31/32/34***).

FLORENCE **ANGELA** MARGARET **MORTIMER** (Great Britain)
Born 21/4/32. Now Mrs Barrett (1967). Britain's first post-war Wimbledon singles champ. Coached by Arthur Roberts at Torquay, she used an armoury of firmly controlled ground- strokes most effectively and considerable determination enabled her to overcome a certain frailty of physique. Her first notable success was the capture of the French title in ***1955*** – the first British victory in Paris since Peggy Scriven won in ***1934*** – and in the same year she won the Wimbledon doubles (with Anne Shilcock). She won the Australian title in ***1958***, after travelling there to recover from illness, and 6 months later was r/u to Althea Gibson at Wimbledon. She won the title in ***1961*** by beating Christine Truman in the first all–British f of the modern Wimbledon. She won 5 rubbers out of 16 in 6 W Cup matches and became W Cup captain ***1964–70*** and Fed Cup captain ***1967–70***.

ILLIE NASTASE (Romania)
Born 19/7/46. One of the most gifted shot-makers and fluid movers in the game's history, he was the first to be ranked No 1 on the ATP computer (***23/08/1973***) and was in top 10 ***1973–77***, but despite his 57 singles and 51 doubles titles, he never quite fulfilled his enormous potential. His two Grand Slam titles were won on different surfaces – on grass in New York in ***1972*** and on clay in Paris the following year. He could also play beautifully indoors as his four Masters titles in ***1971/72/73/75*** testify. Sadly for his many admirers, a childlike and sometimes mischievous streak was his undoing on many occasions, particularly towards the end of his playing days when he fell foul of authority for his behaviour. Throughout his career the showman in him struggled constantly with the athlete so that there was often a lack of steel about his match play. This failing, and an inability to put the ball away with his somewhat lightweight volleys, cost him two chances to win the Wimbledon title – in ***1972*** when Smith beat him and in***1976*** when Borg won the first of his five titles. His lightning reflexes made him an excellent doubles player and he won major titles in Paris (***1970***) and Rome (***1970/72***) with fellow Romanian, Ion Tiriac, at Wimbledon (***1973***) with Connors and in New York (***1975***) also with Connors. He also won two mixed titles at Wimbledon with Rosie Casals (***1970/72***). His biggest disappointment was his failure to lead Romania to victory in the ***1972*** D Cup final against the Americans on clay in Bucharest where his loss to Smith in the opening rubber proved decisive. JB

MARTINA NAVRATILOVA (USA)
Born 18/10/56. Arguably the greatest of all women players, this Czech-born left-hander grew up in Prague but defected to the USA in ***1975*** and became an American citizen on 21st July ***1981***. With her defection she turned professional and embarked upon two decades of conquest that brought her a total of 56 Grand Slam titles (18 singles, 31 doubles, 7 mixed) between ***1975*** and ***1995***. Navratilova's attacking serve-and-volley game was ideally suited to the fast grass of Wimbledon where she reached 12 singles finals and won a record 9 times (***1978/79/82/83/84/85/86/87/90***). She also won 7 of her 9 doubles finals there (***1976*** with Chris Evert, ***1979*** with Billie Jean King, ***1981/82/83/84/86*** with Pam Shriver) and 3 of her 4 mixed finals (***1985*** with Paul McNamee, ***1993*** with Mark Woodforde and ***1995*** with Jonathan Stark) giving her a total of 19 Wimbledon titles, one short of Mrs. King's record of 20 which she had helped the American achieve in ***1979***. This glittering Grand Slam career had begun with a victory over Evonne Cawley at the ***1975*** Australian Open where she won twice more in singles (***1983/84***) from 6 appearances in the final. She won eight Australian doubles titles (***1980*** with Betsy Nagelsen,***1982/83/84/85/87/88/89*** with Shriver), but none in mixed. Slow red clay was the most difficult surface for her and despite appearing in 6 finals at the French Open she was successful only

twice (***1982/84***). However, she won all 7 of her French doubles finals (***1975*** with Evert, ***1982*** with Ann Smith, ***1984/85/86/87/88*** with Shriver) and both mixed finals (***1971*** with Ivan Molina, ***1985*** with Heinz Gunthardt). At the US Open she was in 8 singles finals, winning 4 (***1983/84/86/87***), in 11 doubles finals, winning 9 (***1977*** with Betty Stove, ***1978/80*** with King, ***1983/84/86/87*** with Shriver, ***1989*** with Hana Mandlikova and ***1990*** with Gigi Fernandez), and in 4 mixed finals, winning 2 (***1985*** with Gunthardt, ***1987*** with Emilio Sanchez). Despite this formidable record she never won a calendar-year Grand Slam, though her victory at the French Open in **1984** meant that she held all four major titles at the same time, a feat that earned her a $1 million prize from the ITF. Her 167 singles and 165 doubles titles are a record for men and women as was her winning streak of 74 matches achieved in **1984** between January 16th and December 6th. For a total of 332 weeks she was ranked No.1 in the world and by training intensively and adopting the Haas diet she set new standards of strength and fitness which others have tried to follow. With career prize money of $20,283,727 at the time of her retirement, Navrartilova had won more from her sport than any other female athlete and has been very generous in suporting charities and other deserving causes. Her endorsement income, though considerable, would undoubtedly have been higher had she not made public several lesbian relationships. JB

JOHN DAVID **NEWCOMBE** (Australia)

Born 23/5/44. The supreme exponent of the simple, rugged style in modern tennis. Splendidly confident and with great strength of personality, Newcombe relied upon a heavy service, forceful volleying and solid, powerful groundstrokes. His best singles successes were on grass – Wimbledon ***1967/70/71***, US Championships ***1967/73***, and Australia ***1973/75*** – but he also won, by doggedness and determination, the German (***1968***) and Italian (***1969***) titles. He and Roche formed one of the most successful of modern doubles partnerships, winning Wimbledon in ***1965***, ***1968–70***, and ***1974***. When Roche was injured in ***1966***, Fletcher replaced him at short notice and he and Newcombe won the title. He won the US doubles with Roche ***1967***, with Taylor ***1971***, and with Davidson ***1973***, the French twice with Roche (***1967/69***) and once with Okker (***1973***) and the Australian four times with Roche (***1965/67/71/76***) and once with Anderson (***1973***). In ***1981***, aged 37, he and Stolle (42) took McEnroe/Fleming to 5s tie-break in US Open sf. He first played in the D Cup in ***1963*** when, aged 19, he became the youngest player to compete in a Challenge Round, and finally against Italy in Rome, ***1976***. Perhaps his best performance was in ***1973*** when he and Laver inflicted a 5–0 defeat upon the United States at Cleveland. In 15 ties he won 25 of his 34 rubbers (16–7 singles, 9–2 doubles).

YANNICK NOAH (France)

Born 16/5/60. The son of an African father who had met Yannick's mother when playing soccer for Sedan, he was discovered as a ten-year-old by Arthur Ashe on a goodwill tour in the Cameroons. Sent to the French Federation's training school in Nice, he was coached by Patrice Beust and then sent on to the FFT's school in Paris. A tall athletic figure with a tremendous serve, he was at his best on clay and although he could volley well he preferred to play aggressively from the baseline. He won his first professional title in ***1979*** in Nancy and eventually fulfilled all expectations by winning the French Open in ***1983***, the first Frenchman to do so since Marcel Bernard in ***1946***. The fairy tale had come true. In ***1984*** he teamed with fellow Frenchman, Henri Leconte, to win the French Open doubles title. After leading France to the final of the Davis Cup in ***1982***, when France had lost to the USA 4–1 in Grenoble, he became Davis Cup captain in ***1991*** and was the architect of a famous 3–1 revenge win against the Americans in Lyon, the first French success since ***1932***. JB

BETTY MAY **NUTHALL** (Great Britain)

Born 23/5/11. Died 8/11/83. Became Mrs Shoemaker. An aggressive and attractive competitor, with a remarkable record as a junior, she never progressed beyond qf at Wimbledon but gained her most impressive victories abroad. At 16, after beating Molla Mallory, No. 6 seed, at Wimbledon in ***1927***, she astonished the tennis world by reaching f at F Hills, where Helen Wills beat her 6–1 6–4. In ***1930*** she became the first British player to win that title with 6–4 6–1 victory over Mrs Harper. She won the US doubles ***1930/31/33*** with three different partners – Palfrey, Whittingstall and James and mixed ***1928/29/31*** with Lott and the French doubles ***1931*** with Whittingstall and mixed ***1931/32*** with Spence and Perry. Her only British success in a nat singles event was the capture of the HC title in ***1927***. She won the HC doubles ***1926/28/31/32*** and the mixed in ***1927***. She played in 8 W Cup matches between ***1927–39***, winning 6 rubbers and losing 7.

ALEJANDRO ('**ALEX**') RODRIGUEZ **OLMEDO** (USA)

Born 24/3/36. The son of a groundsman in Peru, this superb natural athlete rose like a comet in ***1958*** to win the D Cup for America in Brisbane almost single-handed. Selected by the captain, Perry T. Jones, Olmedo had rewarded him with two singles wins and a share with Ham Richardson in the doubles win that had sealed the victory. Success in the ***1959*** Australian Championships confirmed the quality of his play as he beat Neale Fraser in four sets. Six months later 'The Chief', as he was popularly known, won the ***1959*** Wimbledon from Rod Laver for the loss of only two sets, with one of the most competent displays of power tennis seen since the war. After taking part in the unsuccessful defence of the D Cup where he lost to Fraser but beat Laver again, he reached the final of the US Championships but failed once more against Fraser. Immediately he turned professional. JB

MANUEL ('**MANOLO**') **ORANTES** (Spain)

Born 6/2/49. A consumate artist on European clay with exquisite touch and gentle, generous manner, he quickly became an international favourite. A left-hander who, after leading Spain to two Galea Cup victories in ***1968/69***, won his first two important titles in ***1972*** – the German and Italian Opens. His best year was ***1975*** for, besides winning a second German title, the Canadian Open and the first of his two US Clay Court crowns (he won the second in ***1977***), he was triumphant on the clay at Forest Hills to win the US Open. After recovering miraculously to defeat Vilas in a night-time semi-final, having trailed one set to two and 0–5 in the fourth, he was back on court 15 hours later to thrash Jimmy Connors 6–4 6–3 6–3 in a near-perfect display of the clay-court art. In ***1976*** he won the Spanish Open and at the year's end won the Masters in Houston against Fibak with another brave recovery, coming back from one set to two and 1–4. He played in the losing Spanish team in the D Cup challenge round of ***1967*** in Brisbane but led his country to victory in the World Team Cup in Dusseldorf 11 years later. JB

MARGARET EVELYN **OSBORNE** (USA)
Born 4/3/18. Now Mrs du Pont (1947). One of the finest of American doubles players and a formidably successful competitor in singles. With her splendidly consistent serving and her strength and skill at the net, she did much to set the pattern for the period of American supremacy in women's tennis, which began in 1946. Won Wimbledon singles in ***1947*** Forest Hills ***1948/49/50*** and Paris in ***1946/49***. She and Louise Brough won the Wimbledon doubles in ***1946/48/49/50/54***. They ruled the US doubles from ***1942–50*** and ***1955–57***, and held the French title ***1946/47/49***. She won the Wimbledon mixed with Neale Fraser in ***1962*** – 15 years after her first singles victory, at the age of 44 years 125 days, to become Wimbledon's oldest champion of either sex in any event.

SARAH HAMMOND **PALFREY** (USA)
Born 18/9/12. Died 27/2/96 became Mrs J. A. Danzig (1951) formerly Mrs M. Fabyan (1934), and Mrs E. T. Cooke (1940). A fine volleyor with a sweeping backhand and a notable doubles player, she partnered Alice Marble to victory at Wimbledon in ***1938/39*** and won the US doubles title 9 times with a variety of partners – Betty Nuthall (***1930***), Helen Jacobs (***1932/34/35***), Alice Marble (***1937/38/39/40***) and Margaret Osborne (***1941***). She won the US singles in ***1941/45*** and was r/u to Helen Jacobs in***1934/35***. She was the US mixed champion on 4 occasions with Perry (***1932***), Maier (***1935***), Budge (***1937***) and Kramer (***1941***). She played in 10 W Cup matches and won 14 rubbers out of 21.

ADRIANO PANATTA (Italy)
Born 9/7/50. Without doubt, ***1976*** was the *annus mirabilis* of Panatta's career. Until then he had always been dashing and stylish, but had never made full use of his talent. In ***1976***, however, he lived dangerously and survived brilliantly. In Rome he became the first home player to win in Italy for 15 years after frustrating Warwick no fewer than 11 times at m-p in the first round. In Paris, against Hutka, he again faced a first-round m-p and again went on to take the championship. Four months later, when Italy won D Cup for the first time, Panatta played a major role in their victory. Paris, Rome and D Cup – this was Panatta's year! He was also the leading player in the Italian teams which reached the ***1977/79/80*** D Cup finals. He reached the French sf in ***1973/75*** and was runner-up in Rome ***1978*** and Hamburg ***1972***.

FRANK ANDREW **PARKER** (USA)
Born 31/1/16. Shrewd, persistent, and accurate in spite of a certain lightness of shot, he shared with Trabert the distinction, rare for an American, of winning the French title twice. At his best on slow courts, he was ranked in the first 10 in the US for 17 consecutive years between ***1933***, the year of the first of his 5 US Clay Court victories, and ***1949*** when he turned pro. His victories in Paris were in ***1948/49***, and in ***1949*** he won the doubles in Paris and Wimbledon with Gonzales. He won the US singles in ***1944/45*** as an Army sergeant and the doubles with Kramer in ***1943***. He played in the D Cup challenge round against Britain in ***1937*** when the US regained the trophy after 10 years and in the ***1939*** and ***1948*** challenge rounds. In 7 ties between ***1932*** and ***1948***, won 12 of 14 singles rubbers.

GERALD LEIGHTON **PATTERSON** (Australia)
Born 17/12/1895. Died 13/6/1967. Formidably aggressive with a cannonball service modelled on McLoughlin's, he was the dominating player when international competition was resumed in 1919. After being r/u to O'Hara Wood in the ***1914*** Australian singles, he became Wimbledon's first post-war champ by defeating Brookes in ***1919***. He lost his Wimbledon title to Tilden in ***1920*** but regained it against Lycett in ***1922***. R/u doubles in***1922*** (O'Hara Wood) and ***1928*** (Hawkes) and won the mixed with Suzanne Lenglen in***1920***. He won the Australian singles in his fourth final in ***1927***. Between ***1919–28*** he played 46 D Cup rubbers for Australia and Australasia, winning 21 out of his 31 singles and 11 of his 15 doubles in 16 ties. He was a nephew of Dame Nellie Melba and was the first man to win the Wimbledon singles by playing through when the Challenge Round was abolished there in ***1922***.

JOHN EDWARD ('**BUDGE**') **PATTY** (USA)
Born 11/2/24. An American who lived in Paris and developed his game there, 'Budge' Patty, with his elegant, effective forehand volley, was one of the great post-war stylists.***1950*** – when he won both the Wimbledon and French singles – was the peak of his career, but his rivalry with Drobny captured the public's imagination. The most notable of their long and dramatic matches was in the third round at Wimbledon in ***1953***. After 4 hours 20 minutes Patty lost 8–6 16–18 3–6 8–6 12–10 after holding 6 m-ps. He had beaten the Czech at Wimbledon in ***1947*** and 3 years later by 6–1 6–2 3–6 5–7 7–5 in his French f. The last of their meetings was

in ***1954***. Drobny, on his way to the title, won a 4-set sf. Patty won his last title there in ***1957*** when he and Mulloy, then aged 43, beat Hoad and Fraser to take the men's doubles. He won the Italian singles ***1954***, and the German singles ***1953/54*** and doubles ***1953/54/55***.

FREDERICK ('**FRED**') JOHN **PERRY** (Great Britain)
Born 18/5/09. Died 2/2/95. A US citizen. The most successful modern British player, and the first man to win all four Grand Slam titles, a feat achieved only by three others – Budge, Emerson and Laver. He was an aggressive competitor with boundless self-confidence and a remarkable running forehand. Won Wimbledon singles ***1934/35/36*** – the first player since A. F. Wilding (***1910–13***) to take the title 3 years in succession – and mixed (with Dorothy Round) ***1935/36***. US singles ***1933/34/36***. French singles ***1935*** and doubles (with G. P. Hughes) ***1933***. Australian singles ***1934*** and doubles (with Hughes) ***1934***. The world no 1 ***1934–36***, he won 45 out of 52 D Cup rubbers, (34–4 singles, 11–3 doubles) between ***1931–36*** leading Britain to victory in ***1933/34/35/36***. Turned pro in ***1936*** and toured with Vines and Tilden, winning US Pro Champ ***1938/41***. Then founded a sports clothing business and became journalist and broadcaster for BBC Radio.

YVON FRANCOIS MARIE **PETRA** (France)
Born 8/3/16 in Indo–China. Died 12/9/84. Wimbledon's first post-war men's singles champion. Reached mixed f at Wimbledon ***1937*** with Simone Mathieu and won French doubles***1938*** with Destremau, defeating Budge and Mako in f. Between ***1942***, when he was released from a prisoner-of-war camp, and ***1945***, he consolidated his reputation as France's most aggressive competitor in wartime domestic competitions. At Wimbledon,***1946***, his strength, flair and, notably, the consistency of his heavy serving gained this formidably built player an unexpected title. Drobny beat Kramer, the favourite, in 4r. Petra disposed of Pails, the other expected finalist, in qf and then won 5s matches against Tom Brown and Geoff Brown. That was the peak of his career. Marcel Bernard beat him in the French sf – played in July that year – and his consolation was a doubles victory, partnered by Bernard, over Morea and Segura in f. Patty beat him easily on the second day at Forest Hills and in ***1947*** he lost to Tom Brown in qf at Wimbledon.

NICOLA PIETRANGELI (Italy)
Born 11/9/33. A master of the European clay court style, he was born in Tunis (of a French father and Russian mother) and between ***1954–72*** played in 164 D Cup rubbers for Italy, more than anyone in history. Won most rubbers (120), played most singles (110) and won most (78), played most doubles (54) and won most (42), and played in most ties (66). Appeared in the ***1960/61*** Challenge Rounds against Australia, but won only one 'dead' singles. Won French singles ***1959/60*** and doubles (with Sirola), Italian singles ***1957/61***, and German singles ***1960***. Reached sf at Wimbledon, ***1960***, and doubles final (with Sirola) ***1956***.

DR JOSHUA PIM (Ireland)
Born 20/5/1869. Died 15/4/1942. A robust, adventurous competitor, regarded by contemporary critics as one of the great geniuses of early tennis. 'When Pim was at his best he was virtually unplayable,' wrote Wallis Myers. 'It is scarcely exaggerating to say that he could hit a coin placed anywhere on the court.' He reached sf at Wimbledon ***1890***, losing to Hamilton, who became Wimbledon's first Irish champ, then lost in ***1891*** to Wilfred Baddeley in the All-Comers' f and again in ***1892*** Challenge Round. He gained his revenge, however, by beating Baddeley in the ***1893/94*** finals. Pim won the Irish title for the 3rd and last time in ***1895*** but then played little first-class tennis until he was controversially picked for the D Cup match against USA at New York in ***1902***. He was preferred to Laurie Doherty, lost both his singles badly and the British Isles were beaten 3–2. 'Although still very good, Pim had no more than a shadow of his former skill, but alas a great deal more than the shadow of his former weight,' wrote Commander Hillyard.

ADRIAN KARL **QUIST** (Australia)
Born 23/1/13. Died 17/11/91. A shrewd, graceful doubles player, whose wins at Wimbledon were separated by a 15 year gap. Won with J. H. Crawford in ***1935*** and, when almost a veteran, with J. E. Bromwich ***1950***. Held Australian title from ***1936–50***, winning twice with D. P. Turnbull (***1936/37***) and 8 times with Bromwich (***1938/39/40/46/47/48/49/50***). Won US doubles (with Bromwich) ***1939***, French doubles (with J. H. Crawford) ***1935***, and Australian singles ***1936/40/48***. Won 42 out of 56 D Cup rubbers in 28 ties between ***1933–48*** (24–10 singles, 19–3 doubles)

WILLIAM CHARLES **RENSHAW** (Great Britain)
Born 3/1/1861. Died 12/8/1904. The first great champion. Learnt on asphalt at school at Cheltenham with twin brother, Ernest, a more graceful but less determined competitor. They were the first spectacular players and their skill – particularly in volleying and smashing – brought crowds to Wimbledon and contributed considerably to the development of lawn tennis as a spectator sport. 'Willie' Renshaw was singles champ at Wimbledon from ***1881–86*** and in ***1889*** and his seven titles remain a record for men. He held the doubles, with Ernest, in ***1884/85/86/88/89***. Ernest won the singles title in ***1888*** and was beaten by William in the challenge rounds of ***1882*** and ***1883***.

NANCY ANN **RICHEY** (USA)
Born 23/8/42. Later Mrs Gunter (1970). A Texan, famous for her shorts and peaked cap, she was, like her brother, George Clifford Richey, a tenacious baseliner, impressive on clay. Her determination occasionally brought unexpected success on grass. She reached the ***1969*** US final, losing 6–2 6–2 to Margaret Court. She

won in Australia ***1967***, beating Lesley Turner, another clay-court specialist, in the final. At Wimbledon she reached qf seven times in nine years ***1964–72*** but was semi-finalist only in ***1968***. She won Wimbledon doubles with Maria Bueno ***1966***. On clay she won French singles ***1968***, beating Ann Jones to avenge a defeat in the ***1966*** final, but the best evidence of her quality was her record in US Clay Courts. She won Indianapolis from ***1963–68*** and even as late as ***1975*** led Chris Evert 7–5 5–0 in the semi-finals there, twice reaching m-p before retiring with cramp at 2–4 in the final set. She played W Cup from ***1962–68*** and three years of Fed Cup between ***1964–69*** winning 15 of her 17 rubbers (10–1 singles, 5–1 doubles).

ROBERT ('**BOBBY**') LARIMORE **RIGGS** (USA)
Born 25/2/18. Died 25/10/95. A shrewd, confident match–player, with remarkable versatility of shot, he won all 3 titles on his first appearance at Wimbledon in ***1939***. He also won Forest Hills in ***1939***, but lost to McNeill in the French f. He turned pro in ***1941*** and later became a notable competitor in veterans' events, but his greatest fame came at the age of 55. Profiting from the Women's Lib controversy, he challenged and beat Margaret Court 6–2 6–1 in a singles match in Ramona, Cal, and then lost to Billie Jean King 6–4 6–3 6–3, before a record television audience of almost 50 million and 30,492 paying spectators at the Houston Astrodome in September ***1973***.

ANTHONY ('**TONY**') DALTON **ROCHE** (Australia)
Born 17/5/45. Strong, rugged and a fine volleyer, he was the left-hander in one of Wimbledon's most successful doubles partnerships. He won the doubles with John Newcombe in ***1965***, from ***1968–70*** (the first hat-trick of titles since the Dohertys ***1903–5***) and in ***1974***. Other doubles victories with Newcombe included US ***1967***, French ***1967/69***, Australia ***1965/67/71/76*** (he also won in ***1977*** with Ashe) and Italy ***1965/71***. He also won Wimbledon mixed doubles with Francoise Durr ***1976***. He did not achieve as much as expected in singles, partly because of injury. The extraordinary operation on his left elbow, performed without knife or anaesthetic in the Philippines by a faith healer, received worldwide publicity. He never reached an Australian final in spite of numerous attempts, but was runner-up to Laver at Wimbledon in ***1968*** and lost two US Open finals: ***1969*** when Laver beat him to complete the Grand Slam and ***1970*** to Rosewall. His most successful year was ***1966*** when he won French and Italian titles. Played Davis Cup ***1964–78*** but did not play singles in a final until he beat Panatta in the opening match ***1977***. His record in 12 ties was 7–3 in singles and 7–2 in doubles.

KENNETH ('**KEN**') ROBERT **ROSEWALL** (Australia)
Born 2/11/34. For a quarter of a century Rosewall's grace and easy, economical style delighted the connoisseurs and the only regret about his long and distinguished career is that, in spite of four finals over a period of 20 years, he never won the Wimbledon singles title. He began in the 1950's as a Hopman prodigy and it was not until the end of ***1979*** that he retired from Grand Prix tennis. In ***1953***, aged 18, he won the Australian and French singles and, with Hoad, the French and Wimbledon doubles. In ***1954*** he lost to Drobny in the Wimbledon final. Hoad beat him in the ***1956*** Wimbledon final, but Rosewall avenged that defeat in the US final, frustrating Hoad in the last leg of his attempt on the Grand Slam. Turning professional in ***1957***, he took over the leadership of the professional circuit from Gonzales until Laver's arrival in ***1963***. Rosewall's skills endured. In ***1968*** he won the first open tournament at Bournemouth and then recaptured some of his former titles. He regained the French singles and doubles (with Stolle) in ***1968***. In ***1970*** – 14 years after his first success and aged 35 – he won the US title again and reached his fourth final at Forest Hills in ***1974***. The gap between his Australian successes was even wider. After his victories in ***1953/55***, he won again in ***1971/72***. But Wimbledon always eluded him. Newcombe beat him in ***1970***, his third final, and Connors overwhelmed him in the ***1974*** final. In the D Cup he won 19 of his 22 rubbers in 11 ties between ***1953*** and ***1956*** (17–2 singles, 2–1 doubles).

DOROTHY EDITH **ROUND** (Great Britain)
Born 13/7/09. Died 12/11/82. Became Mrs D. L. Little (1937). Determined and efficient, possessing a fine forehand drive and shrewd drop-shot, she was one of the two British women's singles champs at Wimbledon between the wars. She gained her first notable victory there against Lili d'Alvarez in ***1931***, was r/u to Helen Wills Moody in ***1933***, then beat Helen Jacobs to win the title in ***1934*** and regained it against Jadwiga Jedrzejowska in ***1937***. She won the Australian singles in ***1935*** and the Wimbledon mixed in ***1934*** (with Miki) and ***1935/36*** (with Perry). She won 4 of her 13 W Cup rubbers between ***1931–36***.

ELIZABETH MONTAGUE **RYAN** (USA)
Born 5/2/1892. Died 6/7/1979. Suzanne Lenglen's doubles partner and the winner of 19 Wimbledon titles. A determined competitor with a cunningly chopped forehand and a great appetite for match-play, she was regarded by contemporaries as 'the best player never to win a great singles Championship'. With a variety of playing partners, she was victorious in the Wimbledon doubles 12 times – ***1914*** with Morton, ***1919/20/21/22/23/25*** with Lenghen, ***1926*** with Browne, ***1927/30*** with Wills Moody, ***1933/34*** with Matthieu. She won 7 mixed titles ***1919/21/23*** with Lycett, ***1927*** with Hunter, ***1928*** with Spence, ***1930*** with Crawford, ***1932*** with Maier. She also won US doubles in ***1926*** with Goss and the French doubles ***1930/32*** with Moody, ***1933/34*** with Matthieu.

GABRIELA **SABATINI** (Argentina)
Born on 16 May 1970 in Buenos Aires, Argentina. One of the most glamorous players ever to reach the heights 'Gaby' first appeared on the scene as an outstanding junior, inspired to take up the game by the example of Argentina's great men's champion Guillermo Vilas whose backhand she copied. The youngest

player ever to win the Orange Bowl 18's when she took the ***1983*** event at the age of 13 years 7 months, she was the No.1 junior on the ITF rankings in ***1994*** and No.1 in Argentina and South America from ***1985-1989***. The youngest semi-finalist (at the time) in the ***1985*** French Open she never did better in Paris during the next 10 consecutive challenges. It was at the ***1990*** US Open that her considerable talent finally came to full flower when she upset the reigning champion and world No.1 Steffi Graf with a brilliant display of all-court tennis. She never reached those heights again and could look back on the ***1988*** US final and the ***1991*** Wimbledon final (when she twice served for the match against Graf) as the other highlights of her 43 Grand Slam appearances. Her ***1988*** doubles win at Wimbledon (with Graf) was her only major doubles success. Elsewhere her ***1987*** and ***1994*** Virginia Slims Championship wins were the best of her 27 career successes that earned her a total of $8.7 million. Her silver medal at the Seoul Olympics in ***1988*** brough her great personal satisfaction. In ***1992*** a rose was named after her and a Gaby Doll was marketed in her name. Towards the end of her career she developed her talent as a singer to make several recordings. JB

MANUEL ('**MANOLO**') **SANTANA** (Spain)

Born 10/5/38. Learnt the game as a ballboy in Madrid and, after a period in which he was the most admired clay court player in Europe, won US singles ***1965***, and Wimbledon singles ***1966***. Possesed a remarkable forehand and great delicacy of touch. Won French singles ***1961/ 64***, defeating Pietrangeli in both finals, and doubles (with Emerson) ***1963***, and South African singles ***1967***. The most successful Spanish player in history, he won 92 D Cup rubbers out of 120 in 46 ties between ***1958–73*** (69–17 singles, 23–11 doubles).

RICHARD ('**DICK**') **SAVITT** (USA)

Born 4/3/27. His talent was discovered in the classic fashion by a complete stranger who saw him playing in a public park, and after a modest junior career he became a powerful exponent of the serve-and-volley game. Concentrating on tennis after a basketball injury in ***1949***, he rose rapidly on the US ranking list, moving up from 16th to 6th after reaching sf at Forest Hills, ***1950***, with victories over Seixas and Bromwich. His remarkable year was ***1951***. He won both the Australian and Wimbledon titles, defeating McGregor in both finals. This was his first trip to Europe and he never achieved the same kind of success again, although he played some memorable matches, notably sf against Rosewall at Forest Hills, ***1956***, and a vain defence of his US indoor title in a three-hour f in ***1959***. He was a member of the US D Cup team in ***1951***, but was not chosen to play in the Challenge Round against Australia.

FREDERICK ('**TED**') RUDOLPH **SCHROEDER** (USA)

Born 20/7/21. A powerful Californian whose aggressive serve-and-volley game brought him much success on fast surfaces. The US National Junior Champion in ***1939***, he won the NCAA Championships from Stanford in ***1942*** and the same year won the US Championships, defeating Frank Parker in the final. In ***1949*** he reached the final again but lost in five sets to Pancho Gonzales. Earlier that same year, on his only visit to Wimbledon he had won the singles in heroic fashion after surviving four five-set matches. In the first round he had beaten his doubles partner, Gardnar Mulloy, 7–5 in the fifth (later they reached the doubles final and lost to Gonzales and Parker). In the quarter-finals he had been m-p down to Frank Sedgman and, despite being foot-faulted on his first serve, had followed in his second serve to hit a winning volley and finally won 9–7 in the final set. In all he played 291 games. Only two champions played more – Boris Becker (292) in ***1985*** and Ashley Cooper (322) in ***1958***. In doubles he won the US Championships with Jack Kramer in ***1940/41/47*** and the mixed with Louise Brough in ***1942***. A distinguished member of the US D Cup team between ***1946–51***, he played in six Challenge Rounds, winning eight of his 11 singles and one of his four doubles. Played in 8 ties, winning 13 of 19 rubbers (11–3 singles, 2–3 doubles). JB

RICHARD ('**DICK**') DUDLEY **SEARS** (USA)

Born 16/10/1861 Died 8/4/1943. The first US Champion in ***1881*** while he was still a 19-year-old student at Harvard, this great Boston athlete was the youngest winner until the slightly younger Oliver Campbell won in ***1890*** aged 19 and a half. (They were both older than Pete Sampras who became the youngest ever winner in ***1990*** aged 19 years, 28 days). Sears retained his title for the next six years, playing through in ***1882/83*** and winning the newly introduced Challenge Round in ***1884/85/86/87***. He also won six doubles titles, five with James Dwight (***1882/83/84/96/97***) and one with Joseph Clark (***1885***). JB

FRANCIS ('**FRANK**') ARTHUR **SEDGMAN** (Australia)

Born 29/10/27. A superb volleyer who seemed to glide about the court, he was Australia's first post-war Wimbledon singles champ and, with Ken McGregor, he achieved the Grand Slam of the 4 major doubles titles in ***1951***. Won Wimbledon singles ***1952*** and doubles (with J. E. Bromwich) ***1948*** and (with McGregor) ***1951/52***. US singles ***1951/52*** and doubles (with Bromwich) ***1950*** and (with McGregor) ***1951***. French doubles (with McGregor) ***1951/52***. Australian singles ***1949/50*** (with McGregor) doubles ***1951/52***. Italian singles and doubles (with McGregor) ***1952***. Won 25 D Cup rubbers out of 28 in 10 ties between ***1949–52***(16–3 singles, 9–0 doubles). Turned pro in ***1953***.

FRANCISCO ('**PANCHO**') **SEGURA** (Ecuador)

Born 20/6/21. An unorthodox showman who made his reputation in his pro years – he achieved little as an amateur. Won the NCAA singles ***1943/44/45***, the only triple winner this century, plus the US Clay Court title in ***1944*** and the US Indoor in ***1946***, but made little mark at Wimbledon, losing to Tom Brown and to Drobny in his two singles appearances. He turned pro in ***1947*** and immediately became one of the great entertainers of the pro game, winning the US Pro title ***1950/51/52***. With his double-fisted forehand, his deadly lobs, his scuttling speed about the court, and his beaming smile, he was a most popular competitor for 20 years. If he did not win as many titles as he deserved, he was always capable of testing players of the quality of Kramer, Rosewall, and Gonzales.

ELIAS VICTOR ('**VIC**') **SEIXAS** (USA)
Born 30/8/23. A doggedly successful American competitor. Won Wimbledon singles ***1953*** and mixed 3 times with Doris Hart (***1953/54/55***) and once with Shirley Fry (***1956***). US singles ***1954*** and doubles (with M. G. Rose) ***1952*** and (with M. A. Trabert) ***1954***. French doubles (with Trabert) ***1954/55***. Played in 7 successive D Cup Challenge Rounds and won 38 out of 55 rubbers in 19 ties between ***1951–57*** (24–12 singles, 14–5 doubles).

MARGARET SMITH (Australia)
Born 16/7/42. Now Mrs Court (1967). In ***1970*** she became the second woman to achieve the Grand Slam of the major singles championships, having brought off a unique mixed doubles slam with Fletcher in ***1963***. A powerful athlete, superbly fit, with a heavy service, great stamina and a formidable reach on the volley, she won a record number of 62 GS titles (24 singles, 19 doubles, 19 mixed) – and would have won more if she had not been afflicted by occasional and often inexplicable losses of confidence. Her major singles successes were Wimbledon ***1963/65/70***, US Championships ***1962/65/69/70/73***, French Championships ***1962/64/69/70/73***, and Australian Championships ***1960–66***, ***1969–71*** and ***1973***. She was also three times the holder of the Italian (***1962/63/64***), German (***1964/65/66***) and South African (***1968/70/71***) titles. In addition, she won the doubles at Wimbledon twice, with Turner (***1964***) and Tegart (***1969***) and the mixed five times, with Fletcher (***1963/65/66/68***) and Riessen (***1975***). She took the US doubles five times – with Ebbern (***1963***), Bueno (***1968***) Dalton (***1970***) and Wade (***1973/75***), and the mixed on eight occasions with Mark (***1961***), Stolle (***1962/65***), Fletcher (***1963***), Newcombe (***1964***) and Riessen (***1969/70/72***). She won the French four times in doubles with Turner (***1964/65***), Tegart (***1966***) and Wade (***1973***) and mixed with Fletcher (***1963/64/65***) and Riessen (***1969***), and she held eight Australian doubles with Reitano (***1961***), Ebbern (***1962/63***), Turner (***1965***), Dalton (***1969/70***), Goolagong (***1971***) and Wade (***1973***) and two mixed titles with Fletcher (***1963/64***). She toured successfully, with the help of her husband, Barry, with two children, but retired in ***1977*** when she found that she was expecting a third baby.

STANLEY ('**STAN**') ROGER **SMITH** (USA)
Born 14/12/46. The very epitome of the All-American boy with his tall straight-backed figure, his fair hair and his clean-cut good looks, he became a national hero in ***1972***, as well as the world's No.1 player, when he won a magnificent Wimbledon final against Nastase and then beat the Rumanian again in the opening rubber of the D Cup final on unfriendly clay in Bucharest to launch the United States towards an improbable victory against the odds. Earlier, in ***1969***, he had won the US Nationals and the following year had beaten Laver and Rosewall to capture the first-ever Masters which, that year, was a round-robin competition. When he won the US Open in ***1971*** on the grass of Forest Hills he was perfecting the serve-and-volley technique that made him such an awkward opponent. Although his groundstrokes were never his strength, he used them intelligently to secure the few breaks of serve that were necessary as he blanketed the net to secure his own service games. His doubles partnership with Lutz was one of the best American pairings there has ever been. They are the only pair to have won US National titles on all four surfaces – grass, clay, hard and indoor. Four times they won the US Open – ***1968/74/78/80*** and in ***1977*** they were successful both in South Africa and the US Pro at Boston. In D Cup they are the only American pair to have won three Challenge Round rubbers and two in the Final Round. Overall his D Cup record is 35 wins and 7 losses in 24 ties between ***1968–79*** (15–4 singles, 20–3 doubles). JB

MICHAEL DETLEF **STICH** (Germany)
Born 18/10/68. Emerging from Boris Becker's shadow in ***1991***, he beat his fellow German in the Wimbledon final with a brilliant display of grass court skill that stamped him as one of the game's great fast-court players. The following year, ***1992***, he teamed with John McEnroe to win the doubles at Wimbledon and then joined Becker to win an Olympic gold medal in Barcelona. But it was not until ***1993*** that he was truly accepted as a great champion by his countrymen. In that *annus mirabilis* he led his country to the final of the World Team Cup, remained undefeated as he beat Sampras to win the ATP Tour World Championship, was a finalist in the Compaq Grand Slam Cup and, in Becker's absence, led Germany to a decisive Davis Cup final win over Australia in Dusseldorf. By winning six of his eight finals that year on four different surfaces he finished as the world's No.2, the highest ranking he ever achieved. In ***1994*** he reached the US Open final but lost to Agassi. Tall, slim and wiry he always looked physically frail and it was injuries to his shoulder and ankle that eventually forced him to retire from the game in ***1996*** after surprising everyone by reaching the French Open final where Kafelnikov beat him. Altogether he recorded 18 singles wins and nine in doubles and in seven years of Davis Cup play had a 35–11 win/loss record (21–9 in singles, 14–2 in doubles) from 17 ties. JB

FREDERICK ('**FRED**') SYDNEY **STOLLE** (Australia)
Born 8/10/38. Former Sydney bank clerk, regarded primarily as doubles specialist, who by diligence and determination became one of the most successful singles players of the 1960s. Powerful serving and volleying, added to dogged consistency in return of service on the backhand, compensated for his lack of mobility and flexibility. Shared with Von Cramm the unlucky distinction of losing in 3 successive Wimbledon singles f,

falling to McKinley (***1963***) and Emerson (***1964/65***). Was also r/u to Lundquist in ***1964*** Italian f, but won French singles ***1965*** and US and German titles ***1966***. Established himself first as a doubles player with Hewitt. They won Australia ***1963/64***, Wimbledon ***1962/64*** and Italy ***1963/64***. With Emerson, who had dominated him in singles, won French and US doubles ***1965*** and Australia, Italy and US ***1966***. In ***1981***, aged 42, he and Newcombe (37) took McEnroe/ Fleming to 5s tie-break in US Open sf. Became contract professional ***1967*** and reached Wimbledon doubles f with Rosewall ***1968***, and won mixed doubles there with Ann Jones in ***1969***. Between ***1964–66*** he won 13 out of his 16 D Cup rubbers in 6 ties (10–2 singles, 3–1 doubles). Coached NY Sets to victory in World Team Tennis competition ***1976***.

ERIC WILLIAM **STURGESS** (South Africa)

Born 10/5/20. South Africa's most successful singles competitor and their nat champ on no fewer than 11 occasions, beginning a sequence of victories in ***1939/40*** and continuing in ***1946***, ***1948–54***, and ***1957***. Outside Johannesburg his major achievement was the capture of the German singles ***1952;*** r/u in Paris ***1947/51*** and lost to Gonzales in ***1948*** US f. Twice he was in Wimbledon sf, but in spite of speed, steadiness, and elegance, he lacked the weight of shot to win in the highest class and his second service was vulnerable. He won the French doubles with Fannin ***1947*** and a number of mixed titles, notably Wimbledon ***1949*** (with Sheila Summers) and ***1950*** (with Louise Brough), and F Hills ***1949*** (with Brough).

MAY GODFREY **SUTTON** (USA)

Born in Plymouth, England, 25/9/1886. Died 4/10/1975. Became Mrs T.C. Bundy (1912). In ***1905*** the first overseas player to win a Wimbledon title. The seventh and youngest child of a British naval officer, Captain A. de G. Sutton, she learnt tennis on asphalt courts after her family moved to California in ***1893***. She was forceful and vigorous with a disconcerting top-spin forehand. F. R. Burrow commented: 'She took a deep breath before every stroke and then hit the ball with all her force to the accompaniment of a very audible expiration.' After winning the US singles and doubles in ***1904*** she went, aged 18, to Wimbledon ***1905*** and defeated the holder, Miss Douglass, in the Challenge Round. Miss Douglass regained the title the following year, but then lost a third battle with the Californian in ***1907***. After winning the US Clay Court singles ***1912***, Miss Sutton married Thomas Bundy, 3 times a US doubles champ. She played doubles in the ***1925*** W Cup and in ***1929*** returned to Wimbledon at 42 to defeat Eileen Bennett, seeded 4, and reach the qf. She was still playing 44 years later. Her daughter Dorothy represented the US 3 times in the W Cup and won the Australian singles ***1938***, and a nephew, John Doeg, was US champ in ***1930***.

WILLIAM ('**BILLY**') FRANKLIN **TALBERT** (USA)

Born 4/9/18. An expert in the practice, technique and strategy of doubles. The best right-court player of his generation, his most important victories were gained with Mulloy, with whom he won the US doubles ***1942/45/46/48***, and a total of 84 out of 90 tournaments in ten years. With a variety of partners, he won US Clay Court doubles ***1942/44/45/46*** and the US Indoor Doubles ***1949/50/51/52/54***. Abroad, with the young Trabert, also from Cincinnati, he won French and Italian doubles ***1950***. He was runner-up to Parker in US singles ***1944/45*** and US Indoor champion ***1948/51***. He won nine of his ten D Cup rubbers ***1946–53***, in 8 ties, (2–0 singles, 7–1 doubles) and from ***1953–57*** he captained the US D Cup team. Later became Tournament Director of the US Open. All this was achieved despite the disability of diabetes.

WILLIAM ('**BILL**') TATEM **TILDEN** (USA)

Born 10/2/1893. Died 5/6/1953. For many critics the greatest player and student of match-strategy in the history of the game who was world No 1 ***1920–25*** and US No 1 ten years in a row ***1920–29***, a record. Tall, with a long reach and a long stride, great strength and versatility of shot, and a powerful sense of drama, Tilden did not win a major title until he was 27. Then won Wimbledon singles ***1920/21/30***, and doubles (with F. T. Hunter) ***1927***, and US singles ***1920/21/22/23/24/25/29***, and doubles (with Richards) ***1918/21/22***, (with Norton) ***1923***, (with Hunter) ***1927***. Was imprisoned for homosexual activities in ***1951***, and died in tragic circumstances two years later, penniless and with few remaining friends. Was first Italian champ in ***1930*** and played D Cup from ***1920–30*** winning 34 rubbers out of 41 and 21 out of 28 in Challenge Rounds. Between ***1920–26*** won 13 successive Challenge Round singles. His final record from 17 ties was 25–5 in singles and 9–2 in doubles. Turned pro in ***1931*** after winning 138 of the 192 tournaments he had contested as an amateur.

MARION ANTHONY ('**TONY**') **TRABERT** (USA)

Born 16/8/30. Won Wimbledon singles ***1955*** and US singles ***1953/55*** without losing a set. Won French singles ***1954/55*** and doubles victories included US in ***1954*** (with E. V. Seixas), French ***1950*** (with W. F. Talbert) and ***1954/55*** (with Seixas) and Italian ***1950*** (with Talbert). Won 27 out of 35 D Cup rubbers in 14 ties between ***1951–55*** (16–5 singles, 11–3 doubles). Served a term as US captain in the ***1970s***. Turned pro in ***1955***.

CHRISTINE CLARA **TRUMAN** (Great Britain)

Born 16/2/41. Now Mrs G. T. Janes (1967). Britain's most popular post-war player. She possessed a powerful forehand, a disconcerting ability to hit her way out of crises, a remarkable capacity for unorthodox volleying, and a temperament and court manners that made her a model for every schoolgirl in the country. She was always regarded as a potential Wimbledon champ and reached sf at the age of 16 at her first Wimbledon, where she lost to Althea Gibson, the eventual winner. Afterwards came a series of spectacular failures until she reached the ***1961*** f, only to fall to Angela Mortimer. Her best performances were a victory over Miss

Gibson in the ***1958*** W Cup match, which helped to give Britain the trophy for the first time since the war, and the capture of the French and Italian singles titles in ***1959***. Won ***1960*** Australian doubles with Maria Bueno. She and her sister, Nell, formed an aggressively effective – and sometimes erratic – doubles partnership. She won 10 rubbers out of 25 in 11 W Cup matches.

WENDY MAY **TURNBULL** (Australia)
Born 26/11/52. Known popularly as 'Rabbit' for her speed about the court, this Australian doubles expert was nevertheless a singles finalist at three of the four Grand Slams and was ranked among the world's top ten for eight years (***1977–1984***). Twice she lost to Chris Evert (French Open ***1977***, US Open ***1979***) and once to Hana Mandlikova (Australian Open ***1980***). For someone whose doubles prowess made her a much sought after partner it is curious that she never won a doubles or mixed title at the Australian Open. Her four ladies doubles successes came in ***1978*** at Wimbledon (with Kerry Reid), in ***1979*** at the French and US Opens (both with Betty Stove), and in ***1982*** at the US Open (with Rosie Casals). In mixed doubles she won five Grand Slam titles – the French Open in ***1979*** (with Bob Hewitt) and ***1982*** (with John Lloyd), the US Open in ***1980*** (with Marty Riessen), and Wimbledon twice, in ***1983*** and ***1984*** (both with John Lloyd). Her last important success came at the Seoul Olympics in ***1988*** where she was a doubles bronze medallist with Liz Smyllie. She appeared in a record 45 Federation Cup ties from ***1977*** contributing 46 wins from her 62 rubbers (17–8 in singles 29–8 in doubles) and later served as Fed Cup captain. She was awarded the OBE in 1984 for services to tennis. JB

LESLEY ROSEMARY **TURNER** (Australia)
Born 16/8/42. Now Mrs W. W. Bowrey (1968). Clever, strong and persistent, she gained her principal successes on European clay courts. In ***1961*** on her first European tour she lost to Maria Bueno in the Italian final and was runner-up again ***1962/64*** before winning the title ***1967/68***. She won the French singles ***1963***, defeating Ann Jones, and ***1965***, beating Margaret Court, and was runner-up ***1962/67***. She reached the Australian final ***1964/67***. In doubles, with Margaret Court, she won Wimbledon ***1964***, Paris ***1964/65*** and Australia ***1965***. Also took the Australian doubles title, with Judy Tegart, ***1964/67*** and the US doubles, with Darlene Hard, ***1961***. Won Wimbledon mixed doubles with Fred Stolle ***1961/64***.

JOHN ('**JOHNNY**') WILLIAM **VAN RYN** (USA)
Born 30/6/05. Formed one of the most famous of all doubles partnerships with Wilmer Allison. Pat Hughes described their combination as 'a perfect blending of styles...Van Ryn dipped the ball over from the right court and his partner stepped in at the psychological moment for the final volley'. George Lott thought that their deep personal friendship and knowledge of each other's movements and reactions played an important part in their success. With Allison, Van Ryn succeeded at Wimbledon in ***1929–30*** and took the US title in ***1931/35***. He won Paris and Wimbledon with Lott in ***1931***. In the ***1929*** D Cup Challenge Round he and Allison beat Cochet and Borotra and in the ***1932*** match they defeated Cochet and Brugnon. He was a member of the US team from ***1928–36*** and won 32 of his 44 rubbers in 24 ties. (18–10 singles, 14–2 doubles).

GUILLERMO VILAS (Argentina)
Born 17/8/52. For a man who had learned his tennis on the slow red clay of Buenos Aires it is remarkable that his first major success should have been to win the ***1974*** Masters title on grass at Kooyong Stadium, Melbourne. This was the only time the tournament was played on grass and his wins over Newcombe, Borg and Nastase were as brilliant as they were unexpected. He proved that this had been no fluke by winning the Australian Open twice, in ***1978*** and ***1979***. A powerfully built left-hander with heavily topped groundstrokes, he specialised in wearing down the opposition, which he did successfully in ***1977*** both at the French Open and the US Open, which for the third and last time was being played on American clay courts. That year he claimed 15 titles altogether. Coached and managed shrewdly by Ion Tiriac, he won 61 of the 103 finals he contested in a long career and in the ***1977/78*** seasons he won 46 consecutive singles matches, a record in the open era. JB

HENRY **ELLSWORTH VINES** (USA)
Born 28/9/11. Died 17/3/94. The possessor of a fine forehand and one of the fastest services of all time. Defeated Bunny Austin in ***1932*** 6–4 6–2 6–0 in one of the shortest Wimbledon f and lost title next year in a classic f against Jack Crawford. Won US singles ***1931/32*** and Australian doubles ***1933*** with Gledhill. Played D Cup ***1932/33***, winning 13 rubbers out of 16, all singles, in 8 ties. Turned pro ***1934***.

BARON **GOTTFRIED** ALEXANDER MAXIMILIAN WALTER KURT **VON CRAMM** (Germany)
Born 7/7/09. Died in car accident in Egypt 9/11/76. An elegant stylist and Germany's most successful pre-war player. Won French singles ***1934/36*** and doubles (with H. Henkel) ***1937***, and German singles ***1932/33/34/35/48/49*** and doubles ***1948/49/53/55***. Like F. S. Stolle, he was losing singles finalist at Wimbledon for 3 successive years – ***1935–37***. Won Wimbledon mixed (with Hilda Krahwinkel) **1933** and US doubles (with Henkel) ***1937***. Won 82 D Cup rubbers out of 102 (58–10 singles, 24–9 doubles) in 37 ties between ***1932–53***.

SARAH **VIRGINIA WADE** (Great Britain)
Born 10/7/45. A spectacular and dramatic competitor, at her 16th attempt she finally achieved her ambition of winning the women's singles at Wimbledon in the Centenary year of ***1977***. Until then her career had been an extravagant mixture of bitter disappointments, many of the worst endured at Wimbledon, and dazzling successes. Her first major success was gained at US Open ***1968*** when she defeated Billie Jean King 6–4 6–2 in the

final. She won the Australian title, beating Evonne Goolagong in ***1972*** and gained her only major clay-court success in ***1971***, when she defeated Helga Masthoff in the Italian final. Her best doubles victories – France ***1973***, US ***1973/75***, Australia ***1975*** and Italy ***1968*** – were won with Margaret Court, but she also succeeded in Rome ***1971*** with Mrs Masthoff and ***1973*** with Olga Morozova. She also holds the record for the most appearances of any player of any nation in both Fed Cup (100 rubbers in 57 ties) and the W Cup (56 rubbers in 20 ties).

MATS ARNE OLOF **WILANDER** (Sweden)
Born 22/8/64. When he won the French Open junior title in 1981, little did anyone suspect that twelve months later, aged 17 years 9 months and 6 days, and unseeded, he would become the youngest ever French Open Champion (***1982***). (He would remain the youngest man to win a Grand Slam singles crown until Boris Becker won Wimbledon in 1985, aged 17 years 7 months. Then Michael Chang lowered the record to 17 years 3 months when he dramatically won the French Open in 1989). His relentless topspin driving, single-handed on the forehand, double-handed on the backhand, plus intense concentration and speedy court coverage (all so reminiscent of his great Swedish predecessor Bjorn Borg), brought him two more successes in Paris (***1985,1988***). It was a mark of his all-round ability that he should have been able to win the Australian Open on grass in ***1983*** with back-to-back wins against McEnroe and Lendl. The following year (***1984***) he won a second Australian title on grass and then won for a third time in ***1988*** when the Championship was played for the first time at the new National Tennis Centre at Flinders Park. When, later in ***1988***, he ended Lendl's streak of 157 consecutive weeks at No.1 to win the US Open title, he became the first man since Connors in ***1974*** to hold three of the four Grand Slam titles in the same year. That win also lifted him to the No.1 world ranking, a position he would hold for 20 weeks. Already in ***1985*** his second French win had given him a fourth Grand Slam title before his 21st birthday – the only man ever to achieve that feat. Altogether he won 33 singles and 7 doubles titles and went on competing spasmodically up to the end of ***1996***. A member of Sweden's successful Davis Cup teams in ***1984*** (d.USA 4–1), ***1985*** (d. W.Germany 3–2) and ***1987*** (d. India 5–0), he won 36 of his 50 singles rubbers and 7 of his 9 doubles rubbers in 26 ties spanning ten years from 1981. JB

ANTHONY FREDERICK **WILDING** (New Zealand)
Born 31/10/1883. Killed in action in Belgium 9/5/1915. Coached by his father, a notable cricketer, he won the champ of Canterbury, New Zealand, at the age of 17 and went to Cambridge Univ for which he played ***1904–05***. The Aus singles champion ***1906–09*** and ***1906*** doubles winner (with Heath), he became one of the great heroes of Edwardian tennis, winning the singles champ at Wimbledon ***1910/11/12/13***. Won doubles (with N. E. Brookes) in ***1907/14*** and (with M. J. G. Ritchie) ***1908/10***. He won 21 of the 30 D Cup rubbers which he played in 11 ties for Australasia between ***1905–14*** (15–6 singles, 6–3 doubles).

HELEN NEWINGTON **WILLS** (USA)
Born 6/10/05. Died 1/1/98. Became Mrs F. S. Moody (1929), later Mrs A. Roark (1939). Lenglen's successor as ruler of Wimbledon. A relentless baseliner, she won the singles 8 times in 9 attempts, losing only to Kitty McKane in 1924. Between ***1927–32*** she won all the major singles champs, except Australia, without losing a set. Won Wimbledon singles ***1927/28/29/30/32 /33/35/38*** and doubles (with Hazel Wightman) ***1924*** and (with Elizabeth Ryan) ***1927/30***. US singles ***1923/24/25/27/28/29/31***, and doubles (with Mrs J. B. Jessup) ***1922***, (with Hazel Wightman) ***1924/28***, and (with Mary K. Browne) ***1925***. French singles ***1928/29/30/32*** and doubles (with Elizabeth Ryan) ***1930/31/32***.

SIDNEY BURR BEARDSLEE **WOOD** (USA)
Born 1/11/11. A nephew of the late Julian Myrick, a former President of the US LTA and the prime mover in ***1913*** in the development of Forest Hills as the national centre of tennis in the US, he made his first appearance at Wimbledon, aged 15, in ***1927***, playing Lacoste on the Centre Court. In ***1931***, aged 19 years and 243 days, he became Wimbledon's second youngest champion at the time. He won by default. Frank Shields fell in 4s of his sf against Borotra and damaged an ankle. Shields won, but was not fit enough to play in f. A shrewd strategist and a graceful stroke-maker, Wood was r/u to Allison at Forest Hills in ***1935*** but lost 6–2 6–2 6–3 in one of the tournament's most disappointing finals. He played in 7 Davis Cup ties, winning 8 out of his 14 rubbers (5–6 singles, 3–0 doubles) between ***1931*** and ***1934***.

NANCYE MEREDITH **WYNNE** (Australia)
Born 10/6/17. Became Mrs.G.F. Bolton (1940). The most successful of Australian champions until the arrival of Margaret Court, Nancy Wynne Bolton's career spanned the years of the Second World War. She won the Australian singles six times (***1937/40/46/47/48/51***) and the doubles on ten occasions, all with her great friend, Thelma Coyne Long (***1936/37/38/39/40/ 47/48/49/ 51/52***), plus four mixed with Colin Long (***1940/46/47/48***). In 1938 she became the first Australian to reach the final of the US Championships, losing to Alice Marble. In ***1947*** she was a quarter-finalist at Wimbledon and a semi-finalist in New York, performances that earned her a world ranking of No.4. JB

Obituaries

PIERRE BABOLAT, who died on 2 September 1998, aged 51, was one of the ill-fated passengers on Swissair flight 111 which crashed after taking off from New York. He was travelling back to his home in Lyon. Since 1985 he had been chairman of the Babolat company that produced among the finest tennis strings, stringing machines and other accessories available in the trade. In 1994 the company produced their first tennis racquet and saw it win a first Grand Slam title when Carlos Moya wielded it at the 1998 French Open.

JOAN BAKER, who died on 2 April 1998 aged 95, was twice the British junior champion (in 1920 and 1921). Born Joan Austin, she was the sister of Bunny Austin, the Davis Cup player who with Fred Perry helped Britain to dominate the Davis Cup competition between 1933 and 1936. Joan's tennis career may not have been as spectacular as that of her more famous brother but she was a Wimbledon doubles finalist in 1923, in partnership with Evelyn Colyer, and won many doubles and mixed titles at home and abroad. Two years later Joan married the British Davis Cup player Randlolph Lycett, an Australian doubles expert who was invited to represent that country in 1911 but did not accept. Lycett died in 1935 and after the war Joan turned to coaching before opening a riding school in Surrey. In 1975 she married Donald Baker. She is survived by a son and a daughter.

GERALD BATTRICK, who died on 26 November 1998 at the age of 51 after a brave fight against brain cancer, was a former British junior champion who won the Plate at Wimbledon in 1968 and two years later earned Davis Cup selection. An astute match player with a superb backhand and great touch, he had wins over Mark Cox, Owen Davidson, Tom Okker, Arthur Ashe and Stan Smith on the Dewar Cup circuit in the 1970's, winning the Aberavon event in 1970, not far from his home town of Bridgend. His capture of the British Hard Court Championships in 1971 was the prelude to an offer from World Championship Tennis. He joined Lamar Hunt's troupe of contract professionals in 1972. By the time he retired from the circuit he had married Carolyn Camp, a Surrey county player and they went to live in Germany where Gerald was engaged as coach by a club in the Hamburg area for whom he played in the Bundesleague. Eventually the call of home brought him back to Bridgend where he set up a successful coaching business which specialised in Summer courses for young Europeans who wanted to combine travel and language tuition with their tennis. He is survived by his wife, his son Jamie, himself a fine tennis player who has inherited the coaching school, and a daughter Amanda.

LILI D'ALVAREZ, who died in Madrid on 8 July 1998 at the age of 93, was the best Spanish woman of the pre-World War II era who for three years in a row was the defeated finalist at Wimbledon. In 1926 she lost a close three-set match against Britain's Kitty Godfree who had won her first title two years earlier, and in 1927 and 1928 she was the victim of America's dominant world champion, Helen Wills. Her skirt-trousers which allowed greater freedom of movement than conventional tennis attire became fashionable among active sportswomen of the period. Born in Rome of Spanish parents on 9 May 1905, she spent her early years in Switzerland where the family had moved because of her mother's poor health. It was there that she developed her natural sporting ability that brought her junior tennis honours as well as a figure skating prize at the age of 11 and the St Moritz gold medal five years later. When she was 18 the family moved again, this time to the Cote d'Azur, where she won the tournaments at Aix-les-Bains and Monte Carlo, the first of many singles, doubles and mixed doubles successes she would enjoy throughout Europe. In 1929, in partnership with Kea Bouman of the Netherlands, she captured the French Ladies Doubles Championship, her only Grand Slam success. In 1931 she turned her hand to journalism covering tennis events as well as Spanish politics for the *Daily Mail*. Following Franco's victory in the Spanish Civil War she won the Spanish Championships of 1941 and one year later decided to retire from the circuit. A devout Catholic, she wrote several books on christian belief and feminism. Always active during a very busy life she had also been successful as a motor-racing driver and as an exponent of the Tango. In 1934 she had married the Count de Valdene but they separated in 1939.

ALLAN HEYMAN who died on 6 September 1998 at the age of 77 had been the President of the International Lawn Tennis Federation (as it was then known) from 1971 to 1974, having been the Danish representative on that body since 1951. The early 1970s was a time of evolution in the sport when the players, released by the arrival of open tennis in 1968 from the shackles of outmoded amateur rules imposed by dictatorial National Associations, were insisting on freedom of action. Heyman, a Danish lawyer who lived in England, became embroiled in controversy when the Yugoslav Federation suspended Nikki Pilic in June 1973 for allegedly refusing to play in a Davis Cup tie, a charge he strenuously denied. The recently formed Association of Tennis Professionals backed Pilic and threatened to withdraw their members from Wimbledon if Pilic was not allowed to play. Heyman would not budge. With the failure of an injunction in the High Court, sought by the ATP to overturn the ITF decision, 93 players did withdraw. This marked the end of the ITF's rigid control of players.

In 1941 Heyman, half Jewish and then living in Denmark, had set off in a boat bound for Sweden with several doctors and rowed for eight hours to escape the German invaders. After the war he qualified first as a Danish lawyer and then read for the English Bar. Called to the Middle Temple in 1951, he spent the rest of his working life in London specialising in Chancery work. He lived in Suffolk and maintained a close connection with his many tennis friends until his death.

SIR FRANCIS RENOUF, who died in October 1998 at the age of 80, was a former New Zealand Universities tennis champion and Oxford Blue who in later life would serve for a time as the President of the New Zealand Tennis Association. A financier nicknamed 'Frank the Bank', he is reputed to have become the wealthiest New Zealander in the world at the height of his stockbroking and merchant banking activities in the 1950's with a personal fortune approaching £100 million. A flamboyant philanthropist, he maintained homes in London and Sydney as well as in New Zealand and always drove Rolls Royce cars. He supported New Zealand tennis by paying for the construction in his native Wellington of a National Tennis Centre which was named after him. In 1987 he was knighted for his services to the game. Renouf had married in 1954 Anne Darkin by whom he had a son and three daughters but they were divorced in 1978. His second wife, Susan, was the daughter of a diplomat and had formerly been married to the racehorse owner and breeder Robert Sangster. Before that she had been the wife of the Australian politician Andrew Peacock who would later become leader of the Liberal party.

Soon after the wedding in 1985 Renouf purchased Robert Sangster's £4 million waterfront home on Point Piper, a spectacular setting on Sydney Harbour which had to be sold when his financial empire was virtually wiped out in the crash of October 1987. His wife claimed that the house was hers, a love token, she said. A very public wrangle ended in divorce from Susan in 1989. The house was sold for a reported £8 million. Renouf's third marriage in 1991 was even shorter. His young and attractive new wife had claimed to be a Russian Countess, Michele Ivan-Zadeb-Griaznoff, but it transpired she was the daughter of Arthur Mainwaring, a retired Australian cab driver. They parted after six weeks and were divorced in 1996.

ROY WILDER who died on 12 January 1998 at the age of 81 was a generous if eccentric philanthropist who adopted the soubriquet 'Friend of Tennis'. A Texan, he was known to every member of the tennis family in the 1950s and 1960s through the regular newsletters he would post to those with whom he had come into contact, however tenuously, in the course of his extensive tennis travels. In the days of amateur tennis he would offer rides from tournament to tournament to grateful overseas competitors on the US Eastern circuit. His card index system was legendary. Spotting an acquaintance in the distance he would hastily consult the cards he always kept carefully in his back pocket before approaching the individual to enquire about the wellbeing of his family and pets by name. He was a lonely but likeable man and something of a mystery, even to those who knew him quite well.

TODD WITSKEN, who died on 1 June 1998 at the age of 34 after a two year battle against brain cancer, had been a member of the US Junior Davis Cup squad in 1983 and 1984 and performed with distinction for USC where he became an All-American. Turning pro in 1986 he immediately came to international notice when he beat Jimmy Connors in straight sets in the third round of the 1986 US Open, a stunning performance that was seen around the world on television. This was the first time since 1972 that Connors had lost at Flushing Meadows before the quarter-finals. Todd reached a career high ranking of 43 in singles and 4 in doubles during the course of a professional career that brought him 11 doubles titles and ended with his retirement in 1993. Born in Indianapolis he lived in Carmel, Indiana, and is survived by his wife Lisa and their four children Tyler, Conner, Tanner and Carlie.

Maiden Names and Married Names

* = since divorced

MAIDEN NAME	*MARRIED NAME(S)*
Adamson, Nellie	Landry, Mme. P.H.
Akhurst, Daphne S.	Cozens, Mrs. R.S.
Alvarez, Elia (Lili) M.	Valdene, Countess, J. de G.
Andrus, Dorothy B.	Burke, Mrs. W.A.
Appel, Elly	Vessies, Mrs. J.
Appelmans, Sabine	Habourdin, Mrs. S.
Arnold, Mimi	Wheeler, Mrs. J.H.
*Arraya, Laura	Gildermeister, Mrs. H.
Aussem, Cilly	Brae, Countess F.M. Della Corte
Austin, Joan W.	Lycett, Mrs. R.
	Chiesman, Mrs. F.R.
	Jepson, Mrs. D.S.
	Baker, Mrs. D.A.
Austin, Tracy A.	Holt, Mrs. S.
Austin, Edith L.	Greville, Mrs. T.G.P.
Baker, Beverley	Beckett, Mrs. S.
	Fleitz, Mrs. J.G.
Barclay, Joyce S.	Williams, Mrs. G.M.
	Hume, Mrs. I.
	Engelfield, Mrs. J.S.
	Sacerdote, Mrs. J.
Barg, Penny	Mager, Mrs. L.
Bartos, Csilla	Serepy, Mrs. D.
Basuki, Yayuk	Suharyadi, Mrs. H.
Baudone, Nathalie	Furlan. Mrs. R.
Bennett, Eileen V.	Fearnley Whittingstall, Mrs. E.O.
	Marsh, Mrs. M.M.
	Akroyd, Mrs. G.
	Forslind, Mrs. C.V.
Betz, Pauline M.	Addie, Mrs. R.R.
Bevis, Mary R.	Hawton, Mrs. K.E.
Bingley, Blanche	Hillyard, Mrs. G.W.
Bjurstedt, A. Margrethe (Molla)	Mallory, Mrs. F.I.
Bloomer, Shirley J.	Brasher, Mrs. C.W.
Bonder, Lisa	Kriess, Mrs. T.
Boothby, P. Dora	Geen, Mrs. A.C.
Boucher, Edith M.	Hannam, Mrs. F.J.
Boulle, Michelle	Rodriguez, Mrs. P.H.
Bowder, Irene E.	Peacock, Mrs. G.E.
Bowes, Beverley	Hackney, Mrs. H.M.
Boyd, Esna	Robertson, Mrs. A.
Broquedis, M. Marguerite	Billout, Mme. J.
	Bordes, Mme. P.R.M.
Brough, A. Louise	Clapp, Mrs. A.T.
Brown, Nina B.	Hamilton, Mrs. E.R.
Browne, Mary K.	Kenneth-Smith, Mrs. K.
Buding, Edda	Duechting, Mrs. E.
Bundy, Dorothy (Dodo) M.	Cheney, Mrs. A.C.
Buxton, Angela	Silk, Mrs. D.W.
Caldwell, Carole A.	Graebner, Mrs. C.E.
Canning, M. Patricia	Todd, Mrs. R.B.

MAIDEN NAME	*MARRIED NAME(S)*
Carillo, Mary	Bowden, Mrs. B.
Carter, Mary M.	Reitano, Mrs. S.J.
Cherneva, Svetlana	Parkhomenko, Mrs. S.
Coghlan, Lorraine G.	Robinson, Mrs. J.D.G.
	Green, Mrs. G.S.
Colyer, Evelyn L.	Munro, Mrs. H.A.
Connolly, Maureen C.	Brinker, Mrs. N.
Connor, Judith N.	Chaloner Mrs. J.D.
Cooper, Charlotte R.	Sterry, Mrs. A.
Cox, Marjorie	Crawford, Mrs. J.H.
Coyne, Thelma D.	Long, Mrs. M.N.
Cross, Edith A.	Jensen, Mrs. C.J.
Csurgo, Virag	Tamas, Mrs. N.
Daniell, Agnes K.R.	Tuckey, Mrs. C.O.
Dechaume, Alexia	Balleret, Mrs. B.
Delhees, Petra	Jauch, Mrs. P.
Douglass, Dorothea K.	Chambers, Mrs. R.Lambert
Durr, Francoise	Browning, Mrs. B.J.
Eastlake-Smith, G.	Lamplough, Mrs. G.
Ebbern, Robin	Vincenzi, Mrs. E.J.
Eisel, Mary Ann	Curtis, Mrs. P.W.
Evert, Chris M.	Lloyd, Mrs. J.M.
	Evert Lloyd, Mrs. C.
	Mill, Mrs. A.R.
Evers, Dianne	Brown, Mrs. D.
Fairbank, Rosalyn	Nideffer, Mrs. R.
Floyd, Donna	Fales, Mrs. H.G.
Forbes, Jean R.	Drysdale, Mrs. E.C.
Fromholtz, Diane L.	Balestrat, Mrs. C.M.
Fry, Joan C.	Lakeman, Mrs. T.A.
Fry, Shirley J.	Irvin, Mrs. K.E.
Fulco, Bettina	Villela, Mrs. P.
Gannon, Joy	Mottram, Mrs. A.J.
Garrison, Zina L.	Jackson, Mrs. W.
Ghiradi, Lea	Rubbi, Mrs. L.
Gibson, Althea	Darben, Mrs. W.A.
	Llewellyn, Mrs. S.
Gillou, Kate	Fenwick, Mme. F.
Goldsack, Elsie A.	Pitman, Mrs. J.B.
	Rowbottom, Mrs. G.F.
	Furlonge, Lady G.W.
Goolagong, Evonne F.	Cawley, Mrs. R.A.
Gourlay, Helen	Cawley, Mrs. R.L.
Groenman, Trudy	Walhof, Mrs. T.
Grossman, Ann	Wunderlich, Mrs. E.
Halard, Julie	Decugis, Mrs. A.
Hall, Eleanor (Nell) M.	Hopman, Mrs. H.C.
Hanks, Carol	Aucamp, Mrs. D.C.
Hantze, Karen J.	Susman, Mrs. J.R.
Hard, Darlene R.	Waggoner, Mrs. R.
Hart, Mary M.	McIlquham, Mrs. C.G.
Haydon, Adrianne (Ann) S.	Jones, Mrs. P.F.
Head, Dorothy	Knode, Mrs. D.P.
Heeley, G.Mary	Cartwright, Mrs. D.F.

MAIDEN NAME	*MARRIED NAME(S)*
Heine, E.A.L. (Bobbie)	Miller, Mrs. J.H.K.
	Davie, Mrs. W.R.
Helgeson, Ginger	Nielsen, Mrs. T.
Herreman, Nathalie	Bagby, Mrs. D.
Hogan, Patti. St.A.	Fordyce, Mrs. I.M.
Holcroft, Phoebe C.	Watson, Mrs. M.R.
	Blakstad, Mrs. W.L.
Hood, Emily	Westacott, Mrs.V.
Hotchkiss, Hazel V.	Wightman, Mrs. G.W.
Housset, Nathalie	Gilbert, Mrs. R.
Howkins, Phyllis, L.	Covell, Mrs. B.C.
Hy, Patricia	Boulais, Mrs. Y.
Jackson, Helen	Atkins, Mrs. H.
Jagerman, Nicole	Muns, Mrs. C.
Jaggard, Michelle	Lie, Mrs. G.
James, Winifred (Freda) A.	Hammersley, Mrs. S.H.
Jedrzejowska, Jadwiga	Gallert, Mrs. A.
Jones, Kimberley	Shaefer, Mrs. L.
Jung, Sylvia	Lafaurie, Mrs. R.
	Henrotin, Mrs. C.F.
	Welton, Mrs. S.
Kiyomura, Ann K.	Hayashi, Mrs. D.
Krahwinkel, Hilde	Sperling, Mrs. S.
Lance, Sylvia	Harper, Mrs. R.
Lehane, Janice (Jan) P.	O'Neill, Mrs. J.J
Lidderdale, Kathleen E.	Bridge, Mrs. A.V.
Lindqvist, Caterina	Ryan, Mrs. W.
Lofdahl, Ingrid A.R.F.	Bentzer, Mrs. J.A.
Louie, Mareen	Harper, Mrs. T.
Lyle, Nancy	Glover, Mrs. P.F.
MacLennan, Frances V.M.	Taylor, Mrs. R.
Madruga, Ivana	Ossies, Mrs. O.
Mandlikova, Hana	Sadlek, Mrs. J.
Marcinkowski, Rita	Baranski, Mrs. A.
May, Kathryn (Kathy)	Teacher, Mrs. B.D.
	Paben, Mrs. D
McCune, Anna V.	Harper, Mrs. L.A.
McInnes, Coral	Buttsworth, Mrs. C.
McKane, Margaret	Stocks, Mrs. A.D.
McKane, Kathleen (Kitty)	Godfree, Mrs. L.A.
Melville, Kerry A.	Reid, Mrs. G.E.
Meshki, Leila	Nadibaidze, Mrs. P.
Metaxa, Doris E.	Howard, Mrs. P.D.
Minter, Anne	Harris, Mrs. G.
Moffitt, Billie Jean	King, Mrs. L.W.
Monami, Dominique	van Roost, Mrs. B.
Moran, Gertrude A.	Corbally, Mrs. T.J.
	Hand, Mrs. E.J.
	Simpson, Mrs. F.M.
Morozova, Olga V.	Rubanov, Mrs. V.B.
Mortimer, F. Angela M.	Barrett, Mrs. J.E.
Morton, Agnes M.	Stewart, Lady H.H.
Mudford, Phyllis E.	King, Mrs. M.R.
Muller, E.Fay	Robinson, Mrs. A.A.
Mundel, Jennifer	Reinbold, Mrs. D.
Mutch, Margaret (Mal)	Molesworth, Mrs. M.
Nagelsen, H. Elizabeth (Betsy)	McCormack, Mrs. M.H.
Nelson, Vicki L.	Dunbar, Mrs. K.
Neumannova, M.	Pinterova, Mrs. M.
Newberry, Janet S.	Wright Mrs. F.I.
Nicholl, Jean	Bostock, Mrs. E.W.A.
Niessen, Helga	Masthoff, Frau H.
Osborne, Margaret E.	duPont, Mrs. W.

MAIDEN NAME	*MARRIED NAME(S)*
Palfrey, Sarah H.	Fabyan, Mrs. M.
	Cooke, Mrs. E.T.
	Danzig, Mrs. J.A.
Pampoulova, Elena	Wagner, Mrs. A.
Paradis, Pascale	Mangon, Mrs. P.
Passemard, Simone	Mathieu, Mme. R.
Peisachov, Paulina	Peled, Mrs. E.
Piatek, Mary Lou	Daniels, Mrs. P.
Piercey, Sheila A.	Summers, Mrs. R.A.
Polzl, Judith	Wiesner, Mrs. H.W.
Prosen, Carol A.	Kalogeropoulos, Mrs. N.
Provis, Nicole A.L.	Bradtke, Mrs. M.R.
Puzejova, Vera	Sukova, Mrs. C.
Quentrec, Karine	Eagle, Mrs. K.
Quertier, Jean	Rinkel, Mrs. I.
Radford, Kristine	Kunce, Mrs. D.
Rajchrtova, Regina	Korda, Mrs. P.
Ramsey, Winifred G.	Beamish, Mrs. A.E.
Raponi, Emilse	Longo, Mrs. N.
Reggi, Raffaela	Concato, Mrs. M.
Reyes, Rosa (Rosie) M.	Darmon, Mrs. P.
Reynolds, Sandra	Price, Mrs. L.E.G.
Richey, Nancy A.	Gunter, Mrs. K.S.
Ridley, Joan C.	O'Meara, Mrs. D.J.P.
Riedl, Iris	Kuhn, Mrs. K.
Rinaldi, Kathy	Stunkel, Mrs. B.
Ritter, Petra	Schwartz, Mrs. P.
Rosenquest, Charlotte(Betty)	Pratt, Mrs. E.C.S.
Round, Dorothy E.	Little, Mrs. D.L.
Rush, Gretchen A.	Magers, Mrs. S.W.
Russell, JoAnne C.	Longdon, Mrs. G.
Sampson, Julia, A.	Haywood, Mrs. D.A.
Saunders, Margaret A.	Michell, Mrs. L.R.C.
Savchenko, Larisa I.	Neiland, Mrs. A.
Sawamatsu, Kazuko	Yoshida, Mrs. M.
Sayers, Elizabeth M.	Smylie, Mrs. P.D.
Schildknecht, Heide	Orth, Frau L.
Schofield, Barbara	Davidson, Mrs. G.
Schuurman, Renee	Haygarth, Mrs. P.
Seeney, Daphne G.	Fancutt, Mrs. T.T.
Shaw, Winnie M.	Wooldridge, Mrs. K.
Shepherd, Dorothy C.	Barron, Mrs. W.P.
Sheriff, Carol	Zeeman, Mrs. C.E.
Sheriff, Gail V.	Chanfreau, Mrs. J.B.
	Lovera, Mrs. J.J.
Shilcock, J. Anne	Spann, Mrs. J.K.
Sigart, Josane	de Meulemeester, Mme. J.
*Simionescu, Mariana	Borg, Mrs. B.
Simpson, Alice M.	Pickering, Mrs. W.H.
*Simpson, Rene	Alter, Mrs. B.
Sloane, Susan	Lundy, Mrs. D.
Slocock, Winifred M.	McNair, Mrs. R.J.
Smith, Margaret	Court, Mrs. B.M.
Spain, Lisa	Short, Mrs. H.
Squire, Mabel B.	Parton, Mrs. E.G.
	Mavrogordato, Mrs. T.M.
St.George, Floris	Conway, Mrs. J.R.
Staley, Jennifer	Hoad, Mrs. L.A.
Stammers, Katherine (Kay) E.	Menzies, Mrs. M.
	Bullitt, Mrs. T.W.

MAIDEN NAME	*MARRIED NAME(S)*
Stevens, Greer R.	Leo-Smith, Mrs. K.
Strnadova, Andrea	Stoltenberg, Mrs. J.
Sutton, May G.	Bundy, Mrs. T.C.
Tegart, Judy A.M.	Dalton, Mrs. D.E.
*Temesvari, Andrea	Trunkos, Mrs. A.
Testud, Sandrine	Magnelli, Mrs. V.
Thomson, Ethel W.	Larcombe, Mrs. D.T.R.
Tomanova, Renata	Roth, Mrs. W.R.
Truman, Christine C.	Janes, Mrs. G.T.
Turner, Lesley R.	Bowrey, Mrs. W.W.
Varner, Margaret	Bloss, Mrs. W.G.
Villagran, Adriana	Reami, Mrs. J.
Walkden, Pat M.	Pretorius, Mrs. Q.C.
Walsh, Sharon A .	Pete, Mrs. M.H.
Ward, Patricia E.	Hales, Mrs. R.
Watanabe, Tina B.	Mochizuki, Mrs. H.A.
Werdel, Marianne	Witmeyer, Mrs. R.
Whitlinger, Tami	Jones, Mrs. K.
Wills, Helen N.	Moody, Mrs. F.S. Roark, Mrs. A.
Wynne, Nancye M.	Bolton, Mrs. G.F.
Zrubakova, Radka	Karabin, Mrs. L.
Zyl, Annette, M. van	Plooy, Mrs. J. du

Finding the burden of being the French Open champion too heavy, the 21-year-old Croatian Iva Majoli saw her world ranking slip from 6 to 25 as a shoulder injury sidelined her in the autumn. (…mmy Hindley)

Championship Rolls

Note: The maiden names of married ladies appearing below can be found on pp 426–428.

AUSTRALIAN CHAMPIONSHIPS

1. Title: Held as the Australasian Championships from 1905 to 1926. In 1927 became the Australian Championships to coincide with the opening of the Kooyong Stadium in Melbourne. **2. Status:** The Championships became open in 1969. **3. Venues:** Since 1905 there have been 86 Championships held in the following cities (there were two Championships in 1977 (Jan and Dec) and from then until 1985 the event was staged in December. In 1986 there was no Championship so that the Jan date could be resumed in 1987): **MELBOURNE (40):** 1905, '14, '24, '27, 30, '33, '35, '39, '48, '50, '53, '57, '61, '65, '68, 1972–present (1927–1987 at Kooyong; since 1988 at the National Tennis Centre, Flinders Park). **SYDNEY (17):** 1908, '19, '22, '25, '28, '31, '34, '37, '40, '47, '51, '54, '58, '62, '66, '70, '71. **ADELAIDE (14):** 1910, '20, '26, '29, '32, '36, '38, '46, '49, '52, '55, '59, '63, '67. **BRISBANE (8):** 1907, '11, '15, '23, '56, '60, '64, '69. **PERTH (3):** 1909, '13, '21. **CHRISTCHURCH, NZL (1):** 1906. **HASTINGS, NZL (1):** 1912. **4. Surface:** Grass 1905–87; Rebound Ace (hard) 1988–present. **5.** Note: The asterisk symbol * denotes best of three sets only.

MEN'S SINGLES

	CHAMPION	*RUNNER-UP*	*SCORE*				
1905	R. W. Heath	A. H. Curtis	4–6	6–3	6–4	6–4	
1906	A. F. Wilding	F. M. B. Fisher	6–0	6–4	6–4		
1907	H. M. Rice	H. A. Parker	6–3	6–4	6–4		
1908	F. B. Alexander	A. W. Dunlop	3–6	3–6	6–0	6–2	6–3
1909	A. F. Wilding	E. F. Parker	6–1	7–5	6–2		
1910	R. W. Heath	H. M. Rice	6–4	6–3	6–2		
1911	N. E. Brookes	H. M. Rice	6–1	6–2	6–3		
1912	J. C. Parke	A. E. Beamish	3–6	6–3	1–6	6–1	7–5
1913	E. F. Parker	H. A. Parker	2–6	6–1	6–3	6–2	
1914	A. O'Hara Wood	G. L. Patterson	6–4	6–3	5–7	6–1	
1915	F. G. Lowe	H. M. Rice	4–6	6–1	6–1	6–4	
1916–18		*Not held*					
1919	A. R. F. Kingscote	E. O. Pockley	6–4	6–0	6–3		
1920	P. O'Hara Wood	R. V. Thomas	6–3	4–6	6–8	6–1	6–3
1921	R. H. Gemmell	A. Hedeman	7–5	6–1	6–4		
1922	J. O. Anderson	G. L. Patterson	6–0	3–6	3–6	6–3	6–2
1923	P. O'Hara Wood	C. B. St John	6–1	6–1	6–3		
1924	J. O. Anderson	R. E. Schlesinger	6–3	6–4	3–6	5–7	6–3
1925	J. O. Anderson	G. L. Patterson	11–9	2–6	6–2	6–3	
1926	J. B. Hawkes	J. Willard	6–1	6–3	6–1		
1927	G. L. Patterson	J. B. Hawkes	3–6	6–4	3–6	18–16	6–3
1928	J. Borotra	R. O. Cummings	6–4	6–1	4–6	5–7	6–3
1929	J. C. Gregory	R. E. Schlesinger	6–2	6–2	5–7	7–5	
1930	E. F. Moon	H. C. Hopman	6–3	6–1	6–3		
1931	J. H. Crawford	H. C. Hopman	6–4	6–2	2–6	6–1	
1932	J. H. Crawford	H. C. Hopman	4–6	6–3	3–6	6–3	6–1
1933	J. H. Crawford	K. Gledhill	2–6	7–5	6–3	6–2	
1934	F. J. Perry	J. H. Crawford	6–3	7–5	6–1		
1935	J. H. Crawford	F. J. Perry	2–6	6–4	6–4	6–4	
1936	A. K. Quist	J. H. Crawford	6–2	6–3	4–6	3–6	9–7
1937	V. B. McGrath	J. E. Bromwich	6–3	1–6	6–0	2–6	6–1
1938	J. D. Budge	J. E. Bromwich	6–4	6–2	6–1		
1939	J. E. Bromwich	A. K. Quist	6–4	6–1	6–3		
1940	A. K. Quist	J. H. Crawford	6–3	6–1	6–2		
1941–45		*Not held*					
1946	J. E. Bromwich	D. Pails	5–7	6–3	7–5	3–6	6–2
1947	D. Pails	J. E. Bromwich	4–6	6–4	3–6	7–5	8–6

	CHAMPION	*RUNNER-UP*	*SCORE*					*FIRST PRIZE (Aus $)*
1948	A. K. Quist	J. E. Bromwich	6–4	3–6	6–3	2–6	6–3	
1949	F. A. Sedgman	J. E. Bromwich	6–3	6–2	6–2			
1950	F. A. Sedgman	K. B. McGregor	6–3	6–4	4–6	6–1		
1951	R. Savitt	K. B. McGregor	6–3	2–6	6–3	6–1		
1952	K. B. McGregor	F. A. Sedgman	7–5	12–10	2–6	6–2		
1953	K. R. Rosewall	M. G. Rose	6–0	6–3	6–4			
1954	M. G. Rose	R. N. Hartwig	6–2	0–6	6–4	6–2		
1955	K. R. Rosewall	L. A. Hoad	9–7	6–4	6–4			
1956	L. A. Hoad	K. R. Rosewall	6–4	3–6	6–4	7–5		
1957	A. J. Cooper	N. A. Fraser	6–3	9–11	6–4	6–2		
1958	A. J. Cooper	M. J. Anderson	7–5	6–3	6–4			
1959	A. Olmedo	N. A. Fraser	6–1	6–2	3–6	6–3		
1960	R. G. Laver	N. A. Fraser	5–7	3–6	6–3	8–6	8–6	
1961	R. S. Emerson	R. G. Laver	1–6	6–3	7–5	6–4		
1962	R. G. Laver	R. S. Emerson	8–6	0–6	6–4	6–4		
1963	R. S. Emerson	K. N. Fletcher	6–3	6–3	6–1			
1964	R. S. Emerson	F. S. Stolle	6–3	6–4	6–2			
1965	R. S. Emerson	F. S. Stolle	7–9	2–6	6–4	7–5	6–1	
1966	R. S. Emerson	A. R. Ashe	6–4	6–8	6–2	6–3		
1967	R. S. Emerson	A. R. Ashe	6–4	6–1	6–4			
1968	W. W. Bowrey	J. M. Gisbert	7–5	2–6	9–7	6–4		
1969	R. G. Laver	A. Gimeno	6–3	6–4	7–5			5,000
1970	A. R. Ashe	R. D. Crealy	6–4	9–7	6–2			3,800
1971	K. R. Rosewall	A. R. Ashe	6–1	7–5	6–3			10,000
1972	K. R. Rosewall	M. J. Anderson	7–6	6–3	7–5			2,240
1973	J. D. Newcombe	O. Parun	6–3	6–7	7–5	6–1		8,750
1974	J. S. Connors	P. Dent	7–6	6–4	4–6	6–3		9,750
1975	J. D. Newcombe	J. S. Connors	7–5	3–6	6–4	7–6		12,489
1976	M. Edmondson	J. D. Newcombe	6–7	6–3	7–6	6–1		32,000
1977	(Jan) R. Tanner	G. Vilas	6–3	6–3	6–3			32,000
1977	(Dec) V. Gerulaitis	J. M. Lloyd	6–3	7–6	5–7	3–6	6–2	28,000
1978	(Dec) G. Vilas	J. Marks	6–4	6–4	3–6	6–3		41,000
1979	(Dec) G. Vilas	J. Sadri	7–6	6–3	6–2			50,000
1980	(Dec) B. Teacher	K. Warwick	7–5	7–6	6–3			65,000
1981	(Dec) J. Kriek	S. Denton	6–2	7–6	6–7	6–4		65,000
1982	(Dec) J. Kriek	S. Denton	6–3	6–3	6–2			70,000
1983	(Dec) M. Wilander	I. Lendl	6–1	6–4	6–4			77,500
1984	(Dec) M. Wilander	K. Curren	6–7	6–4	7–6	6–2		100,000
1985	(Dec) S. Edberg	M. Wilander	6–4	6–3	6–3			100,000
1986	*Not held*							
1987	(Jan) S. Edberg	P. Cash	6–3	6–4	3–6	5–7	6–3	103,875
1988	M. Wilander	P. Cash	6–3	6–7	3–6	6–1	8–6	104,997
1989	I. Lendl	M. Mecir	6–2	6–2	6–2			140,000
1990	I. Lendl	S. Edberg	4–6	7–6	5–2	ret		200,000
1991	B. Becker	I. Lendl	1–6	6–4	6–4	6–4		246,400
1992	J. Courier	S. Edberg	6–3	3–6	6–4	6–2		274,909
1993	J. Courier	S. Edberg	6–2	6–1	2–6	7–5		410,000
1994	P. Sampras	T. Martin	7–6	6–4	6–4			460,000
1995	A. Agassi	P. Sampras	4–6	6–1	7–6	6–4		480,000
1996	B. Becker	M. Chang	6–2	6–4	2–6	6–2		562,000
1997	P. Sampras	C. Moya	6–2	6–3	6–3			585,000
1998	P. Korda	M. Rios	6–2	6–2	6–2			615,000

WOMEN'S SINGLES

	CHAMPION	*RUNNER-UP*	*SCORE*		
1922	Mrs M. Molesworth	Miss E. F. Boyd	6–3	10–8	
1923	Mrs M. Molesworth	Miss E. F. Boyd	6–1	7–5	
1924	Miss S. Lance	Miss E. F. Boyd	6–3	3–6	8–6
1925	Miss D. S. Akhurst	Miss E. F. Boyd	1–6	8–6	6–4
1926	Miss D. S. Akhurst	Miss E. F. Boyd	6–1	6–3	
1927	Miss E. F. Boyd	Mrs S. Harper	5–7	6–1	6–2
28	Miss D. S. Akhurst	Miss E. F. Boyd	7–5	6–2	
9	Miss D. S. Akhurst	Miss L. M. Bickerton	6–1	5–7	6–2
	Miss D. S. Akhurst	Mrs S. Harper	10–8	2–6	7–5

	CHAMPION	*RUNNER-UP*	*SCORE*				FIRST PRIZE *(Aus $)*
1931	Mrs C. Buttsworth	Mrs J. H. Crawford	1–6	6–3	6–4		
1932	Mrs C. Buttsworth	Miss K. Le Mesurier	9–7	6–4			
1933	Miss J. Hartigan	Mrs C. Buttsworth	6–4	6–3			
1934	Miss J. Hartigan	Mrs M. Molesworth	6–1	6–4			
1935	Miss D. E. Round	Miss N. M. Lyle	1–6	6–1	6–3		
1936	Miss J. Hartigan	Miss N. M. Wynne	6–4	6–4			
1937	Miss N. M. Wynne	Mrs V. Westacott	6–3	5–7	6–4		
1938	Miss D. M. Bundy	Miss D. Stevenson	6–3	6–2			
1939	Mrs V. Westacott	Mrs H. C. Hopman	6–1	6–2			
1940	Mrs G. F. Bolton	Miss T. D. Coyne	5–7	6–4	6–0		
1941–45		*Not held*					
1946	Mrs G.F. Bolton	Miss J. Fitch	6–4	6–4			
1947	Mrs G.F. Bolton	Mrs H. C. Hopman	6–3	6–2			
1948	Mrs G.F. Bolton	Miss M. Toomey	6–3	6–1			
1949	Miss D. J. Hart	Mrs G.F. Bolton	6–3	6–4			
1950	Miss A. L. Brough	Miss D. J. Hart	6–4	3–6	6–4		
1951	Mrs G.F. Bolton	Mrs M. N. Long	6–1	7–5			
1952	Mrs M. N. Long	Miss H. Angwin	6–2	6–3			
1953	Miss M. Connolly	Miss J. Sampson	6–3	6–2			
1954	Mrs M. N. Long	Miss J. Staley	6–3	6–4			
1955	Miss B. Penrose	Mrs M. N. Long	6–4	6–3			
1956	Miss M. Carter	Mrs M. N. Long	3–6	6–2	9–7		
1957	Miss S. J. Fry	Miss A. Gibson	6–3	6–4			
1958	Miss A. Mortimer	Miss L. Coghlan	6–3	6–4			
1959	Mrs S. J. Reitano	Miss R. Schuurman	6–2	6–3			
1960	Miss M. Smith	Miss J. Lehane	7–5	6–2			
1961	Miss M. Smith	Miss J. Lehane	6–1	6–4			
1962	Miss M. Smith	Miss J. Lehane	6–0	6–2			
1963	Miss M. Smith	Miss J. Lehane	6–2	6–2			
1964	Miss M. Smith	Miss L. R. Turner	6–3	6–2			
1965	Miss M. Smith	Miss M. E. Bueno	5–7	6–4	5–2	ret	
1966	Miss M. Smith	Miss N. Richey	w.o.				
1967	Miss N. Richey	Miss L. R. Turner	6–1	6–4			
1968	Mrs L. W. King	Mrs B. M. Court	6–1	6–2			
1969	Mrs B. M. Court	Mrs L. W. King	6–4	6–1			2,000
1970	Mrs B. M. Court	Miss K. Melville	6–1	6–3			700
1971	Mrs B. M. Court	Miss E. Goolagong	2–6	7–6	7–5		1,800
1972	Miss S. V. Wade	Miss E. Goolagong	6–4	6–4			1,200
1973	Mrs B. M. Court	Miss E. Goolagong	6–4	7–5			5,700
1974	Miss E. Goolagong	Miss C. M. Evert	7–6	4–6	6–0		9,000
1975	Miss E. Goolagong	Miss M. Navratilova	6–3	6–2			8,115
1976	Mrs R. A. Cawley	Miss R. Tomanova	6–2	6–2			12,000
1977	(Jan) Mrs G. Reid	Miss D. Fromholtz	7–5	6–2			12,000
1977	(Dec) Mrs R. A. Cawley	Mrs R. L. Cawley	6–3	6–0			9,000
1978	(Dec) Miss C. O'Neil	Miss B. Nagelsen	6–3	7–6			6,000
1979	(Dec) Miss B. Jordan	Miss S. Walsh	6–3	6–3			10,000
1980	(Dec) Miss H. Mandlikova	Miss W. M. Turnbull	6–0	7–5			32,000
1981	(Dec) Miss M. Navratilova	Mrs J. M. Lloyd	6–7	6–4	7–5		34,000
1982	(Dec) Mrs J. M. Lloyd	Miss M. Navratilova	6–3	2–6	6–3		40,000
1983	(Dec) Miss M. Navratilova	Miss K. Jordan	6–2	7–6			5,000
1984	(Dec) Mrs J. M. Lloyd	Miss H. Sukova	6–7	6–1	6–3		100,000
1985	(Dec) Miss M. Navratilova	Mrs J. M. Lloyd	6–2	4–6	6–2		100,000
1986		*Not held*					
1987	(Jan) Miss H. Mandlikova	Miss M. Navratilova	7–5	7–6			115,000
1988	Miss S. Graf	Miss C. Evert	6–1	7–6			115,000
1989	Miss S. Graf	Miss H. Sukova	6–4	6–4			135,000
1990	Miss S. Graf	Miss M. J. Fernandez	6–3	6–4			190,000
1991	Miss M. Seles	Miss J. Novotna	5–7	6–3	6–1		246,400
1992	Miss M. Seles	Miss M. J. Fernandez	6–2	6–3			274,909
1993	Miss M. Seles	Miss S. Graf	4–6	6–3	6–2		410,000
1994	Miss S. Graf	Miss A. Sanchez-Vicario	6–0	6–2			460,000
1995	Miss M. Pierce	Miss A. Sanchez-Vicario	6–3	6–2			480,000
1996	Miss M. Seles	Miss A. Huber	6–4	6–1			510,000
1997	Miss M. Hingis	Miss M. Pierce	6–2	6–2			542,000
1998	Miss M. Hingis	Miss C. Martinez	6–3	6–3			572,000

MEN'S DOUBLES

	CHAMPIONS	*RUNNERS-UP*	*SCORE*					
1905	R. Lycett/T. Tachell	E. T. Barnard/B. Spence	11–9	8–6	1–6	4–6	6–1	
1906	R. W. Heath/A. F. Wilding	C. C. Cox/H. A. Parker	6–2	6–4	6–2			
1907	W. A. Gregg/H. A. Parker	H. M. Rice/G. W. Wright	6–2	3–6	6–3	6–2		
1908	F. B. Alexander/A. W. Dunlop	G. G. Sharpe/A. F. Wilding	6–3	6–2	6–1			
1909	J. P. Keane/E. F. Parker	C. Crooks/A. F. Wilding	1–6	6–1	6–1	9–7		
1910	A. Campbell/H. M. Rice	R. W. Heath/J. L. O'Dea	6–3	6–3	6–2			
1911	H. W. Heath/R. Lycett	J. J. Addison/N. E. Brookes	6–2	7–5	6–0			
1912	C. P. Dixon/J. C. Parke	A. E. Beamish/F. G. Lowe	6–4	6–4	6–2			
1913	A. H. Hedemann/E. F. Parker	H. Parker/R. Taylor	8–6	4–6	6–4	6–4		
1914	A. Campbell/G. L. Patterson	R. W. Heath/A. O'Hara Wood	7–5	3–6	6–3	6–3		
1915	H. M. Rice/C. V. Todd	F. G. Lowe/C. St John	8–6	6–4	7–9	6–3		
1916–1918		*Not held*						
1919	P. O'Hara Wood/R. V. Thomas	J. O. Anderson/A. H. Lowe	7–5	6–1	7–9	3–6	6–3	
1920	P. O'Hara Wood/R. V. Thomas	H. Rice/R. Taylor	6–1	6–0	7–5			
1921	S. H. Eaton/R. H. Gemmell	E. Stokes/N. Brearley	7–5	6–3	6–3			
1922	J. B. Hawkes/G. L. Patterson	J. O. Anderson/N. Peach	8–10	6–0	6–0	7–5		
1923	P. O'Hara Wood/C. B. St John	H. Rice/J. Bullough	6–4	6–3	3–6	6–0		
1924	J. O. Anderson/N. E. Brookes	P. O'Hara Wood/G. L. Patterson	6–2	6–4	6–3			
1925	P. O'Hara Wood/G. L. Patterson	J. O. Anderson/F. Kalms	6–4	8–6	7–5			
1926	J. B. Hawkes/G. L. Patterson	J. O. Anderson/P. O'Hara Wood	6–1	6–4	6–2			
1927	J. B. Hawkes/G. L. Patterson	I. McInnes/P. O'Hara Wood	8–6	6–2	6–1			
1928	J. Borotra/J. Brugnon	E. F. Moon/J. Willard	6–2	4–6	6–4	6–4		
1929	J. H. Crawford/H. C. Hopman	R. O. Cummings/E. F. Moon	6–1	6–8	4–6	6–1	6–3	
1930	J. H. Crawford/H. C. Hopman	J. Fitchett/J. B. Hawkes	8–6	6–1	2–6	6–3		
1931	C. Donohoe/R. Dunlop	J. H. Crawford/H. O. Hopman	8–6	6–2	5–7	7–9	6–4	
1932	J. H. Crawford/E. F. Moon	H. C. Hopman/G. L. Patterson	4–6	6–4	12–10	6–3		
1933	K. Gledhill/H. E. Vines	J. H. Crawford/E. F. Moon	6–4	10–8	6–2			
1934	G. P. Hughes/F. J. Perry	A. K. Quist/D. P. Turnbull	6–8	6–3	6–4	3–6	6–3	
1935	J. H. Crawford/V. B. McGrath	G. P. Hughes/F. J. Perry	6–4	8–6	6–2			
1936	A. K. Quist/D. P. Turnbull	J. H. Crawford/V. B. McGrath	6–8	6–2	6–1	3–6	6–2	
1937	A. K. Quist/D. P. Turnbull	J. E. Bromwich/J. E. Harper	6–2	9–7	1–6	6–8	6–4	
1938	J. E. Bromwich/A. K. Quist	H. Henkel/G. Von Cramm	7–5	6–4	6–0			
1939	J. E. Bromwich/A. K. Quist	C. F. Long/D. P. Turnbull	6–4	7–5	6–2			
1940	J. E. Bromwich/A. K. Quist	J. H. Crawford/V. B. McGrath	6–3	7–5	6–1			
1941–1945		*Not held*						
1946	J. E. Bromwich/A. K. Quist	M. Newcombe/L. A. Schwartz	6–3	6–1	9–7			
1947	J. E. Bromwich/A. K. Quist	F. A. Sedgman/G. Worthington	6–1	6–3	6–1			
1948	J. E. Bromwich/A. K. Quist	C. Long/F. A. Sedgman	1–6	6–8	9–7	6–3	8–6	
1949	J. E. Bromwich/A. K. Quist	G. Brown/O. W. Sidwell	1–6	7–5	6–2	6–3		
1950	J. E. Bromwich/A. K. Quist	J. Drobny/E. W. Sturgess	6–3	5–7	4–6	6–3	8–6	
1951	K. B. McGregor/F. A. Sedgman	J. E. Bromwich/A. K. Quist	11–9	2–6	6–3	4–6	6–3	
1952	K. B. McGregor/F. A. Sedgman	D. Candy/M. G. Rose	6–4	7–5	6–3			
1953	L. A. Hoad/K. R. Rosewall	D. Candy/M. G. Rose	9–11	6–4	10–8	6–4		
1954	R. N. Hartwig/M. G. Rose	N. A. Fraser/C. Wilderspin	6–3	6–4	6–2			
1955	E. V. Seixas/M. A. Trabert	L. A. Hoad/K. R. Rosewall	6–4	6–2	2–6	3–6	6–1	
1956	L. A. Hoad/K. R. Rosewall	D. Candy/M. G. Rose	10–8	13–11	6–4			
1957	N. A. Fraser/L. A. Hoad	M. J. Anderson/A. J. Cooper	6–3	8–6	6–4			
1958	A. J. Cooper/N. A. Fraser	R. S. Emerson/R. Mark	7–5	6–8	3–6	6–3	7–5	
1959	R. G. Laver/R. Mark	D. Candy/R. N. Howe	9–7	6–4	6–2			
1960	R. G. Laver/R. Mark	R. S. Emerson/N. A. Fraser	1–6	6–2	6–4	6–4		
1961	R. G. Laver/R. Mark	R. S. Emerson/M. F. Mulligan	6–3	7–5	3–6	9–11	6–2	
1962	R. S. Emerson/N. A. Fraser	R. A. J. Hewitt/F. S. Stolle	4–6	4–6	6–1	6–4	11–9	
1963	R. A. J. Hewitt/F. S. Stolle	K. N. Fletcher/J. D. Newcombe	6–2	3–6	6–3	3–6	6–3	
1964	R. A. J. Hewitt/F. S. Stolle	R. S. Emerson/K. N. Fletcher	6–4	7–5	3–6	4–6	14–12	
1965	J. D. Newcombe/A. D. Roche	R. S. Emerson/F. S. Stolle	3–6	4–6	13–11	6–3	6–4	
1966	R. S. Emerson/F. S. Stolle	J. D. Newcombe/A. D. Roche	7–9	6–3	6–8	14–12	12–10	
1967	J. D. Newcombe/A. D. Roche	W. W. Bowrey/O. K. Davidson	3–6	6–3	7–5	6–8	8–6	
1968	R. D. Crealy/A. J. Stone	T. Addison/R. Keldie	10–8	6–4	6–3			PRIZE
'969	R. S. Emerson/R. G. Laver	K. R. Rosewall/F. S. Stolle	6–4	6–4	*			*(Aus$)*
'70	R. C. Lutz/S. R. Smith	J. G. Alexander/P. Dent	8–6	6–3	6–4			500
1	J. D. Newcombe/A. D. Roche	T. S. Okker/M. C. Riessen	6–2	7–6	*			
	O. K. Davidson/K. R. Rosewall	R. Case/G. Masters	3–6	7–6	6–3*			600
	M. J. Anderson/J. D. Newcombe	J. G. Alexander/P. Dent	6–3	6–4	7–6			
	?. Case/G. Masters	S. Ball/R. Giltinan	6–7	6–3	6–4*			

	CHAMPIONS	*RUNNERS-UP*	*SCORE*	
1975	J. G. Alexander/P. Dent	R. Carmichael/A. J. Stone	6–3 7–6*	
1976	J. D. Newcombe/A. D. Roche	R. Case/G. Masters	7–6 6–4*	
1977	A. R. Ashe/A. D. Roche	C. Pasarell/E. Van Dillen	6–4 6–4*	
1977	(Dec) R. O. Ruffels/A. J. Stone	J. G. Alexander/P. Dent	7–6 7–6*	
1978	(Dec) W. Fibak/K. Warwick	P. Kronk/C. Letcher	7–6 7–5*	
1979	(Dec) P. McNamara/P. McNamee	P. Kronk/C. Letcher	7–6 6–2*	
1980	(Dec) M. R. Edmondson/ K. Warwick	P. McNamara/P. McNamee	7–5 6–4*	
1981	(Dec) M. R. Edmondson/ K. Warwick	H. Pfister/J. Sadri	6–3 6–7 6–3*	24,000
1982	(Dec) J. G. Alexander/J. Fitzgerald	A. Andrews/J. Sadri	6–4 7–6*	28,000
1983	(Dec) M. Edmondson/P. McNamee	S. Denton/S. E. Stewart	6–3 7–6*	30,000
1984	(Dec) M. Edmondson/ S. E. Stewart	J. Nystrom/M. Wilander	6–2 6–2 7–5	38,700
1985	(Dec) P. Annacone/ C. Van Rensburg	M. R. Edmondson/K. Warwick	3–6 7–6 6–4 6–4	34,193
1986		*Not held*		
1987	(Jan) S. Edberg/A. Jarryd	P. Doohan/L. Warder	6–4 6–4 7–6	35,518
1988	R. Leach/J. Pugh	M. J. Bates/P. Lundgren	6–3 6–2 6–3	36,400
1989	R. Leach/J. Pugh	D. Cahill/M. Kratzmann	6–4 6–4 6–4	48,533
1990	P. Aldrich/D. Visser	G. Connell/G. Michibata	6–4 4–6 6–1 6–4	125,000
1991	S. Davis/D. Pate	P. McEnroe/D. Wheaton	6–7 7–6 6–3 7–5	125,000
1992	T. Woodbridge/M. Woodforde	K. Jones/R. Leach	6–4 6–3 6–4	147,500
1993	D. Visser/L Warder	J. Fitzgerald/A. Jarryd	6–4 6–3 6–4	168,000
1994	J. Eltingh/P. Haarhuis	B. Black/J. Stark	6–7 6–3 6–4 6–3	190,000
1995	J. Palmer/R. Reneberg	M. Knowles/D. Nestor	6–3 3–6 6–3 6–2	200,000
1996	S. Edberg/P. Korda	S. Lareau/A. O'Brien	7–5 7–5 4–6 6–1	234,000
1997	T. Woodbridge/M. Woodforde	S. Lareau/A. O'Brien	4–6 7–5 7–5 6–3	244,000
1998	J. Bjorkman/J. Eltingh	T. Woodbridge/M. Woodforde	6–2 5–7 2–6 6–4 6–3	256,000

WOMEN'S DOUBLES

	CHAMPIONS	*RUNNERS-UP*	*SCORE*
1922	E. F. Boyd/M. Mountain	St George/H. S. Utz	3–6 6–4 7–5
1923	E. F. Boyd/S. Lance	M. Molesworth/H. Turner	6–1 6–4
1924	D. S. Akhurst/S. Lance	K. Le Mesurier/M. O'Hara Wood	7–5 6–2
1925	D. S. Akhurst/R. Harper	E. F. Boyd/K. Le Mesurier	6–4 6–3
1926	E. F. Boyd/M. O'Hara Wood	D. S. Akhurst/M. Cox	6–3 6–8 8–6
1927	L. M. Bickerton/M. O'Hara Wood	E. F. Boyd/R. Harper	6–3 6–3
1928	D. S. Akhurst/E. F. Boyd	K. Le Mesurier/D. Weston	6–3 6–1
1929	D. S. Akhurst/L. M. Bickerton	R. Harper/M. O'Hara Wood	6–2 4–6 6–2
1930	E. Hood/M. Molesworth	M. Cox/R. Harper	6–3 0–6 7–5
1931	L. M. Bickerton/R. S. Cozens	A. Lloyd/H. S. Utz	6–2 6–4
1932	C. Buttsworth/J. H. Crawford	K. Le Mesurier/D. Weston	6–2 6–2
1933	M. Molesworth/V. Westacott	J. Hartigan/J. Van Ryn	6–3 6–3
1934	M. Molesworth/V. Westacott	J. Hartigan/U. Valkenborg	6–8 6–4 6–4
1935	E. M. Dearman/N. M. Lyle	L. M. Bickerton/H. C. Hopman	6–3 6–4
1936	T. D. Coyne/N. M. Wynne	M. Blick/K. Woodward	6–2 6–4
1937	T. D. Coyne/N. M. Wynne	H. C. Hopman/V. Westacott	6–2 6–2
1938	T. D. Coyne/N. M. Wynne	D. M. Bundy/D. E. Workman	9–7 6–4
1939	T. D. Coyne/N. M. Wynne	M. Hardcastle/V. Westacott	7–5 6–4
1940	T. D. Coyne/G.F. Bolton	J. Hartigan/E. Niemeyer	7–5 6–2
1941–1945		*Not held*	
1946	M. Bevis/J. Fitch	G. F. Bolton/M. N. Long	9–7 6–4
1947	G.F. Bolton/M. N. Long	M. Bevis/J. Fitch	6–3 6–3
1948	G.F. Bolton/M. N. Long	M. Bevis/N. Jones	6–3 6–3
1949	G.F. Bolton/M. N. Long	D. Hart/M. Toomey	6–0 6–1
1950	L. Brough/D.J. Hart	G. F. Bolton/M. N. Long	6–3 2–6 6–3
1951	G.F. Bolton/M. N. Long	J. Fitch/M. Hawton	6–2 6–1
1952	G.F. Bolton/M. N. Long	R. Baker/M. Hawton	6–1 6–1
1953	M. Connolly/J. Sampson	M. Hawton/B. Penrose	6–4 6–2
1954	M. Hawton/B. Penrose	H. Redick–Smith/J. Wipplinger	6–3 8–6
1955	M. Hawton/B. Penrose	H. C. Hopman/A. Thiele	7–5 6–1
1956	M. Hawton/M. N. Long	M. Carter/B. Penrose	6–3 5–7 9–7
1957	S. J. Fry/A. Gibson	M. Hawton/F. Muller	6–2 6–1
1958	M. Hawton/M. N. Long	L. Coghlan/A. Mortimer	7–5 6–8 6–2

	CHAMPIONS	*RUNNERS-UP*	*SCORE*			FIRST PRIZE *(Aus $)*
1959	S. Reynolds/R. Schuurman	L. Coghlan/M. Reitano	7–5	6–4		
1960	M. E. Bueno/C. Truman	L. Robinson/M. Smith	6–2	5–7	6–2	
1961	M. Reitano/M. Smith	M. Hawton/J. Lehane	6–4	3–6	7–5	
1962	R. Ebbern/M. Smith	D. R. Hard/M. Reintano	6–4	6–4		
1963	R. Ebbern/M. Smith	J. Lehane/L. R. Turner	6–1	6–3		
1964	J. A. M. Tegart/L. R. Turner	R. Ebbern/M. Smith	6–4	6–4		
1965	M. Smith/L. R. Turner	R. Ebbern/B. J. Moffitt	1–6	6–2	6–3	
1966	C. Graebner/N. Richey	M. Smith/L. R. Turner	6–4	7–5		
1967	J. A. M. Tegart/L. R. Turner	L. Robinson/E. Terras	6–0	6–2		
1968	K. Krantzcke/K. Melville	J. A. M. Tegart/L. R. Turner	6–4	3–6	6–2	
1969	B. M. Court/J. A. M. Tegart	R. Casals/L. W. King	6–4	6–4		
1970	B. M. Court/D. Dalton	K. Krantzcke/K. Melville	6–3	6–1		120
1971	B. M. Court/E. F. Goolagong	J. Emmerson/L. Hunt	6–0	6–0		
1972	H. Gourlay/K. Harris	P. Coleman/K. Krantzcke	6–0	6–4		500
1973	B. M. Court/S. V. Wade	K. Harris/K. Melville	6–4	6–4		
1974	E. F. Goolagong/M. Michel	K. Harris/K. Melville	7–5	6–3		
1975	E. F. Goolagong/M. Michel	B. M. Court/O. Morozova	7–6	7–6		
1976	R. A. Cawley/H. Gourlay	W. W. Bowrey/R. Tomanova	8–1	(one set)		
1977	D. Fromholtz/H. Gourlay	B. Nagelsen/G. E. Reid	5–7	6–1	7–5	
1977	(Dec) R. A. Cawley/R. L. Cawley div'd with M. Guerrant/G. E. Reid					
1978	(Dec) B. Nagelsen/R. Tomanova	N. Sato/P. Whytcross	7–5	6–2		
1979	(Dec) D. D. Chaloner/D. R. Evers	L. Harrison/M. Mesker	6–2	1–6	6–0	
1980	(Dec) B. Nagelsen/M. Navratilova	A. Kiyomura/C. Reynolds	6–4	6–4		
1981	(Dec) K. Jordan/A. E. Smith	M. Navratilova/P. H. Shriver	6–2	7–5		13,000
1982	(Dec) M. Navratilova/P. H. Shriver	C. Kohde/E. Pfaff	6–4	6–2		16,000
1983	(Dec) M. Navratilova/P. H. Shriver	A. E. Hobbs/W. M. Turnbull	6–4	6–7	6–2	30,000
1984	(Dec) M. Navratilova/P. H. Shriver	C. Kohde-Kilsch/H. Sukova	6–3	6–4		39,900
1985	(Dec) M. Navratilova/P. H. Shriver	C. Kohde-Kilsch/H. Sukova	6–3	6–4		40,000
1986		*Not held*				
1987	(Jan) M. Navratilova/P. H. Shriver	Z. Garrison/L. McNeil	6–1	6–0		40,000
1988	M. Navratilova/P. H. Shriver	C. Evert/W. M. Turnbull	6–0	7–5		35,000
1989	M. Navratilova/P. H. Shriver	P. Fendick/J. Hetherington	3–6	6–3	6–2	40,000
1990	J. Novotna/H. Sukova	P. Fendick/M. J. Fernandez	7–6	7–6		125,000
1991	P. Fendick/M. J. Fernandez	G. Fernandez/J. Novotna	7–6	6–1		125,000
1992	A. Sanchez-Vicario/H. Sukova	G. Fernandez/Z. Garrison	6–4	7–6		147,500
1993	G. Fernandez/N Zvereva	P. Shriver/E. Smylie	6–4	6–3		168,000
1994	G. Fernandez/N. Zvereva	P. Fendick/M. McGrath	6–3	4–6	6–4	190,000
1995	J. Novotna/A. Sanchez-Vicario	G. Fernandez/N. Zvereva	6–3	6–7	6–4	200,000
1996	S. Rubin/A. Sanchez-Vicario	L. Davenport/M. J. Fernandez	7–5	2–6	6–4	212,000
1997	M. Hingis/N. Zvereva	L. Davenport/L. Raymond	6–2	6–2		225,000
1998	M. Hingis/M. Lucic	L. Davenport/N. Zvereva	6–4	2–6	6–3	237,000

MIXED DOUBLES

	CHAMPIONS	*RUNNERS-UP*	*SCORE*		
1922	J. B. Hawkes/Miss E. F. Boyd	H. S. Utz/Mrs Utz	6–1	6–1	
1923	H. M. Rice/Miss S. Lance	C. St John/Miss M. Molesworth	2–6	6–4	6–4
1924	J. Willard/Miss D. S. Akhurst	G. M. Hone/Miss E. F. Boyd	6–3	6–4	
1925	J. Willard/Miss D. S. Akhurst	R. E. Schlesinger/Mrs R. Harper	6–4	6–4	
1926	J. B. Hawkes/Miss E. F. Boyd	J. Willard/Miss D. S. Akhurst	6–2	6–4	
1927	J. B. Hawkes/Miss E. F. Boyd	J. Willard/Miss Y. Anthony	6–1	6–3	
1928	J. Borotra/Miss D. S. Akhurst	J. B. Hawkes/Miss E. F. Boyd	w.o		
1929	E. F. Moon/Miss D. S. Akhurst	J. H. Crawford/Miss M. Cox	6–0	7–5	
1930	H. C. Hopman/Miss N. Hall	J. H. Crawford/Miss M. Cox	11–9	3–6	6–3
1931	J. H. Crawford/Mrs Crawford	A. Willard/Mrs V. Westacott	7–5	6–4	
1932	J. H. Crawford/Mrs Crawford	J. Satoh/Mrs P. O'Hara Wood	6–8	8–6	6–3
1933	J. H. Crawford/Mrs Crawford	H. E. Vines/Mrs J. Van Ryn	3–6	7–5	13–11
1934	E. F. Moon/Miss J. Hartigan	R. Dunlop/Mrs V. Westacott	6–3	6–4	
935	C. Boussus/Miss L. Bickerton	V. G. Kirby/Mrs Bond	1–6	6–3	6–3
36	H. C. Hopman/Mrs Hopman	A. A. Kay/Miss M. Blick	6–2	6–0	
7	H. C. Hopman/Mrs Hopman	D. P. Turnbull/Miss D. Stevenson	3–6	6–3	6–2
	J. E. Bromwich/Miss J. Wilson	C. Long/Miss N. Wynne	6–3	6–2	
	H. C. Hopman/Mrs Hopman	J. E. Bromwich/Miss J. Wilson	6–8	6–2	6–3
	. Long/Mrs G. F. Bolton	H. C. Hopman/Mrs Hopman	7–5	2–6	6–4
5		*Not held*			
	ong/Mrs G. F. Bolton	J. Bromwich/Miss J. Fitch	6–0	6–4	

	CHAMPIONS	*RUNNERS-UP*	*SCORE*			PRIZE MONEY *(Aus$)*
1947	C. Long/Mrs G. F. Bolton	J. E. Bromwich/Miss J. Fitch	6–3	6–3		
1948	C. Long/Mrs G. F. Bolton	O. W. Sidwell/Mrs M. N. Long	7–5	4–6	8–6	
1949	F. A. Sedgman/Miss D. J. Hart	J. E. Bromwich/Miss J. Fitch	6–1	5–7	12–10	
1950	F. A. Sedgman/Miss D. J. Hart	E. W. Sturgess/Miss J. Fitch	8–6	6–4		
1951	G. A. Worthington/ Mrs M. N. Long	J. May/Miss C. Proctor	6–4	3–6	6–2	
1952	G. A. Worthington/ Mrs M. N. Long	T. Warhurst/Mrs A. R. Thiele	9–7	7–5		
1953	R. N. Hartwig/Miss J. Sampson	H. Richardson/Miss M. Connolly	6–4	6–3		
1954	R. N. Hartwig/Mrs M. N. Long	J. E. Bromwich/Miss B. Penrose	4–6	6–1	6–2	
1955	G. A. Worthington/ Mrs M. N. Long	L. A. Hoad/Miss J. Staley	6–2	6–1		
1956	N. A. Fraser/Miss B. Penrose	R. S. Emerson/Mrs M. Hawton	6–2	6–4		
1957	M. J. Anderson/Miss F. Muller	W. A. Knight/Miss J. Langley	7–5	3–6	6–1	
1958	R. N. Howe/Mrs M. Hawton	A. Newman/Miss A. Mortimer	9–11	6–1	6–2	
1959	R. Mark/Miss S. Reynolds	R. G. Laver/Miss R. Schuurman	4–6	13–11	6–2	
1960	T. Fancutt/Miss J. Lehane	R. Mark/Mrs M. Reitano	6–2	7–5		
1961	R. A. J. Hewitt/Miss J. Lehane	J. Pearce/Mrs M. Reitano	9–7	6–2		
1962	F. S. Stolle/Miss L. R. Turner	R. Taylor/Miss D. R. Hard	6–3	9–7		
1963	K. N. Fletcher/Miss M. Smith	F. S. Stolle/Miss L. R. Turner	7–5	5–7	6–4	
1964	K. N. Fletcher/Miss M. Smith	M. J. Sangster/Miss J. Lehane	6–3	6–2		
1965	J. D. Newcombe/Miss M. Smith div'd with O. K. Davidson/Miss R. Ebbern					
1966	A. D. Roche/Miss J. A. Tegart	W. W. Bowrey/Miss R. Ebbern	6–1	6–3		
1967	O. K. Davidson/Miss L. R. Turner	A. D. Roche/Miss J. A. M. Tegart	9–7	6–4		
1968	R. D. Crealy/Mrs L. W. King	A. J. Stone/Mrs B. M. Court	w.o.			
1969	M. C. Riessen/Mrs B. M. Court div'd with F. S. Stolle/Mrs P. F. Jones					
1969–1986		*Not held*				
1987	S. E. Stewart/Miss Z. Garrison	A. Castle/Miss A. E. Hobbs	3–6	7–6	6–3	13,954
1988	J. Pugh/Miss J. Novotna	Tim Gullikson/ Miss M. Navratilova	5–7	6–2	6–4	13,954
1989	J. Pugh/Miss J. Novotna	S. Stewart/Miss Z. Garrison	6–3	6–4		18,140
1990	J. Pugh/Miss N. Zvereva	R. Leach/Miss Z. Garrison	4–6	6–2	6–3	40,000
1991	J. Bates/Miss J. Durie	S. Davis/Miss R. White	2–6	6–4	6–4	40,000
1992	M. Woodforde/Miss N. Provis	T. Woodbridge/ Miss A. Sanchez-Vicario	6–3	4–6	11–9	62,600
1993	T. Woodbridge/ Miss A. Sanchez-Vicario	R. Leach/Miss Z. Garrison Jackson	7–5	6–4		71,400
1994	A. Olhovskiy/Mrs L. Neiland	T. Woodbridge/Miss H. Sukova	7–5	6–7	6–2	80,000
1995	R. Leach/Miss N. Zvereva	C. Suk/Miss G. Fernandez	7–6	6–7	6–4	83,000
1996	M. Woodforde/Mrs L. Neiland	L. Jensen/Miss N. Arendt	4–6	7–5	6–0	88,000
1997	R. Leach/Miss M. Bollegraf	J. De Jager/Mrs L. Neiland	6–3	6–7	7–5	92,000
1998	J. Gimelstob/Miss V. Williams	C. Suk/Miss H. Sukova	6–2	6–1		92,000

FRENCH CHAMPIONSHIPS

1. Venue and conditions of entry: From 1891 to 1924 the Championships, restricted to members of French clubs, were played at the Stade Francais ground at the Faisanderie in St. Cloud Park. They included the title 'World Clay Court Championship' between 1912 and 1924 when the title was abolished. International from 1925, the Championships were played for three years alternately at the Racing Club at Croix-Catelan in Paris and the Stade Francais at the Faisanderie. Since 1928 the Championships have been played continuously at the Stade Roland Garros, Porte D'Auteuil, Paris. **2. Status:** The Championships became 'Open' in 1968. Since 1991 the Men's Doubles has been reduced to the best of three sets. **3. Surface:** Red clay (Terre Battu).

MEN'S SINGLES

1891	H. Briggs
1892	J. Schopfer
1893	L. Riboulet
1894–96	A. Vacherot
1897–1900	P. Ayme
1901	A. Vacherot
1902	M. Vacherot
1903–04	M. Decugis
1905–06	M. Germot
1907–09	M. Decugis
1910	M. Germot
1911	A. H. Gobert
1912–14	M. Decugis
1915–19	*Not held*
1920	A. H. Gobert
1921	J. Samazeuilh
1922	H. Cochet
1923	P. Blanchy
1924	J. Borotra

	CHAMPION	*RUNNER-UP*	*SCORE*					FIRST PRIZE *(in French francs)*
1925	R. Lacoste	J. Borotra	7–5	6–1	6–4			
1926	H. Cochet	R. Lacoste	6–2	6–4	6–3			
1927	R. Lacoste	W. T. Tilden	6–4	4–6	5–7	6–3	11–9	
1928	H. Cochet	R. Lacoste	5–7	6–3	6–1	6–3		
1929	R. Lacoste	J. Borotra	6–3	2–6	6–0	2–6	8–6	
1930	H. Cochet	W. T. Tilden	3–6	8–6	6–3	6–1		
1931	J. Borotra	C. Boussus	2–6	6–4	7–5	6–4		
1932	H. Cochet	G. De Stefani	6–0	6–4	4–6	6–3		
1933	J. H. Crawford	H. Cochet	8–6	6–1	6–3			
1934	G. von Cramm	J. H. Crawford	6–4	7–9	3–6	7–5	6–3	
1935	F. J. Perry	G. von Cramm	6–3	3–6	6–1	6–3		
1936	G. von Cramm	F. J. Perry	6–0	2–6	6–2	2–6	6–0	
1937	H. Henkel	H. W. Austin	6–1	6–4	6–3			
1938	J. D. Budge	R. Menzel	6–3	6–2	6–4			
1939	W. D. McNeill	R. L. Riggs	7–5	6–0	6–3			
1940–45		*Not held*						
1946	M. Bernard	J. Drobny	3–6	2–6	6–1	6–4	6–3	
1947	J. Asboth	E. W. Sturgess	8–6	7–5	6–4			
1948	F. A. Parker	J. Drobny	6–4	7–5	5–7	8–6		
1949	F. A. Parker	J. E. Patty	6–3	1–6	6–1	6–4		
1950	J. E. Patty	J. Drobny	6–1	6–2	3–6	5–7	7–5	
1951	J. Drobny	E. W. Sturgess	6–3	6–3	6–3			
1952	J. Drobny	F. A. Sedgman	6–2	6–0	3–6	6–4		
1953	K. R. Rosewall	E. V. Seixas	6–3	6–4	1–6	6–2		
1954	M. A. Trabert	A. Larsen	6–4	7–5	6–1			
1955	M. A. Trabert	S. Davidson	2–6	6–1	6–4	6–2		
1956	L. A. Hoad	S. Davidson	6–4	8–6	6–3			
1957	S. Davidson	H. Flam	6–3	6–4	6–4			
1958	M. G. Rose	L. Ayala	6–3	6–4	6–4			
1959	N. Pietrangeli	I. C. Vermaak	3–6	6–3	6–4	6–1		
1960	N. Pietrangeli	L. Ayala	3–6	6–3	6–4	4–6	6–3	
1961	M. Santana	N. Pietrangeli	4–6	6–1	3–6	6–0	6–2	
1962	R. G. Laver	R. S. Emerson	3–6	2–6	6–3	9–7	6–2	
1963	R. S. Emerson	P. Darmon	3–6	6–1	6–4	6–4		
964	M. Santana	N. Pietrangeli	6–3	6–1	4–6	7–5		
'65	F. S. Stolle	A. D. Roche	3–6	6–0	6–2	6–3		
'6	A. D. Roche	I. Gulyas	6–1	6–4	7–5			
'	R. S. Emerson	A. D. Roche	6–1	6–4	2–6	6–2		
	K. R. Rosewall	R. G. Laver	6–3	6–1	2–6	6–2		15,000
	R. G. Laver	K. R. Rosewall	6–4	6–3	6–4			35,000
	Kodes	Z. Franulovic	6–2	6–4	6–0			56,000
	Kodes	I. Nastase	8–6	6–2	2–6	7–5		48,000
	Gimeno	P. Proisy	4–6	6–3	6–1	6–1		48,000
	stase	N. Pilic	6–3	6–3	6–0			70,000
	g	M. Orantes	2–6	6–7	6–0	6–1	6–1	120,000

	CHAMPION	*RUNNER-UP*	*SCORE*					
1975	B. Borg	G. Vilas	6–2	6–3	6–4			120,000
1976	A. Panatta	H. Solomon	6–1	6–4	4–6	7–6		130,000
1977	G. Vilas	B. E. Gottfried	6–0	6–3	6–0			190,000
1978	B. Borg	G. Vilas	6–1	6–1	6–3			210,000
1979	B. Borg	V. Pecci	6–3	6–1	6–7	6–4		208,200
1980	B. Borg	V. Gerulaitis	6–4	6–1	6–2			221,000
1981	B. Borg	I. Lendl	6–1	4–6	6–2	3–6	6–1	250,000
1982	M. Wilander	G. Vilas	1–6	7–6	6–0	6–4		400,000
1983	Y. Noah	M. Wilander	6–2	7–5	7–6			500,000
1984	I. Lendl	J. P. McEnroe	3–6	2–6	6–4	7–5	7–5	1,058,600
1985	M. Wilander	I. Lendl	3–6	6–4	6–2	6–2		1,338,200
1986	I. Lendl	M. Pernfors	6–3	6–2	6–4			1,397,250
1987	I. Lendl	M. Wilander	7–5	6–2	3–6	7–6		1,303,800
1988	M. Wilander	H. Leconte	7–5	6–2	6–1			1,500,240
1989	M. Chang	S. Edberg	6–1	3–6	4–6	6–4	6–2	1,791,390
1990	A. Gomez	A. Agassi	6–3	2–6	6–4	6–4		2,226,100
1991	J. Courier	A. Agassi	3–6	6–4	2–6	6–1	6–4	2,448,000
1992	J. Courier	P. Korda	7–5	6–2	6–1			2,680,000
1993	S. Bruguera	J. Courier	6–4	2–6	6–2	3–6	6–3	2,680,000
1994	S. Bruguera	A. Berasategui	6–3	7–5	2–6	6–1		3,160,000
1995	T. Muster	M. Chang	7–5	6–2	6–4			3,320,000
1996	Y. Kafelnikov	M. Stitch	7–6	7–5	7–6			3,542,000
1997	G. Kuerten	S. Bruguera	6–3	6–4	6–2			3,668,000
1998	C. Moya	A. Corretja	6–3	7–5	6–3			3,852,000

WOMEN'S SINGLES

1897–99	Mlle F. Masson	1906	Mme F. Fenwick	1915–19	*Not held*
1900	Mlle Y. Prevost	1907	Mme De Kermel	1920–23	Mlle S. Lenglen
1901	Mme P. Girod	1908	Mme F. Fenwick	1924	Mlle D. Vlasto
1902–03	Mlle F. Masson	1909–12	Mlle J. Matthey		
1904–05	Mlle K. Gillou	1913–14	Mlle M. Broquedis		

	CHAMPION	*RUNNER-UP*	*SCORE*		
1925	Mlle S. Lenglen	Miss K. McKane	6–1	6–2	
1926	Mlle S. Lenglen	Miss M. K. Browne	6–1	6–0	
1927	Mlle K. Bouman	Mrs G. Peacock	6–2	6–4	
1928	Miss H. N. Wills	Miss E. Bennett	6–1	6–2	
1929	Miss H. N. Wills	Mme R. Mathieu	6–3	6–4	
1930	Mrs F. S. Moody	Miss H. H. Jacobs	6–2	6–1	
1931	Frl C. Aussem	Miss B. Nuthall	8–6	6–1	
1932	Mrs F. S. Moody	Mme R. Mathieu	7–5	6–1	
1933	Miss M. C. Scriven	Mme R. Mathieu	6–2	4–6	6–4
1934	Miss M. C. Scriven	Miss H. H. Jacobs	7–5	4–6	6–1
1935	Mrs H. Sperling	Mme R. Mathieu	6–2	6–1	
1936	Mrs H. Sperling	Mme R. Mathieu	6–3	6–4	
1937	Mrs H. Sperling	Mme R. Mathieu	6–2	6–4	
1938	Mme R. Mathieu	Mme N. Landry	6–0	6–3	
1939	Mme R. Mathieu	Miss J. Jedrzejowska	6–3	8–6	
1940–45		*Not held*			
1946	Miss M. E. Osborne	Miss P. M. Betz	1–6	8–6	7–5
1947	Mrs P. C. Todd	Miss D. J. Hart	6–3	3–6	6–4
1948	Mme N. Landry	Miss S. J. Fry	6–2	0–6	6–0
1949	Mrs W. du Pont	Mme N. Adamson	7–5	6–2	
1950	Miss D. J. Hart	Mrs P. C. Todd	6–4	4–6	6–2
1951	Miss S. J. Fry	Miss D. J. Hart	6–3	3–6	6–3
1952	Miss D. J. Hart	Miss S. J. Fry	6–4	6–4	
1953	Miss M. Connolly	Miss D. J. Hart	6–2	6–4	
1954	Miss M. Connolly	Mme G. Bucaille	6–4	6–1	
1955	Miss A. Mortimer	Mrs D. P. Knode	2–6	7–5	10–8
1956	Miss A. Gibson	Miss A. Mortimer	6–0	12–10	
1957	Miss S. J. Bloomer	Mrs D. P. Knode	6–1	6–3	
1958	Mrs Z. Kormoczy	Miss S. J. Bloomer	6–4	1–6	6–2
1959	Miss C. C. Truman	Mrs Z. Kormoczy	6–4	7–5	
1960	Miss D. R. Hard	Miss Y. Ramirez	6–3	6–4	
1961	Miss A. S. Haydon	Miss Y. Ramirez	6–2	6–1	

	CHAMPION	RUNNER-UP	SCORE			FIRST PRIZE (in French francs)
1962	Miss M. Smith	Miss L. R. Turner	6–3	3–6	7–5	
1963	Miss L. R. Turner	Mrs P. F. Jones	2–6	6–3	7–5	
1964	Miss M. Smith	Miss M. E. Bueno	5–7	6–1	6–2	
1965	Miss L. R. Turner	Miss M. Smith	6–3	6–4		
1966	Mrs P. F. Jones	Miss N. Richey	6–3	6–1		
1967	Mlle F. Durr	Miss L. R. Turner	4–6	6–3	6–4	
1968	Miss N. Richey	Mrs P. F. Jones	5–7	6–4	6–1	5,000
1969	Mrs B. M. Court	Mrs P. F. Jones	6–1	4–6	6–3	10,000
1970	Mrs B. M. Court	Miss H. Niessen	6–2	6–4		17,800
1971	Miss E. Goolagong	Miss H. Gourlay	6–3	7–5		13,500
1972	Mrs L. W. King	Miss E. Goolagong	6–3	6–3		13,500
1973	Mrs B. M. Court	Miss C. M. Evert	6–7	7–6	6–4	25,000
1974	Miss C. M. Evert	Mrs O. Morozova	6–1	6–2		40,000
1975	Miss C. M. Evert	Miss M. Navratilova	2–6	6–2	6–1	40,000
1976	Miss S. Barker	Miss R. Tomanova	6–2	0–6	6–2	30,000
1977	Miss M. Jausovec	Miss F. Mihai	6–2	6–7	6–1	35,000
1978	Miss V. Ruzici	Miss M. Jausovec	6–2	6–2		100,000
1979	Mrs J. M. Lloyd	Miss W. M. Turnbull	6–2	6–0		126,900
1980	Mrs J. M. Lloyd	Miss V. Ruzici	6–0	6–3		178,500
1981	Miss H. Mandlikova	Miss S. Hanika	6–2	6–4		200,000
1982	Miss M. Navratilova	Miss A. Jaeger	7–6	6–1		300,000
1983	Mrs J. M. Lloyd	Miss M. Jausovec	6–1	6–2		375,000
1984	Miss M. Navratilova	Mrs J. M. Lloyd	6–3	6–1		791,600
1985	Mrs J. M. Lloyd	Miss M. Navratilova	6–3	6–7	7–5	1,262,700
1986	Mrs J. M. Lloyd	Miss M. Navratilova	2–6	6–3	6–3	1,278,400
1987	Miss S. Graf	Miss M. Navratilova	6–4	4–6	8–6	1,178,840
1988	Miss S. Graf	Miss N. Zvereva	6–0	6–0		1,463,390
1989	Miss A. Sanchez	Miss S. Graf	7–6	3–6	7–5	1,593,175
1990	Miss M. Seles	Miss S. Graf	7–6	6–4		1,762,900
1991	Miss M. Seles	Miss A. Sanchez-Vicario	6–3	6–4		2,237,000
1992	Miss M. Seles	Miss S. Graff	6–2	3–6	10–8	2,470,000
1993	Miss S. Graf	Miss M. J. Fernandez	4–6	6–2	6–4	2,470,000
1994	Miss A. Sanchez-Vicario	Miss M. Pierce	6–4	6–4		2,930,000
1995	Miss S. Graf	Miss A. Sanchez-Vicario	7–5	4–6	6–0	3,100,000
1996	Miss S. Graf	Miss A. Sanchez-Vicario	6–3	6–7	10–8	3,224,000
1997	Miss I. Majoli	Miss M. Hingis	6–4	6–2		3,450,000
1998	Miss A. Sanchez-Vicario	Miss M. Seles	7–6	0–6	6–2	3,624,000

MEN'S DOUBLES

	CHAMPIONS	RUNNERS-UP	SCORE				
1925	J. Borotra/R. Lacoste	J. Brugnon/H. Cochet	7–5	4–6	6–3	2–6	6–3
1926	H. O. Kinsey/V. Richards	J. Brugnon/H. Cochet	6–4	6–1	4–6	6–4	
1927	J. Brugnon/H. Cochet	J. Borotra/R. Lacoste	2–6	6–2	6–0	1–6	6–4
1928	J. Borotra/J. Brugnon	R. De Buzelet/H. Cochet	6–4	3–6	6–2	3–6	6–4
1929	J. Borotra/R. Lacoste	J. Brugnon/H. Cochet	6–3	3–6	6–3	3–6	8–6
1930	J. Brugnon/H. Cochet	H. C. Hopman/J. Willard	6–3	9–7	6–3		
1931	G. M. Lott/J. Van Ryn	N. G. Farquharson/V. G. Kirby	6–4	6–3	6–4		
1932	J. Brugnon/H. Cochet	M. Bernard/C. Boussus	6–4	3–6	7–5	6–3	
1933	G. P. Hughes/F. J. Perry	V. B. McGrath/A. K. Quist	6–2	6–4	2–6	7–5	
1934	J. Borotra/J. Brugnon	J. H. Crawford/V. B. McGrath	11–9	6–3	2–6	4–6	9–7
1935	J. H. Crawford/A. K. Quist	V. B. McGrath/D. P. Turnbull	6–1	6–4	6–2		
1936	M. Bernard/J. Borotra	G. P. Hughes/C. R. D. Tuckey	6–2	3–6	9–7	6–1	
1937	G. Von Cramm/H. Henkel	N. G. Farquharson/V. G. Kirby	6–4	7–5	3–6	6–1	
1938	B. Destremau/Y. Petra	J. D. Budge/G. Mako	3–6	6–3	9–7	6–1	
1939	C. Harris/W. D. McNeil	J. Borotra/J. Brugnon	4–6	6–4	6–0	2–6	10–8
1940–1945		*Not held*					
1946	M. Bernard/Y. Petra	E. Morea/F. Segura	7–5	6–3	0–6	1–6	10–8
1947	E. Fannin/E. W. Sturgess	T. P. Brown/O. W. Sidwell	6–4	4–6	6–4	6–3	
948	L. Bergelin/J. Drobny	H. C. Hopman/F. A. Sedgman	8–6	6–1	12–10		
949	R. A. Gonzales/F. Parker	E. Fannin/E. W. Sturgess	6–3	8–6	5–7	6–3	
950	W. F. Talbert/M. A. Trabert	J. Drobny/E. W. Sturgess	6–2	1–6	10–8	6–2	
51	K. B. McGregor/F. A. Sedgman	G. Mulloy/R. Savitt	6–2	2–6	9–7	7–5	
52	K. B. McGregor/F. A. Sedgman	G. Mulloy/R. Savitt	6–3	6–4	6–4		
53	L. A. Hoad/K. R. Rosewall	M. G. Rose/C. Wilderspin	6–2	6–1	6–1		
4	E. V. Seixas/M. A. Trabert	L. A. Hoad/K. R. Rosewall	6–4	6–2	6–1		

	CHAMPIONS	*RUNNERS-UP*	*SCORE*					
1955	E. V. Seixas/M. A. Trabert	N. Pietrangeli/O. Sirola	6–1	4–6	6–2	6–4		
1956	D. W. Candy/R. M. Perry	A. J. Cooper/L. A. Hoad	7–5	6–3	6–3			
1957	M. J. Anderson/A. J. Cooper	D. W. Candy/M. G. Rose	6–3	6–0	6–3			
1958	A. J. Cooper/N. A. Fraser	R. N. Howe/A. Segal	3–6	8–6	6–3	7–5		
1959	N. Pietrangeli/O. Sirola	R. S. Emerson/N. A. Fraser	6–3	6–2	14–12			
1960	R. S. Emerson/N. A. Fraser	J. L. Arilla/A. Gimeno	6–2	8–10	7–5	6–4		
1961	R. S. Emerson/R. G. Laver	R. N. Howe/R. Mark	3–6	6–1	6–1	6–4		
1962	R. S. Emerson/N. A. Fraser	W. P. Bungert/C. Kuhnke	6–3	6–4	7–5			
1963	R. S. Emerson/M. Santana	G. L. Forbes/A. Segal	6–2	6–4	6–4			
1964	R. S. Emerson/K. N. Fletcher	J. D. Newcombe/A. D. Roche	7–5	6–3	3–6	7–5		
1965	R. S. Emerson/F. S. Stolle	K. N. Fletcher/R. A. J. Hewitt	6–8	6–3	8–6	6–2		
1966	C. E. Graebner/R. D. Ralston	I. Nastase/I. Tiriac	6–3	6–3	6–0			
1967	J. D. Newcombe/A. D. Roche	R. S. Emerson/K. N. Fletcher	6–3	9–7	12–10			
1968	K. R. Rosewall/F. S. Stolle	R. S. Emerson/R. G. Laver	6–3	6–4	6–3			
1969	J. D. Newcombe/A. D. Roche	R. S. Emerson/R. G. Laver	4–6	6–1	3–6	6–4	6–4	
1970	I. Nastase/I. Tiriac	A. R. Ashe/C. Pasarell	6–2	6–4	6–3			FF8,000
1971	A. R. Ashe/M. C. Riessen	T. W. Gorman/S. R. Smith	6–8	4–6	6–3	6–4	11–9	6,000
1972	R. A. J. Hewitt/F. D. McMillan	P. Cornejo/J. Fillol	6–3	8–6	3–6	6–1		10,000
1973	J. D. Newcombe/T. S. Okker	J. S. Connors/I. Nastase	6–1	3–6	6–3	5–7	6–4	24,000
1974	R. D. Crealy/O. Parun	R. C. Lutz/S. R. Smith	6–3	6–2	3–6	5–7	6–1	30,000
1975	B. E. Gottfried/R. Ramirez	J. G. Alexander/P. Dent	6–2	2–6	6–2	6–4		30,000
1976	F. McNair/S. E. Stewart	B. E. Gottfried/R. Ramirez	7–6	6–3	6–1			47,000
1977	B. E. Gottfried/R. Ramirez	W. Fibak/J. Kodes	7–6	4–6	6–3	6–4		76,000
1978	G. Mayer/H. Pfister	J. Higueras/M. Orantes	6–3	6–2	6–2			84,000
1979	A. A./G. Mayer	R. Case/P. Dent	6–4	6–4	6–4			83,280
1980	V. Amaya/H. Pfister	B. E. Gottfried/R. Ramirez	1–6	6–4	6–4	6–3		89,250
1981	H. Gunthardt/B. Taroczy	T. Moor/E. Teltscher	6–2	7–6	6–3			108,400
1982	S. E. Stewart/F. Taygan	H. Gildemeister/B. Prajoux	7–5	6–3	1–1	ret		160,400
1983	A. Jarryd/H. Simonsson	M. R. Edmondson/S. E. Stewart	7–6	6–4	6–2			262,970
1984	H. Leconte/Y. Noah	P. Slozil/T. Smid	6–4	2–6	3–6	6–3	6–2	423,380
1985	M. R. Edmondson/K. Warwick	S. Glickstein/H. Simonsson	6–3	6–4	6–7	6–3		535,400
1986	J. Fitzgerald/T. Smid	S. Edberg/A. Jarryd	6–3	4–6	6–3	6–7	14–12	558,900
1987	A. Jarryd/R. Seguso	G. Forget/Y. Noah	6–7	6–7	6–3	6–4	6–2	451,000
1988	A. Gomez/E. Sanchez	J. Fitzgerald/A. Jarryd	6–3	6–7	6–4	6–3		520,080
1989	J. Grabb/P. McEnroe	M. Bahrami/E. Winogradsky	6–4	2–6	6–4	7–6		621,024
1990	S. Casal/E. Sanchez	G. Ivanisevic/P. Korda	7–5	6–3				US$151,000
1991	J. Fitzgerald/A. Jarryd	R. Leach/J. Pugh	6–0	7–6				FF1,000,000
1992	J. Hlasek/M. Rosset	C. Adams/A. Olhovskiy	7–6	6–7	7–5			1,100,000
1993	L. Jensen/M. Jensen	M. K. Goellner/D. Prinosil	6–4	6–7	6–4			1,100,000
1994	B. Black/J. Stark	J. Apell/J. Bjorkman	6–4	7–6				1,200,000
1995	J. Eltingh/P. Haarhuis	N. Kulti/M. Larsson	6–7	6–4	6–1			1,364,000
1996	Y. Kafelnikov/D. Vacek	G. Forget/J. Hlasek	6–2	6–3				1,420,000
1997	Y. Kafelnikov/D. Vacek	T. Woodbridge/M. Woodforde	7–6	4–6	6–3			1,508,000
1998	J. Eltingh/P.Haarhuis	M. Knowles/D. Nestor	6–3	3–6	6–3			1,584,000

WOMEN'S DOUBLES

	CHAMPIONS	*RUNNERS-UP*	*SCORE*		
1925	S. Lenglen/D. Vlasto	E. Colyer/K. McKane	6–1	9–11	6–2
1926	S. Lenglen/D. Vlasto	E. Colyer/L. A. Godfree	6–1	6–1	
1927	E. L. Heine/G. Peacock	P. Saunders/P. H. Watson	6–2	6–1	
1928	E. Bennett/P. H. Watson	S. Deve/A. Lafaurie	6–0	6–2	
1929	L. De Alvarez/K. Bouman	E. L. Heine/A. Neave	7–5	6–3	
1930	F. S. Moody/E. Ryan	S. Barbier/S. Mathieu	6–3	6–1	
1931	B. Nuthall/E. F. Whittingstall	C. Aussem/E. Ryan	9–7	6–2	
1932	F. S. Moody/E. Ryan	B. Nuthall/E. F. Whittingstall	6–1	6–3	
1933	S. Mathieu/E. Ryan	S. Henrotin/C. Rosambert	6–1	6–3	
1934	S. Mathieu/E. Ryan	H. H. Jacobs/S. Palfrey	3–6	6–4	6–2
1935	M. C. Scriven/K. Stammers	N. Adamoff/H. Sperling	6–4	6–0	
1936	S. Mathieu/A. M. Yorke	S. Noel/J. Jedrzejowska	2–6	6–4	6–4
1937	S. Mathieu/A. M. Yorke	D. Andrus/S. Henrotin	3–6	6–2	6–2
1938	S. Mathieu/A. M. Yorke	A. Halff/N. Landry	6–3	6–3	
1939	J. Jedrzejowska/S. Mathieu	A. Florian/H. Kovac	7–5	7–5	
1940–1945		*Not held*			
1946	L. Brough/M. Osborne	P. Betz/D. Hart	6–4	0–6	6–1
1947	L. Brough/M. Osborne	D. Hart/P. C. Todd	7–5	6–2	

	CHAMPIONS	*RUNNERS-UP*	*SCORE*			
1948	D. Hart/P. C. Todd	S. Fry/M. A. Prentiss	6–4	6–2		
1949	L. Brough/W. du Pont	J. Gannon/B. Hilton	7–5	6–1		
1950	S. Fry/D. Hart	L. Brough/W. du Pont	1–6	7–5	6–2	
1951	S. Fry/D. Hart	B. Bartlett/B. Scofield	10–8	6–3		
1952	S. Fry/D. Hart	H. Redick-Smith/J. Wipplinger	7–5	6–1		
1953	S. Fry/D. Hart	M. Connolly/J. Sampson	6–4	6–3		
1954	M. Connolly/N. Hopman	M. Galtier/S. Schmitt	7–5	4–6	6–0	
1955	B. Fleitz/D. R. Hard	S. J. Bloomer/P. Ward	7–5	6–8	13–11	
1956	A. Buxton/A. Gibson	D. R. Hard/D. Knode	6–8	8–6	6–1	
1957	S. J. Bloomer/D. R. Hard	Y. Ramirez/R. M. Reyes	7–5	4–6	7–5	
1958	Y. Ramirez/R. M. Reyes	M. K. Hawton/M. N. Long	6–4	7–5		
1959	S. Reynolds/R. Schuurman	Y. Ramirez/R. M. Reyes	2–6	6–0	6–1	
1960	M. E. Bueno/D. R. Hard	R. Hales/A. Haydon	6–2	7–5		
1961	S. Reynolds/R. Schuurman	M. E. Bueno/D. R. Hard	w.o.			
1962	S. Price/R. Schuurman	J. Bricka/M. Smith	6–4	6–4		
1963	P. F. Jones/R. Schuurman	R. A. Ebbern/M. Smith	7–5	6–4		
1964	M. Smith/L. R. Turner	N. Baylon/H. Schultze	6–3	6–1		
1965	M. Smith/L. R. Turner	F. Durr/J. Lieffrig	6–3	6–1		
1966	M. Smith/J. A. M. Tegart	J. Blackman/F. Toyne	4–6	6–1	6–1	
1967	F. Durr/G. Sheriff	A. M. Van Zyl/P. Walkden	6–2	6–2		
1968	F. Durr/P. F. Jones	R. Casals/L. W. King	7–5	4–6	6–4	
1969	F. Durr/P. F. Jones	M. Court/N. Richey	6–0	4–6	7–5	
1970	F. Durr/G. Chanfreau	R. Casals/L. W. King	6–1	3–6	6–3	FF6,000
1971	F. Durr/G. Chanfreau	H. Gourlay/K. Harris	6–4	6–1		4500
1972	L. W. King/B. Stove	W. Shaw/F. E. Truman	6–1	6–2		5,000
1973	M. Court/S. V. Wade	F. Durr/B. Stove	6–2	6–3		7,000
1974	C. Evert/O. Morozova	G. Chanfreau/K. Ebbinghaus	6–4	2–6	6–1	8,000
1975	C. Evert/M. Navratilova	J. Anthony/O. Morozova	6–3	6–2		8,000
1976	F. Bonicelli/G. Lovera	K. Harter/H. Masthoff	6–4	1–6	6–3	8,000
1977	R. Marsikova/P. Teeguarden	R. Fox/H. Gourlay	5–7	6–4	6–2	8,000
1978	M. Jausovec/V. Ruzici	N. Bowey/G. Lovera	5–7	6–4	8–6	20,000
1979	B. Stove/W. M. Turnbull	F. Durr/S. V. Wade	6–4	7–6		42,300
1980	K. Jordan/A. E. Smith	I. Madruga/I. Villagran	6–1	6–0		68,000
1981	R. Fairbank/T. Harford	C. Reynolds/P. Smith	6–1	6–3		80,000
1982	M. Navratilova/A. E. Smith	R. Casals/W. M. Turnbull	6–3	6–4		120,000
1983	R. Fairbank/C. Reynolds	K. Jordan/A. E. Smith	5–7	7–5	6–2	210,000
1984	M. Navratilova/P. H. Shriver	C. Kohde-Kilsch/H. Mandlikova	5–7	6–3	6–2	316,000
1985	M. Navratilova/P. H. Shriver	C. Kohde-Kilsch/H. Sukova	4–6	6–2	6–2	384,300
1986	M. Navratilova/A. Temesvari	S. Graf/G. Sabatini	6–1	6–2		398,200
1987	M. Navratilova/P. H. Shriver	S. Graf/G. Sabatini	6–2	6–1		365,300
1988	M. Navratilova/P. H. Shriver	C. Kohde-Kilsch/H. Sukova	6–2	7–5		453,230
1989	L. Savchenko/N. Zvereva	S. Graf/G. Sabatini	6–4	6–4		552,316
1990	J. Novotna/H. Sukova	L. Savchenko/N. Zvereva	6–4	7–5		US$103,080
1991	G. Fernandez/J. Novotna	L. Savchenko/N. Zvereva	6–4	6–0		FF786,500
1992	G. Fernandez/N. Zvereva	C. Martinez/A. Sanchez-Vicario.	6–3	6–2		865,000
1993	G. Fernandez/N. Zvereva	L. Neiland/J. Novotna	6–3	7–5		944,000
1994	G. Fernandez/N. Zvereva	L. Davenport/L. Raymond	6–2	6–2		1,020,000
1995	G. Fernandez/N. Zvereva	J. Novotna/A. Sanchez-Vicario	6–7	6–4	7–5	1,070,000
1996	L. Davenport/M. J. Fernandez	G. Fernandez/N. Zvereva	6–2	6–1		1,112,800
1997	G. Fernandez/N. Zvereva	M. J. Fernandez/L. Raymond	3–6	6–4	6–1	1,182,400
1998	M. Hingis/J. Novotna	L. Davenport/N. Zvereva	6–1	7–6		1,241,500

IXED DOUBLES

	CHAMPIONS	*RUNNERS-UP*	*SCORE*		
5	J. Brugnon/Miss S. Lenglen	H. Cochet/Miss D. Vlasto	6–2	6–2	
	J. Brugnon/Miss S. Lenglen	J. Borotra/Mrs Le Besnerais	6–4	6–3	
	J. Borotra/Miss M. Broquedis	W. T. Tilden/Miss L. De Alvarez	6–4	2–6	6–2
	H. Cochet/Miss E. Bennett	F. T. Hunter/Miss H. Wills	3–6	6–3	6–3
	Cochet/Miss E. Bennett	F. T. Hunter/Miss H. Wills	6–3	6–2	
	T. Tilden/Miss C. Aussem	H. Cochet/Mrs F. Whittingstall	6–4	6–4	
	B. Spence/Miss B. Nuthall	H. W. Austin/Mrs D. C. Shepherd-Barron	6–3	5–7	6–3
	'erry/Miss B. Nuthall	S. B. Wood/Mrs F. S. Moody	6–4	6–2	
	rawford/Miss M. C. Scriven	F. J. Perry/Miss B. Nuthall	6–2	6–3	
	ra/Miss C. Rosambert	A. K. Quist/Miss E. Ryan	6–2	6–4	
	ard/Miss L. Payot	A. M. Legeay/Mrs S. Henrotin	4–6	6–2	6–4

	CHAMPIONS	RUNNERS-UP	SCORE			
1936	M. Bernard/Miss A. M. Yorke	A. M. Legeay/Mrs S. Henrotin	7–5	6–8	6–3	
1937	Y. Petra/Mrs S. Mathieu	R. Journu/Miss M. Horne	7–5	7–5		
1938	D. Mitic/Mrs S. Mathieu	C. Boussus/Miss N. Wynne	2–6	6–3	6–4	
1939	E. T. Cooke/Mrs S. Fabyan	F. Kukuljevic/Mrs S. Mathieu	4–6	6–1	7–5	
1940–1945		*Not held*				
1946	J. E. Patty/Miss P. M. Betz	T. P. Brown/Miss D. Bundy	7–5	9–7		
1947	E. W. Sturgess/Mrs S. P. Summers	C. Caralulis/Miss J. Jedrzejowska	6–0	6–0		
1948	J. Drobny/Mrs P. C. Todd	F. A. Sedgman/Miss D. Hart	6–3	3–6	6–3	
1949	E. W. Sturgess/Mrs S. P. Summers	G. D. Oakley/Miss J. Quertier	6–1	6–1		
1950	E. Morea/Miss B. Scofield	W. F. Talbert/Mrs P. C. Todd	w.o.			
1951	F. A. Sedgman/Miss D. Hart	M. G. Rose/Mrs M. N. Long	7–5	6–2		
1952	F. A. Sedgman/Miss D. Hart	E. W. Sturgess/Miss S. Fry	6–8	6–3	6–3	
1953	E. V. Seixas/Miss D. Hart	M. G. Rose/Miss M. Connolly	4–6	6–4	6–0	
1954	L. A. Hoad/Miss M. Connolly	R. N. Hartwig/Mrs J. Patorni	6–4	6–3		
1955	G. L. Forbes/Miss D. R. Hard	L. Ayala/Miss J. Staley	5–7	6–1	6–2	
1956	L. Ayala/Mrs M. N. Long	R. N. Howe/Miss D. R. Hard	4–6	6–4	6–1	
1957	J. Javorsky/Miss V. Puzejova	L. Ayala/Miss E. Buding	6–3	6–4		
1958	N. Pietrangeli/Miss S. J. Bloomer	R. N. Howe/Miss L. Coghlan	9–7	6–8	6–2	
1959	W. A. Knight/Miss R. Ramirez	R. G. Laver/Miss R. Schuurman	6–4	6–4		
1960	R. N. Howe/Miss M. Bueno	R. S. Emerson/Miss A. Haydon	1–6	6–1	6–2	
1961	R. G. Laver/Miss D. R. Hard	J. Javorsky/Miss V. Puzejova	6–0	2–6	6–3	
1962	R. N. Howe/Miss R. Schuurman	F. S. Stolle/Miss L. R. Turner	3–6	6–4	6–4	
1963	K. N. Fletcher/Miss M. Smith	F. S. Stolle/Miss L. R. Turner	6–1	6–2		
1964	K. N. Fletcher/Miss M. Smith	F. S. Stolle/Miss L. R. Turner	6–3	6–4		
1965	K. N. Fletcher/Miss M. Smith	J. D. Newcombe/Miss M. Bueno	6–4	6–4		
1966	F. D. McMillan/Miss A. M. Van Zyl	C. Graebner/Mrs P. F. Jones	1–6	6–3	6–2	
1967	O. K. Davidson/Mrs L. W. King	I. Tiriac/Mrs P. F. Jones	6–3	6–1		
1968	J. C. Barclay/Miss F. Durr	O. K. Davidson/Mrs L. W. King	6–1	6–4		*Prize Money*
1969	M. C. Riessen/Mrs. B. M. Court	J. C. Barclay/Miss F. Durr	7–5	6–4		*(FF per team)*
1970	R. A. J. Hewitt/Mrs L. W. King	J. C. Barclay/Miss F. Durr	3–6	6–3	6–2	FF6,000
1971	J. C. Barclay/Miss F. Durr	T. Lejus/Miss W. Shaw	6–2	6–4		4,500
1972	K. Warwick/Miss E. F. Goolagong	J. C. Barclay/Miss F. Durr	6–2	6–4		5,000
1973	J. C. Barclay/Miss F. Durr	P. Dominguez/Miss B. Stove	6–1	6–4		6,000
1974	I. Molina/Miss M. Navratilova	M. Lara/Mrs R. M. Darmon	6–3	6–3		8,000
1975	T. Koch/Miss F. Bonicelli	J. Fillol/Miss P. Teeguarden	6–4	7–6		8,000
1976	K. Warwick/Miss I. Kloss	C. Dowdeswell/Miss L. Boshoff	5–7	7–6	6–2	8,000
1977	J. P. McEnroe/Miss M. Carillo	I. Molina/Miss F. Mihai	7–6	6–3		8,000
1978	P. Slozil/Miss R. Tomanova	P. Dominguez/Miss V. Ruzici	7–6	ret		10,000
1979	R. A. J. Hewitt/Miss W. M. Turnbull	I. Tiriac/Miss V. Ruzici	6–3	2–6	6–3	6,000
1980	W. Martin/Miss A. E. Smith	S. Birner/Miss R. Tomanova	2–6	6–4	8–6	11,000
1981	J. Arias/Miss A. Jaeger	F. D. McNair/Miss B. Stove	7–6	6–4		11,000
1982	J. M. Lloyd/Miss W. M. Turnbull	C. Motta/Miss C. Monteiro	6–2	7–6		13,200
1983	E. Teltscher/Miss B. Jordan	C. Strode/Miss L. Allen	6–2	6–3		20,000
1984	R. L. Stockton/Miss A. E. Smith	L. Warder/Miss A. Minter	6–2	6–4		32,000
1985	H. P. Gunthardt/Miss M. Navratilova	F. Gonzalez/Miss P. Smith	2–6	6–3	6–2	46,000
1986	K. Flach/Miss. K. Jordan	M. R. Edmondson/Miss. R. Fairbank	3–6	7–6	6–3	83,000
1987	E. Sanchez/Miss P. H. Shriver	S. E. Stewart/Miss L. McNeil	6–3	7–6		86,000
1988	J. Lozano/Miss L. McNeil	M. Schapers/Miss B. Schultz	7–5	6–2		120,000
1989	T. Nijssen/Miss M. Bollegraf	H. De la Pena/Miss A. Sanchez-Vicario	6–3	6–7	6–2	135,000
1990	J. Lozano/Miss A. Sanchez-Vicario	D. Visser/Miss N. Provis	7–6	7–6		US$30,000
1991	C. Suk/Miss H. Sukova	P. Haarhuis/Miss C. Vis	3–6	6–4	6–1	FF220,000
1992	T. Woodbridge/ Miss A. Sanchez-Vicario	B. Shelton/Miss L. McNeil	6–2	6–3		242,000
1993	A. Olhovskiy/Miss E. Maniokova	D. Visser/Miss E. Reinach	6–2	4–6	6–4	264,000
1994	M. Oosting/Miss K. Boogert	A. Olhovskiy/Mrs L. Neiland	7–5	3–6	7–5	285,000
1995	M. Woodforde/Mrs L. Neiland	J. De Jager/Miss J. Hetherington	7–6	7–6		300,000
1996	J. Frana/Miss P. Tarabini	L. Jensen/Miss N. Arendt	6–2	6–2		312,000
1997	M. Bhupathi/Miss R. Hiraki	P. Galbraith/Miss L. Raymond	6–4	6–1		330,000
1998	J. Gimelstob/Miss V. Williams	L. Lobo/Miss S. Williams	6–4	6–4		346,000

THE CHAMPIONSHIPS – WIMBLEDON

1. Venue: From 1877–1921 The Championships were played at the Worple Road ground. Since 1922 they have been played at the present ground in Church Road. **2. Title:** For the years 1913, 1914, and 1919–23 inclusive, these records include the 'World's Championship on Grass' granted to the LTA by the ILTF. This title was then abolished. **3. Challenge Round:** Prior to 1922 the holder did not compete in the Championship but met the winner of the All-Comers singles in the Challenge Round. The Challenge Round was abolished in 1922 and the holder subsequently played through. **4. Seeding:** 'Modified seeding' was introduced in 1924. 'Full seeding', as we know it today, was first practised in 1927. **5. Status:** The Championships became 'open' in 1968. (There was a tie-break at 8–all in all sets except the fifth in men's events and the third in women's events and mixed in the years 1971–78. Thereafter the tie-break was played at 6–all.) **6. Surface:** Alone of the four Grand Slams, The Championships have always been played on grass courts. **7.** In the years marked with an asterisk*, the holder(s) did not defend the title.

MEN'S SINGLES

	CHAMPIONS	*RUNNER-UP*	*SCORE*				
1877	S. W. Gore	W. C. Marshall	6–1	6–2	6–4		
1878	P. F. Hadow	S. W. Gore	7–5	6–1	9–7		
1879*	J. T. Hartley	V. St L. Goold	6–2	6–4	6–2		
1880	J. T. Hartley	H. F. Lawford	6–3	6–2	2–6	6–3	
1881	W. Renshaw	J. T. Hartley	6–0	6–1	6–1		
1882	W. Renshaw	E. Renshaw	6–1	2–6	4–6	6–2	6–2
1883	W. Renshaw	E. Renshaw	2–6	6–3	6–3	4–6	6–3
1884	W. Renshaw	H. F. Lawford	6–0	6–4	9–7		
1885	W. Renshaw	H. F. Lawford	7–5	6–2	4–6	7–5	
1886	W. Renshaw	H. F. Lawford	6–0	5–7	6–3	6–4	
1887*	H. F. Lawford	E. Renshaw	1–6	6–3	3–6	6–4	6–4
1888	E. Renshaw	H. F. Lawford	6–3	7–5	6–0		
1889	W. Renshaw	E. Renshaw	6–4	6–1	3–6	6–0	
1890	W. J. Hamilton	W. Renshaw	6–8	6–2	3–6	6–1	6–1
1891*	W. Baddeley	J. Pim	6–4	1–6	7–5	6–0	
1892	W. Baddeley	J. Pim	4–6	6–3	6–3	6–2	
1893	J. Pim	W. Baddeley	3–6	6–1	6–3	6–2	
1894	J. Pim	W. Baddeley	10–8	6–2	8–6		
1895*	W. Baddeley	W. V. Eaves	4–6	2–6	8–6	6–2	6–3
1896	H. S. Mahony	W. Baddeley	6–2	6–8	5–7	8–6	6–3
1897	R. F. Doherty	H. S. Mahony	6–4	6–4	6–3		
1898	R. F. Doherty	H. L. Doherty	6–3	6–3	2–6	5–7	6–1
1899	R. F. Doherty	A. W. Gore	1–6	4–6	6–3	6–3	6–3
1900	R. F. Doherty	S. H. Smith	6–8	6–3	6–1	6–2	
1901	A. W. Gore	R. F. Doherty	4–6	7–5	6–4	6–4	
1902	H. L. Doherty	A. W. Gore	6–4	6–3	3–6	6–0	
1903	H. L. Doherty	F. L. Riseley	7–5	6–3	6–0		
1904	H. L. Doherty	F. L. Riseley	6–1	7–5	8–6		
1905	H. L. Doherty	N. E. Brookes	8–6	6–2	6–4		
1906	H. L. Doherty	F. L. Riseley	6–4	4–6	6–2	6–3	
1907*	N. E. Brookes	A. W. Gore	6–4	6–2	6–2		
1908*	A. W. Gore	H. Roper Barrett	6–3	6–2	4–6	3–6	6–4
1909	A. W. Gore	M. J. G. Ritchie	6–8	1–6	6–2	6–2	6–2
1910	A. F. Wilding	A. W. Gore	6–4	7–5	4–6	6–2	
1911	A. F. Wilding	H. Roper Barrett	6–4	4–6	2–6	6–2	ret
1912	A. F. Wilding	A. W. Gore	6–4	6–4	4–6	6–4	
1913	A. F. Wilding	M. E. McLoughlin	8–6	6–3	10–8		
1914	N. E. Brookes	A. F. Wilding	6–4	6–4	7–5		
1915–18		*Not held*					
1919	G. L. Patterson	N. E. Brookes	6–3	7–5	6–2		
1920	W. T. Tilden	G. L. Patterson	2–6	6–2	6–3	6–4	
1921	W. T. Tilden	B. I. C. Norton	4–6	2–6	6–1	6–0	7–5
1922*	G. L. Patterson	R. Lycett	6–3	6–4	6–2		
1923*	W. M. Johnston	F. T. Hunter	6–0	6–3	6–1		
1924	J. Borotra	R. Lacoste	6–1	3–6	6–1	3–6	6–4
1925	R. Lacoste	J. Borotra	6–3	6–3	4–6	8–6	
1926	J. Borotra	H. Kinsey	8–6	6–1	6–3		
1927	H. Cochet	J. Borotra	4–6	4–6	6–3	6–4	7–5

	CHAMPIONS	*RUNNER-UP*	*SCORE*					FIRST PRIZE (£)
1928	R. Lacoste	H. Cochet	6–1	4–6	6–4	6–2		
1929	H. Cochet	J. Borotra	6–4	6–3	6–4			
1930	W. T. Tilden	W. L. Allison	6–3	9–7	6–4			
1931*	S. B. Wood	F. X. Shields	w.o.					
1932	H. E. Vines	H. W. Austin	6–4	6–2	6–0			
1933	J. H. Crawford	H. E. Vines	4–6	11–9	6–2	2–6	6–4	
1934	F. J. Perry	J. H. Crawford	6–3	6–0	7–5			
1935	F. J. Perry	G. von Cramm	6–2	6–4	6–4			
1936	F. J. Perry	G. von Cramm	6–1	6–1	6–0			
1937*	J. D. Budge	G. von Cramm	6–3	6–4	6–2			
1938	J. D. Budge	H. W. Austin	6–1	6–0	6–3			
1939*	R. L. Riggs	E. T. Cooke	2–6	8–6	3–6	6–3	6–2	
1940–45		*Not held*						
1946	Y. Petra	G.Brown	6–2	6–4	7–9	5–7	6–4	
1947	J. Kramer	T.Brown	6–1	6–3	6–2			
1948	B. Falkenburg	J. Bromwich	7–5	0–6	6–2	3–6	7–5	
1949	T. Schroeder	J. Drobny	3–6	6–0	6–3	4–6	6–4	
1950	B. Patty	F. A.Sedgman	6–1	8–10	6–2	6–3		
1951	D. Savitt	K. B. McGregor	6–4	6–4	6–4			
1952	F. A. Sedgman	J. Drobny	4–6	6–2	6–3	6–2		
1953	V. Seixas	K. Nielsen	9–7	6–3	6–4			
1954	J. Drobny	K. Rosewall	13–11	4–6	6–2	9–7.		
1955	T. Trabert	K. Nielsen	6–3	7–5	6–1			
1956*	L. A. Hoad	K. R. Rosewall	6–2	4–6	7–5	6–4		
1957	L. A. Hoad	A. J. Cooper	6–2	6–1	6–2			
1958*	A. J. Cooper	N. A. Fraser	3–6	6–3	6–4	13–11		
1959*	A. Olmedo	R. G. Laver	6–4	6–3	6–4			
1960*	N. A. Fraser	R. G. Laver	6–4	3–6	9–7	7–5		
1961	R. G. Laver	C. R. McKinley	6–3	6–1	6–4			
1962	R. G. Laver	M. F. Mulligan	6–2	6–2	6–1			
1963*	C. R. McKinley	F. S. Stolle	9–7	6–1	6–4			
1964	R. S. Emerson	F. S. Stolle	6–1	12–10	4–6	6–3		
1965	R. S. Emerson	F. S. Stolle	6–2	6–4	6–4			
1966	M. Santana	R. D. Ralston	6–4	11–9		6–4		
1967	J. D. Newcombe	W. P. Bungert	6–3	6–1	6–1			
1968	R. G. Laver	A. D. Roche	6–3	6–4	6–2			2,000
1969	R. G. Laver	J. D. Newcombe	6–4	5–7	6–4	6–4		3,000
1970	J. D. Newcombe	K. R. Rosewall	5–7	6–3	6–2	3–6	6–1	3,000
1971	J. D. Newcombe	S. R. Smith	6–3	5–7	2–6	6–4	6–4	3,750
1972*	S. R. Smith	I. Nastase	4–6	6–3	6–3	4–6	7–5	5,000
1973*	J. Kodes	A. Metreveli	6–1	9–8	6–3			5,000
1974	J. S. Connors	K. R. Rosewall	6–1	6–1	6–4			10,000
1975	A. R. Ashe	J. S. Connors	6–1	6–1	5–7	6–4		10,000
1976	B. Borg	I. Nastase	6–4	6–2	9–7			12,500
1977	B. Borg	J. S. Connors	3–6	6–2	6–1	5–7	6–4	15,000
1978	B. Borg	J. S. Connors	6–2	6–2	6–3			19,000
1979	B. Borg	R. Tanner	6–7	6–1	3–6	6–3	6–4	20,000
1980	B. Borg	J. P. McEnroe	1–6	7–5	6–3	6–7	8–6	20,000
1981	J. P. McEnroe	B. Borg	4–6	7–6	7–6	6–4		21,600
1982	J. S. Connors	J. P. McEnroe	3–6	6–3	6–7	7–6	6–4	41,667
1983	J. P. McEnroe	C. J. Lewis	6–2	6–2	6–2			66,600
1984	J. P. McEnroe	J. S. Connors	6–1	6–1	6–2			100,000
1985	B. Becker	K. Curren	6–3	6–7	7–6	6–4		130,000
1986	B. Becker	I. Lendl	6–4	6–3	7–5			140,000
1987	P. Cash	I. Lendl	7–6	6–2	7–5			155,000
1988	S. Edberg	B. Becker	4–6	7–6	6–4	6–2		165,000
1989	B. Becker	S. Edberg	6–0	7–6	6–4			190,000
1990	S. Edberg	B. Becker	6–2	6–2	3–6	3–6	6–4	230,000
1991	M. Stich	B. Becker	6–4	7–6	6–4			240,000
1992	A. Agassi	G. Ivanisevic	6–7	6–4	6–4	1–6	6–4	265,000
1993	P. Sampras	J. Courier	7–6	7–6	3–6	6–3		305,000
1994	P. Sampras	G. Ivanisevic	7–6	7–6	6–0			345,000
1995	P. Sampras	B. Becker	6–7	6–2	6–4	6–2		365,000
1996	R. Krajicek	M. Washington	6–3	6–4	6–3			392,500
1997	P. Sampras	C. Pioline	6–4	6–2	6–4			415,000
1998	P. Sampras	G. Ivanisevic	6–7	7–6	6–4	3–6	6–2	435,000

WOMEN'S SINGLES

	CHAMPION	RUNNER-UP	SCORE		
1884	Miss M. Watson	Miss L. Watson	6–8	6–3	6–3
1885	Miss M. Watson	Miss B. Bingley	6–1	7–5	
1886	Miss B. Bingley	Miss M. Watson	6–3	6–3	
1887	Miss C. Dod	Miss B. Bingley	6–2	6–0	
1888	Miss C. Dod	Mrs G. W. Hillyard	6–3	6–3	
1889*	Mrs G. W. Hillyard	Miss H. Rice	4–6	8–6	6–4
1890*	Miss H. Rice	Miss M. Jacks	6–4	6–1	
1891*	Miss C. Dod	Mrs G. W. Hillyard	6–2	6–1	
1892	Miss C. Dod	Mrs G. W. Hillyard	6–1	6–1	
1893	Miss C. Dod	Mrs G. W. Hillyard	6–8	6–1	6–4
1894*	Mrs G. W. Hillyard	Miss L. Austin	6–1	6–1	
1895*	Miss C. Cooper	Miss H. Jackson	7–5	8–6	
1896	Miss C. Cooper	Mrs W. H. Pickering	6–2	6–3	
1897	Mrs G. W. Hillyard	Miss C. Cooper	5–7	7–5	6–2
1898*	Miss C. Cooper	Miss L. Martin	6–4	6–4	
1899	Mrs G. W. Hillyard	Miss C. Cooper	6–2	6–3	
1900	Mrs G. W. Hillyard	Miss C. Cooper	4–6	6–4	6–4
1901	Mrs A. Sterry	Mrs G. W. Hillyard	6–2	6–2	
1902	Miss M. E. Robb	Mrs A. Sterry	7–5	6–1	
1903*	Miss D. K. Douglass	Miss E. W. Thomson	4–6	6–4	6–2
1904	Miss D. K. Douglass	Mrs A. Sterry	6–0	6–3	
1905	Miss M. Sutton	Miss D. K. Douglass	6–3	6–4	
1906	Miss D. K. Douglass	Miss M. Sutton	6–3	9–7	
1907	Miss M. Sutton	Mrs R. Lamb. Chambers	6–1	6–4	
1908*	Mrs A. Sterry	Miss A. M. Morton	6–4	6–4	
1909*	Miss D. P. Boothby	Miss A. M. Morton	6–4	4–6	8–6
1910	Mrs R. Lambert Chambers	Miss D. P. Boothby	6–2	6–2	
1911	Mrs R. Lambert Chambers	Miss D. P. Boothby	6–0	6–0	
1912*	Mrs D. R. Larcombe	Mrs A. Sterry	6–3	6–1	
1913*	Mrs R. Lambert Chambers	Mrs R. J. McNair	6–0	6–4	
1914	Mrs R. Lambert Chambers	Mrs D. R. Larcombe	7–5	6–4	
1915–18		*Not held*			
1919	Mlle S. Lenglen	Mrs R. Lamb. Chambers	10–8	4–6	9–7
1920	Mlle S. Lenglen	Mrs R. Lamb. Chambers	6–3	6–0	
1921	Mlle S. Lenglen	Miss E. Ryan	6–2	6–0	
1922	Mlle S. Lenglen	Mrs F. Mallory	6–2	6–0	
1923	Mlle S. Lenglen	Miss K. McKane	6–2	6–2	
1924	Miss K. McKane	Miss H. N. Wills	4–6	6–4	6–4
1925	Mlle S. Lenglen	Miss J. Fry	6–2	6–0	
1926	Mrs L. A. Godfree	Sta E. De Alvarez	6–2	4–6	6–3
1927	Miss H. N. Wills	Sta E. De Alvarez	6–2	6–4	
1928	Miss H. N. Wills	Sta E. De Alvarez	6–2	6–3	
1929	Miss H. N. Wills	Miss H. H. Jacobs	6–1	6–2	
1930	Mrs F. S. Moody	Miss E. Ryan	6–2	6–2	
1931*	Frl C. Aussem	Frl H. Krahwinkel	6–2	7–5	
1932*	Mrs F. S. Moody	Miss H. H. Jacobs	6–3	6–1	
1933	Mrs F. S. Moody	Miss D. E. Round	6–4	6–8	6–3
1934*	Miss D. E. Round	Miss H. H. Jacobs	6–2	5–7	6–3
1935	Mrs F. S. Moody	Miss H. H. Jacobs	6–3	3–6	7–5
1936*	Miss H. H. Jacobs	Mrs S. Sperling	6–2	4–6	7–5
1937	Miss D. E. Round	Miss J. Jedrzejowska	6–2	2–6	7–5
1938*	Mrs F. S. Moody	Miss H. H. Jacobs	6–4	6–0	
1939*	Miss A. Marble	Miss K. E. Stammers	6–2	6–0	
1940–45		*Not held*			
1946*	Miss P. M. Betz	Miss A. L. Brough	6–2	6–4	
1947*	Miss M. E. Osborne	Miss D. J. Hart	6–2	6–4	
1948	Miss A. L. Brough	Miss D. J. Hart	6–3	8–6	
1949	Miss A. L. Brough	Mrs W. du Pont	10–8	1–6	10–8
1950	Miss A. L. Brough	Mrs W. du Pont	6–1	3–6	6–1
1951	Miss D. J. Hart	Miss S. J. Fry	6–1	6–0	
1952	Miss M. Connolly	Miss A. L. Brough	6–4	6–3	
1953	Miss M. Connolly	Miss D. J. Hart	8–6	7–5	
1954	Miss M. Connolly	Miss A. L. Brough	6–2	7–5	
1955*	Miss A. L. Brough	Mrs J. G. Fleitz	7–5	8–6	

	CHAMPION	RUNNER-UP	SCORE			FIRST PRIZE (£)
1956	Miss S. J. Fry	Miss A. Buxton	6–3	6–1		
1957*	Miss A. Gibson	Miss D. R. Hard	6–3	6–2		
1958	Miss A. Gibson	Miss A. Mortimer	8–6	6–2		
1959*	Miss M. E. Bueno	Miss D. R. Hard	6–4	6–3		
1960	Miss M. E. Bueno	Miss S. Reynolds	8–6	6–0		
1961*	Miss A. Mortimer	Miss C. C. Truman	4–6	6–4	7–5	
1962	Mrs J. R. Susman	Mrs V. Sukova	6–4	6–4		
1963*	Miss M. Smith	Miss B. J. Moffitt	6–3	6–4		
1964	Miss M. E. Bueno	Miss M. Smith	6–4	7–9	6–3	
1965	Miss M. Smith	Miss M. E. Bueno	6–4	7–5		
1966	Mrs L. W. King	Miss M. E. Bueno	6–3	3–6	6–1	
1967	Mrs L. W. King	Mrs P. F. Jones	6–3	6–4		
1968	Mrs L. W. King	Miss J. A. M. Tegart	9–7	7–5		750
1969	Mrs P. F. Jones	Mrs L. W. King	3–6	6–3	6–2	1,500
1970*	Mrs B. M. Court	Mrs L. W. King	14–12	11–9		1,500
1971	Miss E. F. Goolagong	Mrs B. M. Court	6–4	6–1		1,800
1972	Mrs L. W. King	Miss E. Goolagong	6–3	6–3		2,400
1973	Mrs L. W. King	Miss C. M. Evert	6–0	7–5		3,000
1974	Miss C. M. Evert	Mrs O. Morozova	6–0	6–4		7,000
1975	Mrs L. W. King	Mrs R. A. Cawley	6–0	6–1		7,000
1976*	Miss C. M. Evert	Mrs R. A. Cawley	6–3	4–6	8–6	10,000
1977	Miss S. V. Wade	Miss B. F. Stove	4–6	6–3	6–1	13,500
1978	Miss M. Navratilova	Miss C. M. Evert	2–6	6–4	7–5	17,100
1979	Miss M. Navratilova	Mrs J. M. Lloyd	6–4	6–4		18,000
1980	Mrs R. A. Cawley	Mrs J. M. Lloyd	6–1	7–6		18,000
1981	Mrs J. M. Lloyd	Miss H. Mandlikova	6–2	6–2		19,440
1982	Miss M. Navratilova	Mrs J. M. Lloyd	6–1	3–6	6–2	37,500
1983	Miss M. Navratilova	Miss A. Jaeger	6–0	6–3		60,000
1984	Miss M. Navratilova	Mrs J. M. Lloyd	7–6	6–2		90,000
1985	Miss M. Navratilova	Mrs J. M. Lloyd	4–6	6–3	6–2	117,000
1986	Miss M. Navratilova	Miss H. Mandlikova	7–6	6–3		126,000
1987	Miss M. Navratilova	Miss S. Graf	7–5	6–3		139,500
1988	Miss S. Graf	Miss M. Navratilova	5–7	6–2	6–1	148,500
1989	Miss S. Graf	Miss M. Navratilova	6–2	6–7	6–1	171,000
1990	Miss M. Navratilova	Miss Z. Garrison	6–4	6–1		207,000
1991	Miss S. Graf	Miss G. Sabatini	6–4	3–6	8–6	216,000
1992	Miss S.Graf	Miss M. Seles	6–2	6–1		240,000
1993	Miss S. Graf	Miss J. Novotna	7–6	1–6	6–4	275,000
1994	Miss C. Martinez	Miss M. Navratilova	6–4	3–6	6–3	310,000
1995	Miss S. Graf	Miss A. Sanchez-Vicario	4–6	6–1	7–5	328,000
1996	Miss S. Graf	Miss A. Sanchez-Vicario	6–3	7–5		353,000
1997	Miss M. Hingis	Miss J. Novotna	2–6	6–3	6–3	373,000
1998	Miss J. Novotna	Miss N. Tauziat	6–4	7–6		391,500

MEN'S DOUBLES

	CHAMPIONS	RUNNERS-UP	SCORE				
1884	E./W. Renshaw	E. W. Lewis/E. L. Williams	6–3	6–1	1–6	6–4	
1885	E./W. Renshaw	C. E. Farrer/A. J. Stanley	6–3	6–3	10–8		
1886	E./W. Renshaw	C. E. Farrer/A. J. Stanley	6–3	6–3	4–6	7–5	
1887*	P. B-Lyon/W. W. Wilberforce	E. Barratt-Smith/J. H. Crispe	7–5	6–3	6–2		
1888	E./W. Renshaw	P. B-Lyon/W. W. Wilberforce	2–6	1–6	6–3	6–4	6–3
1889	E./W. Renshaw	G. W. Hillyard/E. W. Lewis	6–4	6–4	3–6	0–6	6–1
1890*	J. Pim/F. O. Stoker	G. W. Hillyard/E. W. Lewis	6–0	7–5	6–4		
1891	H./W. Baddeley	J. Pim/F. O. Stoker	6–1	6–3	1–6	6–2	
1892	H. S. Barlow/E. W. Lewis	H./W. Baddeley	4–6	6–2	8–6	6–4	
1893	J. Pim/F. O. Stoker	H. S. Barlow/E. W. Lewis	4–6	6–3	6–1	2–6	6–0
1894*	H./W. Baddeley	H. S. Barlow/C. H. Martin	5–7	7–5	4–6	6–3	8–6
1895	H./W. Baddeley	W. V. Eaves/E. W. Lewis	8–6	5–7	6–4	6–3	
1896	H./W. Baddeley	R. F. Doherty/H. A. Nisbet	1–6	3–6	6–4	6–2	6–1
1897	H. L./R. F. Doherty	H./W. Baddeley	6–4	4–6	8–6	6–4	
1898	H. L./R. F. Doherty	C. Hobart/H. A. Nisbet	6–4	6–4	6–2		
1899	H. L./R. F. Doherty	C. Hobart/H. A. Nisbet	7–5	6–0	6–2		
1900	H. L./R. F. Doherty	H. A. Nisbet/H. Roper Barrett	9–7	7–5	4–6	3–6	6–3
1901	H. L./R. F. Doherty	D. F. Davis/H. Ward	4–6	6–2	6–3	9–7	
1902	F. L. Riseley/S. H. Smith	H. L./R. F. Doherty	4–6	8–6	6–3	4–6	11–9

	CHAMPIONS	*RUNNERS-UP*	*SCORE*					FIRST PRIZE *(£ per team)*
1903	H. L./R. F. Doherty	F. L. Riseley/S. H. Smith	6–4	6–4	6–4			
1904	H. L./R. F. Doherty	F. L. Riseley/S. H. Smith	6–3	6–4	6–3			
1905	H. L./R. F. Doherty	F. L. Riseley/S. H. Smith	6–2	6–4	6–8	6–3		
1906	F. L. Riseley/S. H. Smith	H. L./R. F. Doherty	6–8	6–4	5–7	6–3	6–3	
1907*	N. E. Brookes/A. F. Wilding	K. Behr/B. C. Wright	6–4	6–4	6–2			
1908*	M. J. G. Ritchie/A. F. Wilding	A. W. Gore/H. Roper Barrett	6–1	6–2	1–6	1–6	9–7	
1909*	A. W. Gore/H. Roper Barrett	S. N. Doust/H. A. Parker	6–2	6–1	6–4			
1910	M. J. G. Ritchie/A. F. Wilding	A. W. Gore/H. Roper Barrett	6–1	6–1	6–2			
1911	M. Decugis/A. H. Gobert	M. J. G. Ritchie/A. F. Wilding	9–7	5–7	6–3	2–6	6–2	
1912	C. P. Dixon/H. Roper Barrett	M. Decugis/A. H. Gobert	3–6	6–3	6–4	7–5		
1913	C. P. Dixon/H. Roper Barrett	H. Kleinschroth/F. W. Rahe	6–2	6–4	4–6	6–2		
1914	N. E. Brookes/A. F. Wilding	C. P. Dixon/H. Roper Barrett	6–1	6–1	5–7	8–6		
1915–1918		*Not held*						
1919*	P. O'Hara Wood/R. V. Thomas	R. W. Heath/R. Lycett	6–4	6–2	4–6	6–2		
1920*	C. S. Garland/R. N. Williams	A. R. F. Kingscote/J. C. Parke	4–6	6–4	7–5	6–2		
1921*	R. Lycett/M. Woosnam	A. H./F. G. Lowe	6–3	6–0	7–5			
1922	J. O. Anderson/R. Lycett	P. O'Hara Wood/G.L. Patterson	3–6	7–9	6–4	6–3	11–9	
1923	L. A. Godfree/R. Lycett	E. Flaquer/Count M. De Gomar	6–3	6–4	3–6	6–3		
1924	F. T. Hunter/V. Richards	W. M. Washburn/R. N. Williams	6–3	3–6	8–10	8–6	6–3	
1925	J. Borotra/R. Lacoste	R. Casey/J. Hennessey	6–4	11–9	4–6	1–6	6–3	
1926	J. Brugnon/H. Cochet	H. Kinsey/V. Richards	7–5	4–6	6–3	6–2		
1927	F. T. Hunter/W. T. Tilden	J. Brugnon/H. Cochet	1–6	4–6	8–6	6–3	6–4	
1928	J. Brugnon/H. Cochet	J. B. Hawkes/G. L. Patterson	13–11	6–4	6–4			
1929	W. L. Allison/J. Van Ryn	I. G. Collins/J. C. Gregory	6–4	5–7	6–3	10–12	6–4	
1930	W. L. Allison/J. Van Ryn	J. H. Doeg/G. M. Lott	6–3	6–3	6–2			
1931	G. M. Lott/J. Van Ryn	J. Brugnon/H. Cochet	6–2	10–8	9–11	3–6	6–3	
1932	J. Borotra/J. Brugnon	G. P. Hughes/F. J. Perry	6–0	4–6	3–6	7–5	7–5	
1933	J. Borotra/J. Brugnon	R. Nunoi/J. Satoh	4–6	6–3	6–3	7–5		
1934	G. M. Lott/L. R. Stoefen	J. Borotra/J. Brugnon	6–2	6–3	6–4			
1935	J. H. Crawford/A. K Quist	W. L. Allison/J. Van Ryn	6–3	5–7	6–2	5–7	7–5	
1936	G. P. Hughes/C. R. D. Tuckey	C. E. Hare/F. H. D. Wilde	6–4	3–6	7–9	6–1	5–4	
1937	J. D. Budge/G. Mako	G. P. Hughes/C. R. D. Tuckey	6–0	6–4	6–8	6–1		
1938	J. D. Budge/G. Mako	H. Henkel/G. von Metaxa	6–4	3–6	6–3	8–6		
1939	E. T. Cooke/R. L. Riggs	C. E. Hare/F. H. D. Wilde	6–3	3–6	6–3	9–7		
1940–1945		*Not held*						
1946	T. Brown/J. A. Kramer	G. E. Brown/D. Pails	6–4	6–4	6–2			
1947	R. Falkenburg/J. A. Kramer	A. J. Mottram/O. W. Sidwell	8–6	6–3	6–3			
1948	J. E. Bromwich/F. A. Sedgman	T. Brown/G. Mulloy	5–7	7–5	7–5	9–7		
1949	R. A. Gonzales/F. A. Parker	G. Mulloy/F. R. Schroeder	6–4	6–4	6–2			
1950	J. E. Bromwich/A. K. Quist	G. E. Brown/O. W. Sidwell	7–5	3–6	6–3	3–6	6–2	
1951	K. B. McGregor/F. A. Sedgman	J. Drobny/E. W. Sturgess	3–6	6–2	6–3	3–6	6–3	
1952	K. B. McGregor/F. A. Sedgman	E. V. Seixas/E. W. Sturgess	6–3	7–5	6–4			
1953	L. A. Hoad/K. R. Rosewall	R. N. Hartwig/M. G. Rose	6–4	7–5	4–6	7–5		
1954	R. N. Hartwig/M. G. Rose	E. V. Seixas/M. A. Trabert	6–4	6–4	3–6	6–4		
1955	R. N. Hartwig/L. A. Hoad	N. A. Fraser/K. R. Rosewall	7–5	6–4	6–3			
1956	L. A. Hoad/K. R. Rosewall	N. Pietrangeli/O. Sirola	7–5	6–2	6–1			
1957	G. Mulloy/J. E. Patty	N. A. Fraser/L. A. Hoad	8–10	6–4	6–4	6–4		
1958	S. Davidson/U. Schmidt	A. J. Cooper/N. A. Fraser	6–4	6–4	8–6			
1959	R. Emerson/N. A. Fraser	R. Laver/R. Mark	8–6	6–3	14–16	9–7		
1960	R. H. Osuna/R. D. Ralston	M. G. Davies/R. K. Wilson	7–5	6–3	10–8			
1961	R. Emerson/N. A. Fraser	R. A. J. Hewitt/F. S. Stolle	6–4	6–8	6–4	6–8	8–6	
1962	R. A. J. Hewitt/F. S. Stolle	B. Jovanovic/N. Pilic	6–2	5–7	6–2	6–4		
1963	R. H. Osuna/A. Palafox	J. C. Barclay/P. Darmon	4–6	6–2	6–2	6–2		
1964	R. A. J. Hewitt/F. S. Stolle	R. Emerson/K. N. Fletcher	7–5	11–9	6–4			
1965	J. D. Newcombe/A. D. Roche	K. N. Fletcher/R. A. J. Hewitt	7–5	6–3	6–4			
1966	K. N. Fletcher/J. D. Newcombe	W. W. Bowrey/O. K. Davidson	6–3	6–4	3–6	6–3		
1967	R. A. J. Hewitt/F. D. McMillan	R. Emerson/K. N. Fletcher	6–2	6–3	6–4			
1968	J. D. Newcombe/A. D. Roche	K. R. Rosewall/F. S. Stolle	3–6	8–6	5–7	14–12	6–3	800
1969	J. D. Newcombe/A. D. Roche	T. S. Okker/M. C. Riessen	7–5	11–9	6–3			1,000
1970	J. D. Newcombe/A. D. Roche	K. R. Rosewall/F. S. Stolle	10–8	6–3	6–1			1,000
1971	R. Emerson/R. Laver	A. R. Ashe/R. D. Ralston	4–6	9–7	6–8	6–4	6–4	750
1972	R. A. J. Hewitt/F. D. McMillan	S. R. Smith/E. Van Dillen	6–2	6–2	9–7			1,000
1973	J. S. Connors/I. Nastase	J. R. Cooper/N. A. Fraser	3–6	6–3	6–4	8–9	6–1	1,000
1974	J. D. Newcombe/A. D. Roche	R. C. Lutz/S. R. Smith	8–6	6–4	6–4			2,000
1975	V. Gerulaitis/A. Mayer	C. Dowdeswell/A. J. Stone	7–5	8–6	6–4			2,000

	CHAMPIONS	*RUNNERS-UP*	*SCORE*					
1976	B. E. Gottfried/R. Ramirez	R. L. Case/G. Masters	3–6	6–3	8–6	2–6	7–5	3,000
1977	R. L. Case/G. Masters	J. G. Alexander/P. C. Dent	6–3	6–4	3–6	8–9	6–4	6,000
1978	R. A. J. Hewitt/F. D. McMillan	P. Fleming/J. P. McEnroe	6–1	6–4	6–2			7,500
1979	P. Fleming/J. P. McEnroe	B. E. Gottfried/R. Ramirez	4–6	6–4	6–2	6–2		8,000
1980	P. McNamara/P. McNamee	R. C. Lutz/S. R. Smith	7–6	6–3	6–7	6–4		8,400
1981	P. Fleming/J. P. McEnroe	R. C. Lutz/S. R. Smith	6–4	6–4	6–4			9,070
1982	P. McNamara/P. McNamee	P. Fleming/J. P. McEnroe	6–3	6–2				16,666
1983	P. Fleming/J. P. McEnroe	T. E./T. R. Gullikson	6–4	6–3	6–4			26,628
1984	P. Fleming/J. P. McEnroe	P. Cash/P. McNamee	6–2	5–7	6–2	3–6	6–3	40,000
1985	H. P. Gunthardt/B. Taroczy	P. Cash/J. Fitzgerald	6–4	6–3	4–6	6–3		47,500
1986	J. Nystrom/M. Wilander	G. Donnelly/P. Fleming	7–6	6–3	6–3			48,500
1987	K. Flach/R. Seguso	S. Casal/E. Sanchez	3–6	6–7	7–6	6–1	6–4	53,730
1988	K. Flach/R. Seguso	J. Fitzgerald/A. Jarryd	6–4	2–6	6–4	7–6		57,200
1989	J. B. Fitzgerald/A. Jarryd	R. Leach/J. Pugh	3–6	7–6	6–4	7–6		65,870
1990	R. Leach/J. Pugh	P. Aldrich/D. Visser	7–6	7–6	7–6			94,230
1991	J. B. Fitzgerald/A. Jarryd	J. Franai/L. Lavalle	6–3	6–4	6–7	6–1		98,330
1992	J. P. McEnroe/M. Stich	J. Grabb/R. Reneberg	5–7	7–6	3–6	7–6	19–17	108,570
1993	T. Woodbridge/M. Woodforde	G. Connell/P. Galbraith	7–5	6–3	7–6			124,960
1994	T. Woodbridge/M. Woodforde	G. Connell/P. Galbraith	7–6	6–3	6–1			141,350
1995	T. Woodbridge/M. Woodforde	R. Leach/S. Melville	7–5	7–6	7–6			149,450
1996	T. Woodbridge/M. Woodforde	B. Black/G. Connell	4–6	6–1	6–3	6–2		160,810
1997	T. Woodbridge/M. Woodforde	J. Eltingh/P. Haarhuis	7–6	7–6	5–7	6–3		170,030
1998	J. Eltingh/P. Haarhuis	T. Woodbridge/M. Woodforde	2–6	6–4	7–6	5–7	10–8	178,220

WOMEN'S DOUBLES

	CHAMPIONS	*RUNNERS-UP*	*SCORE*		
1913	R. J. McNair/P. D. H. Boothby	A. Sterry/R. Lambert Chambers	4–6	2–4	ret
1914	A. M. Morton/E. Ryan	F. J. Hannam/D. R. Larcombe	6–1	6–3	
1915–1918		*Not held*			
1919	S. Lenglen/E. Ryan	R. Lambert Chambers/D. R. Larcombe	4–6	7–5	6–3
1920	S. Lenglen/E. Ryan	R. Lambert Chambers/D. R. Larcombe	6–4	6–0	
1921	S. Lenglen/E. Ryan	A. E. Beamish/G. E. Peacock	6–1	6–2	
1922	S. Lenglen/E. Ryan	K. McKane/A. D. Stocks	6–0	6–4	
1923	S. Lenglen/E. Ryan	J. Austin/E. L. Colyer	6–3	6–1	
1924	G. Wightman/H. N. Wills	B. C. Covell/K. McKane	6–4	6–4	
1925	S. Lenglen/E. Ryan	A. V. Bridge/C. G. McIlquham	6–2	6–2	
1926	M. K. Browne/E. Ryan	L. A. Godfree/E. L. Colyer	6–1	6–1	
1927	H. N. Wills/E. Ryan	E. L. Heine/G. Peacock	6–3	6–2	
1928	P. Saunders/M. Watson	E. Bennett/E. H. Harvey	6–2	6–3	
1929	L. R. C. Michell/M. Watson	B. C. Covell/W. P. Shepherd-Barron	6–4	8–6	
1930	F. S. Moody/E. Ryan	E. Cross/S. Palfrey	6–2	9–7	
1931	W. P. Shepherd–Barron/P. E. Mudford	D. Metaxa/J. Sigart	3–6	6–3	6–4
1932	D. Metaxa/J. Sigart	H. H. Jacobs/E. Ryan	6–4	6–3	
1933	R. Mathieu/E. Ryan	W. A. James/A. M. Yorke	6–2	9–11	6–4
1934	R. Mathieu/E. Ryan	D. B. Andrus/S. Henrotin	6–3	6–3	
1935	F. James/K. E. Stammers	R. Mathieu/S. Sperling	6–1	6–4	
1936	F. James/K. E. Stammers	M. Fabyan/H. H. Jacobs	6–2	6–1	
1937	S. Mathieu/A. M. Yorke	M. R. King/J. B. Pittman	6–3	6–3	
1938	M. Fabyan/A. Marble	R. Mathieu/A. M. Yorke	6–2	6–3	
1939	M. Fabyan/A. Marble	H. H. Jacobs/A. M. Yorke	6–1	6–0	
1940–1945		*Not held*			
1946	A. L. Brough/M. E. Osborne	P. M. Betz/D. J. Hart	6–3	2–6	6–3
1947	D. J. Hart/R. B. Todd	A. L. Brough/M. E. Osborne	3–6	6–4	7–5
1948	A. L. Brough/W. du Pont	D. J. Hart/R. B. Todd	6–3	3–6	6–3
1949	A. L. Brough/W. du Pont	G. Moran/R. B. Todd	8–6	7–5	
1950	A. L. Brough/W. du Pont	S. J. Fry/D. J. Hart	6–4	5–7	6–1
1951	S. J. Fry/D. J. Hart	A. L. Brough/W. du Pont	6–3	13–11	
1952	S. J. Fry/D. J. Hart	A. L. Brough/M. Connolly	8–6	6–3	
1953	S. J. Fry/D. J. Hart	M. Connolly/J. Sampson	6–0	6–0	
1954	A. L. Brough/W. du Pont	S. J. Fry/D. J. Hart	4–6	9–7	6–3
1955	A. Mortimer/J. A. Shilcock	S. J. Bloomer/P. E. Ward	7–5	6–1	
1956	A. Buxton/A. Gibson	F. Muller/D. G. Seeney	6–1	8–6	
1957	A. Gibson/D. R. Hard	K. Hawton/M. N. Long	6–1	6–2	
1958	M. E. Bueno/A. Gibson	W. du Pont/M. Varner	6–3	7–5	
1959	J. Arth/D. R. Hard	J. G. Fleitz/C. C. Truman	2–6	6–2	6–3

	CHAMPIONS	*RUNNERS-UP*	*SCORE*			FIRST PRIZE *(£ per team)*
1960	M. E. Bueno/D. R. Hard	S. Reynolds/R. Schuurman	6–4	6–0		
1961	K. Hantz/B. J. Moffitt	J. Lehane/M. Smith	6–3	6–4		
1962	B. J. Moffitt/J. R. Susman	L. E. G. Price/R. Schuurman	5–7	6–3	7–5	
1963	M. E. Bueno/D. R. Hard	R. A. Ebbern/M. Smith	8–6	9–7		
1964	M. Smith/L. R. Turner	B. J. Moffitt/J. R. Susman	7–5	6–2		
1965	M. E. Bueno/B. J. Moffitt	F. Durr/J. Lieffrig	6–2	7–5		
1966	M. E. Bueno/N. Richey	M. Smith/J. A. M. Tegart	6–3	4–6	6–4	
1967	R. Casals/L. W. King	M. E. Bueno/N. Richey	9–11	6–4	6–2	
1968	R. Casals/L. W. King	F. Durr/P. F. Jones	3–6	6–4	7–5	500
1969	B. M. Court/J. A. M. Tegart	P. S. A. Hogan/M. Michel	9–7	6–2		600
1970	R. Casals/L. W. King	F. Durr/S. V. Wade	6–2	6–3		600
1971	R. Casals/L. W. King	B. M. Court/E. Goolagong	6–3	6–2		450
1972	L. W. King/B. Stove	D. E. Dalton/F. Durr	6–2	4–6	6–3	600
1973	R. Casals/L. W. King	F. Durr/B. Stove	6–1	4–6	7–5	600
1974	E. F. Goolagong/M. Michel	H. F. Gourlay/K. M. Krantzcke	2–6	6–4	6–3	1,200
1975	A. Kiyomura/K. Sawamatsu	F. Durr/B. Stove	7–5	1–6	7–5	1,200
1976	C. Evert/M. Navratilova	L. W. King/B. Stove	6–1	3–6	7–5	2,400
1977	R. L. Cawley/J. C. Russell	M. Navratilova/B. Stove	6–3	6–3		5,200
1978	G. E. Reid/W. Turnbull	M. Jausovec/V. Ruzici	4–6	9–8	6–3	6,500
1979	L. W. King/M. Navratilova	B. Stove/W. M. Turnbull	5–7	6–3	6–2	6,930
1980	K. Jordan/A. E. Smith	R. Casals/W. M. Turnbull	4–6	7–5	6–1	7,276
1981	M. Navratilova/P. H. Shriver	K. Jordan/A. E. Smith	6–3	7–6		7,854
1982	M. Navratilova/P. H. Shriver	K. Jordan/A. E. Smith	6–4	6–1		14,450
1983	M. Navratilova/P. H. Shriver	R. Casals/W. M. Turnbull	6–2	6–2		23,100
1984	M. Navratilova/P. H. Shriver	K. Jordan/A. E. Smith	6–3	6–4		34,700
1985	K. Jordan/P. D. Smylie	M. Navratilova/P. H. Shriver	5–7	6–3	6–4	41,100
1986	M. Navratilova/P. H. Shriver	H. Mandlikova/W. M. Turnbull	6–1	6–3		42,060
1987	C. Kohde-Kilsch/H. Sukova	B. Nagelsen/P. D. Smylie	7–5	7–5		46,500
1988	S. Graf/G. Sabatini	L. Savchenko/N. Zvereva	6–3	1–6	12–10	49,500
1989	J. Novotna/H. Sukova	L. Savchenko/N. Zvereva	6–1	6–2		56,970
1990	J. Novotna/H. Sukova	K. Jordan/P. D. Smylie	6–3	6–4		81,510
1991	L. Savchenko/N. Zvereva	G. Fernandez/J. Novotna	6–4	3–6	6–4	85,060
1992	G. Fernandez/N. Zvereva	J. Novotna/L. Savchenko-Neiland	6–4	6–1		93,920
1993	G. Fernandez/N. Zvereva	L. Neiland/J. Novotna	6–4	6–7	6–4	108,100
1994	G. Fernandez/N. Zvereva	J. Novotna/A. Sanchez-Vicario	6–4	6–1		122,200
1995	J. Novotna/A. Sanchez-Vicario	G. Fernandez/N. Zvereva	5–7	7–5	6–4	129,300
1996	M.Hingis/H. Sukova	M. J. McGrath/L. Neiland	5–7	7–5	6–1	139,040
1997	G. Fernandez/N. Zvereva	N. Arendt/M. Bollegraf	6–1	6–2		147,010
1998	M. Hingis/J. Novotna	L. Davenport/N. Zvereva	6–3	3–6	8–6	154,160

MIXED DOUBLES

	CHAMPIONS	*RUNNERS-UP*	*SCORE*		
1913	H. Crisp/Mrs C. O. Tuckey	J. C. Parke/Mrs D. R. Larcombe	3–6	5–3	ret
1914	J. C. Parke/Mrs D. R. Larcombe	A. F. Wilding/Mlle M. Broquedis	4–6	6–4	6–2
1915–1918		*Not held*			
1919	R. Lycett/Miss E. Ryan	A. D. Prebble/Mrs R. Lamb. Chambers	6–0	6–0	
1920	G. L. Patterson/Mlle S. Lenglen	R. Lycett/Miss E. Ryan	7–5	6–3	
1921	R. Lycett/Miss E. Ryan	M. Woosnam/Miss P. L. Howkins	6–3	6–1	
1922	P. O'Hara Wood/Mlle S. Lenglen	R. Lycett/Miss E. Ryan	6–4	6–3	
1923	R. Lycett/Miss E. Ryan	L. S. Deane/Mrs W. P. Shep.–Barron	6–4	7–5	
1924	J. B. Gilbert/Miss K. McKane	L. A. Godfree/Mrs W. P. Shep.d–Barron	6–3	3–6	6–3
1925	J. Borotra/Mlle S. Lenglen	V. L. De Morpurgo/Miss E. Ryan	6–3	6–3	
1926	L. A./Mrs Godfree	H. Kinsey/Miss M. K. Browne	6–3	6–4	
1927	F. T. Hunter/Miss E. Ryan	L. A./Mrs Godfree	8–6	6–0	
1928	P. D. B. Spence/Miss E. Ryan	J. H. Crawford/Miss D. S. Akhurst	7–5	6–4	
1929	F. T. Hunter/Miss H. N. Wills	I. G. Collins/Miss J. Fry	6–1	6–4	
1930	J. H. Crawford/Miss E. Ryan	D. Prenn/Frl H. Krahwinkel	6–1	6–3	
1931	G. M. Lott/Mrs L. A. Harper	I. G. Collins/Miss J. C. Ridley	6–3	1–6	6–1
1932	E. Maier/Miss E. Ryan	H. C. Hopman/Mlle J. Sigart	7–5	6–2	
1933	G. von Cramm/Frl H. Krahwinkel	N. G. Farquharson/Miss M. Heeley	7–5	8–6	
1934	R. Miki/Miss D. E. Round	H. W. Austin/Mrs W. P. Shep.–Barron	3–6	6–4	6–0
1935	F. J. Perry/Miss D. E. Round	H. C./Mrs Hopman	7–5	4–6	6–2
1936	F. J. Perry/Miss D. E. Round	J. D. Budge/Mrs M. Fabyan	7–9	7–5	6–4
1937	J. D. Budge/Miss A. Marble	Y. Petra/Mme R. Mathieu	6–4	6–1	
1938	J. D. Budge/Miss A. Marble	H. Henkel/Mrs M. Fabyan	6–1	6–4	

	CHAMPIONS	*RUNNERS-UP*	*SCORE*			FIRST PRIZE *(£ per team)*
1939	R. L. Riggs/Miss A. Marble	F. H. D. Wilde/Miss N. B. Brown	9–7	6–1		
1940–1945		*Not held*				
1946	T. Brown/Miss A. L. Brough	G. E. Brown/Miss D. Bundy	6–4	6–4		
1947	J. E. Bromwich/Miss A. L. Brough	C. F. Long/Mrs N. M. Bolton	1–6	6–4	6–2	
1948	J. E. Bromwich/Miss A. L. Brough	F. A. Sedgman/Miss D. J. Hart	6–2	3–6	6–3	
1949	E. W. Sturgess/Mrs R. A. Summers	J. E. Bromwich/Miss A. L. Brough	9–7	9–11	7–5	
1950	E. W. Sturgess/Miss A. L. Brough	G. E. Brown/Mrs R.B. Todd	11–9	1–6	6–4	
1951	F. A. Sedgman/Miss D. J. Hart	M. G. Rose/Mrs G. F. Bolton	7–5	6–2		
1952	F. A. Sedgman/Miss D. J. Hart	E. Morea/Mrs M. N. Long	4–6	6–3	6–4	
1953	E. V. Seixas/Miss D. J. Hart	E. Morea/Miss S. J. Fry	9–7	7–5		
1954	E. V. Seixas/Miss D. J. Hart	K. R. Rosewall/Mrs W. du Pont	5–7	6–4	6–3	
1955	E. V. Seixas/Miss D. J. Hart	E. Morea/Miss A. L. Brough	8–6	2–6	6–3	
1956	E. V. Seixas/Miss S. J. Fry	G. Mulloy/Miss A. Gibson	2–6	6–2	7–5	
1957	M. G. Rose/Miss D. R. Hard	N. A. Fraser/Miss A. Gibson	6–4	7–5		
1958	R. N. Howe/Miss L. Coghlan	K. Nielsen/Miss A. Gibson	6–3	13–11		
1959	R. Laver/Miss D. R. Hard	N. A. Fraser/Miss M. E. Bueno	6–4	6–3		
1960	R. Laver/Miss D. R. Hard	R. N. Howe/Miss M. E. Bueno	13–11	3–6	8–6	
1961	F. S. Stolle/Miss L. R. Turner	R. N. Howe/Miss E. Buding	11–9	6–2		
1962	N. A. Fraser/Mrs W. du Pont	R. D. Ralston/Miss A. S. Haydon	2–6	6–3	13–11	
1963	K. N. Fletcher/Miss M. Smith	R. A. J. Hewitt/Miss D. R. Hard	11–9	6–4		
1964	F. S. Stolle/Miss L. R. Turner	K. N. Fletcher/Miss M. Smith	6–4	6–4		
1965	K. N. Fletcher/Miss M. Smith	A. D. Roche/Miss J. A. M. Tegart	12–10	6–3		
1966	K. N. Fletcher/Miss M. Smith	R. D. Ralston/Mrs L. W. King	4–6	6–3	6–3	
1967	O. K. Davidson/Mrs L. W. King	K. N. Fletcher/Miss M. E. Bueno	7–5	6–2		
1968	K. N. Fletcher/Mrs B. M. Court	A. Metreveli/Miss O. Morozova	6–1	14–12		450
1969	F. S. Stolle/Mrs P. F. Jones	A. D. Roche/Miss J. A. M. Tegart	6–2	6–3		500
1970	I. Nastase/Miss R. Casals	A. Metreveli/Miss O. Morozova	6–3	4–6	9–7	500
1971	O. K. Davidson/Mrs L. W. King	M. C. Rieseen/Mrs B. M. Court	3–6	6–2	15–13	375
1972	I. Nastase/Miss R. Casals	K. Warwick/Miss E. Goolagong	6–4	6–4		500
1973	O. K. Davidson/Mrs L. W. King	R. C. Ramirez/Miss J. Newberry	6–3	6–2		500
1974	O. K. Davidson/Mrs L. W. King	M. J. Farrell/Miss L. J. Charles	6–3	9–7		1,000
1975	M. C. Riessen/Mrs B. M. Court	A. J. Stone/Miss B. Stove	6–4	7–5		1,000
1976	A. D. Roche/Miss F. Durr	R. L. Stockton/Miss R. Casals	6–3	2–6	7–5	2,000
1977	R. A. J. Hewitt/Miss G. R. Stevens	F. D. McMillan/Miss B. Stove	3–6	7–5	6–4	3,000
1978	F. D. McMillan/Miss B. Stove	R. O. Ruffels/Mrs L. W. King	6–2	6–2		4,000
1979	R. A. J. Hewitt/Miss G. R. Stevens	F. D. McMillan/Miss B. Stove	7–5	7–6		4,200
1980	J. R. Austin/Miss T. Austin	M. R. Edmondson/Miss D. L. Fromholtz	4–6	7–6	6–3	4,420
1981	F. D. McMillan/Miss B. Stove	J. R. Austin/Miss T. Austin	4–6	7–6	6–3	4,770
1982	K. Curren/Miss A. E. Smith	J. M. Lloyd/Miss W. M. Turnbull	2–6	6–3	7–5	6,750
1983	J. M. Lloyd/Miss W. M. Turnbull	S. Denton/Mrs L. W. King	6–7	7–6	7–5	12,000
1984	J. M. Lloyd/Miss W. M. Turnbull	S. Denton/Miss K. Jordan	6–3	6–3		18,000
1985	P. McNamee/Miss M. Navratilova	J. Fitzgerald/Mrs P. D. Smylie	7–5	4–6	6–2	23,400
1986	K. Flach/Miss K. Jordan	H. P. Gunthardt/Miss M. Navratilova	6–3	7–6		25,200
1987	M. J. Bates/Miss J. M. Durie	D. Cahill/Miss N. Provis	7–6	6–3		27,900
1988	S. E. Stewart/Miss Z. Garrison	K. Jones/Mrs S. W. Magers	6–1	7–6		29,700
1989	J. Pugh/Miss J. Novotna	M. Kratzmann/Miss J. Byrne	6–4	5–7	6–4	34,200
1990	R. Leach/Miss Z. Garrison	J. Fitzgerald/Mrs P. D. Smylie	7–5	6–2		40,000
1991	J. B. Fitzgerald/Mrs P. D. Smylie	J. Pugh/Miss N. Zvereva	7–6	6–2		41,720
1992	C. Suk/Mrs L. Savchenko Neiland	J. Eltingh/Miss M. Oremans	7–6	6–2		46,070
1993	M. Woodforde/Miss M. Navratilova	T. Nijssen/Miss M. Bollegraf	6–3	6–4		53,020
1994	T. Woodbridge/Miss H. Sukova	T. Middleton/Miss L. McNeil	3–6	7–5	6–3	60,000
1995	J. Stark/Miss M. Navratilova	C. Suk/Miss G. Fernandez	6–4	6–4		63,500
1996	C. Suk/Miss H. Sukova	M. Woodforde/Miss L. Neiland	1–6	6–3	6–2	68,280
1997	C. Suk/Miss H. Sukova	A. Olhovskiy/Mrs L. Neiland	4–6	6–2	6–3	72,200
1998	M. Mirnyi/Miss S. Williams	M. Bhupathi/Miss M. Lucic	6–4	6–4		75,700

US CHAMPIONSHIPS

1. Challenge Round: A Challenge Round was introduced in the men's singles in 1884 and discontinued following the 1911 Championship. It was introduced in the women's singles in 1888 and discontinued following the 1919 Championship. In men's doubles it was instituted in 1881 and abolished in 1918, restored in 1919 and finally abolished in 1920. In the years marked with an asterisk (*) the holder did not defend his/her title so the winner of the All-Comers Singles became the champion. From 1891–1901 inclusive (but not in 1893) the women's singles final was contested over five sets. **2. The War Years:** In 1917 a National Patriotic Tournament was held in all five events. The winners were not recognised as National Champions. During World War II (1942–45) all five National Championships were staged together at the West Side Tennis Club, Forest Hills, NY. **3. Last Amateur Events:** During the first two years of Open Tennis (1968–69) a National Amateur Championship was held for all five events at the Longwood Cricket Club, Boston, as well as an Open Championship at Forest Hills, New York (although there was no open mixed in 1968). Thereafter the Amateur event was discontinued. **4. Dress:** The 'predominantly white' clothing rule was last enforced at the 1971 Championships. **5. Prize Money:** Equal prize money for men and women was introduced in 1973. **6. Surfaces:** 1881–1974 Grass; 1975–77 American clay (Har-Tru); 1978–present Hard courts (DecoTurf II). **7. Venues:** *Men's singles:* 1881–1914 The Casino, Newport, RI. 1915–20 West Side Tennis Club, Forest Hills, NY. 1921–23 Germantown Cricket Club, Philadelphia, PA. 1924–77 West Side Tennis Club, Forest Hills, NY. 1978–present National Tennis Center, Flushing Meadows, NY. *Women's singles:* 1887–1920 Philadelphia Cricket Club, PA. 1921–77 West Side Tennis Club, Forest Hills, NY. 1978–present National Tennis Center, Flushing Meadows, NY. *Men's doubles:* 1881–1914 The Casino, Newport, RI. 1915–16 West Side Tennis Club, Forest Hills, NY. 1917–33 Longwood Cricket Club, Boston, MA. 1934 Germantown Cricket Club, Philadelphia, PA. 1935–41 Longwood Cricket Club, Boston, MA. 1942–45 West Side Tennis Club, Forest Hills, NY. 1946–69 Longwood Cricket Club, Boston, MA (1968–69 Amateur). 1968–77 West Side Tennis Club, Forest Hills, NY. 1978–present National Tennis Center, Flushing Meadows, NY. *Women's doubles:* 1887–1920 Philadelphia Cricket Club, PA (1887,1888 non-Championship). 1921–34 West Side Tennis Club, Forest Hills, NY. 1935–41 Longwood Cricket Club, Boston, MA. 1942–45 West Side Tennis Club, Forest Hills, NY. 1946–69 Longwood Cricket Club, Boston, MA (1968–69 Amateur). 1968–77 West Side Tennis Club, Forest Hills, NY. 1978– present National Tennis Center, Flushing Meadows, NY. *Mixed doubles:* 1892–1920 Philadelphia Cricket Club, PA. 1921–34 Longwood Cricket Club, Boston, MA. 1935–66 West Side Tennis Club, Forest Hills, NY. 1967–69 Longwood Cricket Club, Boston, MA. 1969–77 West Side Tennis Club, Forest Hills, NY (not held 1968). 1978–present National Tennis Center, Flushing Meadows, NY. **8. Status:** Since 1993 the men's doubles has been reduced to the best-of-three sets.

MEN'S SINGLES

	CHAMPION	*RUNNER-UP*	*SCORE*				
1881	R. D. Sears	W. E. Glyn	6–0	6–3	6–2		
1882	R. D. Sears	C. M. Clark	6–1	6–4	6–0		
1883	R. D. Sears	J. Dwight	6–2	6–0	9–7		
1884	R. D. Sears	H. A. Taylor	6–0	1–6	6–0	6–2	
1885	R. D. Sears	G. M. Brinley	6–3	4–6	6–0	6–3	
1886	R. D. Sears	R. L. Beeckman	4–6	6–1	6–3	6–4	
1887	R. D. Sears	H. W. Slocum	6–1	6–3	6–2		
1888*	H. W. Slocum	H. A. Taylor	6–4	6–1	6–0		
1889	H. W. Slocum	Q. A. Shaw	6–3	6–1	4–6	6–2	
1890	O. S. Campbell	H. W. Slocum	6–2	4–6	6–3	6–1	
1891	O. S. Campbell	C. Hobart	2–6	7–5	7–9	6–1	6–2
1892	O. S. Campbell	F. H. Hovey	7–5	3–6	6–3	7–5	
1893*	R. D. Wrenn	F. H. Hovey	6–4	3–6	6–4	6–4	
1894	R. D. Wrenn	M. F. Goodbody	6–8	6–1	6–4	6–4	
1895	F. H. Hovey	R. D. Wrenn	6–3	6–2	6–4		
1896	R. D. Wrenn	F. H. Hovey	7–5	3–6	6–0	1–6	6–1
1897	R. D. Wrenn	W. V. Eaves	4–6	8–6	6–3	2–6	6–2
1898*	M. D. Whitman	D. F. Davis	3–6	6–2	6–2	6–1	
1899	M. D. Whitman	J. P. Paret	6–1	6–2	3–6	7–5	
1900	M. D. Whitman	W. A. Larned	6–4	1–6	6–2	6–2	
1901*	W. A. Larned	B. C. Wright	6–2	6–8	6–4	6–4	
1902	W. A. Larned	R. F. Doherty	4–6	6–2	6–4	8–6	
1903	H. L. Doherty	W. A. Larned	6–0	6–3	10–8		
1904*	H. Ward	W. J. Clothier	10–8	6–4	9–7		
1905	B. C. Wright	H. Ward	6–2	6–1	11–9		
1906	W. J. Clothier	B. C. Wright	6–3	6–0	6–4		
1907*	W. A. Larned	R. LeRoy	6–2	6–2	6–4		
1908	W. A. Larned	B. C. Wright	6–1	6–2	8–6		
1909	W. A. Larned	W. J. Clothier	6–1	6–2	5–7	1–6	6–1
1910	W. A. Larned	T. C. Bundy	6–1	5–7	6–0	6–8	6–1
1911	W. A. Larned	M. E. McLoughlin	6–4	6–4	6–2		
1912	M. E. McLoughlin	W. F. Johnson	3–6	2–6	6–2	6–4	6–2
1913	M. E. McLoughlin	R. N. Williams	6–4	5–7	6–3	6–1	
1914	R. N. Williams	M. E. McLoughlin	6–3	8–6	10–8		
1915	W. M. Johnston	M. E. McLoughlin	1–6	6–0	7–5	10–8	

	CHAMPION	*RUNNER-UP*	*SCORE*					*PRIZE MONEY (US$)*
1916	R. N. Williams	W. M. Johnston	4–6	6–4	0–6	6–2	6–4	
1917	R. L. Murray	N. W. Niles	5–7	8–6	6–3	6–3		
1918	R. L. Murray	W. T. Tilden	6–3	6–1	7–5			
1919	W. M. Johnston	W. T. Tilden	6–4	6–4	6–3			
1920	W. T. Tilden	W. M. Johnston	6–1	1–6	7–5	5–7	6–3	
1921	W. T. Tilden	W. M. Johnson	6–1	6–3	6–1			
1922	W. T. Tilden	W. M. Johnston	4–6	3–6	6–2	6–3	6–4	
1923	W. T. Tilden	W. M. Johnston	6–4	6–1	6–4			
1924	W. T. Tilden	W. M. Johnston	6–1	9–7	6–2			
1925	W. T. Tilden	W. M. Johnston	4–6	11–9	6–3	4–6	6–3	
1926	R. Lacoste	J. Borotra	6–4	6–0	6–4			
1927	R. Lacoste	W. T. Tilden	11–9	6–3	11–9			
1928	H. Cochet	F. T. Hunter	4–6	6–4	3–6	7–5	6–3	
1929	W. T. Tilden	F. T. Hunter	3–6	6–3	4–6	6–2	6–4	
1930	J. H. Doeg	F. X. Shields	10–8	1–6	6–4	16–14		
1931	H. E. Vines	G. M. Lott	7–9	6–3	9–7	7–5		
1932	H. E. Vines	H. Cochet	6–4	6–4	6–4			
1933	F. J. Perry	J. H. Crawford	6–3	11–13	4–6	6–0	6–1	
1934	F. J. Perry	W. L. Allison	6–4	6–3	1–6	8–6		
1935	W. L. Allison	S. B. Wood	6–2	6–2	6–3			
1936	F. J. Perry	J. D. Budge	2–6	6–2	8–6	1–6	10–8	
1937	J. D. Budge	C. Von Cramm	6–1	7–9	6–1	3–6	6–1	
1938	J. D. Budge	G. Mako	6–3	6–8	6–2	6–1		
1939	R. L. Riggs	S. W. Van Horn	6–4	6–2	6–4			
1940	W. D. McNeill	R. L. Riggs	4–6	6–8	6–3	6–3	7–5	
1941	R. L. Riggs	F. Kovacs	5–7	6–1	6–3	6–3		
1942	F. R. Schroeder	F. A. Parker	8–6	7–5	3–6	4–6	6–2	
1943	J. R. Hunt	J. A. Kramer	6–3	6–8	10–8	6–0		
1944	F. A. Parker	W. F. Talbert	6–4	3–6	6–3	6–3		
1945	F. A. Parker	W. F. Talbert	14–12	6–1	6–2			
1946	J. A. Kramer	T. P. Brown	9–7	6–3	6–0			
1947	J. A. Kramer	F. A. Parker	4–6	2–6	6–1	6–0	6–3	
1948	R. A. Gonzales	E. W. Sturgess	6–2	6–3	14–12			
1949	R. A. Gonzales	F. R. Schroeder	16–18	2–6	6–1	6–2	6–4	
1950	A. Larsen	H. Flam	6–3	4–6	5–7	6–4	6–3	
1951	F. A. Sedgman	E. V. Seixas	6–4	6–1	6–1			
1952	F. A. Sedgman	G. Mulloy	6–1	6–2	6–3			
1953	M. A. Trabert	E. V. Seixas	6–3	6–2	6–3			
1954	E. V. Seixas	R. N. Hartwig	3–6	6–2	6–4	6–4		
1955	M. A. Trabert	K. R. Rosewall	9–7	6–3	6–3			
1956	K. R. Rosewall	L. A. Hoad	4–6	6–2	6–3	6–3		
1957	M. J. Anderson	A. J. Cooper	10–8	7–5	6–4			
1958	A. J. Cooper	M. J. Anderson	6–2	3–6	4–6	10–8	8–6	
1959	N. A. Fraser	A. Olmedo	6–3	5–7	6–2	6–4		
1960	N. A. Fraser	R. G. Laver	6–4	6–4	9–7			
1961	R. S. Emerson	R. G. Laver	7–5	6–3	6–2			
1962	R. G. Laver	R. S. Emerson	6–2	6–4	5–7	6–4		
1963	R. H. Osuna	F. Froehling	7–5	6–4	6–2			
1964	R. S. Emerson	F. S. Stolle	6–4	6–2	6–4			
1965	M. Santana	E. C. Drysdale	6–2	7–9	7–5	6–1		
1966	F. S. Stolle	J. D. Newcombe	4–6	12–10	6–3	6–4		
1967	J. D. Newcombe	C. Graebner	6–4	6–4	8–6			
1968#	A. R. Ashe	R. C. Lutz	4–6	6–3	8–10	6–0	6–4	
1969#	S. R. Smith	R. C. Lutz	9–7	6–3	6–1			
1968	A. R. Ashe	T. S. Okker	14–12	5–7	6–3	3–6	6–3	14,000
1969	R. G. Laver	A. D. Roche	7–9	6–1	6–2	6–2		16,000
1970	K. R. Rosewall	A. D. Roche	2–6	6–4	7–6	6–3		20,000
1971	S. R. Smith	J. Kodes	3–6	6–3	6–2	7–6		15,000
1972	I. Nastase	A. R. Ashe	3–6	6–3	6–7	6–4	6–3	25,000
1973	J. D. Newcombe	J. Kodes	6–4	1–6	4–6	6–2	6–2	25,000
1974	J. S. Connors	K. R. Rosewall	6–1	6–0	6–1			22,500
1975	M. Orantes	J. S. Connors	6–4	6–3	6–3			25,000
1976	J. S. Connors	B. Borg	6–4	3–6	7–6	6–4		30,000
1977	G. Vilas	J. S. Connors	2–6	6–3	7–5	6–0		33,000
1978	J. S. Connors	B. Borg	6–4	6–2	6–2			38,000

	CHAMPION	*RUNNER-UP*	*SCORE*					
1979	J. P. McEnroe	V. Gerulaitis	7–5	6–3	6–3			39,000
1980	J. P. McEnroe	B. Borg	7–6	6–1	6–7	5–7	6–4	46,000
1981	J. P. McEnroe	B. Borg	4–6	6–2	6–4	6–3		60,000
1982	J. S. Connors	I. Lendl	6–3	6–2	4–6	6–4		90,000
1983	J. S. Connors	I. Lendl	6–3	6–7	7–5	6–0		120,000
1984	J. P. McEnroe	I. Lendl	6–3	6–4	6–1			160,000
1985	I. Lendl	J. P. McEnroe	7–6	6–3	6–4			187,500
1986	I. Lendl	M. Mecir	6–4	6–2	6–0			210,000
1987	I. Lendl	M. Wilander	6–7	6–0	7–6	6–4		250,000
1988	M. Wilander	I. Lendl	6–4	4–6	6–3	5–7	6–4	275,000
1989	B. Becker	I. Lendl	7–6	1–6	6–3	7–6		300,000
1990	P. Sampras	A. Agassi	6–4	6–3	6–2			350,000
1991	S. Edberg	J. Courier	6–2	6–4	6–0			400,000
1992	S. Edberg	P. Sampras	3–6	6–4	7–6	6–2		500,000
1993	P. Sampras	C. Pioline	6–4	6–4	6–3			535,000
1994	A. Agassi	M. Stich	6–1	7–6	7–5			550,000
1995	P. Sampras	A. Agassi	6–4	6–3	4–6	7–5		575,000
1996	P. Sampras	M. Chang	6–1	6–4	7–6			600,000
1997	P. Rafter	G. Rusedski	6–3	6–2	4–6	7–5		650,000
1998	P. Rafter	M. Philippoussis	6–3	3–6	6–2	6–0		700,000

#US Amateur Championships

WOMEN'S SINGLES

	CHAMPION	*RUNNER-UP*	*SCORE*				
1887	Miss E. Hansell	Miss L. Knight	6–1	6–0			
1888	Miss B. L. Townsend	Miss E. Hansell	6–3	6–5			
1889	Miss B. L. Townsend	Miss L. D. Voorhees	7–5	6–2			
1890	Miss E. C. Roosevelt	Miss B. L. Townsend	6–2	6–2			
1891	Miss M. E. Cahill	Miss E. C. Roosevelt	6–4	6–1	4–6	6–3	
1892	Miss M. E. Cahill	Miss E. H. Moore	5–7	6–3	6–4	4–6	6–2
1893*	Miss A. Terry	Miss A. L. Schultz	6–1	6–3			
1894	Miss H. Hellwig	Miss A. Terry	7–5	3–6	6–0	3–6	6–3
1895	Miss J. Atkinson	Miss H. Hellwig	6–4	6–2	6–1		
1896	Miss E. H. Moore	Miss J. Atkinson	6–4	4–6	6–2	6–2	
1897	Miss J. Atkinson	Miss E. H. Moore	6–3	6–3	4–6	3–6	6–3
1898	Miss J. Atkinson	Miss M. Jones	6–3	5–7	6–4	2–6	7–5
1899*	Miss M. Jones	Miss M. Banks	6–1	6–1	7–5		
1900*	Miss M. McAteer	Miss E. Parker	6–2	6–2	6–0		
1901	Miss E. H. Moore	Miss M. McAteer	6–4	3–6	7–5	2–6	6–2
1902	Miss M. Jones	Miss E. H. Moore	6–1	1–0	ret		
1903	Miss E. H. Moore	Miss M. Jones	7–5	8–6			
1904	Miss M. G. Sutton	Miss E. H. Moore	6–1	6–2			
1905*	Miss E. H. Moore	Miss H. Homans	6–4	5–7	6–1		
1906*	Miss H. Homans	Mrs M. Barger-Wallach	6–4	6–3			
1907*	Miss Evelyn Sears	Miss C. Neely	6–3	6–2			
1908	Mrs M. Barger-Wallach	Miss Evelyn Sears	6–3	1–6	6–3		
1909	Miss H. Hotchkiss	Mrs M. Barger-Wallach	6–0	6–1			
1910	Miss H. Hotchkiss	Miss L. Hammond	6–4	6–2			
1911	Miss H. Hotchkiss	Miss F. Sutton	8–10	6–1	9–7		
1912*	Miss M. K. Browne	Miss Eleanora Sears	6–4	6–2			
1913	Miss M. K. Browne	Miss D. Green	6–2	7–5			
1914	Miss M. K. Browne	Miss M. Wagner	6–2	1–6	6–1		
1915*	Miss M. Bjurstedt	Mrs G. W. Wightman	4–6	6–2	6–0		
1916	Miss M. Bjurstedt	Mrs L. H. Raymond	6–0	6–1			
1917	Miss M. Bjurstedt	Miss M. Vanderhoef	4–6	6–0	6–2		
1918	Miss M. Bjurstedt	Miss E. E. Goss	6–4	6–3			
1919	Mrs G. W. Wightman	Miss M. Zinderstein	6–1	6–2			
1920	Mrs F. Mallory	Miss M. Zinderstein	6–3	6–1			
1921	Mrs F. Mallory	Miss M. K. Browne	4–6	6–4	6–2		
1922	Mrs F. Mallory	Miss H. N. Wills	6–3	6–1			
1923	Miss H. N. Wills	Mrs F. Mallory	6–2	6–1			
1924	Miss H. N. Wills	Mrs F. Mallory	6–1	6–3			
1925	Miss H. N. Wills	Miss K. McKane	3–6	6–0	6–2		
1926	Mrs F. Mallory	Miss E. Ryan	4–6	6–4	9–7		
1927	Miss H. N. Wills	Miss B. Nuthall	6–1	6–4			

	CHAMPION	RUNNER-UP	SCORE				FIRST PRIZE (US$)
1928	Miss H. N. Wills	Miss H. H. Jacobs	6–2	6–1			
1929	Miss H. N. Wills	Mrs P. H. Watson	6–4	6–2			
1930	Miss B. Nuthall	Mrs L. A. Harper	6–1	6–4			
1931	Mrs F. S. Moody	Mrs F. Whittingstall	6–4	6–1			
1932	Miss H. H. Jacobs	Miss C. A. Babcock	6–2	6–2			
1933	Miss H. H. Jacobs	Mrs F. S. Moody	8–6	3–6	3–0	ret	
1934	Miss H. H. Jacobs	Miss S. Palfrey	6–1	6–4			
1935	Miss H. H. Jacobs	Mrs S. P. Fabyan	6–2	6–4			
1936	Miss A. Marble	Miss H. H. Jacobs	4–6	6–3	6–2		
1937	Miss A. Lizana	Miss J. Jedrzejowksa	6–4	6–2			
1938	Miss A. Marble	Miss N. Wynne	6–0	6–3			
1939	Miss A. Marble	Miss H. H. Jacobs	6–0	8–10	6–4		
1940	Miss A. Marble	Miss H. H. Jacobs	6–2	6–3			
1941	Mrs E. T. Cooke	Miss P. M. Betz	7–5	6–2			
1942	Miss P. M. Betz	Miss A. L. Brough	4–6	6–1	6–4		
1943	Miss P. M. Betz	Miss A. L. Brough	6–3	5–7	6–3		
1944	Miss P. M. Betz	Miss M. E. Osborne	6–3	8–6			
1945	Mrs E. T. Cooke	Miss P. M. Betz	3–6	8–6	6–4		
1946	Miss P. M. Betz	Miss P. C. Canning	11–9	6–3			
1947	Miss A. L. Brough	Miss M. E. Osborne	8–6	4–6	6–1		
1948	Mrs W. D. du Pont	Miss A. L. Brough	4–6	6–4	15–13		
1949	Mrs W. D. du Pont	Miss D. J. Hart	6–3	6–1			
1950	Mrs W. D. du Pont	Miss D. J. Hart	6–4	6–3			
1951	Miss M. Connolly	Miss S. J. Fry	6–3	1–6	6–4		
1952	Miss M. Connolly	Miss D. J. Hart	6–3	7–5			
1953	Miss M. Connolly	Miss D. J. Hart	6–2	6–4			
1954	Miss D. J. Hart	Miss A. L. Brough	6–8	6–1	8–6		
1955	Miss D. J. Hart	Miss P. E. Ward	6–4	6–2			
1956	Miss S. J. Fry	Miss A. Gibson	6–3	6–4			
1957	Miss A. Gibson	Miss A. L. Brough	6–3	6–2			
1958	Miss A. Gibson	Miss D. R. Hard	3–6	6–1	6–2		
1959	Miss M. E. Bueno	Miss C. C. Truman	6–1	6–4			
1960	Miss D. R. Hard	Miss M. E. Bueno	6–4	10–12	6–4		
1961	Miss D. R. Hard	Miss A. S. Haydon	6–3	6–4			
1962	Miss M. Smith	Miss D. R. Hard	9–7	6–4			
1963	Miss M. E. Bueno	Miss M. Smith	7–5	6–4			
1964	Miss M. E. Bueno	Mrs C. Graebner	6–1	6–0			
1965	Miss M. Smith	Miss B. J. Moffitt	8–6	7–5			
1966	Miss M. E. Bueno	Miss N. Richey	6–3	6–1			
1967	Mrs L. W. King	Mrs P. F. Jones	11–9	6–4			
1968#	Mrs B. M. Court	Miss M. E. Bueno	6–2	6–2			
1969#	Mrs B. M. Court	Miss S. V. Wade	4–6	6–3	6–0		
1968	Miss S. V. Wade	Mrs L. W. King	6–4	6–2			6,000
1969	Mrs B. M. Court	Miss N. Richey	6–2	6–2			6,000
1970	Mrs B. M. Court	Miss R. Casals	6–2	2–6	6–1		7,500
1971	Mrs L. W. King	Miss R. Casals	6–4	7–6			5,000
1972	Mrs L. W. King	Miss K. Melville	6–3	7–5			10,000
1973	Mrs B. M. Court	Miss E. Goolagong	7–6	5–7	6–2		25,000
1974	Mrs L. W. King	Miss E. Goolagong	3–6	6–3	7–5		22,500
1975	Miss C. M. Evert	Mrs R. A. Cawley	5–7	6–4	6–2		25,000
1976	Miss C. M. Evert	Mrs R. A. Cawley	6–3	6–0			30,000
1977	Miss C. M. Evert	Miss W. Turnbull	7–6	6–2			33,000
1978	Miss C. M. Evert	Miss P. Shriver	7–5	6–4			38,000
1979	Miss T. A. Austin	Miss C. M. Evert	6–4	6–3			39,000
1980	Mrs J. M. Lloyd	Miss H. Mandlikova	5–7	6–1	6–1		46,000
1981	Miss T. A. Austin	Miss M. Navratilova	1–6	7–6	7–6		60,000
1982	Mrs J. M. Lloyd	Miss H. Mandlikova	6–3	6–1			90,000
1983	Miss M. Navratilova	Mrs J. M. Lloyd	6–1	6–3			120,000
1984	Miss M. Navratilova	Mrs J. M. Lloyd	4–6	6–4	6–4		160,000
1985	Miss H. Mandlikova	Miss M. Navratilova	7–6	1–6	7–6		187,500
1986	Miss M. Navratilova	Miss H. Sukova	6–3	6–2			210,000
1987	Miss M. Navratilova	Miss S. Graf	7–6	6–1			250,000
1988	Miss S. Graf	Miss G. Sabatini	6–3	3–6	6–1		275,000
1989	Miss S. Graf	Miss M. Navratilova	3–6	7–5	6–1		300,000
1990	Miss G. Sabatini	Miss S. Graf	6–2	7–6			350,000

CHAMPION		RUNNER-UP	SCORE			
1991	Miss M. Seles	Miss M. Navratilova	7–6	6–1		400,000
1992	Miss M. Seles	Miss A. Sanchez-Vicario	6–3	6–3		500,000
1993	Miss S. Graf	Miss H. Sukova	6–3	6–3		535,000
1994	Miss A. Sanchez-Vicario	Miss S. Graf	1–6	7–6	6–4	550,000
1995	Miss S. Graf	Miss M. Seles	7–6	0–6	6–3	575,000
1996	Miss S. Graf	Miss M. Seles	7–5	6–4		600,000
1997	Miss M. Hingis	Miss V. Williams	6–0	6–4		650,000
1998	Miss L. Davenport	Miss M. Hingis	6–3	7–5		700,000

#US Amateur Championships

MEN'S DOUBLES

	CHAMPIONS	RUNNERS-UP	SCORE				
1881	C. M. Clark/F. W. Taylor	A. Van Rensselaer/A. E. Newbold	6–5	6–4	6–5		
1882	J. Dwight/R. D. Sears	W. Nightingale/G. M. Smith	6–2	6–4	6–4		
1883	J. Dwight/R. D. Sears	A. Van Rensselaer/A. E. Newbold	6–0	6–2	6–2		
1884	J. Dwight/R. D. Sears	A. Van Rensselaer/W. V. R. Berry	6–4	6–1	8–10	6–4	
1885	J. S. Clark/R. D. Sears	W. P. Knapp/H. W. Slocum	6–3	6–0	6–2		
1886	J. Dwight/R. D. Sears	G. M. Brinley/H. A. Taylor	7–5	5–7	7–5	6–4	
1887	J. Dwight/R. D. Sears	H. W. Slocum/H. A. Taylor	6–4	3–6	2–6	6–3	6–3
1888	O. S. Campbell/V. G. Hall	C. Hobart/E. P. MacMullen		6–4	6–2	6–4	
1889	H. W. Slocum/H. A. Taylor	O. S. Campbell/V. G. Hall	6–1	6–3	6–2		
1890	V. G. Hall/C. Hobart	C. W. Carver/J. A. Ryerson	6–3	4–6	6–2	2–6	6–3
1891	O. S. Campbell/R. P. Huntington	V. G. Hall/C. Hobart	6–3	6–4	8–6		
1892	O. S. Campbell/R. P. Huntington	V. G. Hall/E. L. Hall	6–4	6–2	4–6	6–3	
1893	C. Hobart/F. H. Hovey	O. S. Campbell/R. P. Huntington	6–3	6–4	4–6	6–2	
1894	C. Hobart/F. H. Hovey	C. B. Neel/S. R. Neel	6–3	8–6	6–1		
1895	M. G. Chace/R. D. Wrenn	C. Hobart/F. H. Hovey	7–5	6–1	8–6		
1896*	C. B./S. R. Neel	M. G. Chace/R. D. Wrenn	6–3	1–6	6–1	3–6	6–1
1897	L. E. Ware/G. P. Sheldon	H. S. Mahony/H. A. Nisbet	11–13	6–2	9–7	1–6	6–1
1898	L. E. Ware/G. P. Sheldon	D. F. Davis/H. Ward	1–6	7–5	6–4	4–6	7–5
1899	D. F. Davis/H. Ward	L. E. Ware/G. P. Sheldon	6–4	6–4	6–3		
1900	D. F. Davis/H. Ward	F. B. Alexander/R. D. Little	6–4	9–7	12–10		
1901	D. F. Davis/H. Ward	L. E. Ware/B. C. Wright	6–3	9–7	6–1		
1902	H. L./R. F. Doherty	D. F. Davis/H. Ward	11–9	12–10	6–4		
1903	H. L./R. F. Doherty	L. Collins/L. H. Waldner	7–5	6–3	6–3		
1904*	H. Ward/B. C. Wright	K. Collins/R. D. Little	1–6	6–2	3–6	6–4	6–1
1905	H. Ward/B. C. Wright	F. B. Alexander/H. H. Hackett	6–3	6–1	6–2		
1906	H. Ward/B. C. Wright	F. B. Alexander/H. H. Hackett	6–3	3–6	6–3	6–3	
1907*	F. B. Alexander/B. C. Wright	W. J. Clothier/W. A. Larned	6–3	6–1	6–4		
1908	F. B. Alexander/H. H. Hackett	R. D. Little/B. C. Wright	6–1	7–5	6–2		
1909	F. B. Alexander/H. H. Hackett	G. J. Janes/M. E. McLoughlin	6–4	6–1	6–0		
1910	F. B. Alexander/H. H. Hackett	T. C. Bundy/T. W. Hendrick	6–1	8–6	6–3		
1911	R. D. Little/G. F. Touchard	F. B. Alexander/H. H. Hackett	7–5	13–15	6–2	6–4	
1912	T. C. Bundy/M. E. McLoughlin	R. D. Little/G. F. Touchard	3–6	6–2	6–1	7–5	
1913	T. C. Bundy/M. E. McLoughlin	C. J. Griffin/J. R. Strachan	6–4	7–5	6–1		
1914	T. C. Bundy/M. E. McLoughlin	G. M. Church/D. Mathey	6–4	6–2	6–4		
1915	C. J. Griffin/W. M. Johnston	T. C. Bundy/M. E. McLoughlin	6–2	3–6	4–6	6–3	6–3
1916	C. J. Griffin/W. M. Johnston	W. Dawson/M. E. McLoughlin	6–4	6–3	5–7	6–3	
1917	F. B. Alexander/ H. A. Throckmorton	H. C. Johnson/I. C. Wright	11–9	6–4	6–4		
1918	V. Richards/W. T. Tilden	F. B. Alexander/B. C. Wright	6–3	6–4	3–6	2–6	6–2
1919	N. E. Brookes/G. L. Patterson	V. Richards/W. T. Tilden	8–6	6–3	4–6	6–2	
1920	C. J. Griffin/W. M. Johnston	W. F. Davis/R. Roberts	6–2	6–2	6–3		
1921	V. Richards/W. T. Tilden	W. M. Washburn/R. N. Williams	13–11	12–10	6–1		
1922	V. Richards/W. T. Tilden	P. O'Hara Wood/G. L. Patterson	4–6	6–1	6–3	6–4	
1923	B. I. C. Norton/W. T. Tilden	W. M. Washburn/R. N. Williams	3–6	6–2	6–3	5–7	6–2
1924	H. O./R. G. Kinsey	P. O'Hara Wood/G. L. Patterson	7–5	5–7	7–9	6–3	6–4
1925	V. Richards/R. N. Williams	J. B. Hawkes/G. L. Patterson	6–2	8–10	6–4	11–9	
1926	V. Richards/R. N. Williams	A. H. Chapin/W. T. Tilden	6–4	6–8	11–9	6–3	
1927	F. T. Hunter/W. T. Tilden	W. M. Washburn/R. N. Williams	10–8	6–3	6–3		
1928	J. F. Hennessey/G. M. Lott	J. B. Hawkes/G. L. Patterson	6–2	6–1	6–2		
1929	J. H. Doeg/G. M. Lott	R. B. Bell/L. N. White	10–8	16–14	6–1		
1930	J. H. Doeg/G. M. Lott	W. L. Allison/J. Van Ryn	8–6	6–3	3–6	13–15	6–4
1931	W. L. Allison/J. Van Ryn	R. B. Bell/G. S. Mangin	6–4	6–3	6–2		
1932	K. Gledhill/H. E. Vines	W. L. Allison/J. Van Ryn	6–4	6–3	6–2		

	CHAMPIONS	*RUNNERS-UP*	*SCORE*					*FIRST PRIZE (US$)*
1933	G. M. Lott/L. R. Stoefen	F. A. Parker/F. X. Shields	11–13	9–7	9–7	6–3		
1934	G. M. Lott/L. R. Stoefen	W. L. Allison/J. Van Ryn	6–4	9–7	3–6	6–4		
1935	W. L. Allison/J. Van Ryn	J. D. Budge/G. Mako	6–2	6–3	2–6	3–6	6–1	
1936	J. D. Budge/G. Mako	W. L. Allison/J. Van Ryn	6–4	6–2	6–4			
1937	G. Von Cramm/H. Henkel	J. D. Budge/G. Mako	6–4	7–5	6–4			
1938	J. D. Budge/G. Mako	J. E. Bromwich/A. K. Quist	6–3	6–2	6–1			
1939	J. E. Bromwich/A. K. Quist	J. H. Crawford/H. C. Hopman	8–6	6–1	6–4			
1940	J. A. Kramer/F. R. Schroeder	G. Mulloy/H. J. Prussoff	6–4	8–6	9–7			
1941	J. A. Kramer/F. R. Schroeder	G. Mulloy/W. Sabin	9–7	6–4	6–2			
1942	G. Mulloy/W. F. Talbert	F. R. Schroeder/S. B. Wood	9–7	7–5	6–1			
1943	J. A. Kramer/F. A. Parker	D. Freeman/W. F. Talbert	6–2	6–4	6–4			
1944	R. Falkenburg/W. D. McNeill	F. Segura/W. F. Talbert	7–5	6–4	3–6	6–1		
1945	G. Mulloy/W. F. Talbert	R. Falkenburg/J. Tuero	12–10	8–10	12–10	6–2		
1946	G. Mulloy/W. F. Talbert	G. Guernsey/W. D. McNeill	3–6	6–4	2–6	6–3	20–18	
1947	J. A. Kramer/F. R. Schroeder	W. F. Talbert/O. W. Sidwell	6–4	7–5	6–3			
1948	G. Mulloy/W. F. Talbert	F. A. Parker/F. R. Schroeder	1–6	9–7	6–3	3–6	9–7	
1949	J. Bromwich/O. W. Sidwell	F. A. Sedgman/G. Worthington	6–4	6–0	6–1			
1950	J. Bromwich/F. A. Sedgman	G. Mulloy/W. F. Talbert	7–5	8–6	3–6	6–1		
1951	K. B. McGregor/F. A. Sedgman	D. Candy/M. G. Rose	10–8	6–4	4–6	7–5		
1952	M. G. Rose/E. V. Seixas	K. B. McGregor/F. A. Sedgman	3–6	10–8	10–8	6–8	8–6	
1953	R. N. Hartwig/M. G. Rose	G. Mulloy/W. F. Talbert	6–4	4–6	6–2	6–4		
1954	E. V. Seixas/M. A. Trabert	L. A. Hoad/K. R. Rosewall	3–6	6–4	8–6	6–3		
1955	K. Kamo/A. Miyagi	G. Moss/W. Quillian	6–3	6–3	3–6	1–6	6–4	
1956	L. A. Hoad/K. R. Rosewall	H. Richardson/E. V. Seixas	6–2	6–2	3–6	6–4		
1957	A. J. Cooper/N. A. Fraser	G. Mulloy/J. E. Patty	4–6	6–3	9–7	6–3		
1958	A. Olmedo/H. Richardson	S. Giammalva/B. McKay	3–6	6–3	6–4	6–4		
1959	R. S. Emerson/N. A. Fraser	E. Buchholz/A. Olmedo	3–6	6–3	5–7	6–4	7–5	
1960	R. S. Emerson/N. A. Fraser	R. G. Laver/R. Mark	9–7	6–2	6–4			
1961	C. McKinley/R. D. Ralston	A. Palafox/R. H. Osuna	6–3	6–4	2–6	13–11		
1962	A. Palafox/R. H. Osuna	C. McKinley/R. D. Ralston	6–4	10–12	1–6	9–7	6–3	
1963	C. McKinley/R. D. Ralston	A. Palafox/R. H. Osuna	9–7	4–6	5–7	6–3	11–9	
1964	C. McKinley/R. D. Ralston	G. Stilwell/M. Sangster	6–3	6–2	6–4			
1965	R. S. Emerson/F. S. Stolle	F. Froehling/C. Pasarell	6–4	10–12	7–5	6–3		
1966	R. S. Emerson/F. S. Stolle	C. Graebner/R. D. Ralston	6–4	6–4	6–4			
1967	J. D. Newcombe/A. D. Roche	O. K. Davidson/W. W. Bowrey	6–8	9–7	6–3	6–3		
1968#	R. C. Lutz/S. R. Smith	R. A. J. Hewitt/R. J. Moore	6–4	6–4	9–7			
1969#	R. D. Crealy/A. Stone	W. W. Bowrey/C. Pasarell	9–11	6–3	7–5			
1968	R. C. Lutz/S. R. Smith	A. R. Ashe/A. Gimeno	11–9	6–1	7–5			
1969	K. R. Rosewall/F. S. Stolle	C. Pasarell/R. D. Ralston	2–6	7–5	13–11	6–3		
1970	P. Barthes/N. Pilic	R. S. Emerson/R. G. Laver	6–3	7–6	4–6	7–6		
1971	J. D. Newcombe/R. Taylor	S. R. Smith/E. Van Dillen	6–7	6–3	7–6	4–6	7–6	2,000
1972	E. C. Drysdale/R. Taylor	O. K. Davidson/J. D. Newcombe	6–4	7–6	6–3			
1973	O. K. Davidson/J. D. Newcombe	R. G. Laver/K. R. Rosewall	7–5	2–6	7–5	7–5		4,000
1974	R. C. Lutz/S. R. Smith	P. Cornejo/J. Fillol	6–3	6–3				4,500
1975	J. S. Connors/I. Nastase	T. S. Okker/M. C. Riessen	6–4	7–6				4,500
1976	T. S. Okker/M. C. Riessen	P. Kronk/C. Letcher	6–4	6–4				10,000
1977	R. A. J. Hewitt/F. D. McMillan	B. E. Gottfried/R. Ramirez	6–4	6–0				13,125
1978	R. C. Lutz/S. R. Smith	M. C. Riessen/S. E. Stewart	1–6	7–5	6–3			15,500
1979	P. Fleming/J. P. McEnroe	R. C. Lutz/S. R. Smith	6–2	6–4				15,750
1980	R. C. Lutz/S. R. Smith	P. Fleming/J. P. McEnroe	7–6	3–6	6–1	3–6	6–3	18,500
1981	P. Fleming/J. P. McEnroe	H. Gunthardt/P. McNamara	w.o.					26,400
1982	K. Curren/S. Denton	V. Amaya/H. Pfister	6–2	6–7	5–7	6–2	6–4	36,000
1983	P. Fleming/J. P. McEnroe	F. Buehning/V. Winitsky	6–3	6–4	6–2			48,000
1984	J. Fitzgerald/T. Smid	S. Edberg/A. Jarryd	7–6	6–3	6–3			64,000
1985	K. Flach/R. Seguso	H. Leconte/Y. Noah	6–7	7–6	7–6	6–0		65,000
1986	A. Gomez/S. Zivojinovic	J. Nystrom/M. Wilander	4–6	6–3	6–3	4–6	6–3	72,800
1987	S. Edberg/A. Jarryd	K. Flach/R. Seguso	7–6	6–2	4–6	5–7	7–6	87,000
1988	S. Casal/E. Sanchez	R. Leach/J. Pugh	w.o.					95,000
1989	J. P. McEnroe/M. Woodforde	K. Flach/R. Seguso	6–4	4–6	6–3	6–3		104,000
1990	P. Aldrich/D. Visser	P. Annacone/D. Wheaton	6–2	7–6	6–2			142,800
1991	J. B. Fitzgerald/A. Jarryd	S. Davis/D. Pate	6–3	3–6	6–3	6–3		163,500
1992	J. Grabb/R. Reneberg	K. Jones/R. Leach	3–6	7–6	6–3	6–3		184,000
1993	K. Flach/R. Leach	M. Damm/K. Novacek	6–7	6–4	6–2			200,000
1994	J. Eltingh/P. Haarhuis	T. Woodbridge/M. Woodforde	6–3	7–6				200,000
1995	T. Woodbridge/M. Woodforde	A. O'Brien/S. Stolle	6–3	6–3				210,000

	CHAMPIONS	*RUNNERS-UP*	*SCORE*	
1996	T. Woodbridge/M. Woodforde	J. Eltingh/P. Haarhuis	4–6 7–6 7–6	240,000
1997	Y. Kafelnikov/D. Vacek	J. Bjorkman/N. Kulti	7–6 6–3	300,000
1998	S. Stolle/C. Suk	M. Knowles/D. Nestor	4–6 7–6 6–2	320,000

#US Amateur Championships

WOMEN'S DOUBLES

	CHAMPIONS	*RUNNERS-UP*	*SCORE*
1887†	E. F. Hansell/L. Knight	L. Allderdice/Church	6–0 6–4
1888†	E. C. Roosevelt/G. W. Roosevelt	A. K. Robinson/V. Ward	3–6 6–3 6–4
1889	M. Ballard/B. L. Townsend	M. Wright/L. Knight	6–0 6–2
1890	E. C. Roosevelt/G. W. Roosevelt	B. L. Townsend/M. Ballard	6–1 6–2
1891	M. E. Cahill/Mrs W. F. Morgan	E. C. Roosevelt/G. W. Roosevelt	2–6 8–6 6–4
1892	M. E. Cahill/A. M. McKinlay	Mrs A. H. Harris/A. R. Williams	6–1 6–3
1893	H. Butler/A. M. Terry	A. L. Schultz/Stone	6–4 6–3
1894	J. P. Atkinson/H. R. Hellwig	A. R. Williams/A. C. Wistar	6–4 8–6 6–2
1895	J. P. Atkinson/H. R. Hellwig	E. H. Moore/A. R. Williams	6–2 6–2 12–10
1896	J. P. Atkinson/E. H. Moore	A. R. Williams/A. C. Wistar	6–4 7–5
1897	J. P. Atkinson/K. Atkinson	F. Edwards/E. J. Rastall	6–2 6–1 6–1
1898	J. P. Atkinson/K. Atkinson	C. B. Neely/M. Wimer	6–1 2–6 4–6 6–1 6–2
1899	J. W. Craven/M. McAteer	M. Banks/E. J. Rastall	6–1 6–1 7–5
1900	H. Champlin/E. Parker	M. McAteer/M. Wimer	9–7 6–2 6–2
1901	J. P. Atkinson/M. McAteer	M. Jones/E. H. Moore	w.o.
1902	J. P. Atkinson/M. Jones	M. Banks/N. Closterman	6–2 7–5
1903	E. H. Moore/C. B. Neely	M. Jones/M. Hall	6–4 6–1 6–1
1904	M. Hall/M. G. Sutton	E. H. Moore/C. B. Neely	3–6 6–3 6–3
1905	H. Homans/C. B. Neely	V. Maule/M. F. Oberteuffer	6–0 6–1
1906	Mrs L. S. Coe/Mrs D. S. Platt	C. Boldt/H. Homans	6–4 6–4
1907	C. B. Neely/M. Wimer	E. Wildey/N. Wildey	6–1 2–6 6–4
1908	M. Curtis/Evelyn Sears	C. B. Neely/M. Steever	6–3 5–7 9–7
1909	H. V. Hotchkiss/E. E. Rotch	D. Green/L. Moyes	6–1 6–1
1910	H. V. Hotchkiss/E. E. Rotch	A. Browning/E. Wildey	6–4 6–4
1911	H. V. Hotchkiss/Eleanora Sears	D. Green/F. Sutton	6–4 4–6 6–2
1912	M. K. Browne/D. Green	Mrs M. Barger-Wallach/Mrs F. Schmitz	6–2 5–7 6–0
1913	M. K. Browne/ Mrs R. H. Williams	D. Green/E. Wildey	12–10 2–6 6–3
1914	M. K. Browne/ Mrs R. H. Williams	Mrs E. Raymond/E. Wildey	8–6 6–2
1915	Eleanora Sears/ Mrs G. W. Wightman	Mrs G. L. Chapman/Mrs M. McLean	10–8 6–2
1916	M. Bjurstedt/Eleanora Sears	Mrs E. Raymond/E. Wildey	4–6 6–2 10–8
1917	M. Bjurstedt/Eleanora Sears	Mrs R. LeRoy/P. Walsh	6–2 6–4
1918	E. E. Goss/M. Zinderstein	M. Bjurstedt/Mrs J. Rogge	7–5 8–6
1919	E. E. Goss/M. Zinderstein	E. Sears/Mrs G. W. Wightman	10–8 9–7
1920	E. E. Goss/M. Zinderstein	H. Baker/E. Tennant	13–11 4–6 6–3
1921	M. K. Browne/ Mrs R. H. Williams	H. Gilleaudeau/Mrs L. G. Morris	6–3 6–2
1922	Mrs J. B. Jessup/H. N. Wills	Mrs F. I. Mallory/E. Sigourney	6–4 7–9 6–3
1923	Mrs B. C. Covell/K. McKane	E. E. Goss/Mrs G. W. Wightman	2–6 6–2 6–1
1924	Mrs G. W. Wightman/ H. N. Wills	E. E. Goss/Mrs J. B. Jessup	6–4 6–3
1925	M. K. Browne/H. N. Wills	Mrs T. C. Bundy/E. Ryan	6–4 6–3
1926	E. E. Goss/E. Ryan	M. K. Browne/Mrs A. H. Chapin	3–6 6–4 12–10
1927	Mrs L. A. Godfree/E. H. Harvey	J. Fry/B. Nuthall	6–1 4–6 6–4
1928	Mrs G. W. Wightman/H. N. Wills	E. Cross/Mrs L. A. Harper	6–2 6–2
1929	Mrs L. R. C. Michell/ Mrs P. H.Watson	Mrs B. C. Covell/ Mrs D. C. Shepherd-Barron	2–6 6–3 6–4
1930	B. Nuthall/S. Palfrey	E. Cross/Mrs L. A. Harper	3–6 6–3 7–5
1931	B. Nuthall/ Mrs E. F. Whittingstall	H. H. Jacobs/D. E. Round	6–2 6–4
1932	H. H. Jacobs/S. Palfrey	A. Marble/Mrs M. Painter	8–6 6–1
1933	F. James/B. Nuthall	Mrs F. S. Moody/E. Ryan	w.o.
1934	H. H. Jacobs/S. Palfrey	Mrs D. B. Andrus/C. A. Babcock	4–6 6–3 6–4
1935	H. H. Jacobs/Mrs M. Fabyan	Mrs D. B. Andrus/C. A. Babcock	6–4 6–2
1936	C. A. Babcock/Mrs J. Van Ryn	H. H. Jacobs/Mrs M. Fabyan	9–7 2–6 6–4
1937	Mrs M. Fabyan/A. Marble	C. A. Babcock/Mrs J. Van Ryn	7–5 6–4

	CHAMPIONS	RUNNERS-UP	SCORE			
1938	Mrs M. Fabyan/A. Marble	J. Jedrzejowska/Mrs R. Mathieu	6–8	6–4	6–3	
1939	Mrs M. Fabyan/A. Marble	Mrs S. H. Hammersley/K. E. Stammers	7–5	8–6		
1940	Mrs M. Fabyan/A. Marble	D. M. Bundy/Mrs J. Van Ryn	6–4	6–3		
1941	Mrs E. T. Cooke/M. E. Osborne	D. M. Bundy/D. J. Hart	3–6	6–1	6–4	
1942	A. L. Brough/M. E. Osborne	P. M. Betz/D. J. Hart	6–7	7–5	6–0	
1943	A. L. Brough/M. E. Osborne	P. M. Betz/D. J. Hart	6–1	6–3		
1944	A. L. Brough/M. E. Osborne	P. M. Betz/D. J. Hart	4–6	6–4	6–3	
1945	A. L. Brough/M. E. Osborne	P. M. Betz/D. J. Hart	6–4	6–4		
1946	A. L. Brough/M. E. Osborne	Mrs P. C. Todd/Mrs M. A. Prentiss	6–1	6–3		
1947	A. L. Brough/M. E. Osborne	Mrs P. C. Todd/D. J. Hart	5–7	6–3	7–5	
1948	A. L. Brough/Mrs W. D. du Pont	Mrs P. C. Todd/D. J. Hart	6–4	8–10	6–1	
1949	A. L. Brough/Mrs W. D. du Pont	S. J. Fry/D. J. Hart	6–4	10–8		
1950	A. L. Brough/Mrs W. D. du Pont	S. J. Fry/D. J. Hart	6–2	6–3		
1951	S. J. Fry/D. J. Hart	N. Chaffee/Mrs P. C. Todd	6–4	6–2		
1952	S. J. Fry/D. J. Hart	A. L. Brough/M. Connolly	10–8	6–4		
1953	S. J. Fry/D. J. Hart	A. L. Brough/Mrs W. D. du Pont	6–2	7–9	9–7	
1954	S. J. Fry/D. J. Hart	A. L. Brough/Mrs W. D. du Pont	6–4	6–4		
1955	A. L. Brough/Mrs W. D. du Pont	S. J. Fry/D. J. Hart	6–3	1–6	6–3	
1956	A. L. Brough/Mrs W. D. du Pont	Mrs B. R. Pratt/S. J. Fry	6–3	6–0		
1957	A. L. Brough/Mrs W. D. du Pont	A. Gibson/D. R. Hard	6–2	7–5		
1958	J. M. Arth/D. R. Hard	A. Gibson/M. E. Bueno	2–6	6–3	6–4	
1959	J. M. Arth/D. R. Hard	S. Moore/M. E. Bueno	6–2	6–3		
1960	M. E. Bueno/D. R. Hard	D. M. Catt/A. A. Haydon	6–1	6–1		
1961	D. R. Hard/L. Turner	E. Buding/Y. Ramirez	6–4	5–7	6–0	
1962	M. E. Bueno/D. R. Hard	Mrs R. Susman/B. J. Moffitt	4–6	6–3	6–2	
1963	R. Ebbern/M. Smith	M. E. Bueno/D. R. Hard	4–6	10–8	6–3	
1964	Mrs R. Susman/B. J. Moffitt	M. Smith/L. Turner	3–6	6–2	6–4	
1965	N. Richey/Mrs C. Graebner	Mrs R. Susman/B. J. Moffitt	6–4	6–4		
1966	M. E. Bueno/N. Richey	R. Casals/Mrs L. W. King	6–3	6–4		
1967	R. Casals/Mrs L. W. King	M. A. Eisel/Mrs D. Fales	4–6	6–3	6–4	
1968#	M. E. Bueno/M. Smith	S. V. Wade/Mrs G. M. Williams	6–3	7–5		
1969#	Mrs B. M. Court/S. V. Wade	Mrs P. W. Curtis/V. Ziegenfuss	6–1	6–3		
1968	M. E. Bueno/Mrs B. M. Court	R. Casals/Mrs L. W. King	4–6	9–7	8–6	
1969	F. Durr/D. R. Hard	Mrs B. M. Court/S. V. Wade	0–6	6–4	6–4	
1970	Mrs B. M. Court/Mrs D. Dalton	R. Casals/S. V. Wade	6–3	6–4		
1971	R. Casals/Mrs D. Dalton	Mrs J. B. Chanfreau/F. Durr	6–3	6–3		
1972	F. Durr/B. Stove	Mrs B. M. Court/S. V. Wade	6–3	1–6	6–3	
1973	Mrs B. M. Court/S. V. Wade	R. Casals/Mrs L. W. King	3–6	6–3	7–5	
1974	R. Casals/Mrs L. W. King	F. Durr/B. Stove	7–6	6–7	6–4	
1975	Mrs B. M. Court/S. V. Wade	R. Casals/Mrs L. W. King	7–5	2–6	7–5	
1976	L. Boshoff/I. Kloss	O. Morozova/S. V. Wade	6–1	6–4		
1977	M. Navratilova/B. Stove	R. Richards/B. Stuart	6–1	7–6		
1978	Mrs L. W. King/M. Navratilova	Mrs G. E. Reid/W. M. Turnbull	7–6	6–4		
1979	B. Stove/W. M. Turnbull	Mrs L. W. King/M. Navratilova	7–5	6–3		
1980	Mrs L. W. King/M. Navratilova	P. H. Shriver/B. Stove	7–6	7–5		
1981	K. Jordan/A. E. Smith	R. Casals/W. M. Turnbull	6–3	6–3		
1982	R. Casals/W. M. Turnbull	B. Potter/S. A. Walsh	6–4	6–4		
1983	M. Navratilova/P. H. Shriver	R. Fairbank/C. Reynolds	6–7	6–1	6–3	
1984	M. Navratilova/P. H. Shriver	A. E. Hobbs/W. M. Turnbull	6–2	6–4		
1985	C. Kohde-Kilsch/H. Sukova	M. Navratilova/P. H. Shriver	6–7	6–2	6–3	
1986	M. Navratilova/P. H. Shriver	H. Mandlikova/W. M. Turnbull	6–4	3–6	6–3	
1987	M. Navratilova/P. H. Shriver	K. Jordan/Mrs P. Smylie	5–7	6–4	6–2	
1988	G. Fernandez/R. White	J. Hetherington/P. Fendick	6–4	6–1		
1989	H. Mandlikova/M. Navratilova	M. J. Fernandez/P. H. Shriver	5–7	6–4	6–4	
1990	G. Fernandez/M. Navratilova	J. Novotna/H. Sukova	6–2	6–4		
1991	P. H. Shriver/N. Zvereva	J. Novotna/L. Savchenko	6–4	4–6	7–6	
1992	G. Fernandez/N. Zvereva	J. Novotna/L. Savchenko Neiland	7–6	6–1		
1993	A. Sanchez-Vicario/H. Sukova	A. Coetzer/I. Gorrochategui	6–4	6–2		
1994	J. Novotna/A. Sanchez-Vicario	K. Maleeva/R. White	6–3	6–3		
1995	G. Fernandez/N. Zvereva	B. Schultz-McCarthy/R. Stubbs	7–5	6–3		FIRST
1996	G. Fernandez/N. Zvereva	J. Novotna/A. Sanchez-Vicario	1–6	6–1	6–4	PRIZE
1997	L. Davenport/J. Novotna	G Fernandez/N. Zvereva	3–6	7–6	6–2	(US$)
1998	M. Hingis/J. Novotna	L. Davenport/N. Zvereva	6–3	6–3		320,000

#US Amateur Championships

†Not recognised as an official championship

MIXED DOUBLES

	CHAMPIONS	*RUNNERS-UP*	*SCORE*			
1887†	J. S. Clark/Miss L. Stokes	E. D. Faries/Miss L. Knight	7–5	6–4		
1888†	J. S. Clark/Miss M. Wright	P. Johnson/Miss A. Robinson	1–6	6–5	6–4	6–3
1889†	A. E. Wright/Miss G. W. Roosevelt	C. T. Lee/Miss B. L. Townsend	6–1	6–3	3–6	6–3
1890†	R. Beach/Miss M. E. Cahill	C. T. Lee/Miss B. L. Townsend	6–2	3–6	6–2	
1891†	M. R. Wright/Miss M. E. Cahill	C. T. Lee/Miss G. W. Roosevelt	6–4	6–0	6–5	
1892	C. Hobart/Miss M. E. Cahill	R. Beach/Miss E. H. Moore	6–1	6–3		
1893	C. Hobart/Miss E. C. Roosevelt	R. N. Willson/Miss E. Bankson	6–1	4–6	10–8	6–1
1894	E. P. Fischer/Miss J. P. Atkinson	G. Remak/Mrs McFadden	8–6	6–2	6–1	
1895	E. P. Fischer/Miss J. P. Atkinson	M. Fielding/Miss A. R. Williams	4–6	6–3	6–2	
1896	E. P. Fischer/Miss J. P. Atkinson	M. Fielding/Miss A. R. Williams	6–2	6–3	6–3	
1897	D. L. Magruder/Miss L. Henson	R. A. Griffin/Miss M. Banks	6–4	6–3	7–5	
1898	E. P. Fischer/Miss C. B. Neely	J. A. Hill/Miss H. Chapman	6–2	6–4	8–6	
1899	A. L. Hoskins/Miss E. J. Rastall	J. P. Gardner/Miss J. W. Craven	6–4	6–0	ret	
1900	A. Codman/Miss M. J. Hunnewell	G. Atkinson/Miss T. Shaw	11–9	6–3	6–1	
1901	R. D. Little/Miss M. Jones	C. Stevens/Miss M. McAteer	6–4	6–4	7–5	
1902	W. C. Grant/Miss E. H. Moore	A. L. Hoskins/Miss E. J. Rastall	6–2	6–1		
1903	H. F. Allen/Miss H. Chapman	W. H. Rowland/Miss C. B. Neely	6–4	7–5		
1904	W. C. Grant/Miss E. H. Moore	F. B. Dallas/Miss M. Sutton	6–2	6–1		
1905	C. Hobart/Mrs Hobart	E. B. Dewhurst/Miss E. H. Moore	6–2	6–4		
1906	E. B. Dewhurst/Miss S. Coffin	J. B. Johnson/Miss M. Johnson	6–3	7–5		
1907	W. F. Johnson/Miss M. Sayres	H. M. Tilden/Miss N. Wildey	6–1	7–5		
1908	N. W. Niles/Miss E. E. Rotch	R. D. Little/Miss L. Hammond	6–4	4–6	6–4	
1909	W. F. Johnson/Miss H. V. Hotchkiss	R. D. Little/Miss L. Hammond	6–2	6–0		
1910	J. R. Carpenter/Miss H. V. Hotchkiss	H. M. Tilden/Miss E. Wildey	6–2	6–2		
1911	W. F. Johnson/Miss H. V. Hotchkiss	H. M. Tilden/Miss E. Wildey	6–4	6–4		
1912	R. N. Williams/Miss M. K. Browne	W. J. Clothier/Miss Evelyn Sears	6–4	2–6	11–9	
1913	W. T. Tilden/Miss M. K. Browne	C. S. Rogers/Miss D. Green	7–5	7–5		
1914	W. T. Tilden/Miss M. K. Browne	J. R. Rowland/Miss M. Myers	6–1	6–4		
1915	H. C. Johnson/Mrs G. W. Wightman	I. C. Wright/Miss M. Bjurstedt	6–0	6–1		
1916	W. E. Davis/Miss Evelyn Sears	W. T. Tilden/Miss F. A. Ballin	6–4	7–5		
1917	I. C. Wright/Miss M. Bjurstedt	W. T. Tilden/Miss F. A. Ballin	10–12	6–1	6–3	
1918	I. C. Wright/Mrs G. W. Wightman	F. B. Alexander/Miss M. Bjurstedt	6–2	6–4		
1919	V. Richards/Miss M. Zinderstein	W. T. Tilden/Miss F. A. Ballin	2–6	11–9	6–2	
1920	W. F. Johnson/Mrs G. W. Wightman	C. Biddle/Mrs F. I. Mallory	6–4	6–3		
1921	W. M. Johnston/Miss M. K. Browne	W. T. Tilden/Miss F. I. Mallory	3–6	6–4	6–3	
1922	W. T. Tilden/Mrs F. I. Mallory	H. Kinsey/Miss H. N. Wills	6–4	6–3		
1923	W. T. Tilden/Mrs F. I. Mallory	J. B. Hawkes/Miss K. McKane	6–3	2–6	10–8	
1924	V. Richards/Miss H. N. Wills	W. T. Tilden/Mrs F. I. Mallory	6–8	7–5	6–0	
1925	J. B. Hawkes/Miss K. McKane	V. Richards/Miss E. H. Harvey	6–2	6–4		
1926	J. Borotra/Miss E. Ryan	R. Lacoste/Mrs G. W. Wightman	6–4	7–5		
1927	H. Cochet/Miss E. Bennett	R. Lacoste/Mrs G. W. Wightman	2–6	6–0	6–2	
1928	J. B. Hawkes/Miss H. N. Wills	G. Moon/Miss E. Cross	6–3	6–3		
1929	G. M. Lott/Miss B. Nuthall	H. W. Austin/Mrs B. C. Lovell	6–3	6–3		
1930	W. L. Allison/Miss E. Cross	F. X. Shields/Miss M. Morrill	6–4	6–4		
1931	G. M. Lott/Miss B. Nuthall	W. L. Allison/Mrs L. A. Harper	6–3	6–3		
1932	F. J. Perry/Miss S. Palfrey	H. E. Vines/Miss H. H. Jacobs	6–3	7–5		
1933	H. E. Vines/Miss E. Ryan	G. M. Lott/Miss S. Palfrey	11–9	6–1		
1934	G. M. Lott/Miss H. H. Jacobs	L. R. Stoefen/Miss E. Ryan	4–6	13–11	6–2	
1935	E. Maier/Mrs M. Fabyan	R. Menzel/Miss K. E. Stammers	6–3	3–6	6–4	
1936	G. Mako/Miss A. Marble	J. D. Budge/Mrs M. Fabyan	6–3	6–2		
1937	J. D. Budge/Mrs M. Fabyan	Y. Petra/Mme S. Henrotin	6–2	8–10	6–0	
1938	J. D. Budge/Miss A. Marble	J. E. Bromwich/Miss T. D. Coyne	6–1	6–2		
1939	H. C. Hopman/Miss A. Marble	E. T. Cooke/Mrs M. Fabyan	9–7	6–1		
1940	R. L. Riggs/Miss A. Marble	J. A. Kramer/Miss D. M. Bundy	9–7	6–1		
1941	J. A. Kramer/Mrs E. T. Cooke	R. L. Riggs/Miss P. M. Betz	4–6	6–4	6–4	
1942	F. R. Schroeder/Miss A. L. Brough	A. D. Russell/Mrs P. C. Todd	3–6	6–1	6–4	
1943	W. F. Talbert/Miss M. E. Osborne	F. Segura/Miss P. M. Betz	10–8	6–4		
1944	W. F. Talbert/Miss M. E. Osborne	W. D. McNeill/Miss D. M. Bundy	6–2	6–3		
1945	W. F. Talbert/Miss M. E. Osborne	R. Falkenburg/Miss D. J. Hart	6–4	6–4		
1946	W. F. Talbert/Miss M. E. Osborne	R. Kimbrell/Miss A. L. Brough	6–3	6–4		
1947	J. Bromwich/Miss A. L. Brough	F. Segura/Miss G. Morgan	6–3	6–1		
1948	T. P. Brown/Miss A. L. Brough	W. F. Talbert/Mrs W. D. du Pont	6–4	6–4		
1949	E. W. Sturgess/Miss A. L. Brough	W. F. Talbert/Mrs W. D. du Pont	4–6	6–3	7–5	
1950	K. B. McGregor/Mrs W. D. du Pont	F. A. Sedgman/Miss D. J. Hart	6–4	3–6	6–3	

	CHAMPIONS	*RUNNERS-UP*	*SCORE*			*FIRST PRIZE (US$)*
1951	F. A. Sedgman/Miss D. J. Hart	M. G. Rose/Miss S. J. Fry	6–3	6–2		
1952	F. A. Sedgman/Miss D. J. Hart	L. A. Hoad/Mrs T. C. Long	6–3	7–5		
1953	E. V. Seixas/Miss D. J. Hart	R. N. Hartwig/Miss J. A. Sampson	6–2	4–6	6–4	
1954	E. V. Seixas/Miss D. J. Hart	K. R. Rosewall/Mrs W. D. du Pont	4–6	6–1	6–1	
1955	E. V. Seixas/Miss D. J. Hart	G. Mulloy/Miss S. J. Fry	7–5	5–7	6–2	
1956	K. R. Rosewall/Mrs W. D. du Pont	L. A. Hoad/Miss D. R. Hard	9–7	6–1		
1957	K. Nielsen/Miss A. Gibson	R. N. Howe/Miss D. R. Hard	6–3	9–7		
1958	N. A. Fraser/Mrs W. D. du Pont	A. Olmedo/Miss M. E. Bueno	6–3	3–6	9–7	
1959	N. A. Fraser/Mrs W. D. du Pont	R. Mark/Miss J. Hopps	7–5	13–15	6–2	
1960	N. A. Fraser/Mrs W. D. du Pont	A. Palafox/Miss M. E. Bueno	6–3	6–2		
1961	R. Mark/Miss M. Smith	R. D. Ralston/Miss D. R. Hard		w.o.		
1962	F. S. Stolle/Miss M. Smith	F. Froehling/Miss L. Turner	7–5	6–2		
1963	K. Fletcher/Miss M. Smith	E. Rubinoff/Miss J. Tegart	3–6	8–6	6–2	
1964	J. D. Newcombe/Miss M. Smith	E. Rubinoff/Miss J. Tegart	10–8	4–6	6–3	
1965	F. S. Stolle/Miss M. Smith	F. Froehling/Miss J. Tegart	5–2	6–2		
1966	O. K. Davidson/Mrs D. Fales	E. Rubinoff/Miss C. A. Aucamp	6–1	6–3		
1967	O. K. Davidson/Mrs L. W. King	S. R. Smith/Miss R. Casals	6–3	6–2		
1968#	P. W. Curtis/Miss M. A. Eisel	R. N. Perry/Miss T. A. Fretz	6–4	7–5		
1969#	P. Sullivan/Miss P. S. A. Hogan	T. Addison/Miss K. Pigeon	6–4	2–6	12–10	
1968		*Not held*				
1969	M. C. Riessen/Mrs B. M. Court	R. D. Ralston/Miss F. Durr	7–5	6–3		
1970	M. C. Riessen/Mrs B. M. Court	F. D. McMillan/Mrs D. Dalton	6–4	6–4		
1971	O. K. Davidson/Mrs L. W. King	R. R. Maud/Miss B. Stove	6–3	7–5		
1972	M. C. Riessen/Mrs B. M. Court	I. Nastase/Miss R. Casals	6–3	7–5		
1973	O. K. Davidson/Mrs L. W. King	M. C. Riessen/Miss B. M. Court	6–3	3–6	7–6	
1974	G. Masters/Miss P. Teeguarden	J. S. Connors/Miss C. M. Evert	6–1	7–6		
1975	R. L. Stockton/Miss R. Casals	F. S. Stolle/Mrs L. W. King	6–3	7–6		
1976	P. Dent/Mrs L. W. King	F. D. McMillan/Miss B. Stove	3–6	6–2	7–5	
1977	F. D. McMillan/Miss B. Stove	V. Gerulaitis/Mrs L. W. King	6–2	3–6	6–3	
1978	F. D. McMillan/Miss B. Stove	R. O. Ruffels/Mrs L. W. King	6–3	7–6		
1979	R. A. J. Hewitt/Miss G. Stevens	F. D. McMillan/Miss B. Stove	6–3	7–5		
1980	M. C. Riessen/Miss W. M. Turnbull	F. D. McMillan/Miss B. Stove	7–5	6–2		
1981	K. Curren/Miss A. E. Smith	S. Denton/Miss J. Russell	6–4	7–6		
1982	K. Curren/Miss A. E. Smith	F. Taygan/Miss B. Potter	6–7	7–6	7–6	
1983	J. Fitzgerald/Miss E. Sayers	F. Taygan/Miss B. Potter	3–6	6–3	6–4	
1984	Tom Gullikson/Miss M. Maleeva	J. Fitzgerald/Miss E. Sayers	2–6	7–5	6–4	
1985	H. Gunthardt/Miss M. Navratilova	J. Fitzgerald/Mrs P. Smylie	6–3	6–4		
1986	S. Casal/Miss R. Reggi	P. Fleming/Miss M. Navratilova	6–4	6–4		
1987	E. Sanchez/Miss M. Navratilova	P. Annacone/Miss B. Nagelsen	6–4	6–7	7–6	
1988	J. Pugh/Miss J. Novotna	P. McEnroe/Mrs P. Smylie	7–5	6–3		
1989	S. Cannon/Miss R. White	R. Leach/Miss M. McGrath	3–6	6–2	7–5	
1990	T. Woodbridge/Mrs P. Smylie	J. Pugh/Miss N. Zvereva	6–4	6–2		
1991	T. Nijssen/Miss M. Bollegraf	E. Sanchez/Miss A. Sanchez-Vicario	6–2	7–6		
1992	M. Woodforde/Miss N. Provis	T. Nijssen/Miss H. Sukova	4–6	6–3	6–3	
1993	T. Woodbridge/Miss H. Sukova	M. Woodforde/Miss M. Navratilova	6–3	7–6		
1994	P. Galbraith/Miss E. Reinach	T. Woodbridge/Miss J. Novotna	6–2	6–4		
1995	M. Lucena/Miss M. McGrath	C. Suk/Miss G. Fernandez	6–4	6–4		
1996	P. Galbraith/Miss L. Raymond	R. Leach/Miss M. Bollegraf	7–6	7–6		
1997	R. Leach/Miss M. Bollegraf	P. Albano/Miss M. Paz	3–6	7–5	7–6	100,000
1998	M. Mirnyi/Miss S. Williams	P. Galbraith/Miss L. Raymond	6–2	6–2		120,000

#US Amateur Championships

†Not recognised as an official championship

GRAND SLAM CUP

A knockout competition launched in 1990 and held in Munich in December until 1977 when it moved to September, for the 16 men who have amassed the most points in the four Grand Slam Championships of Australia, France, Great Britain and the USA. In 1998 a women's event was introduced for eight players and the men's field was reduced from 16 to 12. The competition, administered by the Grand Slam Committee (the four Chairmen) and an Administrator, is promoted by an independent German company and offers prize money of $6 million. A further $2 million goes annually to the Grand Slam Development Fund, administered by the ITF.

MEN'S COMPETITION

	WINNER	*RUNNER-UP*	*SCORE*					*FIRST PRIZE (US$)*
1990	P. Sampras	B. Gilbert	6–3	6–4	6–2			2,000,000
1991	D. Wheaton	M. Chang	7–5	6–2	6–4			2,000,000
1992	M. Stich	M. Chang	6–2	6–3	6–2			2,000,000
1993	P. Korda	M. Stich	2–6	6–4	7–6	2–6	11–9	1,625,000
1994	M. Larsson	P. Sampras	7–6	4–6	7–6	6–4		1,625,000
1995	G. Ivanisevic	T. Martin	7–6	6–3	6–4			1,625,000
1996	B. Becker	G. Ivanisevic	6–3	6–4	6–4			1,875,000
1997	P. Sampras	P. Rafter	6–2	6–4	7–5			2,000,000
1998	M. Rios	A. Agassi	6–4	2–6	7–6	5–7	6–3	1,300,000

WOMEN'S COMPETITION

	WINNER	*RUNNER-UP*	*SCORE*			*FIRST PRIZE (US$)*
1998	V. Williams	P. Schnyder	6–2	3–6	6–2	800,000

GRAND SLAMS

The Grand Slam denotes holding the four championship titles of Australia, France, Wimbledon and the United States in the same year (shown in bold below). The list also includes consecutive wins, not in the same year.

MEN'S SINGLES

J. D. Budge: Wimbledon, US 1937, **Australia, France, Wimbledon, US 1938**
R. G. Laver: **Australia, France, Wimbledon, US 1962**
R. G. Laver: **Australia, France, Wimbledon, US 1969**

WOMEN'S SINGLES

Miss M. Connolly: Wimbledon, US 1952, **Australia, France, Wimbledon, US 1953**
Mrs B. M. Court: US 1969, **Australia, France, Wimbledon, US 1970,** Australia 1971
Miss M. Navratilova: Wimbledon, US, Australia 1983, France, Wimbledon, US 1984
Miss S. Graf: **Australia, France, Wimbledon, US 1988,** Australia 1989, France, Wimbledon, US 1993, Australia 1994

MEN'S DOUBLES

F. A. Sedgman: (With J. E. Bromwich) US 1950, **(with K. McGregor) Australia, France, Wimbledon, US 1951**, Australia, France, Wimbledon 1952
K. McGregor: **(With F. A. Sedgman) Australia, France, Wimbledon, US 1951**, Australia, France, Wimbledon 1952

WOMEN'S DOUBLES

Miss A. L. Brough: (with Mrs W. du Pont) France, Wimbledon, US 1949, (with Miss D. J. Hart) Australia 1950
Miss M. E. Bueno: **(with Miss C. C. Truman) Australia 1960, (with Miss D. R. Hard) France, Wimbledon, US 1960**
Miss M. Navratilova/Miss P. H. Shriver: Wimbledon, US, Australia 1983, **France, Wimbledon, US, Australia 1984,** France 1985; *Wimbledon, US 1986, Australia, France 1987
Miss G. Fernandez/Miss N. Zvereva: France, Wimbledon, US 1992, Australia, France, Wimbledon 1993
Miss M. Hingis: **(with Miss M. Lucic) Australia 1998, (with Miss J. Novotna) France, Wimbledon, US 1998**
** Miss Navratilova also won France 1986 with Miss A. Temesvari.*

MIXED DOUBLES

Miss M. Smith: (With F. S. Stolle) US 1962, **(with K. N. Fletcher) Australia, France, Wimbledon, US 1963**, Australia, France 1964
K. N. Fletcher: **(With Miss M. Smith) Australia, France, Wimbledon, US 1963**, Australia, France 1964
O. K. Davidson: (With Mrs D. Fales) US 1966, **(with Miss L. R. Turner) Australia 1967, (with Mrs L. W. King) France, Wimbledon, US 1967**
Mrs L. W. King: (With O. K. Davidson) France, Wimbledon, US 1967, (with R. D. Crealy) Australia 1968

JUNIOR SINGLES
E. H. Buchholz: **Australia, France, Wimbledon, US 1958** (*Note:* The US event was not then conducted as an international event and entries at all four were by nomination of National Associations.)
S. Edberg: **France, Wimbledon, US, Australia 1983** (*Note:* All Championship events.)

OPEN ERA GRAND SLAM WINNERS

See pp 126–127.

DAVIS CUP

The International Men's Team Championship of the World was initiated in 1900 when the British Isles, then comprising Great Britain and Ireland, challenged the United States for the trophy presented by Dwight F. Davis. The competition was enlarged in 1904 when Belgium and France took part. Each tie has comprised two players engaged in reverse singles plus a doubles match with the best of five sets throughout. In 1989 the tie-break was introduced for all sets except the fifth, in all matches.

From 1900 to 1971 the Champion Nation stood out until challenged by the winner of a knock-out competition between the challenging nations and had the choice of venue. Thereafter the Champion Nation played through. The format was changed in 1981, when the competition became sponsored by NEC and prize money was introduced. The winner of the World Group of the 16 strongest nations became the Champion Nation. Other nations competed in zonal groups, with eight earning the right to play against the eight first round losers in the World Group for places alongside the first round winners of the World Group in the following year's competition. A Zonal Group Three, in which nations from each geographic region play one another on a round-robin basis during one week at one venue to decide promotion to Zonal Group Two, was introduced in 1992. Entries passed the 100 mark for the 1993 competition when 101 nations entered. By 1998 the total had risen to 131.

CHALLENGE ROUNDS (in playing order)
1900 USA (Capt. Dwight Davis) **d. British Isles** (Capt. Arthur Gore) **3–0**, *Boston:* M. D. Whitman d. A. W. Gore 6–1 6–3 6–2; D. F. Davis d. E. D. Black 4–6 6–2 6–4 6–4; Davis/H. Ward d. Black/H. Roper Barrett 6–4 6–4 6–4; Davis div'd with Gore 9–7 9–9.
1901 Not held
1902 USA (Capt: Malcolm Whitman) **d. British Isles** (Capt: William Collins) **3–2**, *Brooklyn, New York:* W. A. Larned lost to R. F. Doherty 6–2 6–3 3–6 4–6 4–6; M. D. Whitman d. J. Pim 6–1 6–1 1–6 6–0; Larned d. Pim 6–3 6–2 6–3; Whitman d. R. F. Doherty 6–1 7–5 6–4; D. F. Davis/H. Ward lost to R. F./H. L. Doherty 6–3 8–10 3–6 4–6.
1903 British Isles (Capt: William Collins) **d. USA** (Capt: William Larned) **4–1**, *Boston:* H. L. Doherty d. R. D. Wrenn 6–0 6–3 6–4; R. F. Doherty lost to W. A. Larnedret'd; R. F./H. L. Doherty d. R. D./G. L. Wrenn 7–5 9–7 2–6 6–3; H. L. Doherty d. Larned 6–3 6–8 6–0 2–6 7–5; R. F. Doherty d. R. D. Wrenn 6–4 3–6 6–3 6–8 6–4.
1904 British Isles (Capt: William Collins) **d. Belgium** (Capt: Paul De Borman) **5–0**, *Wimbledon:* H. L. Doherty d. P. De Borman 6–4 6–1 6–1; F. L. Riseley d. W.Lemaire 6–1 6–4 6–2; R. F./H. L. Doherty d. De Borman/Lemaire 6–0 6–1 6–3; H. L. Doherty w.o. Lemaire; Riseley d. De Borman 4–6 6–2 8–6 7–5.
1905 British Isles (Capt: William Collins) **d. USA** (Capt: Paul Dashiel) **5–0**, *Wimbledon:* H. L. Doherty d. H. Ward 7–9 4–6 6–1 6–2 6–0; S. H. Smith d. W. A. Larned 6–4 6–4 5–7 6–4; R. F./H. L. Doherty d. Ward/B. Wright 8–10 6–2 6–2 4–6 8–6; Smith d. W. J. Clothier 4–6 6–1 6–4 6–3; H. L. Doherty d. Larned 6–4 2–6 6–8 6–4 6–2.
1906 British Isles (Capt: William Collins) **d. USA** (Capt: Beals Wright) **5–0**, *Wimbledon:* S. H. Smith d. R. D. Little 6–4 6–4 6–1; H. L. Doherty d. H. Ward 6–2 8–6 6–3; R. F./H. L. Doherty d. Little/Ward 3–6 11–9 9–7 6–1; Smith d. Ward 6–1 6–0 6–4; H. L. Doherty d. Little 3–6 6–3 6–8 6–1 6–3.
1907 Australasia (Capt: Norman Brookes) **d. British Isles** (Capt: Alfred Hickson) **3–2**, *Wimbledon:* N. E. Brookes d. A. W. Gore 7–5 6–1 7–5; A. F. Wilding d. H. Roper Barrett 1–6 6–4 6–3 7–5; Brookes/Wilding lost to Gore/Roper Barrett 6–3 6–4 5–7 2–6 11–13; Wilding lost to Gore 6–3 3–6 5–7 2–6; Brookes d. Roper Barrett 6–2 6–0 6–3.
1908 Australasia (Capt: Norman Brookes) **d. USA** (Capt: Beals Wright) **3–2**, *Melbourne:* N. E. Brookes d. F. B. Alexander 5–7 9–7 6–2 4–6 6–3; A. F. Wilding lost to B. Wright 6–3 5–7 3–6 1–6; Brookes/Wilding d. Alexander/Wright 6–4 6–2 5–7 1–6 6–4; Brookes lost to Wright 6–0 6–3 5–7 2–6 10–12; Wilding d. Alexander 6–3 6–4 6–1.
1909 Australasia (Capt: Norman Brookes) **d. USA** (Capt: Maurice McLoughlin) **5–0**, *Sydney:* N. E. Brookes d. M. E. McLoughlin 6–2 6–2 6–4; A. F. Wilding d. M. H. Long 6–2 7–5 6–1; Brookes/Wilding d. Long/McLoughlin 12–10 9–7 6–3; Brookes d. Long 6–4 7–5 8–6; Wilding d. McLoughlin 3–6 8–6 6–2 6–3.
1910 Not held
1911 Australasia (Capt: Norman Brookes) **d. USA** (Capt: William Larned) **5–0**, *Christchurch, NZ:* N. E. Brookes d. B. Wright 6–4 2–6 6–3 6–3; R. W. Heath d. W. A. Larned 2–6 6–1 7–5 6–2; Brookes/A. W. Dunlop d. Wright/M. E. McLoughlin 6–4 5–7 7–5 6–4; Brookes d. McLoughlin 6–4 3–6 4–6 6–3 6–4; Heath w.o. Wright.

1912 British Isles (Capt: Charles Dixon) **d. Australasia** (Capt: Norman Brookes) **3–2**, *Melbourne:* J. C. Parke d. N. E. Brookes 8–6 6–3 5–7 6–2; C. P. Dixon d. R. W. Heath 5–7 6–4 6–4 6–4; A. E. Beamish/Parke lost Brookes/A. W. Dunlop 4–6 1–6 5–7; Dixon lost to Brookes 2–6 4–6 4–6; Parke d. Heath 6–2 6–4 6–4.
1913 USA (Capt: Harold Hackett) **d. British Isles** (Capt: Roger McNair) **3–2**, *Wimbledon:* M. E. McLoughlin lost to J. C. Parke 10–8 5–7 4–6 6–1 5–7; R. N. Williams d. C. P. Dixon 8–6 3–6 6–2 1–6 7–5; H. Hackett/McLoughlin d. Dixon/H. Roper Barrett 5–7 6–1 2–6 7–5 6–4; McLoughlin d. Dixon 8–6 6–3 6–2; Williams lost to Parke 2–6 7–5 7–5 4–6 2–6.
1914 Australasia (Capt: Norman Brookes) **d. USA** (Capt: Maurice McLoughlin) **3–2**, *Forest Hills, NY:* A. F. Wilding d. R. N. Williams 7–5 6–2 6–3; N. E. Brookes lost to M. E. McLoughlin 15–17 3–6 3–6; Brookes/Wilding d. T. C. Bundy/McLoughlin 6–3 8–6 9–7; Brookes d. Williams 6–1 6–2 8–10 6–3; Wilding lost to McLoughlin 2–6 3–6 6–2 2–6.
1915–18 Not held
1919 Australasia (Capt: Norman Brookes) **d. British Isles** (Capt: Algernon Kingscote) **4–1**, *Sydney:* G. L. Patterson d. A. H. Lowe 6–4 6–3 2–6 6–3; J. O. Anderson lost to A. R. F. Kingscote 5–7 2–6 4–6; N. E. Brookes/Patterson d. A. E. Beamish/Kingscote 6–0 6–0 6–2; Patterson d. Kingscote 6–4 6–4 8–6; Anderson d. Lowe 6–4 5–7 6–3 4–6 12–10.
1920 USA (Capt: Sam Hardy) **d. Australasia** (Capt: Norman Brookes) **5–0**, *Auckland:* W. T. Tilden d. N. E. Brookes 10–8 6–4 1–6 6–4; W. M. Johnston d. G. L. Patterson 6–3 6–1 6–1; Johnston/Tilden d. Brookes/Patterson 4–6 6–4 6–0 6–4; Johnston d. Brookes 5–7 7–5 6–3 6–3; Tilden d. Patterson 5–7 6–2 6–3 6–3.
1921 USA (Capt: Norris Williams) **d. Japan** (Capt: Ichiya Kumagae) **5–0**, *Forest Hills, NY:* W. M. Johnston d. I. Kumagae 6–2 6–4 6–2; W. T. Tilden d. Z. Schimidzu 5–7 4–6 7–5 6–2 6–1; W. Washburn/R. N. Williams d. Kumagae/Shimidzu 6–2 7–5 4–6 7–5; Tilden d. Kumagae; 9–7 6–4 6–1; Johnston d. Shimidzu 6–3 5–7 6–2 6–4.
1922 USA (Capt: Norris Williams) **d. Australasia** (Capt: James Anderson) **4–1**, *Forest Hills, NY:* W. T. Tilden d. G. L. Patterson 7–5 10–8 6–0; W. M. Johnston d. J. O. Anderson 6–1 6–2 6–3; V. Richards/Tilden lost to P. O'Hara Wood/Patterson 4–6 0–6 3–6; Johnston d. Patterson 6–2 6–2 6–1; Tilden d. Anderson 6–4 5–7 3–6 6–4 6–2.
1923 USA (Capt: Norris Williams) **d. Australia** (Capt: Garald Patterson) **4–1**, *Forest Hills, NY:* W. M. Johnston lost to J. O. Anderson 6–4 2–6 6–2 5–7 2–6; W. T. Tilden d. J. B. Hawkes 6–4 6–2 6–1; Tilden/R. N. Williams d. Anderson/Hawkes 17–15 11–13 2–6 6–3 6–2; Johnston d. Hawkes 6–0 6–2 6–1; Tilden d. Anderson 6–2 6–3 1–6 7–5.
1924 USA (Capt: Norris Williams) **d. Australia** (Capt: Gerald Patterson) **5–0**, *Philadelphia:* W. T. Tilden d. G. L. Patterson 6–4 6–2 6–3; V. Richards d. P. O'Hara Wood 6–3 6–2 6–4; W. M. Johnston/Tilden d. O'Hara Wood/Patterson 5–7 6–3 6–4 6–1; Tilden d. O'Hara Wood 6–2 6–1 6–1; Richards d. Patterson 6–3 7–5 6–4.
1925 USA (Capt: Norris Williams) **d. France** (Capt: Max Decugis) **5–0**, *Philadelphia:* W. T. Tilden d. J. Borotra 4–6 6–0 2–6 9–7 6–4; W. M. Johnston d. R. Lacoste 6–1 6–1 6–8 6–3; V. Richards/R. N. Williams d. Borotra/Lacoste 6–4 6–4 6–3; Tilden d. Lacoste 3–6 10–12 8–6 7–5 6–2; Johnston d. Borotra 6–1 6–4 6–0.
1926 USA (Capt: Norris Williams) **d. France** (Capt: Pierre Gillou) **4–1**, *Philadelphia:* W. M. Johnston d. R. Lacoste 6–0 6–4 0–6 6–0; W. T. Tilden d. J. Borotra 6–2 6–3 6–3; V. Richards/R. N. Williams d. J. Brugnon/H. Cochet 6–4 6–4 6–2; Johnston d. Borotra 8–6 6–4 9–7; Tilden lost to Lacoste 6–4 4–6 6–8 6–8.
1927 France (Capt: Pierre Gillou) **d. USA** (Capt: Charles Garland) **3–2**, *Philadelphia:* R. Lacoste d. W. M. Johnston 6–3 6–2 6–2; H. Cochet lost to W. T. Tilden 4–6 6–2 2–6 6–8; J. Borotra/J. Brugnon lost to F. Hunter/Tilden 6–3 3–6 3–6 6–4 0–6; Lacoste d. Tilden 6–4 4–6 6–3 6–3; Cochet d. Johnston 6–4 4–6 6–2 6–4.
1928 France (Capt: Pierre Gillou) **d. USA** (Capt: Joseph Wear) **4–1**, *Paris:* R. Lacoste lost to W. T. Tilden 6–1 4–6 4–6 6–2 3–6; H. Cochet d. J. Hennessey 5–7 9–7 6–3 6–0; J. Borotra/Cochet d. F. Hunter/Tilden 6–4 6–8 7–5 4–6 6–2; Lacoste d. Hennessey 4–6 6–1 7–5 6–3; Cochet d. Tilden 9–7 8–6 6–4.
1929 France (Capt: Pierre Gillou) **d. USA** (Capt: Fitz-Eugene Dixon) **3–2**, *Paris:* H. Cochet d. W. T. Tilden 6–3 6–1 6–2; J. Borotra d. G. M. Lott 6–1 3–6 6–4 7–5; Borotra/Cochet lost to W. Allison/J. Van Ryn 1–6 6–8 4–6; Cochet d. Lott 6–1 3–6 6–0 6–3; Borotra lost to Tilden 6–4 1–6 4–6 5–7.
1930 France (Capt: Pierre Gillou) **d. USA** (Capt: Fitz-Eugene Dixon) **4–1**, *Paris:* J. Borotra lost to W. T. Tilden 6–2 5–7 4–6 5–7; H. Cochet d. G. M. Lott 6–4 6–2 6–2; J. Brugnon/Cochet d. W. Allison/J. Van Ryn 6–3 7–5 1–6 6–2; Borotra d. Lott 5–7 6–3 2–6 6–2 8–6; Cochet d. Tilden 4–6 6–3 6–1 7–5.
1931 France (Capt: Rene Lacoste) **d. Great Britain** (Capt: Herbert Barrett) **3–2**, *Paris:* H. Cochet d. H. W. Austin 3–6 11–9 6–2 6–4; J. Borotra lost to F. J. Perry 6–4 8–10 0–6 6–4 4–6; J. Brugnon/Cochet d. G. P Hughes/C. H. Kingsley 6–1 5–7 6–3 8–6; Cochet d. Perry 6–4 1–6 9–7 6–3; Borotra lost to Austin 5–7 3–6 6–3 5–7.
1932 France (Capt: Rene Lacoste) **d. USA** (Capt: Bernon Prentice) **3–2**, *Paris:* H. Cochet d. W. Allison 5–7 7–5 3–6 7–5 6–2; J. Borotra d. H. E. Vines 6–4 6–2 2–6 6–4; J. Brugnon/Cochet lost to Allison/J. Van Ryn 3–6 13–11 5–7 6–4 4–6; Borotra d. Allison 1–6 3–6 6–4 6–2 7–5; Cochet lost to Vines 6–4 6–0 5–7 6–8 2–6.
1933 Great Britain (Capt: Herbert Barrett) **d. France** (Capt: Rere Lacoste) **3–2**, *Paris:* H. W. Austin d. A. Merlin 6–3 6–4 6–0; F. J. Perry d. H. Cochet 8–10 6–4 8–6 3–6 6–1; G. P. Hughes/H. G. N. Lee lost to J. Borotra/J. Brugnon 3–6 6–8 2–6; Austin lost to Cochet 7–5 4–6 6–4 4–6 4–6; Perry d. Merlin 4–6 8–6 6–2 7–5.
1934 Great Britain (Capt: Herbert Barrett) **d. USA** (Capt: Norris Williams) **4–1**, *Wimbledon:* F. J. Perry d. S. B. Wood 6–1 4–6 5–7 6–0 6–3; H. W. Austin d. F. X. Shields 6–4 6–4 6–1; G. P. Hughes/H. G. N. Lee lost to G. M. Lott/L. Stoefen 5–7 0–6 6–4 7–9; Perry d. Shields 6–4 4–6 6–2 15–13; Austin d. Wood 6–4 6–0 6–8 6–3.
1935 Great Britain (Capt: Herbert Barrett) **d. USA** (Capt: Joseph Wear) **5–0**, *Wimbledon:* F. J. Perry d. J. D. Budge 6–0 6–8 6–3 6–4; H. W. Austin d. W. Allison 6–2 2–6 4–6 6–3 7–5; G. P. Hughes/C. R. D. Tuckey d. Allison/J. Van Ryn 6–2 1–6 6–8 6–3 6–3; Perry d. Allison 4–6 6–4 7–5 6–3; Austin d. Budge 6–2 6–4 6–8 7–5.
1936 Great Britain (Capt: Herbert Barrett) **d. Australia** (Capt: Cliff Sproule) **3–2**, *Wimbledon:* H. W. Austin d. J. H. Crawford 4–6 6–3 6–1 6–1; F. J. Perry d. A. K. Quist 6–1 4–6 7–5 6–2; G. P. Hughes/C. R. D. Tuckey lost to Crawford/Quist 4–6 6–2 5–7 8–10; Austin lost to Quist 4–6 6–3 5–7 2–6; Perry d. Crawford 6–2 6–3 6–3.
1937 USA (Capt: Walter Pate) **d. Great Britain** (Capt: Herbert Barrett) **4–1**, *Wimbledon:* F. A. Parker lost to H. W. Austin 3–6 2–6 5–7; J. D. Budge d. C. E. Hare 15–13 6–1 6–2; Budge/G. Mako d. C. R. D. Tuckey/F. H. D. Wilde 6–3 7–5 7–9 12–10; Parker d. Hare 6–2 6–4 6–2; Budge d. Austin 8–6 3–6 6–4 6–3.

1938 USA (Capt: Walter Pate) **d. Australia** (Capt: Harry Hopman) **3–2**, *Philadelphia:* R. L. Riggs d. A. K. Quist 4–6 6–0 8–6 6–1; J. D. Budge d. J. E. Bromwich 6–2 6–3 4–6 7–5; Budge/G. Mako lost to Bromwich/Quist 6–0 3–6 4–6 2–6; Budge d. Quist 8–6 6–1 6–2; Riggs lost to Bromwich 4–6 6–4 0–6 2–6.
1939 Australia (Capt: Harry Hopman) **d. USA** (Capt: Walter Pate) **3–2**, *Philadelphia:* J. E. Bromwich lost to R. L. Riggs 4–6 0–6 5–7; A. K. Quist lost to F. A. Parker 3–6 6–2 4–6 6–1 5–7; Bromwich/Quist d. J. R. Hunt/J. Kramer 5–7 6–2 7–5 6–2; Quist d. Riggs 6–1 6–4 3–6 3–6 6–4; Bromwich d. Parker 6–0 6–3 6–1.
1940–45 Not held
1946 USA (Capt: Walter Pate) **d. Australia** (Capt: Gerald Patterson) **5–0**, *Melbourne:* F. R. Schroeder d. J. E. Bromwich 3–6 6–1 6–2 0–6 6–3; J. Kramer d. D. Pails 8–6 6–2 9–7; Kramer/Schroeder d. Bromwich/A. K. Quist 6–2 7–5 6–4; Kramer d. Bromwich 8–6 6–4 6–2 6–4; G Mulloy d. Pails 6–3 6–3 6–4.
1947 USA (Capt: Alrick Man) **d. Australia** (Capt: Roy Cowling) **4–1**, *Forest Hills, NY:* J. Kramer d. D. Pails 6–2 6–1 6–2; F. R. Schroeder d. J. E. Bromwich 6–4 5–7 6–3 6–3; Kramer/Schroeder lost to Bromwich/C. F. Long 4–6 6–2 2–6 4–6; Schroeder d. Pails 6–3 8–6 4–6 9–11 10–8; Kramer d. Bromwich 6–3 6–2 6–2.
1948 USA (Capt: Alrick Man) **d. Australia** (Capt: Adrian Quist) **5–0**, *Forest Hills, NY:* F. A. Parker d. O. W. Sidwell 6–4 6–4 6–4; F. R. Schroeder d. A. K. Quist 6–3 4–6 6–0 6–0; G. Mulloy/W. F. Talbert d. C. F. Long/Sidwell 8–6 9–7 2–6 7–5; Parker d. Quist 6–2 6–2 6–3; Schroeder d. Sidwell 6–2 6–1 6–1.
1949 USA (Capt: Alrick Man) **d. Australia** (Capt: John Bromwich) **4–1**, *Forest Hills, NY:* F. R. Schroeder d. O. W. Sidwell 6–1 5–7 4–6 6–2 6–3; R. A. Gonzales d. F. A. Sedgman 8–6 6–4 9–7; G. Mulloy/W. F. Talbert lost to J. E. Bromwich/Sidwell 6–3 6–4 8–10 7–9 7–9; Schroeder d. Sedgman 6–4 6–3 6–3; Gonzales d. Sidwell 6–1 6–3 6–3.
1950 Australia (Capt: Harry Hopman) **d. USA** (Capt: Alrick Man) **4–1**, *Forest Hills, NY:* F. A. Sedgman d. T. Brown 6–0 8–6 9–7; K. McGregor d. F. R. Schroeder 13–11 6–3 6–4; J. E. Bromwich/Sedgman d. G. Mulloy/Schroeder 4–6 6–4 6–2 4–6 6–4; Sedgman d. Schroeder 6–2 6–2 6–2; McGregor lost to Brown 11–9 10–8 9–11 1–6 4–6.
1951 Australia (Capt: Harry Hopman) **d. USA** (Capt: Frank Shields) **3–2**, *Sydney:* M. G. Rose lost to E. V. Seixas 3–6 4–6 7–9; F. A. Sedgman d. F. R. Schroeder 6–4 6–3 4–6 6–4; K. McGregor/Sedgman d. Schroeder/M. A. Trabert 6–2 9–7 6–3; Rose lost to Schroeder 4–6 11–13 5–7; Sedgman d. Seixas 6–4 6–2 6–2.
1952 Australia (Capt: Harry Hopman) **d. USA** (Capt: Vic Seixas) **4–1**, *Adelaide:* F. A. Sedgman d. E. V. Seixas 6–3 6–4 6–3; K. McGregor d. M. A. Trabert 11–9 6–4 6–1; McGregor/Sedgman d. Seixas/Trabert 6–3 6–4 1–6 6–3; Sedgman d. Trabert 7–5 6–4 10–8; McGregor lost to Seixas 3–6 6–8 8–6 3–6.
1953 Australia (Capt: Harry Hopman) **d. USA** (Capt: Bill Talbert) **3–2**, *Melbourne:* L. A. Hoad d. E. V. Seixas 6–4 6–2 6–3; K. R. Rosewall lost to M. A. Trabert 3–6 4–6 4–6; R. Hartwig/Hoad lost to Seixas/Trabert 2–6 4–6 4–6; Hoad d. Trabert 13–11 6–3 2–6 3–6 7–5; Rosewall d. Seixas 6–2 2–6 6–3 6–4.
1954 USA (Capt: Bill Talbert) **d. Australia** (Capt: Harry Hopman) **3–2**, *Sydney:* M. A. Trabert d. L. A. Hoad 6–4 2–6 12–10 6–3; E. V. Seixas d. K. R. Rosewall 8–6 6–8 6–4 6–3; Seixas/Trabert d. Hoad/Rosewall 6–2 4–6 6–2 10–8; Trabert lost to Rosewall 7–9 5–7 3–6; Seixas lost to R. Hartwig 6–4 3–6 2–6 3–6.
1955 Australia (Capt: Harry Hopman) **d. USA** (Capt: Bill Talbert) **5–0**, *Forest Hills, NY:* K. R. Rosewall d. E. V. Seixas 6–3 10–8 4–6 6–2; L. A. Hoad d. M. A. Trabert 4–6 6–3 6–3 8–6; R. Hartwig/Hoad d. Seixas/Trabert 12–14 6–4 6–3 3–6 7–5; Rosewall d. H. Richardson 6–4 3–6 6–1 6–4; Hoad d. Seixas 7–9 6–1 6–4 6–4.
1956 Australia (Capt: Harry Hopman) **d. USA** (Capt: Bill Talbert) **5–0**, *Adelaide:* L. A. Hoad d. H. Flam 6–2 6–3 6–3; K. R. Rosewall d. E. V. Seixas 6–2 7–5 6–3; Hoad/Rosewall d. S. Giammalva/Seixas 1–6 6–1 7–5 6–4; Hoad d. Seixas 6–2 7–5 6–3; Rosewall d. Giammalva 4–6 6–1 8–6 7–5.
1957 Australia (Capt: Harry Hopman) **d. USA** (Capt: Bill Talbert) **3–2**, *Melbourne:* A. J. Cooper d. E. V. Seixas 3–6 7–5 6–1 1–6 6–3; M. J. Anderson d. B. MacKay 6–3 7–5 3–6 47–9 6–3; Anderson/M. G. Rose d. MacKay/Seixas 6–4 6–4 8–6; Cooper lost to MacKay 4–6 6–1 6–4 4–6 3–6; Anderson lost to Seixas 3–6 6–4 3–6 6–0 11–13.
1958 USA (Capt: Perry Jones) **d. Australia** (Capt: Harry Hopman) **3–2**, *Brisbane:* A. Olmedo d. M. J. Anderson 8–6 2–6 9–7 8–6; B. MacKay lost to A. J. Cooper 6–4 3–6 2–6 4–6; Olmedo/H. Richardson d. Anderson/N. A. Fraser 10–12 3–6 16–14 6–3 7–5; Olmedo d. Cooper 6–3 4–6 6–4 8–6; MacKay lost to Anderson 5–7 11–13 9–11.
1959 Australia (Capt: Harry Hopman) **d. USA** (Capt: Perry Jones) **3–2**, *Forest Hills, NY:* N. A. Fraser d. A. Olmedo 8–6 6–8 6–4 8–6; R. G. Laver lost to B. MacKay 5–7 4–6 1–6; R. S. Emerson/Fraser d. E. Buchholz/Olmedo 7–5 7–5 6–4; Laver lost to Olmedo 7–9 6–4 8–10 10–12; Fraser d. MacKay 8–6 3–6 6–2 6–4.
1960 Australia (Capt: Harry Hopman) **d. Italy** (Capt: Vanni Canapele) **4–1**, *Sydney:* N. A. Fraser d. O. Sirola 4–6 6–3 6–3 6–3; R. G. Laver d. N. Pietrangeli 8–6 6–4 6–3; R. S. Emerson/Fraser d. Pietrangeli/Sirola 10–8 5–7 6–3 6–4; Laver d. Sirola 9–7 6–2 6–3; Fraser lost to Pietrangeli 9–11 3–6 6–1 2–6.
1961 Australia (Capt: Harry Hopman) **d. Italy** (Capt: Vanni Canapele) **5–0**, *Melbourne:* R. S. Emerson d. N. Pietrangeli 8–6 6–4 6–0; R. G. Laver d. O. Sirola 6–1 6–4 6–3; Emerson/N. A. Fraser d. Pietrangeli/Sirola 6–2 6–3 6–4; Emerson d. Sirola 6–2 6–3 4–6 6–2; Laver d. Pietrangeli 6–3 3–6 4–6 6–3 8–6.
1962 Australia (Capt: Harry Hopman) **d. Mexico** (Capt: Franciso Contreras) **5–0**, *Brisbane:* N. A. Fraser d. A. Palafox 7–9 6–3 6–4 11–9; R. G. Laver d. R. H. Osuna 6–2 6–1 7–5; R. S. Emerson/Laver d. Osuna/Palafox 7–5 6–2 6–4; Fraser d. Osuna 3–6 11–9 6–1 3–6 6–4; Laver d. Palafox 6–1 4–6 6–4 8–6.
1963 USA (Capt: Robert Kelleher) **d. Australia** (Capt: Harry Hopman) **3–2**, *Adelaide:* R. D. Ralston d. J. D. Newcombe 6–4 6–1 3–6 4–6 7–5; C. R. McKinley lost to R. S. Emerson 3–6 6–3 5–7 5–7; McKinley/Ralston d. Emerson/N. A. Fraser 6–3 4–6 11–9 11–9; Ralston lost to Emerson 2–6 3–6 6–3 2–6; McKinley d. Newcombe 10–12 6–2 9–7 6–2.
1964 Australia (Capt: Harry Hopman) **d. USA** (Capt: Vic Seixas) **3–2**, *Cleveland, Ohio:* F. S. Stolle lost to C. R. McKinley 1–6 7–9 6–4 2–6; R. S. Emerson d. R. D. Ralston 6–3 6–1 6–3; Emerson/Stolle lost to McKinley/Ralston 4–6 6–4 6–4 3–6 4–6; Stolle d. Ralston 7–5 6–3 3–6 9–11 6–4; Emerson d. McKinley 3–6 6–2 6–4 6–4.
1965 Australia (Capt: Harry Hopman) **d. Spain** (Capt: Jaime Bartroli) **4–1**, *Sydney:* F. S. Stolle d. M. Santana 10–12 3–6 6–1 6–4 7–5; R. S. Emerson d. J. Gisbert 6–3 6–2 6–2; J. D. Newcombe/A. D. Roche d. J. L. Arilla/Santana 6–3 4–6 7–5 6–2; Emerson lost to Santana 6–2 3–6 4–6 13–15; Stolle d. Gisbert 6–2 6–4 8–6.

1966 Australia (Capt: Harry Hopman) **d. India** (Capt: Raj Khanna) **4–1**, *Melbourne:* F. S. Stolle d. R. Krishnan 6–3 6–2 6–4; R. S. Emerson d. J. Mukerjea 7–5 6–4 6–2; J. D. Newcombe/A. D. Roche lost to Krishnan/Mukerjea 6–4 5–7 4–6 4–6; Emerson d. Krishnan 6–0 6–2 10–8; Stolle d. Mukerjea 7–5 6–8 6–3 5–7 6–3.
1967 Australia (Capt: Harry Hopman) **d. Spain** (Capt: Jaime Bartroli) **4–1**, *Brisbane:* R. S. Emerson d. M. Santana 6–4 6–1 6–1; J. D. Newcombe d. M. Orantes 6–3 6–3 6–2; Newcombe/A. D. Roche d. Orantes/Santana 6–4 6–4 6–4; Newcombe lost to Santana 5–7 4–6 2–6; Emerson d. Orantes 6–1 6–1 2–6 6–4.
1968 USA (Capt: Donald Dell) **d. Australia** (Capt: Harry Hopman) **4–1**, *Adelaide:* C. Graebner d. W. W. Bowrey 8–10 6–4 8–6 3–6 6–1; A. R. Ashe d. R. O. Ruffels 6–8 7–5 6–3 6–3; R. C. Lutz/S. R. Smith d. J. G. Alexander/Ruffels 6–4 6–4 6–2; Graebner d. Ruffels 3–6 8–6 2–6 6–3 6–1; Ashe lost to Bowrey 6–2 3–6 9–11 6–8.
1969 USA (Capt: Donald Dell) **d. Romania** (Capt: Georgy Cobzucs) **5–0**, *Cleveland, Ohio:* A. R. Ashe d. I. Nastase 6–2 15–13 7–5; S. R. Smith d. I. Tiriac 6–8 6–3 5–7 6–4 6–4; R. C. Lutz/Smith d. Nastase/Tiriac 8–6 6–1 11–9; Smith d. Nastase 4–6 4–6 6–4 6–1 11–9; Ashe d. Tiriac 6–3 8–6 3–6 4–0 ret.
1970 USA (Capt: Edward Turville) **d. West Germany** (Capt: Ferdinand Henkel) **5–0**, *Cleveland, Ohio:* A. R. Ashe d. W. Bungert 6–2 10–8 6–2; C. Richey d. C. Kuhnke 6–3 6–4 6–2; R. C. Lutz/S. R. Smith d. Bungert/Kuhnke 6–3 7–5 6–4; Richey d. Bungert 6–4 6–4 7–5; Ashe d. Kuhnke 6–8 10–12 9–7 13–11 6–4.
1971 USA (Capt: Edward Turville) **d. Romania** (Capt: Stefan Georgescu) **3–2**, *Charlotte, NC:* S. R. Smith d. I. Nastase 7–5 6–3 6–1; F. A. Froehling d. I. Tiriac 3–6 1–6 6–1 6–3 8–6; Smith/E. Van Dillen lost to Nastase/Tiriac 5–7 4–6 8–6; Smith d. Tiriac 8–6 6–3 6–0; Froehling lost to Nastase 3–6 1–6 6–1 4–6.
Challenge Round abolished

FINAL ROUND SCORES

1972 USA (Capt: Dennis Ralston) **d. Romania** (Capt: Stefan Georgescu) **3–2**, *Bucharest:* S. R. Smith d. I. Nastase 11–9 6–2 6–3; T. Gorman lost to I. Tiriac 6–4 6–2 4–6 3–6 2–6; Smith/E. Van Dillen d. Nastase/Tiriac 6–2 6–0 6–3; Smith d. Tiriac 4–6 6–2 6–4 2–6 6–0; Gorman lost to Nastase 1–6 2–6 7–5 8–10.
1973 Australia (Capt: Neale Fraser) **d. USA** (Capt: Dennis Ralston) **5–0**, *Cleveland, Ohio (indoors):* J. D. Newcombe d. S. R. Smith 6–1 3–6 6–3 3–6 6–4; R. G. Laver d. T. Gorman 8–10 8–6 6–8 6–3 6–1; Laver/Newcombe d. Smith/E. Van Dillen 6–1 6–2 6–4; Newcombe d. Gorman 6–2 6–1 6–3; Laver d. Smith 6–3 6–4 3–6 6–2.
1974 South Africa w.o. India
1975 Sweden (Capt: Lennart Bergelin) **d. Czechoslovakia** (Capt: Antonin Bolardt) **3–2**, *Stockholm (indoors):* O. Bengtson lost to J. Kodes 4–6 6–2 5–7 4–6; B. Borg d. J. Hrebec 6–1 6–3 6–0; Bengtson/Borg d. Kodes/V. Zednik 6–4 6–4 6–4; Borg d. Kodes 6–4 6–2 6–2; Bengtson lost to Hrebec 6–1 3–6 1–6 4–6.
1976 Italy (Capt: Nicola Pietrangeli) **d. Chile** (Capt: Luis Ayala) **4–1**, *Santiago:* C. Barazzutti d. J. Fillol 7–5 4–6 7–5 6–1; A. Panatta d. P. Cornejo 6–3 6–1 6–3; P. Bertolucci/Panatta d. Cornejo/Fillol 3–6 6–2 9–7 6–3; Panatta d. Fillol 8–6 6–4 3–6 10–8; A. Zugarelli lost to B. Prajoux 4–6 4–6 2–6.
1977 Australia (Capt: Neale Fraser) **d. Italy** (Capt: Nicola Pietrangeli) **3–1**, *Sydney:* A. D. Roche d. A. Panatta 6–3 6–4 6–4; J. G. Alexander d. C. Barazzutti 6–2 8–6 4–6 6–2; Alexander/P. Dent lost to P. Bertolucci/Panatta 4–6 4–6 5–7; Alexander d. Panatta 6–4 4–6 2–6 8–6 11–9; Roche div'd with Barazzutti 12–12.
1978 USA (Capt: Tony Trabert) **d. Great Britain** (Capt: Paul Hutchins) **4–1**, *Palm Springs, California:* J. P. McEnroe d. J. M. Lloyd 6–1 6–2 6–2; B. E. Gottfried lost to C. J. Mottram 6–4 6–2 8–10 4–6 3–6; R. C. Lutz/S. R. Smith d. M. Cox/D. A. Lloyd 6–2 6–2 6–3; McEnroe d. Mottram 6–2 6–2 6–1; Gottfried d. J. M. Lloyd 6–1 6–2 6–4.
1979 USA (Capt: Tony Trabert) **d. Italy** (Capt: Vittorio Crotta) **5–0**, *San Francisco (indoors):* V. Gerulaitis d. C. Barazzutti 6–3 3–2 ret; J. P. McEnroe d. A. Panatta 6–2 6–3 6–4; R. C. Lutz/S. R. Smith d. P. Bertolucci/Panatta 6–4 12–10 6–2; McEnroe d. A. Zugarelli 6–4 6–3 6–1; Gerulaitis d. Panatta 6–1 6–3 6–3.
1980 Czechoslovakia (Capt: Antonin Bolardt) **d. Italy** (Capt: Vittorio Crotta) **4–1**, *Prague (indoors):* T. Smid d. A. Panatta 3–6 3–6 6–3 6–4 6–4; I. Lendl d. C. Barazzutti 4–6 6–1 6–1 6–2; Lendl/Smid d. P. Bertolucci/Panatta 3–6 6–3 3–6 6–3 6–4; Smid lost to Barazzutti 6–3 3–6 2–6; Lendl d. G. Ocleppo 6–3 6–3.
1981 USA (Capt: Arthur Ashe) **d. Argentina** (Capt: Carlos Junquet) **3–1**, *Cincinnati (indoors):* J. P. McEnroe d. G. Vilas 6–3 6–2 6–2; R. Tanner lost to J. L. Clerc 5–7 3–6 6–8; P. Fleming/McEnroe d. Clerc/Vilas 6–3 4–6 6–4 4–6 11–9; McEnroe d. Clerc 7–5 5–7 6–3 3–6 6–3; Tanner div'd with Vilas 11–10.
1982 USA (Capt: Arthur Ashe) **d. France** (Capt: Jean-Paul Loth) **4–1**, *Grenoble (indoors):* J. P. McEnroe d. Y. Noah 12–10 1–6 3–6 6–2 6–3; G. Mayer d. H. Leconte 6–2 6–2 7–9 6–4; P. Fleming/McEnroe d. Leconte/Noah 6–3 6–4 9–7; Mayer lost to Noah 1–6 0–6; McEnroe d. Leconte 6–2 6–3.
1983 Australia (Capt: Neale Fraser) **d. Sweden** (Capt: Hans Olsson) **3–2**, *Melbourne:* P. Cash lost to M. Wilander 3–6 6–4 7–9 3–6; J. Fitzgerald d. J. Nystrom 6–4 6–2 4–6 6–4; M. R. Edmondson/P. McNamee d. A. Jarryd/H. Simonsson 6–4 6–4 6–2; Cash d. Nystrom 6–4 6–1 6–1; Fitzgerald lost to Wilander 8–6 0–6 1–6.
1984 Sweden (Capt: Hans Olsson) **d. USA** (Capt: Arthur Ashe) **4–1**, *Gothenburg:* M. Wilander d. J. S. Connors 6–1 6–3 6–3; H. Sundstrom d. J. P. McEnroe 13–11 6–4 6–3; S. Edberg/A. Jarryd d. P. Fleming/McEnroe 7–5 5–7 6–2 7–5; Wilander lost to McEnroe 3–6 7–6 3–6; Sundstrom d. J. Arias 3–6 8–6 6–3.
1985 Sweden (Capt: Hans Olsson) **d. West Germany** (Capt: Wilhelm Bungert) **3–2**, *Munich:* M. Wilander d. M. Westphal 6–3 6–4 10–8; S. Edberg lost to B. Becker 3–6 6–3 5–7 6–8; Wilander/J. Nystrom d. Becker/A. Maurer 6–4 6–2 6–1; Wilander lost to Becker 3–6 6–2 3–6 3–6; Edberg d. Westphal 3–6 7–5 6–4 6–3.
1986 Australia (Capt: Neale Fraser) **d. Sweden** (Capt: Hans Olsson) **3–2**, *Melbourne:* P. Cash d. S. Edberg 13–11 13–11 6–4; P. McNamee lost to M. Pernfors 3–6 1–6 3–6; Cash/J. Fitzgerald d. Edberg/A. Jarryd 6–3 6–4 4–6 6–1; Cash d. Pernfors 2–6 4–6 6–3 6–4 6–3; McNamee lost to Edberg 8–10 4–6.
1987 Sweden (Capt: Hans Olsson) **d. India** (Capt: Vijay Amritraj) **5–0**, *Gothenburg:* M. Wilander d. R. Krishnan 6–4 6–1 6–3; A. Jarryd d. V. Amritraj 6–3 6–3 6–1; Wilander/J. Nystrom d. An./V. Amritraj 6–3 3–6 6–1 6–2; Jarryd d. Krishnan 6–4 6–3; Wilander d. V. Amritraj 6–2 6–0.

1988 West Germany (Capt: Niki Pilic) **d. Sweden** (Capt: Hans Olsson) **4–1**, *Gothenburg:* C.–U. Steeb d. M. Wilander 8–10 1–6 6–2 6–4 8–6; B. Becker d. S. Edberg 6–3 6–1 6–4; Becker/E. Jelen d. Edberg/A. Jarryd 3–6 2–6 7–5 6–3 6–2; Steeb lost to Edberg 4–6 6–8; P. Kuhnen w.o. K. Carlsson.
1989 West Germany (Capt: Niki Pilic) **d. Sweden** (Capt: John Anders Sjogren) **3–2**, *Stuttgart:* C.–U. Steeb lost to M. Wilander 7–5 6–7 7–6 2–6 3–6; B. Becker d. S. Edberg 6–2 6–2 6–4; Becker/E. Jelen d. A. Jarryd/J. Gunnarsson 7–6 6–4 3–6 6–7 6–4; Becker d. Wilander 6–2 6–0 6–2; Steeb lost to Edberg 2–6 4–6.
1990 USA (Capt: Tom Gorman) **d. Australia** (Capt: Neale Fraser) **3–2**, *St Petersburg:* A. Agassi d. R. Fromberg 4–6 6–4 4–6 6–2 6–4; M. Chang d. D. Cahill 6–2 7–6 6–0; R. Leach/J. Pugh d. P. Cash/J. Fitzgerald 6–4 6–2 3–6 7–6; Agassi lost to Cahill 4–6 6–4 ret.; Chang lost to Fromberg 5–7 6–2 3–6.
1991 France (Capt: Yannick Noah) **d. USA** (Capt: Tom Gorman) **3–1**, *Lyon:* G. Forget lost to A. Agassi 7–6 2–6 1–6 2–6; H. Leconte d. P. Sampras 6–4 7–5 6–4; Forget/Leconte d. K. Flach/R. Seguso 6–1 6–4 4–6 6–2; Forget d. Sampras 7–6 3–6 6–3 6–4; Leconte v Agassi not played.
1992 USA (Capt: Tom Gorman) **d. Switzerland** (Capt: Dmitri Sturdza) **3–1**, *Fort Worth:* A. Agassi d. J. Hlasek 6–1 6–2 6–2; J. Courier lost to M. Rosset 3–6 7–6 6–3 4–6 4–6; J. McEnroe/P. Sampras d. Rosset/Hlasek 6–7 6–7 7–5 6–1 6–2; Courier d. Hlasek 6–3 3–6 6–3 6–4; Agassi v Rossi not played.
1993 Germany (Capt: Niki Pilic) **d. Australia** (Capt: Neale Fraser) **4–1**, *Dusseldorf:* M. Stich d. J. Stoltenberg 6–7 6–3 6–1 4–6 6–3; R. Fromberg d. M.-K. Goellner 3–6 5–7 7–6 6–2 9–7; P. Kuhnen/Stich d. T. Woodbridge/M. Woodforde 7–6 4–6 6–3 7–6; Stich d. Fromberg 6–4 6–2 6–2; Goellner d. Stoltenberg 6–1 6–7 7–6.
1994 Sweden (Capt: John Anders Sjogren) **d. Russia** (Capt: Vadim Borisov) **4–1**, *Moscow:* S. Edberg d. A. Volkov 6–4 6–2 6–7 0–6 8–6; M. Larsson d. Y. Kafelnikov 6–0 6–2 3–6 2–6 6–3; J. Apell/J. Bjorkman d. Y. Kafelnikov/A. Olhovskiy 6–7 6–2 6–3 1–6 8–6; Edberg lost to Kafelnikov 6–4 4–6 0–6; Larsson d. Volkov 7–6 6–4.
1995 USA (Capt: Tom Gullikson) **d. Russia** (Capt: Anatoli Lepeshin) **3–2**, *Moscow:* P. Sampras d. A. Chesnokov 3–6 6–4 6–3 6–7 6–4; Y. Kafelnikov d. J. Courier 7–6 7–5 6–3; T. Martin/P. Sampras d. Y. Kafelnikov/A. Olhovskiy 7–5 6–4 6–3; P. Sampras d. Y. Kafelnikov 6–2 6–4 7–6; A. Chesnokov d. J. Courier 6–7 7–5 6–0.
1996 France (Capt: Yannick Noah) **d. Sweden** (Capt: Carl Axel-Hageskog) **3–2**, *Malmo SWE:* C. Pioline d. S. Edberg 6–3 6–4 6–3; T. Enqvist d. A. Boetsch 6–4 6–3 7–6(2); G. Forget/G. Raoux d. J. Bjorkman/N. Kulti 6–3 1–6 6–3 6–3; T. Enqvist d. C. Pioline 3–6 6–7(8) 6–4 6–4 9–7; A. Boetsch d. N. Kulti 7–6(2) 2–6 4–6 7–6(5) 10–8.
1997 Sweden (Capt: Carl-Axel Hageskog) **d. USA** (Capt: Tom Gullikson) **5–0**, *Gothenburg:* J. Bjorkman (SWE) d. M. Chang (USA) 7–5 1–6 6–3 6–3; M. Larsson (SWE) d. P. Sampras (USA) 3–6 7–6(1) 2–1 ret; J. Bjorkman/N. Kulti (SWE) d. T. Martin/J. Stark (USA) 6–4 6–4 6–4; J. Bjorkman (SWE) d. J. Stark (USA) 6–1 6–1; M. Larsson (SWE) d. M. Chang (USA) 7–6(4) 6–7(6) 6–4.
1998 Sweden (Capt: Carl-Axel Hageskog) **d. Italy** (Capt: Paolo Bertulucci) **4–1**, *Milan:* M. Norman (SWE) d. A. Gaudenzi (ITA) 6–7(9) 7–6(0) 4–6 6–3 6–6 ret; M. Gustafsson (SWE) d, D. Sanguinetti (ITA) 6–1 6–4 6–0; J. Bjorkman/N. Kulti (SWE) d. D. Nargiso/D. Sanguinetti (ITA) 7–6(1) 6–1 6–3; M. Gustafsson (SWE) d. G. Pozzi (ITA) 6–4 6–2; D. Nargiso (ITA) d. M. Norman (SWE) 6–3 6–2.

QUALIFIERS FOR WORLD GROUP 1999

Australia	Czech Republic	Great Britain	Russia
Brazil	France	Netherlands	Slovak Republic

FED CUP

Launched in 1963 to celebrate the 50th anniversary of the International Tennis Federation, the Federation Cup (as it was known until 1994) was played annually at one site as a week-long knock-out competition. Each tie comprised two singles rubbers and one doubles. A qualifying competition was introduced in 1992 to accommodate growing numbers. By 1994 there were 73 entries and it was decided to relaunch the competition in 1995 as the Fed Cup, to be played as a season-long home and away zonal competition with the eight top teams contesting the World Group. The final is played in the country of one of the finalists, towards the end of the year. Ties consist of five rubbers, two reverse singles and the doubles. Sponsored first by Colgate (1976–80), then by NEC (1981–94) it has been supported since 1996 by KB (Komereni Banka), one of the largest banks in the Czech Republic.

FINAL ROUNDS

1963 USA (Capt: William Kellog) **d. Australia** (Capt: Nell Hopman) **2–1**, *Queen's Club, London, 18–21 June:* D. R. Hard lost to M. Smith 3–6 0–6; B. J. Moffitt d. L. R. Turner 5–7 6–0 6–3; Hard/Moffitt d. Smith/Turner 3–6 13–11 6–3.
1964 Australia (Capt: Brian Tobin) **d. USA** (Capt: Madge Vosters) **2–1**, *Germanstown Cricket Club, Philadelphia, 2–5 September:* M. Smith d. B. J. Moffitt 6–2 6–3; L. R. Turner d. N. Richey 7–5 6–1; Smith/Turner lost to Moffitt/Mrs J. R. Susman 6–4 5–7 1–6.
1965 Australia (Capt: Margaret Smith) **d. USA** (Capt: Billie Jean Moffitt) **2–1**, *Kooyong Stadium, Melbourne, 12–18 January:* L. R. Turner d. Mrs C. Graebner 6–3 2–6 6–3; M. Smith d. B. J. Moffitt 6–4 8–6; Smith/J. M. Tegart lost to Graebner/Moffitt 5–7 6–4 4–6.
1966 USA (Capt: Ros Greenwood) **d. West Germany** (Capt: Edda Buding) **3–0**, *Turin, 11–15 May:* J. M. Heldman d. H. Niessen 4–6 7–5 6–1; Mrs L. W. King d. E. Buding 6–3 3–6 6–1; Mrs C. Graebner/Mrs King d. Buding/H. Schultse 6–4 6–2.

1967 USA (Capt: Donna Fales) **d. Great Britain** (Capt: Angela Mortimer Barrett) **2–0**, *Rot-Weiss Club, Berlin, 7–11 June:* R. Casals d. S. V. Wade 9–7 8–6; Mrs L. W. King d. Mrs P. F. Jones 6–3 6–4; Casals/Mrs King div'd with Mrs Jones/Wade 6–8 9–7.

1968 Australia (Capt: Margaret Court) **d. Netherlands** (Capt: Jenny Ridderhof) **3–0**, *Stade Roland Garros, Paris, 23–26 May:* K. A. Melville d. M. Jansen 4–6 7–5 6–3; Mrs B. M. Court d. A. Suurbeck 6–1 6–3; Court/Melville d. Suurbeck/L. Venneboer 6–3 6–8 7–5.

1969 USA (Capt: Donna Fales) **d. Australia** (Capt: Wayne Reid) **2–1**, *Athens, 19–25 May:* N. Richey d. K. A. Melville 6–4 6–3; J. M. Heldman lost to Mrs B. M. Court 1–6 6–8; J. Bartkowicz/Richey d. Court/J. M. Tegart 6–4 6–4.

1970 Australia (Capt: Alf Chave) **d. West Germany** (Capt: Edward Dorrenberg) **3–0**, *Freiburg, Germany, 19–24 May:* K. M. Krantzcke d. Mrs H. Hoesl 6–2 6–3; Mrs D. E. Dalton d. H. Niessen 4–6 6–3 6–3; Dalton/Krantzcke d. Hoesl/Niessen 6–2 7–5.

1971 Australia (Capt: Margaret Court) **d. Great Britain** (Capt: Ann Haydon Jones) **3–0**, *Perth, Australia, 26–29 December 1970:* Mrs B. M. Court d. Mrs P. F. Jones 6–8 6–3 6–2; E. F. Goolagong d. S. V. Wade 6–4 6–1; Court/L. Hunt d. W. M. Shaw/Wade 6–4 6–4.

1972 South Africa (Capt: Dr. Jackie Du Toit) **d. Great Britain** (Capt: Virginia Wade) **2–1**, *Ellis Park, Johannesburg, 19–26 March:* Mrs Q. C. Pretorius lost to S. V. Wade 3–6 2–6; B. Kirk d. W. M. Shaw 4–6 7–5 6–0; Kirk/Pretorius d. Wade/Mrs G. M. Williams 6–1 7–5.

1973 Australia (Capt: Vic Edwards) **d. South Africa** (Capt: Dr. Jackie Du Toit) **3–0**, *Bad Homburg, Germany, 30 April–6 May:* E. F. Goolagong d. Mrs Q. C. Pretorius 6–0 6–2; P. Coleman d. B. Kirk 10–8 6–0; Goolagong/J. Young d. Kirk/Pretorius 6–1 6–2.

1974 Australia (Capt: Vic Edwards) **d. USA** (Capt: Donna Fales) **2–1**, *Naples, 13–19 May:* E. F. Goolagong d. J. M. Heldman 6–1 7–5; D. L. Fromholtz lost to C. M. Evert 6–2 5–7 3–6; Goolagong/J. Young d. Heldman/S. A. Walsh 7–5 8–6.

1975 Czechoslovakia (Capt: Vera Sukova) **d. Australia** (Capt: Vic Edwards) **3–0**, *Aix-en-Provence, 6–11 May:* M. Navratilova* d. E. F. Goolagong 6–3 6–4; R. Tomanova d. H Gourlay 6–4 6–2; Navratilova/Tomanova d. D. L. Fromholtz/Gourlay 6–3 6–1.

1976 USA (Capt: Billie Jean King) **d. Australia** (Capt: Neale Fraser) **2–1**, *Spectrum Stadium, Philadelphia, 22–29 August:* R. Casals lost to Mrs G. Reid 6–1 3–6 5–7; Mrs L. W. King d. Mrs E. Cawley 7–6 6–4; Casals/King d. Cawley/Reid 7–5 6–3.

1977 USA (Capt: Vicky Berner) **d. Australia** (Capt: Neale Fraser) **2–1**, *Devonshire Park, Eastbourne, 13–18 June:* Mrs L. W. King d. D. L. Fromholtz 6–1 2–6 6–2; C. M. Evert d. Mrs G. Reid 7–5 6–3; Casals/Evert lost to Reid/W. M. Turnbull 3–6 3–6.

1978 USA (Capt: Vicky Berner) **d. Australia** (Capt: Neale Fraser) **2–1**, *Kooyong Stadium, Melbourne, 27 November–3 December:* T. A. Austin lost to Mrs G. Reid 3–6 3–6; C. M. Evert d. W. M. Turnbull 3–6 6–1 6–1; Evert/Mrs L. W. King d. Reid/Turnbull 4–6 6–1 6–4.

1979 USA (Capt: Vicky Berner) **d. Australia** (Capt: Neale Fraser) **3–0**, *Madrid, 30 April–6 May:* T. A. Austin d. Mrs G. Reid 6–3 6–0; Mrs J. M. Lloyd d. D. L. Fromholtz 2–6 6–3 8–6; R. Casals/Mrs L. W. King d. Reid/W. M. Turnbull 3–6 6–3 8–6.

1980 USA (Capt: Vicky Berner) **d. Australia** (Capt: Mary Hawton) **3–0**, *Rot-Weiss Club, Berlin, 19–25 May:* Mrs J. M. Lloyd d. D. L. Fromholtz 4–6 6–1 6–1; T. A. Austin d. W. M. Turnbull 6–2 6–3; R. Casals/K. Jordan d. Fromholtz/S. Leo 2–6 6–4 6–4.

1981 USA (Capt: Mrs J. M. Lloyd) **d. Great Britain** (Capt: Sue Mappin) **3–0**, *Tokyo, 9–15 November:* A. Jaeger d. S. V. Wade 6–3 6–1; Mrs J. M. Lloyd d. S. Barker 6–2 6–1; R. Casals/K. Jordan d. J. M. Durie/Wade 6–4 7–5.

1982 USA (Capt: Mrs J. M. Lloyd) **d. West Germany** (Capt: Klaus Hofsass) **3–0**, *Santa Clara, California, 19–25 July:* Mrs J. M. Lloyd d. C. Kohde 2–6 6–1 6–3; M. Navratilova d. B. Bunge 6–4 6–4; Lloyd/Navratilova d. Bunge/Kohde 3–6 6–1 6–2.

1983 Czechoslovakia (Capt: Jan Kukal) **d. West Germany** (Capt: Klaus Hofsass) **2–1**, *Zurich, 18–24 July:* H. Sukova d. C. Kohde 6–4 2–6 6–2; H. Mandlikova d. B. Bunge 6–2 3–0 ret; I. Budarova/M. Skuherska lost to E. Pfaff/Kohde 6–3 2–6 1–6.

1984 Czechoslovakia (Capt: Jan Kukal) **d. Australia** (Capt: Judy Dalton) **2–1**, *Sao Paulo, 15–22 July:* H. Sukova lost to A. Minter 5–7 5–7; H. Mandlikova d. E. Sayers 6–1 6–0; Mandlikova/Sukova d. W. Turnbull/Sayers 6–2 6–2.

1985 Czechoslovakia (Capt: Jiri Medonos) **d. USA** (Capt: Tom Gorman) **2–1**, *Nagoya, 7–13 October:* H. Sukova d. E. Burgin 6–3 6–7 6–4; H. Mandlikova d. K. Jordan 7–5 6–1; A. Holikova/R. Marsikova lost to Burgin/Jordan 2–6 3–6.

1986 USA (Capt: Marty Riessen) **d. Czechoslovakia** (Capt: Jiri Medonos) **3–0**, *Prague, 21–27 July:* Mrs J. M. Lloyd d. H. Sukova 7–5 7–6; M. Navratilova d. H. Mandlikova 7–5 6–1; Navratilova/P. H. Shriver d. Mandlikova/Sukova 6–4 6–2.

1987 West Germany (Capt: Klaus Hofsass) **d. USA** (Capt: Marty Riessen) **2–1**, *Vancouver, 27 July–2 August:* C. Kohde-Kilsch lost to P. H. Shriver 0–6 6–7; S. Graf d. C. M. Evert 6–2 6–1; Kohde-Kilsch/Graf d. Evert/Shriver 1–6 7–5 6–4.

1988 Czechoslovakia (Capt: Jiri Medonos) **d. USSR** (Capt: Olga Morozova) **2–1**, *Melbourne, 7–11 December:* R. Zrubakova d. L. Savchenko 6–1 7–6; H. Sukova d. Zvereva 6–3 6–4; J. Novotna/J. Pospisilova lost to Savchenko/Zvereva 6–7 5–7.

1989 USA (Capt: Marty Riessen) **d. Spain** (Capt: Juan Alvarino) **3–0**, *Tokyo, 1–8 October:* C. Evert d. C. Martinez 6–3 6–2; M. Navratilova d. A. Sanchez 0–6 6–3 6–4; Z. Garrison/P. H. Shriver d. Martinez/Sanchez 7–5 6–1.

1990 USA (Capt: Marty Riessen) **d. USSR** (Capt: Olga Morozova) **2–1**, *Atlanta, 22–29 July:* J. Capriati d. L. Meskhi 7–6 6–2; Z. Garrison lost to N. Zvereva 6–4 3–6 3–6; Z. Garrison/G. Fernandez d. N. Zvereva/L. Savchenko 6–4 6–3.

1991 Spain (Capt: Juan Alvarino) **d. USA** (Capt: Marty Riessen) **2–1**, *Nottingham, 22–28 July:* C. Martinez lost to J. Capriati 6–4 6–7 1–6; A. Sanchez d. M. J. Fernandez 6–3 6–4; Martinez/Sanchez d. G. Fernandez/Z. Garrison 3–6 6–1 6–1.

1992 Germany (Capt: Klaus Hofsass) **d. Spain** (Capt: Juan Alvarino) **2–1**, *Frankfurt, 13–19 July:* A. Huber d. C. Martinez 6–3 6–7 6–1; S. Graff d. A. Sanchez-Vic. 6–4 6–2; A. Huber/B. Rittner lost to A. Sanchez-Vicario/ C. Martinez 1–6 2–6.
1993 Spain (Capt: Miguel Margets) **d. Austrialia** (Capt: Wendy Turnbull) **3–0**, *Frankfurt, 19–25 July:* C. Martinez d. M. Jaggard-Lai 6–0 6–2; A. Sanchez-Vicario d. N. Provis 6–2 6–3; Martinez/Sanchez-Vicario d. E.. Smylie/R. Stubbs 3–6 6–1 6–3.
1994 Spain (Capt: Miguel Margets) **d. USA** (Capt: Marty Riessen) **3–0**, *Frankfurt, 18–25 July:* C. Martinez d. M. J. Fernandez 6–2 6–2; A. Sanchez-Vicario d. L. Davenport 6–2 6–1; Martinez/Sanchez-Vicario d. G. Fernandez/M. J. Fernandez 6–3 6–4.
1995 Spain (Capt: Miguel Margets) **d. USA** (Capt: Billie Jean King) **3–2**, *Valencia, 25–26 November:* C. Martinez d. C. Rubin 7–5 6–3; A. Sanchez-Vicario d. M. J. Fernandez 6–3 6–2; C. Martinez d. M. J. Fernandez 6–3 6–4; A. Sanchez-Vicario lost to C. Rubin 6–1 4–6 4–6; V. Ruano/M. A. Sanchez-Vicario lost to L. Davenport/G. Fernandez 3–6 6–7.
1996 USA (Capt: Billie Jean King) **d. Spain** (Capt: Miguel Margets) **5–0**, *Atlantic City, 28–29 September:* M. Seles d. C. Martinez 6–2 6–4; L. Davenport d. A. Sanchez-Vicario 7–5 6–1; M. Seles d. A. Sanchez-Vicario 3–6 6–3 6–1; L. Davenport d. G. Leon Garcia 7–5 6–2; M. J. Fernandez/L. Wild d. G. Leon Garcia/V. Ruano-Pascual 6–1 6–4.
1997 France (Capt: Yannick Noah) **d. Netherlands** (Capt: Fred Hemmes) **4–1**, *Den Bosch, 4–5 October:* S. Testud d. B. Schultz-McCarthy 6–4 4–6 6–3; M. Pierce d. M. Oremans 6–4 6–1; B. Schultz-McCarthy d. M. Pierce 4–6 6–3 6–4; S. Testud d. M. Oremans 0–6 6–3 6–3; A. Fusai/N. Tauziat d. M. Bollegraf/C. Vis 6–3 6–4.
1998 Spain (Capt: Miguel Margets) **d. Switzerland** (Capt: Melanie Molitor) **3–2**, *Geneva, 19–20 September:* A. Sanchez-Vicario d. P. Schnyder 6–2 3–6 6–2; M. Hingis d. C. Martinez 6–4 6–4; M. Hingis d. A. Sanchez-Vicario 7–6 6–3; C. Martinez d. P. Schnyder 6–3 2–6 9–7; C. Martinez/A. Sanchez-Vicario d. M. Hingis/P. Schnyder 6–0 6–2.
** M. Navratilova became a US citizen in 1981.*

OLYMPIC MEDAL WINNERS

1896 Athens
Men's singles: Gold – J Boland (IRL), Silver – D Kasdaglis (GRE). Men's Doubles: Gold – J Boland(IRL) and F Traun (AUT); Silver – D Kasdaglis and D Petrokokkinos (GRE).
1900 Paris
Men's singles: Gold – L Doherty (GBR), Silver – H Mahony (IRL), Bronze – R Doherty (GBR) and A Norris (GBR). Men's doubles: Gold – L and R Doherty (GBR), Silver – M Decugis (FRA) and S De Garmendia (USA), Bronze – A Prevost and G De la Chapelle (FRA); H Mahony (IRL) and A Norris (GBR). Women's singles: Gold – C Cooper (GBR), Silver – H Prevost (FRA), Bronze – M Jones (USA) and H Rosenbaumova (TCH). Mixed doubles: Gold – R Doherty and C Cooper (GBR), Silver – H Mahony (IRL) and H Prevost (FRA), Bronze – A Warden (GBR) and H Rosenbaumova (TCH); L Doherty (GBR) and M Jones (USA).
1904 St Louis
Men's singles: Gold – B Wright (USA), Silver – L LeRoy (USA). Men's doubles: Gold – E Leonard and B Wright (USA), Silver – A Bell and R LeRoy (USA).
1908 London
(Indoors at Queen's Club) Men's singles: Gold – A Gore (GBR), Silver – G Caridia (GBR), Bronze -M Ritchie (GBR). Men's doubles: Gold – A Gore and H Roper Barrett (GBR) SIlver – G Caridia and G Simond (GBR), Bronze – W Bostrom and G Setterwall (SWE). Women's singles: Gold – G Eastlake Smith (GBR), Silver – A Greene (GBR), Bronze Mrs M Adlerstrahle (SWE). (Outdoors at Wimbledon) Men's singles: Gold – M Ritchie (GBR), Silver – O Froitzheim (GER), Bronze – W Eaves (GBR). Men's doubles: Gold – R Doherty and G Hillyard (GBR), Silver – M Ritchie and J Parke (GBR), Bronze – C Cazalet and C Dixon (GBR). Women's singles: Gold – Mrs R Lambert Chambers (GBR), Silver – D Boothby (GBR), Bronze – Mrs R Winch (GBR).
1912 Stockholm
(Indoors) Men's singles: Gold – A Gobert (FRA), Silver – C Dixon (GBR), Bronze -A Wilding (NZL). Men's Doubles: Gold – M Germot and A Gobert (FRA), Silver – C Kempe and G Setterwall (SWE), Bronze – A Beamish and C Dixon (GBR). Women's singles: Gold – Mrs F Hannam (GBR), Silver – S Castenschoild (DEN), Bronze – Mrs E Parton (GBR). Mixed Doubles; Gold – C Dixon and Mrs Hannam (GBR), Silver – H Roper Barrett and F Aitchison (GBR), Bronze – G Setterwall and Mrs H Fick (SWE). (Outdoors). Men's singles: Gold – C Winslow (RSA), Silver – H Kitson (RSA), Bronze – O Kreuzer (GER). Men's doubles: Gold – H Kitson and C Winslow (RSA), Silver – F Pipes and A Zborzil (AUT), Bronze – A Canet and M Meny (FRA). Women's singles: Gold – M Broquedis (FRA), Silver – D Koring (GER), Bronze – M Bjorstedt (NOR). Mixed doubles: Gold – H Schomburgk and D Koring (GER), Silver – G Setterwall and Mrs H Fick (SWE), Bronze – A Canet and M Broquedis (FRA).
1920 Antwerp
Men's singles: Gold – L Raymond (RSA), Silver – I Kumagae (JPN), Bronze – C Winslow (RSA). Men's Doubles: Gold – O Turnbull and M Woosnam (GBR), Silver – S Kashio and Kumagae (JPN), Bronze – P Albarran and M Decugis (FRA). Women's singles: Gold – S Lenglen (FRA) , Silver – E Holman (GBR), Bronze – K McKane (GBR). Women's doubles: Gold – Mrs R McNAir and K McKane (GBR), Silver -MRs A Beamish and E Holman (GBR), Bronze – S Lenglen and E D'Ayen (FRA). Mixed doubles; Gold – M Decugis and S Lenglen (FRA), M Woosnam and K McKane (GBR), Bronze – M Zemla and M Skrobkova (TCH).

1924 Paris
Men's singles: Gold – V Richards (USA), Silver – H Cochet (FRA), Bronze – H De Morpurgo (ITA). Men's doubles: Gold – F Hunter and V Richards (USA), Silver – J Brugnon and H Cochet (FRA), Bronze – J Borotra and H Lacoste (FRA). Women's singles: Gold – H Wills (USA), Silver – J Vlasto (FRA), Bronze -K McKane (GBR). Women's doubles: Gold – Mrs H Wightman and H Wills (USA), Silver – Mrs E Covell and K McKane (GBR), Bronze – Mrs D Shepherd-Barron and E Colyer (GBR). Mixed doubles: Gold – R Williams and Mrs H Wightman (USA), Silver -V Richards and Mrs M Jessup (USA), Bronze – H Timmer and C Bouman (HOL).
1968 Mexico City (Demonstration Sport)
Men's singles: Gold – M Santana(ESP), Silver – M Orantes (ESP), Bronze – H Fitzgibbon (USA). Men's doubles: Gold – R Osuna and V Zarazua (MEX), Silver – J Gisbert and M Santana (ESP), Bronze – P Darmon(FRA) and J Loyo-Mayo (MEX). Women's singles: Gold – H Neissen (GER), Silver – J Bartkowicz (USA), Bronze – J Heldman (USA). Women's doubles: E Buding and H Neissen (GER), Silver – Mrs R Darmon (FRA) and J Heldman (USA), Bronze – J Bartkowicz and V Ziegenfuss (USA). Mixed doubles: Gold – H Fitzgibbon and J Heldman (USA), Silver – J Fassbender and H Neissen (GER), Bronze – J Osborne and J Bartkowicz (USA).
1984 Los Angeles (Demonstration Sport) *6–11 August*. Held at the Los Angeles Tennis Center, UCLA, on hard courts. Men's singles: Gold – S Edberg (SWE), Silver – F Maciel (MEX), Bronze – P Cane (ITA) and J Arias (USA). Women's singles: Gold – S Graf (GER), Silver – S Goles (YUG), Bronze -C Tanvier (FRA) and R Reggi (ITA).
1988 Seoul *20 September–1 October.* Held at Olympic Park Tennis Centre on hard courts
Men's singles: Gold – M Mecir (TCH), Silver – T Mayotte (USA), Bronze – S Edberg (SWE) and B Gilbert (USA). Men's doubles: Gold – K Flach and R Seguso (USA), Silver – S Casal and E Sanchez (ESP), Bronze – S Edberg and A Jarryd (SWE) and M Mecir and M Srejber (TCH). Women's singles: Gold – S Graf (GER), Silver – G Sabatini (ARG), Bronze – Z Garrison (USA) and M Maleeva (BUL). Women's doubles: Gold – P Shriver and Z Garrison (USA), Silver – J Novotna and H Sukova (TCH), Bronze – W Turnbull and E Smylie (AUS) and S Graf and C Kohde-Kilsch (GER).
1992 Barcelona *28 July–8 August*. Held at Vall D'Hebron Tennis Centre on red clay.
Men's singles: Gold – M Rosset (SUI), Silver – J Arrese (ESP), Bronze – G Ivanisevic (CRO) and A Cherkasov (CIS). Men's doubles: Gold – B Becker and M Stich (GER), Silver – W Ferreira and P Norval (RSA), Bronze – G Ivanisevic and G Prpic (CRO) and J Frana and C Miniussi (ARG). Women's singles: Gold – J Capriati (USA), Silver – S Graf (GER), Bronze – M J Fernandez (USA) and A Sanchez-Vicario (ESP). Women's doubles: Gold – M J Fernandez and G Fernandez (USA), Silver – C Martinez and A Sanchez-Vicario (ESP), Bronze – R McQuillan and N Provis (AUS) and L Meskhi and N Zvereva (CIS).
1996 Atlanta *23 July–3 August*. Held at Stone Mountain Park Tennis Center on hard courts.
Men's singles: Gold – A. Agassi (USA), Silver – S. Bruguera (ESP), Bronze – L. Paes (IND). Men's doubles: Gold – T. Woodbridge and M. Woodforde (AUS), Silver – N. Broad and T. Henman (GBR), Bronze – M. Goellner and D. Prinosil (GER). Women's singles: Gold – L. Davenport (USA), Silver – A. Sanchez-Vicario (ESP), Bronze – J. Novotna (CZE). Women's doubles: Gold – G. Fernandez and M. J. Fernandez (USA), Silver – J. Novotna and H. Sukova (CZE), Bronze – C. Martinez and A. Sanchez-Vicario (ESP).

WIGHTMAN CUP

Women's annual team contest between USA and Great Britain, for a silver trophy presented by Mrs Hazel Hotchkiss Wightman in 1923, each match comprising five singles and two doubles, with reverse singles played between the two top players. Discontinued in 1989.
Summary: USA 51 wins; Great Britain 10 wins. (Note: Full match results can be found in previous issues of *World of Tennis* up to 1996.)

EUROPEAN CUP – MEN

Formerly King's Cup. International men's team championship on indoor courts. It was staged on a knock-out basis 1936–38, on a league basis, 1952–74, with ties home and away 1976–83. From 1984 the ties in each division were held concurrently at one venue. The Challenge Round system was used in the two opening years, with 1937 the only Challenge Round.

FINALS
1936 France d. Sweden 4–1, Stockholm: J. Borotra d. K. Schroder 2–6 6–2 6–1 6–3, d. C. Ostberg 6–1 6–3 7–5; B. Destremau d. Schroder 3–6 7–5 6–2 6–4, d. Ostberg 6–2 6–2 6–4; C. Boussus/J. Brugnon lost to Ostberg/ Schroder 2–6 6–3 4–6 6–3 4–6.
1937 France d. Sweden 5–0, *Paris:* B. Destremau d. K. Schroder 8–6 1–6 2–6 11–9 8–6, d. N. Rohlsson 1–6 1–6 6–3 6–1 6–0; Y. Petra d. Rohlsson 6–1 6–4 6–2, d. Schroder 6–3 3–6 6–3 6–4; H. Bolelli/J. Lesueur d. Schroder/H. Wallen 10–8 6–4 6–4.
1938 Germany d. Denmark 5–0, *Hamburg:* R. Menzel d. H. Plougmann 6–3 6–2 8–6; H. Henkel d. I. Gerdes 6–4 6–0 6–3, d. Plougmann 6–2 6–1 6–3; R. Redl d. Gerdes 6–3 6–3 6–2; Henkel/Menzel d. Gerdes/Plougmann 6–0 6–4 6–2.
1939–51 Not held
1952 Denmark d. Sweden 3–2, *Stockholm:* K. Nielsen lost to S. Davidson 3–6 7–9 4–6; T. Ulrich d. T. Johansson 7–5 0–6 6–4 6–2; Nielsen/Ulrich d. Davidson/Johansson 6–2 2–6 4–6 8–6 7–5; Nielsen d. Johansson 6–3 6–4 6–1; Ulrich lost to Davidson 6–4 4–6 1–6 6–1 2–6.

1953 Denmark d. Sweden 3–2, *Copenhagen:* T. Ulrich d. S. Davidson 14–12 11–9 1–6 11–9; J. Ulrich lost to T. Johansson 0–6 2–6 7–9; J. Ulrich/T. Ulrich d. Davidson/N. Rohlsson 6–4 6–4 4–6 3–6 6–3; J. Ulrich lost to Davidson 3–6 4–6 0–6; T. Ulrich d. Johansson 6–3 2–6 6–4 5–7 6–3.
1954 Denmark d. Italy 3–2, *Milan:* T. Ulrich d. G. Merlo 7–5 2–6 9–7 9–7; K. Nielsen lost to O. Sirola 5–7 6–8 8–6 6–2 3–6; Nielsen/Ulrich d. N. Pietrangeli/Sirola 2–6 2–6 11–9 6–1 12–10; Nielsen lost to Pietrangeli 5–7 6–3 9–7 3–6 5–7; Ulrich d. Sirola 7–5 10–8 6–4.
1955 Sweden d. Denmark 4–1, *Copenhagen:* S. Davidson d. J. Ulrich 7–5 12–10 6–1; U. Schmidt lost to K. Nielsen 3–6 2–6 6–4 4–6; Davidson/T. Johansson d. Nielsen/J. Ulrich 11–9 6–3 14–12; Davidson d. Nielsen 8–10 6–2 7–9 12–10 7–5; Schmidt d. J. Ulrich 7–9 3–6 6–0 8–6 6–3.
1956 Sweden d. France 4–1, *Paris:* S. Davidson lost to P. Darmon 7–9 6–2 5–7 6–8; U. Schmidt d. R. Haillet 6–1 /6–2 6–4; Davidson/Schmidt d. Darmon/P. Remy 8–6 3–6 6–1 6–4; Davidson d. Haillet 6–2 2–6 6–4 6–1; Schmidt d. Darmon 6–1 10–8 6–3.
1957 Sweden d. Denmark 3–2, *Copenhagen:* J. E. Lundqvist d. K. Nielsen 4–6 6–3 10–8 6–4; U. Schmidt lost to T. Ulrich 4–6 7–9 2–6; Lundqvist/Schmidt d. J. Ulrich/T. Ulrich 6–3 5–7 6–0 6–3; Lundqvist d. T. Ulrich 7–5 6–1 6–2; Schmidt lost to Nielsen 6–4 4–6 2–6 5–7.
1958 Sweden d. Denmark 3–2, *Stockholm:* B. Folke lost to J. Ulrich 11–13 3–6 4–6; S. Davidson d. K. Nielsen 6–0 6–1 6–4; Davidson/T. Johansson d. Nielsen/J. Ulrich 10–8 1–6 6–3 6–8 6–3; Folke lost to Nielsen 4–6 3–6 3–6; Davidson d. J. Ulrich 6–4 6–3 1–6 6–1.
1959 Denmark won, *Stockholm:* Denmark d. Italy 2–1, lost to Sweden 2–1, d. France 2–1 (12–11 sets); Sweden lost to France 2–1, d. Denmark 2–1, d. Italy 2–1 (10–10 sets); Italy lost to Denmark 2–1, d. France 2–1, lost to Sweden 2–1 (11–11 sets); France d. Sweden 2–1, lost to Italy 2–1, lost to France 2–1 (10–11 sets). Danish team: K. Nielsen and J. Ulrich.
1960 Denmark d. West Germany 3–0, *Paris:* J. Leschly d. B. Nitsche 6–4 8–6; J. Ulrich d. P. Scholl 6–2 6–3; Leschly/J. Ulrich d. Nitsche/Scholl 6–8 6–2 6–0.
1961 Sweden d. Denmark 2–1, *Cologne:* U. Schmidt d. J. Leschly 6–4 6–2; J. E. Lundqvist d. J. Ulrich 6–3 6–1; Lundqvist/Schmidt lost to Leschly/J. Ulrich 5–7 6–4 5–7.
1962 Denmark d. Italy 3–0, *Copenhagen:* J. Leschly d. G. Merlo 6–3 8–6; J. Ulrich d. N. Pietrangeli 6–4 6–2; Leschly/J. Ulrich d. Pietrangeli/O. Sirola 9–7 7–5.
1963 Yugoslavia d. Denmark 3–0, *Belgrade:* Yugoslav team: B. Jovanovic and N. Pilic.
1964 Great Britain d. Sweden 3–0, *Stockholm:* M. J. Sangster d. J. E. Lundquist 13–15 10–8 12–10; R. Taylor d. B. Holmstrom 6–3 9–7; Sangster/R. K. Wilson d. Holmstrom/L. Olander 4–6 12–10 6–4.
1965 Great Britain d. Denmark 2–1, *Torquay:* R. K. Wilson lost to J. Leschly 1–6 4–6; M. Cox d. C. Hedelund 6–4 6–3; A. R. Mills/Wilson d. Leschly/Hedelund 3–6 6–2 6–4 12–10.
1966 Great Britain d. Italy 3–0, *Milan:* R. Taylor d. N. Pietrangeli 6–4 6–4; M. J. Sangster d. G. Maioli 7–9 6–4 11–9; Sangster/R. K. Wilson d. D. Di Maso/Maioli 6–4 6–1.
1967 Great Britain d. Sweden 2–1, *Stockholm:* R. Taylor d. O. Bengtson 2–6 6–3 9–7; R. K. Wilson d. M. Carlstein 8–6 6–2; M. Cox/Taylor lost to Bengtson/B. Homstrom 4–6 7–9.
1968 Sweden d. Netherlands 2–1, *Bratislava:* O. Bengtson lost to T. S. Okker 12–14 4–6; M. Carlstein d. J. Hordjik 6–4 6–3; Bengtson/Carlstein d. N. Fleury/Okker 1–6 4–6 7–5 6–3 6–4.
1969 Czechoslovakia d. Sweden 2–1, *Cologne:* V. Zednik d. H. Zahr 6–4, 7–5; J. Kukal d. O. Bengtson 6–1 5–7 11–9; Kukal/Zednik lost to Bengtson/H. Nerell 4–6 4–6.
1970 France d. Denmark 2–1, *Copenhagen:* J. B. Chanfreau d. J. Ulrich 6–3 8–6; G. Goven lost to J. Leschly 1–6 3–6; Chanfreau/Goven d. Ulrich/Leschly 2–6 6–4 7–5.
1971 Italy d. Spain 2–1, *Ancona:* A. Panatta lost to M. Orantes 2–6 3–6; N. Pietrangeli d. J. Gisbert 7–9 8–6 6–4; Panatta/Pietrangeli d. Gisbert/Orantes 4–6 8–6 6–3 6–4.
1972 Spain d. Hungary 3–0, *Madrid:* A. Gimeno d. S. Baranyi 10–8 6–2; J. Gisbert d. B. Taroczy 6–1 7–9 6–3; J. Herrera/A. Munoz d. R. Machan/Taroczy 6–4 3–6 7–5.
1973 Sweden d. Italy 2–1, *Hannover:* L. Johansson d. A. Zugarelli 6–4 6–3; B. Borg d. A. Panatta 4–6 6–2 8–6; Borg/Johansson lost to P. Bertolucci/Zugarelli 6–3 5–7 4–6.
1974 Italy d. Sweden 3–0, *Ancona:* A. Panatta d. R. Norberg 6–3 6–4; A. Zugarelli d. T. Svensson 6–3 6–4; P. Bertolucci/A. Panatta d. B. Andersson/Norberg 6–2 6–4.
1975 Not held
1976 Hungary 11 wins, Great Britain 10 wins (played entirely as round robin, each tie home and away). Hungarian team: P. Szoke, B. Taroczy. British team: M. Cox, J. M. Lloyd, C. J. Mottram, R. Taylor.
1977 Sweden d. West Germany 5–1, *Berlin:* R. Norberg d. U. Marten 6–2 4–6 6–4; K. Johansson d. K. Meiler 6–4 6–4; O. Bengtson/Norberg d. P. Elter/Meiler 6–2 6–2. *Linkoping:* Norberg d. U. Pinner 7–6 6–2; Johansson d. Meiler 6–7 6–2 6–3; Bengtson/Norberg lost to Elter/Marten 6–3 4–6 4–6.
1978 Sweden d. Hungary 3–3 (9–7 sets), *Uppsala:* T. Svensson d. P. Szoke 6–2 6–4; O. Bengtson lost to B. Taroczy 6–7 6–7; Bengtson/Svensson lost to Szoke/Taroczy 6–7 4–6; *Debrecen:* Svensson d. Szoke 6–2 6–2; Bengtson d. Taroczy 6–4 7–6; Bengtson/Svensson lost to Szoke/Taroczy 3–6 6–3 3–6.
1979 Czechoslovakia d. Hungary 4–2, *Pecs:* I. Lendl lost to J. Benyik 6–7 7–5 6–7; T. Smid d. B. Taroczy 5–7 6–3 6–4; P. Slozil/T. Smid d. P. Szoke/Taroczy 6–4 6–4; *Chrudin:* Lendl lost to Benyik 6–4 2–6 0–6; Smid d. Szoke 6–3 3–6 6–2; Slozil/Smid d. Benyik/Szoke 6–4 6–2.
1980 Czechoslovakia d. Hungary 5–1, *Chrudin:* T. Smid d. R. Machan 6–4 6–2; I. Lendl d. B. Taroczy 6–2 6–1; Smid/P. Slozil d. P. Szoke/Machan 6–4 7–5; *Debreden:* Smid d. J. Benyik 6–2 3–6 6–2; Lendl d. Machan 6–0 6–2; Smid/Slozil lost to Machan/Szoke 6–3 3–6 2–6.
1981 West Germany d. USSR 3–3 (9–7 sets), *Moscow,* **2–1**, *and Hamburg,* **1–2.**
1982 West Germany d. Czechoslovakia 2–1, *Dortmund:* K. Eberhard lost to J. Navratil 4–6 1–6; U. Pinnder d. P. Slozilp 6–4 6–4; C. Zipf/H. D. Beutel d. Navratil/Slozil 6–3 6–4.

1983 West Germany d. Czechoslovakia 2–1, *Uppsala:* H. J. Schwaier lost to L. Pimek 6–4 2–6 3–6; M. Westphal d. J. Navratil 3–6 6–2 6–3; E. Jelen/W. Popp d. Navratil/Piimek 6–1 1–6 7–6.
1984 Czechoslovakia d. Sweden 2–1, *Essen:* M. Mecir d. J. Gunnarsson 7–6 6–4; L. Pimek lost to J. Nystrom 3–6 5–7; Pimek/J. Navratil d. Gunnarsson/Nystrom 3–6 6–2 6–4.
1985 Sweden d. Switzerland 3–0, *Essen:* T. Hogstedt d. R. Stadler 6–3 6–2; J. Gunnarsson d. J. Hlasek 7–5 4–6 6–2; S. Simonsson d. Hlasek/Stadler 6–3 3–6 6–3.
1986 Switzerland d. Czechoslovakia 2–1, *Queen's Club, London:* R. Stadler d. M. Vajda 6–4 7–5; J. Hlasek lost L. Pimek 7–5 3–6 5–7; Hlasek/Stadler d. Pimek/P. Korda 6–2 6–3.
1987 Switzerland d. Great Britain 2–1, *Hannover:* R. Stadler lost to M. J. Bates 6–7 2–6; J. Hlasek d. A. Castle 6–3 6–7 6–2; Hlasek/Stadler d. Bates/Castle 3–6 7–5 6–0.
1988 Czechoslovakia d. Netherlands 2–0, *Zurich:* P. Korda d. M. Oosting 6–3 7–6; doubles not played.
1989 Czechoslovakia d. West Germany 2–1, *Ostrava:* P. Korda lost to C.–U. Steeb 3–6 3–6; M. Srejber d. E. Jelen 7–5 6–3; Srejber/Korda d. P. Kuhnen/Jelen 7–6 7–6.
1990 Germany d. USSR 2–1, *Metz:* U. Riglewski lost to D. Poliakov 7–5 3–6 2–6; M. Stich d. A. Cherkasov 6–3 7–6; Stich/Riglewski d. A. Olhovskiy/V. Gabrichidze 6–3 7–6.
1991 Czechoslovakia d. Netherlands 2–1, *Lengnau:* D. Rikl lost to T. Kempers 6–3 5–7 1–6; M. Damm d. F. Wibier 6–4 6–1; Damm/T. Zdrazila d. Kempers/Wibier 6–3 6–3.
1992 Sweden d. Germany 2–1, *Trieste:* N. Kulti d. M. Goellner 6–4 7–6; T. Enqvist lost to M. Naewie 3–6 4–6; M. Tillstrom/N. Kulti d. M. Naewie/M. Goellner 4–6 6–3 7–6
1993 Sweden d. Germany 2–0, *Trieste:* J. Bjorkman d. J. Renzenbrink 6–1 6–3; N. Kulti d. D. Prinosil 6–4 6–4 (doubles not played).
1994 Italy d. Sweden 2–1, *Trieste:* O. Camporese d. M. Norman 6–2 6–2; C. Caratti lost to T. Johansson 4–6 1–6; Camporese/C. Brandi d. Flyght/Johansson 6–4 6–2.
1995 Italy d. Czech Republic 2–0, *Reggio Calabria:* O. Camporese d. D. Miketa 6–2 6–4; C. Caratti d. Novak 6–7(5–7) 6–4 6–0. Doubles not played.
1996 Sweden d. Italy 2–1, *Reggio Calabria:* G. Galimberti d. T. Johansson 2–6 6–3 6–3; N. Timfjord d. M. Navarra 6–2 6–4; M. Rentröm/N. Timfjord d. M. Navarra/M. Martelli 6–7 6–4 6–1.
1997 Great Britain d. Netherlands 2–1, *Reggio Calabria:* M. Verkerk (NED) d. M. Lee (GBR) 4–6 7–6 6–2; D. Sapsford (GBR) d. P. Wessels (NED) 7–6 6–4; D. Sapsford/M. Lee (GBR) d. T. Kempes/P. Wessels (NED) 6–3 7–5.
1998 Italy d. Bulgaria 2–1, *Montecatini:* G. Galimberti (ITA) d. I. Traykov (BUL) 7–6 6–3; M. Martelli (ITA) d. M. Velev (BUL) 6–2 6–2; doubles not played.

EUROPEAN CUP – WOMEN

A team competition for women launched in 1986 to commemorate the 50th anniversary of the European Cup for men (which had originally been the King's Cup). Ties consist of two singles rubbers and one doubles rubber.

FINALS
1986 Sweden d. W. Germany 2–0 *Eindhoven 27–30 November:* C. Carlsson(SWE) d. A. Betzner (GER) 6–0 6–3; C. Lindqvist (SWE) d. S. Meier (GER) 6–2 7–6. Doubles not played.
1987 France d. Netherlands 2–0 *Lomma-Bjarred 26–29 November:* P. Paradis (FRA) d. M. Mesker (NED) 3–6 7–5 6–2; J. Halard (FRA) d. M. Bollegraf (NED) 6–2 6–4. Doubles not played.
1988 France d. Netherlands 2–1 *Nantes 7–13 November:* K. Quentrec (FRA) d. M. Bollegraf (NED) 6–3 6–4; C. Suire (FRA) d. H. Schultz (NED) 6–2 6–1; Bollegraf/C. Vis (NED) d. Suire/C. Tanvier (FRA) 6–4 4 6–7–6.
1989 USSR d. Great Britain 2–1 *Nantes 23–26 November:* J. Durie (GBR) d. N. Zvereva (URS) 7–6 6–4; L. Meskhi d. C. Wood 6–3 6–1; L. Savchenko/Zvereva (URS) d. Durie/A. Hobbs (GBR) 6–2 6–2.
1990 USSR d. Great Britain 2–1 *Nantes 29 November – 2 December:* Brioukhovets (URS) d. M. Javer (GBR) 7–5 6–3; N. Medvedeva (URS) d. J. Durie 6–3 6–3; Durie/C. Wood (GBR) d. Brioukhovets/ Medvedeva (URS) 7–6 ret.
1991 Netherlands d. Italy 2–0 *Nantes 28 November – 1 December:* M. Oremans d. K. Piccolini 6–4 6–2; S. Rottier (NED) d. L. Ferrando (ITA) 6–1 3–6 7–5. Doubles not played.
1992 Great Britain d. Netherlands 2–1 *Prague, 26–29 November:* C. Wood (GBR) lost to M. Kiene 2–6 3–6; J. Durie (GBR) d. N. Muns Jagerman 7–6 6–4; Durie/Wood d. Kiene/M. Oremans 6–3 6–2.
1993 Germany d. Netherlands 2–0 *Sheffield, 24–28 November:* C. Porwick (GER) d. K. Boogert (NED) 7–5 6–3; B. Rittner (GER) d. S. Rottier (NED) 7–5 6–2. Doubles not played.
1994 Italy d. Germany 2–1 *Aachen, 23–27 November:* M. Babel (GER) d. L. Golarsa (ITA) 6–4 6–2; S. Cecchini (ITA) d. B. Rittner (GER) 6–2 6–4; Cecchini/Golarsa (ITA) d. Rittner/C. Singer (GER) 7–6 6–4.
1995 Belgium d. Netherlands 2–1 *Aachen, 29 November–1 December:* M. Oremans (BEL) d. D. Monami (NED) 6–2 5–7 6–4; S. Appelmans (NED) d. K. Boogert (BEL) 5–7 6–1 6–1; Oremans/C. Vis (BEL) d. Appelmans/ L.Courtois (NED) 6–2 6–4.
1996 Germany d. Netherlands 2–0, *Aachen:* M. Weingartner d. C. Vis 6–0 3–6 6–1; B. Rittner d. M. Oremans 7–5 6–7 6–2; Doubles not played.
1997 Spain d. Italy 2–1, *Barcelona:* G. Leon (ESP) d. F. Perfetti (ITA) 6–4 7–6(3); F. Lubiani (ITA) d. V. Ruano-Pascual (ESP) 4–6 6–4 7–6(6); G. Leon/V. Ruano-Pascual (ESP) d. G. Casoni/F. Perfetti (ITA) 6–2 6–2.
1998 Italy d. Czech Republic 3–0, *Frydlant Nad Ostravici:* G. Pizzichini (ITA) d. M. Pastikova (CZE) 6–3 7–6; F Perfetti (ITA) d. K. Hrdlickova (CZE) 6–1 6–3; G. Casoni/P. Zavagli (ITA) d. D. Bedanova/M. Pastikova (CZE) 6–3 5–7 7–5.

WORLD TEAM CUP

Eight-nation men's team event, qualification by individual ATP rating. Formerly Nations Cup.

FINALS

Played at Kingston, Jamaica

1975 USA d. Great Britain 2–1: R. Tanner (USA) d. R. Taylor (GBR) 6–3 2–6 6–4; A. R. Ashe (USA) lost to C. J. Mottram (GBR) 5–7 7–5 1–6; Ashe/Tanner d. Mottram/Taylor 6–1 1–6 6–4.

***1976–77* Not held**

Played at Dusseldorf

1978 Spain d. Australia 2–1: J. Higueras (ESP) d. J. D. Newcombe (AUS) 6–2 6–3; M. Orantes (ESP) d. P. Dent (AUS) 6–3 6–4; Higueras/ Orantes lost to Dent/Newcombe 6–7 4–6.

1979 Australia d. Italy 2–1: J. G. Alexander (AUS) d. C. Barazzutti (ITA) 6–2 6–0; P. Dent (AUS) lost to A. Panatta (ITA) 3–6 3–6; Alexander/Dent d. P. Bertolucci/Panatta 6–3 7–6.

1980 Argentina d. Italy 3–0: G. Vilas (ARG) d. C. Barazzutti (ITA) 6–3 6–2; J. L. Clerc (ARG) d. A. Panatta (ITA) 7–6 6–3; Clerc/Vilas d. P. A Bertolucci/Panatta 6–2 6–3.

1981 Czechoslovakia d. Australia 2–1: I. Lendl (TCH) lost to P. McNamara (AUS) 3–6 4–6; T. Smid (TCH) d. P. McNamee (AUS) 6–4 7–6; Lendl/Smid d. McNamara/McNamee 6–4 6–3.

1982 USA d. Australia 2–1: G. Mayer (USA) d. K. Warwick (AUS) 7–6 6–2; E. Teltscher (USA) d. P. McNamara (AUS) 6–4 7–6; Mayer/S. E. Stewart lost to M. R. Edmondson/McNamara 1–6 1–6.

1983 Spain d. Australia 2–1: J. Higueras (ESP) d. M. R. Edmondson (AUS) 6–2 6–4; M. Orantes (ESP) d. P. Cash (AUS) 6–3 6–2; A. Gimenez/Higueras lost to Cash/Edmondson 5–7 6–4 1–6.

1984 USA d. Czechoslovakia 2–1: J. P. McEnroe (USA) d. I. Lendl (TCH) 6–3 6–2; J. Arias (USA) lost to T. Smid (TCH) 6–4 6–7 4–6; P. Fleming/McEnroe d. Lendl/Smid 6–1 6–2.

1985 USA d. Czechoslovakia 2–1: J. P. McEnroe (USA) lost to I. Lendl (TCH) 7–6 6–7 3–6; J. S. Connors (USA) d. M. Mecir (TCH) 6–3 3–6 7–5; K. Flach/R. Seguso (USA) d. Lendl/T. Smid 6–3 7–6

1986 France d. Sweden 2–1: H. Leconte (FRA) d. A. Jarryd (SWE) 6–3 3–6 6–1; T. Tulasne (FRA) lost to M. Wilander (SWE) 1–6 4–6; G. Forget/Leconte d. Jarryd/Wilander 6–3 2–6 6–2.

1987 Czechoslovakia d. USA 2–1: M. Mecir (TCH) d. J. P. McEnroe (USA) 7–5 2–6 2–1 disqual.; M. Srejber (TCH) lost to B. Gilbert (USA) 4–6 7–5 4–6; Mecir/T. Smid d. Gilbert/R. Seguso 6–3 6–1.

1988 Sweden d. USA 2–1: S. Edberg (SWE) d. T. Mayotte (USA) 6–4 6–2; K. Carlsson (SWE) d. A. Krickstein (USA) 6–4 6–3; Edberg/A. Jarryd lost to K. Flach/R. Seguso (USA) 7–6 3–6 6–7.

1989 West Germany d. Argentina 2–1: B. Becker (GER) d. G. Perez Roldan (ARG) 6–0 2–6 6–2; C.–U. Steeb (GER) lost to M. Jaite (ARG) 4–6 3–6; Becker/E. Jelen d. J. Frana/G. Luna 6–4 7–5.

1990 Yugoslavia d. USA 2–1: G. Prpic (YUG) d. B. Gilbert (USA) 6–4 6–4; G. Ivanisevic (YUG) d. J. Courier (USA) 3–6 7–5 6–1; Prpic/S. Zivojinovic lost to K. Flach/R. Seguso (USA) 5–7 6–7.

1991 Sweden d. Yugoslavia 2–1: M. Gustafsson (SWE) d. G. Prpic (YUG) 6–2 3–6 6–4; S. Edberg (SWE) d G. Ivanisevic (YUG) 6–4 7–5; Edberg/Gustafsson lost to Prpic/S. Zivojinovic 6–3 3–6 4–6.

1992 Spain d. Czechoslovakia 3–0: E. Sanchez (ESP) d. P. Korda (TCH) 3–6 6–2 7–6; S. Brugera (ESP) d. K. Novacek (TCH) 6–2 6–4; S. Casal/E. Sanchez d. K. Novacek/C. Suk 1–6 6–4 6–3.

1993 USA d. Germany 3–0: P. Sampras (USA) d. M. Stich (GER) 6–4 6–2; M. Chang (USA) d. C.-U. Steeb (GER) 6–3 7–6; P. McEnroe/R. Reneberg (USA) d. P. Kuhnen/M. Stich 6–4 6–3.

1994 Germany d. Spain 2–1: M. Stich (GER) d. S. Bruguera (ESP) 2–6 6–4 6–3; C. Costa (ESP) d. B. Karbacher (GER) 6–2 6–4 6–0; P. Kuhnen/Stich (GER) d. T. Carbonnel/Costa (ESP) 7–5 4–6 6–4.

1995 Sweden d. Croatia 2–1: M. Larsson (SWE) lost to G. Ivanisevic (CRO) 4–6 4–6; S. Edberg (SWE) d. S. Hirszon (CRO) 6–1 6–4; J. Bjorkman/S. Edberg (SWE) d. S. Hirszon/G. Ivanisevic (CRO) 4–6 6–3 6–3.

1996 Switzerland d. Czech Republic 2–1: J. Hlasek (SUI) lost to P. Korda (CZE) 3–6 4–6; M. Rosset (SUI) d. B. Ulihrach (CZE) 7–6 6–2; Hlasek/Rosset (SUI) d. Korda/D. Vacek (CZE) 6–3 6–4.

1997 Spain d. Australia 3–0: F. Mantilla (ESP) d. M. Woodforde (AUS) 7–5 6–2; A. Costa (ESP) d. M. Philippoussis (AUS) 3–6 7–6(3) 7–6(7); T. Carbonell/F.Roig (ESP) d. T. Woodbridge/M. Woodforde (AUS) 6–3 7–5.

1998 Germany d. Czech Republic 3–0: T. Haas (GER) d. S, Dosedel (CZE) 6–1 6–4; N. Kiefer (GER) d. P. Korda (CZE) 7–5 6–3; B. Becker/D. Prinosil (GER) d. C. Suk/D. Vacek (CZE) 6–4 4–6 6–2.

MEN'S GRAND PRIX (1970–1989)

A points-linked circuit of men's tournaments with a bonus pool distributed to the points leaders at the end of the year and a Masters tournament where field varied in size. Full details available in *World of Tennis 1996*, and previous issues.

ATP TOUR CHAMPIONSHIP

A season-ending tournament for the top eight men on the ATP Tour ranking list, played in two round-robin groups of four players each and knock-out semi-finals and final.

SINGLES

	VENUE	*WINNER*	*RUNNER-UP*	*SCORE*	*FIRST PRIZE*
1990	Frankfurt	A. Agassi	S. Edberg	5–7 7–6 7–5 6–2	$950,000
1991	Frankfurt	P. Sampras	J. Courier	3–6 7–6 6–3 6–4	$1,020,000
1992	Frankfurt	B. Becker	J. Courier	6–4 6–3 7–5	$1,020,000
1993	Frankfurt	M. Stich	P. Sampras	7–6 2–6 7–6 6–2	$1,240,000
1994	Frankfurt	P. Sampras	B. Becker	4–6 6–3 7–5 6–4	$1,235,000
1995	Frankfurt	B. Becker	M. Chang	7–6 6–0 7–6	$1,225,000
1996	Hannover	P. Sampras	B. Becker	3–6 7–6 7–6 6–7 6–4	$1,340,000
1997	Hannover	P. Sampras	Y. Kafelnikov	6–3 6–2 6–2	$1,340,000
1998	Hannover	A. Corretja	C. Moya	3–6 3–6 7–5 6–3 7–5	$1,360,000

DOUBLES

	VENUE	*WINNER*	*RUNNER-UP*	*SCORE*	*FIRST PRIZE*
1990	Sanctuary Cove	G. Forget/J. Hlasek	S. Casal/E. Sanchez	6–4 7–6 5–7 6–4	$225,000
1991	Johannesburg	J. Fitzgerald/A. Jarryd	K. Flach/R. Seguso	6–4 6–4 2–6 6–4	$325,000
1992	Johannesburg	T. Woodbridge/M. Woodforde	J. Fitzgerald/A. Jarryd	6–2 7–6 5–7 3–6 6–3	$325,000
1993	Johannesburg	J. Eltingh/P. Haarhuis	T. Woodbridge/ M. Woodforde	7–6 7–6 6–4	$365,000
1994	Jakarta	J. Apell/J. Bjorkman	T. Woodbridge/ M. Woodforde	6–4 4–6 4–6 7–6 7–6	$275,000
1995	Eindhoven	G. Connell/P.Galbraith	J. Eltingh/P. Haarhuis	7–6 7–6 3–6 7–6	$225,000
1996	Hartford	T. Woodbridge/M. Woodforde	S. Lareau/A. O'Brien	6–4 5–7 6–2 7–6	$165,000
1997	Hartford	R. Leach/J. Stark	M. Bhupathi/L. Paes	6–3 6–4 7–6	$145,000
1998	Hartford	J. Eltingh/P. Haarhuis	M. Knowles/D. Nestor	6–4 6–2 7–5	$258,500

WOMEN'S INTERNATIONAL SERIES CHAMPIONSHIPS

(1974–78 Virginia Slims, 1979–82 Avon, 1983–94 Virginia Slims, 1995 Corel, 1996 Chase) Best of 3 sets 1977–1982, best of 5 sets 1983–present.

SINGLES

	VENUE	*WINNER*	*RUNNER-UP*	*SCORE*	*FIRST PRIZE*
1977	Palm Springs	Miss C. M. Evert	Mrs L. W. King	6–2 6–2	$75,000
1978	Palm Springs	Miss C. M. Evert	Miss M. Navratilova	6–3 6–3	$75,000
1979*	Landover, Maryland	Miss M. Navratilova	Miss T. A. Austin	6–2 6–1	$75,000
1980*	Palm Springs	Miss T. A. Austin	Miss A. Jaeger	6–2 6–2	$75,000
1981	East Rutherford, NJ	Miss T. A. Austin	Miss M. Navratilova	2–6 6–4 6–2	$75,000
1982	East Rutherford, NJ	Miss M. Navratilova	Mrs J. M. Lloyd	4–6 6–1 6–2	$75,000
1983*	Madison Sq. Gdn, NY	Miss M. Navratilova	Mrs J. M. Lloyd	6–3 7–5 6–1	$125,000
1984*	Madison Sq. Gdn, NY	Miss M. Navratilova	Miss H. Sukova	6–3 7–5 6–4	$125,000
1985*	Madison Sq. Gdn, NY	Miss M. Navratilova	Miss H. Mandlikova	6–2 6–0 3–6 6–1	$125,000
1986	Madison Sq. Gdn, NY	Miss M. Navratilova	Miss S. Graf	7–6 6–3 6–2	$125,000
1987	Madison Sq. Gdn, NY	Miss S. Graf	Miss G. Sabatini	4–6 6–4 6–0 6–4	$125,000
1988	Madison Sq. Gdn, NY	Miss G. Sabatini	Miss P. H. Shriver	7–5 6–2 6–2	$125,000
1989	Madison Sq. Gdn, NY	Miss S. Graf	Miss M. Navratilova	6–4 7–5 2–6 6–2	$125,000
1990	Madison Sq. Gdn, NY	Miss M. Seles	Miss G. Sabatini	6–4 5–7 3–6 6–4 6–2	$250,000
1991	Madison Sq. Gdn, NY	Miss M. Seles	Miss M. Navratilova	6–4 3–6 7–5 6–0	$250,000
1992	Madison Sq. Gdn, NY	Miss M. Seles	Miss M. Navratilova	7–5 6–3 6–1	$250,000
1993	Madison Sq. Gdn, NY	Miss S. Graf	Miss A. Sanchez-Vic.	6–1 6–4 3–6 6–1	$250,000
1994	Madison Sq. Gdn, NY	Miss G. Sabatini	Miss L. Davenport	6–3 6–2 6–4	$250,000
1995	Madison Sq. Gdn, NY	Miss S. Graf	Miss A. Huber	6–1 2–6 6–1 4–6 6–3	$500,000
1996	Madison Sq. Gdn, NY	Miss S. Graf	Miss M. Hingis	6–3 4–6 6–0 4–6 6–0	$500,000
1997	Madison Sq. Gdn, NY	Miss J. Novotna	Miss M. Pierce	7–6 6–2 6–3	$500,000
1998	Madison Sq. Gdn, NY	Miss M. Hingis	Miss L. Davenport	7–5 6–4 4–6 6–2	$500,000

**Played in the following year*

DOUBLES

	WINNERS	*RUNNERS-UP*	*SCORE*
1977	Miss F. Durr/Miss S. V. Wade	Mrs H. Gourlay Cawley/Miss J. Russell	6–1 4–6 6–4
1978	Mrs L. W. King/Miss M. Navratilova	Mrs G. E. Reid/Miss W. M. Turnbull	6–3 6–4
1979*	Mrs L. W. King/Miss M. Navratilova	Miss R. Casals/Mrs J. M. Lloyd	6–4 6–3

1980*	Miss R. Casals/Miss W. M. Turnbull	Miss C. Reynolds/Miss P. Smith	6–3	4–6	7–6
1991	Miss M. Navratilova/Miss P. H. Shriver	Miss R. Casals/Miss W. M. Turnbull	6–3	6–4	
1982	Miss M. Navratilova/Miss P. H. Shriver	Miss C. Reynolds/Miss P. Smith	6–4	7–5	
1983*	Miss M. Navratilova/Miss P. H. Shriver	Miss J. M. Durie/Miss A. Kiyomura	6–3	6–1	
1984*	Miss M. Navratilova/Miss P. H. Shriver	Miss C. Kohde-Kilsch/Miss H. Sukova	6–7	6–4	7–6
1985*	Miss H. Mandlikova/Miss W. M. Turnbull	Miss C. Kohde-Kilsch/Miss H. Sukova	6–4	6–7	6–3
1986	Miss M. Navratilova/Miss P. H. Shriver	Miss C. Kohde-Kilsch/Miss H. Sukova	7–6	6–3	
1987	Miss M. Navratilova/Miss P. H. Shriver	Miss C. Kohde-Kilsch/Miss H. Sukova	6–1	6–1	
1988	Miss M. Navratilova/Miss P. H. Shriver	Miss L. Savchenko/Miss N. Zvereva	6–3	6–4	
1989	Miss M. Navratilova/Miss P. H. Shriver	Miss L. Savchenko/Miss N. Zvereva	6–3	6–2	
1990	Miss K. Jordan/Mrs P. Smylie	Miss M. Paz/Miss A. Sanchez-Vicario	7–6	6–4	
1991	Miss M. Navratilova/Miss P. H. Shriver	Miss G. Fernandez/Miss J. Novotna	4–6	7–5	6–4
1992	Miss A. Sanchez-Vicario./Miss H. Sukova	Miss J. Novotna/Mrs L. Savchenko-Neil.	7–6	6–1	
1993	Miss G. Fernandez/Miss N. Zvereva	Miss L. Neiland/J. Novotna	6–3	7–6	
1994	Miss G. Fernandez/Miss N. Zvereva	Miss J. Novotna/Miss A. Sanchez-Vicario	6–3	6–7	6–3
1995	Miss J, Novotna/Miss A. Sanchez-Vicario	Miss G. Fernandez/Miss N. Zvereva	6–2	6–1	
1996	Miss L. Davenport/Miss M. J. Fernandez	Miss J. Novotna/Miss A. Sanchez-Vicario	6–2	6–3	
1997	Miss L. Davenport/Miss J. Novotna	Miss A. Fusai/Miss N. Tauziat	6–7	6–3	6–2
1998	Miss L. Davenport/Miss N. Zvereva	Miss A. Fusai/Miss N. Tauziat	6–7	7–5	6–3

* *Played in the following year.*

WORLD CHAMPIONSHIP TENNIS

An independent circuit organised by Lamar Hunt's Dallas-based World Championship Tennis Inc which pre-dated the Grand Prix. The eight-man playoff staged annually in Dallas for the points leaders on the circuit set the standard for professionally promoted tennis tournaments. Begun in 1971, the circuit ended with the 1989 World Championship of Tennis. A doubles event was added in 1973 and continued until 1985. From 1986 the doubles event was incorporated into the Masters Doubles. Final round results and prize money can be found in *World of Tennis 1996* and previous issues.

HOPMAN CUP

A mixed team event which takes place annually at the Burswood Resort, Perth, Western Australia. Each tie consists of a men's singles, a ladies' singles and a mixed doubles. Held annually in January. In 1997 became the ITF's official Mixed Teams Championship.

1989 Czechoslovakia d. Australia 2–0: H.Sukova (TCH) d H.Mandlikova (AUS) 6–4 6–3; M.Mecir/Mandlikova (TCH) d P.Cash/Mandlikova (AUS) 6–2 6–4
1990 Spain d. USA 2–1: A.Sanchez-Vicario (ESP) d P.Shriver (USA) 6–3 6–3; E.Sanchez (ESP) d P.McEnroe (USA) 5–7 7–5 7–5; McEnroe/Shriver (USA) d Sanchez/Sanchez-Vicario (ESP) 6–3 6–2
1991 Yugoslavia d. USA 3–0: M.Seles (YUG) d Z.Garrison (USA) 6–1 6–1; G.Prpic (YUG) d D.Wheaton (USA) 4–6 6–3 7–5; Prpic/Seles (YUG) d Wheaton/Garrison 8–3 (pro set)
1992 Switzerland d. Czechoslovakia 2–1: M.Maleeva-Fragniere (SUI) d H.Sukova (TCH) 6–2 6–4; J.Hlasek (SUI) d K.Novacek (TCH) 6–4 6–4; Novacek/Sukova (TCH) d Hlasek/Maleeva-Fragniere (SUI) 8–4 (pro set)
1993 Germany d. Spain 3–0: S.Graf (GER) d A.Sanchez-Vicario (ESP) 6–4 6–3; M.Stich (GER) d E.Sanchez (ESP) 7–5 6–4; Doubles conceded
1994 Czech Republic d. Germany 2–1: J.Novotna (CZE) d A.Huber (GER) 1–6 6–4 6–3; P.Korda (CZE) d B.Karbacher (GER) 6–3 6–3; Karbacher/Huber (GER) d Korda/Novotna (CZE) 8–3 (pro set)
1995 Germany d. Ukraine 3–0: A.Huber (GER) d N.Medvedeva (UKR) 6–4 3–6 6–4; B.Becker (GER) d A.Medvedev (UKR) 6–3 6–7 6–3; Becker/Huber (GER) wo Medvedev/Medvedeva (UKR) (Medvedev injured)
1996 Croatia d Switzerland 2–1: M.Hingis (SUI) d I.Majoli (CRO) 6–3 6–0; G.Ivanisevic (CRO) d M.Rosset (SUI) 7–6 7–5 ; Ivanisevic/Majoli d Rosset/Hingis (SUI) 3–6 7–6 5–5 ret (Rosset injured)
1997 USA d. South Africa 2–1: C. Rubin (USA) d. A. Coetzer (RSA) 7–5 6–2; W. Ferreira (RSA) d. J. Gimelstob (USA) 6–4 7–6; Gimelstob/Rubin (USA) d. Ferreira/Coetzer (RSA) 3–6 6–2 7–5.
1998 Slovak Republic d. France 2–1: M. Pierce (FRA) d. K. Habsudova (SVK) 6–4 7–5; K. Kucera (SVK) d. C. Pioline (FRA) 7–6 6–4; Kucera/Habsudova (SVK) d. Pioline/Pierce (FRA) 6–3 6–4.

ITF VETERAN WORLD CHAMPIONSHIPS

1981 Sao Paulo, Brazil, 21–26 September

MEN

45 Singles	Sven Davidson	(SWE)
45 Doubles	Sven Davidson	(SWE)
	Hugh Stewart	(USA)
55 Singles	Straight Clark	(USA)
55 Doubles	Straight Clark	(USA)
	Torsten Johansson	(SWE)

WOMEN

40 Singles	Estrella De Molina	(ARG)
40 Doubles	Nancy Reed	(USA)
	M A Plante	(USA)
50 Singles	Amelia Cury	(BRA)

1982 Pörtschach, Austria, 7–13 June

45 Singles	Istvan Gulyas	(HUN)
45 Doubles	Jason Morton	(USA)
	Jim Nelson	(USA)
55 Singles	Robert McCarthy	(AUS)
55 Doubles	Adi Hussmuller	(GER)
	Laci Legenstein	(AUT)
60 Singles	Torsten Johansson	(SWE)
60 Doubles	Torsten Johansson	(SWE)
	Albert Ritzenberg	(USA)
65 Singles	Fritz Klein	(USA)
65 Doubles	Fritz Klein	(USA)
	Jean Becker	(FRA)

40 Singles	Renate Drisaldi	(GER)
40 Doubles	Charleen Hillebrand	(USA)
	Nancy Reed	(USA)
50 Singles	Eva Sluytermann	(GER)
50 Doubles	Eva Sluytermann	(GER)
	I Burmester	(GER)

1983 Bahia, Brazil, 7–13 August

45 Singles	Istvan Gulyas	(HUN)
45 Doubles	Klaus Fuhrmann	(GER)
	Folker Seemann	(GER)
55 Singles	Robert McCarthy	(AUS)
55 Doubles	Laci Legenstein	(AUT)
	Adi Hussmuller	(GER)
65 Singles	Ricardo San Martin	(CHI)
65 Doubles	Federico Barboza	(ARG)
	Hector Hugo Pizani	(ARG)

40 Singles	Helga Masthoff	(GER)
40 Doubles	Helga Masthoff	(GER)
	Heide Orth	(GER)
50 Singles	Ines De Pla	(ARG)
50 Doubles	Gladys Barbosa	(ARG)
	Julia Borzone	(ARG)

1984 Cervia, Italy, 23 May–3 June

35 Singles	Jurgen Fassbender	(GER)
35 Doubles	Gene Malin	(USA)
	Armistead Neely	(USA)
45 Singles	Istvan Gulyas	(HUN)
45 Doubles	Klaus Fuhrmann	(GER)
	Folker Seemann	(GER)
55 Singles	Giuseppe Merlo	(ITA)
55 Doubles	Jason Morton	(USA)
	Hugh Stewart	(USA)
65 Singles	Gardnar Mulloy	(USA)
65 Doubles	Gardnar Mulloy	(USA)
	Fritz Klein	(USA)

40 Singles	Helga Masthoff	(GER)
40 Doubles	Helga Masthoff	(GER)
	Heide Orth	(GER)
50 Singles	Clelia Mazzoleni	(ITA)
50 Doubles	Hana Brabenec	(CAN)
	Pam Wearne	(AUS)

1985 Melbourne, Australia, 25–31 March

35 Singles	Jurgen Fassbender	(GER)
35 Doubles	Jurgen Fassbender	(GER)
	Federico Gadoni	(ITA)
45 Singles	Ian Barclay	(AUS)
45 Doubles	Robert Duesler	(USA)
	Jim Nelson	(USA)
55 Singles	Hugh Stewart	(USA)
55 Doubles	Hugh Stewart	(USA)
	Jason Morton	(USA)
65 Singles	Jim Gilchrist	(AUS)
65 Doubles	Fritz Klein	(USA)
	Albert Ritzenberg	(USA)

40 Singles	Heide Orth	(GER)
40 Doubles	Heide Orth	(GER)
	Judy Dalton	(AUS)
50 Singles	Ilse Michael	(GER)
50 Doubles	Ann Fotheringham	(AUS)
	Helen Polkinghorne	(AUS)

1986 Pörtschach, Austria, 16–22 June

35 Singles	Robert Machan	(HUN)
35 Doubles	Jurgen Fassbender	(GER)
	Hans-Joachim Plotz	(GER)
45 Singles	Jorge Lemann	(BRA)
45 Doubles	Jorge Lemann	(BRA)
	Ivo Ribeiro	(BRA)

40 Singles	Helga Masthoff	(GER)
40 Doubles	Helga Masthoff	(GER)
	Heide Orth	(GER)
50 Singles	Shirley Brasher	(GBR)
50 Doubles	Shirley Brasher	(GBR)
	Lorna Cawthorn	(GBR)

MEN			WOMEN		
55 Singles	Lorne Main	(CAN)			
55 Doubles	Bob Howe	(AUS)			
	Russell Seymour	(USA)			
65 Singles	Torsten Johansson	(SWE)			
65 Doubles	Gardnar Mulloy	(USA)			
	Verne Hughes	(USA)			

1987 Garmisch-Partenkirchen, Germany, 15–21 June

35 Singles	Robert Machan	(HUN)	40 Singles	Marie Pinterova	(HUN)
35 Doubles	Robert Machan	(HUN)	40 Doubles	Marie Pinterova	(HUN)
	Jurgen Fassbender	(GER)		Gail Lovera	(FRA)
45 Singles	Giorgio Rohrich	(ITA)	50 Singles	Shirley Brasher	(GBR)
45 Doubles	Hans Gradischnig	(AUT)	50 Doubles	Shirley Brasher	(GBR)
	Peter Pokorny	(AUT)		Lorna Cawthorn	(GBR)
55 Singles	Istvan Gulyas	(HUN)	60 Singles	Dorothy Cheney	(USA)
55 Doubles	Istvan Gulyas	(HUN)	60 Doubles	Dorothy Cheney	(USA)
	Hugh Stewart	(USA)		Cortez Murdock	(USA)
60 Singles	Bob Howe	(AUS)			
60 Doubles	Andreas Stolpa	(GER)			
	Laci Legenstein	(AUT)			
65 Singles	Alex Swetka	(USA)			
65 Doubles	Bernhard Kempa	(GER)			
	Walter Kessler	(GER)			
70 Singles	Fritz Klein	(USA)			
70 Doubles	Gardnar Mulloy	(USA)			
	Verne Hughes	(USA)			

1988 Huntington Beach, California, USA 21–8 August

35 Singles	Alvin Gardiner	(USA)	40 Singles	Marie Pinterova	(HUN)
35 Doubles	Lajos Levai	(GER)	40 Doubles	Rosie Darmon	(FRA)
	Robert Machan	(HUN)		Gail Lovera	(FRA)
45 Singles	Keith Diepraam	(USA)	50 Singles	Dorothy Matthiessen	(USA)
45 Doubles	Friedhelm Krauss	(GER)	50 Doubles	Dorothy Matthiessen	(USA)
	Gunter Krauss	(GER)		Jane Crofford	(USA)
55 Singles	Istvan Gulyas	(HUN)	60 Singles	Virginia Glass	(USA)
55 Doubles	Sven Davidson	(SWE)	60 Doubles	Dorothy Cheney	(USA)
	Hugh Stewart	(USA)		Cortez Murdock	(USA)
60 Singles	Robert McCarthy	(AUS)			
60 Doubles	Robert McCarthy	(AUS)			
	Bob Howe	(AUS)			
65 Singles	Tom Brown	(USA)			
65 Doubles	Lee Hammel	(USA)			
	Bob Sherman	(USA)			
70 Singles	Fritz Klein	(USA)			
70 Doubles	Glen Hippenstiel	(USA)			
	Geoff Young	(USA)			

1989 Vina del Mar, Chile, 22–29 October

35 Singles	Alvaro Fillol	(CHI)	40 Singles	Marie Pinterova	(HUN)
35 Doubles	Robert Machan	(HUN)	40 Doubles	Marie Pinterova	(HUN)
	Lajos levai	(GER)		Heide Orth	(GER)
45 Singles	Harold Elschenbroich	(GER)	50 Singles	Ilse Michael	(GER)
45 Doubles	Bodo Nitsche	(GER)	50 Doubles	Nancy Reed	(USA)
	Gunter Krauss	(GER)		Barbel Allendorf	(GER)
55 Singles	Istvan Gulyas	(HUN)	60 Singles	Betty Pratt	(USA)
55 Doubles	Chuck De Voe	(USA)	60 Doubles	Dorothy Cheney	(USA)
	John Powless	(USA)		Cortez Murdock	(USA)
60 Singles	Robert McCarthy	(AUS)			
60 Doubles	Robert McCarthy	(AUS)			
	Bob Howe	(AUS)			
65 Singles	Armando Vieira	(BRA)			
65 Doubles	Armando Vieira	(BRA)			
	Sergio Verrati	(FRA)			
70 Singles	Albert Ritzenberg	(USA)			
70 Doubles	Albert Ritzenberg	(USA)			
	Fritz Klein	(USA)			

1990 Umag, Yugoslavia, 26 May–3 June

MEN			WOMEN		
35 Singles	Robert Machan	(HUN)	40 Singles	Marie Pinterova	(HUN)
35 Doubles	Robert Machan	(HUN)	40 Doubles	Barbara Mueller	(USA)
	Lajos Levai	(GER)		Louise Cash	(USA)
45 Singles	Harald Elschenbroich	(GER)	50 Singles	Margit Schultze	(ESP)
45 Doubles	Dick Johnson	(USA)	50 Doubles	Kay Schiavinato	(AUS)
	Jiim Parker	(USA)		Jan Blackshaw	(AUS)
55 Singles	Istvan Gulyas	(HUN)	60 Singles	Louise Owen	(USA)
55 Doubles	Ken Sinclair	(CAN)	60 Doubles	Lurline Stock	(AUS)
	Lorne Main	(CAN)		Dulcie Young	(AUS)
60 Singles	Sven Davidson	(SWE)			
60 Doubles	Sven Davidson	(SWE)			
	Hugh Stewart	(USA)			
65 Singles	Robert McCarthy	(AUS)			
65 Doubles	Oskar Jirkovsky	(AUT)			
	Josef Karlhofer	(AUT)			
70 Singles	William Parsons	(USA)			
70 Doubles	Alex Swetka	(USA)			
	Albert Ritzenberg	(USA)			

1991 Perth, Australia, 17–23 May

35 Singles	Paul Torre	(FRA)	40 Singles	Carol Bailey	(USA)
35 Doubles	Yustedjo Traik	(INA)	40 Doubles	Carol Bailey	(USA)
	Atet Wijono	(INA)		Barbara Mueller	(USA)
45 Singles	Don McCormick	(CAN)	50 Singles	Charleen Hillebrand	(USA)
45 Doubles	Bruce Burns	(AUS)	50 Doubles	Betty Whitelaw	(AUS)
	John Weaver	(AUS)		Jan Blackshaw	(AUS)
55 Singles	Peter Froelich	(AUS)	55 Singles	Carol Wood	(USA)
55 Doubles	Gordon Davis	(USA)	55 Doubles	Carol Wood	(USA)
	Herman Ahlers	(USA)		Margaret Kohler	(USA)
60 Singles	Lorne Main	(CAN)	60 Singles	Betty Pratt	(USA)
60 Doubles	Frank Sedgman	(AUS)	60 Doubles	Ruth Illingworth	(GBR)
	Clive Wilderspin	(AUS)		Ann Williams	(GBR)
65 Singles	Robert McCarthy	(AUS)			
65 Doubles	Robert McCarthy	(AUS)			
	Bob Howe	(AUS)			
70 Singles	Robert Sherman	(USA)			
70 Doubles	Verne Hughes	(USA)			
	Merwin Miller	(USA)			

1992 Palermo, Sicily, 17–23 May

35 Singles	Ferrante Rocchi-Landir	(ITA)	35 Singles	Sally Freeman	(GBR)
35 Doubles	Paul French	(GBR)	35 Doubles	Luisa Figueroa	(ARG)
	Stanislav Birner	(CZE)		Oliveira Villani	(BRA)
45 Singles	Rolf Staguhn	(GER)	40 Singles	Marilyn Rasmussen	(AUS)
45 Doubles	Gary Penberthy	(AUS)	40 Doubles	Marilyn Rasmussen	(AUS)
	Bens De Jell	(NED)		Lesley Charles	(GBR)
50 Singles	Jorge Lemann	(BRA)	45 Singles	Marie Pinterova	(HUN)
50 Doubles	Gerhard Schelch	(AUT)	45 Doubles	Marie Pinterova	(HUN)
	Peter Fuchs	(AUT)		Shirley Brasher	(GBR)
55 Singles	Klaus Fuhrmann	(GER)	50 Singles	Charleen Hillebrand	(USA)
55 Doubles	Hugh Stewart	(USA)	50 Doubles	Charleen Hillebrand	(USA)
	Les Dodson	(USA)		Jacqueline Boothman	(GBR)
60 Singles	Werner Mertins	(GER)	55 Singles	Nancy Reed	(USA)
60 Doubles	Ken Sinclair	(CAN)	55 Doubles	Nancy Reed	(USA)
	Lorne Main	(CAN)		Belmar Gunderson	(USA)
65 Singles	Robert McCarthy	(AUS)	60 Singles	Beverley Rae	(AUS)
65 Doubles	Robert McCarthy	(AUS)	60 Doubles	Beverley Rae	(AUS)
	Bob Howe	(AUS)		Astri Hobson	(AUS)
70 Singles	Robert Sherman	(USA)			
70 Doubles	Robert Sherman	(USA)			
	Mario Isidori	(ITA)			
75 Singles	Gaetano Longo	(ITA)			
75 Doubles	Tiverio De Grad	(ROM)			
	Georg Hunger	(GER)			

1993 Barcelona, Spain, 4–11 April

MEN			WOMEN		
35 Singles	Fernando Luna	(ESP)	35 Singles	Jutta Fahlbusch	(GER)
35 Doubles	Steven Packham	(AUS)	35 Doubles	Jutta Fahlbusch	(GER)
	Tony Luttrell	(AUS)		Dagmar Anwar	(GER)
45 Singles	Robert Machan	(HUN)	40 Singles	Maria Geyer	(AUT)
45 Doubles	Robert Machan	(HUN)	40 Doubles	Elizabeth Craig	(AUS)
	Miodrag Mijuca	(GER)		Carol Campling	(AUS)
50 Singles	Jorge Lemann	(BRA)	45 Singles	Marie Pinterova	(HUN)
50 Doubles	James Parker	(USA)	45 Doubles	Marie Pinterova	(HUN)
	Ken Robinson	(USA)		Tuija Hannuakainen	(FIN)
55 Singles	King Van Nostrand	(USA)	50 Singles	Cathie Anderson	(USA)
55 Doubles	King Van Nostrand	(USA)	50 Doubles	Brigitte Hoffman	(GER)
	Juan Manuel Couder	(ESP)		Siegrun Fuhrmann	(GER)
60 Singles	Lorne Main	(CAN)	55 Singles	Roberta Beltrame	(ITA)
60 Doubles	Lorne Main	(CAN)	55 Doubles	Belmar Gunderson	(USA)
	Ken Sinclair	(CAN)		Nancy Reed	(USA)
65 Singles	Jason Morton	(USA)	60 Singles	Nancy Reed	(USA)
65 Doubles	Laci Legenstein	(AUT)	60 Doubles	Marta Pombo	(ESP)
	Hugh Stewart	(USA)		Ana Maria Estalella	(ESP)
70 Singles	Tom Brown	(USA)	65 Singles	Betty Pratt	(USA)
70 Doubles	Tom Brown	(USA)	65 Doubles	Betty Pratt	(USA)
	Buck Archer	(USA)		Betty Cookson	(USA)
75 Singles	Gordon Henley	(AUS)			
75 Doubles	Albert Ritzenberg	(USA)			
	Mirek Kizlink	(GBR)			

1994 (Group A) Buenos Aires, Argentina, 30 October–6 November

35 Singles	Jose Luis Clerc	(ARG)	35 Singles	Jutta Fahlbusch	(GER)
35 Doubles	Jose Luis Clerc	(ARG)	35 Doubles	Marcela De Gregorio	(ARG)
	Victor Pecci	(PAR)		Beatriz Villaverde	(ARG)
45 Singles	Jairo Velasco	(ESP)	45 Singles	Renata Vojtischek	(GER)
45 Doubles	Jairo Velasco	(ESP)	45 Doubles	Tina Karwasky	(USA)
	Thomaz Koch	(BRA)		Susan Stone	(CAN)
50 Singles	James Parker	(USA)	50 Singles	Louise Cash	(USA)
50 Doubles	James Parker	(USA)	50 Doubles	Carol Campling	(AUS)
	Ken Robinson	(USA)		Elizabeth Craig	(AUS)

1994 (Group B) Los Gatos, California, USA 22–29 May

55 Singles	Gil Howard	(USA)	50 Singles	Petro Kruger	(RSA)
55 Doubles	Klaus Fuhrmann	(GER)	50 Doubles	Ellen Bryant	(USA)
	Leslie Dodson	(USA)		Barbara Mueller	(USA)
60 Singles	King Van Nostrand	(USA)	55 Singles	Rosie Darmon	(FRA)
60 Doubles	Russell Seymour	(USA)	55 Doubles	Dorothy Matthiessen	(USA)
	Whitney Reed	(USA)		Lynn Little	(USA)
65 Singles	Jason Morton	(USA)	60 Singles	Ilse Michael	(GER)
65 Doubles	Jason Morton	(USA)	60 Doubles	Nancy Reed	(USA)
	William Davis	(USA)		Belmar Gunderson	(USA)
70 Singles	Oskar Jirkovsky	(AUT)	65 Singles	Louise Owen	(USA)
70 Doubles	Francis Bushmann	(USA)	65 Doubles	Louise Owen	(USA)
	Vincent Fotre	(USA)		Liz Harper	(USA)
75 Singles	Alex Swetka	(USA)			
75 Doubles	Dan Walker	(USA)			
	Verne Hughes	(USA)			

1995 (Group A), Bad Neuenahr, Germany, 6–13 August

35 Singles	Thibaut Kuentz	(FRA)	35 Singles	Regina Marsikova	(CZE)
35 Doubles	Thibaut Kuentz	(FRA)			
	Stephan Medem	(GER)			
45 Singles	Robert Machan	(HUN)	40 Singles	Renata Vojtishek	(GER)
45 Doubles	Armistead Neely	(USA)	40 Doubles	Renata Vojtishek	(GER)
	Larry Turville	(USA)		Tina Karwasky	(USA)
50 Singles	Giorgio Rohrich	(ITA)	45 Singles	Marie Pinterova	(HUN)
50 Doubles	Jody Rush	(USA)	45 Doubles	Elizabeth Craig-Allan	(AUS)
	Richard Johnson	(USA)		Carol Campling	(AUS)

1995 (Group B), Nottingham, England, 21–28 May

MEN			WOMEN		
55 Singles	Len Saputo	(USA)	50 Singles	Charleen Hillebrand	(USA)
55 Doubles	Leslie Dodson	(USA)	50 Doubles	Elly Keocke	(NED)
	Klaus Fuhrmann	(GER)		Jacqueline Boothman	(GBR)
60 Singles	James Nelson	(USA)	55 Singles	Renate Mayer-Zdralek	(GER)
60 Doubles	James Nelson	(USA)	55 Doubles	Carol Wood	(USA)
	Leonard Lindborg	(USA)		Sinclair Bill	(USA)
65 Singles	Lorne Main	(CAN)	60 Singles	Jennifer Hoad	(ESP)
65 Doubles	Lorne Main	(CAN)	60 Doubles	Rita Lauder	(GBR)
	Ken Sinclair	(CAN)		Ruth Illingworth	(GBR)
70 Singles	Oskar Jirkovsky	(AUT)	65 Singles	Betty Pratt	(USA)
70 Doubles	Brian Hurley	(AUS)	65 Doubles	Louise Owen	(USA)
	Neale Hook	(AUS)		Elaine Mason	(USA)
75 Singles	Robert Sherman	(USA)			
75 Doubles	Mirek Kizlink	(GBR)			
	Antony Starling	(GBR)			

1996 (Group A) Velden, Austria 15–22 September 1996

35 Singles	Greg Neuhart	(USA)	35 Singles	Regina Marsikova	(CZE)
35 Doubles	Greg Neuhart	(USA)	35 Doubles	Regina Marsikova	(CZE)
	Mike Fedderly	(USA)		Jutta Fahlbusch	(GER)
40 Singles	Julio Goes	(BRA)	40 Singles	Renata Vojtischek	(GER)
40 Doubles	Julio Goes	(BRA)	40 Doubles	Renata Vojtischek	(GER)
	Harry Ufer	(BRA)		Tina Karwasky	(USA)
45 Singles	Jairo Velasco	(ESP)	45 Singles	Marie Pinterova	(HUN)
45 Doubles	Jairo Velasco	(ESP)	45 Doubles	Marie Pinterova	(HUN)
	Robert Machan	(HUN)		Heide Orth	(GER)
50 Singles	Peter Pokorny	(AUT)	50 Singles	Eva Szabo	(HUN)
50 Doubles	Ted Hoehn	(USA)	50 Doubles	Carol Campling	(AUS)
	Richard Johnson	(USA)		Elizabeth Craig-Allan	(AUS)

1996 (Group B), Vienna, Austria 26 May–2 June 1996

55 Singles	Giorgio Rohrich	(ITA)	55 Singles	Charleen Hillebrand	(USA)
55 Doubles	Peter Pokorny	(AUT)	55 Doubles	Dorothy Matthiessen	(USA)
	Hans Gradischnig	(AUT)		Sinclair Bill	(USA)
60 Singles	King Van Nostrand	(USA)	60 Singles	Ilse Michael	(GER)
60 Doubles	Jim Nelson	(USA)	60 Doubles	Inge Weber	(CAN)
	Bob Duesler	(USA)		Nancy Reed	(USA)
65 Singles	Lorne Main	(CAN)	65 Singles	Ines De Pla	(ARG)
65 Doubles	Lorne Main	(CAN)	65 Doubles	Ruth Illingworth	(GBR)
	Ken Sinclair	(CAN)		Rita Lauder	(GBR)
70 Singles	Fred Kovaleski	(USA)	70 Singles	Betty Pratt	(USA)
70 Doubles	Fred Kovaleski	(USA)	70 Doubles	Betty Pratt	(USA)
	Bob Howe	(AUS)		Elaine Mason	(USA)
75 Singles	Robert Sherman	(USA)			
75 Doubles	Merwin Miller	(USA)			
	Verne Hughes	(USA)			
80 Singles	Dan Miller	(USA)			
80 Doubles	Dan Miller	(USA)			
	Irving Converse	(USA)			

1997 (Group A) Johannesburg, South Africa 21–28 September 1997

35 Singles	Greg Neuhart	(USA)	35 Singles	Tracy Houk	(USA)
35 Doubles	Chris Loock	(RSA)	35 Doubles	Alexi Beggs	(USA)
	Kobus Visagie	(RSA)		Vikki Beggs	(USA)
40 Singles	Pierre Godfroid	(BEL)	40 Singles	Renata Vojtischek	(GER)
40 Doubles	Pierre Godfroid	(BEL)	40 Doubles	Sherri Bronson	(USA)
	Bruce Osborne	(AUS)		Helle Viragh	(USA)
45 Singles	Frank Puncec	(RSA)	45 Singles	Rita Theron	(RSA)
45 Doubles	Max Bates	(AUS)	45 Doubles	Kerry Ballard	(AUS)
	Andrew Rae	(AUS)		Wendy Gilchrist	(AUS)
50 Singles	Jairo Velasco	(ESP)	50 Singles	Marie Pinterova	(HUN)
50 Doubles	Jairo Velasco	(ESP)	50 Doubles	Elizabeth Craig-Allan	(AUS)
	Luis Flor	(ESP)		Carol Campling	(AUS)

1997 (Group B) Newcastle, New South Wales 14–20 April 1997

MEN			WOMEN		
55 Singles	Bob Howes	(AUS)	55 Singles	Heide Orth	(GER)
55 Doubles	Maurice Broom	(AUS)	55 Doubles	Lyn Wayte	(AUS)
	Max Senior	(AUS)		Margaret Wayte	(AUS)
60 Singles	Klaus Fuhrmann	(GER)	60 Singles	Judith Dalton	(AUS)
60 Doubles	Robert Duesler	(USA)	60 Doubles	Lorice Forbes	(AUS)
	Jim Nelson	(USA)		Peg Hoysted	(AUS)
65 Singles	Russell Seymour	(USA)	65 Singles	Beverley Rae	(AUS)
65 Doubles	William Davis	(USA)	65 Doubles	Ruth Illingworth	(GBR)
	Chuck De Voe	(USA)		Rita Lauder	(GBR)
70 Singles	Laci Legenstein	(AUT)	70 Singles	Twinx Rogers	(RSA)
70 Doubles	Laci Legenstein	(AUT)	70 Doubles	Deedy Krebs	(USA)
	Fred Kovaleski	(USA)		Elaine Mason	(USA)
75 Singles	Robert Sherman	(USA)			
75 Doubles	Robert Sherman	(USA)			
	Ellis Williamson	(USA)			
80 Singles	Alex Swetka	(USA)			
80 Doubles	Alex Swetka	(USA)			
	Gordon Henley	(AUS)			

1998 (Group A) Nottingham, England 27 September–4 October 1998

35 Singles	Nick Fulwood	(GBR)	35 Singles	Tracy Houk	(USA)
35 Doubles	Nick Fulwood	(GBR)	35 Doubles	Susanne Turi	(HUN)
	Brad Properjohn	(AUS)		Kathy Vick	(USA)
40 Singles	Pierre Godfroid	(BEL)	40 Singles	Ros Balodis	(AUS)
40 Doubles	Pierre Godfroid	(BEL)	40 Doubles	Ros Balodis	(AUS)
	Bruce Osbourne	(AUS)		Kaye Nealon	(AUS)
45 Singles	Wayne Cowley	(AUS)	45 Singles	Marlie Buehler	(USA)
45 Doubles	Benson Greatrex	(GBR)	45 Doubles	Elizabeth Boyle	(GBR)
	Philip Siviter	(GBR)		Pauline Fisher	(GBR)
50 Singles	Frank Briscoe	(RSA)	50 Singles	Marie Pinterova	(HUN)
50 Doubles	Keith Bland	(GBR)	50 Doubles	Carol Campling	(AUS)
	Richard Tutt	(GBR)		Elizabeth Craig-Allan	(AUS)

1998 (Group B) Palm Beach Gardens, FL, USA 3–10 May 1998

55 Singles	Bob Howes	(AUS)	55 Singles	Heide Orth	(GER)
55 Doubles	Stasys Labanauskas	(LIT)	55 Doubles	Heide Orth	(GER)
	Peter Pokorny	(AUT)		Rosy Darmon	(FRA)
60 Singles	Bodo Nitsche	(GER)	60 Singles	Judith Dalton	(AUS)
60 Doubles	Henry Leichtfried	(USA)	60 Doubles	Belmar Gunderson	(USA)
	Leonard Lindborg	(USA)		Katie Koontz	(USA)
65 Singles	Jim Perley	(USA)	65 Singles	Clelia Mazzoleni	(ITA)
65 Doubles	Lorne Main	(CAN)	65 Doubles	Astri Hobson	(AUS)
	Kenneth Sinclair	(CAN)		Margaret Robinson	(AUS)
70 Singles	Jason Morton	(USA)	70 Singles	Betty Eisenstein	(USA)
70 Doubles	Jason Morton	(USA)	70 Doubles	Phyllis Adler	(USA)
	Fred Kovaleski	(USA)		Elaine Mason	(USA)
75 Singles	Robert Sherman	(USA)	80 Singles	Alex Swetka	(USA)
75 Doubles	Fran Bushmann	(USA)	80 Doubles	Irving Converse	(USA)
	George Druliner	(USA)		Dan Miller	(USA)

ITALIA CUP

International Men's Team Competition for 35 year age group.

	VENUE	*WINNERS*	*RUNNERS-UP*	*FINAL SCORE*
1982	Cervia (ITA)	Italy	USA	2–1
1983	Cervia (ITA)	West Germany	USA	2–1
1984	Brand (AUT)	West Germany	France	2–1
1985	Reggio Calabria (ITA)	USA	Italy	2–0
1986	Bagnoles De l'Orne (FRA)	West Germany	USA	3–0
1987	Grado (ITA)	USA	Austria	2–1
1988	Bol (YUG)	West Germany	USA	3–0
1989	Mainz (FRG)	West Germany	USA	3–0
1990	Glasgow (GBR)	Spain	Australia	2–1

	VENUE	WINNERS	RUNNERS-UP	FINAL SCORE
1991	Melbourne (AUS)	Australia	Spain	3–0
1992	Ancona, (ITA)	Italy	France	2–1
1993	Barcelona (ESP)	Spain	France	3–0
1994	Rosario, Argentina (ARG)	Germany	USA	2–1
1995	Dormagen (GER)	Germany	USA	2–1
1996	Rome (ITA)	USA	Italy	2–1
1997	Johannesburg (RSA)	USA	Great Britain	2–1
1998	Winchester (GBR)	Great Britain	Italy	2–1

DUBLER CUP

International Men's Team Competition for 45 year age group.

FINALS

	VENUE	WINNERS	RUNNERS-UP	FINAL SCORE
1958	Monte Carlo (FRA)	Italy	West Germany	3–1
1959	Bad Ischl (AUT)	Switzerland	Italy	4–1
1960	Bad Gastain (AUT)	Italy	Switzerland	5–0
1961	Ancona (ITA)	Italy	Austria	4–1
1962	Merano (ITA)	Italy	France	3–2
1963	Merano (FRA)	Italy	Belgium	4–1
1964	Merano (FRA)	Italy	West Germany	5–0
1965	Merano (FRA)	Italy	Sweden	3–0
1966	Florence (ITA)	Sweden	Italy	4–1
1967	Avesta (SWE)	France	Sweden	3–2
1968	Paris (FRA)	USA	France	5–0
1969	St Louis (USA)	USA	Sweden	4–1
1970	Cleveland (USA)	USA	Sweden	4–1
1971	La Costa (USA)	USA	Sweden	3–2
1972	Le Touquet (FRA)	USA	France	4–1
1973	London (GBR)	Australia	USA	3–1
1974	New York (USA)	USA	Australia	3–2
1975	London (GBR)	Australia	USA	5–0
1976	Alassio (ITA)	Italy	Canada	3–2
1977	Barcelona (ESP)	USA	France	4–1
1978	Le Touquet (FRA)	USA	Australia	4–1
1979	Vienna (AUT)	Austria	USA	3–2
1980	Cervia (ITA)	Sweden	Austria	2–1
1981	Buenos Aires (ARG)	USA	Great Britain	2–1
1982	Athens (GRE)	USA	Great Britain	2–1
1983	New York (USA)	USA	West Germany	2–1
1984	Bastad (SWE)	West Germany	USA	3–0
1985	Perth (AUS)	West Germany	Australia	2–1
1986	Berlin (GER)	West Germany	Switzerland	3–0
1987	Portschach (AUT)	Italy	Austria	2–1
1988	Huntington Beach (USA)	USA	West Germany	3–0
1989	Montevideo (URU)	USA	West Germany	2–1
1990	Bol (YUG)	Germany	USA	2–1
1991	Sydney (AUS)	USA	Germany	3–0
1992	Portschach (AUT)	Germany	Spain	2–1
1993	Barcelona (ESP)	Spain	France	2–1
1994	Santiago (CHI)	USA	Chile	2–1
1995	Saarbrucken (GER)	USA	Germany	2–1
1996	Velden (AUT)	USA	Australia	3–0
1997	Pretoria (RSA)	Austria	South Africa	2–1
1998	Dublin (IRL)	USA	Spain	2–1

** From 1958 to 1979 the early rounds were played zonally*

FRED PERRY CUP

International Men's Team Competition for 50 year age group.

	VENUE	WINNERS	RUNNERS-UP	FINAL SCORE
1991	Bournemouth (GBR)	Germany	Great Britain	3–0
1992	Berlin (GER)	Germany	USA	3–0
1993	Royan (FRA)	Germany	USA	2–1

	VENUE	WINNERS	RUNNERS-UP	FINAL SCORE
1994	Buenos Aires (ARG)	France	USA	2–1
1995	Luchow (GER)	France	Germany	2–1
1996	Pörtschach (AUT)	Germany	Austria	2–1
1997	Sun City (RSA)	Spain	Germany	2–1
1998	Glasgow (GBR)	USA	Spain	2–1

AUSTRIA CUP

International Men's Team Competition for 55 year age group.

	VENUE	WINNERS	RUNNERS-UP	FINAL SCORE
1977	Baden (AUT)	Great Britain	Austria	2–1
1978	Brand (AUT)	USA	Sweden	2–1
1979	Brand (AUT)	USA	Sweden	3–0
1980	Brand (AUT)	USA	Sweden	2–1
1981	Portschach (AUT)	USA	Sweden	3–0
1982	Cervia (ITA)	Australia	USA	2–1
1983	New York (USA)	Australia	USA	2–1
1984	Pörtschach (AUT)	USA	Australia	2–1
1985	Perth (AUS)	Australia	USA	3–0
1986	Pörtschach (AUT)	Australia	Canada	2–1
1987	Umag (YUG)	Canada	Australia	3–0
1988	Huntington Beach (USA)	Canada	West Germany	3–0
1989	Buenos Aires (ARG)	Canada	USA	2–1
1990	Pörtschach (AUT)	Canada	USA	3–0
1991	Sydney (AUS)	USA	Australia	3–0
1992	Monte Carlo (FRA)	Germany	USA	3–0
1993	Murcia (ESP)	USA	Australia	3–0
1994	Carmel Valley (USA)	Australia	USA	2–1
1995	Dublin (IRL)	Germany	Austria	2–1
1996	Pörtschach (AUT)	Austria	USA	2–1
1997	Canberra (AUS)	Austria	Germany	2–1
1998	Naples (USA)	USA	Netherlands	3–0

GOTTFRIED VON CRAMM CUP

International Men's Team Competition for 60 year age group.

	VENUE	WINNERS	RUNNERS-UP	FINAL SCORE
1989	Kempten (GER)	Australia	New Zealand	3–0
1990	Ontario (CAN)	USA	Austria	2–1
1991	Adelaide (AUS)	USA	New Zealand	2–1
1992	Bournemouth (GBR)	Canada	USA	2–1
1993	Aix les Bains (FRA)	USA	France	3–0
1994	Burlingame (USA)	USA	Germany	3–0
1995	Pörtschach (AUT)	USA	Germany	3–0
1996	Velden (AUT)	USA	France	3–0
1997	Hamilton (NZL)	USA	Australia	3–0
1998	Fort Lauderdale (USA)	Germany	USA	2–1

BRITANNIA CUP

International Men's Team Competition for 65 year age group.

	VENUE	WINNERS	RUNNERS-UP	FINAL SCORE
1979	London (GBR)	USA	Great Britain	3–0
1980	Frinton-on-Sea (GBR)	USA	Sweden	3–0
1981	London (GBR)	USA	Sweden	3–0
1982	New York (USA)	USA	Canada	3–0
1983	Pörtschach (AUT)	USA	Australia	3–0
1984	Pörtschach (AUT)	USA	Australia	3–0
1985	Pörtschach (AUT)	USA	Australia	3–0
1986	Bournemouth (GBR)	USA	Norway	3–0
1987	Bastad (SWE)	USA	Sweden	2–1
1988	Huntington Beach (USA)	USA	France	3–0
1989	Umag (CRO)	USA	France	3–0

	VENUE	WINNERS	RUNNERS-UP	FINAL SCORE
1990	Bournemouth (GBR)	USA	Australia	2–1
1991	Canberra (AUS)	Austria	Australia	2–1
1992	Seefeld (AUT)	Australia	Austria	2–1
1993	Le Touquet (FRA)	USA	Italy	2–1
1994	Portola Valley (USA)	USA	Austria	2–1
1995	Glasgow (GBR)	USA	Canada	2–1
1996	Villach (AUT)	USA	Canada	2–1
1997	Hamilton (NZL)	USA	Canada	2–1
1998	Palm Beach Gardens (USA)	Canada	USA	3–0

CRAWFORD CUP

International Men's Team Competition for 70 year age group.

	VENUE	WINNERS	RUNNERS-UP	FINAL SCORE
1983	Brand (AUT)	USA	Sweden	3–0
1984	Helsinki (FIN)	USA	Great Britain	3–0
1985	Brand (AUT)	USA	Australia	3–0
1986	Seefeld (AUT)	USA	France	3–0
1987	Pörtschach (AUT)	USA	Great Britain	3–0
1988	Keszthely (HUN)	USA	Great Britain	3–0
1989	Bol (YUG)	USA	Brazil	3–0
1990	Brand (AUT)	USA	Brazil	3–0
1991	Canberra (AUS)	Germany	USA	2–1
1992	Le Touquet (FRA)	USA	Germany	3–0
1993	Menorca (ESP)	USA	France	3–0
1994	Oakland (USA)	Australia	France	2–1
1995	Aix-les-Bains (FRA)	USA	Australia	2–1
1996	Seeboden (AUT)	Austria	USA	2–1
1997	Adelaide (AUS)	Austria	USA	2–1
1998	Pompano Beach (USA)	USA	Austria	2–1

BITSY GRANT CUP

International Men's Team Competition for 75 year age group.

	VENUE	WINNERS	RUNNERS-UP	FINAL SCORE
1994	Mill Valley (USA)	USA	Mexico	3–0
1995	Bournemouth (GBR)	USA	Sweden	3–0
1996	Bad Waltersdorf (AUT)	USA	Germany	3–0
1997	Hobart, Tasmania (AUS)	USA	Australia	3–0
1998	Boca Raton (USA)	USA	Australia	3–0

GARDNAR MULLOY CUP

International Men's Team Competition for 80 year age group.

	VENUE	WINNERS	RUNNERS-UP	FINAL SCORE
1996	Seefeld (AUT)	USA	Mexico	Round Robin
1997	Melbourne (AUS)	USA	Australia	Round Robin
1998	Naples (USA)	USA	Australia	Round Robin

YOUNG CUP

International Women's Team Competition for 40 year age group.

	VENUE	WINNERS	RUNNERS-UP	FINAL SCORE
1977	Malmo (SWE)	Argentina	Germany	3–0
1978	Ancona (ITA)	Italy	Germany	3–0
1979	Cannes (FRA)	West Germany	USA	3–0
1980	Bad Wiessee (GER)	West Germany	Italy	3–0
1981	Bad Wiessee (GER)	France	Italy	2–1
1982	Brand (AUT)	France	Italy	3–0
1983	Cervia (ITA)	West Germany	France	2–1
1984	Cervia (ITA)	USA	France	3–0
1985	Pörtschach (AUT)	West Germany	France	3–0
1986	Brand (AUT)	West Germany	USA	2–1
1987	Venice (ITA)	France	USA	2–1

	VENUE	WINNERS	RUNNERS-UP	FINAL SCORE
1988	Bagnoles De l'Orne (FRA)	Great Britain	West Germany	3–0
1989	Pörtschach (AUT)	France	West Germany	3–0
1990	Keszthely (HUN)	France	USA	3–0
1991	Brisbane (AUS)	Australia	Germany	2–1
1992	Macahide (IRE)	Great Britain	Australia	2–1
1993	Bournemouth (GBR)	USA	Great Britain	2–1
1994	Montivideo (URU)	USA	Germany	2–1
1995	Dortmund (GER)	USA	Germany	2–1
1996	Bad Hofgastein (AUT)	USA	Germany	2–1
1997	Pretoria (RSA)	USA	Germany	3–0
1998	Halton (GBR)	USA	South Africa	3–0

MARGARET COURT CUP

International Women's Team Competition for 45 year age group.

	VENUE	WINNERS	RUNNERS-UP	FINAL SCORE
1994	Perth (AUS)	France	USA	2–1
1995	Gladbeck (GER)	USA	Australia	3–0
1996	Seeboden (AUT)	USA	South Africa	2–1
1997	Pretoria (RSA)	USA	France	3–0
1998	Warwick (GBR)	USA	South Africa	2–1

MARIA ESTHER BUENO CUP

International Women's Team Competition for 50 year age group.

	VENUE	WINNERS	RUNNERS-UP	FINAL SCORE
1983	Pörtschach (AUT)	Great Britain	USA	2–1
1984	Le Touquet (FRA)	USA	France	3–0
1985	Bremen (GER)	USA	Great Britain	3–0
1986	Brand (AUT)	USA	Great Britain	2–1
1987	Helsinki (FIN)	USA	Great Britain	2–1
1988	Bahia (BRA)	USA	Canada	2–1
1989	Bournemouth (GBR)	USA	Great Britain	2–1
1990	Barcelona (ESP)	Australia	Spain	2–1
1991	Perth (AUS)	USA	France	3–0
1992	Bagnoles De L'Orne (FRA)	USA	France	2–1
1993	Barcelona (ESP)	USA	Germany	2–1
1994	San Francisco (USA)	USA	Germany	3–0
1995	Velden (AUT)	Netherlands	USA	2–1
1996	St. Kanzian (AUT)	Australia	Germany	2–1
1997	Pretoria (RSA)	Australia	Germany	2–1
1998	Dublin (IRL)	USA	Australia	2–1

MAUREEN CONNOLLY CUP

International Women's Team Competition for 55 year age group.

	VENUE	WINNERS	RUNNERS-UP	FINAL SCORE
1992	Tyler (USA)	Australia	Great Britain	2–1
1993	Corsica (FRA)	USA	France	3–0
1994	Carmel (USA)	USA	France	2–1
1995	Le Touquet (FRA)	France	South Africa	2–1
1996	Eugendorf (AUT)	France	USA	2–1
1997	Canberra (AUS)	USA	France	3–0
1998	Pompano Beach (USA)	Germany	Great Britain	3–0

ALICE MARBLE CUP

International Women's Team Competition for 60 year age group.

	VENUE	WINNERS	RUNNERS-UP	FINAL SCORE
1988	Pörtschach (AUT)	USA	West Germany	3–0
1989	Brand (AUT)	USA	West Germany	2–1
1990	Paderborn (GER)	USA	Germany	2–1
1991	Perth (AUS)	USA	Great Britain	3–0

	VENUEWINNERS	RUNNERS-UP	FINAL SCORE	
1992	Keszthely (HUN)	Great Britain	USA	2–1
1993	Pörtschach (AUT)	USA	Great Britain	2–1
1994	Carmel Valley (USA)	USA	Great Britain	2–1
1995	Worthing (GBR)	USA	Spain	2–1
1996	Bad Hofgastein (AUT)	USA	Spain	3–0
1997	Adelaide (AUS)	USA	Canada	3–0
1998	Boca Raton (USA)	Australia	USA	2–1

KITTY GODFREE CUP

International Women's Team Competition for 65 year age group.

	VENUE	WINNERS	RUNNERS-UP	FINAL SCORE
1995	Bournemouth (GBR)	USA	Canada	2–1
1996	Brand (AUT)	Great Britain	USA	2–1
	VENUE	WINNERS	RUNNERS-UP	FINAL SCORE
1997	Melbourne (AUS)	Great Britain	USA	2–1
1998	Fort Lauderdale (USA)	Great Britain	USA	2–1

ALTHEA GIBSON CUP

International Women's Team Competition for 70 year age group.

	VENUE	WINNERS	RUNNERS-UP	FINAL SCORE
1998	Palm Beach Gardens (USA)	USA	Germany	Round Robin

AUSTRALIAN INTERNATIONAL JUNIOR CHAMPIONSHIPS

BOYS' SINGLES

1946 F. A. Sedgman
1947 D. Candy
1948 K. B. McGregor
1949 C. Wilderspin
1950 K. R. Rosewall
1951 L. Hoad
1952 K. Rosewall
1953 W. Gilmour
1954 W. A. Knight (GBR)
1955 G. Moss
1956 R. Mark
1957 R. G. Laver
1958 M. Mulligan
1959 E. Buchholz (USA)
1960 W. Coghlan
1961 J. D. Newcombe
1962 J. D. Newcombe
1963 J. D. Newcombe
1964 A. Roche
1965 G. Goven (FRA)
1966 K. Coombes
1967 B. Fairlie (NZL)
1968 P. Dent
1969 A. McDonald
1970 J. Alexander
1971 C. Letcher
1972 P. Kronk
1973 P. McNamee

	WINNER	RUNNER-UP	SCORE		
1974	H. Brittain (AUS)				
1975	B. Drewett (AUS)				
1976	R. Kelly (AUS)	J. Dilouie (USA)	6–2	6–4	
1977	(Jan.) B. Drewett (AUS)	T. Wilkison (USA)	6–4	7–6	
1977	(Dec.) R. Kelly (AUS)				
1978	P. Serrett (AUS)	C. Johnstone (AUS)	6–4	6–3	
1979	G. Whitecross (AUS)	C. Miller (AUS)	6–4	6–3	
1980	C. Miller (AUS)	W. Masur (AUS)	7–6	6–2	
1981	J. Windahl (SWE)	P. Cash (AUS)	6–4	6–4	
1982	M. Kratzman (AUS)	S. Youl (AUS)	6–3	7–5	
1983	S. Edberg (SWE)	S. Youl (AUS)	6–4	6–4	
1984	M. Kratzman (AUS)	P. Flyn (AUS)	6–4	6–1	
1985	S. Barr (AUS)	S. Furlong (AUS)	7–6	6–7	6–3
1986	*Not held*				
1987	J. Stoltenberg (AUS)	T. Woodbridge (AUS)	6–2	7–6	
1988	J. Anderson (AUS)	A. Florent (AUS)	7–5	7–6	
1989	N. Kulti (SWE)	T. Woodbridge (AUS)	6–2	6–0	
1990	D. Dier (GER)	L. Paes (IND)	6–4	7–6	
1991	T. Enqvist (SWE)	S. Gleeson (AUS)	7–6	6–7	6–1
1992	G. Doyle (AUS)	B. Dunn (USA)	6–2	6–0	
1993	J. Baily (GBR)	S. Downs (NZL)	6–3	6–2	
1994	B. Ellwood (AUS)	A. Illie (AUS)	5–7	6–3	6–3
1995	N. Kiefer (GER)	J-M Lee (KOR)	6–4	6–4	
1996	B. Rehnqvist (SWE)	M. Hellstrom (SWE)	2–6	6–2	7–5
1997	D. Elsner (GER)	W. Whitehouse (RSA)	7–6	6–2	
1998	J. Jeanpierre (FRA)	A. Vinciguerra (SWE)	4–6	6–4	6–3

GIRLS' SINGLES

1946	S. Grant	1956	L. Coghlan	1965	K. Melville
1947	J. Tuckfield	1957	M. Rayson	1966	K. Krantzcke
1948	B. Penrose	1958	J. Lehane	1967	A. Kenny
1949	J. Warnock	1959	J. Lehane	1968	L. Hunt
1950	B. McIntyre	1960	L. Turner	1969	L. Hunt
1951	M. Carter	1961	R. Ebbern	1970	E. Goolagong
1952	M. Carter	1962	R. Ebbern	1971	P. Coleman
1953	J. Staley	1963	R. Ebbern	1972	P. Coleman
1954	E. Orton	1964	K. Dening	1973	C. O'Neill
1955	E. Orton				

	WINNER	*RUNNER-UP*	*SCORE*		
1974	J. Walker (AUS)				
1975	S. Barker (GBR)	C. O'Neill (AUS)	6–2	7–6	
WINNER		*RUNNER-UP*	*SCORE*		
1976	S. Saliba (AUS)	J. Fenwick (AUS)	2–6	6–3	6–4
1977	(Jan.) P. Bailey (AUS)	A. Tobin (AUS)	6–2	6–3	
1977	(Dec.) A. Tobin (AUS)	L. Harrison (AUS)	6–1	6–2	
1978	E. Little (AUS)	S. Leo (AUS)	6–1	6–2	
1979	A. Minter (AUS)	S. Leo (AUS)	6–4	6–3	
1980	A. Minter (AUS)	E. Sayers (AUS)	6–4	6–2	
1981	A. Minter (AUS)	C. Vanier (FRA)	6–4	6–2	
1982	A. Brown (GBR)	P. Paradis (FRA)	6–3	6–4	
1983	A. Brown (GBR)	B. Randall (AUS)	7–6	6–3	
1984	A. Croft (GBR)	H. Dahlstrom (SWE)	6–0	6–1	
1985	J. Byrne (AUS)	L. Field (AUS)	6–1	6–3	
1986	*Not held*				
1987	M. Jaggard (AUS)	N. Provis (AUS)	6–2	6–4	
1988	J. Faull (AUS)	E. Derly (FRA)	6–4	6–4	
1989	K. Kessaris (USA)	A. Farley (USA)	6–1	6–2	
1990	M. Maleeva (BUL)	L. Stacey (AUS)	7–5	6–7	6–1
1991	N. Pratt (AUS)	K. Godridge (AUS)	6–4	6–3	
1992	J. Limmer (AUS)	L. Davenport (USA)	7–5	6–2	
1993	H. Rusch (GER)	A. Glass (GER)	6–1	6–2	
1994	T. Musgrave (AUS)	B. Schett (AUT)	4–6	6–4	6–2
1995	S. Drake-Brockman (AUS)	A. Elwood (AUS)	6–3	4–6	7–5
1996	M. Grzybowska (POL)	N. Dechy (FRA)	6–1	4–6	6–1
1997	M. Lucic (CRO)	M.Weingartner (GER)	6–2	6–2	
1998	J. Kostanic (CRO)	W. Prakusya (INA)	6–0	7–5	

BOYS' DOUBLES

	WINNERS	*RUNNERS-UP*	*SCORE*		
1983	J. Harty (AUS)/D. Tyson (AUS)	A. Lane (AUS)/D. Cahill (AUS)	3–6	6–4	6–3
1984	M. Kratzman (AUS)/M. Baroch (AUS)	B. Custer (AUS)/D. Macpherson (AUS)	6–2	5–7	7–5
1985	B. Custer (AUS)/D. Macpherson (AUS)	C. Suk (TCH)/P. Korda (TCH)	7–5	6–2	
1986	*Not held*				
1987	J. Stoltenberg (AUS)/T. Woodbridge (AUS)	S. Barr (AUS)/D. Roe (AUS)	6–2	6–4	
1988	J. Stoltenberg (AUS)/T. Woodbridge (AUS)	J. Anderson (AUS)/R. Fromberg (AUS)	6–3	6–2	
1989	J. Anderson (AUS)/T. Woodbridge (AUS)	J. Morgan (AUS)/A. Kratzmann (AUS)	6–4	6–2	
1990	R. Petterson (SWE)/M. Renstroem (SWE)	R. Janecek (CAN)/E.Munoz De Cote (MEX)	4–6	7–6	6–1
1991	G. Doyle (AUS)/J. Eagle (AUS)	J. Holmes (AUS)/P. Kilderry (AUS)	7–6	6–4	
1992	G. Doyle (AUS)/B. Sceney (AUS)	L. Carrington (USA)/J. Thompson (USA)	6–4	6–4	
1993	L. Rehmann (GER)/C. Tambue (GER)	S. Humphries (USA)/J. Jackson (USA)	6–7	7–5	6–2
1994	B. Ellwood (AUS)/M. Philippoussis (AUS)	J. Delgado (GBR)/R. Kukal (SVK)	4–6	6–2	6–1
1995	L. Borgeois (AUS)/J.-M. Lee (KOR)	N. Kiefer (GER)/U. Seetzen (GER)	6–2	6–1	
1996	D. Bracciali (ITA)/J.-Robichaud (CAN)	M. Lee (GBR)/ J. Trotman (GBR)	6–2	6–4	
1997	D. Sherwood (GBR)/J. Trotman (GBR)	J. Van Der Westhuizen (RSA)/ W. Whitehouse (RSA)	7–6	6–3	
1998	J. Haehnel (FRA)/J. Jeanpierre (FRA)	M. Pehar (CRO)/L. Zovko (CRO)	6–3	6–3	

GIRLS' DOUBLES

	WINNERS	RUNNERS-UP	SCORE		
1983	B. Randall (AUS)/K. Ștaunton (AUS)	J. Byrne (AUS)/J. Thompson (AUS)	3–6	6–3	6–3
1984	L. Field (AUS)/L. Savchenko (URS)	M. Parun (NZL)/J. Masters (AUS)	7–6	6–2	
1985	J. Byrne (AUS)/J. Thompson (AUS)	A. Scott (AUS)/S. McCann (AUS)	6–0	6–3	

	WINNERS	RUNNERS-UP	SCORE		
1986	*Not held*				
1987	N. Provis (AUS)/A. Devries (BEL)	D. Jones (AUS)/G. Dwyer (AUS)	6–3	6–1	
1988	R. McQuillan (AUS)/J. Faull (AUS)	R. Stubbs (AUS)/K. McDonald (AUS)	6–1	7–5	
1989	A. Strnadova (TCH)/E. Sviglerova (TCH)	N. Pratt (AUS)/A. Woolcock (AUS)	6–2	6–0	
1990	L. Zaltz (ISR)/R. Mayer (ISR)	J. Hodder (AUS)/N. Pratt (AUS)	6–4	6–4	
1991	K. Habsudova (TCH/B. Rittner (GER)	J. Limmer (AUS)/A. Woolcock (AUS)	6–2	6–0	
1992	L. Davenport (USA)/N. London (USA)	M. Avotins (AUS)/J. Limmer (AUS)	6–2	7–5	
1993	J. Manta (SUI)/L. Richterova (TCH)	A. Carlsson (SWE)/C. Cristea (ROM)	6–3	6–2	
1994	C. Morariu (USA)/L. Varmuzov (CZE)	Y. Basting(NED)/A. Scheider(GER)	7–5	2–6	7–5
1995	C. Morariu (USA)/L. Varmuzov (CZE)	S. Obata(JPN)/N. Urabe (JPN)	6–1	6–2	
1996	M. Pastikova (CZE)/J. Schonfeldova (CZE)	O. Barabanschikova (BLR)/M. Lucic (CRO)	6–1	6–3	
1997	M. Lucic (CRO)/J. Wohr (GER)	Y-J. Cho (KOR)/S. Hisamatsu (JPN)	6–2	6–2	
1998	E. Dominikovic (AUS)/A. Molik (AUS)	L. Baker (NZL)/R. Hudson (NZL)	6–3	3–6	6–2

FRENCH INTERNATIONAL JUNIOR CHAMPIONSHIPS

BOYS' SINGLES

	WINNER	*RUNNER-UP*	*SCORE*		
1974	C. Casa (FRA)	U. Marten (GER)	2–6	6–1	6–4
1975	C. Roger–Vasselin (FRA)	P. Elter (GER)	6–1	6–2	
1976	H. Gunthardt (SUI)	J. L. Clerc (ARG)	4–6	7–6	6–4
1977	J. P. McEnroe (USA)	R. Kelly (AUS)	6–1	6–1	
1978	I. Lendl (TCH)	P. Hjertquist (SWE)	7–6	6–4	
1979	R. Krishnan (IND)	B. Testerman (USA)	2–6	6–1	6–0
1980	H. Leconte (FRA)	A. Tous (ESP)	7–6	6–3	
1981	M. Wilander (SWE)	J. Brown (USA)	7–5	6–1	
1982	T. Benhabiles (FRA)	L. Courteau (FRA)	7–6	6–2	
1983	S. Edberg (SWE)	F. Fevrier (FRA)	6–4	7–6	
1984	K. Carlsson (SWE)	M. Kratzman (AUS)	6–3	6–3	
1985	J. Yzaga (PER)	T. Muster (AUT)	2–6	6–3	6–0
1986	G. Perez Roldan (ARG)	S. Grenier (FRA)	4–6	6–3	6–2
1987	G. Perez Roldan (ARG)	J. Stoltenberg (AUS)	6–3	3–6	6–1
1988	N. Pereira (VEN)	M. Larsson (SWE)	7–6	6–3	
1989	F. Santoro (FRA)	J. Palmer (USA)	6–3	3–6	9–7
1990	A. Gaudenzi (ITA)	T. Enqvist (SWE)	2–6	7–6	6–4
1991	A. Medvedev (URS)	T. Enqvist (SWE)	6–4	7–6	
1992	A. Pavel (ROM)	M. Navarra (ITA)	7–6	6–3	
1993	R. Carretero (ESP)	A. Costa (ESP)	6–0	7–6	
1994	J. Diaz (ESP)	G. Galimberti (ITA)	6–3	7–6	
1995	M. Zabaleta (ARG)	M. Puerta (ARG)	6–2	6–3	
1996	A. Martin (ESP)	B. Rehnqvist (SWE)	6–3	7–6	
1997	D. Elsner (GER)	L. Horna (PER)	6–4	6–4	
1998	F. Gonzalez (CHI)	J. Ferrero (ESP)	4–6	6–4	6–3

GIRLS' SINGLES

	WINNER	*RUNNER-UP*	*SCORE*		
1974	M. Simionescu (ROM)	S. Barker (GBR)	6–3	6–3	
1975	R. Marsikova (TCH)	L. Mottram (GBR)	6–3	5–7	6–2
1976	M. Tyler (GBR)	M. Zoni (ITA)	6–1	6–3	
1977	A. E. Smith (USA)	H. Strachanova (TCH)	6–3	7–6	
1978	H. Mandlikova (TCH)	M. Rothschild (FRG)	6–1	6–1	
1979	L. Sandin (SWE)	M. L. Piatek (USA)	6–3	6–1	
1980	K. Horvath (USA)	K. Henry (USA)	6–2	6–2	
1981	B. Gadusek (USA)	H. Sukova (TCH)	6–7	6–1	6–4
1982	M. Maleeva (BUL)	P. Barg (USA)	7–5	6–2	
1983	P. Paradis (FRA)	D. Spence (USA)	7–6	6–3	
1984	G. Sabatini (ARG)	K. Maleeva (BUL)	6–3	5–7	6–3
1985	L. Garrone (ITA)	D. Van Rensburg (RSA)	6–1	6–3	
1986	P. Tarabini (ARG)	N. Provis (AUS)	6–3	6–3	
1987	N. Zvereva (URS)	J. Pospisilova(TCH)	6–1	6–0	
1988	J. Halard (FRA)	A. Farley (USA)	6–2	4–6	7–5
1989	J. Capriati (USA)	E. Sviglerova (TCH)	6–4	6–0	
1990	M. Maleeva (BUL)	T. Ignatieva (URS)	6–2	6–3	
1991	A. Smashnova (ISR)	I. Gorrochategui (ARG)	2–6	7–5	6–1
1992	R. De Los Rios (PAR)	P. Suarez (ARG)	6–4	6–0	
1993	M. Hingis(SUI)	L. Courtois (BEL)	7–5	7–5	

	WINNER	RUNNER-UP	SCORE		
1994	M. Hingis (SUI)	S. Jeyaseelan (CAN)	6–3	6–1	
1995	A. Cocheteux (FRA)	M. Weingartner (GER)	7–5	6–4	
1996	A. Mauresmo (FRA)	M. Shaughnessy (USA)	6–0	6–4	
1997	J. Henin (BER)	C. Black (ZIM)	4–6	6–4	6–4
1998	N. Petrova (RUS)	J. Dokic (AUS)	6–3	6–3	

BOYS' DOUBLES

	WINNERS	RUNNERS-UP	SCORE		
1983	M. Kratzman (AUS)/S. Youl (AUS)	A. Chesnokov (URS)/A. Olhovskiy (URS)	6–2	6–3	
1985	P. Korda (TCH)/C. Suk (TCH)	V. Godrichidze (URS)/V. Volkov (URS)	4–6	6–0	7–5
1986	F. Davin (ARG)/G. Perez-Roldan (ARG)	T. Carbonell (ESP)/J. Sanchez (ESP)	7–5	5–7	6–3
1987	J. Courier (USA)/J. Stark (USA)	F. Davin (ARG)/G. Perez-Roldan (ARG)	6–7	6–4	6–3
1988	J. Stoltenberg (AUS)/T. Woodbridge (AUS)	C. Caratti (ITA)/G. Ivanisevic (YUG)	7–6	7–5	
1989	J. Anderson (AUS)/T. Woodbridge (AUS)	L. Herrera (MEX)/M. Knowles (BAH)	6–3	4–6	6–2
1990	S. La Reau (CAN)/P. Le Blanc (CAN)	C. Marsh (RSA)/M. Ondruska (RSA)	7–6	6–7	9–7
1991	T. Enqvist (SWE)/M. Martinelle (SWE)	J. Knowle (AUT)/J. Unterberger (AUT)	6–1	6–3	
1992	E. Abaroa (MEX)/G. Doyle (AUS)	Y. Kafelnikov (CIS)/A. Radulescu (ROM)	7–6	6–3	
1993	S. Downs (NZL)/J. Greenhalgh (NZL)	N. Godwin (RSA)/G. Williams (RSA)	6–1	6–1	
1994	G. Kuerten (BRA)/N. Lapentti (ECU)	M. Boye (FRA)/N. Escude (FRA)	6–2	6–4	
1995	R. Sluiter (NED)/P. Wessels (NED)	J. Gimelstob (USA)/R. Wolters (USA)	7–6	7–5	
1996	S. Grosjean (FRA)/O. Mutis (FRA)	J. Brandt (GER)/D. Elsner (GER)	6–2	6–3	
1997	J. De Armas (VEN)/L. Horna (PER)	A. Di Pasquale (FRA)/J. Jeanpierre (FRA)	6–4	2–6	7–5
1998	J. De Armas (VEN)/F. Gonzalez (CHI)	J. Ferrero (ESP)/F. Lopez (ESP)	6–7	7–5	6–3

GIRLS' DOUBLES

	WINNERS	RUNNERS-UP	SCORE		
1983	C. Anderholm (SWE)/H. Olsson (SWE)	K./M. Maleeva (BUL)	6–4	6–1	
1985	M Perez-Roldan (ARG)/P. Tarabini (ARG)	A. Holikova (TCH)/R. Zrubakova (TCH)	6–3	5–7	6–4
1986	L. Meskhi (URS)/N. Zvereva (URS)	J. Novotna (TCH)/R. Rajchrtova (TCH)	1–6	6–3	6–0
1987	N. Medvedeva (URS)/N. Zvereva (URS)	M. Jaggard (AUS)/N. Provis (AUS)	6–3	6–3	
1988	A. Dechaume (FRA)/E. Derly (FRA)	J. Halard (FRA)/M. Laval (FRA)	6–4	3–6	6–3
1989	N. Pratt (AUS)/S.–T. Wang (TPE)	C. Caverzasio (ITA)/S. Farina (ITA)	7–5	3–6	8–6
1990	R. Dragomir (ROM)/I. Spirlea (ROM)	T. Ignatieva (URS)/I. Soukhova (URS)	6–3	6–1	
1991	E. Bes (ESP)/I. Gorrochategui (ARG)	Z. Malkova (TCH)/E. Martincova (TCH)	6–1	6–3	
1992	L. Courtois (BEL)/N. Feber (BEL)	L. Davenport (USA)/C. Rubin (USA)	6–1	5–7	6–4
1993	L. Courtois (BEL)/N. Feber (BEL)	L. Bitter (NED)/M. Koutstaal (NED)	6–4	7–6	
1994	M. Hingis (SUI)/M. Nedelkova (SVK)	L. Cenkova (CZE)/L. Richterova (CZE)	6–3	6–2	
1995	C. Morariu (USA)/L. Varmuzova (CZE)	A. Canepa (ITA)/G. Casoni (ITA)	7–6	7–5	
1996	A. Canepa (ITA)/G. Casoni (ITA)	A. Kournikova (RUS)/L. Varmuzova (CZE)	6–2	5–7	7–5
1997	C. Black (ZIM)/I. Selyutina (KAZ)	M. Matevzic (SLO)/K. Srebotnik (SLO)	6–0	5–7	7–5
1998	K. Clijsters (BEL)/J. Dokic (AUS)	E. Dementieva (RUS)/N. Petrova (RUS)	6–4	7–6	

WIMBLEDON INTERNATIONAL JUNIOR CHAMPIONSHIPS

The event originated as an invitation tournament, boys' singles in 1947 and girls' singles in 1948. It became a Championship event in 1975.

BOYS' SINGLES

1947 K. Nielsen (DEN)
1948 S. Stockenberg (SWE)
1949 S. Stockenberg (SWE)
1950 J. A. T. Horn (GBR)
1951 J. Kupferburger (RSA)
1952 R. K. Wilson (GBR)
1953 W. A. Knight (GBR)
1954 R. Krishnan (IND)
1955 M. P. Hann (GBR)
1956 R. Holmberg (USA)
1957 J. I. Tattersall (GBR)
1958 E. Buchholz (USA)
1959 T. Lejus (URS)
1960 A. R. Mandelstam (RSA)
1961 C. E. Graebner (USA)
1962 S. Matthews (GBR)
1963 N. Kalogeropoulous (GRE)
1964 I. El Shafei (EGY)
1965 V. Korotkov (URS)
1966 V. Korotkov (URS)
1967 M. Orantes (ESP)
1968 J. G. Alexander (AUS)
1969 B. Bertram (RSA)
1970 B. Bertram (RSA)
1971 R. Kreiss (USA)
1972 B. Borg (SWE)
1973 W. Martin (USA)
1974 W. Martin (USA)

	WINNER	RUNNER-UP	SCORE		
1975	C. J. Lewis (NZL)	R. Ycaza (ECU)	6–1	6–4	
1976	H. Gunthardt (SUI)	P. Elter (FRG)	6–4	7–5	
1977	V. Winitsky (USA)	E. Teltscher (USA)	6–1	1–6	8–6
1978	I. Lendl (TCH)	J. Turpin (USA)	6–3	6–4	
1979	R. Krishnan (IND)	D. Siegler (USA)	6–3	6–4	
1980	T. Tulasne (FRA)	H. D. Beutel (FRG)	6–4	3–6	6–4
1981	M. Anger (USA)	P. Cash (AUS)	7–6	7–5	

	WINNER	RUNNER-UP	SCORE		
1982	P. Cash (AUS)	H. Sundstrom (SWE)	6–4	6–7	6–3
1983	S. Edberg (SWE)	J. Frawley (AUS)	6–3	7–6	
1984	M. Kratzman (AUS)	S. Kruger (RSA)	6–4	4–6	6–3
1985	L. Lavalle (MEX)	E. Velez (MEX)	6–4	6–4	
1986	E. Velez (MEX)	J. Sanchez (ESP)	6–3	7–5	
1987	D. Nargiso (ITA)	J. Stoltenberg (AUS)	7–6	6–4	
1988	N. Pereira (VEN)	G. Raoux (FRA)	7–6	6–2	
1989	N. Kulti (SWE)	T. Woodbridge (AUS)	6–4	6–3	
1990	L. Paes (IND)	M. Ondruska (RSA)	7–6	6–2	
1991	T. Enqvist (SWE)	M. Joyce (USA)	6–4	6–3	
1992	D. Skoch (TCH)	B. Dunn (USA)	6–4	6–3	
1993	R. Sabau (ROM)	J. Szymanski (VEN)	6–1	6–3	
1994	S. Humphries (USA)	M. Philippoussis (AUS)	7–6	3–6	6–4
1995	O. Mutis (FRA)	N. Kiefer (GER)	6–2	6–2	
1996	V. Voltchkov (BLR)	I. Ljubicic (CRO)	3–6	6–2	6–3
1997	W. Whitehouse (RSA)	D. Elsner (GER)	6–3	7–6	
1998	R. Federer (SUI)	I. Labadze (GEO)	6–4	6–4	

GIRLS' SINGLES

1948	O. Miskova (TCH)	1957	M. Arnold (USA)	1966	B. Lindstrom (FIN)
1949	C. Mercelis (BEL)	1958	S. M. Moore (USA)	1967	J. Salome (HOL)
1950	L. Cornell (GBR)	1959	J. Cross (RSA)	1968	K. Pigeon (USA)
1951	L. Cornell (GBR)	1960	K. Hantze (USA)	1969	K. Sawamatsu (JPN)
1952	ten Bosch (HOL)	1961	G. Baksheeva (URS)	1970	S. Walsh (USA)
1953	D. Kilian (RSA)	1962	G. Baksheeva (URS)	1971	M. Kroschina (URS)
1954	V. A. Pitt (GBR)	1963	D. M. Salfati (RSA)	1972	I. Kloss (RSA)
1955	S. M. Armstrong (GBR)	1964	P. Barkowicz (USA)	1973	A. Kiyomura (USA)
1956	A. S. Haydon (GBR)	1965	O. Morozova (URS)	1974	M. Jausovec (YUG)

	WINNER	RUNNER-UP	SCORE		
1975	N. Y. Chmyreva (URS)	R. Marsikova (TCH)	6–4	6–3	
1976	N. Y. Chmyreva (URS)	M. Kruger (RSA)	6–3	2–6	6–1
1977	L. Antonoplis (USA)	Mareen Louie (USA)	6–5	6–1	
1978	T. A. Austin (USA)	H. Mandlikova (TCH)	6–0	3–6	6–4
1979	M. L. Piatek (USA)	A. Moulton (USA)	6–1	6–3	
1980	D. Freeman (AUS)	S. Leo (AUS)	7–6	7–5	
1981	Z. Garrison (USA)	R. Uys (RSA)	6–4	3–6	6–0
1982	C. Tanvier (FRA)	H. Sukova (TCH)	6–2	7–5	
1983	P. Paradis (FRA)	P. Hy (HKG)	6–2	6–1	
1984	A. N. Croft (GBR)	E. Reinach (RSA)	3–6	6–3	6–2
1985	A. Holikova (TCH)	J. Byrne (AUS)	7–5	6–1	
1986	N. Zvereva (URS)	L. Meskhi (URS)	2–6	6–2	9–7
1987	N. Zvereva (URS)	J. Halard (FRA)	6–4	6–4	
1988	B. Schultz (HOL)	E. Derly (FRA)	7–6	6–1	
1989	A. Strnadova (TCH)	M. McGrath (USA)	6–2	6–3	
1990	A. Strnadova (TCH)	K. Sharpe (AUS)	6–2	6–4	
1991	B. Rittner (GER)	E. Makarova (URS)	6–7	6–2	6–3
1992	C. Rubin (USA)	L. Courtois (BEL)	6–2	7–5	
1993	N. Feber (BEL)	R. Grande (ITA)	7–6	1–6	6–2
1994	M. Hingis (SUI)	M-R. Jeon (KOR)	7–5	6–4	
1995	A. Olsza (POL)	T. Tanasugarn (THA)	7–5	7–6	
1996	A. Mauresmo (FRA)	M. Serna (ESP)	4–6	6–3	6–4
1997	C. Black (ZIM)	A. Rippner (USA)	6–3	7–5	
1998	K. Srebotnik (SLO)	K. Clijsters (BEL)	7–6	6–3	

BOYS' DOUBLES

	WINNERS	RUNNERS-UP	SCORE		
1982	P. Cash (AUS)/J. Frawley (AUS)	R. Leach (USA)/J. Ross (USA)	6–3	6–2	
1983	M. Kratzman (AUS)/S. Youl (AUS)	M. Nastase (ROM)/O. Rahnasto (FIN)	6–4	6–4	
1984	R. Brown (USA)/R. Weiss (USA)	M. Kratzman (AUS)/J. Svensson (SWE)	1–6	6–4	11–9
1985	A. Moreno (MEX)/J. Yzaga (PER)	P. Korda (TCH)/C. Suk (TCH)	7–6	6–4	
1986	T. Carbonell (ESP)/P. Korda (TCH)	S. Barr (AUS)/H. Karrasch (CAN)	6–1	6–1	
1987	J. Stoltenberg (AUS)/T. Woodbridge (AUS)	D. Nargiso (ITA)/E. Rossi (ITA)	6–3	7–6	
1988	J. Stoltenberg (AUS)/T. Woodbridge (AUS)	D. Rikl (TCH)/T. Zdrazila (TCH)	6–4	1–6	7–6
1989	J. Palmer (USA)/J. Stark (USA)	J.-L. De Jager (RSA)/W. Ferreira (RSA)	7–6	7–6	
1990	S. Lareau (CAN)/S. LeBlanc (CAN)	C. Marsh (RSA)/M. Ondruska (RSA)	7–6	4–6	6–3

	WINNERS	RUNNERS-UP	SCORE		
1991	K. Alami (MAR)/G. Rusedski (CAN)	J-L. De Jager (RSA)/A. Medvedev (URS)	1–6	7–6	6–4
1992	S. Baldas (AUS)/S. Draper (AUS)	M. Bhupathi (IND)/N. Kirtane (IND)	6–1	4–6	9–7
1993	S. Downs (NZL)/J. Greenhalgh (NZL)	N. Godwin (RSA)/G. Williams (RSA)	6–7	7–6	
1994	B. Ellwood (AUS)/M. Philippoussis (AUS)	V. Platenik(SVK)/R. Schlachter (BRA)	6–2	6–4	
1995	M. Lee (GBR)/G. Trotman (GBR)	A. Hernandez (MEX)/M. Puerta (ARG)	7–6	6–4	
1996	D. Bracciali (ITA)/J. Robichaud (CAN)	D. Roberts (RSA)/W. Whitehouse (RSA)	6–2	6–4	
1997	L. Horna (PER)/N. Massu (CHI)	J. Van Der Westhuizen (RSA)/ W. Whitehouse (RSA)	6–4	6–2	
1998	R. Federer (SUI)/O. Rochus (BEL)	M. Llodra (FRA)/A. Ram (ISR)	6–4	6–4	

GIRLS' DOUBLES

	WINNERS	RUNNERS-UP	SCORE		
1982	B. Herr (USA)/P. Barg (USA)	B. S. Gerken (USA)/G. Rush (USA)	6–1	6–4	
1983	P. Fendick (USA)/P. Hy (HKG)	C. Anderholm (SWE)/H. Olsson (SWE)	6–1	7–5	
1984	C. Kuhlman (USA)/S. Rehe (USA)	V. Milvidskaya (URS)/L. Savchenko (URS)	6–3	5–7	6–4
1985	L. Field (AUS)/J. Thompson (AUS)	E. Reinach (SAF)/J. Richardson (NZL)	6–1	6–2	
1986	M. Jaggard (AUS)/L. O'Neill (AUS)	L. Meskhi (URS)/N. Zvereva (URS)	7–6	6–4	
1987	N. Medvedeva (URS)/N. Zvereva (URS)	I. S. Kim (KOR)/P. M. Modena (HKG)	2–6	7–5	6–0
1988	J. Faull (AUS)/R. McQuillan (AUS)	A. Dechaume (FRA)/E. Derly (FRA)	4–6	6–2	6–3
1989	J. Capriati (USA)/M. McGrath (USA)	A. Strnadova (TCH)/E. Sviglerova (TCH)	6–4	6–2	
1990	K. Habsudova (TCH)/A. Strnadova (TCH)	N. Pratt (AUS)/K. Sharpe (AUS)	6–2	6–4	
1991	C. Barclay (AUS)/L. Zaltz (ISR)	J. Limmer (AUS)/A. Woolcock (AUS)	6–4	6–4	
1992	P. Nelson (USA)/J. Steven (USA)	M. Avotins (AUS)/L. McShea (AUS)	2–6	6–4	6–3
1993	L. Courtois (BEL)/N. Feber (BEL)	H. Mochizuki (JPN)/Y. Yoshida (JPN)	6–3	6–4	
1994	E. De Villiers (RSA)/E. Jelfs (GBR)	C. Morariu (USA)/L. Varmuzova (CZE)	6–3	6–4	
1995	C. Black (ZIM)/A. Olsza (POL)	T. Musgrave (AUS)/J. Richardson (AUS)	6–0	7–6	
1996	O. Barabanschikova (BLR)/A. Mauresmo (FRA)	L. Osterloh (USA)/ S. Reeves (USA)	5–7	6–3	6–1
1997	C. Black (ZIM)/I. Selyutina (KAZ)	M. Matevzic (SLO)/K. Srebotnik (SLO)	3–6	7–5	6–3
1998	E. Dyrberg (DEN)/J. Kostanic (CRO)	P. Rampre (SLO)/I. Tulyaganova (UZB)	6–2	7–6	

US INTERNATIONAL JUNIOR CHAMPIONSHIPS

BOYS' SINGLES

	WINNER	RUNNER-UP	SCORE		
1974	W. Martin (USA)	F. Taygan (USA)	6–4	6–2	
1975	H. Schonfield (USA)	C. J. Lewis (NZL)	6–4	6–3	
1976	Y. Ycaza (ECU)	J. L. Clerc (ARG)	6–4	5–7	6–0
1977	V. Winitsky (USA)	E. Teltscher (USA)	6–4	6–4	
1978	P. Hjertquist (SWE)	S. Simonsson (SWE)	7–6	1–6	7–6
1979	S. Davis (USA)	J. Gunnarsson (SWE)	6–3	6–1	
1980	M. Falberg (USA)	E. Korita (USA)	6–0	6–2	
1981	T. Hogstedt (SWE)	H. Schwaier (FRG)	7–5	6–3	
1982	P. Cash (AUS)	G. Forget (FRA)	6–3	6–3	
1983	S. Edberg (SWE)	S. Youl (AUS)	6–2	6–4	
1984	M. Kratzman (AUS)	B. Becker (FRG)	6–3	7–6	
1985	T. Trigueiro (USA)	J. Blake (USA)	6–2	6–3	
1986	J. Sanchez (ESP)	F. Davin (ARG)	6–2	6–2	
1987	D. Wheaton (USA)	A. Cherkasov (URS)	7–5	6–0	
1988	N. Pereira (VEN)	N. Kulti (SWE)	6–1	6–2	
1989	J. Stark (USA)	N. Kulti (SWE)	6–4	6–1	
1990	A. Gaudenzi (ITA)	M. Tillstroem (SWE)	6–2	4–6	7–6
1991	L. Paes (IND)	K. Alami (MAR)	6–4	6–4	
1992	B. Dunn (USA)	N. Behr (ISR)	7–5	6–2	
1993	M. Rios (CHI)	S. Downs (NZL)	7–6	6–3	
1994	S. Schalken (NED)	M. Tahiri (MAR)	6–2	7–6	
1995	N. Kiefer (GER)	U. Seetzen (GER)	6–3	6–4	
1996	D. Elsner (GER)	M. Hipfl (AUT)	6–3	6–2	
1997	A. Di Pasquale (FRA)	W. Whitehouse (RSA)	6–7	6–4	6–1
1998	D. Nalbandian (ARG)	R. Federer (SUI)	6–3	7–5	

GIRLS' SINGLES

	WINNER	RUNNER-UP	SCORE		
1974	I. Kloss (RSA)	M. Jausovec (YUG)	6–4	6–3	
1975	N. T. Chmyreva (URS)	G. Stevens (RSA)	6–7	6–2	6–2
1976	M. Kruger (RSA)	L. Romanov (ROM)	6–3	7–5	
1977	C. Casabianca (ARG)	L. Antonoplis (USA)	6–3	2–6	6–2

	WINNER	*RUNNER-UP*	*SCORE*		
1978	L. Siegel (USA)	I. Madruga (ARG)	6–4	6–4	
1979	A. Moulton (USA)	M. L. Piatek (USA)	7–6	7–6	
1980	S. Mascarin (USA)	K. Keil (USA)	6–3	6–4	
1981	Z. Garrison (USA)	K. Gompert (USA)	6–0	6–3	
1982	B. Herr (USA)	G. Rush (USA)	6–3	6–1	
1983	E. Minter (AUS)	M. Werdel (USA)	6–3	7–5	
1984	K. Maleeva (BUL)	N. Sodupe (USA)	6–1	6–2	
1985	L. Garrone (ITA)	A. Holikova (TCH)	6–2	7–6	
1986	E. Hakami (USA)	S. Stafford (USA)	6–2	6–1	
1987	N. Zvereva (URS)	S. Birch (USA)	6–0	6–3	
1988	C. Cunningham (USA)	R. McQuillan (AUS)	6–3	6–1	
1989	J. Capriati (USA)	R. McQuillan (AUS)	6–2	6–3	
1990	M. Maleeva (BUL)	N. Van Lottum (FRA)	7–5	6–2	
1991	K. Habsudova (TCH)	A. Mall (USA)	6–1	6–3	
1992	L. Davenport (USA)	J. Steven (USA)	6–2	6–2	
1993	M. F. Bentivoglio (ITA)	Y. Yoshida (JPN)	7–6	6–4	
1994	M. Tu (USA)	M. Hingis (SUI)	6–2	6–4	
1995	T. Snyder (USA)	A. Ellwood (AUS)	6–4	4–6	6–2
1996	M. Lucic (CRO)	M. Weingartner (GER)	6–2	6–1	
1997	C. Black (ZIM)	K. Chevalier (FRA)	6–7	6–1	6–3
1998	J. Dokic (AUS)	K. Srebotnik (SLO)	6–4	6–2	

BOYS' DOUBLES

	WINNERS	*RUNNERS-UP*	*SCORE*		
1982	J. Canter (USA)/M. Kures (USA)	P. Cash (AUS)/J. Frawley (AUS)	7–6	6–3	
1983	M. Kratzman (AUS)/S. Youl (AUS)	P. McEnroe (USA)/B. Pearce (USA)	6–1	7–6	
1984	L. Lavelle (MEX)/M. Nastase (ROM)	J. Ycaza (PER)/A. Moreno (MEX)	7–6	1–6	6–1
1985	J. Blake (USA)/D. Yates (USA)	P. Flynn (USA)/D. McPherson (USA)	3–6	6–3	6–4
1986	T. Carbonell (ESP)/J. Sanchez (ESP)	J. Tarango (USA)/D. Wheaton (USA)	6–4	1–6	6–1
1987	G. Ivanisevic (YUG)/D. Nargiso (ITA)	Z. Ali (IND)/B. Steven (NZL)	3–6	6–4	6–3
1988	J. Stark (USA)/J. Yoncey (USA)	M. Boscatta (ITA)/S. Pescosolido (ITA)	7–6	7–5	
1989	W. Ferreira (RSA)/G. Stafford (RSA)	M. Damm (TCH)/J. Kodes (TCH)	6–3	6–4	
1990	M. Renstroem (SWE)/M. Tillstroem (SWE)	S. LeBlanc (CAN)/G. Rusedski (CAN)	6–7	6–3	6–4
1991	K. Alami (MAR)/J–L. De Jager (RSA)	M. Joyce (USA)/V. Spadea (USA)	6–4	6–7	6–1
1992	J. Jackson (USA)/E. Taino (USA)	M. Rios (CHI)/G. Silberstein (CHI)	6–3	6–7	6–4
1993	N. Godwin (RSA)/G. Williams (RSA)	B. Ellwood (AUS)/J. Sekulov (AUS)	6–3	6–3	
1994	B. Ellwood (AUS)/N. Lapentti (ECU)	P. Goldstein (USA)/S. Humphries (USA)	6–2	6–0	
1995	J-M. Lee (KOR)/J. Robichaud (CAN)	R. Sluiter (NED)/P. Wessels (NED)	7–6	6–2	
1996	B. Bryan (USA)/M. Bryan (USA)	D. Bracciali (ITA)/J. Robichaud (CAN)	5–7	6–3	6–4
1997	F. Gonzalez (CHI)/N. Massu (CHI)	J-R. Lisnard (FRA)/M. Llodra (FRA)	6–4	6–4	
1998	K. Hippensteel (USA)/D. Martin (USA)	A. Ram (ISR)/L. Zovko (CRO)	6–7	7–6	6–2

GIRLS' DOUBLES

	WINNERS	*RUNNERS-UP*	*SCORE*		
1982	P. Barg (USA)/B. Herr (USA)	A. Hulbert (AUS)/B. Randall (AUS)	1–6	7–5	7–6
1983	A. Hulbert (AUS)/B. Randall (AUS)	N. Riva (URS)/L. Savchenko (URS)	6–4	6–2	
1984	G. Sabatini (ARG)/M. Paz (ARG)	S. MacGregor (USA)/S. London (USA)	6–4	3–6	6–2
1985	R. Zrubakova (TCH)/A. Holikova (TCH)	P. Tarabini (ARG)/M. Perez Roldan (ARG)	6–4	2–6	7–5
1986	R. Zrubakova (TCH)/J. Novotna (TCH)	E. Brioukhovets (URS)/L. Meskhi (URS)	6–4	6–2	
1987	M. McGrath (USA)/K. Po (USA)	Il-Soon Kim (KOR)/Shi-Ting Wang (TPE)	6–4	7–5	
1988	M. McGrath (USA)/K. Po (USA)	K. Caverzasio (ITA)/L. Lapi (ITA)	6–3	6–1	
1989	J. Capriati (USA)/M. McGrath (USA)	J. Faull (AUS)/R. McQuillan (AUS)	6–0	6–3	
1990	K. Godridge (AUS)/K. Sharpe (AUS)	E. deLone (USA)/L. Raymond (USA)	4–6	7–5	6–2
1991	K. Godridge (AUS)/N. Pratt (AUS)	A. Carlsson (SWE)/C. Cristea (ROM)	7–6	7–5	
1992	L. Davenport (USA)/N. London (USA)	K. Schlukebit (USA)/J. Steven (USA)	7–5	6–7	6–4
1993	N. London (USA)/J. Steven (USA)	H. Mochizuki (JPN)/Y. Yoshida (JPN)	6–3	6–4	
1994	S. De Beer (RSA)/C. Reuter (NED)	N. De Villiers (RSA) /E. Jelfs (GBR)	4–6	6–4	6–2
1995	C. Morariu (USA)/L. Varmuzova (CZE)	A. Kournikova (RUS)/A. Olsza (POL)	6–3	6–3	
1996	S. De Beer (RSA)/J. Steck (RSA)	P. Rampre (SLO)/K. Srebotnik (SLO)	6–4	6–3	
1997	M. Irvin (USA)/A. Stevenson (USA)	C. Black (ZIM)/I. Selyutina (KAZ)	6–2	7–6	
1998	K. Clijsters (BEL)/E. Dyrberg (DEN)	J. Dokic (AUS)/E. Dominikovic (AUS)	7–6	6–4	

ITALIAN INTERNATIONAL JUNIOR CHAMPIONSHIPS

The event originated as an Under-21 Invitational tournament for boys and girls singles in 1959. It became a Championship event in 1976.

BOYS' SINGLES

	WINNER	*RUNNER–UP*	*SCORE*		
1976	H. Gunthardt (SUI)	F. Luna (ESP)	6–4	6–1	
1977	Y. Noah (FRA)	R. Venter (ESP)	6–4	6–2	
1978	I. Lendl (TCH)	P. Hjertquist (SWE)	2–6	6–2	6–0
1979	H. Simonsson (SWE)	B. Testerman (USA)	6–0	6–3	
1980	T. Tulasne (FRA)	H. Leconte (FRA)	6–2	6–3	
1981	B. Zivojinovic (YUG)	L. Bottazzi (ITA)	7–6	2–6	6–3
1982	G. Forget (FRA)	M. Zampieri (ITA)	6–3	6–4	
1983	M. Fioroni (ITA)	K. Novacek (TCH)	5–7	6–1	6–3
	WINNER	*RUNNER–UP*	*SCORE*		
1984	L. Jensen (USA)	B. Oresar (YUG)	6–4	6–4	
1985	A. Padovani (ITA)	C. Pistolesi (ITA)	6–2	6–1	
1986	F. Davin (ARG)	G. Perez-Roldan (ARG)	6–4	4–6	6–0
1987	J. Courier (USA)	A. Aramburu (PER)	7–6	1–6	6–3
1988	G. Ivanisevic (YUG)	F. Fontang (FRA)	6–3	6–2	
1989	S. Pescosolido (ITA)	F. Santoro (FRA)	6–1	6–0	
1990	I. Baron (USA)	O. Fernandez (MEX)	7–5	6–1	
1991	G. Doyle (AUS)	K. Carlsen (DEN)	1–6	6–3	9–7
1992	Y. Kafelnikov (CIS)	D. Skoch (TCH)	7–6	6–4	
1993	J. Szymanski (VEN)	R. Sabau (ROM)	6–3	6–4	
1994	F. Browne (ARG)	G. Galimberti (ITA)	6–3	6–2	
1995	M. Zabaleta (ARG)	M. Lee (GBR)	6–4	6–2	
1996	O. Mutis (FRA)	D. Sciortino (ITA)	6–1	6–3	
1997	F. Allgauer (ITA)	L. Horna (PER)	6–3	6–4	
1998	G. Coria (ARG)	J. Jeanpierre (FRA)	7–6	6–3	

GIRLS' SINGLES

	WINNER	*RUNNER–UP*	*SCORE*		
1977	H. Strachanova (CZE)	C. Casabianca (ARG)	7–6	6–0	
1978	H. Mandlikova (TCH)	I. Madruga (ARG)	7–6	6–3	
1979	M. L. Piatek (USA)	L. Sandin (SWE)	6–3	3–6	6–3
1980	S. Mascarin (USA)	K. Horvath (USA)	6–4	6–3	
1981	A. Minter (USA)	E. Sayers (AUS)	1–6	6–2	6–3
1982	G. Rush (USA)	B. Herr (USA)	6–7	7–6	6–4
1983	S. Goles (YUG)	A.M. Cecchini (ITA)	6–3	6–4	
1984	G. Sabatini (ARG)	S. Schilder (HOL)	7–6	6–1	
1985	P. Tarabini (ARG)	L. Golarsa (ITA)	6–0	6–1	
1986	B. Fulco (ARG)	P. Tarabini (ARG)	7–6	6–2	
1987	N. Zvereva (URS)	C. Martinez (ESP)	6–3	6–2	
1988	C. Tessi (ARG)	F. Labat (ARG)	3–6	7–6	6–3
1989	F. Labat (ARG)	M. Anderson (RSA)	6–2	6–2	
1990	S. Farina (ITA)	N. Baudone (ITA)	6–1	6–2	
1991	Z. Malkova (TCH)	E. Makarova (URS)	6–2	6–1	
1992	R. De Los Rios (PAR)	N. Feber (BEL)	6–1	7–5	
1993	N. Louarssabichvili (GEO)	J. Lee (USA)	6–4	6–7	7–5
1994	T. Panova (RUS)	S. Ventura (ITA)	1–6	6–3	6–0
1995	A. Kournikova (RUS)	C. Reuter (NED)	6–2	6–0	
1996	O. Barabanschikova (BLR)	S. Drake-Brockman (AUS)	2–6	7–5	6–2
1997	K. Srebotnik (SLO)	T. Pisnik (SLO)	6–1	6–2	
1998	A. Serra-Zanetti (ITA)	A. Vedy (FRA)	6–3	5–7	6–4

BOYS' DOUBLES

	WINNER	*RUNNER–UP*	*SCORE*		
1993	N. London (USA)/J. Steven (USA)	H. Mochizuki (JPN)/Y. Yoshida (JPN)	6–3	6–4	
1976	F. Van Oertzen (BRA)/C.Sacomandi (BRA)	C. Motta (BRA)/H. Roverano (BRA)	6–3	6–2	
1980	S. Giammalva (USA)/M. Anger (USA)	W. Masur (AUS)/C. Miller (AUS)	7–6	6–0	
1981	E. Korita (USA)/J.Brown (USA)	R. Bengston (CAN)/M. Perkins (CAN)	6–2	6–4	
1982	F. Maciel (MEX)/F.Perez (MEX)	M. Kures (USA)/R. Leach (USA)	6–3	7–5	
1983	S. Edberg (SWE)/J.Svensson (SWE)	F. Garcia (ESP)/E. Sanchez (ESP)	6–2	6–3	
1984	A. Moreno (MEX)/J.Yzaga (PER)	A. Antonitsch (AUT)/H. Skoff (AUT)	6–7	7–6	6–4
1985	F. Errard (FRA)/P. Lacombrade (FRA)	G. Saacks (RSA)/D. Shapiro (RSA)	7–6	4–6	6–4

	WINNER	RUNNER–UP	SCORE
1986	F. Davin (ARG)/G. Perez-Roldan (ARG)	A. Mancini (ARG)/N. Pereira (URU)	6–2 6–2
1987	G. Carbonari (ARG)/J.L. Noriega (PER)	L. Bale (RSA)/D. Naikin (RSA)	2–6 6–3 6–4
1988	S. Hirszon (YUG)/G. Ivanisevic (YUG)	M. Boscatto (ITA)/F. Pisilli (ITA)	6–3 6–4
1989	M. Bascatto (ITA)/ S. Pescosolido (ITA)	W. Ferreira (RSA)/ G. Stafford (RSA)	7–5 6–4
1990	W. Bulls (USA)/ B. MacPhie (USA)	J. De Jager (RSA)/ J. De Beer (RSA)	7–6 5–7 6–4
1991	G. Doyle (AUS)/ J. Eagle (AUS)	S. Sargsian (URS)/D. Tomachevitch (URS)	6–1 6–1
1992	M. Bertolini (ITA)/ M. Navarra (ITA)	Y. Kafelnikov (CIS)/ A. Radulescu (ROM)	6–4 4–6 6–4
1993	T. Johansson (SWE)/M. Norman (SWE)	B. Ellwood (AUS)/ J. Sekulov (AUS)	7–6 6–3
1994	B. Ellwood (AUS)/M. Philippoussis (AUS)	A. Hernandez (MEX)/ G. Venegas MEX)	6–2 6–3
1995	G. Canas (ARG)/ M. Garcia (ARG)	S. Grosjean (FRA)/Y. Romero (VEN)	6–2 7–6
1996	M. Lee (GBR)/J. Trotman (GBR)	A. Krasevec (SLO)/G. Krusic (SLO)	7–6 2–6 6–1
1997	J. Van Der Westhuizen (RSA)/ W. Whitehouse (RSA)	F. Gonzalez (CHI)/N. Massu (CHI)	2–0 ret
1998	J. De Armas (VEN)/F. Gonzalez (CHI)	N. Healey (AUS)/A. Kracman (SLO)	2–6 7–5 6–4

GIRLS' DOUBLES

	WINNER	RUNNER–UP	SCORE
1980	B. Moulds (RSA)/ R. Uys (RSA)	K. Horvath (USA)/ P. Murgo (ITA)	4–6 6–2 6–4
1981	H. Sukova (TCH)/ M. Maleeva (BUL)	M. Linstrom (SWE)/ C. Lindquist (SWE)	3–6 6–4 6–4
1982	B. Gerken (USA)/ B. Herr (USA)	B. Randall (AUS)/ E. Minter (AUS)	6–3 6–4
1983	P. Fendick (USA)/ J. Fuchs (USA)	B. Bowes (USA)/ A. Hubert (USA)	6–4 6–4
1984	D. Ketelaar (HOL)/ S. Schilder (HOL)	M. Paz (ARG)/ G. Sabatini (ARG)	5–7 6–4 6–2
1985	P. Tarabini (ARG)/M. Perez-Roldan (ARG)	J. Novotna (TCH)/ R. Rajchrtova (TCH)	6–4 6–4
1986	A. Dechaume (FRA)/S. Niox Chateau (FRA)	E. Derly (FRA)/ F. Martin (FRA)	6–2 6–4
1987	N. Medvedeva (URS)/ N. Zvereva (URS)	P. Miller (URU)/ C. Tessi (ARG)	7–5 6–1
1988	D. Graham (USA)/ A. Grossman (USA)	C. Cunningham (USA)/ A. Farley (USA)	6–2 7–5
1989	R. Bobkova (TCH)/ A. Strnadova (TCH)	N. Baudone (ITA)/ S. Farina (ITA)	5–7 6–4 6–4
1990	T. Ignatieva (URS)/ I. Sukhova (URS)	C. Barclay (AUS)/ J. Stacey (AUS)	5–7 6–2 9–7
1991	B. Martincova (TCH)/ I. Horvat (YUG)	I. Gorrochategui (ARG)/ R. Grande (ITA)	6–3 6–4
1992	N. Feber (BEL)/ L. Courtois (BEL)	M. Avotins (AUS)/ L. McShea (AUS)	6–4 5–7 6–3
1993	C. Moros (USA)/ S. Nickitas (USA)	M. D. Campana (CHI)/ B. Castro (CHI)	7–5 7–5
1994	M. Nedelkova (SVK)/ M. Hasanova (SVK)	K. Mesa (COL)/ C. Giraldo (COL)	1–6 6–3 6–4
1995	A. Canepa (ITA)/ G. Casoni (ITA)	O. Barabanschikova (BLR)/L. Varmuzova (CZE)	6–4 5–7 6–3
1996	A. Canepa (ITA)/G. Casoni (ITA)	S. Drake-Brockman (AUS)/A. Kournikova (RUS)	5–7 6–4 6–3
1997	T. Hergold (SLO)/T. Pisnik (SLO)	S. Bajin (CAN)/I. Visic (CRO)	6–1 6–2
1998	*Finalists:* E. Dyrberg (DEN)/A Vedy (FRA) and M. E. Salemi (ARG)/C. Fernandez (ARG) *Final not played due to rain.*		

NEC WORLD YOUTH CUP

International Team Championship for boys and girls aged 16 and under. Early rounds played zonally.

BOYS' FINALS

1985 Australia d. USA 2–1, *Kobe Japan:* R. Fromberg lost to F. Montana 2–6 2–6, S. Barr d. J. A. Falbo 6–4 6–4; Barr/J. Stoltenberg d. Montana/Falbo 4–6 6–7 7–5.

1986 Australia d. USA 2–1, *Tokyo, Japan:* J. Stoltenberg d. J. Courier 6–2 6–4; R. Fromberg lost to M. Chang 4–6 4–6; Stoltenberg/T. Woodbridge d. Courier/Kass 7–6 6–2.

1987 Australia d. Netherlands 3–0, *Freiburg, West Germany:* T. Woodbridge d. P. Dogger 7–5 3–6 6–2; J. Anderson d. F. Wibier 6–0 6–1; J. Morgan/Woodbridge d. Dogger/Wibier 6–3 6–2.

1988 Czechoslovakia d. USA 2–1, *Perth, Australia:* J. Kodes d. J. Leach 7–6 6–2; M. Damm d. B. MacPhie 6–2 6–7 6–4; Damm/L. Hovorka lost to W. Bull/Leach 4–6 4–6.

1989 West Germany d. Czechoslovakia 2–1, *Asuncion, Paraguay:* S. Gessner lost to L. Thomas 5–7 5–7; G. Paul d. P. Gazda 6–4 6–4; Paul/D. Prinosil d. Gazda/Thomas 7–5 6–1.

1990 USSR d. Australia 2–1, *Rotterdam, Netherlands:* D. Thomashevitch d. T. Vasiliadis 6–3 6–2; A. Medvedev lost to G. Doyle 6–2 4–6 5–7; E. Kafelnikov/Medvedev d. Doyle/B. Sceney 7–6 6–3.

1991 Spain d. Czechoslovakia 2–1, *Barcelona, Spain:* G. Corrales d. D. Skock 7–5 7–5; A. Costa lost to F. Kascak 4–6 5–7; Corrales /Costa d. Kascak/Skock 6–4 6–2.

1992 France d. Germany 2–1, *Barcelona, Spain:* M. Boye d. A. Nickel 7–5 0–6 6–3; N. Escude lost to R. Nicklish 2–6, 6–3, 3–6; Boye/Escude d. Nickel/Nicklish 6–7 6–0 6–3.

1993 France d. New Zealand 2–1, *Wellington, New Zealand:* O. Mutis lost to T. Susnjak 1–6 6–1 3–6; J-F Bachelot d. S. Clark 4–6 6–4 6–4; Mutis/J. Potron d. Clark/N. Nielsen 6–3 6–4.

1994 Netherlands d. Austria 2–1, *Tucson, Arizona:* P. Wessels lost to C. Trimmel 6–4 3–6 5–7; R. Sluiter d. M. Hipfl 7–6 6–1; Sluiter/Wessels d. Hipfl/Trimmel 6–3 6–4.

1995 Germany d. Czech Republic 3–0, *Essen, Germany:* T. Messmer d. P. Kralert 6–3 7–5; D. Elsner d. M. Tabara 6–3 6–4; D. Elsner/T. Zivnicek d. P. Kralert/P. Riha 6–7(4) 6–4 6–4.

1996 France d. Australia 2–1, *Zurich, Switzerland:* J. Haehnel d. N. Healey 6–4 6–2; J. Jeanpierre d. L. Hewitt 6–3 7–5; J. Haehnel/O. Patience lost to N. Healey/L. Hewitt 5–7 6–4 6–7(5).
1997 Czech Republic d. Venezuela 2–0, *Vancouver, Canada:* J. Levinsky d. E. Nastari 6–0 6–2; L. Chramosta d. J. De Armas 7–6(2) 6–2.
1998 Spain d. Croatia 2–1, *Cuneo, Italy:* M. Lopez lost to R. Karanusic 6–3 3–6 3–6; T. Robredo d. M. Radic 6–4 6–4; M. Lopez/T. Robredo d. R. Karanusic/M. Radic 6–4 6–2.

GIRLS' FINALS
1985 Czechoslovakia d. Australia 3–0, *Kobe, Japan:* J. Pospisilova d. S. McCann 6–4 6–4; R. Zrubakova d. N. Provis 7–6 7–5; Pospisilova/Zrubakova d. Provis/W. Frazer 7–5 6–4.
1986 Belgium d. Czechoslovakia 2–1, *Tokyo, Japan:* A. Devries d. R. Zrubakova 6–3 6–4; S. Wasserman d. P. Langrova 6–4 7–5; Devries/C. Neuprez lost to Langrova/Zrubakova 4–6 2–6.
1987 Australia d. USSR 2–1, *Freiburg, West Germany:* J. Faull lost to N. Medvedeva 6–4 2–6 2–6; R. McQuillan d. E. Brioukhovets 3–6 6–2 6–3; Faull/McQuillan d. Brioukhovets/Medvedeva 6–3 6–1.
1988 Australia d. Argentina 3–0, *Perth, Australia:* K. A. Guse d. F. Haumuller 7–6 6–4; L. Guse d. C. Tessi 7–6 1–6 6–2; K. A. Guse/K. Sharpe d. I. Gorrachategui/Tessi 6–0 6–2.
1989 West Germany d. Czechoslovakia 2–1, *Asuncion, Paraguay:* M. Skulj–Zivec d. K. Matouskova 6–0 7–5; A. Huber d. K. Habsudova 6–0 6–3; K. Duell/Skulj–Zivec lost to Habsudova/P. Kucova 3–6 0–6.
1990 Netherlands d. USSR 2–1, *Rotterdam, Netherlands:* P. Kamstra d. I. Soukhova 6–1 7–6; L. Niemantsverdriet lost to T. Ignatieva 0–6 6–1 4–6; Kamstra/Niemantsverdriet d. Ignatieva/Soukhova 6–3 4–6 6–1.
1991 Germany d. Paraguay 2–1, *Barcelona, Spain:* H. Rusch lost to L. Schaerer 6–7 3–6; M. Kochta d. R De los Rios 6–3 6–1; K. Freye/Kochta d. De los Rios/Schaerer 5–7 6–3 6–3.
1992 Belgium d. Argentina 3–0, *Barcelona, Spain:* L. Courtois d. L. Montalvo 6–1 6–3; N. Feber d. L. Reynares 1–6 6–4 6–1; Courtois/S. Deville d. M. Oliva/Montalvo 1–6 7–5 6–4.
1993 Australia d. USA 2–1, *Wellington, New Zealand:* S. Drake-Brockman d. S. Nickitas 6–2 5–7 6–2; A. Ellwood d. A. Basica 6–2 6–1; Ellwood/J. Richardson lost to C. Maros/Nickitas 6–2 5–7 0–6.
1994 South Africa d. France 3–0, *Tucson, Arizona:* J. Steck d. A. Cocheteux 7–5 6–3; S. De Beer d. A. Castera 6–4 6–3; doubles not played.
1995 France d. Germany 2–1, *Essen, Germany:* K. Jagieniak lost to S. Kovacic 4–6 3–6; A. Mauresmo d. S. Klosel 6–0 6–3; K. Chevalier/A. Mauresmo d. C. Christian/S.-Kovacic 6–3 7–5.
1996 Slovenia d. Germany 2–1, *Zurich, Switzerland:* K. Srebotnik d. S. Kovacic 6–1 6–3; P. Rampre lost to J. Wohr 2–6 1–6; P. Rampre/K. Srebotnik d. S. Kovacic/J. Wohr 6–1 6–4.
1997 Russia d. France 2–0, *Vancouver, Canada:* A. Myskina d. S. Schoeffel 6–3 2–6 8–6; E. Dementieva d. S. Rizzi 6–2 4–6 6–4.
1998 Italy d. Slovak Republic 2–1, *Cuneo, Italy:* R. Vinci lost to S. Hrozenska 6–2 2–6 6–8; M. E. Camerin d. D. Hantuchova 6–4 6–2; F. Pennetta/R. Vinci d. D. Hantuchova/S. Hrozenska 6–4 6–1.

WORLD JUNIOR TENNIS COMPETITION

International Team Championship for boys and girls aged 14 and under, known as NTT World Junior Tennis 1991–96.

BOYS' FINALS
1991 Spain d. Italy 2–1, *Yamanakako, Japan:* A. Martin d. C. Zoppi 6–2 7–6; J-A. Saiz d. P. Tabini 6–2 6–1; Martin/J-M. Vincente lost to A. Ciceroni/Tabini 7–5 4–6 6–8.
1992 Austria d. USA 2–1, *Yamanakako, Japan:* K. Trimmel d. C. Brill 4–6 6–2 6–2; M. Hipfl d. G. Adams 6–4 6–0; Trimmel/Hipfl lost to Abrams/R. Bryan 6–1 6–2.
1993 France d. Slovenia 2–1, *Yamanakako, Japan:* J-R. Lisnard d. A. Krasevec 7–6 6–3; A. Di Pasquale d. M. Gregoric 6–1 6–1; A. Di Pasquale/V. Lavergne lost to P. Kralert/J. Krejci 2–6 6–2 6–7.
1994 Italy d. Belgium 2–1, *Yamanakako, Japan:* N. Frocassi lost to O. Rochus 6–7 6–3 3–6; F. Luzzi d. X. Malisse 6–3 7–6; Frocassi/Luzzi d. Malisse/Rochus 6–4 1–6 6–3.
1995 Great Britain d. Germany 3–0, *Yamanakako, Japan:* M. Hilton d. P. Hammer 6–3 4–6 6–4; S. Dickson d. B. Bachert 7–5 6–2; S. Dickson/A. Mackin d. B. Bachert/R. Neurohr 7–5 6–1.
1996 Argentina d. Sweden 3–0, *Nagoya, Japan:* G. Coria d. F. Prpic 6–1 6–1; D. Nalbandian d. J. Johansson 6–3 6–3; G. Coria/A. Pastorino d. J. Johansson/F. Prpic 6–1 6–3.
1997 South Africa d. Czech Republic 2–1, *Nagoya, Japan:* A. Anderson d. M. Kokta 7–5 6–4; D. Stegmann d. J. Masik 6–3 6–0; A. Anderson/R. Blair lost to D. Karol/J. Masik 1–6 0–6.
1998 Austria d. Argentina 3–0, *Nagoya, Japan:* J. Ager d. J. Monaco 6–4 6–4; S. Wiespeiner d. B. Dabul 4–6 6–4 6–1; J. Ager/C. Polessnig d. B. Dabul/J. Ottaviani 6–4 7–5.

GIRLS' FINALS
1991 Czechoslovakia d. Australia 3–0, *Yamanakako, Japan:* L. Cenkova d. A. Ellwood 7–5 6–2; A. Havrlkova d. A. Venkatesan 6–1 6–2; Cenkova/Havrlkova d. Ellwood/E. Knox 6–2 7–6.
1992 USA d. Australia 3–0, *Yamanakako, Japan:* M. Tu d. A. Ellwood 6–4 6–4; A. Basica d. R. Reid 6–3 6–7 6–4; Basica/A. Augustus d. Reid/S. Drake-Brockman 6–2 7–5.
1993 Germany d. USA 2–1, *Yamanakako, Japan:* C. Christian lost to S. Halsell 0–6 3–6; S. Klosel d. K. Gates 6–4 7–6; C. Christian/S. Klosel d. K. Gates/S. Halsell 3–6 6–3 7–5.

1994 Germany d. Czech Republic 2–1, *Yamanakako, Japan:* J. Wohr d. J. Schonfeldova 7–5 6–0; S. Kovacic d. M. Pastikova 6–2 7–5; S. Lozel/Wohr lost to Pastikova/Schonfeldova 4–6 1–6.
1995 Slovenia d. Hungary 2–1, *Yamanakako, Japan:* T. Pisnik d. S. Szegedi 7–6(5) 6–3; Z. Gubacsi d. K. Srebotnik 6–4 3–6 4–6; T. Pisnik/K. Srebotnik d. Z. Gubacsi/I. Szalai 6–3 6–3.
1996 Slovak Republic d. Great Britain 3–0, Nagoya, Japan: S. Hrozenska d. S. Gregg 6–1 6–2; K. Basternakova d. H. Collin 6–3 6–1; S. Hrozenska/Z. Kucova d. H. Collin/H. Reesby 6–4 6–2.
1997 Russia d. Slovak Republic 2–1, *Nagoya, Japan:* L. Krasnoroutskaia d. D. Hantuchova 6–2 6–4; E. Bovina d. M. Babakova 6–4 6–1; G. Fokina/L. Krasnoroutskaia lost to D. Hantuchova/L. Kurhajcova 2–6 6–2 2–6.
1998 Czech Republic d. Russia 2–1, *Nagoya, Japan:* E. Birnerova d. V. Zvonareva 6–3 6–4; P. Cetkovska lost to G. Fokina 2-6 6–2 4–6; E. Birnerova/P. Cetkovska d. G. Fokina/R. Gourevitch 7–5 1–6 6–3.

ORANGE BOWL

International 18 and Under Championship played in Miami each December. There are also events for players aged 16 and under, and 14 and under.

BOYS' SINGLES

	WINNER	*RUNNER-UP*	*SCORE*				
1974	W. Martin (USA)	T. Smid (TCH)	6–7	4–6	6–2	6–1	7–6
1975	F. Luna (ESP)	B. E. Gottfried (USA)	6–4	6–4			
1976	J. P. McEnroe (USA)	E. Teltscher (USA)	7–5	6–1			
1977	I. Lendl (TCH)	Y. Noah (FRA)	4–6	7–6	6–3		
1978	G. Urpi (ESP)	S. Van der Merwe (SAF)	6–3	6–1			
1979	R. Viver (ECU)	P. Arraya (PER)	7–6	6–4			
1980	J. Nystrom (SWE)	C. Castqtellan (ARG)	7–5	7–6			
1981	R. Arguello (ARG)	R. Joaquim (BRA)	6–2	6–1			
1982	G. Forget (FRA)	J. Bardou (ESP)	7–5	2–6	6–1		
1983	K. Carlsson (SWE)	E. Sanchez (ESP)	6–2	6–4			
1984	R. Brown (USA)	J. Berger (USA)	6–3	6–3			
1985	C. Pistolesi (ITA)	B. Oresar (YUG)	6–2	6–0			
1986	J. Sanchez (ESP)	A. Parker (USA)	6–3	6–4			
1987	J. Courier (USA)	A. Cherkasov (URS)	6–3	6–2			
1988	M. Rosset (SUI)	S. Pescosolido (ITA)	7–6	3–6	6–1		
1989	F. Meligeni (ARG)	G. Lopez (ESP)	7–6	7–6			
1990	A. Medvedev (URS)	O. Fernandez (MEX)	6–4	2–6	6–2		
1991	M. Charpentier (ARG)	K. Alami (MAR)	6–4	6–3			
1992	V. Spadea (USA)	G. Etlis(ARG)	7–6	6–3			
1993	A. Costa (ESP)	R. Carretero (ESP)	6–3	6–4			
1994	N. Lapentti (ECU)	G. Kuerten (BRA)	6–3	7–6			
1995	M. Zabaleta (ARG)	T. Haas (GER)	6–2	3–6	6–1		
1996	A. Martin (ESP)	A. Di Pasquale (FRA)	6–0	6–1			
1997	N. Massu (CHI)	R. Rake (USA)	6–1	6–7	6–3		
1998	R. Federer (SUI)	G. Coria (ARG)	7–5	6–3			

GIRLS' SINGLES

	WINNER	*RUNNER-UP*	*SCORE*		
1974	L. Epstein (USA)	C. Penn (USA)	6–1	6–2	
1975	L. Epstein (USA)	S. McInerny (USA)	6–2	6–1	
1976	M. Kruger (SAF)	A. .E. Smith (USA)	2–6	6–3	6–4
1977	A. E. Smith (USA)	H. Strachonova (TCH)	7–6	7–5	
1978	A. Jaeger (USA)	R. Fairbank (SAF)	6–1	6–3	
1979	K. Horvath (USA)	P. Murgo (ITA)	7–5	6–0	
1980	S. Mascarin (USA)	R. Sasak (YUG)	6–3	3–6	6–4
1981	P. Barg (USA)	H. Fukarkova (TCH)	6–2	6–3	
1982	C. Bassett (CAN)	M. Maleeva (BUL)	6–4		ret
1983	D. Spence (USA)	A. Cecchini (ITA)	2–6	7–5	6–4
1984	G. Sabatini (ARG)	K. Maleeva (BUL)	6–1	6–3	
1985	M. J. Fernandez (USA)	P. Tarabini (ARG)	7–5	6–1	
1986	P. Tarabini (ARG)	B. Fulco (ARG)	6–2	6–2	
1987	N. Zvereva (URS)	L. Lapi (ITA)	6–2	6–0	
1988	C. Cunningham (USA)	L. Lapi (ITA)	6–0	6–1	
1989	L. Spadea (USA)	S. Albinus (DEN)	6–0	6–3	
1990	P. Perez (ESP)	S. Ramon (ESP)	6–1	7–6	
1991	E. Likhovtseva (URS)	M-J. Gaidono (ARG)	7–6	6–1	
1992	B. Mulej (SLO)	R. De Los Rios (PAR)	7–5	7–5	
1993	A. Montolio (ESP)	S. Jeyaseelan (CAN)	6–7	6–1	6–1

	WINNER	RUNNER-UP	SCORE
1994	M. Ramon (ESP)	A. Kournikova (RUS)	7–5 6–4
1995	A. Kournikova (RUS)	S. Nacuk (YUG)	6–3 6–2
1996	A. Alcazar (ESP)	K. Srebotnik (SLO)	6–3 6–0
1997	T. Pisnik (SLO)	G. Volekova (SVK)	6–2 6–0
1998	E. Dementieva (RUS)	N. Petrova (RUS)	3–6 6–4 6–0

GALEA CUP AND ANNIE SOISBAULT CUP (Discontinued in 1990)

International Team Championship for men and women respectively aged 20 and under. Full results of final rounds can be found in *World of Tennis 1996* and earlier editions.

VALERIO/GALEA CUP

International Team Championship for boys aged 18 and under. Played zonally with the final stages in Lesa, Italy. Administered by the European Tennis Association.

FINALS

1970 Sweden d. France 4–1: L. Johansson d. F. Caujolle 10–8 6–3; T. Svensson d. E. Naegelen 6–4 6–0; R. Norbeg lost to E. Deblicker 4–6 0–6; M. Stig d. A. Collinot 6–3 6–1; Johansson/Stig d. Deblicker/Naegelen 6–3 6–3.
1971 Italy d. West Germany 4–0: M. Consolini d. U. Pinner 6–2 1–0 ret; N. Gasparini d. R. Gehring 6–1 3–6 6–0; C. Borea d. A. Hongsag 3–6 6–4 6–3; C. Barazzutti v L. Jelitto 5–1 abandoned; Barazzutti/Gasparini d. Gehring/Jelitto 6–4 6–4.
1972 Czechoslovakia d. USSR 3–2: I. Hora lost to V. Borisov 6–4 7–9 5–7; P. Slozil d. A. Machavez 6–2 2–6 6–4; Slozil/J. Granat d. A. Bogomolov/Borisov 6–3 7–5; T. Smid lost to K. Pugaev 3–6 8–6 4–6; Granat d. Bogomolov 6–3 6–4.
1973 Czechoslovakia d. USSR 4–1: A. Jankowski lost to V. Borisov 6–4 2–3 ret; P. Slozil d. A. Machavez 6–3 5–7 6–4: J. Granat d. K. Pugaev 3–6 6–4 6–3; T. Smid d. V. Katsnelson 6–4 6–4; Jankowski/Slozil d. Borisov/Pugaev 6–8 10–8 6–3.
1974 Spain d. Italy 3–2: L. Fargas d. A. Meneschincheri 6–1 6–1; A. Capitan /M. Mir lost to A. Marchetti/A. Vattuone 6–3 4–6 3–6; M. Mir lost to G. Ocleppo 4–6 2–6; A. Torralbo d. Vattuone 9–11 6–4 6–3; Capitan d. G. Marchetti 8–6 3–6 6–3.
1975 Italy d. USSR 3–2: G. Ocleppo d. S. Baranov 7–5 6–5 ret; A. Spiga d. S. Molodoikov 6–4 6–8 6–0; A. Merlone d. V. Gruzman 6–2 0–6 6–3; A. Meneschincheri lost to S. Elerdashvili 9–11 4–6; Ocleppo/Merlone lost to Baranov/Gruzman 5–7 4–6.
1976 West Germany d. France 4–1: P. Elter d. P. Portes 6–3 6–2; W. Popp lost to Y. Noah 3–6 0–6; J. Henn d. J. Kuentz 6–2 6–2; A. Maurer d. G. Geniau 6–4 6–3; Elter/Popp d. G. Moretton/Noah 6–3 3–6 6–3.
1977 Italy d. Rumania 5–0: G. Rinaldini d. E. Pana 6–1 6–1; M. Rivaroli d. L. Mancas 6–2 6–4; N. Canessa d. A. Dirzu 6–3 2–6 6–4; P. Parrini d. F. Segarceanu 6–1 6–0; Canessa/Parrini d. Dirzu/Segarceanu 7–5 6–2.
1978 Sweden d. Italy 3–2: M. Wennberg d. F. Moscino 6–2 6–2; P. Hjertquist/S. Simonsson d. M. Alciati/C. Panatta 6–1 6–3; Hjertquist d. M. Ferrari 6–1 6–3; Simonsson lost to Alciati 4–6 1–6; A. Jarryd lost to Panatta 0–6 1–6.
1979 Sweden d. West Germany 4–1: S. Simonsson d. H. D. Beutel 6–4 6–0; T. Svensson d. C. Zipf 2–6 6–4 6–4; A. Jarryd d. K. Vogel 6–2 7–5; J. Gunnarsson d. A. Schulz 7–5 6–4; Simonsson/Svensson lost to Beutel/Zipf 3–6 6–2 6–8.
1980 Spain d. France 4–1: J. Aguilera d. T. Pham 6–4 1–6 6–3; A. Tous/S. Casal d. J. Potier/J. M. Piacentile 6–2 3–6 6–4; Tous lost to Potier 1–6 6–7; R. Mensua d. P. Kuchna 6–4 6–1; Casal d. Miacentile 6–1 6–1.
1981 Sweden d. Italy 3–2: H. Sundstrom d. S. Ercoli 6–4 6–2; J. Nystrom/M. Tideman lost to L. Botazzi/F. Cancellotti 6–1 3–6 4–6; Nystrom d. Botazzi 6–3 6–2; T. Hogstedt lost to Cancellotti 4–6 1–6; Tideman d. S. Colombo 6–2 7–6.
1982 Italy d. Spain 3–2: S. Ercoli lost to M. Jaite 2–6 6–7; M. Fiorini d. D. De Miguel 6–2 7–5; P. Cane d. E. Sanchez 6–1 3–6 6–4; M. Zampieri lost to J. Bardou 4–6 4–6; Cane/Fioroni d. Bardou/Jaite 4–6 6–3 8–6.
1983 Sweden d. Spain 4–1: J. Svensson d. G. R. Fernando 4–6 6–4 7–5; J./K. Carlsson d. D. De Miguel/J. Bardou 6–2 1–6 6–2; J. Carlsson lost to Bardou 4–6 2–6; K. Carlsson d. E. Sanchez 3–6 6–0 6–1; P. Lundgren d. L. F. Garcia 6–3 6–4.
1984 Italy d. France 3–1: F. Ricci d. G. Tournant 6–4 3–6 7–5; N. Devide d. P. Gardarein 6–3 6–4; I. Cappelloni d. O. Cayla 7–5 7–6; Gardarein/Winogradski d. Devide/Pistolesi 5–7 6–4 6–4.
1985 Italy d. Sweden 3–2: A. Baldoni lost to D. Engel 2–6 1–6; C. Pistolesi/S. Mezzadri d. C. Allgaardh/T. Nydahll 6–4 6–4; Pistolesi d. Allgaardh 6–3 6–4; U. Colombini d. C. Bergstrom 7–6 6–2; O. Càmporese lost to U. Stenlund 0–6 3–6.
1986 Italy d. Spain 3–2: E. Rossi lost to J. Sanchez 6–7 4–6; O. Camporese lost to T. Carbonell 3–6 4–6; U. Pigato d. F. Anda 6–1 6–3; A. Baldoni d. F. Roig 7–5 6–4; Camporese/Rossi d. Carbonell/Sanchez 3–6 6–3 6–4.
1987 Czechoslovakia d. West Germany 2–0: D. Rikl d. C. Arriens 6–1 6–1; T. Zdrazila d. S. Nensel 6–1 4–6 6–2.
1988 Sweden d. Israel 3–0: N. Kulti d. R. Weidenfeld 7–6 6–2; L. Jonsson d. B. Merenstein 6–2 6–1; Kulti/M. Larsson d. Merenstein/O. Weinberg 6–3 3–6 6–4.
1989 Sweden d. West Germany 3–0: O. Kristiansson d. A. Kloodt 6–2 6–3; R. PettersAoson d. R. Leissler 6–2 6–1; D. Geivald/Kristiansson d. Kloodt/Leissler 6–7 6–1 6–2.
1990 Sweden d. USSR 2–1: M. Renstroem d. A. Rybalko 6–3 7–6; O. Ogorodov lost to R. Petterson 6–3 6–7 0–6; Renstroem/M. Tillstroem d. Ogordov/Rybalko 6–2 6–1
1991 Spain d. Germany 2–0: A. Berasategui d. S. Gessner 6–4 6–2; A. Corretja d. G. Paul 6–2 3–6 6–0.
1992 Spain d. Italy 2–0: A. Corretja d. M. Navarra 6–3 6–1; J. Gisbert d. M. Bertolini 6–1 7–6 (doubles not played).
1993 Spain d. Germany 3–0: R. Carretero d. C. Vinck 6–4 6–4; A. Costa d. L. Rehmann 6–3 6–3; G. Corrales/Costa d. Rehmann/Tambue 7–6 7–5.

1994 Spain d. France 2–1: C. Moya d. M. Huard 6–1 6–0; J. Diaz lost to N. Escude 6–3 6–7 2–6; C. Moya/F. Vicente d. J. F. Bachelot/N. Escude 7–5 6–2.
1995 Czech Republic d. Sweden 2–1: J. Vanek d. N. Timfjord 6–4 6–3; M. Tabara d. F. Jonsson 7–5 6–4; O. Fukarek/J. Vanek lost to F. Jonsson/N. Timfjord 6–7 6–3 3–6.
1996 France d. Czech Republic 2–1: S. Grosjean lost to J. Vanek 5–7 4–6; O. Mutis d. M. Tabara 7–6(6) 6–2; S. Grosjean/O. Mutis d. R. Stepanek/J. Vanek 6–0 6–4.
1997 France d. Czech Republic 3–0: J. Jeanpierre d. P. Kralert 6–3 6–2; A. Di Pasquale d. M. Tabara 6–2 6–0; A. Di Pasquale/J. Jeanpierre d. P. Kralert/M. Stepanek 6–3 7–6.
1998 Spain d. France 2–1: F. Lopez lost to J. Haehnel 6–4 1–6 1–6; J. C. Ferrero d. J. Jeanpierre 3–6 6–1 6–4; J. C. Ferrero/F. Lopez d. J. Jeanpierre/M. Llodra 6–2 7–5.

JEAN BOROTRA CUP

International Team Championship for boys aged 16 and under; originally the Jean Becker Cup. Finals played in Le Touquet. Administered by the European Tennis Association.

FINALS
1972 Spain d. France 4–1: M. Mir d. Ph. Gruthchet 6–3 6–2; F. Riba d. C. Freyss 6–2 1–6 6–4; A. Capitan d. R. Brunet 6–3 7–5; Masana/Mir lost to Frantz/Grutchet 6–4 6–7 3–6; Capitan/Riba d. Brunet/Freyss 7–5 3–6 9–7.
1973 Italy d. West Germany 3–2: M. Attolini lost to K. Eberhardt 1–6 1–6; G. Sileo d. P. Elter 7–5 6–4; M. Spiga d. U. Wellerdieck 6–2 7–5; Attolini/Sileo lost to Eberhardt/Elter 0–6 5–7; Mazzocchi/Spiga d. Liebthal/WellerAdieck 6–3 6–2.
1974 West Germany d. Italy 4–1: Buchbinder d. G. Rinaldi 6–2 6–2; P. Elter d. Risi 6–0 6–1; A. Maurer d. Gardi 6–7 7–5 6–1; Buchbinder/W. Popp lost to Gardi/Rinaldi 6–2 6–7 8–10; Elter/Maurer d. Risi/M. Rivarolli 6–0 6–3.
1975 Czechoslovakia d. Italy 3–2: M. Lacek d. G. Rinaldini 7–5 6–1; I. Lendl d. A. Ciardi 6–1 6–3; J. Kucera d. P. Parreni 6–4 6–4; Lacek/Kucera lost to Parreni/A. Rivaroli 4–6 4–6; Lendl/A. Vantuch lost to Ciardi/Rinaldini 6–1 4–6 3–6.
1976 Sweden d. Czechoslovakia 3–2: P. Hjertquist lost to I. Lendl 6–0 3–6 4–6; S. Simonsson d. A. Vikopa 6–3 6–0; H. Johansson d. T. Pitra 6–3 6–2; Simonsson/A. Fritzner lost to Lendl/J. Kerezek 6–4 3–6 1–6; Hjertquist/Johansson d. Pitra/J. Vikopal 6–3 6–2.
1977 Italy d. Sweden 3–2: A. Costa d. A. Jarryd 7–5 6–2; A. Giacomini lost to S. Simonsson 1–6 1–6; A. Moscino d. S. Svensson 6–4 6–4; Giacomini/A. Odling lost to Simonsson/Jarryd 3–6 4–6; Costa/Moscino d. Svensson/M. Wennberg 6–2 6–4.
1978 Sweden d. France 3–2: S. Svensson d. T. Tulasne 6–4 6–2; H. Simonsson lost to J. Potier 6–3 2–6 7–9 disqualified; J. Gunnarsson d. T. Pham 6–2 5–7 6–2; M. Wilander lost to J. L. Cotard 2–6 7–5 4–6; Svensson/ Simonsson d. Cotard/J. M. Piacentile 6–3 6–1.
1979 Sweden d. France 4–1: J. Windahll lost to T. Tulasne 2–6 1–6; M. Wilander d. H. Leconte 6–2 1–6 6–3; T. Hogstedt d. P. Kuchna 6–2 6–1; J. Sjogren d. J. M. Piacentile 6–1 6–1; Hogstedt/Wilander d. Leconte/Piacentile 3–6 6–3 6–4.
1980 Sweden d. Czechoslovakia 3–0: M. Wilander d. M. Mecir 3–6 6–1 6–1; A. Mansson d. K. Novacek 6–3 6–3; H. Sundstrom/Wilander d. Mecir/B. Stankovic 6–3 3–0 ret.
1981 France d. Sweden 3–2: T. Benhabiles d. S. Edberg 6–4 6–4; F. Hamonet d. J. B. Svensson 6–0 6–2; T. Chamsion lost to P. Svensson 3–6 6–2 0–6; O. Cayla lost to A. Henricsson 6–1 4–6 3–6; Hamonet/G. Forget d. Edberg/P. Svensson 6–4 1–6 6–2.
1982 Sweden d. Spain 4–1: J. Svensson d. J. Maso 6–2 6–2; S. Edberg d. F. Garcia 6–4 6–4; P. Svensson d. J. Oltra 6–2 6–1; J. Carlsson lost to S. Castello 5–7 1–6; Edberg/P. Svensson d. Garcia/Oltra 6–2 6–1.
1983 Sweden d. USSR 3–2: D. Engel d. V. Gabritchidze 7–5 6–1; K. Carlsson d. A. Volkov 6–2 6–4; C. Allgaardh d. A. Tchernetsky 7–5 6–3; C. Bergstrom lost to I. Metreveli 6–0 6–7 3–6; Carlsson/Allgaardh d. Volkov/Metreveli 6–3 6–7 6–3.
1984 Italy d. Sweden 4–1: P. Chinellato lost to T. Nydhal 4–6 6–4 3–6; O. Camporese d. H. Holm 6–4 6–0; A. Baldoni d. A. Rosen 6–4 6–0; S. Sorensen d. N. Utgren 6–2 6–4; Baldoni/E. Rossi d. T. Nydal/P. Henricsson 7–6 1–6 6–3.
1985 Sweden d. France 3–2: P. Henricsson lost to A. Boetsch 3–6 2–6; P. Wennberg d. P. Ventura 6–2 6–2; N. Utgren d. S. Blanquie 6–1 6–2; M. Zeile d. C. Sebastiani 6–1 6–3; Henricsson/Utgren lost to Boetsch/R. Pedros 2–6 6–3 4–6.
1986 Italy d. Netherlands 3–2: F. Mordegan lost to P. Dogger 5–7 6–3 1–6; D. Nargiso lost to J. Eltingh 5–7 2–6; C. Caratti d. J. Siemerink 7–5 6–0; R. Furlan d. R. Heethius 7–5 5–7 7–5; Caratti/Nargiso d. Eltingh/Siemerink 4–6 7–5 6–3.
1987 Austria d. Italy 3–2: T. Buchmayer d. F. Pisilli 6–3 6–1; O. Fuchs lost to S. Pescosolido 4–6 1–6; H. Priller d. M. Ardinghi 6–3 6–4; G. Bohm lost to M. Boscatto 6–2 1–6 6–8; Buchmayer/Priller d. Boscatto/Pescosolido 1–6 6–4 6–4.
1988 Sweden d. Czechoslovakia 3–2: J. Alven d. M. Damm 6–1 6–4; R. Pettersson d. J. Kodes 2–6 7–5 6–3; J. Sunnemark lost to L. Hovorka 6–3 0–6 3–6; M. Renstroem d. P. Gazda 6–1 2–6 6–2; Alven/Pettersson lost to Damm/Horkova 0–6 6–3 6–7.
1989 Czechoslovakia d. West Germany 4–1: P. Gazda d. A. Kriebel 7–5 6–3; R. Hanak d. D. Prinosil 6–0 6–4; L. Thomas d. J. Weinzierl 6–2 6–4; B. Galik d. M. Kohlmann 6–4 6–2; Gazda/Thomas lost to M. Kuckenbecker/ Prinosil 6–4 3–6 4–6.
1990 France d. Spain 3–2: N. Kischkewitz d. J. Gisbert 6–4 6–2; P. Lasserre d. A. Corretja 6–4 6–3; J. Hanquez lost to J. Martinez 7–6 5–7 2–6; O. Tauma d. G. Corrales 3–6 6–4 6–0; Kischkewitz/Tauma lost to Corretja/Gisbert 3–6 2–6.
1991 Spain d. Czechoslovakia 4–1: A. Costa d. F. Kascak 6–4 6–2; G. Corrales d. P. Pala 6–7 6–1 6–3; R. Carretero d. D. Skoch 5–7 7–6 7–5; J. Balcells lost to D. Miketa 5–7 6–1 1–6; Corrales/Costa d. Kascak/Pala 6–1 6–4.
1992 France d. Sweden 2–1: N. Escude d. M. Norman 2–6 6–4 6–4; M. Huard lost to A. Stenman 5–7 5–7; Esude/Huard d. Norman/M. Sjoquist 6–2 6–2.

1993 France d. Sweden 2–1: J-F Bachelot lost to F. Jonsson 1–6 6–3 12–14; J. Potron d. N. Timfjord 6–2 6–2; O. Mutis/Potron d. Jonsson/Timfjord 4–6 6–1 6–0.
1994 Spain d. Netherlands 3–0: O. Serrano d. P. Wessels 6–4 1–6 6–3; A. Martin d. R. Sluiter 6–3 6–3; A. Gordon/O. Serrano d. R. Sluiter/P. Wessels 3–6 6–4 14–13.
1995 Germany d. France 2–1: T. Zivnicek d. N. Tourte 6–2 6–2; D. Elsner d. A. Di Pasquale 6–2 0–6 6–2; D. Elsner/T. Messmer lost to A. Di Pasquale/N. Tourte 2–6 2–6.
1996 Belgium d. Russia 2–1: O. Rochus lost to A. Derepasko 6–2 3–6 4–6; X. Malisse d. M. Safin 6–4 6–1; X. Malisse/O. Rochus d. A. Derepasko/K. Ivanov-Smolenski 7–5 6–1.
1997 Spain d. Italy 2–1: T. Robredo lost to F. Volandri 3–6 3–6; F. Lopez d. U. Vico 6–3 4–6 7–5; F. Lopez/T. Robredo d. U. Vico/F. Volandri 4–6 6–1 6–1.
1998 Spain d. France 2–1: D. Ferrer d. N. Mahut 7–6 1–6 8–6; T. Robredo d. P-H. Mathieu 6–3 3–6 6–2; G. Grias/T. Robredo lost to N. Mahut/J. Maigret 4–6 6–3 2–6.

DEL SOL CUP

International Team Championship for boys aged 14 and under. Played in zones with finals in Barcelona. Administered by the European Tennis Association.

FINALS

1979 Italy d. France 3–2: M. Fioroni d. M. Cartier 6–0 6–2; G. Possani d. G. Forget 6–7 7–5 6–3; A. Paris lost to T. Benhabiles 0–6 5–7; L. Baglioni lost to F. Hamonet 0–6 0–6; Possani/Paris d. Benhabiles/Hamonet 6–1 6–4.
1980 Sweden d. Italy 4–1: P. Svensson d. R. Salemme 6–4 7–6; S. Edberg d. F. Ricci 7–5 6–3; R. Lofquist d. F. Filippi 6–3 6–4; J. Svensson lost to P. Poggioli 4–6 2–6; Edberg/P. Svensson d. Filippi/A. Vacca 6–4 6–1.
1981 Sweden d. Israel 3–2: T. Johansson lost to A. Naor 2–6 6–7; C. Allgaardh lost to G. Blom 4–6 6–2 4–6; K. Carlsson d. R. Weinberg 6–0 6–0; C. Bergstrom d. M. Osherov 2–6 7–5 7–5; Allgaardh/Carlsson d. Blom/ Osherov 6–2 6–1.
1982 Sweden d. West Germany 4–1: H. Kolm d. U. Kraft 6–1 6–0; K. Carlsson d. O. Sachau 6–0 6–0; P. Ekstrand lost to I. Kroll 0–6 2–6; T. Nydahl d. C. Guhl 6–0 1–6 6–1; Carlsson/Nydahl d. Guhl/Kraft 6–1 6–4.
1983 Sweden d. West Germany 3–2: U. Persson d. H. Stang 6–2 6–2; P. Henricsson d. P. Pfleger 6–4 6–1; U. Eriksson lost to U. Kraft 7–6 3–6 2–6; P. Wennberg lost to L. Orzessek 2–6 3–6; Henricsson/M. Urgren d. Kraft/Orzessek 6–2 6–3.
1984 West Germany d. Spain 4–1: S. Scheider d. F. Alfonso 6–3 4–6 7–5; F. Loddenkemper/A. Thoms d. J. Olivert/S. Bruguera 6–3 6–2; Loddenkemper d. Olivert 7–6 7–6; D. Richter d. A. Martinez 6–1 7–5; A. Thoms lost to Bruguera 3–6 6–2 4–6.
1985 Austria d. Italy 5–0: G. Bohm d. F. Casa 6–4 6–2; T. Buchmayer/O. Fuchs d. S. Pescosolido/F. Pisilli 6–2 6–3; Buchmayer d. Pescosolido 6–3 4–6 6–4; Fuchs d. Pisilli 6–3 7–6; H. Prilled d. M. Ardinghi 6–2 6–1.
1986 Sweden d. Yugoslavia 4–1: J. Alven d. S. Hirszon 6–3 6–4; R. Pettersson lost to B. Trupy 2–6 3–6; M. Ekstrand d. A. Tonejc 3–6 6–4 6–3; J. Henriksson d. S. Ban 6–4 7–6; Alven/Pettersson d. Hirszon/Trupej 6–2 6–4.
1987 West Germany d. Austria 4–1: J. Weinzierl lost to R. Wawra 3–6 2–6; G. Paul d. N. Patzak 6–0 6–1; S. Petraschek d. J. Knowle 3–6 6–2 6–2; A. Kriebel d. H. Kugler 6–2 6–3; Paul/Petraschek d. Knowle/Wawra 4–6 6–2 6–2.
1988 West Germany d. Spain 3–2: M. Kohlman d. A. Corretja 6–2 6–1; T. Ruhle lost to A. Bragado 0–6 3–6; J. Schors d. J. Martinez 6–2 6–4; G. Hecht lost to J. Velasco 6–0 5–7 1–6; Kohlman/M. Nacke d. Bragado/Corretja 7–6 7–6.
1989 France d. Sweden 4–1: N. Bertsch d. T.A Johansson 7–5 7–6; A. De Cret d. K. Bergh 6–4 6–2; S. Martinez d. P. Salasca 6–2 6–3; M. Dallay d. D. Winberg 7–5 6–4; Bertsch/De Cret lost to Johansson/Salasca 6–4 3–6 1–6 7–6 7–6.
1990 France d. Spain 5–0: M. Boye d. A. Pastor 7–6 3–6 6–4; N. Maurier d. J. Diaz 7–6 6–4; J. Van Lottum d. A. Gandarias 1–6 6–2 6–2; K. Dous d. E. Xapelli 6–4 6–1; Boye/Maurier d. Diaz/Pastor 6–2 6–2.
1991 Spain d. USSR 5–0: J–A. Saiz d. I. Pridankine 7–6 6–1; F. Vincente d. J. Michejev 7–6 6–7 6–4; J. Vincente d. A. Gonopolskij 6–0 6–4; A. Martin d. A. Stoljarov 6–7 6–3 8–6; Martin/J. Vincente d. Pridankine/Stoljarov 7–6 6–3.
1992 Germany d. France 3–1: T. Haas lost to O. Mutis 4–6 4–6; J.-R. Brandt d. J.-R. Lisnard 7–5 6–1; J.-P. Wenner d. J. Barras 6–3 7–6; Brandt/Haas d. M.-O. Baron/Mutis 6–4 6–3.
1993 France d. Italy 4–1: K. Fernandez d. D. Bramanti 7–6 7–5; A Di Pasquale d. F. Allgauer 7–5 6–3; V. Lavergne lost to A. Capodimonte 6–4 3–6 2–6; J-R Lisnard d. D. Sciortino 6–3 6–1; Di Pasquale/Lisnard d. Capodimonte/ Sciortino 6–3 4–6 7–5.
1994 France d. Italy 3–2: N. Senelle d. M. Aprile 6–4 6–3; J. Haenelt d. N. Frocassi 6–4 6–3; A. Rafidison lost to F. Luzzi 3–6 1–6; J. Jeanpierre d. M. Armadroy 6–1 6–1; N. Devilder/J. Jeanpierre lost to N. Frocassi/Luzzi 5–7 2–6.
1995 Great Britain d. Spain 3–2: A. Mackin d. I. Navarro 6–3 6–7(2) 7–5; N. Greenhouse lost to M. Marco w/o; M. Hilton d. F. Lopez 2–6 6–4 6–1; S. Dickson d. T. Robredo 6–1 6–0; S. Dickson/M. Hilton lost to F. Lopez/T. Robredo 5–7 6–4 5–7.
1996 France d. Croatia 4–1: D. Voravoncsa d. V. Sirola 6–0 6–1; P. Capdeville d. M. Ancic 2–6 6–0 6–2; N. Mahut lost to M. Radic 2–6 7–5 3–6; P-H. Mathieu d. R. Karanusic 6–2 6–0; P. Capdeville/P-H. Mathieu d. R. Karanusic/M. Radic 6–3 6–0.
1997 France d. Czech Republic 5–0: N. Beuque d. D. Novak 6–0 7–5; C. Roche d. D. Karol 6–3 6–1; J-M. Ali-Cayol d. M. Kokta 6–2 6–1; J. Maigret d. J. Masik 7–5 6–0; J-M. Ali-Cayol/C. Roche d. D. Karol/J. Masik 7–5 7–6(8).
1998 Germany d. France 3–2: M. Bayer d. M. Auradou 5–7 6–4 6–4; D. Schubert lost to T. Cazes Carrere 1–6 5–7; N. Muschiol lost to R. Gasquet 2–6 6–7; P. Petzschner d. E. Petit 7–5 6–2; P. Petzschner/D. Schubert d. T. Cazes Carrere/ C. Morel 7–5 7–5.

SOISBAULT/REINA CUP

International Team Championship for girls aged 18 and under. Played zonally with the final stages in Spain. Administered by the European Tennis Association.

FINALS

1972 Rumania d. West Germany 3–2: F. Mihai d. A. Spiedel 6–4 7–5; V. Ruzici/M. Simionescu d. B. Portcheller/B. Kasler 8–6 6–1; Ruzici d. Portcheller 2–6 6–0 6–1; Simionescu lost to Kasler 4–6 3–6; M. Neuweiller lost to K. Pohmann 4–6 3–6.

1973 Great Britain d. Spain 4–1: B. L. Thompson d. G. Nogues 6–4 6–4; L. J. Mottram d. J. Mateo 6–3 12–10; S. Barker d. J. Alvarez 7–5 6–0; Barker/Mottram d. Mateo/C. Chillida 6–2 6–2; J. Potterton lost to Chillida 3–6 0–6.

1974 Czechoslovakia d. France 4–1: L. Plchova d. M. Cozaux 6–4 6–1; Y. Brzakova lost to B. Simon 6–8 6–2 4–6; H. Strachonova d. C. Gimmig 6–3 6–0; R. Marsikova d. F. Thibault 8–4 6–4; Brzakova/A. Kulankova d. Thibault/A. Duguy 9–7 4–6 6–4.

1975 Great Britain d. Czechoslovakia 4–1: M. Tyler d. A. Kulhankova 6–1 3–6 6–3; C. Harrison d. J. Kopekova 6–3 6–3; L. J. Mottram d. H. Strachonova 2–6 11–9 6–3; J. Cottrell lost to K. Skronska 1–6 1–6; A. Cooper/Cottrell d. Skronska/Kulhankova 1–6 6–4 6–4.

1976 Great Britain d. Switzerland 3–1: J. M. Durie d. C. Jolissaint 4–6 6–3 6–4; A. Cooper lost to M. Simmen 6–4 0–6 4–6; C. Harrison d. A. Ruegg 6–4 6–7 6–2; M. Tyler d. P. Delhees 6–2 6–2.

1977 Czechoslovakia d. Sweden 5–0: H. Mandlikova d. M. Wiedel 6–2 6–2; I. Budarova d. H. Brywe 6–1 6–1; Mandlikova/Budarova d. A. C. Mansson/A. Nilsson 6–1 6–3; M. Skuherska d. Nilsson 6–0 6–4; H. Strachonova d. Mansson 6–3 7–5.

1978 Czechoslovakia d. Sweden 5–0: M. Skuherska d. L. Jacobson 6–3 6–2; H. Mandlikova d. H. Brywe 6–1 6–1; I. Budarova/Mandlikova d. Jacobson/L. Sandin 6–3 6–1; I. Petru d. A. Nilsson 6–1 6–2; Budarova d. Sandin 6–3 5–7 7–5.

1979 Czechoslovakia d. Switzerland 3–1: I. Bendlova d. P. Frey 6–1 6–1; M. Skuherska/I. Petru lost to C. Jolissaint/I. Villiger 3–6 4–6; Skuherska d. Villiger 3–6 6–1 6–1; I. Novakova d. Jolissaint 6–7 6–3 6–3; Petru v C. Pasquale 5–7 abandoned.

1980 Switzerland d. USSR 3–2: K. Stampfli d. J. Kashevarova 6–3 6–3; I. Villiger/L. Drescher lost to O. Zaitseva/S. Cherneva 4–6 5–7; Villiger d. Zaitseva 6–2 7–5; C. Pasquale lost to Cherneva 4–6 7–5 7–9; Drescher d. J. Salnikova 7–6 6–4.

1981 Sweden d. Czechoslovakia 3–2: B. Bjort d. P. Dutkova 6–2 6–3; M. Lindstrom/C. Lindqvist d. H. Sukova/M. Pazderova 6–3 6–3; C. Jexell lost to Pazderova 6–3 2–6 0–6; Lindqvist d. N. Piskackova 6–2 6–2; Lindstrom lost to Sukova 6–7 3–6.

1982 Italy d. Czechoslovakia 4–1: R. Reggi d. I. Petru 6–3 6–4; N. Virgintino lost to H. Fukarkova 7–5 2–6 3–6; A. Cecchini d. P. Dutkova 7–6 7–6; F. Bonsignori d. A. Souckova 6–3 6–0; Reggi/Virgintino d. Petru/Fukarkova 7–5 4–6 6–2.

1983 Italy d. Czechoslovakia 4–1: L. Ferrando d. A. Souckova 6–0 6–3; B. Romano/N. Virgintino d. A. Holikova/ Souckova 6–3 6–7 6–3; A. M. Cecchini d. O. Votavova 6–7 6–3 6–1; Virgintino d. P. Tesarova 6–3 6–1; S. Dalla Valle lost to Holikova 5–7 3–6.

1984 Sweden d. Czechoslovakia 3–2: H. Dahlstrom d. O. Votavova 6–3 6–3; A. Karlsson d. A. Holikova 6–3 6–0; A. Souckova d. M. Lundquist 7–5 7–5; K. Karlsson d. P. Tesarova 6–1 6–2; Votavova/Holikova d. Lundquist/Olsson 6–4 6–2.

1985 Italy d. Sweden 4–1: L. Lapi lost to C. Dahlman 0–6 1–6; L. Garrone/L. Golarsa d. A. K. Ollson/M. Lundquist 6–1 6–3; Garrone d. H. Dahlstrom 6–2 6–7 6–2; C. Nozzoli d. Ollson 6–4 6–4; Golarsa d. Lundquist 6–2 6–0.

1986 Czechoslovakia d. Sweden 5–0: R. Rajchrtova d. C. Dahlstrom 6–4 6–0; R. Zbrubakova d. J. Jonerup 6–3 6–3; J. Novotna d. M. Stradlund 6–4 6–2; D. Krajcovicova d. M. Ekstrand 6–3 7–5; Novotna/Rajchrtova d. M. Nilsson/ Stradlund 6–0 6–1.

1987 France d. Czechoslovakia 3–0: A. Dechaume d. R. Zrubakova 6–4 6–3; E. Derly d. P. Langrova 7–5 6–1; Dechaume/S. Niox–Chateau d. Langrova/Zrubakova 6–7 6–4 6–3.

1988 Spain d. USSR 2–1: A. Sanchez d. N. Medvedeva 3–6 6–2 6–3; C. Martinez d. E. Brioukhovets 6–2 6–2; Martinez/Sanchez lost to Brioukhovets/Medvedeva 6–7 0–4 ret.

1989 Spain d. Czechoslovakia 3–0: A. Sanchez d. A. Strnadova 6–1 6–3; N. Avila d. J. Dubcova 6–3 6–0; S. Ramon/Sanchez d. K. Balnova/Strnadova 6–4 7–5.

1990 Spain d. France 2–1: P. Perez d. A. Zugasti 6–4 6–0; S. Ramon lost to A. Fusai 6–3 4–6 1–6; Perez/Ramon d. Fusai/Zugasti 7–5 6–2.

1991 Spain d. Sweden 3–0: E. Botini d. A. Carlsson 5–7 6–2 6–4; E. Bes d. M. Vallin 6–2 6–1; Botini/C. Torrens d. Vallin/Carlsson 4–6 7–6 6–2.

1992 Germany d. Spain 2–1: P. Begerow d. E. Bottini 6–2 7–5; K. Freye lost to C. Torrens 2–6 3–6; Freye/S. Wachtershauser d. Bottini/E.Jimenez 2–6 7–5 6–2.

1993 France d. Italy 3–0: S. Pitkowski d. P. Tampieri 6–0 6–0; A. Olivier d. A. Serra-Zanetti 0–6 6–2 6–1; Olivier/C. Toyre d. Serra-Zanetti/Tampieri 8–3.

1994 Italy d. Spain 2–1: F. Lubiani d. M. Ramon 6–4 6–3; A. Serrazanetti lost to M. A. Sanchez 5–7 6–4 1–6; F. Lubiani/A. Serezzanetti d. M. Ramon/M .A. Sanchez 6–0 6–4.

1995 Italy d. Czech Republic 2–1: G. Casoni lost to P. Plackova 3–6 6–4 4–6; A. Canepa d. S. Kleinova 6–2 7–6(2); A. Canepa/G. Casoni d. S. Kleinova/J. Ondrouchova 6–0 6–2.

1996 Slovak Republic d. Spain 2–1: L. Cervanova d. A. Alcazar 7–5 6–4; Z. Valekova lost to M-L. Serna 0–6 1–6; L. Cervanova/Z. Valekova d. A. Alcazar/M-L. Serna 1–6 6–3 10–8.

1997 France d. Czech Republic 2–1: A. Mauresmo d. M. Pastikova 6–3 6–3; N. Dechy d. J. Schonfeldova 6–3 6–4; France defaulted in doubles.
1998 Croatia d. Italy 2–1: D. Krstulovic d. L. Dell'Angelo 6–4 6–4; J. Kostanic lost to A. Serra-Zanetti 1–6 4–6; J. Kostanic/D. Krstulovic d. L. Dell'Angelo/F. Schiavone 6–4 6–7 6–4.

HELVETIE CUP

International Team Championship for girls aged 16 and under. Played zonally with final stages at Leysin, Switzerland.

FINALS

1977 Italy d. Switzerland 3–2: P. Cigognani lost to C. Jolissaint 0–6 3–6; B. Rossi d. I. Villiger 6–3 6–7 8–6; M. Calabria d. K. Stampfli 6–1 6–2; P. Murgo d. C. Pasquale 6–3 6–3; Rossi/Murgo lost to Jolissaint/Villiger 4–6 3–6.
1978 Bulgaria d. West Germany 5–0: M. Condova d. C. Kohde 1–6 6–3 6–1; A. Veltcheva d. Haas 6–3 5–7 6–4; I. Chichkova d. Hammig 6–3 6–0; I. Christova d. Wilmsmeyer 3–6 7–6 6–3; Condova/Veltcheva d. Kohde/Haas 3–6 6–2 6–2.
1979 Sweden d. France 5–0: C. Lindqvist d. I. Vernhes 6–7 6–3 6–0; B. Bjork d. C. Vanier 4–6 6–3 6–3; A. Flodin d. S. Gardette 6–0 6–1; H. Olsson/K. Marivall d. M. Callejo/Vanier 6–3 6–3; Olsson d. Calleja 6–2 6–1.
1980 Sweden d. West Germany 3–2: C. Anderholm d. M. Schropp 6–1 6–2; H. Olsson lost to K. Reuter 5–7 4–6; M. Schultz d. P. Keppeler 6–4 6–4; N. Nielson d. M. Reinhard 6–7 6–3 6–2; Olsson/Schultz lost to Reuter/Reinhard 6–1 4–6 5–7.
1981 Sweden d. Italy 3–2: A. Bjork lost to F. Sollenti 2–6 6–7; H. Olsson/C. Anderholm d. R. Reggi/F. Virgintino 0–6 6–2 6–1; Olsson d. A. M. Cecchini 6–4 7–5; Anderholm d. Reggi 6–3 3–6 6–4; I. Sjogreen lost to Virgintino 0–6 0–6.
1982 USSR d. France 3–2: I. Fishkina d. I. Demongeot 6–1 6–2; L. Savchenko/V. Milvidskaya lost to P. Paradis/N. Phan-Thanh 4–6 7–5 4–6; N. Bykova lost to Paradis 1–6 2–6; Savchenko d. Phan-Thanh 6–2 6–3; Mildvidskaya d. N. Herreman 6–1 6–4.
1983 USSR d. Sweden 3–2: A. Kuzmina d. A. K. Olsson 6–3 1–6 6–3; V. Milvidskaya d. H. Dahlmstrom 3–6 6–2 6–4; I. Fischkina lost to M. Lundquist 4–6 4–6; I. Fateeva lost to E. Helmersson 2–6 3–6; Fishkina/Mildvidskaya d. Dahlstrom/Lundquist 6–4 7–5.
1984 Czechoslovakia d. West Germany 4–1: R. Wlona lost to M. Gartner 7–6 3–6 4–6; J. Novotna/R. Rajchrotova d. S. Meier/R. Weiser 6–0 7–6; Novotna d. Meier 7–5 6–2; Rajchrotova d. Weiser 6–3 4–6 6–1; P. Sedkackova d. S. Hack 6–4 4–6 6–2.
1985 West Germany d. Sweden 4–1: M. Schurhoff d. M. Ekstrand 6–2 4–6 6–4; M. Gartner/S. Hack lost to M. Strandlund/M. Nilsson 3–6 3–6; Gartner/J. Jonerup 7–6 6–2; Hack d. Strandlund 6–1 6–1; W. Probst d. M. Nilsson 6–1 6–1.
1986 Switzerland d. Czechoslovakia 3–1 (one rubber not played)***:*** E. Zardo d. M. Frimmelova 6–4 6–2; M. Strebel d. L. Laskova 7–5 6–1; S. Jaquet v. P. Langrova not played; M. Plocher d. E. Sviglerova 6–4 6–2; Jacquet/Plocher lost to Frimmelova/Langrova 6–0 1–6 5–7.
1987 Netherlands d. Switzerland 3–2: N. Van Dierendonck lost to S. Jacquet 6–7 3–6; B. Sonneveld lost to M. Plocher 6–2 3–6 4–6; Y. Grubben d. G. Villiger 7–5 7–6; E. Haslinghuis d. S. Bregnard 6–1 6–0; Sonneveld/Van Dierendonck d. Jacquet/Plocher 7–5 6–3..
1988 West Germany d. Czechoslovakia 3–2: V. Martinek d. K. Balnova 6–3 6–0; K. Duell lost to A. Strnadova 2–6 3–6; M. Skulj-Zivec d. H. Vildova 7–5 6–1; A. Popp lost to R. Bobkova 4–6 6–1 5–7; C. Hofmann/Martinek d. Balnova/Strnadova 7–5 7–5.
1989 Czechoslovakia d. USSR 3–2: R. Bobkova d. S. Komleva 6–2 6–1; K. Habsudova d. E. Makarova 7–6 6–0; K. Matouskova lost to M. Chirikova 3–6 6–3 5–7; K. Kroupova lost to T. Ignatieva 2–6 2–6; Bobkova/Matouskova d. Chirikova/Komleva 4–6 6–0 8–6.
1990 USSR d. West Germany 3–2: T. Ignatieva d. K. Freye 6–4 4–6 6–3; I. Soukhova d. S. Wachterhauser 7–5 6–2; V. Vitels lost to M. Babel 4–6 0–3 ret.; G. Beleni lost to P. Begerow 3–6 3–6; Ignatieva/Soukhova d. Babel/J. Dobberstein 6–4 6–4.
1991 Czechoslovakia d. Spain 4–1: Z. Malkova d. E. Jiminez 6–4 6–0; E. Martincova lost to M. Cruells 3–6 6–7; E. Hostacova d. A. Ortuno 6–3 7–5; M. Hautova d. A. Montolio 4–6 6–3 6–1; Malkova/Martincova d. Cruells/ Jiminez 6–3 6–1.
1992 Belgium d. Germany 2–1: N. Feber d. A. Glass 6–3 6–2; L. Courtois lost to H. Rusch 6–3 6–7 3–6; Courtoios/Feber d. Glass/C. Muller 6–7 6–3 6–0.
1993 Czech/Slovak Republic d. Netherlands 2–1: L. Cenkova d. C. Reimering 6–3 6–3; A. Havrlikova lost to Y. Basting 3–6 6–1 2–6; Cenkova/L. Richterova d. Basting/D. Haak 6–3 7–5.
1994 France d. Czech Republic 2–1: A. Cocheteaux d. D. Chadkova 6–2 6–3; A. Castera d. S. Kleinova 7–5 1–6 6–0; A. Cocheteaux/I. Taesch lost to D. Chadkova/S. Kleinova 1–6 6–0 2–6.
1995 Czech Republic d. Germany 2–1: J. Lubasova lost to M. Frohlich 6–7(6) 3–6; D. Chladkova d. C. Christian 6–2 7–6(3); D. Chladkova/J. Lubasova d. C. Christian/M. Frohlich 6–2 6–4.
1996 Slovenia d. France 2–1: K. Srebotnik d. K. Chevalier 2–6 7–5 6–2; P. Rampre d. E. le Bescond 6–4 4–6 6–0; M. Matevzic/P. Rampre lost to K. Chevalier/E. le Bescond 6–4 1–6 4–6.
1997 Slovenia d. Spain 2–1: T. Hojnik lost to M. Marrero 3–6 7–6(5) 4–6; T. Pisnik d. L. Dominguez 6–2 6–0; T. Hergold/T. Pisnik d. L. Dominguez/M. Marrero 7–6(4) 6–3.
1998 Slovak Republic d. Italy 3–0: S. Hrozenska d. R. Vinci 6–3 6–4; D. Hantuchova d. F. Pennetta 7–5 3–6 6–2; K. Basternakova/S. Hrozenska d. M. E. Camerin/F. Pennetta 6–4 7–5.

EUROPA CUP

International Team Championship for girls aged 14 and under. Administered by the European Tennis Association.

FINALS

1981 West Germany d. France 3–2, *Winterslag, Belgium:* I. Cueto d. J. Clerin 6–3 2–6 6–1; R. Wieser lost to E. Folcher 1–6 6–3 1–6; S. Graf d. M. Phan-Thanh 7–5 6–3; S. Luidinant d. E. Grousseau 6–2 6–2; Graf/Wieser lost to Folcher/Grousseau 6–4 2–6 1–6.

1982 Sweden d. West Germany 3–2, *Mons, Belgium:* C. Dahlman d. S. Meier 7–5 7–5: H. Dahlstrom d. B. Herget 6–0 6–4; E. Helmersson lost to I. Cueto 3–6 7–6 0–6; I. Mattiasson lost to E. Walliser 5–7 2–6; Dahlstrom/Helmersson d. Cueto/Walliser 6–2 6–2.

1983 West Germany d. France 3–2, *Lee-on-Solent, Hampshire:* N. Vassen d. S. N. Chateau 4–6 6–3 6–2; W. Probst d. M. C. Rolet 7–5 5–7 ret; S. Hack lost to C. Bourdais 6–3 2–6 0–6; M. Gartner d. A. Dechaume 6–4 4–6 7–5; Gartner/Vassen lost to Bourdais/Dechaume 3–6 1–6.

1984 France d. Sweden 4–1: S. Dussault lost to R. Narbe 0–6 6–4 3–6; A. Dechaume/E. Derly d. M. Ekstrand/H. Johnsson 6–3 6–3; Dechaume d. Ekstrand 7–5 6–2; Derly d. Salsgard 6–4 3–6 6–1; M. Laval d. Johnsson 6–4 6–4.

1985 USSR d. Italy 3–2: N. Zvereva d. A. Dell'Orso 6–2 4–6 6–4; T. Tchernysova lost to F. Romano 3–6 2–6; E. Brihovec lost to S. Favini w.o.; A. Blumberga d. G. Boscheiro 6–3 4–6 6–4; Zvereva/Tchernysova d. Boscheiro/Dell'Orso 6–4 6–3.

1986 Netherlands d. Italy 3–2: Y. Grubben lost to Boscheiro 5–7 4–6; N. Van Lottum d. Favini 6–2 6–1; E. Markestein d. Migliori 6–4 6–4; E. Haslinghuis lost to Bertelloni 2–6 2–6; Grubben/Van Lottum d. Boscheiro/Migliori 6–2 6–2.

1987 Czechoslovakia d. Austria 3–2: P. Kucova lost to U. Priller 3–6 0–6; R. Bobkova d. D. Bidmon 6–2 6–4; P. Markova lost to N. Dobrovits 4–6 1–6; K. Matouskova d. S. Suchan 1–6 6–0 10–8; Bobkova/Kucova d. Dobrovits/Priller 6–4 4–6 7–5.

1988 Hungary d. West Germany 3–2: A. Foeldenyi d. A. Huber 6–0 3–6 8–6; B. Bathory lost to K. Denn–Samuel 0–6 3–6; M. Zsoldos d. P. Kemper 6–1 4–6 6–4; K. Kocsis lost to M. Kochta 6–4 1–6 1–6; Foeldenyi/Zsoldos d. Denn–Samuel/Huber 4–6 7–6 6–3.

1989 Czechoslovakia d. Italy 5–0: E. Martiucova d. R. Grande 7–6 6–3; I. Malkova d. G. Pizzichini 6–2 7–5; O. Hostakova d. S. Pifferi 5–7 6–1 7–5; M. Hautova d. A. Serra-Zanetti 6–0 6–2; Malkova/Martiucova d. Grande/Pifferi 6–1 6–4.

1990 Czechoslovakia d. Yugoslavia 3–2: S. Radevicova lost to I. Majoli 2–6 6–4 1–6; Z. Rebekova lost to T. Doric 5–7 4–6; A. Havrlikova d. S. Milas 6–1 6–2; A. Gersi d. D. Karadz 7–6 6–0; Havrlikova/Redevicova d. Doric/Majoli 6–3 7–5.

1991 Germany d. Czechoslovakia 5–0: M. Vladulescu d. A. Havrlikova 6–0 6–3; N. Raidt d. R. Surova 7–6 6–2; S. Schmidle d. K. Bakalarova 6–0 6–4; A. Barna d. R. Pelikanova 6–2 6–4; Barna/T. Karsten d. L. Cenkova/Havrlikova 6–2 6–1.

1992 Czechoslovakia d. France 3–2: L. Varmuzova d. I. Taesch 4–6 6–43 6–4; H. Nagyova lost to A. Castera 3–6 2–6; S. Kleinova lost to E. Curutchet 3–6 6–3 2–6; J. Ondrouchova d. G. Goultefard 6–2 6–2; Kleinova/Ondrouchova d. Castera/Curutchet 3–6 7–5 6–4.

1993 Czech/Slovak Republic d. Germany 3–2: J. Lubasova lost to S. Kovacic 3–6 3–6; D. Chladkova d. M. Weingartner 6–4 6–3; L. Faltynkova lost to M. Frohlich 5–7 3–6; L. Varmuzova d. S. Klosel 6–1 4–6 6–2; Chladkova/Faltynkova d. E. Brunn/Klosel 5–7 6–2 8–6.

1994 Germany d. Czech Republic 3–2: D. Wallenhorst d. D. Luzarova 6–4 6–0; J. Wohr lost to B. Stejsjkalova w/o; S. Losel lost to J. Schonfeldova 7–6 1–6 2–6; S. Kovacic d. M. Pastikova 6–2 6–2; L. Fritz/S. Kovacic d. M. Pastikova/J. Schonfeldova 3–6 6–1 6–1.

1995 Slovenia d. Slovak Republic 4–1: T. Hojnik lost to E. Fislova 2–6 2–6; T. Hergold d. K. Basternakova 1–0 ret; T. Pisnik d. V. Stoklasova 5–7 6–0 10–8; K. Srebotnik d. G. Volekova 6–3 6–1; T. Pisnik/K. Srebotnik d. V. Stoklasova/G. Volekova 2–6 6–1 6–3.

1996 Belgium d. Slovak Republic 3–1: E. Clijsters lost to D. Hantuchova 7–5 1–6 2–6; K. Clijsters d. Z. Kucova; J. Henin d. K. Basternakova 6–3 6–2; K. Clijsters/J. Henin d. S. Hrozenska/K. Basternakova 1–6 7–5 7–5.

1997 Slovak Republic d. Russia 4–1: M. Kunova d. G. Fokina 7–5 6–3; L. Kurhajcova d. I. Murashkintceva 6–1 7–6(4); D. Hantuchova d. L. Krasnoroutskaia 6–3 6–1; M. Babakova lost to E. Bovina 2–6 6–4 4–6; M. Babakova/D. Hantuchova d. E. Bovina/L. Krasnoroutskaia 7–6(3) 6–4.

1998 Russia d. Czech Republic 3–2: R. Gourevitch lost to B. Strucovad 6–4 5–7 1–6; V. Zvonareva lost to P. Ticha 6–4 1–6 2–6; G. Fokina d. E. Birnerova 7–6 2–6 6–3; L. Krasnoroutskaia d. P. Cetkovska 6–2 5–7 6–3; G. Fokina/R. Gourevitch d. P. Cetkovska/P. Ticha 3–6 6–1 6–3.

The International Tennis Federation

Regional Reports • Wheelchair Tennis
ITF Junior Tennis • ITF Vets Tennis
National Association Addresses

Chris Evert (above right) with Judy Dalton, the winning captain of the Australian team that carried off the Alice Marble Cup. (Jeffrey H Friedman)

International Tennis Federation

Bank Lane, Roehampton, London SW15 5XZ
Telephone: 44 181 878 6464 Fax: 44 181 878 7799
Web site http://www.itftennis.com

President: Brian Tobin.

Executive Vice-President: Juan Margets.

Honorary Life President: Philippe Chatrier.

Vice Presidents: Heinz Grimm, Eiichi Kawatei, Eduardo Moline O'Connor.

Honorary Life Vice-President: Pablo Llorens.

Honorary Life Counsellors: Paolo Angeli, Jim Cochrane, Robert A Cookson, Hunter L Delatour, J Howard Frazer, J Randolph Gregson, Gordon Jorgensen, R K Khanna, Stan Malless, David Markin, Enrique Morea, Radmilo Nikolic, Geoff Paish, Alvaro Peña, Francesco Ricci Bitti.

Trustees: Hunter L Delatour, David Jude, Pablo Llorens.

Board of Directors: Brian Tobin, Christian Bimes, Ismail El Shafei, Fathi Farah, Jan Francke, Heinz Grimm, Eiichi Kawatei, Ian King, Julia Levering, Juan Margets, Harry Marmion, Eduardo Moline O'Connor, Geoff Pollard.

Honorary Treasurer: David Jude.

Auditors: Messrs Ernst & Young, London.

Legal Counsel: UK – Townleys, Wedlake Bell.

Committees: Davis Cup, Fed Cup, Finance, Women's Circuit, Junior Competitions, Olympic, Constitutional, Rules of Tennis, Wheelchair, Veterans.

Commissions: Coaches, Media, Medical, Technical.

GRAND SLAM COMMITTEE

Australian Open: Geoff Pollard; ***French Open:*** Christian Bimes;
Wimbledon: John Curry; ***US Open:*** Harry Marmion.
Grand Slam Committee Administrator: William Babcock.

WTA TOUR BOARD OF DIRECTORS

ITF Representative: Ingrid Lofdahl-Bentzer.

ITF MEN'S CIRCUIT JOINT COMMITTEE

ITF Representatives: Juan Duran, Ismail El Shafei, Heinz Grimm, Eiichi Kawatei.

CHALLENGERS JOINT COMMITTEE

ITF Representatives: Ismail El Shafei, Heinz Grimm, Eiichi Kawatei.

SECRETARIAT

Executive Vice-President / General Manager: Juan Margets

Executive Directors: William Babcock, Men's Professional Tournaments/Grand Slam Administrator/Officials • John Garnham, Finance • Thomas Hallberg, Davis Cup Competition/Rules of Tennis • Sally Holdsworth, Administration and Personnel • Deborah Jevans, Fed Cup/Medical (& Olympic Games Administrator) • Jan Menneken, Head of Television • Dave Miley, Development • Christopher Stokes, Marketing.

Managers: Andrew Coe, Technical • Ellen de Lange, Wheelchair • Tony Gathercole, Veterans • Alun James, Communications • Ingrid Lofdahl-Bentzer, Women's Circuit • Jackie Nesbitt, Junior Competitions • Ian Takats, Information Technology.

Administrators: Frances Cason, Finance • Josette Cohen & Frank Couraud, Development • Stefan Fransson, Officiating • Sarah Orr, Men's Professional Tournaments • Tessa Radcliffe, AGM/ Constitutional Committee • Paul Smith, Promomatch• Katie Rowland, Sponsorship Sales • Alison Sowersby, Fed Cup/Olympics/Medical • Barbara Travers, Communications • John Treleven, Computer Rankings.

Regional Reports

Asian Tennis Federation 'ATF'

Despite the Asian financial crisis, devastating floods in China, riots in Indonesia and a number of 'Tiger' economies being reduced to nothing more than whimpering pussy-cats, Asian tennis continued to thrive. It is true that we were forced to cancel a few events but we were also able to add some, like the Hong Kong CMG Asia Open, and two events in China – the Mission Hills Open and Eastcom Cup, plus a new $75,000 women's tournament in India.

India's top doubles pair, Mahesh Bhupathi and Leander Paes, climbed to No.1 on the ATP Tour rankings by claiming victories in Rome, India, Shanghai and the Paris Indoor. Paes has also excelled in singles, winning the Newport tournament and breaking into the seventies on the singles computer rankings.

Indonesia hosted the 1998 ITF World Junior Tennis Competition (Asia/Oceania Qualifying) in May and in October the 9th Asian Coaches Workshop took place in Thailand. The 130 coaches from 31 Asian countries voted it a resounding success.

Sadly we had occasion to say farewell to two old friends of the ATF tennis family – Armando Manzano, a local hero in the Philippines, and Alois Fassbind, Executive Vice-President of the Royal Cliff Beach Resort in Pattaya. It was in Pattaya that the 11th Asian Open Veterans Championships were held during August and won by Hong Kong.

The ATF Seniors Tour events, held respectively in Singapore and Hong Kong, in October and November provided a feast of excellence. Players like Bjorn Borg, Ilie Nastase, Henri Leconte and crowd-pleaser Mansour ('the magician') Bahrami captivated the crowds.

Japan's two leading players, Shuzo Matsuoka and Naoko Sawamatsu, decided to call it a day. After 13 years on the Tour Shuzo decided to marry his girlfriend, the former television newscaster Emiko Taguchi. Naoko won four titles during her seven years on the WTA Tour. We thank them both for their contributions to Asian tennis.

At the ATP Tour World Championship in Hannover, the ITF's administrator Mr S. Uthrapathy received an award for the best new Challenger tournament, Vietnam. Several of our member Associations benefited from Uthra's vast experience on technical matters when he visited them during the year and have since held successful events.

As we head towards the Millennium it is pleasing to report that new facilities have recently been completed in Shanghai and in Thailand. Others in the pipeline include Kuwait, Bangladesh and Palestine.

Pakistan's Shazib Niazi, a member of the 1998 Asian Team to Europe, should be congratulated by all of us. His tournament win in Bruhl was the first by an Asian boy. With other youngsters like Chen Wei Jen of Chinese Taipei, Thailand's Udomchoke Danai and Kannan Vijay of India showing equal promise we can look forward to more tournament wins in the years to come.

Whichever way you look at it, the future of tennis in Asia is bright.

European Tennis Association 'ETA'

The year 1998 can certainly be seen as a successful one for European players at all levels. This is proved by their position at the top of the different rankings (WTA, ATP, Junior, Veterans), not to mention the successes of Spain in the Fed Cup and Sweden once again in the Davis Cup.

The European Men's Champion Clubs Cup was played in Rennes (France) on 1–4 July with 11 teams participating. The final, disputed by two French Clubs, was won by Metz.

The Women's event was contested by nine clubs at the TC Bonnevoie in Luxembourg with Patton Rennes (France) becoming European Champions.

The 1998 European Men's and Women's Team Championships took place at the end of November and in mid-December. A total of 29 teams entered the Women's Championships which was won by Italy. The same country emerged victorious in the Men's Championships from among the 32 teams participating. The Champions Divisions were played in Frydlant and Ostravici (Czech Republic) and Montecatini (Italy).

More playing opportunities than ever were offered to our players in 1998. They included 124 weeks of Satellite Circuits and 134 weeks of Futures Events for Men for total prize money of US$2.4 million. There were 127 women's tournaments, all part of the ITF Women's Circuit, with total prize money of US$2.7 million. In addition, 140 Junior Tournaments were held in the 14 and 16 age groups as part of the ETA Junior Circuit, plus 75 for Veterans in the ETA Veterans Circuit.

This year was also the start of a new administrative structure for the ETA after the retirement of General Secretary Marcel Ferralli. Two Directors were appointed: Olli Mäenpää who is responsible for Marketing & Events and Charlotte Ferrari who has responsibility for administration.

Olli Mäenpää also continues his activity as ITF/ETA Junior/Development Administrator in close co-operation with the ITF Development and Junior Departments. Since he started in 1997 he has visited most ETA member nations, especially those involved in the ITF/ETA Development programme, giving advice in many different fields: administration, coaching, technical matters etc. The total amount distributed for development in Europe during 1998 was US$838,000.

The 1998 meetings and conferences organised by the ETA were all very successful: the Annual General Meeting in Dubrovnik (Croatia) on 27–29 March; the European Tournament Conference in Bergen (Norway) on 24–26 April dealing with entry level tournaments and officiating; the Regional Meeting in Killarney (Ireland) on 8 July; the Coaches Symposium in Paphos (Cyprus) on 26–30 September; the General Secretaries/Top Executives Meeting in Cork (Ireland) on 16–18 October; the Women's Calendar & Men's Satellite Circuits and Futures Meeting in Zürich (Switzerland) on 24 October; the Meeting with Presidents in Zürich (Switzerland) on 31 October; and the Junior General Meeting in Edinburgh (Scotland) on 13–15 November. This busy schedule gives some idea of the number of people involved in improving European tennis.

Every quarter the ETA publishes 'ETA Flash' to report on all its activities. A handbook is also edited once a year with detailed information about the 48 member nations as well as results, rules and so on. The ETA is proud to have been chosen as one of the pilot bodies for the ITF's new Intranet project, launched at the end of 1998.

South American Confederation of Tennis 'COSAT'

The year began with the COSAT 1998 Circuit in 14 & Under,16 & Under and 18 & Under categories. It was another great success, having an average participation of 130 boys and 110 girls at each stage, making a total of 240 players, of which 72% were South American. The circuit was staged over nine continuous weeks in the same number of South American countries. This event gains greater importance each year through the improving level of play among the players and the good organization at every one of its stages.

One of the biggest incentives that the ITF and COSAT offer to 14 and 16-year-old players, is to fund the top 5 ranked players from the COSAT circuit for their participation in six tournaments in Europe. An overseas tour of this sort increases the players' profiles and leaves a good image of South American tennis in Europe.

Once again we staged Professional satellite tournaments for men and women over 62 weeks. For the men there were two US$25,000, six US$15,000 and twenty four US$10,000 prize money tournaments. The women's circuit comprised one US$50,000, ten US$25,000 and thirteen US$10,000 events.

The Ericsson Cup, for the second consecutive year, stands out as one of the most important professional circuits in South America. It has been very successful in six countries and it is important to highlight that this year the circuit has incorporated women's tennis, thus realizing the aspiration of staging high quality competitive tournaments throughout the region.

The South American Championships for boys and girls are valid as qualifiers to the World 14, 16 and 18-year-old Championships. In 1998 they were held in May with the 14 & Under tour being held in Uruguay, the 16 & Under tour in Peru and the 18 & Under in Colombia. The presence of nine countries which are affiliated to COSAT meant that these tournaments were well organized and highly competitive.

COSAT has devoted a great deal of attention to veterans this year with 15 tournaments having taken place in different South American towns. For the second consecutive year, the South American Championships took place in Santa Cruz, Bolivia. Altogether 106 women and 118 men participated there in the different categories, ranging from 35 to 75 years of age.

COSAT has awarded badges and certificates to 136 tennis coaches who passed one of the seven Level I Coaches courses which were held in five different countries – Colombia, Paraguay, Uruguay, Brazil and Peru.

In November, two very successful workshops were held, the first in Guayaquil, Ecuador where 100 professionals and coaches from Venezuela, Colombia, Peru and Ecuador itself attended. The second took place in Santiago, Chile, where 200 professionals from Argentina, Bolivia, Brazil, Chile, Paraguay, Peru and Uruguay attended. Both events enjoyed the presence of high level speakers, enabling us to train and further develop our human talent. Furthermore, in August, two Level I Officiating Courses were held in Uruguay and Paraguay, with the same objectives.

The work carried out by the permanent secretary of COSAT in the city of La Paz, Bolivia, has been tough but very successful, and has allowed COSAT to strengthen itself as an institution.

Oceania Tennis Federation 'OTF'

At the ITF AGM held in Ireland in July, the OTF were pleased that the ITF approved full membership status for Fiji and associate membership status for Norfolk Island and Palau. Fiji has become the third Oceania nation (following Australia and New Zealand) to achieve this recognition, which means that from 1999 it has the right to field its own Davis Cup and Fed Cup teams. With Norfolk Island and Palau being granted associate membership, all OTF member nations are now members of the ITF. The other interesting development is the ITF grant to be allocated to member nations for computer equipment, which will include an enhanced e-mail system to enable quick and easy communication with the ITF/OTF.

The 1998 Fed Cup team emulated the Davis Cup team of last year by earning promotion in next year's competition. The members were Davilyn Godinet (American Samoa), Paiao Short (Cook Islands), Tagifano ('Dengue') So'onalole (Samoa), Adriana Thaggard (Fiji) and the captain, Malcolm Kajer (Cook Islands). The team performed excellently in Bangkok, Thailand to defeat Malaysia and Singapore in the round robin matches. Finishing top in its pool, the team went into the play-offs against India and Tajikstan, needing to win one of those matches to qualify for Regional qualifying Group I in 1999. The team defeated Tajikstan in both singles.

Pacific Oceania's first tie in Group II Davis Cup against Pakistan in Islamabad in April proved to be a tough encounter. The team (in order of merit) consisted of Lency Tenai (Solomon Islands), Lawrence Tere (Papua New Guinea), Sanjeev Tikaram (Fiji), Hitesh Morriswala (Fiji) and the non-playing captain Dave Godinet (American Samoa) plus team manager Barry McMillan (Australia). They found the local clay courts difficult and the opposition more consistent and powerful. Pakistan had been competing in Group II for over 20 years. Although the team lost five rubbers to nil, captain Dave Godinet said in his report that 'this experience is only beneficial if you learn and apply yourself to do better next time'.

Pacific Oceania's Davis Cup team against Qatar in the Group II play-off tie (the loser would return to Group III in 1999) was played in Doha. Jerome Rovo (Vanuatu) made his debut replacing Hitesh Morriswala, who was unavailable due to work commitments. Mike Daws was the Team Manager, while Australian former circuit player, Rob Tucker, accompanied the team as a hitting partner and adviser to team captain, Dave Godinet. In very hot and humid conditions, where the temperature reached 43 °C during the day, the team performed admirably. Although they lost by four rubbers to one, particular reference must be made to Lency Tenai's durability. He played for over 3½ hours in the first singles match, losing in four tight sets. Then he partnered Lawrence Tere in defeating the number one and two players from Qatar 8–6 in the fifth set of the doubles after a further 4½ hours of play. Even more meritorious was the fact that they were down 1–4 in the fourth set and break point on Lency's serve!

As agreed at the last OTF General Meeting, recognised qualifications from coach education providers and regional Olympic courses (if qualifications are attached) would be acknowledged by the OTF. These would include USPTA, USPTR, ITF, TCA and NZPTCA qualifications. To help local coaches attain qualifications, a USPTA course was held in Fiji last September with a further one planned this year.

The ANZ Pacific Tennis Development programme is into its fifth year of operation. In 1998 13 nations were involved with a further two nations set to join in 1999. Apart from providing funds to coaches to teach mini tennis in schools, the programme has also made available special ANZ soft coaching balls and mini tennis nets have been purchased to distribute to nations. The ANZ Bank has been and continues to be a great friend of Oceania.

David Smith (NZ), the OTF's Honorary Development Officer for Officiating, continues to work with member nations in improving the standard of officiating throughout the region. Last year, David (as referee) and a group of chair umpires from Australia and New Zealand officiated at the Mini South Pacific Games in American Samoa, while in August David will undertake a similar task at the Micronesian Games in Palau. He also conducted an abridged Level 1 course for local officials. Rick Ninete (President, Guam NTF) will kindly assist, prior to the Games, in setting up the operations and organization for the Games' tennis event.

The 1998 Pacific Oceania Closed Championships were conducted with the assistance of OTF administrator, Paras Naidu, and officials of the Fiji Tennis Association. This year's results were:

Men's singles: ***Winner:*** Lency Tenai (Solomon Islands) – to hold the Motuliki Kailahi memorial trophy for one year; ***Runner up:*** Lawrence Tere (PNG).
Women's singles: ***Winner:*** Davilyn Godinet (American Samoa) – to hold OTF perpetual trophy for one year; ***Runner up:*** Adriana Thaggard (Fiji)

The Pacific Oceania Junior Circuit (including the North Pacific qualifying event), with legs in Fiji, Samoa and American Samoa, improves in standard each year as does the quality of players who are selected in our Pacific Oceania senior team tour to New Zealand and junior team tour to New Zealand/Australia. The ITF/OTF is also assisting players to travel to other ITF junior events in New Zealand to experience more high level tournament play.

Camps for 14 & Under players and, for the first time, the Pacific Oceania Fed Cup team, were well received and assist Dan O'Connell (ITF Pacific Oceania Development Officer) in talent spotting amongst the younger age groups.

Expert coaching visits to member nations, funded by the Olympic Solidarity, are always welcome, with the excellent new idea this year of the expert 'dropping into' the Regional Training Centre on the way through to pass on his/her knowledge to the Regional scholarship holders.

The OTF Executive Committee has appointed a Regional Advisory Board, consisting of high profile persons who have shown an interest in Oceania tennis affairs. The Committee will, from time to time, seek advice from these 'Board' members, who will add prominence to the various OTF activities. Those appointed are Ashley Cooper (Australia – former Davis Cup player), Michael Grandinetti (Northern Marianas – businessman), Bob Lyon (Australia – ANZ Bank General Manager, Pacific), Jeff Simpson (New Zealand – Davis Cup Captain) and Claudine Toleafoa (Cook Islands/New Zealand – former Fed Cup player).

In elections for the OTF Executive Committee held in January 1999, a proposal will be considered at the 1999 General Meeting to amend the OTF constitution such that the Committee includes at least one person from each of Australia, New Zealand, Melanesia, Micronesia and Polynesia. This will continue to ensure the broadest representation of nations.

Although the ground breaking ceremony for the Pacific Oceania Regional Tennis Centre in Lautoka, Fiji was held last October, construction, to everyone's frustration, has not yet commenced. It is hoped that the centre will be finished early next year. Meanwhile, the ITF, OTF, FTA, Fiji Sports Council and the Northern Club in Lautoka all contributed financially to upgrade the surface and surrounds of the club's courts to help provide, in the interim, a first-class training venue for the Regional scholarship holders. The scholarship programme attracted 11 junior players in 1998, to which are added three Fijian players under the coaching expertise of Pacific Oceania Davis Cup player, Sanjeev Tikaram, and Davis Cup selector, Naga Reddy.

The tragic death last year of Pacific Oceania Davis Cup player, Motuliki Kailahi from Tonga, brought grief to all of Oceania. Davis Cup team mate Sanjeev Tikaram (Fiji), attended the funeral on behalf of the OTF, presenting a wreath to Motuliki's family. As Sanjeev wrote, 'I left with a sad sense of loss. Being at the funeral, it made me realise how important life is and how God plays an important role in our lives'. The OTF is pleased to announce that, with the support of the Tonga Tennis Association and TASANOC, Motuliki's Australia South Pacific 2000 High Performance Athlete grant will be put towards the costs of a practice wall at the Tennis Centre in Tonga (with an appropriate plaque) in memory of Motuliki.

Mike Daws, our Joint Secretary-General, has been seconded by Tennis Australia to the Sydney Olympic Committee for Organising the Games (SOCOG) to manage the Olympic Tennis event and other Test events. The OTF Executive Committee has agreed that Fenton Coull, Mike's successor at Tennis Australia, will temporarily act as Joint Secretary-General until the OTF General Meeting in January, 1999, when elections will be held.

Paras Naidu, the OTF administrator, met with the Joint Secretaries-General in June in Auckland in a mid year meeting, which is planned to be repeated each year to help improve communication and exchange ideas more effectively and efficiently.

Review of Wheelchair Tennis

Ellen de Lange

Nineteen-ninety-eight will be remembered as probably the most significant in the history of wheelchair tennis since the sport began in the late '70s. The merger between the International Wheelchair Tennis Federation (IWTF) and the International Tennis Federation (ITF) was agreed and commenced on 1 January 1998.

The continued support of NEC enabled the ITF's wheelchair tennis department to provide a full programme of activities including the NEC Wheelchair Tennis Tour and the NEC Wheelchair Tennis Masters. Invacare Corporation provided a substantial backing for the Action World Team Cup and for a number of camps for juniors and novice players around the world.

An increased number and quality of tournaments on the NEC Tour provided wheelchair tennis players with a variety of opportunities at all levels. From the start of the season, the competition was fierce and the challenge for ranking points would determine the World Champions at the end of the year. At the ITF World Champions Dinner held during Roland Garros in Paris, the 1997 World Champions Ricky Molier and Chantal Vandierendonck, both from the Netherlands, were presented with their awards alongside their able bodied peers.

In May, a record 32 men's and 16 women's teams participated in the 1998 Action World Team Cup, organised in the Olympic Stadium Vall d'Hebron in Barcelona, Spain. For the first time an invitational event was organised, alongside the main event, for the quadraplegic teams from the USA, Great Britain, France and Japan. This inaugural competition was won by the strong USA team. Very surprisingly in the main event, the final was played between two countries who had never previously progressed beyond the quarter-finals. Germany defeated the Netherlands in a thrilling match. The Dutch still went home with a title when the women's team won the event for a record 13th time against the USA.

Chris Johnson, a member of the British Action World Team Cup team. (Gordon Gillespie)

Development continued to be an important part of the ITF's wheelchair tennis department and thanks to the employment of a new development officer it was possible to visit many new and existing wheelchair tennis countries. Some of these countries now have strong wheelchair tennis programmes in place and are planning to organise an NEC Wheelchair Tennis Tour event within the near future.

In conjunction with the Belgian Open, the ITF once again organised an international junior camp which attracted players and coaches from various countries. The camp provided an excellent opportunity for some of the most promising athletes to be taught by top coaches.

More programmes for quadraplegics were introduced this year to provide a stimulus for growth in this section of wheelchair tennis.

The year concluded with the NEC Wheelchair Tennis Masters in Eindhoven, the Netherlands, for the world's top eight men and women players. The event is fast becoming the most prestigious in the game and two exciting finals brought the season to a fitting end. Ricky Molier, from the Netherlands, finally succeeded on his third attempt, winning the Masters title in an exciting final against Laurent Giammartini from France 7–5 7–5. The 17-year-old Esther Vergeer from the Netherlands finished her phenomenal season with yet another win and her first Masters title in an all-Dutch women's final against Maaike Smit 6–1 7–6.

Wheelchair tennis has many challenges ahead, and the dedicated support from grass roots to international level will be essential to ensure that our sport grows from strength to strength.

Right: *Hector Zuniga, of Argentina, one of the Quad players benefitting from increasing concentration on this area of the game, which is showing significant growth.* (Gordon Gillespie)

Below: *Germany's Wheelchair Championship team that won the trophy: (l to r) Torsten Purschke, Kai Schrameyer, Stefan Bitterauf and Ralph Weisang.* (Gordon Gillespie)

NEC WHEELCHAIR TENNIS RANKING (as of 24 November 1998)

Men's Singles

1	HALL, David	AUS	4102
2	MOLIER, Ricky	NED	3731
3	WELCH, Stephen	USA	3664
4	LEGNER, Martin	AUT	2252
5	GIAMMARTINI, Laurent	FRA	2204
6	GREER, John	USA	1774
7	FOULKS, Michael	USA	1733
8	WEISANG, Ralph	GER	1582
9	DOUGLAS, Scott	USA	1485
10	JOHNSON, David	AUS	1410
11	MISTRY, Jayant	GBR	1243
12	JOHNSON, Paul	CAN	1129
13	SARTOV, Eyal	ISR	1106
14	LACHMAN, Daniel	USA	1056
15	KRUSZELNICKI, Tadeusz	POL	988
16	SAIDA, Satoshi	JPN	885
17	HOSHI, Yoshiteru	JPN	839
18	LARSSON, Niclas	SWE	816
19	PRUITT, Michael	USA	762
20	HATT, Simon	GBR	694

Women's Singles

1	DI TORO, Daniela	AUS	3119
2	VERGEER, Esther	NED	3063
3	SMIT, Maaike	NED	2488
4	PETERS, Sonja	NED	1995
5	CLARK, Sharon	USA	1917
6	AMERYCKX, Brigitte	BEL	1849
7	WALRAVEN, Sharon	NED	1701
8	CHOKYU, Yuka	CAN	1324
9	VANDIERENDONCK, Chantal	NED	1245
10	OHMAE, Chiyoko	JPN	1244
11	LEWELLEN, Hope	USA	895
12	ROLLISON, Patricia	USA	792
13	SIMARD, Helen	CAN	779
14	PUPOVAC, Branka	AUS	738
15	COURTIER, Jacque	NZL	726
16	OLSON, Nancy	USA	700
17	DELL, Kimberly	GBR	670
18	VAN MARUM, Djoke	NED	576
19	SAX-SCHARL, Petra	GER	545
20	ISECKE, Regina	GER	541

Quadraplegic Singles

1	DRANEY, Rick	USA	2919
2	HANSON, Brian	USA	2795
3	ECCLESTON, Mark	GBR	2201
4	VAN ERP, Bas	NED	1988
5	SANDERS, Robert	USA	1543
6	WHALEN, Kevin	USA	783
7	STUDWELL, Chris	USA	675
8	TACHIBANA, Nobuhiro	JPN	672
9	OHASHI, Kazumi	JPN	660
10	KIMURA, Sadahiro	JPN	633
11	TAKASHIMA, Masao	JPN	591
12	SAPPINO, Patrick	FRA	584
13	TAYLOR, Nicholas	USA	580
14	JORDAN, David	USA	503
15	POPPEN, Brent	USA	431
16	KIOKE, Koichi	JPN	429
17	HUMPHREYS, Roy	GBR	389
18	HIRATA, Shinichi	JPN	326
19	EVERETT, Steve	USA	283
20	POLIDORI, Guiseppe	ITA	184

ITF WHEELCHAIR TENNIS WORLD CHAMPIONS

Men

1991	Randy Snow	USA
1992	Laurent Giammartini	FRA
1993	Kai Schrameyer	GER
1994	Laurent Giammartini	FRA
1995	David Hall	AUS
1996	Ricky Molier	NED
1997	Ricky Molier	NED
1998	David Hall	AUS

Women

1991	Chantal Vandierendonck	NED
1992	Monique Kalkman	NED
1993	Monique Kalkman	NED
1994	Monique Kalkman	NED
1995	Monique Kalkman	NED
1996	Chantal Vandierendonck	NED
1997	Chantal Vandierendonck	NED
1998	Daniela Di Toro	AUS

NEC WHEELCHAIR TENNIS TOUR 1998

Dates	*Tournament*	*Grade*	*Singles*	*Doubles*
29 Jan–2 Feb	Sydney Summer Open	CS3	D. Hall d. M. Connell 6–1 7–6	D. Hall/D. Johnson d. M. Legner/M. Connell 6–3 6–4
			D. Di Toro d. C. Ohmae 6–0 6–1	D. Di Toro/R. Hinson d. L. Peeters/B. Pupovac 6–0 6–4
4–7 Feb	Australian Open	CS2	D. Hall d. M. Legner 3–6 6–1 6–0	D. Hall/D. Johnson d. R. Weisang/J. Greer 6–3 6–2
			D. Di Toro d. C. Omae 6–3 6–0	D. Di Toro/ R. Hinson d. C. Omae/Y. Chokyu 7–5 4–6 6–1
10–13 Feb	New Zealand Open	CS4	P. Johnson d. J. Greer 4–6 6–7 7–6	J. Greer/P. Johnson d. J. Ward/C. Tresch 6–1 6–0
			J. Courtier d. B. Pupovac 4–6 7–5 6–3	S. Peters/S. Walraven d. R. Hinson/J. Courtier 6–2 6–2
25–28 Mar	Lipton Champs	CS2	R. Molier d. D. Hall 6–3 7–6 (3)	D. Hall//D. Lachman d. M. Legner/K. Schrameyer 6–3 6–4
			D. Di Toro d. M. Smit 6–1 6–3	D. Di Toro/C. Vandierendonck d. N. Olson/S. Clark 7–6 (7) 6–1
2–5 Apr	Florida Open	CS1	S. Welch d. D. Hall 2–6 6–2 6–4	L. Giammartini/R. Molier d. S. Welch/S. Douglas 3–6 6–3 7–6(5)
			M. Smit d. C. Vandierendonck 6–4 6–1	D. Di Toro/C. Vandierendonck d. H. Lewellen/M. Smit 3–6 6–1 6–1
8–12 Apr	Chilean Open	CS4	M. Foulks d. S. Hatt 6–3 6–3	M. Foulks/S. Hatt d. M. Pruitt/J. Ward 6–4 6–3
13–19 Apr	Argentinean Open	CS4	M. Foulks d. S. Hatt 6–3 6–2	M. Foulks/S. Hatt d. M. Pruitt/S. Wood 6–3 3–6 6–2
17–19 Apr	Lichtenberg Buick-Mazda Champs	CS3	S. Welch d. M. Perron 6–1 6–2	
23–26 Apr	Kobe Open	CS2	J. Greer d. R. Weisang 5–7 6–1 6–4	S. Saida/K. Katou d. J. Greer/C. Turner 7–6 (4) 6–3
			C. Omae d. Y. Chokyu 3–6 6–2 6–4	Y. Chokyu/S. Walraven d. C. Omae/K. Kitamoto 7–5 6–4
12–15 May	Thai Open	CS4	J. Greer d. P. Johnson 6–1 6–4	
			S. Walraven d. J. Laumen 6–2 4–1 ret.	
13–16 May	Slovakia Open	CS4	M. Legner d. R. Weisang 7–5 6–1	L. Shevchick/T. Nijhoff d. M. Legner/R. Weisang 2–6 7–6 6–3
14–17 May	Gateway Classic	Sat	S. Douglas d. M. Haynes 6–2 6–0	
			B. Pyle d. T. Fournier 7–6 7–5	
20–24 May	Japan Open	CS1	R. Molier d. D. Hall 5–7 7–5 6–2	R. Molier/L. Giammartini d. P. Johnson/D. Hall 6–1 6–4
			D. Di Toro d. C. Vandierendonck 7–6 6–3	D. Di Toro/C. Vandierendonck d. C. Ohmae/K. Kitamoto 7–5 6–3
20–24 May	Czech Open	CS3	M. Legner d. E. Sartov 6–4 6–2	M. Legner/R. Weisang d. L. Shevchick/T. Nijhoff 6–0 6–1
27–31 May	Polish Open	CS4	M. Legner d. T. Kruszelnicki 6–3 6–1	M. Legner/M. Brychta d P. Jaroszewski/T. Kruszelnicki 6–1 6–3
28–31 May	USTA National Outdoor Champs	CS1	S. Welch d. R. Molier 6–2 6–0	S. Douglas/S. Welch d. D. Lachman/J. Mistry 6–1 6–2
			S. Clark d. N. Olson 6–2 6–1	S. Clark/N. Olson d. H. Lewellen/S. Peters 7–5 7–5
3–7 Jun	Lakeshore Foundation World Challenge	CS2	R. Molier d. S. Welch 6–4 6–1	S. Douglas/S. Welch d. D. Lachman/M. Legner 7–6 6–2
			S. Peters d. B. Ameryckx 6–1 6–3	Y. Chokyu/H. Simard d. P. Rollison/S. Walraven 6–4 7–6
5–7 Jun	SCTA So Cal Champs	CS4	T. Ambler d. D. MacArthur 6–3 7–5	T. Ambler/T. Lara d. D. Beardon/D. MacArthur 6–2 6–4
2–5 Jul	Dornbirn Cup	CS3	S. Welch d. M. Legner 6–2 6–2	S. Welch/M. Legner d. M. Brychta/T. Kruszelnicki 6–4 6–0
			S. Walraven d. M. Fink 6–4 6–4	B. Pupovac/J. Courtier d. S. Walraven/P. Sax-Scharl 6–1 6–4
7–12 Jul	Dutch Open	CS1	D. Hall d. S. Welch 3–6 6–2 6–2	L. Giammartini/R. Molier d. D. Hall/D. Johnson 7–6 7–5
			E. Vergeer d. D. Di Toro 6–3 6–2	D. Di Toro/C. Vandierendonck d. B. Ameryckx/.D Van Marum 7–6 6–2
14–19 Jul	Belgian Open	CS1	R. Molier d. D. Hall 6–2 6–3	M. Legner/J. Mistry d. L. Giammartini/R. Molier 6–1 6–0
			M. Smit d. B. Ameryckx 6–0 6–3	S. Peters/E. Vergeer d. Y. Chokyu/H. Simard 6–1 7–6

Dates	*Tournament*	*Grade*	*Singles*	*Doubles*
20–26 Jul	British Open	SS	D. Hall d. S. Welch 6–2 6–2	D. Hall/D. Johnson d. L. Giammartini/R. Molier 6–3 6–0
			D. Di Toro d. S. Peters 6–4 6–1	S. Peters/E. Vergeer d. H. Lewellen/M. Smit 6–4 6–0
			R. Draney d. B. Hanson 6–2 3–6 6–4	M. Eccleston/R. Humphrys d. K. Whalen/B. Van Erp 7–5 0–6 6–2
28 Jul–2 Aug	Swiss Open	CS2	R. Molier d. D. Hall 3–6 6–4 6–0	R. Molier/T. Nijhoff d. L. Shevchick/M. Legner 6–0 6–2
			D. Di Toro d. M. Smit 6–1 7–5	M. Smit/E. Vergeer d. D. Di Toro/J. Courtier 6–4 6–3
			B. Van Erp d. M. Eccleston 6–4 6–0	
31 Jul–3 Aug	Japan Cup	CS3	J. Greer d. S. Saida 7–5 3–6 6–3	K. Katou/S. Saida d. J. Greer/R. Julian 6–4 7–5
			N. Kawashima d. S. Khunthasit 6–2 3–6 6–2	K. Kitamoto/C. Ohmae d. N. Kawashima/R. Sakamoto 7–5 4–6 6–1
			K. Ohashi d. N. Tachibana w/o	K. Koike/K. Ohashi d. R. Kakinokihara/H. Nakagawa 6–1 7–5
5–9 Aug	Austrian Open	CS2	D. Hall d. R. Molier 6–1 2–6 7–6	L. Giammartini/R. Molier d. D. Hall/D. Johnson 7–6 6–1
			E. Vergeer d. D. Di Toro 0–6 6–0 7–6	S. Peters/E. Vergeer d. D. Di Toro/H. Lewellen 6–4 3–6 6–1
12–16 Aug	German Open	CS3	R. Weisang d. M. Foulks 6–0 6–0	R. Weisang/M. Legner d. M. Foulks/T Kruszelnicki 6–2 2–6 6–2
			S. Peters d. R. Isecke 6–1 6–1	R. Isecke/D. van Marum d. C. Otterbach/Myung-Hee 6–1 6–3
13–16 Aug	USTA National Indoor Champs	CS3	S. Douglas d. P. Johnson 6–3 6–2	S. Douglas/M. Thompson d. T. Lara/J. Rydberg 6–4 6–1
			H. Lewellen d. K. Korb 6–4 6–2	
26–30 Aug	French Open	CS2	M. Legner d. L. Giammartini 6–3 0–6 6–4	L. Giammartini/J. Mistry d. N. Larsson/M. Legner 4–6 7–6 6–2
			M. Smit d. A. Racineux 6–0 6–2	D. van Marum/M. Smit d. K. Dell/S. Peters 6–2 6–1
2–6 Sep	Citta di Livorno	CS3	R. Molier d. L. Giammartini 4–6 6–4 6–3	R. Molier/L. Giammartini d. L. Shevchick/M. Brychta 6–4 6–3
			B. Ameryckx d. S. Walraven 7–6 7–6	
8–12 Sep	Italian Open	CS4	M. Legner d. L. Giammartini 7–5 7–5	M. Legner/G. Jandrasits d. T. Kruszelnicki/L. Shevchick 4–6 6–0 6–0
7–13 Sep	Southwest Reg Champs	CS2	S. Welch d. S. Douglas 6–3 7–5	S. Douglas/S. Welch d. D. Lachman/S. Hatt 6–1 6–4
			S. Walraven d. S. Clark 6–3 6–4	
17–20 Sep	Panathlon Tenniscup	CS4	M. Legner d. K. Schrameyer 3–6 6–4 6–4	M. Legner/E. Sartov d. R. Ammerlaan/K. Schrameyer 3–2 Ret
18–20 Sep	Santa Rosa Sec Champs	CS3	S. Welch d. J. Greer 6–0 6–1	S. Hatt/D. Johnson d. J. Greer/M. Haynes 6–4 0–6 6–4
18–20 Sep	USPTR/Roho Champs	CS3	S. Douglas d. D. Hall 6–4 6–1	S. Douglas/D Wesley d. P. Johnson/C. McKeage 6–2 6–1
22–27 Sep	Radl Cup	CS3	R. Molier d. L. Giammartini 6–4 7–5	L. Giammartini/R. Molier d. P. Jaroszewski/T. Kruszelnicki 6–4 6–2
			S. Walraven d. C. Otterbach 6–1 6–1	
25–27 Sep	San Diego/Hendrickson Open	CS4	M. Foulks d. D. Johnson 6–4 6–4	M. Foulks/D. Bolton d. T. Lara/S. Hatt 6–2 6–3
			Y. Chokyu d. B. Pupovac 6–4 6–1	
2–4 Oct	Tahoe Donner Intl Champs	CS3	D. Johnson d. M. Foulks 6–1 6–3	M. Foulks/T. Kruszelnicki d. B. Dockerill/S. Hatt 6–1 3–6 6–1
			S. Clark d. Y. Chokyu 3–6 6–0 6–3	Y. Chokyu/P. Rollison d. S. Clark/H. Lewellen 7–6 5–7 6–3
6–9 Oct	Newport Beach	CS4	L. Giammartini d. D. Hall 6–4 3–6 6–3	D. Hall/D. Johnson d. J. Greer/L. Giammartini 6–1 6–4
12–18 Oct	US Open	SS	D. Hall d. S. Welch 3–6 6–1 7–6(4)	S. Douglas/S. Welch d. L. Giammartini/R. Molier 4–6 7–5 7–5
			E. Vergeer d. D. Di Toro 7–5 6–4	S. Peters/E. Vergeer d. H. Lewellen/M. Smit 5–7 7–5 6–4
17–22 Nov	NEC Masters	CS1	R. Molier d. L. Giammartini 7–5 7–5	
			E. Vergeer d. M. Smit 6–0 7–6(6)	

Top left: *The 15-year-old Jelena Dokic exceeded expectations by ending 1998 at the top of the junior rankings.* (Michael Cole)
Top right: *Argentina's David Nalbandian, winner of the US Open junior title and three other ITF ranking tournaments, ended the year at No. 3 in the rankings.* (Michael Cole)
Above: *Julien Jeanpierre, favourite to end 1998 as No. 1 but finishing No. 2.* (Michael Cole)

Review of the Junior Game

Jackie Nesbitt

Junior players captured quite a few headlines on the professional tours in 1998, quite satisfying for the ITF who have now spent 21 years nurturing talented youngsters all over the world. Last year's junior world champions might not have featured in the top stories, but with Cara Black finishing the year with a WTA ranking of 44 and Arnaud Di Pasquale managing an ATP ranking of 81, the outlook looks very promising for both players.

One might be forgiven for not expecting this year's crop of juniors to measure up to the high standards of the previous year, but the 1998 season seems to have produced an even wider spread of talented prospects. Julien Jeanpierre and Katarina Srebotnik started as firm favourites for the world singles titles, having finished just behind Di Pasquale and Black respectively in 1997. Jeanpierre wasted no time in Australia with victory in the Open over Sweden's Andreas Vinciquerra. His semi-final victory over Roger Federer, didn't raise any eyebrows at the time, but the relatively unknown Swiss was to take spectacular revenge by the year's end.

From there on, however, life was to prove very frustrating for Jeanpierre. South American tennis is well and truly on the map thanks to the exploits of Marcelo Rios and the region currently has no less than three top junior boys, Fernando Gonzalez, David Nalbandian and Guillermo Coria, all of whom were to feature in the race for the boys singles crown. Rios's countryman Gonzalez was the first to thwart Jeanpierre's attempt for a second Group A title, defeating him in the final of the Banana Bowl. Argentina's Coria, the closest of the three in playing style to Rios, was next up to defeat Jeanpierre in the final of the Italian Open. Those unexpected defeats, followed by a disappointing showing in Paris, certainly seemed to take the sting from Jeanpierre's game. The young Frenchman was not to feature in any further major finals and ultimately had to watch while his world title hopes rested on the results of others.

The first to claim a second Group A title was actually Gonzalez, who had a terrific run at the French, culminating in a tight three set final victory over Spain's Juan Carlos Ferrero. The grass of Wimbledon not only saw the early demise of Gonzalez and Jeanpierre, but saw the emergence of Federer as a serious title contender, his huge serve aiding him to a straight sets win in the boys' final over the exciting Georgian, Irikl Labadze. At the US Open, revelling in the New York atmosphere, he reached the final. Although he lost to Coria's teammate, David Nalbandian, the big hitting Swiss approached the end of year U.S. circuit full of confidence.

Last minute entrants due to a late withdrawal Federer led unseeded Switzerland to the brink of a major upset in the ITF Sunshine Cup. Following Federer's victory over Spanish number one Ferrero, and with Federer and teammate Jun Kato a set and 5–2 up in the deciding doubles, the top seeds were on the ropes. Unbelievably Ferrero and the outstanding prospect Tommy Robredo, were able to extend the match to three sets, clinching victory 9–7 in the third. Jeanpierre, Gonzalez and the rest were able to heave a sigh of relief as Federer was therefore unable to add to his points tally via the team competitions.

And so, after a year of endeavour, the scene was set for final major of the year. The Orange Bowl played delighted host to all four junior boy Grand Slam winners who, in addition to Coria, would bring to a close a title race of the highest standard. The luckless Jeanpierre had the toughest possible opening round and failed to meet the challenge of Spain's Feliciano Lopez. When Coria beat Gonzalez, Federer needed revenge over Nalbandian to avoid the race continuing to Mexico for the final tournament of the year. Revenge was duly obtained and with victory over Coria in the final, Federer added another Swiss name to the junior roll of honour.

What of Srebotnik? It would not be unfair to say she experienced some bad luck in 1998 – she developed a nasty habit of running into a number of new stars who were having a particularly good run at the majors.

In Australia, Jelena Kostanic proved too tough in the quarter-finals, the young Croatian going on to take the title following victory over Indonesia's unseeded Wynne Prakusya in the final. There was some home cheer for the Australian's, as the then 14 year-old Jelena Dokic reached the last four before narrowly succumbing to Prakusya.

With many top girls mixing professional and junior tournaments, particularly in their final year under 18, Srebotnik did not resurface until the summer season. In the meantime, an all-South American final in the Banana Bowl saw Argentina's Erica Krauth defeat Venezuela's Milagros Sequera in the final. Erica's first major title put her into the top ten along side fellow countrywoman Clarisa Fernandez. Combined with their success in the boys game, the future for Argentine tennis certainly seems bright.

Young Dokic had another good run at the Italian Open. She reached the last four once again before running into an inspired Antonella Serra Zanetti, keen to impress on home soil. Impress she did, although victory over France's Aurelie Vedy was not achieved without a struggle.

Improved progress was achieved in Paris, when Dokic upset both Tina Pisnik and Elena Demetieva to reach her first major final. Spare a thought for Srebotnik who had the misfortune of meeting Nadezhda Petrova in the second round. The young Polish based Russian made the most of her great victory, going on to defeat Kostanic and to thwart Dokic in the final.

With the pack fast closing in on her at the top of the rankings, Srebotnik badly needed a good performance to maintain her position. Following a first round loss the previous year, she would not have had high expectations of Wimbledon, but the grass courts were to prove more accommodating in 1998. Victory over top seeded Evie Dominikovic set her up for a good run, which culminated in her claiming the prestigious girls title by defeating surprise finalist Kim Clijsters.

The unseeded Belgian not only started to show her undoubted talent at Wimbledon, but inadvertently helped Srebotnik's cause by defeating Dokic in the semi-finals in one of the best matches of the Championships.

The chips were down at the U.S. Open as Srebotnik announced that New York would be her final major of the year. Fittingly, both she and Dokic were top seeded and with Srebotnik once again defeating Dominikovic and Dokic overcoming Pisnik, they both reached the final. The Slovenian was expected to win, but they say youth has no respect for age and so it proved as Dokic levelled the Group A tally at one apiece.

One quickly became two, as Dokic claimed her second major title a few weeks later, defeating Slovakia's Daniela Hantuchova in the final of the World Super Junior Championships in Japan, enabling her to rest on her laurels as the world champion elect.

Results from the Orange Bowl could be something of a guide to next year's top performers. Petrova nearly came unstuck in the semi-finals against Slovene Petra Rampre, but progressed as expected. Her opponent in the final also survived a nervy match against Clijsters and surprised her fellow Russian with victory. All but Rampre are eligible for junior tennis next year and are expected to lead the title hunt in what should be another quality year. Having led her country to victory in the ITF Connolly Continental Cup the week prior to the Orange Bowl, it was particularly pleasing to see Demetieva finish the year in great style.

The doubles championships saw a number of outstanding individual performers challenging for the boys and girls titles. In both cases, however, the titles were destined to go to lesser lights in singles terms, but most definitely doubles specialists.

South America's Fernandez and Maria Emilia Salerni paired up for most of the year and for them it was a case of so near yet so far. Together they claimed the Banana Bowl and Orange Bowl titles, but were denied possible bonus points for a third Group A win when rain forced the cancellation of the Italian Open final. In that final they were leading by a set and 5–2 against Denmark's Eva Dyrberg and Belgium's Clijsters and these two, ironically, were to keep them off top spot. It was Dyrberg's victory with Clijsters at the US Open that gave the Danish player her second Group A title, following her win with Kostanic at Wimbledon. Victory in Japan gave Eva the crucial third major win and an unassailable lead at the top of the rankings. Her title will no doubt be a terrific boast for Danish tennis, who also can look forward to the further adventures of Kristian Pless, a top ten boys' singles player in 1998.

The start of Jeanpierre's doubles year mirrored that of his singles exploits when he collected the Australian Open title in company with team mate Jerome Haehnel. There were slim pickings thereafter, with no other major titles going his way until Japan, but that was too late.

Top of the boys doubles tree was to be Venezuela's charismatic Jose De Armas. It was perhaps fitting that De Armas should win the title in a year that saw the loss of long-time Venezuelan Federation President, Fermin Perez. Following wins at the Italian and French Open and the Orange Bowl, he is certainly an outstanding champion. Spare a thought though for Fernando Gonzalez, who partnered Jose to victory in both Milan and Paris, but who missed out on the third major as Croatia's Lovro Zovko formed a new partnership with the Venezuelan at the Orange Bowl to help him clinch his crown.

ITF JUNIOR WORLD RANKINGS 1998 – POINTS EXPLANATION

The ITF Junior Circuit is a world-wide points-linked circuit of 165 tournaments, 6 continental championships and 4 team competitions in 95 countries, under the management of the International Tennis Federation. There are ten separate points categories covering the three types of events. There is no limit to the number of tournaments in which a player may compete each year. The best six results from tournaments (Groups A and 1–5), continental championships (Groups B1–B3) and team competitions (Group C) count towards a player's ranking. To qualify for a final year-end ranking a player must have competed in at least six events, including at least three Group A tournaments and at least three outside his or her own country.

TOURNAMENTS & REGIONAL CHAMPIONSHIPS

Singles

	A	1	2	3	4	5	B1	B2	B3
Winner	250	150	100	60	40	30	180	100	80
Runner-up	180	100	75	45	30	20	120	80	50
Semi-Finalist	120	80	50	30	20	15	80	60	30
Quarter-Finalists *	80	60	30	20	15	10	60	40	15
Losers in last 16 **	50	30	20	15	10	5	30	25	5
Losers in last 32 ***	30	20	–	–	–	–	20	10	–

* only if 16 or more players in draw (excluding withdrawals)
** only if 32 or more players in draw (excluding withdrawals)
*** only if 64 or more players in draw (excluding withdrawals)

Doubles (Each Player)

	A	1	2	3	4	5	B1	B2	B3
Winners	180	100	85	50	30	20	120	80	50
Runners-up	120	75	50	30	20	15	80	60	30
Semi-Finalists *	80	50	30	20	15	10	60	40	15
Quarter-Finalists **	50	30	15	15	10	5	30	25	5
Losers in last 16 ***	30	20	–	–	–	–	20	10	–

* only if 8 or more players in draw (excluding withdrawals)
** only if 16 or more players in draw (excluding withdrawals)
*** only if 32 or more players in draw (excluding withdrawals)

Group A Super Series Bonus Points

	Singles	Doubles
Winner of 3 or more Group A events	200	180

Group C – Team Competitions – Regional Qualifying

	No. 1 Singles Player Win	No. 2 Singles Player Win	Doubles Win Each Player
Final	80	60	60
Semi-Final	60	40	40
Quarter-Final	40	20	20

Group C – Team Competition – Final

	No. 1 Singles Player Win	No. 2 Singles Player Win	Doubles Win Each Player
Final	180	120	120
Semi-Final	120	80	80
Quarter-Final	80	60	60

ITF JUNIOR WORLD RANKING RESULTS 1998

DATE	*TOURNAMENT*	*GRADE*	*BOYS SINGLES FINAL*	*GIRLS SINGLES FINAL*
27–31 Dec	Nigeria	5	C. Anyidoho (GHA) d. J. Igbinovia (NGR) 6–3 6–4	A. Mohammed (GHA) d. S. Ogoe (GHA) 6–2 6–3
29 Dec–4 Jan	Casablanca Cup, Mexico	1	A. Qureshi (PAK) d. A. Derepasko (RUS) 4–6 6–1 6–2	N. Petrova (RUS) d. M. Sequera (VEN) 7–6 6–1
1–7 Jan	Salk Open, Sweden	4	J. Nieminen (FIN) d. J. Kareld (SWE) 6–3 7–6	P. Puheloinen (FIN) d. M. Babakova (SVK) 6–3 6–2
2–6 Jan	Togo	5	J. Igbinovia (NGR) d. C. Anyidoho (GHA)	A. Mohammed (GHA) d. P. Osedumme (NGR) 6–2 6–2
6–10 Jan	Vasteras, Sweden	4	J. Fransson (SWE) d. J. Kareld (SWE) 7–6 6–2	V. Raimrova (CZE) d. P. Navratilova (CZE) 7–6 6–4
6–11 Jan	Coffee Bowl, Costa Rica	1	A. Derepasko (RUS) d. J. Melzer (AUT) 6–2 6–2	M. Buric (GER) d. T. Hergold (SLO) 6–4 2–6 7–6
8–12 Jan	Ghana	5	J. Igbinovia (NGR) d. C. Anyidoho (GHA) 4–6 6–2 6–4	A. Mohammed (GHA) d. L. Nzudie (CMR) 6–4 6–2
9–14 Jan	Victoria, Australia	2	R. Federer (SUI) d. J. Jeanpierre (FRA) 6–4 6–4	J. Dokic (AUS) d. R. Hudson (NZL) 6–3 6–3
12–18 Jan	Pony Malta Cup, Colombia	1	A. Derepasko (RUS) d. I. Kunitcin (RUS) 6–3 6–0	T. Hergold (SLO) d. V. Koksova (CZE) 6–2 6–3
18–24 Jan	Australian Hard Court, Melbourne	1	L. Zovko (CRO) d. J. Jeanpierre (FRA) 1–6 6–1 6–2	K. Srebotnik (SLO) d. A. Serra Zanetti (ITA) 6–3 7–5
19–25 Jan	Cuenca, Ecuador	2	E. Prodom (FRA) d. D. Wright (ECU) 7–5 6–4	V. Krauth (ARG) d. V. Castro (CHI) 0–6 7–6 6–4
19–25 Jan	Moscow, Russia	5	V. Chvets (BLR) d. R. Nourmatov (RUS) 6–7 6–3 7–5	E. Voropaeva (RUS) d. E. Yaryshko (BLR) 3–6 6–3 6–4
24–31 Jan	Inka Bowl, Peru	2	A. Fasching (AUT) d. E. Redondi (ARG) 7–6 6–4	M. Mesa (COL) d. G. Zsiros (HUN) 6–2 7–6
26–31 Jan	Colombo, Sri Lanka	4	S. Zaman (IND) d. R. Saikia (IND) 6–4 6–2	U. Khan (IND) d. M. Sohm (AUT) 6–1 6–4
26 Jan–1 Feb	**Australian Open, Melbourne**	**A**	**J. Jeanpierre (FRA) d. A. Vinciguerra (SWE) 4–6 6–4 6–3**	**J. Kostanic (CRO) d. W. Prakusya (INA) 6–0 7–5**
26 Jan–1 Feb	Bratislava, Slovakia	2	M. Youzhny (RUS) d. F. Babej (SVK) 7–6 6–4	K. Clijsters (BEL) d. V. Raimrova (CZE) 7–5 6–2
2–7 Feb	India I, New Delhi	5	V. Kannan (IND) d. J. Paulsen (DEN) 3–6 6–1 6–3	U. Khan (IND) d. Y. Meusburger (AUT) 6–1 6–3
2–8 Feb	Czech Indoor	2	J. Levinsky (CZE) d. J. Fransson (SWE) 7–5 6–4	M. Buric (GER) d. I. Benesova (CZE) 6–2 5–7 6–1
3–9 Feb	Condor de Plata, Bolivia	3	R. Melo (BRA) d. C. Martin (FRA) 6–2 6–2	G. Zsiros (HUN) d. M. Gaspar (POR) 4–6 6–2 6–4
9–14 Feb	India II, Chandigarh	5	V. Kannan (IND) d. B. Ravikran (IND) 6–2 6–2	U. Khan (IND) d. S. Dhawan (IND) 6–7 6–1 6–4
9–15 Feb	Milo Cup, Chile	2	D. Nalbandian (ARG) d. C. Alvarado (CHI) 6–0 6–2	E. Krauth (ARG) d. C. Fernandez (ARG) 7–6 4–6 6–4
16–22 Feb	Argentina Bowl	2	F. Gonzalez (CHI) d. D. Perez (ARG) 5–7 6–2 7–5	C. Fernandez (ARG) d. E. Krauth (ARG) 6–4 2–6 6–2
16–22 Feb	Bangladesh	5	V. Kannan (IND) d. W. Chang (TPE) 6–4 6–3	G. Sheetal (IND) d. D. Luzarova (CZE) 6–3 2–6 6–3
18–22 Feb	LTA British Indoor, Bisham Abbey	3	A. Vinciguerra (SWE) d. P. Hammer (GER) 1–6 6–4 7–6	K. Koukalova (CZE) d. G. Fattakhetdinova (RUS) 6–1 6–1
18–22 Feb	Smash Open, Finland	5	T. Nieminen (FIN) d. L. Kitski (FIN) 6–3 6–4	P. Puheloinen (FIN) d. A. Eriksson (SWE) 6–3 7–6
23–29 Feb	Dhaka, Bangladesh	3	V. Kannan (IND) d. S. Zaman (IND) 6–0 6–0	U. Khan (IND) d. D. Luzarova (CZE) 6–1 6–3
23 Feb–1 Mch	Uruguay Bowl	2	F. Gonzalez (CHI) d. R. Melo (BRA) 6–1 6–4	E. Krauth (ARG) d. M. E. Salerni (ARG) 4–6 6–1 7–5
25 Feb–1 Mch	Bavarian Junior Challenge	2	L. Uebel (GER) d. J. Melzer (AUT) 3–6 6–0 6–2	E. Dementieva (RUS) d. C. Charbonnier (SUI) 6–1 6–1
2–8 Mch	Kuala Lumpur, Malaysia	3	A. McDade (RSA) d. R. Anderson (RSA) 6–2 4–6 6–1	N. Van De Merwe (RSA) d. J. Wong (SIN) 6–2 6–2
2–8 Mch	Asuncion Bowl, Paraguay	1	E. Massa (ARG) d. R. Melo (BRA) 7–5 6–4	C. Fernandez (ARG) d. D. Hantuchova (SVK) 6–2 6–1
9–14 Mch	Taca 747, El Salvador	5	A. Bogomolov (USA) d. D. Langre (MEX) 6–1 6–2	M. Brito (MEX) d. L. Porros (PAN) 6–2 7–6
9–15 Mch	**Banana Bowl, Brazil**	**A**	**F. Gonzalez (CHI) d. J. Jeanpierre (FRA) 7–6 6–3**	**E. Krauth (ARG) d. M. Sequera (VEN) 6–7 7–5 6–3**
9–13 Mch	Brunei	4	A. McDade (RSA) d. C. Magg (AUT) 6–1 6–0	N. Renken (RSA) d. N. Van Der Merwe (RSA) 7–6 6–3
16–21 Mch	Costa Rican Bowl	5	A. Roddick (USA) d. J. R. Bravo (MEX) 6–3 6–3	M. Strussova (SVK) d. M. E. Brito (MEX) 6–3 5–7 6–2
16–22 Mch	Caracus, Venezuela	1	J. Levinsky (CZE) d. T. Cakl (CZE) 6–1 7–6	M. Sequera (VEN) d. A. Vedy (FRA) 7–5 6–0
16–22 Mch	Singapore	3	J. Melzer (AUT) d. M. Hilton (GBR) 6–4 6–0	J. Schmidt (AUT) d. J. Wong (SIN) 6–4 6–2
16–22 Mch	South American Closed, Brazil	B2	G. Coria (ARG) d. E. Redondi (ARG) 6–3 7–5	C. Fernandez (ARG) d. E. Krauth (ARG) 6–3 4–6 6–1
23–28 Mch	Panama Bowl	5	A. Bohane (USA) d. A. Roddick (USA) 4–6. 6–1 6–2	N. Etienne (HAI) d. M. Strussova (SVK) 6–2 6–1
24–29 Mch	Jakarta, Indonesia	3	F. Widhiyanto (INA) d. J. Melzer (AUT) 6–4 3–6 6–2	M. Gerards (NED) d. O. Mikhailova (RUS) 6–4 6–1
30 Mch–4 Apr	Christchurch, Barbados	5	[illegible]	[illegible]

30 Mch–4 Apr	Dakar, Senegal	5	D. Stegman (RSA) d. A. McDade (RSA) 7–6 6–2	N. Grandin (RSA) d. A. Mojzis (RSA) [illegible]
30 Mch–5 Apr	Mali Milk Cup, Thailand	3	M. Hilton (GBR) d. R. De Voest (RSA) 6–1 7–6	M. Horvath (HUN) d. N. Rencken (RSA) 6–2 6–3
31 Mch–4 Apr	Namangan, Uzbekistan	5	A. Kedriouk (KAZ) d. O. Tereshchuk (UKR) 6–1 6–1	E. Voropaeva (RUS) d. I. Tulyaganova (UZB) 7–5 7–5
1–5 Apr	Umag, Croatia	3	S. Wernhart (AUT) d. N. Fracassi (ITA) 4–3 ret.	L. Bao (SUI) d. P. Novotnikova (CZE) 6–3 6–2
6–12 Apr	African Closed, Senegal	B3	N. McDonald (RSA) d. A. McDade (RSA) 6–0 6–0	N. Grandin (RSA) d. A. Pillay (RSA) 6–4 6–4
6–11 Apr	Sainte Marie, Martinique	5	E. Tanik (TUR) d. J. Benneteau (FRA) (w. o.	M. Strussova (SLO) d. K. Richards (JAM) 3–6 6–4 6–3
6–11 Apr	Haifa, Israel	4	J. Auckland (GBR) d. D. Hanegby (ISR) 4–6 7–5 6–4	A. De Bruyn (RSA) d. A. Andersson (SWE) 6–3 6–1
7–11 Apr	Tashkent, Uzbekistan	5	A. Kedriouk (KAZ) d. S. Pozdnev (RUS) 6–0 6–0	I. Tulyaganova (UZB) d. E. Voropeava (RUS) 6–1 6–3
7–12 Apr	Manila, Philippines	2	D. Udomchoke (THA) d. J. Adaktusson (SWE) 7–5 6–0	M. Clayton (AUS) d. S. Hrozenska (SLO) 6–3 6–2
7–12 Apr	12th Pascuas Bowl, Paraguay	4	I. Gonzalez King (ARG) d. J-P. Menano (BRA) 6–3 6–1	S. Damario (ARG) d. M. A. Garcia (PAR) 6–2 6–3
8–13 Apr	Florence, Italy	2	R. Federer (SUI) d. F. Volandri (ITA) 7–6 6–3	L. Steinbach (GER) d. K. Clijsters (BEL) (w. o.)
13–18 Apr	St Francois, Guadeloupe	5	J. Benneteau (FRA) d. J-J. Rojer (AHO) 7–5 6–4	K. Richards (JAM) d. M. Strussova (SVK) 6–3 6–2
13–17 Apr	Beer Sheva, Israel	4	M. Deri (ISR) d. C. Moore (RSA) 3–6 6–2 7–6	E. Yaryshko (BLR) d. N. Van Der Merwe (RSA) 6–3 6–2
13–19 Apr	Cap D'Ail, France	5	J. Maes (FRA) d. O. Ramos (FRA) 7–6 6–3	A. Kapros (HUN) d. C. Schaul (LUX) 6–2 4–6 6–0
14–19 Apr	Japan Open, Tokyo	1	J. Adaktusson (SWE) d. L. Chramosta (CZE) 7–6 6–4	E. Dominikovic (AUS) d. J. Dokic (AUS) 6–3 6–1
20–26 Apr	Beaulieu Sur Mer, France	4	J. C. Faurel (FRA) d. J. Nieminen (FIN) 6–1 7–5	B. Pirker (AUS) d. A. Dulon (FRA) 6–4 6–0
21–26 Apr	Asian Closed, Japan	B2	W-J. Cheng (TPE) d. D. Udomchoke (THA) 6–1 6–3	N. Li (CHN) d. R. Fujiwara (JPN) 6–0 6–3
27 Apr–1 May	Seoul, Korea	4	Y. W. Lee (KOR) d. J-H Park (KOR) 6–2 6–3	A. Kapros (HUN) d. S-M Im (KOR) 6–1 6–4
27 Apr–3 May	Salsomaggiore, Italy	2	A. Vinciguerra (SWE) d. D. Nalbandian (ARG) 6–3 6–0	C. Fernandez (ARG) d. M. E. Salerni (ARG) 3–6 6–0 6–1
28 Apr–3 May	Slovakia Cup, Bratislava	2	O. Tereshchuk (UKR) d. M. Grolmus (SVK) 6–2 4–6 6–2	K. Basternakova (SVK) d. D. Hantuchova (SVK) 6–1 6–3
4–10 May	Prato, Italy	2	A. Vinciguerra (SWE) d. F. Volandri (ITA) 6–3 6–3	D. Bedanova (CZE) d. M. Gerards (NED) 7–5 7–6
6–10 May	Czech Junior Open, Nymburk	3	V. Hanescu (ROM) d. T. Banczi (SVK) 6–2 2–6 6–2	A. Plackova (CZE) d. A. Mojzis (RSA) 6–3 2–6 6–4
11–17 May	Santa Croce, Austria	1	F. Saretta (BRA) d. G. Coria (ARG) 6–4 6–3	J. Dokic (AUS) d. M. E Salerni (ARG) 6–0 6–3
13–17 May	Raiffeisen Spring Bowl, Austria	3	S. Wernhart (AUT) d. L. Fono (HUN) 6–3 6–4	A. Yaryshka (BLR) d. E. Fislova (SVK) 6–2 7–5
18–24 May	**Italian Junior Open**	**A**	**G. Coria (ARG) d. J. Jeanpierre (FRA) 7–6 6–3**	**A. Serra Zanetti (ITA) d. A. Vedy (FRA) 6–3 5–7 6–4**
25–30 May	Astrid Bowl Charleroi, Belgium	1	I. Labadze (GEO) d. F. Gonzalez (CHI) 7–6 6–1	J. Dokic (AUS) d. K. Clijsters (BEL) 7–6 6–2
31 May–7 Jne	**French Open, Paris**	**A**	**F. Gonzales (CHI) d. J. C. Ferrero (ESP) 4–6 6–4 6–3**	**N. Petrova (RUS) d. J. Dokic (AUS) 6–3 6–3**
1–7 Jne	Canadian Junior Championships	5	H. Choi (CAN) d. V. Capota (CAN) 6–3 6–4	S. Bajin (CAN) d. D. Bechliwanis 6–1 6–1
2–6 Jne	Villach, Austria	3	R. Sproga (LAT) d. M. Polessnig (AUT) 7–5 6–2	I. Benesova (CZE) d. A. Timotic (YUG) 6–2 6–1
10–14 Jne	Frankfurt, Germany	3	D. Dattoli (AUS) d. J. Levinsky (CZE) 6–4 6–3	M. Muller (GER) d. S. Kotschwara (GER) 6–4 6–2
10–14 Jne	Budapest, Hungary	3	K. Beck (SVK) d. M. Polessnig (AUT) 6–4 6–3	T. Nemeth (HUN) d. A. Plackova (CZE) 6–4 6–1
10–14 Jne	Estonia	5	O. Vaskis (LAT) d. S. Zavrazhnov (BLR) 6–2 6–3	K. Kanepi (EST) d. M. Ani (EST) 6–2 1–6 6–2
14–19 Jne	East Molesey, England	2	I. Labadze (GRO) d. W-J. Cheng (TPE) 2–6 6–3 7–5	E. Daniliidou (GRE) d. A. Molik (AUS) 6–0 7–6
15–21 Jne	Ozerov Cup, Russia	5	D. Vlasov (RUS) d. Y. Smirnov (RUS) 7–5 4–6 6–1	M. Samoilenko (RUS) d. G. Fokina (RUS) 7–5 4–6 6–1
21–26 Jne	Roehampton, England	1	A. Qureshi (PAK) d. T. Dent (USA) 6–2 6–4	J. Dokic (AUS) d. E. Dominikovic (AUS) 6–2 6–1
22–28 Jne	Mohammedia, Morroco	5	E. Fowler (RSA) d. Y. Limam (MAR) 6–1 6–4	M. Haddad (MAR) d. S. Bennacer (ALG) 6–3 6–3
23–27 Jne	Danish Junior Tournament	4	A. Hartman (SWE) d. J. Chafai (MAR) 7–6 6–4	A. Abraham (POL) d. I. Collischon (GER) 6–1 6–3
23–28 Jne	Donetsk Cup, Ukraine	5	O. Tereshchuk (UKR) d. I. Bogoomaz (UKR) 6–2 6–0	O. Lazarchuk (UKR) d. D. Tchkouasselli (UKR) 6–2 6–3
27 Jne–5 Jly	**Wimbledon**	**A**	**R. Federer (SUI) d. I. Labadze (GEO) 6–4 6–4**	**K. Srebotnik (SLO) d. K. Clijsters (BEL) 7–6(3) 6–3**
29 Jne–5 Jly	Casablanca, Morocco	4	R. Anderson (RSA) d. M. Belbacha 7–6 6–2 7–5	M. Addou (MAR) d. G. Mhaoud (MAR) 6–4 6–1
30 Jne–4 Jly	Netherlands Antilles	5	S. Martinez (CUB) d. J. Engelhardt (AHO) 6–1 6–3	N. Bogdanovich (CAN) d. A. Longoni (VEN) 6–4 6–0
30 Jne–5 Jly	Van Keeken, Netherlands	2	J. Nieminen (FIN) d. R. Sproga (LAT) 6–3 7–5	A. Kapros (HUN) d. A. Anderson (SWE) 6–4 6–0
6–11 Jly	Darwin, Australia	4	G. Knox (AUS) d. L. Radovanovich (NZL) 6–2 6–3	K. Pinchbeck (AUS) d. M. Adamczak (AUS) 6–4 6–2

DATE	TOURNAMENT	GRADE	BOYS SINGLES FINAL	GIRLS SINGLES FINAL
6–11 Jly	Aruba, West Indies	5	C. Paiz (GUA) d. S. Martinez (CUB) 6–3 7–6 (2)	D. Reynolds (MEX) d. K. Richards (JAM) 4–6 6–2 6–0
7–12 Jly	German Open	1	S. Wauters (BEL) d. M. Polessnig (AUT) 6–4 7–6	M. Buric (GER) d. N. Li (CHN) 6–2 7–5
7–12 Jly	Slovakia	5	L. Dlouhy (CZE) d. J. Mertl (CZE) 6–4 6–4	I. Abramovic (CRO) d. E. Birnerova (CZE) 6–1 6–3
8–12 Jly	Tunis, Tunisia	5	G. Figueiredo (POR) d. S. Lockwood (GBR) 6–1 6–3	M. Hoogland (NED) d. D. Coutry (EGY) 6–3 6–0
13–18 Jly	Winchester, England	5	D. Sanger (GBR) d. J. May (GBR) 7–6 (2) 7–5	K. Vymetal (GBR) d. C. Ito (JPN) 6–3 6–3
13–19 Jly	Copa Merengue, Dominican Rep	4	J. Hernandez (MEX) d. J. Garcia (DOM) 6–2 6–4	D. Reynolds (MEX) d. Z. Reyes (MEX) 1–6 6–2 6–2
13–19 Jly	Malta	5	A. Antonijevic (YUG) d. K. El Dorry (EGY) 6–4 6–1	A. Elazari (ISR) d. A. Edelstein (ISR) 6–4 6–2
14–19 Jly	Swiss Junior Tournament	2	J. Nieminen (FIN) d. O. Rochus (BEL) 6–3 7–5	N. Li (CHN) d. L. Bao (SUI) 2–6 6–2 6–3
14–19 Jly	Auckland, New Zealand	5	A. McNeil (NZL) d. E. Lyndon (NZL) 6–3 7–6	M Adamczak (AUS) d. T. O'Connor (NZL) 4–6 6–0 6–3
20–26 Jly	European Closed, Switzerland	B1	A. Vinciguerra (SWE) d. F. Lopez (ESP) 6–3 2–6 7–6	E. Dyrberg (DEN) d. K. Srebotnik (SLO) 6–4 3–0 ret.
21–26 Jly	Kingston, Jamaica	4	P. Gordon (JAM) d. R. Russell (JAM) 6–4 6–2	Z. Reyes (MEX) d. D. Reynolds (MEX) 2–6 6–3 6–1
22–26 Jly	Plzen, Czech Rep.	3	T. Cakl (CZE) d. T. Hajek (CZE) 6–3 2–6 6–3	K. Koukakova (CZE) d. O. Votavova (CZE) 6–0 7–5
22–26 Jly	Johannesburg, South Africa	4	J. Masson (RSA) d. W. Meyer (RSA) 6–3 6–4	A. Mojzis (RSA) d. N. Grandin (RSA) 6–1 6–1
27–31 Jly	Dublin, Ireland	5	S. Nugent (IRE) d. P. Marx (GER) 6–3 6–1	E. O'Riain (IRE) d. R. Barnes (GBR) 6–4 6–0
27–31 Jly	Vancouver, Canada	5	C. Gostek (CAN) d. S. Rutherford (CAN) 6–4 6–2	N. Bogdanovich (CAN) d. A. Loncaric (CAN) 6–7(7) 6–4 6–4
27Jly–1 Aug	Taca Bowl, El Salvador	4	J-J. Rojer (AHO) d. J. Hernandez (MEX) 6–4 6–3	D. Reynolds (MEX) d. Z. Reyes (MEX) 6–1 7–5
27Jly–2 Aug	Taca Diogo Napoles, Portugal	5	P. Rico (ESP) d. J. L. Lara Salines (ESP) 7–6(6) 6–2	S. Trancoso (FRA) d. A. Velts (KAZ) 6–1 6–4
28 Jly–1 Aug	Pretoria, South Africa	4	R. De Voest (RSA) d. J. Masson (RSA) 6–2 6–0	A. Mojzis (RSA) d. N. Rencken (RSA) 2–6 6–2 6–4
28 Jly–2 Aug	Luxembourg	4	B. Becker (GER) d. U. Kiendl (GER) 7–6 6–2	C. Schaul (LUX) d. E. Birnerova (CZE) 6–1 3–6 6–2
2–4 Aug	European Junior Team Ch'ships	C	Final: SPAIN d. FRANCE 2–1	Final: CROATIA d. ITALY 2–1
2–8 Aug	Gaborone, Botswana	5	P. Nomdo (RSA) d. S. Mitchell (RSA) 6–2 6–1	L. Oosthuizen (RSA) d. K. Berthe (SEN) 6–3 6–1
3–7 Aug	Co. Cork, Ireland	5	R. Green (GBR) d. D. O'Connell (IRE) 3–6 6–2 6–4	A. Kolb (GER) d. A. Barnes (GBR) 6–2 6–2
3–8 Aug	Edmonton, Canada	5	P. Gubenco (CAN) d. S. Tremblay (CAN) 7–5 7–5	K. Krishnamurthy (CAN) d. M Bechliwanis (CAN) 5–7 6–1 6–2
3–9 Aug	JITIC, Guatemala	B3	J-J. Rojer (AHO) d. A. Sanabria (ESA) 6–4 4–6 6–1	D. Reynolds (MEX) d. Z. Reyes (MEX) 6–2 6–4
3–9 Aug	Heliopolis, Egypt	5	D. Stegmann (RSA) d. F. El Idressi (MAR) 4–6 6–4 6–2	F. Esseghir (ALG) d. K. Coetzee (RSA) 6–0 6–2
4–8 Aug	Leiria, Portugal	5	A. Kedryuk (KAZ) d. R. Brooks (GBR) 7–6(5) 6–1	K. Vymetal (GBR) d. M. Brown (GBR) 2–6 7–5 6–2
4–9 Aug	Domzale, Slovenia	4	I. Ogrinc (SLO) d. T. Banczi (SVK) 6–7(6) 6–4 6–1	G. Fokina (RUS) d. L. Dlhopolcova (SVK) 7–5 6–0
7–16 Aug	USTA Closed	1	A. Park (USA) d. Z. Fleishman (USA) 6–1 6–7 6–1	L. Granville (USA) d. W. Laiho (USA) 5–7 6–1 6–4
10–15 Aug	Copa Mundo Maya, Guatemala	5	J. Haro (MEX) d. D. Langre (MEX) 6–4 7–6(1)	D. Reynolds (MEX) d. Z. Reyes (MEX) 6–1 6–2
10–16 Aug	Cairo, Egypt	5	D. Stegmann (RSA) d. H. El Idrissi (MAR) 6–4 5–7 6–1	A. Mojzis (RSA) d. N. Kockott (RSA) 6–4 6–1
11–16 Aug	Vila Do Condo, Portugal	5	A. Kedryuk (KAZ) d. B. Bachert (GER) 1–6 6–3 6–4	K. Srebotnik (SLO) d. D. Krstulovic (CRO) 6–1 6–0
10–16 Aug	St. Lucia, West Indies	5	Y. Sinson (LCA) d. T. Mayers (TRI) 6–4 3–6 6–1	C. Maharaj (TRI) d. I. Perry (ANT) 6–4 6–0
17–21 Aug	Lesotho	5	P-J. Nomdo (RSA) d. M. Westerhoff (RSA) 7–5 6–3	L. Oosthuizen (RSA) d. K. Berthe (SEN) 6–3 6–4
17–21 Aug	Giza, Egypt	4	D. Stegman (RSA) d. M. Ziwar (EGY) 6–2 6–3	D. Milosevic (YUG) d. F. Esseghir (ALG) 7–5 2–6 6–2
17–22 Aug	West Indies	5	O. Posada (VEN) d. T. Mayers (TRI) 6–2 6–1	R. Le Saldo (BAR) d. M. Lopez (VEN) 6–3 6–0
17–23 Aug	Philadelphia, USA	3	N. Rainey (USA) d. R. Steckley (CAN) 6–4 6–1	S. Riske (USA) d. M. Morales (USA) 6–4 6–1
17–23 Aug	Quintana Roo, Mexico	4	J. Haro (MEX) d. D. Langre (MEX) 6–3 6–1	D. Torres (MEX) d. E. Valdez (MEX) 7–5 6–3
18–23 Aug	Windhoek, Namibia	5	T. Samassa (MLI) d. M. Pansy (AUT) 7–6 3–6 7–6	L. Oosthuizen (RSA) d. P. Osedumme (NGR) 6–0 6–4
19–22 Aug	Wels, Austria	4	D. Meffert (GER) d. C. Gard (ROM) 7–6 6–7 7–5	J. Lindstrom (SWE) d. A. Anderrson (SWE) 6–7 6–2 6–4
19–23 Aug	Warsaw, Poland	5	S. Ventura (ESP) d. M. Matkowski (POL) 5–7 7–6 6–2	D. Panova (RUS) d. J. Sakowicz (POL) 6–2 6 –2
24–29 Aug	Damascus, Syria	4	H. El Idrissi (MAR) d. M. Abdul Monem (EGY) [illegible]	[illegible]

24–30 Aug	New Jersey, USA			
26–30 Aug	Balatonboglar, Hungary	3	C. Gard (ROM) d. A. Vlaski (YUG) 6–3 6–4	I. Benesova (CZE) d. S. Kotschwara (GER) 7–5 3–6 7–5
31 Aug–6 Sep	Quebec, Canada	1	D. Nalbandian (ARG) d. O. Rochus (BEL) 7–5 6–3	E. Dominikovic (AUS) d. J. Dokic (AUS) 7–6 6–0
31 Aug–6 Sep	Beirut, Lebanon	5	M. Mamoun (EGY) d. D. Britzen (GER) 6–4 4–6 6–2	M-G. Mikaelian (SUI) d. F. Esseghir (ALG) 6–1 7–5
1–5 Sep	Pago Pago, American Samoa	B3	L. Tere (PNG) d. S. Anesi (SAM) 6–3 6–3	N. Angat (PNG) d. D. Godinet (ASA) 6–4 6–4
2–6 Sep	Timisoara, Romania	5	A. Cruciat (ROM) d. D. Vlassov (RUS) 6–4 6–0	I. Gaspar (ROM) d. Y. Kozhokhina (RUS) 6–4 6–2
2–6 Sep	Corfu, Greece	5	J. G. Berg (SWE) d. E. Aleziou (GRE) 6–3 2–6 6–0	S. Tvaroskova (SVK) d. E. O'Riain (IRL) 7–6 7–5
6–13 Sep	**US Open**	**A**	**D. Nalbandian (ARG) d. R. Federer (SUI) 6–3 7–5**	**J. Dokic (AUS) d. K. Srebotnik (SLO) 6–4 6–2**
8–13 Sep	Sozopol, Bulgaria	5	R. Lukaev (BUL) d. O. Nicodim (ROM) 7–5 6–2	E. Birnerova (CZE) d. M. Penkova (BUL) 6–3 6–2
9–13 Sep	Agrinio, Greece	5	C. Haid (AUT) d. P. Moukhometov (RUS) 6–1 6–1	D. Milosevic (YUG) d. L. Tvaroskova (SVK) 6–3 6–2
6–13 Sep	Nicosia, Cyprus	5	M. Al Moneim (EGY) d. R. Saleh (EGY) 6–2 3–6 2–1 ret.	K. Kanepi (EST) d. Y. Beygelzimer (UKR) 6–2 6–3
14–18 Sep	Tehran, Iran	5	A. Shahgholi (IRI) d. A. Wahla (PAK) 6–4 6–1	—
14–19 Sep	Clermont–Ferand, France	5	C. Deveaux (FRA) d. M. Scott (CAN) 6–4 6–1	C. Schaul (LUX) d. S. Montero (FRA) 7–5 6–2
14–20 Sep	Pancevo, Yugoslavia	5	A. Slovic (YUG) d. B. Pasanski (YUG) 1–6 7–6(2) 6–2	G. Fokina (RUS) d. E. Kozhokhina (RUS) 6–3 6–4
15–20 Sep	New Orleans, USA	2	J. Johansson (SWE) d. A. Kedriouk (KAZ) 7–6(5) 6–2	I. Tulyaganova (UZB) d. M. Horvath (HUN) 6–1 6–0
21–27 Sep	Port Washington, USA	3	J-J. Rojer (AHO) d. C-D. Lee (KOR) 6–1 6–4	Z. Gubacsi (HUN) d. O. Dubovikov (USA) 6–1 6–0
21–27 Sep	Belgrade, Yugoslavia	5	C. Gard (ROM) d. A. Niculescu (ROM) 7–5 6–2	I. Gaspar (ROM) d. K. Palenikova (SVK) 6–3 7–6
21–27 Sep	Santiago, Chile	5	J. Peralta (CHI) d. F. Parada (CHI) 4–6 6–3 7–5	C. S'Algues (URU) d. C. Aravena (CHI) 6–4 6–1
5–10 Oct	Buenos Aires, Argentina	5	L. Childs (GBR) d. S. Decoud (ARG) 6–2 6–2	J. Cravero (ARG) d. G. Dulko (ARG) 7–5 2–6 7–5
5–11 Oct	Causeway Bay, Hong Kong	2	M. Ledvonova (DEN) d. A. Roddick (USA) 6–7 6–1 6–3	D. Bedanova (CZE) v. S. Hrozenska (SVK) not played
12–18 Oct	**Japan**	**A**	**K. Pless (DEN) d. L. Chramosta (CZE) 6–1 6–6 def**	**J. Dokic (AUS) d. D. Hantuchova (SVK) 6–1 6–3**
12–18 Oct	Bahia, Brazil	3	P. Harboe (CHI) d. L. Childs (GBR) 6–3 6–4	C. Seal (GBR) d. E. Baltacha (GBR) 6–4 1–6 6–4
13–18 Oct	Doha, Qatar	5	A. Spaniol (GER) d. A. Banks (GBR) 6–2 6–2	—
19–25 Oct	Bangkok, Thailand	3	F. Prpic (SWE) d. A. Roddick (USA) 3–6 7–6(10) 6–4	S. Viratprasert (THA) d. A. Mojzis (RSA) 6–3 5–7 6–1
19–25 Oct	Porto Alegre, Brazil	3	F. Sareta (BRA) d. P. Custodio (BRA) 6–4 7–5	K. Srebotnik (SLO) d. C. Tiene (BRA) 6–0 6–1
26 Oct–1 Nov	Londrina/Parana, Brazil	5	C. Almeida (BRA) d. J. Montovani (BRA) 6–4 6–1	Y. Beygelzimer (UKR) d. A-P. Novaes (BRA) 6–1 3–6 6–2
3–8 Nov	Chinese Taipei	5	Y. Lu (TPE) d. B. Weir-Smith (RSA) 6–2 7–5	H. Chao (TPE) d. W. Tuan (TPE) 7–6 7–5
9–14 Nov	China	4	W. W ong (HKG) d. W. Wei (CHN) 6–2 6–3	Y.H. Dong (CHN) d. W.N. Liu (CHN) 6–4 6–2
17–21 Nov	Luxembourg Indoor	5	O. Rochus (BEL) d. D. Meffert (GRE) 6–3 6–4	C. Schaul (LUX) d. C. Maes (BEL) 6–1 2–6 6–2
23–29 Nov	Malaysia	3	A. Sigurdson (ISL) d. Hsio Yung Chang (TPE) 6–2 6–1	Ya Ming Lin (CHN) d. S. Stosur (AUS) 7–5 6–2
23–29 Nov	Finland	5	P. Ciorascu (SWE) d. F. Moukhometov (RUS) 6–3 6–3	J. Lindstrom (SWE) d. G. Fokina (RUS) 6–3 6–3
30 Nov–4 Dec	Brunei	4	S. Nugent (IRE) d. A. Vishal Rao (IND) 6–4 6–4	S. Stosur (AUS) d. S. Viratprasert (THA) 7–5 6–3
30 Nov–6 Dec	USA	1	D. Nalbandian (ARG) d. E. Prodon (FRA) 6–3 7–6(5)	V. Razzano (FRA) d. S. Hrozenska (SVK) 6–3 7–5
30 Nov–6 Dec	Pakistan	5	R. Sonchat (THA) d. N. Shahzeb (PAK) 6–1 6–1	A. Kalseriva (KGZ) d. P. Ratanakrong (THA) 7–6(6) 6–0
1–6 Dec	Uganda	5	P. Nomdo (RSA) d. D. Khumalo (ZIM) 6–1 6–0	A. Rafolomanan (MAD) d. M. Rajadarisoa (MAD) 6–0 6–1
7–12 Dec	India	5	S. Nugent (IRE) d. R.K. Bhat (IND) 6–3 6–3	G. Sheetal (IND) d. S. Phadke (IND) 6–1 6–3
7–12 Dec	ITF Sunshine Cup, USA	C	SPAIN	—
7–12 Dec	ITF Connolly Continental Cup, USA	C	—	RUSSIA
7–11 Dec	USA	4	L. Childs (GBR) d. N. Mahut (FRA) 7–6(5) 6–4	K. Clijsters (BEL) d. M. Sequera (VEN) 6–7 6–0 6–1
8–13 Dec	Kenya	5	P. Nomdo (RSA) d. D. Khumalo (ZIM) 4–6 7–6(5) 6–3	A. Rafolomanan (MAD) d. M. Rajadarisoa (MAD) 6–2 6–1
13–20 Dec	Orange Bowl, USA	A	R. Federer (SUI) d. G. Coria (ARG) 7–5 6–3	E. Dementieva (RUS) d. N. Petrova (RUS) 3–6 6–4 6–0
	Yucatan Cup, Mexico	1	A. Roddick (USA) d. S. Pozdnev 6–3 7–6(0)	I. Abramovic (CRO) d. B. Resch (AUT) 6–1 7–6(4)

ITF JUNIOR WORLD RANKINGS 1998

Only those players who qualified for a year-end ranking are listed. The minimum requirements for this were having played six events, three of which were outside their own country and three of which were Group A status.

BOYS' SINGLES

1	Roger Federer	SUI
2	Julien Jeanpierre	FRA
3	David Nalbandian	ARG
4	Fernando Gonzalez	CHI
5	Guillermo Coria	ARG
6	Andreas Vinciguerre	SWE
7	Kristian Pless	DEN
8	Artem Derepasko	RUS
9	Lovro Zovko	CRO
10	Irikli Labadze	GEO
11	Aisam Ul Haq Qureshi	PAK
12	Flavio Saretta	BRA
13	Jarkko Nieminen	FIN
14	Jacob Adaktusson	SWE
15	Ricardo Melo	BRA
16	Ladislav Chramosta	CZE
17	Wei-Jen Cheng	TPE
18	Zachary Fleishman	USA
19	Olivier Rochus	BEL
20	Edgardo Massa	ARG

GIRLS' SINGLES

1	Jelena Dokic	AUS
2	Katarina Srebotnik	SLO
3	Nadejda Petrova	RUS
4	Elena Dementieva	RUS
5	Erica Krauth	ARG
6	Evie Dominikovic	AUS
7	Tina Hergold	SLO
8	Clarissa Fernandez	ARG
9	Mia Buric	GER
10	Milagros Sequera	VEN
11	Kim Clijsters	BEL
12	Antonella Serra-Zanetti	ITA
13	Daniela Hantuchova	SVK
14	Jelena Kostanic	CRO
15	Iroda Tulyaganova	UZB
16	Stanislava Hrozenska	SVK
17	Maria Emilia Salerni	ARG
18	Lydia Steinbach	GER
19	Tina Pisnik	SLO
20	Na Li	CHN

BOYS' DOUBLES

1	Jose De Armas	VEN
2	Fernando Gonzalez	CHI
3	Julien Jeanpierre	FRA
4	David Martin	USA
5	K. J. Hippensteel	USA
6	David Nalbandian	ARG
7	Roger Federer	SUI
8	Jiri Vroka	CZE
9	Andy Ram	ISR
10	Lovro Zovko	CRO
11	Jerome Haehnel	FRA
12	Ladislav Chramosta	CZE
13	Tomas Cakl	CZE
14	Ignacio Gonzalez King	ARG
15	Simon Dickson	GBR
16	Olivier Rochus	BEL
17	Scott Lipsky	USA
18	Igor Kunitcin	RUS
19	Emiliano Redondi	ARG
20	Michael Llodra	FRA

GIRLS' DOUBLES

1	Eva Dryberg	DEN
2	Clarissa Fernandez	ARG
3	Maria Emilia Salerni	ARG
4	Kim Clijsters	BEL
5	Leanne Baker	NZL
6	Daniela Hantuchova	SVK
7	Jelena Dokic	AUS
8	Iroda Tulyaganova	UZB
9	Erica Krauth	ARG
10	Rewa Hudson	NZL
11	Evie Dominikovic	AUS
12	Katarina Basternakova	SLO
13	Eleni Danilidou	GRE
14	Milagros Sequera	VEN
15	Aurelie Vedy	FRA
16	Jelena Kostanic	CRO
17	Tina Hergold	SLO
18	Ansley Cargill	USA
19	Daniela Bedanova	CZE
20	Zsofia Gubacsi	HUN

ITF Vets Tennis

Tony Gathercole

As is obvious above we are now referred to as 'Vets Tennis', with a new logo and it is hoped, an up-to-date image and catchphrase.

This year we had hoped to boast a record of 1000 entries for the two ITF Vets World Championships. We failed! We can still boast, however, an entry of just five short of the magic 1000, which is still a record.

The late April/early May period provided the start to this record activity in Florida, attracting 720 entries for the older Group B events held at the PGA National Health and Racquet Club in Palm Beach Gardens – perhaps better known for its unique golfing events.

As is customary the week before the individual events the ten corresponding team competitions were played at various venues on this very popular US peninsula. The five venues used were well-equipped to host two events at each site. The facility of hosting two events at one site has proved to be not only cost-effective but also means a great deal of social intercourse between players, especially with a men's event and a women's event on the same site. With joint opening ceremonies, official dinners and cocktail parties it has proved to be very popular amongst players and officials.

On the West Coast at the Naples Bath and Tennis Club, the Austria Cup (Men's 55) and the Gardnar Mulloy Cup (Men's 80) were held. On the East Coast events took place at the Ft Lauderdale Tennis Club in Ft Lauderdale; Oaks Racquet Club in Pompano Beach; the Polo Club at Boca Raton and the Ballen Isles Country Club in Palm Beach Gardens. It was a unique experience of American tennis facilities for those who've never competed in this part of the world before.

The US teams are difficult to beat on any courts and on home territory even more of a challenge. Of the ten team competitions the USA won five – the Austria Cup; the Jack Crawford Cup (Men's 70), the Bitsy Grant Cup (Men's 75), the Gardnar Mulloy Cup (Men's 80) and the inaugural Althea Gibson Cup (Women's 70). No other team has managed to claim victory in the Bitsy Grant and Gardnar Mulloy Cups since their inception.

The Von Cramm Cup (Men's 60) was won by Germany for the first time with Canada taking the Britannia Cup (men's 65), also for the first time, from the USA who had been victorious for the past three years. The German Women's 55 team emulated their Men's 60 team by winning the Maureen Connolly Cup for the first time. Another first was the victory by the Australian ladies in the Alice Marble Cup (Women's 60). This was made an additionally memorable occasion when Chris Evert attended the final presentation. Great Britain are also to be congratulated on their three-in-a-row win over the USA in the Kitty Godfree Cup (Women's 65).

As previously mentioned, the PGA National hosted the ITF Vets World Championships with 720 entries. This certainly put the organising committee's abilities to the test. 1107 matches were played in 30 events over 8 days on 29 courts! With such a huge entry, courts were also made available to us at the nearby BallenIsles Country Club who very generously offered their facilities for a second week.

The Tournament Director at the PGA National, Ruth Barnett, even moved out of her own office to accommodate the ITF staff! She is to be congratulated on producing so many volunteers to help run this successful event. All were members of the club and together with her personal staff, comprised a team who made everyone welcome.

The on-court contests were as competitive as ever with many former Fed Cup and Davis Cup players competing. They included Tom Brown (USA) who reached three Wimbledon finals in 1946, finishing runner-up in the men's singles, winning the men's doubles with Jack Kramer and the mixed doubles with Louise Brough. Gardner Mulloy (USA), who holds the record as the oldest player to have won the men's doubles at Wimbledon, after successfully teaming up with Budge Patty in 1957, won the non-championship Men's 85 event and Judy Dalton (Aus), the 1968 Wimbledon finalist, retained the Women's 60 singles.

The younger competitors in the Group A events travelled the length and breadth of the British Isles and Ireland. Team Competitions were held in Warwick, RAF Halton, Glasgow and

The Fred Perry Cup for men's 50s teams was won by the Americans: (Rear, l to r) David Bohannon, Robert Smith (non-playing capt.), Richard Johnson. (Front) Brian Cheyney and James Parker. (ITF)

Winchester, with two in Dublin's fair city. The World Championships then took place in Robin Hood country, at Nottingham. Each of the six team venues in this group had its own unique ambience. There was a bonus at RAF Halton where the British Prime Minister, Mr Tony Blair, himself a member of the Club, opened the event, much to the delight of the teams competing in the Young Cup (Women's 40).

The USA teams were dominant, being victorious in the Fred Perry Cup (Men's 50) for the first time; the Dubler Cup (Men's 45) and the Young Cup (Women's 40) for the 6th time in succession; the Margaret Court Cup (Women's 45) for the 4th time and also the María Esther Bueno Cup (Women's 50). The only trophy they did not claim was the Italia Cup (Men's 35) which was won by Great Britain for the first time under the captaincy of former British Davis Cup player, Jeremy Bates.

Nottingham was not new to organising an ITF Vets World Championships, having previously been host in 1995. The first weekend of the World Championships coincided with the Great Britain/India Davis Cup tie also held at the City of Nottingham Tennis Centre which provided a lively platform for the World Championships. The 275 players were unlucky to suffer with rain and cold conditions. However, this did not in any way affect the quality of play and two exceptional results should be mentioned. Marie Pinterova of Hungary claimed the Women's 50 title for the 2nd year in succession making this her 6th singles title at the World Championships over the past 7 years. A similar feat was achieved by the Australian women's doubles pairing of Carol Campling and Liz Allan who won their sixth doubles title in succession starting off in the Women's 40 and now in the Women's 50.

Results of the World Championships show that Australia claimed five singles titles, USA three, and Great Britain and Belgium one each.

In 1998 a total of 219 teams, from 39 countries and 995 individuals competed at the Championships confirming the increasing popularity of 'Vets Tennis'.

18TH ITF VETS WORLD CHAMPIONSHIPS (GROUP A)

27 September–4 October 1998
Nottingham, England

MEN

35 Singles
Semi-finals: Nick Fulwood (GBR) d. Stefan Heckmanns (GER) 6–2 6–1; Brad Properjohn (AUS) d. Brett Edwards (AUS) 6–7(1) 6–4 6–2. **Final:** Fulwood d. Properjohn 6–3 6–3.

35 Doubles
Semi-finals: Maris Rozentals (LAT)/Alvils Zilgalvis (LAT) d. Nigel Mann (GBR)/Philip Veasey (GBR) 6–1 6–4; Nick Fulwood (GBR)/Brad Properjohn (AUS) d. Kobus Visage (RSA)/ Clive Wilson (RSA) 6–2 6–3.
Final: Fulwood/Properjohn d. Rozentals/Zilgalvis 6–4 7–5.

40 Singles
Semi-finals: Pierre Godfroid (BEL) d. Maris Rozentals (LAT) 6–4 6–7(3) 6–3; Thibaut Kuentz (FRA) d. Julio Goes (BRA) w.o. **Final:** Godfroid d. Kuentz 6–4 6–3.

40 Doubles
Semi-finals: Pierre Godfroid (BEL)/Bruce Osborne (AUS) d. Zachry Bator (USA)/Chris Bennett (USA) 6–4 6–1; Campbell Booth (USA)/Godfrey Evans (GBR) d. Richard Leslie (GBR)/Stephen Alger (GBR) 7–6(5) 7–5.
Final: Godfroid/Osborne d. Booth/Evans 6–1 6–2.

45 Singles
Semi-finals: Wayne Cowley (AUS) d. Paul Torre (FRA) 4–6 4–5 rtd; Andrew Rae (AUS) d. Jan Sie (NED) 7–6(3) 6–3; **Final:** Cowley d. Rae 6–3 6–3.

45 Doubles
Semi-finals: Benson Greatrex (GBR)/Philip Siviter (GBR) d. Phil Landauer (USA)/Neal Newman (USA) 7–5 7–5; Andrew Rae (AUS)/Wayne Cowley (AUS) d. Richard Ballance (GBR)/John Gardiner (GBR) 6–3 6–2.
Final: Greatrex/Siviter d. Rae/Cowley 7–5 6–2.

50 Singles
Semi-finals: Frank Briscoe (RSA) d. Xavier Lemoine (FRA) 7–5 6–7(4) 6–2; John Paish (GBR) d. David Bohannon (USA) 7–6(2) 4–6 6–2; **Final:** Briscoe d. Paish 6–3 6–3.

50 Doubles
Semi-finals: Keith Bland (GBR)/Richard Tutt (GBR) d. Pichet Boratisa (THA)/Zsidislaw Stoltmann (LUX) 6–2 6–0; Henry Michael (AUS)/John Weaver (AUS) d. Frank Briscoe (RSA)/Malcolm Passmore (RSA) 6–4 6–4.
Final: Bland/Tutt d. Michael/Weaver 6–2 6–1.

WOMEN

35 Singles
Semi-finals: Tracy Houk (USA) d. Lisa Prechtel (NED) 6–3 6–3; Anthea Stewart (GBR) d. Karina Elias (GER) 6–0 5–7 6–0. **Final:** Houk d. Stewart 2–6 6–1 6–2.

35 Doubles
Round Robin: Winners: Susanne Turi (HUN)/Kathy Vick (USA). **Runners Up:** Barbara Snapes (GBR)/ Anthea Stewart (GBR).

40 Singles
Semi-finals: Ros Balodis (AUS) d. Elena Poliakova (RUS) 6–3 6–1; Lucille Rijs (RSA) d. Lynette Vermaak (RSA) 6–2 1–6 6–1. **Final:** Balodis d. Rijs 6–2 6–0.

40 Doubles
Semi-finals: Marlie Buehler (USA)/Lynette Vermaak (RSA) d. Nancy Chatlak (USA)/Kathleen Slaysman (USA) 6–1 6–4; Ros Balodis (AUS)/Kaye Nealon (AUS) d. Lucille Rijs (RSA)/Terry Schweitzer (RSA) 6–4 6–3.
Final: Balodis/Nealon d. Buehler/Vermaak 6–2 6–2.
45 Singles
Semi-finals: Rita Theron (RSA) d. Isabella Enz (SUI) 7–6 7–6; Marlie Buehler (USA) d. Eugenia Birukova (ITA) 4–6 6–1 6–4. **Final:** Buehler d. Theron 6–4 6–3.
45 Doubles
Semi-finals: Kerry Ballard (AUS)/Rita Theron (RSA) d. Dianne Grundy (GBR)/Marjory Love (GBR) 6–3 0–6 6–4; Elizabeth Boyle (GBR)/Pauline Fisher (GBR) d. Isabella Enz (SUI)/Margaret Machoian (USA) 6–1 7–5.
Final: Boyle/Fisher d. Ballard/Theron 4–6 6–3 6–4.
50 Singles
Semi-finals: Marie Pinterova (HUN) d. Petro Kruger (RSA) 6–3 6–3; Elizabeth Allan (AUS) d. Trish Faulkner (USA) 6–0 6–1. **Final:** Pinterova d. Allan 6–2 6–2.
50 Doubles
Semi-finals: Carol Campling (AUS)/Elizabeth Allan (AUS) d. Jackie Robinson (GBR)/Jenny Waggott (GBR) 7–5 7–5; Heide Orth (GER)/Marie Pinterova (HUN) d. Louise Cash (USA)/Trish Faulkner (USA) 6–0 6–4.
Final: Campling/Allan d. Orth/Pinterova 6–3 6–1.

18TH ITF VETS WORLD CHAMPIONSHIPS (GROUP B)

3–10 May 1998
Palm Beach Gardens, Florida, USA

MEN

55 Singles
Semi-finals: Robert Howes (AUS) d. Peter Pokorny (AUT) 6–4 6–1; Jimmy Parker (USA) d. Stasys Labanauskas (LTU) 6–0 6–2. **Final:** Howes d. Parker 6–2 6–4.
55 Doubles
Semi-finals: Stasys Labanauskas (LTU)/Peter Pokorny (AUT) d. Ted Hoehn (USA)/Jimmy Parker (USA) 6–3 6–4; Tom Downie (AUS)/Murray French (AUS) d. Bruce Burns (AUS)/Robert Howes (AUS) w.o.
Final: Labanauskas/Pokorny d. Downie/French 6–4 7–6.
60 Singles
Semi-finals: Klaus Fuhrmann (GER) d. Willi Liska (AUT) 6–1 7–6; Bodo Nitsche (GER) d. Donald Shears (GBR) 6–1 7–6. **Final:** Nitsche d. Fuhrmann 6–2 2–6 6–1.
60 Doubles
Semi-finals: Henry Leichtfried (USA)/Leonard Lindborg (USA) d. Jim Nelson (USA)/Robert Duesler (USA) 6–2 2–6 7–5; Herman Ahlers (USA)/Peter Froelich (AUS) d. Leslie Dodson (USA)/Klaus Fuhrmann (GER) 6–2 6–3.
Final: Leichtfried/Lindborg d.Ahlers/Froelich 6–0 7–5.
65 Singles
Semi-finals: Lorne Main (CAN) d. Charles Devoe (USA) 6–3 6–0; Jim Perley (USA) d. Werner Mertins (GER) 6–3 4–6 6–3. **Final:** Perley d. Main 6–1 1–6 6–1.
65 Doubles
Semi-finals: Max Byrne (AUS)/Don Pike (AUS) d. Adrian Alle (AUS)/Neville Langford (AUS) 6–3 6–4; Lorne Main (CAN)/Kenneth Sinclair (CAN) d. Heino Krampe (GER)/Werner Mertins (GER) 4–6 7–6 7–6.
Final: Main/Sinclair d. Byrne/Pike 6–2 6–1.
70 Singles
Semi-finals: Fred Kovaleski (USA) d. Robert McCarthy (AUS) 6–3 6–4; Jason Morton (USA) d. Peter Schoenboerner (GER) 3–6 6–2 6–1. **Final:** Morton d. Kovaleski 6–2 3–6 6–1.
70 Doubles
Semi-finals: Fred Kovaleski (USA)/Jason Morton (USA) d. Adalbert Hussmuller (GER)/Peter Schoenboerner (GER) 7–5 6–2; Robert McCarthy (AUS)/Bernard Lisboa-Pinto (AUS) d. Mario Gonzalez (MEX)/Xavier Sanchez-Cos (MEX) 7–6 6–3. **Final:** Kovaleski/Morton d. McCarthy/ Lisboa-Pinto w/o.
75 Singles
Semi-finals: Tom Brown (USA) d. Newton Meade (USA) 6–2 6–0; Robert Sherman (USA) d. Neville Halligan (AUS) 6–3 6–4. **Final:** Sherman d. Brown 7–5 7–5.
75 Doubles
Semi-finals: Francis Bushmann (USA)/George Druliner (USA) d. Newton Meade (USA)/Richard Sorlien (USA) 6–1 6–2; Mervyn Brown (GBR)/Geoffrey Paish (GBR) d. John Pearce (AUS)/Fred Rodda (AUS) 5–7 6–2 6–2.
Final: Bushmann/Druliner d.Brown/Paish 6–1 6–2.
80 Singles
Semi-finals: Alex Swetka (USA) d. Dan Miller (USA) 7–5 6–4; Federico Barboza (ARG) d. Albert Ritzenberg (USA) 4–6 7–5 6–3. **Final:** Swetka d. Barboza w/o.
80 Doubles
Semi-finals: Gardnar Mulloy (USA)/Alex Swetka (USA) d. George Carter (USA)/Ned Mansfield (USA) 6–4 6–2; Irving Converse (USA)/Dan Miller (USA) d. Trevor Wigmore (AUS)/Frank Kornfeld (AUS) 6–4 6–4.
Final: Converse/Miller d. Mulloy/Swetka 7–5 6–0.

WOMEN

55 Singles

Semi-finals: Heide Orth (GER) d. Rosy Darmon (FRA) 6–0 6–3; Renate Schroeder (GER) d. Charleen Hillebrand (USA) 6–2 1–6 6–4. **Final:** Orth d. Schroeder 6–3 7–6.

55 Doubles

Semi-finals: Rosy Darmon (FRA)/Heide Orth (GER) d. Lynne Nette (AUS)/Elsie Veentjer-Spruyt (NED) 6–3 3–6 6–0; Cathie Anderson (USA)/Sinclair Bill (USA) d. Mary Gordon (AUS)/Linda Pengelly (AUS) 6–0 3–6 7–5. **Final:** Darmon/Orth d. Anderson/Bill 6–0 3–6 7–5.

60 Singles

Semi-finals: Judy Dalton (AUS) d. Doris Devries (USA) 6–3 7–6; Jeannine Lieffrig (RSA) d. Roberta Beltrame (ITA) 6–3 6–2. **Final:** Dalton d. Lieffrig 7–6 6–3.

60 Doubles

Semi-finals: Jeannine Lieffrig (RSA)/Audrey Van Coller (RSA) d. Judy Dalton (AUS)/Carol Wood (USA) 1–6 6–1 6–2; Belmar Gunderson (USA)/Katie Koontz (USA) d. Evelyn Hustwit (CAN)/Inge Weber (CAN) 6–1 5–7 6–3. **Final:** Gunderson/Koontz d. Lieffrig/Van Coller 7–5 6–2.

65 Singles

Semi-finals: Clelia Mazzoleni (ITA) d. Ines Pla (ARG) 6–4 7–5; Rita Lauder (GBR) d. Ana Maria Estalella (ESP) 2–6 7–5 6–4. **Final:** Mazzoleni d. Lauder 6–3 4–4 ret.

65 Doubles

Semi-finals: Lorice Forbes (AUS)/Peg Hoysted (AUS) d. Ruth Illingworth (GBR)/Rita Lauder (GBR) 7–6 6–3; Astri Hobson (AUS)/Margaret Robinson (AUS) d. Mary Ann Plante (USA)/Nancy Reed (USA) 2–6 7–6 7–6. **Final:** Forbes/Hoysted d. Hobson/Robinson 6–4 1–6 6–1.

70 Singles

Semi-finals: Barbara Davidson (USA) d. Elaine Mason (USA) 1–6 6–3 7–5; Betty Eisenstein (USA) Amelia Cury (BRA) 6–2 6–1. **Final:** Eisenstein d. Davidson 4–6 6–0 6–3.

70 Doubles

Semi-finals: Phyllis Adler (USA)/Elaine Mason (USA) d. Twinx Rogers (RSA)/Lurline Stock (AUS) 6–4 6–3; Betty Eisentstein (USA)/Peggy Landtroop (USA) d. Beth Lown (AUS)/Beryl Rocavert (AUS) 6–2 6–1. **Final:** Adler/Mason d. Eisenstein/Landtroop 6–4 7–5.

ITF VETS TEAM COMPETITIONS 1998

WOMEN'S 40

Young Cup, RAF Halton Lawn Tennis Centre, Halton, Buckinghamshire, England

Semi-finals: USA d. Australia 2–1; South Africa d. Argentina 2–1 ***Final:*** USA d. South Africa 3–0 (Diane Fishburne (USA) d. Lucille Rijsa (RSA) 7–5 6–1; Tina Karwasky (USA) d. Lynette Vermaak (RSA) 6–4 6–1; Fishburne/Freeman-Young (USA) d. Rijs/Schweitzer (RSA) 6–3 1–6 6–1).

WOMEN'S 45

Margaret Court Cup, Warwick Boat Club, Warwick, Warwickshire, England

Semi-finals: USA d. New Zealand 3–0; South Africa d. Austria 2–1 ***Final:*** USA d. South Africa 2–1 (Martha Downing (USA) d. Gillian Birch (RSA) 6–2 6–0; Rita Theron (RSA) d. Marlie Buehler (USA) 2–6 7–6 6–3; Bueler/Peltz-Petow (USA) d. Gardiner/Theron (RSA) 6–2 6–3).

WOMEN'S 50

Maria Esther Bueno Cup, Clontarf Lawn Tennis Club, Dublin, Ireland

Semi-finals: USA d. Finland 3–0; Australia d. Germany 3–0 ***Final:*** USA d. Australia 2–1 (Margaret Russo (USA) d. Carol Campling (AUS) 7–6 7–5; Elizabeth Craig-Allan (AUS) d. Trish Faulkner (USA) 6–2 4–6 6–2; Faulkner/Russo (USA) d. Campling/Craig-Allan (AUS) 6–3 6–1).

WOMEN'S 55

Maureen Connolly Cup, Oaks Racquet Club, Pompano Beach, Florida, USA

Final: Germany d. Great Britain 3–0 (Renate Schroder (GER) d. Jacqueline Boothman (GBR) 6–0, 6–1; Heide Orth (GER) d. Frances Taylor (GBR) 6–4, 6–0; Schroder/Orth (GER) d. Taylor/Hill (GBR) 6–2, 6–0).

WOMEN'S 60

Alice Marble Cup, The Polo Club, Boca Raton, Florida, USA

Semi-finals: USA d. Canada 2–1; Australia d. South Africa 2–1 ***Final:*** Australia d. USA 2–1 (Katie Koontz (USA) d. Nola Collins (AUS) 6–2, 6–1; Judy Dalton (AUS) d. Dorothy Matthiessen (USA) 6–1, 6–0; Dalton/Heumiller (AUS) d. Koontz/Matthiessen (USA) 6–3, 6–2).

WOMEN'S 65

Kitty Godfree Cup, Lauderdale Tennis Club, Fort Lauderdale, Florida, USA

Semi-finals: Great Britain d. Canada 3–0; USA d. Australia 2–1 ***Final:*** Great Britain d. USA 2–1 (Ruth Illingworth (GBR) d. Lee Burling (USA) 6–4, 7–6 (3); Rita Lauder (GBR) d. Nancy Reed (USA) 6–1, 6–2; Boswell/Owen (USA) d. Illingworth/Lauder (GBR) 4–6, 6–4 ret).

WOMEN'S 70

Althea Gibson Cup, BallenIsles Country Club, Palm Beach Gardens, Florida, USA
1st placed team: USA. ***2nd placed team:*** Germany. ***3rd placed team:*** Canada. ***4th placed team:*** Australia. ***5th placed team:*** Great Britain. ***6th placed team:*** Brazil.

MEN'S 35

Italia Cup, Winchester Tennis & Squash Club, Winchester, Hampshire, England
Semi-finals: Great Britain d. Germany 2–1; Italy d. USA 2–1 ***Final:*** Great Britain d. Italy 2–1 (Nick Fulwood (GBR) d. Luca Bottazi (ITA) 6–3 5–7 7–5; Simone Colombo (ITA) d. Jeremy Bates (GBR) 6–3 3–6 6–3; Bates/Fulwood (GBR) d. Bottazi/Colombo 4–6 6–1 6–1).

MEN'S 45

Dubler Cup, Lansdowne Lawn Tennis Club, Dublin, Ireland
Semi-finals: USA d. Germany 2–1; Spain d. France 2–1 ***Final:*** USA d. Spain 2–1 (Jim Rombeau (USA) d. Rafael Ruiz (ESP) 6–4 6–1; Jose Moreno (ESP) d. Wesley Jackson (USA) 5–7 6–4 7–5; Turville/Landauer (USA) d.Moreno/Ruiz (ESP) 6–4 6–3).

MEN'S 50

Fred Perry Cup, Whitecraigs Lawn Tennis Club, Glasgow, Scotland
Semi-finals: Spain d. France 3–0; USA d. Germany 2–1 ***Final:*** USA d. Spain 2–1 (Jose Camina (ESP) d. Richard Johnson (USA) 6–3 6–4; Brian Cheney (USA) d. Jairo Velasco (ESP) 7–6 (4) 6–2; Bohannon/Cheney (USA) d. Camina/Gisbert (ESP) 6–2 6–1).

MEN'S 55

Austria Cup, Naples Bath and Tennis Club, Naples, Florida, USA
Semi-finals: Netherlands d. Austria 2–1; USA d. Australia 3–0 ***Final:*** USA d.Netherlands 3–0 (Rob Cadwallader (USA) d. Nico Welschen (NED) 7–5, 6–7 (3), 6–1; Jim Parker (USA) d. Peter Blaas (NED) 6–0, 6–0; Carter/Leichtfried (USA) d. Blaas/Scholtz 6–3, 6–1).

MEN'S 60

Von Cramm Cup, Lauderdale Tennis Club, Fort Lauderdale, Florida, USA
Semi-finals: USA d. France 2–1; Germany d. Sweden 3–0 ***Final:*** Germany d. USA 2–1 (Bodo Nitsche (GER) d. Buddy Lomax 6–1, 2–6, 6–2; Klaus Fuhrmann (GER) d. Jim Perley (USA) 6–3, 6–4; Nelson/Duesler (USA) d. Krauss/Hamm (GER) 6–1, 6–1).

MEN'S 65

Britannia Cup, BallenIsles Country Club, Palm Beach Gardens, Florida, USA
Semi-finals: USA d. Germany 2–1; Canada d. France 3–0 ***Final:*** Canada d. USA 3–0 (Ken Sinclair (CAN) d. Charles DeVoe (USA) 2–6, 6–3, 6–1; Lorne Main (CAN) d. Whitney Reed (USA) 6–3, 6–2; Main/Sinclair (CAN) d. Springer/Davis (USA) 6–3, 3–6, 6–4).

MEN'S 70

Jack Crawford Cup, Oaks Racquet Club, Pompano Beach, Florida, USA
Semi-finals: Austria d. Great Britain 3–0; USA d. Australia 3–0 ***Final:*** USA d. Austria 2–1 (Jason Morton (USA) d. Oskar Jirkovsky (AUT) 6–1, 6–3; Laci Legenstein (AUT) d. Fred Kovaleski (USA) 7–6 (2), 6–1; Kovaleski/Morton (USA) d. Legenstein/Jirkovsky (AUT) 7–6 (5), 6–4).

MEN'S 75

Bitsy Grant Cup, The Polo Club, Boca Raton, Florida, USA
Semi-finals: USA d. Great Britain 3–0; Australia d. Argentina 2–1 ***Final:*** USA d. Australia 3–0 (Robert Sherman (USA) d. Neville Halligan (AUS) 6–3, 6–1; Tom Brown (USA) d. Trevor Millican (AUS) 6–2, 6–0; Bushman/Druliner (USA) d. Millican/Halligan (AUS) 6–2, 7–5).

MEN'S 80

Gardnar Mulloy Cup, Naples Bath and Tennis Club, Naples, Florida, USA
1st placed team: USA. ***2nd placed team:*** Australia. ***3rd placed team:*** Canada. ***4th placed team:*** Mexico. ***5th placed team:*** Germany. ***6th placed team:*** Sweden.

ITF VETS WORLD RANKINGS 1998 (as at 4 January 1999)

MEN

35 AGE GROUP

1	Nick Fulwood (GBR)	570
2	Mike Fedderly (USA)	380
3	Brett Edwards (AUS)	360
4	Neil Smith (AUS)	348
5	Alain Moracchini (FRA)	320
6	Brad Properjohn (AUS)	318
7	Fernando Gambacurta (ITA)	285
8	Wim Groeneveld (NED)	284
9	Juan Plaza (CHI)	280
10=	Stefan Eriksson (GER)	260
10=	Alberto Kuhlmann (BRA)	260
10=	Clive Wilson (RSA)	260

40 AGE GROUP

1	Pierre Godfroid (BEL)	540
2	Ricardo Cano (ARG)	285
3	Joao Arruba Souze (BRA)	260
4	Ervin Berko (HUN)	240
5	Luiz Roberto Lobao (BRA)	205
6	Helmut Kock (AUT)	175
7	Christopher Bennett (USA)	162
8=	Ivan Drcelic (CRO)	142
8=	Gil White (CAN)	142
10	Humberto Morales (BRA)	140

45 AGE GROUP

1	Wayne Cowley (AUS)	600
2	Andrew Rae (AUS)	450
3	Sepp Baumgartner (GER)	420
4	Paul Torre (FRA)	415
5	Wesley Jackson (USA)	365
6	Robert Van Malder (BEL)	360
7	Roger Guedes (BRA)	324
8=	Alfred Klammer (AUT)	320
8=	Pavel Sevcik (GER)	320
8=	Jan Sie (NED)	320

50 AGE GROUP

1	Brian Cheney (USA)	520
2	Frank Briscoe (RSA)	500
3	Daniel Harms (ARG)	480
4	Kenneth Andersson (SWE)	384
5=	Benns de Jel (NED)	360
5=	Michael Mijuca (GER)	360
5=	Peter Pokorny (AUT)	360
8	Terry Smith (AUS)	336
9	John Weaver (AUS)	324
10	Hannes Futterknecht (AUT)	315

55 AGE GROUP

1	James Parker (USA)	550
2	Robert Howes (AUS)	540
3	Peter Pokorny (AUT)	475
4	Jaime Pinto-Bravo (CHI)	420
5	Rob Cadwallader (USA)	390
6	Roberto Aubone (ARG)	380
7=	Bernd Reinholz (GER)	360
7=	Georgio Rohrich (ITA)	360
9	Allan Carter (USA)	324
10=	Stasys Labanauskas (LTU)	320
10=	Bepi Zambon (ITA)	320

60 AGE GROUP

1	Bodo Nitsche (GER)	600
2	Klaus Fuhrmann (GER)	550
3=	Peter Froelich (AUS)	420
3=	Livio Lombardi (ITA)	420
3=	Ricardo Narcio (MEX)	420
6	Heinz Loffler (GER)	375
7=	Robert Duesler (USA)	360
7=	Wilhelm Liska (AUT)	360
7=	Richard Swanton (AUS)	360
10	Fred Farzanegan (USA)	348

65 AGE GROUP

1	Jim Perley (USA)	600
2	Lorne Main (CAN)	550
3	Werner Mertins (GER)	480
4	Juan-Manuel Ruiz (ARG)	420
5=	Charles Devoe (USA)	360
5=	Rene Marik (CZE)	360
7	Kenneth Sinclair (CAN)	350
8	Adolfo Ibarrondo (ARG)	315
9	Heino Krampe (GER)	300
10=	Kenneth Buswell (GBR)	280
10=	Jaime Furio Felipo (ESP)	280
10=	Hans Jell (AUT)	280
10=	Hannes Mentz (RSA)	280

70 AGE GROUP

1	Jason Morton (USA)	600
2	Laci Legenstein (AUT)	520
3	Fred Kovaleski (USA)	510
4	Eduardo Polledo (ARG)	480
5	Adalbert Hussmuller (GER)	420
6	Bernard Lisboa-Pinto (AUS)	400
7=	Oskar Jirkovsky (AUT)	360
7=	Robert Mc Carthy (AUS)	360
7=	Peter Schoenboerner (GER)	360
10	Lionel Matton (FRA)	324

75 AGE GROUP

1	Robert Sherman (USA)	600
2	Tom Brown (USA)	510
3=	Mischa Stachowitsch (AUT)	420
3=	Sergio Verrati (FRA)	420
5=	Cornelis Marre (NED)	360
5=	Andreas Stolpa (GER)	360
7	Elias del Cano (ARG)	343
8=	Hans Borglund (SWE)	324
8=	Francis Bushman (USA)	324
10	Ernst Meidhof (GER)	320

80 AGE GROUP

1	Alex Swetka (USA)	600
2	Gordon Henley (AUS)	480
3	Albert Ritzenberg (USA)	420
4	Dan Miller (USA)	360
5	Trevor Wigmore (AUS)	324
6	Mirek Kizlink (GBR)	320
7	Reg Smith (GBR)	288
8	Gyula Esztergaly (HUN)	276
9	Irving Converse (USA)	264
10	Omar Bergmann (BRA)	255

WOMEN

35 AGE GROUP

1	Tracy Houk (USA)	500
2	Anthea Stewart (GBR)	410
3	Lisa Prechtel (NED)	320
4	Monica Fuentealba (CHI)	310
5	Susanne Turi (HUN)	275
6	Amanda Bishop (GBR)	249
7	Kathy Vick (USA)	240
8	Barbora Koutna (CZE)	210
9	Dora Aner (BRA)	176
10	Adriana Munoz (BRA)	152

40 AGE GROUP

1	Ros Balodis (AUS)	600
2	Beatriz Villaverde (ARG)	435
3=	Ann Etheridge (USA)	420
3=	Helena Poliakova (RUS)	420
5	Lucille Rijs (RSA)	416
6	Gabriela Leinen (GER)	380
7	Tina Karwasky (USA)	370
8=	Diane Fishburne (USA)	360
8=	Renata Vojtischek (GER)	360
10	Eugenvjc Birukova (ITA)	320

45 AGE GROUP

1	Marlie Buehler (USA)	540
2	Rita Theron (RSA)	495
3	Beatriz Chrystman (BRA)	480
4	Eugenvjc Birukova (ITA)	420
5	Isabella Enz (SUI)	360
6	Maria Geyer (AUT)	345
7	Kerry Ballard (AUS)	324
8=	Alena Klein (GER)	320
8=	Patricia Rivera (CHI)	320
10	Marie Annick Morea (ARG)	315

50 AGE GROUP

1	Marie Pinterova (HUN)	600
2	Elizabeth Allan (AUS)	510
3	Trish Faulkner (USA)	480
4=	Ana Maria Arias (CHI)	360
4=	Petro Kruger (RSA)	360
4=	Heide Orth (GER)	360
7=	Mariana Karolyi (HUN)	320
7=	Mary Mc Lean (USA)	320
7=	Renate Schroder (GER)	320
10=	Carol Campling (AUS)	315
10=	Alena Klein (GER)	315

55 AGE GROUP

1	Heide Orth (GER)	600
2	Renate Schroder (GER)	510
3	Charleen Hillebrand (USA)	420
4	Renate Niesler (GER)	380
5=	Renate Mayer-Zdralek (GER)	360
5=	Suella Steel (USA)	360
7	Rosa-Maria Darmon (FRA)	285
8	Cathie Anderson (USA)	284
9	Margaret Bornman (RSA)	279
10	Heidi Attlfellner (USA)	264

60 AGE GROUP

1	Judy Dalton (AUS)	585
2	Janine Lieffrieg (RSA)	450
3=	Roberta Beltrame (ITA)	420
3=	Katie Koontz (USA)	420
3=	Elisabeth Perusch (AUT)	420
6	Paule Ferguson (FRA)	384
7=	Doris Devries (USA)	360
7=	Ilse Michael (GER)	360
9	Lesley Heumiller (AUS)	345
10	Dorothy Matthiessen (USA)	320

65 AGE GROUP

1	Clelia Mazzoleni (ITA)	600
2	Rita Lauder (GBR)	495
3	Lee Burling (USA)	480
4=	Anna-Maria Estalella (ESP)	360
4=	Nancy Reed (USA)	360
6	Rosemarie Nolle (GER)	320
7=	Magdalena Jauch (GER)	315
7=	Monique Kyburz (SUI)	315
9	Erika Steinle (GER)	300
10	Lucette Moreau (FRA)	280

70 AGE GROUP

1	Betty Eisenstein (USA)	540
2	Barbara Davidson (USA)	450
3=	Pinuccia Russo (ITA)	420
3=	Kathe Sorge (GER)	420
5	Lurline Stock (AUS)	384
6=	Amelia Cury (BRA)	360
6=	Elaine Mason (USA)	360
8	Dorothy Knode (USA)	276
9	Ingeborg Haas (GER)	260
10	Maria Frigerio (ITA)	243

National Associations and Voting Rights

Correct at 4 December 1998

Abbreviations

T = Telephone Number **FAX** = Telecopier Number **E-mail** = Internet Address

The date given in parenthesis denotes the foundation date of the National Tennis Association where known.

Full members with voting rights (132)

ALGERIA – ALG (1962) (Votes 1)

Federation Algerienne de Tennis
Centre des Federations Sportives
Cite Olympique B.P. 88 El Biar Algers 16030
T 213 2 924 613 **FAX** 213 2 924 613
Pres: Dr Mohamed Bouabdallah
Sec: Miss Gara

ANDORRA – AND (1986) (Votes 1)

Federacion Andorrana de Tenis Sant Antoni
C/ Verge del Pilar 5 3er Desp. no 10
Andorra la Vella
T 376 861 381 **FAX** 376 868 381
Pres: Mr Antoni Ricart
Sec: Mr Joan Grau

ANTIGUA & BARBUDA – ANT (1982) (Votes 1)

Antigua & Barbuda Tennis Association
PO Box 2758 St John's
T 1 268 460 8585 **FAX** 1 268 462 4811
E-mail elijah@candw.ag
Pres: Mr. Elijah Armstrong
Sec: Mr Ferdinand Peters

ARGENTINA – ARG (1921) (Votes 7)

Asociacion Argentina de Tenis
Avda San-Juan 1307 1148 Buenos Aires
T 54 1 304 2470 **FAX** 54 1 305 0296
Pres: Mr Enrique Morea
Sec: Mr Roberto Fernandaz

ARMENIA – ARM (1940) (Votes 1)

Armenian Tennis Association
Tennis School of Armenia Yerevan 375082
T 3742 345 995 **FAX** 3742 151 069
Pres: Mr Hrachik Israelian
Sec: Mr Hajk Kirakossian

AUSTRALIA – AUS (1904) (Votes 12)

Tennis Australia
Private Bag 6060 Richmond South
Victoria 3121
T 61 392 861 177 **FAX** 61 396 502 743
Pres: Mr Geoff Pollard
Sec: Mr Fenton Coull

AUSTRIA – AUT (1902) (Votes 5)

Osterreichischer Tennisverband
Haeckelstrasse 33 1235 Vienna
T 43 1 865 4506 **FAX** 43 1 865 9806
E-mail oetv@asn.or.at
Pres: Dr Ernst Wolner
Sec: Peter Nader

AZERBAIJAN – AZE (1956) (Votes 1)

Azerbaijan Tennis Federation
Flat 46 44-46 B Madjedov Str Baku 370002
T 994 12 395 172 **FAX** 994 12 394 023
Pres: Mr Nazim Ibraqimov
Sec: Mr Djavanshir Ibragimov

BAHAMAS – BAH (1961) (Votes 1)

The Bahamas Lawn Tennis Association
PO Box N-10169 Nassau
T 1 242 363 2930 **FAX** 1 242 322 8000
E-mail reb@bahamas.net.bs
Pres: Mr Kit Spencer
Sec: Mr R E Barnes

BAHRAIN – BRN (1981) (Votes 1)

Bahrain Tennis Federation
PO Box 26985
T 973 687 236 **FAX** 973 781 533
Pres: Mr Ahmed Al Kalifa
Sec: Mr Mohammad Saleh Abdul Latif

BANGLADESH – BAN (1972) (Votes 1)

Bangladesh Tennis Federation
Tennis Complex Ramna Green Dhaka 1000
T 880 2 506 650 **FAX** 880 2 966 2711
Pres: Mr Syed Chowdhury
Sec: Mr Sanaul Haque

BARBADOS – BAR (1948) (Votes 1)

Barbados Lawn Tennis Association
PO Box 615c Bridgetown
T 1 246 426 6453 **FAX** 1 246 427 8317
Pres: Dr Raymond Forde
Sec: Mrs Jean Date

BELARUS – BLR (1990) (Votes 1)

Tennis Association of the Republic of Belarus
Masherov Avenue 63 Minsk 220035
T 375 172 271 735 **FAX** 375 172 269 823
Pres: Mr Simon Kagan **Sec:** Mr Georgy Matsuk

BELGIUM – BEL (1990) (Votes 1)

Federation Royale Belge de Tennis
Galerie de la Porte Louise 203
(8eme Etage) 1050 Brussels
T 32 2 513 2927 **FAX** 32 2 513 7950
Pres: Mr Pierre De Keghel **Sec:** Mr Walter Goethals

BENIN – BEN (1963) (Votes 1)

Federation Beninoise de Lawn Tennis
BP 2709 Cotonou I
T 229 315 153 **FAX** 229 311 252
Pres: Mr Edgar-Yves Monnou
Sec: Mr Ladami Gafari

BERMUDA – BER (1994) (Votes 1)

Bermuda Lawn Tennis Association
PO Box HM 341
Hamilton HM BX
T 1 441 296 0834 **FAX** 1 441 292 9763
Pres: Mr Colin Smith **Sec:** Ms Airlie Arton

BOLIVIA – BOL (1937) (Votes 1)

Federacion Boliviana de Tennis
Calle Rene Moreno 685 Casilla Postal No. 1041
Santa Cruz
T 591 336 8625 **FAX** 591 336 8625
E-mail: fbtenis@bibosi.scz.entelnet.bo
Pres: Mr Edmundo Rodriguez
Sec: Mr Jaime Guillen

BOSNIA/HERZOGOVINA – BIH (1950) (Votes 1)

Tennis Association of Bosnia and Herzogovina
c/o St Marsala Tita 7/1 71000 Sarajevo
T 387 71 663 514 **FAX** 387 75 251 439
Pres: Mr Tarik Kupusovic **Sec:** Mr Haris Barucija

BOTSWANA – BOT (1964) (Votes 1)

Botswana Tennis Association
PO Box 1174 Gaborone
T 267 373 193 **FAX** 267 373 193
Pres: Dr T John Letsunyane
Sec: Ms Sithembile Keabetswe

BRAZIL – BRA (1956) (Votes 7)

Confederacao Brasileira de Tenis
Av Paulista Nr. 326 – 2° Cj 26/27
01310-902 Sao Paulo
T 55 11 283 1788 **FAX** 55 11 283 0768
E-mail cbt@zaz.com.br
Pres: Mr Nelson Nastas
Sec: Mr Carlos Alberto Martolette

BRUNEI DARUSSALAM – BRU (1967) (Votes 1)

Brunei Darussalam Tennis Association
PO Box 859 Pejabat Pos Gadong
Bandar Seri Bagawan BE 3978
T 673 2 381 205 **FAX** 673 2 381 205
E-mail jstubbs@brunet.bn
Pres: Mr Abdu Bakar Abdul Rahman
Sec: Mr Tom Butcher

BULGARIA – BUL (1930) (Votes 1)

Bulgarian Tennis Federation
Bul. Vasil Levski 75 Sofia 1040
T 359 2 963 1310 **FAX** 359 2 981 5728
E-mail btf@mail.techno-link.com
Pres: Mr Krassimir Angarski
Sec: Mr Chavdar Ganev

CAMEROON – CMR (1966) (Votes 1)

Federation Camerounaise de Tennis
BP 13 001 Douala
T 237 370 790 **FAX** 237 376 218
Pres: Mr Gilbert Kadji
Sec: Mr Victor Momha

CANADA – CAN (1920) (Votes 7)

Tennis Canada
3111 Steeles Avenue West Downsview
Ontario M3J 3H2
T 1 416 665 9777 **FAX** 1 416 665 9017
E-mail commnctn@tenniscanada.com
Pres: Mr Robert H Moffatt
Sec: Ms Kim Ali

CHILE – CHI (1920) (Votes 5)

Federacion de Tenis de Chile
Jose Joaquin Prieto No. 4040, Paradero 7
Gran Avenida Santiago
T 56 25 540 068 **FAX** 56 25 541 078
E-mail ftch@entelchile.net
Pres: Mr Carlos Herrera Arredondo
Sec: Mr Guillermo Toral Bustamante

CHINA HONG KONG – HKG (1909) (Votes 1)

Hong Kong Tennis Association Ltd
Room 1021, Sports House
1 Stadium Path So Kon Po Causeway Bay
T 852 2 504 8266 **FAX** 852 2 512 8649
E-mail: atf@i-wave.net.hk
Pres: Dr Philip Kwok
Sec: Mr Herman Hu

CHINA, PEOPLE'S REPUBLIC OF – CHN (1953) (Votes 1)

Tennis Association of the People's Republic of China
9 Tiyuguan Road Beiijing 100763
T 86 10 6715 8622
FAX 86 10 6711 4096
Pres: Mr Lu Zhenchao
Sec: Mr Zhang Xiaoning

CHINESE TAIPEI – TPE (1973) (Votes 3)

Chinese Taipei Tennis Association
Room 1108, 11th Floor 20 Chu Lun Street Taipei
T 886 2 2772 0298 **FAX** 886 2 2771 1696
E-mail: ctta@email.gcn.net.tw
Pres: Mr P Y Young
Sec: Mr Samuel Mu

COLOMBIA – COL (1932) (Votes 5)

Federacion Colombiana de Tenis
Carrera 8A No 121 – 33 Santafe de Bogota DC
T 571 213 5897 **FAX** 571 213 5784
Pres: Dr Ricardo Mejia Pelaez
Sec: Mr David Murillo

CONGO – CGO (1962) (Votes 1)

Federation Congolaise de Lawn Tennis
BP 550 Brazzaville
T 242 411 222 **FAX** 242 810 330
Pres: Mr Germain Ickonga Akindou
Sec: Mr Antoine Ouabonzi

COSTA RICA – CRC (1960) (Votes 1)

Federacion Costarricense de Tenis
PO Box 326-1005 Barrio Mexico San Jose
T 506 256 5563 **FAX** 506 256 2182
Pres: Mr Reinaldo Brenes-Ross
Sec: Mr Jurgen G Nanne-Koberg

COTE D'IVOIRE – CIV (1969) (Votes 1)

Federation Ivoirienne de Tennis
01 BPV 273 Abidjan 01
T 225 441 354 **FAX** 225 447 434
Pres: Mr Jean-Claude Delafosse **Sec:** Mr Gadjiro

CROATIA – CRO (1922) (Votes 5)

Croatian Tennis Association
HR-10 000 Zagreb Gundulieeva 3
T 385 14 811 968 **FAX** 385 14 811 256
E-mail: hts@zg.tel.hr
Pres: Mr Suad Rizvanbegovic
Sec: Mr Dubravko Lipnjak

CUBA – CUB (1925) (Votes 1)

Federacion Cubana de Tenis de Campo
Calle 13 NR 601 Esq AC Vedado Habana 4
T 53 7 972 121 **FAX** 53 7 972 121
Pres: Mr Rolando Martinez Perez
Sec: Mr Juan Baez

CYPRUS – CYP (1951) (Votes 1)

Cyprus Tennis Federation
Ionos Str. 20 PO Box 3931 Nicosia 1687
T 357 2 666 822 **FAX** 357 2 668 016
Pres: Mr Philios Christodoulou
Sec: Mr Stavros Ioannou

CZECH REPUBLIC – CZE (1906) (Votes 9)

Czech Tenisova Asociace
Ostrov Stvanice 38 170 00 Prague 7
T 420 2 24 810 238 **FAX** 420 2 24 810 301
E-mail: ctatennis@gts.cz
www: www.ctatennis.cz
Pres: Mr Ivo Kaderka **Sec:** Mr Karel Papousek

DENMARK – DEN (1920) (Votes 5)

Dansk Tennis Forbund
Idraettens Hus Broendby Stadion 20
DK-2605 Broendby
T 45 43 262 660 **FAX** 45 43 262 670
E-mail: dktennis@dansktennisforbund.dk
Pres: Mr Peter Schak Larsen
Sec: Mr Niels Persson

DJIBOUTI – DJI (1978) (Votes 1)

Federation Djiboutienne de Tennis
BP 3592 Djibouti
T 253 357 945 **FAX** 253 351 720
E-mail: oned@intnet.dj
Pres: Mr Houmed Houssein
Sec: Mr Chirdon Kaireh Chirdon

DOMINICAN REPUBLIC – DOM (1929) (Votes 1)

Federacion Dominicana de Tennis
Club Deportivo Naco Calle Central
Ens Naco Santo Domingo
T 1 809 549 5031 **FAX** 1 809 549 5131
Pres: Mr Gonzalo Mejia **Sec:** Mr J Ravelo

ECUADOR – ECU (1967) (Votes 3)

Federacion Ecuatoriana de Tenis
Edificio Multi Parqueo Piso 7 Guayaquil
Junin 214 Y Pedro Carbo
T 593 4 518 597 **FAX** 593 4 513 995
E-mail: fetenis@gye.satnet.net
Pres: Mr Jaime Guzman Maspons
Sec: Mrs Nuria Guzman De Ferretti

EGYPT, ARABIAN REPUBLIC OF – EGY (1920) (Votes 5)

Egyptian Tennis Federation
13 Kasr El Nile Street Cairo
T 20 2 574 7697 **FAX** 20 2 575 3235
E-mail: etenis@idsc1.gov.eg
Pres: Mr Mohamed Halawa
Sec: Miss May Elwany

EL SALVADOR – ESA (1949) Votes 1)

Federacion Salvadorena de Tenis
Apartado Postal (01) 110 San Salvador
T 503 278 8087 **FAX** 503 278 8087
Pres: Mr Enrique Molins Rubio
Sec: Mr Jose Martinez

ESTONIA – EST (1932) (Votes 1)

Estonian Tennis Association
Herne Street 28 EE0001 Tallinn
T 372 6 410 404 **FAX** 372 6 410 404
Pres: Mr Jaak Ulman **Sec:** Mr Mati Kuum

ETHIOPIA – ETH (1972) (Votes 1)

Ethiopian Tennis Federation
PO Box 3241 Addis Ababa
T 251 1 152 028 **FAX** 251 1 513 345
Pres: Mr Magussie Mano
Sec: Mr Seifu W/yohannes

FIJI – FIJ (1934) (Votes 1)

Fiji Tennis Association
c/o Mr Paras Naidu PO Box 3664 Lautoka
T 679 315 988 **FAX** 679 302 409
Pres: Mr Cliff Benson
Sec: Mr Paras Naidu

FINLAND – FIN (1911) (Votes 3)

Suomen Tennisliitto
Varikkotie 4 SF – 00900 Helsinki
T 358 9 338 122 **FAX** 358 9 331 105
E-mail: jukka.roiha@lindstrom.fi
Pres: Mr Jukka Roiha **Sec:** Riitta Narhi

FRANCE – FRA (1920) (Votes 12)

Federation Francaise de Tennis
Stade Roland Garros 2 Avenue Gordon Bennett
75016 Paris
T 33 1 4743 4800 **FAX** 33 1 4743 0494
Pres: Mr Christian Bimes
Sec: Mr Jacques Dupre

GEORGIA – GEO (1992) (Votes 1)

Georgian Tennis Federation
K Marjanishvili St 29 Tbilisi
T 995 32 952 781 **FAX** 995 32 953 829
E-mail: geonoc@access.sanet.ge
Pres: Mr Merab Adeishvili
Sec: Mr Zurab Katsarava

GERMANY – GER (1902) (Votes 12)

Deutscher Tennis Bund eV
Hallerstrasse 89 20149 Hamburg
T 49 40 411 780 **FAX** 49 40 411 782 22
E-mail: dtbpress@aol.com
www: www.dtb-tennis.de
Pres: Dr Claus Stauder
Sec: Mr Gunter Sanders

GHANA – GHA (1909) (Votes1)

Ghana Tennis Association
PO Box T-95 Sports Stadium Post Office Accra
T 233 21 667 267 **FAX** 233 21 668 590
Pres: Mr J Stanley-Owusu
Sec: Mr Adam Adbdul Rashid

GREAT BRITAIN – GBR (1888) (Votes 12)

The Lawn Tennis Association
The Queen's Club West Kensington
London W14 9EG
T 44 171 381 7000 **FAX** 44 171 381 5965
www: www.lta.org.uk
Pres: Sir Geoffrey Cass
Sec: Mr John James

GREECE – GRE (1938) (Votes 3)

Hellenic Tennis Federation
Athens Tennis Complex Olympic Stadium
37 Kifissias Str 15123 Maroussi Athens
T 30 16 852 512 **FAX** 30 16 831 865
E-mail: efoa@otenet.gr
Pres: Mr Spyros Zannias
Sec: Mr Ntinos Nikolaidis

GUATEMALA – GUA (1948) (Votes 1)

Federacion Nacionale de Tenis de Guatemala
Section 1551 PO Box 02-5339
Miami, FL 33102-5339
T 502 331 0261 **FAX** 502 331 0261
Pres: Mr Julio Henkle
Sec: Mr Manuel Lucero

HAITI – HAI (1950) (Votes 1)

Federation Haitienne de Tennis
PO Box 1442 Port Au Prince
T 509 451 462 **FAX** 506 491 233
E-mail: abhardware@compa.net
Pres: Mr Maxime Sada
Sec: Mr Jean Pean

HONDURAS – HON (1989) (Votes 1)

Federacion Hondurena de Tenis
PO Box 30152 Toncontin Comayaguela MDC
T 504 2 396 890 **FAX** 504 2 396 890
Pres: Mr Humberto Rodriguez
Sec: Mr Rodulio Perdomo

HUNGARY – HUN (1907) (Votes 5)

Magyar Tenisz Szovetseg
Dozsa Gyorgy ut 1-3 H-1143 Budapest
T 36 1 252 6687 **FAX** 36 1 251 0107
E-mail: tennis@mail.matav.hu
Pres: Dr Janos Berenyi **Sec:** Mr Attila Deak

ICELAND – ISL (1987) (Votes 1)

Icelandic Tennis Association
Ithrotamidstoedinni I Laugardal 104 Reykjavik
T 354 5 813 377 **FAX** 354 5 888 848
Pres: Mr Stefan Eggertsson

INDIA – IND (1920) (Votes 9)

All India Tennis Association
R K Khanna Tennis Stadium
Africa Avenue New Delhi 110 029
T 91 11 617 9062 **FAX** 91 11 617 3159
E-mail: aitaten@del3.vsnl.net.in
Pres: Mr Raj Khanna **Sec:** Mr Ramesh Desai

INDONESIA – INA (1935) (Votes 5)

Indonesian Tennis Association
Gelora Senayan Tennis Stadium Jakarta 10270
T 62 21 571 0298 **FAX** 62 21 570 0157
E-mail: pelti@vision.net.id
Pres: Mr Sarwono Kusumaatmadja
Sec: Mr Zainal Abidin

IRAN, ISLAMIC REPUBLIC OF – IRI (1937) (Votes 3)

Tennis Federation of Islamic Republic of Iran
PO Box 15815 – 1881 Tehran
T 98 21 884 4731
FAX 98 21 884 4731
Pres: Mr Seyed Lankarani
Sec: Mr Hamid R Shayesteh Zad

IRAQ – IRQ (1959) (Votes 1)

Iraqi Tennis Federation
PO Box 441 Baghdad
T 964 17 748 261 **FAX** 964 17 728 424
Pres: Mr Suhail Najim Abdulla
Sec: Mr Manhal Kuba

IRELAND – IRL (1895) (Votes 3)

Tennis Ireland
Argyle Square Donnybrook Dublin 4
T 353 16 681 841 **FAX** 353 16 683 411
E-mail: tennis@iol.ie
Pres: Ms Olwyn Raftery **Sec:** Mr Ciaran O'Donavan

ISRAEL – ISR (1946) (Votes 3)

Israel Tennis Association
2 Shitrit Street Tel Aviv 69482
T 972 36 499 440 **FAX** 972 36 499 144
E-mail: igutenis@netvision.net.il
Pres: Mr David Harnik **Sec:** Mr Yair Engel

ITALY – ITA (1910) (Votes 9)

Federazione Italiana Tennis
Viale Tiziano 74 00196 Rome
T 390 636 858 210 **FAX** 390 636 858 166
E-mail: fit_segr@gisa.net
Pres: Mr Francesco Ricci Bitti
Sec: Mr Claudio Santini

JAMAICA – JAM **(Votes 1)**

Jamaica Lawn Tennis Association
PO Box 175 2a Piccadilly Road Kingston 5
T 1 876 978 2496 **FAX** 1 876 927 9436
E-mail: morgansgroup@cwjamaica.com
Pres: Mr Ken Morgan
Sec: Mrs Jocelin Morgan

JAPAN – JPN (1922) **(Votes 9)**

Japan Tennis Association
c/o Kishi Memorial Hall 1-1-1 Jinnan
Shibuya-Ku Tokyo 8050
T 81 33 481 2321 **FAX** 81 33 467 5192
E-mail: info@jta-tennis.or.jp
Pres: Mr Kiichiro Nakamuta
Sec: Mr Shin-ichi Shimizu

JORDAN – JOR (1980) **(Votes 1)**

Jordan Tennis Federation
PO Box 961046 Amman
T 962 65 682 796 **FAX** 962 65 681 797
Pres: Mr Abdullah Al-Khalil
Sec: Mr Ziad Al-Turk

KAZAKHSTAN – KAZ (1991) **(Votes 1)**

Kazakhstan Tennis Federation
Central Sports Club of the Army 480051 Almaty
T 7 3272 640 469 **FAX** 7 3272 478 971
E-mail: tfkr@imfiko.bishkek.su
Pres: Mr Pavel Novikov
Sec: Mr Valery Kovalev

KENYA – KEN (1922) **(Votes 1)**

Kenya Lawn Tennis Asssociation
PO Box 43184 Nairobi
T 254 2 725 672 **FAX** 254 2 725 672
Pres: Mr James Kenani
Sec: Mr Baldev Aggarwal

KOREA, REPUBLIC OF – KOR (1945) **(Votes 5)**

Korea Tennis Association
Room 108, Olympic Gym No. 2
88-2 Oryun-Dong, Songpa-Gu Seoul 138-151
T 82 2 420 4285 **FAX** 82 2 420 4284
Pres: Mr Doo Hwan Kim
Sec: Mr Yeong-Moo Huh

KUWAIT – KUW (1967) **(Votes 1)**

Kuwait Tennis Federation
PO Box 1462 Hawalli 32015
T 965 539 7260 **FAX** 965 539 0617
Pres: Sheik Ahmed Al-Sabah
Sec: Mr Abdul-Ridha Ghareeb

LATVIA – LAT (1928) **(Votes 1)**

Latvian Tennis Union
Oskara Kalpaka Pr.16 LV 2010 Jurmala
T 371 702 5600 **FAX** 371 702 5601
Pres: Mr Juris Savickis **Sec:** Mr Janis Pliens

LEBANON – LIB (1945) **(Votes 1)**

Federation Libanaise de Tennis
PO Box 11-261 Hamra Beirut
T 961 1 425 873 **FAX** 961 1 426 233
Pres: Mr Riad Haddad
Sec: Mr Nohad V Schoucair

LIECHTENSTEIN – LIE (1968) **(Votes 1)**

Liechtensteiner Tennisverband
Heiligkreuz 28 9490 Vaduz
T 41 75 392 1188 **FAX** 41 75 392 1191
Pres: Mr Joseph Schweiger
Sec: Mr Werner Schachle

LITHUANIA – LTU (1992) **(Votes 1)**

Lithuanian Tennis Union
Sausio 13 Str 2 2050 Vilnius
T 3702 659 229 **FAX** 3702 269 341
Pres: Mr Vytautas Lapinskas
Sec: Mr Minaaugas Dagys

LUXEMBOURG – LUX (1946) **(Votes 1)**

Federation Luxembourgeoise de Tennis
Boite Postale 134 L-4002 Esch-Sur-Alzette
T 352 574 470 **FAX** 352 574 473
Pres: Mr Paul Helminger
Sec: Mr Erny Betzen

MACEDONIA, FORMER YUGOSLAV REPUBLIC OF – MKD (1993) **(Votes 1)**

FYR Macedonian Tennis Association
91000 Skopje Gradski Park 88 Skopje
T 389 91 129 200 **FAX** 389 91 116 146
Pres: Mr George Gurkovic
Sec: Miss Marija Gavrilovska

MADAGASCAR – MAD (1979) **(Votes 1)**

Federation Malgache de Tennis
B P 8410-101 Tsaralalana Antananarivo
T 261 202 235 162 **FAX** 261 202 233 806
E-mail: serge@sinergic.mg
Pres: Mr Serge Ramiandrasoa
Sec: Dr Serge Amdriamampandry

MALAYSIA – MAS (1921) **(Votes 1)**

Lawn Tennis Association of Malaysia
c/o National Tennis Centre Jalan Duta
50480 Kuala Lumpur
T 60 3 651 2377 **FAX** 60 3 651 5041
E-mail: ltam@po.jaring.my
Pres: Mr Abdul Ghafar Baba
Sec: Mr Musaladin Dahalan

MALTA – MLT (1966) **(Votes 1)**

Malta Tennis Federation
PO Box 50 Sliema Post Office Sliema
T 356 330 363 **FAX** 356 345 330
E-mail: mtfinfo@keyworld.net
Pres: Dr Lino Farrugia Sacco
Sec: Mr Michael J Borg Cardona

MEXICO – MEX (1952) **(Votes 7)**

Federacion Mexicana de Tenis
Miguel Angel de Quevedo 953
Mexico City 04330 DF
T 52 5 689 9733 **FAX** 52 5 689 6307
E-mail: fmtmex@mail.internet.com.mx
Pres: Mr Alejandro Hernandez
Sec: Mr Manuel Moctezumam

MOLDOVA – MDA (1953) (Votes 1)

Moldova Republic Tennis Federation
202 Bulevardul Stefan Cel Mare Chisinau 2050
T 3732 638 888 **FAX** 3732 758 888
Pres: Mr Grigorii Kushnir
Sec: Mr Roman Tudoreanu

MONACO – MON (1927) (Votes 1)

Federation Monegasque de Lawn Tennis
27-29 Boulevard de Belgique 98000 Monaco
T 377 93 255 574 **FAX** 377 93 305 482
Pres: Mrs Elisabeth de Massy
Sec: Mr Alain Manigley

MOROCCO – MAR (1957) (Votes 3)

Federation Royale Marocaine de Tennis
Parc de la Ligue Arabe BP 15794 Casablanca
T 212 2 981 266 **FAX** 212 2 981 265
Pres: Mr Mohamed M'Jid
Sec: Mr Hachem Kacimimy

NETHERLANDS – NED (1899) (Votes 9)

Koninklijke Nederlandse Lawn Tennis Bond
PO Box 107 1200 AC Hilversum
T 31 356 264 100 **FAX** 31 356 240 760
E-mail: knltb@worldaccess.nl
Pres: Mr Ruurd de Boer
Sec: Mr H Brouwer

NETHERLANDS ANTILLES – AHO (1941) (Votes 1)

Netherlands Antilles Tennis Association
Louise de Colignylaan 18 PO Box 3571 Curacao
T 599 9 737 3192 **FAX** 599 9 736 9100
Pres: Mr Maximo Rufino Paula
Sec: Mr Hilberto Thomas

NEW ZEALAND – NZL (1886) (Votes 7)

New Zealand Tennis Inc
PO Box 11-541 Manners Street Wellington
T 64 4 476 1115 **FAX** 64 4 471 2152
E-mail: info@tennis.org.nz
Pres: Mr Ian Wells
Sec: Mrs Christine Burr

NIGERIA – NGR (1927) (Votes 3)

Nigeria Tennis Association
National Stadium Surulere PO Box 145 Lagos
T 234 1 264 6444 **FAX** 234 1 545 0104
Pres: Mr Chuka Momah
Sec: Mrs Funmi Koya-Adaku

NORWAY – NOR (1909) (Votes 3)

Norges Tennisforbund
Haslevangen 33 PO Box 287 – Okern Oslo 0511
T 47 2 265 7550 **FAX** 47 2 264 6409
E-mail: tennis@nif.idrett.no
Pres: Mr Jarl Whist
Sec: Mr Jarle Aambo

OMAN – OMA (1986) (Votes 1)

Oman Tennis Association
PO Box 2226 Ruwi Postal Code 112
T 968 751 402 **FAX** 968 751 394
Pres: Mr Rashad Mohammed Al Zubair
Sec: Mr Mohamad Salim Khawwar

PAKISTAN – PAK (1947) (Votes 3)

Pakistan Tennis Federation
39-A Jinnah Stadium Pakistan Sports Complex
Kashmir Highway Islamabad
T 92 519 212 846 **FAX** 92 519 212 846
E-mail: pktenfed@isb.comsats.net.pk
Pres: Mr Anwar Saifullah Khan
Sec: Mr Mohammad Ali Akbar

PANAMA – PAN (1986) (Votes 1)

Federacion Panamena de Tenis
Apartado 6-4965 El Dorado
T 507 232 5196 **FAX** 507 232 6841
Pres: Mrs Norma Maduro
Sec: Mr Rogelio Valenzuela

PARAGUAY – PAR (1920) (Votes 3)

Asociacion Paraguaya de Tenis
Casilla de Correo 1027 Av. Colon 1054
1st Floor Asuncion
T 595 21 503 720 **FAX** 595 21 503 721
Pres: Mr Miguel Carrizosa **Sec:** Mrs Esther Tami

PERU – PER (1930) (Votes 3)

Federacion de Tenis del Peru
Cercado Campo de Marte S/N
Casilla Nro 11-0488 Lima 11
T 511 424 9979 **FAX** 511 431 0533
Pres: Ing. Alfredo Acuna **Sec:** Mr Julio Chang

PHILIPPINES – PHI (1946) (Votes 3)

Philippine Tennis Association
Rizal Memorial Sports Complex
Pablo Ocampo Sr. Street Manila
T 63 2 525 6434 **FAX** 63 2 525 2016
Pres: Colonel Salvador H Andrada
Sec: Mr Romeo Magat

POLAND – POL (1921) (Votes 3)

Polski Zwiazek Tenisowy
Ul. Marszalkowska 2 3rd Floor 00-581 Warsaw
T 48 22 629 2621 **FAX** 48 22 621 8001
Pres: Mr Jacek Durski **Sec:** Ms Regina Sokolowska

PORTUGAL – POR (1925) (Votes 3)

Federacao Portuguesa de Tenis
Rua Actor Chaby Pinheiro, 7-A
2795 Linda-A-Velha
T 351 1 415 1356 **FAX** 351 1414 1520
E-mail: fptenis@mail.telepac.pt
Pres: Dr Paulo Andrade
Sec: Mr Jose Carlos Machado Costa

PUERTO RICO – PUR (1959) (Votes 1)

Asociacion de Tenis de Puerto Rico
PO Box 40456 San Juan 00940-456
T 1 787 724 7782 **FAX** 1 787 724 7990
Pres: Mr Antonio Pavia **Sec:** Dr Jaime Ariza

QATAR – QAT (1984) (Votes 1)

Qatar Tennis and Squash Federation
PO Box 4959 Doha
T 974 409 666 **FAX** 974 832 990
E-mail: mohd.noor@qatar.net.qa
Pres: Mr Ali Hussein Al Fardan
Sec: Mr Mohammad Ismail Moh'd Noor

ROMANIA – ROM (1929) (Votes 1)

Federatia Romana de Tennis
Str Vasile Conta 16 Sector 2 70139 Bucharest
T 40 1 211 7824 **FAX** 40 1 210 7599
Pres: Mr Ilie Nastase
Sec: Prof Lucian Vasiliu

RUSSIA – RUS (1975) (Votes 5)

All Russia Tennis Association
Lutzhnetskaya Nab 8 119871 Moscow
T 7 095 725 4695 **FAX** 7 095 201 0362
Pres: Mr Yaroslav Kalagursky
Sec: Mr Alexander Kalivod

SAINT LUCIA – LCA (1997) (Votes 1)

St Lucia Lawn Tennis Association
PO Box 126 Castries West Indies
T 1 758 450 0106 **FAX** 1 758 450 9277
E-mail: huntet@candw.lc
Pres: Mr John Easter **Sec:** Mr Trevor Hunte

SAN MARINO – SMR (1956) (Votes 1)

Federazione Sammarinese Tennis
Casella Postal No 2 Dogana 47031
T 378 990 578 **FAX** 378 990 584
Pres: Mr Remo Raimondi
Sec: Mr Christian Forcellini

SAUDI ARABIA, KINGDOM OF – KSA (1956) (Votes 1)

Saudi Arabian Tennis Federation
PO Box 29454 Riyadh 11457
T 966 1 482 0188 **FAX** 966 1 482 2829
Pres: Mr Abdulaziz S Kridis
Sec: Mr Rasheed Abu Rasheed

SENEGAL – SEN (1960) (Votes 1)

Federation Senegalaise de Tennis
BP 510 Dakar
T 221 820 3269 **FAX** 221 820 3269
E-mail: jjntab@senelec.sn
Pres: Mr Diagna N'diaye
Sec: Mr Jean Jacques Ntab

SINGAPORE – SIN (1928) (Votes 1)

Singapore Lawn Tennis Association
Unit 10 National Stadium
15 Stadium Road 397718
T 65 348 0124 **FAX** 65 348 2414
E-mail: slta@pacific.net.sg
Pres: Mr S Uthrapathy **Sec:** Mr Tay Mah Keong

SLOVAK REPUBLIC – SVK (1968) (Votes 3)

Slovak Tennis Association
Junacka 6 832 80 Bratislava
T 421 7 49249 134 **FAX** 421 7 49249 561
E-mail: stz@mbox.bts.sk
Pres: Mr Tibor Macko **Sec:** Mr Lubomir Palenik

SLOVENIA – SLO (1946) (Votes 1)

Slovene Tennis Association
Vurnikova 2/Vi1000 Ljubljana
T 386 611 337 170 **FAX** 386 611 334 281
E-mail: teniska.zveza@sting.si
Pres: Dr Drasko Veselinovic
Sec: Mr Tone Preseren

SOUTH AFRICA, REPUBLIC OF – RSA (1991) (Votes 9)

South African Tennis Association
PO Box 15978 Doornfontein Johannesburg 2028
T 27 11 402 3616 **FAX** 27 11 402 0242
E-mail: satennis@icon.co.za
www: www.tennisnet.co.za
Pres: Mr Gordon Forbes
Sec: Mr Hardie Botha

SPAIN – ESP (1901) (Votes 9)

Real Federacion Espanola de Tenis
Avda Diagonal 618 3 D 08021 Barcelona
T 34 93 200 5355 **FAX** 34 93 202 1279
Pres: Mr Augustin Pujol Niubo
Sec: Mr Thomas Garcia Balmaseda

SRI LANKA – SRI (1915) (Votes 1)

Sri Lanka Tennis Association
45 Sir Marcus Fernando Mawatha Colombo 7
T 94 1 686 174 **FAX** 96 1 686 174
E-mail: naro@sri.lanka.net
Pres: Mr John Rajapakse
Sec: Mr Gihan Dalpethado

SUDAN – SUD (1956) (Votes 1)

Sudan Lawn Tennis Association
PO Box 3792 Africa House Khartoum
T 249 11 770 246 **FAX** 246 11 781 818
Pres: Mr Hassab Elrasoul Mohamed Eltayeb
Sec: Mr Nour Eldine Elsadig

SWEDEN – SWE (1906) (Votes 9)

The Swedish Tennis Association
Box 27915 S-115 94 Stockholm
T 46 86 679 770 **FAX** 48 86 646 606
E-mail: info@tennis.se
Pres: Mr Jan Francke **Sec:** Mr Anders Wetterberg

SWITZERLAND – SUI (1896) (Votes 7)

Swiss Tennis Association
Solothurnstrasse 112 2501 Biel
T 41 32 344 0707 **FAX** 41 32 344 0700
Pres: Mrs Christine Ungricht
Sec: Mr Pierre-Alain Morard

SYRIA – SYR (1953) (Votes 1)

Syrian Arab Tennis Federation
PO Box 967 421 Baramke Damascus
T 963 11 212 5026 **FAX** 963 11 212 3346
Pres: Mr Mustafa Hendi **Sec:** Mr Safa Sarakbi

TAJIKISTAN – TJK (1992) (Votes 1)

National Tennis Federation of
the Republic of Tajikistan
Tennis Palace A/B 308 Dushanbe 734001
T 7 3372 360 606 **FAX** 7 3372 217 815
Pres: Mr Amircul Azimov **Sec:** Mr Vazirbek Nazirov

THAILAND – THA (1927) (Votes 3)

The Lawn Tennis Association of Thailand
110-119 Nightingale Sports Complex
Raminthra Road (Km 11) Bangkok 10230
T 66 2 917 8771 **FAX** 66 2 917 9116
Pres: General Akaradej Sasiprapha
Sec: Gen Wichar Siritham

TOGO – TOG (1955) (Votes 1)

Federation Togolaise de Tennis
BP 12720 Lome
T 228 215 181 **FAX** 228 222 397
E-mail: fttennis@togo-imet.com
Pres: Mr Kouassi Luc Dofontien
Sec: Mr Koffi Galokpo

TRINIDAD AND TOBAGO – TRI (1951) (Votes 1)

The Tennis Association of Trinidad and Tobago
21 Taylor Street Woodbrook, Port of Spain
Trinidad West Indies
T 1 868 625 3939 **FAX** 1 686 625 3939
Pres: Mr Earle James **Sec:** Ms Sadie Robarts

TUNISIA – TUN (1954) (Votes 1)

Federation Tunisienne de Tennis
BP 350 El Menzah 1004 Tunis
T 216 1 844 144 **FAX** 216 1 798 844
Pres: Mr Tarak Cherif **Sec:** Mr Mahmoud Azzouz

TURKEY – TUR (1923) (Votes 3)

Turkiye Tenis Federasyonu
Ulus Is Hani Ankara
T 90 312 310 7345 **FAX** 90 312 311 254
Pres: Mr Sadi Toker **Sec:** Mr Yener Dogru

UGANDA – UGA (1948) (Votes 1)

Uganda Tennis Association
PO Box 9825 Kampala
T 256 41 258 183 **FAX** 256 41 258 188
Pres: Prof Frederick Ssempebwa
Sec: Mr Gideon M Karyoko

UKRAINE – UKR (1946) (Votes 1)

Ukrainian Tennis Federation
A/C B-2 PO 252001 Kiev
T 38 044 224 8782 **FAX** 38 044 290 4062
Pres: Mr German Benyaminov
Sec: Mr Volodimir Gerashchenko

UNITED ARAB EMIRATES – UAE (1982) (Votes 1)

United Arab Emirates Tennis Association
PO Box 22466 Dubai
T 971 4 690 393 **FAX** 971 4 669 390
E-mail: jstubbs@emirates.net.ae
Pres: Sheikh Hasher Al-Maktoum
Sec: Mr Nasser Madani

UNITED STATES OF AMERICA – USA (1881) (Votes 12)

United States Tennis Association
70 West Red Oak Lane White Plains
New York NY 10604
T 1 914 696 7000 **FAX** 1 914 696 7167
Pres: Dr Harry A Marmion
Sec: Mr Michael Kohlhoff

UNITED STATES VIRGIN ISLANDS – ISV (1973) (Votes 1)

Virgin Islands Tennis Association
PO Box 306715 St Thomas Usvi 00803-6715
T 1 340 776 1010 **FAX** 1 340 776 2185
Pres: Mr Wilbur Callender
Sec: Ms Delores Stephen Rivas

URUGUAY – URU (1915) (Votes 3)

Asociacion Uruguaya de Tenis
Galicia 1392 CP 11.200 Montevideo
T 598 2 901 5020 **FAX** 598 2 902 1809
Pres: Sr Gilberto Saenz
Sec: Sr Elbio Arias

UZBEKISTAN – UZB (1992) (Votes 1)

Uzbekistan Tennis Federation
Troitskoe Chausse 22, House 7
Tashkent 700142
T 7 3712 642 720 **FAX** 7 3712 890 053(s)
E-mail: prescup1@mail.uznet.net
Pres: Mr R Innoyatov
Sec: Mr I Shepelev

VENEZUELA – VEN (1927) (Votes 5)

Federacion Venezolana de Tenis
Calle Apartado 70539 Caracas 1070-A
T 58 29 797 095 **FAX** 58 29 792 694
E-mail: fevtnis@ibm.net
Pres: Mr Pablo Jose Fermin Perez
Sec: Ms Rebeca Torrealba

YUGOSLAVIA – YUG (1922) (Votes 3)

Tenis Savez Yugoslavije
Aleksandra Stamboliskog 26
11000 Beograd
T 38 111 667 540 **FAX** 38 111 667 540
E-mail: yugtenis@verat.net.
Pres: Mr Radoman Bozovic
Sec: Mr Dejan Simic

ZAMBIA – ZAM (1975) (Votes 1)

Zambia Lawn Tennis Association
c/o Ndola Tennis Club
PO Box 70436 Ndola
T 260 1 221 792 **FAX** 260 1 226 260
E-mail: bwalyap@nchnet.zccm.zm
Pres: Mr Henry Musenge
Sec: Mr Mike Kamungu

ZIMBABWE – ZIM (1904) (Votes 1)

Tennis Zimbabwe
PO Box A575 Avondale Harare
T 263 4 229 938 **FAX** 263 4 224 079
Pres: Mr Paul Chingoka
Sec: Ms Gladys Mutyiri

Associate Members without voting rights (69)

AFGHANISTAN – AFG (1963)

Afghan Lawn Tennis Association
House No. 400 Street No. 89
Sector G-9/4 Islamabad
T 92 51 260 987 **FAX** 92 51 299 756
E-mail: pricom@meganet.com.pk
Pres: Mr Homayun Paravanta
Sec: Mr Muhammad Khalil

ALBANIA – ALB (1996)

Federata Shqiptare E Tenisit
Kartografike sh. A Rruga Tirana
T 355 422 5925 **FAX** 355 422 5925
Pres: Mr Perlat Voshtina
Sec: Mr Arben Alushi

AMERICAN SAMOA – ASA (1985)

American Samoa Tennis Association
PO Box PPB Pago Pago 96799
T 684 644 5251 **FAX** 684 644 5005
Pres: Mr Perelini Perelini
Sec: Dr Jerome Amoa

ANGOLA – ANG (1983)

Federacao Angolana de Tenis
Cidadeia Desportive PO Box 3677 Luanda
T 244 2 337 412 **FAX** 244 2 332 388
Pres: Mr Luis Rosa Lopes
Sec: Mr Francisco Barros

ARUBA – ARU (1954)

Aruba Lawn Tennis Bond
Fergusonstraat Nr 40-A PO Box 1151 Oranjestad
T 2978 59 310 **FAX** 2978 34 670
Pres: Mr Lucas Rasmijn
Sec: Ms Barbara Kroonenberg

BELIZE – BIZ (1910)

Belize Tennis Association
PO Box 365 Belize City
T 501 277 070 **FAX** 501 275 593
Pres: Mr Edward Nabil Musr Sr
Sec: Mr Clement Usher

BHUTAN – BHU (1976)

Bhutan Tennis Federation
PO Box 103 Thimphu
T 975 222 138 **FAX** 975 223 937
Pres: Mr Dasho Passang Dorji
Sec: Mr Tshering Namgay

BRITISH VIRGIN ISLANDS – IVB (1983)

British Virgin Islands Lawn Tennis Association
PO Box 948 Road Town Tortola
T 1 284 494 3650 **FAX** 1 284 494 5671
Pres: Mr Lloyd Black **Sec:** Mr Clive Gumbs

BURKINA FASO – BUR (1970)

Federation Burkinabe de Tennis
01 BP 45 Ouagadougou 1
T 226 312 733 **FAX** 226 314 863
Pres: Mr Zambo Martin Zongo
Sec: Mr Andre Batiana

BURUNDI – BDI (1993)

Federation de Tennis du Burundi
BP 2221 Bujumbura
T (257) 221 095 **FAX** (257) 222 247
Pres: Mr Edouard Hicintuka
Sec: Mrs Dominique Niyonizigiye

CAMBODIA – CAM (1996)

The Tennis Federation of Cambodia
No 12 St 254 Senei Vinna Vau Oum
Khan Daun Penh Sangkat Chaktomuk
Phnom Penh
T 855 23 362 578 **FAX** 855 23 362 580
E-mail: p.i.g.@bigpond.com.kh
Pres: Mr Cham Prasidh
Sec: Mr Tep Rithivit

CAPE VERDE ISLANDS – CPV (1986)

Federacao Cabo-Verdiana de Tenis
Ministerio da Informacao Cultura E Desportos
Rua 5 de Julho Praia
T 238 613 309 **FAX** 238 621 312
Pres: Mr Hugo Almeida
Sec: Mr Antonio Ferreira

CAYMAN ISLANDS – CAY (1973)

Tennis Federation of the Cayman Islands
PO Box 219 GT Grand Cayman
British West Indies
T 1 345 949 7000 **FAX** 1 345 949 8154
Pres: Mr Chris Johnson
Sec: Mr John Smith

CENTRAL AFRICAN REPUBLIC – CAF (1990)

Federation Centrafricaine de Tennis
BP 804 Bangui R C A
T 236 611 805 **FAX** 236 615 660
Pres: Mr I Kamach
Sec: Mr Jean Ombi

COMOROS – COM (1985)

Federation Comorienne de Tennis
BP 701 Moroni
T 269 732 113 **FAX** 269 733 166
Pres: Mr Youssouf Ali
Sec: Mr Youssouf Ahamada

CONGO, DEMOCRATIC REPUBLIC OF – ZAI (1984)

Federation Congolaise Democratique
de Lawn Tennis
BP 20750 Kin 15 Kinshasa
T 243 881 0013 **FAX** 243 881 0034
Pres: Mr Kanyama Mishindu
Sec: Mr Eleko Botuna Bo'Osisa

COOK ISLANDS – COK (1947)

Tennis Cook Islands
PO Box 780 Rarotonga
T 682 22 327 **FAX** 682 23 602
Pres: Mrs June Baudinet
Sec: Ms Elizabeth Ponga

DOMINICA – DMA (1960)

Dominica Lawn Tennis Association
PO Box 1593 Roseau
T 1 767 448 2681 **FAX** 1 767 448 7010
Pres: Mr Kenny Alleyne
Sec: Mr Thomas Dorsett

EQUATORIAL GUINEA – GEQ (1992)

Equatorial Guinea Tennis Federation
PO Box 980 B.N Malabo
T 240 9 2866 **FAX** 240 9 3313
Pres: Mr Enrique Mercader Costa
Sec: Mr Francisco Sibita

ERITREA – ERI (1998)

Eritrean Tennis Federation
PO Box 5853 Asmara
T 291 1 121 284 **FAX** 291 1 127 255
Pres: Mr Daniel Haile
Sec: Mr Belai G Egzabiher

GABON – GAB (1988)

Federation Gabonaise de Tennis
PO Box 4241 Libreville
T 241 724 707 **FAX** 241 764 472
Pres: Mr Samuel Minkomi Ndong
Sec: Mr Jean-Bernard Romporouet

GAMBIA – GAM (1938)

Gambia Lawn Tennis Association
PMB 664 Serekunda
T 220 495 834 **FAX** 220 496 270
E-mail: gnosc@commit.gm
Pres: Mr Charles Thomas
Sec: Mr Geoffrey Renner

GRENADA – GRN (1973)

Grenada Tennis Association
PO Box 514 St George's
T 1 473 440 3343 **FAX** 1 473 440 9094
Pres: Mr Ken Aberdeen
Sec: Mr Wayne Murray

GUAM – GUM (1973)

Tennis Association of Guam
PO Box 21809 GMF 96921
T 1 671 472 6270 **FAX** 1 671 472 8719
Pres: Mr Torgun Smith
Sec: Mr Rick Ninete

GUINEE-CONAKRY – GUI (1980)

Federation Guineenne de Tennis
BP 4897
T 224 444 019 **FAX** 224 411 926
Pres: Mme Magass-Malado Diallo
Sec: Mr Baba Bayo

GUYANA – GUY (1933)

Guyana Lawn Tennis Association
PO Box 10205 Georgetown
T 592 256 846 **FAX** 592 267 446
Pres: Mr Wilfred Lee
Sec: Mrs Marcia Moore

KIRIBATI – KIR (1979)

Kiribati Tennis Association
PO Box 80 Antebuka Tarawa
T 686 28071 **FAX** 686 28202
Pres: Mr Peter Itibita

KOREA, DEMOCRATIC PEOPLE'S REPUBLIC – PRK (1945)

Tennis Association of Democratic People's Rep of Korea
Kumsong Mangyongdae District Pyongyang
T 850 2 18000 x 8164 **FAX** 520 2 381 4403
Pres: Mr Kim Su Ik
Sec: Mr Ri Won Gun

KYRGHYZSTAN – KGZ (1992)

Kyrghyzstan Tennis Federation Kyrghyzstan
Moskovskey Str 121/58 Bishkek 720000
T 996 312 214 756 **FAX** 996 312 214 756
Pres: Mr Nikolai Tanaev
Sec: Mr Valentin Akinshin

LAOS, DEMOCRATIC PEOPLE'S REPUBLIC – LAO (1998)

Laos Tennis Federation
PO Box 6280 Vientiane
T 856 212 956 **FAX** 856 21 215 274
Pres: Mr Kikham Vongsay
Sec: Mr Khounno Phonesomdeth

LESOTHO – LES (1920)

Lesotho Lawn Tennis Association
PO Box 156 Maseru 100
T 266 317 340 **FAX** 266 310 047
Pres: Mr P M Morolong
Sec: Mr Clement M Nots'I

LIBERIA – LBR (1987)

Liberia Tennis Association
PO Box 1742 1000 Monrovia
T 231 227 124 **FAX** 231 226 253
Pres: Mr Siake Toure
Sec: Mr Edmund Dassin

LIBYA – LBA (1996)

Libyan Arab Tennis & Squash Federation
PO Box 879 – 2729 Tripoli
T 218 21 333 9150 **FAX** 218 21 333 9150
Pres: Mr Abdul-Hamid M Shamash
Sec: Mr Abdulssalam A Bellel

MALAWI – MAW (1966)

Lawn Tennis Association of Malawi
PO Box 1417 Blantyre
T 265 623 670 **FAX** 265 620 549
Pres: Mr Albert Banda
Sec: Mrs Auttie Sibley

MALDIVES – MDV (1983)

Tennis Association of the Maldives
PO Box 20175 Male
T 960 317 018 **FAX** 960 310 325
Pres: Mr Ahmed Aslam

MALI – MLI (1963)

Federation Malienne de Tennis
Ministere des Affaires Etrangeres Koulouba
T 223 226 740 **FAX** 223 229 350
Pres: Mr Mohamed Traore

MARSHALL ISLANDS – MSH (1996)

Marshall Island Tennis Federation
PO Box 197 Marjuro MH96960
T 692 625 3396 **FAX** 692 625 3389
Pres: Mr Oscar Debrum
Sec: Ms Netty Nathan

MAURITANIA – MTN (1989)

Federation Mauritanienne de Tennis
BP 654 Nouakchott
T FAX only **FAX** 222 251 410
Pres: Mr Isaac Ould Rajel
Sec: Mr Cheickh Ould Horomtala

MAURITIUS – MRI (1910)

Mauritius Lawn Tennis Association
La Croix Street Curepipe
T 230 670 2603 **FAX** 230 370 2539
Pres: Mrs Francoise Desvaux de Marigny
Sec: Mr Akhtar Toorawa

MICRONESIA, FEDERATED STATES OF – FSM (1985)

Federated States of Micronesia
Lawn Tennis Association
PO Box PS319 Paliker Pohnpei FM 96941
T 691 320 619 **FAX** 691 320 8915
E-mail: fsmnoc@mail.fm
Pres: Mr Richard Alex
Sec: Mr James Tobin

MONGOLIA – MGL (1990)

Mongolian Tennis Association
PO Box 522 Ulaanbaatar 44
T 976 1 372 980 **FAX** 976 1 372 980
E-mail: ganbaatar@mail.parl.gov.mn
Pres: Mr A Ganbaatar
Sec: Janchiv Batjargal

MOZAMBIQUE – MOZ (1979)

Federacao Mocambicana de Tenis
Caixa Postal 4351 Maputo
T 258 1 42 7027 **FAX** 258 1 30 5855
Pres: Mr Arao Nhancale
Sec: Mr Albino Nguenha

MYANMAR – MYA (1949)

Myanmar Tennis Federation
627-635 Merchant Street PO Box No 204 Yangon
T 95 1 283 656 **FAX** 95 1 283 961
Pres: Mr U Ba Tun
Sec: Dr Myint Soe

NAMIBIA – NAM (1930)

Namibia Tennis Association
PO Box 479 Windhoek 9000
T 264 61 244 495 **FAX** 264 61 251 718
E-mail: idcnam@iafrica.com.na
Pres: Dr Pietie Loubser
Sec: Mrs Carien du Plessis

NAURU – NRU (1992)

Nauru Tennis Association
PO Box 274
T 674 444 3706 **FAX** 674 444 3200
Pres: Chief Paul Aingimea
Sec: Mr Preston Itaia

NEPAL – NEP (1968)

All Nepal Tennis Association
PO Box 3943 Kathmandu
T 977 1 426 002 **FAX** 977 1 416 427
Pres: Mr Siddheshwar K Singh
Sec: Mr Ramji Thapa

NICARAGUA – NCA (1994)

Federacion Nicaraguense de Tenis
PO Box 2878 Sucursal Jorge Navarro Managua
T 505 265 1572 **FAX** 505 278 7039
Pres: Mr Ricardo Fuentes
Sec: Mr Jose Antonio Arguello

NIGER – NIG (1988)

Federation Nigerienne de Tennis
Stade du 29 Juillet 1991 Avenue du Zarmaganda
BP 10 788 Niamey
T 227 735 893 **FAX** 227 732 876
E-mail: bdaniger@intnet.ne
Pres: Mr Ahmed Ousman Diallo
Sec: Mr Boubacar Djibo

NORFOLK ISLANDS – NFK (1998)

Norfolk Islands Tennis Association
Queen Elizabeth Avenue Norfolk Island
South Pacific Ocean
T (6723) 229 66 **FAX** (6723) 224 71
Pres: Mr Thomas Greening
Sec: Ms Lyn Sterling

NORTHERN MARIANA ISLANDS – NMA

Northern Mariana Islands Tennis Association
PO Box 10,000 Saipan MP 96950-9504
T 670 234 8438 **FAX** 670 234 5545
Pres: Mr Mike Walsh **Sec:** Mr Ed Johnson

PALAU, DEMOCRATIC REPUBLIC OF – PAL (1998)

Palau Amateur Tennis Association
PO Box 9 Koror 96940
T (608) 488 2690 **FAX** (680) 488 1310
Pres: Mr Presley Etibeck **Sec:** Mr Jay Olegerill

PALESTINE – PLE (1998)

Palestinian Tennis Association
Beit Sahour PO Box 131
T 972 2 277 5244
FAX 972 2 277 5245
E-mail: medrish@p.ol.com
Pres: Mr Issa Rishmawi
Sec: Mrs Samar Mousa Araj

PAPUA NEW GUINEA – PNG (1963)

Papua New Guinea Lawn Tennis Association
PO Box 5656 Boroko
T 675 321 1533 **FAX** 675 321 3001
E-mail: tennispng@dg.com.pg
Pres: Mr Robert Aisi

RWANDA – RWA (1984)

Federation Rwandaise de Tennis
BP 362 Kigali
T 250 77458 **FAX** 250 76853
E-mail: thierryn@usa.net
Pres: Dr Charles Ruadkubana
Sec: M Isidore Sezirahiga

SAINT KITTS – SKN (1962)

St Kitts Lawn Tennis Association
PO Box 717 Basseterre
T 1 869 465 0791 **FAX** 1 869 465 5501
Pres: Mr Raphael Jenkins
Sec: Ms Connie Marsham

SAINT VINCENT & THE GRENADINES – VIN (1972)

St Vincent & the Grenadines Lawn Tennis Association PO Box 589 Halifax Street St. Vincent
T 1 784 457 2210 **FAX** 1 784 456 2259
E-mail: bollers@caribsurf.com
Pres: Mr Michael Nanton
Sec: Mr Grahame Bollers

SEYCHELLES – SEY (1955)

Seychelles Tennis Association
PO Box 602 Victoria Mahe
T 248 323 908 **FAX** 248 324 066
Pres: Mr Guy Robert
Sec: Mr John Adam

SIERRA LEONE – SLE (1965)

Sierra Leone Lawn Tennis Association
National Sports Council PO Box 1181 Freetown
T 232 22 40562 **FAX**
Pres: Mr Henry Moore
Sec: Mr E T Ngandi

SOLOMON ISLANDS – SOL (1993)

Solomon Islands Tennis Association
PO Box 111 Honiara
T 677 21 616 **FAX** 677 25 498
Pres: Mr Ranjit Hewagama
Sec: Mr Asery Kukui

SOMALIA – SOM

The Somali Tennis Association
c/o 5 Gabalaya Street 11567 El Borg Cairo
T 252 1 280 042 **FAX** 252 1 216 516
Pres: Mr Osman Mohiadin Moallim
Sec: Mr Abdurahman Warsame Abdulle

SURINAM – SUR (1936)

Surinaamse Tennisbond
PO Box 2087 Paramaribo-Zuid
T 597 476 703 **FAX** 597 471 047
E-mail: hindori@cq-link.sr
Pres: Mr Manodj Hindori
Sec: Ms Ann Meyer

SWAZILAND – SWZ (1968)

Swaziland National Tennis Union
PO Box 2397 Manzini
T 268 54564 **FAX** 268 40063
Pres: Mr J M Silaula
Sec: Mr Bennie Pool

TANZANIA – TAN

Tanzania Lawn Tennis Association
PO Box 965 Dar Es Salaam
T 255 51 133 730 **FAX** 255 51 113 043
E-mail: rugimbana@ud.co.tz
Pres: Mr Richard Rugimbana
Sec: Mr Godfrey Zimba

TONGA – TGA (1959)

Tonga Tennis Association
PO Box 816 Nuku'alofa
T 676 23933 **FAX** 676 24127
Pres: Mr Fuka Kitekeiaho
Sec: Ms Kiu Tatafu

TURKMENISTAN – TKM (1992)

Turkmenistan Tennis Association
30 Mkrn Pr 2 Bulvarny 744020 Ashgabat
T 993 12 247 825 **FAX** 993 12 395 970
Pres: Mr Berdimurad Redjepov
Sec: Mr Bjashimov Serdar

VANUATU – VAN (1990)

Federation de Tennis de Vanuatu
BP 563 Port Vila
T 678 22087 **FAX** 678 22698 (& Tel)
Pres: Mme Evelyne Jacobe
Sec: Mr Michel Mainguy

VIETNAM – VIE (1989)

Vietnam Tennis Federation
36 Tran Phu Street Hanoi
T 84 4 845 3272 **FAX** 84 4 823 2455
Pres: Mr Le Thanh Binh
Sec: Mr Vu Nhu Y

WESTERN SAMOA – SAM (1955)

Western Samoa Lawn Tennis Association
PO Box 1297 Apia
T 685 21145 **FAX** 685 21145
Pres: Mr Waikaremoaana Soonalole
Sec: Ms Helen Mihaljevich

YEMEN – YEM (1902)

Yemen Tennis Federation
PO Box 19816 Sanaa
T 967 1 274 561 **FAX** 967 1 268 456
Pres: Mr Mohamed Hajar
Sec: Mr S Al-Altherah

Affiliated Regional associations

ASIAN TENNIS FEDERATION (ATF)

10th Floor Manulife Tower 169 Electric Road
North Point China Hong Kong
T 852 2 521 8226 **FAX** 852 2 512 8649
E-mail: atf@i-wave.net.hk
Pres: Mr Eiichi Kawatei
Sec: Mr Herman Hu

CONFEDERACION DE TENIS DE CENTROAMERICA CARIBE (COTECC)

c/o Federacion Dominicana de Tenis
Club Deportivo Naco Ens Naco Calle Central
Santo Domingo Dominican Republic
T 1 809 549 5031 **FAX** 1 809 549 5131
Pres: Mr Gonzalo Mejia
Sec: Mr Frank Liautaud

CONFEDERACION SUDAMERICANA DE TENIS (COSAT)

Calle Mexico No. 1638 Casilla 14752 La Paz Bolivia
T 591 2 361 799 **FAX** 591 2 378 769
E-mail: seccosat@ceibo.entelnet.bo
Pres: Mr Vincente Calderon Zeballos
Sec: Mr Miguel Carrizosa Galiano

EUROPEAN TENNIS ASSOCIATION (ETA)

Seltisbergerstrasse 6
CH-4059 Basle Switzerland
T 41 61 331 76 75 **FAX** 41 61 331 72 53
E-mail: etatennis.com
Pres: Mr Francesco Ricci Bitti
Sec: Mrs Charlotte Ferrari

OCEANIA TENNIS FEDERATION (OTF)

Private Bay 6060 Richmond South 3121
Victoria Australia
T 61 3 9286 1177
FAX 61 3 9650 2743
Pres: Mr Geoff Pollard
Sec: Mr Patrick O'Rourke

Publications to mark the Davis Cup Centenary

The ITF has commissioned a number of publications to commemorate 100 years of the Davis Cup. Available to order are:

☐ ***Davis Cup: Celebrating One Hundred Years of International Tennis***
by Richard Evans
UK £18.50 Europe £19.00 Rest of World £25.00

☐ ***Dwight Davis: the Man and the Cup***
by Nancy Kriplen
Available from March 1999
UK £18.50 Europe £19.00
Rest of World £25.00

☐ ***Davis Cup by NEC: The Year in Tennis 1998***
by Christopher Clarey
Available from March 1999
UK £25.00 Europe £27.00
Rest of World £32.00

THE DAVIS CUP
CELEBRATING 100 YEARS OF INTERNATIONAL TENNIS
RICHARD EVANS
FOREWORD BY JOHN McENROE
ITF

DWIGHT DAVIS
The Man and the Cup
NANCY KRIPLEN

DAVIS CUP NEC
THE YEAR IN TENNIS
ITF

Prices include postage and packing and payment can be made by cheque or credit card (no cash please).

Please indicate in the tick boxes above which book(s) you would like to order.

Cheque: Sterling draft, drawn on an English bank and made payable to: ITF Licensing (UK) Ltd.

Credit card: Please fill in the voucher below and return by fax or mail.

Orders to: Communications Department, International Tennis Federation, Bank Lane, Roehampton, London SW15 5XZ, United Kingdom. Fax +44 181 392 4747.

EUROCARD MasterCard VISA DELTA SWITCH

I wish to pay by Eurocard/MasterCard/Visa/Delta/Switch
I authorise you to debit my account with the amount of £ ______________

My Card Number is:

Issue Number:
(Switch badged cards only) ☐☐ **Expiry date of card:** ☐☐☐☐

Name (as on card) ______________

Cardholder's address ______________

____

Signature ______________ Telephone ______________

PHOTOCOPY THIS PAGE AND POST OR FAX TO THE ITF

Index